PSTricks
Graphics and PostScript for LaTeX

PSTricks
Graphics and PostScript for LaTeX

Herbert Voss

UIT
CAMBRIDGE, ENGLAND

Published by
UIT Cambridge Ltd.
PO Box 145
Cambridge
CB4 1GQ
England

Tel: +44 1223 302 041
Web: www.uit.co.uk

ISBN 978-1-906860-13-4

Copyright © 2011 Herbert Voss
All rights reserved.
This book was previously published in German by
Lehmanns Media (**www.lob.de**) in 2008.

The right of Herbert Voss to be identified as the author of this work has been asserted by him in accordance with the Copyright, Designs and Patents Act 1988.

The programs and instructions in this book have been included for their instructional value. Neither the publisher nor the author offers any warranties or representations in respect of their fitness for a particular purpose, nor do they accept accept any liability for any loss or damage arising from their use.

The publication is designed to provide accurate and authoritative information in regard to the subject matter covered. Neither the publisher nor the author makes any representation, express or implied, with regard to the accuracy of information contained in this book, nor do they accept any legal responsibility or liability for any errors or omissions that may be made. This work is supplied with the understanding that UIT Cambridge Ltd and its authors are supplying information, but are not attempting to render engineering or other professional services. If such services are required, the assistance of an appropriate professional should be sought.

Many of the designations used by manufacturers and sellers to distinguish their products are claimed as trade-marks. UIT Cambridge Ltd acknowledges trademarks as the property of their respective owners.

10 9 8 7 6 5 4 3 2

Contents

1	**Introduction**	3
1.1	The history	3
1.2	The core	4
1.3	Getting to grips with PSTricks	5
1.4	Knowing its limitations	5
1.5	Using this book	5
2	**First steps**	7
2.1	Colours	8
2.2	Setting parameters and star versions	21
2.3	Coordinates	22
2.4	Measures and lengths	22
2.5	pspicture environment	24
2.6	Whitespace	30
3	**The Coordinate System**	31
3.1	Grids	33
3.2	Parameters	33
3.3	Command \psgrid	37
3.4	Special cases	40
3.5	Examples	41
4	**Lines and polygons**	43
4.1	Parameters	43
4.2	\psline	52
4.3	\qline	53

4.4	\pspolygon.	53
4.5	\psframe and \psTextFrame.	54
4.6	\psdiamond.	55
4.7	\pstriangle.	55

5 Circles, ellipses, and curves — 57
5.1	Parameters	57
5.2	Circles and ellipses	60
5.3	Curves	65

6 Dots — 69
6.1	Parameters	69
6.2	\psdot and \psdots.	72
6.3	T_EXnicalities.	72

7 Filling — 79
7.1	Parameters	79
7.2	"Semi-transparent" colours.	89
7.3	Circular colour gradients	90

8 Arrows — 91
8.1	Parameters	92
8.2	Extensions.	96

9 Labels — 103
9.1	Alignment reference points.	103
9.2	Angle of rotation.	104
9.3	Label separation	104
9.4	\rput.	105
9.5	\multirput and \rmultiput.	105
9.6	\uput.	106
9.7	\Rput.	107
9.8	\cput.	108
9.9	\multips	108

10 Boxes — 109
10.1	Parameters	110
10.2	Commands	111
10.3	Box size.	113
10.4	Clipping	114
10.5	Rotating and scaling	116
10.6	Mathematics and verbatim boxes	118
10.7	Examples.	119

11	**Custom styles and objects**	**121**
11.1	Custom styles	121
11.2	Custom objects	122
11.3	\pscustom	122

12	**Coordinates**	**139**
12.1	Defining Points	139
12.2	Angle specifications	144
12.3	Obsolete commands	145
12.4	Examples for \SpecialCoor	146

13	**Overlays**	**147**
13.1	Slides	147
13.2	Overwriting	148

14	**Basics**	**151**
14.1	Header files	151
14.2	Special commands	152
14.3	"Low-level" commands	157
14.4	"High-level" commands	160
14.5	"key value" interface	162

15	**pst-plot: Plotting functions and data**	**165**
15.1	Coordinate axes	166
15.2	Plot styles	197
15.3	Plotting functions	203
15.4	Plotting data	212
15.5	Examples	224

16	**pst-node: Nodes and connections**	**225**
16.1	Node names	226
16.2	Parameters	226
16.3	Nodes	236
16.4	Connections using \nc commands	241
16.5	Connections using \pc commands	252
16.6	Label	253
16.7	Special cases	256
16.8	\psmatrix	257
16.9	TeX and PostScript	262
16.10	Examples	263

17 pst-tree: Trees — 265
- 17.1 Parameters for tree nodes — 266
- 17.2 Tree nodes — 277
- 17.3 Labels — 280
- 17.4 \skiplevel and \skiplevels — 283
- 17.5 Problems — 284
- 17.6 Examples — 284

18 pst-text – Manipulate text and characters — 287
- 18.1 Text manipulations — 287
- 18.2 Character manipulations — 290
- 18.3 Examples — 293

19 pst-fill – Filling and tiling — 295
- 19.1 Parameters — 296
- 19.2 \psboxfill — 300
- 19.3 Examples — 300

20 pst-coil – Coils, springs, and zigzag lines — 303
- 20.1 Parameters — 303
- 20.2 Commands — 309
- 20.3 Node connections — 310
- 20.4 Examples — 312

21 pst-eps – Exporting PSTricks environments — 313
- 21.1 TeXtoEPS — 314
- 21.2 \PSTtoEPS — 314
- 21.3 Parameters — 315
- 21.4 Example — 315

22 pst-grad and pst-slpe – Colour gradients and shadows — 317
- 22.1 pst-grad — 317
- 22.2 pst-slpe — 320
- 22.3 pst-blur – Blurred shadows — 328
- 22.4 Examples — 331

23 Three-dimensional figures — 333
- 23.1 pst-3d – Shadows, tilting, and three-dimensional illustrations — 334
- 23.2 pst-ob3d – Simple three-dimensional objects — 346
- 23.3 pst-gr3d – Three-dimensional grids — 348
- 23.4 pst-fr3d – Buttons with 3D effects — 355
- 23.5 pst-3dplot – 3D parallel projection of functions and data — 358

23.6	`pst-solides3d` — perspective 3D views.	391
23.7	Examples.	443

24 `pst-circ` – Creation of circuits — 445
24.1	How it works.	445
24.2	Parameters.	446
24.3	The objects.	447
24.4	Logical elements.	457
24.5	Examples.	462

25 `pst-geo` – Geographic projections — 465
25.1	Installation.	466
25.2	Parameters.	467
25.3	`pst-map2d`.	476
25.4	`pst-map3d`.	478
25.5	`pst-map2dII`.	487
25.6	`pst-map3dII`.	489
25.7	\mapput and \pnodeMap.	491
25.8	Examples.	494

26 `pst-barcode` – Bar codes — 497
26.1	The options.	497
26.2	Types of bar code.	499

27 `pst-bar` – bar charts — 509
27.1	Data.	509
27.2	Parameters.	509
27.3	Commands.	513

28 Mathematical functions — 517
28.1	`pst-math` – Extended PostScript functions.	517
28.2	`pst-func` – Special functions.	519

29 `pst-eucl` – Euclidean geometry — 551
29.1	Parameters.	551
29.2	Commands.	563
29.3	Examples.	580

30 `pstricks-add` – Extended basic functions — 581
30.1	Mathematical functions at TeX level.	581
30.2	New commands.	584
30.3	Node types and lines.	596
30.4	Commands and options to plot data and functions.	601

Contents

31 `pst-labo` – Chemical instruments — 619
- 31.1 Parameters — 619
- 31.2 Predefined colours and styles — 632
- 31.3 Commands — 633
- 31.4 Examples — 639

32 UML diagrams — 641
- 32.1 `pst-uml` — 641
- 32.2 `uml` — 652

33 Further PSTricks packages — 659
- 33.1 Linguistics — 659
- 33.2 Mathematics — 666
- 33.3 Natural sciences — 683
- 33.4 Information technology — 724
- 33.5 Miscellaneous — 731
- 33.6 `multido` — 738

34 Special applications… — 739
- 34.1 Gouraud shading — 739
- 34.2 Animations — 741

35 PSTricks in presentations — 747
- 35.1 powerdot — 747
- 35.2 beamer — 766

36 Examples — 769

A Tables — 819
- A.1 Summary of parameters — 819
- A.2 Summary of all commands — 831

B PostScript — 839
- B.1 The mathematical PostScript functions — 839
- B.2 The non-mathematical PostScript functions — 840
- B.3 The PostScript definitions of `pstricks.pro` — 844
- B.4 The names of the PSTricks dictionaries — 845

C Known problems — 847
- C.1 `pstricks` — 847
- C.2 `pst-plot` — 848
- C.3 `pst-node` — 849

D	**PDF output**	**851**
D.1	ps2pdf	852
D.2	pst-pdf	852
D.3	auto-pst-pdf	855
D.4	pdftricks	855
E	**Errors and help**	**857**
E.1	Frequent errors	857
E.2	Help	858
E.3	Packages	858

Index of Commands and Concepts	**867**
People	**903**

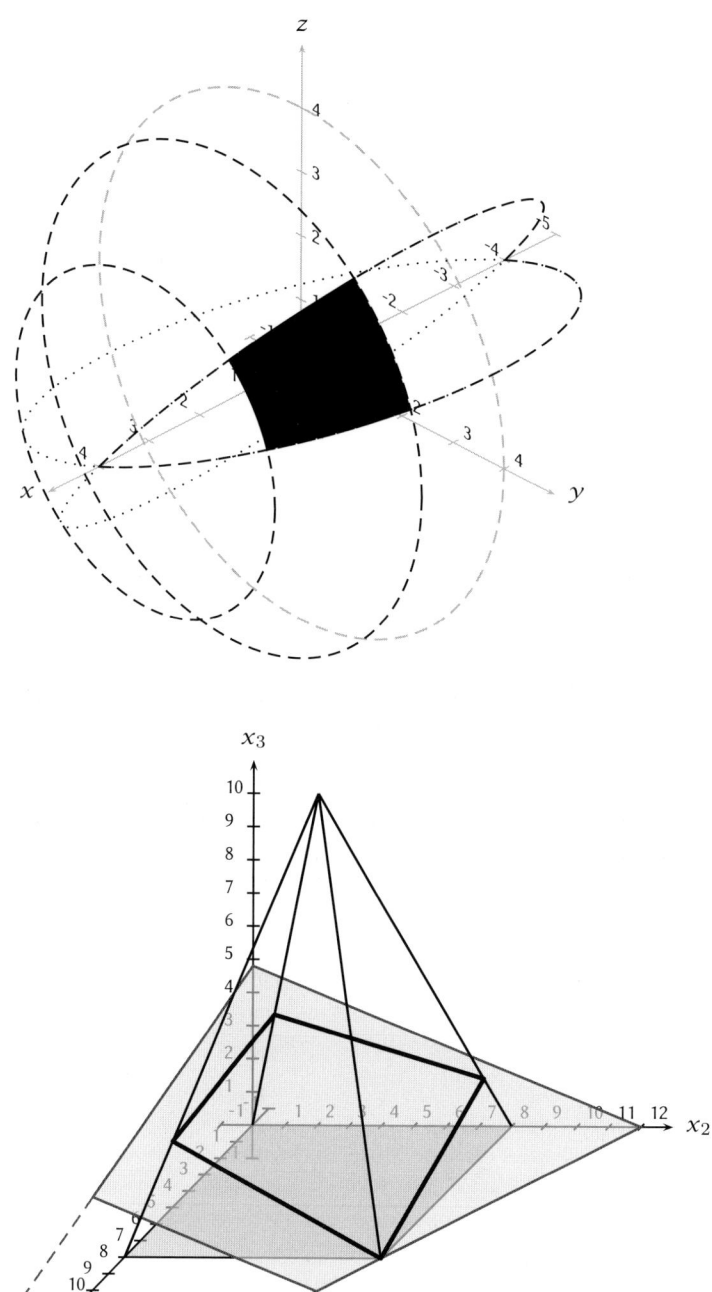

Preface

"PSTricks–more than an old hat" was the title of a presentation at the DANTE e.V. conference in Darmstadt. [54] It was meant to underline the fact that PSTricks, one of the first packages developed for Plain TeX, has not lost any of its relevance and professionalism over recent years. The quality of the figures that can be produced with PSTricks is second to none. Nevertheless everything has its limits: the figures have to be input completely in TeX and therefore in textual form – and nobody creates blueprints for a gas turbine plant or the layout for the next generation of processors as text. However, for research and teaching this isn't necessarily a problem – often the aim is to create figures that are less demanding, but still sufficiently complex, for use in handouts, publications (papers or books), and theses of various kinds, to name but a few examples. The functionality that PSTricks offers with respect to the professionalism of the output is almost unrivalled, as it is backed by the old, but graphically very powerful, PostScript programming language. However, the current documentation of PSTricks has grown old and incomplete, so this publication provides help with the basic PSTricks package and the ever-growing number of add-on packages, commands, and parameters that are in use nowadays.

TeX lives and dies with the enthusiasm of its developers and the positive feedback of its users. It was Timothy Van Zandt who began developing PSTricks in the early 1990s when he wrote some commands to support seminar classes – and, as so often happens, it "started slowly, but then...". At some point, when his enthusiasm for PSTricks was interfering negatively with "official breadwinning", Timothy stopped the more-or-less finished work on the very comprehensive basic PSTricks framework. Now it is of course a major task to develop something, but maintaining it is no less difficult and time-consuming. For years Denis Girou has been fixing bugs and answering questions quickly and comprehensively on the PSTricks mailing list. Besides that, he also developed a number of additional packages. Without Denis, PSTricks would not be what it is today.

All examples in the book are available as stand-alone documents from one of the CTAN mirrors `http://mirror.ctan.org/info/examples/PSTricks-EN/`. The used document classes like `exaarticle`, can simply be changed to the corresponding standard LaTeX classes,

e. g. `article`. However, the example classes are also available from CTAN – they are part of the example directory. All examples and classes can be downloaded as a tarzip file.

Special thanks go to Lars Kotthoff, who translated this book from the German edition, and thanks also to Joel J. Adamson, David Arnold, Bruce Burlton, Gerry Coombes, Mike Daven, Juan-Pablo Férnandez, Malcom Field, Shane Gibney, Manjusha Joshi, Vafa Khalidi, Hubert Lam, Zbigniew Nitecki, Bill O'Connor, Rich Shepard, Ciaran Taylor, Boris Veytsman, and Lakhinder Walia. And last but not least a big thanks to Catherine Jagger for her excellent job of proof reading.

Berlin, April 2011 Herbert Voß

Chapter 1

Introduction

1.1 The history. 3
1.2 The core. 4
1.3 Getting to grips with PSTricks. 5
1.4 Knowing its limitations 5
1.5 Using this book. 5

Graphical capabilities were not a major consideration when TeX was developed. The system's rudimentary graphical elements were extended with the introduction of LaTeX, but only very recently has the development of the `pict2e` package [41] expanded the functionality enough to meet normal expectations and requirements. Early on, however, the idea was put forward to use the graphical capabilities of the "old" PostScript programming language – PostScript was after all intended to be the standard output format of TeX (apart from the "intermediate format" DVI).

PSTricks is a collection of PostScript-based TeX commands that are compatible with most TeX formats like Plain TeX, LaTeX, LuaTeX and ConTeXt. PSTricks provides these formats with the capability to use colour, figures, transformations, trees, overlays, and so on.

1.1 The history

PSTricks is one of the older packages created to enhance the graphical capabilities of Plain TeX.

> I started in 1991. Initially I was just trying to develop tools for my own use. Then I thought it would be nice to package them so that others could use them. It soon became tempting to add lots of features, not just the ones I needed. When this became so interesting that it interfered with my "day job", I gave up the project "cold turkey", in 1994.
>
> [Timothy Van Zandt]

This will sound familiar for many package developers, most of whom work (or worked) voluntarily. Developing an idea often starts quite moderately, and at some point gathers

1 Introduction

enough momentum from the TeX community to carry on "on its own". Altruistic developers are vital for the further development of TeX if it wants to stay at a high level of software development.

After Timothy Van Zandt left, Sebastian Rahtz and Denis Girou took over the task of looking after PSTricks and fixing bugs. New packages (cf. chapter 33) are still being developed – just one indication that PSTricks still can't be called "old hat". [54]

1.2 The core

Similar to TeX and LaTeX, the core of PSTricks is in a quasi-frozen state, and isn't going to change in the near future. The core consists of the packages listed in Table 1.1, all of which can be found in the CTAN[1] directory CTAN: /graphics/pstricks/generic/. The generic path name indicates that the packages are compatible with Plain TeX and can be included either through the \input command, or for LaTeX through the corresponding \usepackage command. The corresponding style files are in the directory CTAN: /graphics/pstricks/latex/.

Table 1.1: The base packages and config files of PSTricks

package name	date	property
Changes	2010	log
pst-fp.tex	2010	floating point arithmetic
pst-key.tex	1998	default key handling
pstricks.con	2010	PSTricks config file (dvips version)
pstricks.tex	2010	the base package
pstricks97.tex	1999	version 97 patch 14
config files		
distiller.cfg	2008	
dvips.cfg	2010	default
dvipsone.cfg	1994	
textures.cfg	1997	
vtex.cfg	2003	
xdvipdfmx.cfg	2008	for XeTeX/XeLaTeX

The base packages are part of every established TeX distribution, so you don't need to do anything else to be able to work with them. For further information about these and other packages see Chapter 33. The files with the extension .cfg are special configuration files. You will only need one of these – depending on the system being used. Most distributions already provide the correct base setting, as for example do MiKTeX and TeX Live. If not, you will have to rename the required config file as pstricks.con.

---

[1] CTAN: Comprehensive TeX Archive Network

1.3 Getting to grips with PSTricks

You can find basic information about the package in the README file that comes with it; it also contains updates about recent problems with using PSTricks.

Few users these days are completely familiar with the vast array of options available with PSTricks commands or with their use. This book provides a comprehensive reference guide. The index contains every command mentioned together with their options, and can be used as a starting point alongside the table of contents and the compilation of options in the appendix (Section A.1 on page 819) when looking for information.

For reasons of compatibility, there is a TEX version (file extension .tex) and a LATEX version (file extension .sty) for almost every PSTricks package. Both are in principle equivalent; the LATEX style file usually only loads the TEX version with the \input command. The pstricks.sty file is different however, as it does a number of basic tests (cf. Chapter 2 on page 7). .sty and .tex

PSTricks makes heavy use of PostScript functions, which are handed to PostScript through the \special command of the dvips program, that is, the DVIPS driver. This means that in principle all of PostScript is available from (LA)TEX. In principle, because one restriction has to be made; the communication between TEX and PostScript is unidirectional, i.e. only in this direction (Section 16.9 on page 262). Only with additional and relatively cumbersome tricks is it possible to pass information back from PostScript to TEX. This includes the PostScript error messages, which are not known when TEX is run. Only the PostScript interpreter is able to provide further information.

The TEX log file contains **no** information whatsoever about potential PostScript errors, which only occur when the PostScript file is executed! If in doubt, the explicit execution of the PostScript file with GhostScript can be helpful.

1.4 Knowing its limitations

The package's name, PSTricks, is basically an abbreviation of PostScript tricks, so as you might expect output in PostScript format is the rule (file extension .ps). There are nevertheless options to achieve output in the popular PDF format; they are detailed in appendix D on page 851.

While many of the PSTricks packages could be characterized as professional, they aren't in fact as robust as programs like AutoCAD, AutoSketch, etc. The application of PSTricks is only sensible if the required figure does not exceed a complexity that varies from package to package. Users have to decide for themselves what to use PSTricks for and what not.

1.5 Using this book

Every section in this book has at least one example where possible. This is often quite difficult, as the commands that are required for a non-trivial example may not have been introduced up to that point. This is why there are many cross-references to where the commands or packages are discussed in full elsewhere in the book.

Default values for parameters are always in italics, optional parameters are additionally in a grey box . For the inputs, the conventions detailed in Table 1.2 have been used. Note

1 Introduction

that for boolean variables, specifying "keyword" is equivalent to specifying "keyword=true", though the contrary is not the case i. e. not specifying "keyword" results in the default setting, which is either true or false depending on the parameter.

The use of PSTricks, TeX, and colour does sometimes create problems. If you are using LaTeX, avoid unnecessary confusion when using colour-specific commands by using the syntax of the xcolor/color package and not the PSTricks-specific one. However TeX users must use the PSTricks-specific syntax.

Table 1.2: Input conventions

example	meaning
name	name of a parameter or an option
parameter	field for options or parameters
arrows	specification of the start/end of the line/curve
text	arbitrary alphanumeric text
material	arbitrary material, possibly a \parbox has to be used if the material contains line breaks
boolean	false or true
value	numeric value without unit
value unit	numeric value **with** unit
value `unit`	numeric value **with or without** unit
value1 value2	two numeric values, separated by a space
value1 `value2`	optional second numeric value
angle	angle, corresponds to a numeric value in degrees
colour	colour name, which has to be defined by PSTricks or xcolor/color
length	a length register, defined with \newlength
x, y	coordinate pair (point)
x_1, y_1	first coordinate pair (point) of several
x_n, y_n	nth coordinate pair (nth point) of several

Chapter 2

First steps

2.1 Colours 8
2.2 Setting parameters and star versions 21
2.3 Coordinates 22
2.4 Measures and lengths 22
2.5 pspicture environment 24
2.6 Whitespace 30

To get started with PSTricks you first of all need to know about loading packages. Then to draw graphics you need to understand how to use and define colours, lengths, angles and coordinates. This chapter covers the defaults and options for each of these topics, as well as introducing the pspicture environment. To enable us to show you examples, we have to use some commands that are covered in later chapters, including \psline (cf. Section 4.2 on page 52), \psframebox (cf. Section 10.2.1 on page 111), and \psaxes (cf. Section 15.1 on page 166).

To load PSTricks packages, use the usual syntax; Table 2.1 shows an overview for the different base systems.

syntax	system
\input{*pstricks*}	for Plain TeX
\usepackage [settings] {*pstricks*}	for LaTeX
\usemodule[*pstric*]	for ConTeXt

Table 2.1: Loading of PSTricks packages for different TeX systems.

Almost all PSTricks packages are compatible with Plain TeX; therefore the LaTeX style files in general just load the corresponding TeX file. The pstricks.sty file is an exception; as well as loading pstricks.tex, it performs several tests and subsequently some modifications, especially with regard to colour management. The following optional settings are used by pstricks.sty, whereas all other settings are passed on to color or xcolor:

2 First steps

noxcolor   Load the `color` package instead of its successor, the `xcolor` package.

plain   Only do a \input{*pstricks*}, do not perform any of the colour command modifications. Only the PSTricks-specific commands for defining colours are available (cf. Section 2.1).

distiller   Redefines the line and area transparency commands for the application of Adobe Distiller.

The `pst-all` package loads all the base packages of PSTricks. However, which packages are base packages is just historical; the list doesn't follow any inner logic. On the other hand there is not much point in extending the list to load all the packages – there are too many of them now and some conflict with one another, which then make errors harder to trace.

Table 2.2: Package order in `pst-all`

```
[ ... ]
\ProvidesPackage{pst-all}[2008/01/01 the main pstricks tools]
\RequirePackage{pstricks}   % important
% this loads the xcolor package and pstricks in the right order
% and does some modification to the colour handling. Look at the
% pstricks documentation for the options.
%
\RequirePackage{pst-plot}              \RequirePackage{pst-node}
\RequirePackage{pst-tree}              \RequirePackage{pst-grad}
\RequirePackage{pst-coil}              \RequirePackage{pst-text}
\RequirePackage{pst-3d}                \RequirePackage{pst-eps}
\RequirePackage[tiling]{pst-fill}      \RequirePackage{pstricks-add}
\RequirePackage{multido}
\endinput
```

Don't use `pst-all` for larger projects – just load the packages you require one by one. Then you'll be able to correct errors during a TEX run more easily. The next section deals with this in more detail.

2.1 Colours

It is well-known that TEX itself doesn't know anything about colours. In the past this has led to problems using several packages. PSTricks itself resorts to the capabilities of PostScript and defines five greyscale values and six colours (Table 2.3).

Table 2.3: The predefined greyscale values and colours of PSTricks

greyscale values	`black, darkgray, gray, lightgray, white`
colours	`red, green, blue, cyan, magenta, yellow`

You can use these within PSTricks without any additional packages by using commands named as listed above, since they are defined at the PostScript level (cf. example 02-01-1).

However, when working with LaTeX bear the following in mind: the short forms used to set the colour, like \red, are still supported by PSTricks, but avoid potential conflict problems by using the \color (or \textcolor) command instead (cf. Section 2.1.1 on the following page).

Use the following PSTricks commands to define new colours:

\newgray{*anotherGray*}{*value*}
\newrgbcolor{*anotherRGB*}{*value1 value2 value3*}
\newhsbcolor{*anotherHSB*}{*value1 value2 value3*}
\newcmykcolor{*anotherCMYK*}{*value1 value2 value3 value4*}

In a few cases these definitions don't work with the xcolor package; therefore pstricks.sty performs some modifications so that LaTeX users can use the xcolor commands safely instead.

To avoid complications, bear in mind the following points:

▷ Always load the pstricks package **before** any other package based on PSTricks. Using LaTeX, pstricks.sty loads both pstricks.tex **and** xcolor (or alternatively color if that option is specified), so you don't have to load a colour package in addition. This is not relevant for TeX users, who have to use the colour definitions of PSTricks anyway.

▷ The RGB colour model is supported by all implementations of PostScript. HSB and CMYK are not supported in all Level 1 implementations of PostScript, but this shouldn't cause a problem nowadays as printers almost invariably support Level 2 or Level 3.

▷ Some packages provide their own colour management rather than relying completely on the xcolor/color packages, which can then lead to conflicts with PSTricks (cf. Section 14.2.5 on page 154). For example, using the prosper document class, derived from seminar, frequently causes problems with PSTricks and the definition of colours; instead use a newer and conflict-free class like beamer[1] or the successor to prosper, powerdot[2] (cf. Chapter 35.1 on page 747).

This is red using the PSTricks syntax, not anymore.

```
\input{pstricks}% Do not load a colour package!

This is {\red red using the PSTricks
syntax}, not anymore.
```

2.1.1 Using xcolor

There is an important difference between the xcolor package (by Uwe Kern) and the color package (by David Carlisle) when using the dvips option. color additionally activates the dvipsnames option to load the predefined DVIPS colours when one of the dvips, oztex, or xdvi drivers is selected. However, if you then compile the document with pdftex, the colours will be undefined. xcolor avoids this problem by requiring that when you want to use the corresponding predefined (named) colours you must specify when loading the package the dvipsnames option (and its associated prologue option, which tells xcolor to write the xcolor.pro header file to the PostScript output, cf. Table 2.4 on the next page).

\usepackage[*dvipsnames,prologue*]{*xcolor*}

---

[1] CTAN://tex-archive/macros/latex/contrib/beamer/
[2] CTAN://tex-archive/macros/latex/contrib/powerdot/

Table 2.4: Summary of package options for xcolor

option	meaning
natural	(default) Use all colours within their model, except RGB (converted to rgb), HSB (converted to hsb), and Gray (converted to gray).
rgb	Converts all colours to the rgb model.
cmy	Converts all colours to the cmy model.
cmyk	Converts all colours to the cmyk model.
hsb	Converts all colours to the hsb model.
gray	Converts all colours to the gray model.
RGB	Converts all colours to the RGB model (and then to the rgb model).
HTML	Converts all colours to the HTML model (and then to the rgb model).
HSB	Converts all colours to the HSB model (and then to the hsb model).
Gray	Converts all colours to the Gray model (and then to the gray model).
dvipsnames	Loads the predefined DVIPS colours.
svgnames	Loads the predefined SVG colours.
x11names	Loads the predefined Unix/X11 colours.
prologue	Writes the list of colour names (dvipsnames) in the PostScript header (required for the document creation via DVIPS).
kernelfbox	Use the original LaTeX command.
table	Loads the colortbl package for coloured table rows.
hyperref	Support for the hyperref package.
showerrors	(default) Output error messages for undefined colours.
hideerrors	Only output error messages when an undefined colour is used and set it to black.

A compilation of the available colour names for the dvipsnames and svgnames colour models are shown in tables ?? and ?? on page ??. Note: to create a table with coloured rows such as this one, you must set the table option when loading the pstricks package, which then passes the option on to xcolor. The syntax is:

\usepackage[dvipsnames,prologue,table]{pstricks}

Use of predefined colours

On the lines of the colour definitions of PSTricks there are also some predefined colours for xcolor that don't depend on the colour model. All drivers obviously support the colours black and white as well as red, green, and blue for RGB support. When additionally the CMYK model is supported, the colours cyan, magenta, and yellow are also predefined.

\color{*name*}
\textcolor{*name*}{*text*}

2.1 Colours

The first form works basically like a switch and defines a new active foreground colour until either a new \color command is encountered or the local group ends. Use the second form when only small sections of text need to be set to a different colour; in principle it is equivalent to the command sequence {\color{*name*}... *Text*...}.

To select one of the set of named colours supplied by the underlying colour driver, for example the predefined colour SpringGreen from dvips, use \color[named]{*SpringGreen*}. You can avoid having to specify the [*named*] option every time you want to use the colour by setting up an alias (cf. Section 2.1.1 on the next page).

Creating colours through numerical values

When the predefined colours don't suffice, you can create additional colours by choosing a particular colour model (rgb, cmyk, etc.) and then specifying a colour by its numerical values within that model.

```
\color [model] {specification}
\textcolor [model] {specification}{text}
```

Both colour commands can take an optional argument to allow you to specify the colour model. The specification is not given as a name, but as comma-separated colour values.

Table 2.5: Supported colour models (L, M, N are integers)

name	primary colour(s)	parameter range	default
rgb	red, green, blue	$[0,1]^3$	
cmy	cyan, magenta, yellow	$[0,1]^3$	
cmyk	cyan, magenta, yellow, black	$[0,1]^4$	
hsb	hue, saturation, brightness	$[0,1]^3$	
gray	gray	$[0,1]$	
RGB	Red, Green, Blue	$\{0,1,\ldots,L\}^3$	$L = 255$
HTML	RRGGBB	$\{000000,\ldots,\text{FFFFFF}\}$	
HSB	Hue, Saturation, Brightness	$\{0,1,\ldots,M\}^3$	$M = 240$
Gray	Gray	$\{0,1,\ldots,N\}$	$N = 15$
wave	lambda (measured in nm)	$[363, 814]$	

The following examples set colours from different models explicitly, first with color loaded and then with xcolor loaded. The second example also uses one of the predefined colours mentioned previously.

Now the text is green and now a bit magenta and now blue and now green again.

```
\usepackage[noxcolor]{pstricks}% load color.sty

Now the text is \color[rgb]{0,1,0} green and now
\textcolor[cmyk]{0,1,0,0}{a bit magenta} and
{\color[rgb]{0,0,1}now blue} and now green again.
```

2 First steps

1. magenta cmyk and black
2. predefined blue grey text

```
\usepackage{pstricks}% loads xcolor
\begin{enumerate}
\item \textcolor[cmyk]{0,1,0,0}{magenta cmyk}
    and black
\item \color[gray]{0.2}\textcolor{blue}{%
    predefined blue} grey text
\end{enumerate}
```

02-01-3

Fundamentally, using colours in specific models doesn't facilitate the exchange of documents; the end result in PostScript or PDF form is highly dependent on which drivers are used. To be safe, define your own colours in the preamble and subsequently use them by name.

Defining colours

xcolor provides several commands to define additional colours:

```
\providecolor [type] {name}{model}{colour specification}
\definecolor [type] {name}{model}{colour specification}
\colorlet{name} [num model] {colour}
```

Unlike command names, colour names may contain numbers, which means you can choose helpful colour names like *Grey30*. xcolor even allows you to use additional characters – but for compatibility with other packages or with future developments it's better to avoid using them.

Let's see how these commands work by defining new colours *MyOrange*, *Blue*, *MyGrey*, *MyBlack*, and *MyRGBO* for general use:

```
\definecolor{MyOrange}{cmyk}{0,0.42,1,0}
\definecolor[named]{Blue}{rgb}{0,0,0.8}
\providecolor{MyGrey}{gray}{0.75}
\definecolor{MyBlack}{named}{Black}
\colorlet{MyRGBO}[rgb]{MyOrange}
```

The \providecolor command is like the familiar LaTeX command \providecommand. If you try to use it to define a new colour by a name that is already in use for a colour or colour definition, you'll get an error message and the existing definition is not redefined or overwritten. This is not the case with \definecolor. *MyBlack* is really just an alias for the named colour *black*, but this is useful as it saves you specifying named each time you want to use the colour. The \colorlet command uses the colour *MyOrange* as defined above in the CMYK colour model as base. It is converted into the RGB model and then called *MyRGBO*.

Once defined, as in the following example, these new colours are then available in addition to the basic predefined colours and to the named colours defined by the dvips program loaded by setting the dvipsnames and prologue package options.

2.1 Colours

```
\usepackage[dvipsnames,prologue]{xcolor}
\definecolor{MyOrange}{cmyk}{0,0.42,1,0}
\definecolor[named]{Blue}{rgb}{0,0,0.8}
\definecolor{MyGrey}{gray}{0.75}
\definecolor{MyBlack}{named}{Black}
\colorlet{MyRGBO}[rgb]{MyOrange}
\newcommand*\col[1]{\color{#1}\rule{3cm}{5mm}}

{\col{MyOrange}}\\{\col{Blue}}\\
{\col{MyGrey}}\\{\col{MyBlack}}\\{\col{MyRGBO}}
```

Colour series (or colorsets) are useful when you want to use colour gradients. xcolor has three commands for defining colour series:

> \providecolorset [type] {model}{prefix}{suffix}{set specification}
> \definecolorset [type] {model}{prefix}{suffix}{set specification}
> \definecolorseries{name}{base model} [method] {b model}
> {b specification} [s model] {s specification}

The first two are just extended versions of \definecolor:

```
\definecolorset{rgb}{}{}{red,1,0,0;green,0,1,0;blue,0,0,1}
\providecolorset{rgb}{}{H}{red,0.5,0,0;green,0,0.5,0;blue,0,0,0.5}
```

The first example defines the RGB base colours and the second one three new base colours with the suffix H – *redH*, *greenH*, and *blueH*. As with \providecolor, \providecolorset has the advantage that existing colours are never overwritten when you specify a name that has already been used. Here that means that you couldn't use \providecolorset in the first example as the three RGB base colours red, green, and blue are already defined by PSTricks as well as by xcolor. However, in the second example you could use either \providecolorset or \definecolorset because the colour names do not already exist.

```
\usepackage{xcolor}
\definecolorset{rgb}{}{}{%
    red,1,0,0;green,0,1,0;blue,0,0,1}
\providecolorset{rgb}{}{H}{%
    red,0.5,0,0;green,0,0.5,0;blue,0,0,0.5}
\newcommand*\col[1]{\color{#1}\rule{3cm}{5mm}}

{\col{red}}\\{\col{green}}\\
{\col{blue}}\\[4pt]
{\col{redH}}\\{\col{greenH}}\\{\col{blueH}}
```

Using the third method, \definecolorseries, you can specify a whole colour series, with a start colour, end colour, and the number of steps. This example creates a series from black to white in 200 steps:

```
\definecolorseries{testA}{rgb}{last}{black}{white}
\resetcolorseries[200]{testA}%  defines the series with 200 colors
```

2 First steps

As you can see, you actually need a pair of commands: the \definecolorseries command takes care of the "logic" definition of the series, whereas \resetcolorseries does the "physical" definition by computing the intermediate steps and defining all intermediate colours internally in a kind of field. It is possible to access particular colours in the field at all times: \testA!![*Index*]

The way to determine the intermediate values depends on the chosen method:
▷ {*b model*}{*b specification*} Specification of the first colour.
▷ {*s model*}{*s specification*} Computation of the intermediate values depending on method:

- last: Specification of the last colour, e.g. [rgb]{0.1,0.5,0.5}.
- step, grad: The optional argument is meaningless and {*s specification*} is a vector whose dimension is fixed by the {*base model*}, e.g. [hsb]{0.1,-0.2,0.3}.

The details of the computation of the intermediate values are described in the documentation of xcolor. [39]

Here is the output from our example of going from black to white in 200 steps, and also an example of defining a colour series by using the step option.

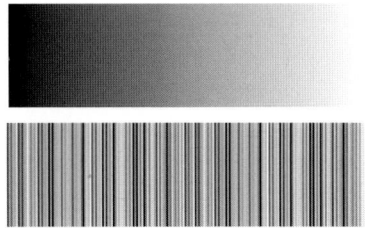

```
\usepackage{xcolor,multido}
\definecolorseries{testA}%
    {rgb}{last}{black}{white}
\resetcolorseries[200]{testA}%200 colour steps
\definecolorseries{testB}{rgb}{step}[rgb]{%
    0.95,0.85,0.55}{0.17,0.47,0.37}
\resetcolorseries[200]{testB}
\linethickness{0.004\linewidth}

\multido{\nC=1+1}{200}{\hspace{.004\linewidth}%
    \color{testA!![\nC]}\line(0,1){40}}\\[5pt]
\multido{\nC=1+1}{200}{\hspace{.004\linewidth}%
    \color{testB!![\nC]}\line(0,1){40}}
```

02-01-6

The last option is definitely the easiest way of defining a colour series. Here are two more examples illustrating its use; the first references the CMYK colour model and the second one the HSB colour model.

```
\usepackage{xcolor,multido}
\definecolorseries{testC}{cmyk}{last}{white}[cmyk]{1,0,0,0}
\resetcolorseries[10]{testC}
\definecolorseries{testM}{cmyk}{last}{white}[cmyk]{0,1,0,0}
\resetcolorseries[10]{testM}
\definecolorseries{testY}{cmyk}{last}{white}[cmyk]{0,0,1,0}
\resetcolorseries[10]{testY}
\definecolorseries{testK}{cmyk}{last}{white}[cmyk]{0,0,0,1}
\resetcolorseries[10]{testK} \setlength{\fboxsep}{2mm}
\makebox[30mm][l]{cyan (C):}%
\multido{\nColr=0+1}{10}{\colorbox{testC!![\nColr]}{0.\nColr}}\\
\makebox[30mm][l]{magenta (M):}%
\multido{\nColr=0+1}{10}{\colorbox{testM!![\nColr]}{0.\nColr}}\\
\makebox[30mm][l]{yellow (Y):}%
\multido{\nColr=0+1}{10}{\colorbox{testY!![\nColr]}{0.\nColr}}\\
```

2.1 Colours

```
\makebox[30mm][l]{black (K):}%
\multido{\nColr=0+1}{10}{\colorbox{testK!![\nColr]}{0.\nColr}}
```

cyan (C):	0.0	0.1	0.2	0.3	0.4	0.5	0.6	0.7	0.8	0.9
magenta (M):	0.0	0.1	0.2	0.3	0.4	0.5	0.6	0.7	0.8	0.9
yellow (Y):	0.0	0.1	0.2	0.3	0.4	0.5	0.6	0.7	0.8	0.9
black (K):	0.0	0.1	0.2	0.3	0.4	0.5	0.6	0.7	0.8	

02-01-7

```
\usepackage{xcolor,multido}
\definecolorseries{testH}{hsb}{last}[hsb]{0,1,1}[hsb]{1,1,1}
\resetcolorseries[10]{testH}
\definecolorseries{testS}{hsb}{last}[hsb]{.1,0,1}[hsb]{.1,1,1}
\resetcolorseries[10]{testS}
\definecolorseries{testB}{hsb}{last}[hsb]{1,1,0}[hsb]{1,1,1}
\resetcolorseries[10]{testB} \setlength{\fboxsep}{2mm}
\makebox[30mm][l]{hue (H):}%
\multido{\nColr=0+1}{10}{\colorbox{testH!![\nColr]}{0.\nColr}}\\
\makebox[30mm][l]{saturation (S):}%
\multido{\nColr=0+1}{10}{\colorbox{testS!![\nColr]}{0.\nColr}}\\
\makebox[30mm][l]{brightness (B):}%
\multido{\nColr=0+1}{10}{\colorbox{testB!![\nColr]}{\color{white}0.\nColr}}\\
```

hue (H):	0.0	0.1	0.2	0.3	0.4	0.5	0.6		0.8	0.9
saturation (S):	0.0	0.1	0.2	0.3	0.4	0.5	0.6	0.7	0.8	0.9
brightness (B):	0.0	0.1	0.2	0.3	0.4	0.5	0.6	0.7	0.8	0.9

02-01-8

Remember that there is a fundamental difference between the definition of a colour series and a single colour: \definecolor only has local scope within the group whereas \definecolorseries always has global scope.

Colour specification

The main advantage of xcolor over the old color package is the many ways of specifying colours in xcolor, The specification can primarily be by name or by expression.

xcolor defines the currently active colour – the *current color* in PostScript – as the dot (.), which can be referred to like a normal colour name. In the following example the colour is repeatedly set to 80% (\color{.!80}) of its current value, which in the end would lead to white. The following \colorbox uses the colour that is complementary to the current colour (specified by -.) for the background so that the index \iCol is readable.

```
\usepackage{pstricks,multido}
\newcommand\CBox[1]{%
  \color{.!80}\colorbox{.}{{\color{-.}#1}}}
\multido{\iCol=1+1}{11}{\CBox{\large\iCol}}
```

Specify a colour by expression using the following syntax:

prefixname! value1! name1! ... ! valueN! nameNsuffix

prefix If the prefix is a minus sign ("−") then the colour is converted to the complementary colour.

name Model and colour parameters of *name* define a temporary colour \temp.

value1!name1 The new colour results from *value1*% of the colour *temp* and (100 − *value1*)% of the colour *name1*, saved as a new temporary colour \temp. This step is repeated for all additional *!value!name*. If a *suffix* has been specified, the temporary colour corresponds to the colour series *name*.

suffix May have one of the forms !!+, !!++, !!+++, ... The number of plus signs (+) refers to the underlying colour series.

```
\usepackage{xcolor}
Current colour test with \texttt{\string\definecolorseries}:    \par
\color{blue}    \definecolorseries{foo}{rgb}{last}{.}{-.}
\resetcolorseries[5]{foo}
\def\test{\hbox to 2em{{\color{foo!!+}\vrule width 2em height 2ex}}}
Test\test\test\test\test\test\test Test                \par
\resetcolorseries[5]{foo}
\def\test{\hbox to 2em{{\color{foo!!++}\vrule width 2em height 2ex}}}
Test\test\test\test\test\test\test Test                \par
\resetcolorseries[5]{foo}
\def\test{\hbox to 2em{{\color{foo!![2]}\vrule width 2em height 2ex}}}
Test\test\test\test\test\test\test Test
```

Current colour test with \definecolorseries:
Test   Test
Test   Test
Test   Test

Table 2.6 on the facing page shows some examples of colour expressions and the corresponding RGB code expression. The latter half of the table shows the application of the complementary colours. The sum of a colour and its complementary colour yields white with the RGB value "1 1 1".

Each successive *!value!name* in a colour expression is evaluated in turn using the following formula until the final colour is determined:

$$\vec{c} = (1 - p) \cdot \vec{e} + p \cdot (x, y, z) \tag{2.1}$$

where p is the numeric percentage (*value*), $\vec{e}$ is the unit vector, and (x, y, z) is the given RGB triple of *name*. *red!75* yields $\vec{c} = (1 − 0.75) \cdot \vec{e} + 0.75 \cdot (1, 0, 0) = (1, 0.25, 0.25)$, which is

2.1 Colours

colour expression	RGB triple		
red	1	0	0
red!75	1	0.25	0.25
red!75!blue!100	0.75	0	0.25
red!75!blue!40	0.9	0.6	0.7
red!75!blue!40!yellow!50	0.95	0.8	0.55
-red	0	1	1
-red!75	0	0.75	0.75
-red!75!blue!100	0.25	1	0.75
-red!75!blue!40	0.1	0.4	0.3
-red!75!blue!40!yellow!50	0.05	0.2	0.45

Table 2.6: Colour expressions and the corresponding RGB triple

commonly denominated as 75% of red. The third row of the table with the colour expression red!75!blue!100 becomes a colour vector resulting from the sum of $\vec{c} = 0.75(1,0,0) + (1 - 0.75)(0,0,1) = (0.75, 0, 0.25)$. In other words: 75% of red and 25% of blue. A value of !100 doesn't change the colour because it produces the vector sum $\vec{c} = 1 \cdot (x_1, y_1, z_1) + 0 \cdot (x_2, y_2, z_2) = (x_1, y_1, z_1)$. Here is the colour computation for the fourth row of Table 2.6 in detail:

$$(\text{red!75!blue}) = 0.75(1,0,0) + (1 - 0.75)(0,0,1) \qquad (2.2)$$
$$= 0.75, 0, 0.25 = \vec{c}_{\text{temp}} \qquad (2.3)$$
$$(0.75, 0, 0.25)!40 = (1 - 0.4)\vec{e} + 0.4 \cdot (0.75, 0, 0.25) \qquad (2.4)$$
$$= 0.6\vec{e} + (0.3, 0, 0.1) \qquad (2.5)$$
$$= (0.9, 0.6, 0.7) = \vec{c} \qquad (2.6)$$

The following example shows an application of the colour expressions within PSTricks

```
\usepackage{pstricks}

\psframebox[linecolor={red!70!green},
    fillcolor=yellow!90!cyan, fillstyle=solid,
    doubleline=true,doublesep=5pt,framesep=10pt,
    doublecolor=-yellow!90!cyan]{%
    \Large PST\textcolor{%
        red!72.75}{PST}\color{-green}PST}
```

Table 2.7 shows further examples of colour expressions, by making use of the \colorbox command (which we cover in Section 2.1.3 on page 19). For example, the syntax for the final colour swatch is:

\fcolorbox{black}{-red!75!green!50!blue!25!gray}{}

In addition to the "normal" colour expressions, xcolor also knows about "extended" colour expressions, which refer to a mixture of colours:
core model,sum!:expr1,fac1;expr2,fac2;...;exprN,facN

2 First steps

Table 2.7: Examples of colour expressions

■	red	□	-red
■	red!75	□	-red!
■	red!75!green	□	-red!75!green
■	red!75!green!50	■	-red!75!green!50
■	red!75!green!50!blue	■	-red!75!green!50!blue
■	red!75!green!50!blue!25	■	-red!75!green!50!blue!25
■	red!75!green!50!blue!25!gray	■	-red!75!green!50!blue!25!gray

Every colour in the expression comes with a factor that determines the weight of the colour. To achieve such an extended colour definition, every colour is converted to the base mode and then multiplied by the following factor (where *dec* is a real decimal value):

$$\frac{\text{dec}_i}{\sum_{i=0}^{n} \text{fac}_i}, \quad \text{with} \quad i \in [1; n] \tag{2.7}$$

Table 2.8: Examples of extended colour expressions

■	red	□	-red
□	rgb:red,1;white,2	□	cmyk:red,2;white,2
■	rgb:red,5;green,2;yellow,10	■	cmyk:red,5;green,2;yellow,10
■	rgb,11:red,5;green,2;cyan,1	■	cmyk,11:red,5;cyan,2;cyan,1

Colours in boxes

Colours used or defined inside a \savebox are always saved within the box. They are local to the box and override the current colour outside the box.

```
\usepackage{xcolor}
\newsavebox{\X}
\sbox{\X}{[black] and \color[cmyk]{0,0.6,0.8,0}[orange]}
Begin with \usebox{\X} and back to black.\\
\color{green}Begin with green, see \usebox{\X} and green again.
```

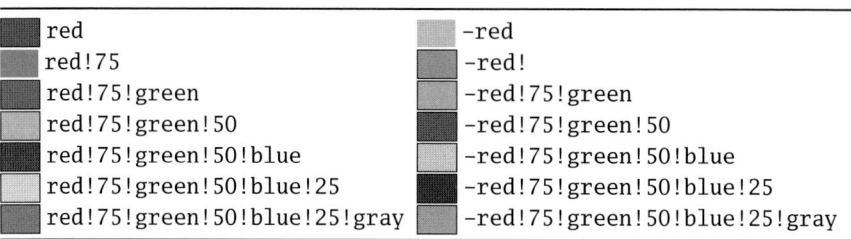

Begin with [black] and [orange] and back to black.
Begin with green, see [black] and [orange] and green again.

Problems can occur When a \savebox is processed with Plain TeX. You are more likely to avoid these if you only use LaTeX commands. The problems are discussed in detail in [76] and [66].

2.1.2 Page background colour

```
\pagecolor{name}
```

The background colour of the whole page can be changed with \pagecolor, which uses the same syntax as \color. The current page as well as all pages after the current page are set to the given background colour. This definition is always global so doesn't make sense within a minipage or group.

2.1.3 Box background colour

There are two commands to set the background colour of a box, \colorbox and \fcolorbox (which, like the familiar \fbox command, sets the colour of the frame as well).

```
\colorbox{background colour}{text}
\fcolorbox{frame colour}{background colour}{text}
```

```
\usepackage{xcolor}
\definecolor{light}{gray}{.80}
\definecolor{dark}{gray}{.20}
\colorbox{red}{black on red}\hfill%
\fcolorbox{red}{cyan}{black -- text, cyan -- background, red -- frame}\\
\colorbox{light}{\textcolor{dark}{light background}}\hfill%
\fcolorbox{red}{cyan}{\color{white}white -- text, cyan --
background,
    red -- frame}\\
\colorbox{dark}{\textcolor{white}{dark background}}
```

02-01-13

The following examples use the familiar \fboxrule and \fboxsep parameters to determine respectively the line width and the distance between the text inside the box and the frame.

```
\usepackage{xcolor}
\setlength\fboxsep{10pt}\setlength\fboxrule{6pt}
\colorbox{yellow}{Fun with PSTricks}\quad
\fcolorbox{red}{yellow}{Fun with PSTricks}\\[5pt]
\setlength\fboxrule{1pt}\setlength\fboxsep{5pt}
\colorbox{green}{Fun with PSTricks}\quad
\fcolorbox{red}{green}{Fun with PSTricks}
```

02-01-14

2 First steps

2.1.4 Determining colour values

The \convertcolorspec command in the xcolor package converts a colour value from one colour model into its closest corresponding value in a different colour model. If for example you want to use a colour similar to a given HTML page, first find out the colour's number in the HTML model and then this command transforms the values into another specified model and outputs the result. Here is the syntax:

\convertcolorspec{*existing model*}{*specification*}{*desired model*}\{*name*}

```
HTML colour 006666
rgb  :  0,0.4,0.4
cmyk :  0.4,0,0,0.6
hsb  :  0.5,1,0.4
```

```
\usepackage{xcolor}

\definecolor{HTMLcolour}{HTML}{006666}% #006666
\ttfamily{\color{HTMLcolour}HTML colour 006666}\\
rgb : \convertcolorspec{HTML}{006666}{rgb}\RGBcolour
\RGBcolour\\
cmyk: \convertcolorspec{HTML}{006666}{cmyk}\RGBcolour
\RGBcolour\\
hsb : \convertcolorspec{HTML}{006666}{hsb}\RGBcolour
\RGBcolour
```

02-01-15

2.1.5 xcolor and PSTricks

Here are a couple of specific points to remember when using xcolor with PSTricks:

When defining a colour in an optional argument of a command, you must enclose the colour values in curly braces if a colour model is specified as well, as shown in the second and third example. If the curly braces are missing, the argument isn't read correctly and you'll get an error message.

- \psset{*linecolor=green!50*}
- \psset{*linecolor={[rgb]{0.5,1,0.5}}*}% Note the braces!
- \psframebox[*linecolor={[rgb]{0.5,1,0.5}}*]{*foo*}

In addition to the colour models specified in Table 2.5 on page 11 PSTricks has a specific one, ps. This is not a colour model in the ordinary sense because it leaves the colour values unchanged and simply passes them through to PostScript. This allows for calculations with the colour values in PostScript before they are used.

\definecolor [ps] {*name*}{*base model*}{*PostScriptcode*}

The specification of the base model directly refers to the PostScript command like setrgbcolor. If for example a "colour" *foo* is defined as
 \definecolor[*ps*]{*foo*}{*cmyk*}{*bar*}
a \psline[*linecolor=foo*](x_3, y_3) of xcolor only passes the argument with the PostScript command: bar setcmykcolor. This only works if you have defined bar in PostScript beforehand.

```
\usepackage{pstricks}
\newcount\WL \unitlength.75pt
\def\WaveToPS#1{%
  \definecolor{tmp}{wave}{#1}\extractcolorspec{tmp}\tmp
  \expandafter\convertcolorspec\tmp{rgb}\tmp \expandafter\WaveToPSi\tmp,}
\def\WaveToPSi#1,#2,#3,{\pstVerb{/Red {#1} def /Green {#2} def /Blue {#3} def}}
%
\pstVerb{/Corr {dup 0 gt {Gamma exp} if } def }
\definecolor[ps]{lambda}{rgb}{Red Corr Green Corr Blue Corr}
\begin{picture}(510,70)(310,-10)\sffamily\tiny
  \linethickness{1.25\unitlength}\WL=360
  \pstVerb{/Gamma .8 def}\multiput(320,0)(1,0){456}{%
    \WaveToPS{\the\WL}{\color{lambda}\line(0,1){50}}\global\advance\WL1}%
  \linethickness{0.25\unitlength}\WL=360
  \multiput(320,0)(20,0){23}{%
    \picture(0,0)
      \line(0,-1){5}\multiput(5,0)(5,0){3}{\line(0,-1){2.5}}%
      \put(0,-10){\makebox(0,0){\the\WL}}\global\advance\WL20
    \endpicture}%
\end{picture}
```

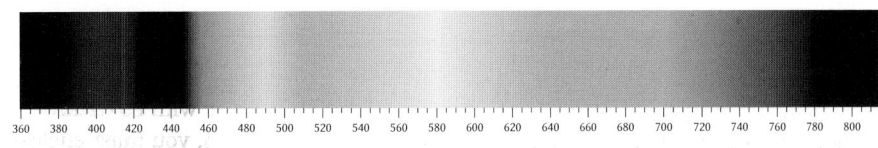

2.2 Setting parameters and star versions

PSTricks makes heavy use of the "key-value" interface (cf. Section 14.5 on page 162) for the specification of parameters and options. This makes life easy as you can change settings globally with the \psset command. The syntax is:

```
\psset [package] {name1=value1,name2=value2,...}
```

You can specify a package in the optional argument in a case where different packages have parameters of the same name. In general, package authors try to choose parameter names that aren't used with a different meaning in another package at the same time. However if this does occur, the optional package specification limits the scope of the affected parameter to the specified package.

Alternatively you can specify parameters through the optional argument in the familiar LaTeX way (shown here for \psline, which is covered in detail in Section 4.2 on page 52):

```
\psline [settings] (...)(...)
```

Remember, parameters passed through the optional argument of a command are **local**, but global for deeper levels. Parameters set with \psset are **global** within the group and deeper levels. However, you can use \psset to set parameters locally by forming a group. The following two instructions are equivalent:

```
\psline[linewidth=5pt](3,3)
{\psset{linewidth=5pt}\psline(3,3)}
```

For historical reasons PSTricks also has another way of specifying options – with curly braces:

\psline [settings] {arrow type} (...)(...)

Having so many methods to specify settings doesn't always improve readability of the code – the user could have specified the arrow type in curly braces, in square braces, or through \psset. The starred version of a PSTricks command in principle creates an inverse display of the respective object, filled with the current line colour (linecolor). Table 2.9 summarizes what the parameters are changed to when a starred version is used:

Table 2.9: Effects of the starred version options for PSTricks commands like \psframe*, \pspolygon*, etc

keyword	value
linewidth	0pt
fillcolor	\pslinecolor
fillstyle	solid
linestyle	none

For further details of parameter values for filling areas, see Chapter 7 on page 79. Most PSTricks commands (except for those whose names begin with \q) have a starred version, though their existence is for software engineering reasons without necessarily having any logical justification. Therefore the starred versions of several commands are meaningless in practice.

2.3 Coordinates

Here is a quick introduction to coordinates, which are discussed in more detail in Chapter 3 on page 31. Coordinates almost always occur in pairs (x, y) and are only extended to a triple (x, y, z) for packages that support three dimensions. A coordinate pair usually consists of two numerical values; the unit for the values is whatever has been currently defined as the unit of measurement (the default is cm, cf. Section 2.4). If you want to use a different unit of measurement, you can specify any valid unit explicitly within a coordinate pair, for example: \psline(0.1in,1)(3mm,300pt) Here the x value of the first coordinate pair is measured in inches and the y value in cm (unless previously redefined). The second pair refers to values in mm and points. This "normal" specification of coordinates is sufficient for handling Cartesian coordinates, but for other forms (such as polar coordinates) you can extend the specification by switching to "special" coordinates (cf. Chapter 12 on page 139).

2.4 Measures and lengths

2.4.1 Lengths

The predefined unit measure is 1cm. This can be changed separately for x and y directions, either with \psset or locally with corresponding command options. Table 2.10 gives a summary of the various length units.

2.4 Measures and lengths

option name	meaning	default	length register
xunit	*x* axis	1 cm	\psxunit
yunit	*y* axis	1 cm	\psyunit
runit	radius (radian)	1 cm	\psrunit
unit	everything	1 cm	\psunit

Table 2.10: Length units and their corresponding register names in PSTricks

length unit

The instruction \psset{*xunit=1cm, yunit=1cm, runit=1cm*} is therefore identical to \psset{*unit=1cm*} by definition and vice versa.[3] This means that by changing unit you can scale a whole pspicture environment. (For more information on the pspicture environment, see Section 2.5 on the next page.)

2.4.2 Angles

```
\degrees                               % identical to \degrees[360]
\degrees[value for full circle]
\radian                                % identical to \degrees[6.28319]
```

The default of 360 degrees for a full circle isn't very useful when creating a pie diagram where the values for the slices are specified in percentages. Instead, you can change the angular unit from 360 degrees to 100 degrees by setting \degrees[100], and then use the percentage values without transformation to draw the corresponding sectors of a circle. This is used for example in the \psChart command from the pstricks-add package (cf. Section 30.2.3 on page 586). To set radian measure, you can use the special command \radian.

Here is an example with a circle divided into 14 sections (cf. Section 6.2 on page 72 for details of the \psdot command and Section 30.2.7 on page 595 for details of the \psforeach command):

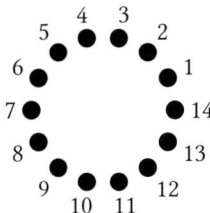

```
\usepackage{pstricks}
\SpecialCoor

\begin{pspicture}(-1.2,-1.2)(1.2,1.2)
\degrees[14]
\psforeach{\iA}{1,2,...,14}{%
    \psdot[dotscale=2](1;\iA)%
    \uput{6pt}[\iA](1;\iA){\iA}}
\end{pspicture}
```

2.4.3 Extensions

PSTricks provides the following two commands for changing length registers, similar to those provided by LaTeX:

```
\pssetlength{length register}{value unit }
\psaddtolength{length register}{value unit }
```

---
[3] The unit cm was chosen arbitrarily here, it could have been any other valid unit.

2 First steps

The advantage compared to (LA)TEX is that values without a unit as well as values with a unit can be specified. If the explicit specification of a unit is missing, PSTricks chooses the current measure with the predefined unit cm.

2.5 pspicture environment

```
\usepackage{pstricks}
Usually you will want to display a PSTricks figure in its own space and not on top
of the current text. PSTricks has a special environment for doing this. If,
however, you did want to overlay the figure, this is very easy as shown here by the
dashed line that occurs on top of the text.
\psline[linewidth=1.5pt,linestyle=dashed,dotscale=2]{-|}(0,1.5)
```

Usually you will want to display a PSTricks figure in its own space and not on top of the current text. PSTricks has a special environment for doing this. If, however, you did want to overlay the figure, this is very easy as shown here by the dashed line that occurs on top of the text.

02-05-1

The pspicture environment reserves the necessary space for the figure. The syntax alternatives for TEX and for LATEX are:

\pspicture * [settings] (xMin,yMin)(xMax,yMax)...\endpspicture *
\pspicture * [settings] (xMax,yMax)...\endpspicture
\begin{pspicture * } [settings] (xMin,yMin)(xMax,yMax)...\end{pspicture * }
\begin{pspicture * } [settings] (xMax,yMax)...\end{pspicture * }

```
\usepackage{pstricks,pst-plot}
\raggedright The reserved box, by definition, sits on the baseline of the current
line of text, as you can see with this
\psframebox[framesep=0]{%
   \begin{pspicture}(-1,-0.5)(1.5,1)
      \psaxes[labels=none]{->}(0,0)(-1,-0.5)(1.5,1)
   \end{pspicture}},
whose \textbf{internal} origin may be somewhere completely different, even outside
the box. In this example it is at \Largrfix{1,0.5}, measured from the lower left
corner of the box.
```

The reserved box, by definition, sits on the baseline of the current line of text, as you can see with this ▯, whose **internal** origin may be somewhere completely different, even outside the box. In this example it is at (1,0.5), measured from the lower left corner of the box.

02-05-2

2.5 pspicture environment

This example has also demonstrated a frame and axes; they have however nothing to do with the pspicture environment in general (\psframebox ⇒ Section 10.2.1 on page 111, \psaxes ⇒ Section 15.1 on page 166). Obviously you'll normally use pspicture in its own section – when used within a paragraph the resulting line spacing is not desirable.

A box defined by a pspicture environment has by definition no depth and is in principle simply a placeholder. It is up to you to make sure that the space reserved through the specification of the coordinates is large enough to contain the figure. If the above example were used with incorrect coordinates, the reserved space would be either too big (there would be unnecessary empty space) or too small (the figure and the text would overlap). The latter is shown in the following example; the requested space of size (-1,-0.5)(1.5,1) is far too small for the coordinate plane (-1,-1)(2,2).

```
\usepackage{pstricks,pst-plot}
\raggedright The reserved box, by definition, sits on the baseline of the current
line of text, as you can see with this
\psframebox[framesep=0]{%
   \begin{pspicture}(-1,-0.5)(1.5,1)
     \psaxes[labels=none]{->}(0,0)(-1,-1)(2,2)
   \end{pspicture}}, whose \textbf{internal} origin may be somewhere completely
different, even outside the box. In this example it is at \Largrfix{1,0.5},
measured from the lower left corner of the box.
```

02-05-3

The reserved box, by definition, sits on the baseline of the current line of text, as you can see with this ⎿▕▁▁⏌, whose **internal** origin may be somewhere completely different, even outside the box. In this example it is at (1,0.5), measured from the lower left corner of the box.

▷ If only one pair of coordinates is specified, these are taken as the maximum coordinates and the space reserved is expanded automatically to the rectangle (0,0)(xMax,yMax). Note that PSTricks does not check whether the combination of the individual values makes sense or not.

▷ If no length unit is specified, the numbers represent multiples of either 1 cm or the last value set with \psset{[x/y]unit=value}, where different values are possible for [x/y]unit.

▷ The coordinates only specify the reserved space visible to TeX; they have no effect on the output, which could also lie outside this space (as with the axes in the example above).

▷ The starred version deletes everything outside the borders specified by the minimum and maximum coordinates (clipping) and uses \pstVerb and \pstverbscale (cf. Section 14.2.6 on page 154) so we can write PostScript code directly. The clipping can be particularly useful when computing and displaying mathematical functions, as it means you don't need to know the expected extreme values exactly, e. g. if plotting $y = (x-1)^3$.

2 First steps

You can change a length unit within a pspicture environment, without it affecting the coordinates already set for the reserved space. However, if the length unit is changed **before** the start of the environment, the coordinates of the pspicture also refer to the changed scale. This example shows both options – completely different values are specified for the pspicture environment, but the results are the same. The advantage of the second alternative is that the value specifications for the pspicture environment and the following commands refer to the same units.

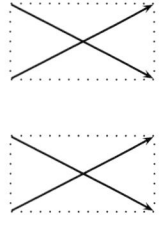

```
\usepackage{pstricks}

\psframebox[framesep=0pt,linestyle=dotted]{%
\begin{pspicture}(2,1)% cm is default
    \psset{xunit=0.5mm,yunit=2mm}
    \psline{->}(40,5)\psline{->}(0,1cm)(40,0)
\end{pspicture}}\\[20pt]
\psset{xunit=0.5mm,yunit=2mm}% changes the default!
\psframebox[framesep=0pt,linestyle=dotted]{%
\begin{pspicture}(40,5)% default for x and y is different
    \psline{->}(40,5)\psline{->}(0,1cm)(40,0)
\end{pspicture}}
```

02-05-4

The coordinates of the pspicture environment have different meanings for TeX and PostScript; for TeX they just specify the size of the box, whose lower left corner is on the baseline. For PostScript the coordinates determine the origin of the coordinate system, starting from the lower left corner. You must bear in mind that there is no "communication" between TeX and PostScript so you must take care that PostScript gets all the information it needs to display the figure as desired.

PostScript is only geared to the current point, which also corresponds to the origin of the coordinate system if the pspicture environment is not used. Therefore the \psframebox command is without effect in the following example because it refers to the TeX box, which has a width and a height of zero if no space has been reserved.

```
\usepackage{pst-plot}
\raggedright Without a space reserved through a \TeX{} box, the current point becomes by
definition the origin of the coordinate system for PostScript and the graphic overwrites
the text $\rightarrow$ \psframebox[framesep=0]{\psaxes[labels=none]{->}(0,0)(-1,-1)(2,2)%
\psplot[linewidth=1.5pt,linecolor=red!60,algebraic]{-1}{1.5}{x^2-0.5}} because PostScript
doesn't know whether space there has been reserved or not from \TeX. Therefore the current
point also remains unchanged by PostScript; \TeX\ simply carries on writing\ldots{}
Nevertheless, this ``overpainting'' can be used in a sensible way for overlays.
```

02-05-5

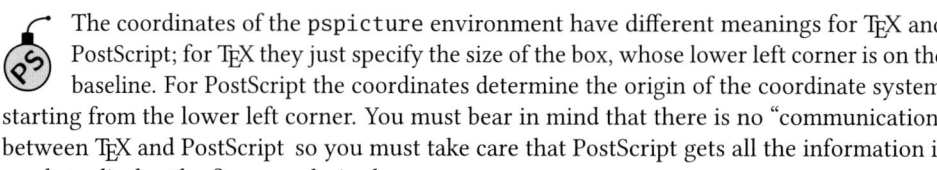

Without a space reserved through a TeX box, the current point becomes by definition the origin of the coordinate system for PostScript and the graphic overwrites the text → because PostScript doesn't know whether space there has been reserved or not from TeX. Therefore the current point also remains unchanged by PostScript; TeX simply carries on writing... Nevertheless, this "overpainting" can be used in a sensible way for overlays.

2.5 pspicture environment

For more details on overlays, see Chapter 13 on page 147.

2.5.1 Options

Table 2.11 shows the two options that are available for the pspicture environment. All other options can be used for commands inside the environment, but they aren't valid for pspicture itself.

name	meaning	default
shift	absolute vertical offset	0pt
showgrid	draw coordinate grids	false

Table 2.11: Special optional arguments for the pspicture environment

Both options are only available for PSTricks versions >=1.12 (13/Oct/2005). An optional argument for the vertical offset was always possible, though with a different syntax and different effects. This often led to misunderstandings; after the change the commonly used syntax for optional parameters is now employed.

shift

The shift option denotes vertical offset from the baseline of the text, which also corresponds to the lower line of the whole pspicture environment. The default value is 0 pt; −0.5 cm would move the box vertically 0.5 cm down, as shown in the example below. If no unit is specified for the shift option, the current one is assumed, which is usually cm. In absolute terms, of course, the baseline doesn't stay at the same height because the height of the line has to be adjusted within the page to fit the pspicture.

```
\usepackage{pstricks}
\textcolor{red}{\rule{5mm}{1pt}}%
\begin{pspicture}[shift=0.5cm](-0.6,-0.5)(0.6,0.75)
  \psframe[linecolor=blue](-0.5,-0.5)(0.6,0.75)\rput(0,0){0.5cm}
\end{pspicture}\textcolor{red}{\rule{10mm}{1pt}}%
\begin{pspicture}(-0.6,-0.5)(0.6,0.75)
  \psframe[linecolor=blue](-0.6,-0.5)(0.6,0.75)\rput(0,0){without}
\end{pspicture}\textcolor{red}{\rule{10mm}{1pt}}%
\begin{pspicture}[shift=-0.5cm](-0.6,-0.5)(0.6,0.75)
  \psframe[linecolor=blue](-0.6,-0.5)(0.6,0.75)\rput(0,0){-0.5cm}
\end{pspicture}\textcolor{red}{\rule{10mm}{1pt}}%
\begin{pspicture}[shift=*](-0.6,-0.5)(0.6,0.75)
  \psframe[linecolor=blue](-0.6,-0.5)(0.6,0.75)\rput(0,0){*}
\end{pspicture}\textcolor{red}{\rule{10mm}{1pt}}
```

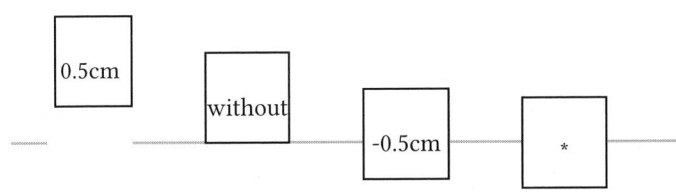

2 First steps

The specification of shift=* since version 1.20 centres the pspicture environment vertically, which corresponds to a vertical offset up or down of half the box height. This option achieves the behaviour of older versions of PSTricks.

shift=*

To get the internal baseline of a PSTricks box to the same height as the text baseline, move it down by the first y value of the box size, as shown in the next example. Here the \psyunit command is useful as it means you don't need to know the current unit. The first arrow is 0.3 units above the baseline, the second one on the baseline because of the option [shift=-0.3\psyunit]. Alternatively we could have used shift=*.

```
\usepackage{pstricks}

\rule{1cm}{.1pt}gjg%
\pspicture(-.25,-.3)(.25,.25)
\psline{<->}(-.25,0)(.25,0)
\endpspicture%
gjg\rule{1cm}{.1pt}gjg%
\pspicture[shift=-0.3\psyunit](-.25,-.3)(.25,.25)
\psline{<->}(-.25,0)(.25,0)
\endpspicture%
gjg\rule{1cm}{.1pt}
```

02-05-7

The shift option is only relevant for the outermost pspicture environment as you can move nested environments about arbitrarily with the \rput command (cf. Section 9.4 on page 105).

shift basically corresponds to the LaTeX \raisebox command, though when using \fbox to give a pspicture environment a frame it's better to use \raisebox, as shown with the two rectangles on the right in the following example. This is because \fbox preserves the baseline, so using shift results in the frame assuming undesired lengths. Using \raisebox gives the box a "positive" depth and the moves the frame with the box. (For more information on the \psgrid command used here, see Section 3.1.)

```
\usepackage{pstricks,array,calc}
\psset{gridlabels=7pt}% default value
L\_\_%
\fbox{\begin{pspicture}(-1,-1)(1,1)              \psgrid \end{pspicture}}\_\_%
\fbox{\begin{pspicture}[shift=*](-1,-1)(1,1)     \psgrid \end{pspicture}}\_\_%
\fbox{\begin{pspicture}[shift=-2cm](-1,-1)(1,1)\psgrid \end{pspicture}}\_\_%
\fbox{\begin{pspicture}[shift=1.5](-1,-1)(1,1) \psgrid \end{pspicture}}\_\_%
\raisebox{0.5\height}{%
  \fbox{\begin{pspicture}(-1,-1)(1,1)
        \psgrid
        \end{pspicture}}}\_\_R

\medskip
\begin{tabular}{@{L\_\_}*5{>{\ttfamily}p{2cm+2\fboxsep+2\fboxrule}@{\_\_}}@{R}}
  & shift=* & shift=-2cm & shift=1.5 & \textbackslash raisebox
\end{tabular}
```

2.5 pspicture environment

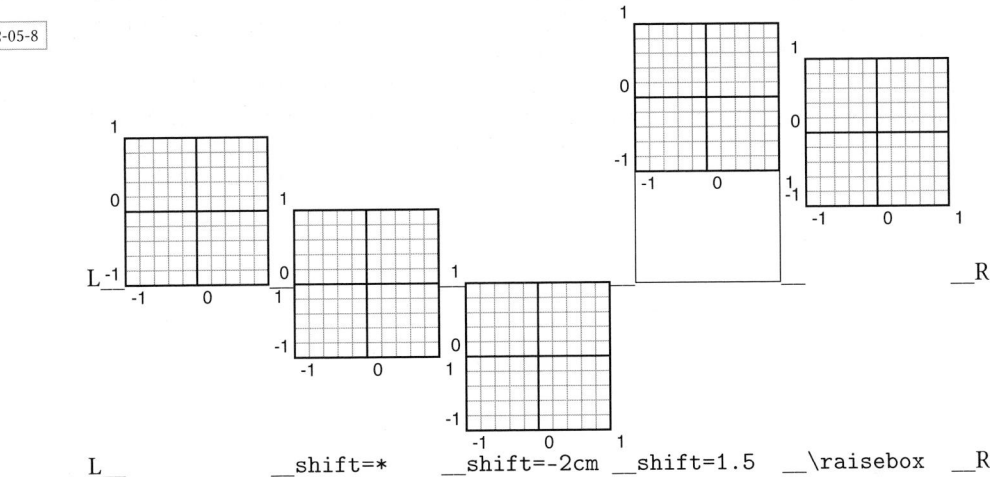

You can use the shift option inside a table to set a pspicture environment to the same height as the other columns.

```
\usepackage{pstricks}
\begin{tabular}{p{3cm}|c|l}
\texttt{p}--column & \texttt{c}--column & \texttt{l}--column\\\hline
 \makeatletter\@minipagetrue\makeatother
\begin{enumerate} \item Item 1 \item Item 2 \item Item 3 \end{enumerate}
  \texttt{enumerate}   &
  \begin{pspicture}[shift=-2.1](1,2.5)(4,5)
    \psline{<->}(1,2.5)(4,5)  \psline{<->}(4,2.5)(1,5)
  \end{pspicture} &
  \begin{minipage}[t]{3cm} \raggedright
    \begin{itemize} \item Item 1 \item Item 2 \end{itemize}
  \texttt{itemize}
\end{minipage}
\end{tabular}
```

p-column	c-column	l-column
1. Item 1		• Item 1
2. Item 2		• Item 2
3. Item 3		itemize
enumerate		

showgrid
Graphical figures are often displayed on a coordinate grid. The showgrid option switches on the grid, created with the \psgrid command (cf. Section 3.3). pstricks has an internal style for a grid defined as gridstyle:

2 First steps

\newpsstyle{gridstyle}{subgriddiv=0,gridcolor=lightgray,griddots=10}

Section 3.2 explains the grid parameters that are used to define the grid style; Section 11.1 describes the \newpsstyle command. You can override the internal style of the coordinate grid at any time. The three examples below show the internal grid style and then two other grid options.

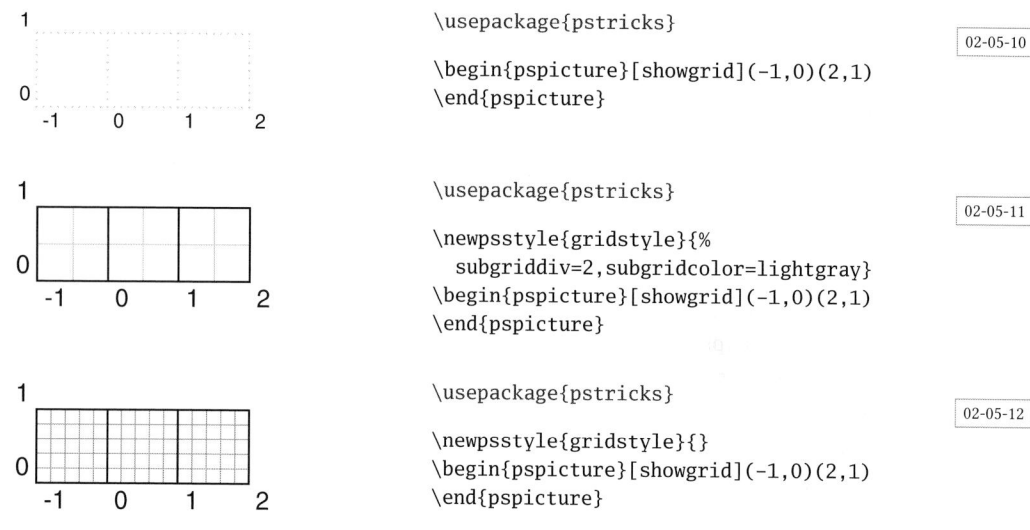

```
\usepackage{pstricks}

\begin{pspicture}[showgrid](-1,0)(2,1)
\end{pspicture}
```
02-05-10

```
\usepackage{pstricks}

\newpsstyle{gridstyle}{%
    subgriddiv=2,subgridcolor=lightgray}
\begin{pspicture}[showgrid](-1,0)(2,1)
\end{pspicture}
```
02-05-11

```
\usepackage{pstricks}

\newpsstyle{gridstyle}{}
\begin{pspicture}[showgrid](-1,0)(2,1)
\end{pspicture}
```
02-05-12

The following example does 'nothing'; it reserves only space for a box but draws nothing in it. This is the reason why the output file has a bounding box with the values %%BoundingBox: 72 72 72 72, which makes no real sense.

```
\usepackage{pstricks}

\begin{pspicture}(-1,0)(2,1)
\end{pspicture}% EPS without meaningful bounding box
```
02-05-13

Using the \psgrid command is equivalent to using the optional showgrid argument after redefining gridstyle to an empty value (see Example 02-05-12).

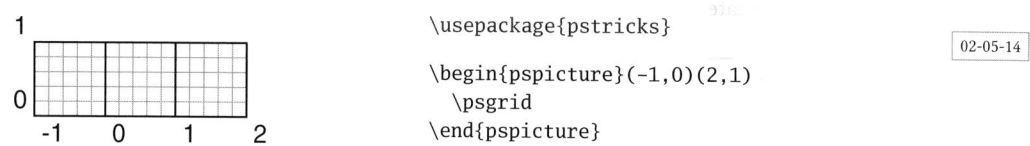

```
\usepackage{pstricks}

\begin{pspicture}(-1,0)(2,1)
    \psgrid
\end{pspicture}
```
02-05-14

2.6 Whitespace

Within a pspicture environment, all whitespace between PSTricks objects is removed. Outside this environment every object is treated as a single character; therefore additional whitespace is not removed. This may not always be what you want, for example within a picture LaTeX environment. In such cases you can remove or insert additional whitespace with \KillGlue and \DontKillGlue (cf. Section 14.2.2 on page 152).

Chapter 3

The Coordinate System

3.1 Grids. 33
3.2 Parameters. 33
3.3 Command \psgrid. 37
3.4 Special cases. 40
3.5 Examples 41

In general everything is based on a Cartesian coordinate system as this is understood by PostScript. This chapter covers how to set the origin, axes, and grid of the system, in terms of both its format and its display options.

The origin of the coordinate system is determined by the choice of the pspicture environment, but you can move it locally to any position with the origin option, giving complete flexibility for whatever use you want. You can also swap the axes with the swapaxes option, which can be very handy when the inverse function is easier to compute than the function you actually require (see the example on the next page). Table 3.1 shows the syntax of these options, which are usable with all commands in principle, but exclusively refer to the underlying coordinate system.

Table 3.1: Parameters for the coordinate system

name	type	default
origin	{xValue unit, yValue unit}	{0pt,0pt}
swapaxes	boolean	false

 The origin option has only been used in the way shown here since PSTricks version 1.12; in previous versions the parameter origin wasn't assigned correctly. Also note that this option only affects commands that were defined as PSTricks objects, for example \psdot.[1]

---
[1] A PSTricks object is a command defined internally using the \pst@object command.

3 The Coordinate System

This is illustrated in the following example, which first of all draws coordinate axes fixed by the coordinates of a pspicture environment and a parabola $y = (x + 0.5)^2 - 0.5$ (solid lines in each case) and then draws the axes and parabola again with dotted lines, this time with the additional option origin={0.25,-0.5}, but without changes to the other values. Compared to the main coordinate system the origin of the dashed system moves from $(0; 0)$ to $(0.25; -0.5)$. However, the coordinate labels are not shifted; the labelling occurs at the TEX level and is therefore unaffected by the movement!

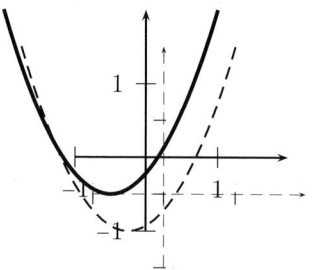

```
\usepackage{pstricks,pst-plot}

\begin{pspicture}(-1,-1)(2,2)
  \psaxes{->}(0,0)(-1,-1)(2,2)
  \psparabola[linewidth=1.5pt](1,2)(-0.5,-0.5)
  \psset{linestyle=dashed}
  \psparabola[origin={0.25,-0.5}](1,2)(-0.5,-0.5)
  \psaxes[origin={0.25,-0.5},
         linewidth=0.2pt]{->}(0,0)(-1,-1)(2,2)
\end{pspicture}
```

03-00-1

The swapaxes option is important as PostScript only provides one trigonometric inverse function, the arc tangent (atan). All the other inverse functions have to be defined through the tangent. In the following example swapaxes is used to display the function $y = \arccos x$ by simply showing the cosine function with swapped axes. Hence no mathematical conversions are necessary; the only thing to think about is the defined interval for the segment of the function that you want to plot.

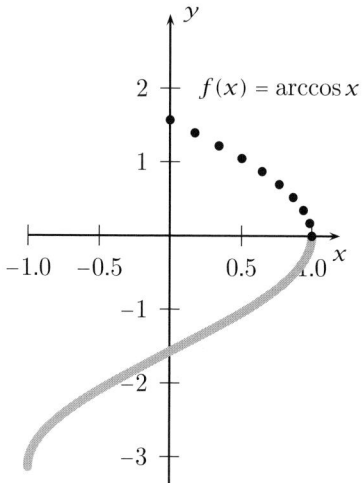

```
\usepackage{pstricks,pst-plot}

\psset{xunit=2,plotpoints=200,
       plotstyle=dots}
\begin{pspicture}(-1.1,-3.5)(1.2,3.1)
  \psaxes[Dx=0.5]{->}%
        (0,0)(-1,-3.5)(1.2,3)[$x$,-90][$y$,0]
  \rput[l](0.2,2){$f(x)=\arccos x$}
  \psset{yunit=2,xunit=0.5,swapaxes=true}
  \psplot[linecolor=red]{-3.1415}{0}%
        {x RadtoDeg cos}
  \psplot[plotstyle=dots,plotpoints=10]%
        {0}{1.5707}{x RadtoDeg cos}
\end{pspicture}
```

03-00-2

Alternatively you could use the relatively new PSTricks package pst-math (cf. Section 28.1 on page 520), which provides support for mathematical functions that are not directly supported by PostScript. [35]

3.1 Grids

You can create various Cartesian coordinate grids using the many possibilities offered by PSTricks. However this flexibility does mean that you are faced with a relatively large number of parameters that can be adjusted. The pstricks-add package provides even more options, especially useful when you need logarithmic axes or decimal labels. If all figures are to be identical in terms of the grid, you can automate the creation of grids. This is done by defining a new grid style (for which you have to use \newpsstyle{*gridstyle*} instead of the usual \psset command) and then using the showgrid option, which was already dealt with in Section 2.5.1 on page 29.

3.2 Parameters

Table 3.2 shows all parameters associated with \psgrid, the command for drawing coordinate grids (cf. Section 3.3 on page 37).

Table 3.2: Summary of all parameters for \psgrid

name	type	default
gridwidth	value unit	0.8pt
gridcolor	colour	black
griddots	value	0
gridlabels	value unit	10pt
gridlabelcolor	colour	black
subgriddiv	value	5
subgridwidth	value unit	0.4pt
subgridcolor	colour	gray
subgriddots	value	0

The following examples look at each parameter in turn, assuming default values for all the other parameters; for space reasons only small grids are used, and hence the labels usually appear to be too large.

3.2.1 gridwidth

gridwidth determines the width of the main grid lines. If you are not sure what width to choose, it is better to set it too small rather than too large, but make sure it is larger than the subgrid lines (subgridwidth, cf. Section 3.2.8 on page 36).

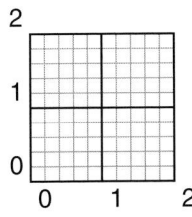

```
\usepackage{pstricks}

\begin{pspicture}(2,2)
    \psgrid% default for the line is 0.8pt
\end{pspicture}
```

3 The Coordinate System

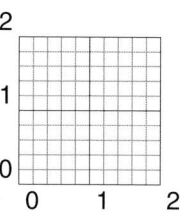

```
\usepackage{pstricks}

\begin{pspicture}(2,2)
    \psgrid[gridwidth=0.1pt]
\end{pspicture}
```

03-02-2

3.2.2 gridcolor

gridcolor determines the colour of the main grid lines and is useful if you want to highlight them.

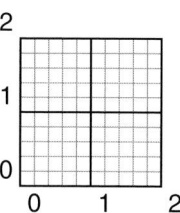

```
\usepackage{pstricks}

\begin{pspicture}(2,2)
    \psgrid[gridcolor=blue]
\end{pspicture}
```

03-02-3

3.2.3 griddots

griddots determines the number of dots per unit if you want to use dotted lines for the main grid lines instead of solid lines. This is particularly useful when you don't want the grid to stand out. If using this format, bear in mind that for the dots to be visible you must assign the value zero or one to subgriddiv (cf. Section 3.2.7 on the facing page) so that no subgrid lines are drawn; otherwise the dots would be covered by the subgrid.

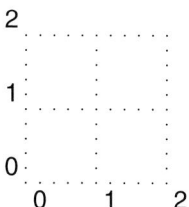

```
\usepackage{pstricks}

\begin{pspicture}(2,2)
    \psgrid[griddots=5,subgriddiv=0]
\end{pspicture}
```

03-02-4

3.2.4 gridlabels

gridlabels determines the font size of the labels.

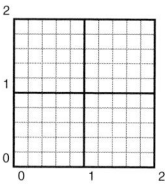

```
\usepackage{pstricks}

\begin{pspicture}(2,2)
    \psgrid[gridlabels=5pt]
\end{pspicture}
```

03-02-5

3.2 Parameters

3.2.5 gridfont

Unlike the labels on \psaxes, which are written at TeX level, the labels of the coordinate grid are written at PostScript level. This means that you can only use PostScript fonts for the labels. The default font is Helvetica, but you can change this through the gridfont option. Usually only the following PostScript fonts are available:

Helvetica (default) – Helvetica-Narrow – Times-Roman – Courier – AvantGarde – NewCenturySchlbk – Palatino-Roman – Bookman-Demi – ZapfDingbats – Symbol

```
\usepackage{pstricks}
\begin{pspicture}[showgrid=true](3,2)\end{pspicture}\qquad % Helvetica is the default
\begin{pspicture}(3,2)\psgrid[gridfont=AvantGarde-Demi]\end{pspicture}\qquad
\begin{pspicture}(3,2)\psgrid[style=gridstyle,gridfont=ZapfDingbats]\end{pspicture}
```

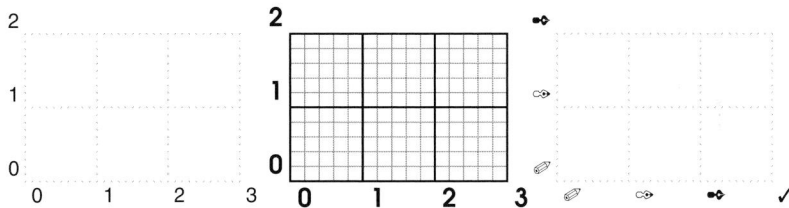

3.2.6 gridlabelcolor

gridlabelcolor determines the font colour of the labels.

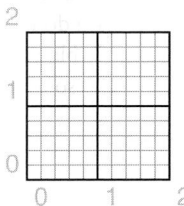

```
\usepackage{pstricks,pst-plot}

\begin{pspicture}(2,2)
    \psgrid[gridlabelcolor=cyan]
\end{pspicture}
```

3.2.7 subgriddiv

subgriddiv determines the number of divisions between two integer numbers. For large scales you may want many more divisions. subgriddiv=0 and subgriddiv=1 are identical and result in no subgrid lines being drawn.

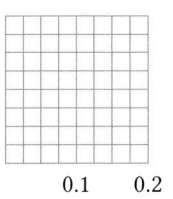

```
\usepackage{pstricks}

\psset{unit=10}
\begin{pspicture}(0.2,0.2)
    \psgrid[gridlabels=0pt,subgriddiv=40]
    \uput[-90](0.1,0){0.1}
    \uput[-90](0.2,0){0.2}
\end{pspicture}
```

The values of xunit and yunit are used to determine the divisions. This can lead to massive problems if the defined unit is very small and \psgrid is called with absolute

3 The Coordinate System

observe scale
coordinates; for example \psgrid(*10cm,10cm*). If, for example, the unit were defined as 1pt, there would be difficulties as this would mean the distance between two main labels would be only 1 pt, and in a 10 cm×10 cm square there would be approximately 280 labels and about 1400 divisions. In fact PSTricks limits the maximum number of divisions; in the current version the limit is about 500. The solution is to switch locally to a different scale: \psgrid[*unit=1cm*](10cm,10cm).

change unit locally
Setting the base unit to unit=1pt is quite useful, for example when labelling existing figures with measures in pt, so it's worth looking at this further. For all three grids in example 03-02-9 a \begin{pspicture}(50,50) reserves a box of size 50 pt×50 pt. In the first case a coordinate grid with a subdivision of subgriddiv=2 is created, resulting in what appears to be a solid black square as three lines are drawn per main unit of 1 pt≈0.35 mm. If instead we switch *locally* to another unit, such as 10 pt≈3.5 mm, the desired result is achieved, as long as we also remember to adjust the coordinates accordingly either by setting them to $\frac{1}{10}$ of their original value or by specifying them with the unit pt.

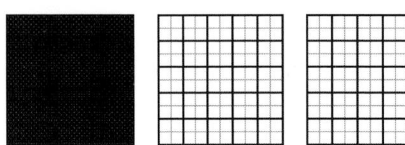

```
\usepackage{pstricks}

\psset{unit=1pt}%     very small base unit
\begin{pspicture}(50,50)% 50 main divisions
    \psgrid[gridlabels=0pt,subgriddiv=2]
\end{pspicture}\quad
\begin{pspicture}(50,50)
    \psgrid[unit=10pt,% different unit for psgrid
        gridlabels=0pt,subgriddiv=2](5,5)
\end{pspicture}\quad
\begin{pspicture}(50,50)
    \psgrid[unit=10pt,% different unit for psgrid
        gridlabels=0pt,subgriddiv=2](50pt,50pt)
\end{pspicture}
```

03-02-9

3.2.8 subgridwidth

subgridwidth determines the width of the subgrid lines. As with the main grid lines, if you are not sure what width to choose, it is better to set it too small rather than too large. In particular make sure it is smaller than the superposed main grid lines.

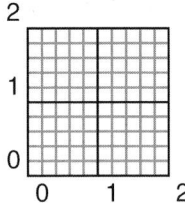

```
\usepackage{pstricks}

\begin{pspicture}(2,2)
    \psgrid[subgridwidth=1pt]
\end{pspicture}
```

03-02-10

3.2.9 subgridcolor

subgridcolor determines the colour of the subgrid lines and can be used to highlight them. They are perceived only as greyscale in the following example.

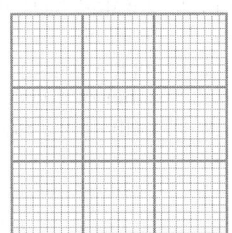

```
\usepackage{pstricks}

\definecolor{orange}{cmyk}{0,0.61,0.87,0}
\begin{pspicture}(3,3)
  \psgrid[subgriddiv=10,gridlabels=0,
     gridwidth=1pt,gridcolor=orange,
     subgridwidth=0.1pt,subgridcolor=orange]
\end{pspicture}
```

3.2.10 subgriddots

subgriddots determines the number of dots per division unit if you want to use dotted lines for the subgrid instead of solid lines. This is particularly useful when you don't want the grid to be emphasized.

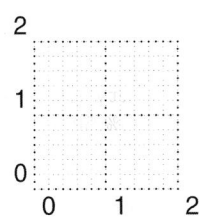

```
\usepackage{pstricks}

\begin{pspicture}(2,2)
    \psgrid[griddots=10,subgriddots=3]
\end{pspicture}
```

3.3 Command \psgrid

We have already mentioned that \psgrid is the only command that draws a grid. However, as there are so many grid options available through the various parameters, it is often convenient to define a separate command to draw the particular style of grid that you want to use. You can do this either with the starred version of the default LaTeX \newcommand

```
\newcommand*\myGrid{\psgrid[subgriddiv=0,griddots=10,gridlabels=7pt]}
```

or with the PSTricks \newpsobject command (cf. Section 11.2 on page 122). Both are shown in the following example.

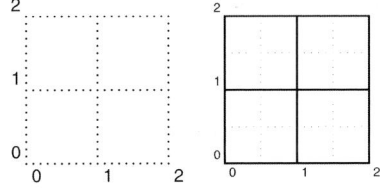

```
\usepackage{pstricks}

\newcommand*\Grid{\psgrid[subgriddiv=0,
    griddots=10,gridlabels=7pt]}
\newpsobject{psGrid}{psgrid}{subgriddots=5,
    subgriddiv=2,gridlabels=5pt}
\begin{pspicture}(0,-.2)(2,2)\Grid  \end{pspicture}
\qquad
\begin{pspicture}(0,-.2)(2,2)\psGrid\end{pspicture}
```

Alternatively, rather than defining a new command you can overwrite the internally defined style gridstyle and then just activate the grid when you want it using the showgrid option of the pspicture environment (cf. Section 2.5.1 on page 29).

The \psgrid command is a powerful tool for drawing coordinate grids. The syntax is very easy though:

3 The Coordinate System

```
\psgrid [settings]
\psgrid [settings] (x,y)
\psgrid [settings] (x₁,y₁)(x₂,y₂)
\psgrid [settings] (x₀,y₀)(x₁,y₁)(x₂,y₂)
```

A Cartesian coordinate system is assumed by definition.

▷ If coordinate pair is specified at all, \psgrid takes the coordinates determined by the pspicture environment. If \psgrid is not being used within a pspicture environment, a 10×10 coordinate grid with the current scale is assumed.

▷ If only one coordinate pair is specified, the origin is set to (0,0) automatically.

▷ The specification of two coordinate pairs fixes the lower left and the upper right corners of the coordinate grid.

▷ If three coordinate pairs are specified, the first pair determines the intersection point of the coordinate axes and the other two again the lower left and the upper right corners of the coordinate grid.

The \psgrid command only works with integer coordinate values for the grids it draws, so if it is given decimal coordinate values it rounds them up to the next integer before drawing the grid. If you don't manipulate the scale factors so that you can give \psgrid integer coordinate values, you may get unexpected results. In the following example space for a box of width 3 cm and height 2.5 cm is reserved. \psgrid however needs a width of 4 cm and a height of 2 cm because of the rounding of the values. This needs to be taken into account or your graphic could overlap your text.

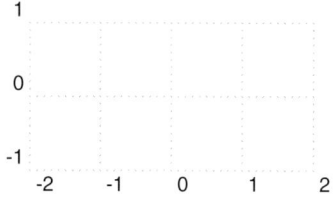

```
\usepackage{pstricks}

\begin{pspicture}[showgrid]%
    (-1.5,-1.25)(1.5,1.25)
\end{pspicture}
```

03-03-2

The following examples show some possible variants of \psgrid. The use of

```
\psset{gridlabels=7pt,subgriddiv=2}
```

is only repeated each time for clarity; in a real document it would be set globally and then be valid for all grids.

The grid labels are usually set on the right below the respective point for the horizontal axis and on the left above for the vertical axis. However, if you give \psgrid the two coordinate pairs that fix the lower left and the upper right corners of the coordinate grid in the opposite order, the labels for the horizontal values changes to left above and for the vertical values to right below. This is illustrated in three of these examples (Examples 03-03-6, 03-03-7, and 03-03-10).

3.3 Command \psgrid

03-03-3

```
\usepackage{pstricks}

\psset{gridlabels=7pt,subgriddiv=2}
\begin{pspicture}(-1,-1)(2,2)
    \psgrid
\end{pspicture}
```

03-03-4

```
\usepackage{pstricks}

\psset{gridlabels=7pt,subgriddiv=2}
\begin{pspicture}(-1,-1)(2,2)
    \psgrid(2,1)
\end{pspicture}
```

03-03-5

```
\usepackage{pstricks}

\psset{gridlabels=7pt,subgriddiv=2}
\begin{pspicture}(-1,-.25)(2,2)
    \psgrid(1,2)
\end{pspicture}
```

03-03-6

```
\usepackage{pstricks}

\psset{gridlabels=7pt,subgriddiv=2}
\begin{pspicture}(-1,-.25)(2,1.25)
    \psgrid(2,1)(0,0)
\end{pspicture}
```

03-03-7

```
\usepackage{pstricks}

\psset{gridlabels=7pt,subgriddiv=2}
\begin{pspicture}(-1,-.25)(2,2)
    \psgrid(1,2)(0,0)
\end{pspicture}
```

03-03-8

```
\usepackage{pstricks}

\psset{gridlabels=7pt,subgriddiv=2}
\begin{pspicture}(-1,-1)(2,2)
    \psgrid(-1,-1)(2,2)
\end{pspicture}
```

3 The Coordinate System

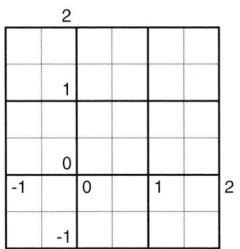

```
\usepackage{pstricks}

\psset{gridlabels=7pt,subgriddiv=2}
\begin{pspicture}(-1,-1)(2,2)
    \psgrid(0,0)(-1,-1)(2,2)
\end{pspicture}
```
03-03-9

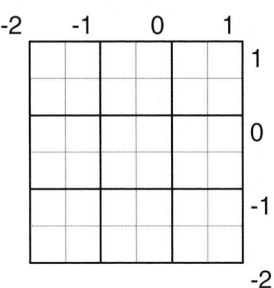

```
\usepackage{pstricks}

\psset{gridlabels=7pt,subgriddiv=2}
\begin{pspicture}(-1,-1)(2,2)
    \psgrid(0,0)(2,2)(-1,-1)
\end{pspicture}
```
03-03-10

3.4 Special cases

PSTricks allows negative units as well as positive ones, which leads to a diagonally moved coordinate origin with negative axes:

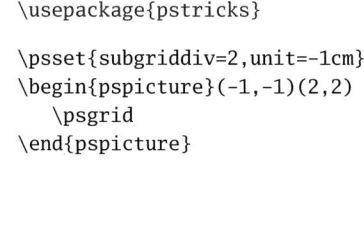

```
\usepackage{pstricks}

\psset{subgriddiv=2,unit=-1cm}
\begin{pspicture}(-1,-1)(2,2)
    \psgrid
\end{pspicture}
```
03-04-1

If you are using \psgrid together with \psaxes (cf. Section 15.1 on page 166), you get duplicate labels of the coordinates unless you suppress the output of one set of labels through the corresponding option for that command:

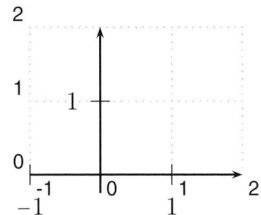

```
\usepackage{pst-plot}

\begin{pspicture}[showgrid](-1,-0.5)(2,2)
    \psaxes{->}(0,0)(-1,-0.25)(2,2)
\end{pspicture}
```
03-04-2

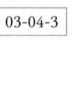
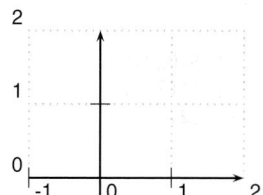

```
\usepackage{pst-plot}

\begin{pspicture}[showgrid](-1,-0.5)(2,2)
    \psaxes[labels=none]{->}(0,0)(-1,-0.25)(2,2)
\end{pspicture}
```

3.5 Examples

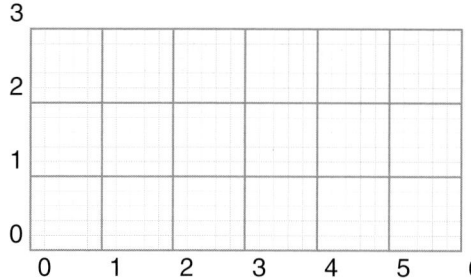

```
\usepackage{pstricks}

\begin{pspicture}(6,3)
    \psgrid[subgriddiv=5,griddots=0,
        subgridwidth=0.1pt,
        subgridcolor=black!15,
        gridcolor=black!50]
\end{pspicture}
```

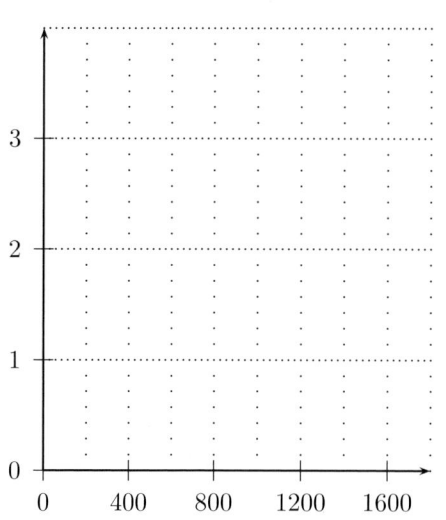

```
\usepackage{pst-plot}

\psset{xunit=0.03mm,yunit=15mm}
\begin{pspicture}(-0.25,-0.25)(1950,4)
    \psgrid[subgriddiv=0,
        griddots=7,
        gridlabels=0pt,
        xunit=200](9,4)
    \psaxes[Dx=400]{->}(1800,4)
\end{pspicture}
```

If you want to overwrite an existing graphic (as in the next example[2]) or to create an overlay (cf. Chapter 13 on page 147), it can be useful to have a coordinate grid to determine specific positions in the figure. This example just shows the creation of the grid overlay and the application of different scales for pspicture and \psgrid. A coordinate grid in cm scale is applied to the figure without knowing the exact measures of the scaled figure by using the

---

[2]The graphic tiger.eps is publicly available at CTAN.

3 The Coordinate System

\wd and \ht commands.[3] For an example of using a grid with an overlay, see Section 13.2 on page 148.

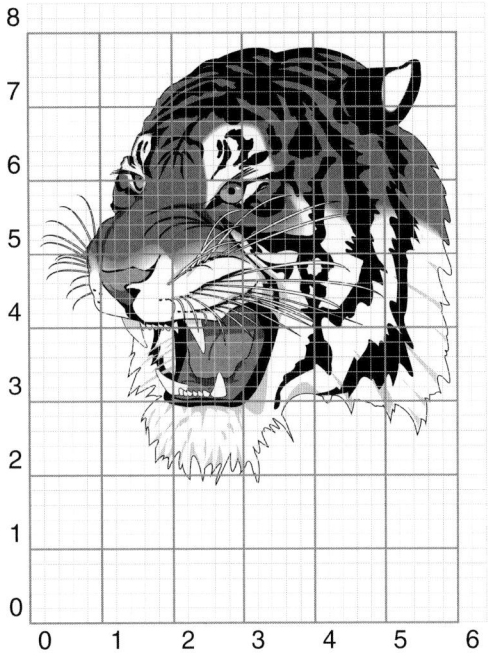

```
\usepackage{pstricks,graphicx}
\newsavebox\IBox

\savebox\IBox{%
  \includegraphics[scale=0.3]{figures/tiger}}
\psset{unit=1pt}
\begin{pspicture}(\wd\IBox,\ht\IBox)
  \rput[lb](0,0){\usebox\IBox}
  \psgrid[unit=1cm,subgriddiv=5,griddots=0,
    subgridwidth=0.1pt,
    subgridcolor=black!15,
    gridcolor=black!50](\wd\IBox,\ht\IBox)
\end{pspicture}
```

03-05-3

---

[3]\wd\box yields the width of a box, \ht\box the height, and \dp\box the depth.

Chapter 4

Lines and polygons

4.1 Parameters. 43
4.2 \psline 52
4.3 \qline 53
4.4 \pspolygon. 53
4.5 \psframe and \psTextFrame 54
4.6 \psdiamond. 55
4.7 \pstriangle 55

Lines are a fundamental feature in any graphical software and PSTricks is no exception. Accordingly the set of parameters that you can use to define lines is extensive; they are summarized in Table 4.1 and then explained one by one. Once we've covered the available options for line formats, we then discuss the straight line commands, starting with the basic \psline command (for drawing single lines or *polylines*, composed of several line segments) and moving on to polygons (\pspolygon, \pstriangle, \psdiamond) and frames (\psframe and (\psTextFrame). Curved lines are dealt with in Chapter 5.

4.1 Parameters

Table 4.1 lists all the parameters available for working with lines. You can also use many of them for commands that are not line-specific, such as \pscircle.

Table 4.1: Summary of all parameters for lines and polygons

name	type	default
linewidth	*value unit*	0.8pt
linecolor	*colour*	black
linestyle	none|solid|dotted|dashed	solid
linejoin	0|1|2	0
linecap	0|1|2	0
dash	*value unit value unit* ...	5pt 3pt

continuation...

4 Lines and polygons

... continuation

name	type	default
dotsep	*value* unit	3pt
doubleline	*boolean*	false
doublesep	*value* unit	1.25\pslinewidth
doublecolor	*colour*	white
dimen	*outer|inner|middle*	outer
arrows	*arrow type*	–
showpoints	*boolean*	false
linearc	*value* unit	0pt
framearc	*value*	0
cornersize	*relative|absolute*	relative
gangle	*angle*	0
border	*value* unit	0pt
bordercolor	*colour*	white
shadow	*boolean*	false
shadowsize	*value* unit	3pt
shadowangle	*angle*	−45
shadowcolor	*colour*	darkgray
linetype	*value*	0
liftpen	*0|1|2*	0

The following sections give examples to each of these parameters, covered in the order listed above. To find out about the parameters available for filling an area enclosed by lines, see Chapter 7 on page 79.

4.1.1 linewidth

In principle you can set a line to have any arbitrary line width. The actual limitations in terms of the largest and the smallest widths possible are determined by the underlying PostScript driver, which TeX and PostScript know nothing about, so at this stage there is no check on the feasibility of the line width. Beware of using lines that are too thin: they may end up being invisible or looking wrong when PDF output is viewed onscreen, due to the limit of the monitor resolution; only a printout shows the correct line width.

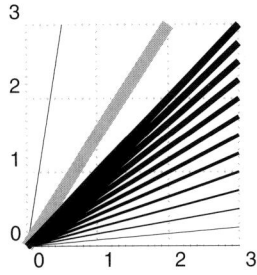

```
\usepackage{pstricks,multido}

\begin{pspicture}[showgrid](3,3)
    \psline[linewidth=0.01pt](0.5,3)
    \psline[linewidth=5pt,linecolor=red](2,3)
    \multido{\rA=0.0+0.25}{13}{%
        \psline[linewidth=\rA pt](3,\rA)}
\end{pspicture}
```

04-01-1

4.1.2 `linecolor`

As mentioned in Section 2.1 on page 8, without loading any external packages PSTricks already knows 11 colours. You can extend this number arbitrarily as described in Chapter 2.

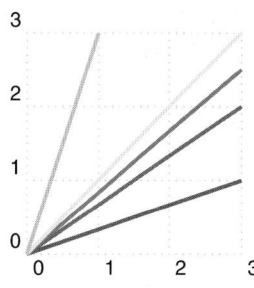

```
\usepackage{pstricks}

\begin{pspicture}[showgrid,
    linewidth=1.5pt](3,3)
\psline[linecolor=blue](3,1)
\psline[linecolor=red](3,2)
\psline[linecolor=magenta](3,2.5)
\psline[linecolor=yellow](3,3)
\definecolor{LColor}{rgb}{0.1,1,0.1}
\psline[linecolor=LColor](1,3)
\end{pspicture}
```

4.1.3 `linestyle`

Line styles can be solid, dashed, or dotted. Also, you can set the line style to none, as in the first \psline command in this example, which results in no line being drawn. This is not as pointless as it sounds – this value is useful if you want to fill an area without a borderline or draw the endpoints (nodes) of a line without drawing the actual line.

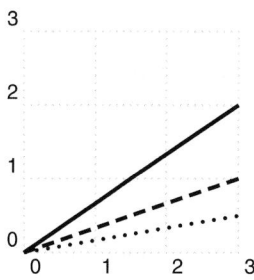

```
\usepackage{pstricks}

\begin{pspicture}[showgrid](3,3)
\psset{linewidth=1.5pt}
\psline[linestyle=none](3,3)%<-- no line!
\psline[linestyle=solid](3,2)
\psline[linestyle=dashed](3,1)
\psline[linestyle=dotted](3,0.5)
\end{pspicture}
```

4.1.4 `linejoin`

When two line ends meet, PostScript can't know automatically how to join them as there are several possible ways. It is controlled at PostScript level by the `setlinejoin` command. The corresponding parameter can be given to PostScript from TeX with the `linejoin` option. Only values of 0, 1, and 2 have any effect on the output. This parameter has most significance when dealing with thick lines and small connection angles.

since version 1.20

0 The borders of both lines are extended up to the intersection point (default).
1 The outline is drawn with an arc.
2 The outline is drawn with a horizontal line.

4 Lines and polygons

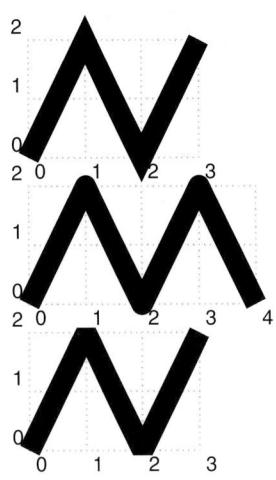

```
\usepackage{pstricks}

\psset{linewidth=3mm,unit=0.8}
\begin{pspicture}[showgrid](3,2)
  \psline(0,0)(1,2)(2,0)(3,2)
\end{pspicture}\\[10pt]
\begin{pspicture}[showgrid](4,2)
  \psline[linejoin=1](0,0)(1,2)(2,0)(3,2)(4,0)%
\end{pspicture}\\[10pt]
\begin{pspicture}[showgrid](3,2)
  \psline[linejoin=2](0,0)(1,2)(2,0)(3,2)%
\end{pspicture}
```

04-01-4

4.1.5 linecap

since version 1.20 How thick lines end is also significant. You can choose from three `linecap` options, with possible values of 0, 1, and 2.

- **0** The lines are cut off at the coordinates (default).
- **1** Semicircles with radius half of the line width (0.5\pslinewidth) are appended to the end of the lines.
- **2** The lines are extended by half the line width.

The following example shows the effect of each value of `linecap`, but also shows that you can achieve the same effect without using `linecap` by setting the line ends to *arrow symbols* (cf. Table 8.2 on page 93). The examples below use exaggerated line widths to emphasize the effect. In reality, the style of line end used is not always apparent when looking at a figure.

```
\usepackage{pstricks}

\begin{pspicture}(4,4)
  \psline[linestyle=dashed](0,4)
  \psline[linestyle=dashed](4,0)(4,4)
  \psset{linewidth=5mm}
  \psline[arrows=C-C](0,3.75)(4,3.75)
  \psline[linecap=2](0,3)(4,3)     \uput{10pt}[0](4,3){2}
  \psline[arrows=c-c](0,2.25)(4,2.25)
  \psline[linecap=1](0,1.5)(4,1.5)\uput{10pt}[0](4,1.5){1}
  \psline[arrows=-](0,0.75)(4,0.75)
  \psline(4,0)                     \uput{10pt}[0](4,0){0}
\end{pspicture}
```

04-01-5

Using the `linecap` option only makes sense in very special cases. One such occurrence would be when filling a space bordered by a thick line: arrows are in principle not part of the current path, so the fill option only refers to part of the line, where as this is not the case with

4.1 Parameters

`linecap`, as then the line end is part of the current path. The following example shows first of all a curve created by a thick line ending with arrow symbols, and then the effect of fill on the inside of this curve. The third figure shows the correct fill, achieved when the `linecap` option is used instead.

```
\usepackage{pstricks}

\def\curve{\pscurve(-.1,.1)(-.15,.15)(0,.2)(.15,.15)(.1,.1)}
\psset{unit=5cm,linewidth=5mm}
\begin{pspicture}(-0.2,-0.6)(0.2,0.5)%
\rput(0,.2){\psset{arrows=c-c}\curve}
\rput(0,-.2){%
  \psset{fillstyle=solid,fillcolor=red,arrows=c-c}%
  \curve}
\rput(0,-.6){%
  \psset{fillstyle=solid,fillcolor=red,linecap=1}%
  \curve}
\end{pspicture}
```

For dashed lines, `linecap` affects every line segment and not just the beginning and end of the whole line:

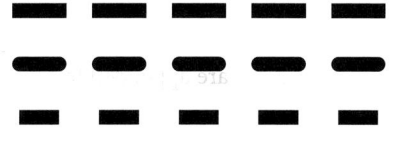

```
\usepackage{pstricks}

\psset{linewidth=2mm,linestyle=dashed,
       dash=5mm 5mm}
\psline[linecap=2](5,0)\\[3mm]
\psline[linecap=1](5,0)\\[3mm]
\psline[linecap=0](5,0)
```

4.1.6 dash

The `dash` parameter is only applicable when the dashed line style has been specified. The first value of the dash parameter defines the length of the dash and the second value the length of the space to the next dash. This example produces a series of lines, each line having a space between dashes that is 1.5 pt greater than the spacing in the previous line.

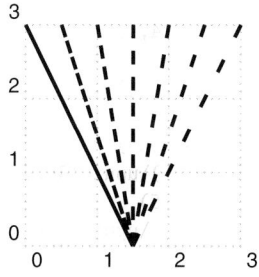

```
\usepackage{pstricks,multido}

\begin{pspicture}[showgrid](3,3)
  \psset{linewidth=1.5pt,linestyle=dashed}
  \multido{\rA=0.0+1.5,\rB=0.0+0.5}{7}{%
    \psline[dash=5pt \rA pt](1.5,0)(\rB,3)}
\end{pspicture}
```

By default, the dashed line style only uses a maximum of four values supplied in the dash parameter (first dash length, first space length, second dash length, second space length, and then the cycle repeats). However, the `pstricks-add` package refers to the PostScript

4 Lines and polygons

definition, and under that definition the number of intervals is in principle unlimited. The fourth line in this example takes advantage of this flexibility. The option can also be applied to any other line or curve command.

```
\usepackage{pstricks-add}

\begin{pspicture}(4,1.5)
  \psset{linestyle=dashed,linewidth=2pt}
  \psline[dash=3mm 3mm 1mm 1mm](0,1.5)(4,1.5)
  \psline[dash=5mm 2mm 0.1 0.2](0,1)(4,1)
  \psline[dash=5mm 1mm 1mm 1mm](0,0.5)(4,0.5)
  \psline[dash=5mm 1mm 1mm 1mm 1mm 1mm
    1mm 1mm 1mm 1mm](4,0)
\end{pspicture}
```

04-01-9

4.1.7 dotsep

The `dotsep` parameter is only applicable when the line style `dotted` has been specified. The size of the individual dots is controlled by the value of `linewidth`; it does not depend on the parameters `dotsize` and `dotscale`, which refer to the \psdot command (cf. Section 6.2 on page 72).

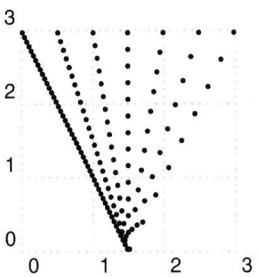

```
\usepackage{pstricks,multido}

\begin{pspicture}[showgrid](3,3)
  \psset{linewidth=2pt,linestyle=dotted}
  \multido{\rA=0.0+1.5,\rB=0.0+0.5}{7}{%
    \psline[dotsep=\rA pt](1.5,0)(\rB,3)}
\end{pspicture}
```

04-01-10

4.1.8 doubleline, doublesep, doublecolor

The `doubleline` command creates a double line when set to "true". Then `doublecolor` and `doublesep` control the width and fill of the space between the lines; the line colour and line width are still set with `linecolor` and `linewidth`.

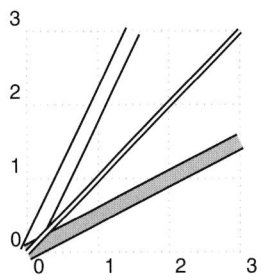

```
\usepackage{pstricks-add}

\begin{pspicture}[showgrid](3,3)
  \psset{doubleline=true}
  \psline[doublesep=5pt](1.5,3)
  \psline[doublesep=5pt,doublecolor=cyan](3,1.5)
  \psline(3,3)
\end{pspicture}
```

04-01-11

4.1.9 dimen

This option is only used with closed polylines like \psframe (cf. Section 4.5 on page 54), \pscircle, \psellipse, and \pswedge (for more information on these commands see Chapter 5 on page 57). dimen determines whether the specified coordinates refer to a point on the inner edge, the outer edge, or in the middle of the line enclosing the object. The following figure illustrates the three settings.

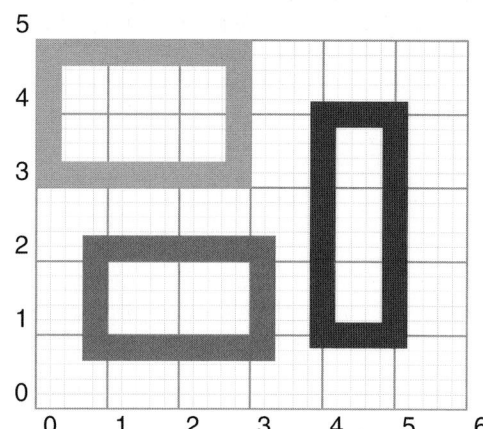

```
\usepackage{pstricks-add}

\begin{pspicture}(6,5)
  \psgrid[subgriddiv=5,griddots=0,
    subgridwidth=0.1pt,
    subgridcolor=black!15,
    gridcolor=black!50]
  \psset{linewidth=10pt}
  \psframe[dimen=outer,
    linecolor=black!40](0,3)(3,5)
  \psframe[dimen=inner,
    linecolor=black!60](1,1)(3,2)
  \psframe[dimen=middle,
    linecolor=black!80](4,1)(5,4)
\end{pspicture}
```

For \pswedge, the dimen option only affects the radial lines; the middle of the line forming the arc is always the defined distance from the specified coordinate point.

4.1.10 arrows

PSTricks already has a large number of predefined arrows and line end markers, which are summarized in Table 8.2 on page 93. You can set these arrows for most line and curve commands using either the key-value interface or the corresponding option, as shown below for \psline:

```
\psline [arrows=arrow type] (x,y)...
\psline {arrow type} (x,y)...
```

"*arrow type*" designates an expression of the form "*start arrow-end arrow*", where the specification of both *start arrow* and *end arrow* are optional. arrows=- or {-} result in a line or curve without arrows at the ends, which corresponds to the general default.

Because of the different ways to specify line ends, it is possible to give conflicting specifications. However, the last specification always takes precedence. For example: a \psline[arrows=->]{-}(3,0) has therefore the same effect as a \psline(3,0) because the options are read internally in the same order. "-" overwrites all previous definitions.

If you've created a polyline, the arrow specification refers to the start (first line) and the end (last line) of the . \pspolygon creates closed polylines (polygons) by definition by drawing a line from the first to the last point. Therefore arrow specification doesn't make sense here at all.

4 Lines and polygons

4.1.11 showpoints

showpoints is primarily of interest for bezier curves and other commands that draw curves, in order for you to be able to see where the actual points are. However, it can also be a useful option for polylines.

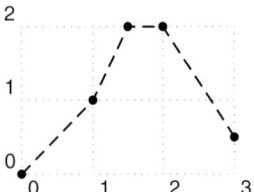

```
\usepackage{pstricks-add}

\begin{pspicture}[showgrid](3,2)
    \psline[showpoints=true,linestyle=dashed]%
        (0,0)(1,1)(1.5,2)(2,2)(3,0.5)
\end{pspicture}
```

04-01-13

You can change the size of the dots with the dotsize and dotscale parameters (cf. Chapter 6 on page 69).

4.1.12 linearc

You can create sophisticated curving polylines using the linearc option. In principle it only makes sense with polylines and polygons. The value of linearc determines the radius of the circle around which the line is "bent", as shown in this example.

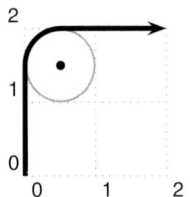

```
\usepackage{pstricks}

\begin{pspicture}[showgrid](2,2)
    \pscircle[linecolor=red](0.5,1.5){0.5}
    \psdot(0.5,1.5)
    \psline[linearc=0.5,linewidth=2pt]{->}(0,0)(0,2)(2,2)
\end{pspicture}
```

04-01-14

The first figure in the next example shows a polyline with the same start and end point; the linearc parameter is not applied to this point and the lines are connected normally here. The \pspolygon command behaves differently; it assumes a closed polyline by definition and applies linearc to all vertices (cf. Section 4.4 on page 53).

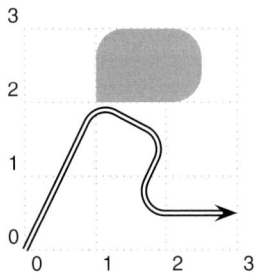

```
\usepackage{pstricks}

\begin{pspicture}[showgrid](3,3)
    \psline*[linecolor=red,linearc=0.4]%
        (1,2)(2.5,2)(2.5,3)(1,3)(1,2)
    \psline[linearc=0.3,doubleline=true]%
        {->}(0,0)(1,2)(2,1.5)(1.5,0.5)(3,0.5)
\end{pspicture}
```

04-01-15

4.1.13 framearc

This parameter is like linearc, but is used for closed areas (frames), i.e. primarily \psframe (Section 4.5 on page 54) and \pspolygon (Section 4.4 on page 53). framearc only takes values between 0 and 1, where 1 refers to half the length of the shortest side. In the case of a square, a value of 1 results in a circle.

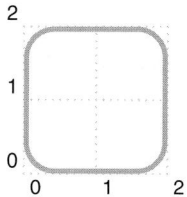

```
\usepackage{pstricks}

\begin{pspicture}[showgrid](2,2)
    \psframe[linewidth=2pt,framearc=0.4,
        linecolor=red](2,2)
\end{pspicture}
```

4.1.14 cornersize

In order for any two-dimensional polyline or shape to exhibit the same behaviour at all its corners, you can set cornersize to either relative or absolute. relative refers to half of the shortest side, whereas absolute causes the absolute value of linearc to be taken into account instead of framearc.

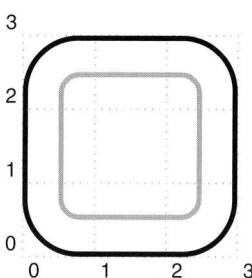

```
\usepackage{pstricks}

\begin{pspicture}[showgrid](3,3)
    \psframe[linewidth=2pt,linearc=0.25,
        cornersize=absolute,
        linecolor=red](0.5,0.5)(2.5,2.5)
    \psframe[linewidth=2pt,framearc=0.5,
        linecolor=blue](3,3)
\end{pspicture}
```

4.1.15 border, bordercolor

The border parameter is used to draw intersections of polylines without them actually crossing, by regarding one of the lines as above the other and fitting it with a circumferential frame. bordercolor determines the colour.

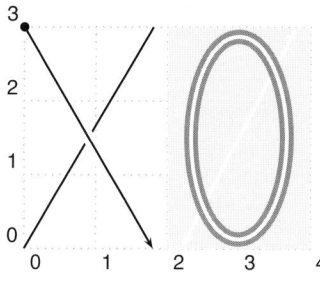

```
\usepackage{pstricks}

\begin{pspicture}[showgrid](4,3)
\psline(0,0)(1.8,3)
\psline[border=2pt]{*->}(0,3)(1.8,0)
\psframe*[linecolor=gray!10](2,0)(4,3)
\psset{linecolor=white}
\psline[linewidth=1.5pt]{<->}(2.2,0)(3.8,3)
\psellipse[linewidth=1.5pt,bordercolor=gray,
    border=2pt](3,1.5)(.7,1.4)
\end{pspicture}
```

4.1.16 shadow, shadowsize, shadowangle, shadowcolor

Shadow effects are mainly used to emphasize certain regions. It is important to choose the size of the shadow carefully. In principle creating shadows only makes sense for closed polylines, as it then creates closed areas. When shadows are created for lines, they are essentially just drawn again, which is also possible with the doubleline option. More information about how PSTricks achieves the shadow effect can be found in Chapter 11.3.16 on page 133.

4 Lines and polygons

```
\usepackage{pstricks}

\begin{pspicture}(2,1)
 \pspolygon[linearc=2pt,shadow=true,shadowangle=45](0,0)%
   (0,1.1)(0.2,1.1)(0.2,1.2)(0.8,1.2)(0.8,1.05)(2,1.05)(2,0)
\end{pspicture}
```

4.1.17 linetype

The dashed and dotted line styles can only connect to existing paths (lines or curves) without gaps if they know about the current *state of the path*, i.e. the type of the line/curve that was drawn before. This is especially important for \pscustom (cf. page 121), where arbitrary line and curve types can be connected. The linetype parameter lets you specify the line type for the current curve (Table 4.2).

Table 4.2: Possible values for linetype

value	type
0	open curve without arrows
-1	open curve with arrow at the start
-2	open curve with arrow at the end
-3	open curve with arrows at the start and end
1	closed curve with different segments
n>1	closed curve with n similar segments

4.1.18 liftpen

The liftpen parameter controls the behaviour when drawing open curves. This is especially relevant to \pscustom (cf. Section 11.3.2 on page 124, which also has examples).

4.2 \psline

The syntax for lines and for polylines that result from a series of coordinates is:

```
\psline * [settings] {arrow type} (x,y)
\psline * [settings] {arrow type} (x₁,y₁)(x₂,y₂)...(xₙ,yₙ)
```

Internally the specified points are processed in reverse order (LIFO principle). This is important to know when using \pscustom to create closed polylines or curves. The starred version results in a closed polyline by drawing a line from the point specified last to the first one. After that the whole area is *filled* with the line colour.

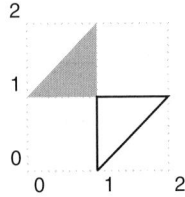

```
\usepackage{pstricks}

\begin{pspicture}[showgrid](2,2)
  \psline*[linecolor=red](0,1)(1,2)(1,1)
  \psline[linecolor=blue](1,0)(1,1)(2,1)(1,0)
\end{pspicture}
```

4.3 \qline

If you enter only one coordinate pair for \psline, the line is drawn from the current point to the specified point. If a pspicture environment exists, the current point is always set to the coordinate origin (0,0). As the following example shows, arrow specifications have no effect with the starred version of \psline. This is only shown for the sake of completeness; the starred version is basically useless when you only specify one or two coordinates.

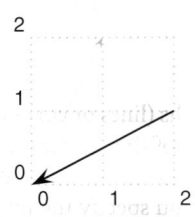

```
\usepackage{pstricks}

\begin{pspicture}[showgrid](2,2)
    \psset{arrowscale=2}
    \psline*[linecolor=red]{->}(1,2)% pointless
    \psline[linecolor=blue]{<-}(2,1)
\end{pspicture}
```

4.3 \qline

This is the minimal version (quick line) of \psline; it doesn't evaluate any local options and you have to specify *exactly* two points:

```
\qline(x₁,y₁)(x₂,y₂)
```

\qline does recognize all parameters set with \psset, since these specifications are globally valid for the current environment and deeper levels.

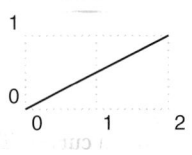

```
\usepackage{pstricks}

\begin{pspicture}[showgrid](2,1)
    \qline(0,0)(2,1)
\end{pspicture}
```

4.4 \pspolygon

In contrast to \psline, \pspolygon always creates a *closed* polyline (polygon). Any arrow specifications are therefore ignored.

```
\pspolygon * [settings] (x₁,y₁)(x₂,y₂)
\pspolygon * [settings] (x₁,y₁)(x₂,y₂)...(xₙ,yₙ)
```

If the end point does not match the start point, then the polyline closes itself by joining the two points with a direct line; however, if only two points are given, (0,0) is added as the start *and* end point by default. The starred version fills the inside of the polygon with the current line colour and the current filling pattern.

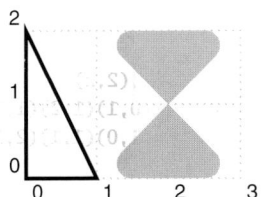

```
\usepackage{pstricks}

\begin{pspicture}[showgrid](3,2)
    \pspolygon[linewidth=1.5pt](0,2)(1,0)
    \pspolygon*[linearc=.2,linecolor=cyan,
        swapaxes=true](0,1)(0,3)(2,1)(2,3)
\end{pspicture}
```

4 Lines and polygons

4.5 \psframe and \psTextFrame

\psframe draws the horizontal rectangle defined by two diagonally opposite points.

```
\psframe * [settings] (x,y)
\psframe * [settings] (x_1,y_1)(x_2,y_2)
\psTextFrame * [settings] (x_1,y_1)(x_2,y_2){text}
```

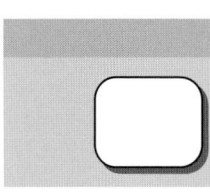

If only one point is specified for \psframe, the second point is automatically assumed to be $(0,0)$. The starred version fills the inside of the rectangle with the current line colour and filling pattern. The special options framearc and cornersize are designed primarily for use with this command.

```
\usepackage{pstricks}

\begin{pspicture}(3,2)
  \psframe*[shadowsize=15pt,linecolor=lightgray,
    shadow=true,shadowcolor=red,shadowangle=90](3,1.75)
  \psframe[fillcolor=white,fillstyle=solid,
    framearc=0.5,shadow=true](1.25,0.25)(2.8,1.5)
\end{pspicture}
```

04-05-1

```
\usepackage{pstricks}

\begin{pspicture}[showgrid](3,3)
  \rput(0,1){\psframe*[linecolor=lightgray](1,1)}
  \rput(0,2){\psframe(1,1)}
  \rput(2,0){\psframe(1,1)}
  \rput(2,2){\psframe*[linecolor=red!30](1,1)}
\end{pspicture}
```

04-05-2

line breaks   If you want line breaks inside \psTextFrame, you have to use a \parbox in the usual manner; you can't put them directly in the *text* argument. The ref option changes the alignment of the text relative to the box (cf. Table 9.1 on page 104). The rot option rotates *text* (positive values give angle of rotation counterclockwise). The command itself is in fact a combination of \psframe and \rput (cf. Section 9.4 on page 105).

```
\usepackage{pstricks}
\begin{pspicture}(0,-0.5)(8,6)
\psTextFrame[linecolor=lightgray,ref=l](0,0.5)(4,1.5){hello}
\psTextFrame[linecolor=blue](2,4)(4,6){\color{blue}hello}
\psTextFrame*[linecolor=red!40,ref=lB](7,4)(8,6){\Huge H}
\psTextFrame*[linecolor=blue!40,ref=rt](7,1)(8,3){\Huge H}
\psTextFrame[linestyle=dashed](4.5,0)(6.5,6){\parbox{2cm}{\centering
   Here comes text in a \texttt{\textbackslash parbox} that spans several lines
   but still appears vertically and horizontally centred.}}
\psTextFrame*[linecolor=cyan!20,rot=90](.5,2)(1.5,6){\parbox{4cm}{\centering
   Here comes text spanning several lines that is also rotated.}}
\end{pspicture}
```

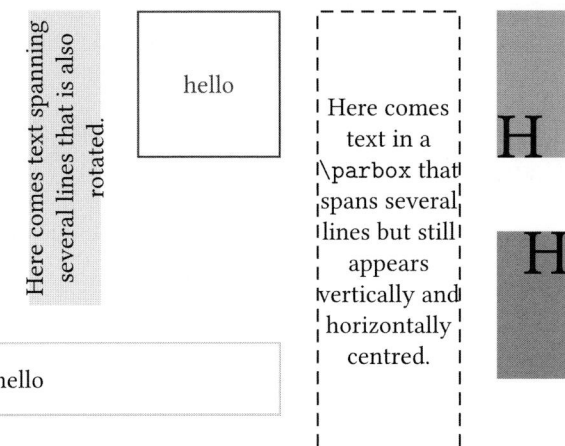

4.6 \psdiamond

\psdiamond draws the horizontal diamond defined by a centre point and the lengths of the horizontal and vertical diagonals. dx and dy specify only half the the lengths, respectively.

```
\psdiamond * [settings] (dx,dy)
\psdiamond * [settings] (x_M,y_M)(dx,dy)
```

If only one pair of numbers is specified, these are taken as the diagonal half-lengths and the coordinate origin (0,0) is automatically assumed to be the centre point, regardless of whether this point is inside or outside the PSTricks box. The starred version fills the inside of the diamond with the current line colour and the current filling pattern. Use the gangle=*angle* parameter to rotate the diamond arbitrarily.

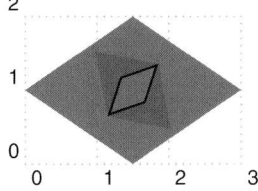

```
\usepackage{pstricks}

\begin{pspicture}[showgrid](3,2)
    \psdiamond*[linecolor=cyan](1.5,1)(1.5,1)
    \psdiamond*[linecolor=red,gangle=45]%
        (1.5,1)(0.5,0.75)
    \psdiamond[fillstyle=solid,fillcolor=cyan,
        gangle=-45](1.5,)(0.25,0.5)
\end{pspicture}
```

4.7 \pstriangle

\pstriangle draws the isosceles triangle defined by the centre point of a horizontal base line, the length of this base line and the vertical height of the triangle, where dx and dy specify the whole length of the base line and the height, respectively.

4 Lines and polygons

```
\pstriangle * [settings] (dx,dy)
\pstriangle * [settings] (xM,yM)(dx,dy)
```

If only one pair of numbers is specified, the coordinate origin (0,0) is automatically assumed to be the centre point of the base line, regardless of whether this point is inside or outside the PSTricks box. The starred version fills the inside of the triangle with the current line colour and the current filling pattern. You can rotate the triangle arbitrarily with the gangle=angle parameter.

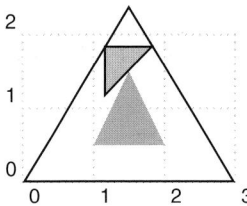

```
\usepackage{pstricks}

\begin{pspicture}[showgrid](3,2.4)
    \pstriangle[linecolor=blue](1.5,0)(3,2.4)
    \pstriangle*[linecolor=red](1.5,0.5)(1,1)
    \pstriangle[fillstyle=solid,fillcolor=cyan,%
        gangle=45](1.5,1.5)(1,0.5)
\end{pspicture}
```

04-07-1

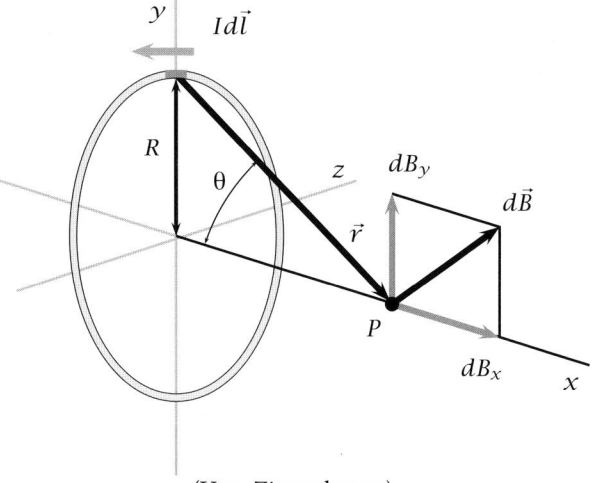

04-07-2

(Uwe Ziegenhagen)

Chapter 5

Circles, ellipses, and curves

5.1 Parameters.. 57
5.2 Circles and ellipses 60
5.3 Curves.. 65

Everything that is not a polyline is formally referred to as a curve (or *polycurve*, if composed of several curve segments). This covers circles and ellipses, or parts thereof as special cases. Again we look first at the available parameters, and then the various circle, ellipse, and curve commands themselves, including \pscircle, \psarc, and \pscurve.

5.1 Parameters

The parameters presented in Table 4.1 on page 43 that refer to lines in general and to filling are also valid for circles, ellipses, and curves. Table 5.1 lists the additional parameters that are available.

name	type	default
arcsep	*value unit*	0pt
arcsepA	*value unit*	0pt
arcsepB	*value unit*	0pt
curvature	*value1 value2 value3*	1 0.1 0

Table 5.1: Summary of additional parameters for circles, ellipses, and curves

arcsep is only a shorthand for setting arcsepA (point A) and arcsepB (point B) simultaneously. An example for each of the parameters is presented below; the order follows the order in Table 5.1.

5 Circles, ellipses, and curves

5.1.1 arcsep, arcsepA, and arcsepB

The three versions of arcsep are useful when you want a line segment to end exactly at the outer edge of another line or point rather than in the centre. This is particularly important when the line or curve ends with an arrow because usually you don't want its tip to overlap with another line or point. This option doesn't always work flawlessly, as can be seen in the following example where the upper line overlaps the edge of the circle, though adjusting the angle would remedy this. Note that this example uses polar coordinates by switching to the special coordinates option \SpecialCoor (cf. Chapter 12 on page 139).

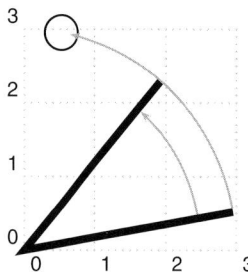

```
\usepackage{pstricks}
\SpecialCoor

\begin{pspicture}[showgrid](3,3)
    \psline[linewidth=3pt,linecolor=blue]%
        (3;50)(0,0)(3;10)
    \psarc[arcsep=3pt,linecolor=red]{->}{2.5}{10}{50}
    \pscircle(3;80){0.25}
    \psarc[arcsepA=3pt,arcsepB=0.25cm,%
        linecolor=red]{->}{3}{10}{80}
\end{pspicture}
```

05-01-1

5.1.2 curvature

This parameter controls the appearance of all curves that – apart from the Bezier curve – contain all specified points. The curve is determined by an interpolation polynomial of second order ($y = ax^2 + bx + c$). The curvature parameter controls the curvature of the curve.

First of all, before we look at this parameter in more detail, it's important to note that when a curve is drawn from A via C to B it is done so by making the gradient at point C perpendicular to the bisecting line of the angle ∢ABC. The bisecting line in the example below is depicted as a dashed line. This behaviour does not depend on the scale or on the values of the curvature parameter.

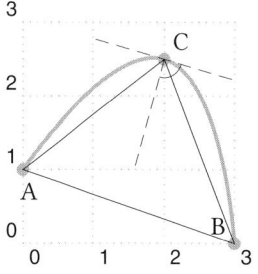

```
\usepackage{pstricks}

\begin{pspicture}[showgrid](3,3)
    \pscurve[showpoints=true,linecolor=red,%
        linewidth=1.5pt](0,1)(2,2.5)(3,0)
    \pspolygon[linewidth=0.3pt](0,1)(2,2.5)(3,0)
    \rput[lC]{-105.7}(2,2.5){%
        \psset{linewidth=0.2pt}
        \psline[linestyle=dashed](0,-1)(0,1)
        \psline[linestyle=dashed](0,0)(1.5,0)
        \psarc(0,0){0.25}{0}{90}}
    \uput[-75](0,1){A}
    \uput[135](3,0){B}
    \uput[45](2,2.5){C}
\end{pspicture}
```

05-01-2

You won't often need to change the default values of the curvature parameter (curvature=1 0.1 0) as they usually produce satisfactory curves, unless you are drawing

5.1 Parameters

curves with a very steep gradient towards the centre point (cf. Section 15.2.2 on page 199). Nevertheless, let's look at the effects of changing the three parts of the parameter in turn.

Each of the three values must lie within the interval $[-1;+2]$. The first parameter determines the initial gradient of the curve; if the value is less than zero, it is smaller than the gradient of the line segment $\overline{AC}$. For values greater than zero the behaviour is reversed; the gradient is larger than that of the segment $\overline{AC}$. Example 05-01-3 draws a series of curves for inital parameter values $\{2; 1; 0; -0.5; -1\}$. For a value of 0 the curve corresponds to a normal polyline; for negative values the curve inserts a loop in order to fulfill the gradient condition at point C mentioned above.

05-01-3

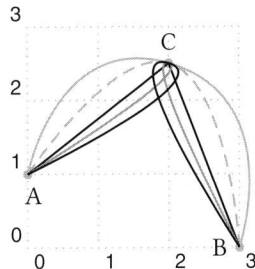

```
\usepackage{pstricks}

\begin{pspicture}[showgrid](3,3)
    \pscurve[showpoints=true,linecolor=red,%
        linestyle=dashed](0,1)(2,2.5)(3,0)
    \pscurve[linecolor=green,curvature=2 0.1 0]%
        (0,1)(2,2.5)(3,0)
    \pscurve[linecolor=blue,curvature=0.0 0.1 0]%
        (0,1)(2,2.5)(3,0)
    \pscurve[linecolor=gray,curvature=-0.5 0.1 0]%
        (0,1)(2,2.5)(3,0)
    \pscurve[linecolor=black,curvature=-1.0 0.1 0]%
        (0,1)(2,2.5)(3,0)   \uput[-75](0,1){A}
    \uput[180](3,0){B}\uput[90](2,2.5){C}
\end{pspicture}
```

The second parameter affects the gradient to the left and the right of the intermediate point, but only has any effect if the gradient $\overline{AC}$ or $\overline{BC}$ is greater than $45°$. Point C has been moved up in the following example to show the outcomes of setting the parameter to values $\{2; 0; -0.5; -1\}$. As can be seen from the figure, it behaves symmetrically around the centre point.

05-01-4

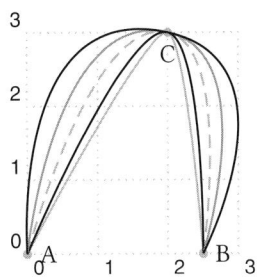

```
\usepackage{pstricks}

\begin{pspicture}[showgrid](3,3)
    \pscurve[showpoints=true,linecolor=red,%
        linestyle=dashed](0,0)(2,3)(2.5,0)
    \pscurve[linecolor=green,curvature=1 2.0 0]%
        (0,0)(2,3)(2.5,0)
    \pscurve[linecolor=blue,curvature=1 1 0]%
        (0,0)(2,3)(2.5,0)
    \pscurve[linecolor=gray,curvature=1 -0.5 0]%
        (0,0)(2,3)(2.5,0)
    \pscurve[linecolor=black,curvature=1 -1.0 0]%
        (0,0)(2,3)(2.5,0)   \uput[0](0,0){A}
    \uput[0](2.5,0){B}\uput[-90](2,3){C}
\end{pspicture}
```

The last parameter affects the gradient in every point. For a value of zero the behaviour described above occurs. If the value is equal to -1, the gradient at point C is parallel to the line $\overline{AB}$, as shown by the green curve in the following example. In contrast to the second

5 Circles, ellipses, and curves

parameter, it now behaves asymmetrically around the centre point: if the curve moves up on the left side, it moves down on the right side.

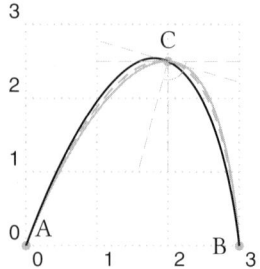

```
\usepackage{pstricks}

\begin{pspicture}[showgrid](3,3)
    \pscurve[showpoints=true,linecolor=red,%
        linestyle=dashed](0,0)(2,2.5)(3,0)
    \pscurve[linecolor=green,curvature=1 0.1 -1](0,0)(2,2.5)(3,0)
    \pscurve[linecolor=blue,curvature=1 0.1 2](0,0)(2,2.5)(3,0)
    \rput[lC]{-105.7}(2,2.5){\psset{linewidth=0.2pt,linecolor=red}
        \psline[linestyle=dashed](0,-1)(0,1)
        \psline[linestyle=dashed](0,0)(1.5,0)
        \psarc(0,0){0.25}{0}{90}}
    \rput[lC]{-90}(2,2.5){\psset{linewidth=0.2pt,linecolor=green}
        \psline[linestyle=dashed](0,-1)(0,1)
        \psline[linestyle=dashed](0,0)(1.5,0)
        \psarc(0,0){0.25}{0}{90}}   \uput[45](0,0){A}
    \uput[180](3,0){B}\uput[90](2,2.5){C}
\end{pspicture}
```

05-01-5

The third value influences the behaviour of the curve when it is scaled proportionally with the unit parameter. The first and second values have no effect in this case.

5.2 Circles and ellipses

PSTricks distinguishes between circles and ellipses, despite the circle in fact only being a special case of an ellipse. In both cases, you can draw the entire shape or just sectors and segments.

5.2.1 \pscircle

\pscircle * [settings] {radius}
\pscircle * [settings] (x_M, y_M) {radius}

If the centre of the circle is not specified, the coordinate origin (0,0) is automatically assumed. The starred version fills the inside of the circle with the current line colour and filling pattern.

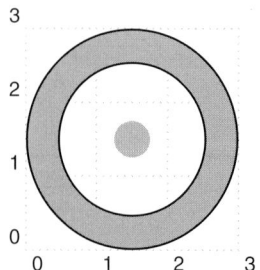

```
\usepackage{pstricks}

\begin{pspicture}[showgrid](3,3)
    \pscircle[linecolor=blue,doubleline=true,
        doublecolor=red,doublesep=12pt](1.5,1.5){1.5}
    \pscircle*[linecolor=green](1.5,1.5){0.25}
\end{pspicture}
```

05-02-1

5.2.2 \pscircleOA

`\pscircleOA * [settings] ` $(x_M, y_M)(x_A, y_A)$

This command draws a circle with its centre at the first specified point and with its circumference passing through the second specified point, which can be any arbitrary point on the circle. The radius is determined automatically by the distance between the two points. The starred version fills the inside of the circle with the current line colour and filling pattern.

```
\usepackage{pstricks}

\begin{pspicture}[showgrid](-1,-1)(5,5)
\pscircleOA*[linecolor=black!40](1,1)(2,2.4)
\psdot[dotscale=1.5,dotstyle=+](1,1)
\psdot[dotscale=1.5](2,2.4)
\pscircleOA[linecolor=blue](2,2)(3,4)
\psdot[dotscale=1.5,dotstyle=+](2,2)
\psdot[dotscale=1.5](3,4)
\pscircleOA[linewidth=2pt](3,3)(2,4)
\psdot[dotscale=1.5,dotstyle=+](3,3)
\psdot[dotscale=1.5](2,4)
\pscircleOA*[opacity=0.3,
    linecolor=red](2.5,2.5)(2,4.5)
\psdot[dotscale=1.5,dotstyle=+](2.5,2.5)
\psdot[dotscale=1.5](2,4.5)
\end{pspicture}
```

5.2.3 \qdisk

\qdisk is basically the minimal version of the starred circle command. It doesn't evaluate any local options, so parameters can only be set through \psset, and you have to specify both the centre point and the radius.

`\qdisk` (x_M, y_M){*radius*}

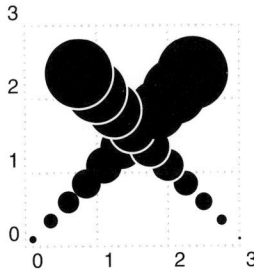

```
\usepackage{pstricks,multido}

\begin{pspicture}[showgrid](3,3)
    \multido{\rA=0.1+0.25,\rB=0.05+0.05,%
      \rC=3.0+-0.25}{10}{%
      \qdisk(\rA,\rA){\rB}%
      \pscircle[linecolor=white,
          fillcolor=black,
          fillstyle=solid](\rC,\rA){\rB}
    }
\end{pspicture}
```

5.2.4 \psarc

Use \psarc both to draw arcs and to draw circle segments by using the filling function. The arc is drawn mathematically in a positive sense, i.e. counter clockwise.

5 Circles, ellipses, and curves

```
\psarc * [settings]  {arrows}  {radius}{angle1}{angle2}
\psarc * [settings]  {arrows} (x_M,y_M){radius}{angle1}{angle2}
```

If the centre point of the circle is not specified, the coordinate origin (0,0) is assumed by default. The starred version fills the area that is enclosed by the arc and the secant connecting the ends of the arc with the current line colour and filling pattern. The showpoints=true option behaves differently from usual when used with \psarc; it draws dashed lines from the centre point to the starting point and endpoint of the arc.

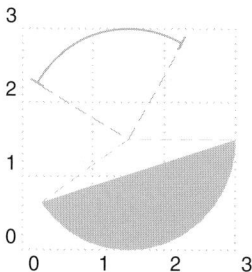

```
\usepackage{pstricks}

\begin{pspicture}[showgrid](3,3)
    \psarc*[showpoints,linecolor=cyan]%
           (1.5,1.5){1.5}{215}{0}
    \psarc[showpoints,linecolor=red]{|-|}%
          (1.5,1.5){1.5}{60}{150}
\end{pspicture}
```

05-02-4

5.2.5 \psarcn

\psarcn is virtually identical to \psarc; the only difference is that the arc is drawn clockwise, or mathematically in a negative sense. You can't achieve this effect with \psarc by just swapping the angles – it still draws counterclockwise. \psarcn is very useful, especially with \pscustom (cf. page 121), which among other things deals with the drawing of closed polylines.

```
\psarcn * [settings]  {arrows}  {radius}{angle1}{angle2}
\psarcn * [settings]  {arrows} (x_M,y_M){radius}{angle1}{angle2}
```

If no centre point for the circle is specified, (0,0) is assumed by default. The starred version fills the area enclosed by the arc and the secant connecting the ends of the arc with the current line colour and filling pattern. As with \psarc, the showpoints=true option behaves differently to usual, drawing dashed lines from the centre point to the starting point and endpoint of the arc. In the example below, these lines aren't visible as the starred version of the command fills the area with solid colour.

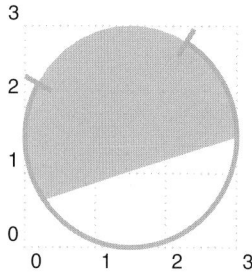

```
\usepackage{pstricks}

\begin{pspicture}[showgrid](3,3)
    \psarcn*[showpoints,linecolor=cyan]%
            (1.5,1.5){1.5}{215}{0}
    \psarcn[linecolor=red,linewidth=2pt]{|-|}%
           (1.5,1.5){1.5}{60}{150}
\end{pspicture}
```

05-02-5

5.2.6 \pswedge

\pswedge draws a circle sector starting at the first specified angle counterclockwise to the second angle.

```
\pswedge * [settings] {radius}{angle1}{angle2}
\pswedge * [settings] (xM,yM){radius}{angle1}{angle2}
```

If no centre point is specified, (0,0) is assumed by default. The starred version fills the inside of the circle sector with the current line colour and filling pattern.

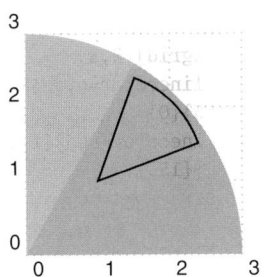

```
\usepackage{pstricks}

\begin{pspicture}[showgrid](3,3)
    \pswedge*[linecolor=red]{3}{0}{30}
    \pswedge*[linecolor=green]{3}{30}{60}
    \pswedge*[linecolor=cyan]{3}{60}{90}
    \pswedge(1,1){1.5}{20}{70}
\end{pspicture}
```

5.2.7 \psellipse

As mentioned earlier, the circle is a special case of an ellipse. Therefore the only difference between \pscircle and \psellipse is the extended radius specification: in the case of an ellipse you need to specify the lengths of the semi major and semi minor axes.

```
\psellipse * [settings] (a,b)
\psellipse * [settings] (xM,yM)(a,b)
```

If the centre of the ellipse is not specified, the coordinate origin (0,0) is assumed by default. The starred version fills the inside of the ellipse with the current line colour and filling pattern.

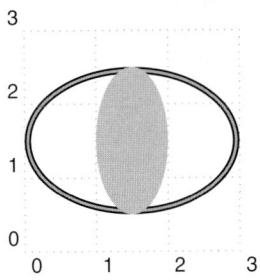

```
\usepackage{pstricks}

\begin{pspicture}[showgrid](3,3)
    \psellipse[linecolor=blue,doubleline=true,
        doublecolor=red](1.5,1.5)(1.5,1)
    \psellipse*[linecolor=cyan](1.5,1.5)(0.5,1)
\end{pspicture}
```

5.2.8 \psellipticarc

You can use \psellipticarc to draw ellipse arcs, and also to draw ellipse sectors by using the filling function. The ellipse arc is drawn in a mathematically positive sense, i.e. counterclockwise.

5 Circles, ellipses, and curves

```
\psellipticarc * [settings] {arrows} (a,b){angle1}{angle2}
\psellipticarc * [settings] {arrows} (xM,yM)(a,b){angle1}{angle2}
```

If the centre of the ellipse is not specified, the coordinate origin (0,0) is assumed by default. The starred version fills the area enclosed by the ellipse arc and the lines connecting the endpoints of the ellipse arc with the centre point with the current line colour and filling pattern. The showpoints option again behaves differently from usual; dashed lines are drawn from the centre point to the starting point and endpoint. Again in the example below these lines are not visible as the starred version of the command fills the area with solid colour.

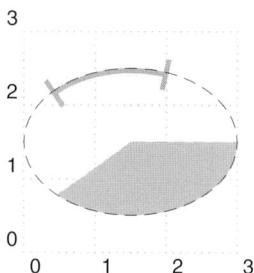

```
\usepackage{pstricks}

\begin{pspicture}[showgrid](3,3)
    \psellipticarc*[showpoints,
        linecolor=cyan](1.5,1.5)(1.5,1){215}{0}
    \psellipticarc[linecolor=red,
        linewidth=2pt]{|-|}(1.5,1.5)(1.5,1){60}{150}
    \psellipse[linestyle=dashed,
        linewidth=0.1pt](1.5,1.5)(1.5,1)
\end{pspicture}
```

05-02-8

5.2.9 \psellipticarcn

\psellipticarcn is virtually identical to \psellipticarc; the only difference is that the ellipse arc is drawn clockwise. You can't achieve this effect with \psellipticarc by just swapping the angles – it still draws counterclockwise. \psellipticarcn is very useful, especially with \pscustom (cf. page 121), which among other things deals with the drawing of closed polylines.

```
\psellipticarcn * [settings] {arrows} (a,b){angle1}{angle2}
\psellipticarcn * [settings] {arrows} (xM,yM)(a,b){angle1}{angle2}
```

If the centre of the ellipse is not specified, the coordinate origin (0,0) is assumed by default. The starred version fills the area enclosed by the ellipse arc and the lines connecting the endpoints of the ellipse arc with the centre point with the current line colour and filling pattern. As with \psellipticarc, the showpoints=true option behaves differently to usual, drawing dashed lines from the centre point to the starting point and endpoint of the arc. Again in the example below these lines are not visible as the starred version of the command fills the area with solid colour.

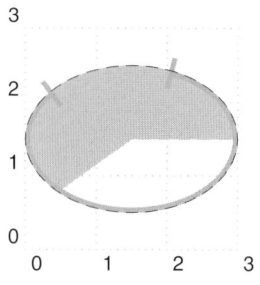

```
\usepackage{pstricks}

\begin{pspicture}[showgrid](3,3)
    \psellipticarcn*[showpoints=true,
        linecolor=cyan](1.5,1.5)(1.5,1){215}{0}
    \psellipticarcn[linecolor=red,
        linewidth=2pt]{|-|}(1.5,1.5)(1.5,1){60}{150}
    \psellipse[linestyle=dashed,
        linewidth=0.1pt](1.5,1.5)(1.5,1)
\end{pspicture}
```

05-02-9

5.2.10 \psellipticwedge

This command is virtually identical to \pswedge (Section 5.2.6 on page 63); the only difference is that it draws a sector of an ellipse rather than a sector of a circle.

```
\psellipticwedge * [settings] (a,b){angle1}{angle2}
\psellipticwedge * [settings] (x_M,y_M)(a,b){angle1}{angle2}
```

If the centre of the ellipse is not specified, the coordinate origin (0,0) is assumed by default. The starred version fills the inside of the ellipse sector with the current line colour and filling pattern.

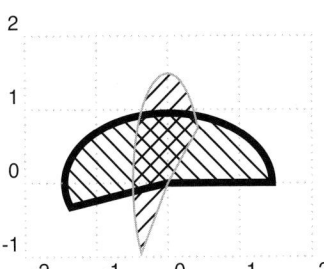

```
\usepackage{pstricks}

\begin{pspicture}[showgrid](-2.2,-1)(2.2,2)
    \psellipticwedge[fillstyle=vlines,
        linewidth=0.1](0,0)(1.5,1){0}{200}
    \psellipticwedge[fillstyle=hlines,
        linecolor=red](0,0)(0.5,1.5){30}{220}
\end{pspicture}
```

5.3 Curves

5.3.1 \psbezier and \pscbezier

Bezier curves are an important tool when drawing non-linear curves. PostScript itself has an internal command available to draw Bezier curves. PSTricks uses exactly the same algorithm to draw the curve, which is based on four points: a starting point, endpoint, and two middle *interpolation points* that usually just specify the curvature of the curve.[1]

```
\psbezier * [settings] {arrows} (x_1,y_1)(x_2,y_2)(x_3,y_3)
\psbezier * [settings] {arrows} (x_0,y_0)(x_1,y_1)(x_2,y_2)(x_3,y_3)
```

\pscbezier only differs in that it always closes the series of curves; the c in the name of the command stands for "closed". Therefore arrow options are not applicable here.

If only three points are given, the current point is assumed to be the starting point by default; if the Bezier curve doesn't connect to an existing series of curves, then the coordinate origin (0,0) is assumed by default. The starred version of \pscbezier fills the enclosed area with the current line colour and filling pattern. The starred version of \psbezier draws a connecting line from the end of the curve to the beginning before filling the enclosed area. So the starred versions of \psbezier and \pscbezier in fact produce identical results.

Within a \pscustom command a second or subsequent Bezier curve is assumed to start at the current point, so only requires three coordinate pairs.

---

[1] Bezier curves of a higher order are provided by the package pst-func, cf. Section 28.2.2 on page 524.

5 Circles, ellipses, and curves

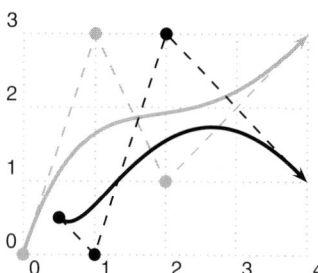

```
\usepackage{pstricks}

\begin{pspicture}[showgrid](4,3)
    \psbezier[linewidth=1.5pt,linecolor=red,
        showpoints=true]{->}(1,3)(2,1)(4,3)
    \psbezier[linewidth=1.5pt,linecolor=blue,
        showpoints=true]{->}(0.5,0.5)(1,0)(2,3)(4,1)
\end{pspicture}
```

05-03-1

The use of the starred version doesn't necessarily make sense as the resulting area is not always meaningful.

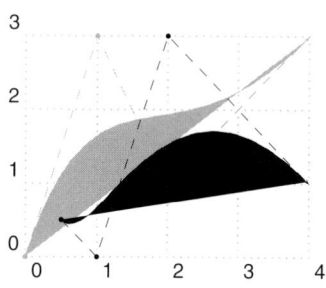

```
\usepackage{pstricks}% \psbezier

\begin{pspicture}[showgrid](4,3)
    \psbezier*[linewidth=1.5pt,linecolor=red,
        showpoints=true]{->}(1,3)(2,1)(4,3)
    \psbezier*[linewidth=1.5pt,linecolor=blue,
        showpoints=true]{->}(0.5,0.5)(1,0)(2,3)(4,1)
\end{pspicture}
```

05-03-2

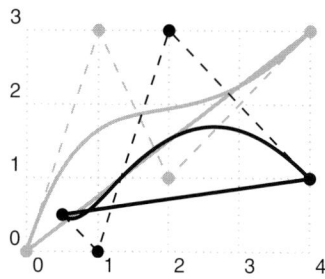

```
\usepackage{pstricks}

\begin{pspicture}[showgrid](4,3)
    \pscbezier[linewidth=1.5pt,linecolor=red,
        showpoints=true](1,3)(2,1)(4,3)
    \pscbezier[linewidth=1.5pt,linecolor=blue,
        showpoints=true](0.5,0.5)(1,0)(2,3)(4,1)
\end{pspicture}
```

05-03-3

5.3.2 \psparabola

This command requires the specification of the apex $S(x_S; y_S)$ and an arbitrary point on the curve $P(x_P; y_P)$ to draw a parabola. Starting at point P, the parabola is drawn through the apex and round as far as the mirror point of P.

\psparabola * [settings] {arrows} (x_P,y_P)(x_S,y_S)

The starred version fills the area starting at the apex up to ($y = y_P$) with the current line colour and filling pattern.

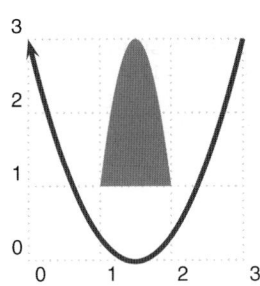

```
\usepackage{pstricks}

\begin{pspicture}[showgrid](3,3)
    \psparabola*[linecolor=cyan](1,1)(1.5,3)
    \psparabola[linecolor=blue,
        linewidth=2pt]{->}(3,3)(1.5,0)
\end{pspicture}
```

5.3.3 \pscurve

\pscurve requires the specification of at least three points on the curve in order to create the interpolation polynomial of second order that PSTricks uses to connect the points. Note: PSTricks does not produce an error message if fewer coordinate pairs are specified! However, the PostScript interpreter usually will point out that there is an error when it tries to display the output. ok

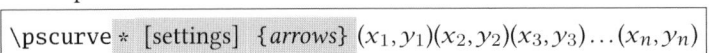

The starred version fills the area that results from connecting the endpoint of the curve with the starting point with the current line colour and filling pattern.

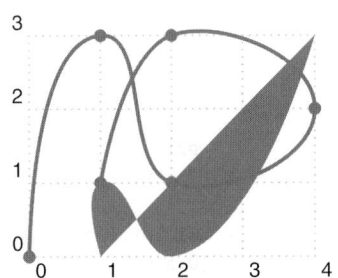

```
\usepackage{pstricks}

\begin{pspicture}[showgrid](4,3)
    \pscurve*[linecolor=cyan,
        linewidth=1.5pt](1,0)(1,1)(2,0)(4,3)
    \pscurve[linecolor=red,
        linewidth=1.5pt,showpoints=true]%
        (0,0)(1,3)(2,1)(4,2)(2,3)(1,1)
\end{pspicture}
```

5.3.4 \psecurve

\psecurve is an abbreviation for "end curve". It draws a curve connecting specified points like \pscurve, except that it doesn't plot the starting point and endpoint. This command also requires at least three points in order to create the interpolation polynomial (and again PSTricks doesn't produce an error message if fewer than three coordinate pairs are specified), but specifying only three points makes little sense anyway for \psecurve as it only plots the curve for $n - 2$ points! Using \psecurve, you can give the curve a defined behaviour at the "visible" endpoints (such as making the curve have a particular gradient at its start or end) as the true first and last points are not drawn; this isn't possible with \pscurve.

The following example plots a five-point curve using a seven-point specification in a \psecurve command, and also plots \pscurve with the same five points for comparison purposes. Another illustration of the \psecurve command is shown in Example 36-00-52 on page 789.

5 Circles, ellipses, and curves

```
\psecurve * [settings] {arrows} (x₁,y₁)(x₂,y₂)(x₃,y₃)...(xₙ,yₙ)
```

The starred version fills the area that results from connecting the endpoint of the curve with the starting point with the current line colour and filling pattern.

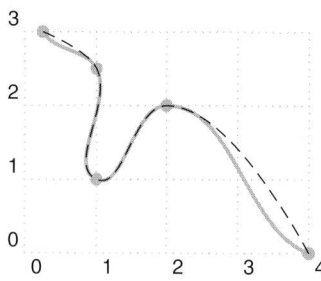

```
\usepackage{pstricks}

\begin{pspicture}[showgrid](4,3)
    \psecurve[showpoints=true,linecolor=red,
        linewidth=1.5pt]%
        (.125,5)(.25,3)(1,2.5)(1,1)(2,2)(4,0)(8,.125)
    \psecurve[linecolor=blue,
        linewidth=0.5pt,linestyle=dashed]%
        (0.25,3)(1,2.5)(1,1)(2,2)(4,0)
\end{pspicture}
```

05-03-6

5.3.5 \psccurve

\psccurve is an abbreviation of "closed curve". It creates a closed curve by extending the curve from the endpoint to the starting point. Again it requires at least three points in order to create the interpolation polynomial and, as with the other curve commands, PSTricks doesn't produce an error message if fewer than three coordinate pairs are specified!

```
\psccurve * [settings] (x₁,y₁)(x₂,y₂)(x₃,y₃)...(xₙ,yₙ)
```

The starred version fills the area that results from connecting the endpoint of the curve with the starting point with the current line colour and filling pattern.

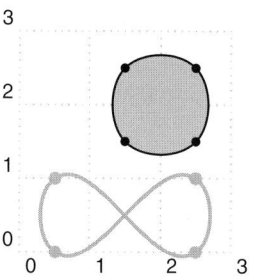

```
\usepackage{pstricks}

\begin{pspicture}[showgrid](3,3)
    \psccurve*[linecolor=cyan]%
        (1.5,1.5)(2.5,1.5)(2.5,2.5)(1.5,2.5)
    \psccurve[showpoints=true]%
        (1.5,1.5)(2.5,1.5)(2.5,2.5)(1.5,2.5)
    \psccurve[showpoints=true,linecolor=red,
        linewidth=1.5pt](.5,0)(2.5,1)(2.5,0)(.5,1)
\end{pspicture}
```

05-03-7

Chapter 6

Dots

6.1 Parameters. 69
6.2 \psdot and \psdots 72
6.3 T_EXnicalities 72

This section deals with any object that can be referenced through the dotstyle option, which defines it as a dot. Some of the 'dots', such as the vertical bar, would be better known as symbols since they can take on arbitrary forms and sizes – especially the symbols of the ZapfDingbats font as you can easily access the individual symbols through \ding{*number of character*}. As usual we look first at the available parameters and then at the \psdot and \psdots commands themselves. The final section in the chapter looks at defining new dots. Remember that the definitions of dot style and size affect the showpoints option (cf. Section 4.1.11 on page 50).

6.1 Parameters

The following table shows the parameters that affect the dot commands.

name	type	default
dotstyle	*style name* (cf. Table 6.2)	*
dotsize	*value unit* [*value*]	2pt 2
dotscale	*value1 value2*	1
dotangle	*angle*	0

Table 6.1: Summary of all parameters for dots with the \psdot and \psdots commands

6.1.1 dotstyle

There are many predefined styles for drawing dots, all of which are summarized in Table 6.2. The third column shows the corresponding starred version, which fills 'open' symbols with

6 Dots

the current line colour (available from PSTricks version 1.13). For presentation purposes, we've enlarged the symbols using dotscale=1.5 (cf. Section 6.1.3 on the next page). There are no limits to the additional symbols that you can define (cf. Section 6.3 on page 72).

Table 6.2: Summary of dot styles, where a preceeding B indicates a version with bold lines

name	\psdot	\psdot*	name	\psdot	\psdot*
*	● ● ●	● ● ●	o	○ ○ ○	● ● ●
Bo	○ ○ ○	● ● ●	x	× × ×	× × ×
+	+ + +	+ + +	B+	+ + +	+ + +
Add	+ + +	+ + +	BoldAdd	+ + +	+ + +
Oplus	⊕ ⊕ ⊕	● ● ●	BoldOplus	⊕ ⊕ ⊕	● ● ●
SolidOplus	⊕ ⊕ ⊕	● ● ●	Hexagon	○ ○ ○	● ● ●
BoldHexagon	○ ○ ○	● ● ●	SolidHexagon	● ● ●	● ● ●
asterisk	✳ ✳ ✳	✳ ✳ ✳	Basterisk	✳ ✳ ✳	✳ ✳ ✳
Asterisk	✳ ✳ ✳	✳ ✳ ✳	BoldAsterisk	✳ ✳ ✳	✳ ✳ ✳
SolidAsterisk	✴ ✴ ✴	● ● ●	oplus	⊕ ⊕ ⊕	⊕ ⊕ ⊕
otimes	⊗ ⊗ ⊗	⊗ ⊗ ⊗	Otimes	⊗ ⊗ ⊗	● ● ●
BoldOtimes	⊗ ⊗ ⊗	● ● ●	SolidOtimes	⊗ ⊗ ⊗	● ● ●
Mul	× × ×	× × ×	BoldMul	× × ×	× × ×
|	| | |	| | |	B|	| | |	| | |
Bar	| | |	| | |	BoldBar	| | |	| | |
Bullet	● ● ●	● ● ●	Circle	○ ○ ○	● ● ●
BoldCircle	○ ○ ○	● ● ●	square	□ □ □	■ ■ ■
Bsquare	□ □ □	■ ■ ■	square*	■ ■ ■	■ ■ ■
Square	□ □ □	■ ■ ■	BoldSquare	□ □ □	■ ■ ■
SolidSquare	■ ■ ■	■ ■ ■	diamond	◇ ◇ ◇	◆ ◆ ◆
Bdiamond	◇ ◇ ◇	◆ ◆ ◆	diamond*	◆ ◆ ◆	◆ ◆ ◆
Diamond	◇ ◇ ◇	◆ ◆ ◆	BoldDiamond	◇ ◇ ◇	◆ ◆ ◆
SolidDiamond	◆ ◆ ◆	◆ ◆ ◆	triangle	△ △ △	▲ ▲ ▲
Btriangle	△ △ △	▲ ▲ ▲	triangle*	▲ ▲ ▲	▲ ▲ ▲
Triangle	△ △ △	▲ ▲ ▲	BoldTriangle	△ △ △	▲ ▲ ▲
SolidTriangle	▲ ▲ ▲	▲ ▲ ▲	pentagon	⬠ ⬠ ⬠	⬟ ⬟ ⬟
Bpentagon	⬠ ⬠ ⬠	⬟ ⬟ ⬟	pentagon*	⬟ ⬟ ⬟	⬟ ⬟ ⬟
Pentagon	⬠ ⬠ ⬠	⬟ ⬟ ⬟	BoldPentagon	⬠ ⬠ ⬠	⬟ ⬟ ⬟
SolidPentagon	⬟ ⬟ ⬟	⬟ ⬟ ⬟	Hexagon	○ ○ ○	● ● ●
BoldHexagon	○ ○ ○	● ● ●	SolidHexagon	● ● ●	● ● ●
Octogon	○ ○ ○	● ● ●	BoldOctogon	○ ○ ○	● ● ●
SolidOctogon	● ● ●	● ● ●			

6.1 Parameters

6.1.2 dotsize

dotsize controls the height of the symbol, or the diameter in the case of circles. It is composed of the normal size specification and additionally (additively) an optional number that is a multiple of linewidth (cf. Section 4.1.1). This combination gives you the option of setting the symbol size with reference only to the linewidth if desired, as is done in the first of these two examples.

```
\usepackage{pstricks,pst-node}

\psdot[dotsize=0pt 10,dotstyle=square](0,0)%
\psdot[dotsize=0pt 10,dotstyle=square](2,0)%
\pcline[nodesep=5\pslinewidth,
    linewidth=10\pslinewidth](0,0)(2,0)
```

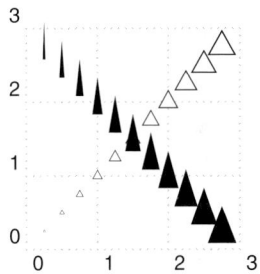

```
\usepackage{pstricks,multido}

\begin{pspicture}[showgrid](3,3)
    \multido{\nA=1+1,\rA=0.0+0.25}{12}{%
        \psdot[dotsize=\nA pt,dotstyle=o](\rA,\rA)}
    \psset{fillcolor=cyan}
    \multido{\nA=1+1,\rA=0.0+0.25,\rB=3+-0.25}{12}{%
        \psdot[dotsize=\nA pt \nA,dotstyle=o](\rA,\rB)}
\end{pspicture}
```

6.1.3 dotscale

dotscale uses one or two values to control the Scaling of dots. If you only specify one value, this scales the dot retaining its aspect ratio; otherwise the first value specifies the scaling in the horizontal direction and the second one in the vertical direction.

```
\usepackage{pstricks,multido}

\begin{pspicture}[showgrid](3,3)
    \multido{\rA=0.25+0.25}{11}{%
        \psdot[dotscale=\rA,dotstyle=triangle](\rA,\rA)}
    \multido{\rA=0.25+0.25,\rB=2.75+-0.25}{11}{%
        \psdot*[dotscale=\rA\space 4,
            dotstyle=triangle](\rA,\rB)}
\end{pspicture}
```

6.1.4 dotangle

After the application of other parameters such as dotsize and dotscale, you can then also rotate the symbol by the angle dotangle. The direction of the rotation is mathematically positive, i.e. counterclockwise commencing from the positive x direction.

71

6 Dots

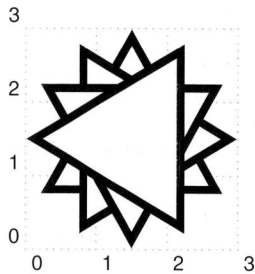

```
\usepackage{pstricks,multido}

\begin{pspicture}[showgrid](3,3)
    \multido{\nA=0+30}{12}{%
        \psdot[dotsize=2.25cm,dotstyle=triangle,
            dotangle=\nA](1.5,1.5)}
\end{pspicture}
```

06-01-5

6.2 \psdot and \psdots

As we said at the beginning of the chapter, any object that can be referenced through the dotstyle parameter (cf. Section 6.1.1 on page 69) is by definition a 'dot', so can be used with the \psdot and \psdots commands.

```
\psdot * [settings]
\psdot * [settings] (x,y)
\psdots * [settings] (x_1,y_1)(x_2,y_2)...(x_n,y_n)
```

```
\usepackage{pstricks}

\begin{pspicture}[showgrid](3,2)
    \psdot*[dotstyle=pentagon,dotscale=5](1.5,1.5)
    \psdots[dotsize=.4cm,dotstyle=square,
        linecolor=red](0,0)(0.5,0)(1,1)(1.5,1)(2,2)(2.5,2)
    \psdots*(2.5,0.6)\psdot(2.5,0.2)
\end{pspicture}
```

06-02-1

If no coordinates are specified, the current TeX coordinates are assumed by default, which correspond to the position of the text or to the coordinate origin (0,0) within a pspicture environment.

6.3 TeXnicalities

You can use the following commands to define customized dots.

```
\newpsfontdot{Name}[xS xW yW yS xO yO]{font name}{<n>}
\newpsfontdot{Name}[xS xW yW yS xO yO]{PSTricksDotFont}{(x)}
\newpsfontdotH{Name}[xSxW yW yS xO yO]{PSTricksDotFont}{(x)}{(y)}
```

The values of the second argument correspond to the elements of the *transformation matrix*, which are explained in Table 6.3, along with the other arguments.

Which PostScript fonts are available depends on the loaded driver and on the printer's character sets. Alternatively you can use the PSTricks internal PostScript font, PSTricksDotFont. Its characters are defined in the header file pst-dots.pro. To use a character from this font, you must specify its position number within the 256 characters of the font through the

6.3 TeXnicalities

Table 6.3: The parameters of the \newpsfontdot command

xS	x scale factor	xW	x shearing factor
yS	y scale factor	yW	y shearing factor
x0	x offset	y0	y offset
font name	PSTricks or PostScript font	n	character number (hexadecimal)
PSTricksDotFont	—	(x)	abbreviation character1
		(y)	abbreviation character2

corresponding ASCII character, for example (A) for the 65th character (for more details on this see page 74).

Using \newpsfontdotH, you can define new characters by overlaying two existing characters. One use for this is to overlay two symbols of different colours to achieve the impression of a 'dot' with line and fill colour chosen separately.

The PSTricksDotFont font is formally a Type 3 font, despite it being called a vector font! The definition of Type 3 only says that the font doesn't follow the Type 1 conventions – it does not indicate that it is a bitmap font that becomes pixellated at high magnifications. All the symbols defined in PSTricks have vector characters, even though they appear as Type 3 fonts in the font list. This is important to remember as many printers insist that the document contains bitmap fonts. The reason for the Type 3 convention is that for normal Type 1 characters it is not possible to choose line and fill colours separately.

In the following example we define and use three new symbols CircMultiply, CircPlus, and Flower in different variants. The symbols all come from the standard PostScript character sets: the first two are from the Symbol font (numbers 196 and 197) and the third one is from the ZapfDingbats font (number 96). [40] (The symbols also have internal definitions, which are used below.)

```
\usepackage{pstricks}
\newpsfontdot{CircMultiply}[2 0 0 2 -.78 -.7]{Symbol}{<C4>}
\newpsfontdot{CircPlus}[2 0 0 2 -.78 -.7]{Symbol}{<C5>}
\newpsfontdot{CircPlus45}[2 2 -2 2 -.78 -.7]{Symbol}{<C5>}
\newpsfontdot{Flower}[2 0 0 2 -.78 -.7]{ZapfDingbats}{<60>}
% ... see the TeX code for other definitions ...

\begin{pspicture}[showgrid](4,4)
  \psset{dotscale=2.5}          \psdot[dotstyle=Flower](4,0)
  \psdot[dotstyle=Flower45](4,1) \psdot[dotstyle=Flower90](4,2)
  \psdot[dotstyle=Flower135](4,3)\psdot[dotstyle=Flower180](4,4)
  \psdots[dotstyle=hFlower](0,0) \psdot[dotstyle=vFlower](1,1)
  \psdot[dotstyle=hvFlower](0,1) \psdot[dotstyle=xsFlower](2,2)
  \psdot[dotstyle=ysFlower](3,3) \psdot[dotstyle=dxyFlower](2,3)
  \psdot[dotstyle=ysFlower](2,4) \psdot[dotstyle=CircPlus](3,0)
  \psdots[dotstyle=CircPlus45](3,2)(1,2)(2,1)
  \psdots[dotstyle=CircMultiply](0,3)(0,4)(1,4)
\end{pspicture}
```

6 Dots

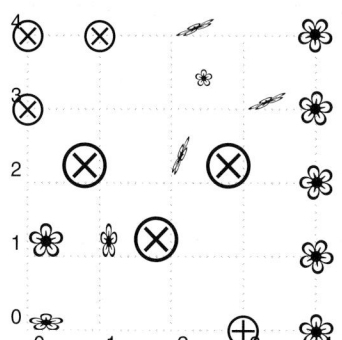

Finding the correct values for \newpsfontdot primarily depends on the base character itself and ultimately requires manual tuning; it is usually easier for axially symmetric characters.

Softfont   Usually there is a normal, bold, and solid variant for each character, which is attributed to the internal PSTricksDotFont font (which is a Softfont so is loaded into the printer's memory). Therefore three characters have to be defined; this is illustrated here using the example of an octagon, which we created as an example of adding a self-defined symbol while writing this book.

```
\newpsfontdot {SolidOctogon}[1 0 0 1 0 0]{PSTricksDotFont}{(g)}
\newpsfontdotH{Octogon}      [1 0 0 1 0 0]{PSTricksDotFont}{(f)}{(g)}
\newpsfontdotH{BoldOctogon} [1 0 0 1 0 0]{PSTricksDotFont}{(F)}{(g)}
```

SolidOctogon is a filled octagon. Octogon is a normal non-filled octagon, created from the overlay of two filled octagon characters, the larger of which is filled with the line colour, and the smaller of which is filled with white. BoldOctogon is similarly created from the overlay of two filled octagon characters, though the inner one is smaller in this case, which gives the impression of a bold character.

So even before creating these definitions, we had to define and map these characters in the PSTricksDotFont character set. The first step was to refer to the pst-dots.pro file, which lists all the predefined slots, to find three available slots. We found slots 103, 102, and 70 were available, corresponding to the characters (g), (f), and (F) in ASCII.

Next step was to add to pst-dots.pro both the specifications of the slots in the list of characters and the definition of the character itself. The specification of the slot is relatively easy:

```
...
dup (f) 0 get /Octogon put       % 2008-04-18 hv
dup (F) 0 get /BoldOctogon put   % 2008-04-18 hv
dup (g) 0 get /SolidOctogon put  % 2008-04-18 hv
...
```

The encoding vector that is already on the stack is *dup*licated; (f) 0 get places the ASCII code of the character (f) on the stack; and /Octogon put moves the name of the character to the appropriate position in the encoding vector.

The definition of the character uses the standard PostScript commands. Bear in mind when defining characters that PostScript assumes a 1000×1000 dot matrix; larger characters have to be scaled accordingly. The path for an octagon is:

```
/OctogonPath {
    550 dup 22.5 tan mul              % 8 * 45 angle triangles
    dup neg dup add /xMove exch def   % base side=xMove
    exch moveto                       % move to starting point
    7 { xMove 0 rlineto 45 rotate } repeat closepath } def
```

We use the fact that for one of the eight triangles in the octagon $\tan(22.5°) \cdot 550 \approx 227.82$ to control the path in PSTricks.

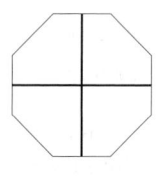

```
\usepackage{pstricks}

\psset{unit=0.05pt}% for pspicture and \psline
\begin{pspicture}(-550,-550)(550,550)
\psline(-550,0)(550,0)\psline(0,-550)(0,550)
\pscustom{
   \scale{0.05}%  for PS
   \moveto(227.82pt, 550pt)
   \code{7 \pslbrace -455.84 0 rlineto
         45 rotate \psrbrace repeat}
   \closepath \stroke[linewidth=2pt] }
\end{pspicture}
```

That has defined the path for an octagon, but we must also define the use of this path for the individual characters. Appropriate scales and and subsequent `fill` (or `eofill` in this case – cf. Section 7.1.3 on page 81) also need to be defined, otherwise the most recently used fill will be used. [40]

So `SolidOctogon` is a single octagon path, whereas `Octogon` and `BoldOctogon` comprise two octagon paths at different scales and with different fills.

```
/SolidOctogon { OctogonPath fill                                  } def
/Octogon {      OctogonPath .89 .89 scale OctogonPath eofill } def
/BoldOctogon {  OctogonPath .79 .79 scale OctogonPath eofill } def
```

This can be easily tested, for example for the normal and bold octagon:

```
\usepackage{pstricks}
\psset{unit=0.05pt}% for pspicture
\begin{pspicture}(-550,-550)(550,550)
\pscustom{ \scale{0.05} \moveto( 227.82pt, 550pt)
  \code{7 \pslbrace -455.84 0 rlineto 45 rotate \psrbrace repeat}
  \closepath   % now no fill!
  \scale{0.89} % now only 98%
  \moveto( 227.82pt, 550pt)
  \code{7 \pslbrace -455.84 0 rlineto 45 rotate \psrbrace repeat}
  \closepath \code{ eofill } \stroke }
\end{pspicture} \qquad \begin{pspicture}(-550,-550)(550,550)
\pscustom{ \scale{0.05} \moveto( 227.82pt, 550pt)
```

6 Dots

```
    \code{7 \pslbrace -455.84 0 rlineto 45 rotate \psrbrace repeat}
    \closepath \scale{0.79} \moveto( 222.82pt, 550pt)
    \code{7 \pslbrace -455.84 0 rlineto 45 rotate \psrbrace repeat}
    \closepath \code{ eofill } \stroke }
\end{pspicture}\\[10pt]
```

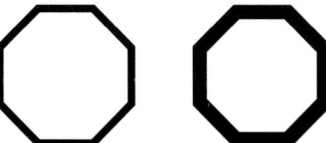

06-03-3

This completes the process for defining new 'dot' characters; to view the results of the definitions, look at the octagons in Table 6.2 on page 70. The effect of the dot matrix is shown in the following example.

```
\usepackage{pstricks}
\psset{dotscale=5}
\begin{pspicture}[showgrid](0,0.55)(4,3.49)
  \psdots[dotstyle=diamond](1,3)(2,3)(3,3)
  \psdots[dotstyle=diamond*](1,2)(2,2)(3,2)
  \psdots[dotstyle=Bdiamond](1,1)(2,1)(3,1)
\end{pspicture}
\qquad
\newpsfontdot{diamond}[1.9 -0.4 -0.9 1.5 -0.8 -0.70775]{Symbol}{<E0>}
\newpsfontdot{diamond*}[2.3 -0.6 0.8 2.3 -0.8533 -0.5336]{Symbol}{<A8>}
\newpsfontdotH{Bdiamond}[2.0 0.2 -0.5 -0.75 0.1 0.1     ]{PSTricksDotFont}{(D)}{(l)}
\begin{pspicture}[showgrid](0,0.55)(4,3.49)
  \psdots[dotstyle=diamond](1,3)(2,3)(3,3)
  \psdots[dotstyle=diamond*](1,2)(2,2)(3,2)
  \psdots[dotstyle=Bdiamond](1,1)(2,1)(3,1)
\end{pspicture}
\par\bigskip
\newpsfontdot{diamond}[1.5 0.0 0.0 1.9 -0.4598 -0.70775]{Symbol}{<E0>}
\newpsfontdot{diamond*}[2 0.0 0.0 2.3 -0.8533 -0.5336   ]{Symbol}{<A8>}
\newpsfontdotH{Bdiamond}[1.0 0.2 0.5 0.75 -0.1 0.1      ]{PSTricksDotFont}{(D)}{(l)}
\begin{pspicture}[showgrid](0,0.55)(4,3.49)
  \psdots[dotstyle=diamond](1,3)(2,3)(3,3)
  \psdots[dotstyle=diamond*](1,2)(2,2)(3,2)
  \psdots[dotstyle=Bdiamond](1,1)(2,1)(3,1)
\end{pspicture}
\qquad
\newpsfontdotH{diamond}[1.9 0.0 0.0 1.0 0.0 0.25]{PSTricksDotFont}{(d)}{(l)}
\newpsfontdot{diamond*}[0.5 0.0 0.0 1.0 0.0 0.0 ]{PSTricksDotFont}{(l)}
\newpsfontdotH{Bdiamond}[1.0 0.2 0.5 0.75 0.0 0.0]{PSTricksDotFont}{(D)}{(l)}
\begin{pspicture}[showgrid](0,0.55)(4,3.49)
  \psdots[dotstyle=diamond](1,3)(2,3)(3,3)
  \psdots[dotstyle=diamond*](1,2)(2,2)(3,2)
  \psdots[dotstyle=Bdiamond](1,1)(2,1)(3,1)
\end{pspicture}
```

06-03-4

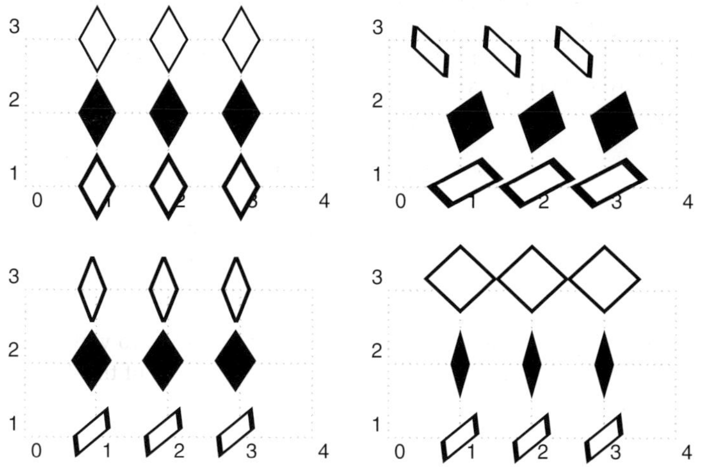

06-03-5

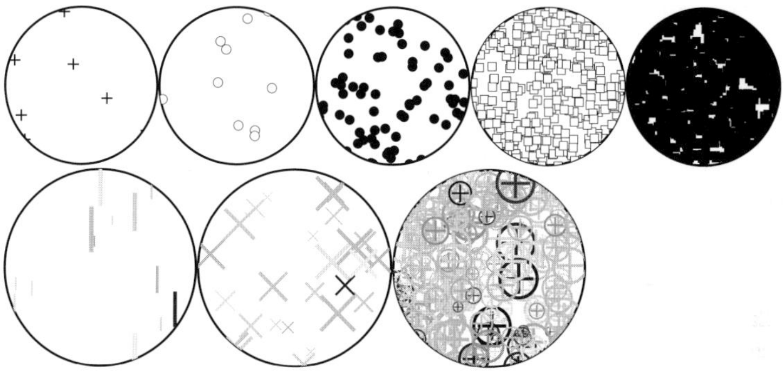

06-03-6

```
\usepackage{pstricks-add}

\psset{unit=2.5cm}
\begin{pspicture}(1,1)
  \psRandom(1,1){\pscircle(0.5,0.5){0.5}}
\end{pspicture}
```

06-03-7

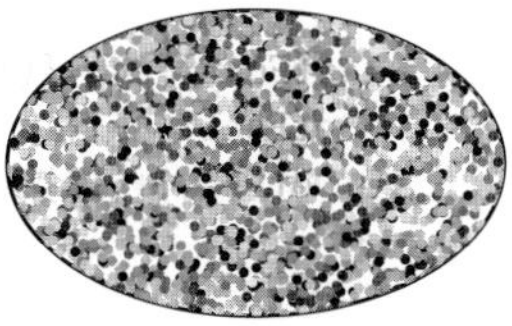

```
\usepackage{pstricks-add}

\psset{unit=3.5cm}
\begin{pspicture}(1,1)
 \psRandom[dotsize=2pt,randomPoints=5000,color,
    fillstyle=solid](1,1){%
      \psellipse(0.5,0.5)(0.5,0.3){0.5}}
\end{pspicture}
```

6 Dots

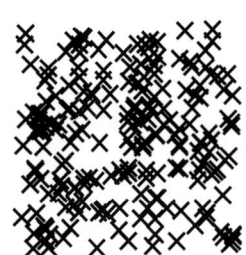

```
\usepackage{pstricks-add}

\psset{unit=3cm}
\begin{pspicture}(1,1)
  \psRandom[randomPoints=200,dotsize=8pt,
     dotangle=45,dotstyle=+]{}
\end{pspicture}
```

06-03-8

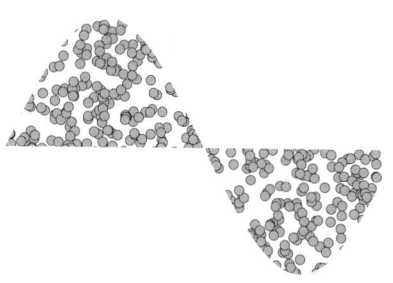

```
\usepackage{pstricks-add}

\psset{unit=1.75cm}
\begin{pspicture}(0,-1)(3,1)
  \psRandom[dotsize=4pt,dotstyle=o,
    linecolor=blue,fillcolor=red,
    fillstyle=solid,
    randomPoints=1000](0,-1)(3,1){%
    \psplot[linestyle=none]%
      {0}{3.14}{ x 114 mul sin }}
\end{pspicture}
```

06-03-9

Chapter 7

Filling

7.1 Parameters. 79
7.2 "Semi-transparent" colours 89
7.3 Circular colour gradients 90

As a rule, only areas that are formed by a closed polyline can be filled with a colour or a pattern. If you specify filling for a non-closed polyline through an appropriate parameter, a line is drawn automatically from the last point to the first point – which usually leads to undesired results. This chapter looks at the parameters available for filling areas without loading additional packages, and then discusses a couple of tricks for creating fills that are not quite all they appear! The gradient fill style is covered in Chapter 22.1 on page 317 as it requires either the `pst-grad` or `pst-slpe` package to be loaded. Filling with patterns or tiles is described in Chapter 19 on page 295 as it requires the `pst-fill` package.

When using one of the options for making transparent lines, curves, or areas described below, you must bear in mind that PostScript itself doesn't support transparency. Therefore the output has to be in PDF format version 1.4 or higher. This is especially important for TeX systems in Linux because the ps2pdf programme usually creates PDF output of version 1.2, which is unable to process transparency. So you must either specify version=14 when running ps2pdf, use ps2pdf14 instead, or use ps2pdfwr as long as the command line option dCompatibilityLevel=1.4 is passed. If you want to use Adobe's Distiller to create PDF output instead of using ghostscript, you must specify the `distiller` option when loading PSTricks. Users of pure TeX must manually copy the corresponding code from `pstricks.sty` and paste it into `pstricks.tex` or another file. LaTeX users can disable transparency completely by setting the `vtex` package option as the VTeX system doesn't support transparency.

7.1 Parameters

Table 7.1 on the following page summarizes all important parameters when dealing with transparent lines and curves and transparent or non-transparent area fills. The following sections look at each parameter in turn, in the order listed in the table.

7 Filling

Table 7.1: Summary of all parameters for filling areas

name	value	default
fillcolor	colour	white
psscale	value	1
fillstyle	none|solid|vlines|vlines*|hlines|hlines*|eofill penrose|penrose*|crosshatch|crosshatch*|boxfill|shape	none
shapealpha	value	0.6
hatchsep	value unit	4pt
hatchsepinc	value unit	0pt
hatchwidth	value unit	0.8pt
hatchwidthinc	value unit	0pt
hatchcolor	colour	black
hatchangle	angle	45
addfillstyle	none|solid|vlines|vlines*|hlines|hlines*| penrose|penrose*|crosshatch|crosshatch*|boxfill	none
opacity	0...1	1
strokeopacity	0...1	1

7.1.1 fillcolor

fillcolor determines the fill colour for the fill styles solid, shape, vlines*, hlines*, and crosshatch*.

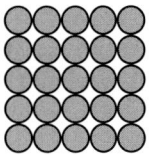

```
\usepackage{pstricks,multido}

\begin{pspicture}(2,2)
\multido{\rRow=0.2+0.4}{5}{\multido{\rCol=0.2+0.4}{5}{%
    \pscircle[fillstyle=solid,fillcolor=red](\rRow,\rCol){0.2}}}
\end{pspicture}
```

07-01-1

7.1.2 psscale

The value of psscale scales the fill pattern only on PostScript level. It hasn't any effect on TEX level for labels, etc. For an example of it in use, see Example 07-01-10 on page 83.

7.1.3 fillstyle

none

This fill style fills an area with "no" style. This might appear to be contradictory, but this option can be useful when disabling the filling of parts of a whole area in complex PSTricks figures for testing purposes.

solid

solid is the default fill style and fills the whole area with the current fill colour. If the fill colour is the same as the line colour, then this corresponds to using the starred version.

7.1 Parameters

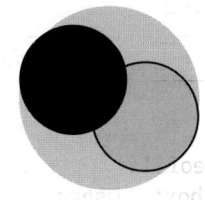

```
\usepackage{pstricks}

\begin{pspicture}(2.5,2.5)
    \pscircle*[linecolor=black!30](1.25,1.25){1.25}
    \pscircle[fillstyle=solid,fillcolor=red](1.75,1){0.75}
    \pscircle*(0.75,1.5){0.75}
\end{pspicture}
```

eofill

eofill specifies the "even–odd" rule for filling a closed object.

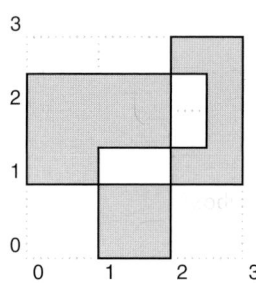

```
\usepackage{pstricks}

\begin{pspicture}[showgrid](3,3)
    \pspolygon[fillstyle=eofill,
            fillcolor=blue!30]%
    (0,1)(3,1)(3,3)(2,3)(2,0)(1,0)(1,1.5)%
    (2.5,1.5)(2.5,2.5)(0,2.5)
\end{pspicture}
```

vlines and vlines*

vlines stands for *vertical lines* and fills the whole area with vertical lines of the current fill colour (while leaving the rest of the area transparent). The rotation angle hatchangle (cf. Section 7.1.9 on page 86) is set to $45°$ by definition; if actual vertical lines are desired, it has to be corrected accordingly.

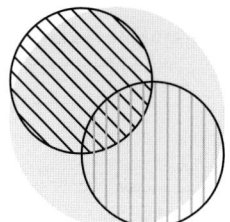

```
\usepackage{pstricks}

\begin{pspicture}(3,3)
    \pscircle*[linecolor=gray!20](1.5,1.5){1.5}
    \pscircle[fillstyle=vlines](1,2){1}
    \pscircle[fillstyle=vlines,hatchcolor=red,
            hatchangle=0](2,1){1}
\end{pspicture}
```

While the vlines option creates a transparent filling, the starred version vlines* behaves in the opposite way – first the background is filled with the colour defined through fillcolor and then this is overlaid with the "normal" vlines style.

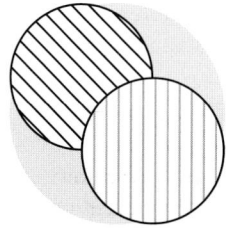

```
\usepackage{pstricks}

\begin{pspicture}(3,3)
    \pscircle*[linecolor=gray!20](1.5,1.5){1.5}
    \pscircle[fillstyle=vlines*](1,2){1}
    \pscircle[fillstyle=vlines*,hatchcolor=red,
            hatchangle=0](2,1){1}
\end{pspicture}
```

7 Filling

hlines and hlines∗

hlines (horizontal lines) works analogously to vlines and vlines∗ so no further explanations are necessary.

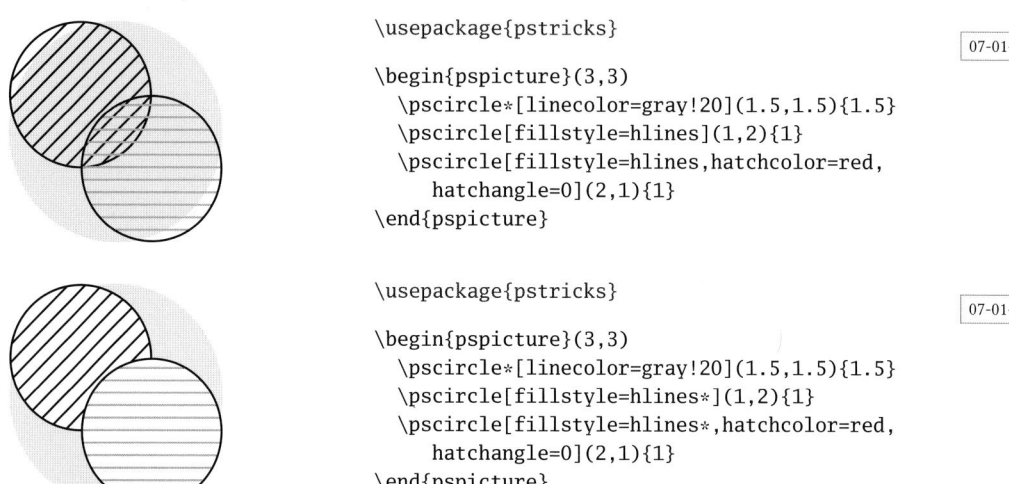

```
\usepackage{pstricks}

\begin{pspicture}(3,3)
  \pscircle*[linecolor=gray!20](1.5,1.5){1.5}
  \pscircle[fillstyle=hlines](1,2){1}
  \pscircle[fillstyle=hlines,hatchcolor=red,
      hatchangle=0](2,1){1}
\end{pspicture}
```

07-01-6

```
\usepackage{pstricks}

\begin{pspicture}(3,3)
  \pscircle*[linecolor=gray!20](1.5,1.5){1.5}
  \pscircle[fillstyle=hlines*](1,2){1}
  \pscircle[fillstyle=hlines*,hatchcolor=red,
      hatchangle=0](2,1){1}
\end{pspicture}
```

07-01-7

crosshatch and crosshatch∗

crosshatch (crossed lines) is a combination of vlines and hlines, and also works analogously.

```
\usepackage{pstricks}

\begin{pspicture}(3,3)
  \pscircle*[linecolor=gray!20](1.5,1.5){1.5}
  \pscircle[fillstyle=crosshatch](1,2){1}
  \pscircle[fillstyle=crosshatch,hatchcolor=red,
      hatchangle=0](2,1){1}
\end{pspicture}
```

07-01-8

```
\usepackage{pstricks}

\begin{pspicture}(3,3)
  \pscircle*[linecolor=gray!20](1.5,1.5){1.5}
  \pscircle[fillstyle=crosshatch*](1,2){1}
  \pscircle[fillstyle=crosshatch*,
      hatchcolor=red,hatchangle=0](2,1){1}
\end{pspicture}
```

07-01-9

penrose and penrose∗

The penrose fill style was named after Roger Penrose and creates a non-periodic tiling. For more information on this topic, see Chapter 19 on page 295. The only parameters that affect this fill style are hatchcolor and psscale. The starred version penrose∗ works either in combination with a non-white fillcolor or when the background colour is not white.

7.1 Parameters

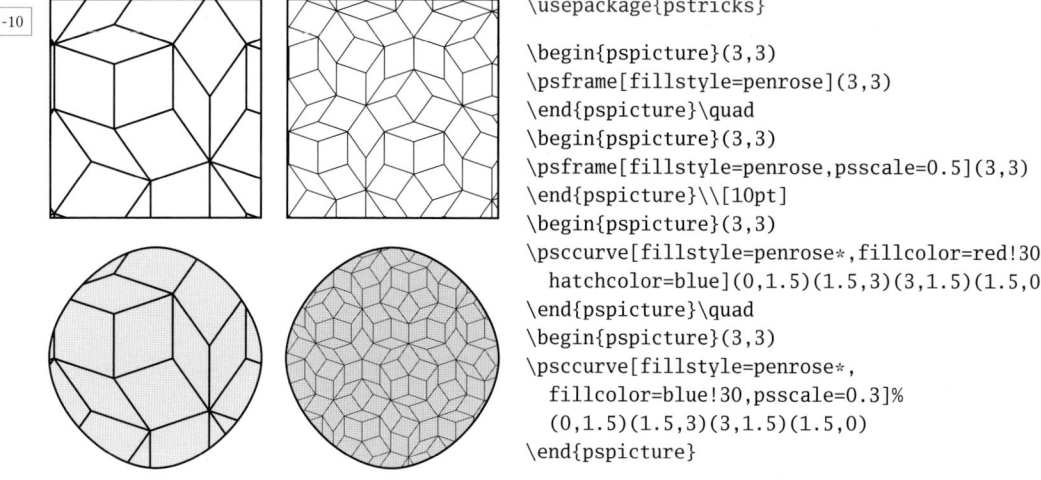

```
\usepackage{pstricks}

\begin{pspicture}(3,3)
\psframe[fillstyle=penrose](3,3)
\end{pspicture}\quad
\begin{pspicture}(3,3)
\psframe[fillstyle=penrose,psscale=0.5](3,3)
\end{pspicture}\\[10pt]
\begin{pspicture}(3,3)
\psccurve[fillstyle=penrose*,fillcolor=red!30,
   hatchcolor=blue](0,1.5)(1.5,3)(3,1.5)(1.5,0)
\end{pspicture}\quad
\begin{pspicture}(3,3)
\psccurve[fillstyle=penrose*,
   fillcolor=blue!30,psscale=0.3]%
   (0,1.5)(1.5,3)(3,1.5)(1.5,0)
\end{pspicture}
```

boxfill

boxfill refers to the tilings available from the `pst-fill` package, so we won't discuss it further here except to give an example. For more information, see Chapter 19 on page 295.

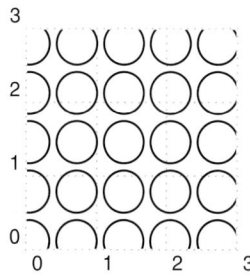

```
\usepackage{pstricks,pst-fill}

\def\Circle{%
   \pspicture(0.6,0.6)%
      \pscircle(0.3,0.3){0.3}
   \endpspicture}
\begin{pspicture}[showgrid](3,3)
   \psboxfill{\Circle}
   \psframe[fillstyle=boxfill](3,3)
\end{pspicture}
```

shape and shapealpha

Using the shape fill style and the specification of a value for the *blendmode*, various types of transparent fill are possible. Alternative transparency options are available using the `strokeopacity` and `opacity` commands (cf. Sections 7.1.11 on page 87 and 7.1.12 on page 88). GhostScript supports four different modes for *blendmode*, which can be specified by assigning a numeric value to the blendmode option. *from version 1.20*

/Normal->0   /Compatible->1   /Screen->2   /Multiply->3

Acrobat's Distiller supports additional modes, but these are too complex to be dealt with in this book. Remember that you must specify the `distiller` option when loading PSTricks if you want to use Distiller rather than GhostScript for PDF output. The default value for shapealpha is 0.6, which corresponds to a "normal" transparency.

7 Filling

```
\usepackage{pst-fill}  \psset{unit=0.65}
\begin{pspicture}(5,5)% default blendmode
  \psframe*[linecolor=red](0,1)(3,4)
  \psframe[fillcolor=blue,fillstyle=shape](2,2)(5,5)
  \psframe[fillcolor=green,fillstyle=shape](1,0)(4,3)
  \pscircle[fillcolor=cyan,fillstyle=shape,shapealpha=0.3](1.5,3.5){1.25}
  \rput(1.5,3.5){\huge\textbf{0}}
\end{pspicture}
\begin{pspicture}(5,5)
  \psset{blendmode=1}% type /Compatible
  \psframe*[linecolor=red](0,1)(3,4)
  \psframe[fillcolor=blue,fillstyle=shape](2,2)(5,5)
  \psframe[fillcolor=green,fillstyle=shape](1,0)(4,3)
  \pscircle[fillcolor=cyan,fillstyle=shape,shapealpha=0.3](1.5,3.5){1.25}
  \rput(1.5,3.5){\huge\textbf{1}}
\end{pspicture}
\begin{pspicture}(5,5)
  \psset{blendmode=2}% type /Screen
  \psframe*[linecolor=red](0,1)(3,4)
  \psframe[fillcolor=blue,fillstyle=shape](2,2)(5,5)
  \psframe[fillcolor=green,fillstyle=shape](1,0)(4,3)
  \pscircle[fillcolor=cyan,fillstyle=shape,shapealpha=0.3](1.5,3.5){1.25}
  \rput(1.5,3.5){\huge\textbf{2}}
\end{pspicture}
\begin{pspicture}(5,5)
  \psset{blendmode=3}% type /Multiply
  \psframe*[linecolor=red](0,1)(3,4)
  \psframe[fillcolor=blue,fillstyle=shape](2,2)(5,5)
  \psframe[fillcolor=green,fillstyle=shape](1,0)(4,3)
  \pscircle[fillcolor=cyan,fillstyle=shape,shapealpha=0.3](1.5,3.5){1.25}
  \rput(1.5,3.5){\huge\textbf{3}}
\end{pspicture}
```

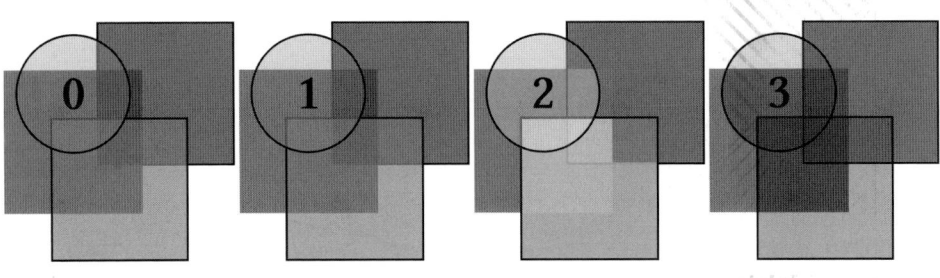

7.1.4 hatchsep

hatchsep determines the distance between two adjacent lines for the vlines, hlines, and crosshatch fill styles, and their starred versions. In the example below both of the "incomplete" polylines are closed by PSTricks to get a definite fill area, which it does by creating a line (which is not displayed) from the endpoint to the starting point.

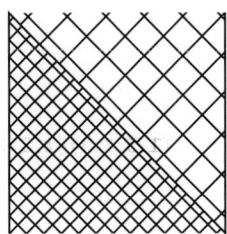

```
\usepackage{pstricks}

\begin{pspicture}(3,3)
  \psline[fillstyle=crosshatch](0,0)(0,3)(3,0)
  \psline[fillstyle=crosshatch,hatchsep=10pt]%
      (3,3)(3,0)(0,3)
\end{pspicture}
```

7.1.5 hatchsepinc

hatchsepinc lets you gradually increase the distance between each pair of adjacent lines by setting an increment for the line distance for the vlines, hlines, and crosshatch fill styles, and their starred versions.

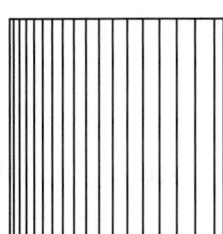

```
\usepackage{pstricks}

\begin{pspicture}(3,3)
  \psframe[fillstyle=vlines,hatchangle=0,
     hatchsep=1pt,hatchsepinc=0.175pt](3,3)
\end{pspicture}
```

7.1.6 hatchwidth

hatchwidth determines the line width for the vlines, hlines, and crosshatch fill styles, and their starred versions. Again in the example both "incomplete" polylines of \psline are closed by PSTricks to get a definite fill area, by creating a line (which is not displayed) from the endpoint to the starting point.

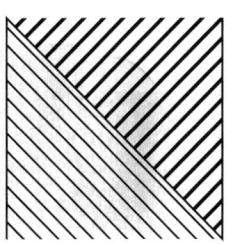

```
\usepackage{pstricks}

\begin{pspicture}(3,3)
  \psline[fillstyle=vlines](0,0)(0,3)(3,0)
  \psline[fillstyle=hlines,hatchwidth=1.5pt]%
      (3,3)(3,0)(0,3)
\end{pspicture}
```

7.1.7 hatchwidthinc

hatchwidthinc lets you gradually increment the line width for the fill styles vlines, hlines, and crosshatch, and their starred versions. This option can be used to achieve a continuous increase of the width of single lines. Internally PSTricks tries to keep the ratio of the line width to the distance between the lines constant, which means that hatchsep, too, is changed dynamically and can't be specified as a constant. Only the start value can be chosen freely (as shown in this example).

7 Filling

```
\usepackage{pstricks}

\begin{pspicture}(3,3)
  \psframe[fillstyle=vlines,
    hatchsep=1pt,hatchwidthinc=0.5pt](3,3)
\end{pspicture}
```

7.1.8 hatchcolor

hatchcolor determines the line colour for the vlines, hlines, and crosshatch fill styles, and their starred versions. Again in the example both "incomplete" polylines of \psline are closed by PSTricks to get a definite fill area, by creating a line (which is not displayed) from the endpoint to the starting point.

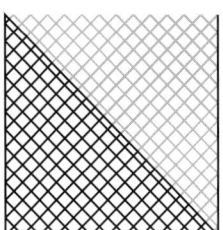

```
\usepackage{pstricks}

\begin{pspicture}(3,3)
  \psline[fillstyle=crosshatch,
    hatchcolor=blue](0,0)(0,3)(3,0)
  \psline[fillstyle=crosshatch,
    hatchcolor=red](3,3)(3,0)(0,3)
\end{pspicture}
```

7.1.9 hatchangle

hatchangle determines the gradient of the lines for the vlines, hlines, and crosshatch fill styles, and their starred versions. Because of rounding problems not all angle specifications work; the existing code would have to be modified to allow for any arbitrary angle. Again in the example both "incomplete" polylines of \psline are closed by PSTricks to get a definite fill area, by creating a line (which is not displayed) from the endpoint to the starting point.

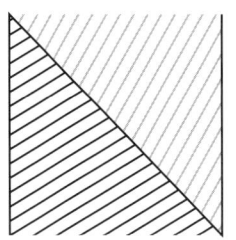

```
\usepackage{pstricks}

\begin{pspicture}(3,3)
  \psline[fillstyle=hlines,hatchcolor=blue,
    hatchangle=30](0,0)(0,3)(3,0)
  \psline[fillstyle=hlines,hatchcolor=red,
    hatchangle=60](3,3)(3,0)(0,3)
\end{pspicture}
```

7.1.10 addfillstyle

addfillstyle adds an additional fill style on top of the existing fill. This creates many possibilities for filling areas, especially when \psboxfill is used in a combination with addfillstyle. However, you need to apply the styles in the right order: the "normal" fill style *must* be assigned before addfillstyle, and the boxfill fill style **must** be assigned to addfillstyle.

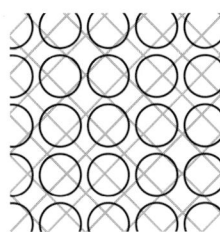

```
\usepackage{pstricks,pst-fill}

\def\Circle{\pspicture(0.6,0.6)%
    \pscircle(0.3,0.3){0.3}\endpspicture}
\begin{pspicture}(3,3)
  \psboxfill{\Circle}
  \psframe[fillstyle=crosshatch,
    addfillstyle=boxfill,
    hatchsep=10pt,hatchcolor=red](3,3)
\end{pspicture}
```

7.1.11 strokeopacity

PostScript itself does not provide functions that support transparency. With the help of ghostscript or Distiller, however, you can achieve transparency of lines and areas for PDF output. Remember that if you want to use Adobe's Distiller, you must specify the distiller option when loading PSTricks When using the VTEX compiler, you must load PSTricks with the vtex option, as VTEX does not (currently) support transparency at all.

since version 1.20

VTEX

strokeopacity allows you to set transparency for lines. This option is independent from the opacity option (cf. next section), which sets transparency when filling areas. The "strength" of the transparency is defined by a numeric value between 0 (total transparency) and 1 (no transparency). The default value is 1, corresponding to normal behaviour with no transparency.

```
\usepackage{pstricks}
\psset{unit=0.75}

\begin{pspicture}[linewidth=1cm](4,4)
  \psline[linecolor=red](0,0)(4,4)
  \psline[linecolor=blue,strokeopacity=0.5](0,4)(4,0)
  \psline[linecolor=green,
    strokeopacity=0.5](0,3.5)(4,3.5)
  \psline[linecolor=yellow,
    strokeopacity=0.5](0,0.5)(4,0.5)
\end{pspicture}
```

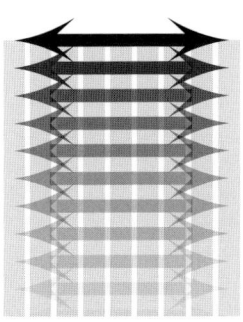

```
\usepackage{pstricks,multido}
\psset{unit=0.75}

\begin{pspicture}[linewidth=3mm](4,5.5)
  \multido{\rA=0.0+0.5}{9}{%
    \psline[linecolor=red!40](\rA,0)(\rA,5)}
  \multido{\rA=0.0+0.5,\rB=0.0+0.1}{11}{%
    \psline[arrows=<D-D>,linecolor=blue,
      linewidth=5pt,arrowscale=1.5,
      strokeopacity=\rB](0,\rA)(4,\rA)}
\end{pspicture}
```

7 Filling

7.1.12 opacity

When using the solid fill style, you can assign a value between 0 and 1 to the opacity option to achieve total, partial, or no transparency. The default value is 1, corresponding to no transparency.

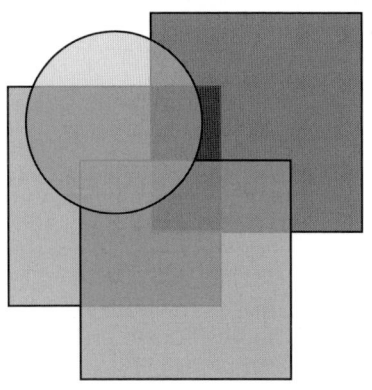

```
\usepackage{pstricks,multido}

\begin{pspicture}(5,5)
 \psset{fillstyle=solid}
 \psframe[fillcolor=red](0,1)(3,4)
 \psframe[fillcolor=blue,opacity=0.7](2,2)(5,5)
 \psframe[fillcolor=green,opacity=0.7](1,0)(4,3)
 \pscircle[fillcolor=cyan,
     opacity=0.5](1.5,3.5){1.25}
\end{pspicture}
```

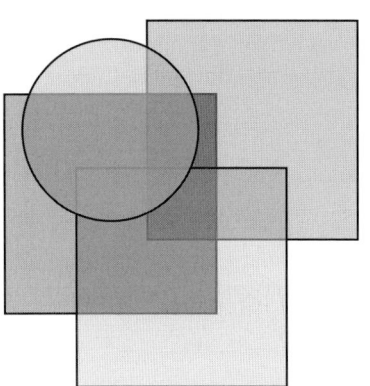

```
\usepackage{pstricks,multido}

\begin{pspicture}(5,5)
 \psset{fillstyle=solid}
 \psframe[fillcolor=red](0,1)(3,4)
 \psframe[fillcolor=blue,opacity=0.3](2,2)(5,5)
 \psframe[fillcolor=green,opacity=0.3](1,0)(4,3)
 \pscircle[fillcolor=cyan,
     opacity=0.5](1.5,3.5){1.25}
\end{pspicture}
```

Remember that the transparency of lines and curves doesn't depend on the fill function so has to be set separately through strokeopacity; different values for both options are possible.

```
\usepackage{pstricks}
\psset{unit=0.75}

\begin{pspicture}[linewidth=1cm](4,4)
  \psline[linecolor=red](0,0)(4,4)
  \pscircle*[opacity=0.5](2,2){2}
  \psline[linecolor=blue,
     strokeopacity=0.6](0,4)(4,0)
\end{pspicture}
```

7.2 "Semi-transparent" colours

 Transparent fill styles should be displayable by all current PDF viewers, independent of the underlying operating system. However, as we mentioned at the beginning of this chapter, the output has to be in PDF format version 1.4 or higher, so you must either use ps2pdfwr with the command line option dCompatibilityLevel=1.4, use ps2pdf14 (which automatically takes this option into account), or specify version=14 when running ps2pdf. Also remember that when using Adobe's Distiller, you must load pstricks with the distiller option specified, because the default GhostScript commands have no effect here.

7.2 "Semi-transparent" colours

If the methods presented in this chapter for creating transparent colours are not available, you can create the optical illusion of "transparency" with a narrow line pattern. With the help of the fill style options, you can put the fill lines so close together that they no longer look like a line pattern, but the underlying colour remains visible. To achieve this, it is best to set up a small command \defineTColor to define a corresponding new style (cf. Section 11.1 on page 121).

```
%% defining a "transparent colour"
\def\defineTColor#1#2{%
  \newpsstyle{#1}{%
    fillstyle=vlines,hatchcolor=#2,
    hatchwidth=0.1\pslinewidth,
    hatchsep=1\pslinewidth}%
}
```

When the pstricks-add package (cf. Chapter 30 on page 581) is loaded, this command is already available, although it is still possible to overwrite the definition. The parameters are the style name (#1) and the base colour (#2), which has to be defined. Bear in mind that moiré effects can occur when printing the figure as the lines may be superimposed badly. Alternatives are to use different angles of fill lines or the crosshatch fill style. For a more in-depth look at transparent colours, see Section 34.1 on page 739.

```
\usepackage{pstricks-add}

\defineTColor{tRot}{red}
\defineTColor{tCyan}{cyan}
\begin{pspicture}(0,-0.25)(5,5.25)
  \rput(2.5,2.5){%
    \psframebox[doubleline=true,
       framearc=0.3]{%
        \Huge\textsf{ PostScript}}}
  \rput{-40}(1,1){%
    \psframe[style=tRot](2.5,4)}
  \rput{40}(2.5,1){%
    \psframe[style=tCyan](2.5,4)}
\end{pspicture}
```

7 Filling

7.3 Circular colour gradients

You need pst-slpe (cf. Section 22.2 on page 320) to achieve circular colour gradients, but you can create the illusion of a circular colour gradient in an easy way with a series of overlaid fills, as shown in this example .

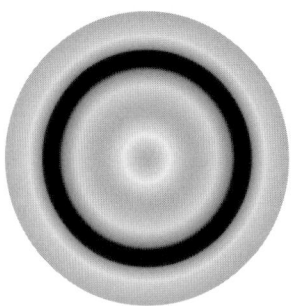

```
\usepackage{pstricks,multido}

\begin{pspicture}(-3,-3)(3,3)
\psset{unit=2}%
\multido{\rHue=0.01+0.01}{100}{%
  \pscircle[linewidth=0.01,
    linecolor={[hsb]{\rHue,1,1}}]{\rHue}}
\end{pspicture}
```

07-03-1

The Example 07-03-1 can be defined as a macro and then be used in conjunction with psclip as a fill style (cf. Section 10.4.2 on page 115).

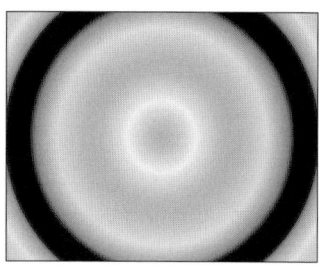

```
\usepackage{pstricks,multido}
\def\kreisFuellung#1{\psset{unit=#1}%
  \begin{pspicture}(-1,-1)(1,1)
    \multido{\rHue=0.01+0.01}{100}{%
      \pscircle[linewidth=0.01,
        linecolor={[hsb]{\rHue,1,1}}]{\rHue}}
  \end{pspicture}}

\begin{pspicture}(4.4,3.4)
\begin{psclip}{\psframe(4.4,3.4)}
    \rput(2.2,1.7){\kreisFuellung{3}}
\end{psclip}
\end{pspicture}
```

07-03-2

Chapter 8

Arrows

8.1 Parameters. 92
8.2 Extensions 96

PSTricks provides a large number of predefined "arrows", which are summarized in Table 8.2. By the term "arrow", we mean any method of beginning and ending lines, which includes regular arrows and other line end markers. You can specify "arrows" for any "open" polyline or curve; this refers to the definition of the command and therefore includes the case where a polyline has the same start and end point. There are three ways to specify an "arrow": through the key-value interface; through the special {*arrows*} option, if applicable under the respective command (cf. Section 4.1.10 on page 49); and globally through \psset (cf. Section 2.2 on page 21).

```
\psline{->}(3,3)
\psline[arrows=->](3,3)
{ \psset{arrows=->}\psline(3,3) }
```

All three ways are equivalent; remember that the specification with \psset has to be put into a group to keep the change local. If several definitions occur at the same time, only the last one is valid, as shown in the following example. For the final line, the arrow -> is defined first and then <-. The order is relevant because the order of the options during input corresponds to this order, so it is the second (final) option that is used.

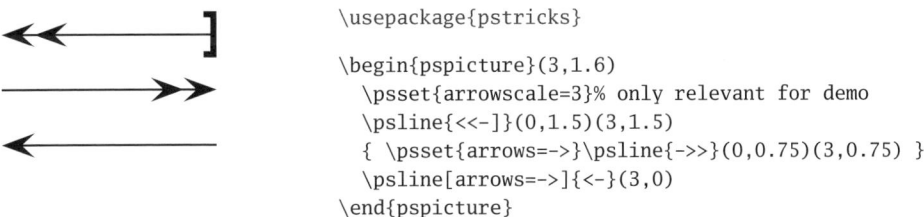

```
\usepackage{pstricks}

\begin{pspicture}(3,1.6)
  \psset{arrowscale=3}% only relevant for demo
  \psline{<<-]}(0,1.5)(3,1.5)
  { \psset{arrows=->}\psline{->>}(0,0.75)(3,0.75) }
  \psline[arrows=->]{<-}(3,0)
\end{pspicture}
```

You can use various parameters to influence line endings. Table 8.1 on the following page summarizes the options available without additional packages. The following sections

8 Arrows

then look at each one in turn, in the order presented in the table. The final sections in this chapter look at defining your own arrows, special options for multiarrows, and extra arrow possibilities that are available when the `pstricks-add` package is loaded.

8.1 Parameters

The first four parameters in Table 8.1 influence the style and specification of the tip of the regular arrow, while the next three influence the size ratio of T-bars and square and round brackets. You can use the final parameter, `arrowscale`, with all "arrows".

Table 8.1: Summary of all parameters available for arrows (with the base packages loaded)

name	type	default
arrows	*style* (cf. Table 8.2)	–
arrowsize	*value unit value*	1.5pt 2
arrowlength	*value*	1.4
arrowinset	*value*	0.4
tbarsize	*value unit value*	2pt 5
bracketlength	*value*	0.15
rbracketlength	*value*	0.15
arrowscale	*value1 value2*	1

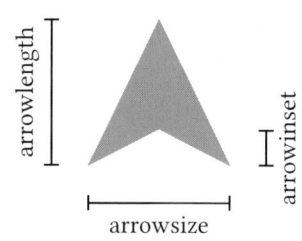

8.1.1 arrows

Table 8.2 on the next page lists the predefined styles for line beginnings and endings, with examples and the necessary code. You can mix almost all types or arrows arbitrarily.

 The "-]" arrow type has to be enclosed in curly braces if you are specifying it through the general optional argument i. e. `\psline[arrows={-]}](...` – otherwise the square bracket is interpreted as the closing bracket for the argument! Curly braces are not required for "[-", but we suggest you use them there too for consistency.

The following example shows the different effects that occur depending on whether you choose an ending that is defined to align with the point where the line itself is defined to end or an ending that is centred on the point where the line itself is defined to end. A similar example was given earlier when discussing the `linecap` option (cf. Section 4.1.5 on page 46).

```
\usepackage{pstricks}

\begin{pspicture}(3,3)
\psset{linewidth=0.5cm,linecolor=black!50}
\psline(0.25,0.25)(0.25,2.25)\rput(0.25,-0.25){-}
\psline{c-c}(1,0.25)(1,2.25)\rput(1,-0.25){c-c}
\psline{cc-cc}(1.75,0.25)(1.75,2.25)
\rput(1.75,-0.25){cc-cc}
\psline{C-C}(2.5,0.25)(2.5,2.25)\rput(2.5,-0.25){C-C}
\end{pspicture}
```

8.1 Parameters

Table 8.2: Summary of possible arrows

type	example	code	description
-		\psline{-}(1.3,0)	no arrow
<->		\psline{<->}(1.3,0)	standard arrows
>-<		\psline{>-<}(1.3,0)	inverted arrows
<<->>		\psline{<<->>}(1.3,0)	double arrows
>>-<<		\psline{>>-<<}(1.3,0)	inverted double arrows
<D-D>		\psline{<D-D>}(1.3,0)	Bézier arrows
D>-<D		\psline{D>-<D}(1.3,0)	inverted Bézier arrows
<D<D-D>D>		\psline{<D<D-D>D>}(1.3,0)	double Bézier arrows
|-|		\psline{|-|}(1.3,0)	bars, aligned with ends
|*-|*		\psline{|*-|*}(1.3,0)	bars, centric with ends
[-]		\psline{[-]}(1.3,0)	square brackets
]-[		\psline{]-[}(1.3,0)	inverted square brackets
(-)		\psline{(-)}(1.3,0)	rounded corners
)-(		\psline{)-(}(1.3,0)	inverted rounded corners
o-o		\psline{o-o}(1.3,0)	circles, centric with ends
-		\psline{*-*}(1.3,0)	discs, centric with ends
oo-oo		\psline{oo-oo}(1.3,0)	circles, aligned with ends
-		\psline{**-**}(1.3,0)	discs, aligned with ends
|<->|		\psline{|<->|}(1.3,0)	bars and arrows
|>-<|		\psline{|>-<|}(1.3,0)	bars and inverse arrows
c-c		\psline{c-c}(1.3,0)	rounded ends, centric with ends
cc-cc		\psline{cc-cc}(1.3,0)	rounded ends, aligned with ends
C-C		\psline{C-C}(1.3,0)	square ends

Examples for mixed combinations

8 Arrows

8.1.2 arrowsize

arrowsize specifies the width of an arrowhead, in the form length plus multiple of the line width (linewidth). This means you can choose to specify the width of the arrow only in terms of the current line width, which is saved in \pslinewidth.

```
width = value[unit] + value * \pslinewidth
```

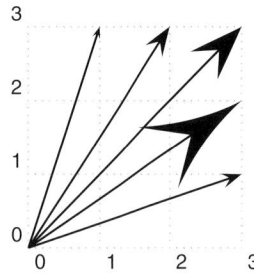

```
\usepackage{pstricks}

\begin{pspicture}[showgrid](3,3)
  \psline{->}(1,3)
  \psline[arrows=->,arrowsize=0pt 10](2,3)
  \psline[arrows=->,arrowsize=15pt](3,3)
  \psline[arrows=-D>,arrowsize=1](3,2)
  \psline[arrows=->,arrowsize=.2cm](3,1)
\end{pspicture}
```

08-01-4

8.1.3 arrowlength

arrowlength specifies the length of an arrowhead as a multiple of the arrow width (arrowsize), which means that the ratio is preserved if the scale is altered through a change of unit.

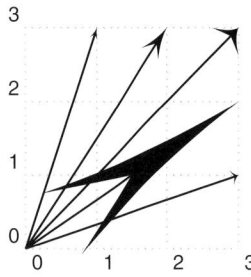

```
\usepackage{pstricks}

\begin{pspicture}[showgrid](3,3)
  \psset{arrows=-D>}
  \psline(1,3)
  \psline[arrowsize=0pt 10,arrowlength=1.5](2,3)
  \psline[arrowsize=15pt,arrowlength=0.5](3,3)
  \psline[arrowsize=1,arrowlength=3](3,2)
  \psline[arrowsize=.2cm,arrowlength=0.5](3,1)
\end{pspicture}
```

08-01-5

8.1.4 arrowinset

arrowinset specifies the depth of an arrowhead's tails as a proportion of the arrow length (arrowlength), which means that the ratio is preserved if the scale is altered through a change of unit. arrowinset takes a value between 0 (no inset – a triangular arrow) and 1 (fully inset – an arrowhead of single line width).

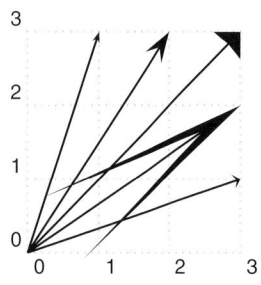

```
\usepackage{pstricks}

\begin{pspicture}[showgrid](3,3)
  \psline{->}(1,3)
  \psline[arrows=->,arrowsize=0pt 10,arrowlength=1.5](2,3)
  \psline[arrows=->,arrowsize=15pt,arrowlength=0.5,
    arrowinset=0.1](3,3)
  \psline[arrowsize=1,arrowlength=3,arrowinset=0.8]{->}(3,2)
  \psline[arrowsize=.2cm,arrowlength=0.5,
    arrowinset=0.5]{->}(3,1)
\end{pspicture}
```

08-01-6

8.1.5 tbarsize

Now we are dealing with line endings that meet the line at right angles at the endpoint, such as bars and square or round brackets. tbarsize controls the perpendicular dimension (width) of these line endings, in the form length plus multiple of the line width (linewidth). This means you can choose to specify the perpendicular width only in terms of the current line width, which is saved in \pslinewidth.

```
perpendicular width = value[unit] + value*\pslinewidth
```

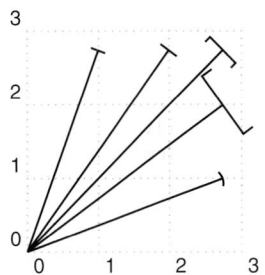

```
\usepackage{pstricks}

\begin{pspicture}[showgrid](3,3)
    \psline{-|}(1,2.75)
    \psline[arrows=-|,tbarsize=0pt 10](2,2.75)
    \psline[arrows={-]},tbarsize=15pt](2.75,2.75)
    \psline[arrows=-[,tbarsize=1](2.75,2)
    \psline[arrows=-),tbarsize=0.2cm](2.75,1)
\end{pspicture}
```

8.1.6 bracketlength

bracketlength specifies the length of a square bracket (its dimension parallel to the line) as a multiple of the bracket width, which means that the ratio is preserved if the scale is altered through a change of unit.

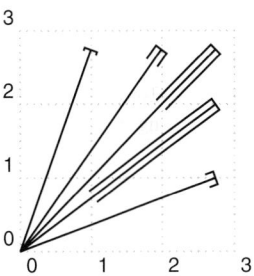

```
\usepackage{pstricks}

\begin{pspicture}[showgrid](3,3)
    \psline{{-]}}(1,2.75)
    \psline[arrows={-]},bracketlength=1](2,2.75)
    \psline[arrows={-]},bracketlength=5](2.75,2.75)
    \psline[arrows={-]},bracketlength=10](2.75,2)
    \psline[arrows={-]},bracketlength=0.5](2.75,1)
\end{pspicture}
```

8.1.7 rbracketlength

rbracketlength specifies the length of a round bracket (its dimension parallel to the line) as a multiple of the bracket width, which means that the ratio is preserved if the scale is altered through a change of unit.

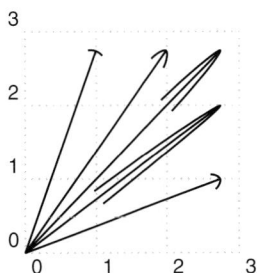

```
\usepackage{pstricks}

\begin{pspicture}[showgrid](3,3)
    \psline{-)}(1,2.75)
    \psline[arrows=-),rbracketlength=1](2,2.75)
    \psline[arrows=-),rbracketlength=5](2.75,2.75)
    \psline[arrows=-),rbracketlength=10](2.75,2)
    \psline[arrows=-),rbracketlength=0.5](2.75,1)
\end{pspicture}
```

8 Arrows

8.1.8 arrowscale

arrowscale specifies the scale factor that the requested "arrow" is scaled by. If only one value is specified, the arrow is scaled retaining the ratio of its width and length; otherwise the first parameter specifies the scale factor for the arrow's width and the second one for the arrow's length.

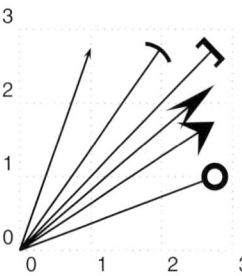

```
\usepackage{pstricks}

\begin{pspicture}[showgrid](3,3)
  \psline{{->}}(1,2.75)
  \psline[arrows=-),arrowscale=2](2,2.75)
  \psline[arrows={-]},arrowscale=2 3](2.75,2.75)
  \psline[arrows=->,arrowscale=3 5](2.75,2.25)
  \psline[arrows=->,arrowscale=5 3](2.75,1.75)
  \psline[arrows=-o,arrowscale=3](2.75,1)
\end{pspicture}
```

8.2 Extensions

You can create new arrow types arbitrarily. The easiest way is to define arrows using predefined symbols from fonts. For example, we can use the new symbols defined in Section 6.3 on page 72 as "arrows" by defining corresponding arrow types. The arrows are referred to symbolically as "cm" and "cp" in the following example and used in the usual way. There is a problem through – the line always refers to the centre of the symbol. To avoid this, a custom definition as PSTricks font helps.

```
\usepackage{pstricks}
\makeatletter  % C4=196 and  C5=197
\newpsfontdot{CirclePlus}[2 0.0 0.0 2 -0.78 -0.7]{Symbol}{<C5>}
\newpsfontdot{CircleMultiply}[2 0.0 0.0 2 -0.78 -0.7]{Symbol}{<C4>}
\@namedef{psas@cm}{\psk@dotsize \psds@CircleMultiply 0 0 Dot}
\@namedef{psas@cp}{\psk@dotsize \@nameuse{psds@CirclePlus} 0 0 Dot}
\makeatother
\psline[arrowscale=2]{cm-cm}(0,0.5)(2,0.5)
\psline[arrowscale=4,linecolor=red]{cm-cp}(3,0.5)(5,0.5)
  \psline[arrowscale=3,linecolor=blue]{cm->}(6,0.5)(8,0.5)
```

Situations where the symbol can't be taken from a font and has to be drawn "by hand" are a bit more involved. The following example illustrates the process, in this case defining a line end in the form of a rectangle, which is assigned the arrow symbol "B" for "box".

```
\usepackage{pstricks}
\makeatletter                          % definition of new "arrows" B-B
\edef\pst@arrowtable{\pst@arrowtable,B-B} % add to table
\def\tx@ABox{ABox } %                  internal PostScript name ABox
\@namedef{psas@B}{%                    internal macro name
  /ABox { %                            PostScript procedure
    CLW mul add dup CLW sub 2 div %take line width into account
    /x ED mul %                        save x value
    /y ED %                            y as well
    /z CLW 2 div def %                 reserve
    x neg y moveto %                   starting point
    x neg CLW 2 div L %                lineto
    x CLW 2 div L  %                   lineto
    x y L %                            lineto
    x neg y L %                        lineto
    closepath %                        close line
    stroke 0 y moveto %                draw and go to line end
  } def
  \psk@bracketlength \psk@tbarsize \tx@ABox % width height ABox
}
\newpsfontdot{CircleMultiply}[2 0.0 0.0 2 -0.78 -0.7]{Symbol}{<C4>} % 196
\newpsfontdot{CirclePlus}[2 0.0 0.0 2 -0.78 -0.7]{Symbol}{<C5>} % 197
\@namedef{psas@cm}{\psk@dotsize \psds@CircleMultiply 0 0 Dot}
\@namedef{psas@cp}{\psk@dotsize \@nameuse{psds@CirclePlus} 0 0 Dot}
\makeatother
\begin{pspicture}[showgrid](4,4)
  \psset{arrowscale=3,arrows=B-cp}
  \psline[bracketlength=2](1,1)(4,4)
  \psarc[linecolor=red](0,0){2}{0}{90}
  \psarc[arrowsize=2mm,linecolor=blue]{cm-cp}(1,1){2}{20}{70}
\end{pspicture}\hspace{1cm}
\begin{pspicture}[showgrid](4,4)
  \psset{arrowscale=3,arrows=B->}      \psline(3,3)
  \psarc[linecolor=red,tbarsize=20pt](0,0){2}{0}{90}
  \psarc[tbarsize=0.5cm,bracketlength=0.3,linecolor=blue](1,1){2}{20}{70}
\end{pspicture}
```

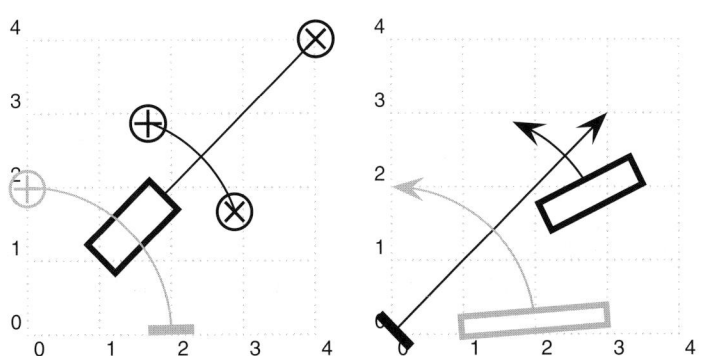

8 Arrows

8.2.1 "Hook" arrow type

In addition to the arrows listed in Table 8.2 on page 93, the `pstricks-add` package provides the additional arrows summarized in Table 8.3.

Table 8.3: Summary of arrows for "hook" line and curve endings.

type	example	code
h-h		`\psline{h-h}(0,1ex)(1.3,1ex)`
H-H		`\psline{H-H}(0,1ex)(1.3,1ex)`

You can control the length and width of the h arrow type with the usual parameters, but the H arrow type (curved hook arrow) is modified through the options summarized in Table 8.4. If a line begins with a right hook, it ends with a left hook, and vice versa (by changing the sign of the hookwidth parameter).

Table 8.4: Summary of the parameters for the "hook" arrow type with the short form H.

name	default	description
hooklength	3mm	length of the arc
hookwidth	1mm	width of the arc

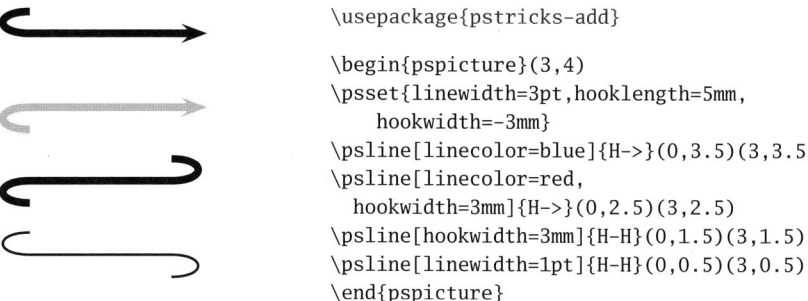

```
\usepackage{pstricks-add}

\begin{pspicture}(3,4)
\psset{linewidth=3pt,hooklength=5mm,
    hookwidth=-3mm}
\psline[linecolor=blue]{H->}(0,3.5)(3,3.5)
\psline[linecolor=red,
   hookwidth=3mm]{H->}(0,2.5)(3,2.5)
\psline[hookwidth=3mm]{H-H}(0,1.5)(3,1.5)
\psline[linewidth=1pt]{H-H}(0,0.5)(3,0.5)
\end{pspicture}
```

The following two examples illustrate the use of hooked arrows in conjunction with the `\ncline` command (cf. Section 16.2.4 on page 229). This command is similar to `\psline` but connects nodes instead of points. In these examples the nodes are positions in a matrix.

```
\usepackage{pstricks-add}
\psset{arrowsize=8pt,arrowlength=1,linewidth=1pt,nodesep=2pt,shortput=tablr}
\begin{psmatrix}[colsep=12mm,rowsep=10mm]
        &  & $R_2$           \\
        &  & 0     &  & $R_3$\\
$e_b:S$ & 1 &     & 1 & 0    \\
        &  & 0               \\
        &  & $R_1$           \\
\end{psmatrix}
\ncline{h-}{1,3}{2,3}<{$e_{r2}$}>{$f_{r2}$}\ncline{-h}{2,3}{3,2}<{$e_1$}
\ncline{-h}{3,1}{3,2}^{$e_s$}_{$f_{s}$}\ncline{-h}{3,2}{4,3}>{$e_3$}<{$f_3$}
\ncline{-h}{4,3}{3,4}>{$e_4$}<{$f_4$}  \ncline{-h}{3,4}{2,3}>{$e_2$}<{$f_2$}
\ncline{-h}{3,4}{3,5}^{$e_5$}          \ncline{-h}{3,5}{2,5}<{$e_{r3}$}>{$f_{r3}$}
\ncline{-h}{4,3}{5,3}<{$e_{r1}$}>{$f_{r1}$}
```

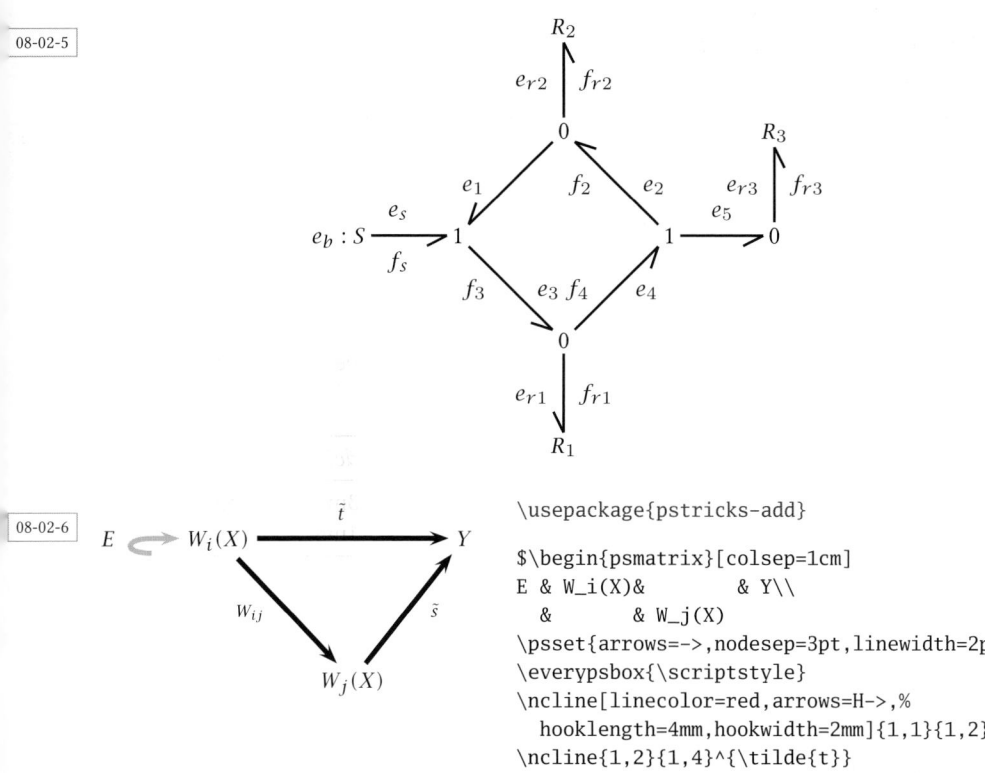

```
\usepackage{pstricks-add}

$\begin{psmatrix}[colsep=1cm]
E  &  W_i(X)&           & Y\\
   &        & W_j(X)
\psset{arrows=->,nodesep=3pt,linewidth=2pt}
\everypsbox{\scriptstyle}
\ncline[linecolor=red,arrows=H->,%
    hooklength=4mm,hookwidth=2mm]{1,1}{1,2}
\ncline{1,2}{1,4}^{\tilde{t}}
\ncline{1,2}{2,3}<{W_{ij}}
\ncline{2,3}{1,4}>{\tilde{s}}
\end{psmatrix}$
```

8.2.2 Multiarrows

For the two arrow types << and >>, the `pstricks-add` package provides two nArrows parameters that let you choose the number of arrows drawn at the line ends. nArrowsA affects line ends with outward-pointing arrows (->>), and nArrowsB affects line ends with inward-pointing arrows (-<<). If the parameter is empty, the arrow behaves in the standard way as a double arrow, as described in Section 8.1.1. Multiarrows are not possible for any other arrow type; none of the nArrow parameters have any effect on them.

There is no formal limit to the number of multiarrows you can set; PSTricks does not check the parameter in any way; it simply repeats the algorithm the specified number of times. However, using a large number of arrows usually looks strange, as in some of the examples in Table 8.5.

8.2.3 ArrowInside and arrowfill options

With `pstricks-add` loaded, you can also add arrows along lines and curves, not just at the ends. Table 8.6 on the next page summarizes the available parameters and Table 8.7 on page 101 gives examples.

8 Arrows

Table 8.5: Examples for multiarrows

code	output
`\psline{->>}(0,1ex)(2.3,1ex)`	
`\psline[nArrowsA=3]{->>}(0,1ex)(2.3,1ex)`	
`\psline[nArrowsA=5]{->>}(0,1ex)(2.3,1ex)`	
`\psline{<<-}(0,1ex)(2.3,1ex)`	
`\psline[nArrowsA=3]{<<-}(0,1ex)(2.3,1ex)`	
`\psline[nArrowsA=5]{<<-}(0,1ex)(2.3,1ex)`	
`\psline{<<->>}(0,1ex)(2.3,1ex)`	
`\psline[nArrowsA=3]{<<->>}(0,1ex)(2.3,1ex)`	
`\psline[nArrowsA=5]{<<->>}(0,1ex)(2.3,1ex)`	
`\psline{<<-|}(0,1ex)(2.3,1ex)`	
`\psline[nArrowsA=3]{<<-<<}(0,1ex)(2.3,1ex)`	
`\psline[nArrowsA=5]{<<-o}(0,1ex)(2.3,1ex)`	
`\psline[nArrowsA=3,nArrowsB=4]{<<-<<}(0,1ex)(2.3,1ex)`	
`\psline[nArrowsA=3,nArrowsB=4]{>>->>}(0,1ex)(2.3,1ex)`	
`\psline[nArrowsA=1,nArrowsB=4]{>>->>}(0,1ex)(2.3,1ex)`	

pstricks-add also provides the new ArrowFill parameter. Arrows are basically filled polylines, but using this parameter prevents them from being filled – the arrows are then pure polylines. You can use this option both on arrows at the ends of a line or curve and also on inner arrows, though remember that the underlying line or curve shows through the arrow in this case.

Table 8.6: Parameters for inner and filled arrows

name	default	description
ArrowInside	{}	inner arrow type
ArrowInsidePos	0.5	relative or absolute position of the first arrow
ArrowInsideNo	1	number of arrows, spread evenly on the line
ArrowInsideOffset	0	relative offset of the first arrow
ArrowFill	true	filled or not

If you specify a value between 0 and 1 for the arrow position through ArrowInsidePos, this is taken as a relative value of the arrow's position along the line from the start point; for example, ArrowInsidePos=0.1 means that the first arrow is 10% of the way along the total length of the line or curve. If you specify a value greater than 1, then this is taken as an absolute value in the unit pt; for example, ArrowInsidePos=10 means that the first arrow is 10 pt from the start of the line or curve. This combination of meanings doesn't cause any problems, as absolute lengths of less than 5 pt don't make sense in practice.

Any positive value is also valid for the offset (ArrowInsideOffset), although it is always taken as a relative value to the length of the line; for example, the specification ArrowInsideOffset=1.5 means that the first arrow is actually drawn at a position 1.5

times the length of the line from the position otherwise defined for it, i.e. outside the line in this case. This situation is shown in the second example below: a single inside arrow is specified, which would normally be positioned 0.5 of the way along the length of the line, but the additional specification of an offset of 0.6 leads to the arrow being drawn outside the line.

Table 8.7: Options for "inside" arrows

name	example
ArrowInside	\psline[ArrowInside=->](0,0)(2,0)
ArrowInsidePos	\psline[ArrowInside=->, ArrowInsidePos=0.25](0,0)(2,0)
ArrowInsidePos	\psline[ArrowInside=->, ArrowInsidePos=10](0,0)(2,0)
ArrowInsideNo	\psline[ArrowInside=->, ArrowInsideNo=2](0,0)(2,0)
ArrowInsideOffset	\psline[ArrowInside=->, ArrowInsideNo=2, ArrowInsideOffset=0.1](0,0)(2,0)
ArrowInside	\psline[ArrowInside=->]{->}(0,0)(2,0)
ArrowInsidePos	\psline[ArrowInside=->, ArrowInsidePos=0.25]{->}(0,0)(2,0)
ArrowInsidePos	\psline[ArrowInside=->, ArrowInsidePos=10]{->}(0,0)(2,0)
ArrowInsideNo	\psline[ArrowInside=->, ArrowInsideNo=2]{->}(0,0)(2,0)
ArrowInsideOffset	\psline[ArrowInside=->,ArrowInsideNo=2, ArrowInsideOffset=0.1]{->}(0,0)(2,0)
ArrowFill	\psline[arrowscale=3, ArrowFill=false]{<->>}(0,0)(2,0)

Let's look at some examples. The last two are particularly interesting as they show the behaviour for curves where the course of the curve has to be determined iteratively internally as it is not fixed in the beginning.

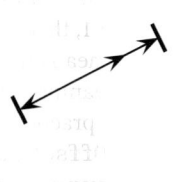

```
\usepackage{pstricks-add}

\begin{pspicture}(2,1)
\psline[arrowscale=2,ArrowInside=->,
    ArrowInsideOffset=0.25]{|<->|}(2,1)
\end{pspicture}
```

8 Arrows

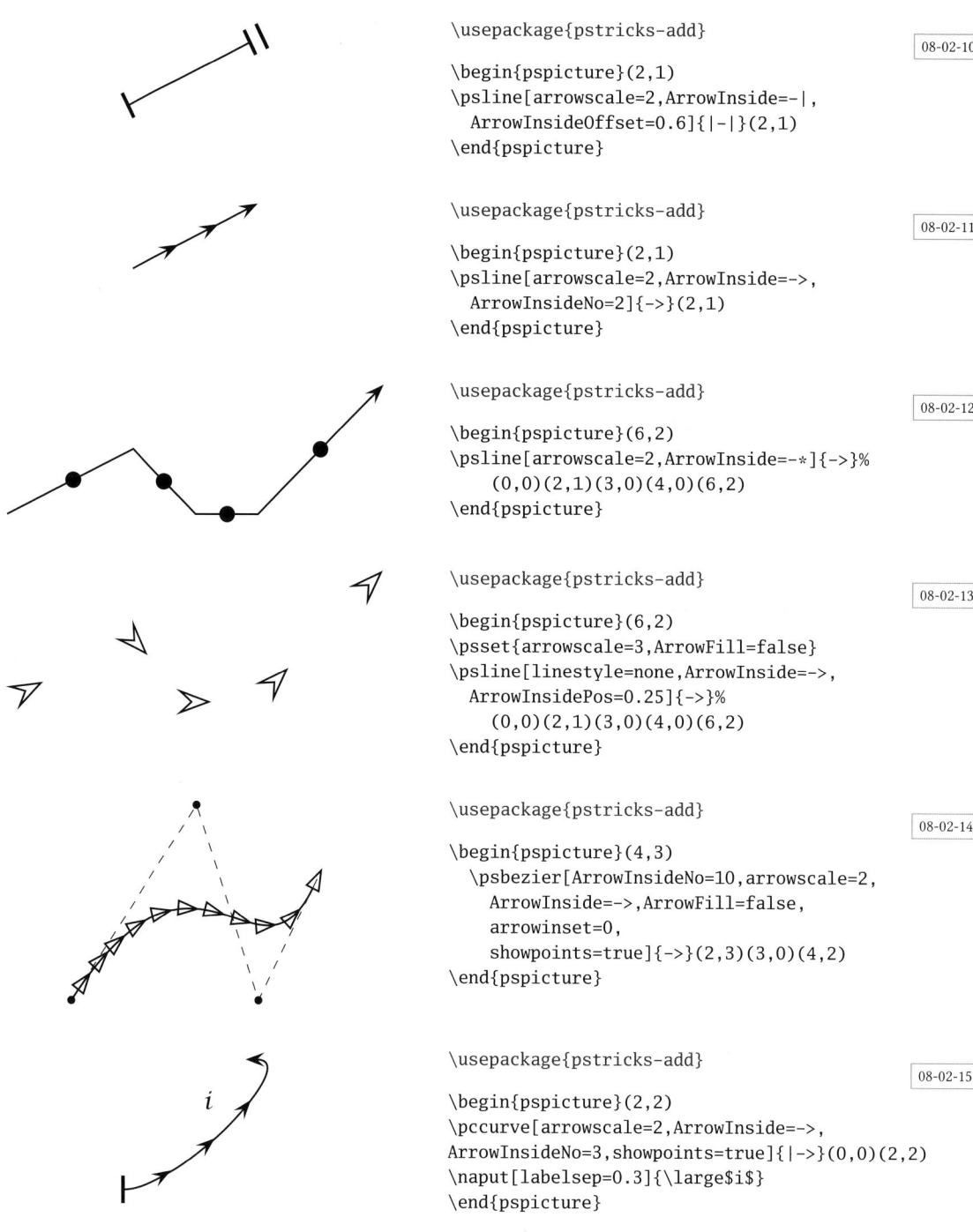

```
\usepackage{pstricks-add}

\begin{pspicture}(2,1)
\psline[arrowscale=2,ArrowInside=-|,
   ArrowInsideOffset=0.6]{|-|}(2,1)
\end{pspicture}
```

08-02-10

```
\usepackage{pstricks-add}

\begin{pspicture}(2,1)
\psline[arrowscale=2,ArrowInside=->,
   ArrowInsideNo=2]{->}(2,1)
\end{pspicture}
```

08-02-11

```
\usepackage{pstricks-add}

\begin{pspicture}(6,2)
\psline[arrowscale=2,ArrowInside=-*]{->}%
    (0,0)(2,1)(3,0)(4,0)(6,2)
\end{pspicture}
```

08-02-12

```
\usepackage{pstricks-add}

\begin{pspicture}(6,2)
\psset{arrowscale=3,ArrowFill=false}
\psline[linestyle=none,ArrowInside=->,
   ArrowInsidePos=0.25]{->}%
    (0,0)(2,1)(3,0)(4,0)(6,2)
\end{pspicture}
```

08-02-13

```
\usepackage{pstricks-add}

\begin{pspicture}(4,3)
  \psbezier[ArrowInsideNo=10,arrowscale=2,
    ArrowInside=->,ArrowFill=false,
    arrowinset=0,
    showpoints=true]{->}(2,3)(3,0)(4,2)
\end{pspicture}
```

08-02-14

```
\usepackage{pstricks-add}

\begin{pspicture}(2,2)
\pccurve[arrowscale=2,ArrowInside=->,
ArrowInsideNo=3,showpoints=true]{|->}(0,0)(2,2)
\naput[labelsep=0.3]{\large$i$}
\end{pspicture}
```

08-02-15

Chapter 9

Labels

9.1 Alignment reference points 103
9.2 Angle of rotation 104
9.3 Label separation 104
9.4 \rput 105
9.5 \multirput and \rmultiput 105
9.6 \uput 106
9.7 \Rput 107
9.8 \cput 108
9.9 \multips 108

PSTricks commands that position labels or arbitrary objects all end in put and largely share the same syntax, with small variations in the interpretation of the parameters. Each command provides varying levels of control over the location, alignment and rotation of the label relative to the point that is being labelled. This chapter begins by discussing these variables, and then looks at \rput, \uput, and the other object-positioning commands that are available.

9.1 Alignment reference points

Every object has a certain width, height, and depth relative to the baseline of a line. To positioned the object with a specific alignment with reference to the point (x, y), you have to specify the *alignment reference point* of the object. This is normally defined to be the centre of the baseline of the object (box), but you can change it by specifying a character for the vertical and the horizontal alignment. Table 9.1 summarizes all possible values, with the figure illustrating their use. You can either use each horizontal/vertical alignment specification alone or paired with a vertical/horizontal alignment i.e. a maximum of two specifications (one horizontal and one vertical, in either order) at a time. If, for example, you want the top left corner of a label to adjoin (x, y), then the alignment reference point for the label is tl.

9 Labels

Table 9.1: Summary of the alignment reference points and their respective position in a box

horizontal		vertical
l	left	t	top
r	right	b	bottom
		B	baseline

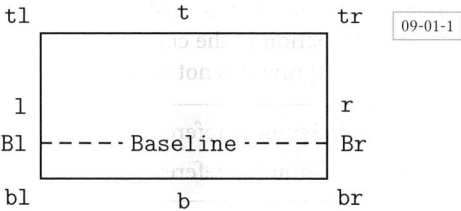

9.2 Angle of rotation

To specify an angle of rotation, you can either specify an angle in degrees, with zero degrees lying along the positive x axis and positive angles measured counterclockwise from there (by normal mathematical convention), or you can use the abbreviations listed in Table 9.2, representing the cardinal directions (N, S, E, and W) or a relative direction of rotation (U, L, D, and R).

Table 9.2: Summary of the short forms for the angle of rotations

character	U	L	D	R	N	W	S	E
meaning	up	left	down	right	north	west	south	east
angle of rotation	0	90	180	270	*0	*90	*180	*270

If you prefix an angle with an asterisk (star), PSTricks ignores all previous rotations and executes the starred angle independently. This is illustrated by the alignment of the second "top right" label in the following example.

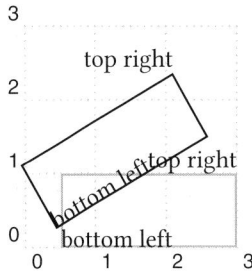

```
\usepackage{pstricks}

\begin{pspicture}[showgrid](3,3)
  \psframe[linecolor=red](0.5,0)(3,1)
  \rput[lb](0.5,0){bottom left}
  \rput[br]{*0}(3,1){top right}
  \rput{30}(0,0){%
    \psframe(0.5,0)(3,1)
    \rput[lb](0.5,0){bottom left}
    \rput[br]{*0}(3,1){top right}}
\end{pspicture}
```

9.3 Label separation

When dealing specifically with labels, you can sometimes use the labelsep parameter to control the distance of a label from an object. The default value is 5pt. However, this parameter has no effect on the \rput command, though it is used by other packages, e.g. pst-plot. The value of the parameter is saved in the \pslabelsep length command, which you can then use for your own purposes.

9.4 \rput

The \rput command is used frequently as it enables you to place an arbitrary object at an arbitrary position in the coordinate system with ease. When using the starred version, the object's background is not transparent.

```
\rput * [alignment reference point]  {rotation} {object}
\rput * [alignment reference point]  {rotation} (x,y){object}
```

If you specify a coordinate pair, then both the alignment reference point and the angle of rotation are optional. However, if you don't specify a coordinate pair (in which case the origin is used by default), it is then expected that an angle of rotation is specified. There are many possibilities for using \rput; we just give one example here but the command is used in many other examples in this book.

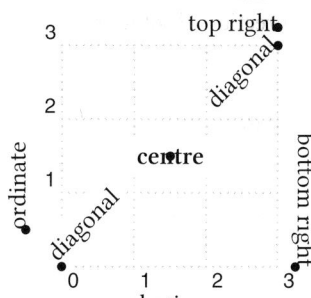

```
\usepackage{pstricks}

\begin{pspicture}[showgrid](-0.48,-0.48)(3,3)
 \rput[lb]{L}(-0.5,0.5){ordinate}  \psdot(-.5,.5)
 \rput(1.5,-0.5){abscissa}          \psdot(1.5,-.5)
 \rput[rB](3,3.2){top right}       \psdot(3,3.25)
 \rput[rb]{R}(3.2,0){bottom right}\psdot(3.25,0)
 \rput*[lb]{45}{diagonal}           \psdot(0,0)
 \rput[rB]{45}(3,3){diagonal}       \psdot(3,3)
 \rput*(1.5,1.5){\textbf{centre}}  \psdot(1.5,1.5)
\end{pspicture}
```

9.5 \multirput and \rmultiput

\multirput is based on \rput, but it is executed n times where each time the current point is moved by the values (dx,dy).

```
\multirput * [alignment reference point]  {rotation} (x,y)(dx,dy){n}{object}
```

The specification of the alignment reference point and the angle of rotation are optional again. A common use for \multirput is for adding axis ticks or numbering. Axis ticks are created in the following example.

```
\usepackage{pstricks}
\begin{pspicture}(4,4)
  \psline{->}(4,0)\psline{->}(0,4)
  \multirput(0,0)(0.25,0){15}{\psline[linewidth=0.1pt](0,-0.1)}
  \multirput(0,0)(0,0.25){15}{\psline[linewidth=0.1pt](-0.1,0)}
  \multirput(0,0)(0.5,0){8}{\psline(0,-0.15)}
  \multirput(0,0)(0,0.5){8}{\psline(-0.15,0)}
  \uput[0](4,0){$x$}\uput[90](0,4){$y$}
\end{pspicture}
```

9 Labels

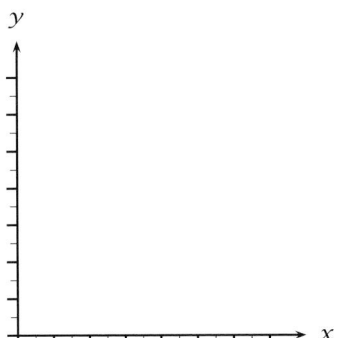

The \rmultiput command from the pstricks-add package places an object at multiple locations that aren't necessarily related. The parameters are identical to \rput, except that the rotation and reference point have to be specified by the optional rot and ref arguments (cf. Section 9.4). \rmultiput lets you specify multiple points anywhere in the coordinate system for the location of the object, unlike \multirput, which creates a series of objects a fixed distance apart.

\rmultiput * [settings] {object}(x_1,y_1)(x_2,y_2)...(x_n,y_n)

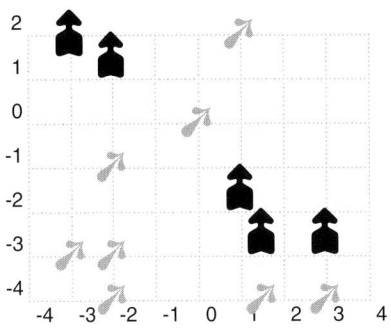

```
\usepackage{pstricks-add,pifont}

\psset{unit=0.6}
\def\bigDingA{\textcolor{red}{%
    \psscalebox{2}{\ding{250}}}}
\def\bigDingB{\psscalebox{2}{\ding{253}}}
\begin{pspicture}[showgrid](-4,-4)(4,2)
\rmultiput[rot=45]{\bigDingA}(-2,-4)(-2,-3)%
    (-3,-3)(-2,-1)(0,0)(1,2)(1.5,-4)(3,-4)
\rmultiput[rot=90,ref=lC]{\bigDingB}%
    (-2,1)(-3,1.5)(-2,1)(1,-2)(1.5,-3)(3,-3)
\end{pspicture}
```

9.6 \uput

Using \rput can be a bit cumbersome in certain circumstances, for example when labelling axis ticks. \rput can only place a label (or object) at a certain point, with a limited set of options for specifying its alignment and choice of its angle of rotation. However, \uput is much more powerful: it places a label or object at a certain distance (label distance) in any specified direction (angle) and at any angle of rotation (rotation) relative to *any given point* (x,y).

Hence \rput is placing an object at an absolute coordinate, taking into account the angle of rotation and alignment, whereas \uput places an object at any specified distance/angle/rotation relative to another point.

9.7 \Rput

\uput * {label distance} [angle] {rotation} (x,y){object}

As we mentioned in Section 9.3, you can also set the distance of the label through the labelsep parameter, which is valid with the \uput command.

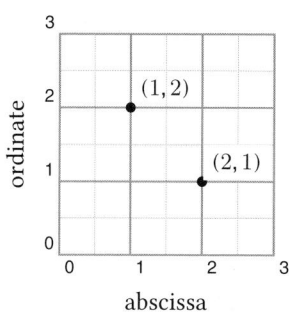

```
\usepackage{pstricks}

\begin{pspicture}(-0.45,-0.45)(3,3)
    \psgrid[subgriddiv=2,gridcolor=black!50,
        subgridcolor=black!20,gridlabels=7pt](3,3)
    \uput{0.5}[180]{90}(0,1.5){ordinate}
    \uput{0.5}[-90](1.5,0){abscissa}
    \qdisk(1,2){2pt}\uput[45](1,2){\small $(1,2)$}
    \qdisk(2,1){2pt}\uput*[45](2,1){\small $(2,1)$}
\end{pspicture}
```

You can specify the reference angle (indicating the direction of the object from the coordinate point) in degrees in the normal manner or by using the abbreviations summarized in Table 9.3.

Table 9.3: Summary of the abbreviations for the reference angles

character	r	u	l	d	ur	ul	dl	dr
meaning	right	up	left	down	up right	up left	down left	down right
corresponding angle	0	90	180	270	45	135	225	315

9.7 \Rput

\Rput is an obsolete command that has been superseded by \uput. In contrast to \uput, it uses the syntax of the \rput command for the reference angles (cf. Table 9.4).

\Rput * {label distance} [angle] {rotation} (x,y){object}

command	short form							
\uput	r	u	l	d	ur	ul	dr	dl
\Rput	l	b	r	t	bl	br	tr	rl

Table 9.4: Comparison of the short forms of the reference angles for the \uput and \Rput commands

This table makes it clear that \rput defines alignment by considering which part of the label or object should adjoin the coordinate point, whereas \uput considers the position of the label or object relative to the coordinate point. In our example above the point labels were *up right* from the points, but when the example is recreated below with the \uput commands replaced by \Rput, the labels' positions using \rput's syntax are specified through setting the *bottom left* of the labels to adjoin the point. \Rput also changes the location of the other labels.

9 Labels

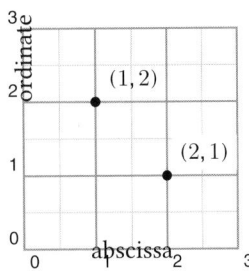

```
\usepackage{pstricks}

\begin{pspicture}(3,3)
  \psgrid[subgriddiv=2,gridcolor=black!50,
    subgridcolor=black!20,gridlabels=7pt](3,3)
  \Rput{0.5}[l]{90}(0,1.5){ordinate}
  \Rput{0.5}[-90](1.5,0){abscissa}
  \qdisk(1,2){2pt}\Rput[lb](1,2){\small $(1,2)$}
  \qdisk(2,1){2pt}\Rput*[lb](2,1){\small $(2,1)$}
\end{pspicture}
```

9.8 \cput

\cput combines the two commands \pscirclebox (cf. Section 10.2.4 on page 112) and \rput. The alignment reference point of \cput is always the centre of the label; this can't be changed.

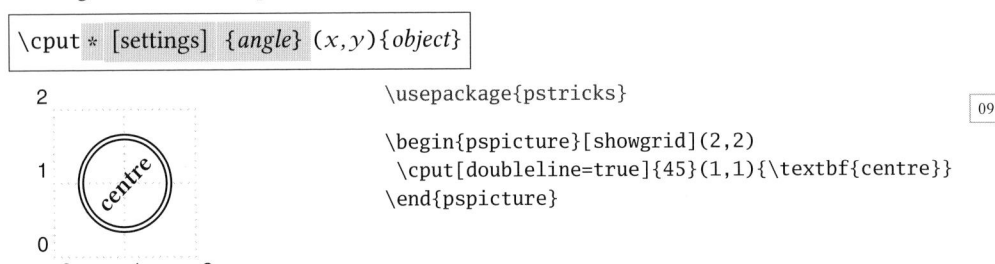

```
\usepackage{pstricks}

\begin{pspicture}[showgrid](2,2)
  \cput[doubleline=true]{45}(1,1){\textbf{centre}}
\end{pspicture}
```

9.9 \multips

If you want to draw a certain graphical object repeatedly, it is easier to use \multips rather than \multirput. With \multips you don't specify an alignment reference point, but otherwise the syntax is identical to \multirput; however, there is no starred version.

\multips {*rotation*} (*x,y*)(*dx,dy*){*n*}{*object*}

```
\usepackage{pstricks}

\def\myCoil{\pscurve(-0.5,0.5)(-0.1,0.45)(0.3,0)%
  (0,-0.5)(-0.3,0)(0.1,0.45)(0.5,0.5)}%
\begin{pspicture}[unit=0.5,linewidth=1.5pt](2,0.5)
  \multips(0,0)(1,0){4}{\myCoil}
\end{pspicture}
```

Chapter 10

Boxes

10.1 Parameters 110
10.2 Commands 111
10.3 Box size 113
10.4 Clipping 114
10.5 Rotating and scaling 116
10.6 Mathematics and verbatim boxes 118
10.7 Examples 119

This chapter discusses the creation of boxes to contain arbitrary objects. It looks first at the parameters and commands for boxes and then deals with using boxes for clipping, shading, rotating and scaling. Most of the examples contain text objects, but it is possible to enclose many other objects, though there are some issues to consider that are mentioned below and dealt with in further detail at the end of the chapter.

Almost all PSTricks box commands provide a parameter for text that is processed in a restricted horizontal mode (LR mode, for short). In this mode, the argument (consisting of characters and other boxes) is merged more or less into a long line; line breaks or display style formulae are not catered for. This is not really a restriction, as it is easy, for example, to insert a \parbox or minipage. Hence there is essentially no command or complex object that can't be used in the argument of a LR box.

Another point to note is that the LR box commands in PSTricks have some slightly different characteristics from those in LaTeX. In LaTeX commands such as \fbox process their contents in text mode, even if math mode was active before the box. However, PSTricks preserves contents in math mode, and also tries to save whichever mode is currently active. TeX knows about the four math styles \textstyle, \displaystyle, \scriptstyle, and \scriptscriptstyle; PSTricks supports switching between one of these math styles in math mode and the normal text mode (cf. Section 10.6 on page 118).

10 Boxes

10.1 Parameters

You can use most of the line and fill parameters (cf. Table 4.1 on page 43) for boxes, and Table 10.1 lists the additional parameters that are available.

Table 10.1: Summary of the additional parameters for boxes

name	type	default
framesep	value unit	3 pt
boxsep	boolean	true
trimode	L|*L|R|*R|D|*D|U|*U	U

10.1.1 framesep

framesep controls the distance between the edge of the box and the enclosed object; it is like \fboxsep in LaTeX.

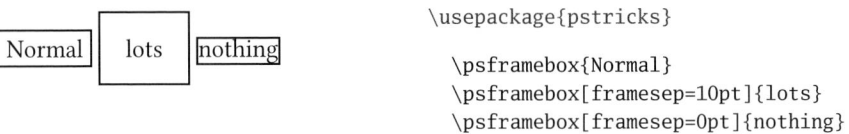

```
\usepackage{pstricks}

\psframebox{Normal}
\psframebox[framesep=10pt]{lots}
\psframebox[framesep=0pt]{nothing}
```

10.1.2 boxsep

boxsep is a boolean parameter that determines whether the size of the box takes on the size of the outer frame (i.e. boxsep=true) or the size of the enclosed object (i.e. boxsep=false). This is only valid with the \psframebox, \pscirclebox, and \psovalbox commands. For all other commands, the box is always the size of the outer frame. The following example initially uses boxsep=true (which is the default setting) and then repeats the commands with boxsep=false.

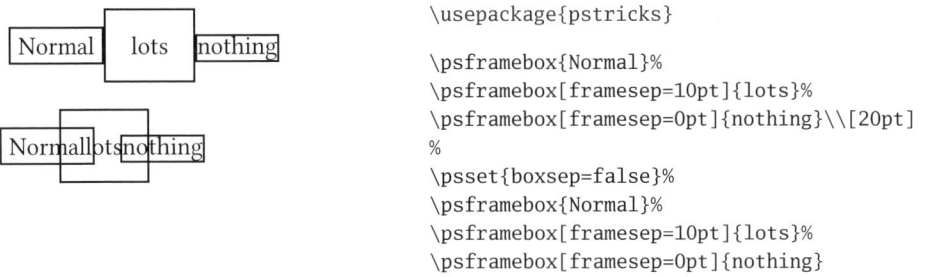

```
\usepackage{pstricks}

\psframebox{Normal}%
\psframebox[framesep=10pt]{lots}%
\psframebox[framesep=0pt]{nothing}\\[20pt]
%
\psset{boxsep=false}%
\psframebox{Normal}%
\psframebox[framesep=10pt]{lots}%
\psframebox[framesep=0pt]{nothing}
```

Setting boxsep=false makes the frame invisible to TeX. This is useful when you are in the middle of a paragraph or figure and want to highlight something with a frame (such as in the example in Section 10.2.5 on page 113), since the frame of the box is inserted without additional space around it.

10.1.3 trimode

Triangular frames (cf. Section are always isosceles triangles with their base set horizontally or vertically, the only question is which way the "tip" of the triangle points. This is controlled by the trimode parameter. Table 10.2 lists the parameter's values with examples; the default value is U (tip pointing upwards). The starred version shrinks the horizontal width of the triangle to create more acutely-angled triangles (or less acutely-angled if their tip is side-pointing).

Table 10.2: trimode parameter for use with triangular frames (\pstribox[trimode=...]{...})

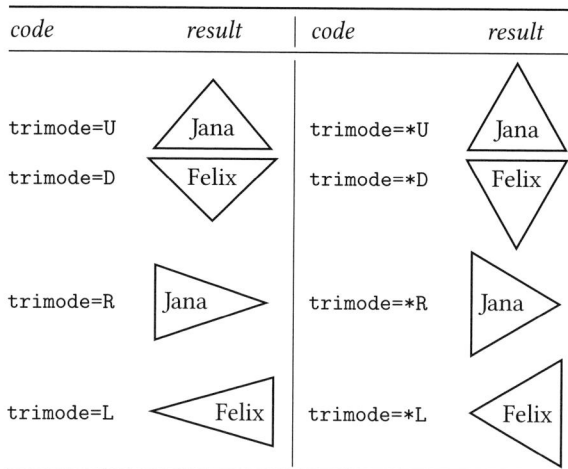

10.2 Commands

10.2.1 \psframebox

\psframebox is the simplest of all available boxes.

\psframebox * [settings] {contents}

In contrast to the normal behaviour of starred versions, the starred version of \psframebox fills the background with the fillcolor rather than with the linecolor. Therefore this is an easy way to create labels and markings with a white background.

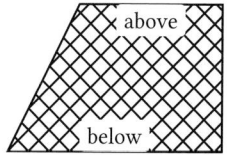

```
\usepackage{pstricks}

\begin{pspicture}(3,2)
  \pspolygon[fillcolor=lightgray,fillstyle=crosshatch,
      hatchsep=5pt](0,0)(3,0)(3,2)(1,2)
  \rput[b](1.5,0){\psframebox*[framearc=.3]{\small below}}
  \rput[t](2,2){\psframebox*[framearc=.3]{\small above}}
\end{pspicture}
```

10.2.2 \psdblframebox

\psdblframebox is almost identical to \psframebox except that it creates a double frame.

\psdblframebox * [settings] {contents}

This example uses a \parbox inside the frame, which then permits line breaks within the text, as mentioned in the opening section of this chapter.

```
\usepackage{pstricks}

\psdblframebox[framearc=0.25,framesep=10pt]{%
    \parbox{3.5cm}{This is a normal
    \texttt{psdblframebox}
    which has a line break because
    of using a \texttt{parbox}!}}
```

 Beware when using framearc value that the frame could overwrite the enclosed text. This is because the text is aligned within the strictly **rectangular** dimensions (i.e. the extended corners without arcs) of the frame box. So if framesep is too small or framearc is too large, you will not get a desirable result.

10.2.3 \psshadowbox

\psshadowbox is identical to using the \psframebox command with option shadow=true.

\psshadowbox * [settings] {contents}

```
\usepackage{pstricks}

\psshadowbox{\texttt{\textbackslash psshadowbox}}
\psframebox[shadow=true]{%
    \texttt{\textbackslash psframebox}}
```

10.2.4 \pscirclebox

\pscirclebox creates a circular frame large enough to contain the dimensions of the inner rectangular box. However, this often results in the frame being unnecessarily large, especially when using \parbox or tabular, as the borders, framesep and \fboxsep/\tabcolsep all add to the dimensions of the inner rectangular box. To reduce this effect, we use @{}c@{} in the following example to set the spacing outside the table to zero.

\pscirclebox * [settings] {contents}

```
\usepackage{pstricks}

\_\quad\pscirclebox{\rule{1pt}{1cm}}\kern1cm%
\pscirclebox{\begin{tabular}{@{}c@{}}%
    A very big\\circle%
\end{tabular}}\kern1cm\_
```

\cput provides an alternative to \pscirclebox if you are placing the contents at a specific location (cf. Section 9.8 on page 108).

10.2.5 \psovalbox

\psovalbox creates a frame in the shape of an oval or rather an ellipse with a horizontal axis, so is different from just using \psframebox with rounded corners. As with \pscirclebox, the oval box will often be too big when working with a \parbox or tabular.

\psovalbox * [settings] {contents}

10-02-5

The introductory price of this book is just €29.95, which is very affordable!

```
\usepackage{pstricks,eurosym}

\parbox{4cm}{The introductory price of this book
  is just \psovalbox[boxsep=false,
    linecolor=darkgray]{\euro{}29.95,}
  which is very affordable!}
```

10.2.6 \psdiabox

\psdiabox creates a frame in the shape of a diamond where the width is equal to twice the height.

\psdiabox * [settings] {contents}

10-02-6

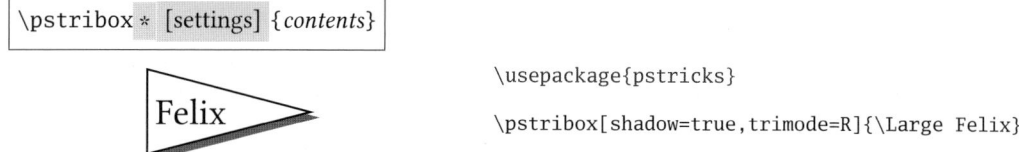

```
\usepackage{pstricks}

\psdiabox[shadow=true]{\Large Jana}
```

10.2.7 \pstribox

\pstribox creates a frame in the shape of an isosceles triangle, with its orientation controlled by the special trimode parameter discussed in Section 10.1.3 on page 111. The width of the triangle is equal to either the height or twice the height, depending on whether the value of trimode is preceded by an asterisk.

\pstribox * [settings] {contents}

10-02-7

```
\usepackage{pstricks}

\pstribox[shadow=true,trimode=R]{\Large Felix}
```

10.3 Box size

None of the box commands discussed in this chapter have inbuilt parameters for specifying the size of the box. If you do require a specific box size, put the contents of the box inside a \makebox (if you just need to control the width) or inside a \parbox (which has parameters for specifying both width and height). The following two sections contain examples of each method.

Note that for circular "boxes" of a uniform size you can use \cnode, which has an inbuilt parameter for setting the radius. Here is a quick example, but the command is covered in more detail in Section 16.3.4 on page 238.

10 Boxes

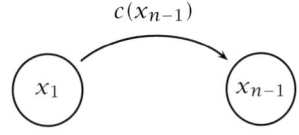

```
\usepackage{pst-node}

\begin{pspicture}(-0.25,-0.25)(3.25,0.5)
   \psset{nodesep=3pt,shortcut=nab}
   \cnode(0,0){0.5cm}{A}\rput(0,0){$x_1$}
   \cnode(3,0){0.5cm}{B}\rput(3,0){$x_{n-1}$}
   \ncarc[arcangle=40]{->}{A}{B}^{$c(x_{n-1})$}
\end{pspicture}
```

10.3.1 Constant width

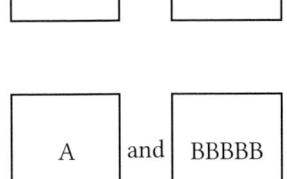

```
\usepackage{pstricks}

\def\bBox#1#2{\makebox[#1]{#2}}
\psframebox{\bBox{1.3cm}{A}} and
\psframebox{\bBox{1.3cm}{BBBBB}}
```

10.3.2 Constant width and height

You can centre the contents of a box vertically by using the optional argument of the \parbox and horizontally by using either a \makebox or the \centering command.

```
\usepackage{pstricks}

\def\bhBox#1#2{\parbox[c][#1][c]{#1}{%
   \makebox[#1]{#2}}}
\psframebox{\bhBox{1.3cm}{A}} and %
\psframebox{\bhBox{1.3cm}{BBBBB}}
```

```
\usepackage{pstricks}

\def\bhpBox#1#2{\parbox[c][#1][c]{#1}{%
   \centering #2}}
\psframebox{\bhpBox{1.3cm}{A}} and %
\psframebox{\bhpBox{1.3cm}{BBBBB}}
```

10.4 Clipping

10.4.1 \clipbox

This command places arbitrary objects into a horizontal box and clips the object when it exceeds a specified dimension.

\clipbox[*value unit*]{*contents*}

The default value of the optional parameter is 0pt (i. e. clips nothing from the box contents). In the following example, we draw a box and overlapping line, and then redraw them using the \clipbox command, with optional value 0pt, so the section of the line inside the frame is shown in full. The second line of boxes shows clipping at 10pt (part of the line is shown outside the box) and at −10pt (only part of the line is shown inside the box). Finally we show that the version with clipping at 0pt can also be produced by using the starred version of the pspicture environment .

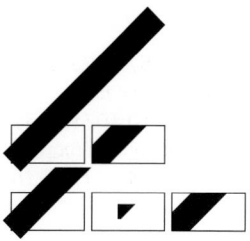

```
\usepackage{pstricks}
\newcommand*\exa[1][0pt]{%
  \fbox{\clipbox[#1]{\begin{pspicture}(1,0.5)
    \psline(2,2)\end{pspicture}}}}

\psset{linewidth=10pt}
\fbox{\pspicture(1,.5)\psline(2,2)\endpspicture}
\exa\\[10pt]
\exa[10pt] \exa[-10pt]
\fbox{\pspicture*(1,.5)\psline(2,2)\endpspicture}
```

10.4.2 \psclip

This clipping box cuts arbitrary material along any curve.

\psclip{*border curve*} … *material*… \endpsclip	% TeX version
\begin{psclip}{*border curve*} … *material*… \end{psclip}	% LaTeX version

```
\usepackage{pstricks}
\begin{pspicture}(-2,-2)(2,1.5)
\psclip{ \pscircle[linestyle=none](0.5\wd\TBox,-0.15\ht\TBox){1.5cm} }
  \usebox\TBox
\endpsclip
\end{pspicture}
\begin{pspicture}(-2,-2)(2,1.5)
\psclip{ \pscurve[linestyle=dashed](-1.5,-1.5)(0,1.5)(1.5,-1.5)(-1.5,-1.5)}
  \rput(0,0){\usebox\TBox}
\endpsclip
\end{pspicture}
```

Often a specific area between different mathematical functions needs to be shaded. To do this, use the \pscustom command (cf. Section 11.3 on page 122) and subsequently fill or clip the area. In the following example the two functions define a path that clips everything outside this path from the shaded frame (-2,0)(2,5).

10 Boxes

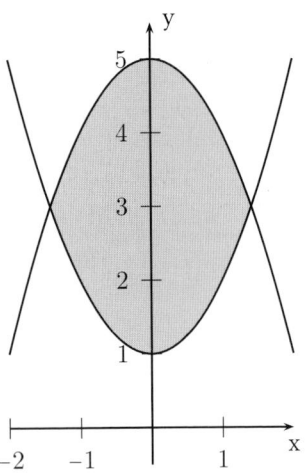

```
\usepackage{pstricks,pst-plot}

\begin{pspicture}(-2,-0.5)(2,5.5)
   \psclip{%
      \pscustom[linestyle=none]{%
         \psplot{-2}{2}{x dup mul 1 add}}
      \pscustom[linestyle=none]{%
         \psplot{2}{-2}{x dup mul neg 5 add}}%
   }% end of \psclip
      \psframe*[linecolor=lightgray](-2,0)(2,5)
   \endpsclip
   \psaxes{->}(0,0)(-2,-0.5)(2,5.5)
   \psplot{-2}{2}{x dup mul 1 add}
   \psplot{2}{-2}{x dup mul neg 5 add}
   \uput[-90](2,0){x}
   \uput[0](0,5.5){y}
\end{pspicture}
```

The clipping commands are not particularly robust. In particular, problems arise when \psclip and \endpsclip don't end on the same page. The use of \AltClipMode forces the use of gsave and grestore (cf. Section 11.3.9 on page 129). This is especially advisable if nested clipping commands are used inside a pspicture* environment.

10.5 Rotating and scaling

10.5.1 Rotating

You can rotate horizontal boxes to the left, right or upside down either by using one of a set of three commands with teh following syntax:

```
\psrotateleft{contents}
\psrotateright{contents}
\psrotatedown{contents}
```

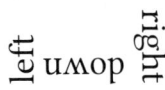

```
\usepackage{pstricks}

\Large\psrotateleft{\Large left}
\psrotatedown{\Large down}
\psrotateright{\Large right}
```

Alternatively you can use one of an equivalent set of environments, with the following internal definitions:

```
\pslongbox{Rotateleft}{\psrotateleft}
\pslongbox{Rotateright}{\psrotateright}
\pslongbox{Rotatedown}{\psrotatedown}
```

The advantage of the environments is that you can use verbatim mode (\verb and verbatim environment), which isn't permitted as a parameter to a command.

10.5 Rotating and scaling

10-05-2

Question: Which commands create a new page?
Answer:
\clearpage and \newpage

```
\usepackage{pstricks}

Question: Which commands create a new page?\\
Answer:

\begin{Rotatedown}%
\verb+\clearpage+ and \verb+\newpage+%
\end{Rotatedown}
```

10-05-3

Felix
Jana
Felix
Jana

```
\usepackage{pstricks}

\psrotateright{\Huge\texttt{Felix}}
\begin{Rotateright}
  \Huge\verb+Jana+%
\end{Rotateright}\psrotateleft{\Huge\texttt{Felix}}
\begin{Rotateleft}
  \Huge\verb+Jana+
\end{Rotateleft}
```

Note that if you are using a version of PSTricks prior to 1.12, the above command names don't have the \ps prefix.

10.5.2 \psscalebox and \psscaleboxto

There are two commands for scaling objects, with the following syntax:

```
\psscalebox{value1  value2 }{contents}
\psscaleboxto(dx,dy){contents}
```

The first command works in the familiar way: if only one scaling factor is given, it scales the object in proportion. If two values are given, separate horizontal and vertical scalings are performed. A negative value both scales and mirrors the object: \psscalebox{-1 1}{word} → bɿow; this example corresponds to \reflectbox from the graphicx package.

\psscaleboxto on the other hand does not scale by a factor, but to the two values specified (measured in the current PSTricks dimension). Here, too, there are two equivalent environments, with which you can use \verb. The definitions are:

```
\pslongbox{Scalebox}{\psscalebox}
\pslongbox{Scaleboxto}{\psscaleboxto}
```

10-05-4

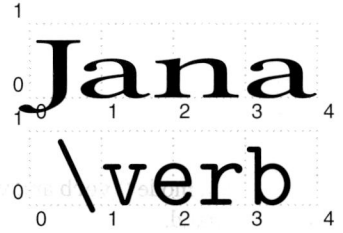

```
\usepackage{pstricks}

\begin{pspicture}[showgrid](4,1)
  \psscaleboxto(4,1){Jana}
\end{pspicture}\\[12pt]
\begin{pspicture}[showgrid](4,1)
  \begin{Scaleboxto}(4,1) \verb+\verb+
  \end{Scaleboxto}
\end{pspicture}
```

If you are using a version of pstricks.tex older than 1.10, the above command names don't have the \ps prefix. This can lead to a conflict with the graphicx package, which also defines a \scalebox command (albeit with different syntax). The pstricks.sty package automatically defines the two PSTricks commands as \psscalebox and \psscaleboxto so that the conflict is avoided. With more recent versions of PSTricks (>1.10), the command names are prefixed with \ps so no further problems arise.

10.6 Mathematics and verbatim boxes

In the introduction to this chapter and in the previous sections, we've mentioned briefly that there are problems with vertical and "verbatim" material. We look at these situations in more detail here.

10.6.1 Mathematics mode

When using math mode, we often want to use vertical material, such as adding a superscript and a subscript to a letter or adding limits above and below an integral sign. However, it's not straightforward to use \fbox to frame these objects as TeX switches back to text mode at the beginning of \fbox; that means that we have to remember to enclose the objects inside the \fbox in math mode again manually: $f(x)=\fbox{$x^2_3$}$ $f(x) = \boxed{x_3^2}$. PSTricks solves this problem by providing a switch that makes sure that this happens automatically:

| \psmathboxtrue   \psmathboxfalse |

By specifying \psmathboxtrue, you can use the \psframebox command in math mode without having to mark its argument with $...$:

$f(x) = \boxed{x_3^2}$

```
\usepackage{pstricks}

\psmathboxtrue $f(x) = \psframebox{x^2_3}$
```

10-06-1

This behaviour can be reversed with \psmathboxfalse; the example above would then generate an error message.

In inline math there is another problem: limits also revert to text style rather than display style. This can be avoided either by switching to \displaystyle style prior to the \psmathbox or by using the following declaration:

| \everypsbox{*code*} |

This declaration makes PSTricks add the specified code prior to **every** box. In this case the code would be \displaystyle. There are many other uses for this command, not just for math mode.

$f(x) = \boxed{\int_a^b \frac{x^2}{3}\,dx}$

```
\usepackage{pstricks}

\psmathboxtrue $f(x)=\psframebox{\int_a^b\frac{x^2}{3}\,dx}$
```

10-06-2

$f(x) = \boxed{\int\limits_a^b \frac{x^2}{3}\,dx}$

```
\usepackage{pstricks}

\everypsbox{\displaystyle}
$f(x)=\psframebox{\int\limits_a^b\frac{x^2}{3}\,dx}$
```

10-06-3

10.6.2 Verbatim mode

In the previous sections we've covered several examples of using "verbatim" material within PSTricks environments in the LR box. Instead of using these environments, there is a switch to make PSTricks handle using \verb inside "normal" box commands, similar to the one just discussed for math mode.

```
\psverbboxtrue
\psverbboxfalse
```

By setting \psverbboxtrue, you can use the \psframebox command together with \verb without having to revert to using an environment:

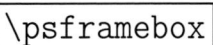   \usepackage{pstricks}

\psverbboxtrue\Large\psframebox{\verb+\psframebox+}

This behaviour can be reverted with \psverbboxfalse; the example above would then generate an error message.

10.7 Examples

Figure 10.1: Demonstration of a clipping path

10 Boxes

Abstract
Lorem ipsum dolor sit amet, urna augue. Luctus sollicitudin, accusantium nostrum. Scelerisque duis eget nonummy, rhoncus

Abstract
Lorem ipsum dolor sit amet, urna augue. Luctus sollicitudin, accusantium nostrum. Scelerisque duis eget nonummy, rhoncus
Lorem ipsum dolor sit amet, urna augue. Luctus sollicitudin, accusantium nostrum. Scelerisque duis eget nonummy, rhoncus

10-07-

Some text in a box

Some text in a box with linearcs only on the left side

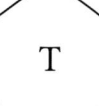
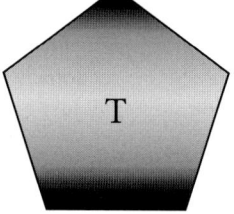

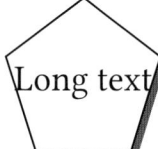

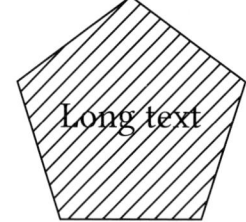

Chapter 11

Custom styles and objects

11.1 Custom styles 121
11.2 Custom objects 122
11.3 \pscustom 122

As well as the many predefined styles and commands that PSTricks offers for creating graphical objects, it also lets you define your own styles, commands, and functionalities. The first two sections in this chapter discuss creating new styles and styled objects, though these are basically just quick ways of reusing a certain specification rather than having to apply it parameter-by-parameter at each use. Then we look at the much more powerful \pscustom command, which lets you perform a wide range of previously undefined functions, allowing for arbitrary area borders for filling and clipping. There are several special commands that can only be used with \pscustom, which are covered in turn, followed by examples.

11.1 Custom styles

If you want to use certain combinations of parameters (cf. Section 2.2 on page 21) repeatedly, you can define special styles for them. Then each time you want to use this style combination, you just specify this new style (using the style keyword) when passing the parameters to a command, rather than having to apply each component of the style separately.

> \newpsstyle{*name*}{*list of parameters*}
> \addtopsstyle{*name*}{*list of parameters*}

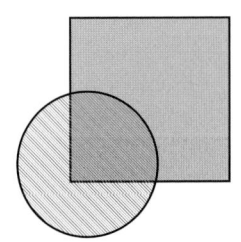

```
\usepackage{pstricks}

\newpsstyle{TransparentMagenta}{%
  fillstyle=vlines,hatchcolor=magenta,
  hatchwidth=0.1\pslinewidth,hatchsep=1\pslinewidth}
\begin{pspicture}(3,3)
  \psframe[fillstyle=solid,fillcolor=cyan](0.75,0.75)(3,3)
  \pscircle[style=TransparentMagenta](1,1){1}
\end{pspicture}
```

11 Custom styles and objects

The idea illustrated in the above example of defining a new style in order to create the illusion of a "transparent" colour was also mentioned earlier in Section 7.2 on page 89.

```
\usepackage{pstricks}

\newpsstyle{Fiber}{linewidth=2pt}
\begin{pspicture}(4,4)
  \psline[style=Fiber](0,0)(4,1)
  \addtopsstyle{Fiber}{linecolor=green}
  \psline[style=Fiber](0,1)(4,2)
  \addtopsstyle{Fiber}{linestyle=dotted}
  \psline[style=Fiber](0,2)(4,3)
  \addtopsstyle{Fibber}{linecolor=red}
  \psline[style=Fibber](0,3)(4,4)
\end{pspicture}
```

11.2 Custom objects

The previous section provided an easy way to use the same style combination repeatedly with different objects. However, if you are dealing with the same *object* repeatedly, life is even easier if you define a new command for that object with its style parameters, rather than having to add the style to the object each time you use it.

```
\newpsobject{name}{name of object}{list of parameters}
```

In the example below the new commands are based on \psline.

```
\usepackage{pstricks}
\newpsobject{LineA}{psline}{linewidth=1.5pt}
\newpsobject{LineB}{LineA}{linestyle=dashed,
  dash=3pt 1.5pt}
\newpsobject{LineC}{LineB}{dash=5pt 2pt}
\newpsobject{LineD}{LineB}{dash=5pt 1pt 1pt 1pt}
\newpsobject{LineE}{LineB}{dash=2pt 1pt}

\begin{pspicture}(4,4)
\LineA(0,0)(4,0)\LineB(0,1)(4,1)\LineC(0,2)(4,2)
\LineD(0,3)(4,3)\LineE(0,4)(4,4)
\end{pspicture}
```

11.3 \pscustom

PSTricks offers many ways to create graphical objects, but you will still find situations where none of the existing commands meet your needs. In these cases, working with \pscustom is usually the answer. Here is the syntax:

```
\pscustom * [settings] {arbitrary code}
```

The starred version fills the background with the current line colour as usual.

11.3 \pscustom

\pscustom creates an arbitrary closed path through a series of lines or curves of whatever form. \pscustom starts the path; the last closing brace terminates it. You can fill or tile the closed path with any colour or pattern through the filling function. You don't need to create line or curve segments that connect to each other. Usually \pscustom automatically joins them up to form a closed polycurve.

There are several special PostScript commands that you can **only** use with \pscustom; we discuss them in the following sections. PSTricks itself uses them frequently as special PSTricks compatible versions. This has the advantage that no additional use of the \special command is necessary. These additional commands influence the PostScript output virtually without any control by PSTricks so it is useful to have some basic knowledge of PostScript as a programming language before using them. Because of the PostScript-specific code, the current scale doesn't apply for these commands; only two units are valid, the common PostScript unit bp (big points) or pt.

The \pscustom command uses \pstverb (cf. Section 14.2.6 on page 154) and \pstunit (cf. Section 2.4 on page 22), which write \special into the DVI file. The length of the argument is system-specific; problems can arise when putting many small polycurves together within \pscustom because these are all arguments of a single \special command. Also beware that PSTricks objects defined through the special command sequence \begin@SpecialObj...\end@SpecialObj can't be used within the argument of \pscustom. PSTricks outputs a corresponding error message in this case.

11.3.1 Parameters

Because \pscustom refers to a **single** closed path, it (generally) only takes notice of parameters referring to the whole path, i. e. assigned to \pscustom rather than to its component commands. It is therefore advisable as a rule not to use any parameters with the commands within \pscustom. There are a few exceptions to this, for example when adding arrows; these are pointed out separately in the examples in the following sections. The next example illustrates this behaviour: \psline is executed outside and inside \pscustom to create an upper and lower triangle respectively, both of which we want filled. In the left example, the lower triangle is not filled, however, as the linewidth, linecolor, and fillstyle parameters were assigned to \psline itself inside \pscustom; in the correct example, the lower triangle is filled, as the parameters were specified through the optional argument of \pscustom.

```
\usepackage{pstricks}
\begin{pspicture}[showgrid](3,3)
\psline[linewidth=2pt,linecolor=blue,fillstyle=vlines](0,1)(2,3)(0,3)
\pscustom{\psline[linewidth=2pt,linecolor=blue,fillstyle=hlines](1,0)(3,2)(3,0)}
\end{pspicture}\qquad
\begin{pspicture}[showgrid](3,3)
\psline[linewidth=2pt,linecolor=blue,fillstyle=vlines](0,1)(2,3)(0,3)
\pscustom[linewidth=2pt,linecolor=blue,fillstyle=hlines]{\psline(1,0)(3,2)(3,0)}
\end{pspicture}
```

11 Custom styles and objects

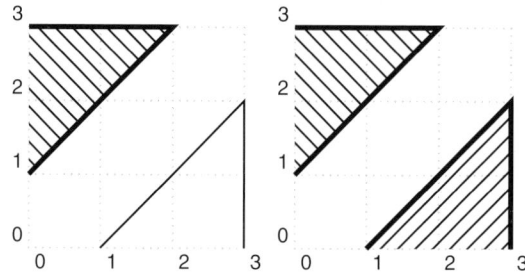

As mentioned in Section 4.1.17 on page 52, there can be problems using the dashed and dotted line styles with \pscustom as they don't know anything about an existing path when assigned to \pscustom. To avoid problems, you also need to give \pscustom the linetype parameter for the existing line style as listed in Table 4.2 on page 52.

 Note that shadow, border, doubleline, and showpoints are **not** available with the \pscustom command. Also, the origin and swapaxes parameters only affect \pscustom itself.

11.3.2 Open and closed curves

As we have said before, PSTricks distinguishes between closed curves and open curves. The actual primary purpose of \pscustom is for connecting open lines and curves. As \pscustom itself creates closed polylines and polycurves, it makes little sense to use closed lines or curves within \pscustom – and in fact we recommend you avoid it as unexpected side effects can result.

In principle \pscustom draws a direct line from the end of the last-drawn line/curve to the start of the next line or curve if it defines an **end arrow**; if not, \pscustom doesn't connect the lines/curves. This is shown in the following example where in the red (outer) curve a connection is made from the first arc to the second one because it has an end arrow.

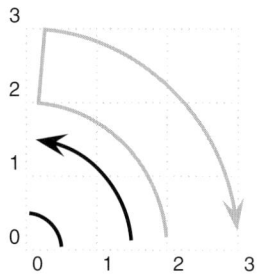

```
\usepackage{pstricks}

\begin{pspicture}[showgrid](3,3)
\psset{linewidth=1.5pt,arrowscale=2}
\pscustom[linecolor=red]{%
  \psarc(0,0){2}{5}{85}\psarcn{->}(0,0){3}{85}{5}}
\pscustom[linecolor=blue]{%
  \psarc(0,0){0.5}{5}{85}\psarcn{<-}(0,0){1.5}{85}{5}}
\end{pspicture}
```

The above example assumes that the arrow is defined locally as it is only valid for a single polycurve.

 The \psline, \pscurve, and \psbezier commands start at the current point when their parameters are "incomplete", i.e. insufficient coordinate points are given. Normally PSTricks sets the starting point to the coordinate origin in these cases for \psline and \psbezier, but if the commands are within \pscustom it continues from the end of the previous line or curve. In the following example this behaviour results in a polyline whereas, without \pscustom, the commands would produce two independent lines starting at the coordinate origin and no curve would be drawn as \pscurve is specified with fewer than three coordinate pairs.

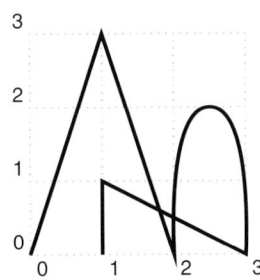

```
\usepackage{pstricks}

\begin{pspicture}[showgrid](3,3)
\pscustom[linewidth=1.5pt]{%
  \psline(1,3)\psline(2,0)
  \pscurve(2.5,2)(3,0)
  \psline(1,1)(1,0)}
\end{pspicture}
```

Note that \psgrid, \psdots, \qline, \qdisk are **not** available within \pscustom. Also, bear in mind that we recommend you **not** to include closed lines or curves within \pscustom.

11.3.3 liftpen

The liftpen parameter, mentioned briefly in Chapter 4, is a powerful tool for controlling the connection of several partial lines or curves within \pscustom.

Table 11.1: Meaning of the liftpen parameter

value	meaning
0	If a new polyline or polycurve does not start at the current point, a line is drawn from the current point to the starting point of the line or curve (default behaviour). If there is a line or curve with incomplete coordinates, the current point is included as the starting point.
1	The current point is not taken into account when the specification of coordinates is incomplete; instead the coordinate origin is included as the starting point (only applies to \psline, \psbezier, and \pscurve).
2	Single polylines or polycurves are treated as individual units; they don't use the current point as starting point (with incomplete coordinates) and no line is drawn from the current point to the starting point of the next object.

The commands within \pscustom in the next example are almost identical to those in the previous example, the only difference being that this time the second and third commands have liftpen=1 as parameter. This means that the second line doesn't use the endpoint of the first line as its starting point, but uses the coordinate origin instead. Also, no \pscurve is drawn in this case as with liftpen=1 the current point is not added to the incomplete coordinates. The current point therefore remains at $(2,0)$, so the connecting line to the last \psline command's starting point $(1,1)$ begins from there. The original result is shown with dashed lines for comparison.

11 Custom styles and objects

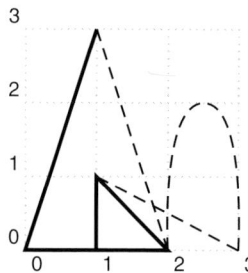

```
\usepackage{pstricks}

\begin{pspicture}[showgrid](3,3)
  \pscustom[linewidth=1.5pt]{%
    \psline(1,3)\psline[liftpen=1](2,0)
    \pscurve[liftpen=1](2.5,2)(3,0)
    \psline(1,1)(1,0)}
  \psline[linestyle=dashed](1,3)(2,0)
  \pscurve[linestyle=dashed](2,0)(2.5,2)(3,0)
  \psline[linestyle=dashed](3,0)(1,1)
\end{pspicture}
```

The same example with complete coordinates for \pscurve yields:

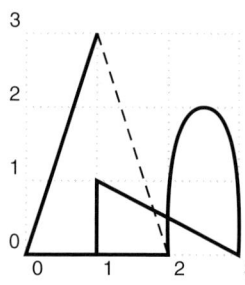

```
\usepackage{pstricks}

\begin{pspicture}[showgrid](3,3)
  \pscustom[linewidth=1.5pt]{%
    \psline(1,3)\psline[liftpen=1](2,0)
    \pscurve[liftpen=1](2,0)(2.5,2)(3,0)
    \psline(1,1)(1,0)}
  \psline[linestyle=dashed](1,3)(2,0)
\end{pspicture}
```

Let's look at another example that compares results for the different values of liftpen. It uses the \psplot command, provided by the pst-plot package (cf. Chapter 15 on page 165).

```
\usepackage{pstricks,pst-plot}
\begin{pspicture}[showgrid](3,3)
\pscustom[fillcolor=lightgray,fillstyle=solid]{%
  \psplot{0}{2.6}{x RadtoDeg 2 mul sin 2 add}
  \pscurve(3,1)(2,0)(1,1)(0,0)}
\end{pspicture}\quad
\begin{pspicture}[showgrid](3,3)
  \pscustom[fillcolor=lightgray,fillstyle=solid]{%
    \psplot{0}{2.6}{x RadtoDeg 2 mul sin 2 add}
    \pscurve[liftpen=1](3,1)(2,0)(1,1)(0,0)}
\end{pspicture}\quad
\begin{pspicture}[showgrid](3,3)
  \pscustom[fillcolor=lightgray,fillstyle=solid]{%
    \psplot{0}{2.6}{x RadtoDeg 2 mul sin 2 add}
    \pscurve[liftpen=2](3,1)(2,0)(1,1)(0,0)}
\end{pspicture}
```

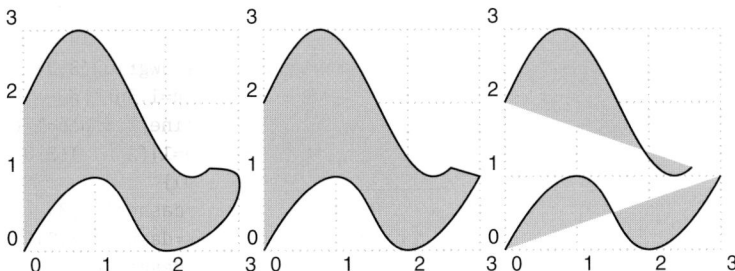

The left example (liftpen=0) uses the endpoint of the first curve (\psplot) as starting point of the next curve (\pscurve). The example in the middle (liftpen=1) does **not** use the endpoint of the first curve (\psplot) as the starting point of the next curve (\pscurve); instead it draws a connecting line from the endpoint of the first curve to the starting point of the second curve. In the right example (liftpen=2) neither of the above occur: two individual units are created instead.

11.3.4 \moveto

The \moveto command moves the current point to the new coordinates (x, y) without drawing a line.

```
\moveto(x,y)
```

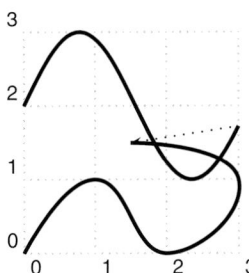

```
\usepackage{pstricks,pst-plot}
\SpecialCoor

\begin{pspicture}[showgrid](3,3)
  \pscustom[linewidth=1.5pt]{%
    \psplot{0}{3}{x 180 mul 1.57 div sin 2 add}
    \moveto(1.5,1.5)\pscurve(3,1)(2,0)(1,1)(0,0)}
  \psline[linestyle=dotted]{->}%
    (! 3 dup 180 mul 1.57 div sin 2 add)(1.5,1.5)
\end{pspicture}
```

11.3.5 \newpath

\newpath is identical to the PostScript command newpath. The current path is deleted and a new one started; all information about the old path is lost. In the following example the first curve is not drawn for this reason.

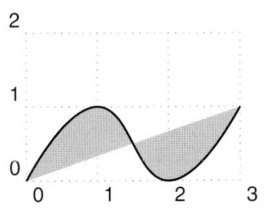

```
\usepackage{pstricks,pst-plot}

\begin{pspicture}[showgrid](3,2)
\pscustom[fillcolor=lightgray,fillstyle=solid]{%
  \psplot{0}{3}{x 180 mul 1.57 div sin 2 add}
  \newpath
  \pscurve(3,1)(2,0)(1,1)(0,0) }
\end{pspicture}
```

11.3.6 \closepath

\closepath is the counterpart to \newpath, and similarly it is identical to the PostScript command closepath. The current path is closed by connecting the starting point and the endpoint. When using \moveto many different parts may exist; they are all treated separately. The starting point is made the current point; after that all information about the old path is lost.

The following example determines the starting point (0, 2) as the new current point after the application of \closepath; this makes the next curve look completely different as it uses this point as its starting point.

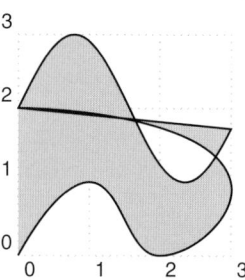

```
\usepackage{pstricks,pst-plot}

\begin{pspicture}[showgrid](3,3)
    \pscustom[fillcolor=lightgray,
        fillstyle=solid]{%
    \psplot{0}{3}{x 180 mul 1.57 div sin 2 add}
    \closepath
    \pscurve(3,1)(2,0)(1,1)(0,0)}
\end{pspicture}
```

11.3.7 \stroke

The \stroke command lets you pass special parameters to single sections within the \pscustom command in order to affect the drawing of the previously created polyline or polycurve.

\stroke [settings]

Inserting a \stroke command does not replace the \stroke command carried out by PSTricks itself in the PostScript code at the end of a \pscustom command. This means that if you don't choose a larger line width for your command it will be completely overwritten. The next example illustrates how to create special lines from several colours by adding extra \stroke commands in red, blue, and green of decreasing thickness. Finally the white line defined by the \pscustom command is added.

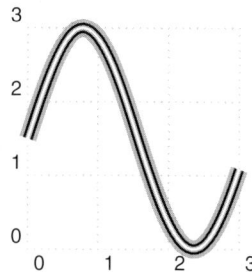

```
\usepackage{pstricks,pst-plot}

\begin{pspicture}[showgrid](3,3)
    \pscustom[linecolor=white]{%
    \psplot{0}{3}{x 180 mul 1.57 div sin
        1.5 mul 1.5 add}
    \stroke[linecolor=red,linewidth=7pt]
    \stroke[linecolor=blue,linewidth=4pt]
    \stroke[linecolor=green,linewidth=2pt]}
\end{pspicture}
```

11.3.8 \fill

\fill, analogous to \stroke, lets you pass special parameters to single sections within the \pscustom command in order to affect the fill of the polyline or polycurve created previously.

11.3 \pscustom

\fill [settings]

Again \fill does not replace the \fill carried out by PSTricks in the PostScript code at the end of a \pscustom command. As this fills the area with the current fill colour and fill style at the end anyway, possible applications of \fill are limited.

```
\usepackage{pstricks}
\begin{pspicture}(2.5,11.25)(3.4,12.5)
\pscustom{\moveto(2.6,11.75)
 \curveto(2.66,11.43)(2.89,11.14)(3.07,11.18)
 \curveto(3.24,11.21)(3.35,11.56)(3.28,11.88)
 \fill[fillstyle=solid,fillcolor=red]
 \curveto(3.22,12.20)(2.98,12.49)(2.81,12.45)
 \curveto(2.64,12.42)(2.53,12.06)(2.60,11.75)}
\end{pspicture} \qquad
\begin{pspicture}(2.5,11.25)(3.4,12.5)
\pscustom[fillstyle=solid,fillcolor=red]{\moveto(2.6,11.75)
 \curveto(2.66,11.43)(2.89,11.14)(3.07,11.18)
 \curveto(3.24,11.21)(3.35,11.56)(3.28,11.88)
 \curveto(3.22,12.20)(2.98,12.49)(2.81,12.45)
 \curveto(2.64,12.42)(2.53,12.06)(2.60,11.75)}
\end{pspicture}
```

11.3.9 \gsave and \grestore

\gsave saves the current PostScript stack referring to the graphical output (path specifications, colour, line width, coordinate origin, etc.). \grestore restores all these values. The next example uses \gsave to save a plotted path, then defines an enclosed area with borders that are not visible and fills it, and then uses \grestore to restore the plotted path.

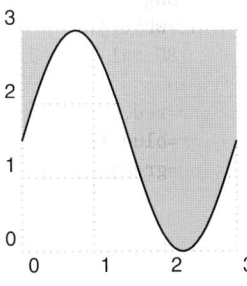

```
\usepackage{pstricks,pst-plot}

\begin{pspicture}[showgrid](3,3)
  \pscustom{%
    \psplot{0}{3}{x 180.0 mul 1.5 div
      sin 1.5 mul 1.5 add}
    \gsave
      \psline(3,3)(0,3)% is _not_ drawn
      \fill[fillcolor=lightgray,fillstyle=solid]
    \grestore }
\end{pspicture}
```

11 Custom styles and objects

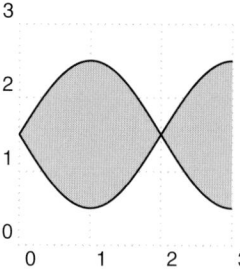

```
\usepackage{pst-plot}\SpecialCoor

\begin{pspicture}[showgrid](3,3)
  \pstVerb{/rad {180.0 mul 2 div} def}
  \pscustom[plotpoints=200]{%
    \psplot{0}{3}{x rad sin 1.5 add}
    \gsave
    \psline(! 3 dup rad sin 1.5 add)%
              (!3 dup rad sin neg 1.5 add)
    \psplot{3}{0}{x rad sin neg 1.5 add}
    \fill[fillcolor=lightgray,fillstyle=solid]
    \grestore
    \psplot[liftpen=2]{3}{0}{x rad sin neg 1.5 add}}
\end{pspicture}
```

> Note that \gsave and \grestore commands must be used **in pairs**; they can be arbitrarily nested.

11.3.10 \translate

\translate moves the coordinate origin to (x, y) for all subsequent graphical operations.

$\boxed{\texttt{\textbackslash translate}(x, y)}$

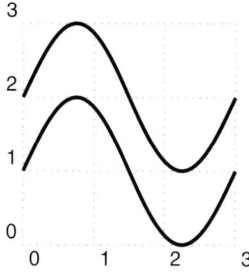

```
\usepackage{pstricks,pst-plot}

\begin{pspicture}[showgrid](3,3)
  \pscustom[linewidth=1.5pt]{%
    \translate(0,1)
    \psplot{0}{3}{x 180.0 mul 1.5 div sin}
    \translate(0,1)
    \psplot[liftpen=2]{0}{3}{x 180.0 mul 1.5 div sin}}
\end{pspicture}
```

11.3.11 \scale

Unlike other length assignments, \scale takes only dimensionless values, which are assumed to have unit pt.

$\boxed{\texttt{\textbackslash scale}\{\textit{value1}\ \textit{value2}\ \}}$

It behaves in the usual way, scaling the \pscustom object by *value1* horizontally and by *value2* vertically, or if no second value is specified, scaling it proportionally by *value1*. As can be seen from the example, you can also usenegative values, which correspond to scaling and mirroring.

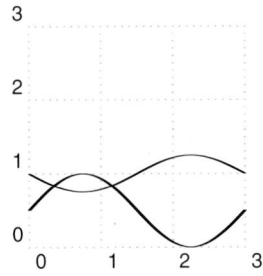

```
\usepackage{pstricks,pst-plot}

\begin{pspicture}[showgrid](3,3)
 \pscustom[linewidth=1.5pt]{%
    \scale{1 0.5}
    \translate(0,1)
    \psplot{0}{3}{x 180.0 mul 1.5 div sin}
    \translate(0,1)
    \scale{1 -0.5}
    \psplot[liftpen=2]{0}{3}{x 180.0 mul 1.5 div sin}}
\end{pspicture}
```

11.3.12 \rotate

\rotate{*angle in degrees*}

\rotate rotates the \pscustom object by the desired angle, which has to be specified in degrees to be compliant with PostScript.

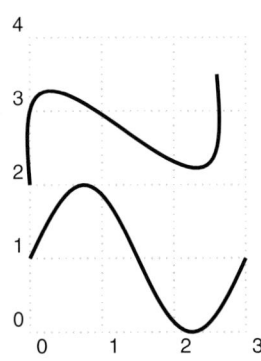

```
\usepackage{pstricks,pst-plot}

\begin{pspicture}[showgrid](3,4)
 \pscustom[linewidth=1.5pt]{%
    \translate(0,1)
    \psplot[liftpen=2]{0}{3}{
      x 180.0 mul 1.5 div sin}
    \translate(0,1)
    \rotate{30}
    \psplot[liftpen=2]{0}{3}{
      x 180.0 mul 1.5 div sin}
  }
\end{pspicture}
```

11.3.13 \swapaxes

In Chapter 3 on page 31 we discussed using \swapaxes as a parameter. This just swaps the *x-y* axes, which is equivalent to \rotate{-90} \scale{-1 1}. You can achieve greater effects by using \swapaxes within a \pscustom command.

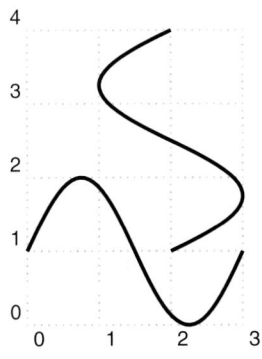

```
\usepackage{pstricks,pst-plot}

\begin{pspicture}[showgrid](3,4)
 \pscustom[linewidth=1.5pt]{%
    \translate(0,1)
    \psplot{0}{3}{x 180.0 mul 1.5 div sin}
    \translate(2,0)
    \swapaxes
    \psplot[liftpen=2]{0}{3}%
      {x 180.0 mul 1.5 div sin}}
\end{pspicture}
```

11.3.14 \msave and \mrestore

These commands can be used to save and restore the currently valid coordinate system. In contrast to \gsave and \grestore all other parameters such as line type, line width, etc. are not affected by this.

The example draws the first sine function with the coordinate origin at \translate(0,1.5); after that the state of the coordinate system is saved. Then \translate(1,2) moves the origin from its current position of (0,1.5) to the absolute coordinates (0,3.5). Then another sine function is drawn. Afterwards the old state is restored with the \mrestore command; the coordinate origin is at (0,1.5) again and the following cosine function refers to it again.

```
\usepackage{pstricks,pst-plot}

\begin{pspicture}[showgrid](3,4)
  \pscustom[linewidth=1.5pt]{%
    \translate(0,1.5)
    \psplot{0}{3}{x 180.0 mul 1.5 div sin}%
    \msave
      \translate(1,2) \scale{1 0.5}
      \psplot[liftpen=2]{-1}{2}%
        {x 180.0 mul 1.5 div sin}
    \mrestore
    \psplot[liftpen=2]{0}{3}%
      {x 180.0 mul 0.5 div cos}}
\end{pspicture}
```

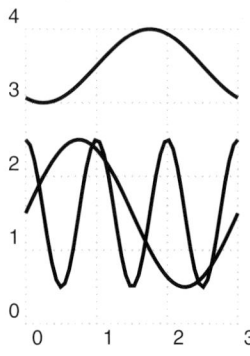

Note that the \msave and \mrestore commands must be used **in pairs**. They can be arbitrarily nested with themselves or with \gsave and \grestore, but the nesting has to be balanced pairwise.

11.3.15 \openshadow

\openshadow creates a copy of the current path using the specified shadow-parameters. In contrast to \closedshadow (discussed next), the original path is not filled with a colour by default - it stays "open". You can set it to be filled though, if desired.

\openshadow [settings]

```
\usepackage{pstricks,pst-plot}

\begin{pspicture}[showgrid](3,4)
  \pscustom{%
    \translate(0,3)
    \psplot{0}{3}{x 180.0 mul 1.5 div sin}
    \openshadow[shadowsize=6pt]}
  \pscustom[fillcolor=black!20,fillstyle=solid]{%
    \translate(0,1)
    \psplot{0}{3}{x 180.0 mul 1.5 div sin}
    \openshadow[shadowsize=6pt]}
\end{pspicture}
```

11.3.16 \closedshadow

\closedshadow creates a shadow of the area defined by the current path as if this area were not transparent.

\closedshadow [settings]

```
\usepackage{pstricks,pst-plot}

\begin{pspicture}(3,2)
  \pscustom{\translate(0,1)
    \psplot{0}{3}{x 180.0 mul 1.5 div sin}
    \closedshadow[shadowsize=6pt]}
\end{pspicture}
```

It's useful to bear in mind how the shadow is created: PSTricks simply copies the closed path, translates it according to the specifications of shadowsize and shadowangle, fills it with shadowcolor, and fills the old path again with fillcolor, which is set to white by default. If the second filling is suppressed (corresponds to \openshadow), it results in the complete shadow copy shown in the left example below, in contrast to the correct result next to it on the right.

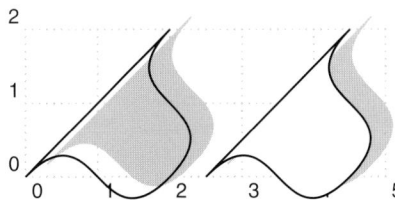

When specifying a fillcolor other than white for \pscustom, you must also remember to pass the right fill colour to the \closedshadow command. The following examples show some of the possibilities:

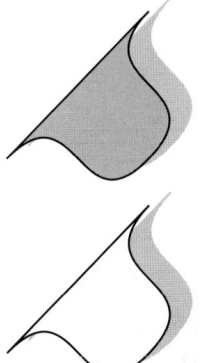

```
\usepackage{pstricks}

\begin{pspicture}(0,-0.25)(2.5,2)
\pscustom[shadowcolor=black!30,fillcolor=red]{%
  \psbezier(0,0)(1,1)(1,-1)(2,0)\psbezier(3,1)(1,1)(2,2)
  \closepath
  \closedshadow[shadowsize=10pt,shadowangle=30]}
\end{pspicture}\\[10pt]
\begin{pspicture}(0,-0.25)(2.5,2)
\pscustom[shadowcolor=black!30,fillcolor=red]{%
  \psbezier(0,0)(1,1)(1,-1)(2,0)\psbezier(3,1)(1,1)(2,2)
  \closepath
  \closedshadow[shadowsize=10pt,shadowangle=30,
    fillcolor=white]}
\end{pspicture}
```

11.3.17 \movepath

\movepath translates the current path by (dx, dy); after that, the orginal path is lost. \gsave and \grestore can be used to save and restore the original path, however.

`\movepath(dx,dy)`

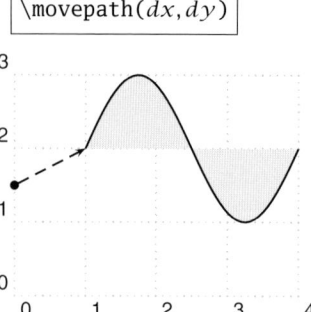

```
\usepackage{pstricks,pst-plot}

\begin{pspicture}[showgrid](4,3)
  \pscustom[fillcolor=black!10,
      fillstyle=solid]{%
    \translate(0,1.5)
    \psplot{0}{3}{x 180.0 mul 1.5 div sin}
    \movepath(1,0.5)}
  \psline[linestyle=dashed]{*->}(0,1.5)(1,2)
\end{pspicture}
```

11.3.18 \lineto

\lineto corresponds to \psline$(x,y)$ in principle; it always draws a line to (x,y) starting from the current point (which therefore has to exist).

`\lineto(x,y)`

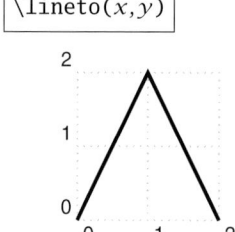

```
\usepackage{pstricks}

\begin{pspicture}[showgrid](2,2)
  \pscustom[linewidth=1.5pt]{%
    \psline(0,0)(1,2)\lineto(2,0)}
\end{pspicture}
```

11.3.19 \rlineto

\rlineto corresponds to \lineto$(x,y)$ in principle, except that the pair of values indicate a relative translation from the current point.

`\rlineto(dx,dy)`

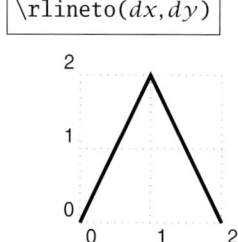

```
\usepackage{pstricks}

\begin{pspicture}[showgrid](2,2)
  \pscustom[linewidth=1.5pt]{%
    \psline(0,0)(1,2)\rlineto(1,-2)}
\end{pspicture}
```

11.3.20 \curveto

\curveto corresponds to \psbezier$(x_1,y_1)(x_2,y_2)(x_3,y_3)$ in principle; it takes the current point as the first one (which therefore has to exist).

$\boxed{\texttt{\textbackslash curveto}(x_1,y_1)(x_2,y_2)(x_3,y_3)}$

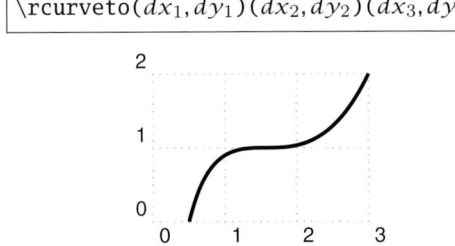

```
\usepackage{pstricks}

\begin{pspicture}[showgrid](3,2)
    \pscustom[linewidth=1.5pt]{%
        \moveto(0.5,0)\curveto(1,2)(2,0)(3,2)}
\end{pspicture}
```

11.3.21 \rcurveto

\rcurveto corresponds to \curveto$(x_1,y_1)(x_2,y_2)(x_3,y_3)$ in principle, except that *each* pair of values indicates a coordinate pair by a relative translation from the (same) current point.

$\boxed{\texttt{\textbackslash rcurveto}(dx_1,dy_1)(dx_2,dy_2)(dx_3,dy_3)}$

```
\usepackage{pstricks}

\begin{pspicture}[showgrid](3,2)
    \pscustom[linewidth=1.5pt]{%
        \moveto(0.5,0)
        \rcurveto(0.5,2)(1.5,0)(2.5,2)}
\end{pspicture}
```

11.3.22 \code

\code inserts the PostScript code given as parameter directly into the PostScript output. This command is identical to \addto@pscode and should be preferred over using \special in **all** cases. Another example for \code can be found in Section 15.4.5 on page 215.

$\boxed{\texttt{\textbackslash code}\{\textit{PostScript code}\}}$

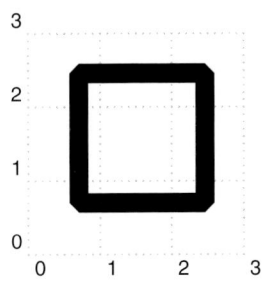

```
\usepackage{pstricks}

\begin{pspicture}[showgrid](3,3)
    \pscustom{%
        \code{%
            newpath
            20 20 moveto 0 50 rlineto
            50 0 rlineto 0 -50 rlineto
            -50 0 rlineto closepath
            2 setlinejoin 7.5 setlinewidth stroke}}
\end{pspicture}
```

11.3.23 \dim

\dim converts the current PSTricks unit to pt, in such a way that you can do calculations in the units specified by the pspicture environment, and then it puts the result on the PostScript stack.

11 Custom styles and objects

```
\dim{value unit}
```

In this example translation dimensions are given in pairs and put on the stack, then the code references them (using LIFO) to create the path.

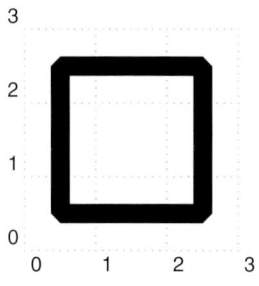

```
\usepackage{pstricks}

\begin{pspicture}[showgrid](3,3)
    \pscustom{%
        \code{newpath}
        \dim{0cm}\dim{-2cm}  \dim{2cm}\dim{0cm}
        \dim{0cm}\dim{2cm}   \dim{0.5cm}\dim{0.5cm}
        \code{
            moveto rlineto rlineto rlineto closepath
            2 setlinejoin 7.5 setlinewidth
            stroke}}
\end{pspicture}
```

11.3.24 \coor

\coor converts the specified coordinates from the PSTricks unit to pt, in such a way that you can do calculations in the units specified by the pspicture environment, and then it puts the result on the PostScript stack. Using \coor with several coordinates is simpler than repeatedly using \dim; \coor internally uses the \pst@@getcoor{#1} command, which is called recursively when more than one coordinate pair is supplied.

```
\coor(x₁,y₁)(x₂,y₂)...(xₙ,yₙ)
```

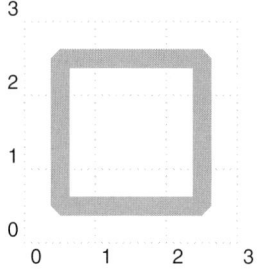

```
\usepackage{pstricks}

\begin{pspicture}[showgrid](3,3)
    \pscustom[linecolor=red]{%
        \code{newpath}\coor(0,-2)(2,0)(0,2)(0.5,0.5)
        \code{ moveto rlineto rlineto rlineto
            closepath
            2 setlinejoin 7.5 setlinewidth stroke}}
\end{pspicture}
```

11.3.25 \rcoor

\rcoor is in principle identical to \coor except that the coordinates are put on the stack in reverse order (reverse coor).

11.3 \pscustom

$\boxed{\texttt{\textbackslash rcoor}(x_1,y_1)(x_2,y_2)\ldots(x_n,y_n)}$

```
\usepackage{pstricks}

\begin{pspicture}[showgrid](3,3)
 \pscustom{%
   \code{newpath}\rcoor(0.5,0.5)(0,2)(2,0)(0,-2)
   \code{ moveto rlineto rlineto rlineto
     closepath
     2 setlinejoin 7.5 setlinewidth stroke}}
\end{pspicture}
```

11.3.26 \file

$\boxed{\texttt{\textbackslash file}\{\textit{filename}\}}$

\file inserts the contents of a file without any expansion as PostScript code. Only comment lines starting with "%" are ignored. The following example reads the contents of the file file.ps previously written with filecontents and executes the corresponding commands.

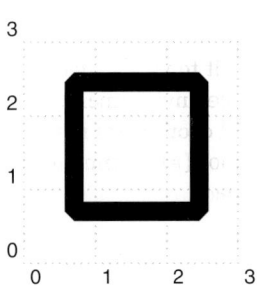

```
\usepackage{pstricks}
\begin{filecontents*}{data/file.ps}
newpath 20  20 moveto    0 50 rlineto 50 0 rlineto
0 -50 rlineto -50 0 rlineto closepath
2 setlinejoin 7.5 setlinewidth stroke
\end{filecontents*}

\begin{pspicture}[showgrid](3,3)
 \pscustom{\file{data/file.ps}}
\end{pspicture}
```

11.3.27 \arrows

\arrows defines the type of line ends to insert at the beginning and end of the line or curve.

$\boxed{\texttt{\textbackslash arrows}\{\textit{arrow type}\}}$

Internally the two PostScript procedures ArrowA and ArrowB are used; parameters are to be given as follows:

```
x2 y2 x1 y1 ArrowA
x2 y2 x1 y1 ArrowB
```

Both draw an arrow from (x_2, y_2) to (x_1, y_1). ArrowA sets the current point to the end of the arrow and leaves (x_2, y_2) on the stack. On the other hand, ArrowB does not change the current point, but leaves the four values x2 y2 x1' y1' on the stack, where (x'_1, y'_1) is the point where a line or curve connects.

11 Custom styles and objects

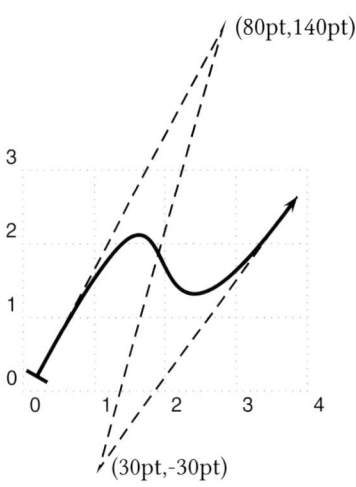

```
\usepackage{pstricks}

\SpecialCoor
\begin{pspicture}[showgrid](4,3)
\pscustom[linewidth=1.5pt]{%
   \arrows{|->}
   \code{%
      80 140 5 5 ArrowA     % 80 140 on the stack
      30 -30 110 75 ArrowB  % 30 -30 105.41 68.986
      curveto}}             % curve for three points
   \psline[linestyle=dashed]%
      (5pt,5pt)(80pt,140pt)(30pt,-30pt)(110pt,75pt)
\uput[0](80pt,140pt){(80pt,140pt)}
\uput[0](30pt,-30pt){(30pt,-30pt)}
\end{pspicture}
```

11.3.28 \setcolor

\setcolor sets the current colour and uses \pst@usecolor internally.

| \setcolor{*colour name*} |

```
\usepackage{pstricks}

\begin{pspicture}[showgrid](3,3)
\pscustom{%
   \code{newpath}
   \rcoor(0.5,0.5)(0,2)(2,0)(0,-2)
   \setcolor{red}
   \code{ moveto rlineto rlineto rlineto
      closepath
      2 setlinejoin 7.5 setlinewidth stroke}}
\end{pspicture}
```

138

Chapter 12

Coordinates

12.1 Defining Points 139
12.2 Angle specifications 144
12.3 Obsolete commands 145
12.4 Examples for \SpecialCoor 146

It is possible to switch arbitrarily between "normal" and "special" defined coordinates within a document or a pspicture environment. This chapter looks at the special forms that are available.

```
\SpecialCoor  % activates special coordinates
\NormalCoor   % only (x,y) pairs are allowed
```

When \SpecialCoor is activated, coordinates are examined for the type of the values internally before processing them. This can take a while if extensive calculations of points is involved, so if you are dealing with Cartesian coordinates it makes more sense to use \NormalCoor. Nowadays, however, with the power of modern computers, there isn't really any problem with activating \SpecialCoor globally.

12.1 Defining Points

When \SpecialCoor is activated, the additional functionality listed in Table 12.1 becomes available. The following sections look at each form in turn, giving examples.

Table 12.1: Valid coordinate forms when \SpecialCoor is activated

syntax	explanation	example
(x,y)	Cartesian coordinates (default).	$(2,-3)$

continued...

12 Coordinates

... continued

syntax	explanation	example
$(r;\alpha)$	Polar coordinates.	$(2;-60)$
(! PS code)	The argument has to yield two values for x y on the stack. Apart from that condition, any arbitrary PostScript code is possible. The values are specified in *user coordinates* and then they are converted internally to PostScript coordinates (pt) taking \psxunit and \psyunit into account.	(! 2 sin -20 cos)
(* x {Algebraic expression})	This is the alternative to the ! operator; again it has to yield two values on the stack after evaluating the input x {f(x)}; the mathematical expression must be given in algebraic form. You must enclose f(x) in curly braces if the expression itself contains parentheses.	(* Pi {sin(x)^2-2cos(x)})
(*pair1*|*pair2*)	The *x* value of the first coordinate pair is taken, the *y* value from the second pair. In this example the polar coordinates (*2;35*) are converted to Cartesian coordinates before combining.	(2;35|3,-4)
(*node name*)	The geometric centre of an arbitrary node defined before.	(A)
([*parameter*]*node name*)	The coordinates are determined by the geometric centre of the node, translated relatively by the values specified with the parameters, which refer to the angle (angle), horizontal translation (nodesep), and vertical translation (offset).	([nodesep=-1]A)
([*parameter*]{*node 2*}*node 1*)	The coordinates are determined by the geometric centre of node 1, translated relatively by the values specified with the parameters, which refer to the angle (angle), horizontal translation (nodesep and [X|Y]nodesep), and vertical translation (offset), which is given by a virtual connecting line between node 2 and node 1.	([nodesep=-1]{B}A)

12.1.1 Polar coordinates

Polar coordinates are specified in the usual notation: (*radius;angle*). The \runit scale (cf. Section 2.4 on page 22) applies to the radius and for the angle the scale is determined by the \degrees[*full circle*] command (cf. Section 2.4.2 on page 23).

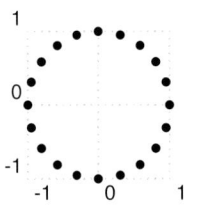

```
\usepackage{pstricks,multido}
\SpecialCoor

\begin{pspicture}[showgrid](-1,-1)(1,1)
    \multido{\iAngle=0+18}{20}{\psdot(1;\iAngle)}
\end{pspicture}
```

12-01-1

12.1.2 Coordinates calculated with PostScript

There are two possibilities for calculated coordinates: either a pure PostScript version or a modified one that allows the specification of a function in algebraic notation.

(!PS code): The PostScript code has to put a pair of numbers x y on the stack. The coordinates refer to the scale specified by the user through [x|y]unit; for example cm. The next example shows the conversion of given polar coordinates into a x y pair of numbers; there is in fact a separate PostScript procedure for this however.

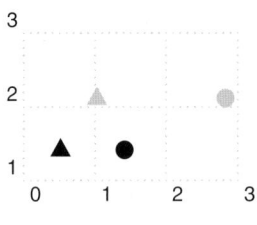

```
\usepackage{pstricks}\SpecialCoor

\begin{pspicture}[showgrid](0,1)(3,3)
    \psset{dotscale=2,xunit=2,yunit=1.5}
    \psdot(2;45)
    \psdot[linecolor=cyan](!2 45 cos mul 2 45 sin mul)
    \psset{dotstyle=triangle*}
    \psdot(1.5;70)
    \psdot[linecolor=cyan](!1.5 70 cos mul 1.5 70 sin mul)
\end{pspicture}
```

The next example uses the rand function of PostScript which yields a random real number that is then restricted to the interval [0..3] by the subsequent operations. Also the colour of the dot is determined randomly.

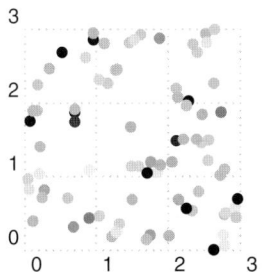

```
\usepackage{pstricks}
\SpecialCoor

\begin{pspicture}[showgrid](3,3)
    \psset{dotscale=1.25}
    \multips(0,0){80}{%
        \psdot(! rand 301 mod 100 div
            rand 301 mod 100 div rand 101
            mod 100 div 1 1 sethsbcolor)}
\end{pspicture}
```

(*x {Algebraic expression}): x stands for the *x* coordinate; you must give it as a numeric value or an internally defined constant (for example π), with no space inserted between the * and the value. *Algebraic expression* stands for a function in *algebraic* notation; don't forget to enclose it in curly braces if the expression itself contains parentheses. Unlike the pure PostScript notation, this version expects angle specifications in radian.

*No space between * and the x value!*

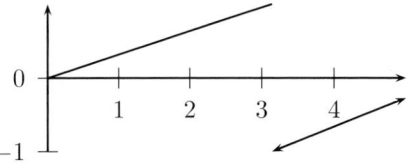

```
\usepackage{pst-plot}\SpecialCoor

\begin{pspicture}(0,-1)(5,1)
    \psaxes{->}(0,0)(0,-1)(5,1)
    \psline(0,0)(*Pi {sqrt(abs(cos(x)))})
    \psline{<->}(*Pi {cos(x)})(*5 {sin(x)*cos(x)})
\end{pspicture}
```

12.1.3 Double coordinates

(*point1|point2*): The possibility of combining a coordinate pair from two defined points is especially useful when making connections when you don't necessarily know both coordinates. The *x* coordinate is taken from the first point and the *y* coordinate from the second one. In the following example we simulate this sort of situation: nodes A and B are set to be the centres of the words PSTricks and PS, whose coordinates are not known exactly. Nevertheless it is possible to draw vertical lines which keep the x coordinate without further ado by using double coordinates.

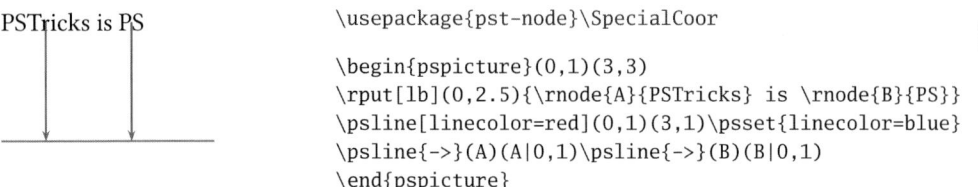

```
\usepackage{pst-node}\SpecialCoor

\begin{pspicture}(0,1)(3,3)
\rput[lb](0,2.5){\rnode{A}{PSTricks} is \rnode{B}{PS}}
\psline[linecolor=red](0,1)(3,1)\psset{linecolor=blue}
\psline{->}(A)(A|0,1)\psline{->}(B)(B|0,1)
\end{pspicture}
```

Alternatively you could have defined new nodes in order to use the nodesep option with \ncline (cf. Section 16.2.4 on page 229).

12.1.4 Relative translations

The next coordinate form lets you do horizontal and vertical translations relative to a target point, using nodesep and offset, two parameters from the pst-node package (cf. Section 16.2 on page 226). The four lines drawn in the next example are explained individually in Table 12.2.

Table 12.2: Meaning of the parameters for relative translations of points

number	command	explanation
I	`\psline([nodesep=1]A)`	line from $(0,0)$ to $(x_A + 1, y_A)$
II	`\psline[linestyle=dashed]([nodesep=-1]A)`	line from $(0,0)$ to $(x_A - 1, y_A)$
III	`\psline[linestyle=dotted,linewidth=0.08]([offset=1]A)`	line from $(0,0)$ to $(x_A, y_A + 1)$
IV	`\psline[linewidth=1.5pt]([nodesep=-1,offset=-1]A)`	line from $(0,0)$ to $(x_A - 1, y_A - 1)$

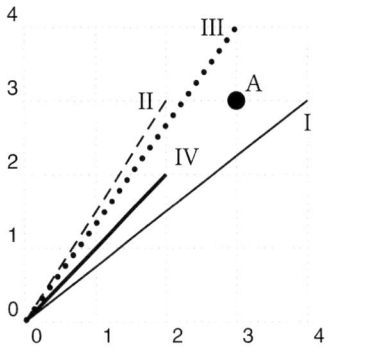

```
\usepackage{pstricks,pst-node}
\SpecialCoor

\begin{pspicture}[showgrid](4,4)
\pnode(3,3){A}\psdot[dotscale=2](A)\uput[45](A){A}
\psline([nodesep=1]A)\uput[-90](4,3){I}
\psline[linestyle=dashed]([nodesep=-1]A)
\uput[180](2,3){II}
\psline[linestyle=dotted,linewidth=0.08]%
       ([offset=1]A)\uput[180](3,4){III}
\psline[linewidth=1.5pt]([nodesep=-1,offset=-1]A)
\uput[45](2,2){IV}
\end{pspicture}
```

A similar effect occurs with the angle parameter (also from the pst-node package); the specification of an angle corresponds to an additional rotation. The meanings of the individual parameters in the following example are listed in Table 12.3.

12.1 Defining Points

Table 12.3: Meaning of the parameters for relative translations of points with angle specification

no.	command	explanation
I	`\psline([nodesep=1,angle=-45]A)`	
		line from $(0,0)$ to $(1;-45°)$ with A as centre
II	`\psline[linestyle=dashed]([nodesep=-1,angle=-45]A)`	
		line from $(0,0)$ to $(-1;-45°)$ with A as centre
III	`\psline[linestyle=dotted,linewidth=0.08]([offset=1,angle=-45]A)`	
		line from $(0,0)$ to $(1;-45°)$ with A as centre and an offset of 1
IV	`\psline[linewidth=1.5pt]([offset=1,angle=135]A)`	
		line from $(0,0)$ to $(1;135°)$ with A as centre

```
\usepackage{pstricks,pst-node}\SpecialCoor

\begin{pspicture}[showgrid](4,4)
\pnode(3,3){A}\psdot[dotscale=2](A)\uput[135](A){A}
\pscircle[linestyle=dotted](A){1}
\psline([nodesep=1,angle=-45]A)\uput[0](3.5,2){I}
\psline[linestyle=dashed]([nodesep=-1,angle=-45]A)
\uput[-45](2,4){II}
\psline[linestyle=dotted,linewidth=1.5pt]%
       ([offset=1,angle=-45]A)\uput[-225](4,4){III}
\psdot([offset=1]A)\uput[90]([offset=1]A){III'}
\psline[linewidth=1.5pt]([offset=1,angle=135]A)
\uput[0](2,2){IV}
\end{pspicture}
```

The second version of this coordinate form is a bit more complicated; it takes an extra point into account for the relative translation. This case is especially useful when extending lines beyond the endpoint of a segment. Table 12.4 provides additional explanations for the individual lines in the example below.

Table 12.4: Meaning of the parameters for relative point translations referring to a third point

command	explanation
`\psline[linestyle=dashed,dash=.4 .1](B)([nodesep=-2.5]{B}A)`	
	Line from (B) to $(x_A + \Delta x, y_A + \Delta y)$ where $\sqrt{(\Delta x)^2 + (\Delta y)^2} = 2.5$ applies and the endpoint is on the extension of the segment $\overline{AB}$.
`\psline(A)`	
	"Normal" line from $(0,0)$ to (A).
`\psline[linestyle=dashed]([nodesep=-1]{B}A)`	
	Line from $(0,0)$ to $(x_A + \Delta x, y_A + \Delta y)$ where $\sqrt{(\Delta x)^2 + (\Delta y)^2} = 1$ applies and the endpoint is on the extension of the segment $\overline{AB}$.

12 Coordinates

command	explanation
`\psline[linewidth=1.5pt]([Ynodesep=-1]{B}A)`	Line from $(0,0)$ to $(x_A + \Delta x, y_A - 1)$ where Δx is chosen such that the endpoint is on the extension of the line $\overline{AB}$.
`\psline[linestyle=dotted,linewidth=1.5pt]([Xnodesep=1]{B}A)`	Line from $(0,0)$ to $(x_A - 1, y_A)$ where Δy is chosen such that the endpoint is on the line $\overline{AB}$.

```
\usepackage{pstricks-add}\SpecialCoor
\begin{pspicture}[showgrid](5,5)
  \pnode(3,3){A}\psdot[dotscale=2](A)\uput[45](A){A}
  \pnode(0,5){B}\psdot[dotscale=2](B)\uput[45](B){B}
  \psline[linestyle=dashed,dash=0.4 0.1](B)([nodesep=-2.5]{B}A)
  \psline(A)\psline[linestyle=dashed]([nodesep=-1]{B}A)
  \psline[linewidth=1.5pt]([Ynodesep=-1]{B}A)
  \psline[linestyle=dotted,linewidth=1.5pt]([Xnodesep=1]{B}A)
\end{pspicture}
```

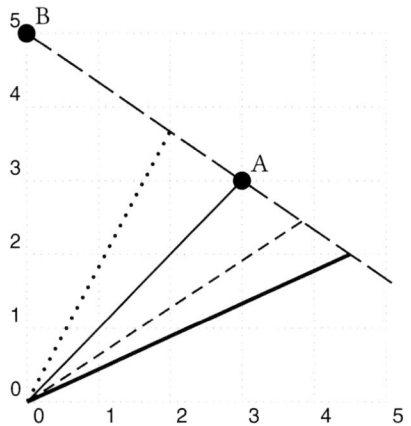

Load pstricks-add This example uses the `pstricks-add` package, which corrects a mistake in the original PSTricks package concerning allocation of horizontal and vertical translation. Because this "mistake" has always been present, the decision has been taken not to correct it in order to retain compatibility with old PSTricks figures. So don't forget to load `pstricks-add` if you want to use this coordinate form.

12.2 Angle specifications

`\SpecialCoor` also provides additional ways to specify angles, which are summarized in Table 12.5 on the next page. Don't forget that angles always have to be given in curly braces.

In the example below the first `\psarc` command is given (-1,1) instead of an explicit angle specification. This corresponds to an angle of $\alpha = \arctan \frac{1}{-1} = 135°$. Note that this illustrates that the point $P(-1, 1)$ itself doesn't need to be part of the arc.

144

12.3 Obsolete commands

Table 12.5: Ways of specifying an angle when \SpecialCoor is activated

syntax	explanation	example
{*angle*}	Numeric value (default); this refers to the specification of \degrees (cf. Section 2.4.2 on page 23).	{90}
{*!PS*}	PostScript code, which has to yield a value for α on the stack. Apart from that requirement, any code is possible.	{! 1 -2 atan}
{(*x,y*)}	Coordinate pair, which is converted into the respective angle ($\tan \alpha = \frac{y}{x}$).	{(3,-4)}

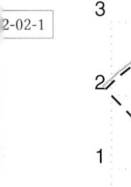
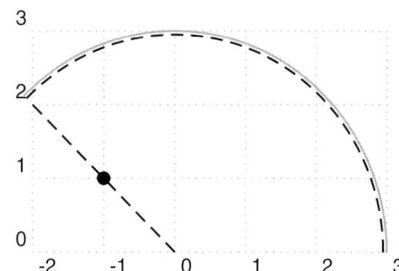

```
\usepackage{pstricks}
\SpecialCoor

\begin{pspicture}[showgrid](-2,0)(3,3)
  \psarc[linecolor=red](0,0){3}{0}{(-1,1)}
  \psarc[linestyle=dashed](0,0){2.95}{0}{135}
  \psdot[dotscale=1.5](-1,1)
  \psline[linestyle=dashed](-2,2)
\end{pspicture}
```

12.3 Obsolete commands

In principle PSTricks supports switching between Cartesian coordinates and polar coordinates through two specific commands. However, you should avoid using these commands now, as the same can be achieved with \SpecialCoor and \NormalCoor and also polar coordinates are displayed in a different way.

```
\Cartesian
\Cartesian(xunit,yunit)
\Polar
```

The only useful application of \Cartesian is as a quick way to specify the scale as \Cartesian(1,0.5) is equivalent to
    \psset{xunit=1,yunit=0.5}.

12 Coordinates

12.4 Examples for \SpecialCoor

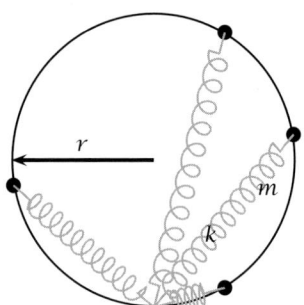

```
\usepackage{pstricks,pst-node,pst-coil}
\SpecialCoor

\begin{pspicture}(-2,-2)(2,2)
  \pscircle{2}
  \pnode(2;-90){O}\pnode(2;10){A}
  \pnode(2;60){B}\pnode(2;190){C}
  \pnode(2;-60){D}
  \qdisk(A){3pt}\qdisk(B){3pt}
  \qdisk(C){3pt}\qdisk(D){3pt}
  \psset{coilarm=3mm,coilwidth=3mm}
  \nccoil[linecolor=red]{-}{O}{A}
  \nccoil[coilheight=1.4,linecolor=red]{-}{O}{B}
  \nccoil[coilheight=.9,linecolor=red]{-}{O}{C}
  \nccoil[coilheight=.5,linecolor=red]{-}{O}{D}
  \rput(1.6,-.4){$m$}\rput(.8,-1){$k$}
  \psline[linewidth=1.5pt]{<-}(-2,0)(0,0)
  \rput(-1,.2){$r$}
\end{pspicture}
```

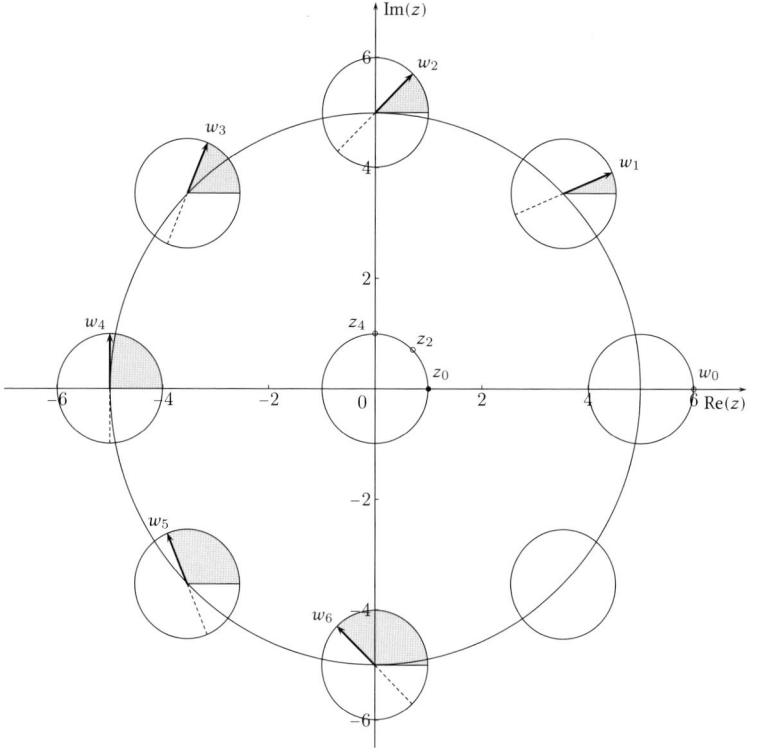

Figure 12.1: Application of polar coordinates (Ulrich Dirr)

Chapter 13

Overlays

13.1 Slides. 147
13.2 Overwriting 148

"Real" overlays are used to put an object like a grid on top of an existing EPS figure, or amend some textual or graphic labels. In both cases a second object is put on top of an existing object. This is primarily of interest when creating slides or presentations – for example those used in the PSTricks compatible `seminar` document class.

This class should not be used anymore however — the successor package powerdot and the powerdot class (cf. Section 35.1 on page 747) are much better. [14]

13.1 Slides

Using the overlay commands, you can put several boxes on top of one another.

```
\overlaybox              % TeX version
... material ...
\endoverlaybox

\begin{overlaybox}       % LaTeX version
... material ...
\end{overlaybox}

\psoverlay{name}
\putoverlaybox{name}
```

name designates the slide (box) so must be unique. As the next example shows, the result is boxes of the same size (overlays) with the text at the correct position so they can be placed on top of each other (using \rput commands).

```
\usepackage{pstricks}

\begin{overlaybox} \psoverlay{all}%
    \psframebox[framearc=0.15,linewidth=1.5pt]{%
        \psoverlay{main}%
        \parbox{3cm}{Herbert {\psoverlay{one} Voss\\
            {\psoverlay{two} Berlin}}}}
\end{overlaybox}\par
\putoverlaybox{main}\par
\putoverlaybox{one}\par
\putoverlaybox{two}

\vspace{1cm}
\rput[lb](0,0){\putoverlaybox{main}}%
\rput[lb](0,0){\putoverlaybox{one}}%
\rput[lb](0,0){\putoverlaybox{two}}
```

13.2 Overwriting

A common situation for using overlays is the supplementary labelling or dimensioning of existing figures, which only have to be available in an (LA)TEX or pdfLATEX compatible format. To determine the size of the figure and the coordinates to start with, the figure is saved in a box with \savebox. In the following example figure, we want to add labels and dimensions at the left and upper sides, so when setting the dimensions of the environment these sides are enlarged to give us some space. The size of the pspicture environment used in this example, as specified by the coordinates (-2,0)(1.1\wd\IBox,1.4\ht\IBox), corresponds widthwise to 2 units plus 1.1 times the width of the picture and heightwise to 1.4 times the height of the picture. These values are used only because we want to add space for labels around the picture; if you wanted all labels to sit within the figure, then make the size of the environment exactly equal to the size of the figure.[1] A coordinate grid is then put on top of the figure with \psgrid (cf. Section 3.1 on page 33), though this is only temporary and is removed at the end. To make sure that the image fits properly, we set the position parameter for the \rput command to lb, which corresponds to putting the lower left corner of the figure at the origin.

Now we can use the appropriate PSTricks commands with the right coordinates to add labels and dimensions. For labels, it's always best to use the starred versions as long as they don't write over the picture. Finally we remove \psgrid and the result is the final figure of Example 13-02-2 on page 150.

```
\usepackage{pstricks,pst-node,graphicx}
\newsavebox\IBox
\sbox\IBox{\includegraphics[scale=0.75]{figures/overlay50}}
\begin{pspicture}(-2,0)(1.1\wd\IBox,1.4\ht\IBox)
  \rput[lb](0,0){\usebox\IBox}
  \psgrid[gridcolor=black!50,subgridcolor=black!15]
  \pnode(-0.5,0){A}\pnode(-0.5,\ht\IBox){B} \ncline{->}{A}{B}
```

---

[1] \wd\box yields the width of a box, \ht\box the height, and \dp\box the depth.

```
\ncput*[nrot=:U]{molecular weight}
\pnode(0,1.05\ht\IBox){A}\pnode(\wd\IBox,1.05\ht\IBox){B}
\rput*[rC](-1,.3\ht\IBox){\small$13$db}
\rput*[rC](-1,.65\ht\IBox){\small$38$db}
\rput*[rC](-1,.8\ht\IBox){\small$76$db}
\ncline{->}{A}{B}
\ncput*{\small molecular weight in the complex}
\rput*[rC]{-90}(0.1\wd\IBox,1.1\ht\IBox){\small$-100$kDa}
\rput*[rC]{-90}(0.8\wd\IBox,1.1\ht\IBox){\small$-800$kDa}
\psline[linewidth=0.1pt,arrowscale=2]{|-|}(4,1)(5,1)
\uput[-90](4.5,1){\small 1$\mu$m}
\end{pspicture}
```

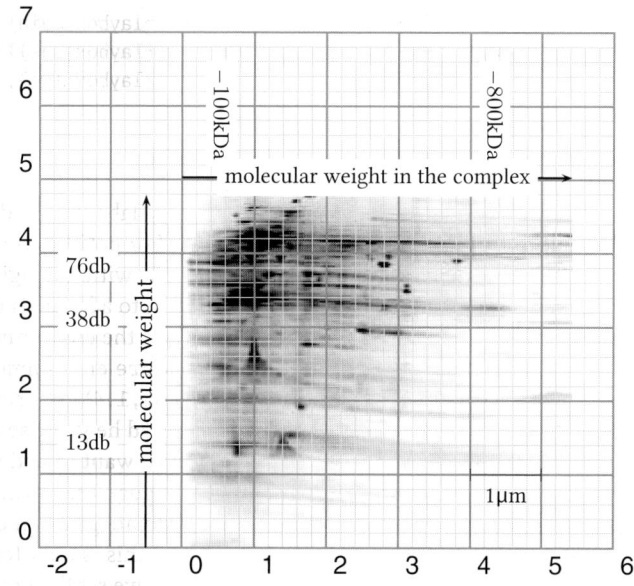

The title of the fifth German edition of this book (http://www.lob.de/isbn/9783865412807) was created using this overlay technique. The base was the title of the first edition with the picture and ISBN removed. After that the new elements were simply added as overlays with \rput.

```
\psset{unit=1pt}%
\begin{pspicture}(12pt,0)(1200pt,795pt)
\rput[lb](0,0){\includegraphics[width=1200pt,height=795pt]{Titel}}
\rput(293,120){\psframe[fillcolor=white,
    fillstyle=solid](-1.75cm,-1.3cm)(1.75cm,1.3cm)}
\rput(293,120){\includegraphics[scale=0.8]{ISBN}}
\rput(34cm,11cm){\includegraphics{bsp}}
\rput[lb](24.15cm,14cm){\huge\sffamily\color{white} 5th edition}
\end{pspicture}
```

13 Overlays

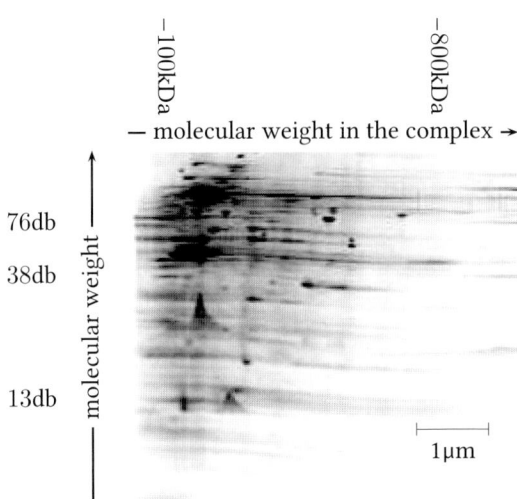

Figure 13.1: "Final results" of the overlay

```
\usepackage{pstricks,pst-node,graphicx}
\newsavebox\IBox
\sbox\IBox{%
  \includegraphics{figures/rose}}

\color{red}\fboxsep=0pt\fbox{%
\begin{pspicture}(\wd\IBox,\ht\IBox)
\rput[lb](0,0){\usebox\IBox}
\rput[rt](\wd\IBox,\ht\IBox){%
  \includegraphics[width=1.5cm]{figures/rose}}
\end{pspicture}}
```

Figure 13.2: Overlay "on itself..."

Chapter 14

Basics

14.1 Header files 151
14.2 Special commands 152
14.3 "Low-level" commands 157
14.4 "High-level" commands. 160
14.5 "key value" interface 162

This chapter deals with some of the basics of PSTricks that are not of importance for every user and are usually only encountered when creating complex figures. Those wanting to develop their own commands or PSTricks packages will, however, find the information in this chapter useful.

14.1 Header files

A PostScript header (prologue) corresponds to a TeX command file or a style file principally in LaTeX, although it doesn't contain (LA)TeX source code, but pure PostScript. The header is put at the beginning of the PostScript file and contains definitions and procedures that can be referred to in the file. The inclusion of such header files happens through the \special command on the side of TeX; for PSTricks \pstheader can be used:

\special{header=file name}	% TeX
\pstheader{file name}	% PSTricks

In principle there is no need to create and load a prologue file when developing packages. Nevertheless many PSTricks packages use this mechanism because this way pure PostScript code can be moved easily away from TeX, and the compilation process is also faster. All header files have the extension .pro for "prologue" and can usually be found in the directory \$TEXMF/dvips/pstricks/, \$TEXMF/dvips/pst-xxx/, \$TEXMFLOCAL/dvips/pstricks/, \$TEXMFLOCAL/dvips/pst-xxx/, \$TEXMFHOME/dvips/pst-xxx/, or \$TEXMFHOME/dvips/pstricks/. The following prologue files are currently on CTAN:

14 Basics

```
   1869 14. Feb 01:13 pst-3d.pro           24795 16. Feb 01:35 pst-3dplot.pro
    467  9. Jan 2006  pst-bar.pro         282741 13. Aug 2009 pst-barcode.pro
   3401 30. Jan 2009  pst-bezier.pro        2212 15. Jan 2007 pst-blur.pro
    748 29. Feb 2008  pst-circ.pro          2663  2. Feb 00:42 pst-coil.pro
2460104 27. Feb 2008  pst-coxeter.pro       4676  9. Jan 2006 pst-eucl.pro
   8980 11. Feb 00:56 pst-fractal.pro      45088 24. Jun 2008 pst-fun.pro
  11484 10. Feb 01:48 pst-func.pro          6106  3. Sep 2009 map3dII.pro
   6230  9. Jan 2006  map3d.pro             6106  3. Sep 2009 pst-map3dII.pro
  18795  3. Sep 2009  pst-map3d.pro         2782  9. Jan 2006 pst-ghsb.pro
   7384 28. Jul 2007  pst-grad.pro         52651 16. Nov 20:53 pst-psm.pro
   2600  9. Jan 2006  pst-light3d.pro       9649 28. Aug 2009 pst-math.pro
  29130 12. Dez 02:03 pst-mirror.pro       16545 12. Feb 00:45 pst-node.pro
   4697 16. Nov 20:58 pst-optexp.pro       28990 12. Feb 00:48 pst-algparser.pro
   6817 12. Feb 00:48 pst-dots.pro         12327 26. Nov 2008 pstricks97.pro
  26603 12. Feb 00:48 pstricks.pro          5064 12. Feb 00:46 pstricks-add.pro
   4912 22. Sep 2008  pst-slpe.pro        255551 26. Jul 2009 solides.pro
 256787 28. Okt 2007  pst-spectra.pro       2598 30. Nov 2006 pst-text.pro
  57107  2. Apr 2007  pst-vue3d.pro         2055 22. Jan 2007 xcolor.pro
```

These files are the primary reason why TEX files that contain PostScript-compatible source code can't be compiled directly with pdfTEX. [96]

14.2 Special commands

14.2.1 \PSTricksoff

This command turns off all PSTricks-specific properties so that the document can be viewed with any DVI viewer (e.g. xdvi). Also it should then be possible to create a PDF without any problems.

```
\PSTricksOff
```

This is a good way of getting a quick overview of just the text, especially when using PSTricks commands frequently, but it is only a temporary solution – the PostScript-specific commands are "switched off":

```
\def\PSTricksOff{%
  \def\pstheader##1{}\def\pstverb##1{}\def\pstVerb##1{}\PSTricksfalse}
```

In most cases you will need to use alternative ways of exporting to DVI or PDF (cf. Section D on page 851). A corresponding \PSTricksOn command does not exist.

14.2.2 \KillGlue and \DontKillGlue

Within a pspicture environment, all the whitespace between PSTricks objects is removed. This usually variable space is referred to as "glue" in TEX terminology. Outside the pspicture environment, every object is treated as a separate character – additional space is not removed. This behaviour can end up not producing the desired effect, for example in a picture LaTeX environment. In such cases you can override the default behaviour and use the \KillGlue and \DontKillGlue switches to specify space being ignored or taken into account respectively.

14.2 Special commands

\KillGlue   \DontKillGlue

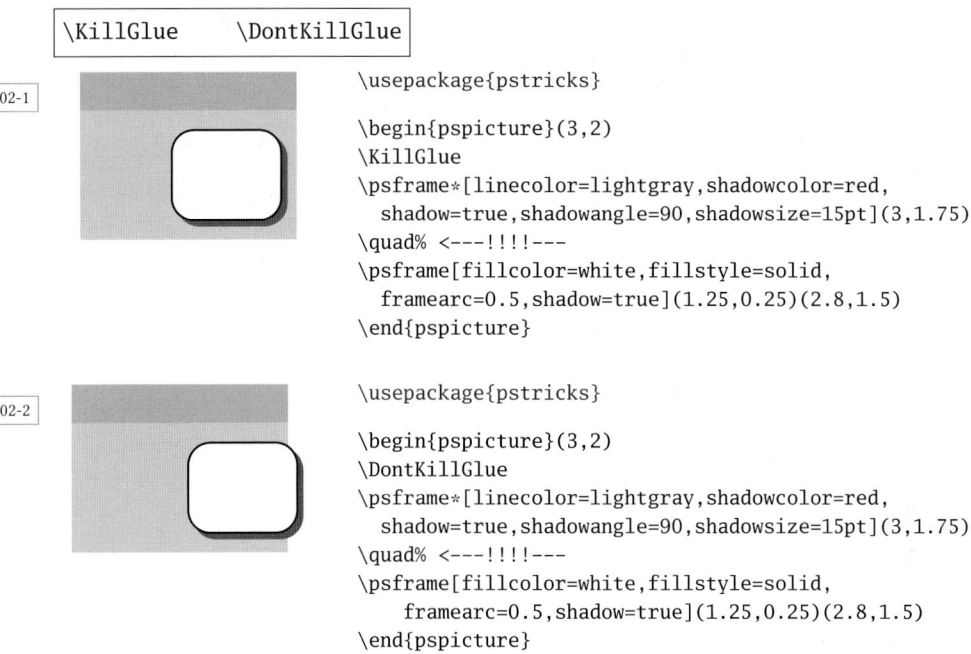

```
\usepackage{pstricks}

\begin{pspicture}(3,2)
\KillGlue
\psframe*[linecolor=lightgray,shadowcolor=red,
    shadow=true,shadowangle=90,shadowsize=15pt](3,1.75)
\quad% <---!!!!---
\psframe[fillcolor=white,fillstyle=solid,
    framearc=0.5,shadow=true](1.25,0.25)(2.8,1.5)
\end{pspicture}
```

```
\usepackage{pstricks}

\begin{pspicture}(3,2)
\DontKillGlue
\psframe*[linecolor=lightgray,shadowcolor=red,
    shadow=true,shadowangle=90,shadowsize=15pt](3,1.75)
\quad% <---!!!!---
\psframe[fillcolor=white,fillstyle=solid,
    framearc=0.5,shadow=true](1.25,0.25)(2.8,1.5)
\end{pspicture}
```

14.2.3 \pslbrace and \psrbrace

These two commands only make sense in conjunction with PostScript input.

```
\pslbrace
\psrbrace
```

They are virtually identical to { and } except that they are written directly into the PostScript output so don't serve any additional purpose in TeX-specific parts. For PostScript the role of these braces is the same as for (LA)TeX; it is however sometimes more difficult to get them into the PostScript output because TeX usually interprets { and } as an argument or group delimiter and doesn't pass them on to PostScript in that case.

14.2.4 \space

This straightforward command is only defined in TeX, but is mentioned here nevertheless. It simply inserts a space and has no additional function, but it is of vital importance within PostScript-specific code when a TeX command is used that eats the following space; this space could well be required by PostScript as a separator between values or variables, however, so using this command we can reinsert the space.

```
\space
```

If, for example, we have the following PostScript sequence within special coordinates (cf. Section 12.1.2 on page 141):

```
\psk@lineAngle abs 0 gt { ... } if
```

14 Basics

TEX would expand it to the expression:

```
20abs 0 gt gt { ... } if
```

During the expansion of \psk@lineAngle to the replacement text the space following the command was eaten as terminator. This results in a faulty PostScript instruction as 20abs is not a PostScript command. If the \space command is applied, however, the space is not eaten because a new command automatically terminates the preceding one. \space itself inserts a space and is defined in PSTricks or latex.ltx:

```
\psk@lineAngle\space abs 0 gt gt { ... } if
```

When inputting PostScript code, you must take care to insert a space in front of the % character for comments; otherwise the following like is appended to the current one which can lead to errors again (cf. example 14-03-1 on page 158):

```
\psk@lineAngle\space abs 0 gt gt { ... } if% ...   WRONG!
\psk@lineAngle\space abs 0 gt gt { ... } if % ...  CORRECT!
```

14.2.5 \altcolormode

We have mentioned before that the collaboration between (LA)TEX, the color and xcolor packages, and PSTricks is not flawless because TEX doesn't understand colours at all and the syntax of the packages and PSTricks is different. Problems with colours are bound to occur if you don't keep certain criteria in mind.

```
\altcolormode
```

When an erroneous colour can't be removed, you can activate this command, which saves the entire PostScript state with gsave before setting a colour and reverts the old state with grestore before any new colour setting.

14.2.6 \pstverb and \pstVerb

```
\pstverb{PS-Code}
\pstVerb{PS-Code}
\code{PS-Code}
\pstverbscale
```

The next example shows the difference between the \pstverb and \pstVerb commands. The *two* visible squares are important – read the text after the code to find out why!

14.2 Special commands

```
(pstverb)
\pstverb{newpath 100 -100 moveto
   50 0 rlineto   0 50 rlineto
  -50 0 rlineto 0 -50 rlineto
   1 1 0 setrgbcolor gsave fill grestore}%
\pstVerb{newpath 100 -100 moveto
   50 0 rlineto   0 50 rlineto
  -50 0 rlineto 0 -50 rlineto
     1 0 0 setrgbcolor gsave fill grestore}
(pstVerb)
```

(pstverb) (pstVerb)
In theory both commands should draw the same size square since the absolute coordinates are identical, placed logically in the middle of the "(pstverb) (pstVerb)" text. However, what in fact we get is a large yellow square in the middle of this paragraph, a small, red one at the top left of this example page, and the "(pstverb) (pstVerb)" text output concatenated at the current text position. Furthermore, after the red square is drawn, the font is set to red (1 0 0) – only a \black switches this back. The fact that the two squares are different sizes is in fact not a difference in the commands themselves but with the dvips programme – it does not reset all values correctly.

With VTEX both squares in Example 14-02-3 would be the same size, albeit still at different positions. So \pstVerb allows us to write PSTricks-compatible PostScript code in the PostScript output, whereas \pstverb writes only local PostScript-compatible code, which is embedded in gsave – grestore. Both commands correspond to the \special commands that have a driver-specific syntax however and are summarized in Table 14.1 for the currently known drivers.

Both commands are defined in the pstricks.con configuration file, which is part of every PSTricks distribution. It assumes use of the dvips driver by definition. When using a different driver, the corresponding file, for example vtex.cfg, has to be renamed to pstricks.con. Nowadays it's fairly safe to assume that distributions rename the appropriate file themselves.

There are in fact several commands that allow us to write PostScript code directly.

The following example uses some of the trigonometric constants. Instead of defining them as numerical values or within the argument of \psplot, they are written to the PostScript output before the pspicture environment with \pstVerb. Thus they only have to be defined once and not repeatedly for every point to be calculated. Note that this wouldn't work with \pstverb as the locally-defined values would not be known to PSTricks. The constants defined internally by the pstricks.pro file are listed in Appendix B.

14 Basics

Table 14.1: Driver-specific definitions

driver	command definition
dvips	`\gdef\pstverb#1{\special{" #1}}`
	`\def\pstVerb#1{\special{ps:  #1}}`
dvipsone	`\gdef\pstverb#1{\special{" #1}}`
	`\def\pstVerb#1{\special{ps::  #1}}`
VTEX	`\gdef\pstverb#1{\special{pS*GS @beginspecial @setspecial #1%`
	`@endspecial GR }}`
	`\def\pstVerb#1{\special{pS: #1}}`
textures	`\def\pstverb#1{\special{postscript #1 }}`
	`\def\pstVerb#1{\special{rawpostscript #1}}`
xdvipdfmx	`\def\pstverb#1{\special{pst:    #1}}`
	`\def\pstVerb#1{\immediate\special{PST: #1}}`

Table 14.2: The PostScript-related commands of the driver

command	meaning
`\addto@pscode`	PSTricks internal command that adds PostScript code to a valid object.
`\code`	cf. Section 11.3.22 on page 135
`\pstverb`	Writes to the PostScript output, but puts everything into a PSTricks compatible gsave – grestore environment, such that after this command nothing is known about the PSTricks-specific things defined in this command anymore.
`\pstVerb`	Writes to the PostScript output, but doesn't change the current state of the graphic plane (origin, scale, etc.).
`\pst@Verb`	Like \pstVerb, but the code is executed within the PSTricks dictionary, within `pstricks.pro`.
`\pstverbscale`	If it is part of the argument of \pstVerb, the TEX coordinate system with its origin is assumed.

```
\usepackage{pstricks,pst-plot}
\psset{yunit=3.5,plotpoints=200}
\begin{pspicture}(-0.5,-0.75)(5,0.75)
  \pstVerb{
    /euler 2.7183 def
    /pi 3.1416 def
    /rad {180 div pi mul } def
    /deg {pi div 180 mul } def
  }
  \psplot[linewidth=1pt,plotpoints=200]{0}{5}{ euler x neg exp x 6 mul deg sin mul }
  \psaxes[linewidth=0.1pt]{->}(0,0)(0,-0.5)(5,0.8)
\end{pspicture}
```

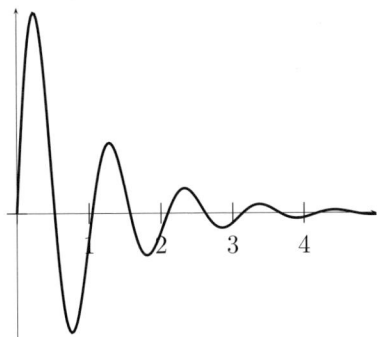

All the constants used in this example are already defined in `pstricks.pro` with a different spelling; in real applications those should be used. The above definitions are only examples.

14.2.7 `\pst@def`

This command is only meant for internal use, but it does have a certain significance: it defines another TeX command itself, which saves PostScript code passed as second argument.

```
\makeatletter \pst@def{name}<... PostScript code...> \makeatother
```

Note that the acute brackets are mandatory as delimiters here! At (LA)TeX level there is also the command name `\tx@name`, shown below:

```
\@ifundefined{pst@def}{\def\pst@def#1<#2>{\@namedef{tx@#1}{#2\space}}}{}
```

Note that the last space (`\space`) was put there on purpose to achieve correct delimiting to other PostScript functions (cf. Section 14.2.4 on page 153 and the examples in Section 15.4.5 on page 215).

14.3 "Low-level" commands

PSTricks knows four different types of objects:

`\begin@OpenObj`	... `\end@OpenObj`	% with arrows
`\begin@AltOpenObj`	... `\end@AltOpenObj`	% without arrows
`\begin@ClosedObj`	... `\end@ClosedObj`	
`\begin@SpecialObj`	... `\end@SpecialObj`	

The naming in principle refers to the created path. This section looks at the composition of these types of objects.

Drawing a hexagon with PSTricks is no problem, but does require several lines of code. When using it repeatedly, it's quicker to define a custom command `\psHexagon`. This command requires one special option to specify whether the radius refers to the inner or outer circle; since this is a yes/no question, we can define a Boolean variable using the key-value interface (cf. Section /vrefsec:basics:keyvalue).

```
\define@boolkey[psset]{}[Pst@]{HRInner}[true]{}
\psset{HRInner=false}
```

The step is to define a \psHexagon command for the object that has the following syntax:

| \psHexagon * [settings] {radius} |
| \psHexagon * [settings] (x,y){radius} |

The code for defining this command is given in the following example. Some procedures are used that are part of the pstricks.pro header file. \pst@object{psHexagon} defines the command \psHexagon

as a PSTricks object. You can then apply this command to draw the new object in exactly the same way as all the other object commands dealt with already – it automatically reads an optional * and optional arguments in square brackets before it continues with calling the \psHexagon@i command. The suffix @i is added by the object, so you have to make sure that your code has defined at least this command (cf. Section 14.3.1 on the next page). Further explanations can be found in Table 14.3 on the facing page and in [92].

```
\usepackage{pstricks,pst-xkey}\makeatletter
\define@boolkey[psset]{}[Pst@]{HRInner}[true]{}   % a boolean key
\psset{HRInner=false,unit=0.7}% unit only reduced for display in this book
\def\psHexagon{\pst@object{psHexagon}}%    defined it as an object
\def\psHexagon@i{\@ifnextchar({\psHexagon@ii}{\psHexagon@ii(0,0)}}% set default centre
\def\psHexagon@ii(#1)#2{%
  \begin@ClosedObj%                            closed object, i.e. can be filled
    \pst@@getcoor{#1}%                         get centre
    \pssetlength\pst@dimc{#2}%                 set radius to pt
    \addto@pscode{%                            PostScript
      \pst@coor T %                            xM yM new origin
      \psk@dimen CLW mul %                     set line width
      /Radius \pst@number\pst@dimc\space % save radius
        \ifPst@HRInner\space 3 sqrt 2 div div \fi def % adjust radius if inner
      /angle \ifPst@HRInner 30 \else 0 \fi def % starting angle
      Radius angle PtoC moveto %               go to the first point
      6 {/angle angle 60 add def %             set alpha to alpha+60
        Radius angle PtoC L %                  draw line to the next point
      } repeat %                               repeat
      closepath }%                             object closed / end pscode
    \def\pst@linetype{3}%                      set line type
    \showpointsfalse%                          do not show support points
  \end@ClosedObj\ignorespaces}%                eat spaces
\makeatother
\begin{pspicture}(-3,-3)(3,3)
\psHexagon[linewidth=3pt,linecolor=red]{2.5}
\pscircle[linestyle=dashed,linecolor=red]{2.5}
\psHexagon[linewidth=3pt,linecolor=blue,HRInner=true]{2.5}
\pscircle[linestyle=dashed,linecolor=blue]{2.17}
\end{pspicture}\hspace{1cm}
\begin{pspicture}[showgrid](-3,-3)(3,3)
```

14.3 "Low-level" commands

```
\psHexagon[doubleline=true](2,2){1}\psHexagon*[linecolor=gray!15,
   HRInner=true](2,-2){1}
\psHexagon[doubleline=true,doublesep=0.5,linecolor=magenta]{2}
\psHexagon*(-2.5,2.5){0.5}\psHexagon[border=3pt,HRInner=true](-1,-1){2}
\end{pspicture}
```

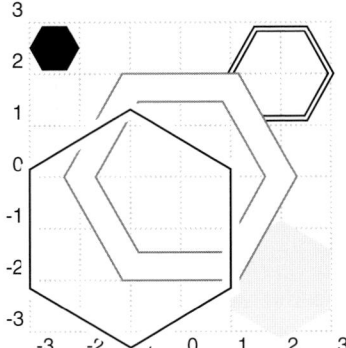

short form	long form
T	/T /translate load def
CLW	/CLW /currentlinewidth load def
PtoC	/PtoC {2 copy cos mul 3 1 roll sin mul} def
L	/L /lineto load def
sqrt	square root
moveto	change current position
repeat	repeat loop
closepath	close current path

Table 14.3: Explanation of the used PostScript procedures from Example 14-03-1

14.3.1 PSTricks objects

In Example 14-03-1 in the previous section, the \psHexagon command was defined as a PSTricks object through \pst@object. There are similarities between this and object-oriented programming, even if TeX or PostScript are not particularly intended for this. By defining a command as an object, you save having to write the code to read options and the starred version.

```
\newif\if@star
\def\pst@ifstar#1{\@ifnextchar*{\@startrue\def\next*{#1}\next}{\@starfalse#1}}
\def\pst@object#1{%
   \pst@ifstar{\@ifnextchar[{\pst@@object{#1}}%
      {\def\pst@par{}\@nameuse{#1@i}}}}
\def\pst@@object#1[#2]{%
   \def\pst@par{#2}%
   \@ifnextchar+{\@nameuse{#1@i}}{\@nameuse{#1@i}}}
```

The list of optional assignments is saved in \pst@par here and a possible starred version in the Boolean \if@star variable. After that the *name of object*@i command is called automatically, which can read further parameters and call one of the object environments listed in Section 14.3 on page 157. The \pst@@object command has only historic meaning; the "+" option is not used anymore.

The code below is an example of the internal structure of a "closed" PSTricks object, which differs from an "open" object only in that no line endings (arrows) are intended. Example 14-03-1 on page 158 is a practical application of such a type of object and Example 14-04-1 on the next page illustrates the definition of an object without referring to a particular type.

```
\def\begin@ClosedObj{%
    \leavevmode%                                    enter horizontal mode
    \pst@killglue%                                  ignore space
    \begingroup%                                    keep everything local
        \use@par%                                   activate local options
        \solid@star%                                test for starred version
        \ifpsdoubleline \pst@setdoublesep \fi%      set separation if double line
        \init@pscode}%                              initialize PS code
\def\end@ClosedObj{%
    \ifpsshadow \pst@closedshadow \fi%              check for shadow option
    \ifdim\psk@border\p@>\z@ \pst@addborder \fi%    check for border>0pt
    \psk@fillstyle%                                 set fill option
    \pst@stroke%                                    draw path
    \ifpsdoubleline \pst@doublestroke \fi%          check for double line
    \ifshowpoints\pst@OpenShowPoints\fi%            check for show points
    \use@pscode%                                    execute PS code
    \endgroup\ignorespaces}%                        ignore spaces
```

14.4 "High-level" commands

"High-level" commands are applications of existing low- or high-level commands to build a new command. The pst-circ package [36] is a prime example: it defines virtually no low-level commands but a large number of new high-level commands. Normally packages are a combination of both types. As an example, we will define a command that determines the focal point of a given triangle and saves it in a node name. The focal point of a triangle is the intersection of the median lines. Let the triangle ABC be given by the coordinates of its corners (though they could be given as node names as well). Let (x_A, y_A) be the coordinates of A, (x_B, y_B) the coordinates of B, and (x_C, y_C) the coordinates of C. The coordinates of the focal point are the arithmetic mean of the three corners (you can find the proof of this in any book on trigonometry):

$$x_S = (x_A + x_B + x_C)/3 \qquad (14.1)$$
$$y_S = (y_A + y_B + y_C)/3 \qquad (14.2)$$

This can be incorporated easily into a new command. To determine the coordinates the PSTricks-internal \pst@getcoor command is used:

\pst@getcoor{*x,y*}*command*

14.4 "High-level" commands

\pst@getcoor primarily fulfils the task of returning the coordinates in normal form x y – when \SpecialCoor is active (Chapter 12 on page 139), they can be available in many forms. [92] Three auxiliary commands are created to contain the coordinates in PostScript-compatible format, and then the \focalPoint command is defined for creating a node at the focal point. Using \focalPoint is now simple, as shown in the example below.

```
\usepackage{pstricks,pst-node}  \SpecialCoor
\makeatletter
\define@boolkey[psset]{}[Pst@]{showFP}[true]{}% mark focal point?
\psset{showFP}                           % true as default
\def\focalPoint{\@ifnextchar[{\focalPoint@i}{\focalPoint@i[]}}
\def\focalPoint@i[#1](#2)(#3)(#4)#5{{    % everything stays local
  \psset{#1}                             % set parameters
  \pst@getcoor{#2}\pst@tempA% point A    % get coordinates as x y
  \pst@getcoor{#3}\pst@tempB% point B    %
  \pst@getcoor{#4}\pst@tempC% point C    %
  \pnode(!                               % set node
    \pst@tempA /YA exch \pst@number\psyunit div def
    /XA exch \pst@number\psxunit div def % x y in user coordinates
    \pst@tempB /YB exch \pst@number\psyunit div def
    /XB exch \pst@number\psxunit div def
    \pst@tempC /YC exch \pst@number\psyunit div def
    /XC exch \pst@number\psxunit div def
    XA XB XC add add 3.0 div             % xSP
    YA YB YC add add 3.0 div             % ySP
  ){#5}                                  % #5 = node name
  \ifPst@showFP\qdisk(#5){2pt}\fi\ignorespaces}
\makeatother
\begin{pspicture}[showgrid](4,4)  \psset{linewidth=2pt}
  \pspolygon[linecolor=red](0,0)(2,4)(4,0)%
  \focalPoint[showFP=true,linecolor=red](0,0)(2,4)(4,0){SP1}%
  \pnode(0,0){A}\pnode(0,4){B}\pnode(4,2){C}%
  \pspolygon[linecolor=blue](A)(B)(C)\focalPoint(A)(B)(C){SP2}%
  {\psset{linecolor=blue}\qdisk(SP2){2pt}}
  \ncline[linewidth=0.2pt]{<->}{SP1}{SP2}%
\end{pspicture}
```

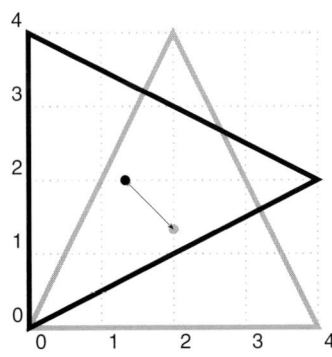

14.5 "key value" interface

The pst-xkey package by Hendri Adriaens, which is an extended version of the old pst-key, is loaded automatically with virtually any PSTricks package because it provides excellent support for passing parameters. It is based on the xkeyval package, [3] but has been specially adapted for PSTricks. These adaptations are not of importance to the normal user so this section is only of interest for those who want to extend existing packages or write new ones. In principle all parameters are set through the \psset command; however, when using pst-xkey you can alternatively change only particular parameters (where parameters in different packages have the same name) by referring to the "family name", for example \psset[pst-solides3d]{xMax=3}. \psset{xMax=3}, on the other hand, changes all existing parameters with the name xMax. In PSTricks the family name should always be the same as the name of the package for reasons of consistency or empty if it can't be assigned in a meaningful way. More information on the use of "families" can be found in [3] or in the individual packages.

In principle a single type of parameter would be enough to cover all cases. PSTricks already provides the functionality to assess the validity of parameters on input and make corresponding corrections. It is therefore advisable to differentiate between parameters according to their meaning and to define them accordingly, as discussed in the following sections.

14.5.1 Boolean

The syntax for a Boolean parameter is:

`\define@boolkey[psset]{package name}[prefix]{name}[default]{commands}`

The definition from Section 14.4 on page 160 can serve as an example:

```
\define@boolkey[psset]{}[Pst@]{showFP}[true]{}% mark focal point?
\psset{showFP=false}                          % set default value
```

The specification [*true*] does not refer to the default value, but to what is to be assumed if only the name of the parameter is specified in the input: \focalpoint[*showFP*] is expanded to showFP=true. The \PST@ prefix is arbitrary, but its use both provides a certain uniformity and prevents conflicts with other packages that might have the same names. For simple use as a Boolean variable, the last parameter in the definition may remain empty; in this case nothing but the assignment of the variables is to be done. Within TeX, you can use the variable as usual:

```
\ifPst@showFP ... code for true ...
\else         ... code for false ...
\fi
```

14.5.2 Integer

The syntax for an integer parameter is:

`\define@key[psset]{package name}{name}{\pst@getint{#1}{\psk@name}}`

```
\define@key[psset]{pstricks-add}{trigLabelBase}{%
  \pst@getint{#1}{\psk@trigLabelBase}}
\psset[pstricks-add]{trigLabelBase=0}
```

The value of the parameter as well as the name of the command that is to save this value are passed to `\pst@getint`. If the input is erroneous, the default value of the next smaller whole number of the rounded parameter is assumed, e.g. 10.3 would yield the value 10.

14.5.3 Real
The syntax for a real parameter is:

```
\define@key[psset]{package name}{name}{\pst@checknum{#1}{\psk@name}}
```

```
\define@key[psset]{pstricks-add}{transpalpha}{%
  \pst@checknum{#1}\psk@transpalpha}
\psset[pstricks-add]{transpalpha=1}
```

`\pst@checknum` checks whether it is a valid value and saves it in the `\psk@name` command.

14.5.4 Length
The syntax for a length parameter is:

```
\define@key[psset]{package name}{name}{\pst@getlength{#1}{\psk@name}}
```

```
\define@key[psset]{}{XnodesepA}{\pst@getlength{#1}\psk@nodesepA%
  \def\psk@nodeseptypeA{2 }}
\psset{XnodesepA=5pt}
```

`\pst@getlength` checks that it is a valid numerical value and whether a unit has been specified. If not, the current unit is assumed and converted to pt internally. Here no family is specified since this parameter was defined in PSTricks already and is only redefined here.

14.5.5 String
The syntax for a string parameter is:

```
\define@key[psset]{package name}{name}{\def\psk@name{#1}}
```

```
\define@key[psset]{pstricks-add}{lineAngle}{%
  \psset{armB=0.5}\def\psk@lineAngle{#1}}
\psset[pstricks-add]{lineAngle=0}
```

This is the most simple type; it doesn't do anything but save the parameter in the specified command. Nevertheless it can also be used to read angles as PSTricks has its own command to validate the input; the above definition can be refined as below:

```
\define@key[psset]{pstricks-add}{lineAngle}{%
  \pst@getangle{#1}\psk@lineAngle\psset{armB=0.5}}
\psset[pstricks-add]{lineAngle=0}
```

14 Basics

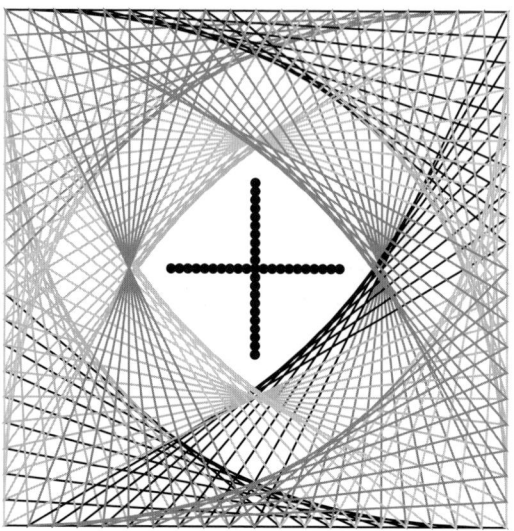

Figure 14.1: "Baubles" with the focal point command

Chapter 15
pst-plot: Plotting functions and data

15.1 Coordinate axes. 166
15.2 Plot styles. 197
15.3 Plotting functions 203
15.4 Plotting data. 212
15.5 Examples 224

The pst-plot package offers additional commands that make it easier to create coordinate axes and plot functions or sets of data. [82, 80, 79] pst-plot works with two-dimensional pairs of data. Functions are plotted over a specified interval, with the number of coordinate points to be computed (and plotted) controlled by the plotpoints parameter (cf. Section 15.2.1 on page 198). These points are then joined up using a designated plot style. To display (x, y, z) data triples or three-dimensional functions, you need pst-3dplot or pst-solides3d (cf. Section 23.5 on page 358 and Section 23.6 on page 391). [81, 87]

The first section of this chapter looks at the \psaxes command for create coordinate axes, and its corresponding parameters, which are divided into two batches: those available since the original version of the pst-plot package, and the additional ones now available with the current version of pst-plot loaded. The options now include plotting logarithmic and trigonometric graphs. Then we look at the plotting commands themselves, starting with the parameters available to all of these commands. Then we look at the function-plotting commands \psplot and \parametricplot, covering the parameters specific to them, how to express the functions in their arguments, and more advanced possibilities. Finally we look at the data-plotting commands \fileplot, \dataplot, and \listplot and the other commands and parameters associated with these.

15 pst-plot: Plotting functions and data

15.1 Coordinate axes

In principle you can use the normal line commands to draw coordinate axes, but the \psaxes command makes it much easier. The syntax is:

```
\psaxes [settings] {arrows} (x₂,y₂)
\psaxes [settings] {arrows} (x₁,y₁)(x₂,y₂)
\psaxes [settings] {arrows} (x₀,y₀)(x₁,y₁)(x₂,y₂)
```

All coordinates have to be specified in Cartesian form; you can't use special forms here (cf. Chapter 12 on page 139). Figure 15.1 illustrates how the specified coordinates points define the axes drawn; only the point (x_2, y_2) is required – the other two default to the coordinate origin $(0,0)$ if not specified. The available options for *arrows* are as listed in Table 8.2 on page 93.

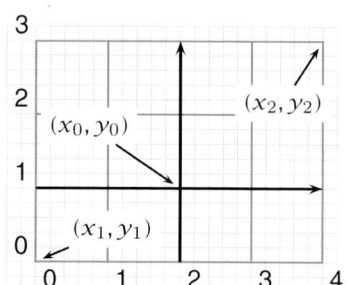

Figure 15.1: Reference points when drawing coordinate axes

Table 15.1 shows a summary of the basic parameters you can use when creating coordinate axes; they are explained in detail in the following sections. Extensions can be found in Section 15.1.11 on page 176. When labelling the axes, you can also use labelsep (cf. Section 9.3 on page 104).

Table 15.1: Summary of the basic \psaxes parameters

name	type	default
axesstyle	axes|frame|none	axes
Ox	value	0
Oy	value	0
Dx	value	1
Dy	value	1
dx	value unit	0 pt
dy	value unit	0 pt
labels	all|x|y|none	all
showorigin	boolean	true
ticks	all|x|y|none	all
tickstyle	full|top|bottom	full
ticksize	value unit	3pt

15.1.1 axesstyle

axes

axes is the most commonly used axes style: two lines are drawn and the coordinate origin is specified by (x_0, y_0). The placement of the labels depends on the alignment of the axes. Note that we chose (-0.5,-0.5) as the bottom left point of the pspicture environment so that the axis labels were inside it.

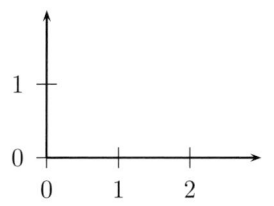

```
\usepackage{pstricks,pst-plot}

\begin{pspicture}(-0.5,-0.5)(3,2)
    \psaxes[axesstyle=axes]{->}(3,2)
\end{pspicture}
```

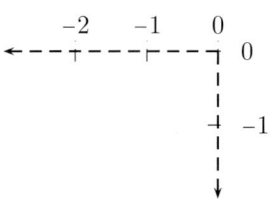

```
\usepackage{pstricks,pst-plot}

\begin{pspicture}(0.5,0.5)(-3,-2)
    \psaxes[axesstyle=axes,
        linestyle=dashed]{->}(-3,-2)
\end{pspicture}
```

frame

When using the frame axes style, it makes sense to put the coordinate origin in one of the corners.

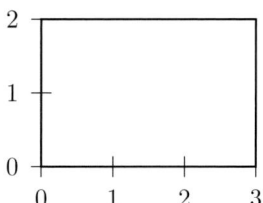

```
\usepackage{pstricks,pst-plot}

\begin{pspicture}(-0.5,-0.5)(3,2)
    \psaxes[axesstyle=frame]{->}(3,2)
\end{pspicture}
```

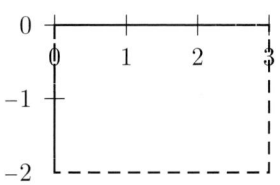

```
\usepackage{pstricks,pst-plot}

\begin{pspicture}(-0.5,0.5)(3,-2)
    \psaxes[axesstyle=frame,
        linestyle=dashed]{->}(3,-2)
\end{pspicture}
```

none

At first glance, the none axes style appears pointless; however, it provides you with the option to draw axis labels and then use custom commands for the lines.

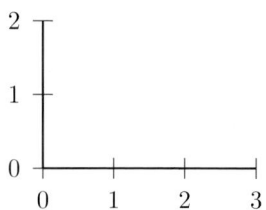

```
\usepackage{pstricks,pst-plot}

\begin{pspicture}(-0.5,-0.5)(3,2)
    \psaxes[axesstyle=none]{->}(3,2)
\end{pspicture}
```

15.1.2 0x and 0y

0x and 0y determine the coordinate origin, which is at (0,0) by default. In principle any real numbers can be given here; however, as PSTricks uses \multido for the labels, this can lead to incorrect results as \multido implements floating-point arithmetic in a rudimentary manner, which can lead to large inaccuracies.

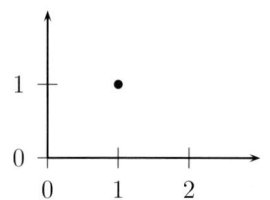

```
\usepackage{pstricks,pst-plot}

\begin{pspicture}(-0.5,-0.5)(3,2)
    \psaxes{->}(3,2)
    \psdot(1,1)
\end{pspicture}
```

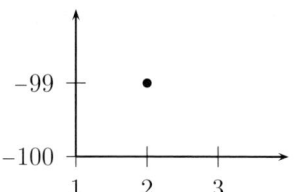

```
\usepackage{pstricks,pst-plot}

\begin{pspicture}(-0.5,-0.5)(3,2)
    \psaxes[Ox=1,Oy=-100]{->}(3,2)
    \psdot(1,1)
\end{pspicture}
```

15.1.3 Dx and Dy

Dx and Dy determine the difference in value between two consecutive labels. This difference refers to the current unit, so only a number is given. Any real number is valid; negative values reverse the numbering, as shown in the third example below.

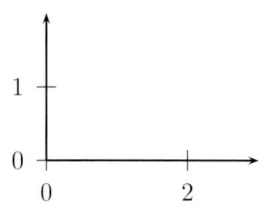

```
\usepackage{pstricks,pst-plot}

\begin{pspicture}(-0.5,-0.5)(3,2)
    \psaxes[Dx=2]{->}(3,2)
\end{pspicture}
```

15.1 Coordinate axes

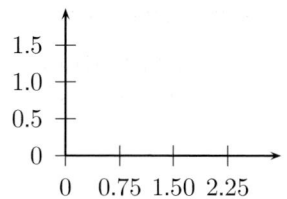

```
\usepackage{pstricks,pst-plot}

\begin{pspicture}(-0.5,-0.5)(3,2)
    \psaxes[Dx=0.75,Dy=0.5]{->}(3,2)
\end{pspicture}
```

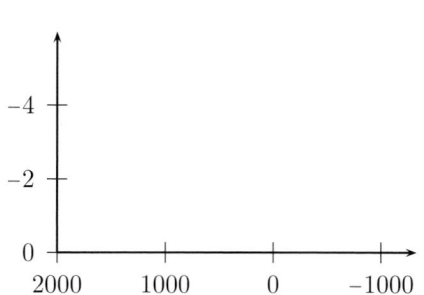

```
\usepackage{pstricks,pst-plot}

\begin{pspicture}(-0.5,-1)(5,3)
    \psaxes[Dy=-2,dy=1,Ox=2000,
        Dx=-1000,dx=1.5]{->}(5,3)
\end{pspicture}
```

15.1.4 dx and dy

dx and dy determine the physical distance between two consecutive labels; you need to state a unit if you want to define an absolute value (e. g. 1.25cm). So, for example, if you set dx to 2 and Dx to 5, the labels will be 0,5,10... with each label set 2 current units apart. The default values of 0 pt are not as ridiculous as they sound; the trigger the following internal substitution:

$$dx = 0 \to dx = Dx \times psxunit \qquad (15.1)$$
$$dy = 0 \to dy = Dy \times psyunit \qquad (15.2)$$

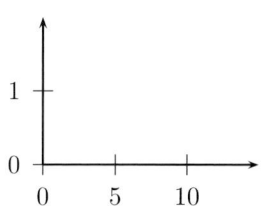

```
\usepackage{pstricks,pst-plot}

\begin{pspicture}(-0.5,-0.5)(3,2)
    \psaxes[Dx=5,dx=1]{->}(3,2)
\end{pspicture}
```

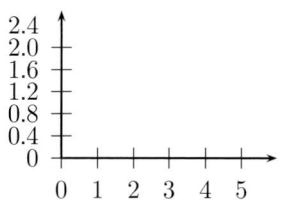

```
\usepackage{pstricks,pst-plot}

\begin{pspicture}(-0.5,-0.5)(3,2)
    \psaxes[Dx=1,dx=0.5,
        Dy=0.4,dy=0.3]{->}(3,2)
\end{pspicture}
```

169

15 pst-plot: Plotting functions and data

15.1.5 labels

The `labels` parameter lets you specify which of the axes gets labels; there are four options, discussed below. You can also control the distance of the labels from the axes with the `labelsep` parameter (cf. Section 9.3 on page 104), and change the label style with the `labelFontSize` parameter (cf. page 178).

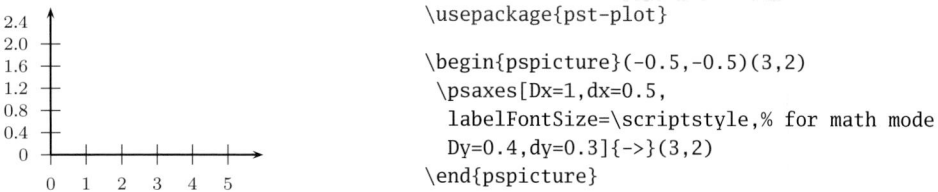

```
\usepackage{pst-plot}

\begin{pspicture}(-0.5,-0.5)(3,2)
    \psaxes[Dx=1,dx=0.5,
        labelFontSize=\scriptstyle,% for math mode
        Dy=0.4,dy=0.3]{->}(3,2)
\end{pspicture}
```

By default the labels are printed in math mode, with the four font styles \displaystyle, \scriptstyle, and \scriptscriptstyle available. You can change to text mode by using the mathLabel parameter (cf. page 177); then the usual text mode styles are available, such as \tiny or \small. In the above example we used the default math mode for the labels, so \scriptstyle was the best choice for the font style. Section 15.1.10 on page 174 shows how to define special labels, and the pstricks-add package (cf. Chapter 30 on page 581) provides further ways to influence the label style.

all

`labels=all` is the default, as used in all the examples given so far in this chapter.

x

`labels=x` means that only the x axis is labelled.

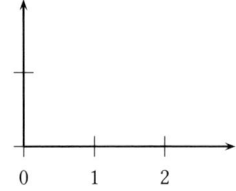

```
\usepackage{pstricks,pst-plot}

\begin{pspicture}(-0.5,-0.5)(3,2)
    \psaxes[labels=x]{->}(3,2)
\end{pspicture}
```

y

`labels=y` means that only the y axis is labelled.

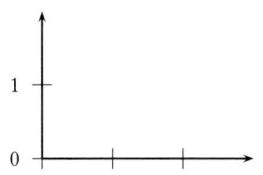

```
\usepackage{pstricks,pst-plot}

\begin{pspicture}(-0.5,-0.5)(3,2)
    \psaxes[labels=y]{->}(3,2)
\end{pspicture}
```

none

`labels=none` means neither axes has labels, but the ticks are still drawn. This is useful when you want to do the labelling manually, as in the second example below.

15.1 Coordinate axes

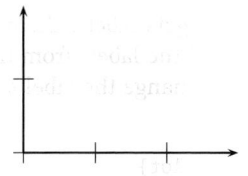

```
\usepackage{pstricks,pst-plot}

\begin{pspicture}(-1,-1)(3,2)
    \psaxes[labels=none]{->}(3,2)
\end{pspicture}
```

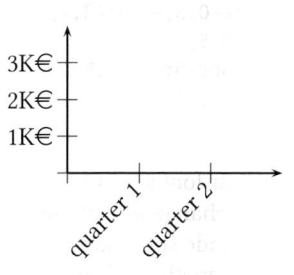

```
\usepackage{pstricks,pst-plot,eurosym}

\begin{pspicture}(-1,-1)(3,2)
    \psaxes[labels=none,Dy=0.5]{->}(3,2)
    \rput[rC]{45}(1,-0.2){quarter 1}
    \rput[rC]{45}(2,-0.2){quarter 2}
    \rput[rC](-0.2,0.5){1K\euro}
    \rput[rC](-0.2,1){2K\euro}
    \rput[rC](-0.2,1.5){3K\euro}
\end{pspicture}
```

15.1.6 showorigin

When set to false, the showorigin switch prevents the labelling of the origin; in the following example the label 0 is missing on both axes.

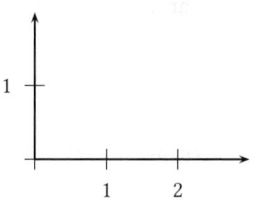

```
\usepackage{pstricks,pst-plot}

\begin{pspicture}(-0.5,-0.5)(3,2)
    \psaxes[showorigin=false]{->}(3,2)
\end{pspicture}
```

15.1.7 ticks

The ticks option specifies which of the axes get ticks.

all

ticks=all is the default, as used in all the examples given so far in this chapter.

x

ticks=x means that only the x axis gets ticks.

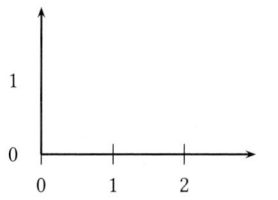

```
\usepackage{pstricks,pst-plot}

\begin{pspicture}(-0.5,-0.5)(3,2)
    \psaxes[ticks=x]{->}(3,2)
\end{pspicture}
```

15 pst-plot: Plotting functions and data

y
ticks=y means that only the y axis gets ticks.

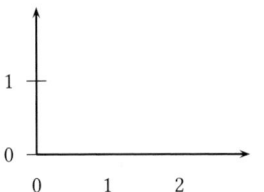

```
\usepackage{pstricks,pst-plot}

\begin{pspicture}(-0.5,-0.5)(3,2)
    \psaxes[ticks=y]{->}(3,2)
\end{pspicture}
```

none
ticks=none means that the axes are both drawn without the ticks (but with labels). This is useful when the figure shows a purely qualitative relationship.

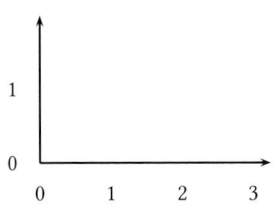

```
\usepackage{pstricks,pst-plot}

\begin{pspicture}(-0.5,-0.5)(3.25,2)
    \psaxes[ticks=none]{->}(3.25,2)
\end{pspicture}
```

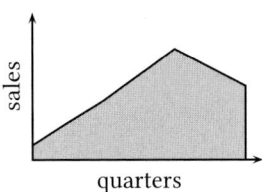

```
\usepackage{pstricks,pst-plot}

\begin{pspicture}(-0.5,-0.5)(3.25,2)
    \psaxes[ticks=none,labels=none]{->}(3.25,2)
    \uput[-90](1.5,0){quarters}
    \uput[180]{90}(0,1){sales}
    \pspolygon[fillcolor=lightgray,
        fillstyle=solid]%
            (0,0)(0,0.2)(1,0.8)(2,1.5)(3,1)(3,0)
\end{pspicture}
```

15.1.8 tickstyle
tickstyle specifies the style of the ticks.

full
tickstyle=full is the default, as used in all the examples given so far in this chapter that have ticks.

bottom
tickstyle=bottom means that ticks are only drawn on the left for the y axis and below the x axis. If one axis points in a negative direction, the ticks remain on the same side of each axis. However, this changes when both axes point in a negative direction, when the labels switch to the other side of the ticks.

15.1 Coordinate axes

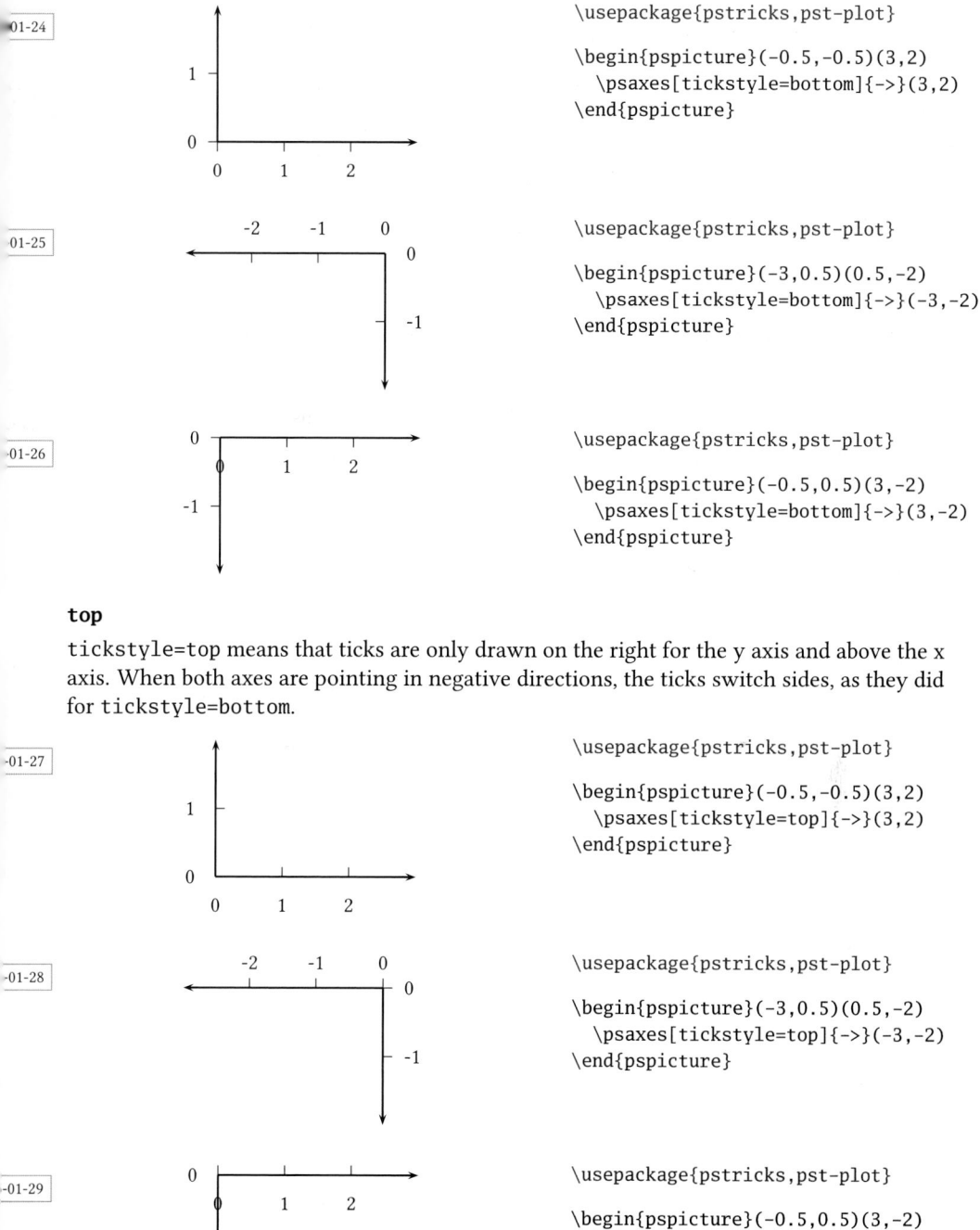

```
\usepackage{pstricks,pst-plot}

\begin{pspicture}(-0.5,-0.5)(3,2)
    \psaxes[tickstyle=bottom]{->}(3,2)
\end{pspicture}
```

```
\usepackage{pstricks,pst-plot}

\begin{pspicture}(-3,0.5)(0.5,-2)
    \psaxes[tickstyle=bottom]{->}(-3,-2)
\end{pspicture}
```

```
\usepackage{pstricks,pst-plot}

\begin{pspicture}(-0.5,0.5)(3,-2)
    \psaxes[tickstyle=bottom]{->}(3,-2)
\end{pspicture}
```

top

`tickstyle=top` means that ticks are only drawn on the right for the y axis and above the x axis. When both axes are pointing in negative directions, the ticks switch sides, as they did for `tickstyle=bottom`.

```
\usepackage{pstricks,pst-plot}

\begin{pspicture}(-0.5,-0.5)(3,2)
    \psaxes[tickstyle=top]{->}(3,2)
\end{pspicture}
```

```
\usepackage{pstricks,pst-plot}

\begin{pspicture}(-3,0.5)(0.5,-2)
    \psaxes[tickstyle=top]{->}(-3,-2)
\end{pspicture}
```

```
\usepackage{pstricks,pst-plot}

\begin{pspicture}(-0.5,0.5)(3,-2)
    \psaxes[tickstyle=top]{->}(3,-2)
\end{pspicture}
```

15.1.9 ticksize

ticksize specifies the length of a half tick mark (one drawn only on one side of an axis) or half the length of a full tick mark. The value refers to the current unit.

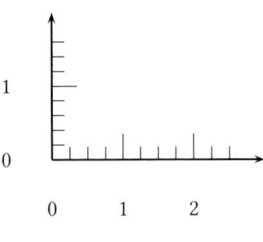

```
\usepackage{pst-plot}

\begin{pspicture}(-0.5,-0.5)(3,2)
    \psaxes[ticks=none,labelsep=12pt]{->}(3,2)
    \psset{linewidth=0.1pt,axesstyle=none,
            tickstyle=bottom,ticksize=5pt,labels=none}
    \psaxes[ticks=x,Dx=0.25]{->}(2.5,1.75)
    \psaxes[ticks=y,Dy=0.2](2.5,1.75)
    \psset{linewidth=0.4pt,ticksize=10pt}
    \psaxes[ticks=x](2.5,1.75)\psaxes[ticks=y](2.5,1.75)
\end{pspicture}
```

As the following example shows, you can use ticks as a way of creating a grid: you can mark the whole axis area by setting tickstyle accordingly.

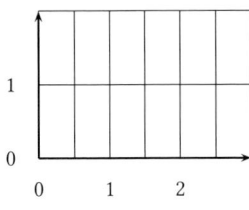

```
\usepackage{pst-plot}

\begin{pspicture}(-0.5,-0.5)(3,2)
    \psaxes[ticks=none]{->}(3,2)
    \psset{linewidth=0.1pt}%
    \psaxes[axesstyle=none,tickstyle=top,
        ticksize=3,ticks=y,labels=none]{->}(3,2)
    \psaxes[axesstyle=none,tickstyle=top,ticksize=2,
        ticks=x,Dx=0.5,labels=none](3,2)
\end{pspicture}
```

15.1.10 Special labels

Often you want to label axes not with numeric values, but with symbols or text labels; for example the names of the months. The second example in Section 15.1.5 on page 170 showed one way of achieving this. The arrayjob package by Jiang Zhuhan provides further support and simplifies the labelling of the axes by letting you define arbitrary alphanumeric labels. [33]

Another option is to work with the \ifcase command, which essentially provides the same possibilities without having to load an external package. The commands that put commands are used again; PSTricks defines them as virtually empty and therefore they can be overwritten easily.

```
\usepackage{pstricks,pst-plot}
\def\month#1{%
   \ifcase#1\or January\or February\or March\or April\or May\or June\or
      July\or August\or September\or October\or November\or December\fi}
\def\Level#1{\ifcase#1\or little\or medium\or much\fi}
\makeatletter
\def\pst@@@vlabel#1{\footnotesize\Level{#1}}
\def\pst@@@hlabel#1{\rput[rb]{30}{\footnotesize\month{#1}}}
\makeatother
```

```
\psset{unit=0.8}
\begin{pspicture}(-0.5,-1)(13,4)
  \psaxes[showorigin=false]{->}(13,4)
\end{pspicture}
```

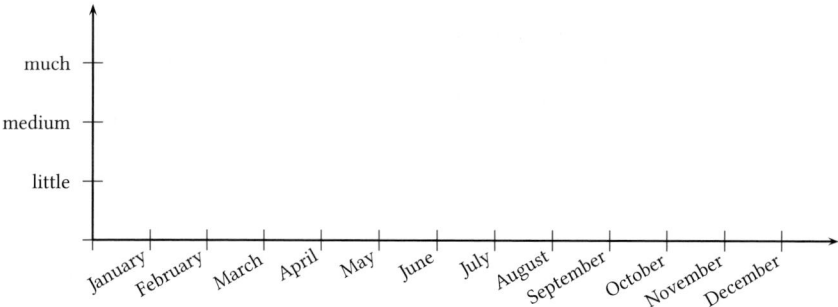

You can achieve the same effect with angular units in radian measure by changing the scale locally.

Assuming that a sine function in the interval $[0; 3\pi]$ is to be drawn, you could take 6 length units for 3π and the scale factor would be $\frac{\pi}{2}$. The whole x axis would have a length of at least $6 \times \frac{\pi}{2} \approx 9.4248$ cm (assuming the scale is 1 cm). At each unit a multiple of $\frac{\pi}{2}$ has to be marked on the axis. You can use the modulo function defined by pstricks-add (cf. Chapter 30 on page 581) to label the axis in a sensible way, with some knowledge of TeX. \psplot is called with the normal scale, so the function only needs to be plotted for the interval $[0; 2\pi]$.

```
\usepackage{pstricks,pst-plot}
\makeatletter
\def\pst@@@hlabel#1{\small%
    \pst@mod{#1}{2}\tempa%              0 or 1
    \ifnum1>\tempa%                     odd value?
        \count1=#1\divide\count1 by 2%  #1/2
        $\the\count1\pi$%               n*pi
    \else$\frac{#1}{2}\pi$\fi}%         n/2*pi
\makeatother
\begin{pspicture}(-0.5,-1.25)(10,1.25)
  \psaxes[xunit=1.570796,showorigin=false]{->}(0,0)(-0.5,-1.25)(6.4,1.25)
  \psplot[linecolor=red,linewidth=1.5pt]{0}{9.4247}{x RadtoDeg sin}
\end{pspicture}
```

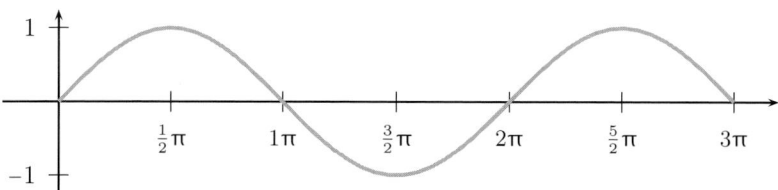

In fact the pstricks-add package already provides an option for trigonometric labels (cf. Section 15.1.12 on page 193).

15 pst-plot: Plotting functions and data

15.1.11 Extensions

A lot of the extensions for axis labels provided by the pstricks-add package (cf. Chapter 30 on page 581) are now also available with pst-plot itself. The new options are summarized in Table 15.2, and then discussed in detail in the following sections.

The \psaxes command itself is extended as well, with two optional arguments to simplify axis labelling:

\psaxes [settings] {arrows} (x_2,y_2) [xLabel,angle] [yLabel,angle]
\psaxes [settings] {arrows} $(x_1,y_1)(x_2,y_2)$ [xLabel,angle] [yLabel,angle]
\psaxes [settings] {arrows} $(x_0,y_0)(x_1,y_1)(x_2,y_2)$ [xLabel,angle] [yLabel,angle]

If only one optional argument is specified, it is taken as referring to the x axis. The angle specifies where the label is positioned relative to the endpoint of the respective axis (with the distance of the label from the endpoint controlled through the labelsep parameter, cf. Section 9.3 on page 104).

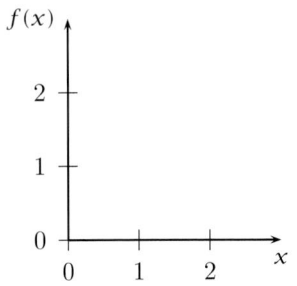

```
\usepackage{pst-plot}

\begin{pspicture}(-0.5,-0.5)(3,3)
\psaxes{->}(3,3)[$x$,-90][$f(x)$,180]
\end{pspicture}
```

Table 15.2: Parameters for \psaxes with latest version of pst-plot

name	type	default
mathLabel	boolean	true
labelFontSize	length command	{}
comma	boolean	false
xyAxes	boolean	true
xAxis	boolean	true
yAxis	boolean	true
xyDecimals	value|{}	{}
xDecimals	value|{}	{}
yDecimals	value|{}	{}
ticks	all|x|y|none	all
labels	all|x|y|none	all
ticksize	length length	-4pt 4pt
xticksize	length length	-4pt 4pt
yticksize	length length	-4pt 4pt

continued...

15.1 Coordinate axes

... continued

name	type	default
subticks	value	0
xsubticks	value	0
ysubticks	value	0
subticksize	value	0.75
xsubticksize	value	0.75
ysubticksize	value	0.75
tickcolor	colour	black
xtickcolor	colour	black
ytickcolor	colour	black
subtickcolor	colour	darkgray
xsubtickcolor	colour	darkgray
ysubtickcolor	colour	darkgray
tickstyle	full|top|bottom|inner[1]	full
ticklinestyle	solid|dashed|dotted|none	solid
subticklinestyle	solid|dashed|dotted|none	solid
logLines	all|x|y|none	none
xylogBase	value|{}	{}
xlogBase	value|{}	{}
ylogBase	value|{}	{}
tickwidth	length	0.5\pslinewidth
subtickwidth	length	0.25\pslinewidth
xlabelFactor	arbitrary	{}
ylabelFactor	arbitrary	{}
xAxisLabel	arbitrary	{}
yAxisLabel	arbitrary	{}
xAxisLabelPos	(x,y)|(c,y)|{}	{}
yAxisLabelPos	(x,y)|(x,c)|{}	{}
xlabelPos	bottom | axis | top	bottom
ylabelPos	left | axis | right	left
trigLabels	boolean	false
trigLabelBase	integer	0

Most of the parameters defined in older versions of the pst-plot package (as listed in Table 15.1 on page 166) still work. However, the Lkeyword[pst-plot]tickstyle option isn't available in its original form anymore; the new extensions modify it to support just the inner style. Instead, you can create all the other styles with the extended functions of the ticksize option.

mathLabel

As mentioned in Section 15.1.5 on page 170, labels are set in math mode by default, which means that you don't have to use $...$ to enclose the values for parameters like

---
[1]The option inner is only effective for axesstyle=frame

labelFontSize (cf. Section 15.1.11) and xylabelFactor (cf. Section 15.1.11 on page 192). You can reverse this with mathLabel=false, enabling you to set labels in text mode.

```
\usepackage{pst-plot}
\begin{pspicture}(-0.5,-0.5)(4,4)
\psaxes[labelFontSize=\scriptstyle,ylabelFactor=\times10^6]{->}(4,4)
\end{pspicture}\qquad
\begin{pspicture}(-0.5,-0.5)(4,4)
\psaxes[mathLabel=false,labelFontSize=\small,xlabelFactor=$\times10^6$]{->}(4,4)
\end{pspicture}
```

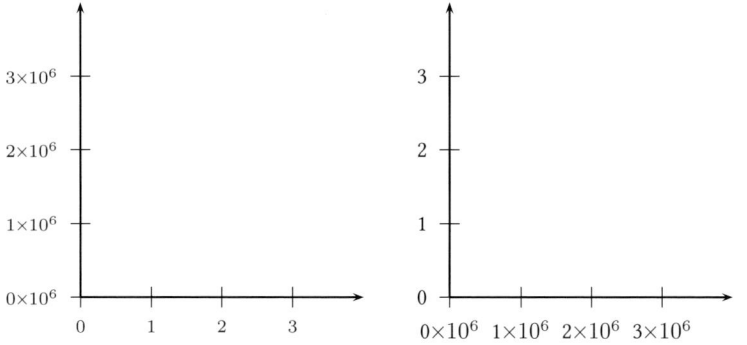

labelFontSize

The labelFontSize parameter is empty by default, but you can use it to change the font size of the axis labels from the currently valid one by assigning one of the font size commands specified by the document class. Note that which text commands are valid for labelFontSize at any time depends on the setting of mathLabel, which toggles between text and math mode as mentioned above. Table 15.3 summarizes the standard font commands that you might want to use for labelling axes; the text mode sizes that aren't relevant here are not listed.

Table 15.3: Summary of the relevant commands for setting the font size via the labelFontSize parameter

text	math
\tiny	\scriptscriptstyle
\scriptsize	\scriptstyle
\footnotesize	\displaystyle
\small	\textstyle
\normalsize	

15.1 Coordinate axes

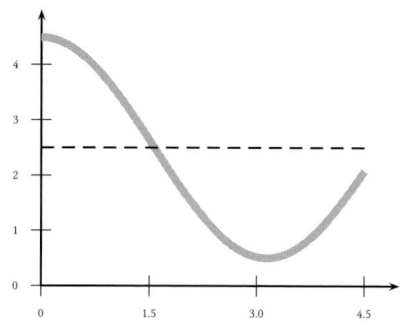

```
\usepackage{pst-plot}

\psset{yunit=0.75}
\begin{pspicture}(-0.5,-0.5)(5,5)
    \psaxes[Dx=1.5,mathLabel=false,
        labelFontSize=\tiny]{->}(5,5)
    \psplot[linecolor=red,
        linewidth=3pt]{0}{4.5}%
            {x RadtoDeg cos 2 mul 2.5 add}
    \psline[linestyle=dashed](0,2.5)(4.5,2.5)
\end{pspicture}
```

comma

If the comma option is set to true, commas are used instead of points when specifying decimals.

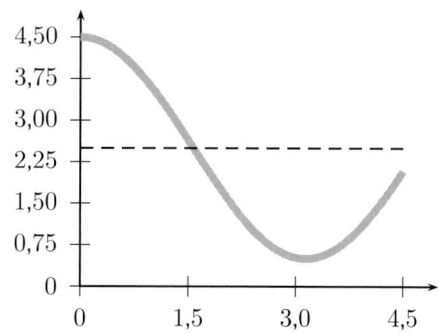

```
\usepackage{pst-plot}

\psset{yunit=0.75}
\begin{pspicture}(-0.5,-0.5)(5,5)
    \psaxes[Dx=1.5,Dy=0.75,comma]{->}(5,5)
    \psplot[linecolor=red,
        linewidth=3pt]{0}{4.5}%
            {x RadtoDeg cos 2 mul 2.5 add}
    \psline[linestyle=dashed](0,2.5)(4.5,2.5)
\end{pspicture}
```

xyAxes, xAxis, and yAxis

These options control which axes are drawn. The boolean xyAxes option draws either both axes or neither, while setting xAxis and yAxis to true or false draws or omits one axis.

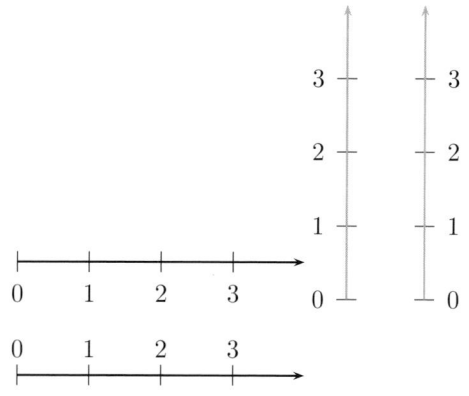

```
\usepackage{pst-plot}

\begin{pspicture}(4,1)
\psaxes[yAxis=false,
    linecolor=blue]{->}(0,0.5)(4,0.5)
\end{pspicture}
\begin{pspicture}(1,4)
\psaxes[xAxis=false,
    linecolor=red]{->}(0.5,0)(0.5,4)
\end{pspicture}
\begin{pspicture}(1,4)
\psaxes[xAxis=false,linecolor=red,
    ylabelPos=right]{->}(0.5,0)(0.5,4)
\end{pspicture}\\[0.5cm]
\begin{pspicture}(4,1)
\psaxes[yAxis=false,linecolor=blue,
    xlabelPos=top]{->}(0,0.5)(4,0.5)
\end{pspicture}
```

15 pst-plot: Plotting functions and data

As these examples show, a single y axis has the labels on the left side by default. There are several ways to change this: through the labelsep parameter (cf. Section 9.3 on page 104); through the trick of keeping a very short and therefore invisible x axis; or through the ylabelPos parameter. The latter can be seen in the example on the right. You can switch the x axis labels similarly.

xlabelPos and ylabelPos

If an axis points in the negative direction it may be useful to change the position of the labels. xlabelPos and ylabelPos set the position of labels for the x and y axis respectively, with possible values bottom (default), axis, or top for the x axis and left (default), axis, or right for the y axis. Bear in mind that the value of labelsep is taken into account for placing the labels and it is set by default to 0.

labelsep

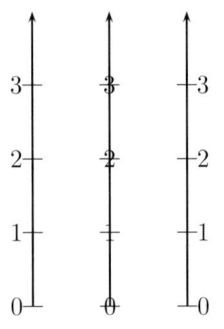

```
\usepackage{pst-plot}
\psset{labelsep=0pt}
\begin{pspicture}(1,4)
    \psaxes[xAxis=false]{->}(0.5,0)(0.5,4)
\end{pspicture}
\begin{pspicture}(1,4)
    \psaxes[xAxis=false,
        ylabelPos=axis]{->}(0.5,0)(0.5,4)
\end{pspicture}
\begin{pspicture}(1,4)
    \psaxes[xAxis=false,
        ylabelPos=right]{->}(0.5,0)(0.5,4)
\end{pspicture}
```

15-0?

```
\usepackage{pst-plot}
\psset{labelsep=0pt}
\begin{pspicture}(4,1) \psaxes[yAxis=false]{->}(0,0.5)(4,0.5) \end{pspicture}\quad
\begin{pspicture}(4,1) \psaxes[yAxis=false,xlabelPos=axis]{->}(0,0.5)(4,0.5)
\end{pspicture}\quad
\begin{pspicture}(4,1) \psaxes[yAxis=false,xlabelPos=top]{->}(0,0.5)(4,0.5)
\end{pspicture}
```

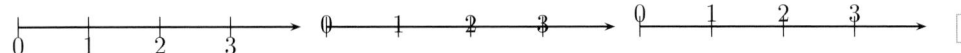

15-01

xyDecimals, xDecimals, and yDecimals

Axis labels are created without any formatting by default; the number of decimal places is determined at random. Using these parameters, you can specify a defined number of decimal places for one or both axes. The syntax is:

    xyDecimals=*Integer*   xDecimals=*Integer*   yDecimals=*Integer*

xyDecimals controls the setting for both axes simultaneously. An empty assignment {} restores the default behaviour.

15.1 Coordinate axes

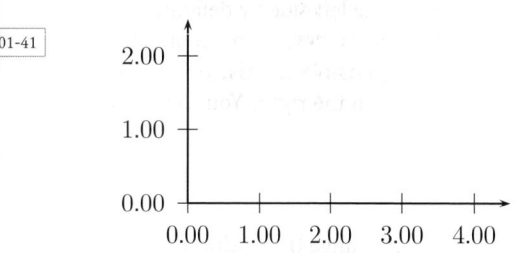

```
\usepackage{pst-plot}

\begin{pspicture}(-1.5,-0.5)(5,2.5)
    \psaxes[xyDecimals=2]{->}(0,0)(4.5,2.5)
\end{pspicture}
```

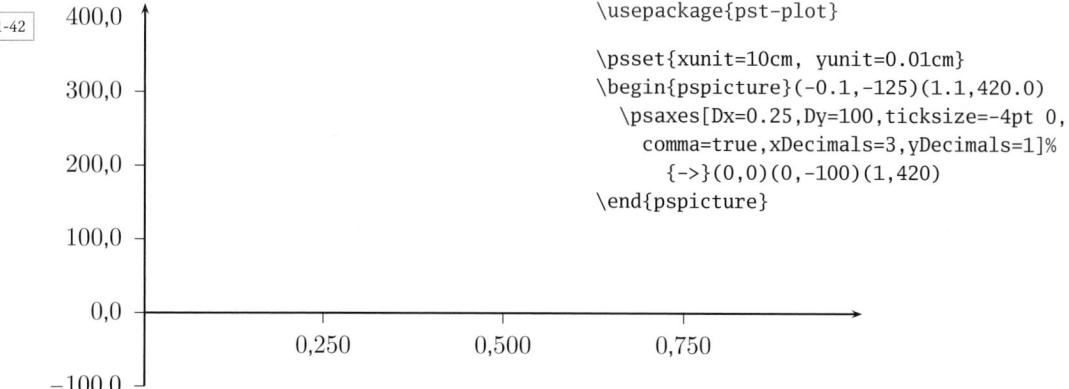

```
\usepackage{pst-plot}

\psset{xunit=10cm, yunit=0.01cm}
\begin{pspicture}(-0.1,-125)(1.1,420.0)
    \psaxes[Dx=0.25,Dy=100,ticksize=-4pt 0,
        comma=true,xDecimals=3,yDecimals=1]%
            {->}(0,0)(0,-100)(1,420)
\end{pspicture}
```

ticksize, xticksize, and yticksize
In the latest version of the pst-plot package, the tickstyle option no longer works as described in Section 15.1.8 on page 172. Instead, use the new ticksize, xticksize, and yticksize parameters to set a more detailed specification of the axis ticks. tickstyle itself does still exist, and its new meaning is covered on page 184.

ticksize=*value unit*	ticksize=*value unit value unit*
xticksize=*value unit*	xticksize=*value unit value unit*
yticksize=*value unit*	yticksize=*value unit value unit*

The three parameters set the tick size on both axes, the *x* axis, or the *y* axis, respectively. The assigned value can consist of up to two specifications: a negative value to set the length of the ticks to the left of the *y* axis or below the *x* axis (depending on which axis is being specified) and a positive value to set the length of the ticks to the right or on top of the respective axes. If only one value is specified, it can be positive or negative, depending on which side of the axis you want the ticks. For example, ticksize=-6pt 3 results in an axis tick of length 6pt+3\psunit in total, starting 6pt to the left of or below the axis and finishing 3\psunit on the other side of the axis.

15 pst-plot: Plotting functions and data

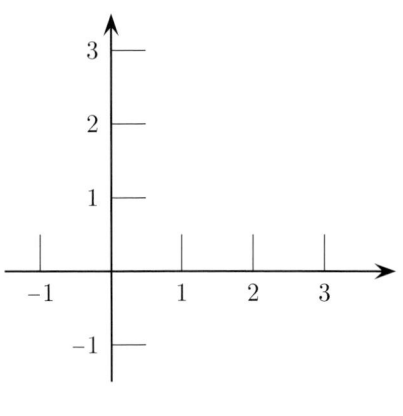

```
\usepackage{pst-plot}

\psset{arrowscale=2}
\begin{pspicture}(-1.5,-1.5)(4,3.5)
    \psaxes[ticksize=0.5cm]%
        {->}(0,0)(-1.5,-1.5)(4,3.5)
\end{pspicture}
```

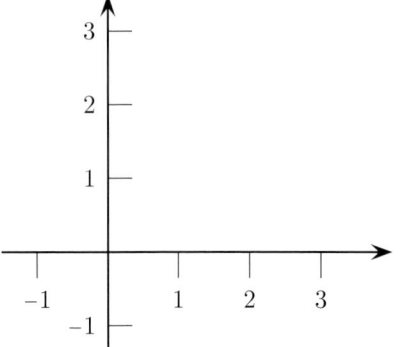

```
\usepackage{pst-plot}

\psset{arrowscale=2}
\begin{pspicture}(-1.5,-1.5)(4,3.5)
    \psaxes[xticksize=-10pt 0,
        yticksize=0 10pt]%
        {->}(0,0)(-1.5,-1.5)(4,3.5)
\end{pspicture}
```

As with the old `tickstyle` option, you can use the new `ticksize` parameters as an easy way to achieve a grid, by extending the axis ticks accordingly.

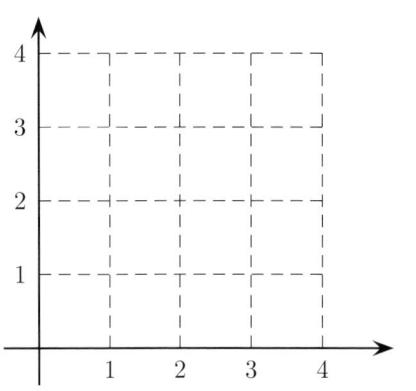

```
\usepackage{pst-plot}

\psset{arrowscale=2}
\begin{pspicture}(-.5,-.5)(5,4.5)
    \psaxes[ticklinestyle=dashed,
        ticksize=0 4cm]%
        {->}(0,0)(-.5,-.5)(5,4.5)
\end{pspicture}
```

subticks, xsubticks, and ysubticks

subticks specifies the number of subticks in the interval between two ticks; it is set to 0 by default. You can use xsubticks and ysubticks to set it for one axis only. The subticks are

182

never labelled; if you do want them to be labelled, you have to use \uput (cf. Section 9.6 on page 106). The syntax for the subticks parameters is:

subticks=<value>, xsubticks=<value>, ysubticks=<value>

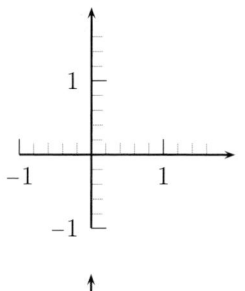

```
\usepackage{pst-plot}

\psset{ticksize=6pt}
\begin{pspicture}(-1,-1)(2,2)
  \psaxes[ticks=all,
    subticks=5]{->}(0,0)(-1,-1)(2,2)
\end{pspicture}
```

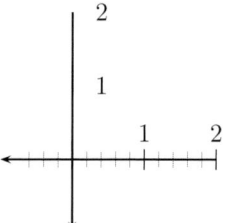

```
\usepackage{pst-plot}

\begin{pspicture}(-1,-1)(2,2)
  \psaxes[ticks=y,
    subticks=5]{->}(0,0)(-1,-1)(2,2)
\end{pspicture}
```

If you set ticks to a certain axis, so that the other axis will remain tick free, you can then use either subticks or its axis-specific equivalent to control the subticks on the required axis.

```
\usepackage{pst-plot}

\begin{pspicture}(-1,-1)(2,2)
  \psaxes[ticks=x,
    subticks=5]{->}(0,0)(2,2)(-1,-1)
\end{pspicture}
```

subticksize, xsubticksize, and ysubticksize

These options are equivalent to the ones for the main ticks, except that the length of the subticks is given as a proportion of the length of the main ticks. Therefore the value specified must be in the interval $[0; 1]$. subticksize sets the values for both axes whereas the other two are valid only for the respective axis. The syntax for these parameters is:

subticksize=<value>, xsubticksize=<value>, ysubticksize=<value>

```
\usepackage{pst-plot}
\psset{yunit=1.5cm,xunit=3cm}
\begin{pspicture}(-1,-2.75)(3.2,.5)
  \psaxes[xticksize=-2.5 0.5,ticklinestyle=dashed,
    subticks=5,xsubticksize=1,ysubticksize=0.75,xsubticklinestyle=dotted,
    xsubtickwidth=1pt,subtickcolor=gray]{->}(0,0)(-1,-2.5)(3.1,0.5)
\end{pspicture}
```

15 pst-plot: Plotting functions and data

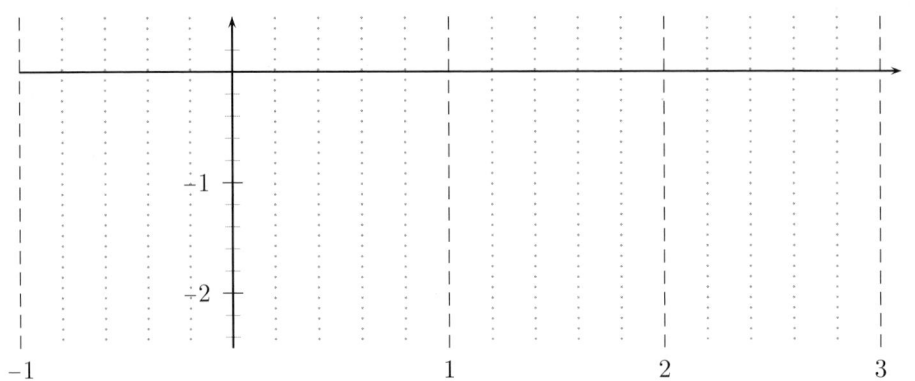

tickcolor and subtickcolor

tickcolor and subtickcolor set the values globally for both axes. As usual there are axis-specific variants of each parameter, with prefix 'x' or 'y'. The syntax for all six parameters is:

tickcolor=*colour*   xtickcolor=*colour*   ytickcolor=*colour*
subtickcolor=*colour*   xsubtickcolor=*colour*   ysubtickcolor=*colour*

When specifying colours, you can use the xcolor syntax (cf. Section 2.1.1 on page 9).

```
\usepackage{pst-plot}
\begin{pspicture}(0,-0.2)(10,1)
\psaxes[yAxis=false,ticksize=0 10mm,subticks=10,subticksize=0.75,
  subtickcolor=black!50,tickwidth=1pt,subtickwidth=0.5pt](10.01,0)
\end{pspicture}
```

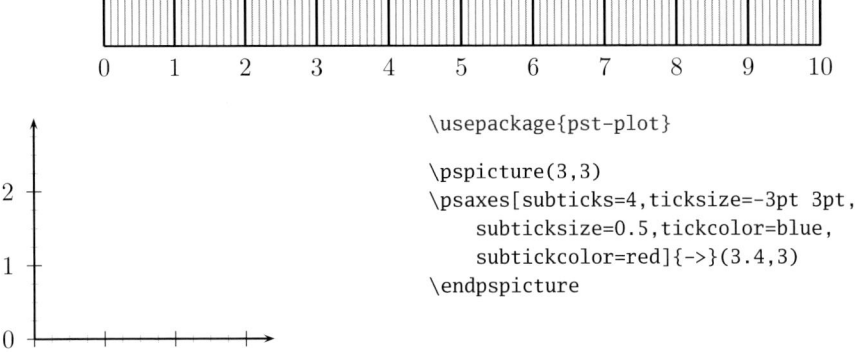

```
\usepackage{pst-plot}
\pspicture(3,3)
\psaxes[subticks=4,ticksize=-3pt 3pt,
    subticksize=0.5,tickcolor=blue,
    subtickcolor=red]{->}(3.4,3)
\endpspicture
```

tickstyle

As mentioned earlier, the original values for the tickstyle option described in Section 15.1.8 on page 172 are no longer active if you have loaded a current version of pst-plot. However, a new value inner is defined which, in conjunction with the axis style frame, creates partitions on all four sides of the frame.

15.1 Coordinate axes

```
\usepackage{pst-plot}
\begin{pspicture}(-0.3,-0.3)(5,5)
\psaxes[axesstyle=frame,ticksize=0 5pt,subticks=10,subticksize=0.75,tickstyle=inner,
   subtickcolor=black!50,tickwidth=1pt,subtickwidth=0.5pt](5,5)
\end{pspicture}\qquad\begin{pspicture}(-0.3,-0.3)(5,5)
\psaxes[axesstyle=frame,logLines=all,xylogBase=10,ticksize=0 5pt,subticksize=0.75,
   tickstyle=inner,subticks=10,subtickcolor=black!50,tickwidth=1pt,
   subtickwidth=0.5pt](5,5)
\end{pspicture}
```

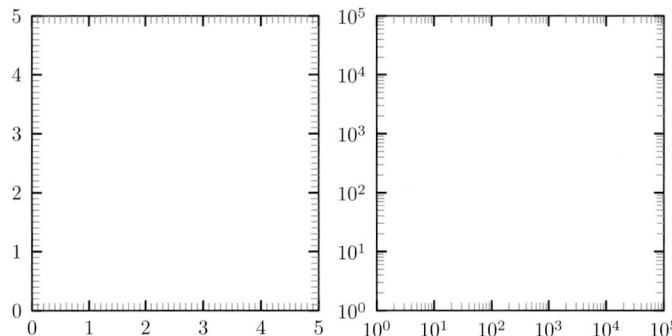

For more details on drawing logarithmic axes, as used in the second part of the previous example, see page 190.

```
\usepackage{pst-plot}
\def\data{0 0 1 4 1.5 1.75 2.25 4 2.75 7 3 9} \psset{lly=-0.5cm}
\begin{psgraph}[axesstyle=none,ticks=none,labels=none](0,0)(3.0,9.0){12cm}{5cm}
\pscustom[fillstyle=solid,fillcolor=red!30,linestyle=none]{%
   \listplot{\data}\psline(3,9)(3,0)}
\pscustom[fillstyle=solid,fillcolor=blue!20,linestyle=none]{%
   \listplot{\data}\psline(3,9)(0,9)}
\listplot[linewidth=2pt]{\data}
\psaxes[axesstyle=frame,ticksize=0 5pt,xsubticks=20,ysubticks=4,
     tickstyle=inner,dy=2,Dy=2,tickwidth=1.5pt,subtickcolor=black](0,0)(3,9)
\rput*(2.5,3){level 1}\rput*(1,7){level 2}
\end{psgraph}
```

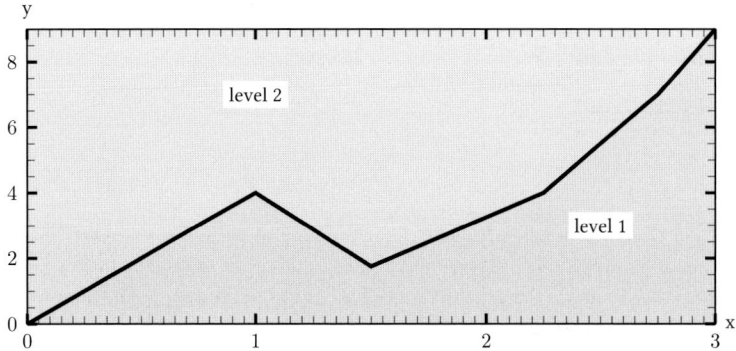

185

15 pst-plot: Plotting functions and data

ticklinestyle and subticklinestyle

The ticklinestyle and subticklinestyle create solid, dashed, or dotted ticks and subticks for both axes. ticklinestyle and subticklinestyle again set the values for both axes. As usual there are axis-specific variants of each parameter, with prefix 'x' or 'y'. The syntax for all six parameters is:

ticklinestyle=solid|dashed|dotted|none   subticklinestyle=...
xticklinestyle=...   xsubticklinestyle=...
yticklinestyle=...   ysubticklinestyle=...

The assignment of the line style none is again pointless in principle and is equivalent to specifying [sub]ticklines=0.

```
\usepackage{pst-plot}
\psset{unit=4cm}
\pspicture(-0.15,-0.15)(2.5,1)
  \psaxes[axesstyle=frame,logLines=y,xticksize=0 1,xsubticksize=1,
    ylogBase=10,tickcolor=red,subtickcolor=blue,tickwidth=1pt,
    subticks=20,xsubticks=10,xticklinestyle=dashed,
    xsubticklinestyle=dashed](2.5,1)
\endpspicture
```

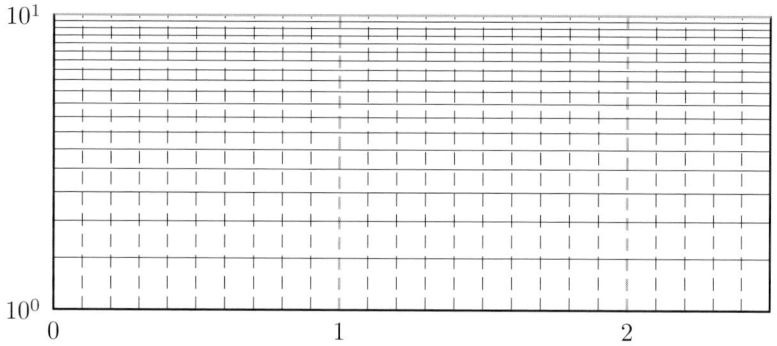

For more details on drawing logarithmic axes, as used in the previous example, see page 190.

tickwidth and subtickwidth

You can use the tickwidth and subtickwidth options to alter the line width of axis divisions.

tickwidth=*value unit*

subtickwidth=*value unit*

```
\usepackage{pst-plot}
\def\Psaxes[#1](#2)(#3)(#4){\pspicture(5,1)\psaxes[#1](#2)(#3)(#4)\endpspicture}
\psset{arrowscale=2.5,yAxis=false,arrows=-D>}
\Psaxes[subticks=8](0,0)(-5,-1)(5,1)\\[4pt]
\Psaxes[subticks=4,ticksize=-4pt 0,xlabelPos=top](0,0)(5,1)(-5,-1)\\[-10pt]
\Psaxes[subticks=4,ticksize=-10pt 0](0,0)(-5,-5)(5,5)\\[4pt]
\Psaxes[subticks=10,ticksize=0 -10pt](0,0)(-5,-5)(5,5)\\[5pt]
```

15.1 Coordinate axes

```
\Psaxes[subticks=4,ticksize=0 10pt,xlabelPos=bottom](0,0)(5,5)(-5,-5)\\[4pt]
\Psaxes[subticks=4,ticksize=0 -10pt,xlabelPos=top](0,0)(5,5)(-5,-5)\\[-3pt]
\Psaxes[subticks=0](0,0)(-5,-5)(5,5)\\[4pt]
\Psaxes[subticks=0,tickcolor=red,linecolor=blue,xlabelPos=top](0,0)(5,5)(-5,-5)\\
\Psaxes[subticks=5,tickwidth=2pt,subtickwidth=1pt](0,0)(-5,-5)(5,5)\\[5pt]
\Psaxes[subticks=0,tickcolor=red,xlabelPos=top](0,0)(5,5)(-5,-5)
```

```
\usepackage{pst-plot}
\psset{xAxis=false,arrowscale=2.5,arrows=-D>}
\psaxes[subticks=8]{->}(0,0)(-5,-5)(5,5)\hspace*{2em}
\psaxes[subticks=4,ylabelPos=right,ylabelPos=left]{->}(0,0)(5,5)(-5,-5)\hspace*{3em}
\psaxes[subticks=4,ticksize=0 4pt]{->}(0,0)(-5,-5)(5,5)\hspace*{3em}
\psaxes[subticks=4,ticksize=-4pt 0]{->}(0,0)(-5,-5)(5,5)\hspace*{1em}
\psaxes[subticks=4,ticksize=0 4pt,ylabelPos=right]{->}(0,0)(5,5)(-5,-5)\hspace*{3em}
\psaxes[subticks=4,ticksize=-4pt 0,linecolor=red,
   ylabelPos=right]{->}(0,0)(5,5)(-5,-5)\hspace*{5em}
\psaxes[subticks=0]{->}(0,0)(-5,-5)(5,5)\hspace*{1em}
\psaxes[subticks=0,tickcolor=red,linecolor=blue,
   ylabelPos=right]{->}(0,0)(5,5)(-5,-5)\hspace*{5em}
\psaxes[subticks=5,tickwidth=2pt,subtickwidth=1pt]{->}(0,0)(-5,-5)(5,5)
\hspace*{1em}
\psaxes[subticks=5,tickcolor=red,tickwidth=2pt,ticksize=10pt,
   subtickcolor=blue,subticksize=0.75,ylabelPos=right]{->}(0,0)(5,5)(-5,-5)
```

15 pst-plot: Plotting functions and data

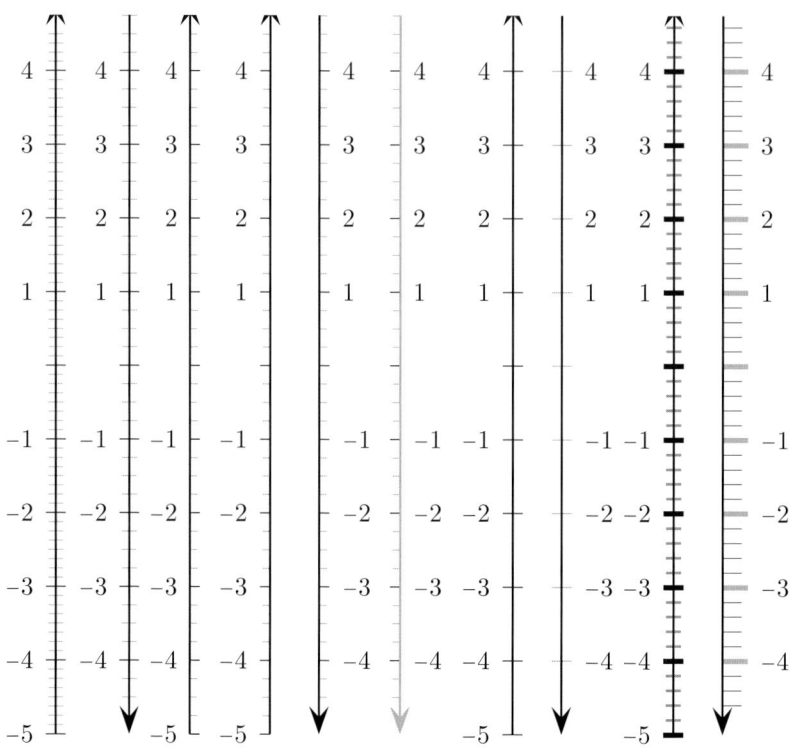

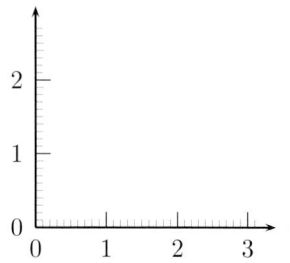

```
\usepackage{pst-plot}

\pspicture(3,3.25)
  \psaxes[subticks=10,ticksize=0 6pt,
    subticksize=0.5]{->}(3.4,3)
\endpspicture
```

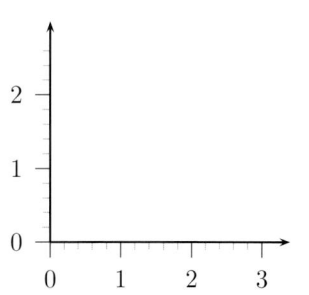

```
\usepackage{pst-plot}

\pspicture(3,3.25)
  \psaxes[subticks=5,ticksize=-6pt 0,
    subticksize=0.5]{->}(3.4,3)
\endpspicture
```

15.1 Coordinate axes

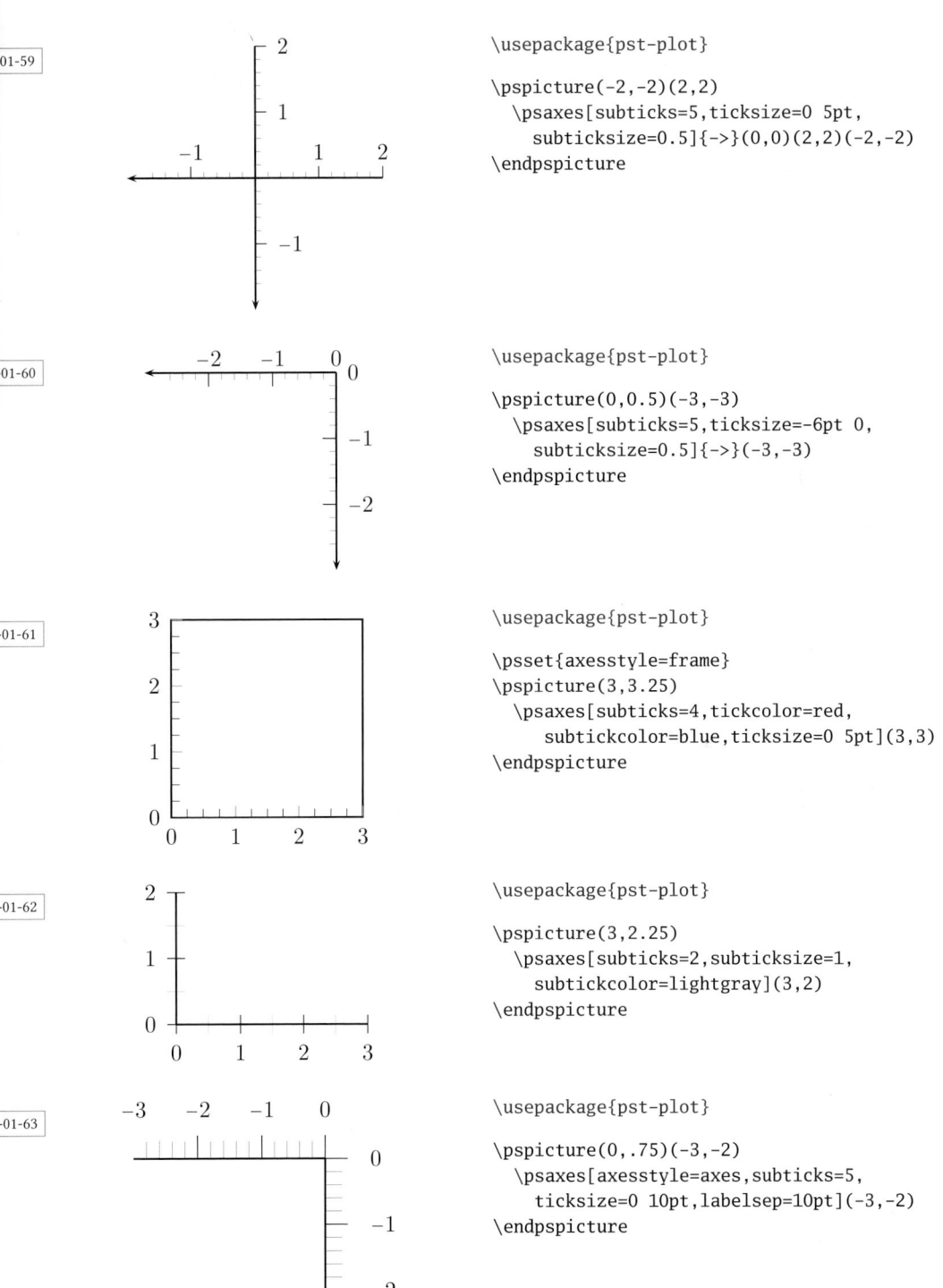

```
\usepackage{pst-plot}

\pspicture(-2,-2)(2,2)
  \psaxes[subticks=5,ticksize=0 5pt,
    subticksize=0.5]{->}(0,0)(2,2)(-2,-2)
\endpspicture
```

```
\usepackage{pst-plot}

\pspicture(0,0.5)(-3,-3)
  \psaxes[subticks=5,ticksize=-6pt 0,
    subticksize=0.5]{->}(-3,-3)
\endpspicture
```

```
\usepackage{pst-plot}

\psset{axesstyle=frame}
\pspicture(3,3.25)
  \psaxes[subticks=4,tickcolor=red,
    subtickcolor=blue,ticksize=0 5pt](3,3)
\endpspicture
```

```
\usepackage{pst-plot}

\pspicture(3,2.25)
  \psaxes[subticks=2,subticksize=1,
    subtickcolor=lightgray](3,2)
\endpspicture
```

```
\usepackage{pst-plot}

\pspicture(0,.75)(-3,-2)
  \psaxes[axesstyle=axes,subticks=5,
    ticksize=0 10pt,labelsep=10pt](-3,-2)
\endpspicture
```

logLines, xylogBase, xlogBase, and ylogBase

Using these commands you can draw logarithmic graphs. The syntax for logLines, which creates logarithmic axes, is similar to some options of the PSTricks base package:

logLines=all|x|y|none

Earlier examples have already used the logLines option (Example 15-01-52 on page 185 and Example 15-01-54 on page 186). The difficulty with logarithmic lines isn't so much the drawing of the lines themselves, which is entirely controlled by PostScript, but the labels. The values setting the lengths of the axes are now interpreted as exponents, so integer values only make sense here.

The following example on the left draws a double logarithmic axis with \psaxes(5,5), which runs through the powers $0\ldots5$, while in the example on the right, the x axis runs through $-1\ldots4$ and the y axis through $-2\ldots3$.

Three more commands enable you to set the base for the logarithm, either through xylogBase for both axes or through xlogBase or ylogBase for just one axis. If this specification is missing, the default labels are set.

xylogBase=*value*   xlogBase=*value*   ylogBase=*value*

```
\usepackage{pst-plot}
\pspicture(-0.3,-0.5)(5,5)\psaxes[logLines=all,subticks=5,xylogBase=10](5,5)
\endpspicture\qquad
\pspicture(-0.3,-0.5)(5,5)
  \psaxes[subticks=10,axesstyle=frame,xylogBase=e,logLines=all,
    ticksize=0 5pt,tickstyle=inner,Ox=-1,Oy=-2](5,5)
\endpspicture
```

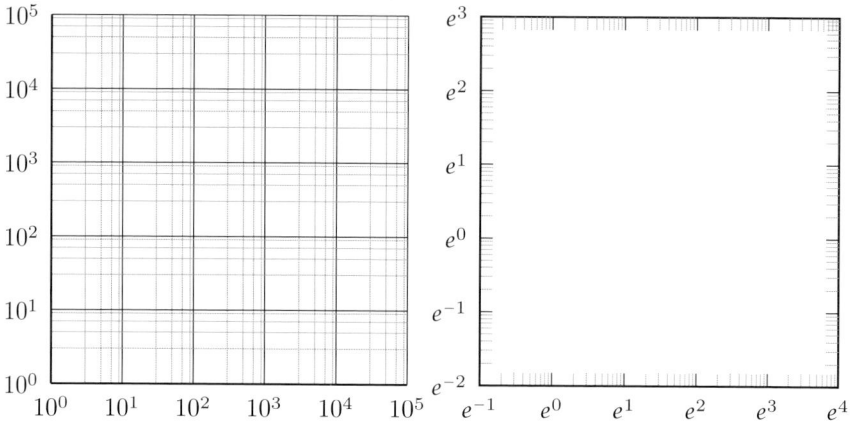

```
\usepackage{pst-plot}
\psset{unit=4}
\pspicture(-0.1,-0.1)(3,1.2)
  \psaxes[axesstyle=frame,logLines=x,xlogBase=10,Dy=0.5,
    subtickcolor=black!50,tickwidth=1pt,subticks=10](3,1)
\endpspicture
```

15.1 Coordinate axes

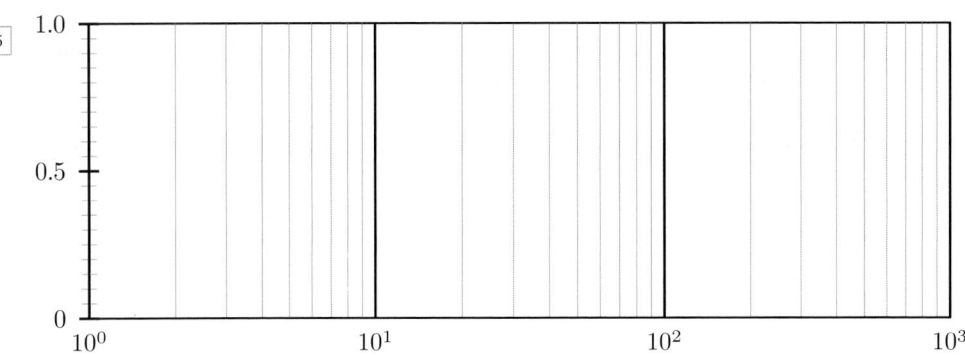

You can choose the intersection point of the coordinates through 0x and 0y as usual, and set arbitrary labels of the axes. In the following example the exponent of the y axis doesn't start at −3, but through 0y= −1 at this value and accordingly goes up to a maximal exponent of 3.

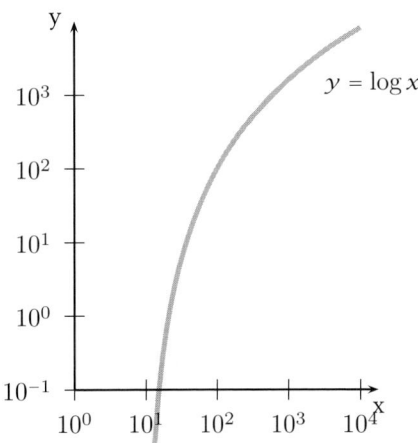

```
\usepackage{pst-plot}

\begin{pspicture}(-1.75,-3.5)(3.5,2.25)
    \psplot[linewidth=2pt,linecolor=red]%
        {0.11}{3}{x 4 exp log}
    \psaxes[xylogBase=10,Oy=-1]%
        {->}(-1,-3)(3.25,2)
    \uput[-90](3.25,-3){x}
    \uput[180](-1,2){y}
    \rput[lb](2.5,1){$y=\log x$}
\end{pspicture}
```

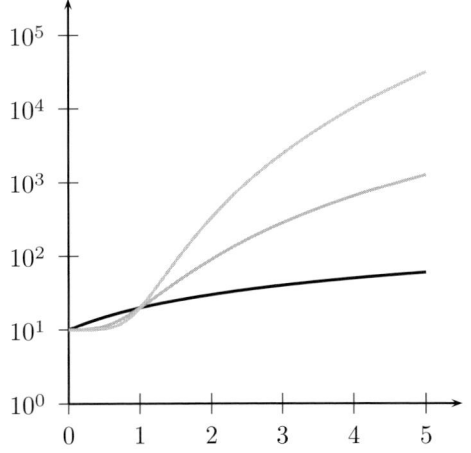

```
\usepackage{pst-plot}

\begin{pspicture}(-0.75,-1.25)(5.5,4.5)
    \psaxes[ylogBase=10]%
        {->}(0,-1)(0,-1)(5.5,4.5)
    \psset{linewidth=1.2pt}
    \psplot{0}{5}{x x cos add log}
    \psplot[linecolor=red]{0}{5}%
        {x 3 exp x cos add log}
    \psplot[linecolor=cyan]{0}{5}%
        {x 5 exp x cos add log}
\end{pspicture}
```

15 pst-plot: Plotting functions and data

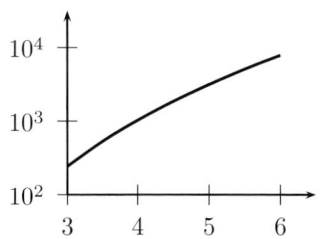

```
\usepackage{pst-plot}

\begin{pspicture}(2.25,1.75)(6.5,4.5)
    \psaxes[ylogBase=10,Ox=3,Oy=2]%
        {->}(3,2)(3,2)(6.5,4.5)
    \psplot[linewidth=1.2pt]{3}{6}%
        {x 5 exp x cos add log}
\end{pspicture}
```

15-01-

xlabelFactor and ylabelFactor

By default, labels are real numbers in decimal notation, and in principle it isn't possible to use exponential notation as TeX doesn't have a corresponding internal representation (unlike the axis ticks, the labels are set at the TeX level). However, you can use the xlabelFactor and ylabelFactor options to simulate an equivalent representation.

xlabelFactor=<arbitrary>

 math mode!   The defined string of text is put after every number, which can be used to create the impression of exponential notation. You must take care that the font and font style (math or text mode) are the same for both the labels set internally and the additional text.

```
\usepackage{pst-plot}
\readdata{\data}{demo1.dat}
\pstScalePoints(1,0.000001){}{} \psset{llx=-1.5cm,lly=-.2cm,ury=.2cm}
\psgraph[ylabelFactor=\times10^6,Dx=5,Dy=100,ticksize=-5pt 0]{->}(0,0)(25,650){8cm}{4cm}
    \listplot[linecolor=red,showpoints=true]{\data}
\endpsgraph
```

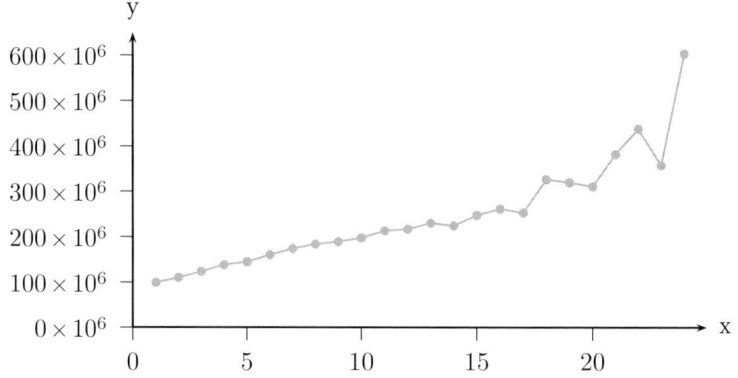

15-01-6

This example deals with data with extremely large y values, which are scaled with the \pstScalePoints command (cf. page 223) so that the figure can be drawn using smaller values to avoid any TeX errors with using too large values. Applying xlabelFactor=$\times10^6$ when labelling the axis makes the graph look like the original values of the data have been handled.

15.1.12 Axes with trigonometric units

A common situation is the need to partition axes using angular units. This is relatively easy for degrees, and one way to do it for radians is to create a custom label definition (as shown in Section 15.1.10 on page 174). However, it is easier to set units in radians automatically by using the trigLabels option.

    trigLabels=boolean   trigLabelBase=integer

Together with the option trigLabelBase which is the denominator of the fraction, one can set any possible values. When using trigLabels, you must take care that when displaying the x axis with the \psaxes command the correct measure is set with xunit: it has to be a multiple or fraction of π. In the first example it is set to $\frac{\pi}{2} \approx 1.571$. For the \psplot command, the normal axis division is applied as multiples of π (radian) and an interval of $[0..3\pi] \approx [0..9.42]$ is used.

measure

```
\usepackage{pst-plot}
\begin{pspicture}(-0.5,-1.25)(10,1.25)
  \psplot[linecolor=red,linewidth=1.5pt,plotpoints=500]{0}{9.42}{x RadtoDeg sin}
  \psaxes[xunit=1.571,showorigin=false,trigLabels]{->}(0,0)(-0.5,-1.25)(6.4,1.25)
\end{pspicture}
```

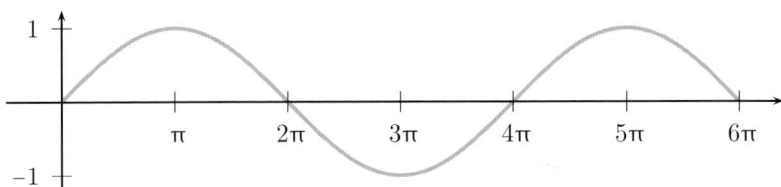

```
\usepackage{pst-plot}
\begin{pspicture}(-0.5,-1.25)(10,1.25)
  \psplot[linecolor=red,linewidth=1.5pt,plotpoints=500]{0}{9.42}{x dup add RadtoDeg sin}
  \psaxes[xunit=0.785,showorigin=false,trigLabels]{->}(0,0)(-1,-1.25)(12.8,1.25)
\end{pspicture}
```

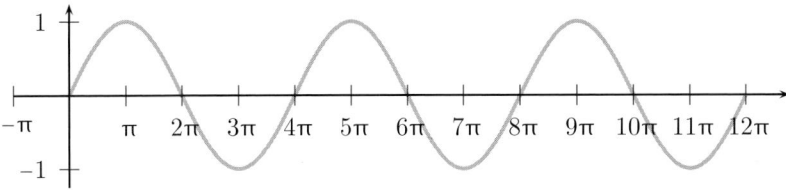

```
\usepackage{pst-plot}
\begin{pspicture}(-0.5,-1.25)(10,1.25)
  \psplot[linecolor=red,linewidth=1.5pt,plotpoints=500]{0}{9.42}{x dup add RadtoDeg sin}
  \psaxes[xunit=0.785,showorigin=false,trigLabels,Dx=2]{->}(0,0)(-1,-1.25)(12.8,1.25)
\end{pspicture}
```

15 pst-plot: Plotting functions and data

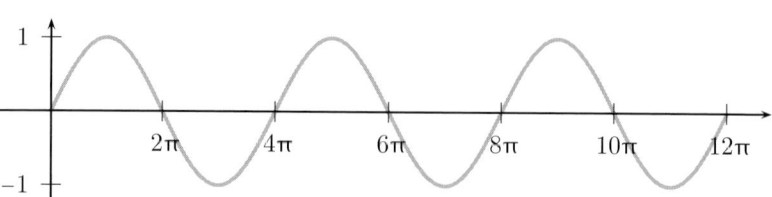

To achieve other divisions, pst-plot already offers the following constants:

```
\def\psPiFour{12.566371}      \def\psPiTwo{6.283185}
\def\psPi{3.14159265}         \def\psPiH{1.570796327}
\newdimen\pstRadUnit          \pstRadUnit=1.047198cm % this is pi/3
\newdimen\pstRadUnitInv       \pstRadUnitInv=0.95493cm % this is 3/pi
```

Using the length \pstRadUnit simplifies axis division:

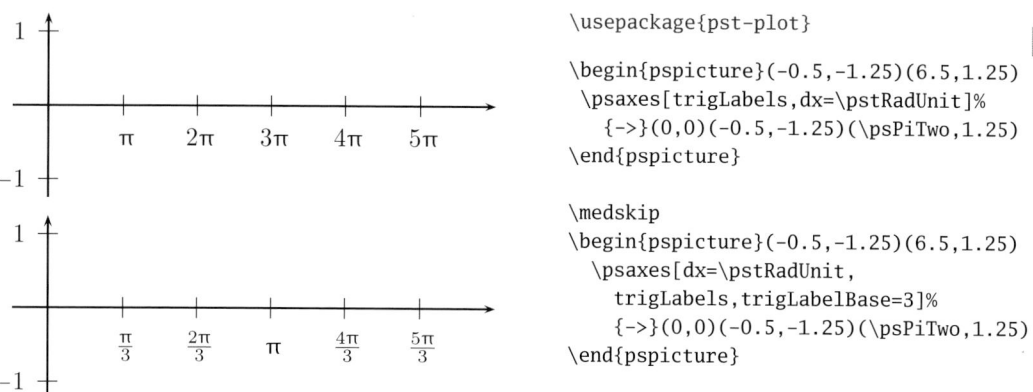

```
\usepackage{pst-plot}

\begin{pspicture}(-0.5,-1.25)(6.5,1.25)
\psaxes[trigLabels,dx=\pstRadUnit]%
    {->}(0,0)(-0.5,-1.25)(\psPiTwo,1.25)
\end{pspicture}

\medskip
\begin{pspicture}(-0.5,-1.25)(6.5,1.25)
    \psaxes[dx=\pstRadUnit,
        trigLabels,trigLabelBase=3]%
        {->}(0,0)(-0.5,-1.25)(\psPiTwo,1.25)
\end{pspicture}
```

Alternatively you can set with the macro \psset the general unit to radian beforehand by setting \psset{xunit=\pstRadUnit}; Once you've done that, the pspicture environment also gets the correct coordinates: six length units on the x axis correspond to 6π. With trigLabelBase=3 the value is reduced to 2π, etc.

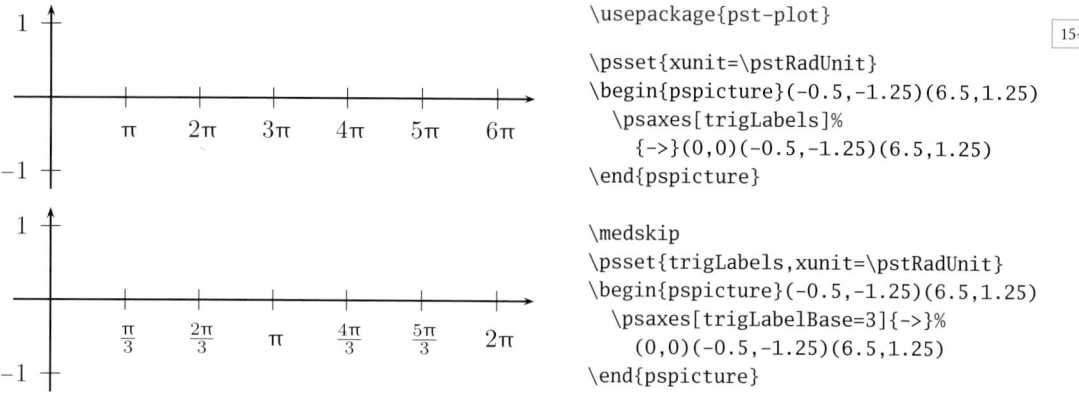

```
\usepackage{pst-plot}

\psset{xunit=\pstRadUnit}
\begin{pspicture}(-0.5,-1.25)(6.5,1.25)
    \psaxes[trigLabels]%
        {->}(0,0)(-0.5,-1.25)(6.5,1.25)
\end{pspicture}

\medskip
\psset{trigLabels,xunit=\pstRadUnit}
\begin{pspicture}(-0.5,-1.25)(6.5,1.25)
    \psaxes[trigLabelBase=3]{->}%
        (0,0)(-0.5,-1.25)(6.5,1.25)
\end{pspicture}
```

15.1 Coordinate axes

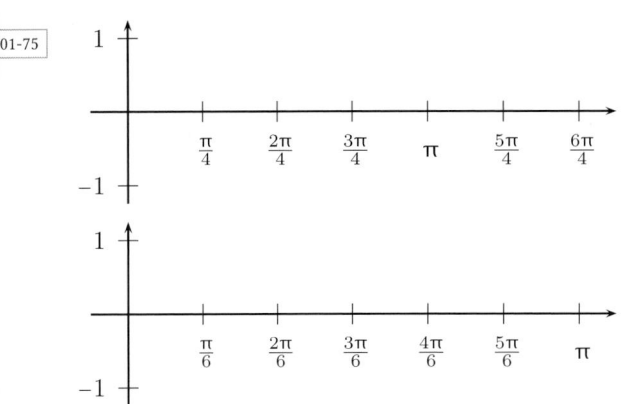

```
\usepackage{pst-plot}

\psset{trigLabels,xunit=\pstRadUnit}
\begin{pspicture}(-0.5,-1.25)(6.5,1.25)
  \psaxes[trigLabelBase=4]%
    {->}(0,0)(-0.5,-1.25)(6.5,1.25)
\end{pspicture}

\medskip
\psset{trigLabels,xunit=\pstRadUnit}
\begin{pspicture}(-0.5,-1.25)(6.5,1.25)
  \psaxes[trigLabelBase=6]%
    {->}(0,0)(-0.5,-1.25)(6.5,1.25)
\end{pspicture}
```

When plotting trigonometric functions, you must bear in mind that \psplot doesn't honour the trigLabels option if it is given different values locally in its own parameters. The following example resets the x unit for \psplot locally to 1 cm as it is used on the PostScript side.

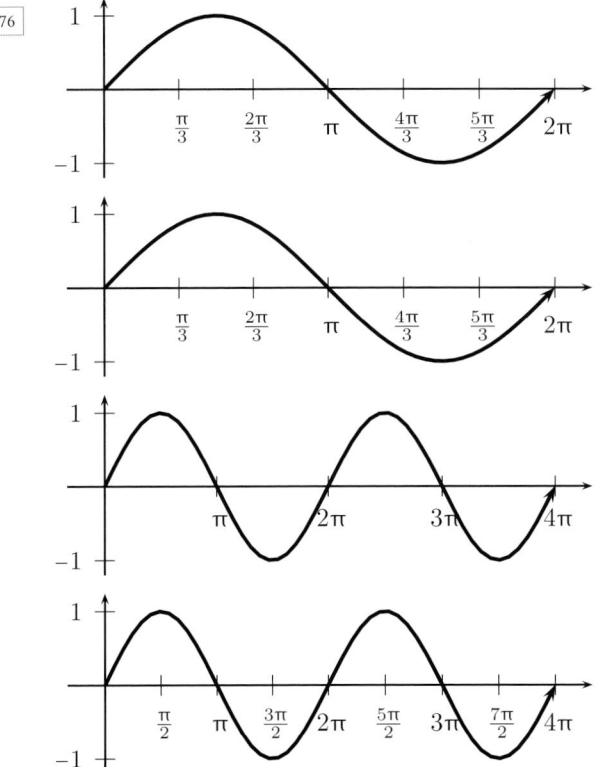

```
\usepackage{pst-plot}

\psset{trigLabels,xunit=\pstRadUnit,
    arrows=->}
\begin{pspicture}(-0.5,-1.2)(6.5,1.25)
\psaxes[trigLabelBase=3]%
    (0,0)(-0.5,-1.2)(6.5,1.25)
\psplot[xunit=1cm,linewidth=1.5pt]%
    {0}{\psPiTwo}{x RadtoDeg sin}
\end{pspicture}\par\medskip
\begin{pspicture}(-0.5,-1.2)(6.5,1.25)
\psaxes[trigLabelBase=3]%
    (0,0)(-0.5,-1.2)(6.5,1.25)
\psplot[linewidth=1.5pt]%
    {0}{6}{x Pi 3 div mul RadtoDeg sin}
\end{pspicture}\par\medskip
\begin{pspicture}(-0.5,-1.2)(6.5,1.25)
\psaxes[dx=1.5](0,0)(-.5,-1.2)(6.5,1.25)
\psplot[xunit=.5cm,linewidth=1.5pt]%
    {0}{\psPiFour}{x RadtoDeg sin}
\end{pspicture}\par\medskip
\begin{pspicture}(-0.5,-1.2)(6.5,1.25)
\psaxes[dx=0.75,trigLabelBase=2]%
    (0,0)(-0.5,-1.2)(6.5,1.25)
\psplot[xunit=.5cm,linewidth=1.5pt]%
    {0}{\psPiFour}{x RadtoDeg sin}
\end{pspicture}
```

There is one more method for setting the labels (though it requires significant knowledge about the inner workings) using xunit and dx. Specifying \psset{xunit=1.57079} sets the

15 pst-plot: Plotting functions and data

x unit to $\frac{\pi}{2}$ and specifying \psset{dx=0.6667} sets a tick and a label every $\frac{2}{3}$ of the current unit. In the following example the length of the axis is 6.4 units, which corresponds to $6.4 \times 1.571\,\text{cm} \approx 10\,\text{cm}$. The function is plotted in the interval 0 to $3\pi \approx 9.425$.

```
\usepackage{pst-plot}
\begin{pspicture}(-0.5,-1.25)(10,1.25)
  \psaxes[xunit=1.570796327,showorigin=false,trigLabels,
    trigLabelBase=3,dx=0.666667]{->}(0,0)(-0.5,-1.25)(6.4,1.25)
  \psplot[linecolor=red,linewidth=1.5pt]{0}{9.424777961}{
    x RadtoDeg dup sin exch 1.1 mul cos add}
\end{pspicture}
```

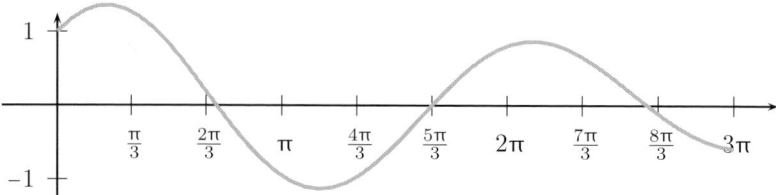

```
\usepackage{pst-plot}
\begin{pspicture}(-0.5,-1.25)(10,1.25)
  \psaxes[trigLabels,xunit=\psPi,dx=0.25]{->}(0,0)(-0.25,-1.25)(3.2,1.25)
  \psplot[xunit=0.25,plotpoints=500,linecolor=red,linewidth=1.5pt]{0}{37.70}{
    x RadtoDeg dup sin exch 1.1 mul cos add}
\end{pspicture}
```

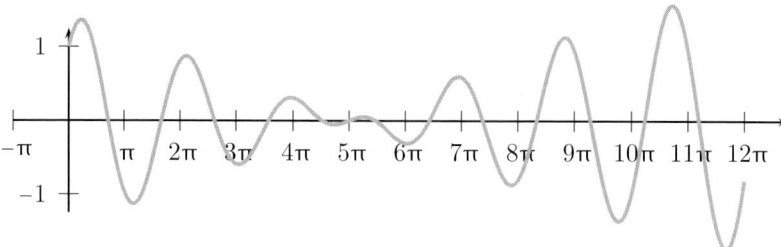

```
\usepackage{pst-plot}
\begin{pspicture}(-0.5,-2)(10,2)
  \psplot[xunit=0.0625,linewidth=1.5pt,
    plotpoints=5000]{0}{150.80}{x RadtoDeg dup sin exch 1.1 mul cos add}
  \psaxes[trigLabels,xunit=\psPi,dx=0.5,Dx=8,subticks=2]{->}(0,0)(-0.1,-2)(3.2,2)
\end{pspicture}
```

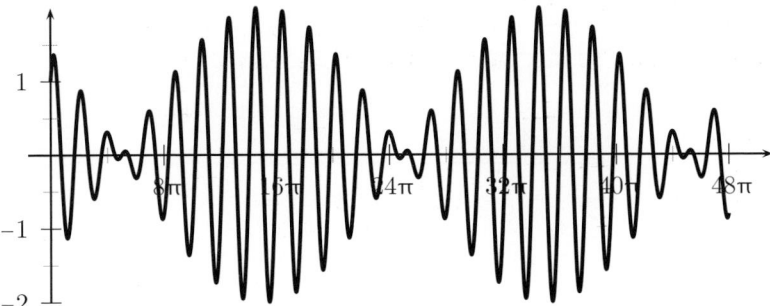

```
\usepackage{pst-plot}
\begin{pspicture}(-7,-1.5)(7,1.5)
  \psaxes[trigLabels,xunit=\psPi]{->}(0,0)(-2.2,-1.5)(2.2,1.5)
  \psplot[linewidth=1.5pt,plotpoints=1000]{-7}{7}{x dup add RadtoDeg sin}
\end{pspicture}

\medskip
\begin{pspicture}(-7,-1.5)(7,1.5)
  \psaxes[trigLabels,trigLabelBase=2,dx=\psPiH,
    xunit=\psPi]{->}(0,0)(-2.2,-1.5)(2.2,1.5)
  \psplot[linewidth=1.5pt,plotpoints=1000]{-7}{7}{x dup mul RadtoDeg sin}
\end{pspicture}
```

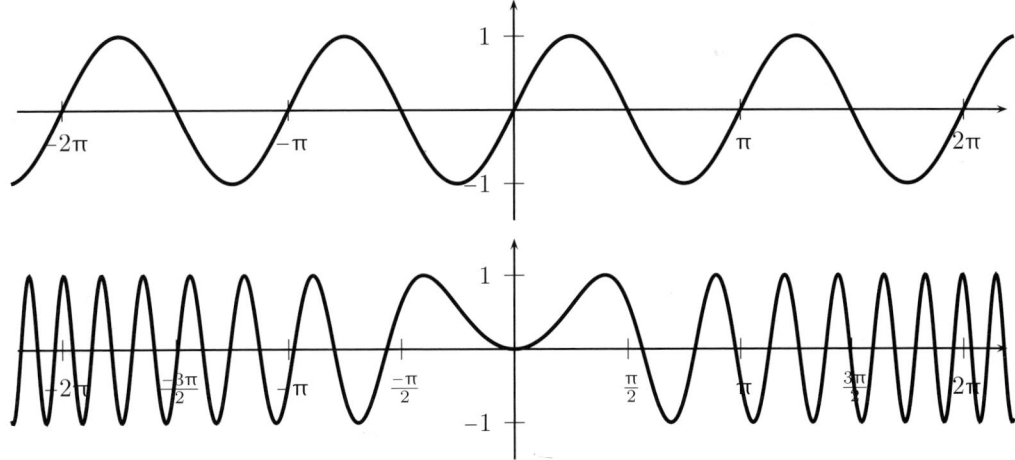

15.2 Plot styles

Table 15.4 shows a summary of the special parameters you can use with any of the plotting commands in pst-plot (cf. Sections 15.3 on page 203 and 15.4 on page 212). The following sections look at the parameters in detail.

15 pst-plot: Plotting functions and data

Table 15.4: Summary of the special parameters for the plotting commands in pst-plot. For older versions the values LineToXAxis, LineToYAxis, and bar need the package pstricks-add.

name	type	default
plotpoints	value	50
plotstyle	dots|line|polygon|curve|ecurve|ccurve| LineToXAxis|LineToYAxis|bar	line
barwidth	value	2.5mm

15.2.1 plotpoints

The plotpoints parameter controls the number of points plotted for the function within the specified interval, which has a major effect on how the curve displays. The default of 50 points is enough for many functions, but it is also frequently too few. With modern computers, specifying values of 5000 and more is no problem. On the other hand, when dealing with functions with very small gradients, you could choose to plot fewer points. Another factor to bear in mind is the printer resolution.

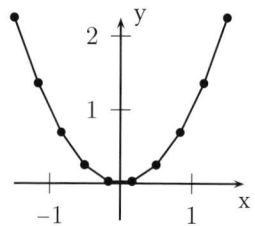

```
\usepackage{pst-plot}

\begin{pspicture}(-1.75,-0.5)(1.75,2.3)
  \psaxes{->}(0,0)(-1.5,-0.5)(1.75,2.25)
  \uput[-90](1.75,0){x} \uput[0](0,2.25){y}
  \psplot[plotpoints=10,
    showpoints=true]{-1.5}{1.5}{x dup mul}
\end{pspicture}
```

15.2.2 plotstyle

As can be seen from the following examples, dots is a distinct plot style, but line and polygon are very similar, and there is virtually no difference between how curve, ecurve, and ccurve are displayed. This is usually the case when functions are plotted. Whichever plot style is selected, the number of coordinates plotted is controlled by the plotpoints parameter (cf. Section 15.2.1).

dots

With the dots plot style, the plotted coordinates are only marked by points. You can alter the appearance of the points through the parameters in Table 6.1 on page 69, or define new symbols (cf. Section 6.3 on page 72).

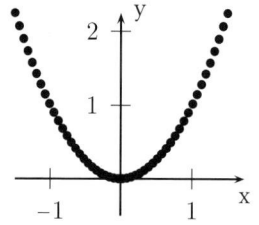

```
\usepackage{pst-plot}

\begin{pspicture}(-1.75,-0.5)(1.75,2.3)
  \psaxes{->}(0,0)(-1.5,-0.5)(1.75,2.25)
  \uput[-90](1.75,0){x} \uput[0](0,2.25){y}
  \psplot[plotstyle=dots]{-1.5}{1.5}{x dup mul}
\end{pspicture}
```

line

With the line plot style, the plotted coordinates are connected by secants (lines). You can alter the appearance of the lines through the parameters in Table 4.1 on page 43.

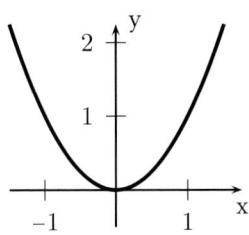

```
\usepackage{pst-plot}

\begin{pspicture}(-1.75,-0.5)(1.75,2.3)
\psaxes{->}(0,0)(-1.5,-0.5)(1.75,2.25)
\uput[-90](1.75,0){x} \uput[0](0,2.25){y}
\psplot[plotstyle=line,linewidth=1.5pt]%
    {-1.5}{1.5}{x dup mul}
\end{pspicture}
```

polygon

The polygon plot style behaves like the \pspolygon line command (cf. Section 4.4 on page 53): the polygon is closed by connecting the endpoint and the starting point with a line.

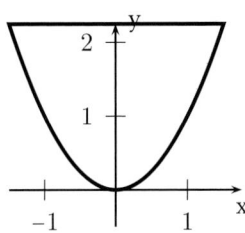

```
\usepackage{pst-plot}

\begin{pspicture}(-1.75,-0.5)(1.75,2.3)
\psaxes{->}(0,0)(-1.5,-0.5)(1.75,2.25)
\uput[-90](1.75,0){x} \uput[0](0,2.25){y}
\psplot[plotstyle=polygon,linewidth=1.5pt]%
    {-1.5}{1.5}{x dup mul}
\end{pspicture}
```

curve

The curve plot style behaves like the \pscurve command (cf. Section 5.3.3 on page 67). There can be problems when the curve is very steep, in which case you have to adjust the curvature parameter (cf. Section 5.1.2 on page 58). The following examples illustrate a steep curve before and after curvature adjustment.

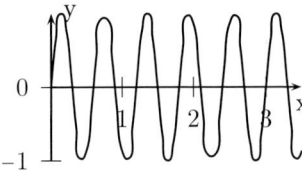

```
\usepackage{pst-plot}

\begin{pspicture}(0,-1)(3.5,1)
    \psaxes{->}(0,0)(0,-1)(3.5,1)
    \uput[-90](3.5,0){x} \uput[0](0,1){y}
    \psplot[plotstyle=curve]{0}{3.5}%
        { x 360 mul 0.6 div sin }
\end{pspicture}
```

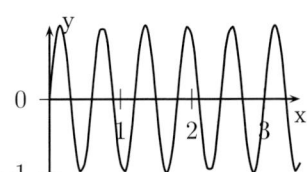

```
\usepackage{pst-plot}

\begin{pspicture}(0,-1)(3.5,1)
    \psaxes{->}(0,0)(0,-1)(3.5,1)
    \uput[-90](3.5,0){x} \uput[0](0,1){y}
    \psplot[plotstyle=curve,curvature=1 1 -1]%
        {0}{3.5}{x 360 mul 0.6 div sin}
\end{pspicture}
```

ecurve

The ecurve plot style behaves like the \psecurve command (cf. Section 5.3.4 on page 67), so the endpoints of the curve are not plotted. Again there can be problems when the curve is very steep, in which case you have to adjust the curvature parameter (cf. Section 5.1.2 on page 58). The following examples illustrate a steep curve before and after curvature adjustment.

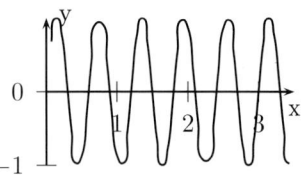

```
\usepackage{pst-plot}

\begin{pspicture}(0,-1)(3.5,1)
    \psaxes{->}(0,0)(0,-1)(3.5,1)
    \uput[-90](3.5,0){x} \uput[0](0,1){y}
    \psplot[plotstyle=ecurve]{0}{3.5}%
        {x 360 mul 0.6 div sin}
\end{pspicture}
```

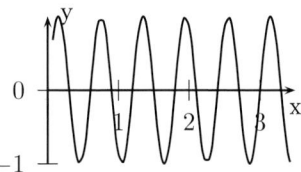

```
\usepackage{pst-plot}

\begin{pspicture}(0,-1)(3.5,1)
    \psaxes{->}(0,0)(0,-1)(3.5,1)
    \uput[-90](3.5,0){x} \uput[0](0,1){y}
    \psplot[plotstyle=ecurve,curvature=1 1 -1]%
        {0}{3.5}{x 360 mul 0.6 div sin}
\end{pspicture}
```

ccurve

The ccurve plot style behaves like the \psccurve command (cf. Section 5.3.5 on page 68): the curve is closed by connecting the endpoint and the starting point with a curve. Again there can be problems when the curve is very steep, in which case you have to adjust the curvature parameter (cf. Section 5.1.2 on page 58). The following examples illustrate a steep curve before and after curvature adjustment.

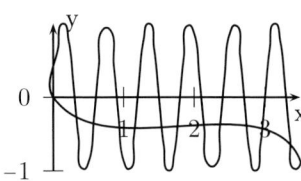

```
\usepackage{pst-plot}

\begin{pspicture}(0,-1)(3.5,1)
    \psaxes{->}(0,0)(0,-1)(3.5,1)
    \uput[-90](3.5,0){x} \uput[0](0,1){y}
    \psplot[plotstyle=ccurve]{0}{3.5}%
        {x 360 mul 0.6 div sin}
\end{pspicture}
```

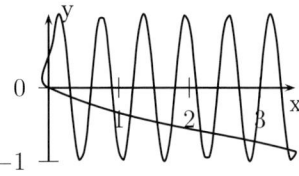

```
\usepackage{pst-plot}

\begin{pspicture}(0,-1)(3.5,1)
    \psaxes{->}(0,0)(0,-1)(3.5,1)
    \uput[-90](3.5,0){x} \uput[0](0,1){y}
    \psplot[plotstyle=ccurve,curvature=1 1 -1]%
        {0}{3.5}{x 360 mul 0.6 div sin}
\end{pspicture}
```

15.2 Plot styles

LineToXAxis and LineToYAxis

The LineToXAxis and LineToYAxis plot styles are available if you load version 1.01 or later of the pst-plot package. They draw lines from the function value to the respective axis.

```
\usepackage{pst-plot}
\psset{xunit=0.0333cm,yunit=2.5cm}
\begin{pspicture}(0,-1.2)(400,1.4)
  \psline{->}(0,0)(390,0)\psline{->}(0,-1.1)(0,1.2)
  \psplot[plotstyle=LineToXAxis,linestyle=dashed,plotpoints=50,
    showpoints=true,dotstyle=o,dotsize=0.2]{0}{360}{x sin}
\end{pspicture}
```

```
\usepackage{pst-plot}
\psset{xunit=0.0333cm,yunit=2.5cm}
\begin{pspicture}(0,-1.2)(400,1.4)
  \psline{->}(0,0)(390,0)\psline{->}(0,-1.1)(0,1.2)
  \psplot[plotstyle=LineToYAxis,linestyle=dashed,plotpoints=50,
    showpoints=true]{0}{360}{x cos}
\end{pspicture}
```

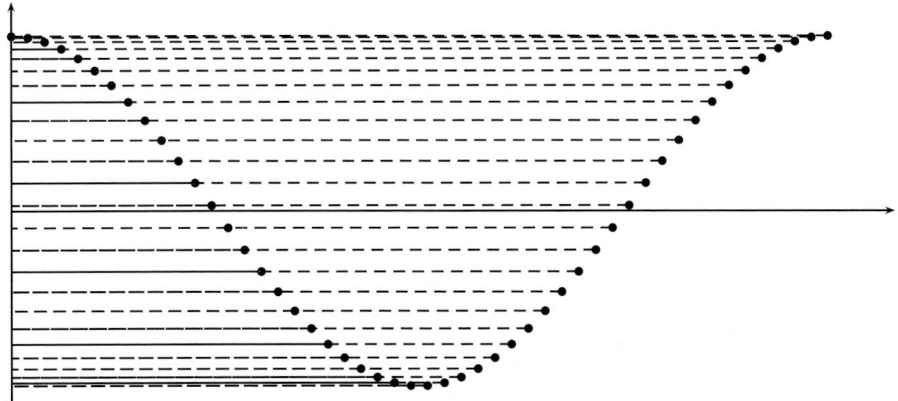

15 pst-plot: Plotting functions and data

bar and barwidth

The bar style, available only in the current version of pst-plot, draws rudimentary bar diagrams. The width of the individual bars can be adjusted through the barwidth parameter, which is only valid with this plot style; the default value for barwidth is 2.5 mm.

    barwidth=<value>[unit]

You can use all the usual filling parameters (cf. Section 4.1 on page 43) for the bars and also give them a shadow.

```
\usepackage{pst-plot}
\psset{xunit=.4cm,yunit=.3cm}
\begin{pspicture}(-2.25,-1.25)(29,12)
 \psaxes[axesstyle=axes,Ox=1466,Oy=0,Dx=4,Dy=2,ylabelFactor={\,\%}]{-}(29,12)
 \listplot[shadow=true,linecolor=blue,plotstyle=bar,barwidth=0.3cm,
          fillcolor=red,fillstyle=solid]{\barData}   \rput{90}(-3,6.25){amount}
\end{pspicture}
```

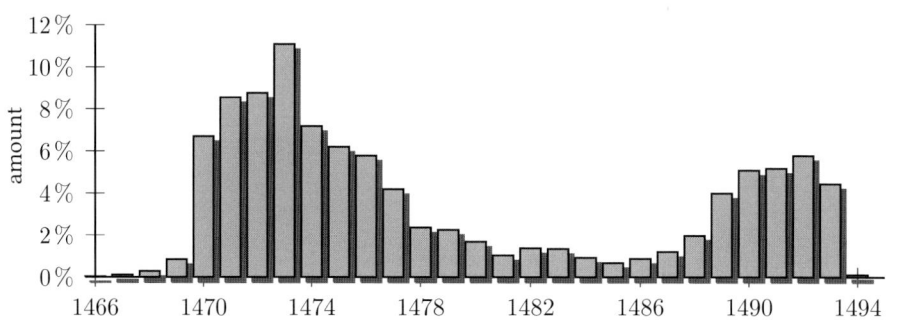

15-02-

```
\usepackage{pst-plot}
\psset{xunit=.4cm,yunit=.3cm}
\begin{pspicture}(-2.25,-1.25)(29,12)
 \psaxes[axesstyle=axes,Ox=1466,Oy=0,Dx=4,Dy=2,ylabelFactor={\,\%}]{-}(29,12)
 \listplot[linecolor=blue,plotstyle=bar,barwidth=0.3cm,fillcolor=red,
          fillstyle=crosshatch]{\barData}   \rput{90}(-3,6.25){amount}
\end{pspicture}
```

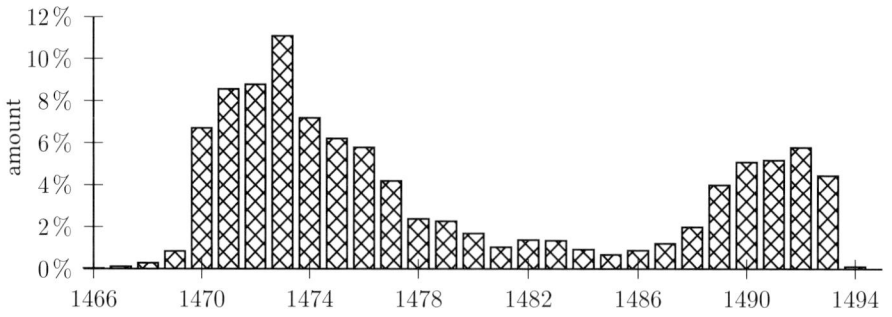

15-02-

15.3 Plotting functions

```
\usepackage{pst-plot}
\psset{xunit=.4cm,yunit=.3cm}
\begin{pspicture}(-2.25,-1.25)(29,12)
  \psaxes[axesstyle=axes,Ox=1466,Oy=0,Dx=4,Dy=2,ylabelFactor={\,\%}]{-}(29,12)
  \listplot[linecolor=blue,plotstyle=bar,barwidth=0.3cm,fillcolor=red,
           fillstyle=vlines]{\barData}
  \listplot[showpoints=true]{\barData}  \rput{90}(-3,6.25){amount}
\end{pspicture}
```

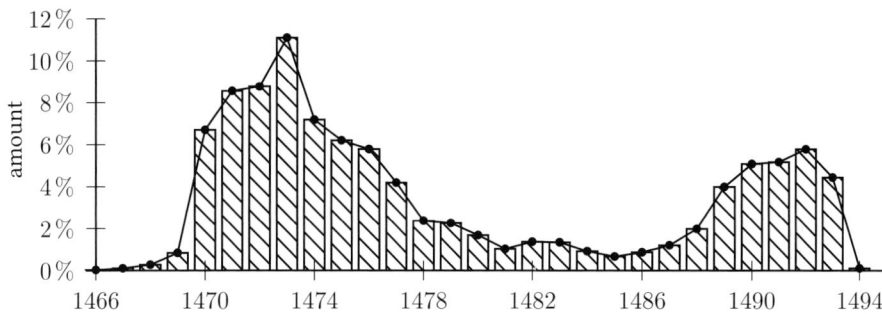

15.3 Plotting functions

The syntax of the commands for plotting functions is:

`\psplot` [settings] {*xmin*}{*xmax*}{*function f(x)*}
`\parametricplot` [settings] {*tmin*}{*tmax*}{*functions x(t) y(t)*}

By definition the name of the variable for \psplot is x and for \parametricplot it is t. It isn't easy to change these names, but this doesn't impose any restrictions on possible applications.

Here $[x_{min}; x_{max}]$ and $[t_{min}; t_{max}]$ describe the respective definition interval (start and end value) over which the function is to be evaluated; these can also be described by normal PostScript code (cf. Section 12.1.2 on page 141). Of the parameters listed in Table 15.4, only plotpoints (cf. Section 15.2.1 on page 198) is really of interest in connection with functions, as it is unusual to use anything other than plotstyle=line to join the computed points. plotpoints defaults to plotting 50 nodes in the specified interval, but it is usually a good idea to increase this to about 200 to avoid getting a polyline rather than a curve.

There is only one difference between the two commands: \psplot plots the input variable (x) against the one variable (y) output by the function argument, whereas \parametricplot uses the input variable (t) to output two variables (x and y) from the functions in the argument. You can use the x and t variables repeatedly within an expression; it is only when the closing parenthesis for the function expression is encountered that the coordinates for the point of the graph are assumed to be ready.

PostScript works with the stack system, also referred to as **RPN** (Reverse Polish Notation), which is the internal standard for all computers. If you use an HP calculator, you will already be familiar with it. The normal notation for the multiplication "$a * b =$" becomes

15 pst-plot: Plotting functions and data

"a<enter>b<enter>*". The parameters (variables) always have to be put onto the stack first (symbolized by <enter>) before one of the mathematical functions can be called. After the operation has been called, the result is on top of the stack. Once the complete function argument has been processed, the \psplot and \parametricplot commands always refer to the one or two elements at the top of the stack.

PSTricks expects the mathematical functions to be described in RPN notation. If you aren't familiar with this stack-oriented processing or have a problem with the notation for a particular expression, you can use a so-called infix/postfix converter, which transforms "normal" (infix) mathematical expressions into ones in RPN notation (postfix). [56] Both the pst-infixplot package and pstricks itself provide facilities to describe functions algebraically (cf. Sections 33.2.1 on page 666 and 15.3.3 on page 207).

 Note that neither command displays any error messages. This is particularly relevant for those mathematical functions whose domains aren't within the real numbers: if any value of the input variable results in **one** erroneous argument, for example $\sqrt{-1}$, the whole graph is not drawn!

Bear in mind that the immediate application of PostScript commands to display mathematical relations doesn't necessarily provide any benefits in the final printout over using programmes such as gnuplot. Furthermore it isn't always easy to solve mathematical problems with the PostScript commands.

15.3.1 \psplot

This section looks at the use of PostScript and algebraic notation for math functions. To help you understand the notation, each function is given in normal notation, in algebraic notation, and in PostScript notation. The following example illustrates $y(x) = \sin x$.

function	algebraic	PostScript
$y(x) = \sin x$	sin(x)	x sin

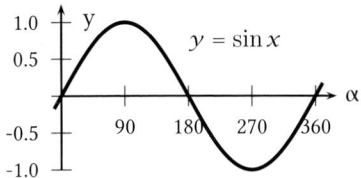

```
\usepackage{pst-plot}

\psset{xunit=0.01cm,yunit=1cm}
\begin{pspicture}(-80,-1.25)(410,1.25)
\psaxes[showorigin=false,
    Dx=90,Dy=0.5]{->}(0,0)(0,-1)(390,1.25)
\uput{.3}[0](370,0){$\alpha$}\uput{.3}[0](0,1){y}
\psplot[plotstyle=curve,
    linewidth=1.5pt]{-10}{370}{x sin}
\rput[l](180,0.75){$y=\sin x$}
\end{pspicture}
```

The next example shows a parabola of third order and its inverse function. The differentiation between the intervals is not necessary if exponential notation with $y = x^{\frac{1}{3}}$ is chosen.

15.3 Plotting functions

function	algebraic	PostScript
$y(x) = x^3$	x^3	x 3 exp
$y^{-1}(x) = \begin{cases} +\sqrt[3]{\|x\|} & x > 0 \\ -\sqrt[3]{\|x\|} & x < 0 \end{cases}$	x^(1/3)	x 0.333 exp (inverse function)

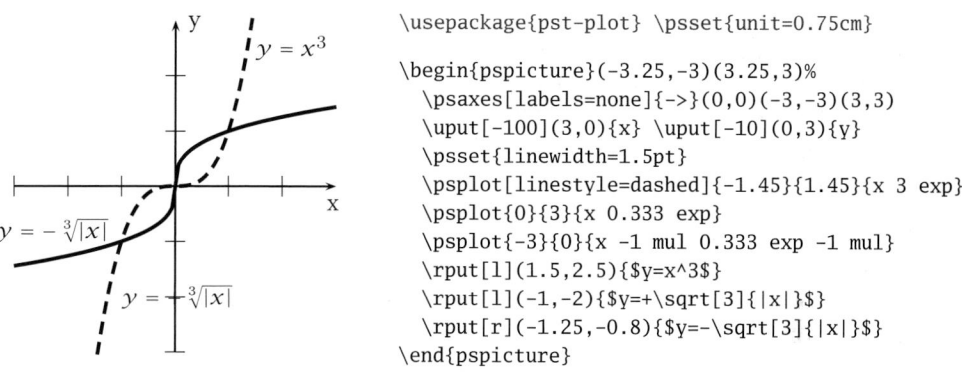

```
\usepackage{pst-plot} \psset{unit=0.75cm}

\begin{pspicture}(-3.25,-3)(3.25,3)%
  \psaxes[labels=none]{->}(0,0)(-3,-3)(3,3)
  \uput[-100](3,0){x} \uput[-10](0,3){y}
  \psset{linewidth=1.5pt}
  \psplot[linestyle=dashed]{-1.45}{1.45}{x 3 exp}
  \psplot{0}{3}{x 0.333 exp}
  \psplot{-3}{0}{x -1 mul 0.333 exp -1 mul}
  \rput[l](1.5,2.5){$y=x^3$}
  \rput[l](-1,-2){$y=+\sqrt[3]{|x|}$}
  \rput[r](-1.25,-0.8){$y=-\sqrt[3]{|x|}$}
\end{pspicture}
```

The following example shows an application that comes from power electronics. The graphic representation of the relative mean value of the current is shown for control of the direction of the current by a Thyristor pair. The φ parameter corresponds to the phase shift between current and voltage. The independent variable α shows the delay angle. PostScript expects the arguments of trigonometric functions to be given in degrees; relative angles must also be in degrees. So the expression $\frac{\alpha}{\pi}$ has to be replaced by $\frac{\alpha}{180}$.

function	$\dfrac{I(\alpha)}{I_0} = \begin{cases} \sqrt{1 - \frac{\alpha}{\pi} + \frac{1}{2\pi}\sin 2\alpha} & \varphi = 0 \\ \sqrt{\left(2 - \frac{2\alpha}{\pi}\right)(2 + \cos 2\alpha) + \frac{3}{\pi}\sin 2\alpha} & \varphi = \frac{\pi}{2} \end{cases}$	
algebraic	sqrt(1-x/Pi+sin(2*x)/(2*Pi))	$\varphi = 0$
	sqrt((2-2*x/Pi)*(2+cos(2*x))+3*sin(2*x)/Pi)	$\varphi = \frac{\pi}{2}$
PostScript	1 x 180 div sub 1 6.28 div x 2 mul sin mul add sqrt	$\varphi = 0$
	2 x 90 div sub x 2 mul cos 2 add mul x 2 mul sin 3 3.15 div mul add sqrt	$\varphi = \frac{\pi}{2}$

```
\usepackage{pst-plot} \psset{xunit=0.02cm,yunit=3cm}
\begin{pspicture}(-0.1,-0.1)(190,1.1)
  \psgrid[subgriddiv=0,griddots=5,gridlabels=0pt,xunit=30,yunit=0.2](6,5)
  \psaxes[linewidth=1pt,ticks=none,Dx=30,Dy=0.2]{->}(190,1.1)%
    [$\mathbf{\alpha}$,0][$\mathbf{I/I_0}$,90]
  \psplot[linewidth=1.5pt,algebraic,xunit=57.325]{0}{Pi}{sqrt(1-x/Pi+sin(2*x)/(2*Pi))}
  \psplot[linewidth=1.5pt,linestyle=dashed]{90}{180}{
    2 x 90 div sub x 2 mul cos 2 add mul x 2 mul sin 3 3.15 div mul add abs sqrt}
  \rput*(40,0.85){$\varphi=0$}  \rput*(125,0.9){$\varphi=\pi/2$}
\end{pspicture}
```

205

15 pst-plot: Plotting functions and data

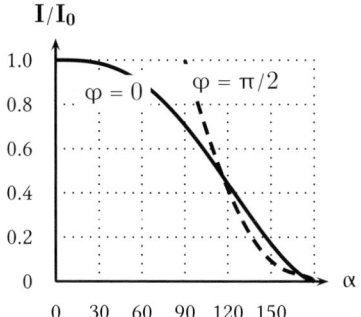

15.3.2 \parametricplot

The Lissajous figures known from physics or electronics are a typical use for equations in parametric form. The figure below is based on the following equations:

function	algebraic	PostScript
$x = \sin 1.5t$	sin(1.5*t)	t 1.5 mul sin
$y = \sin\left(2t + \frac{\pi}{3}\right)$	sin(2*t+Pi/3)	t 2 mul 60 add sin

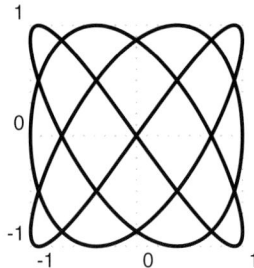

```
\usepackage{pst-plot}

\psset{unit=1.5cm}
\begin{pspicture}[showgrid](-1.1,-1.1)(1.1,1.1)
    \parametricplot[plotstyle=curve,algebraic,
        linewidth=1.5pt,plotpoints=200]{-6.28}{6.28}%
        {sin(1.5*t) | sin(2*t+Pi/3)}
\end{pspicture}
```

Because of the "length" of the graph, `plotpoints` is set to 200 so that the "corners" with high curvature appear smooth.

A strophoid results from the following parametric display, where a has to be substituted by a numeric value:

function	$x(t) = \dfrac{a\left(t^2 - 1\right)}{t^2 + 1}$
	$y(t) = \dfrac{at\left(t^2 - 1\right)}{t^2 + 1}$
algebraic	a*(t^2-1)/(t^2+1)
	a*t*(t^2-1)/(t^2+1)
PostScript	t t mul 1 sub a mul t t mul 1 add div
	t t mul 1 sub t mul a mul t t mul 1 add div

15.3 Plotting functions

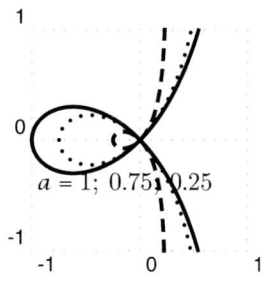

```
\usepackage{pst-plot}

\psset{unit=1.5}
\begin{pspicture}[showgrid](-1.2,-1.2)(1.2,1.2)
   \psset{plotpoints=200,linewidth=1.5pt}
   \def\PSfunc{t t mul 1 sub \param\space mul
      t t mul 1 add div t t mul 1 sub t mul
      \param\space mul t t mul 1 add div}
   \def\param{1}\parametricplot{-1.85}{1.85}{\PSfunc}
   \def\param{0.25}\parametricplot[linestyle=dashed]%
      {-4.5}{4.5}{\PSfunc}
   \def\param{0.75}\parametricplot[linestyle=dotted]%
      {-2.1}{2.1}{\PSfunc}
   \rput[l](-0.95,-0.4){$a=1;\ 0.75;\ 0.25$}
\end{pspicture}
```

15.3.3 Advanced possibilities

There are a few other important parameters that are specific to the plotting of functions. The syntax is summarized in Table 15.5, and the following sections look at the parameters in detail.

name	type	default
algebraic	boolean	false
polarplot	boolean	false
yMaxValue	value	

Table 15.5: Summary of the additional parameters for plotting functions in pst-plot

algebraic

In principle there is no reason to insert mathematical functions in anything other than RPN notation (Reverse Polish Notation, or postfix notation). For many uses, however, this notation is unusual and not particularly easy for complex function expressions. The algebraic option lets you input expressions in algebraic form (or infix notation). Table 15.6 gives some examples, with the syntax of postfix and infix notation shown side-by-side.

RPN	algebraic
x ln	ln(x)
x cos 2.71 x neg 10 div exp mul	cos(x)*2.71^(-x/10)
1 x div cos 4 mul	4*cos(1/x)
t cos t sin	cos(t)|sin(t)

Table 15.6: Juxtaposition of postfix and infix notation for describing functions

Algebraic form uses all basic arithmetic operations +-*/, the power operator ^, and the functions summarized in Table 15.7. The notation follows the usual one for algebraic expressions $3 + 4 \times 5^5 = 3 + (4 \times (5^5))$ and is processed internally from left to right. One point to remember, however, is that trigonometric functions in algebraic notation expect their arguments to be given in radian.

15 pst-plot: Plotting functions and data

Table 15.7: Valid functions when using algebraic notation.

name	meaning
sin, cos, tan, acos, asin	argument in radian for sin, cos, tan
log, ln	decimal and natural logarithm
ceiling	round up to next integer
floor	round down to next integer
truncate	truncate decimal digits
round	mathematical rounding
sqrt	square root
abs	absolute value
fact	factorial
Sum	sum (cf. Page 210)
IfTE	a simple "case" structure (cf. Page 209)

```
\usepackage{pst-plot}
\psset{yunit=4}\begin{pspicture}(-0.5,-0.4)(10cm,0.5)
  \psaxes[dy=.2,Dy=.2]{->}(0,0)(0,-0.4)(10,0.5)\psset{algebraic,plotpoints=51}
  \psplot[linecolor=cyan,linewidth=2pt]{0}{10}{sin(x)*cos(x)^2}%
  \psplot[linecolor=red,showpoints=true]{0}{10}{sin(x)*cos(x)^2}
\end{pspicture}
```

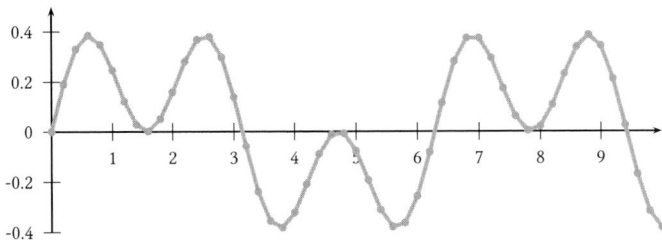

```
\usepackage{pst-plot}
\psset{yunit=0.7}\begin{pspicture}(0,-3.25)(10,3.5)
  \psaxes{->}(0,0)(0,-3)(10,3.25) \psset{algebraic,plotpoints=501}
  \psplot[linecolor=cyan,linewidth=3\pslinewidth]{0.05}{10}{ln(x)}%
  \psplot[linecolor=yellow,linewidth=3\pslinewidth]{0}{10}{3*cos(x)*2.71^(-x/10)}
  \psplot[linecolor=blue,showpoints,plotpoints=51]{0}{10}{3*cos(x)*2.71^(-x/10)}
\end{pspicture}
```

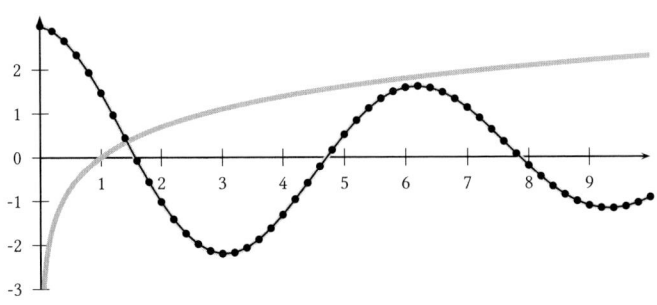

When giving functions in algebraic form for the \parametricplot command, you must separate the two parts of the function $x = f(t)$ and $y = f(t)$ by a vertical bar |, as in the following example:

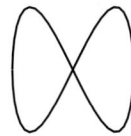

```
\usepackage{pst-plot}

\begin{pspicture}(-0.75,-0.75)(0.75,0.75)
\parametricplot[algebraic,linewidth=1pt]{-3.14}{3.14}%
   {cos(t)|sin(2*t)}
\end{pspicture}
```

The IfTE function

The IfTE function models a simple *case* structure ('if then else') at PostScript level. The only issue is that the number of nodes has to be chosen such that the interval borders are reached exactly (or the end and start points would be connected); The alternative is to use a very large number of nodes, which should result in the correct display in any case. You can use showpoints to view the computed nodes in the DVI output if there is an error in conversion by dvips.

IfTE(*condition,true part,false part*)

You can nest the IfTE function arbitrarily, and any number of cases are theoretically possible, however complex. It's a good idea to observe a certain methodical style in construction, however, to avoid or help find mistakes.

```
\usepackage{pst-plot}
\psset{yunit=4cm,xunit=1cm}
\begin{pspicture}(-5.75,-1)(5.75,1.1)\psaxes{->}(0,0)(-5.5,-.1)(5.5,1.1)
  \psplot[algebraic,plotpoints=51,linewidth=1.5pt,
    showpoints=true]{-5}{5}{IfTE(x<-1.0,-sin(x+1),IfTE(x<1.0,(1-x^2)/2,sin(x-1)))}
  \uput*[90](0,0.5){$y=\frac{1-x^2}{2}$}
  \uput[90](2.6,1){$y=\sin (x-1)$}\uput[90](-2.6,1){$y=-\sin (x+1)$}
\end{pspicture}%
```

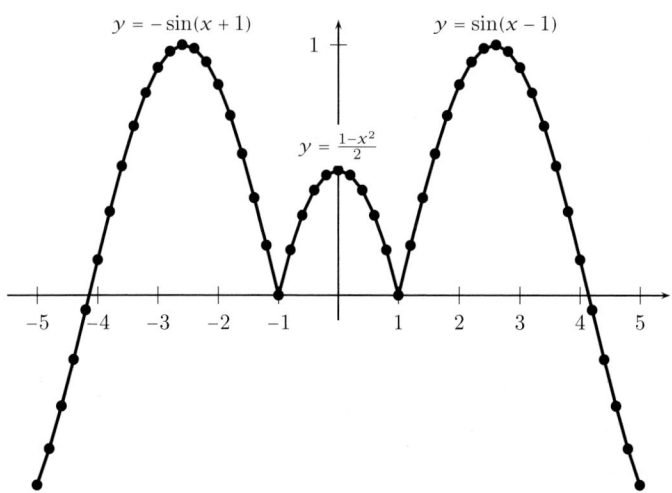

15 pst-plot: Plotting functions and data

Sum function
PostScript itself does not have its own sum function; instead it is defined in the prologue file. This means that it is not available in TeX, but in PostScript and you can therefore use it without the backslash characteristic for a command.

| Sum(*index name,start,step,end,function*) |

As an example, let's look at the general series expansion of the cosine function; the mathematical background can be found in textbooks.

$$\cos(x) = \sum_{n=0}^{+\infty} \frac{(-1)^n x^{2n}}{(2n)!} = 1 - \frac{x^2}{2!} + \frac{x^4}{4!} - \frac{x^6}{6!} + - \ldots \tag{15.3}$$

In the example graphic, the first ten expansions of the series are shown in different shades of grey. It starts with $n = 0$ (the horizontal line $y = 1$), then $n = 1$ (the translated and compressed parabola $y = 1 - \frac{x^2}{2}$), etc.

```
\usepackage{pst-plot}
\psset{algebraic,plotpoints=501, yunit=2,linewidth=1pt}
\begin{pspicture*}(-6,-1.5)(6,1.5)
  \psaxes{->}(0,0)(-7,-1.5)(7,1.5)
  \psline[linecolor=black!15](-6,1)(6,1)
  \psplot[plotpoints=51,showpoints=true]{-6}{6}{cos(x)}
  \multido{\nA=1+1,\nB=20+5}{10}{%
    \psplot[linecolor=black!\nB]{-6}{6}{%
      Sum(ijk,0,1,\nA,(-1)^ijk*x^(2*ijk)/fact(2*ijk))}}
  \uput[180](2,1.1){$n=0$}\uput[0](0.9,-1){$n=1$}\uput[180](3.5,1.2){$n=2$}
\end{pspicture*}
```

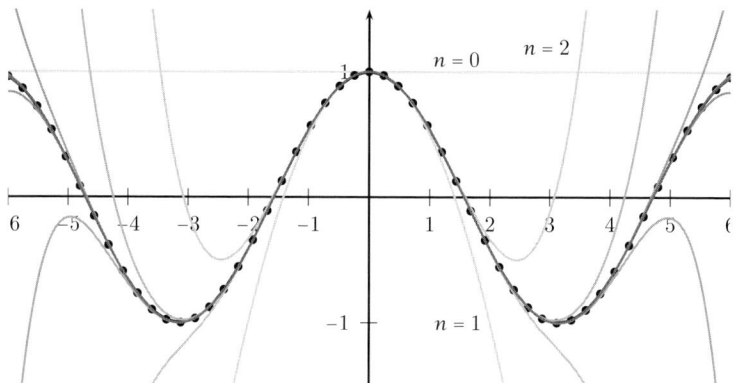

Functions in polar coordinates
Using the polarplot option, you can use polar coordinates in functions with the \psplot command. This is independent from the axes, which are still available as a Cartesian coordinate system. The computation of the coordinates is done internally depending on the angle α ($r = f(\alpha)$), though α is named x here as we are using \psplot. For a unit circle, the expres-

sion is $r = \sqrt{\sin^2 x + \cos^2 x}$, or in RPN notation x sin dup mul x cos dup mul add sqrt. The polarplot option changes the general syntax of \psplot, as shown here:

`\psplot [polarplot,...] {start angle}{end angle}{r(alpha)}`

The following examples (by Ulrich Dirr) show three different equations.

$$r = \frac{-3\sin(\varphi)\cos(\varphi)}{\sin^3(\varphi) + \cos^3(\varphi)} \qquad r = 2 \times \cos(\varphi)\sin(\varphi) \qquad r = 8 \times \sin(2,5 \times \varphi) \qquad (15.4)$$

```
\usepackage{pst-plot}
\psset{unit=0.5cm,polarplot}
\begin{pspicture}*(-5.1,-5.1)(3.1,3.1)
  \psaxes[labelsep=.75mm,ticksize=2pt,arrowlength=1.75,linewidth=0.17mm]%
      {->}(0,0)(-4.99,-4.99)(3,3)[$x$,-90][$y$,0]
  \psset{linewidth=.35mm}
  \def\Func{neg x sin mul x cos mul x sin 3 exp x cos 3 exp add div}
  \psplot[linecolor=red]{140}{310}{3 \Func} \psplot[linecolor=cyan]{140}{310}{6 \Func}
  \psplot[linecolor=blue]{140}{310}{9 \Func}
\end{pspicture} \psset{unit=1cm}
\begin{pspicture}(-2.5,-2.5)(2.5,2.5)% Ulrich Dirr
 \psaxes[labelsep=.75mm,arrowlength=1.75,
     ticksize=2pt,linewidth=0.17mm]{->}(0,0)(-2,-2)(2,2)[$x$,-90][$y$,0]
 \psset{linewidth=.35mm,plotstyle=curve}
 \psplot[linecolor=red]{0}{360}{x cos 2 mul x sin mul}
 \psplot[linecolor=green]{0}{360}{x cos 3 mul x sin mul}
 \psplot[linecolor=blue]{0}{360}{x cos 4 mul x sin mul}
\end{pspicture} \psset{plotpoints=200,unit=0.25cm}
\begin{pspicture}(-8.5,-8.5)(9,9)% Ulrich Dirr
 \psaxes[Dx=2,dx=2,Dy=2,dy=2,labelsep=.75mm,arrowlength=1.75,ticksize=2pt,
     linewidth=0.17mm]{->}(0,0)(-8.5,-8.5)(9,9)[$x$,-90][$y$,0]
 \psplot[linecolor=blue,linewidth=.35mm,plotstyle=curve]{0}{720}{8 2.5 x mul sin mul}
\end{pspicture}
```

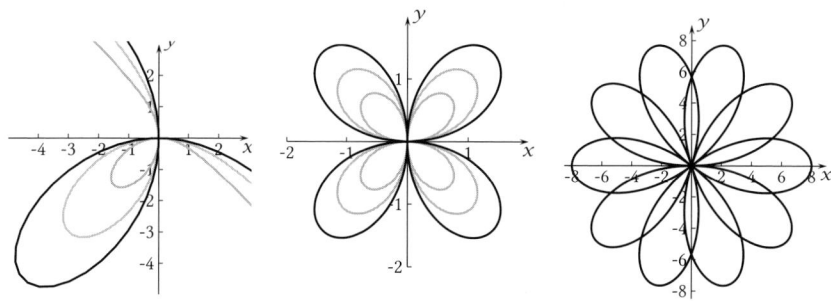

Using yMaxValue for functions with vertical asymptotes

A function with one or more vertical asymptotes, such as $f(x) = x^{-1}$, is not straightforward, as you can't plot it with a continuous curve. However, the yMaxValue keyword lets you

15 pst-plot: Plotting functions and data

specify the greatest *y* value for the plotted curve. For all other values higher or lower than the given yMaxValue the command uses the moveto PostScriptfunction instead of the default lineto or curveto to prevent the curve being drawn for such values.

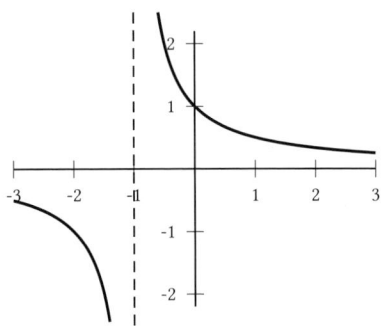

```
\usepackage{pst-plot}

\begin{pspicture}(-3,-2.2)(3,2.2)
\psaxes(0,0)(-3,-2.2)(3,2.2)
\psplot[algebraic,linewidth=1.4pt,
    plotpoints=201,yMaxValue=2.5]%
    {-3}{3}{1/(x+1)}
\psline[linestyle=dashed]%
    (-1,2.5)(-1,-2.5)
\end{pspicture}
```

15.4 Plotting data

The pst-plot package provides three commands for plotting data, and two additional commands for handling the data:

\fileplot * [settings] {file name}	\dataplot * [settings] {command name}
\listplot * [settings] {list of values}	\readdata{command name}{file name}
\savedata{command name}[list of values]	

The starred versions aren't of much interest as you don't usually want to extend the series of data to a closed curve and fill it with the current line colour.

15.4.1 Data structure

You have to arrange the external data in pairs of numeric values, separated in one of the following four ways:

```
x y
x,y
(x,y)
{x,y}
```

Enclosing the whole data set in square brackets significantly speeds up processing as PostScript reads the data as an array; however, you have to put "[" at the beginning of every line. On the other hand, device-specific restrictions apply to how much data TeX can read at once. Another way to avoid memory problems is to use the \PSTtoEPS command (cf. Section 21 on page 313).

Data files may not contain any characters other than the numeric values, the delimiters and the comment character "%" commonly used in TeX.

Note that the tabulator (\t or \009) often used as a data separator is *not* allowed, but you can replace it by a space when using Unix-compatible tools, as shown here:

```
tr '\t' ' ' < inFile > outFile+
```

15.4.2 \readdata and \savedata

These two commands assign a data set to a command name, ready for use with one of the data-plotting tools. The application of these commands is very simple. \readdata expects two parameters, the name of a command and a file name, for example:

\readdata{\feigenbaum}{feigenbaum.data}

If no absolute path is given in the file name, it is relative to the current directory. \savedata expects the name of a command and a list of values.

The following example looks at how to handle data given as pairs of values with an associated error margin. What we want to do is display the error margin data next to the actual data. Usually PSTricks is only able to read data as pairs or triples of numbers (⇒ Section 23.5 on page 358), but if you use the \readdata command, **any** list of values can be read and saved in the given command in the following form:

D <value1> D <value2> D <value3> ...

In this form the values can be processed arbitrarily; \@ifnextchar D can check whether more data is available at any time. On the PostScript side, D is defined as an empty procedure /D {} def; this can be changed at any time for given requirements though. The example is based on the following data, all of which has the structure x y dmin dmax:

```
-0.7   -0.4       0.1   0.5
-0.43   3         0     0.4
 1      4.6      -0.5   0.2
 1.2    2.3      -0.2   0.2
 1.7    3.9      -0.1   1
 2.7   -1.1      -0.2   0.3
 3.98  -0.7      -0.4   0
 4.5    0.7539   -0.5   0.4
```

dmax specifies the maximum error above and dmin below, in the same measure as the actual values. After reading the data with \readdata{\Data}{*dataError.dat*}, the \Data command contains the whole data set from the dataError.dat file in the form:

D -0.7 D -0.4 D 0.1 D 0.5 D -0.43 D 3 D 0 D 0.4 D 1 D 4.6 D -0.5 D 0.2
D 1.2 D 2.3 D -0.2 D 0.2 D 1.7 D 3.9 D -0.1 D 1 D 2.7 D -1.1 D -0.2 D 0.3
D 3.98 D -0.7 D -0.4 D 0 D 4.5 D 0.7539 D -0.5 D 0.4

For control purposes, using \show\Data writes the data set into the log file automatically. Now we need to plot the data: to each single point we want to add a vertical line of the form \psline{|-|}(x,y+dmax)(x,y+dmin). The D in the data is filtered out by reading a batch of eight variables from the \Data command but only making use of every second one. The coordinates for the error bars are determined by using the special PostScript coordinates. The corresponding output is shown below.

15 pst-plot: Plotting functions and data

```
\usepackage{pstricks,pst-plot}
\SpecialCoor\makeatletter
\def\errorLine{\@ifnextchar[{\pst@errorLine}{\pst@errorLine[]}}
\def\pst@errorLine[#1](#2)#3#4{{%
  \def\pst@tempa{#1}\ifx\pst@tempa\@empty\else\psset{#1}\fi
  \pst@getcoor{#2}\pst@tempb
  \psline{|-|}(!\pst@tempb\space pop \pst@number\psxunit div
     \pst@tempb\space exch pop \pst@number\psyunit div #3\space add)
  (!\pst@tempb\space pop \pst@number\psxunit div
     \pst@tempb\space exch pop \pst@number\psyunit div #4\space add )}}
\def\GetCoordinates#1{\expandafter\GetCoordinates@i#1}
\def\GetCoordinates@i #1{\GetCoordinates@ii#1}
\def\GetCoordinates@ii#1 #2 #3 #4 #5 #6 #7 #8 {%
  \DoCoordinate{#2}{#4}\errorLine[linecolor=red,linewidth=1.5pt](#2,#4){#6}{#8}% <<<<<
  \@ifnextchar D{\GetCoordinates@ii}{}}
\makeatother
\readdata{\Data}{dataError.dat}\psset{dotscale=2,yunit=0.7}%
\begin{pspicture}(-1,-2)(5,5.5)
  \psaxes(0,0)(-1,-2)(5,5)\def\DoCoordinate#1#2{\psdot(#1,#2)}\GetCoordinates{\Data}
\end{pspicture}
```

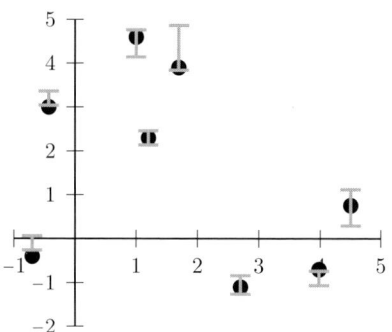

15.4.3 \fileplot

\fileplot is the easiest of the three data-plotting commands to use and is applicable when you want to plot pairs of numbers (x,y) saved in an external file. However, \fileplot does come with several restrictions: "curve" plot styles are not possible and arrows, linearc, and showpoints parameter specifications are ignored.

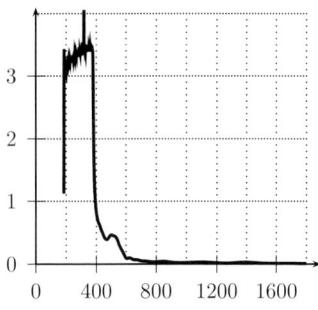

```
\usepackage{pstricks,pst-plot}

\psset{xunit=0.025mm}
\begin{pspicture}(-200,-0.5)(1900,4.25)
  \fileplot[plotstyle=line,linewidth=1.5pt]%
     {fileplot.data}
  \psaxes[dx=400,Dx=400]{->}(1900,4.1)
  \psgrid[griddots=10,subgriddiv=0,%
       xunit=0.5cm,gridlabels=0pt](9,4)
\end{pspicture}
```

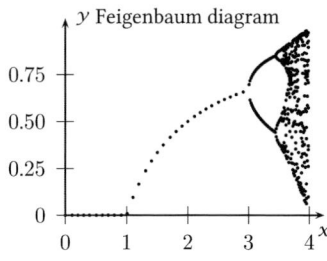

```
\usepackage{pstricks,pst-plot}

\psset{yunit=3cm}
\begin{pspicture}(-0.75,-0.1)(4.25,1.05)
  \fileplot[plotstyle=dots,dotsize=1.5pt]%
      {feigenbaum.data}
  \psaxes[Dy=0.25]{->}(4.25,1.05)%
      [$x$,-90][$y$,0]
  \rput[l](0.5,1.05){Feigenbaum diagram}
\end{pspicture}
```

15.4.4 \dataplot

Like \fileplot, \dataplot requires an external data set, though in this case not as a file but as a command. The reading and saving of an external file into a command can be done with \readdata (cf. Section 15.4.2 on page 213).

The number of read files and the amount of the data is limited only by available memory. \dataplot allows simple overlays. The next example shows two separate data files plotted in the same coordinate system.

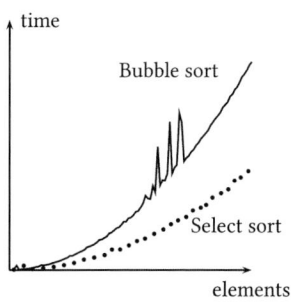

```
\usepackage{pstricks,pst-plot}

\psset{xunit=0.0004cm,yunit=0.004cm}
\begin{pspicture}(0,-50)(10000,1050)
  \readdata{\bubble}{bubble.data}
  \readdata{\select}{select.data}
  \psaxes[ticks=none,labels=none]{->}%
      (10000,1000)[elements,-90][time,0]
  \dataplot[plotstyle=line]{\bubble}
  \dataplot[linestyle=dotted,
      plotstyle=line,linewidth=2pt]{\select}
  \rput[l](4500,800){Bubble sort}
  \rput[l](7500,180){Select sort}
\end{pspicture}
```

In principle there is no real difference between the \dataplot or \fileplot commands in terms of the final graphic created. However, for large data sets, \dataplot processes and displays the data faster, but it uses more memory than \fileplot. Internally, \dataplot uses the \listplot commands, described in the next section, if parameters are given. This means that overall it only makes sense to use \dataplot when drawing polylines, when the greater speed is handy.

15.4.5 \listplot

unlike the previous commands, the argument of \listplot is expanded by TeX first if it is a TeX command but otherwise is passed on to PostScript unchanged. Therefore you can put entire PostScript programmes into the argument of \listplot. The following example shows the development of the Hénon attractor. The figure below contains an additional "DRAFT" note enforced by PostScript code in addition to the normal data set.

15 pst-plot: Plotting functions and data

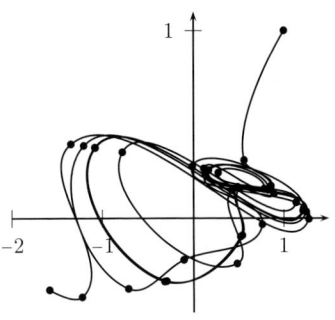

```
\usepackage{pstricks,pst-plot}

\psset{xunit=1.5cm, yunit=3cm}
\begin{pspicture}(-2,-0.5)(2.25,1.1)
    \psaxes{->}(0,0)(-2,-0.5)(1.5,1.1)
    \listplot[showpoints=true,
        plotstyle=curve]{\henon}
\end{pspicture}
```

```
\newcommand{\DataA}{ [ ... data ... ]
    gsave          % save state
    /Helvetica findfont 40 scalefont setfont
    45 rotate      % rotate 45 degrees
    0.9 setgray    % 1 is white
    -60 10 moveto (DRAFT) show grestore }
```

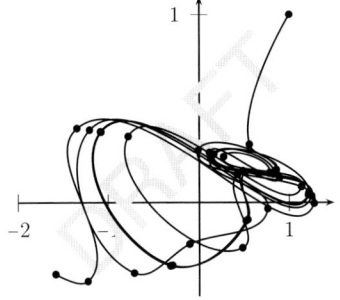

```
\usepackage{pstricks,pst-plot}
% see example file for preamble

\psset{xunit=1.5cm, yunit=3cm}
\begin{pspicture}(-2,-0.5)(2.25,1.1)
    \psaxes{->}(0,0)(-2,-0.5)(1.5,1.1)
    \listplot[showpoints=true,%
        plotstyle=curve]{\dataA}
\end{pspicture}
```

An alternative to manipulating the data set of \listplot is to change the corresponding function from pst-plot. If for example you want to swap the (x,y) values and rotate the graph by $45°$ (which corresponds to a rotation and subsequent mirroring), you can redefine ScalePoints to achieve this as follows:

15.4 Plotting data

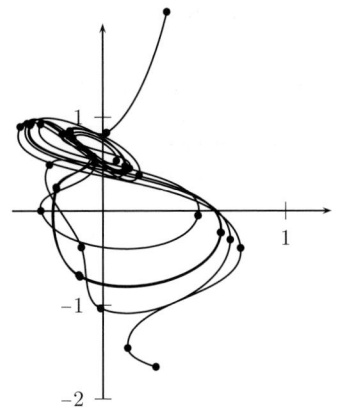

```
\usepackage{pstricks,pst-plot}
\makeatletter
\pst@def{ScalePoints}<%
    45 rotate % rotate by 45 degrees
    /y ED /x ED
    counttomark dup dup cvi eq not {exch pop} if
    /m exch def /n m 2 div cvi def
    n {exch % swap x y
        y mul m 1 roll x mul m 1 roll
        /m m 2 sub
        def } repeat>
\makeatother

\psset{yunit=1.5cm, xunit=3cm}
\begin{pspicture}(-0.5,-2)(1.25,2)
\psaxes{->}(0,0)(-0.5,-2)(1.25,2)
\listplot[showpoints,plotstyle=curve]{\henon}
\end{pspicture}
```

With \pscustom and the \code command, you can perform virtually any manipulation at PostScript level, without having to interfere with the \listplot command. The next example puts the *y* coordinate next to the points after drawing the data.

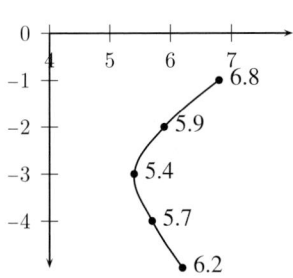

```
\usepackage{pst-plot} \psset{yunit=0.75cm}
\makeatletter
\def\plotValues#1{%
    \pscustom{\code{ /xOffset 5 def /yOffset -2 def
        /Times findfont 11 scalefont setfont
        /Feld [ #1 ] def /cnt 0 def
        Feld length 2 div cvi {
            /x Feld cnt get def /y Feld cnt 1 add get def
            x \pst@number\psxunit mul xOffset add
            y \pst@number\psyunit mul yOffset add
            moveto x 10 string cvs show
            /cnt cnt 2 add def } repeat }}}
\makeatother
\def\dataV{6.8 -1 5.9 -2 5.4 -3 5.7 -4 6.2 -5}

\begin{pspicture}(3.5,0.5)(8,-5.5)
\psaxes[Ox=4]{->}(4,0)(8,-5)
\listplot[plotstyle=curve,showpoints]{\dataV}
\plotValues{\dataV}
\end{pspicture}
```

15.4.6 Additional functionality

The latest version of pst-plot provides several new options, especially when plotting external data.

15 pst-plot: Plotting functions and data

New options for \readdata and \listplot

Usually the \readdata command reads an external file line by line and interprets it as a data set. This isn't always exactly what you want, for example the data may come with an introductory text (header) which needs to be ignored, or the data set could be very large and reading every nth value would be enough. Therefore the options summarized in Table 15.8 were introduced; an empty assignment {} means that the default is to ignore the option. These options are only available for the \listplot command; this is essentially no restriction, however, as reading data with \readdata is not a problem anymore given the performance of modern computers. You can't use these options with \dataplot because it doesn't use the data as a list; this shouldn't be a problem though. [80]

Table 15.8: Summary of the new parameters for \readdata and \listplot

name	default	remarks
ignoreLines	0	ignore the first ignoreLines lines of the data file, e.g. a header line
nStart	1	start saving values with the nStartth one
nEnd	{}	stop reading with the nEndth one
nStep	1	step
xStart	{}	start saving when the value read is at least as big as xStart
xEnd	{}	stop reading when the value read is at least as big as xEnd
yStart	{}	same for the y axis
yEnd	{}	same for the y axis
xStep	0	absolute step
plotNo	1	the plotNoth value is assumed to be the plotted y value
plotNoMax	1	number of all y values (without the x value) in the current data set
ChangeOrder	false	process data set in reverse order

ignoreLines — The ignoreLines parameter ignores the first n lines of a file. In the following example the setting ignoreLines=2 tells \readdata to skip the two comment lines at the start of the file.

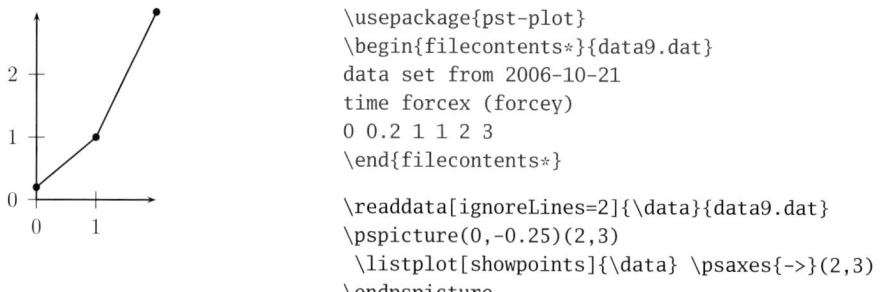

```
\usepackage{pst-plot}
\begin{filecontents*}{data9.dat}
data set from 2006-10-21
time forcex (forcey)
0 0.2 1 1 2 3
\end{filecontents*}

\readdata[ignoreLines=2]{\data}{data9.dat}
\pspicture(0,-0.25)(2,3)
  \listplot[showpoints]{\data} \psaxes{->}(2,3)
\endpspicture
```

nStart *nEnd* — The nStart and nEnd parameters are straightforward. For nStart, \listplot only plots from the nStartth value onwards, and for nEnd, it stops plotting the data when it reaches the nEndth value. The file in the following example contains 1000 lines of data altogether, but the graph only displays the data from line 200 to line 800:

15.4 Plotting data

```
\usepackage{pst-plot}
\readdata{\data}{data.dat} \psset{xunit=0.11mm,yunit=0.00015mm}
\begin{pspicture}(-80,-30000)(1000,260000)
\psaxes[axesstyle=frame,Dx=100,dx=100,Dy=50,dy=50000,ylabelFactor=$\times10^3$,subticks=4,
    ticksize=0 5pt,tickstyle=inner,labelFontSize=\footnotesize,mathLabel=false](1000,250000)
\listplot[nStart=200,nEnd=800,linewidth=2pt,linecolor=blue]{\data}
\end{pspicture}
```

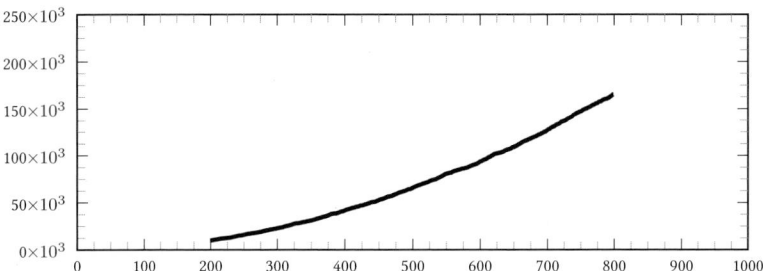

The nStep parameter just plots every nth line of the data set. Using the same file as in the previous example, this time we display only every 50th line. For comparison purposes, the entire data set is also plotted (with a grey line); note that it is plotted first so as not to overwrite the other points.

nStep

```
\usepackage{pst-plot}
\readdata{\data}{data.dat}   \psset{xunit=0.11mm,yunit=0.00015mm}
\begin{pspicture}(-80,-30000)(1000,310000)
\psaxes[axesstyle=frame,Dx=100,dx=100,Dy=50,dy=50000,ylabelFactor=$\times10^3$,subticks=4,
    ticksize=0 5pt,labelFontSize=\footnotesize,mathLabel=false,tickstyle=inner](1000,300000)
\listplot[linewidth=1pt,linecolor=black!30]{\data}      % all
\listplot[nStep=50,linewidth=2pt,plotstyle=dots]{\data}% every 50th
\end{pspicture}
```

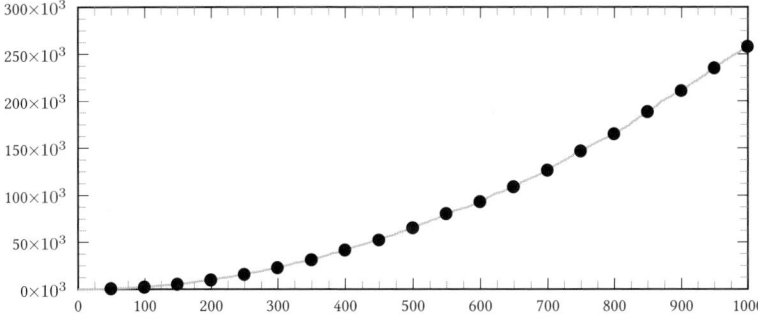

The xStart and xEnd options start and stop the plotting of data when the x variable reaches the specified value; this is useful if you don't know how far into the data set this occurs, i.e. the index of the data points that you want to start or end with are unknown. You can create a zoom effect on a graph by using these options. In the following example we want to display the area in the interval $0.355 < x < 0.700$ again but magnified, so we use

xStart
xEnd

15 pst-plot: Plotting functions and data

the options xStart=0.355, xEnd=0.7 to specify which part is redrawn. This section of the data is then replotted with a different scale with \rput and moved to a different part of the coordinate system.

```
\usepackage{pst-plot}
\psset{xunit=10cm, yunit=0.01cm}
\readdata{\data}{data3.dat}
\begin{pspicture}(-0.1,-100)(1.1,630.0)
  \psaxes[Dx=0.25,Dy=100,dy=100\psyunit,ticksize=-4pt 0,
    labelFontSize=\footnotesize,mathLabel=false]{->}(0,0)(0,-100)(1.1,520)
  \uput[0](1.1,0){\textsf{t [s]}}
  \rput(-0.125,200){\psrotateleft{\small\sffamily flow [ml/s]}}
  \listplot[linewidth=2pt, linecolor=blue]{\data}
  \rput[lb](0.2,300){%
    \pscustom[yunit=0.04cm,linewidth=1pt]{%
      \listplot[xStart=0.355,xEnd=0.7]{\data}% start at x>=0.355
      \psline(.7,-2.57)(.7,0)(0.355,0)
      \fill[fillstyle=hlines,fillcolor=gray,hatchwidth=0.4pt,
          hatchsep=1.5pt]
      \psline[linewidth=0.5pt]{->}(0.7,0)(0.9,0)
  }}
  \psline[linewidth=.01]{->}(0.55,300)(0.4,20)
  \psline[linewidth=.01]{->}(0.75,290)(0.8,440)
  \rput(.8,470){\footnotesize\sffamily leak volume}
  \psline[linewidth=.01]{->}(0.6,200)(.8,100)
  \rput[l](.8,100){\footnotesize\sffamily closing volume}
\end{pspicture}
```

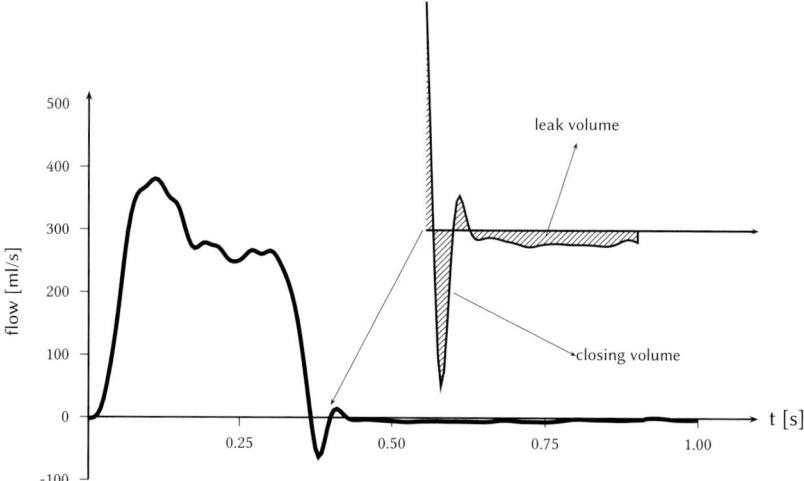

The yStart and yEnd options work in an identical fashion:

yStart
yEnd

15.4 Plotting data

```
\usepackage{pst-plot}
\readdata{\data}{data.dat}
\psset{xunit=0.11mm,yunit=0.00015mm}
\begin{pspicture}(-80,-30000)(1000,260000)
  \psaxes[axesstyle=frame,Dx=100,dx=100,Dy=50,dy=50000,ylabelFactor=$\times10^3$,
    subticks=4,ticksize=0 5pt,tickstyle=inner,labelFontSize=\footnotesize,
    mathLabel=false](1000,250000)
  \psset{linewidth=0.1pt, linestyle=dashed,linecolor=red}
  \psline(0,40000)(1000,40000)   \psline(0,175000)(1000,175000)
  \listplot[yStart=40000,yEnd=175000,linewidth=2pt,plotstyle=dots]{\data}
\end{pspicture}
```

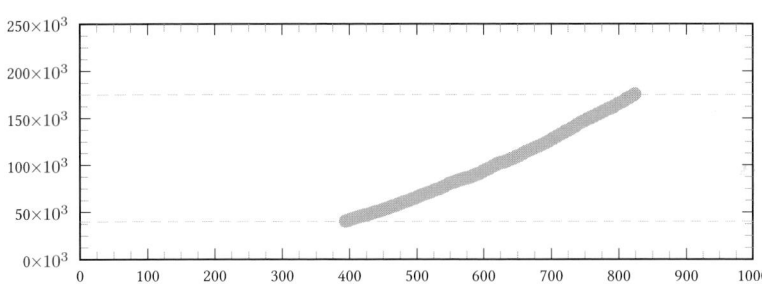

With the optional argument xStep you can set the absolute step width for the *x* values. *xStep*

```
\usepackage{pst-plot}
\readdata{\data}{data.dat}    \psset{xunit=0.11mm,yunit=0.00015mm}
\begin{pspicture}(-80,-30000)(1000,260000)
  \psaxes[Dx=100,dx=100,Dy=50,dy=50000,ylabelFactor=$\times10^3$,subticks=4,
      ticksize=0 5pt,labelFontSize=\footnotesize,mathLabel=false](1000,250000)
  \listplot[xStep=75,plotstyle=bar,fillstyle=solid,fillcolor=blue!30,barwidth=5mm]{\data}
\end{pspicture}
```

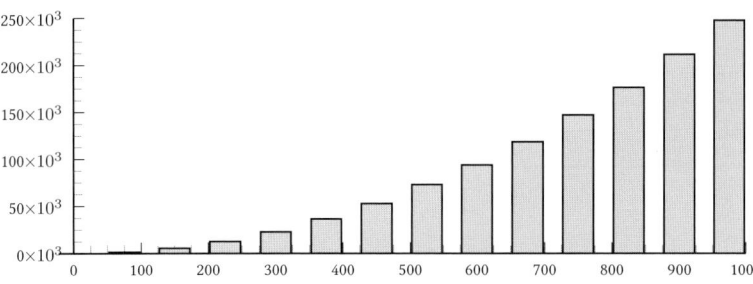

Another type of situation that the new parameters help you handle is when dealing with *plotNo*
data sets that assign several *y* values to every *x* value: *plotNoMax*

```
x y1 y2 y3 y4 ... yMax
x y1 y2 y3 y4 ... yMax
...
```

These data sets require the `plotNo` and `plotNoMax` options, as otherwise the data is assumed to be structured in pairs. You specify which of the *y* values you want to plot with

221

15 pst-plot: Plotting functions and data

plotNo, and to make the structure of the data unambiguous for \listplot you also have to specify the maximum number of available y values with plotNoMax. There is no upper limit to the number of y values that can be handled. As an example, consider the following data file, which consists of lines of the form x y1 y2 y3; the word "line" does not have any real meaning here, however, as in this situation all the data could in fact be given on a single line.

```
[% file data.dat
0      0        3.375     0.0625    10    5.375    7.1875    4.5
20     7.1875   8.375     6.25      30    5.75     7.75      6.6875
40     2.1875   5.75      5.9375    50   -1.9375   2.1875    4.3125
60    -5.125   -1.8125    0.875     70   -6.4375  -5.3125   -2.6875
80    -4.875   -7.1875   -4.875     90    0       -7.625    -5.625
100    5.5     -6.3125   -5.8125   110    6.8125  -2.75     -4.75
120    5.25     2.875    -0.75
]%
```

In the following figure three different graphs are created from this data, one for each pair of $(x; y_i)$, where $i \in \{1; 2; 3\}$.

```
\usepackage{pst-plot}
\readdata\Data{dataMul.dat} \psset{xunit=0.1cm, yunit=0.3cm}
\begin{pspicture}(-6,-7.5)(125,10)
  \psaxes[Dx=10,Dy=2.5,labelFontSize=\footnotesize,
    mathLabel=false]{->}(0,0)(0,-7.5)(120,8.5)
  \psset{linewidth=2pt}
  \listplot[linecolor=green,plotNo=1,plotNoMax=3]{\Data}
  \listplot[linecolor=red,plotNo=2,plotNoMax=3]{\Data}
  \listplot[linecolor=blue,plotNo=3,plotNoMax=3]{\Data}
\end{pspicture}
```

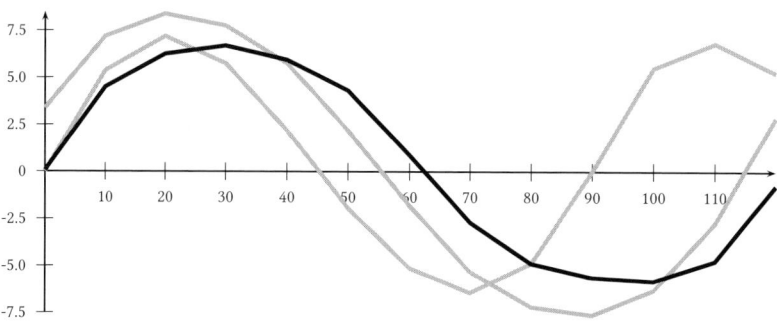

15-04-

ChangeOrder If you want to fill the area between two curves drawn from data sets, you first of all have to create a closed polyline, but this can be tricky if the x values are the same in both data sets. The ChangeOrder option reverses the order of the data in a particular set, which then makes the two sets easy to close within a \pscustom command. As we mentioned earlier, you can't usually pass parameters that refer to line or fill styles to commands within \pscustom, but that is not a problem here as the ChangeOrder option is not directly referring to filling.

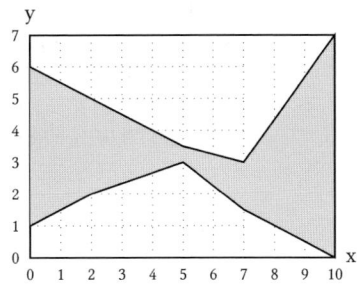

```
\usepackage{pst-plot}

\psset{lly=-10pt}\readdata{\data}{data10.dat}
\begin{psgraph}[axesstyle=frame,ticksize=0 7,
    ticklinestyle=dotted,mathLabel=false,
    labelFontSize=\footnotesize]%
    (0,0)(10,7){2in}{1.4in}
\pscustom[fillstyle=solid,fillcolor=red!20]{%
    \listplot[plotNo=2,plotNoMax=2]{\data}
    \listplot[plotNo=1,plotNoMax=2,
      ChangeOrder]{\data}}
\end{psgraph}
```

\pstScalePoints

\pstScalePoints expects two parameters for scaling and another two parameters for arbitrary manipulation of the values. All of the parameters are only evaluated definitively in PostScript.

\pstScalePoints(*xScale,yScale*){*xPS*}{*yPS*}

Note that \pstScalePoints is only valid with the \listplot command; it is not effective for the other two plot commands. The order of evaluation of the parameters is always the PostScript code first, then the scaling. In principle the scale parameters aren't necessary as scaling can also be done through the PostScript commands. However they do simplify using \pstScalePoints.

The following example uses \pstScalePoints(1,0.5){}{3 add} to add 3 to each y value **before** multiplying it by 0.5. This corresponds to the grey curve in the following example; the first y value is 1.5= $(0+3) \times 0.5$.

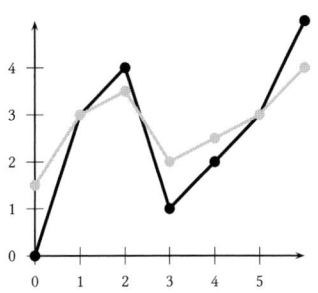

```
\usepackage{pst-plot}

\def\data{ 0 0 1 3 2 4 3 1 4 2 5 3 6 5 }
\psset{unit=0.75}
\begin{pspicture}(-0.5,-0.5)(6,5)
\psaxes[labelFontSize=\footnotesize,
    mathLabel=false]{->}(0,0)(6,5)
\psset{linewidth=1.5pt}
\listplot[showpoints=true]{\data}
\pstScalePoints(1,0.5){}{3 add}
\listplot[showpoints=true,
    linecolor=black!40]{\data}
\end{pspicture}
```

Changes through \pstScalePoints always have global effect and therefore affect all subsequent \listplot commands. It's therefore a good idea to reset everything at the end with \pstScalePoints(1,1){}{}.

15.5 Examples

The plotting of axes is one of the most sophisticated things that PSTricks offers – even if it doesn't look like it at first glance. As soon as very large numbers are involved, however, the lack of floating point arithmetic quickly causes problems and you have to make use of everything that PSTricks has to offer to work a way round. The first example has the following data:
0.003472 -13.159 0.003332 -12.859 0.003246 -11.27

The example shows several methods for creating an *x* axis; because of the very small *x* values, it makes sense here to draw the *x* axis with "normal" values and adapt the data by scaling it. Also it shows the basic procedure for handling negative *y* values, which you can align upwards downwards.

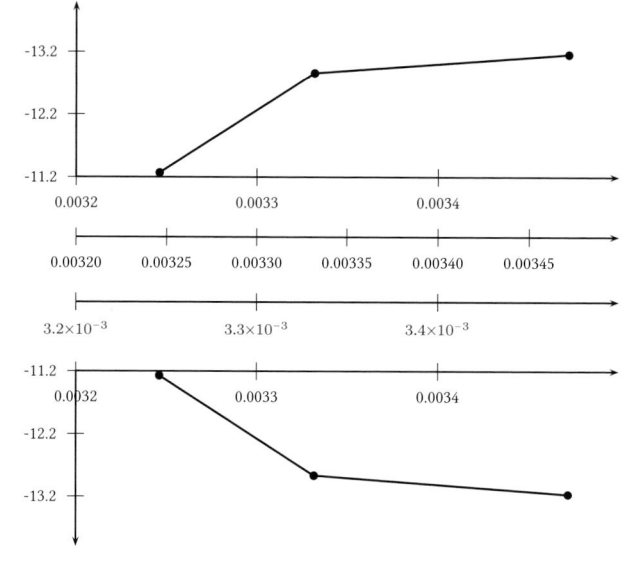

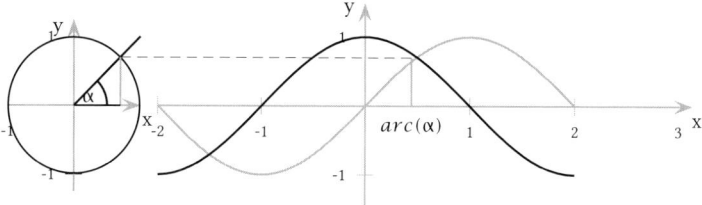

Chapter 16

pst-node: Nodes and connections

16.1 Node names 226
16.2 Parameters 226
16.3 Nodes 236
16.4 Connections using \nc commands 241
16.5 Connections using \pc commands 252
16.6 Label 253
16.7 Special cases 256
16.8 \psmatrix 257
16.9 TEX and PostScript 262
16.10 Examples 263

The pst-node package is much better at handling nodes and connections than the pstricks base package, which provides some commands for drawing arbitrary connecting lines but is lacking commands to put and save nodes.

```
\usepackage{pst-node}
\section{\texttt{pst-node}: Nodes and \protect\rnode{A}{connections}}
In principle it is concerned with the placing of nodes, such as \verb+\rnode{A}{connections}+
on the first line of this chapter, and with the creation of
connections, such as from \rnode{B}{here}\ncarc[arcangle=-100,linestyle=dashed,
   arrowscale=2]{->}{B}{A} to the node defined above.
```

16 pst-node: Nodes and connections

In principle it is concerned with the placing of nodes, such as \rnode{A}{connections} on the first line of this chapter, and with the creation of connections, such as from here to the node defined above.

 You don't need to know the exact coordinates of the nodes: instead you define a name for the node and pst-node saves the coordinates in a "dictionary", which is essentially a two-dimensional field, mapping node name→coordinates. In principle there are no restrictions on the placement of nodes, although everything has to happen on one page of output – PostScript is a page-description language.

Most node commands let you name the node and place material or an object at the node. This material then sits within the node's surrounding box. You can draw connections between nodes that start and end either at the edge of the surrounding box or at the centre of the node. This is reflected in the two groups of connection commands, the former prefixed by \nc and the latter prefixed by \pc. There are many parameters for controlling nodes and connections, listed in Table 16.1 and explained one by one in the following sections. Different effects are also achieved depending on whether the connection starts at node A and finishes at node B or vice versa. Keep in mind that "above" and "below" refer to the default direction of the connection running from "left to right"from the start node to the finish node. Also the direction of the connection also affects how some angles are measured. This chapter looks at the parameters for node and connection commands, and then covers the commands themselves, before moving on to putting labels on the connections and using the nodes and connections in a psmatrix environment.

16.1 Node names

A node name consists of a finite number of alphanumeric characters and should start with a letter. All node names of PSTricks are prefixed with N@ at the PostScript level; the restriction that the name has to start with a letter is just a safety precaution at the LaTeX level where commands may only contain alphanumeric characters. Nevertheless, none of the eight PostScript-specific active characters may be used – (){}/[]<space>. Node commands are usually fragile; when used in captions, indexes, etc. put a \protect in front of the node command (or a \noexpand if you are using TeX).

16.2 Parameters

Table 16.1 shows a summary of the parameters valid for pst-node.

16.2 Parameters

Table 16.1: Summary of the parameters for pst-node

name	type	default	name	type	default
href	value	0	vref	value unit	0.7ex
radius	value unit	0.25cm	framesize	value unit value unit	10pt
nodesep	value unit	0pt	nodesepA	value unit	0pt
nodesepB	value unit	0pt	Xnodesep	value unit	0pt
XnodesepA	value unit	0pt	XnodesepB	value unit	0pt
Ynodesep	value unit	0pt	YnodesepA	value unit	0pt
YnodesepB	value unit	0pt	arcangle	angle	8
arcangleA	angle	8	arcangleB	angle	8
angle	angle	0	angleA	angle	0
angleA	angle	0	arm	value unit	10pt
armA	value unit	10pt	armB	value unit	10pt
loopsize	value unit	1cm	ncurv	value	0.67
ncurvA	value	0.67	ncurvB	value	0.67
boxsize	value unit	0.4cm	offset	value unit	0pt
offsetA	value unit	0pt	offsetB	value unit	0pt
ref	reference	c	rot	rotation	0
nrot	rotation	0	npos	value	{}
tpos	value	0.5	shortput	nab|tablr|tab|none	none

16.2.1 href and vref

The href and vref parameters are only meaningful for the \Rnode command (cf. 16.3.2 on page 237), where by definition the centre of the node is the middle of the base line of the surrounding box. You can use these parameters to move this centre. href moves it by the href multiple of half the box width of the node. Using href without vref has no visible effect if the connecting line is horizontal. In contrast to href, vref determines this point with an absolute value relative to the base line (vref=0 pt). If relative units like ex or em are used, the relation stays the same even for different font sizes.

\Rnode

```
\usepackage{pstricks,pst-node}
\psscalebox{0.8}{\BildI}\\[12pt]
\psscalebox{0.8}{\BildII}\\[12pt]
\psscalebox{0.8}{%
 \begin{pspicture}[showgrid](7,4)%
  \rput[lb](0,0){\Rnode{A}{\Square}\hspace{3cm}\Rnode[href=4,vref=3cm]{B}{\Square}}
  \psframe*[linecolor=black!20](4,3)(5,4)   \psframe*[linecolor=black!20](6,3)(7,4)
  \psline[arrows=->](4.5,3.5)(6.5,3.5)
  \uput[-90](5.5,3.5){href}
  \pcline[linecolor=red,linestyle=dotted,linewidth=2pt](A)(B)
  \ncline[linecolor=red,style=line]{A}{B}
```

```
    \pnode(4,0.7ex){C}
    \pcline{->}(4.5,0.5)(4.5,3.5)
    \uput[0](3.5,2){vref}
    \pcline[linecolor=white](3.5,0.5)(3.5,1)
    \ncline[linecolor=blue,style=line]{A}{C}
\end{pspicture}}
```

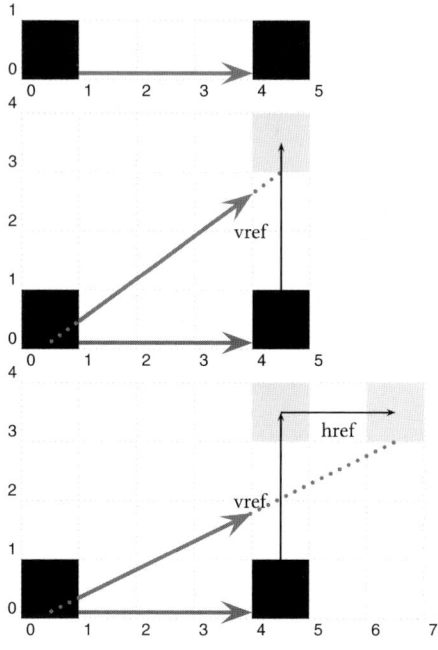

16.2.2 radius

Use the radius parameter when you want to display nodes by circles of the same size.

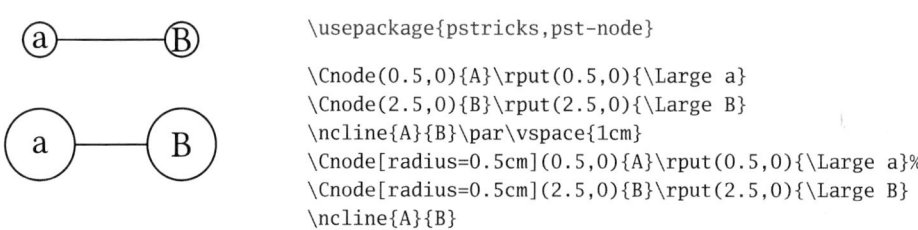

```
\usepackage{pstricks,pst-node}

\Cnode(0.5,0){A}\rput(0.5,0){\Large a}
\Cnode(2.5,0){B}\rput(2.5,0){\Large B}
\ncline{A}{B}\par\vspace{1cm}
\Cnode[radius=0.5cm](0.5,0){A}\rput(0.5,0){\Large a}%
\Cnode[radius=0.5cm](2.5,0){B}\rput(2.5,0){\Large B}
\ncline{A}{B}
```

16.2.3 framesize

The framesize parameter only takes effect when using \fnode (cf. Section 16.3.12 on page 241). You can specify one or two values as an argument: if two are given, these set the width and height of the frame; if only one is given, it sets both dimensions, creating a square frame.

16.2 Parameters

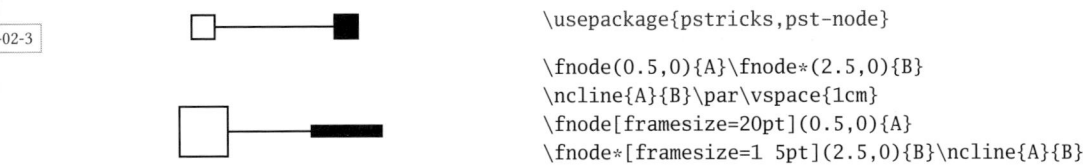

```
\usepackage{pstricks,pst-node}

\fnode(0.5,0){A}\fnode*(2.5,0){B}
\ncline{A}{B}\par\vspace{1cm}
\fnode[framesize=20pt](0.5,0){A}
\fnode*[framesize=1 5pt](2.5,0){B}\ncline{A}{B}
```

16.2.4 nodesep, nodesepA, and nodesepB

Usually the connection stops at the outer box of the node. The nodesep parameters influence this in both ways. Positive values stop the connection short, and negative values continue the connection into the box. nodesep always refers to both nodes, nodesepA to the first one, and nodesepB to the second one.

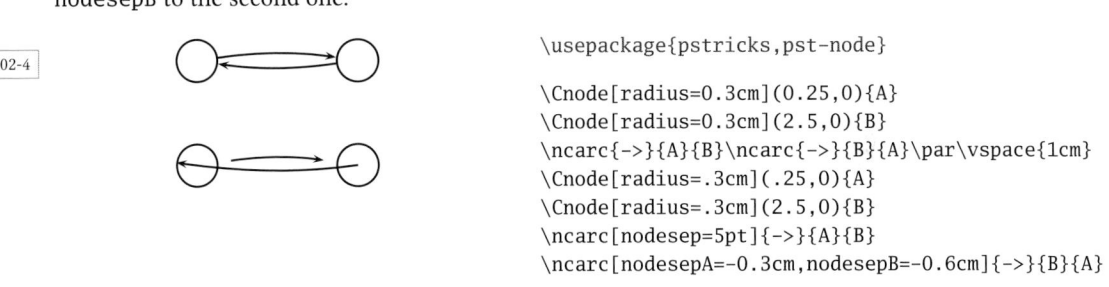

```
\usepackage{pstricks,pst-node}

\Cnode[radius=0.3cm](0.25,0){A}
\Cnode[radius=0.3cm](2.5,0){B}
\ncarc{->}{A}{B}\ncarc{->}{B}{A}\par\vspace{1cm}
\Cnode[radius=.3cm](.25,0){A}
\Cnode[radius=.3cm](2.5,0){B}
\ncarc[nodesep=5pt]{->}{A}{B}
\ncarc[nodesepA=-0.3cm,nodesepB=-0.6cm]{->}{B}{A}
```

16.2.5 Xnodesep, XnodesepA, XnodesepB, Ynodesep, YnodesepA, and YnodesepB

The [XY]nodesep parameters also control how far the connection reaches, but whereas nodesep refers to the distance along the connecting line from the outer box, these parameters refer to the horizontal and/or vertical distance from the centre of the node (cf. Section 12.1.4 on page 142 about relative translation). The example below shows two connecting lines of different lengths: the line from A to B stop 0.25cm from the outer box of the node, while the line from C to D stops 0.25cm vertically before the node centres. These parameters are particularly handy when using special coordinates.

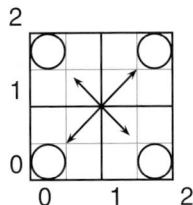

```
\usepackage{pstricks,pst-node}

\begin{pspicture}(2,2)\psgrid[subgriddiv=2]
  \cnode(0.25,1.75){0.25cm}{A}\cnode(1.75,0.25){0.25cm}{B}
  \ncline[nodesep=.25]{<->}{A}{B}
  \cnode(1.75,1.75){0.25cm}{C}\cnode(0.25,0.25){0.25cm}{D}
  \ncline[Ynodesep=.25]{<->}{C}{D}
\end{pspicture}
```

16.2.6 arcangle, arcangleA, and arcangleB

arcangle determines the start angle of the connection, measured from the centre of the node with respect to the line connecting the nodes (see Example 16-04-26 on page 251). In the example in Section 16.2.4, the connections are relatively close together, but you can change this with the arcangle parameter. arcangle always refer to both nodes, arcangleA to the

229

16 pst-node: Nodes and connections

first node, and arcangleB to the second node. By choosing the angles appropriately, you can create arbitrary curves, as in the example below.

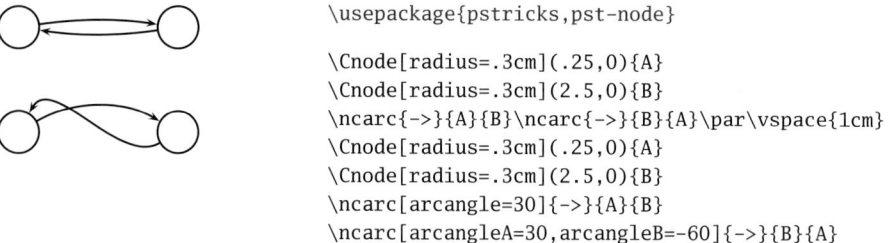

```
\usepackage{pstricks,pst-node}

\Cnode[radius=.3cm](.25,0){A}
\Cnode[radius=.3cm](2.5,0){B}
\ncarc{->}{A}{B}\ncarc{->}{B}{A}\par\vspace{1cm}
\Cnode[radius=.3cm](.25,0){A}
\Cnode[radius=.3cm](2.5,0){B}
\ncarc[arcangle=30]{->}{A}{B}
\ncarc[arcangleA=30,arcangleB=-60]{->}{B}{A}
```

16.2.7 angle, angleA, and angleB

angle specifies the angle between the connection and the horizontal line through the node. angle refers to both nodes, angleA to the first node, and angleB to the second node. By choosing the angles appropriately, you can create arbitrary curves.

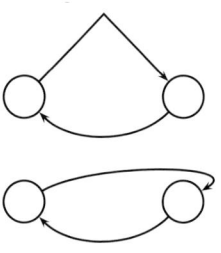

```
\usepackage{pstricks,pst-node}

\Cnode[radius=.3cm](.25,0){A}
\Cnode[radius=.3cm](2.5,0){B}
\ncangle[angleA=45,angleB=135]{->}{A}{B}%
\nccurve[angleB=-45,angleA=-135]{->}{B}{A}
\par\vspace{1cm}
\Cnode[radius=.3cm](.25,0){A}
\Cnode[radius=.3cm](2.5,0){B}
\nccurve[angle=30]{->}{A}{B}
\nccurve[angleB=-45,angleA=-135]{->}{B}{A}
```

16.2.8 arm, armA, and armB

arm specifies the length of the straight line starting from the node – the arm – before the connection may take another path. arm refers to both nodes, armA to the first node, and armB to the second node.

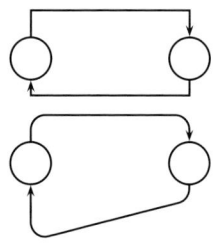

```
\usepackage{pstricks,pst-node}

\psset{radius=0.3cm}\Cnode(.25,0){A}
\Cnode(2.5,0){B}\ncbar[angle=90]{->}{A}{B}
\ncbar[angle=-90,arm=.2cm]{->}{B}{A}\par\vspace{1cm}
\Cnode(.25,0){A}\Cnode(2.5,0){B}
\psset{linearc=.2cm}\ncdiag[angle=90]{->}{A}{B}%
\ncdiag[angle=-90,armA=.2cm,armB=.75cm]{->}{B}{A}
```

16.2.9 loopsize

loopsize determines the "height" of the connection that is designated for \ncloop.

16.2 Parameters

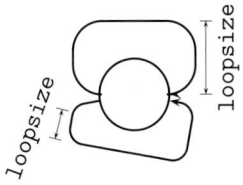

```
\usepackage{pstricks,pst-node}

\Cnode[radius=0.5cm](1.5,0){A}%
\ncloop[angleA=0,angleB=180,linearc=0.4cm]{<-}{A}{A}
\psline[linewidth=0.1pt,tbarsize=5pt]{|<->|}(2.5,0)(2.5,1)
\uput[0]{90}(2.5,0.5){\texttt{loopsize}}
\ncloop[angleB=-10,angleA=-170,linearc=0.2cm,
    loopsize=0.5cm]{->}{A}{A}
\psline[linewidth=.1pt,tbarsize=5pt]{|<->|}(.4,-.6)(.5,-.2)
\uput[180]{70}(.5,-0.25){\texttt{loopsize}}
```

16.2.10 ncurv, ncurvA, and ncurvB

ncurv influences the shape of the bezier curve (cf. Section 5.3.1 on page 65) drawn by \nccurve to connect the nodes. The smaller the value of ncurv, the "tighter" the curve drawn, eventually tending to a straight line. ncurv refers to both nodes, ncurvA to node A, and ncurv to node B.

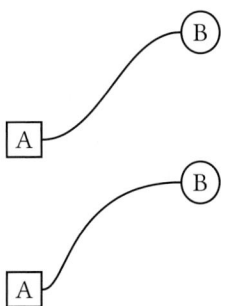

```
\usepackage{pstricks,pst-node}

\begin{pspicture}(3,2)
  \rput[bl](0,0){\rnode{A}{\psframebox{A}}}
  \rput[tr](3,2){\ovalnode{B}{B}}
  \nccurve[angleB=180]{A}{B}
\end{pspicture}\par
\begin{pspicture}(3,2)
  \rput[bl](0,0){\rnode{A}{\psframebox{A}}}
  \rput[tr](3,2){\ovalnode{B}{B}}
  \nccurve[angleB=180,ncurvA=0.3,ncurvB=1.3]{A}{B}
\end{pspicture}
```

16.2.11 boxsize

boxsize refers exclusively to the \ncbox and \ncarcbox connection types and specifies half the width of the box.

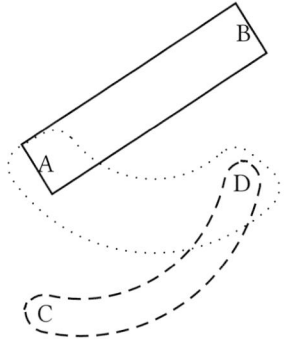

```
\usepackage{pstricks,pst-node}

\begin{pspicture}(3,2)
  \rput[bl](0,0){\rnode{A}{A}}
  \rput[tr](3,2){\rnode{B}{B}}  \ncbox{A}{B}
\end{pspicture}\par
\begin{pspicture}(3,2)
  \rput[bl](0,0){\rnode{C}{C}}
  \rput[tr](3,2){\rnode{D}{D}}
  \ncarcbox[nodesep=5pt,linearc=0.3,arcangle=45,
    boxsize=0.25cm,linestyle=dashed]{C}{D}
\end{pspicture}
\ncarcbox[nodesep=5pt,linearc=0.3,arcangle=45,
    boxsize=0.5cm,linestyle=dotted]{A}{D}
```

231

16 pst-node: Nodes and connections

16.2.12 offset, offsetA, and offsetB

offset moves the connecting line parallel to its original path. This is primarily of use with double straight line connections. offset refers to both nodes, offsetA to the first node, and offsetB to the second node. Note that offset is not available for \ncarcbox.

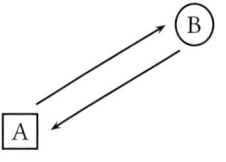

```
\usepackage{pstricks,pst-node}

\begin{pspicture}(3,3)
    \rput[bl](0,0){\rnode{A}{\psframebox{A}}}
    \rput[tr](3,2){\ovalnode{B}{B}}
    \psset{offset=0.2,nodesep=2pt}
    \ncline{->}{A}{B} \ncline{->}{B}{A}
\end{pspicture}
```

16-02

16.2.13 ref

ref refers to the reference points given in Table 9.1 on page 104 and is only meaningful for labels that are put with \ncput. The parameter determines how the label is put in the centre of the connecting line. rb means that the lower right corner of the label will be exactly at the centre of the connecting line.

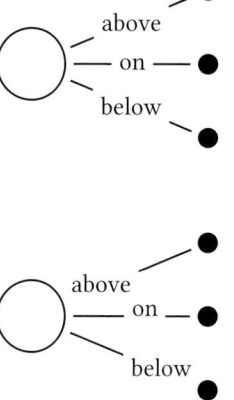

```
\usepackage{pstricks,pst-node}

\cnode(0.5,0){.5cm}{root}%
\cnode*(3,1){4pt}{A}\cnode*(3,0){4pt}{B}%
\cnode*(3,-1){4pt}{C}
\psset{nodesep=3pt}
\ncline{root}{A}   \ncput*{above}
\ncline{root}{B}   \ncput*{on}
\ncline{root}{C}   \ncput*{below}
\par\vspace{3cm}
\cnode(.5,0){.5cm}{root}\cnode*(3,1){4pt}{A}%
\cnode*(3,0){4pt}{B}\cnode*(3,-1){4pt}{C}
\psset{nodesep=3pt}
\ncline{root}{A}   \ncput*[ref=rt]{above}
\ncline{root}{B}   \ncput*[ref=lb]{on}
\ncline{root}{C}   \ncput*[ref=lt]{below}
```

16-02-

16.2.14 rot

rot rotates a label relative to its own centre or relative to another point. rot can take any value that is valid for \rput (cf. Section 9.3 on page 107). rot only affects the \nput command (cf. Section 16.6.3 on page 255).

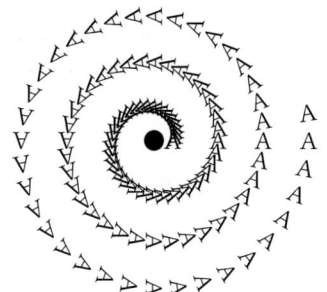

```
\usepackage{pstricks,pst-node,multido}

\begin{pspicture}(4.5,3.5)
  \cnode*(2,2){4pt}{A}
  \multido{\nA=0+10,\rB=0+0.5}{110}{%
    \nput[rot=\nA,%
      labelsep=\rB pt]{\nA}{A}{A}}
\end{pspicture}
```

16.2.15 nrot

nrot lets you rotate labels before placing them. The rotation is specified relative to the connecting line, either in degrees or in the shorthand forms listed in Table 9.2. The specification must be in the form {:*angle*} or {:*shorthand*}.

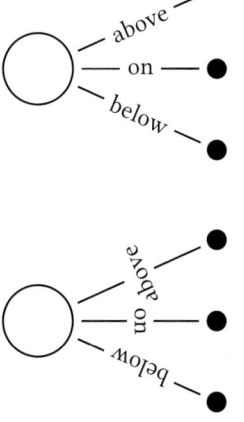

```
\usepackage{pstricks,pst-node}

\cnode(0.5,0){.5cm}{root}%
\cnode*(3,1.1){4pt}{A}\cnode*(3,0){4pt}{B}%
\cnode*(3,-1.1){4pt}{C}
\psset{nodesep=3pt}
\ncline{root}{A}  \ncput*[nrot=:U]{above}
\ncline{root}{B}  \ncput*[nrot=:U]{on}
\ncline{root}{C}  \ncput*[nrot=:U]{below}
\par\vspace{3cm}
\cnode(0.5,0){.5cm}{root}%
\cnode*(3,1.1){4pt}{A}\cnode*(3,0){4pt}{B}%
\cnode*(3,-1.1){4pt}{C}
\psset{nodesep=3pt}
\ncline{root}{A}  \ncput*[nrot=:L]{above}
\ncline{root}{B}  \ncput*[nrot=:R]{on}
\ncline{root}{C}  \ncput*[nrot=:D]{below}
```

16.2.16 tpos

tpos specifies the relative position of a label within a line segment of a straight connecting line of one of the series of \tXput commands.

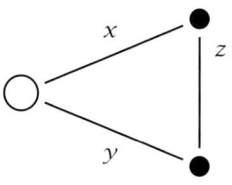

```
\usepackage{pstricks,pst-node}

\cnode(0.5,0){.25cm}{root}
\cnode*(3,1){4pt}{A}\cnode*(3,-1){4pt}{C}
\psset{nodesep=3pt,shortput=tablr}
\ncline{root}{A}^{$x$}\ncline{root}{C}_{$y$}
\ncline{A}{C}>[tpos=0.2]{$z$}
```

16.2.17 npos

Any connection between two nodes consists of at least one segment (using \ncline, \nccurve, or \ncarc) and at most five segments (in the case of \ncloop). npos lets you choose in which segment to place a label. The value is given as a decimal number, with the number before the decimal point specifying the $n + 1$th segment and the number after the point specifying the relative position within the segment. For example, 1.6 means that the label is placed in the second segment at a distance of 60% of the length of the segment from the beginning of the segment. Table 16.2 gives the number of segments for the different connection types and the possible values for npos.

Table 16.2: Comparison of the different node connections with regards to the number of segments

connection	segment	region	default	connection	segment	region	default
\ncline	1	$0 \leq npos \leq 1$	0.5	\nccurve	1	$0 \leq npos \leq 1$	0.5
\ncarc	1	$0 \leq npos \leq 1$	0.5	\ncbar	3	$0 \leq npos \leq 3$	1.5
\ncdiag	3	$0 \leq npos \leq 3$	1.5	\ncdiagg	2	$0 \leq npos \leq 2$	0.5
\ncangle	3	$0 \leq npos \leq 3$	1.5	\ncangles	4	$0 \leq npos \leq 4$	1.5
\ncloop	5	$0 \leq npos \leq 5$	2.5	\nccircle	1	$0 \leq npos \leq 1$	0.5

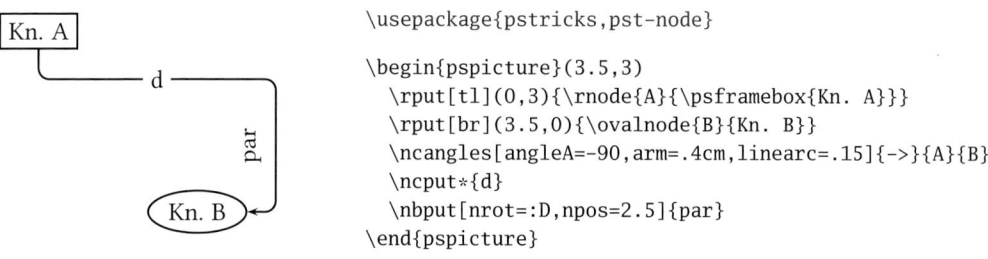

```
\usepackage{pstricks,pst-node}

\begin{pspicture}(3.5,3)
  \rput[tl](0,3){\rnode{A}{\psframebox{Kn. A}}}
  \rput[br](3.5,0){\ovalnode{B}{Kn. B}}
  \ncangles[angleA=-90,arm=.4cm,linearc=.15]{->}{A}{B}
  \ncput*{d}
  \nbput[nrot=:D,npos=2.5]{par}
\end{pspicture}
```

For closed connections like \ncbox and \ncarcbox, the individual segments are counted clockwise, starting at the lower side of the box.

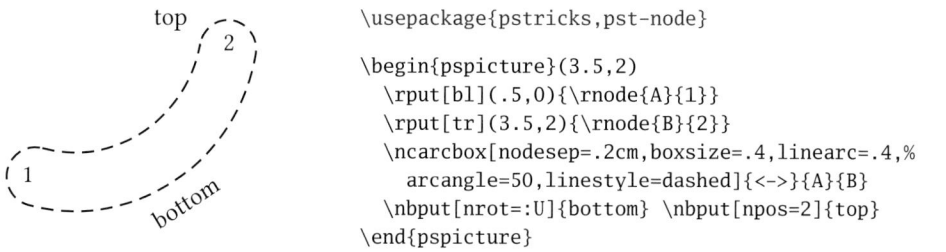

```
\usepackage{pstricks,pst-node}

\begin{pspicture}(3.5,2)
  \rput[bl](.5,0){\rnode{A}{1}}
  \rput[tr](3.5,2){\rnode{B}{2}}
  \ncarcbox[nodesep=.2cm,boxsize=.4,linearc=.4,%
            arcangle=50,linestyle=dashed]{<->}{A}{B}
  \nbput[nrot=:U]{bottom} \nbput[npos=2]{top}
\end{pspicture}
```

16.2.18 shortput

The shortput parameter enables various sets of short forms for you to use when placing labels; it is never necessary to use them as you can always use the corresponding long forms. There are four settings for shortput: none, nab, tablr, and tab.

none No short forms are available.

nab The following short forms are available:

short form	long form	short form	long form
^{*Text*}	\naput{*Text*}	_{*Text*}	\nbput{*Text*}

You must put the short forms **immediately** after a connection; the notation is simplified.

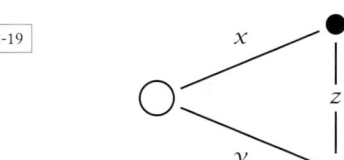

```
\usepackage{pstricks,pst-node}

\cnode(0.5,0){.25cm}{root}
\cnode*(3,1){4pt}{A}\cnode*(3,-1){4pt}{C}
\psset{nodesep=3pt,shortput=nab}
\ncline{root}{A}^{$x$} \ncline{root}{C}_{$y$}
\ncline{A}{C}\ncput*{$z$}
```

If the short form symbols are put in parentheses, PSTricks is prevented from expanding them to the corresponding long forms. If you want to use different symbols for the short form commands, you can change them with the following command:

`\MakeShortNab{`*symbol1*`}{`*symbol2*`}`

tablr The following short forms are available:

short form	long form	short form	long form
^{*text*}	\taput{*text*}	_{*text*}	\tbput{*text*}
<{*text*}	\tlput{*text*}	>{*text*}	\trput{*text*}

You must put the short forms **immediately** after a connection; the notation is simplified.

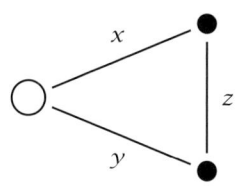

```
\usepackage{pst-node}

\cnode(0.5,0){.25cm}{root}
\cnode*(3,1){4pt}{A}\cnode*(3,-1){4pt}{C}
\psset{nodesep=3pt,shortput=tablr}
\ncline{root}{A}^{$x$}\ncline{root}{C}_{$y$}
\ncline{A}{C}>{$z$}
```

Here, too, you can change the symbols for the short forms with a command:

`\MakeShortTablr{`*symbol1*`}{`*symbol2*`}{`*symbol3*`}{`*symbol4*`}`

tab This is a simplified form of `tablr`:

short form	long form	short form	long form
^{*text*}	\taput{*text*}	_{*text*}	\tbput{*text*}

You must put the short forms **immediately** after a connection; the notation is simplified. The previous example would be almost identical here, except that the <> symbols could not now be used as short forms.

16 pst-node: Nodes and connections

16.3 Nodes

The pst-node package provides a large number of different commands for creating node connections. In fact, it isn't always easy to work out which is the right connection to use for a specific problem.

16.3.1 \rnode

This is the simplest form of a node command. Its syntax is:

\rnode[*reference point*]{*name*}{*material*}

The required arguments are a name for the node and the material to be placed at the node; this material, as usual, sits within a surrounding box with the same reference points as for \rput (hence the style of the name of this type of node). You can use these reference points in the optional parameter to specify the centre of the node. The possible reference points are summarized in Table 9.1 on page 104. If the optional parameter is missing, the node is placed at the centre of the surrounding box.

```
\usepackage{pstricks,pst-node}

\rnode{A}{\Large g}\hspace{2cm}\rnode{B}{\Large G}
\ncline{A}{B}\par
\rnode[lB]{A}{\Large g}\hspace{2cm}\rnode[lB]{B}{\Large G}
\ncline{A}{B}
```

You can nest \rnode commands arbitrarily; even for a single character of material, you can for example put nodes into each of the four corners of the surrounding box.

```
\usepackage{pstricks,pst-node}

\rnode[lb]{A}{\rnode[rb]{B}{\rnode[rt]{C}{\rnode[lt]{D}{\Huge g}}}}
\psset{nodesep=5pt}
\ncline{A}{B}\ncline{B}{C}\ncline{C}{D}\ncline{D}{A}
```

You can use the same idea to "circle" arbitrary areas. Through the command definition of a fourfold node, you can back every region with the four corner nodes, and can then connect them with a closed curve with the \psccurve command (cf. Section 5.3.5 on page 68). Using this method of creating an "all around definition" of nodes, you can achieve virtually any curve.

```
\usepackage{pstricks,pst-node}
\def\DefNodes#1#2{\rnode[tl]{#1-tl}{\rnode[tr]{#1-tr}{%
      \rnode[bl]{#1-bl}{\rnode[br]{#1-br}{#2}}}}}
\LARGE\[ \frac{\DefNodes{A}{A_1}+\DefNodes{B}{B_1}+C_1}
        {\DefNodes{D}{D_1}+\DefNodes{E}{E_1}+\DefNodes{F}{F_1}} \]
\psccurve[linecolor=red,linestyle=dashed,fillstyle=hlines,hatchcolor=yellow]%
    (D-bl)(A-tl)(A-tr)([angle=-90,nodesep=0.1]B-bl)
    ([angle=-90,nodesep=0.1]B-br)(F-tr)(F-br)(F-bl)
    ([angle=90,nodesep=0.1]E-tr)([angle=90,nodesep=0.1]E-tl)(D-br)(D-bl)
```

16.3 Nodes

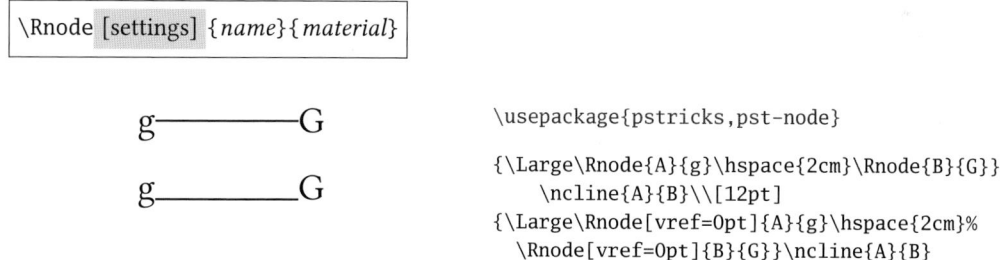

16.3.2 \Rnode

The only difference between \Rnode and \rnode is the location of the centre. For \Rnode, the settings specify a change of position relative to the base line of the surrounding box, using the vref parameter. This means that you can connect nodes with lines parallel to the base line even if the actual centres of the nodes are at different heights above the base line (cf. Section 16.2.1 on page 227).

\Rnode [settings] {name}{material}

```
\usepackage{pstricks,pst-node}

{\Large\Rnode{A}{g}\hspace{2cm}\Rnode{B}{G}}
    \ncline{A}{B}\\[12pt]
{\Large\Rnode[vref=0pt]{A}{g}\hspace{2cm}%
    \Rnode[vref=0pt]{B}{G}}\ncline{A}{B}
```

16.3.3 \pnode

The \pnode command defines a node with zero radius, which is primarily of use in line graphics. You can also use this command to put a node at an arbitrary position in text, as done in the subsection header (\subsection{\protect\pnode(0,0){A}}; then you can achieve similar effects to that in Example 16-00-1 on page 225). \protect has to be specified because of the fragility of the \pnode command.

\pnode{name}   \pnode(x,y){name}

The second version with coordinates makes it possible to place arbitrary nodes, independent of the current point. If, for example, you want to determine the centre between two arbitrary nodes, this is easily done using \pnode with \SpecialCoor active (cf. Chapter 12 on page 139). \pnode(! instructs PSTricks that the coordinates are now computed in PostScript code and x y will be on top of the stack at the end. The following example shows a simple definition and application of a \nodeBetween command.

16 pst-node: Nodes and connections

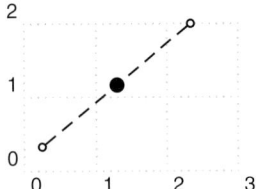

```
\usepackage{pstricks,pst-node}\SpecialCoor
\makeatletter \def\nodeBetween(#1)(#2)#3{%
  \pst@getcoor{#1}\pst@tempa\pst@getcoor{#2}\pst@tempb
  \pnode(! \pst@tempa /YA exch \pst@number\psyunit div def
    /XA exch \pst@number\psxunit div def
    \pst@tempb /YB exch \pst@number\psyunit div def
    /XB exch \pst@number\psxunit div def
    XB XA add 2 div YB YA add 2 div){#3}}\makeatother

\begin{pspicture}[showgrid](3,2)
\psline[linestyle=dashed]{o-o}(0.25,0.33)(2.333,2)
\nodeBetween(0.25,0.33)(2.333,2){centre}\pscircle*(centre){3pt}
\end{pspicture}
```

16.3.4 \cnode

```
\usepackage{pst-node}
\def\Lcs#1{\texttt{\textbackslash#1}}
\Lcs{cnode}, in contrast to \Lcs{pnode}, creates a circular node with defined
radius. Again you can put the node anywhere within text
\makebox[2ex]{\cnode{1ex}{A}} (\verb+\cnode{2ex}{A}+). The centre of the node is
on the base line. Note that \Lcs{cnode} doesn't reserve any space, so it's a good idea
to put it inside a \Lcs{makebox} when using it in text.
\begin{center}
\begin{pspicture}[showgrid](2,2)
  \cnode[linecolor=red](1,1){3pt}{B}
  \nccurve[arrows=->,linestyle=dashed,angleA=-90,angleB=200]{A}{B}
\end{pspicture}
\end{center}
```

\cnode, in contrast to \pnode, creates a circular node with defined radius. Again you can put the node anywhere within text ○ (\cnode{2ex}{A}). The centre of the node is on the base line. Note that \cnode doesn't reserve any space, so it's a good idea to put it inside a \makebox when using it in text.

| \cnode * [settings] {radius}{name} | \cnode * [settings] (x,y){radius}{name} |

16.3.5 \Cnode

\Cnode is very similar to \cnode except that you have to specify the radius with the radius parameter in the optional argument. This is useful in large documents where all nodes have the same size as you can use \psset to specify the radius beforehand.

16.3 Nodes

```
\Cnode * [settings] {name}
\Cnode * [settings] (x,y){name}
```

The starred version fills the node, in the usual manner.

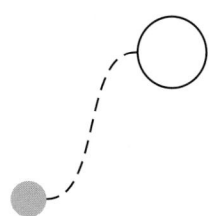

```
\usepackage{pstricks,pst-node}

\begin{pspicture}(3,3)
  \Cnode*[linecolor=red](0.25,0.5){A}
  \Cnode[linecolor=blue,radius=0.5](2.25,2.5){B}
  \nccurve[linestyle=dashed,angleB=180]{A}{B}
\end{pspicture}
```

16.3.6 \circlenode

\circlenode corresponds to \pscirclebox (cf. Section 10.2.4 on page 112) except that the box is given the meaning of a node at the same time. The size of the circle is only affected by its content. The starred version fills the node, in the usual manner.

```
\circlenode * [settings] {name}{material}
```

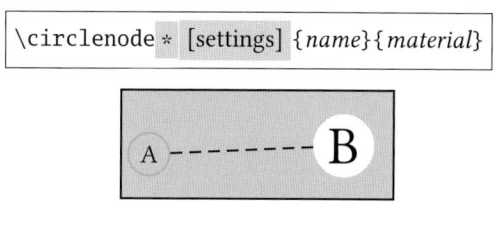

```
\usepackage{pstricks,pst-node}

\psframe[fillcolor=lightgray,
         fillstyle=solid](-0.1,1)(3.75,-0.5)
\circlenode[linecolor=red]{A}{A}%
\hspace{2cm}%
\circlenode*{B}{\huge B}
\ncline[linestyle=dashed]{A}{B}
```

16.3.7 \cnodeput

\cnodeput corresponds to \cput and is a combination of \rput and \circlenode – \rput{<angle>}{\circlenode{<name>}{<material>}}. The starred version fills the node, in the usual manner.

```
\cnodeput * [settings] (x,y){name}{material}
\cnodeput * [settings] {angle}(x,y){name}{material}
```

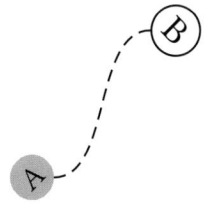

```
\usepackage{pstricks,pst-node}

\begin{pspicture}(3,3)
  \cnodeput*[fillcolor=red]{45}(0.25,0.5){A}{\large A}
  \cnodeput[linecolor=blue]{-45}(2.25,2.5){B}{\Large B}
  \nccurve[linestyle=dashed,angleB=180]{A}{B}
\end{pspicture}
```

16.3.8 \ovalnode

\ovalnode corresponds to \psovalbox (cf. Section 10.2.5 on page 113) except that the box is given the meaning of a node at the same time. The size of the oval is only affected by its content. The starred version fills the node, in the usual manner.

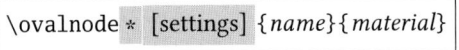

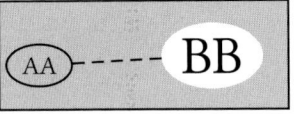

```
\usepackage{pstricks,pst-node}

\psframe[fillcolor=lightgray,%
    fillstyle=solid](-0.1,1)(4,-0.5)
\ovalnode{A}{AA}\hspace{1.25cm}%
\ovalnode*{B}{\huge BB}%
\ncline[linestyle=dashed]{A}{B}%
```

16.3.9 \dianode

\dianode corresponds to \psdiabox (cf. Section 10.2.6 on page 113) except that the box is given the meaning of a node at the same time. The size of the diamond is only affected by its content. The starred version fills the node, in the usual manner.

\dianode * [settings] {name}{material}

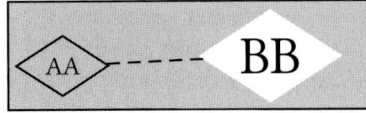

```
\usepackage{pstricks,pst-node}

\psframe[fillcolor=lightgray,
    fillstyle=solid](-0.1,1)(5,-0.5)
\dianode{A}{AA}\hspace{1.25cm}%
\dianode*{B}{\huge BB}%
\ncline[linestyle=dashed]{A}{B}%
```

16.3.10 \trinode

\trinode corresponds to \pstribox (cf. Section 10.2.7 on page 113) except that the box is given the meaning of a node at the same time. The size of the triangle is only affected by its content. The starred version fills the node, in the usual manner.

\trinode * [settings] {name}{material}

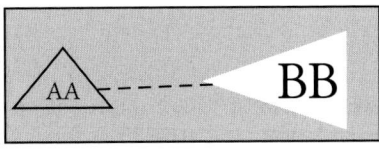

```
\usepackage{pstricks,pst-node}

\psframe[fillcolor=lightgray,
    fillstyle=solid](-0.1,1.25)(5.2,-0.6)
\trinode{A}{AA}\hspace{1.25cm}%
\trinode*[trimode=L]{B}{\huge BB}%
\ncline[linestyle=dashed]{A}{B}%
```

16.3.11 \dotnode

\dotnode corresponds to \psdot (cf. Section 6.2 on page 72) except that the box is given the meaning of a node at the same time. The size of the symbols is controlled by the dotsize and dotscale parameters (cf. Sections 6.1.2 on page 71 and 6.1.3 on page 71).

```
\dotnode [settings] (x,y){name}
```

```
\usepackage{pstricks,pst-node}

\begin{pspicture}[showgrid](3,3)
    \dotnode[linecolor=red,dotscale=3](0.25,0.5){A}
    \dotnode*[linecolor=blue,dotstyle=triangle*](2.5,2.5){B}
    \ncline[nodesep=5pt]{A}{B}
    \dotnode[dotscale=3,dotstyle=pentagon*](0.25,2.5){A}
    \dotnode[linecolor=blue,
        dotscale=2,dotstyle=triangle*](2.5,0.5){B}
    \ncline[nodesep=5pt]{A}{B}
\end{pspicture}
```

16.3.12 \fnode

\fnode corresponds to \psframe, except that the frame size has to be defined by the framesize parameter (cf. Section 16.2.3 on page 228).

```
\fnode * [settings] {name}        \fnode * [settings] (x,y){name}
```

If you don't specify a coordinate pair, the centre of the frame is set to the current coordinates. The starred version fills the node, in the usual manner.

```
\usepackage{pstricks,pst-node}

\begin{pspicture}[showgrid](3,3)
    \fnode(0.25,0.5){A}
    \fnode*(2.5,2.5){B}
    \ncline{A}{B}
    \fnode[framesize=0.25](0.25,2.5){A}
    \fnode*[framesize=1,linecolor=cyan](2.5,0.5){B}
    \ncline{A}{B}
\end{pspicture}
```

16.4 Connections using \nc commands

This group of connection commands all start with \nc and most of them have the same syntax. A line or curve is drawn from node A to node B, startign and ending at the outer box of the nodes. The nc connections are always aligned to the centre of a node. However, specifying nodesep or angles refers to the frame of the box. Using starred versions is always possible, but they don't always make sense. At first the differences between the connection commands can be confusing, so it's worth doing a little bit of experimenting to figure out the pros and cons of each individual connection type. For the remainder of this chapter, Node A and node B always specify the order of the nodes, where the order is significant for the example.

16.4.1 \ncline

This is the simplest of all connection types; it draws a straight line from one node to the other.

16 pst-node: Nodes and connections

```
\ncline * [settings] {arrows} {nodeA}{nodeB}
```

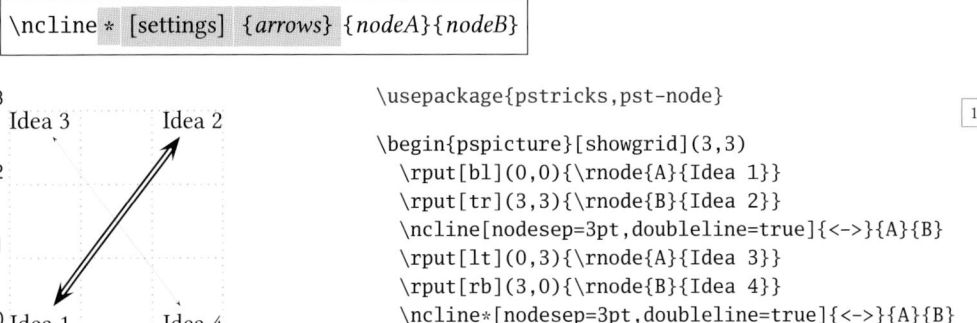

```
\usepackage{pstricks,pst-node}

\begin{pspicture}[showgrid](3,3)
    \rput[bl](0,0){\rnode{A}{Idea 1}}
    \rput[tr](3,3){\rnode{B}{Idea 2}}
    \ncline[nodesep=3pt,doubleline=true]{<->}{A}{B}
    \rput[lt](0,3){\rnode{A}{Idea 3}}
    \rput[rb](3,0){\rnode{B}{Idea 4}}
    \ncline*[nodesep=3pt,doubleline=true]{<->}{A}{B}
\end{pspicture}
```

16-0

16.4.2 \ncarc

This draws a curve; the angle of the gradient to the straight line at the beginning is equal to arcangle (cf. Section 16.2.6 on page 229).

```
\ncarc * [settings] {arrows} {nodeA}{nodeB}
```

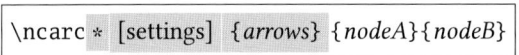

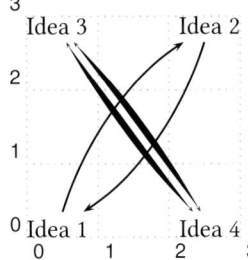

```
\usepackage{pstricks,pst-node}

\begin{pspicture}[showgrid](3,3)
    \rput[bl](0,0){\rnode{A}{Idea 1}}
    \rput[tr](3,3){\rnode{B}{Idea 2}}\psset{nodesep=3pt}
    \ncarc[arcangle=20]{->}{A}{B}\ncarc[arcangle=20]{->}{B}{A}
    \rput[lt](0,3){\rnode{A}{Idea 3}}
    \rput[rb](3,0){\rnode{B}{Idea 4}}
    \ncarc*{<->}{A}{B}\ncarc*{<->}{B}{A}
\end{pspicture}
```

16-04

16.4.3 \ncdiag

\ncdiag draws a line made up of three segments. This type of connection doesn't make sense with nodes that are on the same vertical or horizontal line. The arm parameter (cf. Section 16.2.8 on page 230) controls the lengths of the initial and final segments, which in turn determine the length and angle of the middle segment.

```
\ncdiag * [settings] {arrows} {nodeA}{nodeB}
```

The first example shows that for this command the starred version is pretty useless. As mentioned in the opening to this section, this is true for many of the connections, so for the remainder of this chapter we will only give an example with the starred version if using it makes sense.

242

16.4 Connections using \nc commands

Idea 3, Idea 2, Idea 1, Idea 4

```
\usepackage{pstricks,pst-node}

\begin{pspicture}(3,3)
    \rput[bl](0,0){\ovalnode{A}{Idea 1}}
    \rput[tr](3,3){\ovalnode{B}{Idea 2}}
    \ncdiag[angleA=90,angleB=-90]{->}{A}{B}
    \rput[lt](0,3){\rnode{A}{Idea 3}}
    \rput[rb](3,0){\rnode{B}{Idea 4}}
    \ncdiag*[angleA=-90,angleB=90]{->}{A}{B}
\end{pspicture}
```

Idea 3, Idea 2, Idea 1, Idea 4

```
\usepackage{pstricks,pst-node}

\begin{pspicture}(3,3)
    \rput[bl](0,0){\ovalnode{A}{Idea 1}}
    \rput[tr](3,3){\ovalnode{B}{Idea 2}}
    \ncdiag[angleA=90,angleB=-90,arm=1.25cm]{->}{A}{B}
    \rput[lt](0,3){\rnode{A}{Idea 3}}
    \rput[rb](3,0){\rnode{B}{Idea 4}}
    \ncdiag[angleA=-90,angleB=90,arm=0]{->}{A}{B}
\end{pspicture}
```

As the last example shows, specifying arm=0 just creates a straight line. You might think that you may as well use \ncline, but there is an advantage in some cases to using \ncdiag here, for example if you want to align a connecting line not directly to the centre of a node, as \ncdiag lets you still use the angle option to align the line with a different point at the node. The next examples illustrate the effect of using \ncdiag in this situation:

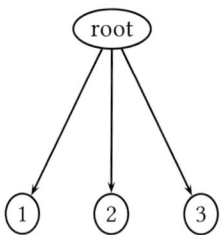

```
\usepackage{pstricks,pst-node}

\begin{pspicture}(2.75,3)
    \rput(1.5,2.8){\ovalnode{A}{root}}
    \rput[lb](0,0){\ovalnode{B}{1}}
    \rput[b](1.5,0){\ovalnode{C}{2}}
    \rput[rb](3,0){\ovalnode{D}{3}}
    \ncline{->}{A}{B}\ncline{->}{A}{C}\ncline{->}{A}{D}
\end{pspicture}
```

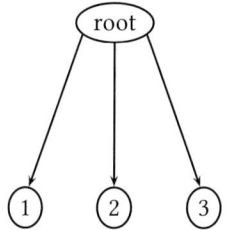

```
\usepackage{pstricks,pst-node}

\begin{pspicture}(2.75,3)
    \rput(1.5,2.8){\ovalnode{A}{root}}
    \rput[lb](0,0){\ovalnode{B}{1}}
    \rput[b](1.5,0){\ovalnode{C}{2}}
    \rput[rb](3,0){\ovalnode{D}{3}}
    \ncdiag[arm=0,angleA=80,angleB=-160]{<-}{B}{A}
    \ncline{->}{A}{C}
    \ncdiag[arm=0,angleA=100,angleB=-20]{<-}{D}{A}
\end{pspicture}
```

243

16 pst-node: Nodes and connections

None of the parameters listed in Table 16.1 permits you to control connections so that ones next to each other can be made to have parallel connecting lines, as found on circuit path diagrams for example. However, the pstricks-add package defines an additional lineAngle option for use with \ncdiag, which lets you specify the angle of the centre line.

lineAngle=angle

This means that the three segments are entirely defined by the specified length of the first "arm" (armA) and the specified angle of the second arm. The command then calculates the lengths of the second and third arms. Specifying armB via a parameter has no effect, as it is determined by the command and overwritten. However, specifying armB=0 is still possible if you don't want the third segment to join the outer box heading directly for the centre of the node.

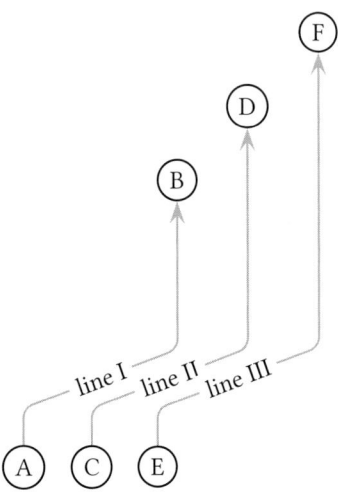

```
\usepackage{pstricks-add}

\begin{pspicture}(5,6)
    \circlenode{A}{A}\quad\circlenode{C}{C}%
        \quad\circlenode{E}{E}
    \rput(0,4){\circlenode{B}{B}}
    \rput(1,5){\circlenode{D}{D}}
    \rput(2,6){\circlenode{F}{F}}
    \psset{arrowscale=2,linearc=0.2,
        linecolor=red,armA=0.5,
        angleA=90,angleB=-90}
    \ncdiag[lineAngle=20]{->}{A}{B}
    \ncput*[nrot=:U]{line I}
    \ncdiag[lineAngle=20]{->}{C}{D}
    \ncput*[nrot=:U]{line II}
    \ncdiag[lineAngle=20]{->}{E}{F}
    \ncput*[nrot=:U]{line III}
\end{pspicture}
```

You can also use the lineAngle parameter with the corresponding \pcdiag command (cf. Section 16.5 on page 252).

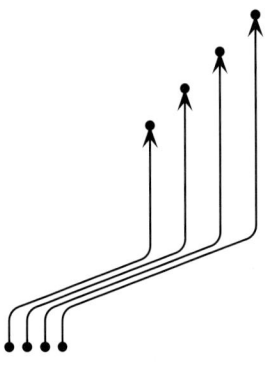

```
\usepackage{pstricks-add}

\begin{pspicture}(4,4.5)
\cnode*(0,0){2pt}{A}   \cnode*(0.25,0){2pt}{C}
\cnode*(0.5,0){2pt}{E}\cnode*(0.75,0){2pt}{G}
\cnode*(2,3){2pt}{B}   \cnode*(2.5,3.5){2pt}{D}
\cnode*(3,4){2pt}{F}   \cnode*(3.5,4.5){2pt}{H}
{\psset{arrowscale=2,linearc=0.2,
    linecolor=blue,armA=0.5, angleA=90,angleB=-90}
\pcdiag[lineAngle=20]{->}(A)(B)
\pcdiag[lineAngle=20]{->}(C)(D)
\pcdiag[lineAngle=20]{->}(E)(F)
\pcdiag[lineAngle=20]{->}(G)(H)}
\end{pspicture}
```

16.4.4 \ncdiagg

\ncdiagg is similar to \ncdiag except that an "arm" is only drawn for the first node, so the connection consists of two line segments.

| \ncdiagg * [settings] {arrows} {nodeA}{nodeB} |

In principle, \ncdiagg should be equivalent to using \ncdiag with armB=0. However, as the following example shows, this is not the case because angleB=0 still applies to \ncdiag while \ncdiagg makes this angle variable to align the connection with the centre of the node.

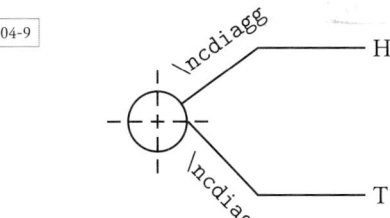

```
\usepackage{pstricks,pst-node}
\SpecialCoor

\begin{pspicture}(-0.2,-1)(3,1)
\cnode{12pt}{a}
\pcline[nodesep=20pt,linestyle=dashed](a)(a)
\rput{90}(a){\pcline[nodesep=20pt,
    linestyle=dashed](a)(a)}
\rput[l](3,1){\rnode{b}{H}}
\rput[l](3,-1){\rnode{c}{T}}
\ncdiagg[angleA=180,armA=1.5,
    nodesepA=3pt]{b}{a}
\nbput[nrot=:D,npos=1.3]{\CMD{ncdiagg}}
\ncdiag[angleA=180,armA=1.5,armB=0,
    nodesepA=3pt]{c}{a}
\naput[nrot=:D,npos=1.3]{\CMD{ncdiag}}
\end{pspicture}
```

You can also use \ncdiagg to draw a single line that starts at the first node at a specific angle (with armA=0) and aims at the centre of the second node.

The lineAngle option from the pstricks-add package (cf. Section 16.4.3 on page 242) also works with \ncdiagg (and \pcdiagg, cf. Section 16.5 on page 252) for creating parallel connecting segments. Here are two more examples using lineAngle:

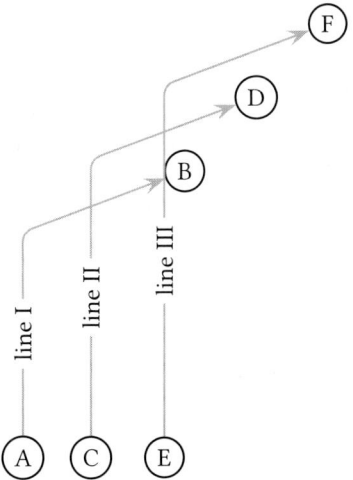

```
\usepackage{pstricks-add}

\begin{pspicture}(4,6)
    \circlenode{A}{A}\quad\circlenode{C}{C}
    \quad\circlenode{E}{E}
    \rput(0,4){\circlenode{B}{B}}
    \rput(1,5){\circlenode{D}{D}}
    \rput(2,6){\circlenode{F}{F}}
    {\psset{arrowscale=2,linearc=0.2,
        linecolor=red,armA=0.5,angleA=90}
    \ncdiagg[lineAngle=-160]{->}{A}{B}
    \ncput*[nrot=:U]{line I}
    \ncdiagg[lineAngle=-160]{->}{C}{D}
    \ncput*[nrot=:U]{line II}
    \ncdiagg[lineAngle=-160]{->}{E}{F}
    \ncput*[nrot=:U]{line III}}
\end{pspicture}
```

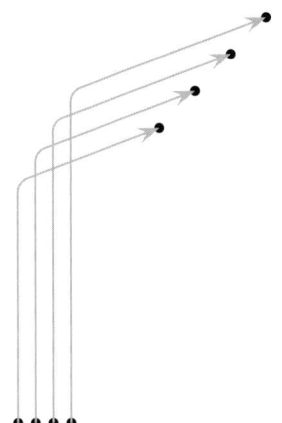

```
\usepackage{pstricks-add}

\begin{pspicture}(4,6)
  \cnode*(0,0){2pt}{A}    \cnode*(0.25,0){2pt}{C}
  \cnode*(0.5,0){2pt}{E}\cnode*(0.75,0){2pt}{G}
  \cnode*(2,4){2pt}{B}    \cnode*(2.5,4.5){2pt}{D}
  \cnode*(3,5){2pt}{F}    \cnode*(3.5,5.5){2pt}{H}
  {\psset{arrowscale=2,linearc=0.2,
      linecolor=red,armA=0.5, angleA=90}
  \pcdiagg[lineAngle=20]{->}(A)(B)
  \pcdiagg[lineAngle=20]{->}(C)(D)
  \pcdiagg[lineAngle=20]{->}(E)(F)
  \pcdiagg[lineAngle=20]{->}(G)(H)}
\end{pspicture}
```

16.4.5 \ncbar

\ncbar is similar to \ncdiag except that the angles between the individual segments are always 90°. If the "arms" are of different lengths or a starting angle that is not a multiple of 90° is used, then a "skewed" results occurs. Note that the starting angle and the end angle must be the same, so you can only change it for both nodes at once, i.e. angleA and angleB must have the same values (cf. Section 16.2.7 on page 230).

\ncbar * [settings] {arrows} {nodeA}{nodeB}

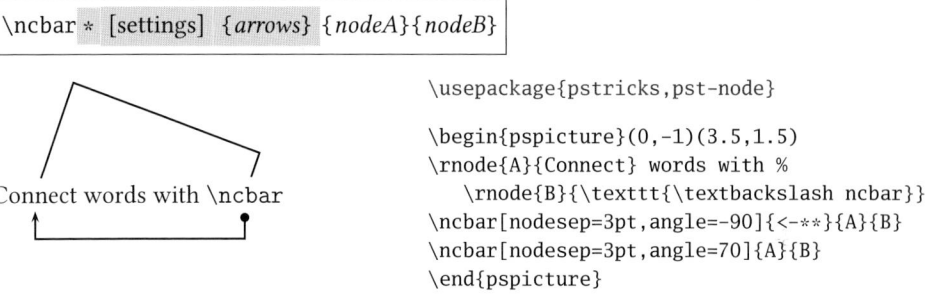

```
\usepackage{pstricks,pst-node}

\begin{pspicture}(0,-1)(3.5,1.5)
\rnode{A}{Connect} words with %
    \rnode{B}{\texttt{\textbackslash ncbar}}
\ncbar[nodesep=3pt,angle=-90]{<-**}{A}{B}
\ncbar[nodesep=3pt,angle=70]{A}{B}
\end{pspicture}
```

16.4.6 \ncbarr

The \ncbar command described above connects two nodes with a maximum of three line segments, whereas the pstricks-add package provides an additional \ncbarr command that uses five segments. This leads to an S-shaped connection; all segments are perpendicular lines. Therefore the starting angle angleA has to be either 0° or 180°. All other values are set to zero internally. The centre line is symmetric to the two nodes.

\ncbarr [settings] {nodeA}{nodeB}

In contrast to the general definition of \nc connections, arrows have to be specified within the setting parameters for \ncbarr rather than as a separate arrows argument.

16.4 Connections using \nc commands

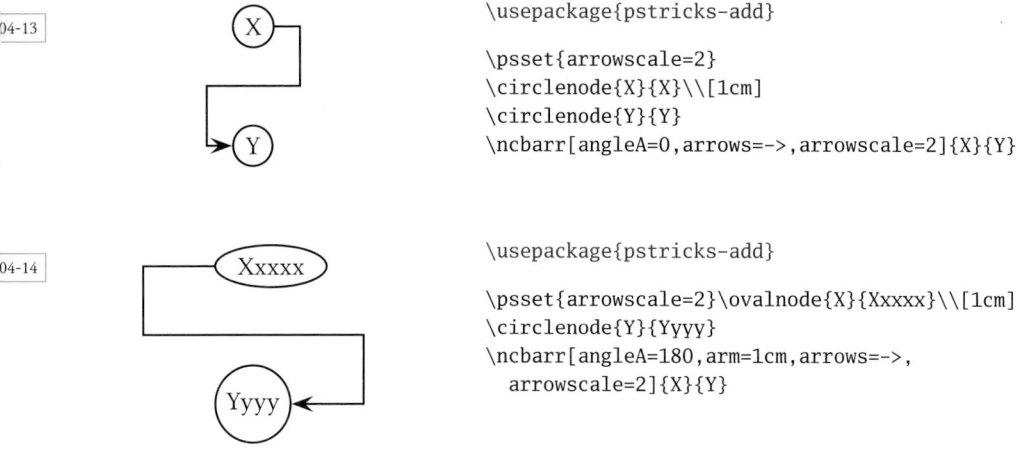

```
\usepackage{pstricks-add}

\psset{arrowscale=2}
\circlenode{X}{X}\\[1cm]
\circlenode{Y}{Y}
\ncbarr[angleA=0,arrows=->,arrowscale=2]{X}{Y}
```

```
\usepackage{pstricks-add}

\psset{arrowscale=2}\ovalnode{X}{Xxxxx}\\[1cm]
\circlenode{Y}{Yyyy}
\ncbarr[angleA=180,arm=1cm,arrows=->,
    arrowscale=2]{X}{Y}
```

It is not possible to rotate the whole figure because nodes don't work within \rput or similar commands that support rotation (cf. Section C.3.1 on page 849).

Note that a similar \pcbarr connection doesn't exist, but it is simple to define it if you have need of it.

16.4.7 \ncangle

\ncangle is similar to \ncdiag except that the lengths of the arms and the angles are calculated so that they take the correct values depending on the parameters.

\ncangle * [settings] {arrows} {nodeA}{nodeB}

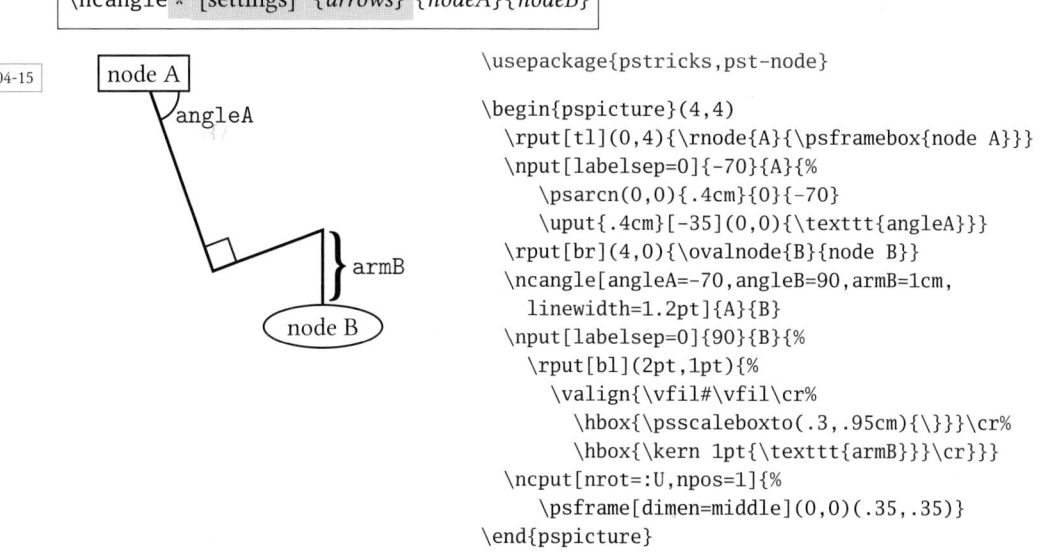

```
\usepackage{pstricks,pst-node}

\begin{pspicture}(4,4)
  \rput[tl](0,4){\rnode{A}{\psframebox{node A}}}
  \nput[labelsep=0]{-70}{A}{%
      \psarcn(0,0){.4cm}{0}{-70}
      \uput{.4cm}[-35](0,0){\texttt{angleA}}}
  \rput[br](4,0){\ovalnode{B}{node B}}
  \ncangle[angleA=-70,angleB=90,armB=1cm,
      linewidth=1.2pt]{A}{B}
  \nput[labelsep=0]{90}{B}{%
    \rput[bl](2pt,1pt){%
      \valign{\vfil#\vfil\cr%
        \hbox{\psscaleboxto(.3,.95cm){\}}}\cr%
        \hbox{\kern 1pt{\texttt{armB}}}\cr}}}
  \ncput[nrot=:U,npos=1]{%
      \psframe[dimen=middle](0,0)(.35,.35)}
\end{pspicture}
```

247

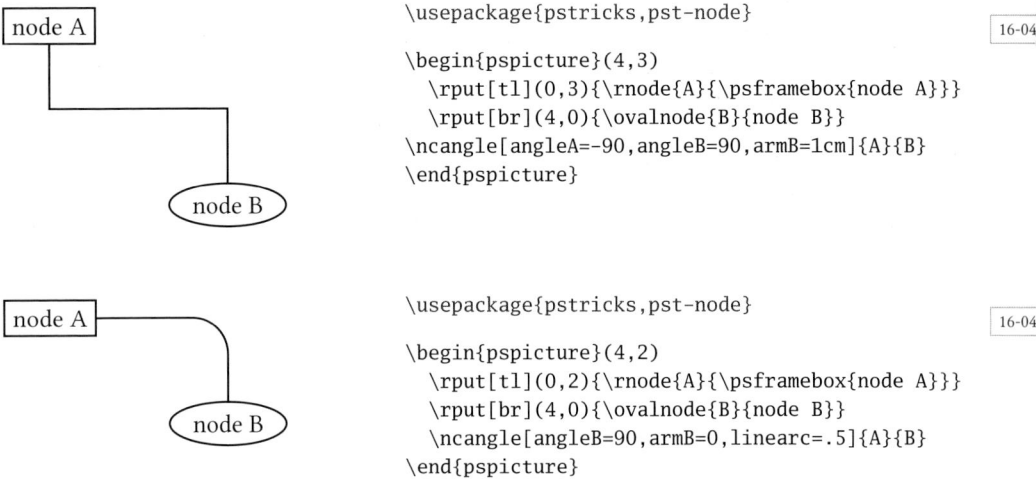

```
\usepackage{pstricks,pst-node}

\begin{pspicture}(4,3)
  \rput[tl](0,3){\rnode{A}{\psframebox{node A}}}
  \rput[br](4,0){\ovalnode{B}{node B}}
  \ncangle[angleA=-90,angleB=90,armB=1cm]{A}{B}
\end{pspicture}
```

```
\usepackage{pstricks,pst-node}

\begin{pspicture}(4,2)
  \rput[tl](0,2){\rnode{A}{\psframebox{node A}}}
  \rput[br](4,0){\ovalnode{B}{node B}}
  \ncangle[angleB=90,armB=0,linearc=.5]{A}{B}
\end{pspicture}
```

16.4.8 \ncangles

\ncangles is the "plural" of \ncangle so to speak; it can have up to four line segments altogether. The length of armA is fixed by default (cf. Section 16.2.8 on page 230). The connection to armB is done via two line segments that are perpendicular where they join each other (unless only a single line segment is necessary to fit in with the parameters). The angle that the second to last segment has to armB is determined from the values of the other parameters.

`\ncangles * [settings] {arrows} {nodeA}{nodeB}`

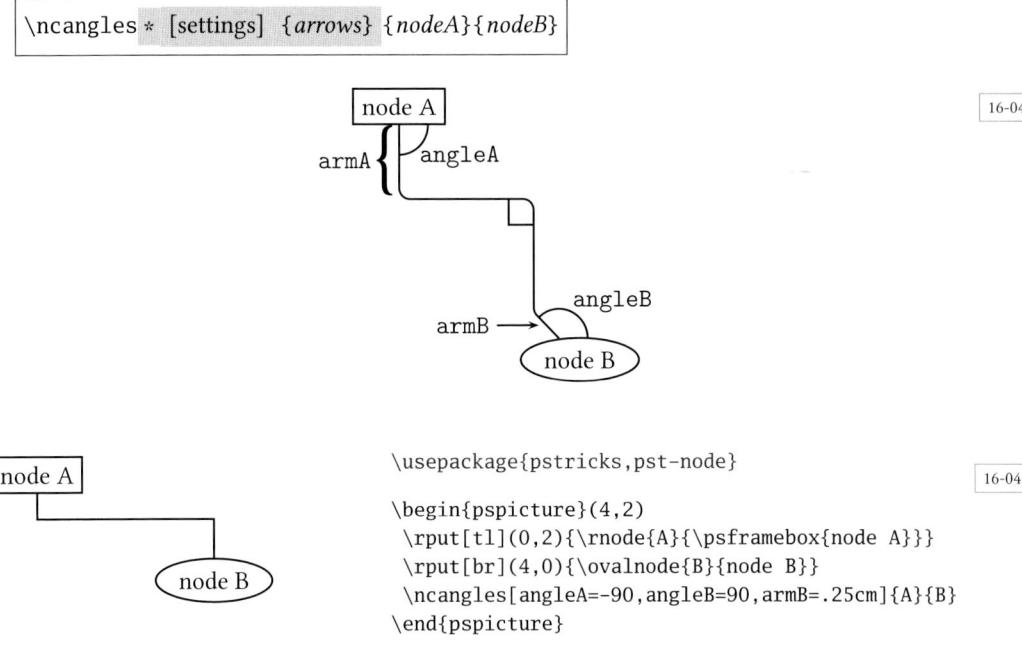

```
\usepackage{pstricks,pst-node}

\begin{pspicture}(4,2)
  \rput[tl](0,2){\rnode{A}{\psframebox{node A}}}
  \rput[br](4,0){\ovalnode{B}{node B}}
  \ncangles[angleA=-90,angleB=90,armB=.25cm]{A}{B}
\end{pspicture}
```

16.4.9 \ncloop

\ncloop differs from the similar \ncangle and \ncangles commands in that it has five line segments. The first segment takes the specified value of armA, the next line segment is added such that the penultimate line segment meets the armB segment at an angle of 90° and the next segment is added after length loopsize (cf. Section 16.2.9 on page 230), again at an angle of 90°. All changes of direction are done counterclockwise, which determines whether the whole line is drawn above or below. A loop can end at the node it started at by specifying the same start and end node. If this should be similar to a circle however, it's better to use \nccircle instead (Section 16.4.11 on the following page).

\ncloop * [settings] {arrows} {nodeA}{nodeB}

```
\usepackage{pstricks,pst-node}

\rnode[lB]{A}{\psframebox{\Huge loooop}}
\ncloop[angleB=180,loopsize=1,arm=.5,
    linearc=.2]{->}{A}{A}
\ncput[npos=3.5,nrot=:U]{\psline{|<->|}%
    (0.5,-0.2)(-0.5,-0.2)}
\nbput[npos=3.5,nrot=:D,labelsep=.35cm]{%
    {\small\texttt{loopsize}}}
```

The inner angles of the loop are by default always of 90°. If the starting angle is different to 0° or 180°, then the end angle is also modified so that both together add up to 180°. However, this is a special case.

```
\usepackage{pstricks,pst-node}

\hspace*{0.5cm}\rnode{A}{\psframebox{%
    \large\textbf{beginning}}} of the
\rnode{B}{\psframebox{\large\textbf{end}}}
\ncloop[angleA=180,loopsize=0.9,arm=0.5,
    linearc=.2]{->}{A}{B}}
\ncput[npos=1.5,nrot=:U]{%
    \psline{|<->|}(.45,-.2)(-.45,-.2)}
\nbput[npos=1.5,nrot=:D,labelsep=.35cm]%
    {\small\texttt{loopsize}}
\ncloop[angleA=10,angleB=180,%
    linecolor=cyan,linearc=.2]{->}{B}{A}
```

You can use \ncloop to create "railroad diagrams", by reaching both nodes from the same side by specifying an appropriate angle.

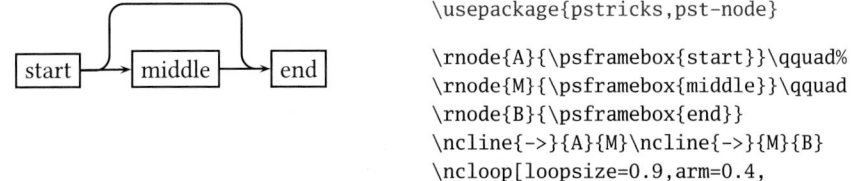

```
\usepackage{pstricks,pst-node}

\rnode{A}{\psframebox{start}}\qquad%
\rnode{M}{\psframebox{middle}}\qquad
\rnode{B}{\psframebox{end}}
\ncline{->}{A}{M}\ncline{->}{M}{B}
\ncloop[loopsize=0.9,arm=0.4,
    linearc=.2,angleB=180]{->}{A}{B}
```

16.4.10 \nccurve

\nccurve creates a bezier curve between two nodes. You can modify the curve through the angleA, angleB, and ncurv parameters (cf. Section 16.2.10 on page 231).

\nccurve * [settings] {arrows} {nodeA}{nodeB}

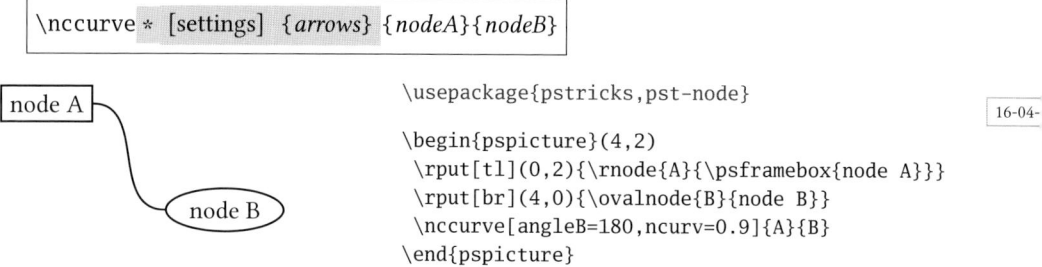

```
\usepackage{pstricks,pst-node}

\begin{pspicture}(4,2)
  \rput[tl](0,2){\rnode{A}{\psframebox{node A}}}
  \rput[br](4,0){\ovalnode{B}{node B}}
  \nccurve[angleB=180,ncurv=0.9]{A}{B}
\end{pspicture}
```

16-04-

16.4.11 \nccircle

\nccircle draws a circle passing through the centre of a node. It only ever refers to one node, but requires an additional radius parameter. Its syntax is:

\nccircle * [settings] {arrows} {node}{radius}

You can modify \nccircle through the angleA and radius parameters. The starred version is useful here, filling the circle in the usual manner.

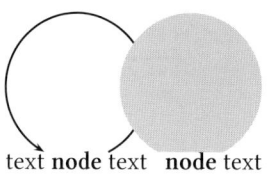

```
\usepackage{pstricks,pst-node}

\begin{pspicture}(5.5,2)
   text \rnode{A}{\textbf{node}} text%
   \nccircle[nodesep=3pt]{->}{A}{1cm}%
   \kern0.7em\rnode{A}{\textbf{node}} text
   \nccircle*[linecolor=lightgray,
       nodesep=3pt]{A}{1cm}
\end{pspicture}
```

16-04-2

16.4.12 \ncbox

\ncbox creates a box enclosing two nodes. You do have to take care, however, that the node contents really are contained in the box: the boxsize (cf. Section 16.2.11) and nodesep parameters (cf. 16.2.4) offer an easy way to control this.

\ncbox [settings] {nodeA}{nodeB}   \ncbox* [settings] {nodeA}{nodeB}

In contrast to the general definition of \nc connections, arrows are not available for \ncbox. The starred version is useful here, filling the box in the usual manner. The next example makes use of the border parameter to illustrate the overlay effect (cf. Section 4.1.15).

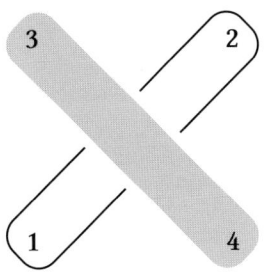

```
\usepackage{pstricks,pst-node}

\begin{pspicture}(3,3)\large\bfseries
    \psset{nodesep=3pt,linearc=0.3}
    \rput[bl](0,0){\rnode{A}{1}}
    \rput[tr](3,3){\rnode{B}{2}}
    \ncbox{A}{B}\rput[lt](0,3){\rnode{A}{3}}
    \rput[rb](3,0){\rnode{B}{4}}
    \ncbox*[border=4pt,
        linecolor=lightgray]{->}{A}{B}
    \rput[lt](0,3){\rnode{A}{3}}
    \rput[rb](3,0){\rnode{B}{4}}
\end{pspicture}
```

16.4.13 \ncarcbox

\ncarcbox encloses the nodes in a curved box that is essentially part of a circle, with a line width of boxsize. Again you must take care that the node contents are contained in the box: the boxsize (cf. Section 16.2.11) and nodesep parameters (cf. 16.2.4) offer an easy way to control this.

| \ncarcbox * [settings] {nodeA}{nodeB} |

As with \ncarcbox, arrows are not available for \ncarcbox. The starred version is useful here, filling the box in the usual manner. The angles are counted counterclockwise, so an angle of arcangle=−30 leads to the arc being drawn the other way when the nodes are switched in addition to a gradient of 30° between line $\overline{AB}$ and the starting gradient, as in the example below. This example also makes use of the border parameter to illustrate the overlay effect (cf. Section 4.1.15 on page 51).

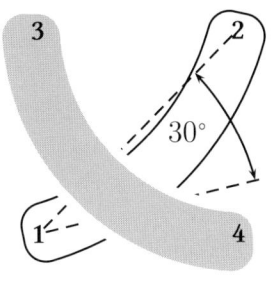

```
\usepackage{pstricks,pst-node,textcomp}
\SpecialCoor

\begin{pspicture}(-0.5,0)(3,3) \large\bfseries
    \psset{nodesep=3pt,linearc=0.3}
    \rput[bl](0,0){\rnode{A}{1}}
    \rput[tr](3,3){\rnode{B}{2}}
    \ncarcbox[arcangle=30]{A}{B}
    \pcline[linestyle=dashed](A)(B)
    \pcline[linestyle=dashed,nodesepB=-0.2](A)(3,0.8)
    \psarc{<->}(0,0){3.25}{15}{45}
    \rput(2.2,1.5){$30^\circ$}
    \pnode(0,3){A}\pnode(3,0){B}
    \ncarcbox*[border=4pt,linecolor=lightgray,
        arcangle=45]{A}{B}
    \rput[lt](A){3}\rput[rb](B){4}
\end{pspicture}
```

16 pst-node: Nodes and connections

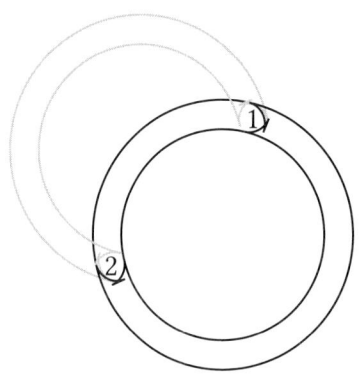

```
\usepackage{pstricks,pst-node}

\begin{pspicture}(0.5,0)(4,3)  \large
  \psset{nodesep=3pt,linearc=0.3,boxsize=2mm}
  \rput(3,3){\rnode{A}{1}}
  \rput(1,1){\rnode{B}{2}}
  \ncarcbox[arcangle=60]{A}{B}
  \ncarcbox[arcangle=-60,linecolor=lightgray]{A}{B}
  \ncarcbox[arcangle=-60,linecolor=blue]{B}{A}
\end{pspicture}
```

16-04

16.5 Connections using \pc commands

This group of connection commands all start with \pc and most of them have the same syntax.

\pc???? * [settings] {arrows}(nodeA)(nodeB)

They have the same behaviour as the corresponding \nc commands (cf. previous section) except that the \pc connections **always** start and end at the centre of the node and not at the surrounding box. Therefore we are primarily dealing with lines and curves here, which also becomes clear from having to enclose coordinates or node names in parentheses () now. Table 16.3 shows a summary of the \pc commands; note that \ncbarr and \nccirclebox don't have \pc equivalents.

Table 16.3: Comparison of the pc and nc connections

name	corresponding nc connection
\pcline [settings] {arrows} $(x_1,y_1)(x_2,y_2)$	\ncline
\pcarc [settings] {arrows} $(x_1,y_1)(x_2,y_2)$	\ncarc
\pcdiag [settings] {arrows} $(x_1,y_1)(x_2,y_2)$	\ncdiag
\pcdiagg [settings] {arrows} $(x_1,y_1)(x_2,y_2)$	\ncdiagg
\pcbar [settings] {arrows} $(x_1,y_1)(x_2,y_2)$	\ncbar
\pcangle [settings] {arrows} $(x_1,y_1)(x_2,y_2)$	\ncangle
\pcangles [settings] {arrows} $(x_1,y_1)(x_2,y_2)$	\ncangles
\pcloop [settings] {arrows} $(x_1,y_1)(x_2,y_2)$	\ncloop
\pccurve [settings] {arrows} $(x_1,y_1)(x_2,y_2)$	\nccurve
\pcbox [settings] $(x_1,y_1)(x_2,y_2)$	\ncbox
\pcarcbox [settings] $(x_1,y_1)(x_2,y_2)$	\ncarcbox

16.6 Label

When special coordinates are activated with \SpecialCoor (cf. Chapter 12 on page 139), you can pass node names as coordinates for other commands as well, e.g. \psframe. Here you can also refer to a point by its node name directly, like \psline(3,3)(A).

The two examples below correspond to those given in Section 16.4.3 on page 242. You can use the nodesep parameter to extend the start and the end of the connection (negative values) or shorten them (positive values).

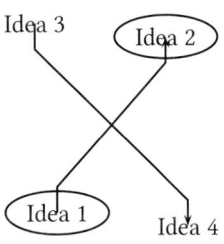

```
\usepackage{pstricks,pst-node}
\SpecialCoor

\begin{pspicture}(3,3)
  \rput[bl](0,0){\ovalnode{A}{Idea 1}}
  \rput[tr](3,3){\ovalnode{B}{Idea 2}}
  \pcdiag[angleA=90,angleB=-90]{->}(A)(B)
  \rput[lt](0,3){\rnode{A}{Idea 3}}
  \rput[rb](3,0){\rnode{B}{Idea 4}}
  \pcdiag[angleA=-90,angleB=90]{->}(A)(B)
\end{pspicture}
```

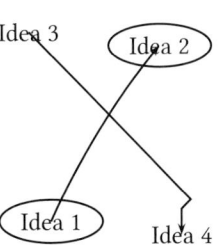

```
\usepackage{pstricks,pst-node}
\SpecialCoor

\begin{pspicture}(3,3)
  \rput[bl](0,0){\ovalnode{A}{Idea 1}}
  \rput[tr](3,3){\ovalnode{B}{Idea 2}}
  \pcarc{->}(A)(B)
  \rput[lt](0,3){\rnode{A}{Idea 3}}
  \rput[rb](3,0){\rnode{B}{Idea 4}}
  \pcangles[angleA=-45,angleB=90]{->}(A)(B)
\end{pspicture}
```

16.6 Label

In Chapter 9 on page 103 we covered several commands to place labels at arbitrary positions. However, in the context of connections, there are a few special commands. After a connection has been drawn, the coordinates of the two nodes are available until a new connection is drawn. This information is useful when placing labels, but it does mean that the label commands must follow straight after the connection commands.

This chapter has already shown many examples for placing labels, while discussing possible parameters. Here we will only cover the commands specific to dealing with nodes.

16.6.1 \n-label

The \n-label commands always refer to the visible length of the connection; the actual centres of the nodes are of no interest. The label is placed in the centre of this visible connection by default, but this can be changed with the npos parameter.

253

16 pst-node: Nodes and connections

```
\ncput * [settings] {material}
\naput * [settings] {material}
\nbput * [settings] {material}
```

Here c means **on** the line (centre), a means **above** the line, and b means **below** the line. The starred versions are not transparent, overwriting the line to make the label more visible.

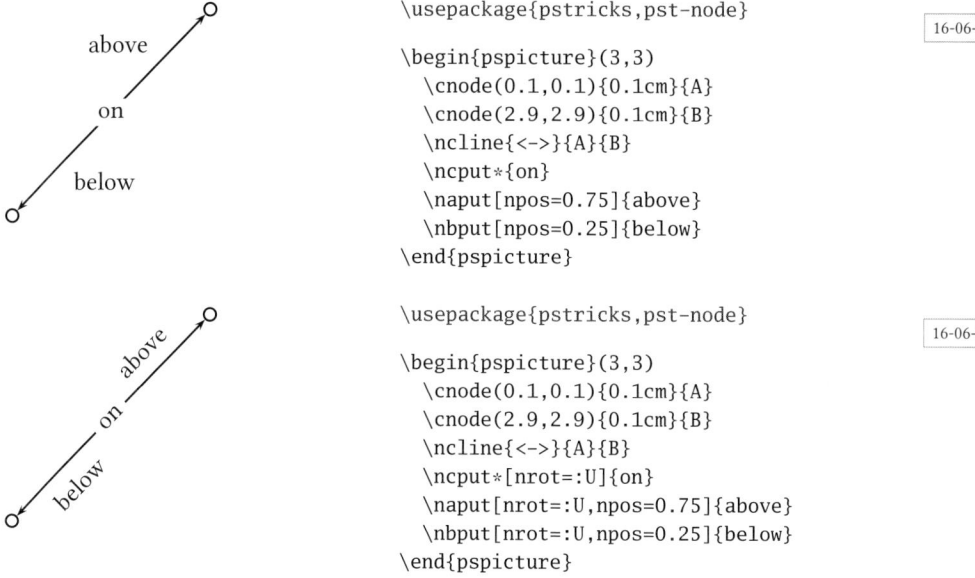

```
\usepackage{pstricks,pst-node}

\begin{pspicture}(3,3)
    \cnode(0.1,0.1){0.1cm}{A}
    \cnode(2.9,2.9){0.1cm}{B}
    \ncline{<->}{A}{B}
    \ncput*{on}
    \naput[npos=0.75]{above}
    \nbput[npos=0.25]{below}
\end{pspicture}
```

```
\usepackage{pstricks,pst-node}

\begin{pspicture}(3,3)
    \cnode(0.1,0.1){0.1cm}{A}
    \cnode(2.9,2.9){0.1cm}{B}
    \ncline{<->}{A}{B}
    \ncput*[nrot=:U]{on}
    \naput[nrot=:U,npos=0.75]{above}
    \nbput[nrot=:U,npos=0.25]{below}
\end{pspicture}
```

Keep in mind that "above" and "below" refer to the default direction of the connection from "left to right". If the nodes are swapped in the last example, "above" and "below" are swapped as well. You could easily correct this by replacing the angle specification :U (up) with :D (down).

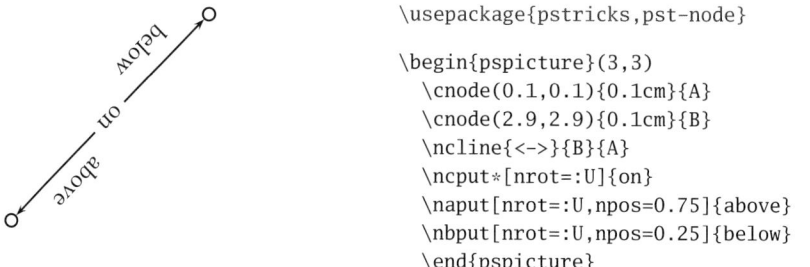

```
\usepackage{pstricks,pst-node}

\begin{pspicture}(3,3)
    \cnode(0.1,0.1){0.1cm}{A}
    \cnode(2.9,2.9){0.1cm}{B}
    \ncline{<->}{B}{A}
    \ncput*[nrot=:U]{on}
    \naput[nrot=:U,npos=0.75]{above}
    \nbput[nrot=:U,npos=0.25]{below}
\end{pspicture}
```

16.6.2 \t label

These commands always refer to the centres of the nodes, independent of which type of connection command has been used. The following example illustrates this difference; \thput places the label nearer the large node than \ncput places the label (as \ncput doesn't take any notice of the radius of the node).

16.6 Label

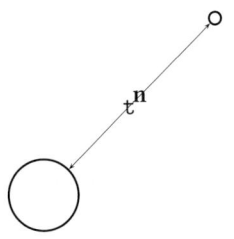

```
\usepackage{pstricks,pst-node}

\begin{pspicture}(3,3)
    \cnode(0.5,0.5){0.5cm}{A}
    \cnode(2.9,2.9){0.1cm}{B}
    \ncline[linewidth=0.1pt]{<->}{A}{B}
    \ncput{\textbf{n}}
    \thput{\texttt{t}}
\end{pspicture}
```

The \t?put commands are primarily meant for trees and commutative diagrams; therefore there are additional left/right commands, and different commands for centring horizontally and vertically.

\tvput * [settings] {material}		\thput * [settings] {material}	
\taput * [settings] {material}		\tbput * [settings] {material}	
\tlput * [settings] {material}		\trput * [settings] {material}	

v means **centred vertically** on the line.
h means **centred horizontally** on the line.
a means **above** the line.
b means **below** the line.
l means **left** of the line.
r means **right** of the line.

The starred versions are not transparent, they allow overwriting the line to make the label more visible. In the next example, the nodes are defined with \Rnode in order to get horizontal connecting lines between nodes of different heights (cf. Section 16.3.2 on page 237).

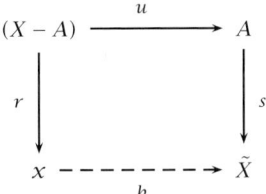

```
\usepackage{pstricks,pst-node}

$\arraycolsep=1.1cm
\begin{array}{@{}cc@{}}
    \Rnode{a}{(X-A)} & \Rnode{b}{A} \\[1.5cm]
    \Rnode{c}{x} & \Rnode{d}{\tilde{X}}
\end{array}
\psset{nodesep=5pt,arrows=->}
\everypsbox{\scriptstyle}
\ncline{a}{c}                       \tlput{r}
\ncline{a}{b}                       \taput{u}
\ncline[linestyle=dashed]{c}{d}  \tbput{b}
\ncline{b}{d}                       \trput{s}$
```

16.6.3 \nput – node labels

\nput is identical to \uput in principle (cf. Section 9.6 on page 106) except that it places a label at a node rather than at a point.

16 pst-node: Nodes and connections

```
\nput [settings] {reference angle}{node name}{material}
\nput* [settings] {reference angle}{node name}{material}
```

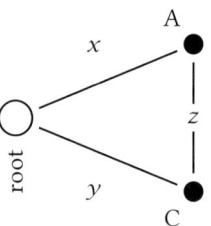

```
\usepackage{pstricks,pst-node}

\cnode(0.5,0){.25cm}{root}
\nput[rot=90]{-90}{root}{root}
\cnode*(3,1){4pt}{A}   \nput{130}{A}{A}
\cnode*(3,-1){4pt}{C}  \nput{-130}{C}{C}
\psset{nodesep=3pt,shortput=nab,labelsep=10pt}
\ncline{root}{A}^{$x$}\ncline{root}{C}_{$y$}
\ncline{A}{C}\ncput*{$z$}
```

16-06-

16.6.4 Obsolete commands

There are a few other commands provided by pst-node for placing labels, which although still supported should not be used anymore:

```
\lput [reference angle] {rotation}(x,y){material}
\Lput{label distance} [reference angle] {rotation}(x,y){material}
\mput [reference angle] {material>}
\Mput{label distance} [reference angle] {material}
\aput [label distance] {rotation angle}(x,y){material}
\Aput [label distance] {material}
\bput [label distance] {rotation angle}(x,y){material}
\Bput [label distance] {material}
```

16.7 Special cases

Sometimes you want to start or end several connections at the same node. With offset, you can easily "separate" two connections of the same type, as in this example:

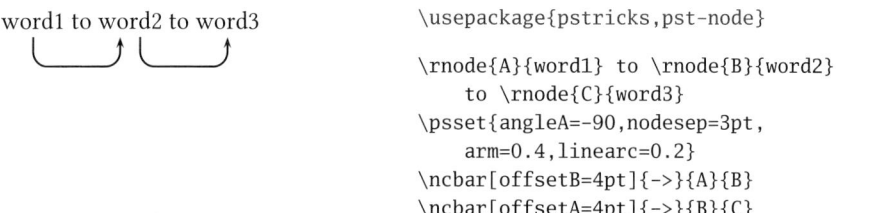

```
\usepackage{pstricks,pst-node}

\rnode{A}{word1} to \rnode{B}{word2}
    to \rnode{C}{word3}
\psset{angleA=-90,nodesep=3pt,
    arm=0.4,linearc=0.2}
\ncbar[offsetB=4pt]{->}{A}{B}
\ncbar[offsetA=4pt]{->}{B}{C}
```

16-07-1

If connections point to two objects that have box frames of different sizes, the connections don't end at the same height, as shown here:

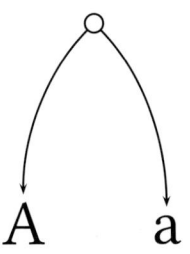

```
\usepackage{pstricks,pst-node}

\begin{pspicture}(-0.5,0)(3,3) \Huge
    \cnode(1,3){4pt}{A}
    \rput[B](0,0){\Rnode{B}{A}}
    \rput[B](2,0){\Rnode{C}{a}}
    \psset{angleA=90,armA=1,nodesepA=3pt}
    \nccurve[angleB=-135]{<-}{B}{A}
    \nccurve[angleB=-45]{<-}{C}{A}
\end{pspicture}
```

Using nodesep doesn't really help here as the difference between small and large letters is not known exactly. However, as the lower nodes are defined with \Rnode, the node centre is relative to the base line (cf. Section 16.3.2 on page 237), so you can specify the same distance to it for both small and large letters. Now you have to choose the equivalent \pc connection instead of the \nc connection so that it refers to the centre of the node. That way you get connections of the same length, as shown here:

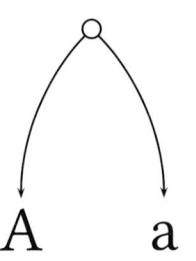

```
\usepackage{pstricks,pst-node}
\SpecialCoor

\begin{pspicture}(3,3)
    \cnode(1,3){4pt}{A}
    \rput[B](0,0){\Rnode[vref=20pt]{B}{\Huge A}}
    \rput[B](2,0){\Rnode[vref=20pt]{C}{\Huge a}}
    \psset{angleA=90,nodesepB=4pt}
    \pccurve[angleB=-135]{<-}(B)(A)
    \pccurve[angleB=-45]{<-}(C)(A)
\end{pspicture}
```

Alternatively you could use the \nc variants in conjunction with the Ynodesep parameter, which determines absolute distances from the centre. This option is shown here:

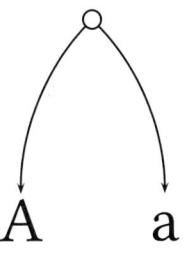

```
\usepackage{pstricks,pst-node}

\begin{pspicture}(-0.5,0)(3.5,3) \Huge
    \cnode(1,3){4pt}{A}
    \rput[B](0,0){\Rnode{B}{A}}
    \rput[B](2,0){\Rnode{C}{a}}
    \psset{angleA=90,YnodesepA=1ex}
    \nccurve[angleB=-135]{<-}{B}{A}
    \nccurve[angleB=-45]{<-}{C}{A}
\end{pspicture}
```

16.8 \psmatrix

We have said before that you can place nodes at any arbitrary position of a document, within text, tables or other objects, with the only caveat being that node connections have to refer to nodes that are defined on the same TeX page. If this requirement is satisfied, even connections from normal text to a floating environment are possible.

This facility for the arbitrary placement of nodes makes it possible to base larger projects on a matrix and refer to individual cells by their row and column numbers. Instead of the node name, {*row,column*} are given. In principle, you could use any `matrix` or `array` environment of (LA)TEX, but the `psmatrix` environment offers the best support.

`\psmatrix` [settings] ... `\endpsmatrix`	% TEX version
`\begin{psmatrix}` [settings] ... `\end{psmatrix}`	% LATEX version

▷ The `\psmatrix` command is based on `array`, but you can use it outside math mode as well. If the cells contain mostly mathematic expressions, `\psmatrix` can also be part of a corresponding environment or command. For normal font, you can use `\mathrm` or `\text` from amsmath.

▷ You can nest the `\psmatrix` command, but make sure that all node connections are made within the depth where the nodes they connect are defined. Every entry can be defined to be a node itself. This can be used to achieve individual styles.

▷ At the beginning of each row, `\psrowhook#` is called and at the beginning of each column `\pscolhook#`; where # stands for the respective row or column number as a Roman numeral, e.g. *vi* for the sixth row or column.

The following sections look at the special parameters for using nodes in a `psmatrix` environment, the multicolumn `\psscancommand`, and the `\psrowhook` and `\pscolhook` commands. Examples are given along the way.

16.8.1 Parameters

Table 16.4 summarizes the parameters you can use with `psmatrix`.

Table 16.4: Summary of the parameters for using nodes with `\psmatrix`

name	type	default
mnode	R|r|C|f|p|circle|Circle|oval|dia|tri|dot|none	R
emnode	R|r|C|f|p|circle|Circle|oval|dia|tri|dot|none	none
name	*name*	
nodealign	boolean	false
mcol	l|r|c	c
rowsep	*value* *unit*	1.5 cm
colsep	*value* *unit*	1.5 cm
mnodesize	*value* *unit*	-1 pt

mnode determines the type of the nodes. You can set it globally for the whole matrix and change it locally for a particular node. The node type specifications are listed in Table 16.5 and refer to the node types dealt with in Section 16.3 on page 236.

16.8 \psmatrix

Table 16.5: Summary of the abbreviations used by mnode for node types

mnode	node type	mnode	node type
R	\Rnode	r	\rnode
C	\Cnode	f	\fnode
p	\pnode	circle	\circlenode
Circle	\Circlenode	oval	\ovalnode
dia	\dianode	tri	\trinode
dot	\dotnode	none	no node

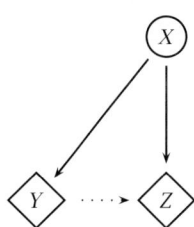

```
\usepackage{pstricks,pst-node}

$\psmatrix[mnode=dia,colsep=1cm]
       & [mnode=circle] X \\
    Y & Z
\endpsmatrix
\psset{nodesep=3pt,arrows=->}
\ncline{1,2}{2,1}
\ncline{1,2}{2,2}
\ncline[linestyle=dotted]{2,1}{2,2}$
```

emnode determines the node type for empty cells. The node type specifications are the same as for , listed in Table 16.5. Again you can set globally for the whole matrix and change it locally, though the latter doesn't make a lot of sense as this would make the cell non-empty. There may be problems with nodes for empty cells, especially in the rightmost columns, as pst-node doesn't work correctly here, as shown in the example below.

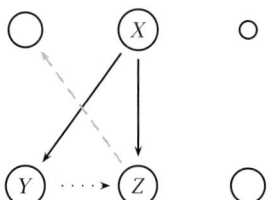

```
\usepackage{pstricks,pst-node}

\psset{linestyle=solid}
$\psmatrix[mnode=circle,emnode=C,colsep=1cm]
       & X & \\
    Y & Z &
\endpsmatrix
\psset{nodesep=3pt,arrows=->}
\ncline{1,2}{2,1} \ncline{1,2}{2,2}
\ncline[linestyle=dotted]{2,1}{2,2}
\ncline[linestyle=dashed,
    linecolor=red]{->}{2,2}{1,1}$
```

name lets you assign a name to a cell. You can then use the node name to make connection rather than specifying the cell's coordinates. Note that the node names (and the assigned coordinates) are valid until they are reassigned, regardless of whether a new \psmatrix is started. The node name **must** be specified at the beginning of a cell, though this can lead to problems if you are using an older package version. If, for example, the following structure is given:

line end

```
    ... & ... & ... \\
[name=K21] & ...
```

it is equivalent to \\[name=K21] for TeX and the [name=K21] is interpreted as optional line feed with a corresponding error message. TO avoid this problem you either have to use a current version of pst-node or terminate the line in one of the following ways:
▷ \\[0pt] or
▷ \\\space

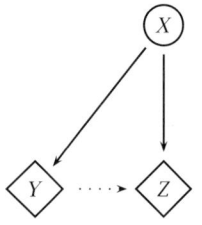

```
\usepackage{pstricks,pst-node}

$ \psmatrix[mnode=dia,colsep=1cm]
    & [mnode=circle,name=X] X \\[0pt]
    [name=Y] Y & [name=Z] Z
  \endpsmatrix
  \psset{nodesep=3pt,arrows=->}
  \ncline{X}{Y}  \ncline{X}{Z}
  \ncline[linestyle=dotted]{Y}{Z} $
```

nodealign The base line of a node is normally the bottom line of the node. Setting nodealign=true changes this to align the centre of the node with the base line instead. Usually this has little effect on \psmatrix because every cell as a whole is de facto the content of the node.

aa **X** bb **X** cc

```
\usepackage{pstricks,pst-node}

aa\rule{1em}{0.5pt}\rnode{X}{\Huge X}%
  \rule{1em}{0.5pt}bb%
\psset{nodealign}%
\rule{1em}{0.5pt}\rnode{X}{\Huge X}%
  \rule{1em}{0.5pt}cc
```

mcol determines horizontal alignment within cells. Again you can set it globally for the whole matrix and change it locally.

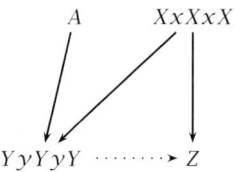

```
\usepackage{pstricks,pst-node}

$ \psmatrix[colsep=1cm,mcol=c]
    [name=A,mcol=r] A & [name=X] XxXxX \\[0pt]
    [name=Y] YyYyY   & [name=Z] Z
  \endpsmatrix
  \psset{nodesep=3pt,arrows=->}
  \ncline{X}{Y} \ncline{X}{Z} \ncline{A}{Y}
  \ncline[linestyle=dotted]{Y}{Z} $
```

rowsep and colsep These parameters correspond to the \arraycolsep and \arraystretch values, and specify the **additional** vertical and horizontal space between individual cells. You can choose any value, including negative ones.

$$ab$$
$$cd$$

```
\usepackage{pstricks,pst-node}

$ \psmatrix[colsep=0pt,rowsep=0pt]
    a & b \\ c & d
  \endpsmatrix $
```

mnodesize Usually the width of a column is determiend by the longest entry it contains, as common with array. However, you can use mnodesize to set all columns to the same width (though if that width isn't sufficient for them all, some columns may still be wider).

```
                                        \usepackage{pstricks,pst-node}
    111      a    bbbb
                                        \psmatrix[colsep=0pt,rowsep=12pt,mnodesize=1cm]
     2       c    ddddd                     111 & a & bbbb \\ 2   & c & ddddd
                                        \endpsmatrix
```

16.8.2 Multicolumn

psmatrix also supports the \multispan command known from TeX and the \multicolumn command known from LaTeX. The syntax is different though:

`\psspan{n}`

n determines the number of the columns to be combined. You must specify \psspan **at the end** of the cell that is to contain the following $n - 1$ cells as well.

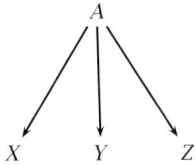

```
                               \usepackage{pstricks,pst-node}
                               $ \psmatrix[colsep=1cm]
                                    [name=A] A \psspan{3} \\[0pt]
                                    [name=X] X  & [name=Y] Y  & [name=Z] Z
                               \endpsmatrix $
                               \psset{nodesep=3pt,arrows=->}
                               \ncline{A}{X}\ncline{A}{Y}\ncline{A}{Z}
```

16.8.3 \psrowhook and \pscolhook

Before opening a psmatrix environment, you can define actions to be performed for a certain row or column before the actual row or column is processed. You assign the action to the individual row or column by appending lowercase **Roman** numerals to the respective command:

`\psrowhook`*row number*`{ ... }`
`\pscolhook`*column number*`{ ... }`

For example, the valid command name for the second row is \psrowhookii and for the eleventh column is \pscolhookxi; the first row and column is i because of the missing Roman zero. Note that there is no inbuilt check as to whether there are that many rows and columns – you must get it right yourself.

```
    A    B    C         \usepackage{pstricks,pst-node}
                        \def\psrowhookii{\huge}
                        \def\pscolhookiii{\green}
    a    b    c
                        \psmatrix[colsep=0.5cm,rowsep=0.5cm]
                            A & B & C \\
    1    2    3             a & b & c \\
                            1 & 2 & 3 \\
                            I & II & \color{blue}III
    I    II   III       \endpsmatrix
```

16 pst-node: Nodes and connections

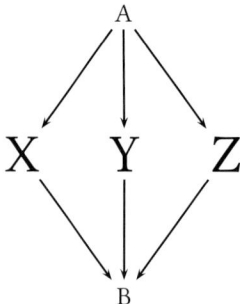

```
\usepackage{pstricks,pst-node}
\def\psrowhookii{\huge}

\psmatrix[colsep=1cm]
    [name=A]A \psspan{3}\\[0pt]
    [name=X] X  & [name=Y] Y  & [name=Z] Z\\
                & [name=B]B
\endpsmatrix
\psset{nodesep=3pt,arrows=->}
\ncline{A}{X} \ncline{A}{Y} \ncline{A}{Z}
\ncline{X}{B} \ncline{Y}{B} \ncline{Z}{B}
```

16-0

16.9 TeX and PostScript

The relationship between TeX and PostScript is quite one-sided; you can pass any information at any time from TeX to PostScript, and every PostScriptspecific piece of information is written into the DVI file as \special. There is no easy way, however, to get information back from PostScript– it's made impossible by the intermediate step from TeX to DVI. One possibility is to write PostScript information to a file and read it when re-running TeX. Alternatively, you can use VTeX, although then you won't be able to compile the TeX document with a different system. VTeX creates a PDF file directly and can return some information through the integrated "distiller" GeX after processing by PostScript.

```
\usepackage{pst-node}
```
Especially when defining nodes such as `\Lcs{cnode}\{3pt\}\{A\}`, `\cnode*{3pt}{A}` the coordinates aren't known explicitly as the nodes appear in the middle of text or are the result of a temporary calculation, but sometimes you do want to know those coordinates. This isn't possible at \TeX{} level as explained before, so we have to fall back on the possibilities that PSTricks offers.

```
\bigskip
\begin{pspicture}[showgrid](1,1)
  \Cnode*[radius=0.1](0.5,0.5){B}
  \makeatletter
  \psline[arrowscale=2,linestyle=dashed]{->}(B)(!%
    tx@NodeDict begin
      /N@B load GetCenter /yB ED /xB ED % centre of node B
      /N@A load GetCenter /yA ED /xA ED % centre of node A
      xA xB sub 0.7 mul xB add \pst@number\psxunit div
      yA yB sub 0.7 mul yB add \pst@number\psyunit div
    end)
  \makeatother
\end{pspicture}
```

16.10 Examples

Especially when defining nodes such as \cnode{3pt}{A}, the coordinates aren't known explicitly as the nodes appear in the middle of text or are the result of a temporary calculation, but sometimes you do want to know those coordinates. This isn't possible at TEX level as explained before, so we have to fall back on the possibilities that PSTricks offers.

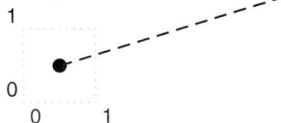

The above example draws a line from the node in the grid (node B) towards the node defined at the beginning of this section that is exactly 0.7 times the distance between the two nodes. As you can see, the arrow points directly towards node A. The example uses the tx@NodeDict dictionary to be able to refer to the corresponding procedures. ED (exchange and define variable) corresponds to exch def and is defined in pstricks.pro. Although this is pure PostScript code, \psline has to be embedded in \makeatletter...\makeatother in the example above because at this point it is still TEX code, which is expanded before passing it on to PostScript.

16.10 Examples

```
\usepackage{pstricks,pst-node}
\def\ncIII#1#2#3#4#5#6#7{
  \ncline[linecolor=#5,linewidth=2pt]{#1}{#2}
  \ncline[linecolor=magenta,offset=2mm,arrows=<-,nodesepA=4mm]{#1}{#2}
  \ncline[linecolor=magenta,offset=-2mm,arrows=->]{#1}{#2}
  \ncline[linecolor=#6,linewidth=2pt]{#1}{#3}
  \ncline[linecolor=magenta,offset=2mm,arrows=<-,nodesepA=4mm]{#1}{#3}
  \ncline[linecolor=magenta,offset=-2mm,arrows=->,nodesepA=4mm]{#1}{#3}
  \ncline[linecolor=#7,linewidth=2pt]{#1}{#4}
  \ncline[linecolor=magenta,offset=2mm,arrows=<-]{#1}{#4}
  \ncline[linecolor=magenta,offset=-2mm,arrows=->,nodesepA=4mm]{#1}{#4}}
\psset{fillstyle=solid,fillcolor=black!30}
\begin{psmatrix}[colsep=0.75cm]
 & & & & & [name=a]\psframebox{\textcolor{red}{\textbf{7}}} \\
 & [name=b]\pscirclebox{7} & & & & [name=c]\pscirclebox{4} & & & &
                                  [name=d]\pscirclebox{1}\\[0pt]
[name=e]\psframebox{9} & [name=f]\psframebox{8} & [name=g]\psframebox{7} & &
[name=h]\psframebox{6} & [name=i]\psframebox{5} & [name=j]\psframebox{4} & &
[name=k]\psframebox{6} & [name=l]\psframebox{5} & [name=m]\psframebox{4}
\end{psmatrix}
\ncIII{a}{b}{c}{d}{cyan}{black}{black}
\ncIII{b}{e}{f}{g}{cyan}{black}{black}
\ncIII{c}{h}{i}{j}{black}{black}{black}
\ncIII{d}{k}{l}{m}{black}{black}{black}
```

16 pst-node: Nodes and connections

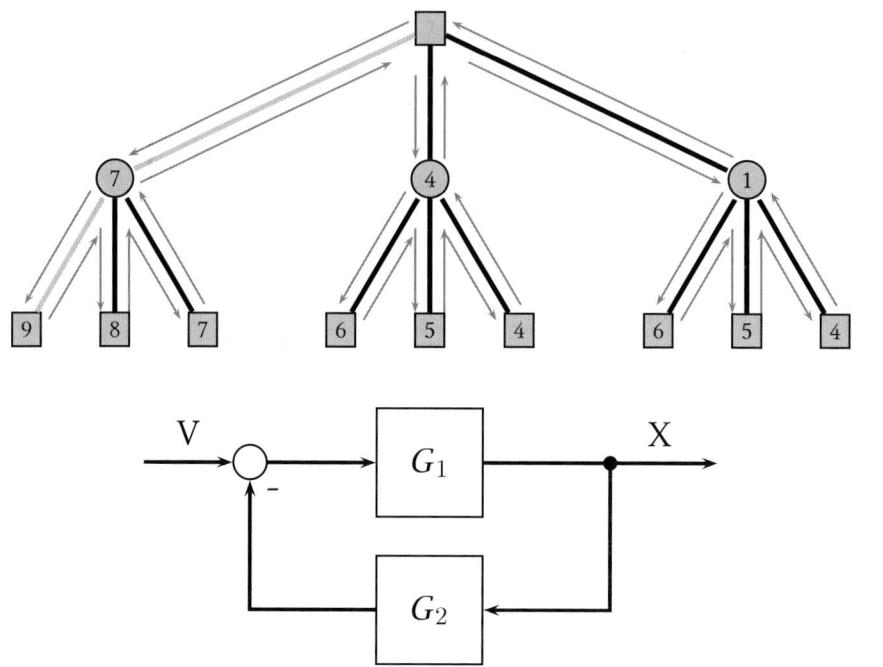

Figure 16.1: Block diagrams

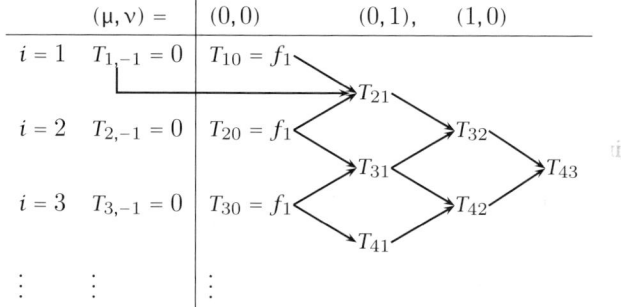

Figure 16.2: Connections within a table

Chapter 17

pst-tree: Trees

17.1 Parameters for tree nodes 266
17.2 Tree nodes 277
17.3 Labels 280
17.4 \skiplevel and \skiplevels 283
17.5 Problems 284
17.6 Examples 284

We've seen that pstricks and pst-node provide commands for drawing frames, circles, ovals, etc. that can then be connected with arbitrary lines. However, for drawing arbitrary trees, there is significantly better support in the pst-tree package, which uses pst-node itself (Chapter 16 on page 225). The basic syntax of a tree is:

\pstree [settings] {root}{children}	% TeX
\psTree [settings] {root} children \endpsTree	% TeX
\begin{psTree} [settings] {root} children \end{psTree}	% LaTeX

As far as the contents are concerned, there is no difference between the two command versions \pstree and \psTree or the psTree environment – the latter is merely the "long" version.[1] Both the commands put the whole tree into a box whose base line intersects the centre of the root (which is on the base line of the current line). Therefore the tree is created top-down. 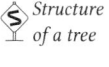 *Structure of a tree*

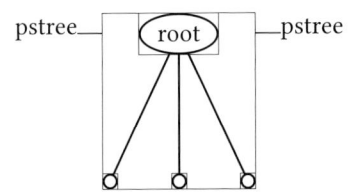

```
\usepackage{pst-tree}

\psset{showbbox=true}%
pstree\rule{1em}{0.5pt}%
\pstree[radius=3pt]{\Toval{root}}{\TC\TC\TC}%
\rule{1em}{0.5pt}pstree
```

---
[1]Commands defined as "long" may also contain paragraphs.

17 pst-tree: Trees

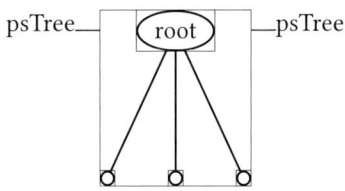

```
\usepackage{pst-tree}

psTree\rule{1em}{0.5pt}%
\psset{showbbox=true}%
\begin{psTree}[radius=3pt]{\Toval{root}}
    \TC\TC\TC
\end{psTree}%
\rule{1em}{0.5pt}psTree
```

If there are difficulties with the vertical line space, you can put the \pstree command or the psTree environment into a pspicture environment or alternatively add extra vertical whitespace with \vspace.

From now on we refer to trees and tree connections as tree objects. A tree's root should be a single tree object; children can be any tree object. Subtrees are created recursively; in this case one of the main tree's children is a new root, as shown in the following example:

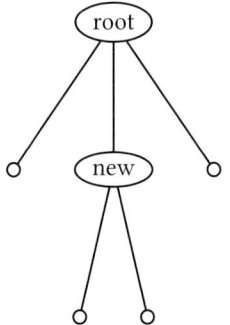

```
\usepackage{pst-tree}

\pstree[radius=3pt]{\Toval{root}}{%
    \TC%                               child 1,1
    \pstree{\Toval{new}}{%             child 1,2 (new root)
        \TC\TC}%                       children 2,1 and 2,2
    \TC%                               child 1,3
}%
```

The example above shows that when creating complex trees, it is a good idea to follow a certain formatting style in the code for visual clarity. Otherwise it is very difficult to detect errors.

The following sections look at the parameters available for drawing trees, and the alternatives for nodes and labels.

17.1 Parameters for tree nodes

Table 17.1 shows a summary of the special parameters valid for pst-tree.

Table 17.1: Summary of the parameters available with pst-tree

name	type	default
fansize	value *unit*	1cm
treemode	D|U|R|L	D
treeflip	boolean	false
treesep	value *unit*	0.75cm

continued...

17.1 Parameters for tree nodes

... continued

name	type	default
thistreesep	value unit	{}
treefit	loose|tight	tight
thistreefit	value unit	{}
treenodesize	value unit	-1pt
thistreenodesize	value unit	{}
levelsep	* value unit	2cm
thislevelsep	* value unit	{}
edge	command	\ncline
showbbox	boolean	false
bbl	value unit	{}
bbr	value unit	{}
bbh	value unit	{}
bbd	value unit	{}
xbbl	value unit	0
xbbr	value unit	0
xbbh	value unit	{}
xbbd	value unit	{}

17.1.1 fansize

You can symbolize bunches of connections with a triangle, the size of the base side of which is determined by fansize. You can modify the triangle with the nodesep (cf. Section 16.2.4 on page 229) and offset parameters (cf. Section 16.2.12 on page 232).

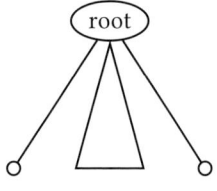

```
\usepackage{pst-tree}

\pstree[radius=3pt]{\Toval{root}}{%
    \TC%
    \Tfan%
    \TC%
}%
```

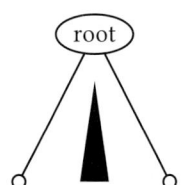

```
\usepackage{pst-tree}

\pstree[radius=3pt]{\Toval{root}}{%
    \TC%
    \Tfan*[fansize=0.4cm,nodesepA=10pt]%
    \TC%
}%
```

17.1.2 treemode

The treemode parameter determines the direction of the main tree or the subtrees as they move from the root to the children: (D)own, (L)eft, (R)ight, or (U)p.

```
\usepackage{pst-tree}
\begin{pspicture}(-0.75,0.25)(0.75,-4.2)
  \pstree{\pstree[treemode=L]{\Toval{root}}{\TC*}}{%
    \pstree[treemode=L]{\Toval{left}}{\TC\TC}%
    \pstree{\Toval{new}}{\TC\TC}%
    \pstree[treemode=R]{\Toval{right}}{%
      \TC%
      \pstree[treemode=U]{\Toval{right}}{\TC*\TC*}%
    }
  }
\end{pspicture}
```

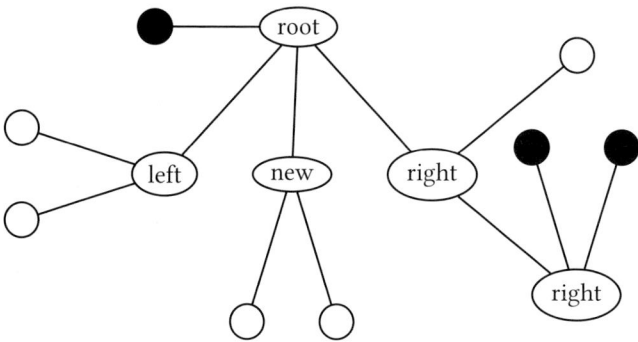

17.1.3 treeflip

Usually all nodes within a single generation are aligned from left to right or from top to bottom. You can reverse this order by setting treeflip=true, either locally or globally. In the second example below, you can tell that the order of the numbered nodes has just been changed locally as the order A-B is the same as in the first example.

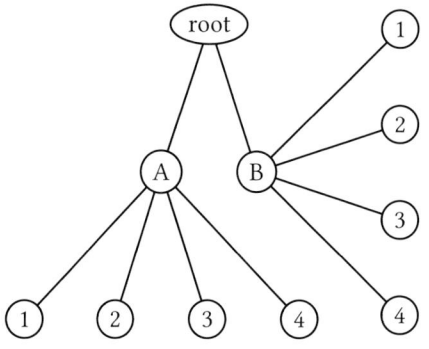

```
\usepackage{pst-tree}

\pstree{\Toval{root}}{%
  \pstree{\Tcircle{A}}{%
    \Tcircle{1}\Tcircle{2}
    \Tcircle{3}\Tcircle{4}
  }%
  \pstree[treemode=R]{\Tcircle{B}}{%
    \Tcircle{1}\Tcircle{2}
    \Tcircle{3}\Tcircle{4}
}}
```

17.1 Parameters for tree nodes

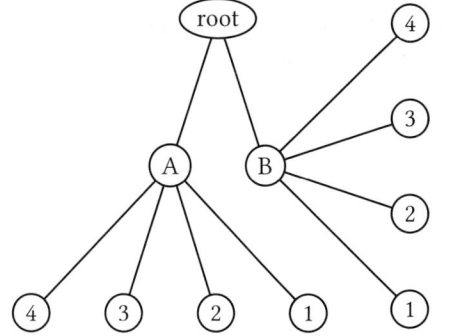

```
\usepackage{pst-tree}

\pstree{\Toval{root}}{%
   \pstree[treeflip=true]{\Tcircle{A}}{%
      \Tcircle{1}\Tcircle{2}
      \Tcircle{3}\Tcircle{4}
   }%
   \pstree[treeflip=true,%
      treemode=R]{\Tcircle{B}}{%
      \Tcircle{1}\Tcircle{2}
      \Tcircle{3}\Tcircle{4}
   }
}
```

17.1.4 treesep and thistreesep

The treesep parameter controls the distance between the tree nodes. This enables you to make a whole tree smaller and narrower, which can be desirable with large tree structures.

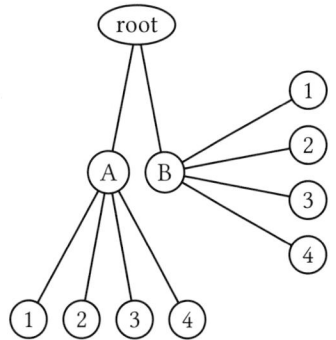

```
\usepackage{pst-tree}

\pstree[treesep=0.2cm]{\Toval{root}}{%
   \pstree{\Tcircle{A}}{%
      \Tcircle{1}\Tcircle{2}
      \Tcircle{3}\Tcircle{4}}%
   \pstree[treemode=R]{\Tcircle{B}}{%
      \Tcircle{1}\Tcircle{2}
      \Tcircle{3}\Tcircle{4}}%
}
```

thistreesep limits the change to a single level.

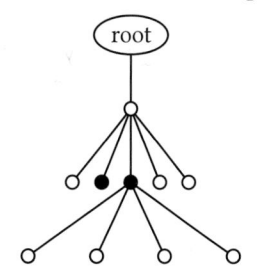

```
\usepackage{pst-tree}

\pstree[levelsep=1cm,
   radius=3pt]{\Toval{root}}{%
   \pstree[thistreesep=0.2cm]{\TC}{%
      \TC\TC*
      \pstree{\TC*}{\TC\TC\TC\TC}%
      \TC\TC
}}
```

17.1.5 treefit and thistreefit

PSTricks determines the distance between the end nodes depending on their contents. We have just discussed that the treesep parameter sets this distance globally or locally; however, you can also tell PSTricks always to increase the distance.

▷ With treefit=tight (default), the minimal distance between nodes at the same level is treesep; greater separation is only used if this is necessary to stop the contents of the nodes from overlapping. The first example below uses this default setting.

269

17 pst-tree: Trees

▷ With `treefit=loose`, the distance between the vertical lines through **all** nodes at all levels is at least equal to `treesep`. This can lead to nodes at a higher level being further apart than nodes at a deeper level, as shown in the second example below.

▷ Note that if **all** nodes are at the same level, there is no difference between `loose` and `tight`.

```
\usepackage{pst-tree}

\pstree[treesep=0.5,radius=3pt]{\Toval{root}}{%
  \pstree{\TC}{%
    \TC*
    \pstree{\TC}{\TC*\TC*\TC*\TC*}%
    \TC*
    \TC*}
}
```

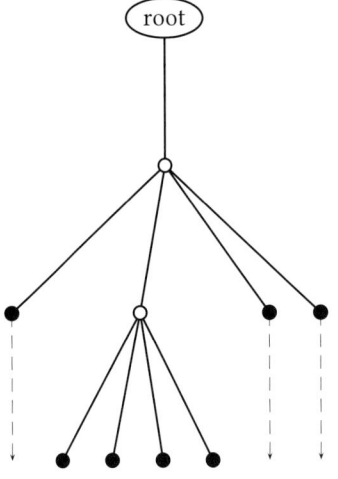

```
\usepackage{pst-tree}
\SpecialCoor

\pstree[treesep=0.5,radius=3pt,%
    treefit=loose]{\Toval{root}}{%
  \pstree{\TC}{%
    \TC*\rnode{A}{}
    \pstree{\TC}{%
      \TC*\TC*\TC*
      \rnode{D}{\TC*}
    }%
    \TC*\rnode{B}{}
    \TC*\rnode{C}{}%
}}
\psset{linestyle=dashed,linewidth=0.2pt,
    arrows=->}
\pcline(A)(A|D)
\pcline(B)(B|D)
\pcline(C)(C|D)
```

You can make changes that are local to a particular subtree by using `thistreefit`:

```
\usepackage{pst-tree}
\pstree[levelsep=1cm,radius=3pt]{\Toval{root}}{%
  \pstree[thistreefit=loose]{\TC}{%
    \TC\TC*
    \pstree{\TC*}{\TC\TC\TC\TC}%
```

```
        \TC\TC}
\pstree[thistreefit=tight]{\TC}{%
        \TC\TC*
        \pstree{\TC*}{\TC\TC\TC\TC}%
        \TC\TC}}
```

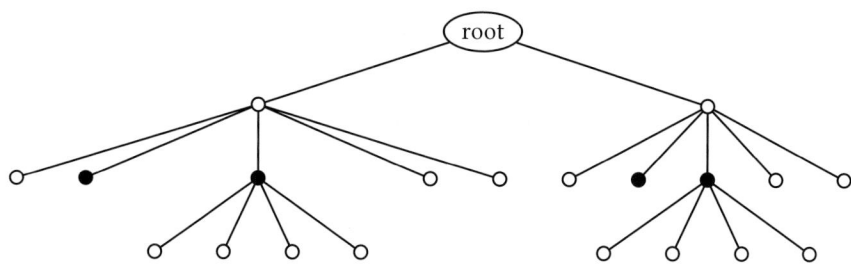

17.1.6 treenodesize and thistreenodesize

If in any particular level there is an odd number of nodes with contents of different widths, the central line of the tree is often not vertical, which doesn't look good. You can use the treenodesize parameter to set the box to a fixed width large enough to contain the contents of the central node (or for horizontal trees, a fixed height and depth) such that the alignment becomes symmetric and the central line vertical (or horizontal). In some cases this method still doesn't yield the desired result; then you have to resort to inserting (positive or negative) whitespace manually with \tspace (cf. Section 17.2.6 on page 279).

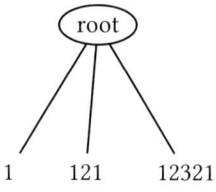

```
\usepackage{pst-tree}

\pstree[nodesepB=4pt]{\Toval{root}}{%
    \TR{1}
    \TR{121}
    \TR{12321}}
```

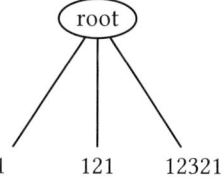

```
\usepackage{pst-tree}

\pstree[nodesepB=4pt,treenodesize=0.3cm]{%
    \Toval{root}}{%
    \TR{1}
    \TR{121}
    \TR{12321}}
```

You can make changes that are local to a particular subtree by using thistreenodesize, for instance the spacing of the nodes in the first subtree of the following example is larger than that of the second subtree.

17 pst-tree: Trees

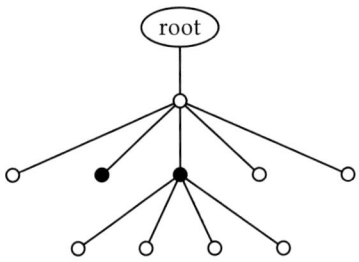

```
\usepackage{pst-tree}

\pstree[levelsep=1cm,radius=3pt]{%
    \Toval{root}}{%
        \pstree[thistreenodesize=0.25cm]{\TC}{%
            \TC\TC*
            \pstree{\TC*}{\TC\TC\TC\TC}%
            \TC\TC}
}
```

17.1.7 levelsep and thislevelsep

The `levelsep` parameter determines the vertical (or horizontal) distance between two levels, with reference to the respective centres of the nodes at each level. However, if the value of the parameter is prefixed with an asterisk, the value measures from the lower edge of the current box to the upper edge of the successor box, which makes the distance within individual levels variable.

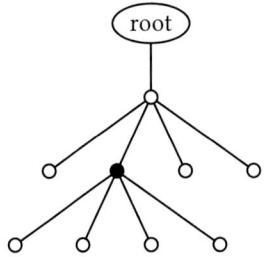

```
\usepackage{pst-tree}

\pstree[levelsep=1cm,radius=3pt]{\Toval{root}}{%
    \pstree{\TC}{%
        \TC
        \pstree{\TC*}{\TC\TC\TC\TC}%
        \TC\TC
}}
```

This parameter is particularly useful for improving the display of horizontal trees. The following example is first of all created with `levelsep=3cm`. The lengths of the lines are not optimal, due to the different lengths of the names.

```
\usepackage{pst-tree}
\SpecialCoor
\psset{nodesep=5pt}
\pstree[treemode=R,levelsep=3cm]{\rnode{A}{}\Tr{\rnode{A}{}Friedrich Wilhelm}}{%
    \pstree{\Tr{Friedrich I.}}{%
        \Tr{\rnode{C}{}Friedrich Wilhelm I.} \Tr{Friedrich}}
    \pstree{\Tr{\rnode{B}{}Albrecht Friedrich}}{%
        \Tr{Wilhelm Heinrich} \Tr{Friedrich}}}
\psset{arrowscale=2,linewidth=0.2pt}
\pcline[linestyle=dashed](A)(A|0,-1)\pcline[linestyle=dashed](B)(B|0,-1)
\pcline[linestyle=dashed](C)(C|0,-1)\pnode(A|0,-0.8){A1}\pnode(B|0,-0.8){A2}
\ncline[arrows=<->]{A1}{A2}\ncput*{\texttt{levelsep}}
\pnode(C|0,-0.8){A3}\ncline[arrows=<->]{A2}{A3}\ncput*{\texttt{levelsep}}
```

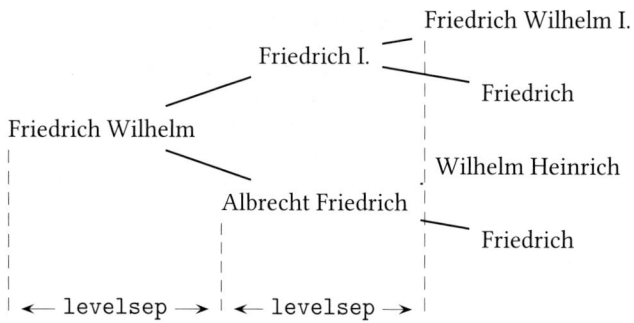

The display is improved by specifying \levelsep=*1cm.

```
\usepackage{pst-tree}
\SpecialCoor
\pstree[treemode=R,levelsep=*1cm]{\Tr{Friedrich Wilhelm\rnode{A}{}}}{%
  \pstree{\Tr{Friedrich I.}}{%
    \Tr{Friedrich Wilhelm I.}
    \Tr{Friedrich}}
  \pstree{\Tr{\rnode{B1}{}Albrecht Friedrich\rnode{C}{}}}{%
    \Tr{\rnode{B2}{}Wilhelm Heinrich}
    \Tr{Friedrich}}}
\psset{arrowscale=2,linewidth=0.2pt}
\pcline[linestyle=dashed](A)(A|0,-1)   \pcline[linestyle=dashed](B1)(B1|0,-1)
\pcline[linestyle=dashed](B2)(B2|0,-1)\pcline[linestyle=dashed](C)(C|0,-1)
\pcline{<->}(A|0,-0.8)(B1|0,-0.8)\ncput*{\footnotesize 1cm}
\pcline{<->}(B2|0,-0.8)(C|0,-0.8)\ncput*{\footnotesize 1cm}
```

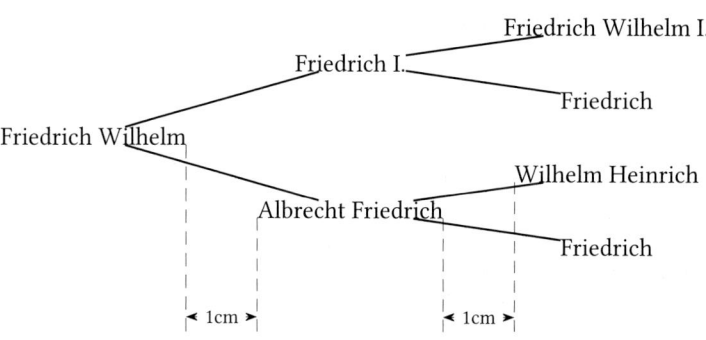

You can make changes that are local to a particular subtree by using thislevelsep.

17 pst-tree: Trees

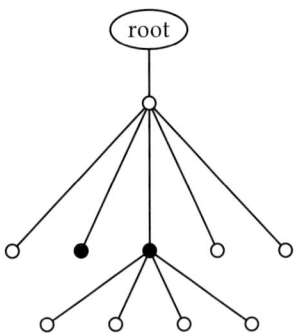

```
\usepackage{pst-tree}

\pstree[levelsep=1cm,radius=3pt]{\Toval{root}}{%
    \pstree[thislevelsep=2cm]{\TC}{%
        \TC\TC*
        \pstree{\TC*}{\TC\TC\TC\TC}%
        \TC\TC}}
```

 Remember that PSTricks needs at least two (LA)TEX runs to determine the right distance. It saves the values of the intermediate calculations in the .aux file (LATEX) or \jobname.tmp.

17.1.8 edge

At the end of any definition of a new tree node, \pssucc (successor) is set to the name of the node just defined and \pspred (predecessor) to the name of the parent node pointing to the new node. This makes it possible to draw an arbitrary line/curve between these two nodes:

    \ncline{\pspred}{\pssucc}

In fact pst-tree defines its own command for this:

    \psedge{\pspred}{\pssucc}

By default, \psedge is identical to \ncline and draws straight lines to connect nodes, but you can easily redefine it, as in the following example where the default is for curves to be drawn instead of lines. You can also use the edge option to change the connection style locally by passing a predefined command as value; this is also illustrated in the following example where a dashed connecting curve is predefined as \psedgeDash and then called locally by edge for nodes 3 and 4.

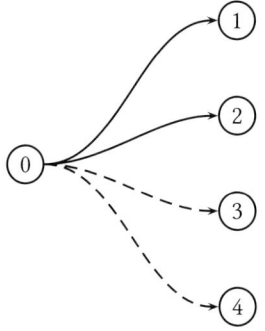

```
\usepackage{pst-tree}
\def\psedge#1#2{%
    \nccurve[angleA=0,angleB=180]{->}{#1}{#2}}
\def\psedgeDash#1#2{%
    \nccurve[angleA=0,angleB=180,%
        linestyle=dashed]{->}{#1}{#2}}

\pstree[treemode=R,levelsep=3cm]{\Tcircle{0}}{%
    \Tcircle{1}
    \Tcircle{2}
    \Tcircle[edge=\psedgeDash]{3}
    \Tcircle[edge=\psedgeDash]{4}}
```

The last example in Section 17.1.7 on page 272 looks better if we use \ncdiagg for the connections (cf. Section 16.4.4 on page 245). Here it is redrawn:

17.1 Parameters for tree nodes

```
\usepackage{pst-tree}
\SpecialCoor
\def\edgeCyan#1#2{\ncdiagg[angleA=180,arm=0pt,nodesep=2pt,linecolor=cyan]{#2}{#1}}
\def\edgeBlue#1#2{\ncdiagg[angleA=180,arm=0pt,nodesep=2pt,linecolor=blue]{#2}{#1}}
\pstree[treemode=R,levelsep=*1cm]{\Tr{Friedrich Wilhelm\rnode{A}{}}}{%
  \pstree{\Tr[edge=\edgeCyan]{Friedrich I.}}{%
    \Tr[edge=\edgeCyan]{Friedrich Wilhelm I.}
    \Tr[edge=\edgeCyan]{Friedrich}}
  \pstree{\Tr[edge=\edgeBlue]{\rnode{B1}{}Albrecht Friedrich\rnode{C}{}}}{%
    \Tr[edge=\edgeBlue]{\rnode{B2}{}Wilhelm Heinrich}
    \Tr[edge=\edgeBlue]{Friedrich}}}
\psset{arrowscale=2,linewidth=0.2pt}
  \pcline[linestyle=dashed](A)(A|0,-1)    \pcline[linestyle=dashed](B1)(B1|0,-1)
  \pcline[linestyle=dashed](B2)(B2|0,-1)\pcline[linestyle=dashed](C)(C|0,-1)
  \psline{<->}(A|0,-0.8)(B1|0,-0.8)       \psline{<->}(B2|0,-0.8)(C|0,-0.8)
```

If you don't want to define commands outside `\pstree`, you can also assign them directly to edge. Note that if the commands have parameters themselves, the whole definition has to be enclosed in {}.

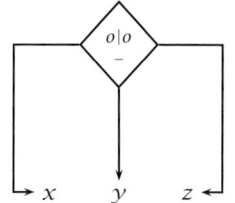

```
\usepackage{pst-tree,amsmath}

\pstree[nodesepB=3pt,arrows=->,levelsep=2cm]{%
  \Tdia{$\substack{o|o\\\_}$}}{%
    \TR[edge={\ncbar[angle=180,armB=0.3cm]}]{$x$}
    \TR{$y$}
    \TR[edge={\ncbar[armB=0.3cm]}]{$z$}}
```

17.1.9 showbbox

Labels are always set independently of the respective box size, which means that sometimes they don't fit inside the normal box. If you are using `\psframebox`, this yields an ugly result, as can be seen in the following example:

17 pst-tree: Trees

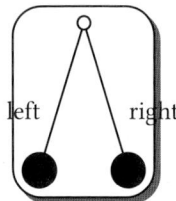

```
\usepackage{pst-tree}

\psshadowbox[framearc=0.4]{%
    \psset{tpos=.6}%
    \pstree{\Tc{3pt}}{%
        \TC*^{left}
        \TC*_{right}}%
}
```

Setting showbbox=true shows the frame of the current box, which then enables you to to correct the problem using the box options shown in the next section with the same example.

17.1.10 bb? and xbb?

As seen in some of the previous examples, it is sometimes difficult to specify the size of the bounding box correctly. pst-tree offers eight parameters altogether for influencing the box surrounding the node; these are in two groups of four based on the following structures:

\bb?   The bounding box is set to the specified values.
\xbb?   The bounding box is enlarged or shrunk by the specified values.
The final character of the parameter name specifies (l)eft, (r)ight, (h)eight, or (d)epth.

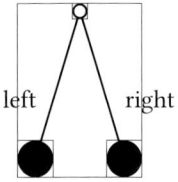

```
\usepackage{pst-tree}

\psset{tpos=.6,showbbox}%
\pstree{\Tc{3pt}}{%
    \TC*^{left}
    \TC*_{right}}
```

```
\usepackage{pst-tree}

\psset{tpos=.6,showbbox}%
\pstree[xbbl=15pt,xbbr=20pt]{\Tc{3pt}}{%
    \TC*^{left}
    \TC*_{right}}
```

With the surrounding box enlarged, you can now use commands like \psshadowbox successfully as well:

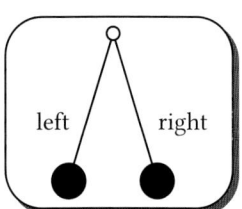

```
\usepackage{pst-tree}

\psshadowbox[fillcolor={[rgb]{1,1,0.8}},
    fillstyle=solid,framearc=0.4]{%
    \psset{tpos=.6}%
    \pstree[xbbl=15pt,xbbr=20pt]{\Tc{3pt}}{%
        \TC*^{left}
        \TC*_{right}%
}}
```

17.2 Tree nodes

There are corresponding commands in pst-tree for most of the node commands introduced in Chapter 16 on page 225; they are summarized in Table 17.2.

A few general differences in their behaviour are described below:

▷ All tree node commands have an optional argument even if the original definition from pst-node doesn't permit one.

▷ Tree node commands don't have an argument for the node name.

▷ Tree node commands are always placed automatically; they can't be specified by coordinates.

▷ You have to set reference points for \Tr through the ref parameter.

Apart from these differences, the behaviour of the commands inherited from pst-node is as expected, so we won't discuss them any further in this chapter. However, there are also a few additional tree node commands, which we cover in the following sections.

Table 17.2: Tree nodes derived from pst-node

name	starred version	long form
\Tp [settings]	yes	\pnode
\Tc [settings] {value unit}	yes	\cnode
\TC [settings]	yes	\Cnode
\Tf [settings]	yes	\fnode
\Tdot [settings]	yes	\dotnode
\Tr [settings] {material}	yes	\rnode
\TR [settings] {material}	yes	\Rnode
\Tcircle [settings] {material}	yes	\circlenode
\TCircle [settings] {material}	yes	\Circlenode
\Toval [settings] {material}	yes	\ovalnode
\Tdia [settings] {material}	yes	\dianode
\Ttri [settings] {material}	yes	\trinode

17.2.1 \TR and \Tr

Figure 17.1 doesn't show the difference between \Tr and \TR clearly. In Section 16.3.2 on page 237 we described the difference between \rnode and \Rnode – the centre of the node is the geometric centre of the box for \rnode and it is the centre of the base line within the box for \Rnode. The same applies to \Tr and \TR, so for vertical tree structures in particular it's better to use \TR to make sure the text is aligned horizontally on the same base line. The next two examples illustrate the different results from using \Tr and \TR:

17 pst-tree: Trees

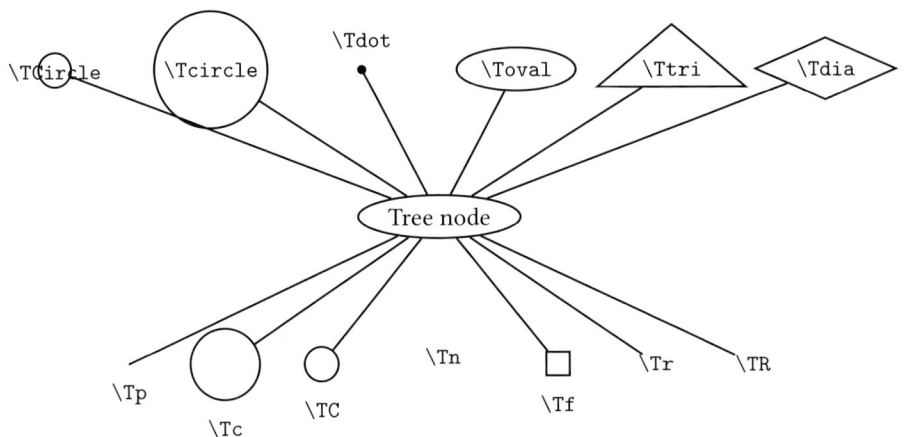

Figure 17.1: Summary of the different tree nodes

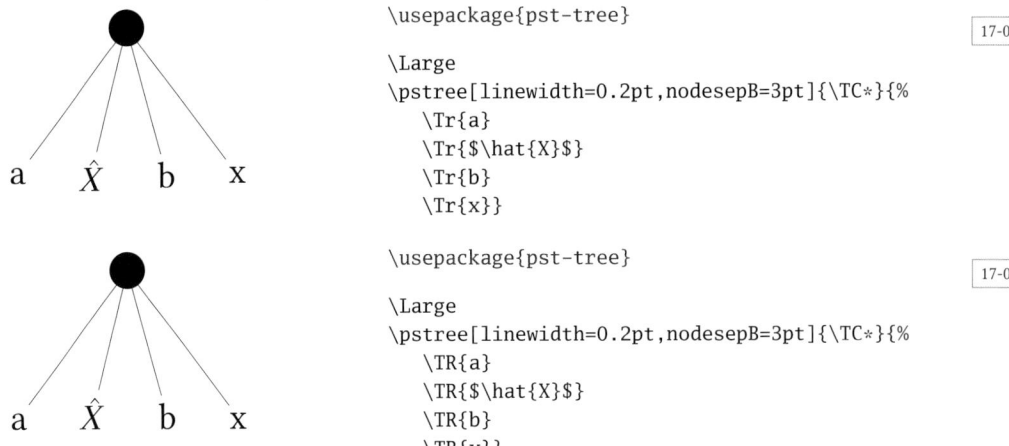

```
\usepackage{pst-tree}

\Large
\pstree[linewidth=0.2pt,nodesepB=3pt]{\TC*}{%
    \Tr{a}
    \Tr{$\hat{X}$}
    \Tr{b}
    \Tr{x}}
```

```
\usepackage{pst-tree}

\Large
\pstree[linewidth=0.2pt,nodesepB=3pt]{\TC*}{%
    \TR{a}
    \TR{$\hat{X}$}
    \TR{b}
    \TR{x}}
```

17.2.2 \Tn – null nodes

If you want to reserve space for a future node or separate groups of nodes, you can use the null node command. It does nothing but claim the space. It has no argument for containing material, but it can be followed by arbitrary material, for example text to be placed at the end of the invisible line. The following example has two empty nodes:

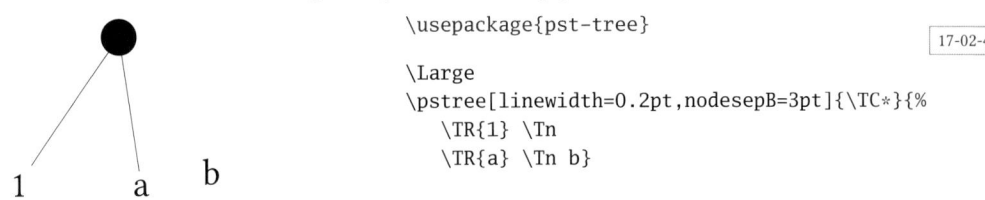

```
\usepackage{pst-tree}

\Large
\pstree[linewidth=0.2pt,nodesepB=3pt]{\TC*}{%
    \TR{1} \Tn
    \TR{a} \Tn b}
```

17.2.3 \Tfan

Another special node command is \Tfan, which you can use for example to symbolize how a tree would be continued if it weren't about to get too large. \Tfan doesn't have any arguments, despite appearances in the following example – the braces are only to separate it from the following commands. \uput refers to the current point, which is set to (0,0) after \Tfan.

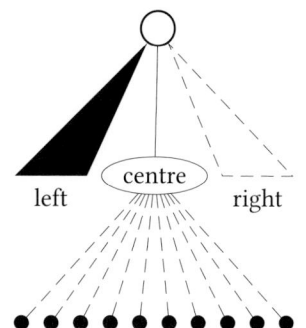

```
\usepackage{pst-tree}

\pstree[treesep=0.2cm,linewidth=0.2pt,%
    radius=3pt]{\TC}{%
  \Tfan*{\uput[-90](0,0){left}}
  \pstree[linestyle=dashed]{\Toval{centre}}{%
    \TC*\TC*\TC*\TC*\TC*\TC*\TC*\TC*\TC*\TC*}
  \Tfan[linestyle=dashed]{\uput[-90](0,0){right}}
}
```

17.2.4 \pssucc

After the definition of a tree node, \pssucc contains the internal name of the new node.

17.2.5 \pspred

After the definition of a tree node, \pspred contains the internal name of the predecessor pointing to the new node.

17.2.6 \tspace

In situations where the methods described previously in this chapter for sorting out spacing issues don't lead to the result you want, you can use \tspace to insert whitespace manually.

`\tspace{value unit}`

```
\usepackage{pst-tree}

\begin{pspicture}(0,0.25)(0.5,-2)
\pstree[nodesepB=4pt]{\Toval{root}}{%
  \TR{1} \tspace{10pt}
  \TR{121} \TR{12321} }
\end{pspicture}
```

17.2.7 \psedge

\psedge has been discussed already in Section 17.1.8 on page 274, with examples illustrating its use. We give the syntax again here for completeness:

`\psedge{nodeA}{nodeB}{connection command}`

You can also define \psedge to be empty if no connecting lines are desired: \def\psedge#1#2{}. The two nodes #1 and #2 default to \pspred and \pssucc.

17.3 Labels

Immediately after defining a node (with the exception of the root), you must create the connecting line from the predecessor to this current node. Because the commands used internally are from pst-node, the coordinates of the two nodes \pssucc and \pspred are still available after the connection is created. Therefore the label commands from pst-node can also be used (cf. Section 16.6 on page 253). This makes it easy to create vertical or horizontal labels, especially with the \t?put variants (cf. Section 16.6.2 on page 254).

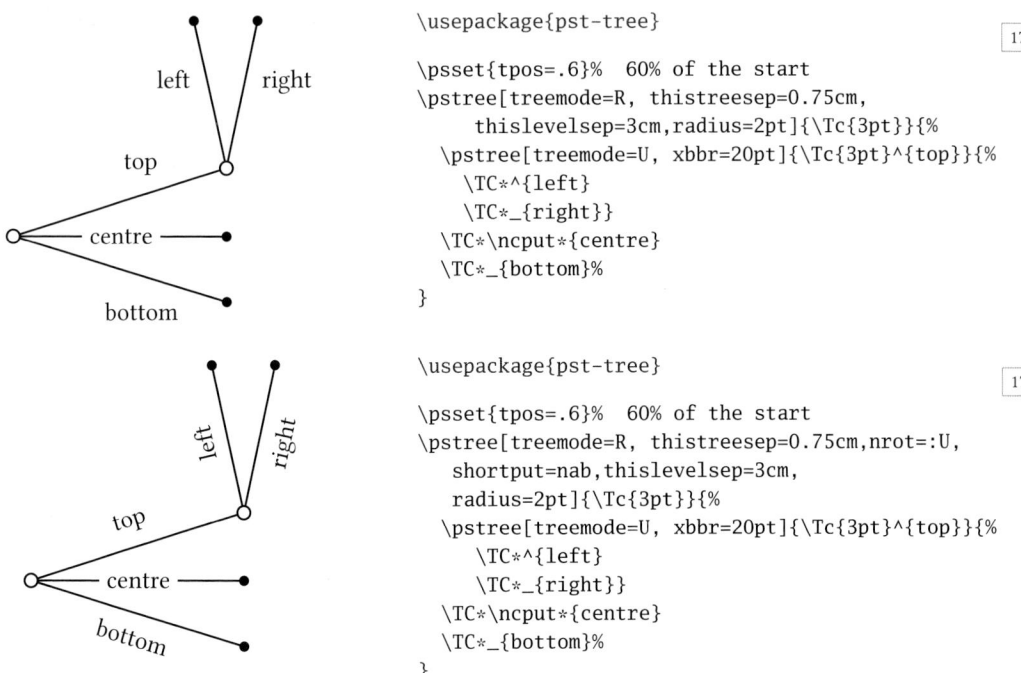

```
\usepackage{pst-tree}

\psset{tpos=.6}%  60% of the start
\pstree[treemode=R, thistreesep=0.75cm,
        thislevelsep=3cm,radius=2pt]{\Tc{3pt}}{%
    \pstree[treemode=U, xbbr=20pt]{\Tc{3pt}^{top}}{%
        \TC*^{left}
        \TC*_{right}}
    \TC*\ncput*{centre}
    \TC*_{bottom}%
}
```

```
\usepackage{pst-tree}

\psset{tpos=.6}%  60% of the start
\pstree[treemode=R, thistreesep=0.75cm,nrot=:U,
        shortput=nab,thislevelsep=3cm,
        radius=2pt]{\Tc{3pt}}{%
    \pstree[treemode=U, xbbr=20pt]{\Tc{3pt}^{top}}{%
        \TC*^{left}
        \TC*_{right}}
    \TC*\ncput*{centre}
    \TC*_{bottom}%
}
```

The \nput command for labelling nodes is available as well (cf. Section 16.6.3 on page 255). In this case the single node referred to is always \pssucc. Additionally, pst-tree defines the following special option:

~ * [settings] {*material*}

In principle this corresponds to \nput, but is meant exclusively for use with tree connections. You can use this short form in combination with other short or long forms without restrictions, placing two labels in a single step, as long as you always remember that the ~ character must be used first after the node command.

The following example shows virtually every possible combination of labels. Here are some notes on the code:

- shortput=nab   Command to substitute the short forms with the \n?put long forms (cf. Section 16.2.18 on page 234).
- nrot=:U   All labels are to appear parallel to the line (cf. Section 16.2.15 on page 233).
- ~{B}^{top}   A combination of label commands: the node is labelled "B" and the connection from the predecessor is labelled "top" above the connecting line.

17.3 Labels

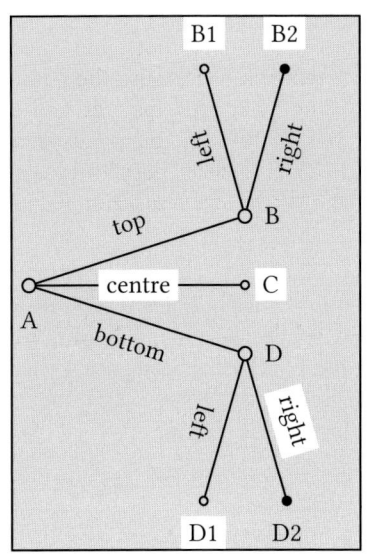

```
\usepackage{pst-tree}

\psset{tpos=.6}%   60% of the start
\psframebox[fillstyle=solid,
    fillcolor=black!15]{%
\pstree[treemode=R,thistreesep=0.7cm,
    shortput=nab,nrot=:U,
    thislevelsep=3cm,
    radius=2pt]{\Tc{3pt}~{A}}{%
\pstree[treemode=U,xbbr=20pt]{%
    \Tc{3pt}~{B}^{top}}{%
        \TC~*{B1}^{left}
        \TC*~*{B2}_{right}}
\TC~*{C}\ncput*{centre}
\pstree[treemode=D,xbbr=20pt]{%
    \Tc{3pt}~{D}_{bottom}}{%
        \TC~*{D1}_{left}
        \TC*~{D2}^*{right}}
}}
```

17.3.1 \MakeShortTnput

Similar to Sections 16.2.18 on page 234 and 16.2.18 on page 235, the special "~" command can be reassigned to be a different character, a longer name, or a command for pst-tree as well.

\MakeShortTnput{*Character/command*}

For example \MakeShortTnput{\tnput} would assign "~" as a short form for \tnput in order to avoid the problems that exist when using the "~" command.

17.3.2 Label parameters

name	type	default
tnpos	l|r|a|b	{}
tnsep	*value unit*	{}
tnheight	*value unit*	\ht\strutbox
tndepth	*value unit*	\dp\strutbox
tnyref	*number*	{}

Table 17.3: Summary of the parameters for labels with pst-tree

Each parameter is discussed in turn in the following sections.

tnpos

The tnpos option aligns labels: (l)eft, (r)ight, (a)bove, or (b)elow.

17 pst-tree: Trees

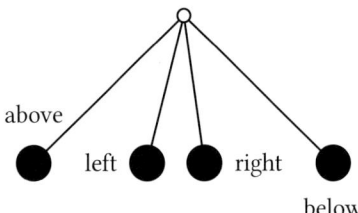

```
\usepackage{pst-tree}

\pstree[treesep=0.3cm]{\Tc{3pt}}{%
    \TC*~[tnpos=a]{above}
    \TC*~[tnpos=l]{left}
    \TC*~[tnpos=r]{right}
    \TC*~[tnpos=b]{below}}
```

tnsep

Usually PSTricks assumes `labelsep` for the distance between the label and the edge of the node. However, setting a value for `tnsep` means PSTricks takes this value instead. By default, the distance is measured from the edge of the node, but if you specify a negative value, the distance is measured from the centre of the node instead.

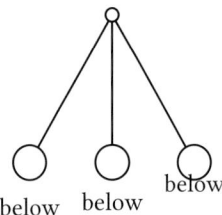

```
\usepackage{pst-tree}

\pstree[treesep=0.3cm]{\Tc{3pt}}{%
    \TC~{below}
    \TC~[tnsep=3pt]{below}
    \TC~[tnsep=-3pt]{below}}
```

tnheight and tndepth

By default, labels are positioned on the same horizontal base line. Sometimes, however, you might want to align them at the nodes. In this case setting `tnheight=0pt` makes the label boxes have no height, but only depth, and therefore all the labels are positioned the same distance from the nodes. `tndepth` works similarly for horizontal trees. The following examples illustrate the effect of `tnheight=0pt`.

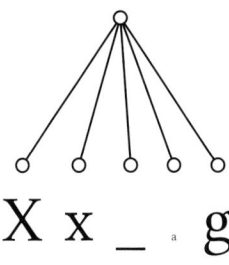

```
\usepackage{pst-tree}

\Huge
\pstree[treesep=0.3cm,
        radius=3pt]{\Tc{3pt}}{%
    \TC~{X}
    \TC~{x}
    \TC~{\_}
    \TC~{\tiny a}
    \TC~{g}
}
```

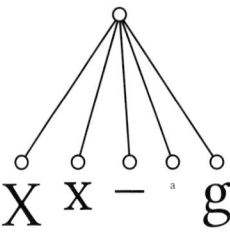

```
\usepackage{pst-tree}

\Huge
\pstree[treesep=0.3cm,radius=3pt,
        tnheight=0pt]{\Tc{3pt}}{%
    \TC~{X}   \TC~{x}   \TC~{\_}
    \TC~{\tiny a}  \TC~{g}
}
```

17.4 \skiplevel and \skiplevels

tnyref
If tnyref is empty (i.e. {}), the vref parameter (cf. Section 16.2.1 on page 227) controls the vertical placement of a label by defining the vertical distance from the base line to the upper edge of the surrounding box. If instead you set 0 <tnyref< 1, this places the label at that relative position along the vref distance.

```
\usepackage{pst-tree}
\psset{treesep=0.5,levelsep=0.75,labelsep=5pt,treenodesize=0.4}
\LARGE
\pstree[treemode=L,angleB=-90,angleA=90]{%
   \pstree[treemode=R,angleA=-90,angleB=90]{\TC*}{
     \TC~{j}\TC~{G}\TC~{X}\TC~{g}\TC~{\_}\TC~{H}}%
}{\TC~{G}\TC~{g}\TC~{j}\TC~{X}\TC~{\_}\TC~{H}}
%
\qquad    \psset{tnyref=0.3}% <-----
\pstree[treemode=L,angleB=-90,angleA=90]{%
   \pstree[treemode=R,angleA=-90,angleB=90]{\TC*}{
     \TC~{j}\TC~{G}\TC~{X}\TC~{g}\TC~{\_}\TC~{H}}%
}{\TC~{G}\TC~{g}\TC~{j}\TC~{X}\TC~{\_}\TC~{H}}
```

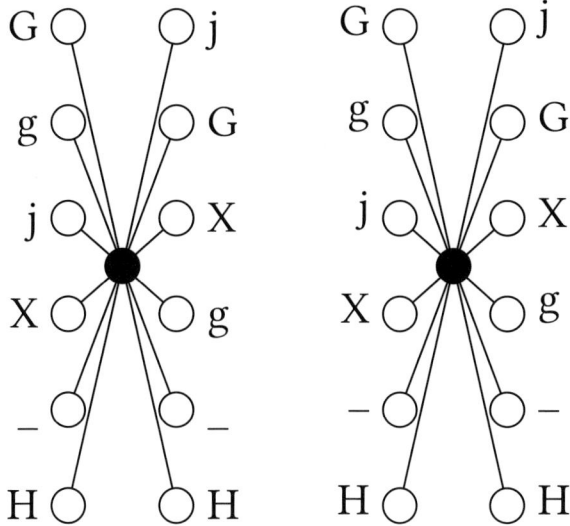

17.4 \skiplevel and \skiplevels

Usually connections are made from one level to the next, but the \skiplevel and \skiplevels commands are handy if you want to skip levels and make connections to the current nodes from the predecessors of their predecessor. The syntax for the commands is:

17 pst-tree: Trees

```
\skiplevel [settings] {node/subtree}   % TeX
\skiplevels [settings] {int}
... node/subtrees...
\endskiplevels                         % TeX

\begin{skiplevels} [settings] {int}
... node/subtrees...
\end{skiplevels}                       % LaTeX
```

\skiplevels is equivalent to nested skiplevel commands; you can use either, depending on which seems most suitable at the time.

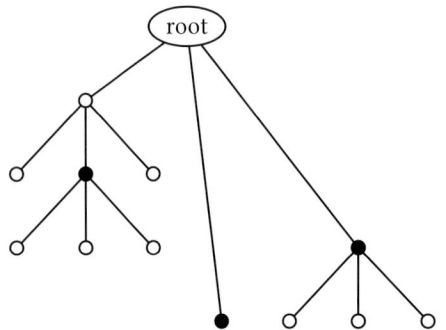

```
\usepackage{pst-tree}

\pstree[levelsep=1cm,radius=3pt]{%
   \Toval{root}}{%
   \pstree{\TC}{%
     \TC
     \pstree{\TC*}{\TC\TC\TC}
     \TC}
   \skiplevels{2}
   \skiplevel{\TC*}
     \pstree{\TC*}{\TC\TC\TC}
   \endskiplevels}
```

17.5 Problems

If you want to draw a single connection with a different type of line, you may find that when you change the parameters they end up referring either to the node as well as the connection or in fact just to the node itself. To separate the parameters for the connection from applying to the node, you have to work with the edge option, which can be used to modify a single connecting line (cf. Section 17.1.8 on page 274).

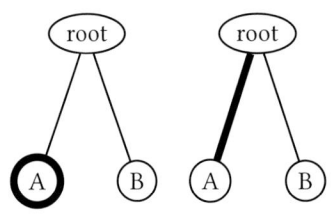

```
\usepackage{pst-tree}

\pstree{\Toval{root}}{%
   \Tcircle[linewidth=3pt]{A}
   \Tcircle{B}}\quad
\def\thickline#1#2{%
   \ncline[linewidth=3pt]{#1}{#2}}
\pstree{\Toval{root}}{%
   \Tcircle[edge=\thickline]{A}
   \Tcircle{B}}
```

17.6 Examples

You can make multi-line labels by using a \parbox or a \shortstack command, as shown in the following example.

```
\usepackage{pst-tree}
\pstree{\Tcircle{P}}{%
  \Tdot~[tnpos=l]{\shortstack{Do\\Nothing}}
  \Tdot~[tnpos=r]{\kern1em\shortstack{Sue\\No Offer\\Pursue Suit}}
  \Tdot~[tnpos=r]{\shortstack{Sue\\No Offer\\Drop Suit}}
  \Tcircle{D}_{\shortstack{Sue\\Offer\\Settlement}}
  \Tdot~[tnpos=r]{Accept}
}
```

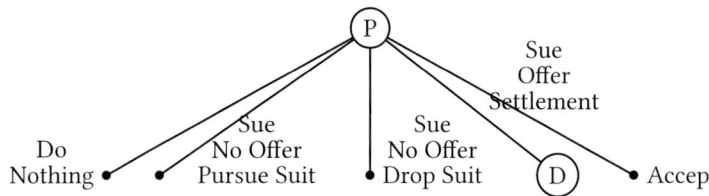

pst-node defines the name option especially for the \psmatrix command, but it is also handy for working with trees as you can use it to assign symbolic names to nodes and then refer to them afterwards. The syntax is shown for the example of the \TC node but is identical for all other node types:

```
\TC[name=node name]
```

```
\usepackage{pst-tree}
\psset{dotsize=4pt}
\pstree[thislevelsep=0,edge=none,levelsep=2.5cm]{\Tn}{%
    \pstree{\TR{Player 1}}{\pstree{\TR{Player 2}}{\TR{Player 3}}}
    \psset{edge=\ncline}
    \pstree{\pstree[treemode=R]{\Tcircle{\Large A}}{\Tdot~{(0,0,0)}^{N}}}{%
      \pstree{\Tcircle[name=A]{\Large B}^{L}}{%
        \Tdot ~{(-10,10.-10)} ^{l}
        \pstree{\Tcircle[name=C]{\Large D} _{r}}{%
          \Tdot ~{(3,8,-4)} ^{c}
          \Tdot ~{(-8,3,4)} _{d}}}
      \pstree{\Tcircle[name=B]{\Large C}_{R}}{%
        \Tdot ~{(10,-10.0)} ^{l}
        \pstree{\Tcircle[name=D]{\Large E}_{r}}{%
          \Tdot ~{(4,8,-3)} ^{c}
          \Tdot ~{(0,-5,0)} _{d}}%
      }%
    }%
}
\psset{linearc=0.3,boxsize=0.5,linestyle=dashed,nodesep=0.4,arcangle=20}
\ncbox[linecolor=red]{A}{B}
\ncarcbox[linecolor=blue]{D}{C}
```

17 pst-tree: Trees

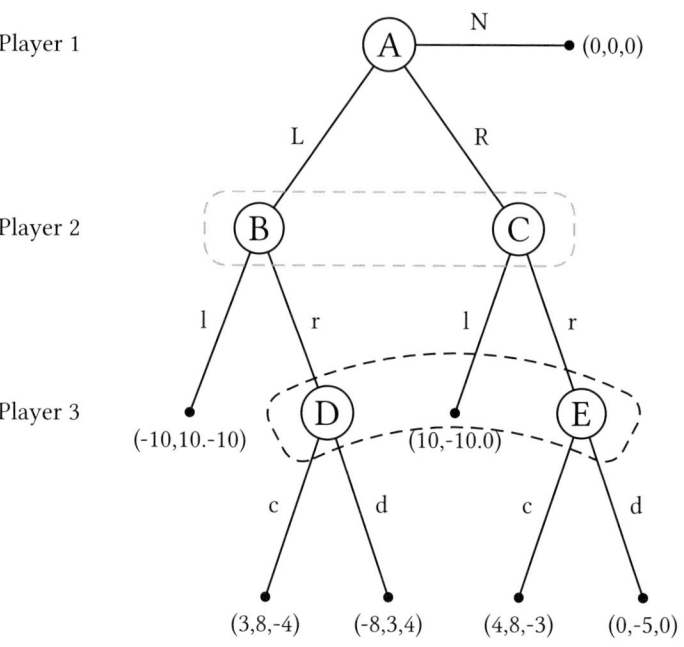

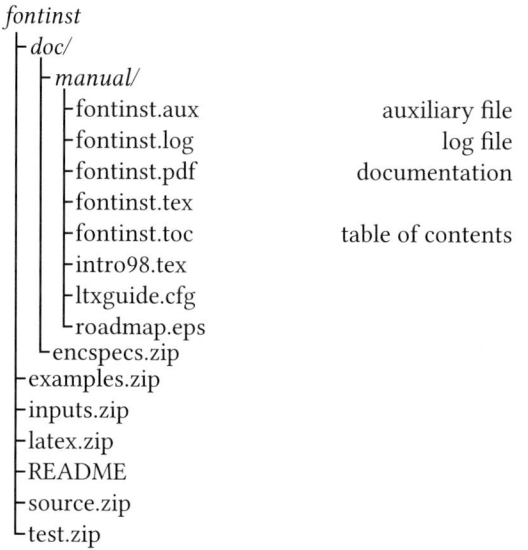

Figure 17.2: List of a file directory (Idea: Walter Schmidt)

Chapter 18

pst-text – Manipulate text and characters

18.1 Text manipulations. 287
18.2 Character manipulations. 290
18.3 Examples 293

In principle PostScript doesn't know lines as such, but only paths, which can have any arbitrary course. If you want to align arbitrary text along such a path, use the pst-text package. As well as providing excellent support for placing text on paths, the package is also useful for other character manipulations, such as making a path from the outlines of multiple characters. Some examples of filling these outline characters are shown at the end of this chapter, though further possibilities are provided by the pst-text package (cf. Chapter 19 on page 295). Note that not every dvi or dvips driver produces the correct results; it is only guaranteed when using Rokicki's dvips programme, which is part of virtually any freely available TEX distribution.

18.1 Text manipulations

The pst-text package defines only a single command in practice.

\pstextpath [position] (x,y){graphics path}{text}

The parameters and arguments are discussed in Table 18.1.

PostScript doesn't reserve any space for the output, which means that the current text is overwritten unless sufficient space is available from TEX. This is not a problem as long as you insert either a vertical space (\vspace) or a pspicture environment.

Table 18.1: Explanation of the parameters and arguments of \pstextpath

option	meaning
position	specifies the alignment of the text referring to the path: l Text starts at the beginning of the path (default). c Text is symmetric to the centre of the path. r Text ends at the end of the path. This option has no effect if the text is longer than the path – in this case the path is filled with text and the rest of the text is omitted.
(x,y)	is an offset and specifies how much the individual characters are to be translated horizontally and vertically relative to the path. (x,y) have to be Cartesian coordinates; the support for special coordinates offered by PSTricks (cf. Chapter 12 on page 139) is not available here. The specifications refer to the current scale. The default is (0,\TPoffset), where \TPoffset is set to a length of −0.7 ex.
graphics path	is any arbitrary object that creates a path.
text	is the text to align along the path. It may only consist of alphanumeric characters – no commands are allowed. However, you can put the text in a \parbox.

```
\usepackage{pstricks,pst-text}

\begin{pspicture}(-2,-2.2)(2,2.2)
    \psset{linewidth=0.2pt}
    \pstextpath[c](0,0){\pscircle{1.8}}%
        {\Large Now we are just writing text in a circle.}
\end{pspicture}
```

18-01-1

This first example shows a relatively simple application of the command. If you don't want the path itself to be drawn, just set the line style to none. The following example shows an application of the offset option. Since the text is written in a circle, a positive value for \TPoffset achieves a translation towards the centre (vertically relative to the path). Note that the angles where the text begins and ends remain the same; this is because every single character is translated separately, with the result that the text becomes more bunched.

```
\usepackage{pstricks,pst-text}

\begin{pspicture}(-2,-2.2)(2,2.2)
    \psset{linewidth=0.2pt}
    \pstextpath[c](0,2ex){\pscircle{1.8}}%
        {\Large Now we are just writing text in a circle.}
\end{pspicture}
```

18-01-2

18.1.1 Examples

With \pscustom (cf. Chapter 11 on page 121), there are unlimited possibilities for a path. The following example again uses a circle, but creates a figure of eight, composed of parts of four circles to get a path without interruptions. In the second example a square is appended to the circle instead. The starting point of the path in both cases is the circle at $0°$, which we have marked with ⇒.

```
\usepackage{pstricks,pst-text}

\psset{unit=0.75,linestyle=none}
\begin{pspicture}(-2,-4)(2,4)
\pstextpath[l](0,0){%
   \pscustom{%
     \psarcn(0,2){2}{0}{-90}\psarc(0,-2){2}{90}{0}
     \psarc(0,-2){2}{0}{90}
     \psarcn(0,2){2}{-90}{0}}}{%
     \large $\Rightarrow$Now we just want to write
     some text in the form of quite a large EIGHT,
     but in the right direction.}
\end{pspicture}
```

In the example above the top circle looks larger than the bottom one, despite them having the same radius. This is because we set an offset of $(0, 0)$ so the text is written above the path, which means it is on the outside of the circle for the top one and on the inside for the bottom one because of the change of direction.

```
\usepackage{pstricks,pst-text}

\begin{pspicture}(-2,-3.25)(2,3.25)
\psset{linestyle=none}
\pstextpath[l](0,0){%
   \pscustom[unit=0.75]{%
     \psarcn(0,2){2}{0}{-90}
     \pspolygon(0,0)(-1.7,0)(-1.7,-3.4)%
        (1.7,-3.4)(1.7,0)(0,0)
     \psarcn(0,2){2}{-90}{0}
   }}{\large $\Rightarrow$Now we just want to write
   some text in the form of quite a large EIGHT,
   but in the right direction.}
\end{pspicture}
```

Placing text along a path consumes a lot of memory and processing power on the PostScript side; even on fast machines it can take a few seconds before results are shown for longer texts. This is the case with the following example:

```
\usepackage{pstricks,pst-text,pst-plot}
```

18 pst-text – Manipulate text and characters

```
\begin{pspicture}(-4.5,-2.5)(4.5,3)   \psset{linestyle=none}
\pstextpath(0,0){%
  \parametricplot[plotstyle=curve,%
    plotpoints=500]{0}{3000}{%
      /r {t 1000 div} def t sin r 1.75 mul mul t cos r mul }}{\TeXt}
\end{pspicture}
```

18-01-

18.2 Character manipulations

As with placing text along paths, when manipulating characters the same caveat about the dvips driver applies that we mentioned in the introduction to this chapter; correct results are only guaranteed when using Rokicki's dvips programme. Furthermore, for character manipulations only the outline fonts of PostScript are supported.

18.2.1 \pscharpath

This command has a similar name as \pstextpath, but a completely different meaning.

\pscharpath * [settings] {*text*}

You can use all PSTricks parameters with this command, though not all of them make sense or have an effect. The text may only contain alphanumeric characters; no commands are possible. Usually it's easiest to define a custom font size before using the command; the best way to do this is with \DeclareFixedFont, which works very quickly as it simply specifies the sizes without searching font tables.

```
\usepackage{pstricks,pst-text,pst-grad}
\DeclareFixedFont{\RM}{T1}{ptm}{b}{n}{2cm}
\pscharpath{\RM TeXnic}\pscharpath[linecolor=lightgray]{\RM TeXnic}\\
\psset{fillstyle=gradient,gradbegin=red,gradend=cyan}
\pscharpath[gradangle=90]{\RM TeXnic}%
\pscharpath[linestyle=none,gradangle=-90]{\RM TeXnic}
```

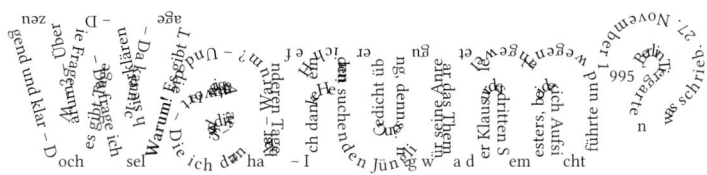

Usually the character path – the outer line of the characters in the example below – is deleted after the \pscharpath command terminates. However, by using the starred version it is saved for use in other things, in this case as a path along which \pstextpath places text.

```
\usepackage{pstricks,pst-text}
\DeclareFixedFont{\SF}{T1}{phv}{b}{n}{2.4cm}
\pstextpath(0,-1ex){\pscharpath*[linestyle=none]{\SF Warum?}}{\scriptsize\TeXt}
```

18.2.2 \pscharclip

\pscharclip is virtually identical to \pscharpath except that the clipping path is set to the current path. This can be used to write "inside" text.

| \pscharclip * [settings] {text}...\endpscharclip | % TEX |
| \begin{pscharclip * } [settings] {text}...\end{pscharclip} | % LATEX |

It is not always easy to get the "base" (or "underlying" text) to align properly; the following example is worked through step by step to show you how to proceed. It's a good idea to put the whole thing within a pspicture* environment, as this gives you unambiguous coordinates to work with and means you can set the environment's dimensions to show only the interesting area. Let's set a font size of 3cm and make the entire image cover the whole width of the page:

```
\begin{pspicture*}(\linewidth,3cm)
...
\end{pspicture*}
```

Now we can place the large text exactly in the centre with a \rput command:

```
\usepackage{pstricks,pst-text}
\DeclareFixedFont{\RM}{T1}{ptm}{b}{n}{3cm}
\begin{pspicture*}[showgrid](\linewidth,3cm)
  \begin{pscharclip}[linewidth=0.1pt]{\rput(0.5\linewidth,1.5){\RM PSTricks}}%
  \end{pscharclip}
\end{pspicture*}
```

18 pst-text – Manipulate text and characters

The underlying text is best created as a `minipage` (of width `\linewidth`) so that it can be moved to arbitrary positions. Because this text is subject to the clipping path, its length is not important as long as it covers the whole area. If the text is to be rotated, you must take care that the whole area remains covered; reducing the width of the `minipage` might help, as done in the example here. In the second example we also rotate the `minipage`, ignore the line colour, and halve the line spacing (using the `setspace` package).

```
\usepackage{pstricks,multido,setspace}
\DeclareFixedFont{\Rm}{T1}{ptm}{m}{n}{2mm}
\begin{pspicture*}[showgrid](\linewidth,3cm)
  \rput{60}(0.5\linewidth,1.5){%
    \begin{minipage}{0.6\linewidth}
      \setstretch{0.5}\color{red}\multido{\i=1+1}{500}{\Rm PSTricks }
    \end{minipage}}
\end{pspicture*}
```

Now both objects can be put on top of each other; because of the clipping path, only the inside of the large characters appears transparent:

```
\usepackage{pstricks,pst-text,multido,setspace}
\DeclareFixedFont{\RM}{T1}{ptm}{b}{n}{3cm}
\DeclareFixedFont{\Rm}{T1}{ptm}{m}{n}{2mm}
\begin{pspicture*}(\linewidth,3cm)
  \begin{pscharclip}[linewidth=0.1pt]{\rput(0.5\linewidth,1.5){\RM PSTricks}}%
    \rput{60}(0.5\linewidth,1.5){%
      \begin{minipage}{0.6\linewidth}
        \setstretch{0.5}\color{red}\multido{\i=1+1}{500}{\Rm PSTricks }
      \end{minipage}}
  \end{pscharclip}
\end{pspicture*}
```

And finally, we can set the clipping path to not be visible:

```
\usepackage{pstricks,pst-text,multido,setspace}
\DeclareFixedFont{\RM}{T1}{ptm}{b}{n}{3cm}\DeclareFixedFont{\Rm}{T1}{ptm}{m}{n}{2mm}
\begin{pspicture*}(\linewidth,3cm)
  \begin{pscharclip}[linewidth=0.1pt,linestyle=none]{%
    \rput(0.5\linewidth,1.5){\RM PSTricks}}%
    \rput{-60}(0.5\linewidth,1.5){\begin{minipage}{0.6\linewidth}
       \setstretch{0.5}\multido{\i=1+1}{500}{\Rm  PSTricks }
     \end{minipage}}
  \end{pscharclip}
\end{pspicture*}
```

18.3 Examples

In principle any text can be subjected to \pscharclip; using a figure can sometimes lead to interesting effects. Alternatively, \pscharpath can be used in conjunction with \psboxfill (cf. Section 19 on page 295) as in the third example below.

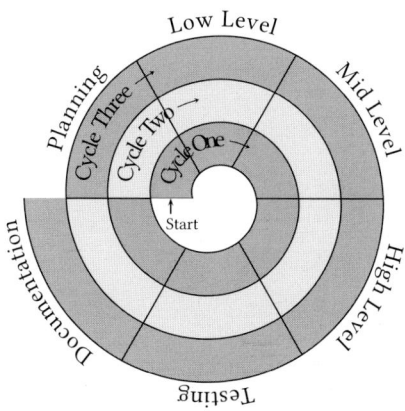

Figure 18.1: Application of the \pstextpath and \parametricplot commands (Ewan Todd)

18 pst-text – Manipulate text and characters

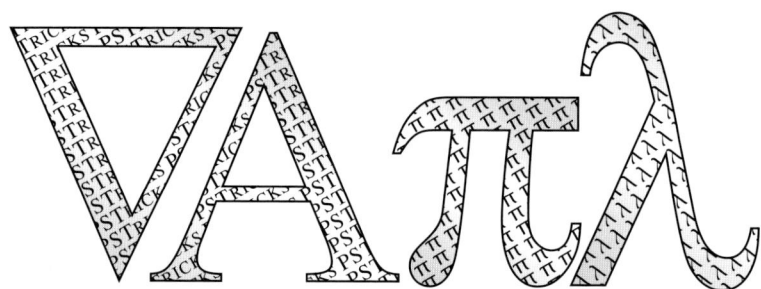

Figure 18.2: Application of the symbol font

Figure 18.3: \pstextpath and \pscharpath

Chapter 19

pst-fill – Filling and tiling

19.1 Parameters 296
19.2 \psboxfill 300
19.3 Examples 300

We discussed some examples for filling outline fonts with the help of the pst-text package in Section 18.2 on page 290, but the best support for filling and tiling is provided by the pst-fill package.

The difference between filling and tiling is that filling covers an area with a colour, a colour pattern, or a picture pattern, without any control of the underlying coordinate system, while tiling takes into account the geometry of the underlying area, so can achieve symmetry for example. Tiling is an age-old topic in mathematics but is not necessarily easy to understand. [72, 75, 27] The pst-fill package doesn't claim to help in all situations. In particular, it is restricted to monohedral tilings, ones created from many repetitions of a single base pattern (or prototile); it can't cope with tilings that are created from several base patterns (n-hedral). However, you can sometimes get round this by first of all using \multido or \multiput (cf. Section 9.5 on page 105) to create an individual base pattern, and then you can create a monohedral tiling from this.

pst-fill has two different modes **manual** and **automatic**. Both fill the whole area starting from a point and clip overlaying parts afterwards.

manual mode To fill an area, the pattern is placed n times and written to the PostScript output correspondingly often.

automatic mode To fill an area, the pattern is placed n times but only written once to the PostScript output. The repetition is done by PostScript itself. Since the information about the point of origin is lost with this method, it can only be used for filling with subsequent clipping, but not for tiling.

In principle there are no reasons to prefer manual mode. You can switch on automatic mode by loading pst-fill with the option tiling or for TeX by defining the \PstTiling command after reading pst-fill.tex.

19 pst-fill – Filling and tiling

```
\usepackage[tiling]{pst-fill}%     LaTeX
\input pstricks.tex%               TeX
\def\PstTiling{true}
```

For most of the examples, we use one of the patterns defined below, unless specified otherwise.

```
\newcommand{\FSquare}{%
  \begin{pspicture}(0.5,0.5)
    \psframe[dimen=middle](0.5,0.5)
  \end{pspicture}}
\newcommand\FHexagon{%
  \begin{pspicture}(0.433,0.375)%
    \pspolygon(0.25;30)(0.25;90)%
      (0.25;150)(0.25;210)(0.25;270)(0.25;330)
  \end{pspicture}}
```

```
\newcommand{\FRectangle}{%
  \begin{pspicture}(0.5,0.75)
    \psframe[dimen=middle](0.5,0.75)
  \end{pspicture}}
```

19.1 Parameters

Table 19.1 shows a summary of the special parameters valid for pst-fill. Each parameter is discussed in turn in the following sections.

Table 19.1: Summary of the special parameters valid for pst-fill

name	type	default
fillangle	angle	0
fillsep[1]	value unit	0 pt
fillsepx[2]	value unit	0 pt
fillsepy[2]	value unit	0pt
fillcycle	value	0
fillcyclex[2]	value	0
fillcycley[2]	value	0
fillmove	value unit	0 pt
fillmovex[2]	value unit	0pt
fillmovey[2]	value unit	0pt
fillsize	auto$\vert\{(x_0,y_0)(x_1,y_1)\}$	auto
fillloopadd[2]	value	0
fillloopaddx[2]	value	0
fillloopaddy[2]	value	0
PstDebug[2]	0$\vert$1	0

---

[1]Without the tiling option the default value is set to 2 pt.
[2]Only available with the tiling option.

19.1.1 fillangle

`fillangle` specifies the angle of the pattern, measured as usual from 0° at the horizontal line.

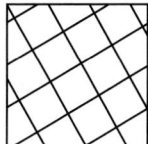

```
\usepackage[tiling]{pst-fill}

\psboxfill{\FSquare}
\begin{pspicture}(2,2)
  \psframe[fillstyle=boxfill,fillangle=30](2,2)
\end{pspicture}
```

19.1.2 fillsep, fillsepx, and fillsepy

`fillsep` specifies the distance between the individual patterns. This can also take negative values, as shown in the following example.

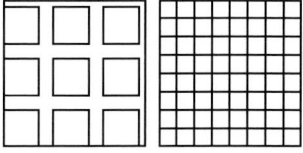

```
\usepackage[tiling]{pst-fill}

\psboxfill{\FSquare}
\begin{pspicture}(2,2)
  \psframe[fillstyle=boxfill,fillsep=0.2cm](2,2)
\end{pspicture}~
\begin{pspicture}(2,2)
  \psframe[fillstyle=boxfill,fillsep=-0.25cm](2,2)
\end{pspicture}
```

`fillsepx` and `fillsepy` are identical to `fillsep` except that they only refer to one side. These parameters are only available in `tiling` mode.

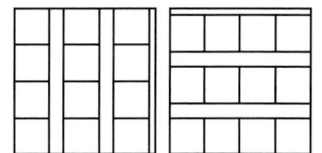

```
\usepackage[tiling]{pst-fill}

\psboxfill{\FSquare}
\begin{pspicture}(2,2)
  \psframe[fillstyle=boxfill,fillsepx=0.2cm](2,2)
\end{pspicture}~
\begin{pspicture}(2,2)
  \psframe[fillstyle=boxfill,fillsepy=0.2cm](2,2)
\end{pspicture}
```

19.1.3 fillcycle, fillcyclex, and fillcycley

`fillcyclex` specifies the distance by which every other row is translated. The specified value becomes the denominator of the fraction that controls the translation. A value of 2 means a translation of $\frac{1}{2} = 0.5$, i.e. a shift of 50% of the width of a pattern to the right. Negative values are also possible. `fillcycley` works similarly for columns, with positive values translating upwards, and `fillcycle` refers to alternate rows and columns. Note that `fillcyclex` and `fillcycley` are only available in `tiling` mode.

19 pst-fill – Filling and tiling

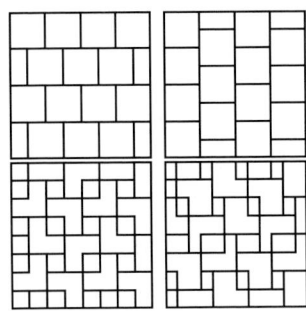

```
\usepackage[tiling]{pst-fill}

\psboxfill{\FSquare}
\begin{pspicture}(2,2)
    \psframe[fillstyle=boxfill,fillcyclex=2](2,2)
\end{pspicture}~
\begin{pspicture}(2,2)
    \psframe[fillstyle=boxfill,fillcycley=2](2,2)
\end{pspicture}\par
\begin{pspicture}(2,2)
    \psframe[fillstyle=boxfill,fillcycle=2](2,2)
\end{pspicture}~
\begin{pspicture}(2,2)
    \psframe[fillstyle=boxfill,fillcyclex=3,
        fillcycley=-2](2,2)
\end{pspicture}
```

19.1.4 fillmove, fillmovex, and fillmovey

fillmove specifies the translation between two consecutive patterns. This is in contrast to fillcycle where every other pattern is translated by the same value. To make this clearer, we use a rectangle as filling pattern in the examples below. fillmovex translates only in the x direction and fillmovey only in the y direction; these parameters are only available in tiling mode. Again, negative values are possible.

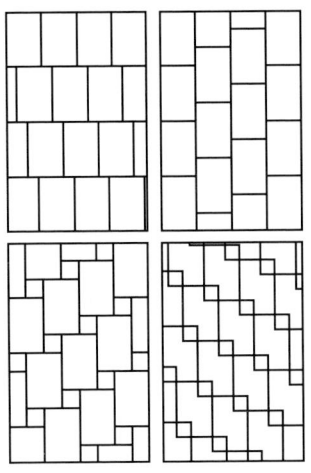

```
\usepackage[tiling]{pst-fill}

\psboxfill{\FRectangle}
\begin{pspicture}(2,3.1)
    \psframe[fillstyle=boxfill,fillmovex=0.15](2,3)
\end{pspicture}~
\begin{pspicture}(2,3.1)
    \psframe[fillstyle=boxfill,fillmovey=0.25](2,3)
\end{pspicture}

\begin{pspicture}(2,3.1)
    \psframe[fillstyle=boxfill,fillmove=0.25](2,3)
\end{pspicture}~
\begin{pspicture}(2,3.1)
    \psframe[fillstyle=boxfill,fillmovex=0.2,
        fillmovey=-0.2](2,3)
\end{pspicture}
```

19.1.5 fillsize

fillsize specifies the type of filling: it is either set to automatic mode, or if manual mode is to be used it is set to the coordinates of the fill area. auto is the default value when you have specified the tiling package option. It tiles an area of (-15cm,-15cm)(15cm,15cm), with the patterns aligned such that they appear symmetric within the visible area. Only in special cases would you want to choose manual mode, for example when using an EPS figure as the pattern. The coordinates defining the area are specified as $(x_0, y_0)(x_1, y_1)$. If only one pair of values is given, (x_0, y_0) is automatically set to $(0,0)$ and the specified value is taken as (x_1, y_1).

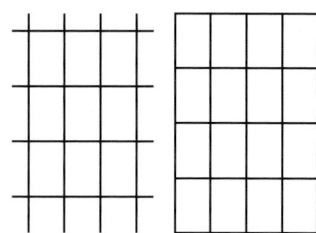

```
\usepackage[tiling]{pst-fill}

\psboxfill{\FRectangle}
\begin{pspicture}(2.1,3.2)
  \psframe[fillstyle=boxfill,
    fillsize={(-0.25,-0.25)(4,4)}](2,3)
\end{pspicture}~
\begin{pspicture}(2.1,3.1)
  \psframe[fillstyle=boxfill](2,3)
\end{pspicture}
```

19.1.6 fillloopadd, fillloopaddx, and fillloopaddy

All of these parameters are only available in tiling mode and only make sense with complex patterns where one or more rows are missing. fillloopadd and its counterparts let you specify how many rows and/or columns are to be added.

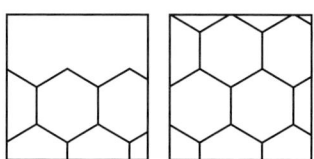

```
\usepackage[tiling]{pst-fill}

\psboxfill{\FHexagon}
\begin{pspicture}(2.1,2.1)
  \psframe[fillstyle=boxfill,fillcyclex=2](2,2)
\end{pspicture}~
\begin{pspicture}(2.1,2.1)
  \psframe[fillstyle=boxfill,
    fillcyclex=2,fillloopaddy=1](2,2)
\end{pspicture}
```

19.1.7 PstDebug

PstDebug is not an actual debugger, but it does show you the process of tiling, which means that problems with special patterns can be sorted out more easily. This parameter is only available in tiling mode. The default setting of PstDebug=0 means that the option is turned off. The following examples are identical to the previous ones except that the additional PstDebug=1 option is used to turn on the option.

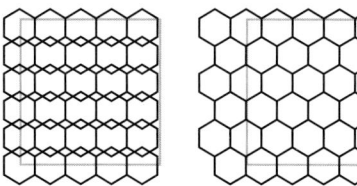

```
\usepackage[tiling]{pst-fill}

\psboxfill{\FHexagon}
\begin{pspicture}(-0.5,-0.5)(2.5,2.5)
  \psframe[linecolor=red,
    fillstyle=boxfill,PstDebug=1](2,2)
\end{pspicture}~
\begin{pspicture}(-0.5,-0.5)(2.5,2.5)
  \psframe[linecolor=red,fillstyle=boxfill,
    fillcyclex=2,PstDebug=1](2,2)
\end{pspicture}
```

19 pst-fill – Filling and tiling

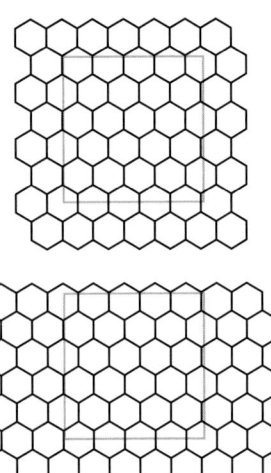

```
\usepackage[tiling]{pst-fill}

\psboxfill{\FHexagon}
\begin{pspicture}(-0.5,-0.5)(2.5,2.5)
  \psframe[linecolor=red,fillstyle=boxfill,
    fillcyclex=2,fillloopaddy=1,PstDebug=1](2,2)
\end{pspicture}\\[5pt]
\begin{pspicture}(-0.5,-0.5)(2.5,2.5)
  \psframe[linecolor=red,fillstyle=boxfill,
    fillcyclex=2,fillloopadd=1,PstDebug=1](2,2)
\end{pspicture}
```

19.2 \psboxfill

In principle, you can give the \psboxfill command anything as its argument, for example a figure that has to be scaled accordingly.

\psboxfill{*object*}

The object is always included again at its original size, however, which means that the PostScript files become very large when the object is an image. You can find further examples in the documentation of the pst-fill package. [20]

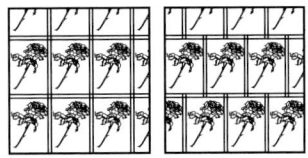

```
\usepackage[tiling]{pst-fill}
\usepackage{graphicx}

\psboxfill{\includegraphics[scale=0.15]{figures/rose}}
\begin{pspicture}(2.1,2.1)
  \psframe[fillstyle=boxfill,fillloopadd=1](2,2)
\end{pspicture}~\begin{pspicture}(2.1,2.1)
  \psframe[fillstyle=boxfill,fillcyclex=2,
    fillloopadd=1](2,2)
\end{pspicture}
```

19.3 Examples

The next example shows how to use the pst-fill package to create the same effect as we created with \pscharclip (cf. Section 18.2.2 on page 291). Again you have to take care to overlap the different objects properly.

```
\usepackage[tiling]{pst-fill}
\usepackage{pst-text}
\DeclareFixedFont{\SF}{T1}{phv}{b}{n}{3.5cm}
\DeclareFixedFont{\Rm}{T1}{ptm}{m}{n}{3mm}
```

19.3 Examples

```
\psboxfill{\Rm PSTricks!}
\begin{pspicture*}(\linewidth,4)
  \rput(\linewidth,2){\pscharpath[linestyle=none,fillstyle=solid,
     addfillstyle=boxfill,fillangle=60,
     fillsep=0.7mm]{\rput(-0.5\linewidth,0){\SF DANTE}}}
\end{pspicture*}
```

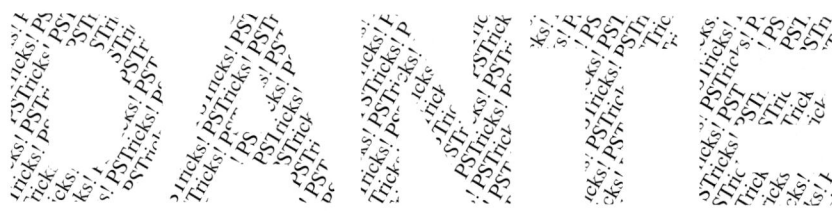

Interesting tilings often arise when playing around with simple base patterns that allow many manipulations because of their symmetry.

```
\usepackage[tiling]{pst-fill}
\usepackage{pst-text}
\FArcL\ \psboxfill{\FArcL}
\begin{pspicture}(2.1,2.1)
  \psframe[fillstyle=boxfill](2,2)
\end{pspicture}
\begin{pspicture}(2.1,2.1)
  \psframe[fillstyle=boxfill,fillcyclex=2](2,2)
\end{pspicture}
\begin{pspicture}(2.1,2.1)
  \psframe[fillstyle=boxfill,fillcyclex=2,fillangle=45](2,2)
\end{pspicture}
```

```
\usepackage[tiling]{pst-fill}
\FArcLW\ \psboxfill{\FArcLW}
\begin{pspicture}(2.1,2.1)
  \psframe[fillstyle=boxfill](2,2)
\end{pspicture}
\begin{pspicture}(2.1,2.1)
  \psframe[fillstyle=boxfill,fillcyclex=4](2,2)
\end{pspicture}~
\begin{pspicture}(2.1,2.1)
  \psframe[fillstyle=boxfill,fillcyclex=2,fillangle=45](2,2)
\end{pspicture}
```

19 pst-fill – Filling and tiling

```
\usepackage[tiling]{pst-fill}
\newcommand\SheepHead[1]{%
  \begin{pspicture}(3,1.5)
    \pscustom[liftpen=2,fillstyle=solid,fillcolor=#1]{
      \pscurve(0.5,-0.2)(0.6,0.5)(0.2,1.3)(0,1.5)(0,1.5)(0.4,1.3)(0.8,1.5)(2.2,1.9)
        (3,1.5)(3,1.5)(3.2,1.3)(3.6,0.5)(3.4,-0.3)(3,0)(2.2,0.4)(0.5,-0.2)}
    \pscircle*(2.65,1.25){0.12\psunit} % Eye
    \psccurve*(3.5,0.3)(3.35,0.45)(3.5,0.6)(3.6,0.4)% Muzzle
    \pscurve(3,0.35)(3.3,0.1)(3.6,0.05)% Mouth
    \pscurve(2.3,1.3)(2.1,1.5)(2.15,1.7)\pscurve(2.1,1.7)(2.35,1.6)(2.45,1.4)
  \end{pspicture}}
\psboxfill{\pspicture(0.25,0.25)\psframe[linecolor=black!15](0.25,0.25)\endpspicture}
\psboxfill{\psset{unit=0.5}\SheepHead{yellow}\SheepHead{cyan}}
\begin{pspicture}(10,5)
  \psframe[fillstyle=boxfill,fillcyclex=2,fillloopadd=1](10,5)
\end{pspicture}
```

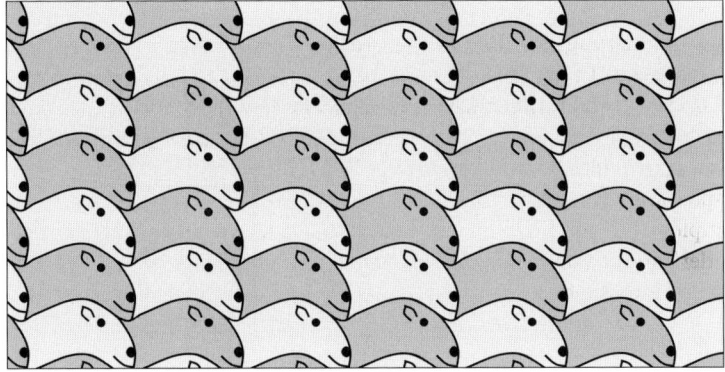

Chapter 20

pst-coil – Coils, springs, and zigzag lines

20.1 Parameters 303
20.2 Commands 309
20.3 Node connections 310
20.4 Examples 312

Coils, springs, and zigzag lines are not the most frequently needed items when creating figures, so the pst-coil package is not widely known. Nevertheless, when these are needed, the package is very useful for creating coil-shaped connections. You can also use these lines for node connections (cf. Chapter 16 on page 225), which is shown at the end of this chapter. The package also provides the \pssin command for drawing sine curves.

This chapter looks first at the package's special parameters and commands, before giving further examples of its application. The parameters for the coil variants in particular are easier to understand if you bear in mind that we are dealing here with three-dimensional helixes projected into the two-dimensional paper plane. This will be explained in more detail as we go on.

20.1 Parameters

Table 20.1 shows a summary of the special parameters valid for pst-coil. Each parameter is then discussed in turn in the following sections.

Table 20.1: Summary of the special parameters valid for pst-coil

name	type	default
coilwidth	value unit	1cm
coilheight	value	1

continued...

20 pst-coil – Coils, springs, and zigzag lines

... continued

name	type	default
coilarm	value unit	0.5cm
coilarmA	value unit	0.5cm
coilarmB	value unit	0.5cm
coilaspect	angle	45
coilinc	angle	45
ppoints	value	360
periods	* * value unit	1
amplitude	value	1
function	PS code	sin

20.1.1 coilwidth

coilwidth specifies the diameter of the coil or the height of a zigzag line. The diameter corresponds to the height for an upright parallel projection across the length.

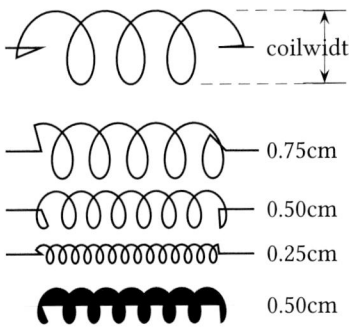

```
\usepackage{pst-coil}

\begin{pspicture}(0,-5)(5,5)
    \pscoil(0,4)(3.5,4)
    \uput*[0](3.5,4){coilwidth}
    \pscoil[coilwidth=0.75cm](0,2.6)(3.6,2.6)
    \uput*[0](3.5,2.6){0.75cm}
    \pscoil[coilwidth=0.5cm](0,1.8)(3.5,1.8)
    \uput*[0](3.5,1.8){0.50cm}
    \pscoil[coilwidth=0.25cm](0,1.2)(3.5,1.2)
    \uput*[0](3.5,1.2){0.25cm}
    \pscoil*[coilwidth=0.5cm](0,0.5)(3.5,0.5)
    \uput*[0](3.5,0.5){0.50cm}
    \Markierung
\end{pspicture}
```

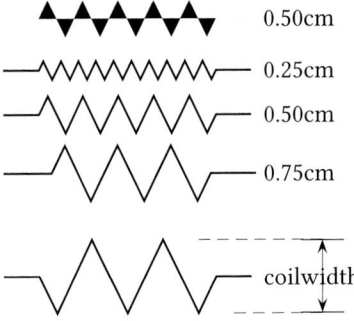

```
\usepackage{pst-coil}

\begin{pspicture}(0,-5)(5,5)
    \pszigzag(0,-4)(3.5,-4)
    \uput*[0](3.5,-4){coilwidth}
    \pszigzag[coilwidth=0.75cm](0,-2.6)(3.6,-2.6)
    \uput*[0](3.5,-2.6){0.75cm}
    \pszigzag[coilwidth=0.5cm](0,-1.8)(3.5,-1.8)
    \uput*[0](3.5,-1.8){0.50cm}
    \pszigzag[coilwidth=0.25cm](0,-1.2)(3.5,-1.2)
    \uput*[0](3.5,-1.2){0.25cm}
    \pszigzag*[coilwidth=0.5cm](0,-0.5)(3.5,-0.5)
    \uput*[0](3.5,-0.5){0.50cm}
    \Markierung
\end{pspicture}
```

20.1.2 coilheight

In contrast to `coilwidth`, `coilheight` is not a length but only a factor, where the distance between two windings or jags is defined as $dx = coilheight \times coilwidth$. This doesn't result in the same physical distance on paper, however, because of the internal three-dimensional representation of the coil; it is not seen directly at $90°$, but from an aspect of $45°$ (cf. Section 20.1.4 on the following page).

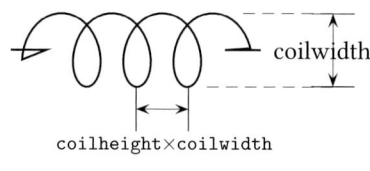

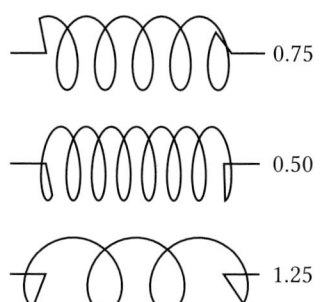

```
\usepackage{pst-coil}

\begin{pspicture}(0,-4)(5,4.5)
\pscoil(0,4)(3.5,4)
\uput*[0](3.5,4){coilwidth}
\pscoil[coilheight=0.75](0,1.5)(3.6,1.5)
\uput*[0](3.5,1.5){0.75}
\pscoil[coilheight=0.5](0,0)(3.5,0)
\uput*[0](3.5,0){0.50}
\pscoil[coilheight=1.25](0,-1.5)(3.5,-1.5)
\uput*[0](3.5,-1.5){1.25}
\pscoil*[coilheight=0.5](0,-3)(3.5,-3)
\uput*[0](3.5,-3){0.50}
\Markierung
\end{pspicture}
```

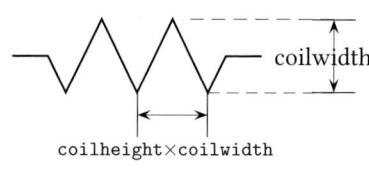

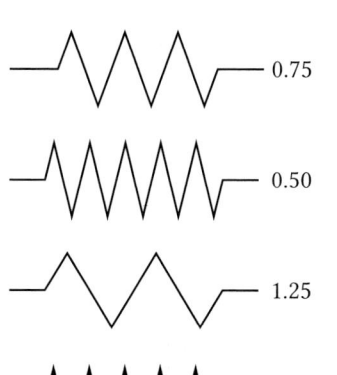

```
\usepackage{pstricks,pst-coil}

\begin{pspicture}(0,-4)(5,4.5)
\pszigzag(0,4)(3.5,4)
\uput*[0](3.5,4){coilwidth}
\pszigzag[coilheight=0.75](0,1.5)(3.6,1.5)
\uput*[0](3.5,1.5){0.75}
\pszigzag[coilheight=0.5](0,0)(3.5,0)
\uput*[0](3.5,0){0.50}
\pszigzag[coilheight=1.25](0,-1.5)(3.5,-1.5)
\uput*[0](3.5,-1.5){1.25}
\pszigzag*[coilheight=0.5](0,-3)(3.5,-3)
\uput*[0](3.5,-3){0.50}
\Markierung
\end{pspicture}
```

20.1.3 `coilarm`, `coilarmA`, and `coilarmB`

`coilarm` specifies the length of the lines added to the left and right. `coilarmA` and `coilarmB` just change the length at the left or right end respectively. Negative values are possible, but usually don't make much sense; the negative value in the example below extends the line back to the specified starting point or endpoint, i.e. gives the line a negative "direction". Note that this parameter is not available for `\psCoil` (cf. Section 20.2.2 on page 310).

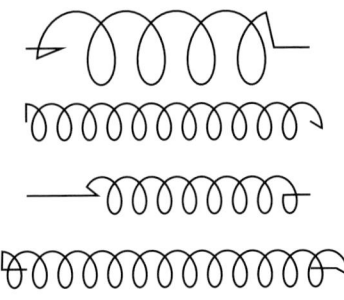

```
\usepackage{pstricks,pst-coil}

\begin{pspicture}(4,4.5)
\pscoil(0,4)(4,4)
\psset{coilwidth=0.5}
\pscoil[coilarm=0](0,3)(4,3)
\pscoil[coilarmA=1cm,coilarmB=0.2cm](0,2)(4,2)
\pscoil[coilarm=-10pt](0,1)(4,1)
\end{pspicture}
```

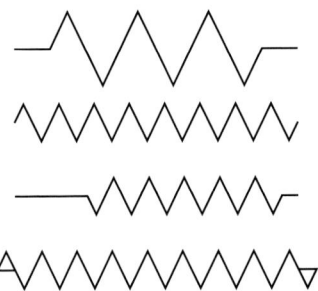

```
\usepackage{pstricks,pst-coil}

\begin{pspicture}(0,0.5)(4,4)
\pszigzag(0,4)(4,4)
\psset{coilwidth=0.5}
\pszigzag[coilarm=0](0,3)(4,3)
\pszigzag[coilarmA=1cm,coilarmB=0.2cm](0,2)(4,2)
\pszigzag[coilarm=-10pt](0,1)(4,1)
\end{pspicture}
```

20.1.4 `coilaspect`

In Section 20.1.2 on the preceding page we already mentioned the three-dimensional representation of the coil. If you were to look at a coil at an angle perpendicular to its centre-line, you would not see the windings at all. Therefore, the default "viewing angle" is $45°$, but you can change this with `coilaspect`. `coilaspect=0` yields a sine curve. Note that this parameter is only available for the coil variants.

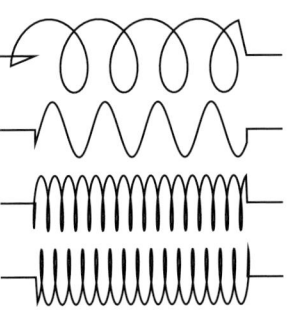

```
\usepackage{pstricks,pst-coil}

\begin{pspicture}(4,4.5)
\pscoil(0,4)(4,4)
\psset{coilwidth=0.75}
\pscoil[coilaspect=0](0,3)(4,3)
\pscoil[coilaspect=30,coilheight=0.3](0,2)(4,2)
\pscoil[coilaspect=-30,coilheight=0.3](0,1)(4,1)
\end{pspicture}
```

20.1.5 coilinc

The curve is drawn with the `lineto` procedure of PostScript, where `coilinc` specifies the rotation angle after which the next point is calculated in degrees. We have already mentioned that the calculation happens as a three-dimensional spiral and it is only projected onto the two-dimensional plane at the end. Large angles of `coilinc` yield a polyline, whereas small angles produce a harmonic curve – at the expense of increased processing requirements. `coilinc` makes no sense for zigzag lines; this parameter is only available for the `coil` variants.

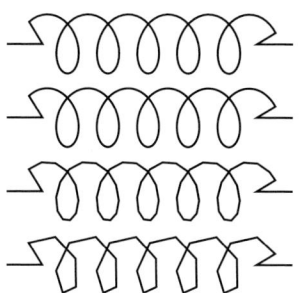

```
\usepackage{pstricks,pst-coil}

\begin{pspicture}(4,4.5)
\psset{coilwidth=0.8}
\pscoil(0,4)(4,4)
\psset{coilinc=0}
\pscoil[coilinc=5](0,3)(4,3)
\pscoil[coilinc=30](0,2)(4,2)
\pscoil[coilinc=60](0,1)(4,1)
\end{pspicture}
```

20.1.6 ppoints

By default the connection between the starting point and endpoint is divided into 360 segments. `ppoints` lets you change the number of segments, which is useful for long distances where you should specify a large number.

```
\usepackage{pst-coil}

\begin{pspicture}(5,2)
\pssin[ppoints=2000,
    periods=30](0,1)(5,1)
\end{pspicture}
```

20.1.7 periods

A curve from point A to point B is by default one period, which is of a relative period length `periods=1`. With a setting of `periods=3.3`, a curve is drawn with 3.3 periods for the same length.

```
\usepackage{pst-coil}

\begin{pspicture}(5,2)
\pssin[linecolor=blue](0,1)(5,1)
\pssin[periods=3.3](0,1)(5,1)
\end{pspicture}
```

The value of `periods` is taken as a relative value if no unit is specified and otherwise as an absolute value.

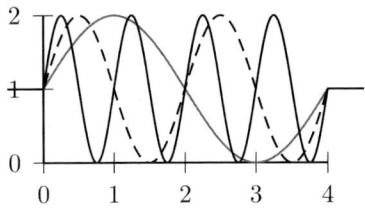

```
\usepackage{pst-plot,pst-coil}

\begin{pspicture}(5,2)
\psaxes(5mm,0)(4.5,2)
\psset{coilarm=5mm}
\pssin[linecolor=blue](0,1)(5,1)
\pssin[periods=1cm](0,1)(5,1)
\pssin[periods=2cm,linestyle=dashed](0,1)(5,1)
\end{pspicture}
```

If an absolute value of periods is preceded by a star, the value is truncated to get an even number of periods.

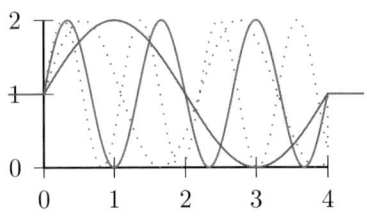

```
\usepackage{pst-plot,pst-coil}

\begin{pspicture}(5,2)
\psset{coilarm=5mm}
\psaxes(5mm,0)(4.5,2)
\pssin[periods=1.1cm,linestyle=dotted,
    linecolor=red](0,1)(5,1)
\pssin[periods=*1.1cm,linecolor=red](0,1)(5,1)
\pssin[periods=2.2cm,linestyle=dotted,
    linecolor=blue](0,1)(5,1)
\pssin[periods=*2.2cm,linecolor=blue](0,1)(5,1)
\end{pspicture}
```

If an absolute value of periods is preceded by two stars, the value is rounded to the closest value up or down that gives an even number of periods.

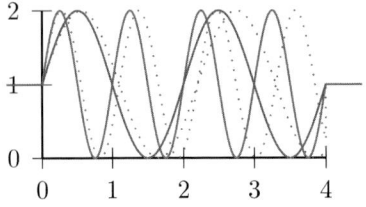

```
\usepackage{pst-plot,pst-coil}

\begin{pspicture}(5,2)
\psset{coilarm=5mm}
\psaxes(5mm,0)(4.5,2)
\pssin[periods=1.1cm,linestyle=dotted,
    linecolor=red](0,1)(5,1)
\pssin[periods=**1.1cm,linecolor=red](0,1)(5,1)
\pssin[periods=2.2cm,linestyle=dotted,
    linecolor=blue](0,1)(5,1)
\pssin[periods=**2.2cm,linecolor=blue](0,1)(5,1)
\end{pspicture}
```

20.1.8 amplitude

The amplitude of the sine curve is preset to \psyunit, but you can change this with amplitude. This parameter is only valid with the \pssin command.

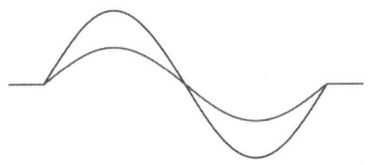

```
\usepackage{pst-coil}

\begin{pspicture}(5,2)
\pssin[linecolor=blue](0,1)(5,1)
\pssin[amplitude=0.5,
    linecolor=red](0,1)(5,1)
\end{pspicture}
```

20.1.9 function

When using the \pssin command, a sine curve $y = sin(x)$ is drawn by default as the connection between the two points. However, you can use the function parameter to specify any periodic function as the connection. The function has to be defined in PostScript notation (cf. Section 15.3 on page 203) with an x value ready on top of the stack. In the following example we use the function $y = cos(x \times \sin(x))$ together with the default sine curve.

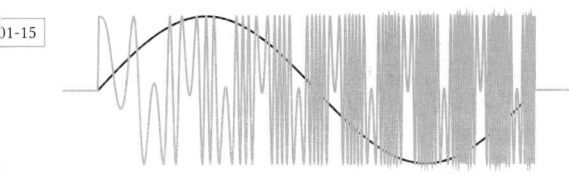

```
\usepackage{pst-coil}

\begin{pspicture}(\linewidth,2)
\pssin[linecolor=blue](0,1)(\linewidth,1)
\pssin[function=dup sin mul cos,
    linecolor=red,ppoints=10000,
    periods=6](0,1)(\linewidth,1)
\end{pspicture}
```

20.2 Commands

pst-coil defines four commands for the creation of coils or zigzag lines.

| \pscoil * [settings] {arrows} (x_0,y_0) (x_1,y_1) |
| \psCoil * [settings] {angle1}{angle2} |
| \pszigzag * [settings] {arrows} (x_0,y_0) (x_1,y_1) |
| \pssin * [settings] {arrows} (x_0,y_0) (x_1,y_1) |

If only one coordinate pair is given, the first point is automatically assumed to be the coordinate origin $(0,0)$. You can specify arrows either with the dedicated parameter or with the optional parameter arrows=*arrows* (cf. Chapter 8 on page 91). For \psCoil, the coils are always drawn without "arms". The starred versions fill the coil or zigzag, but this is fairly meaningless; there were a few examples in Section 20.1 on page 303.

20.2.1 \pscoil

\pscoil is in fact just a polyline with very small segments, so you can use all the usual parameters for lines (cf. Chapter 4 on page 43).

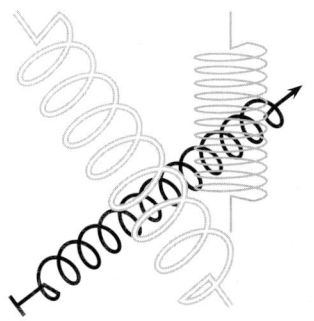

```
\usepackage{pstricks,pst-coil}

\begin{pspicture}(4,4)
\pscoil[coilarm=.5cm,linewidth=1.5pt,
    coilwidth=.5cm]{|->}(4,3)
\pscoil[linecolor=red,
    coilheight=0.25](3,4)(3,1)
\pscoil[doubleline=true,linecolor=cyan,
    coilheight=0.75](0,4)(3,0)
\end{pspicture}
```

20.2.2 \psCoil

\psCoil requires two angles as its arguments; these angles are measured along the coil with one winding equal to an angle of 360. The command draws an invisible coil from the current point to {*angle1*} and then draws the real coil from {*angle1*} to {*angle2*}. This means that you can specify exactly how many windings are drawn. You have to work inside an \rput command (cf. Section 9.4 on page 105) to place the coil at a particular position.

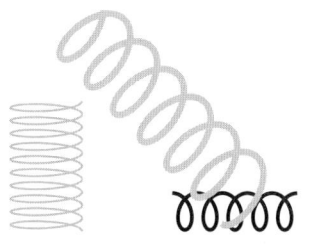

```
\usepackage{pstricks,pst-coil}

\begin{pspicture}(4,3)
\rput{-90}(0,1.5){\psCoil[linecolor=red,
    coilheight=0.25]{0}{3600}}
\psCoil[linewidth=1.5pt,coilwidth=.5cm]{1800}{3600}
\rput{-45}(0,3){\psCoil[doubleline=true,
    linecolor=cyan,coilheight=0.75]{400}{2700}}
\end{pspicture}
```

20.2.3 \pszigzag

The \pszigzag command is the "two-dimensional" variant and therefore its application is much simpler. The linearc option (cf. Section 4.1.12 on page 50) can yield good results for \pszigzag. A zigzag always starts and ends at its geometric centre, so any coilarm specification for the lengths of the arms is not an absolute one.

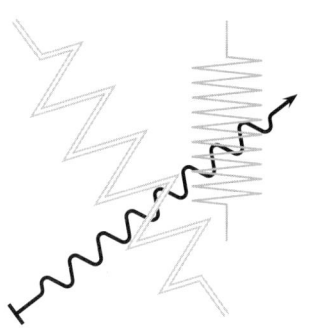

```
\usepackage{pstricks,pst-coil}

\begin{pspicture}(4,4)
\pszigzag[coilarm=.5cm,linewidth=1.5pt,
    coilwidth=.5cm,linearc=0.08]{|->}(4,3)
\pszigzag[linecolor=red,
    coilheight=0.2](3,4)(3,1)
\pszigzag[doubleline=true,
    linecolor=cyan,coilheight=0.75](0,4)(3,0)
\end{pspicture}
```

20.2.4 \pssin

The \pssin command creates sine curves; examples of its use have already been covered in the preceding sections that dealt with its parameters.

20.3 Node connections

If both the pst-node package (cf. Chapter 16 on page 225) and the pst-coil package are loaded, four special commands for node connections are available. These are prefixed \nc or \pc in the style familiar from pst-node. The syntax is:

20.3 Node connections

```
\nccoil  * [settings]  {arrows}  {nodeA}{nodeB}
\nczigzag * [settings]  {arrows}  {nodeA}{nodeB}
\pccoil  * [settings]  {arrows}  (nodeA)(nodeB)
\pczigzag * [settings]  {arrows}  (nodeA)(nodeB)
\ncsin   * [settings]  {arrows}  {nodeA}{nodeB}
\pcsin   * [settings]  {arrows}  (nodeA)(nodeB)
```

These connections behave in the same way as those dealt with in Sections 16.4 on page 241 and 16.5 on page 252:

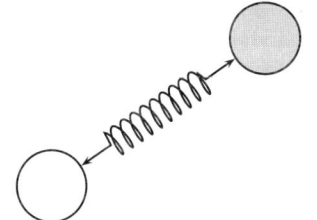

```
\usepackage{pstricks,pst-coil,pst-node}

\begin{pspicture}(4,3)
\cnode(0.5,0.5){0.5}{A}\cnode[fillstyle=solid,
   fillcolor=lightgray](3.5,2.5){0.5}{B}
\nccoil[coilwidth=0.4,coilaspect=35,%
   coilheight=0.5]{<->}{A}{B}
\end{pspicture}
```

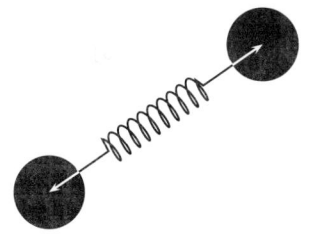

```
\usepackage{pstricks,pst-coil,pst-node}
\SpecialCoor

\begin{pspicture}(4,3)
\cnode*(0.5,0.5){0.5}{A}\cnode*(3.5,2.5){0.5}{B}
\pccoil[coilwidth=0.4,coilaspect=35,
   coilheight=0.5,linecolor=white]{<->}(A)(B)
\nccoil[coilwidth=0.4,coilaspect=35,
   coilheight=0.5]{A}{B}
\end{pspicture}
```

311

20.4 Examples

Figure 20.1: "Doodles"

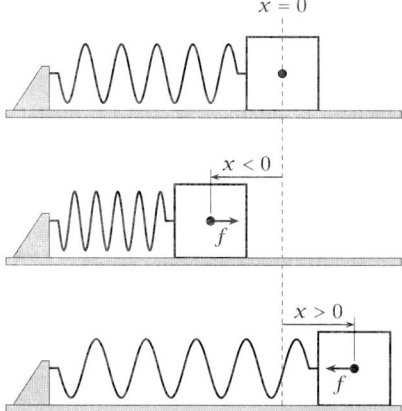

Figure 20.2: Application of the \pscoil command (Eugene Ressler)

Chapter 21

pst-eps – Exporting PSTricks environments

21.1 TeXtoEPS 314
21.2 \PSTtoEPS 314
21.3 Parameters 315
21.4 Example 315

In principle it is fairly easy to save individual PSTricks figures as PostScript files, but the approach commonly described in the literature (via dvips) isn't always successful. To construct a PSTricks figure properly for saving as a PostScript file, the following points are important:
▷ Create a frame with \fbox around the PSTricks object.
▷ Make the frame by setting \color{*white*}.
▷ Set \fboxsep to 0 pt to get no additional margin.
▷ Choose \pagestyle{*empty*} to suppress the page number.
   Now you can create an EPS file with

```
dvips spirale.dvi -E -o spirale.eps
```

which corrects the bounding box (%%BoundingBox: 148 456 364 668 for Figure 21.1; also see Section D.2.4 on page 854). You can then include the file as a normal figure in the document. Figure 21.1 shows a figure created in such a way.

\fbox has to be used in this approach as dvips doesn't see graphic elements as borders so can't determine the correct bounding box from them. Try converting the example without using \fbox to see the difference. dvips doesn't have any problems determining the correct bounding box when \fbox is used, however, as this is a text element and has an unambiguous border at the text level.

This method is quite efficient for converting a few figures, but is onerous when a large number of figures are required. The pst-eps package automates this process of saving PostScript files. Practical applications for pst-eps also arise when calculating individual

21 pst-eps – Exporting PSTricks environments

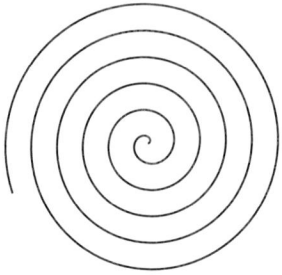

Figure 21.1: The EPS file created with dvips and the "–E" option

objects is very expensive on processing power, for example with three-dimensional objects such as cylinders or spheres. Instead of recalculating everything every time the document is translated, you can export the figure as an EPS file during the first run and then simply include it in subsequent runs. However, this package has been superseded now by other methods (cf. Chapter D on page 851) so we will only cover it briefly in this book.

21.1 TeXtoEPS

This command makes the trick with \fbox shown above superfluous and gives dvips the opportunity to determine the bounding box correctly.

\TeXtoEPS...\endTeXtoEPS	% TeX
\begin{TeXtoEPS}...\end{TeXtoEPS}	% LaTeX

Here is Example 21-00-1 rewritten using the TeXtoEPS environment:

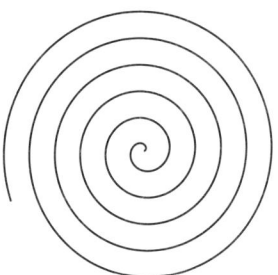

```
\usepackage{pstricks,pst-plot,pst-eps}

\begin{TeXtoEPS}
  \begin{pspicture}(-2,-2)(2,2)
    \parametricplot[plotpoints=1000]{0}{2000}{
      t dup cos 1000 div mul t
      dup sin 1000 div mul}
  \end{pspicture}
\end{TeXtoEPS}
```

Again the DVI file is converted with dvips as described above; this time we get a correct bounding box – %%BoundingBox: 71 509 286 721 – which only differs in its absolute values, not in the relative ones, from the values above.

21.2 \PSTtoEPS

\PSTtoEPS saves a pspicture environment to an external file.

21.3 Parameters

\PSTtoEPS [settings] {file name}{graphic object}

This command again has the problem that the bounding box can't be determined correctly, but you can get round this by specifying it through the appropriate parameters (Table 21.3). The file is created immediately, so you can include it as an EPS file immediately thereafter, as in the following example:

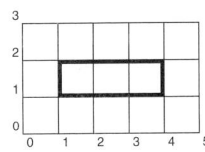

```
\usepackage{pstricks,pst-plot,pst-eps,graphicx}

\PSTtoEPS[bbllx=-0.5,bblly=-0.5,bburx=5.3,bbury=3.4,
    checkfile,headers=all,makeeps=all*]{rahmen.eps}{%
\psgrid[subgriddiv=0](5,3)
\psframe[linecolor=blue,linewidth=0.1](1,1)(4,2)}
\includegraphics[scale=0.5]{rahmen}
```

21.3 Parameters

Table 21.3 shows a summary of the special parameters for pst-eps. As we are only covering this package briefly in this book, we won't go into detail about these parameters.

Table 21.1: Summary of the special parameters for pst-eps

name	type	default
bbllx	value unit	0pt
bblly	value unit	0pt
bburx	value unit	0pt
bbury	value unit	0pt
makeeps	none|new|all|all*	new
checkfile	boolean	true
headerfile	file name	{}
headers	none|all|user	none
GraphicsRef	{x_0, y_0}	{}
Translation	{x,y}	{}
Rotation	value	{}
Scale	value1 value2	{}

21.4 Example

The following figure was created during the compilation run and included here immediately afterwards with \includegraphics.

```
\usepackage{pstricks,pst-plot,pst-eps,graphicx,multido}
\def\particle#1#2{%
  \pscircle[fillstyle=solid,fillcolor=black](#1,#2){2pt} %particle
  \pscircle[linestyle=dotted,dotsep=1.5pt,linewidth=0.5pt,linecolor=gray](#1,#2){6pt}}
```

```
\PSTtoEPS[bbllx=-1cm,bblly=-0.5cm,bburx=7cm,bbury=7cm]{figures/image1.eps}{%
  \begin{pspicture}(-1,-0.5)(7,7)
    \psset{linewidth=2pt}
    \psframe[linecolor=white](-1,-0.5)(7,7)
    \psgrid[subgriddiv=0,griddots=10,gridlabels=0,gridcolor=lightgray](0,0)(6,6)%grid
    \psline[linewidth=1.5pt]{-}(-1,6)(7,6) %boundary
    \psdots[dotscale=1,dotstyle=o,fillstyle=solid,fillcolor=red](3,6.5)   %photon
    \psline[linewidth=0.5pt]{->}(3,6.5)(3,5.5) %direction
    \multido{\ia=0+1}{7}{\multido{\ib=0+1}{7}{\particle{\ia}{\ib}}}
  \end{pspicture}}
\begin{figure}[htb]
\centering
\fbox{\includegraphics[scale=0.8]{figures/image1}}
\caption{Figure creation on the fly}
\end{figure}
```

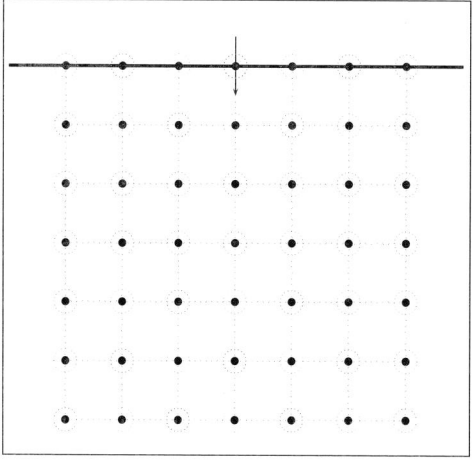

Figure 1: Figure creation on the fly

Chapter 22

pst-grad and pst-slpe — Colour gradients and shadows

22.1 pst-grad 317
22.2 pst-slpe 320
22.3 pst-blur – Blurred shadows 328
22.4 Examples 331

pst-grad is one of the older and smaller packages, and provides just one fill style (fillstyle=gradient) for colour gradients. In principle you can create colour gradients with the commands provided by PSTricks, but using pst-grad means that the intermediate colour values don't have to be calculated manually internally. The HSB and RGB colour models are supported by pst-grad.

The pst-slpe package fills the gaps not covered by pst-grad, including creating circular colour gradients (cf. Section 7.3 on page 90) and applying several user-defined colours for a gradient. pst-slpe also supports linear gradients, so there is no need to load pst-grad as well.

At the end of this chapter, we also cover the pst-blur package by Martin Giese, which supports the creation of blurred shadows.

22.1 pst-grad

22.1.1 Parameters

Table 22.1 on the following page shows a summary of the special parameters for pst-grad. These parameters are only available when using fillstyle=gradient.

22 pst-grad and pst-slpe – Colour gradients and shadows

Table 22.1: Summary of the parameters for pst-grad

name	type	default
gradbegin	colour	gradbegin
gradend	colour	gradend
gradlines	value	500
gradmidpoint	value	0.9
gradangle	angle	0
gradientHSB	boolean	false
GradientCircle	boolean	false
GradientScale	value	1.0
GradientPos	(x,y)	$(0,0)$

gradbegin

gradbegin designates both the parameter and the name of the start colour, which can be a bit confusing. The internal definition of that colour is in PSTricks notation, but you should avoid this if you are a LaTeX user. It's best to use the color/xcolor syntax (cf. Section 2.1 on page 8). The gradbegin colour is preset as \newrgbcolor{gradbegin}{0 .1 .95}. You can change the start colour either by redefining the preset colour or by assigning a start colour through the parameter.

```
\newrgbcolor{gradbegin}}\Largb{0 0 1} % obsolete TeX syntax
\definecolor{gradbegin}{rgb}{0, 0, 1} % needs color/xcolor package
\psset{gradbegin=blue}
```

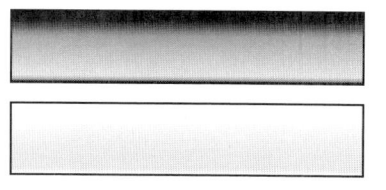

```
\usepackage{pstricks,pst-grad}

\begin{pspicture}(5,2.25)
\psframe[fillstyle=gradient,gradbegin=white](5,1)
\definecolor{gradbegin}{rgb}{0, 1, 1}
\psframe[fillstyle=gradient](0,1.25)(5,2.25)
\end{pspicture}
```

Remember that for the best results you should define the gradbegin colour as an RGB colour and avoid CMYK or greyscales. Also not that ConTeXt users can change the colour with \definecolor{gradbegin}{r=0,g=0,b=1}.

gradend

The gradend is reached **not** at the end of the frame, but at a certain point within the frame called the gradmidpoint (described below). Again it is ambiguously both a parameter and the name of a colour, preset in this case to \newrgbcolor{gradend}{0 1 1}. You can change gradend in similar ways to those described above for gradbegin.

```
\newrgbcolor{gradend}{1 0 0}      % obsolete TeX syntax
\definecolor{gradend}{rgb}{1, 0, 0} % needs color/xcolor package
\psset{gradend=red}
```

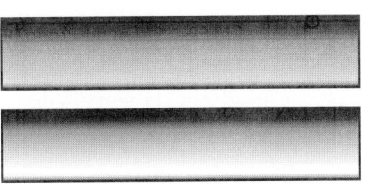

```
\usepackage{pstricks,pst-grad}

\begin{pspicture}(5,2.25)
\psframe[fillstyle=gradient,
    gradend=white](5,1)
\definecolor{gradend}{rgb}{1, 0, 0}
\psframe[fillstyle=gradient](0,1.25)(5,2.25)
\end{pspicture}
```

Remember that for the best results you should define the gradend colour as an RGB colour and avoid CMYK or greyscales.

gradlines

A colour gradient is really just a sequence of coloured lines. The width of these lines is limited only in absolute terms by the resolution of the monitor or printer. By default there are 500 lines, but you can alter this through gradlines.

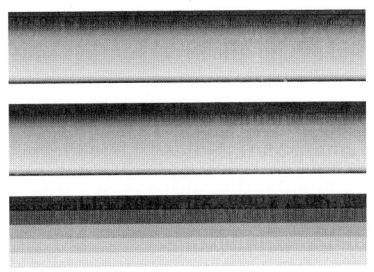

```
\usepackage{pstricks,pst-grad}

\begin{pspicture}(5,3.5)
\psset{fillstyle=gradient,linestyle=none}
\psframe[gradlines=5](5,1)
\psframe(0,1.25)(5,2.25)
\psframe[gradlines=1000](0,2.5)(5,3.5)
\end{pspicture}
```

gradmidpoint

This option designates the relative point within the frame where the gradend colour is reached. After this point it continues in reverse order. As it is a relative point, the option must have a value in the interval [0..1]. The default value is 0.9. A value of 0 means that the gradend colour is reached immediately, and the frame just displays the reversed gradient back to the gradbegin colour.

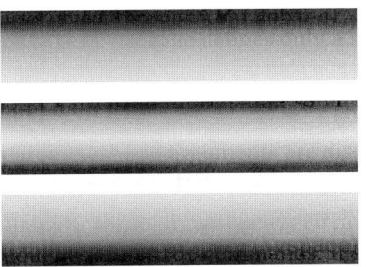

```
\usepackage{pstricks,pst-grad}

\begin{pspicture}(5,3.5)
\psset{fillstyle=gradient,linestyle=none}
\psframe[gradmidpoint=0](5,1)
\psframe[gradmidpoint=0.5](0,1.25)(5,2.25)
\psframe[gradmidpoint=1](0,2.5)(5,3.5)
\end{pspicture}
```

gradangle

gradangle specifies the angle of the gradient lines.

22 pst-grad and pst-slpe – Colour gradients and shadows

```
\usepackage{pstricks,pst-grad}

\begin{pspicture}(5,3.5)
\psset{fillstyle=gradient,linestyle=none,
    gradmidpoint=0.5}
\psframe[gradangle=0](5,1)
\psframe[gradangle=45](0,1.25)(5,2.25)
\psframe[gradangle=90](0,2.5)(5,3.5)
\end{pspicture}
```

gradientHSB

gradientHSB is a Boolean variable, specifying that the HSB colour scheme be used if it is set to true.

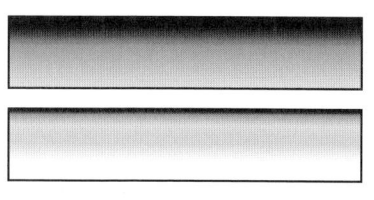

```
\usepackage{pstricks,pst-grad}

\begin{pspicture}(5,2.25)
\psset{gradientHSB=true,gradmidpoint=1}
\psframe[fillstyle=gradient,gradend=white](5,1)
\newrgbcolor{gradend}{1 0 0}
\psframe[fillstyle=gradient](0,1.25)(5,2.25)
\end{pspicture}
```

GradientCircle, GradientScale, and GradientPos

The GradientCircle option creates circular colour gradients; the radius is determined by GradientScale and the centre by GradientPos. The specification of the coordinates refers to the underlying coordinate system, which is usually given by the pspicture environment.

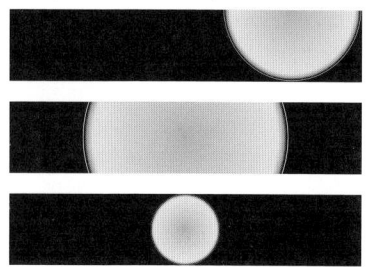

```
\usepackage{pstricks,pst-grad}

\begin{pspicture}(5,3.5)
\psset{fillstyle=gradient,linestyle=none}
\psframe[GradientCircle=true](5,1)%
\psframe[GradientCircle=true,
    GradientScale=3](0,1.25)(5,2.25)%
\psframe[GradientCircle=true,GradientScale=2,%
    GradientPos={(4,3.5)}](0,2.5)(5,3.5)%
\end{pspicture}
```

22.2 pst-slpe

22.2.1 Fill styles

Table 22.2 shows a list of all the new fill styles defined by the pst-slpe package for use with the fillstyle parameter (cf. Section 7.1.3 on page 80).

When interpolating linearly, the change of colour from for example red $(1,0,0)$ to green $(0,1,0)$ is done linearly with $(1-dz,0,0)$ and $(0,dz,0)$, where dz is the step $(0 < dz < 1)$. In most cases this transition is fine, but in some cases you might prefer to interpolate via intermediate colours – e.g. via yellow $(1,1,0)$ and brown $(0.5,0.5,0)$. This method is used if you choose the plural form of one of the fill styles.

22.2 pst-slpe

name	description
slope	linear interpolation
slopes	additionally with intermediate colours
ccslope	circular with linear interpolation
ccslopes	additionally with intermediate colours
radslope	radial with linear interpolation
radslopes	additionally with intermediate colours

Table 22.2: Summary of the fill styles defined by pst-slpe

The following sections discuss each fill style in turn.

slope and slopes

The slope fill style corresponds to the gradient style of the pst-grad package (cf. Section 22.1 on page 317), while slopes is only supported by pst-slpe.

```
\usepackage{pstricks,pst-slpe}

\begin{pspicture}(5,3.5)
  \psframe[fillstyle=slope](5,1.5)
  \psframe[fillstyle=slopes](0,2)(5,3.5)
\end{pspicture}
```

ccslope and ccslopes

These fill styles make circular colour gradients.

 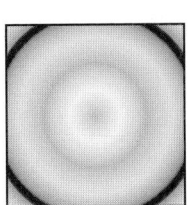

```
\usepackage{pstricks,pst-slpe}

\begin{pspicture}(5.5,2.5)
  \psframe[fillstyle=ccslope](2.5,2.5)
  \psframe[fillstyle=ccslopes](3,0)(5.5,2.5)
\end{pspicture}
```

radslope and radslopes

These fill styles make radial colour gradients.

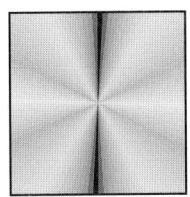 

```
\usepackage{pstricks,pst-slpe}

\begin{pspicture}(5.5,2.5)
  \psframe[fillstyle=radslope](2.5,2.5)
  \psframe[fillstyle=radslopes](3,0)(5.5,2.5)
\end{pspicture}
```

22.2.2 Parameters

Table 22.3 shows a list of the available parameters. The following sections cover each one in turn. From now on we give colour specifications in PSTricks syntax, as they are specified in the package itself. LaTeX users should by all means use the syntax of color/xcolor (cf. Section 2.1 on page 8).

Table 22.3: Summary of the parameters available with the pst-slpe package

name	type	default
slopebegin	colour	slopebegin
slopeend	colour	slopeend
slopecolors	colour list	0.0 1 0 0
		0.4 0 1 0
		0.8 0 0 1
		1.0 0 1 0
slopesteps	value	100
slopeangle	angle	0
slopecenter	x y	0.5 0.5
sloperadius	value unit	0
fading	boolean	false
startfading	0	
endfading	1	

slopebegin

slopebegin designates the parameter as well as the name of the start colour, which can be a bit confusing. The color is preset by \newrgbcolor{slopebegin}{0.9 1 0}. Therefore you can change this start colour either by redefining it or by assigning it through the parameter.

```
\newrgbcolor{slopebegin}{0 0 1}        % obsolete \TeX syntax
\definecolor{slopebegin}{rgb}{0, 0, 1} % needs the color/xcolor package
\psset{slopebegin=blue}
```

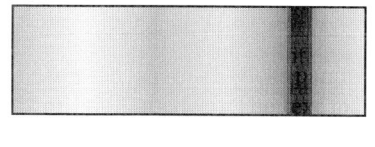
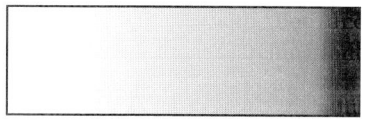

```
\usepackage{pstricks,pst-slpe}

\begin{pspicture}(5,3.5)
  \psframe[fillstyle=slope,
    slopebegin=white](5,1.5)
  \definecolor{slopebegin}{rgb}{0,1,1}
  \psframe[fillstyle=slopes](0,2)(5,3.5)
\end{pspicture}
```

slopeend

The slopeend is reached at the end of the frame. Again it is ambiguously both a parameter and the name of a colour, preset in this case to \newrgbcolor{slopeend}{1 0 0}. You can change slopeend in similar ways to those described above for slopebegin.

```
\newrgbcolor{slopeend}{1 0 0}       % obsolete \TeX\ syntax
\definecolor{slopeend}{rgb}{1,0,0} % needs the color/xcolor package
\psset{slopebegin=red}
```

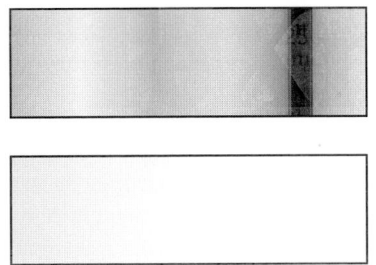

```
\usepackage{pstricks,pst-slpe}

\begin{pspicture}(5,3.5)
    \psframe[fillstyle=slope,
        slopeend=white](5,1.5)
    \definecolor{slopeend}{rgb}{1,0,0}
    \psframe[fillstyle=slopes](0,2)(5,3.5)
\end{pspicture}
```

slopecolors

slopecolors defines the colour list for non-linear interpolations between slopebegin and slopeend. slopecolors is used if you have chosen one of the plural versions of the fill options from Table 22.2. The list of colours consists of a one-dimensional coordinate and the corresponding colour. The list is terminated with the number of interpolation points (colours).

```
\usepackage{pstricks,pst-plot,pst-slpe}
\begin{pspicture}(0,-0.25)(\linewidth,0.75cm)
    \psaxes[axesstyle=frame,tickstyle=bottom](\linewidth,0.5cm)
    \psframe[fillstyle=slopes](\linewidth,0.5cm)
\end{pspicture}
```

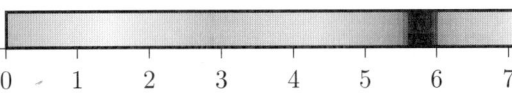

The example above shows the default gradient, a rainbow. This is defined by the following colour list:

```
0.0 1 0 0 % start colour red
0.4 0 1 0 % intermediate colour at 40% green
0.8 0 0 1 % intermediate colour at 80% blue
1.0 1 0 1 % end colour purple
4         % number of steps
```

The four interpolation points refer to the entire x width of the area to fill and are adapted if necessary. For the example above, the x axis can be taken directly as a scale for the colour points.

```
\usepackage{pstricks,pst-plot,pst-slpe}
\begin{pspicture}(0,-0.25)(\linewidth,0.75cm)
\psset{slopecolors= 0.0  1.0 1.0 0.9
                    8.5  0.5 1.0 0.5
                   12.5  0.0 0.5 0.5
                    3}
```

22 pst-grad and pst-slpe – Colour gradients and shadows

```
\psaxes[axesstyle=frame,tickstyle=bottom](\linewidth,0.5cm)
\psframe[fillstyle=slopes](\linewidth,0.5cm)
\end{pspicture}
```

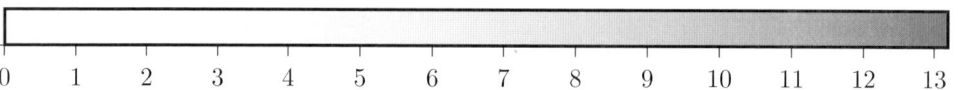

slopesteps

A colour gradient is really just a sequence of coloured lines. The width of these lines is limited only in absolute terms by the resolution of the monitor or printer. By default there are 100 lines, but you can alter this through slopesteps.

```
\usepackage{pstricks,pst-slpe}

\begin{pspicture}(5,4)
  \psset{fillstyle=slope,linestyle=none}
  \psframe[slopesteps=5](5,1)
  \psframe(0,1.5)(5,2.5)
  \psframe[slopesteps=1000](0,3)(5,4)
\end{pspicture}
```

slopeangle

slopeangle determines the angle of the gradient lines. For the radslope[s] fill style, the gradient is rotated by the specified angle. This parameter has no effect with ccslope[s].

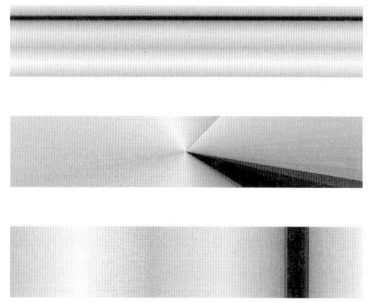

```
\usepackage{pstricks,pst-slpe}

\begin{pspicture}(5,4)
  \psset{fillstyle=slopes,linestyle=none}
  \psframe[slopeangle=0](5,1)
  \psframe[fillstyle=radslopes,
    slopeangle=45](0,1.5)(5,2.5)
  \psframe[slopeangle=90](0,3)(5,4)
\end{pspicture}
```

slopecenter

slopecenter determines the centre for the radslope[s] and ccslope[s] fill styles. The coordinates denote a relative position within the current bounding box. To make sure that the box is defined unambiguously, it is a good idea to use \pscustom (cf. Chapter 11 on page 121). In the following examples the centre is set to 60% of the width and 25% of the height.

22.2 pst-slpe

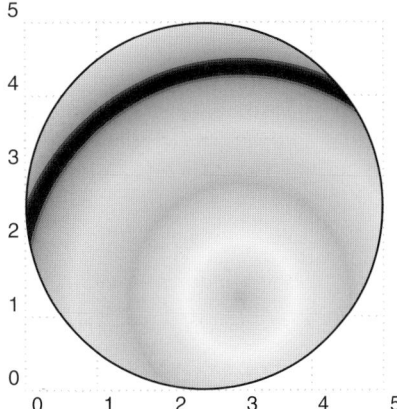

```
\usepackage{pstricks,pst-slpe}

\begin{pspicture}[showgrid](5,5)
    \pscustom[fillstyle=ccslopes,
        slopecenter={0.6 0.25}]{%
        \pscircle(2.5,2.5){2.5}}
\end{pspicture}
```

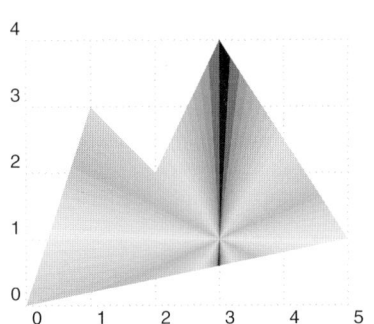

```
\usepackage{pstricks,pst-slpe}

\begin{pspicture}[showgrid](5,4)
    \pscustom[fillstyle=radslope,
        linestyle=none,slopecenter=0.6 0.25]{%
        \psline(0,0)(1,3)(2,2)(3,4)(5,1)(0,0)}
\end{pspicture}
```

sloperadius

For circular and radial gradients, the default behaviour is for the colour gradient to start with the first colour at the centre of the bounding box and reach the last colour at the box's edge, such that the entire area is filled. You can change this behaviour through the sloperadius parameter, which specifies the maximum radius; any visible area outside the circle defined by this radius is filled with the last colour.

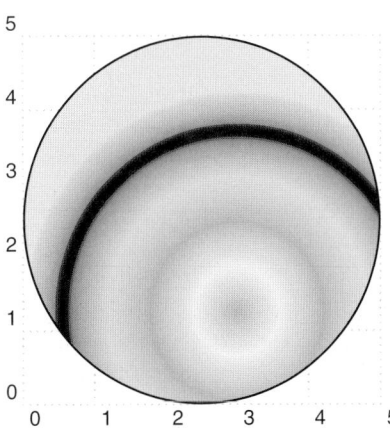

```
\usepackage{pstricks,pst-slpe}

\begin{pspicture}[showgrid](5,5)
    \pscustom[fillstyle=ccslopes,
        slopecenter={0.6 0.25},
        sloperadius=3cm]{%
        \pscircle(2.5,2.5){2.5}}
\end{pspicture}
```

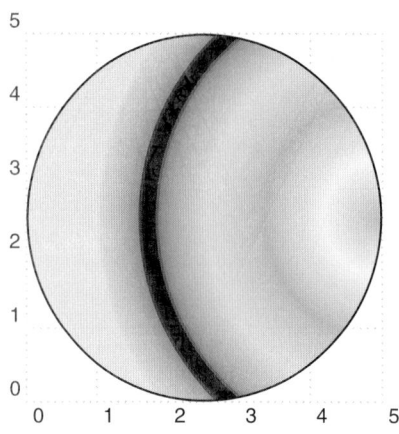

```
\usepackage{pstricks,pst-slpe}

\begin{pspicture}[showgrid](5,5)
  \pscustom[fillstyle=ccslopes,
      slopecenter={1 0.5},
      sloperadius=4cm]{%
      \pscircle(2.5,2.5){2.5}}
\end{pspicture}
```

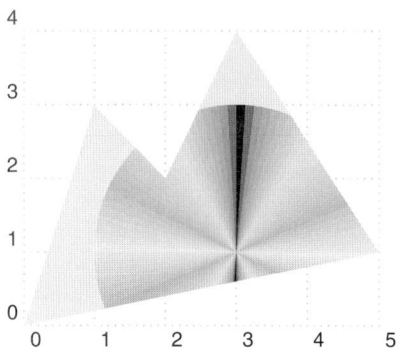

```
\usepackage{pstricks,pst-slpe}

\begin{pspicture}[showgrid](5,4)
  \pscustom[fillstyle=radslope,
     linestyle=none,slopecenter=0.6 0.25,
     sloperadius=2cm]{%
     \psline(0,0)(1,3)(2,2)(3,4)(5,1)(0,0)}
\end{pspicture}
```

fading, startfading, and endfading

since version 1.3 With pst-slpe package versions 1.3 and later, there are linear and radial "fade out" effects available, which you can use to create transparency in a number of ways. The fade out is activated by fading=true; the start and end values for the transparency are specified through startfading and endfading. The default values are 0 and 1 respectively, which correspond to no and total transparency.

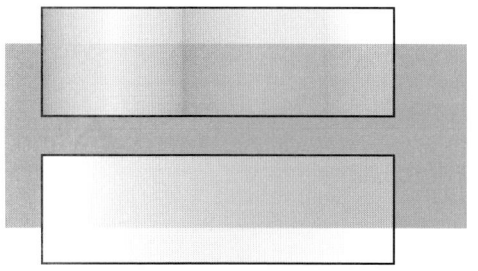

```
\usepackage{pstricks,pst-slpe}

\begin{pspicture}(5,3.5)
\psframe*[linecolor=black!40](-.5,.5)(6,3)
\psframe[fillstyle=slope,fading,
    slopebegin=white](5,1.5)
\definecolor{slopebegin}{rgb}{0,1,1}
\psframe[fading,
    fillstyle=slopes](0,2)(5,3.5)
\end{pspicture}
```

`\usepackage{pstricks,pst-slpe}`

22.2 pst-slpe

```
\LARGE\psset{fading,endfading=0.75,linecolor=black!40}
\begin{tabular}{cc}
\psframe*(-0.3,-0.25)(3.5,20pt)\psframebox[fillstyle=slope]{\st{slope}} &\qquad
\psframe*(-0.3,-0.25)(3.5,20pt)\psframebox[fillstyle=slopes]{\st{slopes}} \\[3ex]
\psframe*(-0.3,-0.25)(3.5,20pt)\psframebox[fillstyle=ccslope]{\st{ccslope}} &\qquad
\psframe*(-0.3,-0.25)(3.5,20pt)\psframebox[fillstyle=ccslopes]{\st{ccslopes}} \\[3ex]
\psframe*(-0.3,-0.25)(3.5,20pt)\psframebox[fillstyle=radslope]{\st{radslope}} &\qquad
\psframe*(-0.3,-0.25)(3.5,20pt)\psframebox[fillstyle=radslopes]{\st{radslopes}}\\[3ex]
\end{tabular}
```

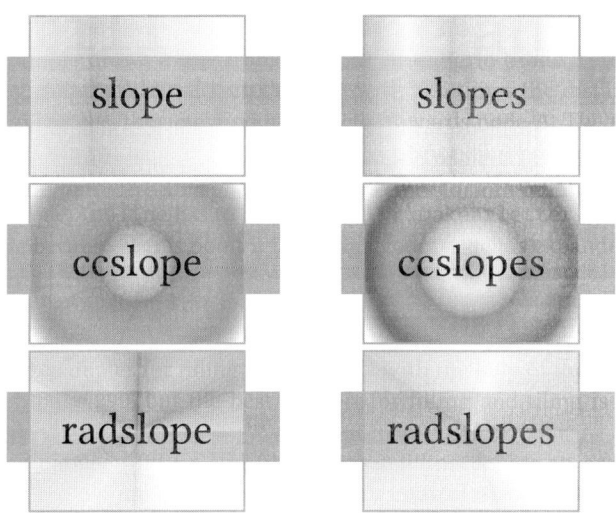

22.2.3 Commands

The package provides the \psBall command primarily for the itemize environment in presentations, as you can use it to make coloured balls with a 3D effect.

\psBall [settings] {colour}{radius}
\psBall [settings] (x,y){colour}{radius}

```
\usepackage{pst-slpe}

\begin{pspicture}(-0.5,-0.5)(5,0.5)
\psBall{black}{2ex}
\psBall(1,0){blue}{3ex}
\psBall(2.5,0){red}{4ex}
\psBall(4,0){green!50!blue!60}{5ex}
\end{pspicture}
```

The default parameters for \psBall are:

```
sloperadius=0.075radius
fillstyle=ccslope
slopebegin=white
```

```
slopeend=colour
slopecenter=0.4 0.6
linestyle=none
```

You can overwrite these as described above to achieve different effects. You don't have to use the command within a `pspicture` environment. If you do use it directly in text, bear in mind that by default it is put into a box of size 0pt and if you don't specify coordinates, it is output symmetric to the current point.

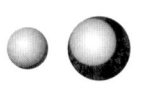
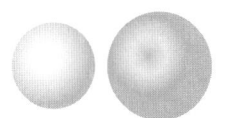

```
\usepackage{pst-slpe}

\begin{pspicture}(-0.5,-0.5)(5,0.5)
\psBall{black}{2ex}
\psBall[sloperadius=10pt](1,0){blue}{3ex}
\psBall(2.5,0){red}{4ex}
\psBall[slopebegin=red](4,0){green!50!blue!60}{5ex}
\end{pspicture}
```

22.3 pst-blur – Blurred shadows

In Section 4.1.16 on page 51 and Chapter 23.1 on page 334, we discuss several possibilities for creating shadows of a single shadow colour. However, the pst-blur package by Martin Giese supports the creation of blurred shadows, which makes a much better impression. [16] Prerequisite is a closed area, so no open polylines can have blurred shadows. pst-blur creates these shadows in the same way as described for \closedshadow in Section 11.3.16 on page 133.

22.3.1 Parameters

Table 22.4 shows a summary of the special parameters for pst-blur. You can also use the shadow, shadowsize, shadowangle, and shadowcolor parameters described in Section 4.1.16 on page 51 with pst-blur. Figure 22.1 illustrates some of these parameters, and the ones specific to pst-blur are discussed inthe following sections.

Table 22.4: Summary of the special parameters for the pst-blur package

name	type	default
blur	boolean	false
blurradius	value unit	1.5pt
blurbg	colour	white
blursteps	value	20

blur

The setting blur=true is the prerequisite for activating the package. Otherwise shadows are created normally as described in Section 4.1.16. However, shadow=true has to be valid as well, otherwise blur doesn't have any effect.

22.3 pst-blur – Blurred shadows

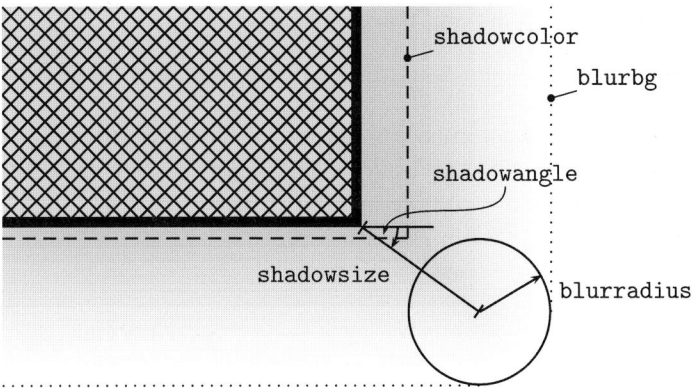

Figure 22.1: Parameters for blurred shadows (Martin Giese)

blurradius

As shown in Figure 22.1, `blurradius` specifies the radius of the rounded corners. The combination of `blurradius` and `shadowsize` (cf. Section 4.1.16) determines the size of the area covered by the blurred shadow. As can be seen from the following examples, if `blurradius` becomes too large relative to `shadowsize`, the optical impression is negated.

```
\usepackage{pstricks,pst-blur}

\begin{pspicture}(4,4.25)
  \psset{shadow=true,blur=true,shadowsize=10pt,
      linecolor=lightgray}
  \psframe(3.5,1)
  \psframe[blurradius=5pt](0,1.5)(3.5,2.5)
  \psframe[blurradius=10pt](0,3.25)(3.5,4.25)
\end{pspicture}
```

blurbg

`blurbg` determines the background colour, i.e. the final shadow colour. The shadow starts at `shadowcolor` and ends at `blurbg`. In principle you can specify any colour here, which can create completely different shadow effects:

```
\usepackage{pstricks,pst-blur}
\begin{pspicture}(8,2)
  \psset{shadow=true,blur=true,shadowsize=10pt,
      blurradius=5pt,linestyle=none,linecolor=lightgray}
  \psframe[shadow=false](2,2)\pscircle[linestyle=solid](0.8,1.2){0.75}
  \psframe*[shadow=false](4,0)(6,2)
  \pscircle[linestyle=solid,fillcolor=yellow,blurbg=lightgray](4.8,1.2){0.75}
```

```
\psframe*[linecolor=red,shadow=false](2,0)(4,2)
\pscircle[linestyle=solid,fillcolor=blue,blurbg=red](2.8,1.2){0.75}
\psframe*[linecolor=cyan,shadow=false](6,0)(8,2)
\pscircle[linestyle=solid,fillcolor=magenta,blurbg=cyan](6.8,1.2){0.75}
\end{pspicture}
```

blursteps

This parameter specifies how many steps the shadow colour is divided into, starting with shadowcolor and ending with blurbg. The larger the number of intermediate steps, the longer the time to calculate them, but the more even the shadow gradient.

```
\usepackage{pstricks,pst-blur}

\begin{pspicture}(4,4.25)
  \psset{shadow=true,blur=true,shadowsize=15pt,
    blurradius=10pt,linecolor=lightgray}
  \psframe(3.5,1)
  \psframe[blursteps=5](0,1.5)(3.5,2.5)
  \psframe[blursteps=50](0,3.25)(3.5,4.25)
\end{pspicture}
```

22.3.2 \psblurbox

pst-blur has one specific command, \psblurbox, which creates a framed box with a blurred shadow in the middle of text.

\psblurbox [settings] {material}

The following example compares \psblurbox to the outputs of \psframebox and \psshadowbox from the basic PSTricks package when used in conjunction with pst-blur.

```
\usepackage{pst-blur}
\def\Lcs#1{\texttt{\textbackslash#1}}
```
If the \psframebox[shadow=true,blur=true]{\Lcs{psframebox}} is used in normal text with the \texttt{blur=true} option, the result is usually bad because \TeX{} doesn't take into account that, because of the shadow, the line spacing needs to be larger for this line. The result with a \psshadowbox[blur=true]{\Lcs{psshadowbox}} using the option \texttt{blur=true} is a bit different, although it is still not satisfactory -- it adjusts for the \texttt{shadowsize} but not for the \texttt{blurradius}. \psblurbox{\Lcs{psblurbox}} on the other hand takes care of

the line spacing. However, for this command you can't change the shadow angle of `\texttt{shadowangle=45}`.

If the `\psframebox` is used in normal text with the blur=true option, the result is usually bad because TeX doesn't take into account that, because of the shadow, the line spacing needs to be larger for this line. The result with a `\psshadowbox` using the option blur=true is a bit different, although it is still not satisfactory – it adjusts for the shadowsize but not for the blurradius. `\psblurbox` on the other hand takes care of the line spacing. However, for this command you can't change the shadow angle of shadowangle=45.

22.4 Examples

$$F(x) = \int f(x)dx$$

$$F(x) = \int f(x)dx$$

$$x_1 = x_0 - \frac{F(x_0)}{F'(x_0)} \ge x_0 \quad (1)$$

```
\usepackage{pst-blur,amsmath}

\psblurbox{\parbox{0.9\linewidth}{%
    \[F(x)=\int f(x)dx\]}}

\medskip
\psblurbox[blurbg=red]{%
    \parbox{0.9\linewidth}{%
        \[F(x)=\int f(x)dx\]}}

\bigskip
\psblurbox[blurbg=blue!30!red!80,
    blurradius=5pt]{%
        \parbox{0.9\linewidth}{%
            \begin{align}
                x_1 &= x_0-\frac{F(x_0)}%
                    {F^\prime(x_0)}\ge x_0
            \end{align}}}
```

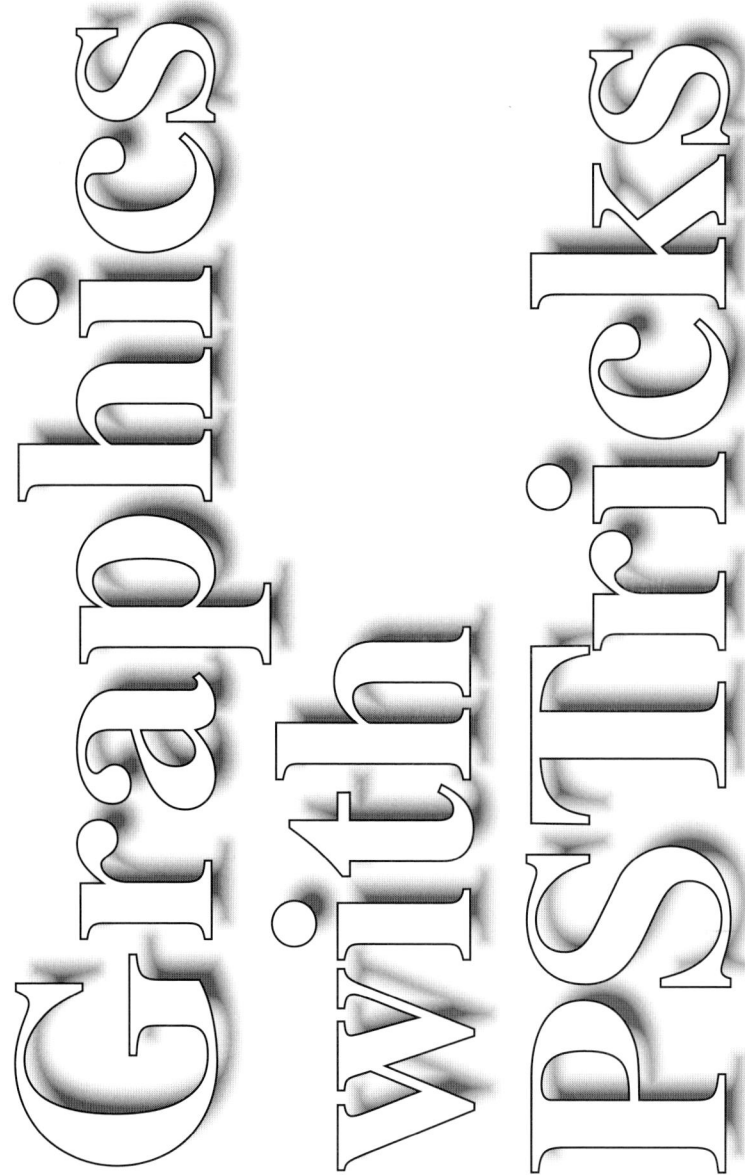

Figure 22.2: Shadow plays...

Chapter 23

Three-dimensional figures

23.1 pst-3d – Shadows, tilting, and three-dimensional illustrations 334
23.2 pst-ob3d – Simple three-dimensional objects 346
23.3 pst-gr3d – Three-dimensional grids. 348
23.4 pst-fr3d – Buttons with 3D effects 355
23.5 pst-3dplot – 3D parallel projection of functions and data. 358
23.6 pst-solides3d — perspective 3D views 391
23.7 Examples 443

PSTricks has several additional packages that help you draw three-dimensional figures and mathematical functions with two variables. A summary is shown in Table 23.1. In some cases, the functionality of packages overlaps – parallel development is not uncommon in the TeX world.

package	contents	page
pst-3d	basic 3D operations	334
pst-ob3d	3D basic objects	346
pst-gr3d	3D grids	348
pst-fr3d	3D framed boxes	355
pst-3dplot	3D plots	358
pst-solides3d	3D views	391
pst-map3d	3D geographical projections	478
pst-map3dII	3D geographical projections	489
pst-light3d	3D light effects	??

Table 23.1: Summary of the packages with 3D support

23 Three-dimensional figures

23.1 pst-3d – Shadows, tilting, and three-dimensional illustrations

pst-3d contains the pre-stage of three-dimensional illustrations – using tilting and the formation of shadows to give a 3D appearance. It is one of the older packages, but nevertheless is worth discussing in detail.

23.1.1 Shadows

pst-3d defines the \psshadow command with the following syntax:

\psshadow [settings] {*material*}

The material can be anything of a text-like character – text, rules, and mathematical expressions in inline-mode.

```
\usepackage{pstricks,pst-3d}

\psset{Tshadowcolor=black!25}
\psshadow[]{\Huge shadow}\\[10pt]
\psshadow{\Huge $f(x)=x^2$}\\[15pt]
\psshadow[Tshadowsize=2.5]{%
    \rule{2cm}{10pt}}\\
```

Parameters

Table 23.2 lists the additional parameters that are available for \psshadow; shadow, shadowsize, shadowangle, and shadowcolor can also be used where meaningful (cf. Section 4.1.16 on page 51).

Table 23.2: Summary of all shadow parameters

name	type	default
Tshadowangle	angle	60
Tshadowcolor	colour	lightgray
Tshadowsize	value	1

Tshadowangle The Tshadowangle option specifies the angle between the horizontal line and the shadow. Therefore the angle $90°$ corresponds to the text itself. Negative angles cause the shadow to protrude from the paper plane. Values of $0°$ and $180°$ are not allowed.

```
\usepackage{pstricks,pst-3d}
\psset{Tshadowcolor=black!60}
{\huge\psshadow{shadow} \psshadow[Tshadowangle=30]{shadow}
\psshadow[Tshadowangle=70]{shadow} \psshadow[Tshadowangle=-30]{shadow}}
```

23.1 pst-3d – Shadows, tilting, and three-dimensional illustrations

Tshadowcolor   The Tshadowcolor option determines the colour of the shadow.

```
\usepackage{pstricks,pst-3d}
{\huge\psshadow{shadow} \psshadow[Tshadowcolor=red]{shadow}
\psshadow[Tshadowcolor=green]{shadow} \psshadow[Tshadowcolor=blue]{shadow}}
```

shadow shadow shadow shadow

Tshadowsize   The Tshadowsize option specifies the size of the shadow as a scaling factor.

```
\usepackage{pstricks,pst-3d}
{\huge\psshadow{shadow} \psshadow[Tshadowsize=-2]{shadow}
\psshadow[Tshadowsize=2]{shadow} \psshadow[Tshadowsize=3.5]{shadow}}
```

shadow shadow shadow shadow

23.1.2 Tilting

By tilting objects, you can simulate the perspective of a three-dimensional object. pst-3d defines two commands for this.

```
\pstilt [settings] {angle}{material}
\psTilt [settings] {angle}{material}
```

Figure 23.1 shows the difference between these two commands. In principle you can pass anything as the argument for tilting, though it's best to put vertical material, such as out-of-line formulae, into a \parbox (cf. Example 23-01-7 and 23-01-12 on page 337). Angles of 0° and 180° are not allowed.

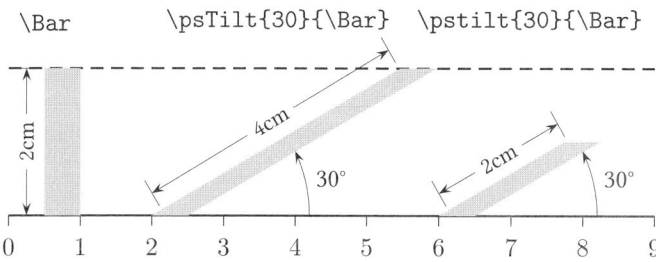

Figure 23.1: Demonstration of the difference between \pstilt and \psTilt

23 Three-dimensional figures

\pstilt

\pstilt tilts objects such that their original height appears as the length of the tilted object – the object becomes smaller. The hypotenuse of the triangle of base point, height, and perpendicular now corresponds to the old height (cf. Figure 23.1). Here the length is taken from the centre of the base side.

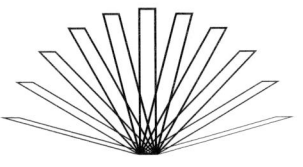

```
\usepackage{pstricks,pst-3d,multido}

\def\Bar{\psframe(0,0)(0.25,2)}
\begin{pspicture}(5,2)
  \multido{\nA=15+15}{11}{\rput(2.5,0){\pstilt{\nA}{\Bar}}}
\end{pspicture}
```

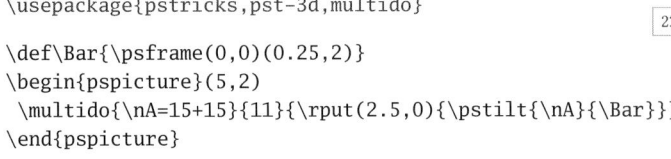

```
\usepackage{pstricks,pst-3d}

\pstilt{60}{\parbox{0.5\linewidth}{%
  \[f(x)=\int_1^{\infty}\frac{1}{x}\,dx=1\]}}
```

```
\usepackage{pstricks,pst-3d,pst-plot}

\pstilt{60}{\begin{pspicture}(-0.5,-0.5)(2,2)
  \psaxes[axesstyle=frame](2,2)
\end{pspicture}}
```

```
\usepackage{pstricks,pst-3d,graphicx}

\pstilt{-30}{\includegraphics[scale=0.5]{rose}}
```

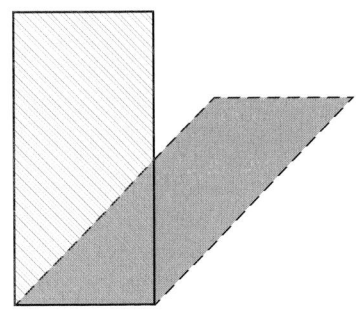

```
\usepackage{pstricks,pst-3d,multido}

\newpsstyle{TransparencyCyan}{%
  fillstyle=vlines,hatchwidth=0.1\pslinewidth,
  hatchcolor=cyan,hatchsep=1.5\pslinewidth}
\begin{pspicture}(2,4)
  \rput[lb](0,0){\pstilt{45}{%
    \psframe[linestyle=dashed,
      fillstyle=solid,fillcolor=red](2,4)}}
  \psframe[style=TransparencyCyan](0,0)(2,4)
\end{pspicture}
```

\psTilt

\psTilt tilts objects such that they keep their original height – in theory the object could become infinitely long if \psTilt is set to a tiny angle (cf. Figure 23.1 on the preceding page).

23.1 pst-3d – Shadows, tilting, and three-dimensional illustrations

```
\usepackage{pstricks,pst-3d,multido}
\def\Bar{\psframe(0,0)(0.25,2)}
\begin{pspicture*}(\linewidth,2)
  \multido{\nA=10+10}{17}{\rput(0.5\linewidth,0){\psTilt{\nA}{\Bar}}}
\end{pspicture*}
```

```
\usepackage{pstricks,pst-3d,multido}

\psTilt{60}{\parbox{0.5\linewidth}{%
   \[f(x)=\int_1^{\infty}\frac{1}{x}\,dx=1\]}}
```

```
\usepackage{pstricks,pst-3d,pst-plot}

\psTilt{60}{%
  \begin{pspicture}(-0.5,-0.5)(2,2)
    \psaxes[axesstyle=frame](2,2)
  \end{pspicture}}
```

```
\usepackage{pstricks,pst-3d,graphicx}

\psTilt{-30}{\includegraphics[scale=0.5]{rose}}
```

```
\usepackage{pstricks,pst-3d,multido}

\newpsstyle{TransparencyCyan}{%
    fillstyle=vlines,hatchcolor=cyan,
    hatchwidth=0.1\pslinewidth,
    hatchsep=1.5\pslinewidth}
\begin{pspicture}(2,4)
  \rput[lb](0,0){\psTilt{45}{%
    \psframe[linestyle=dashed,
      fillstyle=solid,fillcolor=red](2,4)}}
  \psframe[style=TransparencyCyan](0,0)(2,4)
\end{pspicture}
```

Application example for \pstilt and \psTilt

The rotating package provides commands to rotate text to make slanting table headings, for example. However, if you want to frame the headings you are better off using \pstilt or \psTilt instead. The example below shows an application using each command in turn.

23 Three-dimensional figures

```
\usepackage{pst-3d}

\begin{tabular}{l}
\pstilt{60}{%
 \begin{tabular}{|p{1em}|p{1em}|p{1em}|}\hline
   \psrotateleft{column 1\ } & \psrotateleft{column 2\ } &
   \psrotateleft{column 3\ }
 \end{tabular}}\\
\begin{tabular}{|p{1em}|p{1em}|p{1em}|}\hline
 1 & 2 & 3 \\\hline  4 & 5 & 6 \\\hline
\end{tabular}
\end{tabular}
```

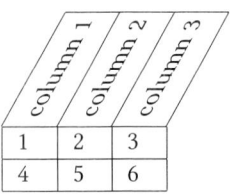

```
\usepackage{pst-3d}

\begin{tabular}{c}
\kern2.2em\psTilt{60}{%
 \begin{tabular}{|p{1em}|p{1em}|p{1em}|}\hline
   \psrotateleft{column 1\ } & \psrotateleft{column 2\ } &
   \psrotateleft{column 3\ }
 \end{tabular}}\\\noindent
\begin{tabular}{|p{1em}|p{1em}|p{1em}|}\hline
 1 & 2 & 3 \\\hline  4 & 5 & 6 \\\hline
\end{tabular}
\end{tabular}
```

23.1.3 Three-dimensional illustrations

pst-3d only supports central projections, which restricts how geometric objects like spheres or cylinders can be displayed. Although pst-3d only actually defines a single command for 3D projections, it is a very effective package to use and also serves as base for other packages. [87]

\ThreeDput

pst-3d only defines this one command, but you can use it to achieve a virtually arbitrary display of line- or plane-like objects in three-dimensional space.

> \ThreeDput [settings] (x, y, z) {material}

If no coordinates are specified, $(0, 0, 0)$ is assumed to be the coordinate origin for \ThreeDput. The material can be anything that you can put into a box. If it is vertical material in the TeX sense, it has to be put into a \parbox or minipage. The material has its own origin, for example:

```
\psframe(2,2)%            origin is bottom left (0,0)
\psframe(-1,-1)(1,1)%     origin is at the centre (0,0)
arbitrary text%           origin is at the centre of the base line
```

23.1 pst-3d – Shadows, tilting, and three-dimensional illustrations

\ThreeDput places the coordinate origin of the material at the point specified in its argument, though this is not necessarily the visible, geometric centre. In the following example, the smaller square with centre $(0,0)$ is put at the coordinates $(4,4,0)$.

Note that to simplify the source code of the examples, we use the \IIIDKOSystem example command to draw the coordinate axes and grid.

```
\usepackage{pstricks,pst-3d,multido}
\begin{pspicture}(0,-0.75)(5,4.5)
    \psset{viewpoint=1 -1 0.75} \IIIDKOSystem[subgriddiv=0,gridcolor=black!50]{5}
    \ThreeDput{\psframe*[linecolor=gray!20](3,3)}
    \ThreeDput(1.5,1.5,0){\Huge bottom}
    \ThreeDput(0,0,1.5){\psframe*[linecolor=gray!25](3,3)}
    \ThreeDput(1.5,1.5,1.5){\Huge centre}
    \ThreeDput(0,0,3){\psframe*[linecolor=gray!15](3,3)}
    \ThreeDput(1.5,1.5,3){\Huge top}
    {\psset{subgriddiv=0,gridcolor=black!50}\xzEbene{5}}
    \ThreeDput(4,4,0){\psframe*[linecolor=gray!5](-1,-1)(1,1)}
    \ThreeDput(4,4,0){\psdot[dotscale=3]}
\end{pspicture}
```

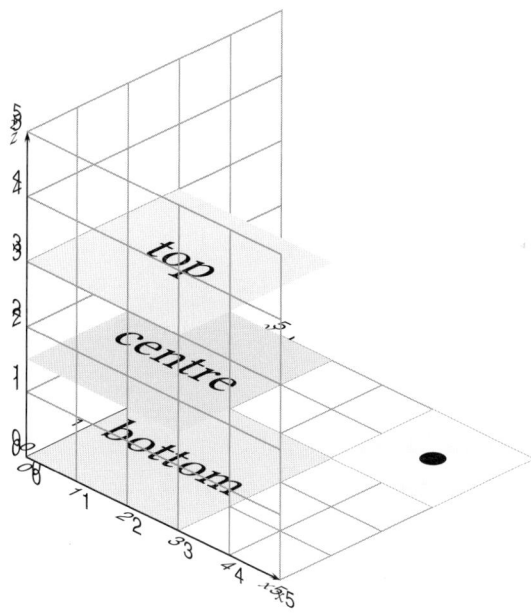

The \ThreeDput command is very versatile; you can determine the position in three-dimensional space unambiguously by specifying the normal vector $\vec{n}$ (cf. page 343) and a point $P(x, y, z)$ of the line or plane. Making planes different shades of grey enhances the three-dimensional effect, as shown in the following example.

```
\usepackage{pstricks,pst-3d,multido}
\begin{pspicture}(-4.5,-3)(3,4.75)
\psset{viewpoint=1 1.5 0.8}
```

23 Three-dimensional figures

```
\IIIDKOSystem[gridlabels=0pt,subgriddiv=0,gridcolor=black!50]{5}
\ThreeDput[normal=0 0 1]{% xy plane
    \psline[linewidth=3pt,linecolor=blue]{->}(4,4)(4,5.5)
    \uput[90](4,5.5){\psrotateleft{\textcolor{blue}{$\vec{n}_A$}}}}
\ThreeDput[normal=0 -1 0]{%   xz plane
    \psline[linewidth=3pt,linecolor=green]{->}(4,0)(5.5,0)
    \uput[90](5.5,0){\psscalebox{-1 1}{\textcolor{green}{$\vec{n}_B$}}}}
\ThreeDput[normal=1 0 0]{%  yz plane
    \psline[linewidth=3pt,linecolor=red]{->}(0,4)(0,5.5)
    \uput[0](0,5.5){$\vec{n}_{top}$}} % cube and axes
\ThreeDput[normal=0 0 1](0,0,4){\psframe*[linecolor=gray!25](4,4)
    \rput(2,2){\Huge\textbf{TOP}}}
\ThreeDput[normal=0 1 0](4,4,0){\psframe*[linecolor=gray!5](4,4)
    \rput(2,2){\Huge\textbf{side A}}}
\ThreeDput[normal=1 0 0](4,0,0){\psframe*[linecolor=gray!15](4,4)
    \rput(2,2){\Huge\textbf{side B}}}
% Die kleinen Achsen
\ThreeDput[normal=0 0 1](0,0,4){\psline(4,0)\uput[90](3,0){X$_{top}$}
    \psline(0,4)\uput[0](0,3){Y$_{top}$}}
\ThreeDput[normal=0 1 0](4,4,0){\psline(4,0)\uput[90](3,0){X$_{A}$}
    \psline(0,4)\uput[0](0,3){Y$_{A}$}}
\ThreeDput[normal=1 0 0](4,0,0){\psline(4,0)\uput[90](3,0){X$_{B}$}
    \psline(0,4)\uput[0](0,3){Y$_{B}$}}
\end{pspicture}
```

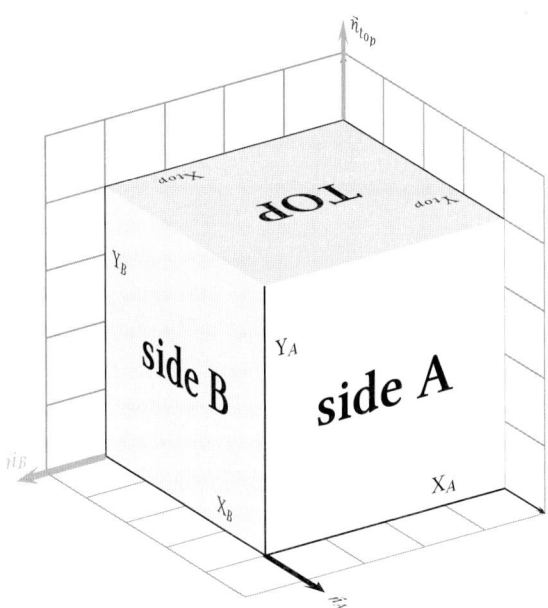

3D parameters

Table 23.3 shows a summary of the additional parameters that can be used for 3D illustrations with pst-3d.

name	type	default
viewpoint	valuex valuey valuez	1 -1 1
viewangle	angle	0
normal	valuex valuey valuez	0 0 1
embedangle	angle	0

Table 23.3: Summary of the additional 3D parameters

viewpoint The view point from which we "see" a 3D object is a major factor in its display. viewpoint specifies the (x y z) coordinates of the direction, or vector, of the viewpoint. Because of the parallel projection, the length of the vector is unimportant: (1 0.5 1.5) and (2 1 3) achieve the same illustrations. Figure 23.2 shows how someone would look at an illustration with that viewpoint vector – though the actual figure itself is seen from another direction of course.

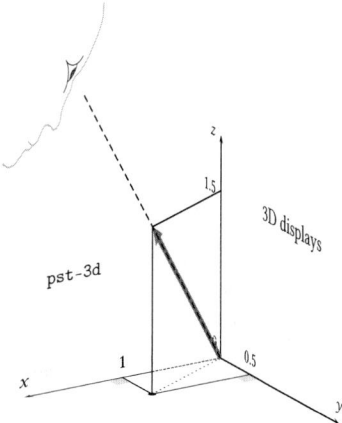

Figure 23.2: Specifying the viewpoint

The actual viewpoint defined for Figure 23.2 was viewpoint=3 5 2. If instead you wanted to view it from greater height up the z axis for example, you could choose the setting viewpoint=1 1 3. The observer moves from the centre (origin) by one unit in the x and y directions respectively and three units in the z direction.

Beware that you can't specify zero for any of the values of viewpoint as otherwise a division by zero would be attempted internally. Specifying 0.001 instead is good enough to achieve a similar effect while not dividing by zero.

There are particular values for viewpoint that often produce good results for viewing three-dimensional illustrations. One for example is viewpoint=1 1 0.5, which corresponds to a horizontal rotation by 45° and a vertical rotation by about 20°. Another good one is

23 Three-dimensional figures

viewpoint=1.5 1 0.5, which corresponds to a horizontal rotation by $33°$ and the same vertical rotation. Each of these is used in the following examples.

```
\usepackage{pstricks,pst-3d,multido}
\begin{pspicture}(-3,-1.75)(3,4)
    \psset{unit=0.75,viewpoint=1 1 0.5}
    \IIIDKOSystem[subgriddiv=0,gridcolor=black!40]{5}
\end{pspicture}\hfill
\begin{pspicture}(-3,-1.75)(2.2,3.5)
    \psset{unit=0.75,viewpoint=1 1.5 0.5,gridlabels=6pt}
    \IIIDKOSystem[subgriddiv=0,gridcolor=black!40]{5}
\end{pspicture}
```

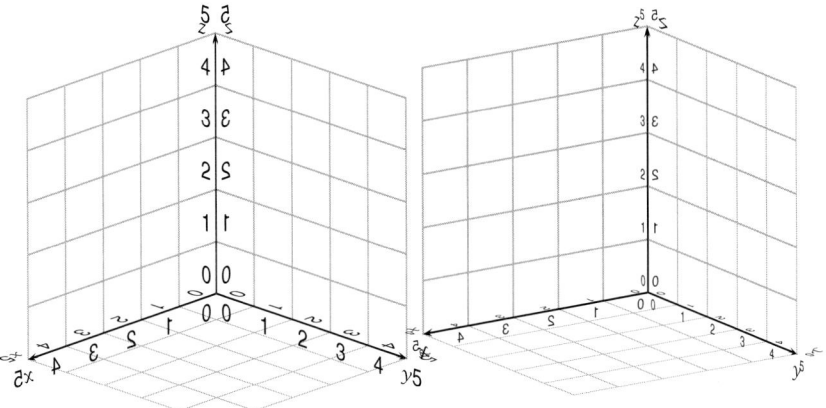

viewangle In addition to the viewpoint, everything can be rotated by an angle viewangle. There are other ways to achieve this, such as using \rotatebox, but this method has some advantages here, including being able to define a plane for the view.

Each of the examples below has a rectangle in the xy plane to avoid confusion between top and bottom with these "wire frame models".

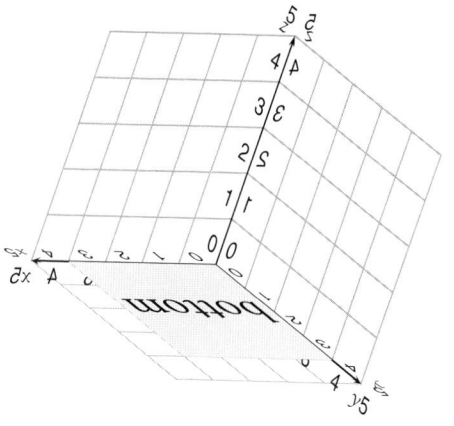

```
\usepackage{pstricks,pst-3d}

\begin{pspicture}(-3,-2.25)(-3,3.25)
    \psset{unit=0.7,viewpoint=1 1 0.5,
        viewangle=20}
    \IIIDKOSystem[subgriddiv=0,
        gridcolor=black!40]{5}
    \ThreeDput(0,0,0){%
        \psframe*[linecolor=gray!20](4,4)}
    \ThreeDput(2,2,0){\Huge bottom}
\end{pspicture}
```

23.1 pst-3d – Shadows, tilting, and three-dimensional illustrations

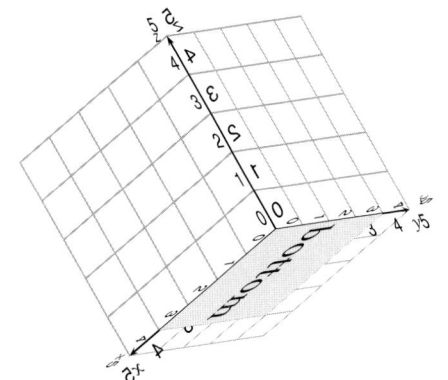

```
\usepackage{pst-3d}

\begin{pspicture}(-4,-2.25)(2.25,2.75)
    \psset{unit=0.7,viewpoint=1 1.5 0.5,
      viewangle=-30}
    \IIIDKOSystem[subgriddiv=0,
      gridcolor=black!40]{5}
    \ThreeDput(0,0,0){%
      \psframe*[linecolor=gray!20](4,4)}
    \ThreeDput(2,2,0){\Huge bottom}
\end{pspicture}
```

normal   normal specifies the direction of the normal vector, which is perpendicular to the corresponding plane. The normal vector specifies the orientation of an object in three-dimensional space unambiguously.

```
\usepackage{pstricks,pst-3d}
\begin{pspicture}(-4,-1.5)(3,5)
    \psset{viewpoint=1 1.5 0.5} \IIIDKOSystem[subgriddiv=0,gridcolor=black!40]{5}
    \ThreeDput(0,0,0){\psframe*[linecolor=gray!20](4,4)}
    \ThreeDput(2,2,0){\huge\psrotatedown{xy plane}}
    \ThreeDput[normal=0 -1 0](0,0,0){\psframe*[linecolor=gray!15](4,4)}
    \ThreeDput[normal=0 1 0](2,0,2){\huge xz plane}
    \ThreeDput[normal=1 0 0](0,0,0){\psframe*[linecolor=gray!10](4,4)}
    \ThreeDput[normal=1 0 0](0,2,2){\huge yz plane}
    \ThreeDput[normal=0 0 1](0,0,0){\psline{->}(0,0)(0,5)\psline{->}(0,0)(5,0)}% xy
    \ThreeDput[normal=0 1 0](0,0,0){\psline{->}(0,0)(0,5)}% xz
\end{pspicture}
```

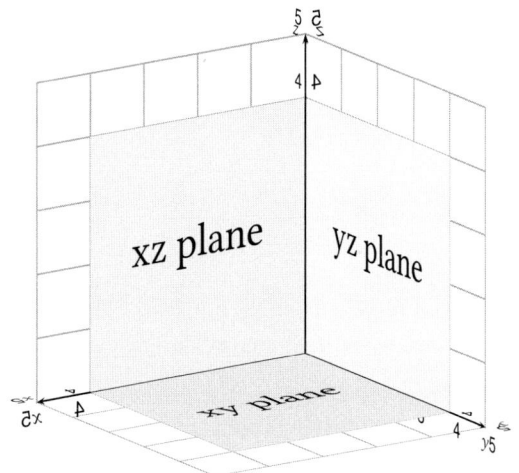

23 Three-dimensional figures

Without an allocation through the normal vector the example above would have been much harder to create. Let's step through the code and explain it:

`\psset{viewpoint=1 1.5 0.5}`
    The `viewpoint` is set to the point $P(1, 1.5, 0.5)$.

`\DreiDKOSystem{5}`
    First the coordinate system with the grid is drawn such that axes and grids remain visible on the planes for a better optical attribution.

`\ThreeDput(0,0,0){\psframe*[linecolor=gray!20](4,4)}`
    This draws a square with sides of length four, with its bottom left corner at the coordinate origin. No normal vector was specified here, so the default value $\vec{n} = (0, 0, 1)$ is assumed and the square is placed in the first quadrant of the xy plane.

`\ThreeDput(2,2,0){\huge\psrotatedown{xy plane}}`
    This puts the text into the xy plane, centred at $(2, 2, 0)$ and rotated by $180°$.

`\ThreeDput[normal=0 -1 0](0,0,0){\psframe*[linecolor=gray!15](4,4)}`
    This draws a square with sides of length four, with its bottom left corner at the coordinate origin. Because the normal vector is the "negative" y axis, however, the square is placed in the first quadrant of the xz plane. With `normal=0 1 0` it would have been placed in the second quadrant.

`\ThreeDput[normal=0 1 0](2,0,2){\huge xz plane}`
    This puts the text into the xz plane, centred at $(2, 0, 2)$. Because the xz plane is seen from behind from the viewpoint, the normal vector of the plane has to be reversed to avoid the text being seen from "behind".

`\ThreeDput[normal=1 0 0](0,0,0){\psframe*[linecolor=gray!10](4,4)}`
    This draws a square with sides of length four, with its bottom left corner at the coordinate origin. The normal vector is the "positive" x axis, so the square is placed in the first quadrant of the yz plane.

`\ThreeDput[normal=1 0 0](0,2,2){\huge yz plane}`
    This puts the text into the yz plane centred at $(0, 2, 2)$. Because the text is written on the "positive" side of the plane, the normal vector remains the same.

`\ThreeDput[normal=0 0 1](0,0,0)`
    The coordinate axes have been overwritten by the three planes, so we need to draw them again, starting with the xy axes.

`\ThreeDput[normal=0 1 0](0,0,0)`
    And finally redrawing the z axis.

embedangle

`viewangle` performs a rotation perpendicular to the plane of the observer; `embedangle` performs a rotation perpendicular to the normal vector. The angle is specified in the mathematical sense, counterclockwise.

23.1 pst-3d – Shadows, tilting, and three-dimensional illustrations

```
\usepackage{pstricks,pst-3d}
\def\tBlack#1#2{\psframe[style=#2](2,2)%
    \rput(1,1){\textcolor{#1}{\textbf{PSTricks}}}}
\newpsstyle{SolidYellow}{fillstyle=solid,fillcolor=yellow}% text
\newpsstyle{TransparencyRed}{fillstyle=vlines,hatchcolor=red,
    hatchwidth=0.1\pslinewidth,hatchsep=1\pslinewidth}% Text
\newpsstyle{TransparencyBlue}{fillstyle=vlines,hatchcolor=gray!25,
    hatchwidth=0.1\pslinewidth,hatchsep=1\pslinewidth}
\begin{pspicture}(-1.2,-2)(4.8,3.7)
\ThreeDput{\psgrid[subgriddiv=0](-2,0)(4,3)} % embedangle=0
\ThreeDput(-1,0,0){\tBlack{black}{SolidYellow}}
\ThreeDput(2,0,0){\tBlack{black}{SolidYellow}}
\ThreeDput[embedangle=50](-1,0,0){\tBlack{gray}{TransparencyRed}}
\ThreeDput[embedangle=50](2,0,0){\tBlack{gray}{TransparencyBlue}}
% the normal vectors
\ThreeDput[normal=0 1 0](-1,0,0){\psline[linewidth=0.1,linecolor=red](0,4)}
\ThreeDput[normal=0 1 0](2,0,0){\psline[linewidth=0.1,linecolor=blue](0,4)}
\end{pspicture}
%
\psset{viewpoint=1 1 100}
\begin{pspicture}(-2.5,-4.75)(2.8,1.6)
\ThreeDput{\psgrid[subgriddiv=0](-2,0)(4,3)} % embedangle=0
\ThreeDput(-1,0,0){\tBlack{black}{SolidYellow}}
\ThreeDput(2,0,0){\tBlack{black}{SolidYellow}}
\ThreeDput[embedangle=50](-1,0,0){\tBlack{gray}{TransparencyRed}}
\ThreeDput[embedangle=50](2,0,0){\tBlack{gray}{TransparencyBlue}}
% the normal vectors
\ThreeDput[normal=0 1 0](-1,0,0){\psline[linewidth=0.1,linecolor=red](0,4)}
\ThreeDput[normal=0 1 0](2,0,0){\psline[linewidth=0.1,linecolor=blue](0,4)}
\end{pspicture}
```

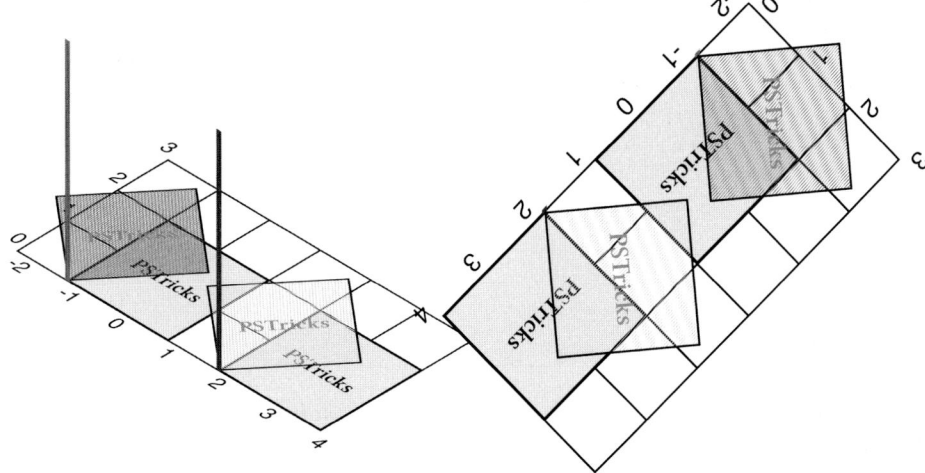

23 Three-dimensional figures

23.2 pst-ob3d – Simple three-dimensional objects

pst-ob3d only provides commands for simple three-dimensional objects, namely cuboids and die, but if this is all you need, it makes sense to use this package rather than the extended packages like pst-solides3d (cf. Section 23.6 on page 391) or pst-3dplot (cf. Section 23.5 on page 358).

23.2.1 Parameters

Table 23.4 shows a summary of the special parameters for pst-ob3d. Each one is then explained in turn below.

Table 23.4: Summary of the special parameters for pst-ob3d

name	type	default
PstDebug	0|1	0
OnlyVisibleFaces	boolean	false
RandomFaces	boolean	false
Corners	boolean	false
CornersColor	colour	black
CornersLength	value	0.15

PstDebug

Switching PstDebug from "off" (0) to "on" (1) lets you mark the side planes to get a better overview of the position of the cuboid or cube in space.

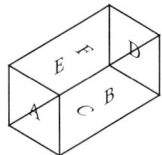
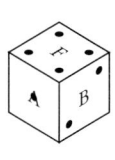

```
\usepackage{pstricks,pst-ob3d}

\begin{pspicture}(4,1.25)
  \rput(-.25,-0.3){%
    \PstCube[PstDebug=1]{1}{2}{1}}
  \rput(3,0){\PstDie[PstDebug=1]}
\end{pspicture}
```

23-02-1

OnlyVisibleFaces

OnlyVisibleFaces is a boolean variable controlling the visibility of the edges on the far side of the cuboid. OnlyVisibleFaces=true makes the cuboid appear solid.

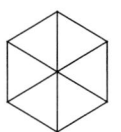
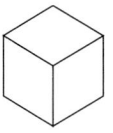

```
\usepackage{pstricks,pst-ob3d}

\begin{pspicture}(4,1.25)
  \rput(1,0){\PstCube{1}{1}{1}}
  \rput(3,0){%
    \PstCube[OnlyVisibleFaces=true]%
      {1}{1}{1}}
\end{pspicture}
```

23-02-2

23.2 pst-ob3d – Simple three-dimensional objects

RandomFaces

The keyword RandomFaces has only a meaning for dies to simulate a throw of them. The hazard is managed by the package random from Donald Arseneau. The random seed is set by using the time when the compilation occur. It can also be set by the TeX counter randomi.

```
\usepackage{pstricks,pst-ob3d}
\PstDie[dotscale=2,RandomFaces]
\hspace*{2cm}
\PstDie[dotscale=2,fillstyle=solid,fillcolor=cyan,RandomFaces]
\hspace*{2cm} \randomi=12345
\PstDie[dotscale=1.5,fillstyle=solid,fillcolor=magenta,RandomFaces]
```

Corners, CornersColor, and CornersLength

Corners determines whether the corners of the cuboid are "cut off". If you set Corners=true, you can use the other two parameters to control the size and colour of the corners. The value of CornersLength is multiplied by the unit values for each direction. It must rather be a number between 0 and 0.5, otherwise the results will look strange.

```
\usepackage{pstricks,pst-ob3d}
\begin{pspicture}(10,1.25)
\rput(1,0){\PstCube{1}{1}{1}}
\rput(3,0){\PstCube[OnlyVisibleFaces=true,Corners=true]{1}{1}{1}}
\rput(5,0){\PstCube[Corners=true,CornersColor=blue,
   fillstyle=solid,fillcolor=cyan,viewpoint=1 2 1]{1}{1}{1}}
\rput(7,0){\PstCube[Corners=true,CornersLength=0.1,
   fillstyle=solid,fillcolor=cyan,viewpoint=2 1 1]{1}{1}{1}}
\rput(9,0.2){\PstCube[Corners=true,fillstyle=solid,fillcolor=cyan,
   viewpoint=2 1 1]{1}{1}{1}}
\end{pspicture}
```

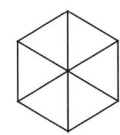 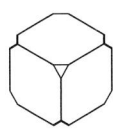 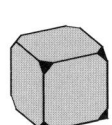 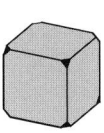 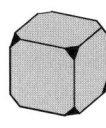

23.2.2 Commands

pst-ob3d provides two commands:

\PstCube{*x length*}{*y length*}{*z length*}   \PstDie [settings]

\PstDie is by default a unit cube, though you can make it larger or smaller by setting the optional local unit parameter, as in the following example.

23 Three-dimensional figures

```
\usepackage{pstricks,pst-ob3d}
\begin{pspicture}(-1,-0.5)(\linewidth,1.7)
  \psset{fillstyle=solid,fillcolor=yellow,RandomFaces=true}
  \rput(0,0){\PstDie[viewpoint=1 -5 1]}\rput(1.5,0){\PstDie[viewpoint=1 -3 1]}
  \rput(3,-0.5){\PstDie[unit=1.5,dotscale=2,viewpoint=1 -1 1]}
  \rput(4.5,0){\PstDie[viewpoint=1 -0.3 1]}\rput(6,0){\PstDie[viewpoint=1 0.3 1]}
  \rput(7.5,0){\PstCube[viewpoint=1 1 1,fillcolor=magenta]{2}{1}{1}}
  \rput(9,0){\PstCube[viewpoint=1 3 3,fillcolor=cyan]{2}{1}{1}}
\end{pspicture}
```

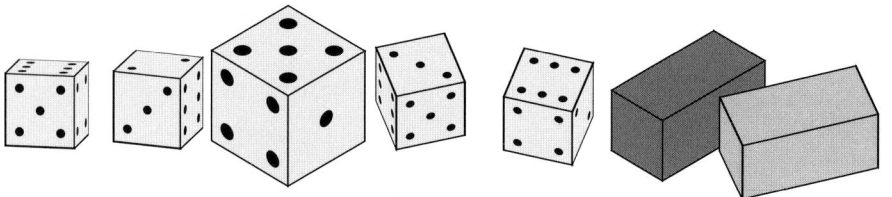

23.3 pst-gr3d – Three-dimensional grids

The pst-gr3d package is based on pst-3d, but simplifies its use significantly. Three-dimensional grid models have many practical applications, so this package can be a real help. You can achieve the same functionality with most of the other 3D packages, but not in this grid-optimized form. [22] The package provides the \PstGridThreeD command for creating 3D grids, which is based on the \ThreeDput command from pst-3d (cf. Section 23.1.3) in conjunction with \psgrid from the pstricks base package (cf. Section 3.1 on page 33). It also provides special parameters and additional commands for modifying the grid.

23.3.1 Parameters

You can use the special parameters listed in Table 23.5 as well as the ones defined already in Section 23.1.3 on page 338.

Table 23.5: Summary of the additional parameters available with pst-gr3d

name	type	default
PstDebug	0|1	0
PstPicture	boolean	true
GridThreeDXUnit	values	1
GridThreeDYUnit	values	1
GridThreeDZUnit	values	1
GridThreeDXPos	values	0
GridThreeDYPos	values	0
GridThreeDZPos	values	0
GridThreeNodes	boolean	false

PstDebug

Switching `PstDebug` from "off" (0) to "on" (1) shows the corresponding bounding box, which can be useful if there are problems with placing the object.

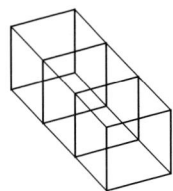

```
\usepackage{pstricks,pst-gr3d}

\PstGridThreeD(3,1,1)
```

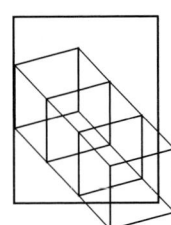

```
\usepackage{pstricks,pst-gr3d}

\psset{PstDebug=1}
\PstGridThreeD(3,1,1)
```

Bear in mind that the `pst-fill` package (cf. Section 19.1.7 on page 299) also has a PstDebug option, and these overlap when both packages are used at the same time. However, as long as you load `pst-fill` **before** loading `pst-gr3d`, the option works as expected.

PstPicture

The Boolean variable `PstPicture` determines whether or not the grid is inserted into a pspicture environment. The default value is true, to reserve the necessary space. If a different viewpoint (cf. Section 23.1.3 on page 341) is being used, however, this may not be appropriate, because then the figure will be a different size when viewed from that observation angle so won't necessarily fit into the pspicture environment, whose size is determined internally.

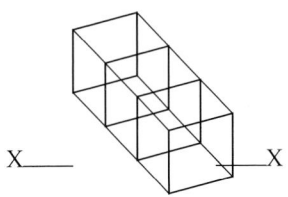

```
\usepackage{pstricks,pst-gr3d}

X\rule{20pt}{0.5pt}\PstGridThreeD(3,1,1)%
\rule{20pt}{0.5pt}X
```

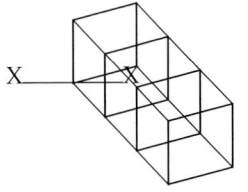

```
\usepackage{pstricks,pst-gr3d}

X\rule{20pt}{0.5pt}%
\PstGridThreeD[PstPicture=false](3,1,1)%
\rule{20pt}{0.5pt}X
```

23 Three-dimensional figures

As the first example shows, the internally-determined size of the pspicture environment is not optimal: the line that corresponds to the base line restarts inside the figure. In the second example no pspicture environment is created to reserve space; the line representing the base line carries straight on, inside the figure.

GridThreeDXUnit, GridThreeDYUnit, GridThreeDZUnit

These parameters denote the scale factors for the three dimensions. These factors have to be **integer** numbers; decimal values are not allowed.

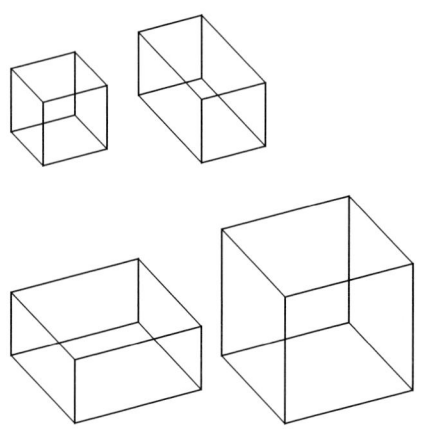

```
\usepackage{pstricks,pst-gr3d}

\psset{griddots=0}
\PstGridThreeD(1,1,1)\hspace{20pt}
\PstGridThreeD[GridThreeDXUnit=2](1,1,1)
\par
\PstGridThreeD[GridThreeDXUnit=2,
   GridThreeDYUnit=2](1,1,1)\hspace{25pt}
\PstGridThreeD[GridThreeDXUnit=2,
   GridThreeDYUnit=2,
   GridThreeDZUnit=2](1,1,1)
```

23-03-

GridThreeDXPos, GridThreeDYPos, GridThreeDZPos

These three parameters translate the corner of the coordinate grid, which is normally at $(0,0,0)$, by the specified values, which have to be **integer** numbers. Decimal values are not allowed, but negative integer numbers are possible. In the example below, the cuboid is translated by two units in the x direction, one unit in the y direction, and three units in the z direction. Most of the source code is not essential here; it only serves to illustrate the process.

Specifying PstPicture=false in the source code is important here as otherwise the grid would be placed in a new pspicture environment. This would inevitably lead to an offset of the cuboid here because the coordinate origins would not be the same anymore.

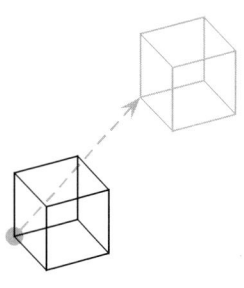

```
\usepackage{pstricks,pst-gr3d}

\SpecialCoor
\psset{GridThreeDNodes=true,arrowscale=2}
\def\PstGridThreeDHookEnd{%
   \ThreeDput(0,0,0){\rnode{A}{}}
   \ThreeDput(2,1,3){\rnode{B}{}}%
   \pcline[linestyle=dashed]{*->}(A)(B)%
   \PstGridThreeD[PstPicture=false,gridcolor=black,
      GridThreeDXPos=0,GridThreeDYPos=0,
      GridThreeDZPos=0](1,1,1)}
\PstGridThreeD[linecolor=red,gridcolor=red,
   GridThreeDXPos=2,GridThreeDYPos=1,
   GridThreeDZPos=3](1,1,1)
```

23-03-6

GridThreeDNodes

This Boolean variable determines whether or not each grid point gets a node name. The default for this option is false because the required memory is significant for large grids. The names of the nodes are generated in matrix format Gr3dNodexyz. The name Gr3dNode is followed by a three-digit number that corresponds to the coordinates, for example Gr3dNode132 is the node reached when moving one unit in the x direction, three units in the y direction, and two units in the z direction. The node names remain available after the \PstGridThreeD command, so you can reference them for many applications, such as for arbitrary node connections as in the example below. They are always global and are overwritten by subsequent applications of \PstGridThreeD.

```
\usepackage{pstricks,pst-gr3d,pst-node,multido}\SpecialCoor
\PstGridThreeD[GridThreeDNodes=true,unit=2.5](2,3,2)
\multido{\ix=0+1}{3}{%
    \multido{\iy=0+1}{4}{%
        \multido{\iz=0+1}{3}{%
            \rput*(Gr3dNode\ix\iy\iz){\footnotesize $\ix\iy\iz$}}}}
\psset{linecolor=blue,linestyle=dashed,linewidth=0.3pt,arrowscale=2,nodesep=8pt}
\pcline{->}(Gr3dNode000)(Gr3dNode202)\pccurve{->}(Gr3dNode000)(Gr3dNode232)
```

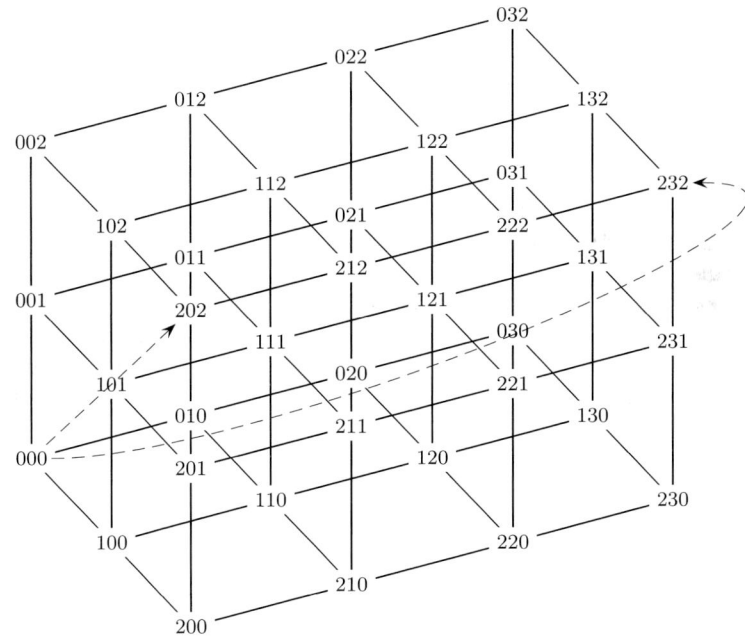

23.3.2 Commands

\PstGridThreeD is the main grid-drawing command provided by the pst-gr3d package, but there are several other commands that are always called during the creation of a grid. These default to the empty commands, but by redefining them you can create many variations on the basic grid. The following sections discuss each command in turn.

23 Three-dimensional figures

\PstGridThreeD

\PstGridThreeD [settings] (x,y,z)

This command is equivalent to calling \ThreeDput{\psgrid} several times with \multido (cf. Section 33.6 on page 738) to draw the grids. Therefore you can't change the form of the grid with the parameters for lines, but have to use the parameters for \psgrid summarized in Table 3.2 on page 33. \PstGridThreeD requires the specification of xyz, which denotes the volume of grid unit cubes to be drawn.

In the following example viewpoint=1.2 -0.6 0.8 is used for the grids; this is not a limitation however – it can always be changed.

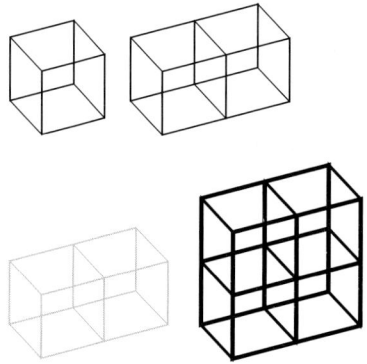

```
\usepackage{pstricks,pst-gr3d}

\PstGridThreeD(1,1,1)\qquad
\PstGridThreeD[griddots=0](1,2,1)

\PstGridThreeD[gridcolor=cyan,
    griddots=0](1,2,1)\qquad
\PstGridThreeD[griddots=0,
    gridwidth=2pt](1,2,2)
```

\PstGridThreeDHookEnd

It isn't straightforward to work with combinations of commands that each end with \psgrid, especially when embedding everything in a pspicture environment. This is where \PstGridThreeDHookEnd comes into play.

\PstGridThreeDHookEnd{}

pst-gr3d always calls this command **before** the end of the pspicture environment; by default it's an empty command, but you can redefine it to do virtually anything. If for example you want to highlight a certain area in a created grid with colour, you can define \PstGridThreeDHookEnd to draw that area again with another colour. Again it is important to set the PstPicture option to false within this command so as not to open a new pspicture environment.

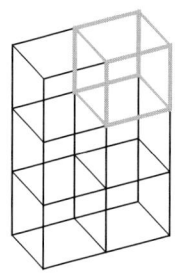

```
\usepackage{pstricks,pst-gr3d,pst-node,multido}

\def\PstGridThreeDHookEnd{%
    \PstGridThreeD[PstPicture=false,griddots=0,
        gridcolor=red,gridwidth=2pt,
        GridThreeDYPos=1,GridThreeDZPos=2](1,1,1)}%
\PstGridThreeD(1,2,3)
```

23.3 pst-gr3d – Three-dimensional grids

\PstGridThreeDHookXFace, \PstGridThreeDHookYFace, and \PstGridThreeDHookZFace

In contrast to \PstGridThreeDHookEnd, these commands are called when the corresponding coordinate is drawn. You can use them to interfere with the creation of the grid, such as colouring a certain face. Again all commands default to be empty but can be redefined arbitrarily.

```
\PstGridThreeDHookXFace{}    \PstGridThreeDHookYFace{}
\PstGridThreeDHookZFace{}
```

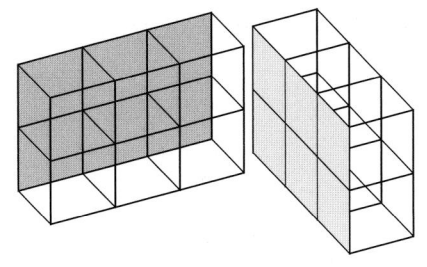

```
\usepackage{pstricks,pst-gr3d}

\def\PstGridThreeDHookXFace{%
  \ifnum\multidocount=1
    \psframe*[linecolor=cyan](3,2)\fi}
\def\PstGridThreeDHookYFace{\psset{griddots=0}}
\PstGridThreeD(1,3,2)\def\PstGridThreeDHookXFace{}~
\def\PstGridThreeDHookYFace{\ifnum\multidocount=2
  \psframe*[linecolor=yellow](-3,0)(0,2)\fi}
\PstGridThreeD(3,1,2)
```

\PstGridThreeDHookNode

This command is called **after** the definition of a node and again defaults to be empty. You can redefine it to set any symbol as the node marker.

```
\PstGridThreeDHookNode{}
```

There is one special case: if you want to draw all nodes with a small circle, use the internally-defined \PstGridThreeDNodeProcessor command inside your definition of \PstGridThreeDHookNode, and it will do exactly that. Its syntax is:

```
\PstGridThreeDNodeProcessor{colour}
```

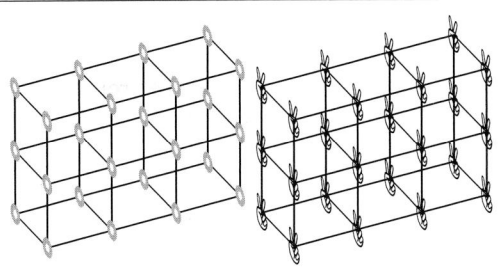

```
\usepackage{pstricks,pst-gr3d,pifont}

{\def\PstGridThreeDHookNode{%
    \PstGridThreeDNodeProcessor{red}}
  \PstGridThreeD(1,3,2)}\quad
\def\PstGridThreeDHookNode{%
  \psscalebox{2}{\ding{44}}}
\PstGridThreeD(1,3,2)
```

```
\usepackage{pst-gr3d}\SpecialCoor
\def\PstGridThreeDHookEnd{{\psset{PstPicture=false,gridwidth=0.1}
  {\def\PstGridThreeDHookNode{\PstGridThreeDNodeProcessor{blue}}
    \PstGridThreeD[gridcolor=blue,GridThreeDZPos=3](0,7,0)}
  {\def\PstGridThreeDHookNode{\PstGridThreeDNodeProcessor{red}}
    \PstGridThreeD[gridcolor=red,GridThreeDXPos=1,GridThreeDZPos=1](0,3,1)}
  {\def\PstGridThreeDHookNode{\PstGridThreeDNodeProcessor{green}}
    \PstGridThreeD[gridcolor=green,GridThreeDYPos=6](1,1,1)}}}
```

23 Three-dimensional figures

```
\PstGridThreeD[gridwidth=0.04,GridThreeDNodes=true](1,7,3)
\rput([Rx=0.15,angle=140]Gr3dNode033){\psline[linecolor=blue]{<-}(0.8;150)}
\rput([Rx=0.95,angle=140]Gr3dNode033){\shortstack{1d grid\\\small (X=8,Y=1,Z=1)}}
\rput([Rx=0.15,angle=-50]Gr3dNode121){\psline[linecolor=red]{<-}(1.2;-50)}
\rput([Rx=1.5,angle=-55]Gr3dNode121){\shortstack{2d grid\\\small (X=4,Y=2,Z=1)}}
\rput([Rx=0.05,angle=-80]Gr3dNode160){\psline[linecolor=green]{<-}(0.8;-80)}
\rput([Rx=0.3,angle=-80]Gr3dNode160){\shortstack{3d grid\\\small (X=2,Y=2,Z=2)}}
```

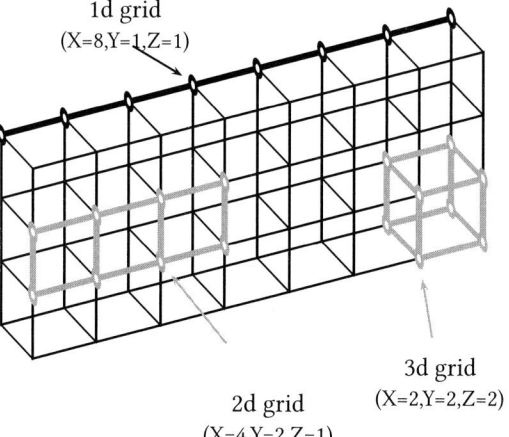

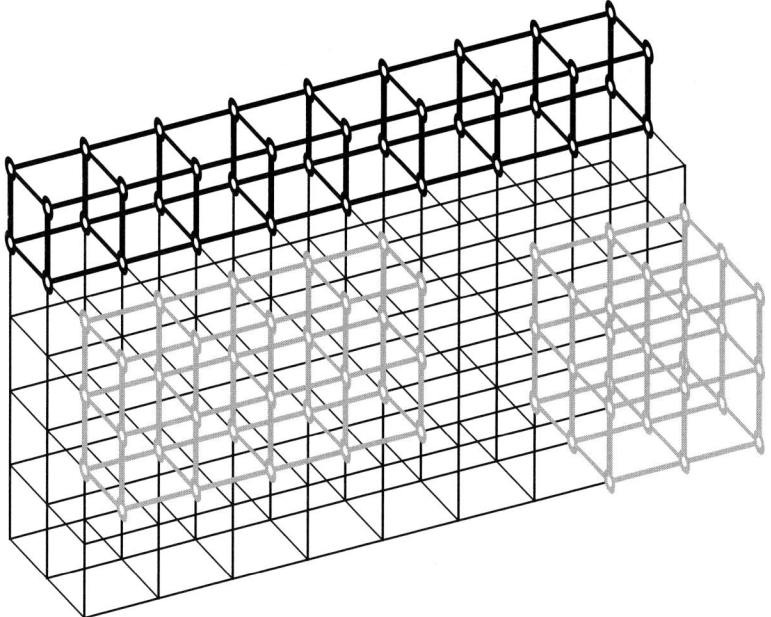

Figure 23.3: Extension of the grid size (Denis Girou)

23.4 pst-fr3d – Buttons with 3D effects

The `pst-fr3d` package by Denis Girou is in principle an extension of the `\psframebox` command (cf. Section 10.2.1 on page 111) – it create buttons (or boxes) with 3D effects. [21] The size of the frame is determined by its content, but you can use the usual methods to change it.[1] The buttons are especially suited for presentations where links to further slides are to be inserted.

23.4.1 Parameters

Table 23.6 summarizes the special parameters, and then each is discussed in turn below. In addition to those parameters, you can also use the following parameters defined in the standard package: `linestyle`, `linecolor`, `doubleline`, and `doublecolor`. Each of these is preset internally by the package to the usual values. Avoid using `border`, `linearc`, and `shadow` as the results can be unexpected.

name	type	default
FrameBoxThreeDOn	boolean	true
FrameBoxThreeDOpposite	boolean	false
FrameBoxThreeDColorHSB	value value value	0 0 0.5
FrameBoxThreeDBrightnessDistance	-1...1	0.15

Table 23.6: Summary of the additional parameters for the pst-fr3d package

FrameBoxThreeDOn

The Boolean variable `FrameBoxThreeDOn` simulates the on/off state of a button through a corresponding shadow. The "on" state (default setting of `true`) displays a pressed and therefore lowered button.

```
\usepackage{pst-fr3d}

\PstFrameBoxThreeD[FrameBoxThreeDOn=false]{\Large off}
\quad\PstFrameBoxThreeD{\Large on}% on is default
```

FrameBoxThreeDOpposite

By default, the colours of the left and lower sides of the button match, as do those of the right and upper sides. Setting `FrameBoxThreeDOpposite=true` changes this so that opposite sides match in colour, i.e. left and right, and top and bottom.

```
\usepackage{pstricks,pst-fr3d}
\newcommand\Button{\textcolor{white}{\textbf{Button}}}
\psset{linewidth=0.2}
\PstFrameBoxThreeD{\Button}
\PstFrameBoxThreeD[FrameBoxThreeDOn=false]{\Button}
\PstFrameBoxThreeD[FrameBoxThreeDOpposite=true]{\Button}
\PstFrameBoxThreeD[FrameBoxThreeDColorHSB=0.7 0.4 0.8,FrameBoxThreeDOn=false,
     FrameBoxThreeDOpposite=true]{\Button}
```

---

[1] For example you can enlarge the content by drawing invisible lines with \rule or \vphantom.

23 Three-dimensional figures

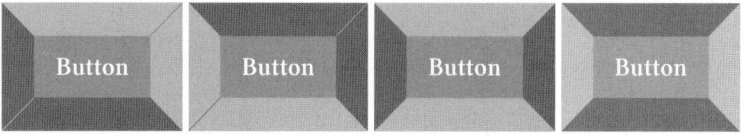

FrameBoxThreeDColorHSB

The colour of the buttons has to specified in the HSB colour model (Hue, Saturation, Brightness, cf. Table 2.5 on page 11). You can assign this as real numeric values separated by spaces to the FrameBoxThreeDColorHSB parameter. Only the inside of the button actually takes this colour; the border colours are determined from the B value of this colour based on the value of FrameBoxThreeDBrightnessDistance (explained in the next section). Note that a negative value for B results in the inside of the button not being filled with any colour.

```
\usepackage{pst-fr3d}   \psset{doublesep=0.1}
\PstFrameBoxThreeD[FrameBoxThreeDColorHSB=0.1 0.3 0.5]{Button}
\PstFrameBoxThreeD[FrameBoxThreeDColorHSB=0.6 0.3 0.5]{Button}
\PstFrameBoxThreeD[FrameBoxThreeDColorHSB=0.4 0.1 0.5]{\Huge$\frac{1}{\sqrt{3}}$}
\PstFrameBoxThreeD[FrameBoxThreeDColorHSB=0.9 0.5 0.5]{%
   \psovalbox[fillstyle=solid,fillcolor=yellow]{Button}}
\PstFrameBoxThreeD[FrameBoxThreeDColorHSB=0.4 0.7 0.2]{%
   \PstFrameBoxThreeD[FrameBoxThreeDColorHSB=0.4 0.7 0.5]{%
      \PstFrameBoxThreeD[FrameBoxThreeDColorHSB=0.4 0.7 0.8]{Button}}}%
```

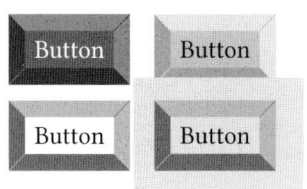

```
\usepackage{pstricks,pst-fr3d}   \psset{doublesep=0.2}
\PstFrameBoxThreeD[FrameBoxThreeDColorHSB=0 0 0.3]{%
   \color{white}Button}\quad
\PstFrameBoxThreeD[FrameBoxThreeDColorHSB=0 0 .7]{Button}\\[5
\PstFrameBoxThreeD[FrameBoxThreeDColorHSB=0 0 -1]{Button}\qua
\psframe*[linecolor=black!15](-0.3,-0.65)(2.1,0.9)
\PstFrameBoxThreeD[FrameBoxThreeDColorHSB=0 0 -1]{Button}
```

FrameBoxThreeDBrightnessDistance

The FrameBoxThreeDBrightnessDistance option alters the "shadow effect" on the frame by changing the relation between the border colours and the main colour FrameBoxThreeDColorHSB. A negative value has the same effect as FrameBoxThreeDOn=false; a 0 value achieves no shadow effect – the inside and the outside have the same colour. The maximum value is 1.

```
\usepackage{pst-fr3d}   \psset{doublesep=0.2}
\PstFrameBoxThreeD[FrameBoxThreeDColorHSB=0.8 0.3 0.6]{\textbf{Button}}
\PstFrameBoxThreeD[FrameBoxThreeDColorHSB=0.8 0.3 0.6,
```

```
    FrameBoxThreeDBrightnessDistance=0.3]{\textbf{Button}}
\PstFrameBoxThreeD[FrameBoxThreeDColorHSB=0.8 0.3 0.6,
    FrameBoxThreeDBrightnessDistance=0.5]{\textbf{Button}}
\PstFrameBoxThreeD[FrameBoxThreeDColorHSB=0.8 0.3 0.8,
    FrameBoxThreeDBrightnessDistance=0.3]{\textbf{Button}}
\PstFrameBoxThreeD[FrameBoxThreeDColorHSB=0.8 0.3 0.6,
    FrameBoxThreeDBrightnessDistance=-0.2]{\textbf{Button}}
```

23.4.2 Command

There is only one command defined in this package:

\PstFrameBoxThreeDMacro [settings] {*material*}

You can put anything in the *material* argument, though line breaks are only possible by using an appropriate \parbox or table.

```
\usepackage{pstricks,pst-tree,pst-fr3d}
\newcommand{\MyNode}[2]{%
  \TR{\PstFrameBoxThreeD[FrameBoxThreeDOn=#2,FrameBoxThreeDColorHSB=0.2 0.8 0.5,
    FrameBoxThreeDBrightnessDistance=0.2]{\textcolor{white}{#1}}}}
\renewcommand{\psedge}[2]{\ncangle{#2}{#1}}
\psset{angleB=-90,angleA=90,levelsep=2,treesep=3}
\pstree{\MyNode{Jana}{true}}{%
  \pstree{\MyNode{Felix}{true}}{%
    \pstree{\MyNode{Beate}{false}}{%
      \MyNode{Otto}{false}}
    \MyNode{Waltraudt}{false}}
  \MyNode{Herbert}{false}}
```

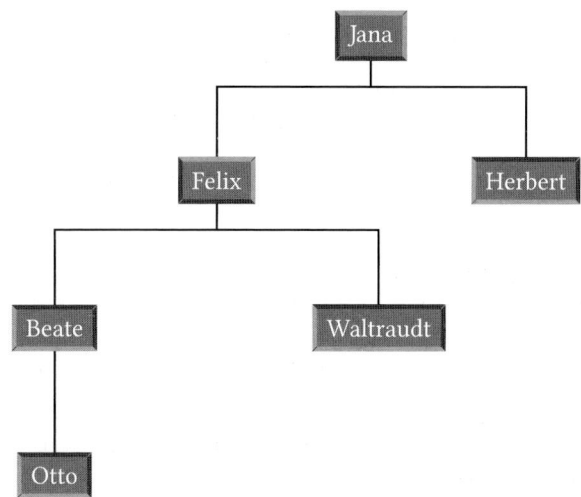

23.5 pst-3dplot – 3D parallel projection of functions and data

pst-3dplot supports the display (in two dimensions) of three-dimensional mathematical functions and the plotting of three-dimensional data sets. It is based on the pst-plot package (cf. Chapter 15 on page 165) and in principle uses the same syntax. Furthermore pst-3dplot provides commands for the parallel projection of simple three-dimensional points, lines, curves, and objects. The main difference between this package and the pst-3d and pst-solides3d packages (cf. Section 23.1 on page 334, cf. Section 23.6 on page 391) is the lack of the viewpoint option. This simplifies use, but also restricts the possibilities.

23.5.1 The parallel projection

Figure 23.4 shows a three-dimensional point $P(x,y,z)$ in a Cartesian coordinate system (x,y,z) with a transformation to the two-dimensional point $P^*(x^*,y^*)$ of the coordinate system (x_E, y_E).

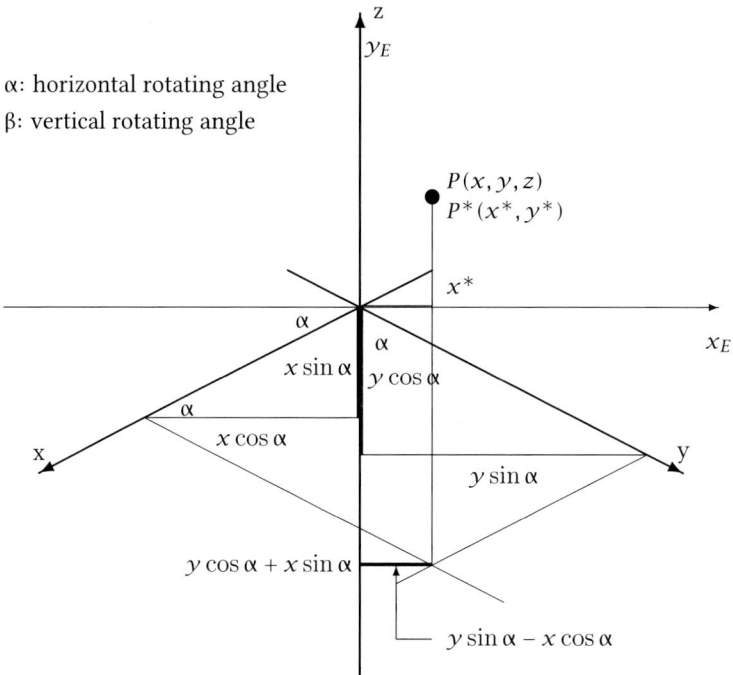

Figure 23.4: Coordinates in a three-dimensional Cartesian coordinate system

The angle α shows the horizontal rotation across the z axis and is measured counterclockwise in the z direction. The angle β is the vertical rotation referring to the paper plane. In Figure 23.5 below, $\alpha = \beta = 0$ such that the viewpoint is directly above the y axis which is orthogonal to the paper plane. Figure 23.6 shows the same arrangement, only this time from the side with an angle of β > 0.

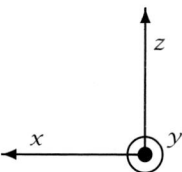

Figure 23.5: Coordinate system for α = β = 0 (y axis is orthogonal to the paper plane)

The two-dimensional coordinate x^* is the difference between the two horizontal lengths $y \sin \alpha$ and $x \cos \alpha$ (Figure 23.4):

$$x^* = -x\alpha + y \sin \alpha \qquad (23.1)$$

The z coordinate has no effect on x^* as the rotation is done from the paper plane; it only affects the value of y^*. Figure 23.6 shows the meaning of the angle β; this figure follows from Figure 23.5 when rotating the coordinate system by 90° horizontally to the left and vertically by β to the left as well.

The value of the projected z coordinate is $z^* = z \cos \beta$. In Figure 23.4 it can be seen that the point $P(x, y, z)$ is on an ellipse if β is constant and α is changed consistently.

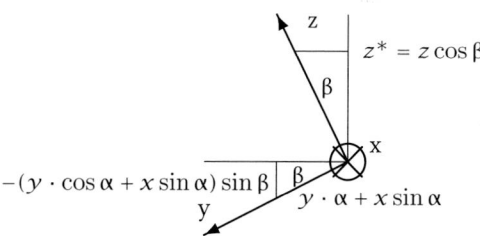

Figure 23.6: Coordinate system for α = 0 and β > 0 (x axis goes in direction of the paper plane)

The vertical change of P is the difference between the two "orthogonal" lines $y \cos \alpha$ and $x \sin \alpha$. These are rotated by the angle β, so have to be multiplied by $\sin \beta$ to get the correct value. We get the following transformation equation:

$$\begin{aligned} x_E &= -x \cos \alpha + y \sin \alpha \\ y_E &= -(x \sin \alpha + y \cos \alpha) \sin \beta + z \cos \beta \end{aligned} \qquad (23.2)$$

or in matrix form:

$$\begin{pmatrix} x_E \\ y_E \end{pmatrix} = \begin{pmatrix} -\cos \alpha & \sin \alpha & 0 \\ -\sin \alpha \sin \beta & -\cos \alpha \sin \beta & \cos \beta \end{pmatrix} \begin{pmatrix} x \\ y \\ z \end{pmatrix} \qquad (23.3)$$

23 Three-dimensional figures

23.5.2 Parameters

Table 23.7 lists the parameters available with pst-3dplot. Each one is then discussed in turn in the following sections.

Table 23.7: Summary of the parameters for the pst-3dplot package

name	type	default	meaning
Alpha	angle	45	rotation angle of the coordinate system
Beta	angle	30	tilting angle of the coordinate system
xMin	number	-1	smallest x value
xMax	number	4	largest x value
yMin	number	-1	smallest y value
yMax	number	4	largest y value
zMin	number	-1	smallest z value
zMax	number	4	largest z value
drawing	boolean	true	draw coordinate axes
drawCoor	boolean	false	show the xyz coordinates
IIIDticks	boolean	true	axis divisions
IIIDlabels	boolean	false	axis labels
IIIDxTicksPlane	xy|xz|yz	xy	
IIIDyTicksPlane	xy|xz|yz	yz	
IIIDzTicksPlane	xy|xz|yz	yz	
xThreeDunit	value	1	scale factor in x direction
yThreeDunit	value	1	scale factor in y direction
zThreeDunit	value	1	scale factor in z direction
xPlotpoints	number	25	interpolation values in x direction
yPlotpoints	number	25	interpolation values in y direction
beginAngle	angle	0	start angle for the arc
endAngle	angle	360	end angle for the arc
linejoin	1|2|3	1	PS option for line connections
nameX	string	x	x axis label
nameY	string	y	y axis label
nameZ	string	z	z axis label
spotX	angle	180	rotation angle for the x axis label
spotY	angle	0	rotation angle for the y axis label
spotZ	angle	90	rotation angle for the z axis label
plane	plane	xy	name of the plane
pOrigin	reference point	c	reference point
hiddenLine	boolean	false	use "hidden line"
drawStyle	grid type	xLines	type of plot
visibleLineStyle	line style	solid	line style for visible lines
invisibleLineStyle	line style	dashed	line style for hidden lines
SphericalCoor	boolean	false	spherical coordinates
rotX	angle	0	rotation about the x axis
rotY	angle	0	rotation about the y axis
rotZ	angle	0	rotation about the z axis
RotSequence	order	xyz	rotation order
increment	angle	10	distance between grid lines

continued...

23.5 pst-3dplot – 3D parallel projection of functions and data

... continued

name	type	default	meaning
SegmentColor	colour	[cmyk]{.2,.6,1,0}	colour of the segment
xyzLight	x y z	1 1 2	position of the light source

Alpha and Beta

Alpha and Beta determine the rotation of the coordinate system in the horizontal and vertical direction, as illustrated in figures 23.4 to 23.6 on page 359.

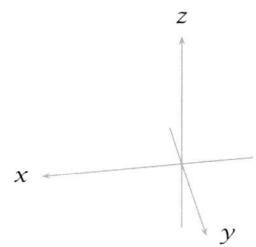

```
\usepackage{pstricks,pst-3dplot}

\begin{pspicture}(-2,-1)(1,2)
    \psset{Alpha=10,Beta=30,xMax=2,yMax=2,zMax=2}
    \pstThreeDCoor
\end{pspicture}
```

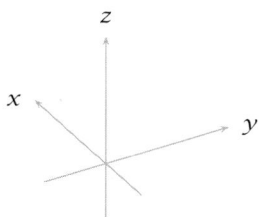

```
\usepackage{pstricks,pst-3dplot}

\begin{pspicture}(-1,-1)(2,2)
    \psset{Alpha=60,Beta=-30,xMax=2,yMax=2,zMax=2}
    \pstThreeDCoor
\end{pspicture}
```

xMin, xMax, yMin, yMax, zMin, and zMax

These values determine the visible area of the three-dimensional coordinate system; examples of their use were shown above.

drawing and drawCoor

You can use this to suppress the drawing of the coordinate axes, though they are still created internally for reference in calculations. The keyword drawCoor can be used to visualize the coordinates of a given point by dashed lines from the point to the coordinate axes.

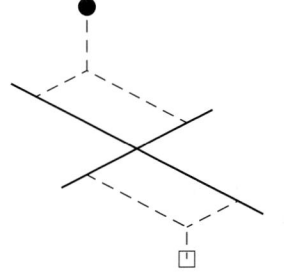

```
\usepackage{pstricks,pst-3dplot}

\begin{pspicture}(-1.5,0)(1,1.75)
\pstThreeDCoor[drawing=false]
\pstThreeDDot[drawCoor,dotscale=2](-1,-2,1)
\pstThreeDDot[drawCoor,dotscale=2,
    dotstyle=square](1,2,-0.5)
\pstThreeDLine(-1.5,0,0)(1.5,0,0)
\pstThreeDLine(0,-2.5,0)(0,2.5,0)
\end{pspicture}
```

23 Three-dimensional figures

IIIDticks and IIIDlabels

These are boolean variables controlling whether or not axis ticks and labels are displayed.

```
\usepackage{pstricks,pst-3dplot}
\pspicture(-2,-2)(1,3)\pstThreeDCoor[IIIDticks,IIIDlabels]\endpspicture\quad
\pspicture(-5,-2)(0,3)\psset{Alpha=-30,Beta=30}\pstThreeDCoor[IIIDticks,IIIDlabels]
\endpspicture
```

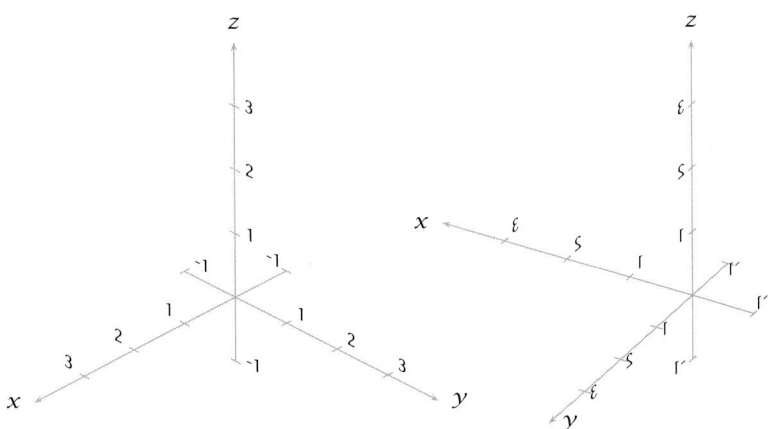

Note that ticks and labels are done in the xy plane for the x axis and in the yz plane for the y and z axes by default. This is independent of the values chosen for rotation and tilting angles.

You can change the font plane of the labels for each axis through the IIIDxTicksPlane, IIIDyTicksPlane, and IIIDzTicksPlane parameters.

Possible values are xy, xz, and yz. You can change the distance of the labels from the axis using IIIDxticksep, IIIDyticksep, and IIIDzticksep. You can also use Dx and Dy from the standard pst-plot package (cf. Section 15.1.3 on page 168) in the usual manner, plus the additional Dz variant. The planecorr parameter controls whether labels are rotated automatically to make them more readable; it can be set to none (default), normal, and xyrot.

The rotation and tilting angles of the 3D coordinate system in the following examples is chosen on purpose to create a disadvantageous display with the default label settings (on the left). The centre coordinate system improves readability with the planecorr=normal option, and the right one has a more or less optimal configuration through the use of the other parameters.

```
\usepackage{pstricks,pst-3dplot}
\psset{Alpha=-60,Beta=60,IIIDticks,IIIDlabels}
\begin{pspicture}(-1,-2.25)(0,3)\pstThreeDCoor[Dx=2,Dy=1,Dz=0.25]\end{pspicture}
\begin{pspicture}(-4,-2.25)(0,3)
  \pstThreeDCoor[planecorr=normal,IIIDzticksep=-0.4,Dx=2,Dy=1,Dz=0.25]
\end{pspicture}
\begin{pspicture}(-4,-2.25)(0,3)
  \pstThreeDCoor[IIIDyTicksPlane=xy,IIIDyticksep=-0.4,IIIDzticksep=-0.4,
    planecorr=xyrot,Dx=2,Dy=1,Dz=0.25]
\end{pspicture}
```

23.5 pst-3dplot – 3D parallel projection of functions and data

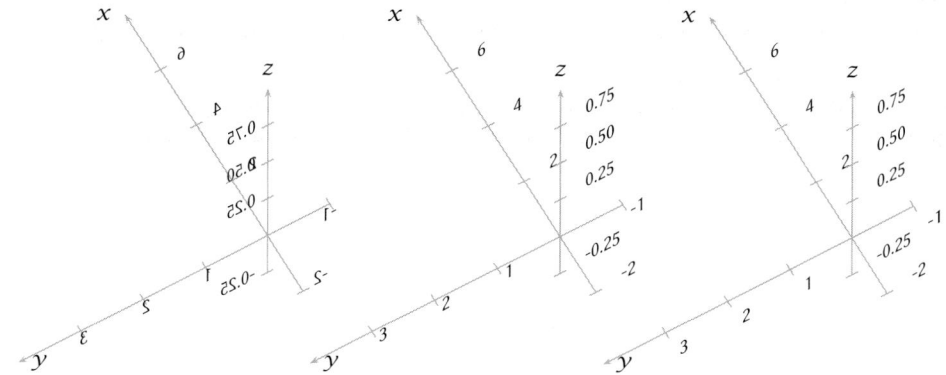

You can alter the font and font size of the labels by redefining the appropriate command: \def\psxyzlabel#1{\bgroup\footnotesize\textsf{#1}\egroup}. Instead of using the the label setting of pst-3dplot you can also use the commands \multido and \pstThreeDPut (23.5.4 on page 377). \pstThreeDPut puts its argument at a three-dimensional position, but always in the observer plane.

xThreeDunit, yThreeDunit, and zThreeDunit

These parameters modify the scale in any single dimension. Note that they are not available for spherical coordinates (cf. page 370).

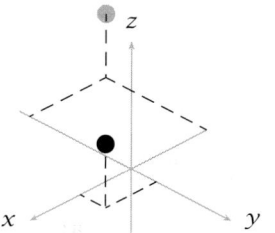

```
\usepackage{pst-3dplot}

\begin{pspicture}(-2,-1)(1,2)
\psset{xMin=-1.5,xMax=2,yMin=-2.2,yMax=2,zMax=2}
\pstThreeDCoor
\psset{drawCoor,dotscale=2}\pstThreeDDot(1,.5,1)
\pstThreeDDot[linecolor=red,yThreeDunit=2](-1.5,-1,1)
\end{pspicture}
```

xPlotpoints and yPlotpoints

yPlotpoints and xPlotpoints determine the number of points plotted depending to the axis. This has a major impact on the appearance of functions; the correct values can sometimes only be determined by trial and error. The examples use the following function:

```
\usepackage{pst-3dplot}
\def\func{ x 3 exp x y 4 exp mul add x 5 div sub 10 mul
  2.729 x dup mul y dup mul add neg exp mul
  2.729 x 1.225 sub dup mul y dup mul add neg exp add }
\psscalebox{0.75}{\begin{pspicture}(-4,-3)(4,4)
  \psset{Alpha=45,Beta=15}
  \psplotThreeD[plotstyle=curve,yPlotpoints=10,xPlotpoints=10,
     linewidth=0.5pt,hiddenLine](-3,3)(-3,3){\func}
  \pstThreeDCoor[xMin=-1,xMax=5,yMin=-1,yMax=5,zMin=-1,zMax=3.5]
\end{pspicture}}\hfill
```

23 Three-dimensional figures

```
\psscalebox{0.75}{\begin{pspicture}(-4,-3)(4,4)
  \psset{Alpha=45,Beta=15}
  \psplotThreeD[plotstyle=curve,yPlotpoints=20,xPlotpoints=50,
      linewidth=0.5pt,hiddenLine](-3,3)(-3,3){\func}
  \pstThreeDCoor[xMin=-1,xMax=5,yMin=-1,yMax=5,zMin=-1,zMax=3.5]
\end{pspicture}}
```

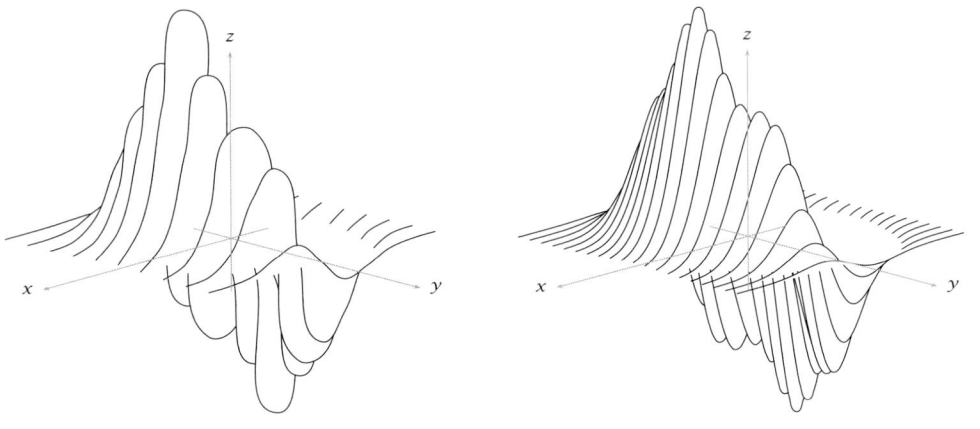

beginAngle and endAngle

These two parameters control the start and end angles when drawing three-dimensional ellipses and arcs (cf. page 383).

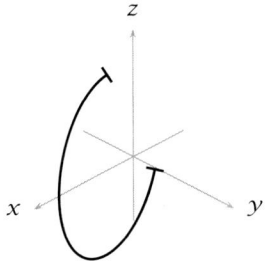

```
\usepackage{pstricks,pst-3dplot}

\begin{pspicture}(-2,-1.25)(2,1.75)
  \pstThreeDCoor[xMin=-1,xMax=2,yMin=-1,
     yMax=2,zMin=-1,zMax=2]
  \pstThreeDEllipse[beginAngle=30,endAngle=270,
     arrows=|-|,linewidth=1pt]%
     (1,0.5,0.5)(-0.5,0.5,0.5)(0.5,0.5,-1)
\end{pspicture}
```

linejoin

Especially when drawing triangles with acute angles, it is sometimes desirable to alter how the line ends meet. The values for linejoin are 0|1|2 as for the PostScript setlinejoin command (cf. Section 4.1.4 on page 45).

23.5 pst-3dplot – 3D parallel projection of functions and data

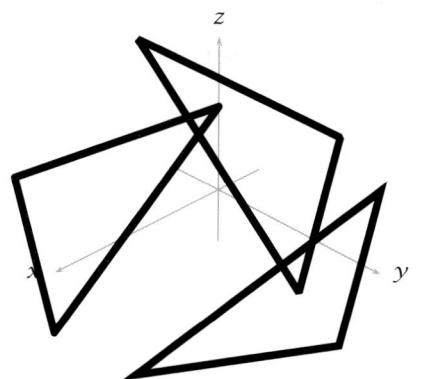

```
\usepackage{pstricks,pst-3dplot}

\psset{unit=0.80}
\begin{pspicture}(-3,-4)(3,3.25)
    \pstThreeDCoor[xMax=4,zMax=3]
    \psset{linewidth=3pt}
    \pstThreeDTriangle[linejoin=0]%
        (3,1,-2)(1,4,-1)(-2,2,0)
    \pstThreeDTriangle[linejoin=1]%
        (3,-1,-2)(1,-4,-1)(-2,-2,0)
    \pstThreeDTriangle[linejoin=2]%
        (-1,1,-2)(-4,-1,-1)(-2,-4,0.5)
\end{pspicture}
```

nameX, nameY, and nameZ

Usually the axes are named x, y, and z, but you can use these parameters to change this.

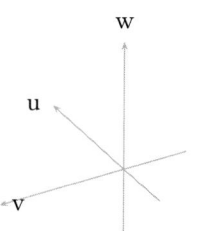

```
\usepackage{pstricks,pst-3dplot}

\begin{pspicture}(-2,-0.5)(1,2)
    \psset{Alpha=-60,Beta=30,
        xMax=2, yMax=2,zMax=2}
    \pstThreeDCoor[nameX=u,nameY=v,nameZ=w]
\end{pspicture}
```

spotX, spotY, and spotZ

In the previous example the configuration of the labels was not optimal. These parameters can improve this, by specifying the angle by which a label is rotated, in a similar manner to the \uput command (cf. Section 9.6 on page 106).

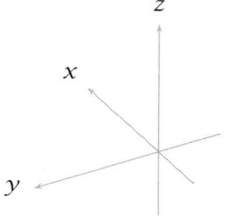

```
\usepackage{pstricks,pst-3dplot}

\begin{pspicture}(-2,-0.5)(1,2)
    \psset{Alpha=-60,Beta=30,linecolor=blue,
        xMax=2,yMax=2,zMax=2}
    \pstThreeDCoor[spotX=135,spotY=180]
\end{pspicture}
```

plane

plane specifies the plane that is written in by the \pstPlanePut command. Possible values are xy|xz|yz.

23 Three-dimensional figures

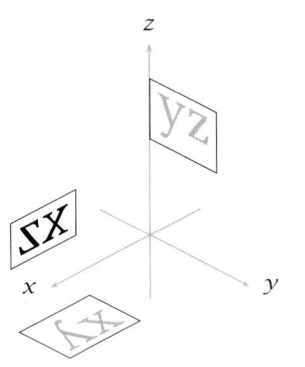

```
\usepackage{pstricks,pst-3dplot}

\begin{pspicture}(-2,-2)(1,3)
  \psset{xMax=3.5,yMax=3,zMax=3}
  \pstThreeDCoor\psset{pOrigin=lb}
  \pstPlanePut(1,0,0){\fbox{\Huge\red xy}}
  \pstPlanePut[plane=xz](0,2,0)%
    {\fbox{\Huge\blue xz}}
  \pstPlanePut[plane=yz](0,0,2)%
    {\fbox{\Huge\green yz}}
\end{pspicture}
```

pOrigin

pOrigin is the positional parameter that is passed on to \rput. This affects \pstThreeDPut exclusively; the values are determined by the specifications of \rput (cf. Section 9.1 on page 103).

```
\usepackage{pstricks,pst-3dplot}

\begin{pspicture}(-2,-1.5)(1,3)
  \pstThreeDCoor[xMax=2,yMax=2,zMax=3]
  \pstPlanePut[pOrigin=c](0,0,-1){%
    \fbox{\Huge\red xy}}
  \pstPlanePut[plane=xz,
    pOrigin=rb](0,0,0)%
    {\fbox{\Huge\blue xz}}
  \pstPlanePut[plane=yz,
    pOrigin=lb](0,0,1.5)%
    {\fbox{\Huge\green yz}}
\end{pspicture}
```

hiddenLine

The hiddenLine=true option creates a plotted 3D function that looks solid. It makes a rudimentary hidden-line algorithm possible by first drawing the function with the \pscustom command and then filling it with the hiddenStyle fill style:

\newpsstyle{*hiddenStyle*}{*fillstyle=solid,fillcolor=white*}

You can of course overwrite this style arbitrarily. The curves are created back to front because due to the fill function everything which is "below" the previous curve is overwritten. Examples are given below and in Section 23.5.6 on page 385.

drawStyle

drawStyle determines the style of how a plotted 3D function is drawn. Possible values are:
  xLines | yLines | xyLines | yxLines

These values refer to how the three-dimensional function is created. This is always done with a lattice model (or wire frame). For xLines, the lines are drawn in the x direction, while yxLines means that they are first drawn in y direction and then in the x direction. The following figures all make use of the function given earlier in Section 23.5.2.

23.5 pst-3dplot – 3D parallel projection of functions and data

```
\usepackage{pstricks,pst-3dplot}
\begin{pspicture}(-6,-3)(6,4)  \psset{Beta=15}
  \psplotThreeD[plotstyle=line,drawStyle=xLines,yPlotpoints=50,xPlotpoints=50,
     linewidth=0.2pt](-4,4)(-4,4){\func}
  \pstThreeDCoor[xMax=5,yMax=5,zMax=3.5]
\end{pspicture}
```

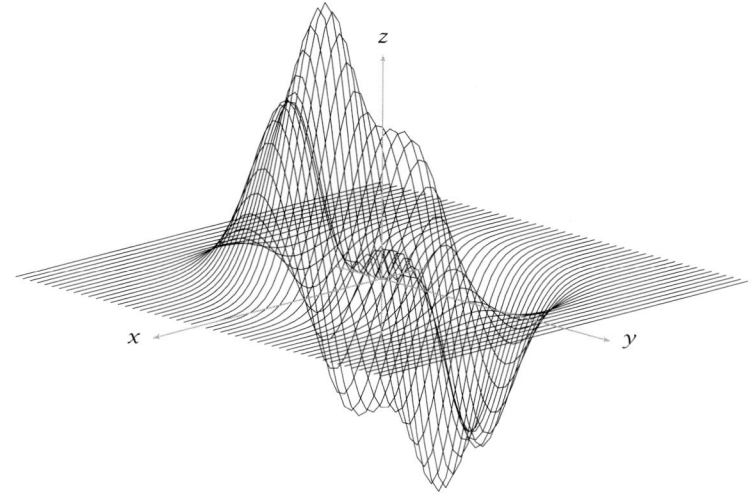

```
\usepackage{pstricks,pst-3dplot}
\begin{pspicture}(-6,-3)(6,4)  \psset{Beta=15}
  \psplotThreeD[plotstyle=curve,drawStyle=yLines,hiddenLine=true,
     yPlotpoints=50,xPlotpoints=50,linewidth=0.2pt](-4,4)(-4,4){\func}
  \pstThreeDCoor[xMax=5,yMax=5,zMax=3.5]
\end{pspicture}
```

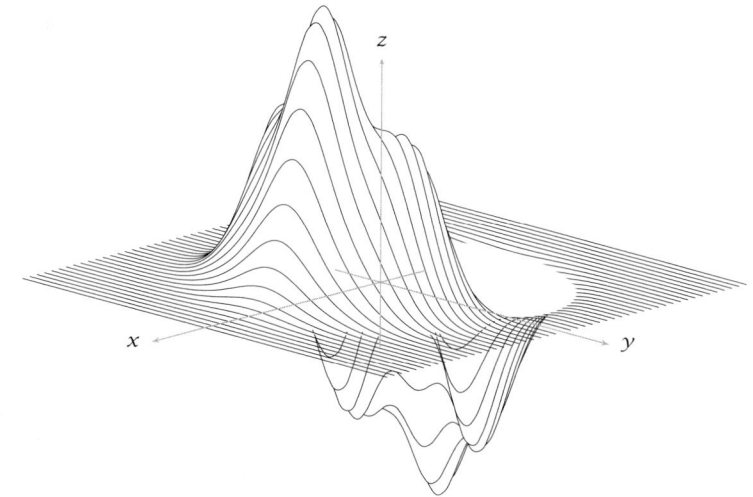

23 Three-dimensional figures

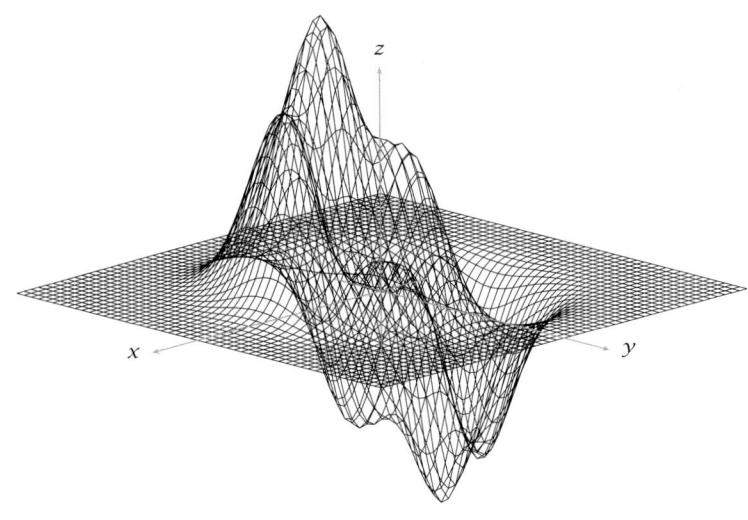

```
\usepackage{pstricks,pst-3dplot}
\psscalebox{0.8}{%
\begin{pspicture}(-6,-3)(6,4)   \psset{Beta=15}
  \psplotThreeD[plotstyle=curve,drawStyle=xyLines,hiddenLine=true,
    yPlotpoints=50,xPlotpoints=50,linewidth=0.2pt](-4,4)(-4,4){\func}
  \pstThreeDCoor[xMax=5,yMax=5,zMax=3.5]
\end{pspicture}}
```

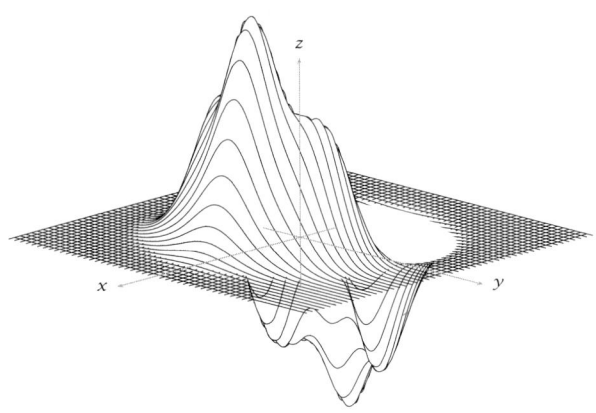

```
\usepackage{pstricks,pst-3dplot}
\psscalebox{0.8}{%
\begin{pspicture}(-6,-3)(6,4)   \psset{Beta=15}
  \psplotThreeD[plotstyle=curve,drawStyle=yxLines,hiddenLine=true,
    yPlotpoints=50,xPlotpoints=50,linewidth=0.2pt](-4,4)(-4,4){\func}
  \pstThreeDCoor[xMax=5,yMax=5,zMax=3.5]
\end{pspicture}}
```

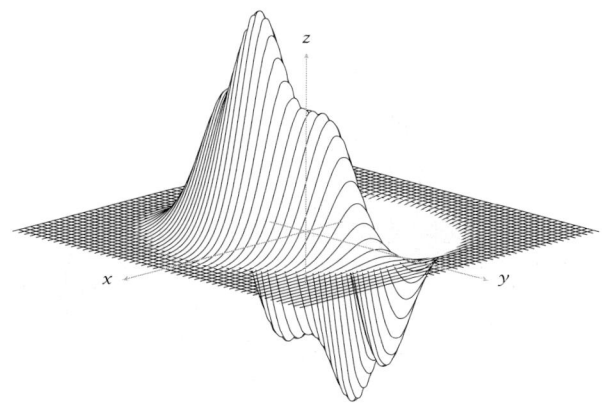

visibleLineStyle and invisibleLineStyle

These two parameters refer to drawing 3D objects. The drawing commands try to detect hidden lines and draw them with the invisibleLineStyle (which is set to default to dashed), while visible ones are drawn with the visibleLineStyle (which is set to default to solid).

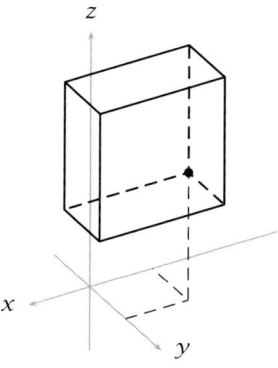

```
\usepackage{pstricks,pst-3dplot}

\begin{pspicture}(-1,-1)(3,3.25)
  \psset{Alpha=30}
  \pstThreeDCoor[xMin=-3,xMax=1,yMax=2,zMax=4]
  \pstThreeDBox(-1,1,2)(0,0,2)(2,0,0)(0,1,0)
  \pstThreeDDot[drawCoor=true,linecolor=blue](-1,1,2)
\end{pspicture}
```

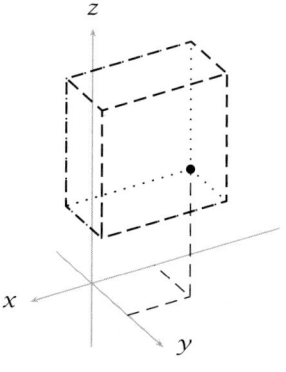

```
\usepackage{pstricks,pst-3dplot}

\begin{pspicture}(-1,-1)(3,3.5)
  \psset{Alpha=30,invisibleLineStyle=dotted,
    visibleLineStyle=dashed}
  \pstThreeDCoor[xMin=-3,xMax=1,yMax=2,zMax=4]
  \pstThreeDBox(-1,1,2)(0,0,2)(2,0,0)(0,1,0)
  \pstThreeDDot[drawCoor=true,linecolor=blue](-1,1,2)
\end{pspicture}
```

23 Three-dimensional figures

SphericalCoor

If this parameter is set to `true`, the triples of numbers are interpreted as spherical coordinates in the usual notation (r, θ, ϕ).

```
\usepackage{pstricks,pst-3dplot}
\def\oA{\pstThreeDLine[linecolor=blue,linewidth=3pt,arrows=c-> ](0,0,0)(1,60,70)}
\def\oB{\pstThreeDLine[linecolor=red,linewidth=3pt,arrows=c->](0,0,0)(1,10,50)}
\def\oAB{\pstThreeDEllipse[beginAngle=58,endAngle=90](0,0,0)(1,140,40)(1,10,50)}
\begin{pspicture}(-4.8,-1.75)(4.8,3.75)
\psset{unit=4cm,drawCoor,beginAngle=90,endAngle=180,linestyle=dotted}
\pstThreeDCoor[drawing=true, linewidth=1pt,linecolor=black,%
   linestyle=solid,xMin=0,xMax=1.1, yMin=0,yMax=1.1, zMin=0,zMax=1.1]
\pstThreeDEllipse(0,0,0)(-1,0,0)(0,1,0)  \pstThreeDEllipse(0,0,0)(-1,0,0)(0,0,1)
\pstThreeDEllipse[beginAngle=0,endAngle=90](0,0,0)(0,0,1)(0,1,0)
\psset{SphericalCoor,linestyle=solid}
\pstThreeDDot[dotstyle=none](1,10,50)   \pstThreeDDot[dotstyle=none](1,60,70)
\pscustom[fillstyle=crosshatch,hatchcolor=yellow,linestyle=none]{\oB\oAB\oA}
\oA \oB \oAB
\pstThreeDPut[origin=lb](1.1,60,70){$\vec\Omega_1$}
\pstThreeDPut[origin=rb](1.2,10,50){$\vec\Omega_2$}
\pstThreeDPut[origin=lb](1,10,65){$\gamma_{12}$}
\end{pspicture}
```

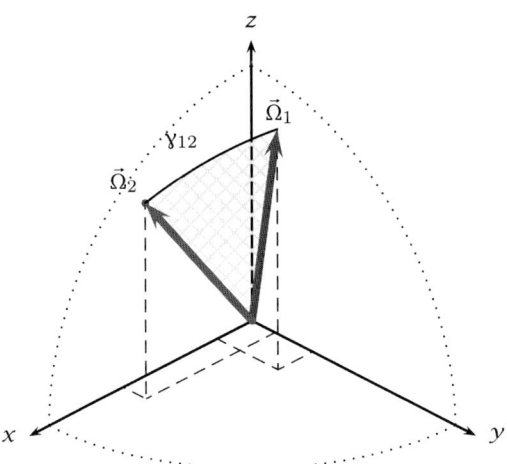

rotX, rotY, and rotZ

These rotation parameters specify the angle by which the three-dimensional object is rotated around the respective axis. The default order of rotation corresponds to the alphabetic order X|Y|Z, but you can change this through the `RotSequence` parameter discussed next.

23.5 pst-3dplot – 3D parallel projection of functions and data

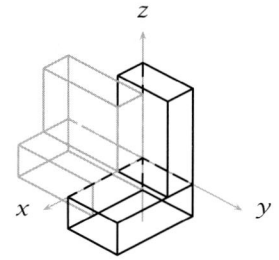

```
\usepackage{pst-3dplot}

\begin{pspicture}(-2,-1.5)(2,2)%
    \pstThreeDCoor[xMin=0,xMax=2,yMax=2,zMax=2]%
    \pstThreeDBox(0,0,0)(.5,0,0)(0,1,0)(0,0,1.5)
    \pstThreeDBox[RotX=90,linecolor=red]%
        (0,0,0)(.5,0,0)(0,1,0)(0,0,1.5)
    \pstThreeDBox[RotX=90,RotY=90,linecolor=green]%
        (0,0,0)(.5,0,0)(0,1,0)(0,0,1.5)
    \pstThreeDBox[RotX=90,RotY=90,RotZ=90,
        linecolor=blue](0,0,0)(.5,0,0)(0,1,0)(0,0,1.5)
\end{pspicture}%
```

RotSequence

By default objects are rotated in order *x*-*y*-*z* around the axes; the whole rotation is not commutative however – therefore changing the rotation order achieves a different outcome. Six combinations are possible: xyz|xzy|zxy|zyx|yxz|yzx. The default order of rotation corresponds to the alphabetic order X|Y|Z, but you can change this through the RotSequence parameter by assigning it one of these values.

```
\usepackage{pst-3dplot,pst-grad}
\psset{unit=1.5,linewidth=1.5pt}
\begin{pspicture}(-2,-1.75)(2,2)
   \pstThreeDCoor[xMin=0,xMax=2,yMin=0,yMax=2,zMin=0,zMax=2]
   \psset{RotX=90,RotY=90,RotZ=90}
   \pstThreeDBox[linecolor=red](0,0,0)(.5,0,0)(0,1,0)(0,0,1.5)
   \pstThreeDBox[RotSequence=xzy,linecolor=yellow](0,0,0)(.5,0,0)(0,1,0)(0,0,1.5)
   \pstThreeDBox[RotSequence=zyx,linecolor=green](0,0,0)(.5,0,0)(0,1,0)(0,0,1.5)
   \pstThreeDBox[RotSequence=zxy,linecolor=blue](0,0,0)(.5,0,0)(0,1,0)(0,0,1.5)
   \pstThreeDBox[RotSequence=yxz,linecolor=cyan](0,0,0)(.5,0,0)(0,1,0)(0,0,1.5)
   \pstThreeDBox[RotSequence=yzx,linecolor=magenta](0,0,0)(.5,0,0)(0,1,0)(0,0,1.5)
   \pstThreeDBox[fillstyle=gradient,RotX=0,RotY=0,RotZ=0](0,0,0)(.5,0,0)(0,1,0)(0,0,1.5)
\end{pspicture}
```

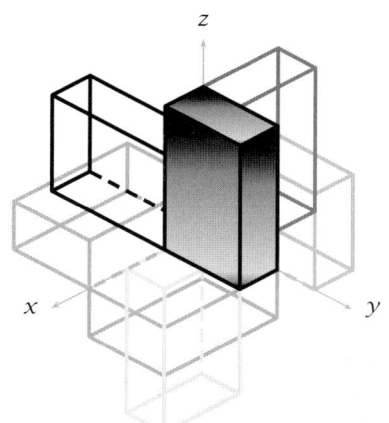

23 Three-dimensional figures

increment

The `increment` option determines the size of a sphere or paraboloid segment in degrees and defaults to $10°$, meaning that 36 segments are drawn altogether.

```
\usepackage{pstricks,pst-3dplot}
\begin{pspicture}(-3,-1.5)(7.5,3)
  \psset{Alpha=60,Beta=10}
  \pstThreeDCoor[xMax=5,yMax=8,zMax=3]
  \pstThreeDPut(4,4,0){\pstParaboloid[increment=20]{2}{3}}
  \pstThreeDDot[drawCoor](4,4,0)
  \pstThreeDPut(2,7,2){\pstParaboloid[increment=6]{1.5}{1.5}}
  \pstThreeDDot[drawCoor](2,7,2)
\end{pspicture}%
```

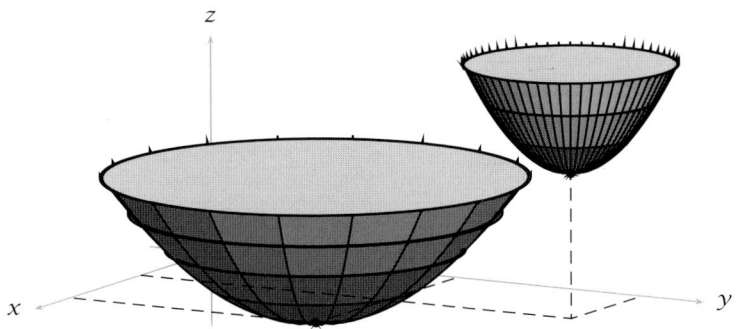

SegmentColor

The individual segments of a sphere or paraboloid are coloured in a 3D manner, i.e. as if lit from a light source, with the colour shade never constant. The colour is specified through SegmentColor, which applies for the object as a whole, despite the name of the option suggesting otherwise.

Remember that you must specify the colour in the CMYK colour model as the filling is done at the PostScript level. To get the xcolor package to parse the colour correctly, it has to be enclosed in parentheses: SegmentColor={[cmyk]{c,m,y,k}}.

```
\usepackage{pstricks,pst-3dplot}
\begin{pspicture}(-3,-2)(8,7)
  \psset{Alpha=60,Beta=20}
  \pstThreeDCoor[xMax=5,yMax=8,zMax=7]
  \pstThreeDSphere(4,4,4){2}
  \pstThreeDDot[drawCoor](4,4,4)
  \pstThreeDSphere[SegmentColor={[cmyk]{0.1,0.7,0.9,0.3}}](2,7,7){1.5}
  \pstThreeDDot[drawCoor](2,7,7)
\end{pspicture}%
```

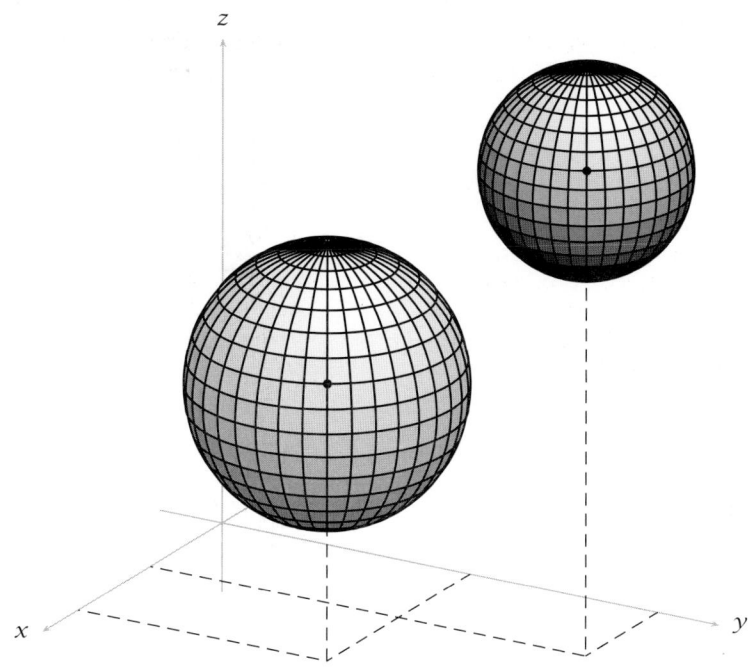

Spheres and paraboloids are filled with a colour by default; to suppress this, specify white as the fill colour with SegmentColor={[cmyk]{0,0,0,0}}.

To ensure the results are as expected, use at least version 2.06 of xcolor and version 1.71 of pst-3dplot, both available on CTAN.

xyzLight

As we said above, SegmentColor refers to a light source; xyzLight specifies the position of the light source, and defaults to $(1, 1, 2)$.

```
\usepackage{pst-3dplot}
\begin{pspicture}(-3,-2)(8,5)
  \psset{Alpha=60,Beta=20}
  \pstThreeDCoor[xMax=5,yMax=8,zMax=5]
  \pstThreeDSphere(4,4,3){2}
  \pstThreeDDot[drawCoor](4,4,3)
  \pstThreeDSphere[xyzLight=0 1 0](2,7,5){1.5}
  \pstThreeDDot[drawCoor](2,7,5)
\end{pspicture}
```

23 Three-dimensional figures

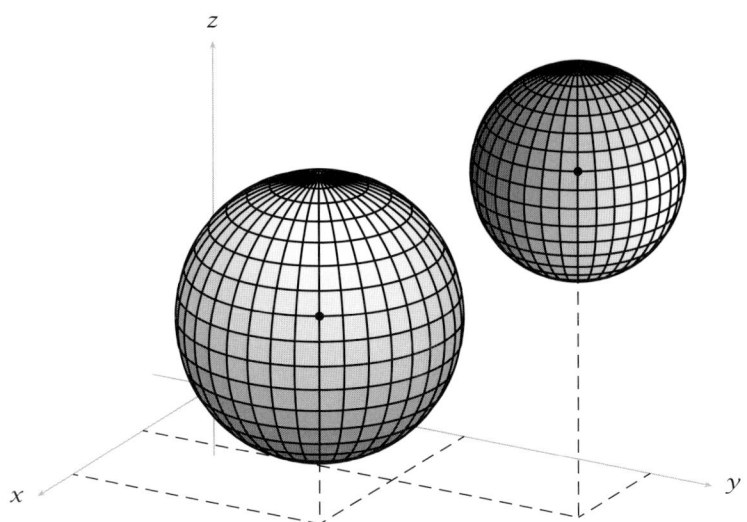

23.5.3 Coordinate axes

The syntax to create coordinate axes is:

`\pstThreeDCoor [settings]`

With the default values for the parameters, you get the following coordinate plane:
xMin=-1,xMax=4,yMin=-1, yMax=4,zMin=-1,zMax=4, Alpha=45,Beta=30

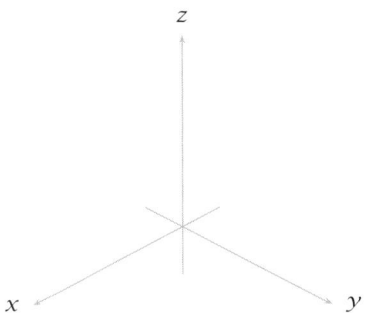

```
\usepackage{pstricks,pst-3dplot}

\psset{unit=0.75}
\begin{pspicture}(-3,-1)(3,3.25)
    \pstThreeDCoor
\end{pspicture}
```

The angles Alpha and Beta determine the display of all commands, so it's best to set them globally with \psset, as done in the following examples.

23.5 pst-3dplot – 3D parallel projection of functions and data

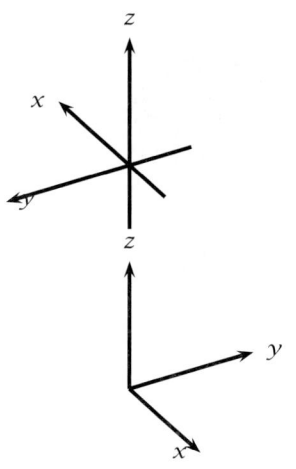

```
\usepackage{pstricks,pst-3dplot}

\begin{pspicture}(-2,-1)(1,2)
  \psset{Alpha=-60,Beta=30}
  \pstThreeDCoor[linewidth=1.5pt,linecolor=blue,
    xMax=2,yMax=2,zMax=2]
\end{pspicture}

\begin{pspicture}(-2,-1)(1,2)
  \psset{Alpha=120,Beta=30}
  \pstThreeDCoor[linewidth=1.5pt,linecolor=blue,
    xMin=0,xMax=2,yMin=0,yMax=2,zMin=0,zMax=2]
\end{pspicture}
```

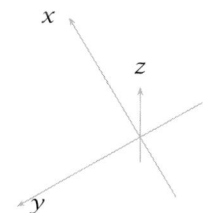

```
\usepackage{pstricks,pst-3dplot}

\begin{pspicture}(-2,-1)(1,2)
  \psset{Alpha=-60,Beta=70}
  \pstThreeDCoor[xMax=2,yMax=2,zMax=2]
\end{pspicture}
```

So far in this chapter we have dealt with the default method for arranging the three-dimensional coordinate system, namely with rotation angle α and tilting angle β. However, this is in fact only one of the possibilities for arranging the system. The pst-3dplot package supports additional arrangements, but these are currently only experimental. You can activate one of these arrangements by assigning the appropriate number to the coorType parameter. The different values are explained below, followed by examples:

coorType=0 The default behaviour as described before.

coorType=1 The y–z axes are orthogonal and the angle between the x axis and the y axis is given by α. β has no meaning.

coorType=2 The y–z axes are orthogonal and the angle between the x and the y axis is $135°$; the x axis is shortened by $1/\sqrt{2}$. The angle α is only of interest for labels and β has no meaning.

coorType=3 The y–z axes are orthogonal and the angle between the x and the y axis is $45°$; the x axis is shortened by $1/\sqrt{2}$. The angle α is only of interest for labels and β has no meaning.

coorType=4 The trimetric projection; the direction of viewing is such that all three axes of space appear unequally foreshortened.

23 Three-dimensional figures

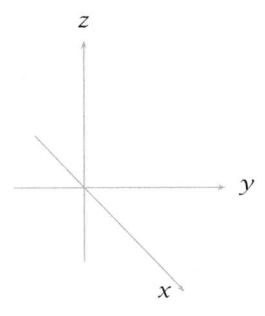

```
\usepackage{pst-3dplot}

\psset{coorType=1}
\begin{pspicture}(-2,-3)(3,3)
\pstThreeDCoor[xMax=2,yMax=2,zMax=2]
\end{pspicture}
```

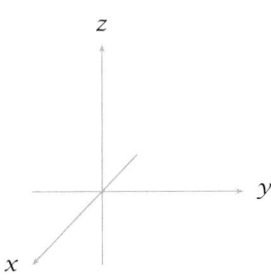

```
\usepackage{pst-3dplot}

\psset{coorType=2}
\begin{pspicture}(-2,-2)(3,3)
\pstThreeDCoor[xMax=2,yMax=2,zMax=2]
\end{pspicture}
```

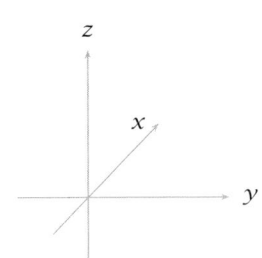

```
\usepackage{pst-3dplot}

\psset{coorType=3}
\begin{pspicture}(-2,-2)(3,3)
\pstThreeDCoor[xMax=2,yMax=2,zMax=2]
\end{pspicture}
```

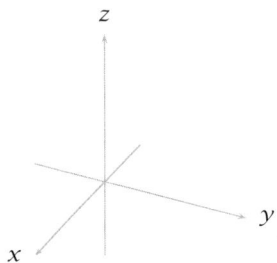

```
\usepackage{pst-3dplot}

\psset{coorType=4}
\begin{pspicture}(-2,-2)(3,3)
\pstThreeDCoor[xMax=2,yMax=2,zMax=2]
\end{pspicture}
```

23.5.4 General commands
\pstThreeDPut

The syntax for \pstThreeDPut is similar to the \rput command (cf. Section 9.4 on page 105):

\pstThreeDPut [settings] (x, y, z){material}

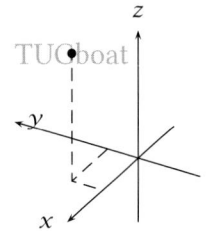

```
\usepackage{pstricks,pst-3dplot}

\begin{pspicture}(-2,-1)(1,2)
  \psset{Alpha=-60,Beta=-30}
  \pstThreeDCoor[linecolor=blue,
    xMax=2,yMax=2,zMax=2]
  \pstThreeDPut(1,0.5,2){\red\large TUGboat}
  \pstThreeDDot[drawCoor=true](1,0.5,2)
\end{pspicture}
```

Internally \pstThreeDPut defines a two-dimensional node temp@pstNode and then uses the \rput command. Therefore the three-dimensional coordinates of such nodes are not known after their definition.

\pstThreeDNode

The syntax for a node is:

\pstThreeDNode(x, y, z){node name}

(*x,y,z*) is saved as a two-dimensional node internally. Therefore it can't be substituted for the coordinate triple (*x,y,z*) in the sense of the special coordinates of PSTricks (cf. Chapter 12 on page 139). If *A* and *B* are two nodes defined like this, then \psline{A}{B} draws a line from *A* to *B* – you don't need to use the pst-3dplot line command.

\pstThreeDDot

The syntax for a dot is:

\pstThreeDDot [settings] (x, y, z)

You can draw dots with the lines to their coordinates (dashed lines) using the drawCoor parameter.

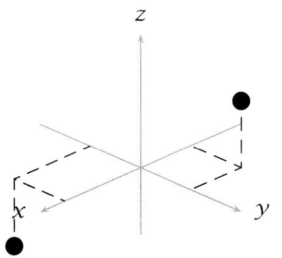

```
\usepackage{pstricks,pst-3dplot}

\begin{pspicture}(-2,-1.5)(2,2)
  \psset{xMin=-2,xMax=2,yMin=-2,yMax=2,
    zMax=2,Beta=25}
  \pstThreeDCoor
  \psset{dotstyle=*,dotscale=2,drawCoor=true}
  \pstThreeDDot(-1,1,1)\pstThreeDDot(1.5,-1,-1)
\end{pspicture}
```

23 Three-dimensional figures

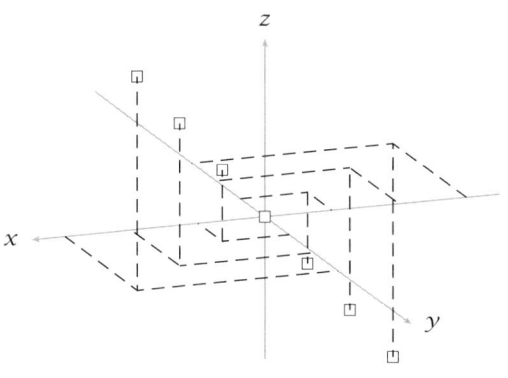

```
\usepackage{pst-3dplot,multido}

\begin{pspicture}(-4,-2)(3,3.25)
  \psset{xMin=-3.5,xMax=3.5,
      yMin=-7,yMax=6,zMin=-2,
      zMax=2.5,Alpha=20,Beta=15}
  \pstThreeDCoor
  \psset{dotstyle=square,
      dotsize=5pt,linecolor=blue,
      drawCoor=true}
  \multido{\n=-3+1}{7}{%
      \pstThreeDDot(\n,\n,\n)}
\end{pspicture}
```

\pstThreeDLine

The syntax for drawing a line is:

\pstThreeDLine [settings] $(x_1, y_1, z_1)(x_2, y_2, z_2)$

All parameters that are available for lines in general are valid with it.

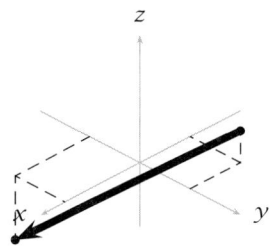

```
\usepackage{pstricks,pst-3dplot}

\psset{xMin=-2,xMax=2,yMin=-2,yMax=2,zMax=2}
\begin{pspicture}(-2,-2)(2,2.25)
  \pstThreeDCoor
  \psset{dotstyle=*,drawCoor=true}
  \pstThreeDDot(-1,1,0.5)
  \pstThreeDDot(1.5,-1,-1)
  \pstThreeDLine[linewidth=3pt,
      arrows=->](-1,1,0.5)(1.5,-1,-1)
\end{pspicture}
```

```
\usepackage{pstricks,pst-3dplot}
\def\Name#1{\ifcase#1\or HP\or Hm.t\or zA\or zA.t\or jtj\or mw.t\or sn\or sn.t\fi}
\begin{pspicture}(-9,-2)(1.2,11)  \psset{yunit=0.25,Alpha=10,origin=cB}
\pstThreeDLine(1,10,0)(8,10,0)
\multido{\iA=1+1}{8}{\pstThreeDLine(\iA,10,0)(\iA,10.5,0)%
    \pstPlanePut[plane=xz,planecorr=normal,origin=lB](\iA,10,-1.5){\Name{\iA}}}
%
\pstThreeDLine(8,1,0)(8,10,0)
\multido{\iA=1+1}{10}{\pstThreeDLine(8,\iA,0)(8.25,\iA,0)
    \pstPlanePut[plane=xz,planecorr=normal](8.75,\iA,-0.5){\iA}}
\multido{\iA=1+2}{5}{\pstThreeDLine[linestyle=dashed,linewidth=0.5pt](8,\iA,0)(1,\iA,0)}
%
\pstThreeDLine(8,1,0)(8,1,40)
\multido{\iA=0+5}{9}{\pstThreeDLine(8,1,\iA)(8.2,1,\iA)
    \pstPlanePut[plane=xz,planecorr=normal](8.75,0,\iA){\iA}}
\pstThreeDLine[linestyle=dashed,arrows=->](1,1,45)(1,1,50)
\pstPlanePut[plane=xz,planecorr=normal](1,1,50){445}
```

```
\rput(-3.5,-8){person}\rput{90}(-9,16){frequency}
\rput[c]{-37}(-8,-6){\tabular[t]{@{}c@{}}Position in the script\endtabular}
\psset{opacity=0.7}
\pscustom[fillstyle=solid,fillcolor=black!30,linestyle=none]{%
   \pstThreeDLine(1,1,0)(1,1,45)(1,2,7)( 1,3,1)( 1,4,1)( 1,5,0)%
               ( 1,6,1)(1,7,1)(1,8,0)(1,9,0)(1,10,0)(1,1,0)}
\pstThreeDLine(1,1,45)(1,2,7)(1,3,1)(1,4,1)(1,5,0)(1,6,1)%
              (1,7,1)(1,8,0)(1,9,0)(1,10,0)(1,1,0)
\pscustom[fillstyle=solid,fillcolor=blue!50,linestyle=none]{%
   \pstThreeDLine(2,1,0)(2,2,38)(2,3,13)(2,4,4)(2,5,1)(2,6,0)%
               (2,7,5)(2,8,1)(2,9,3)(2,10,0)(2,1,0)}
\pstThreeDLine(2,1,0)(2,2,38)(2,3,13)(2,4,4)(2,5,1)(2,6,0)(2,7,5)(2,8,1)(2,9,3)(2,10,0)
%
\pscustom[fillstyle=solid,fillcolor=red!50,linestyle=none]{%
   \pstThreeDLine(3,1,0)(3,1,2)(3,2,30)(3,3,30)(3,4,20)(3,5,14)(3,6,8)%
               (3,7,9)(3,8,3)(3,9,2)(3,10,2)(3,10,0)(3,1,0)}
\pstThreeDLine(3,1,2)(3,2,30)(3,3,30)(3,4,20)(3,5,14)(3,6,8)(3,7,9)
              (3,8,3)(3,9,2)(3,10,2)(3,10,0)
%
\pscustom[fillstyle=solid,fillcolor=green!50,linestyle=none]{%
   \pstThreeDLine(4,1,0)(4,2,9)(4,3,11)(4,4,14)(4,5,13)(4,6,11)
               (4,7,7)(4,8,5)(4,9,4)(4,10,4)(4,10,0)(4,1,0)}
\pstThreeDLine(4,1,0)(4,2,9)(4,3,11)(4,4,14)(4,5,13)(4,6,11)(4,7,7)(4,8,5)(4,9,4)(4,10,4)
%
\pscustom[fillstyle=solid,fillcolor=cyan!50,linestyle=none]{%
   \pstThreeDLine(5,1,0)(5,2,11)(5,3,10)(5,4,5)(5,5,3)(5,6,3)%
               (5,7,1)(5,8,1)(5,9,2)(5,10,1)(5,10,0)(5,1,0)}
\pstThreeDLine(5,1,0)( 5,2,11)(5,3,10)(5,4,5)(5,5,3)(5,6,3)(5,7,1)(5,8,1)(5,9,2)(5,10,1)
%
\pscustom[fillstyle=solid,fillcolor=gray!50,linestyle=none]{%
   \pstThreeDLine(6,1,0)(6,2,5)(6,3,7)(6,4,6)(6,5,6)(6,6,1)%
               (6,7,1)(6,8,1)(6,9,2)(6,10,3)(6,10,0)(6,1,0)}
\pstThreeDLine(6,1,0)(6,2,5)(6,3,7)(6,4,6)(6,5,6)(6,6,1)(6,7,1)(6,8,1)(6,9,2)(6,10,3)
%
\pscustom[fillstyle=solid,fillcolor=yellow!70,linestyle=none]{%
   \pstThreeDLine(7,1,0)(7,2,10)(7,3,6)(7,4,11)(7,5,12)(7,6,11)%
               (7,7,8)(7,8,5)(7,9,4)(7,10,4)(7,10,0)(7,1,0)}
\pstThreeDLine(7,1,0)(7,2,10)(7,3,6)(7,4,11)(7,5,12)(7,6,11)(7,7,8)(7,8,5)(7,9,4)(7,10,4)
%
\pscustom[fillstyle=solid,fillcolor=lime!70,linestyle=none]{%
\pstThreeDLine(8,1,0)(8,2,8)(8,3,9)(8,4,8)(8,5,3)(8,6,8)(8,8,6)%
              (8,8,3)(8,9,2)(8,10,4)(8,10,0)(8,1,0)}
\pstThreeDLine(8,1,0)(8,2,8)(8,3,9)(8,4,8)(8,5,3)(8,6,8)(8,8,6)(8,8,3)(8,9,2)(8,10,4)
\end{pspicture}
```

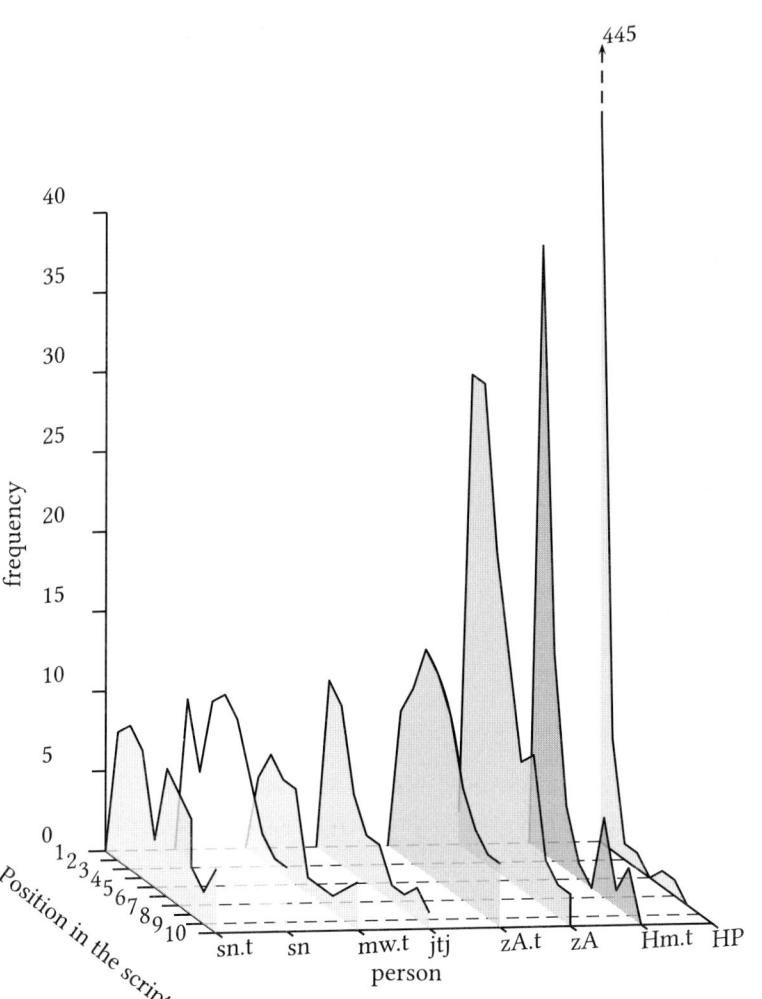

23.5.5 Simple geometric objects
\pstThreeDTriangle

A triangle is specified by its three vertices:

```
\pstThreeDTriangle [settings] (P_1)(P_2)(P_3)
```

If fillstyle has a value other than none, then the triangle is filled with the current fill colour – anything behind it is no longer visible.

23.5 pst-3dplot – 3D parallel projection of functions and data

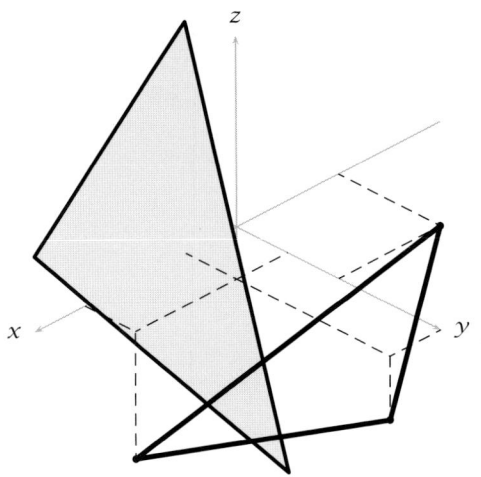

```
\usepackage{pstricks,pst-3dplot}

\begin{pspicture}(-3,-4)(3,3.25)
    \pstThreeDCoor[xMin=-4,zMax=3]
    \pstThreeDTriangle[fillcolor=yellow,
        fillstyle=solid,linecolor=blue,
        linewidth=1.5pt]%
        (5,1,2)(3,4,-1)(-1,-2,2)
    \pstThreeDTriangle[drawCoor=true,
        linecolor=black,linewidth=2pt]%
        (3,1,-2)(1,4,-1)(-2,2,0)
\end{pspicture}
```

\pstThreeDSquare

The syntax for a rectangle (or square) is:

\pstThreeDSquare [settings] $(\vec{o})(\vec{u})(\vec{v})$

A rectangle is just a closed polyline that starts and ends at point P_o (defined by the support vector $\vec{o}$) and is determined by two direction vectors, which also specify the lengths of the sides. You can fill rectangles with colours or patterns in the usual manner.

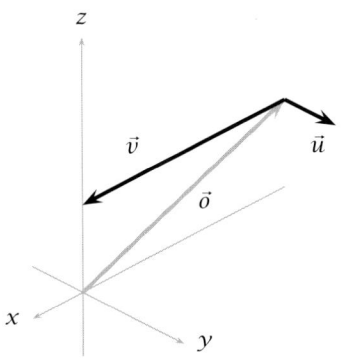

```
\usepackage{pstricks,pst-3dplot}

\begin{pspicture}(-1,-1)(4,4)
\pstThreeDCoor[xMin=-4,xMax=1,yMax=2,zMax=4]
\psset{arrows=->,arrowsize=0.2,
    linecolor=blue,linewidth=1.5pt}
\pstThreeDLine[linecolor=green](0,0,0)(-2,2,3)
\uput[45](1.5,1){$\vec{o}$}
\pstThreeDLine(-2,2,3)(2,2,3)
\uput[0](3,2){$\vec{u}$}
\pstThreeDLine(-2,2,3)(-2,3,3)
\uput[180](1,2){$\vec{v}$}
\end{pspicture}
```

23 Three-dimensional figures

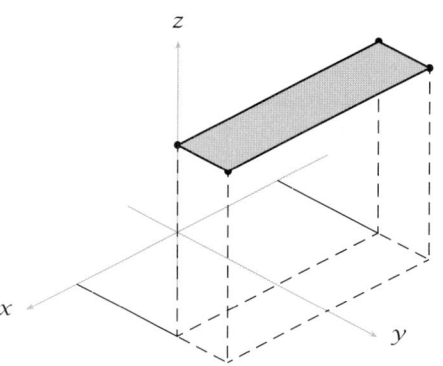

```
\usepackage{pstricks,pst-3dplot}

\begin{pspicture}(-2,-2)(4,3)
  \pstThreeDCoor[xMin=-3,xMax=3,
     yMax=4,zMax=3]
  \pstThreeDSquare[drawCoor,
     fillstyle=solid,
     fillcolor=red!60,]%
     (-2,2,3)(4,0,0)(0,1,0)
\end{pspicture}
```

\pstThreeDBox

A box or cuboid is based on rectangles so has similar syntax:

$$\boxed{\texttt{\textbackslash pstThreeDBox [settings] }(\vec{o})(\vec{u})(\vec{v})(\vec{w})}$$

You have to specify the support vector $\vec{o}$ and three direction vectors $\vec{u}$, $\vec{v}$, and $\vec{w}$, whose norm specifies the lengths of the sides.

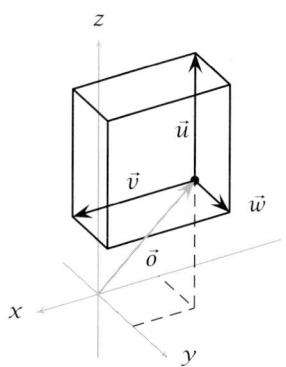

```
\usepackage{pstricks,pst-3dplot}

\begin{pspicture}(-1,-1)(3,4.25)
  \psset{Alpha=30,Beta=30}
  \pstThreeDCoor[xMin=-3,xMax=1,yMax=2]
  \pstThreeDBox(-1,1,2)(0,0,2)(2,0,0)(0,1,0)
  \pstThreeDDot[drawCoor=true](-1,1,2)
  \psset{arrows=->,arrowsize=0.2}
  \pstThreeDLine[linecolor=green](0,0,0)(-1,1,2)
  \uput[0](0.5,0.5){$\vec{o}$}
  \uput[0](0.9,2.25){$\vec{u}$}
  \uput[90](0.5,1.25){$\vec{v}$}
  \uput[45](2,1.){$\vec{w}$}
  \pstThreeDLine[linecolor=blue](-1,1,2)(-1,1,4)
  \pstThreeDLine[linecolor=blue](-1,1,2)(1,1,2)
  \pstThreeDLine[linecolor=blue](-1,1,2)(-1,2,2)
\end{pspicture}
```

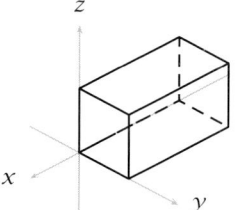

```
\usepackage{pstricks,pst-3dplot}

\begin{pspicture}(-1,-1)(3,3.25)
  \pstThreeDCoor[xMin=-3,xMax=1,yMax=2,
     zMax=2]
  \pstThreeDBox(-2,0,0)(0,0,1)(2,0,0)(0,1,0)
\end{pspicture}
```

\pstThreeDEllipse and \pstThreeDCircle

Based on the two-dimensional form, the equation of an ellipse in three-dimensional space is:

$$e : \vec{x} = \vec{c} + \cos\alpha \vec{u} + \sin\alpha \vec{v}, \qquad 0 \leq \alpha \leq 360° \qquad (23.4)$$

where $\vec{c}$ is the centre of the ellipse and $\vec{u}$ and $\vec{v}$ are the orthogonal vectors of the semiaxes. Therefore the syntax of the ellipse command is:

```
\pstThreeDEllipse [settings] (c̄)(ū)(v̄)
```

Specify $\vec{c}$, $\vec{u}$, and $\vec{v}$ in (x,y,z) notation. If the beginAngle and endAngle parameters (cf. page 364) are set to their default values of 0° and 360°, a complete ellipse is drawn; otherwise an arc is drawn.

\pstThreeDEllipse is in fact a version of the \parametricplotThreeD command (cf. Section 23.5.6 on page 389). It sets the number of interpolation points to 50, but for very thin ellipses you may need to increase the number of interpolation points.

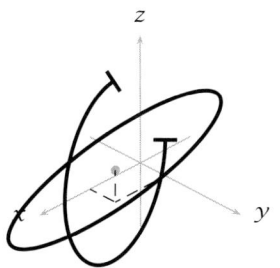

```
\usepackage{pstricks,pst-3dplot}

\psset{xMin=-1,xMax=2,yMin=-1,yMax=2,zMin=-1,zMax=2}
\begin{pspicture}(-2,-2)(2,2)
  \pstThreeDCoor
  \pstThreeDDot[linecolor=red,%
    drawCoor=true](1,0.5,0.5)% center
  \psset{linecolor=blue, linewidth=1.5pt}
  \pstThreeDEllipse(1,0.5,0.5)(-0.5,1,0.5)(1,-0.5,-1)
  % settings for an arc
  \psset{beginAngle=0,endAngle=270,arrows=|-|}
  \pstThreeDEllipse(1,0.5,0.5)(-0.5,0.5,0.5)(0.5,0.5,-1)
\end{pspicture}
```

The circle is, of course, just a special case of the ellipse with $|\vec{u}| = |\vec{v}| = r$. The \pstThreeDCircle command is in principle nothing but a synonym for \pstThreeDEllipse. In the example below, the circle was drawn with 20 points and the showpoints=true option specified.

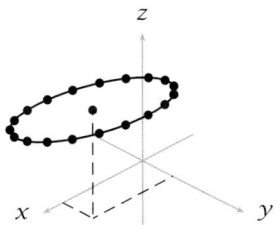

```
\usepackage{pstricks,pst-3dplot}

\begin{pspicture}(-2,-1)(2,2)
  \pstThreeDCoor[xMax=2,yMax=2,zMax=2]
  \psset{plotpoints=20,showpoints=true}
  \pstThreeDCircle%
    (1.6,.6,1.7)(.8,.4,.8)(.8,-.8,-.4)
  \pstThreeDDot[drawCoor=true](1.6,.6,1.7)
\end{pspicture}
```

\pstParaboloid

The surface of a paraboloid is approximated by rectangles. This can be used to achieve fills. The syntax for the creation of a paraboloid is

23 Three-dimensional figures

\pstParaboloid [settings] {height}{radius}

The apex of the paraboloid is always at the coordinate origin, but can be translated to any arbitrary position with the \pstThreeDPut command. You can choose the two arguments freely, though they do depend on each other – the specified radius depends on the height and vice versa.

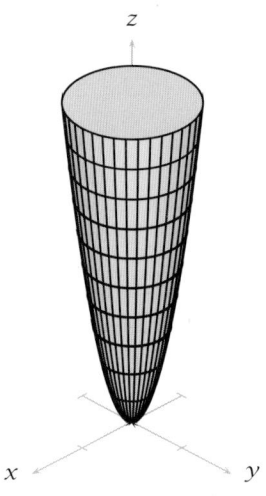

```
\usepackage{pstricks,pst-3dplot}

\begin{pspicture}(-2,-1)(2,5)
    \pstThreeDCoor[xMax=2,yMax=2,
        zMin=0,zMax=6,IIIDticks]
    \pstParaboloid{5}{1}% height 5 and radius 1
\end{pspicture}
```

```
\usepackage{pstricks,pst-3dplot}
\begin{pspicture}(-.5\linewidth,-1)(.5\linewidth,5)
    \pstParaboloid[showInside=false,SegmentColor={[cmyk]{0.8,0.1,.11,0}}]{3}{5}
    \pstThreeDCoor[xMax=3,yMax=3,zMax=6,IIIDticks]
\end{pspicture}
```

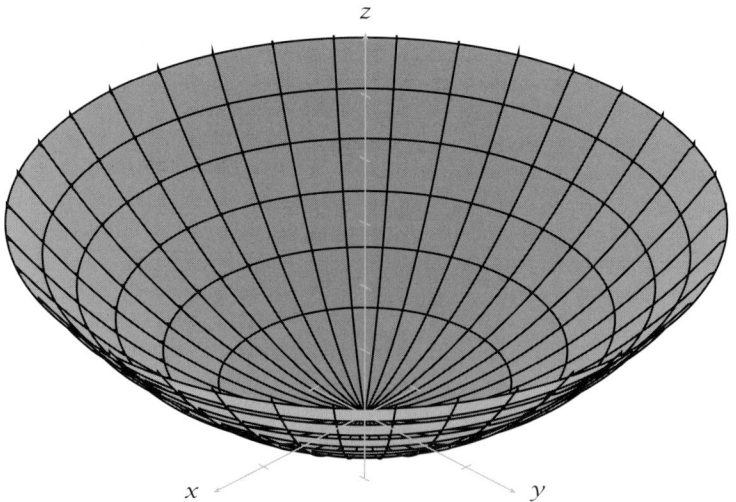

23.5 pst-3dplot – 3D parallel projection of functions and data

\pstThreeDSphere

Like the paraboloid, the surface of a sphere is approximated by rectangles. The syntax for creating spheres is:

\pstThreeDSphere [settings] $(x,y,z)\{radius\}$

(x,y,z) is the centre of the sphere.

```
\usepackage{pstricks,pst-3dplot}
\begin{pspicture}(-5,-5)(3,6) \psset{Alpha=20,Beta=35}
 \pstThreeDCoor[xMax=5,yMin=-2,yMax=8,zMax=7]
 \pstThreeDDot[drawCoor](4,4,4)\pstThreeDDot[drawCoor](2,7,7)
 \pstThreeDDot[drawCoor](2,-2,4)\pstThreeDSphere(4,4,4){2}
 \pstThreeDSphere[SegmentColor={[cmyk]{0,0,0,0}},linecolor=black](2,7,7){1.5}
 \pstThreeDSphere[linecolor=black,SegmentColor={[cmyk]{.8,.1,.11,0}}](2,-2,4){1.5}
\end{pspicture}
```

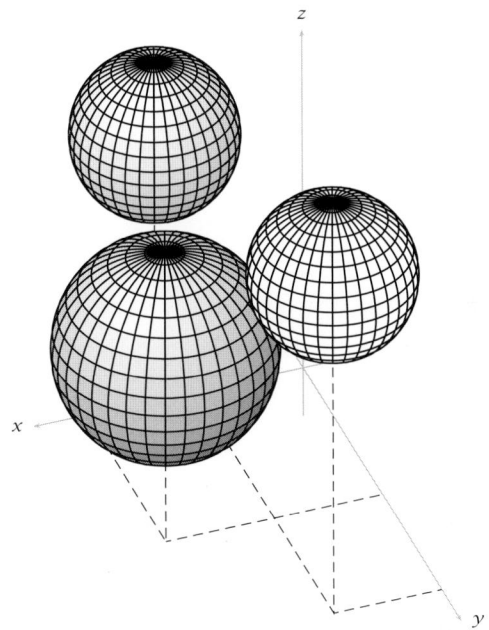

23.5.6 Plotting functions in 3D

There are two different commands for creating mathematical functions, similar to pst-plot (cf. Section 15.3 on page 203) but here dependent on two variables $z = f(x,y)$. pst-3dplot doesn't support the algebraic option of the pstricks-add package to avoid having to describe functions in infix notation. With the infix-RPN package (cf. Section 33.2.1 on page 666), however, you can transform an expression into PostScript-compatible postfix notation. \infixtoRPN{$(x\hat{}2)^*y$} converts the expression and saves it in the \RPN command, which can then be used as input for the function: \psplotThreeD(...)(...){\RPN}.

23 Three-dimensional figures

\psplotThreeD

This command has a different syntax than its equivalent in the pst-plot package, but is used in the same way.

\psplotThreeD [settings] (x_{min}, x_{max}) (y_{min}, y_{max}) {*function expression*}

x and y are the only valid variable names and you have to specify the function expression in PostScript notation. For example {x dup mul y dup mul add sqrt} is equivalent to the mathematical expression $\sqrt{x^2 + y^2}$. The old plotpoints option from pst-plot is replaced with xPlotpoints and yPlotpoints (cf. page 363), allowing you to set these separately. The default values for these parameters is 50. The hiddenLine option (cf. page 366) implements a rudimentary hidden line algorithm by drawing the curve from back to front and filling it with the current fill colour. By default hiddenLine is set to false.

```
\usepackage{pstricks,pst-3dplot}
\begin{pspicture}(-6,-3)(6,4)
  \psset{Alpha=45,Beta=15}
  \psplotThreeD[plotstyle=curve,yPlotpoints=50,xPlotpoints=80,
      linewidth=0.5pt](-4,4)(-4,4){\func}
  \pstThreeDCoor[xMax=5,yMax=5,zMax=3.5]
\end{pspicture}
```

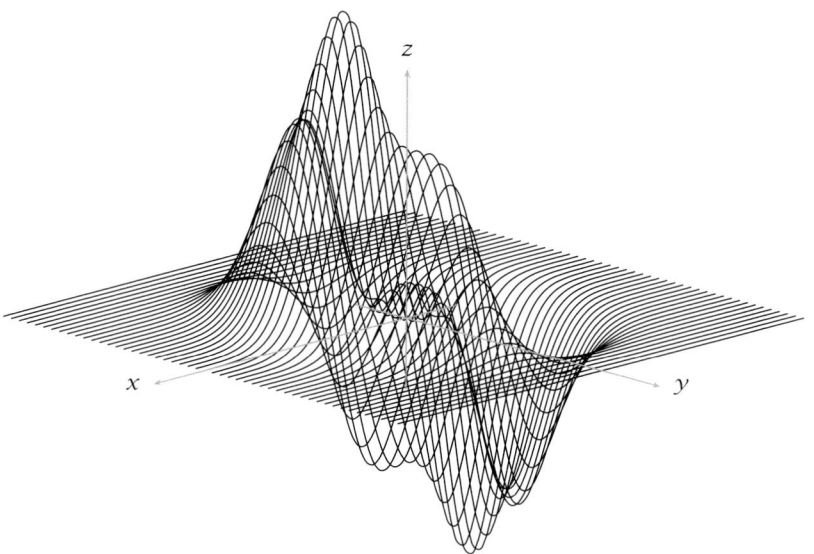

The equation 23.5 is depicted in the following examples.

$$z = 10\left(x^3 + xy^4 - \frac{x}{5}\right)e^{-(x^2+y^2)} + e^{-((x-1.225)^2+y^2)} \tag{23.5}$$

```
\usepackage{pstricks,pst-3dplot}
```

23.5 pst-3dplot – 3D parallel projection of functions and data

```
\begin{pspicture}(-6,-3)(6,4)   \psset{Alpha=45,Beta=15}
  \psplotThreeD[plotstyle=curve,yPlotpoints=50,xPlotpoints=80,
     linewidth=0.5pt,hiddenLine=true](-4,4)(-4,4){\func}
  \pstThreeDCoor[xMax=5,yMax=5,zMax=3.5]
\end{pspicture}
```

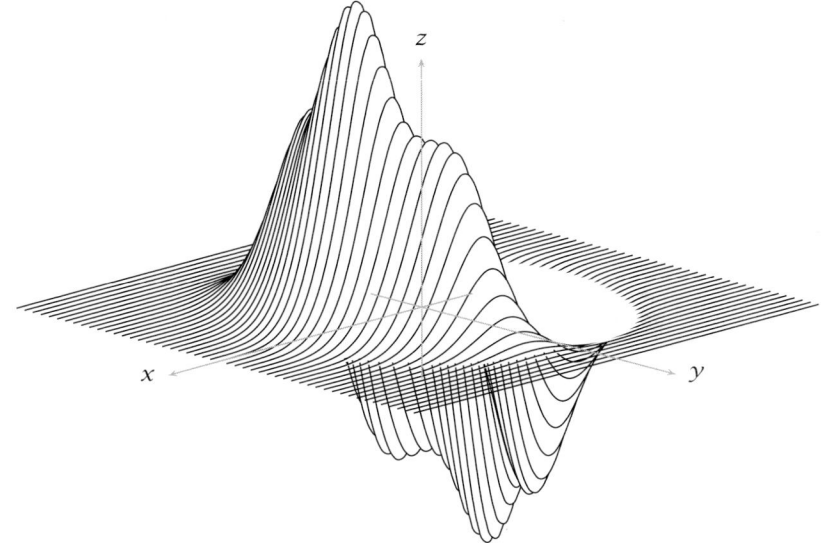

The function is primarily determined by two loops:

```
for (float y=yMin; y<yMax; y+=dy)
    for (float x=xMin; x<xMax; x+=dx)
        z=f(x,y);
```

The inner loop is incrementing the x values; therefore a closed curve can only be created in this direction, as at the end of the part of a curve in x direction the current point is reset to the beginning. Hence too few yPlotpoints are not really a problem, but too few xPlotpoints cause a curve similar to a polygon line.

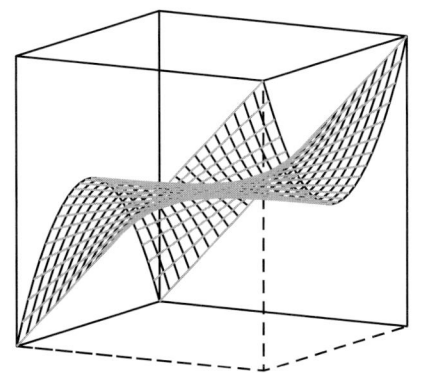

```
\usepackage{pstricks,pst-3dplot}

\psset{unit=2cm,Beta=10,Alpha=60}
\begin{pspicture}(-1.25,-1.2)(1,1.2)
\pstThreeDCoor[xMax=2.5,yMax=2.5,zMax=2.5,
    drawing=false]
\pstThreeDBox(1,1,-1)(-2,0,0)(0,-2,0)(0,0,2)
\psplotThreeD[linecolor=blue,drawStyle=xyLines]%
    (-1,1)(-1,1){x 2 exp y mul}
\psplotThreeD[linecolor=red,drawStyle=yLines]%
    (-1,1)(-1,1){x 2 exp y mul}
\end{pspicture}
```

23 Three-dimensional figures

To fill three-dimensional surfaces with a pattern or a colour, you need a closed polyline, but just creating a three-dimensional surface with an xy grid doesn't produce this. What you in fact need to do is to draw the border curves for the function by setting one of the values of xPlotpoints or yPlotpoints to one, as shown in the example below. If you create these border lines in the correct order for making a closed polyline, and set them inside a \pscustom command, you can add a fill style for the surface.

```
\usepackage{pstricks,pst-3dplot,pst-grad}
\def\func{x dup mul y dup mul 2 mul add x 6 mul sub y 4 mul sub 3 add 10 div}
\psset{unit=1cm,linewidth=1.5pt}
\begin{pspicture}(-1,-1)(10,9)
  \psset{Beta=20,Alpha=160,subticks=7}
  \pstThreeDCoor[xMin=0,yMin=0,zMin=0,xMax=7,yMax=7,zMax=7,linewidth=1pt]
  \psset{linewidth=0.1pt,linecolor=gray}
  \pstThreeDPlaneGrid(0,0)(7,7)
  \pstThreeDPlaneGrid[planeGrid=xz,planeGridOffset=7](0,0)(7,7)
  \pstThreeDPlaneGrid[planeGrid=yz](0,0)(7,7)
  {\psset{linewidth=1.5pt}
   \pscustom[fillstyle=gradient,plotstyle=curve]{
    \psplotThreeD[xPlotpoints=200,yPlotpoints=1,drawStyle=xLines](0,7)(0,0){\func}
    \psplotThreeD[xPlotpoints=1,yPlotpoints=200,drawStyle=yLines](7,7)(0,7){\func}
    \psplotThreeD[xPlotpoints=200,yPlotpoints=1,drawStyle=xLines](7,0)(7,7){\func}
    \psplotThreeD[xPlotpoints=1,yPlotpoints=200,drawStyle=yLines](0,0)(7,0){\func}}}
  \pstThreeDPlaneGrid[planeGrid=yz,planeGridOffset=7](0,0)(7,7)
\end{pspicture}
```

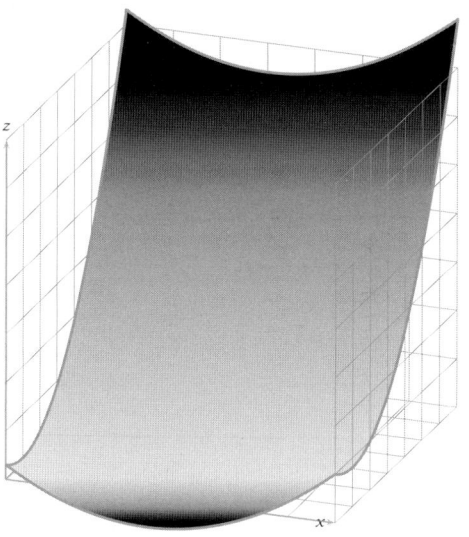

23-05-5

23.5 pst-3dplot – 3D parallel projection of functions and data

\parametricplotThreeD

The syntax for \parametricplotThreeD is:

```
\parametricplotThreeD [settings] (t1,t2) (u1,u2) {x(t,u) y(t,u) z(t,u)}
```

$$x = f(t,u) \qquad y = f(t,u) \qquad z = f(t,u) \qquad (23.6)$$

The only variable names possible are t and u, and the function is evaluated for the intervals $[t_1, t_2]$ and $[u_1, u_2]$. The order is unimportant, and u is not needed at all if you are only wanting to draw a curve rather than a surface. The three function terms must put the three values x, y, and z on the stack.

For example to draw a spiral, the following functions in parameter representation are required:

$$x = r\cos t \qquad y = r\sin t \qquad z = t/600 \qquad (23.7)$$

The t value is divided by 600 because angle specifications are to be done in degrees in PostScript. Furthermore only the t variable is required here because it is a curve.

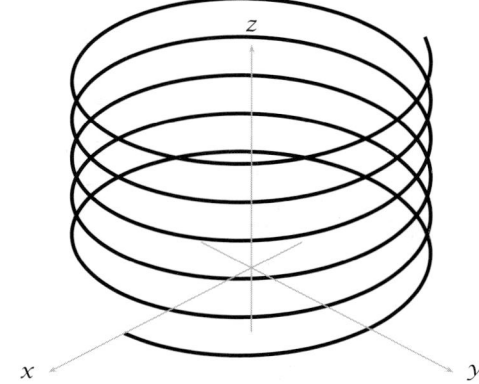

```
\usepackage{pstricks,pst-3dplot}

\begin{pspicture}(-3,-2)(3,4.2)
\parametricplotThreeD[
  xPlotpoints=200,
  linecolor=blue,linewidth=1.5pt,
  plotstyle=curve](0,1950){
    2.5 t cos mul
    2.5 t sin mul
    t 600 div}
\pstThreeDCoor[xMax=4,
  yMax=4,zMax=3.5]
\end{pspicture}
```

23.5.7 Plotting data in 3D

The structure of the data files has to be similar to that described in Section 15.4.1 on page 212. For example:

```
0.0000   1.0000   0.0000      -0.4207   0.9972   0.0191   ....
0.0000,  1.0000,  0.0000      -0.4207,  0.9972,  0.0191   ....
( 0.0000,1.0000,0.0000)       (-0.4207,0.9972,0.0191)     ....
{ 0.0000,1.0000,0.0000}       {-0.4207,0.9972,0.0191}     ....
```

\fileplotThreeD

The syntax is trivial and the same as in the two-dimensional case (cf. Section 15.4.3 on page 214):

23 Three-dimensional figures

`\fileplotThreeD` [settings] {*file name*}

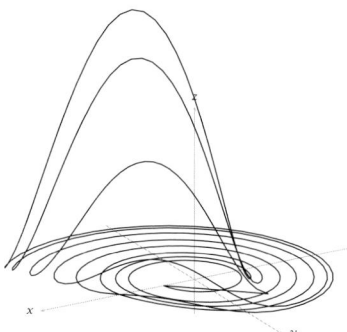

```
\usepackage{pstricks,pst-3dplot,graphicx}

\resizebox{6cm}{!}{%
\begin{pspicture}(-6,-3)(6,9.5)
  \psset{xunit=0.5cm,yunit=0.5cm,Alpha=30,
      Beta=20}% the global parameters
  \pstThreeDCoor[xMin=-10,xMax=10,
      yMin=-10,yMax=10,zMin=-2,zMax=10]
  \fileplotThreeD[plotstyle=polygon]%
      {data3D.Roessler}
\end{pspicture}}
```

\dataplotThreeD

The syntax is:

`\dataplotThreeD` [settings] {*data command*}

The data command containing all the data can be created with \readdata, as described in Section 15.4.4.

`\readdata`{*command name*}{*file name*}

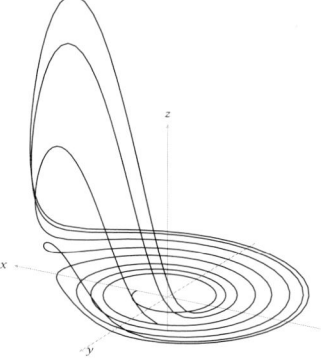

```
\usepackage{pstricks,pst-3dplot,graphicx}

\resizebox{5.5cm}{!}{%
\readdata{\dataThreeD}{data3D.Roessler}
\begin{pspicture}(-6,-3)(5,11)
 \psset{xunit=0.5cm,yunit=0.5cm,
   Alpha=-30,Beta=20}
 \pstThreeDCoor[%
   xMin=-10,xMax=10,
   yMin=-10,yMax=10,
   zMin=-2,zMax=10]
 \dataplotThreeD[plotstyle=line]%
     {\dataThreeD}
\end{pspicture}}
```

\listplotThreeD

The syntax is:

`\listplotThreeD` [settings] {*data command*}

There is no real difference for the user between \listplotThreeD and \dataplotThreeD. You can use \listplotThreeD to insert additional PostScript code to PostScript via TeX. There is a corresponding example in Section 15.4.5 on page 215.

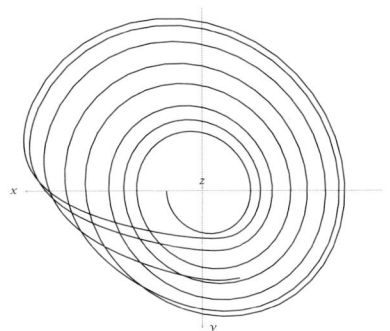

```
\usepackage{pstricks,pst-3dplot,graphicx}

\resizebox{5cm}{!}{%
\readdata{\dataThreeD}{data3D.Roessler}
\begin{pspicture}(-5,-4)(5,4.5)
  \psset{unit=0.5cm,Alpha=0,Beta=90}
  \pstThreeDCoor[xMin=-10,xMax=10,
     yMin=-10,yMax=7.5,
     zMin=-2,zMax=10]
  \listplotThreeD[plotstyle=line]%
     {\dataThreeD}
\end{pspicture}}
```

23.6 pst-solides3d — perspective 3D views

The three-dimensional view of a graphical object or landscape is one of the most interesting things in computer graphics and therefore has a large number of applications, including 3D games. Animation isn't needed when publishing printed matter – simple 3D views are often enough – but even these can be demanding graphically and aren't always easy to create.

The pst-solides3d package [78] by Jean-Paul Vignault, Manuel Luque, and Arnaud Schmittbuhl is the successor to the nowadays more or less obsolete pst-vue3d package. The basis of the new pst-solides3d package are the ideas and PostScript programmes of Bill Casselmann [11], which have been extended by several PostScript procedures by Jean-Paul Vignault. The PostScript version was published some time ago under the name *BBgraf* (http://melusine.eu.org/syracuse/bbgraf/). The documentation of the PostScript functions is at http://melusine.eu.org/syracuse/texpng/jpv/guide_jps/guide_util.pdf. The pst-solides3d package basically offers an interface for using this PostScript library. In particular, it supports perspective views including hidden surfaces and lines of various objects, which is a major extension. However, this increases the mathematical requirements and therefore also the computation times and the size of the PostScript files; conversion to PDF with ps2pdf can take a particularly long time.

The package's main command is \psSolid, and there are a lot of additional parameters available for it, which are listed in Table 23.12 on page 422. The rest of this introductory section discusses a few useful concepts, naming the corresponding parameters where appropriate, but otherwise we deal with the parameters right at the end of the chapter after covering the commands. You'll find that several of the terms used in this package are in French, which is a reflection of its origins.

The viewpoint (vanishing point), explained earlier in Figure 23.2 on page 341, is specified by setting the optional argument viewpoint=<x y z>. It is also possible to specify the *spherical* viewpoint in spherical coordinates by calling the PostScript function rtp2xyz after specifying *coordinates* the three values *radius, rotation angle,* and *tilting angle* (r,θ,φ).

23 Three-dimensional figures

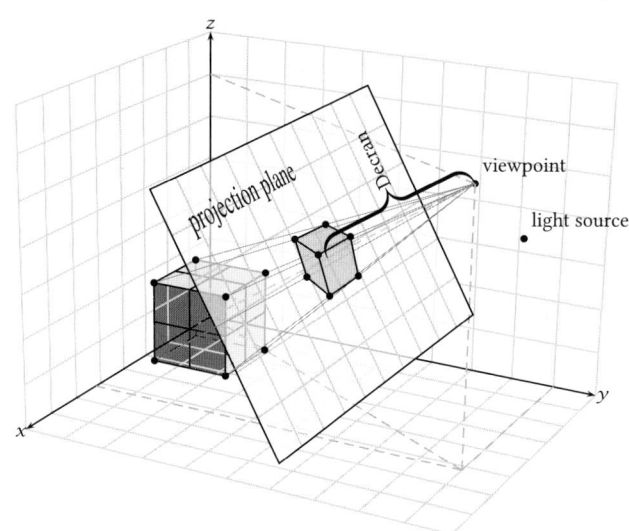

Example 23-06-1 demonstrates the view of a three-dimensional object. The object, here the blue cube, is seen from the viewpoint V. Perpendicular to the connecting line $\overline{OV}$ (coordinate origin–viewpoint), there is the virtual two-dimensional screen (projection plane), which has a default distance of Decran=50 to the viewpoint V. This value may be positive as well as negative. Independent of the viewpoint, a light source can be placed by assigning xyz coordinates to the lightsrc parameter to make shadows possible. By default, there is no light source.

light source

A smaller value for Decran achieves a smaller image with the same z coordinate; a larger value achieves a larger image. The construction follows the simple laws of the intercept theorems, independent of the values of viewpoint and Decran; viewpoint=0 0 0 and Decran=0 do not make sense, however. Furthermore, drawing axes with \psaxes from the pst-plot package doesn't depend on the value of Decran as that command doesn't evaluate this parameter.

negative values possible

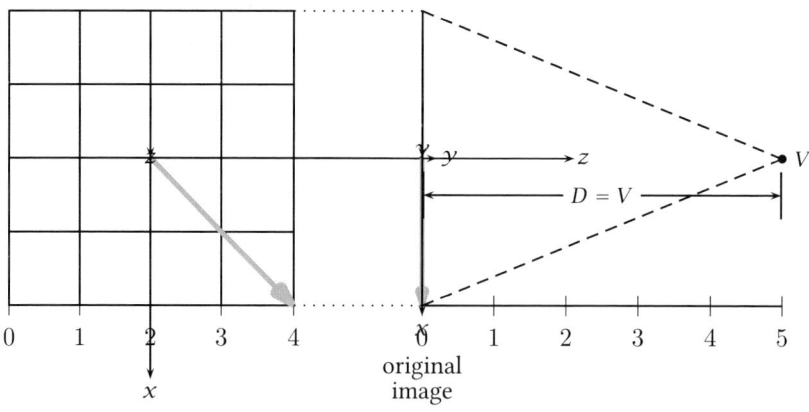

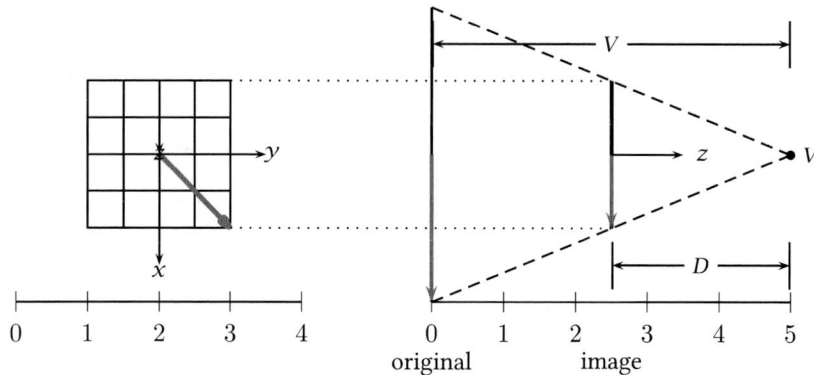

The viewpoint can move arbitrarily around the original image in all three dimensions, as illustrated in the following set of examples. The current coordinates of the viewpoint are given in the centre of each figure. Display problems only arise if a surface defined with just a front face is viewed from behind. This is the case in the final graphic, where the grille object is no longer visible when viewed from behind. The problem is resolved by setting the object to be transparent with action=draw (cf. Section 23.6.9 on page 428).

The first view is at viewpoint=0 0 20, square on above the centre of the image, but because of the centric perspective we aren't directly above the individual objects – only the line connecting the viewpoint and the centre of the image is perpendicular to the image plane. In the following images the x coordinate is increased 10 units at a time. Because we are increasing the x coordinate while keeping the z coordinate the same, everything stays parallel to the y axis. The distance between viewpoint and coordinate origin increases ($d = \sqrt{x_V^2 + y_V^2 + z_V^2}$) while the value of Decran stays the same. This results in a smaller image each time we move.

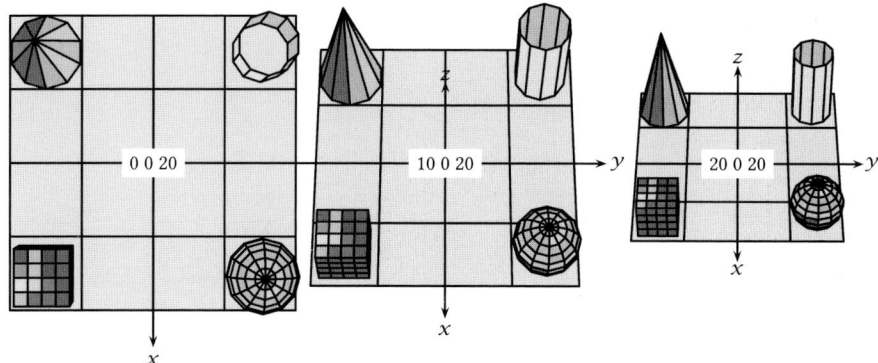

The second row of examples continue from the last one above, but this time changing the y coordinate in three steps. In the right image, the viewpoint is viewpoint=20 20 20 and the view angle is 45°.

23 Three-dimensional figures

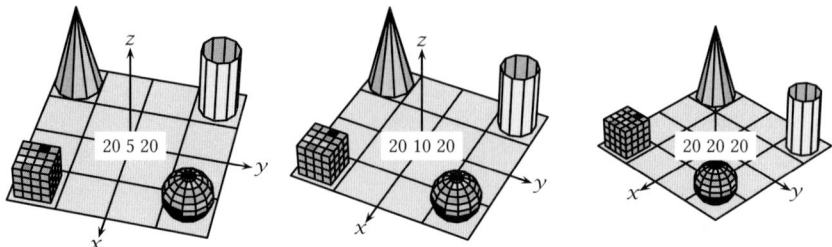

The examples in the third row each continue from the last one above, but this time they show the effect of negative values for the individual coordinates. In the first image, the sign of the x coordinate is changed; we see the image from the same distance from the other x side. The next two examples change the sign of the y and z coordinates, respectively.

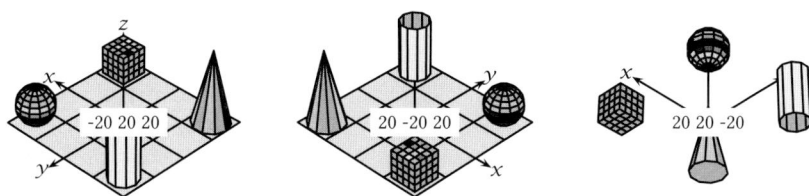

You can change the light source locally for individual objects with `lightsrc`, or switch it off by assigning an empty value to the parameter, as demonstrated for the cone in the following example. Because of this, the transparent light cone can be drawn with a lighter colour. In practice the outer surface of the cone visible here would be outside the actual light cone.

```
\usepackage{pst-solides3d,pstricks-add}
\psset{unit=0.8}
\begin{pspicture}(-3,-3)(3,9)\psset{viewpoint=50 10 15,lightsrc=8 8 8}
\psSolid[object=sphere,r=4,fillcolor=blue!60!yellow!90,ngrid=36 36,
        intersectiontype=1,intersectionplan={[1 1 1 -2]},intersectioncolor=(jaune),
        intersectionlinewidth=1](0,0,0)
\psSolid[object=cone,r=3.944,h=12.7,linecolor=yellow,fillcolor=yellow!40,
        opacity=0.4,lightsrc={},RotX=-35.26,RotY=-45,RotZ=-90,
        ngrid=12 36](0.667,0.667,0.667)
\psPoint(8,8,8){ls}
\uput[45](ls){light source}
\rput(ls){$\bullet$}
\axesIIID[showOrigin=false](4,4,4)(11,6,6)
\end{pspicture}
```

23.6 pst-solides3d — perspective 3D views

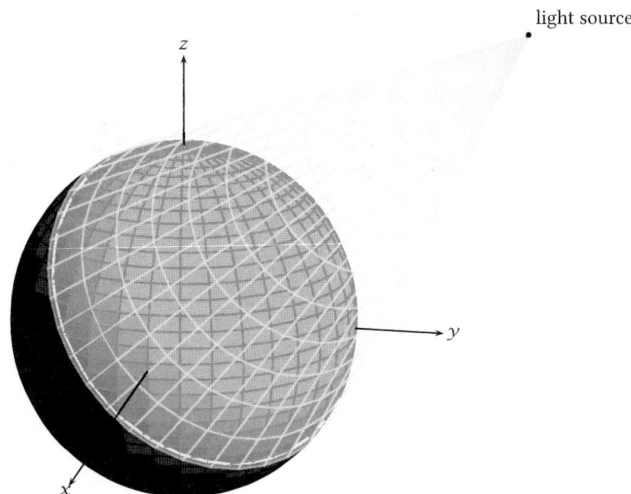

If the coordinates of the light source are set to the coordinates of the viewpoint through `lightsrc=viewpoint`, no shadows occur, and the visible surfaces are all created with the same brightness, which you can change through the `lightintensity` parameter (default 2).

```
\usepackage{pst-solides3d}
\psset{viewpoint=20 10 40 rtp2xyz,lightsrc=viewpoint,Decran=28,ngrid=36 36,grid=false}
\begin{pspicture}(-2,-2)(2,2)\psSolid[object=sphere,r=1]\rput(0,0){2}\end{pspicture}
\begin{pspicture}(-2,-2)(2,2)\psSolid[object=sphere,r=1,lightintensity=1]\rput(0,0){1}
\end{pspicture}
\begin{pspicture}(-2,-2)(2,2)\psSolid[object=sphere,r=1,lightintensity=0.8]\rput(0,0){0.8}
\end{pspicture}
```

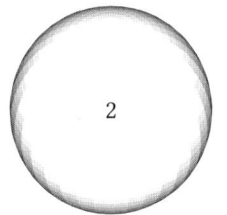 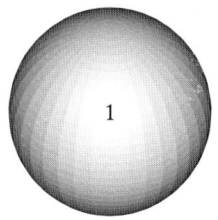 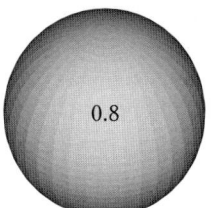

23.6.1 \psSolid

The number of available commands is relatively small; most of the objects are created by assigning a parameter at PostScript level. \psSolid is the main command of the package and can display all three-dimensional objects through its many optional parameters (cf. Table 23.12 on page 422).

`\psSolid [settings] ($x_0, y_0, z_0$)`

The optional (x_0, y_0, z_0) triple specifies the reference point of the object within the current three-dimensional coordinate system, for example the location for the centre of a sphere. If

23 Three-dimensional figures

this argument is missing, the coordinate origin is taken by default. The following summary shows the basic objects, though you can make your own custom creations with other values too.

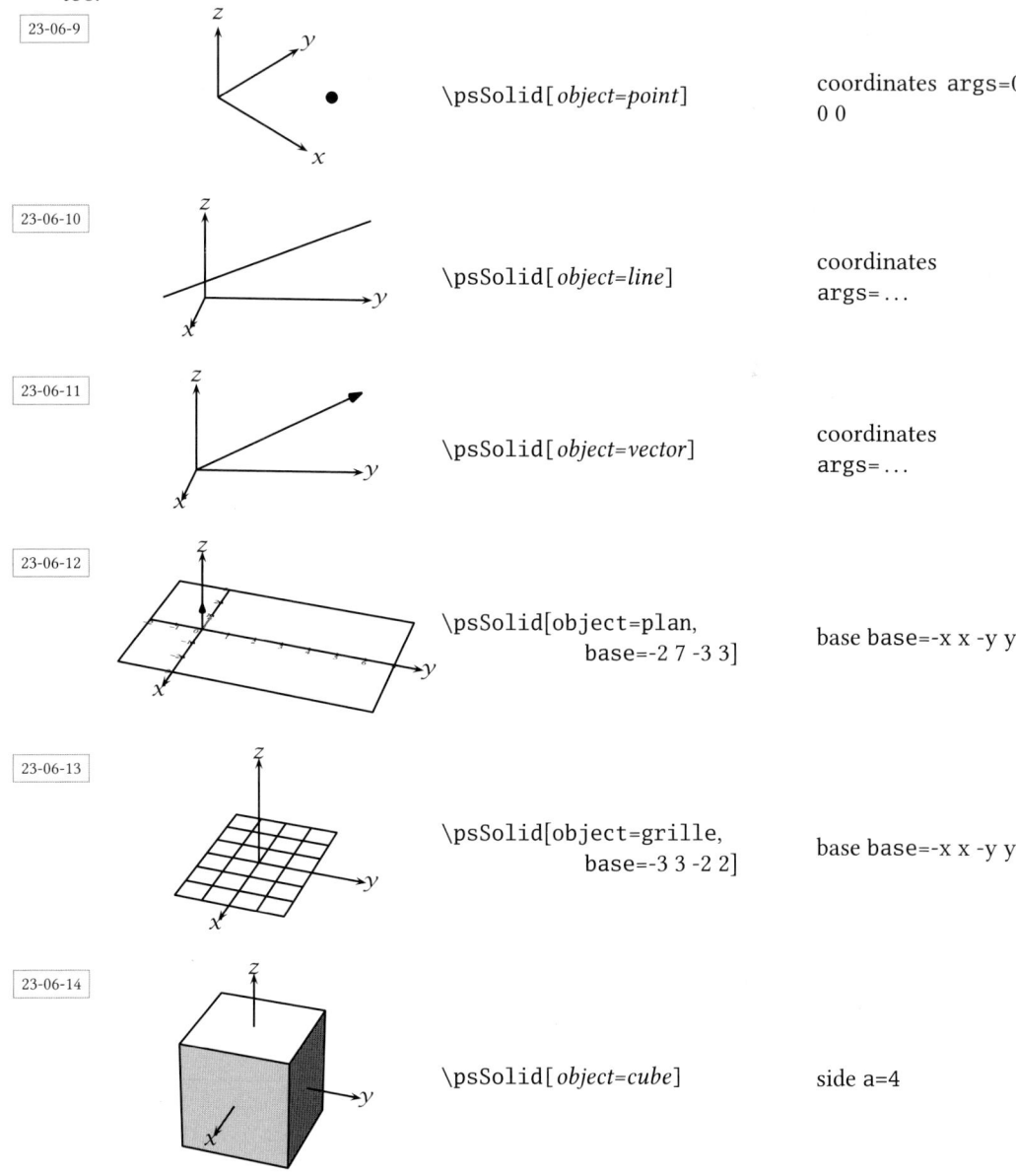

23.6 pst-solides3d — perspective 3D views

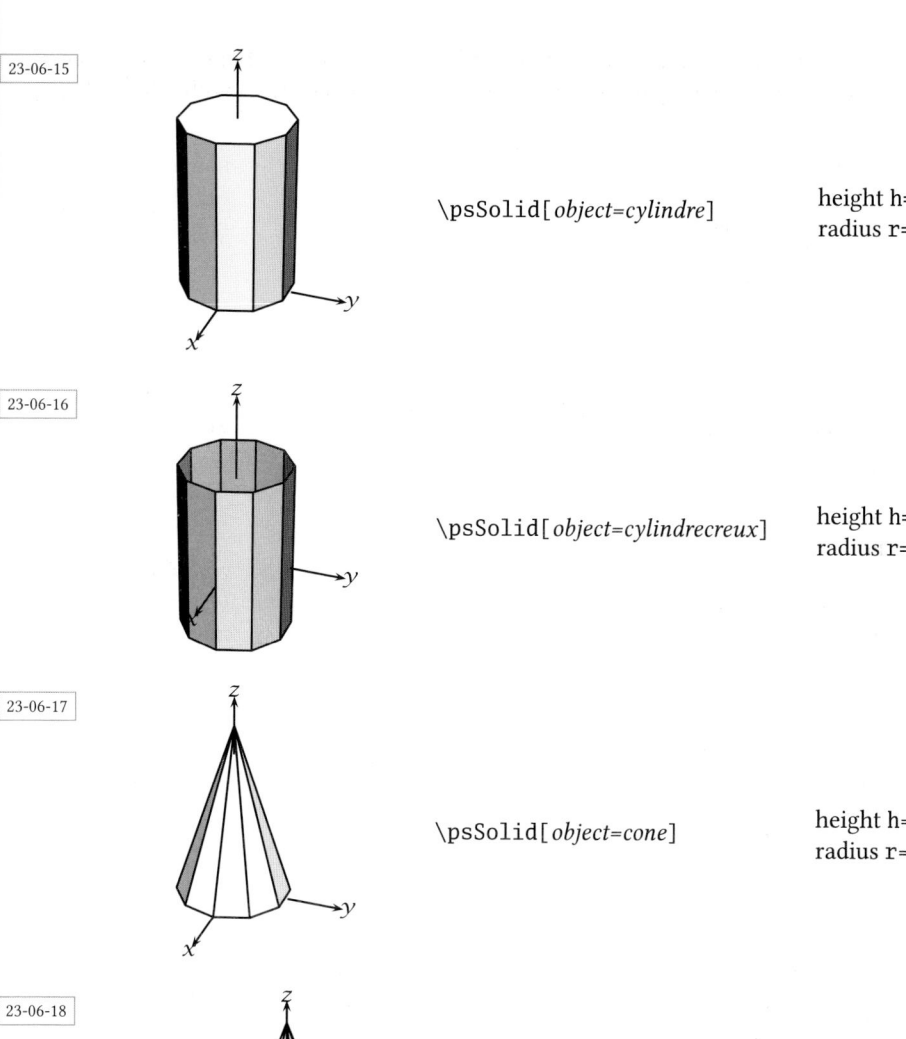

23-06-15   \psSolid[object=cylindre]   height h=6 radius r=2

23-06-16   \psSolid[object=cylindrecreux]   height h=5 radius r=2

23-06-17   \psSolid[object=cone]   height h=5 radius r=2

23-06-18   \psSolid[object=conecreux]   height h=6 radius r=2

23 Three-dimensional figures

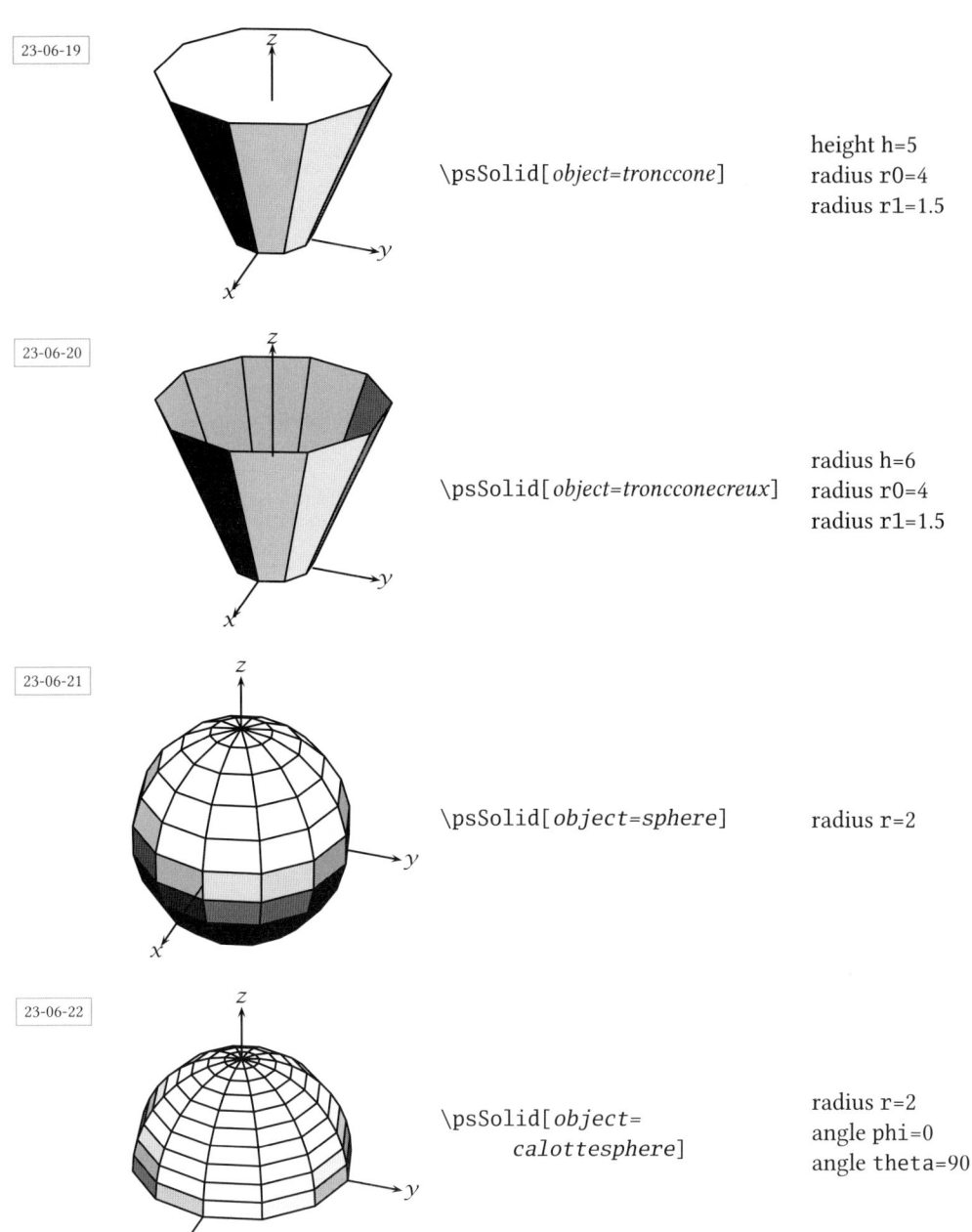

23-06-19	`\psSolid[object=tronccone]`	height h=5 radius r0=4 radius r1=1.5
23-06-20	`\psSolid[object=troncconecreux]`	radius h=6 radius r0=4 radius r1=1.5
23-06-21	`\psSolid[object=sphere]`	radius r=2
23-06-22	`\psSolid[object=calottesphere]`	radius r=2 angle phi=0 angle theta=90

23.6 pst-solides3d — perspective 3D views

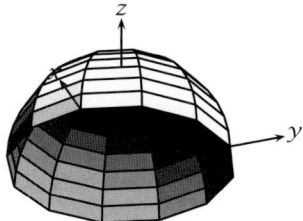

\psSolid[*object=*
calottespherecreuse]
radius r=2
angle phi=0
angle theta=90

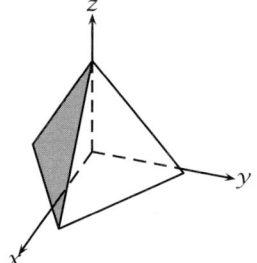

\psSolid[*object=tetrahedron*]   side a=4

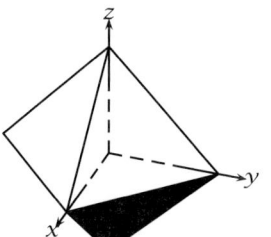

\psSolid[*object=octahedron*]   side a=4

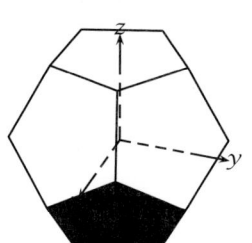

\psSolid[*object=dodecahedron*] side a=4

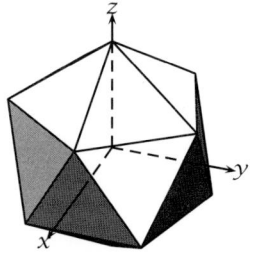

\psSolid[*object=icosahedron*] side a=4

23 Three-dimensional figures

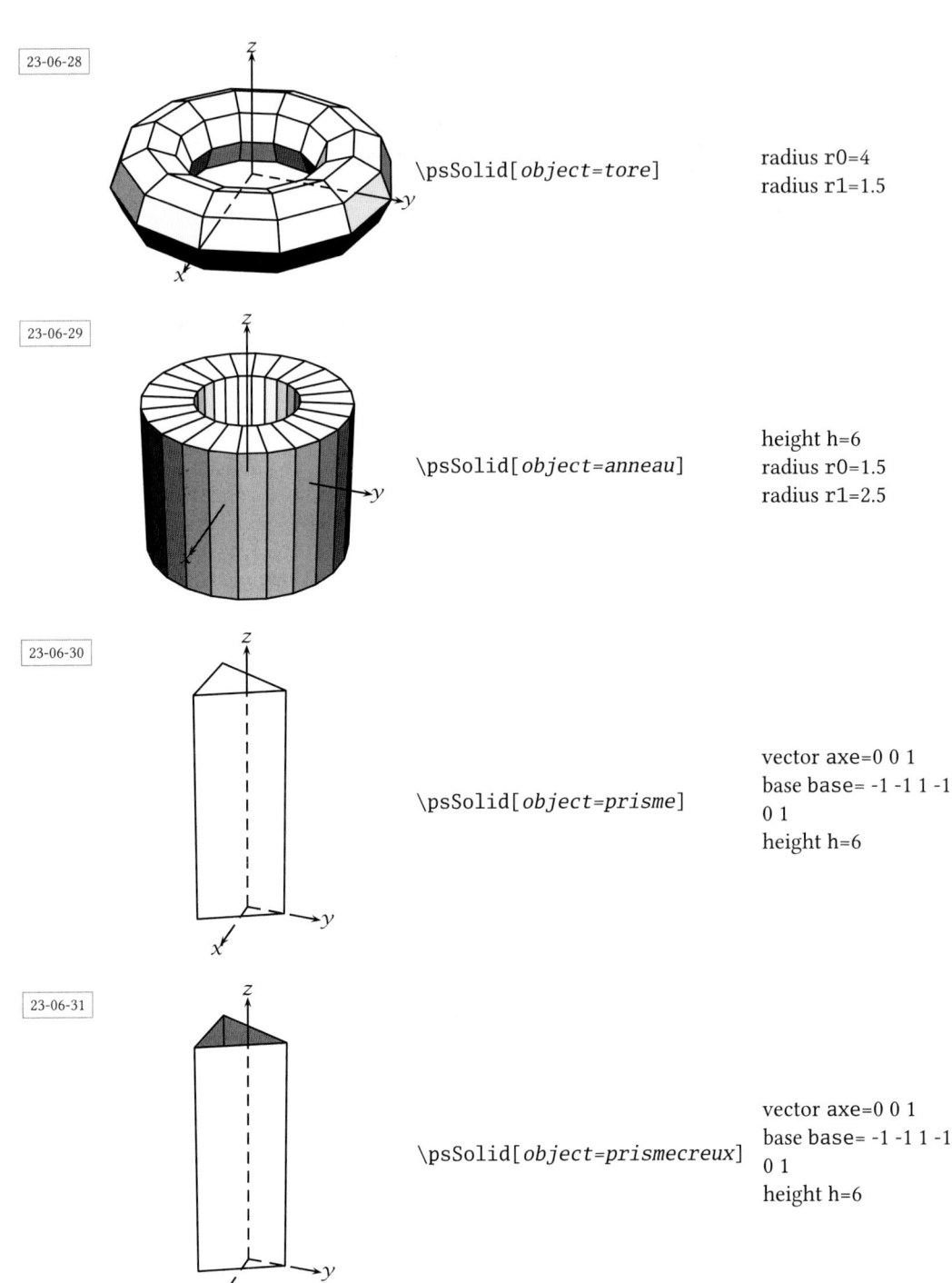

23-06-28

\psSolid[object=tore]

radius r0=4
radius r1=1.5

23-06-29

\psSolid[object=anneau]

height h=6
radius r0=1.5
radius r1=2.5

23-06-30

\psSolid[object=prisme]

vector axe=0 0 1
base base= -1 -1 1 -1 0 1
height h=6

23-06-31

\psSolid[object=prismecreux]

vector axe=0 0 1
base base= -1 -1 1 -1 0 1
height h=6

23.6 pst-solides3d — perspective 3D views

23-06-32

`\psSolid[object=`
`    parallelepiped]`

side a=4
side b=4
side c=4

23-06-33

`\psSolid[object=face]`

points base=...

23-06-34

`\psSolid[object=`
`    polygoneregulier,`
`    ngrid=...]`

radius r=2

23-06-35

`\psSolid[object=ruban]`

points base=...
height h=4
direction axe=0 0 1
elements ngrid=1

23-06-36

`\psSolid[object=courbe`
`    function=...`
`    range=...`

points base=...
height h=4
direction axe=0 0 1
elements ngrid=1

23-06-37

`\psSolid[object=surface`
`    function=...`
`    ngrid=dx dy]`

function
function=...
interval range=...
step ngrid=dx dy

23 Three-dimensional figures

23-06-38

```
\psSolid[object=surface*
         function=...
         ngrid=...]
```

function
function=...
parameters r=1

23-06-39

```
\psSolid[object=
         surfaceparametree
         function=...
         base=0 1 02 pi mul
         ngrid=20
```

base base=...
function
function=*name*
intervals ngrid=1

23-06-40

`\psSolid[object=pie]`

angle phi=0
angle theta=*90*
height h=6
radius r=1

23-06-41

`\psSolid[object=fusion]`

base base=*names*

23-06-42

`\psSolid[object=geode]`

grid ngrid=m n

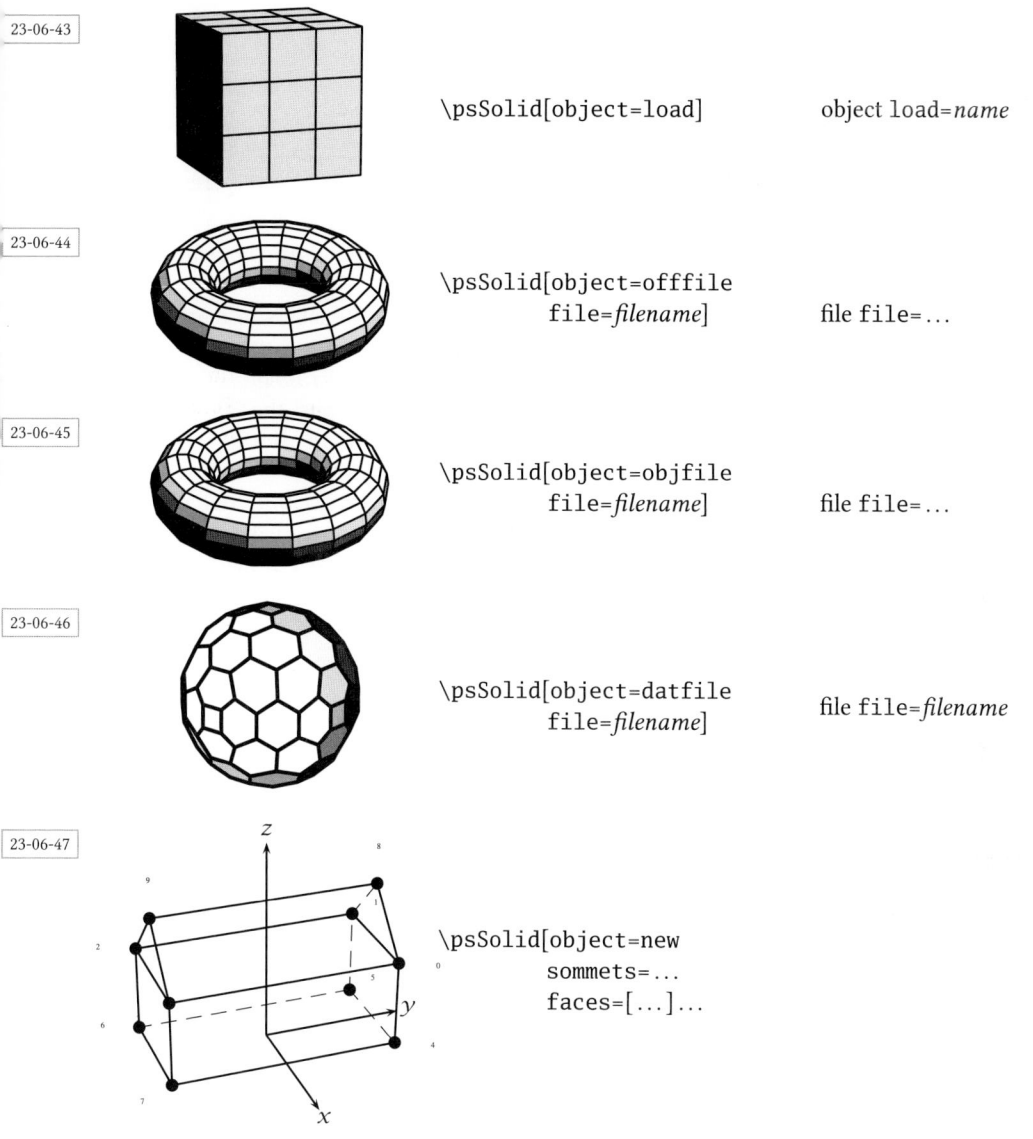

23.6.2 \axesIIID

The \axesIIID draws the coordinate axes.

\axesIIID [settings] (x_0, y_0, z_0) (x_1, y_1, z_1)

The axes are drawn as dashed lines from the coordinate origin to the point $P_0(x_0, y_0, z_0)$ (if two triples are specified) and as solid lines from there to $P_1(x_1, y_1, z_1)$. You can suppress the dashed lines with showOrigin=false, but you can't hide the solid lines; coordinate axes are *Axes not as hidden lines!*

23 Three-dimensional figures

always drawn on top of an already existing illustration – the hidden line algorithm is not used! Table 23.8 summarizes the relevant parameters.

Table 23.8: Summary of the relevant parameters for the \axesIIID command

name	type	default	meaning
showOrigin	boolean	true	This setting draws dashed lines from the coordinate origin to the first triple of the command (where two triples are specified).
mathLabel	boolean	true	This setting draws the labels in math mode; you must the mathLabel setting into account when assigning commands to axisemph.
axisnames	{x,y,z}	{x,y,z}	This parameter specifies the axis labels; you must enclose them in braces, for example axisnames={u,v,w}.
axisemph	command	{}	This setting specifies the font size or font style. Different commands are valid, depending on whether you've chosen text or math mode through mathLabel. The options are listed in Table 15.3 on page 178.
labelsep	value unit	10pt	This specifies the distance of the axis labels (in the direction of the axis) from the tip of the axis.

```
\usepackage{pst-solides3d}
\begin{pspicture}(-2,-1.2)(2,2.2)\axesIIID(0.4,0.4,0.4)(0.7,0.7,0.7)\end{pspicture}
\begin{pspicture}(-2,-1.2)(2,2.2)
\axesIIID[mathLabel=false](0.4,0.4,0.4)(0.7,0.7,0.7)
\end{pspicture}
\begin{pspicture}(-2,-1.2)(2,2.2)
\axesIIID[axisemph=\bfseries,mathLabel=false](0.4,0.4,0.4)(0.7,0.7,0.7)
\end{pspicture}
```

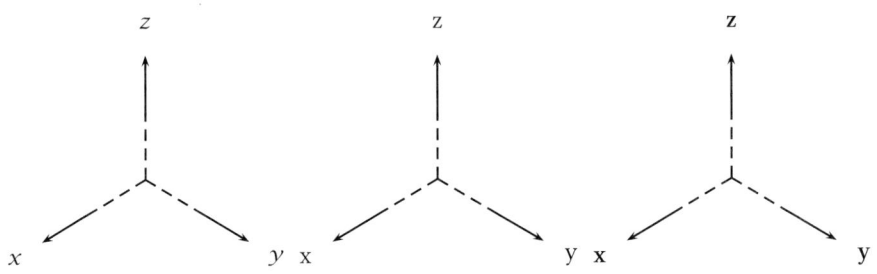

```
\usepackage{pst-solides3d}
\begin{pspicture}(-2,-1.2)(2,2.2)
\axesIIID[showOrigin=false,axisemph=\scriptstyle](0.4,0.4,0.4)(0.7,0.7,0.7)\psdot(0)
```

```
\end{pspicture}\begin{pspicture}(-2,-1.2)(2,2.2)
\axesIIID[axisnames={a,b,c},axisemph={\mbox{\boldmath}\color{red}}](0,0,0)(0.7,0.7,0.7)
\end{pspicture}\begin{pspicture}(-2,-1.2)(2,2.2)
\axesIIID[axisemph={\displaystyle},
   axisnames={\vec{u},\vec{v},\vec{w}}](0,0,0)(0.7,0.7,0.7)
\end{pspicture}
```

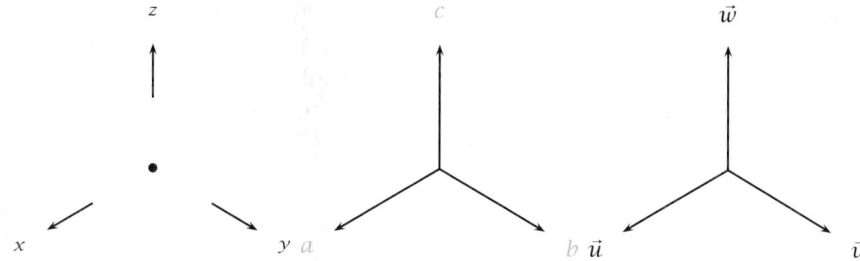

```
\usepackage{pst-solides3d}
\begin{pspicture}(-2,-1.2)(2,2.2)
\axesIIID[axisnames={\mathcal{U},\mathcal{V},\mathcal{W}}](0,0,0)(0.7,0.7,0.7)
\end{pspicture}
\begin{pspicture}(-2,-1.2)(2,2.2)
\axesIIID[axisnames={1,2,3},labelsep=2pt,arrows=-,linecolor=blue](0,0,0)(0.7,0.7,0.7)
\end{pspicture}
\begin{pspicture}(-2,-1.2)(2,2.2)
\axesIIID[axisnames={1,2,3},labelsep=2pt,arrows=-|,
   showOrigin=false,linecolor=blue](0.4,0.4,0.4)(0.7,0.7,0.7)\psdot(0)
\end{pspicture}
```

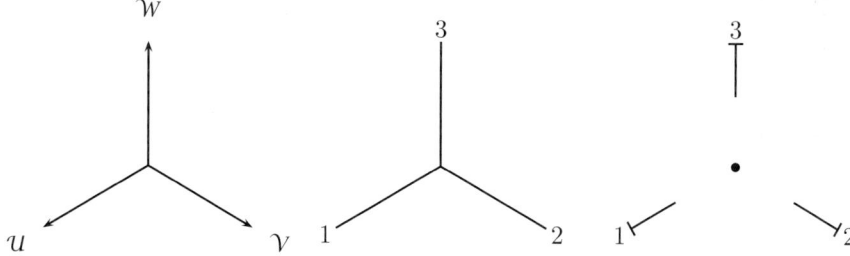

23.6.3 \gridIIID

The \gridIIID command creates a two or three dimensional grid depending on the current setting of the three axes.

\gridIIID [settings] $(x_{min}, x_{max})(y_{min}, y_{max})$ [dx,dy,dz]

The two required arguments for \gridIIID denote the x and y intervals, respectively. The z axis gets an interval of $[-4\ldots 4]$ by default, though you can change this interval using the zMin and zMax parameters. The labels aren't drawn at the actual coordinate axes, but outside

23 Three-dimensional figures

the grid. You can use [dx,dy,dz] to specify the length of each individual axis. These are drawn as dashed lines within a grid and solid lines outside. The default lengths are [2,2,3]. Table 23.9 summarizes the other parameters that are valid.

Table 23.9: Summary of the available parameters for the \gridIIID command

name	type	default	meaning
spotX	r|u|l|d| ul|cl|bl|dl|ub|cb| bb|db|uc|cc|bc|dc| ur|cr|br|dr	dr	position of x label
spotY	ditto	dl	position of y label
spotZ	ditto	1	position of z label
Zmin	value	-4	min coordinate
Zmax	value	4	max coordinate
stepX	value	1	x step of the tick marks
stepY	value	1	y step of the tick marks
stepZ	value	1	z step of the tick marks
ticklength	value	0.2	length of the tick marks

```
\usepackage{pst-solides3d}
\psset{Decran=15,viewpoint=20 10 10}
\begin{pspicture}(-3,-2.5)(2.5,3) \gridIIID(-3,3)(-3,3) \end{pspicture}
\begin{pspicture}(-4,-2.5)(2,3.5) \gridIIID[Zmin=0,Zmax=0](-3,3)(-3,3) \end{pspicture}
```

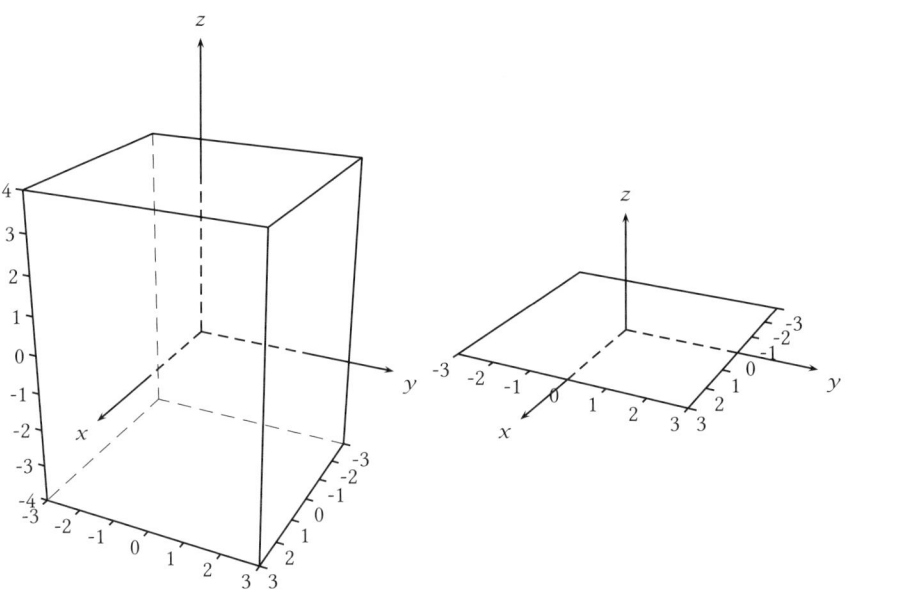

23-06-

The coordinate labels are always put on top of the current image; the hidden line algorithm is not used for the labels. Sometimes you'll need to change the order of \gridIIID and other commands to prevent overwriting.

```
\usepackage{pst-solides3d}\psset{Decran=15,viewpoint=20 10 10}
\begin{pspicture}(-3,-2.5)(2.5,3)
  \gridIIID[Zmin=-2,stepX=2,stepY=2,stepZ=4](-3,3)(-3,3)[3,2,2]
\end{pspicture}
\begin{pspicture}(-4,-2.5)(2,3.5)
  \gridIIID[Zmin=0,Zmax=0,stepX=2,stepY=2](-3,3)(-3,3)[1,2,2.5]
\end{pspicture}
```

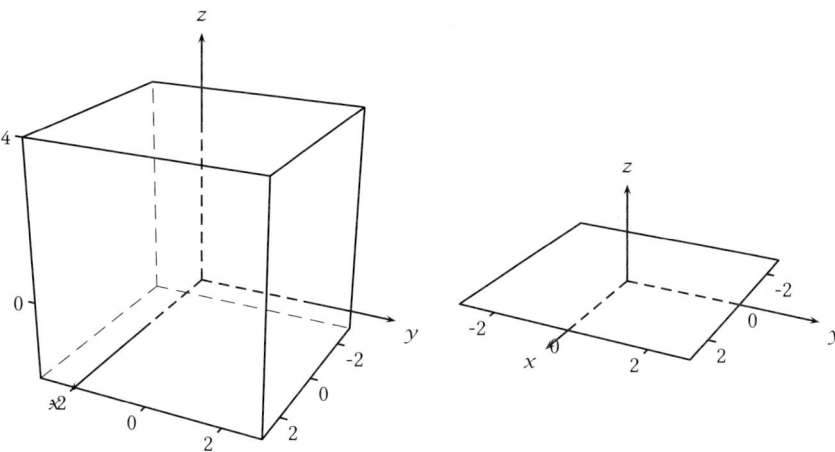

23.6.4 \psPoint

The \psPoint command puts a 3D node; internally only the two-dimensional screen coordinates are saved.

\psPoint [settings] (x, y, z){node name}

You can specify a viewpoint for the command as usual, but no other options have any effect.

```
\usepackage{pst-solides3d}
\begin{pspicture}(-4,-4)(4,5)
  \psset{Decran=20,viewpoint=100 50 20 rtp2xyz}
  \axesIIID[labelsep=5pt](0,0,0)(20,20,10)
  \psPoint(-4.79,2.06,0){C1}\psPoint(-4.79,15.76,0){Ox}\psPoint(8.43,5.57,0){C2}
  \psPoint(-14.14,3.34,0){H3}     \psPoint(14.14,-2.94,8.90){H6}
  \psPoint(14.14,-2.94,-8.90){H7} \psPoint(6.43,-16.29,0){H8}
  \psline(C1)(H3)\psline(C2)(H7)  \psline(C2)(H8)\psline(C1)(C2)
  \psline[doubleline=true](C1)(Ox)\psline(C2)(H6)
  \uput[r](H3){$\mathrm{H_1}$}       \uput[l](H6){$\mathrm{H_2}$}
  \uput[l](H7){$\mathrm{H_3}$}       \uput[l](H8){$\mathrm{H_4}$}
  \uput{0.25}[u](C1){$\mathrm{C_1}$} \uput{0.25}[d](C2){$\mathrm{C_2}$}
  \uput{0.25}[r](Ox){$\red\mathrm{O}$}
  \psdots[dotstyle=o,dotsize=0.3](H3)(H6)(H7)(H8)
  \psdots[dotsize=0.4](C1)(C2)\psdot[linecolor=red,dotsize=0.4](Ox)
\end{pspicture}
```

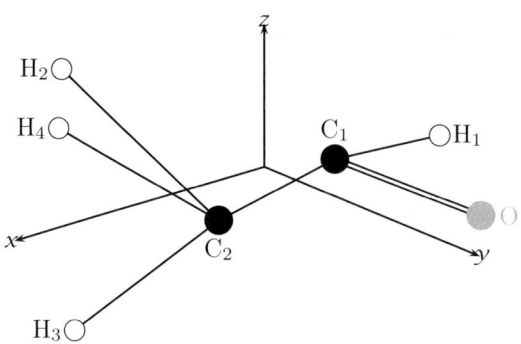

23.6.5 \psLineIIID and \psPolygonIIID

The \psLineIIID and \psPolygonIIID commands work in the same way as the standard \psline and \pspolygon commands (cf. Section 4.2 and 4.4). In principle the number of parameters you can use is unlimited. You can create polylines with \psLineIIID, but they won't necessarily be closed, whereas \psPolygonIIID always creates a closed polyline.

\psLineIIID [settings] {arrows} $(x_1, y_1, z_1)(x_2, y_2, z_2) \ldots (x_n, y_n, z_n)$
\psPolygonIIID [settings] {arrows} $(x_1, y_1, z_1)(x_2, y_2, z_2) \ldots (x_n, y_n, z_n)$

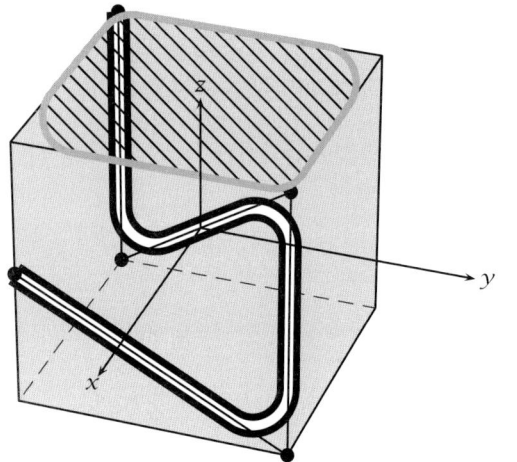

```
\usepackage{pst-solides3d}

\psset{viewpoint=50 20 30 rtp2xyz,
    Decran=50}
\begin{pspicture}(-3,-4)(4,4)
\psSolid[object=cube,a=4,action=draw*,
    fillcolor=green!40]
\psLineIIID[linecolor=blue,linewidth=0.1,
    linearc=0.5,doubleline=true]%
    (-2,-2,2)(-2,-2,-2)(2,2,2)(2,2,-2)(2,-2,0)
\psLineIIID[dotsize=0.2,showpoints=true]%
    (-2,-2,2)(-2,-2,-2)(2,2,2)(2,2,-2)(2,-2,0)
\psPolygonIIID[linecolor=red,fillstyle=vlines
    linearc=0.5,linewidth=0.1]%
    (-2,-2,2)(-2,2,2)(2,2,2)(2,-2,2)
\axesIIID(4,4,2)
\end{pspicture}
```

23.6.6 Point transformation with \psTransformPoint

\psTransformPoint [settings] $(x, y, z)(dx, dy, dz)${name}

To transform point $P(x, y, z)$, you can rotate it by assigning values to the optional RotX, RotY, and RotZ parameters and then translate it by (dx, dy, dz). The order of the rotation is x-y-z by definition. The result of the transformation is saved in the node *name*.

23.6 pst-solides3d — perspective 3D views

In the following example, the second, equal-sized cube with its centre at $M(7.5, 11.25, 10)$ is created by rotation about all three axes. However, the coordinates of the corresponding point A' aren't known. Using \psTransformPoint, we first rotate the original point A by the same angles and then translate it by the centre vector of the second cube. Now the node A' is set to the coordinates of the corner.

```
\usepackage{pst-solides3d}
\begin{pspicture}(-2,-4)(6,6)
\psset{unit=0.75,viewpoint=40 20 40,Decran=40}
\psSolid[object=cube,a=4,action=draw*,linecolor=red]% kleiner Würfel
\psPoint(2,2,2){A}
\psSolid[object=cube,a=4,action=draw*,RotX=-30,RotY=60,RotZ=-60](7.5,11.25,10)% großer
\psTransformPoint[RotX=-30,RotY=60,RotZ=-60](2 2 2)(7.5,11.25,10){A'}
\psdot(A')\psline[linecolor=blue,arrowsize=0.3]{o->}(A)(A')
\uput[-90](A'){$\mathbf{A'}$}\uput[u](A){$\mathbf{A}$}
\psLineIIID[linecolor=blue,linestyle=dashed,arrowsize=0.3]{->}(0,0,0)(7.5,11.25,10)
\psset{solidmemory,action=none}
\psSolid[object=cube,a=4,name=A1](0,0,0)
\psSolid[object=plan,definition=solidface,args=A1 0,name=P0]
\psset{fontsize=100}
\psProjection[object=texte,linecolor=red,text=A,plan=P0]
\psSolid[object=cube,a=4,RotX=-30,RotY=60,RotZ=-60,name=A2](7.5,11.25,10)
\psSolid[object=plan,definition=solidface,args=A2 0,name=P'0]
\psProjection[object=texte,text=A,plan=P'0]
\axesIIID(2,2,2)(10,12,8)
\end{pspicture}
```

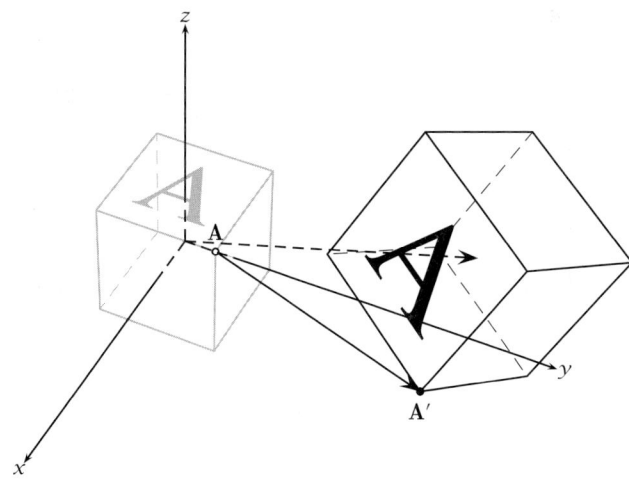

23.6.7 Projections with \psProjection

The \psProjection command allows projections of two-dimensional objects in an arbitrary plane in three-dimensional space, which has to be defined beforehand through the \psSolid command.

23 Three-dimensional figures

```
\psProjection [settings] (x,y)
```

Table 23.10 summarizes the parameters available for this command; there is more detail on the new parameters in Table 23.12 on page 422. The object is defined by the parameter of the same name and are already listed in Section 23.6.1 on page 395.

Table 23.10: Summary of the available parameters for the \psProjection command

name	type	default	name	type	default
object	object name		definition	object name	
args	value value		text	string	
pos	ul|cl|bl|dl| ur|cr|br|dr uc|cc|bc|dc| ur|cr|br|dr	bl	name	string	
			plan	object	–
			path	PS code	–
planmarks	boolean	false	showBase	boolean	
base	$x_0\ x_1\ y_0\ y_1$	-3 3 -2 2	range	$x_0\ x_1\ y_0\ y_1$	-3 3 -2 2
fontsize	value		resolution	value	
function	function	–	transform	PS code	–

Let's look first at the case where the definition parameter is set to equation. The plane is then given by the equation $rx + sy + tz + b = 0$. In the following example, the normal vector points in the x direction (1 0 0) and the plane intersects the origin (as the fourth variable is zero); this corresponds to the equation $x = 0$. Additionally, the plane is rotated by 90°. It is assigned the arbitrarily-chosen object name Ebene, which is referred to by \psProjection.

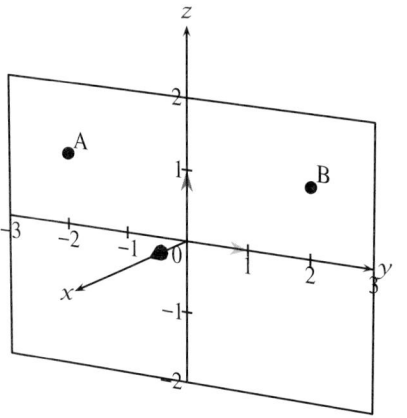

```
\usepackage{pst-solides3d}

\begin{pspicture}(-3,-3)(4,3.5)%
\psset{viewpoint=50 30 15,Decran=60,
    solidmemory}
\psSolid[object=plan,definition=equation,ngrid=,
    args={[1 0 0 0] 90},name=Ebene,planmarks,showBase]
\psset{plan=Ebene}
\psProjection[object=point,args=-2 1,text=A,pos=ur]
\psProjection[object=point,text=B,pos=ur](2,1)
\axesIIID(3,3,3)
\end{pspicture}
```

23-06-5

When projecting vectors, several values for the definition parameter are available:

23.6 pst-solides3d — perspective 3D views

definition=vecteur	The vector $\vec{AB}$ requires two arguments, args=A B.
definition=orthovecteur	The orthogonal vector to $\vec{u}$ of the same length requires one argument, args=u.
definition=normalize	The normal vector $\|\vec{u}\|^{-1}\vec{u}$, if $\vec{u} \neq \vec{0}$; $\vec{0}$ requires one argument, args=u.
definition=addv	The vector addition $\vec{u} + \vec{v}$ requires two arguments, args=u v.
definition=subv	The vector subtraction $\vec{u} - \vec{v}$ requires two arguments, args=u v.
definition=mulv	The scalar vector multiplication $c\vec{u}$ requires two arguments, args=u c.

```
\usepackage{pst-solides3d}
\begin{pspicture}(-3,-3)(4,3.5)
\psset{viewpoint=50 30 15,Decran=60,solidmemory}
\psSolid[object=plan,definition=equation,args={[1 0 0 0] 90},planmarks,name=Ebene]
\psset{plan=Ebene}
\psProjection[object=point,args=-2 0.75,name=A,text=A,pos=dl]
\psProjection[object=vecteur,args=1 1,name=U](1,0)
\psProjection[object=vecteur,definition=orthovecteur,linestyle=dashed,args=U,name=V](1,0)
\psProjection[object=vecteur,linecolor=blue,definition=normalize,args=U](A)
\psProjection[object=vecteur,definition=addv,args=U V](1,0)
\axesIIID(4,2,2)(5,4,3)
\end{pspicture}
```

When projecting lines several values for the definition parameter are available, which refer to common definitions of a line. The last three expect a defined line d as an object beforehand.

definition=horizontale	A horizontal line with $y = b$, given by args=b.
definition=verticale	A vertical line $x = a$, given by args=a.
definitio=paral	A line parallel to $d = f(x)$ that intersects point A, given by args=d A. You must have defined the line d as an object beforehand.

23 Three-dimensional figures

definition=perp	A line perpendicular to $d = f(x)$ that intersects point A, given by args=d A. You must have defined the line d as an object beforehand.
definition=mediatrice	A vertical line through the centre of an interval $[AB]$, given by args=A B.
definition=bissectrice	A bisectrix of $\widehat{ABC}$, given by args=A B C.
definition=axesymdroite	A line symmetric to d referring to the symmetry axis D, given by args=d D.
definition=rotatedroite	A line d rotated about the point I by the angle r (in degrees), given by args=d I r.
definition=translatedroite	A line d translated by the vector $\vec{u}$, given by args=d u.

```
\usepackage{pst-solides3d}
\begin{pspicture}(-3,-3)(4,3.5)   \psset{viewpoint=50 30 15,Decran=60,solidmemory}
\psSolid[object=plan,definition=equation,args={[1 0 0 0] 90},planmarks,name=Plain]
\psset{plan=Plain}
\psProjection[object=point,name=A,text=A,pos=ur](-2,1.25)
\psProjection[object=point,name=B,text=B,pos=ur](1,.75)
\psProjection[object=droite,linecolor=blue,args=0 0 1 .5,name=c]% 4 coordinates
\psProjection[object=droite,linecolor=red, args=A B,name=d]% two given points
\psProjection[object=droite,linecolor=blue,linestyle=dashed,definition=perp,args=c A]
\psProjection[object=droite,linecolor=red,linestyle=dashed,definition=axesymdroite,args=
\end{pspicture}
```

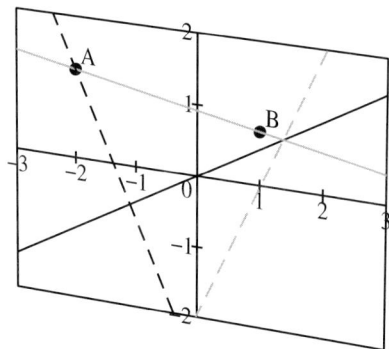

The only difference between the objects object=droite and object=line is that you can describe lines by arbitrarily many points, making polylines. The line object type therefore requires the coordinates or names of points in its argument – args=A_0 A_1 ... A_n. The same applies for the polygone object, which is then closed at the end by connecting the last point to the first point by a direct line (unlike the polyline, which is not closed automatically). The following definitions exist for polygons; you can also apply all but hompol to the line object.

definition=translatepol	A polygon pol translated by the vector $\vec{u}$, given by args=pol u.
definition=rotatepol	A polygon pol rotated about the point I by the angle α (in degrees), given by args=pol I α.

definition=hompol	A polygon *pol* stretched by α with the stretch centre *I*, given by args=pol I α.
definition=sympol	A polygon *pol* symmetric to the point *I*, given by args=pol I.
definition=axesympol	A symmetric polygon referring to the symmetry axis *D*, given by args=pol D.

```
\usepackage{pst-solides3d}
\begin{pspicture}(-3,-3)(4,3.5)
\psset{lightsrc=50 20 20,Decran=60,viewpoint=50 30 15,solidmemory}
\psSolid[object=plan,definition=equation,name=Plain,args={[1 0 0 0] 90},
   base=-3.2 3.2 -2.2 2.2,planmarks]  \psset{plan=Plain}
\psSolid[object=plan,args=Plain,plangrid,linecolor=gray!40,action=none]
\psProjection[object=line,args=-1 0 -3 1 1 2,name=P]
\psProjection[object=line,args=P -1 0 -45,definition=rotatepol,linecolor=blue]
\psProjection[object=line,linestyle=dashed,definition={2 -2 addv} papply,args=P]
\axesIIID(6,4,3)
\end{pspicture}
```

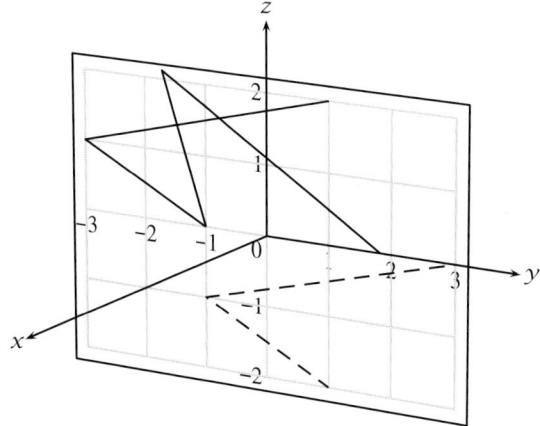

```
\usepackage{pst-solides3d}
\begin{pspicture}(-3,-3)(4,3.5)
\psset{lightsrc=50 20 20,Decran=60,viewpoint=50 30 15,solidmemory}
\psSolid[object=plan,definition=equation,args={[1 0 0 0] 90},name=Plain,
   base=-3.2 3.2 -2.2 2.2,planmarks]  \psset{plan=Plain}
\psSolid[object=plan,args=Plain,plangrid,linecolor=gray!40,action=none]
\psProjection[object=polygone,args=-1 0 -3 1 0 2,name=P]
\psProjection[object=polygone,args=P -1 0 -45,definition=rotatepol,linecolor=blue]
\psProjection[object=polygone,fillstyle=hlines,hatchcolor=yellow,linestyle=dashed,
   definition={2 -2 addv} papply,args=P]  \axesIIID(4,2,2)(5,4,3)
\end{pspicture}
```

23 Three-dimensional figures

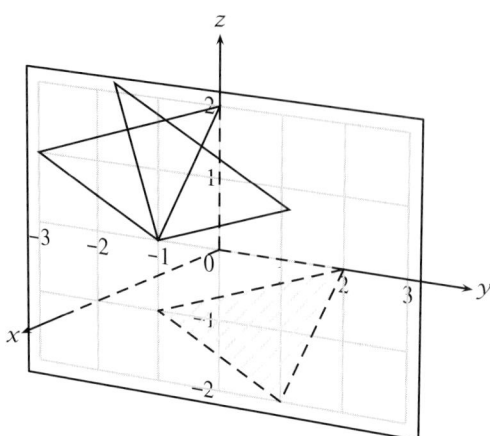

When projecting circles or arcs using the cercle object type, there are two different values for the definition parameter available:

definition=ABcercle   A circle intersecting the three points A, B, and C, given by args=A B C.

definition=diamcercle   A circle with diameter $\overline{AB}$, given by args=A B.

```
\usepackage{pst-solides3d}
\begin{pspicture}(-3,-3)(4,3.5)  \psset{viewpoint=50 30 15,Decran=60,solidmemory}
\psSolid[object=plan,definition=equation,args={[1 0 0 0] 90},planmarks,name=Plain]
\psset{plan=Plain}
\psProjection[object=point,name=A,text=A,pos=ur](-2,1.25)
\psProjection[object=cercle,args=A 1,range=180 360]
\psProjection[object=cercle,args=1 1 .5,linecolor=blue]
\psProjection[object=point,name=a,text=A,pos=ul](0,0)
\psProjection[object=point,name=b,text=B,pos=ur](1.5,-1.5)
\psProjection[object=point,name=c,text=C,pos=ul](0,-1.5)
\psProjection[object=cercle,args=a b c,definition=ABcercle,linestyle=dashed,
    fillstyle=solid,fillcolor=green!35]
\end{pspicture}
```

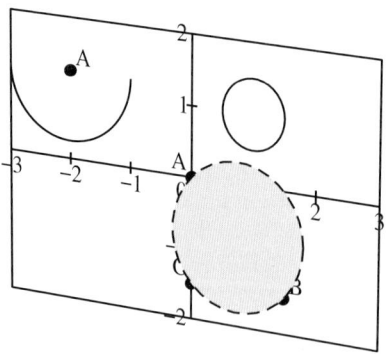

23.6 pst-solides3d — perspective 3D views

You can use the rightangle object type to mark right angles, as shown in the following example. object=rightangle requires three points in its args parameter.

```
\usepackage{pst-solides3d}
\begin{pspicture}(-3,-2.5)(3.5,2.5)%
\psset{lightsrc=viewpoint,viewpoint=50 30 15,Decran=40,solidmemory,fontsize=15}
\psSolid[object=plan,definition=equation,args={[1 0 1 0] 90},base=-4 4 -3 3,
    fillcolor=white,linecolor=gray!30,planmarks,name=Plain]
\psset{plan=Plain,visibility=false}
\psProjection[object=droite,definition=horizontale,args=-1,name=d]% straight d
\psProjection[object=point,args=-2 1,name=M,text=M,pos=ul]
\psProjection[object=point,definition=orthoproj,args=M d,name=H,text=H,pos=dr]
\psProjection[object=point,definition=xdpoint,args=2 d,name=H',action=none,
    text=d,pos=ur]% determine H'
\psProjection[object=line,args=M H]
\psProjection[object=rightangle,args=M H H']% mark right angle
\axesIIID(8,5,3)
\end{pspicture}
```

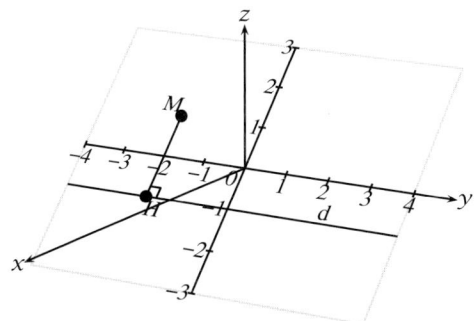

You can project functions using the \defFunction command.

```
\defFunction [settings] {function name}(x){f(x)}{}{}
\defFunction [settings] {function name}(t){x(t)}{y(t)}{}
\defFunction [settings] {function name}(t){x(t)}{y(t)}{z(t)}
```

For all of these commands, PostScript notation is the default for the description of the function, but you can change it to algebraic by setting the algebraic keyword in the optional argument. The first command defines $f(x)$ – see first example below, the second one defines $f(x(t), y(t))$ – see second example below, and the third one defines $f(x(t), y(t), z(t))$, which works similarly to the second command so we don't give a separate example. You can use any arbitrary letter instead of the variable t, but it must correspond to the first parameter, which is given in round brackets before the function descriptions begin. Note that there are always three function definitions whatever the type of function, meaning that the second and third definitions may be empty braces.

23 Three-dimensional figures

```
\usepackage{pst-solides3d}
\begin{pspicture}[viewpoint=50 30 15,Decran=60,solidmemory](-3,-3)(4,3.5)
\defFunction[algebraic]{1_sin}(x){2*sin(1/x)}{}{} % function defined as y=f(x)
\psSolid[object=plan,definition=equation,args={[1 0 0 0] 90},base=-3.2 3.2 -2.2 2.2,
    planmarks,showBase,name=Plain]   \psset{plan=Plain}
\psSolid[object=plan,args=Plain,linecolor=gray!40,plangrid,action=none]
\psProjection[object=courbe,linecolor=red,range=-3 3,resolution=720,function=1_sin]
\axesIIID(4,2,2)(5,4,3)
\end{pspicture}
```

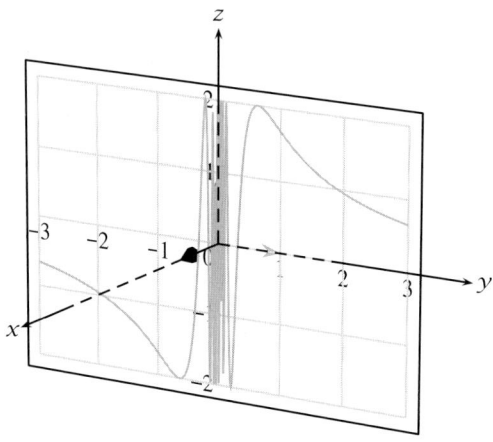

```
\usepackage{pst-solides3d}
\begin{pspicture}[viewpoint=50 30 15,Decran=60,solidmemory](-3,-3)(4,3.5)
\defFunction[algebraic]{F}(t){2*sin(0.57735*t)}{2*sin(0.707*t)}{}
\psSolid[object=plan,definition=equation,args={[1 0 1 0] 90},base=-3.2 3.2 -3 3,
    planmarks,name=Plain]   \psset{plan=Plain}
\psSolid[object=plan,args=Plain,linecolor=gray!40,plangrid,action=none]
\psProjection[object=courbeR2,range=-25.12 25.12,resolution=720,normal=1 1 2,
    linecolor=red,function=F]   \axesIIID(7,4,3)
\end{pspicture}
```

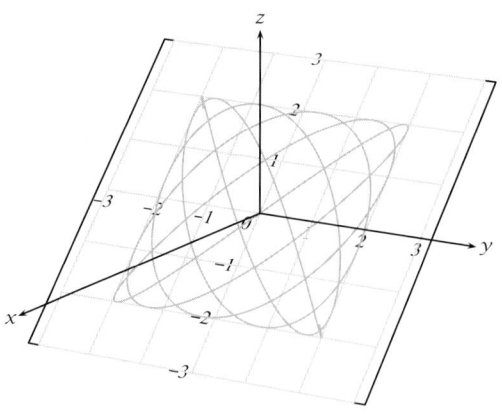

23.6 pst-solides3d — perspective 3D views

Several of the earlier examples in this section have used the \psProjection command to position text (letters), but you can also transfer longer text using object=texte, as shown below:

```
\usepackage{pst-solides3d}
\begin{pspicture}(-3,-3)(4,3.5)%
\psset{lightsrc=50 20 20,Decran=60,viewpoint=50 30 15,solidmemory}
\psSolid[object=plan,definition=equation,args={[1 0 1 0] 90},planmarks,
  base=-3.2 3.2 -2.5 2.5,name=Plain]
\psset{plan=Plain}
\psSolid[object=plan,args=Plain,plangrid,linecolor=gray!40,action=none]
\psProjection[object=texte,fontsize=50,linecolor=cyan,text=Jana](0,1)
\psProjection[object=texte,fontsize=50,text=PSTricks,phi=180](0,-1)
\end{pspicture}
```

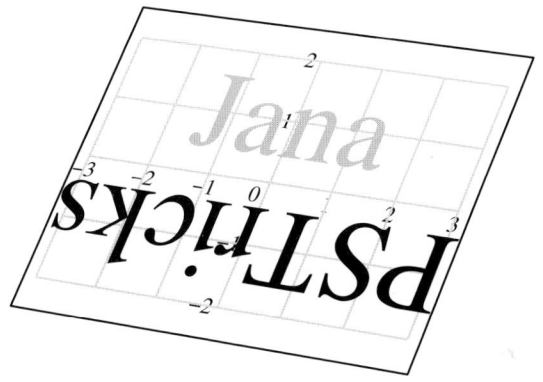

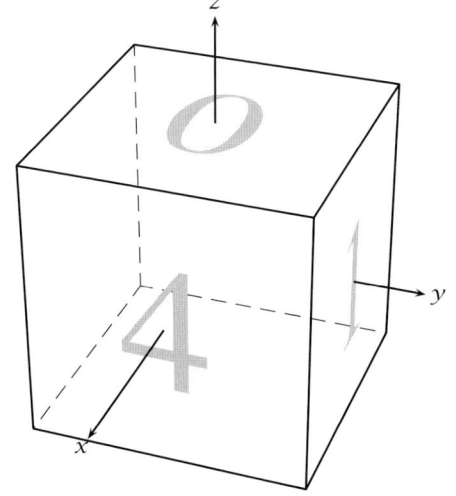

```
\usepackage{pst-solides3d}

\begin{pspicture}(-3,-4)(4,5)
\psset{unit=0.5,fontsize=150,Decran=50,
  viewpoint=50 20 30 rtp2xyz,solidmemory}
\psSolid[object=cube,a=8,action=draw,name=A]
\psSolid[object=plan,action=none,
  definition=solidface,args=A 0,name=P0]
\psProjection[object=texte,text=0,
  plan=P0,linecolor=cyan]
\psSolid[object=plan,action=none,
  definition=solidface,args=A 1,name=P1]
\psProjection[object=texte,text=1,
  plan=P1,phi=180,linecolor=cyan]
\psSolid[object=plan,action=none,
  definition=solidface,args=A 4,name=P4]
\psProjection[object=texte,text=4,
  plan=P4,phi=-90,linecolor=cyan]
\axesIIID[showOrigin=false](4,4,4)(9,6,7)
\end{pspicture}
```

23.6.8 Display of mathematic functions with \psSurface

Examples 23-06-37, 23-06-38, and 23-06-36 on page 401 have already shown how to calculate and display two- and three-dimensional functions with the \psSolid command. The \psSurface command doesn't provide any additional functionality, but makes the display of functions easier.

> \psSurface [settings] $(x_0, x_1)(y_0, y_1)\{function\ z = f(x, y)\}$

You have to give the function in PostScript notation by default, or alternatively set the algebraic option to give it in algebraic notation. Tables 23.11 and 23.12 on page 422 summarize the meaningful parameters for the \psSurface command. Options for the coordinate grid can be found in Table 23.9 on page 406.

Table 23.11: Summary of parameters for the \psSurface command

name	type	default	meaning
algebraic	boolean	false	Determines equation notation
ngrid	n0 n1	–	dx and dy, if < 0; N_x and N_y, if > 0 (number of steps)
grid	boolean	true	Shows/hides grid lines
axesboxed	boolean	false	Encloses surface in coordinate axes box

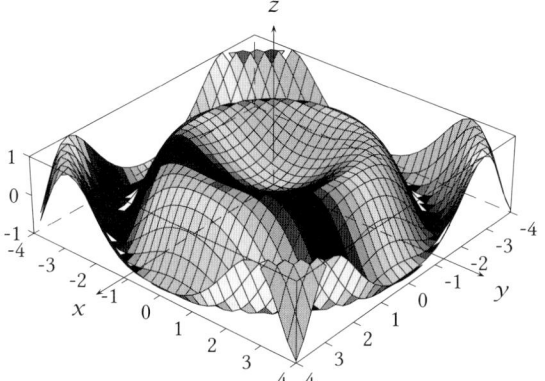

```
\usepackage{pst-solides3d}

\psset{viewpoint=50 40 30 rtp2xyz,
    Decran=30,lightsrc=viewpoint}
\begin{pspicture}(-6,-2)(7,4)
\psSurface[ngrid=0.25 0.25,incolor=yellow,
    linewidth=0.01,axesboxed,algebraic,
    hue=0 1,Zmin=-1,Zmax=1](-4,-4)(4,4)%
    {sin((x^2+y^2)/3)}
\end{pspicture}
```

23-06-6

23.6 pst-solides3d — perspective 3D views

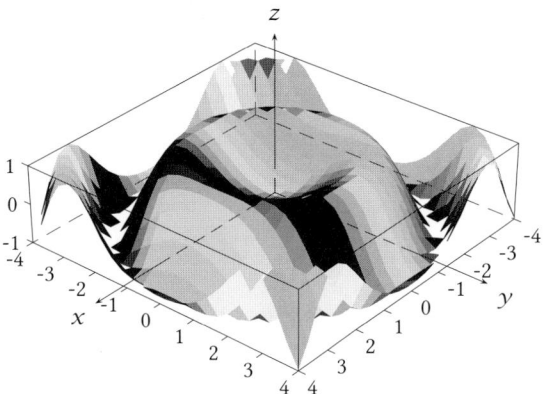

```
\usepackage{pst-solides3d}

\psset{lightsrc=30 30 25,
  viewpoint=50 40 30 rtp2xyz,Decran=30}
\begin{pspicture}(-6,-2)(7,4)
\psSurface[fillcolor=red!50,ngrid=25 25,
  incolor=yellow,linewidth=0.01,grid,
  axesboxed,hue=0 1,Zmin=-1,Zmax=1]%
  (-4,-4)(4,4){ y dup mul x dup mul
    add 3 div RadtoDeg sin }
\end{pspicture}
```

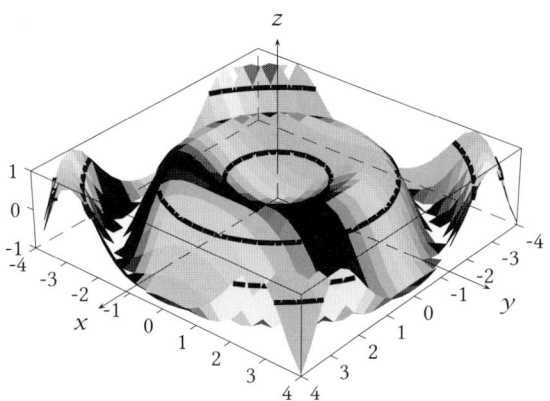

```
\usepackage{pst-solides3d}

\psset{lightsrc=30 30 25,algebraic,
  viewpoint=50 40 30 rtp2xyz,Decran=30}
\begin{pspicture}(-6,-2)(7,4)
\psSurface[fillcolor=red!50,ngrid=25 25,
  intersectionplan={[0 0 1 -0.5]},
  intersectioncolor=(noir),grid,
  intersectionlinewidth=2,Zmin=-1,
  Zmax=1,intersectiontype=0,
  incolor=yellow,linewidth=0.01,
  axesboxed,hue=0 1,](-4,-4)(4,4)%
  { sin((x^2+y^2)/3) }
\end{pspicture}
```

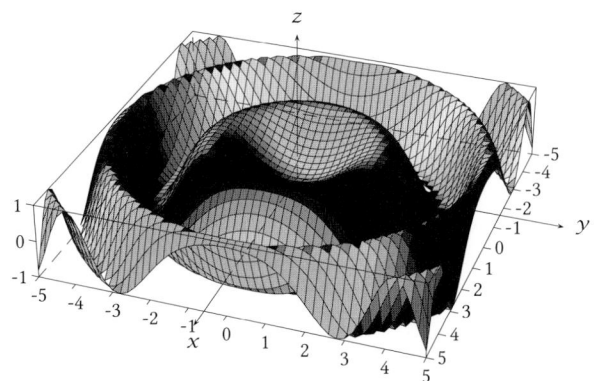

```
\usepackage{pst-solides3d}

\psset{lightsrc=30 -10 10,algebraic,
  viewpoint=50 20 30 rtp2xyz,
  Decran=30}
\begin{pspicture}(-2,-2)(4,4)
\psSurface[ngrid=.2 .2,axesboxed,
  Zmin=-1,Zmax=1,linewidth=0.01,
  spotX=r,spotY=d,spotZ=l,hue=0 1]%
  (-5,-5)(5,5){ sin((x^2+y^2)/3) }
\end{pspicture}
```

23 Three-dimensional figures

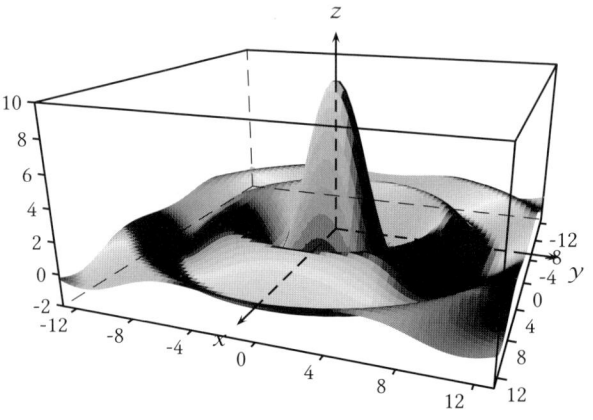

```
\usepackage{pst-solides3d}

\psset{lightsrc=30 -10 10,
    viewpoint=50 20 20 rtp2xyz,
    Decran=10}
\begin{pspicture}(-4,-2)(4,4)
\psSurface[ngrid=0.4 0.4,algebraic,
    axesboxed,Zmin=-2,Zmax=10,
    grid=false,ticklength=0.5,
    stepX=4,stepY=4,stepZ=2,hue=0 1]%
    (-13,-13)(13,13)%
    {10*sin(sqrt((x^2+y^2)))%
        /(sqrt(x^2+y^2)) }
\end{pspicture}
```

```
\usepackage{pst-solides3d}
\psset{lightsrc=30 30 25,viewpoint=50 40 20 rtp2xyz,Decran=20}
\begin{pspicture}(-6,-8)(7,8)
\psSurface[ngrid=.25 .25,inouthue=1 0 0.5 1,linewidth=0.01,axesboxed,algebraic]%
    (-4,-4)(4,4){ ((y^2)-(x^2))/4 }
\end{pspicture}
```

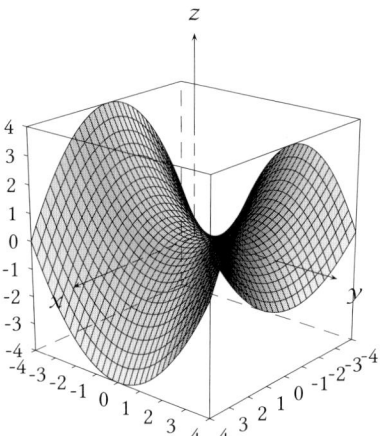

```
\usepackage{pst-solides3d}
\def\NormalSin#1#2#3{%
 \psset{linecolor=#3}%
 \pstVerb{
    /xP #1 def
    /yP #2 def
    /zP 2 #1 Sin mul #2 Sin mul def
    /normaleX 2 #1 Cos mul #2 Sin mul neg def
    /normaleY 2 #2 Cos mul #1 Sin mul neg def
```

```
    /Norme normaleX dup mul normaleY dup mul add 1 add sqrt def
    /Nx normaleX Norme div def
    /Ny normaleY Norme div def
    /Nz 1 Norme div def }%
\psSolid[object=vecteur,args=Nx Ny Nz](xP,yP,zP)}
\psset{viewpoint=50 20 20 rtp2xyz,Decran=50}
\begin{pspicture}(-3,-3)(3,4)
\psSurface[algebraic,ngrid=0.2 0.2,incolor=yellow!20,axesboxed,Zmin=-2,Zmax=2,
    fillcolor=blue!20](-3,-3)(3,3){2*sin(x)*sin(y)}%
\NormalSin{1.57}{0.75}{red}%
\NormalSin{1.57}{1.57}{blue}%
\NormalSin{2}{1.57}{green}%
\NormalSin{-1.57}{-1.57}{magenta}
\end{pspicture}
```

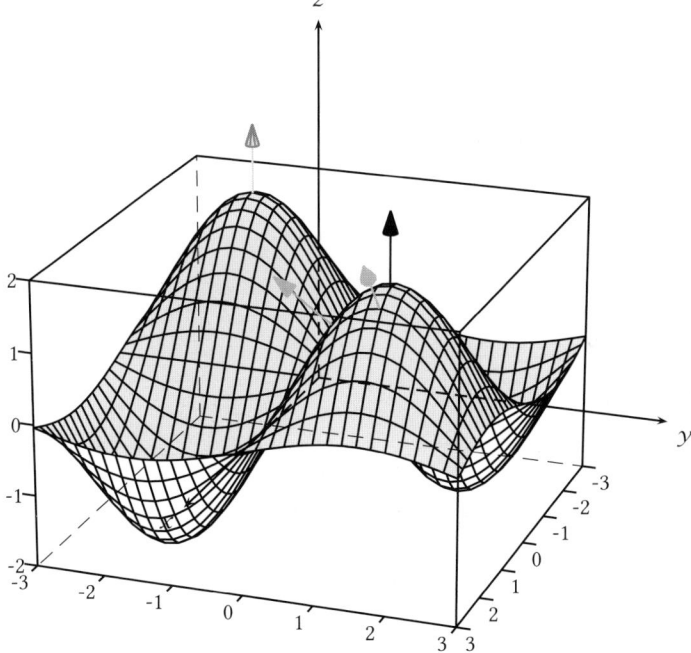

23.6.9 Parameters

There are a large number of optional parameters in the pst-solides3d package, so it is easy to lose the plot. Table 23.12 on the next page shows a summary of all the parameters that are relevant for the \psSolid command, in alphabetical order. The columns [object=...] and [definition=...] point to additional required specifications. If there are several alternative values for the parameters, they are given as a comma-separated list. The following sections then discuss the new parameters, grouped by theme.

23 Three-dimensional figures

Table 23.12: Summary of all parameters for the \psSolid command

name	meaning	[object=...]	[definition=...]	type	default
a	Edge length of a cube or radius of the surrounding sphere of a regular polyhedron.	cube, tetrahedron, octahedron, dodecahedron, icosahedron		value	2
a, b, c	Edge length of a cuboid.	parallelepiped		value	4
action	Specification of the drawing algorithm – transparent, coloured with dashed hidden lines, coloured without hidden lines and surfaces, or write internal data to external files.			none, draw, draw*, draw**, writeobj, writeoff, writesolid	draw**
affinage	Specifies the polygon faces that aren't filled (creating holes).			all, i_0 $i_1 \ldots i_n$	
affinagecoeff	The coefficient for the relative size of the individual openings (holes).			value	0.8
affinagerm	Removes the centre element by default.			boolean	true
args	The argument list for different objects.		equation	plan	$[a\ b\ c\ d]$, $[a\ b\ c\ d]\alpha$
			normalpoint	plan	$x_0\ y_0\ z_0$ $[a\ b\ c]$,
					$x_0\ y_0\ z_0$ $[a\ b\ c\ \alpha]$,
					$x_0\ y_0\ z_0$ $[u_x\ u_y\ u_z\ a\ b\ c]$,
					$x_0\ y_0\ z_0$ $[u_x\ u_y\ u_z\ a\ b\ c\ \alpha]$
			solidface		$S\ i$
args			addv3d	point	$x\ y\ z,\ P$
			barycentre3d	point	$x_1\ y_1\ z_1\ x_2\ y_2\ z_2,\ u\ v$
			hompoint3d	point	$[A\ i_A\ B\ i_B]$
			isobarycentre3d	point	$P\ A\ k$
			milieu3d	point	$[A_0\ A_1 \ldots A_n]$
					$A\ B$

continued...

23.6 pst-solides3d — perspective 3D views

... continued

name	meaning	[object=...]	[definition=...]	type	default
		point	mulv3d	$x\ y\ z\ k,\ u\ k$	
		point	normalize3d	$x\ y\ z,\ u$	
		point	orthoprojplane3d	$P\ A\ v$	
		point	rotate0point3d	$P\ \alpha_x\ \alpha_y\ \alpha_z$	
		point	scale0point3d	$x\ y\ z\ k_x\ k_y\ k_z,$ <Name> $k_x\ k_y\ k_z$	
		point	solidcentreface	$S\ i$	
		point	solidgetsommet	$S\ i$	
		point	subv3d	$x_1\ y_1\ z_1\ x_2\ y_2\ z_2,\ u\ v$	
		point	sympoint3d	$P\ A$	
		point	translatepoint3d	$P\ v$	
		point	vectprod3d	$x_1\ y_1\ z_1\ x_2\ y_2\ z_2,\ u\ v$	
args		vecteur		$x\ y\ z,$ $x_1\ y_1\ z_1\ x_2\ y_2\ z_2\ addv3d,$ $x_1\ y_1\ z_1\ x_2\ y_2\ z_2\ subv3d,$ $x\ y\ z\ k\ mulv3d,$ $x\ y\ z\ normalize3d,$ $x_1\ y_1\ z_1\ x_2\ y_2\ z_2\ vectprod3d$ $x_A\ y_A\ z_A\ x_B\ y_B\ z_B,\ A\ B$	
args		vecteur3d			
axe	Position of the symmetry axis for the objects cylinder, prism, and band.	cylindre prisme ruban		$x\ y\ z$	0 0 1
axesboxed	xyz axis division of the surrounding cuboid of a three-dimensional function.			boolean	false
base	The base of a two-dimensional base/surface.	face, prisme, ruban fusion grille surfaceparametree		$x_1\ y_1\ x_2\ y_2\ \ldots x_n\ y_n$ $S_1\ S_2$ $x_0\ x_1\ y_0\ y_1$ $u_{\min}\ u_{\max}\ v_{\min}\ v_{\max}$	-1 -1 1 -1 0 1
biface	Definition of a face with front and back.	face		boolean	true

continued...

23 Three-dimensional figures

... continued

name	meaning	[object=...]	[definition=...]	type	default
chanfrein	Symmetric flattening of the edges (edge trimming).			boolean	true
chanfreincoeff	Relative value for the symmetric flattening of the edges.			value	0.2
deactivatecolor	Do not use colour.			boolean	false
decal	The starting value for the internal sorting of the edge points.			value	-2
definition	Object-dependent specification of the definition[2]				
dualreg	Connects the centre points of neighbouring faces (creates the dual object).[3]	geode		boolean	false
faces	Specification of the faces of a newly-defined object.	new		$[i_1 \ldots i_n][i'_1 \ldots i'_m]\ldots$	
fcol	Specification of the colour of individual faces.			$i_0\ (colour_0)\ i_1\ (colour_1)\ldots$	
fcolor	Specification of the colour when the affinagerm parameter is set.			colour	
file	Specification of the file type for action=writesolid.	datfile, objfile, offfile		name	
fillcolor	The default fill colour.			colour	
function	Specification of the defined PostScript function name.	cone, courbe, courbeR2, cylindre, surfaceparametree		name	
grid	Drawing of the polygon lines.			boolean	true
h	Height of specific objects.	cone, cylindre, prisme, tronccone		value	6

continued...

[2]Details are given individually for each parameter in the fourth column of this table.
[3]Also see http://www.platonicsolids.info.

23.6 pst-solides3d — perspective 3D views

...continued

name	meaning	[object=...]	[definition=...]	type	default
hollow	Whether a face should appear "transparent".	cone, cylindre, prisme, tronccone		boolean	false
hue	Specification of a colour gradient for the outer surface filling.			$h_0\,h_1, h_0\,h_1\,s\,b$, $h_0\,s_0\,b_0\,h_1\,s_1\,b_1$ (hsb), $r_0\,g_0\,b_0\,r_1\,g_1\,b_1$, $c_0\,m_0\,y_0\,k_0\,c_1\,m_1\,y_1\,k_1$, $(colour_1)\,(colour_2)$	
incolor	The default fill colour for the inside of an object.			colour	green
inhue	Specification of a colour gradient for the inside of an object.			see hue	
inouthue	Specification of a colour gradient for the inside and outside of an object.			see hue	
intersectioncolor	Colour of the intersection line between plane an object; a colour can be given to every intersection line.			$(colour_1)\ldots(colour_n)$	(rouge)
intersectionlinewidth	Similarly for line width.			$w_1\ldots w_n$	1
intersectionplan	Specification of the intersection plane(s).			name(s), $[a_1\,b_1\,c_1\,d_1]$ ... $[a_n\,b_n\,c_n\,d_n]$	
labelsep	Distance of the axis names from the ends of the axes.			value unit	10pt
lightintensity	Intensity of the light source.			value	2
lightsrc	Coordinates of the light source; an empty argument disables the light source.			viewpoint, x y z	20 30 50
load	Loads a saved object.	load		name	

continued...

23 Three-dimensional figures

... continued

name	meaning	[object=...]	[definition=...]	type	default
mode	Division of the polygon grid (0–coarse; 4–fine).			0,1,2,3,4	0
name	Name of an object.			String	
ngrid	Polygon grid.	cube, prisme, prismecreux, cone, conecreux, cylindre, cylindrecreux, tore, tronccone, troncconecreux		n_1	
		grille, surface, surface*, surfaceparametree		$n_1\ n_2$	
				$n_1, n_1\ n_2$	
num	Numbering of the corners.			$all, i_0 \ldots i_n$	
opacity	Transparency for the fill colour (0–complete; 1–none).			$0 \ldots 1$	1
origine	Origin of the plane.	plan		$x_0\ y_0\ z_0$	0 0 0
phi	General angle specification for a segment of a sphere.			angle	0
plangrid	Grid for the plane.	plan		boolean	false
plansection	List of equations for the intersection planes.			$[a_1\ b_1\ c_1\ d_1]\ldots$ $[a_n\ b_n\ c_n\ d_n]$	
plansepare	Equation of the plane that splits an object into two halves.[4]			$[a_1\ b_1\ c_1\ d_1]$	
RotX, RotY, RotZ	Rotation angle.			angle	0
r	Radius of a function "snake".	courbe		value	2
r0	Inner radius of an object.	tore, tronccone, troncconecreux		value	1.5
r1	Outer radius of an object.	tore, tronccone, troncconecreux		value	4
range	Domain of a function.	cercle, courbe, courbeR2		$t_{\min}\ t_{\max}$	-5 5

continued...

[4]To be able to refer to the halves, you have to specify an object name (name=...), which is then appended the suffixes 0 and 1.

... continued

name	meaning	[object=...]	[definition=...]	type	default
resolution	Number of interpolation points for the function.	courbe, courbeR2, ruban		n	36
rm	Specification of the polygon faces not to be filled.			$i_0 \ldots i_n$	
section	The coordinates of the corners for the cross-section of a ring.[5]	anneau		$x_1\ y_1 \ldots x_n\ y_n$	
show	Output of the internal face numbers of the polylines.			$all,\ i_0 \ldots i_n$	
showBase	Draws the unit vectors e_x, e_y, and e_z.			boolean	false
sommets	List of the corner points.		new	$x_1\ y_1\ z_1 \ldots x_n\ y_n\ z_n$	
theta	General angle specification for a sphere.			angle	0
transform	Transformation equations for the corner points of an object.			PS code, function name	
trunc	List of the corner points that are to be "cut off".			$all,\ i_0 \ldots i_n$	
trunccoeff	Relative value for the "cutting off".			value	0.2
viewpoint	Specification of the viewpoint.			$x\ y\ z,\ r\ \theta\ \phi\ rtp2xyz$	10 10 10
visibility	Visibility of the text that is assigned to a non-visible face.			boolean	true

---

[5]The PostScript stack is only expected to provide $2n$ values; intermediate calculations are therefore possible as well.

23 Three-dimensional figures

Actions

The action parameter determines how an object is processed internally. action may take one of the following values:

none	The object only remains in memory; no output occurs.
draw	The object is output in the form of a wire model; the lines that wouldn't be visible are drawn as dashed lines (as in the lefthand cube in the examples below).
draw*	Like the option without the star except that the faces are filled with the specified colour, taking into account any specified light source to create shadows (as in the central cube in the examples below).
draw**	Like the option with one star except that it takes into account hidden faces (as in the righthand cube in the examples below).
draw*	Like the option without the star except that the faces are filled with the specified colour (as in the central cube in the examples below).
draw**	Takes into account hidden faces and the data of a present light source; shadows are created (as in the righthand cube in the examples below).
writesolid	Creates the following files:
	▷ <Name>-sommets.dat → a list of the corners
	▷ <Name>-faces.dat → a list of the polygon faces
	▷ <Name>-couleurs.dat → a list of the colours of the faces
	▷ <Name>-io.dat → the borders of the faces for the inside and outside
writeobj	Writes external data in the .obj file format[6]
writeoff	Writes external data in the .off file format[7]

```
\usepackage{pst-solides3d}
\psset{Decran=6,lightsrc=15 -10 30,viewpoint=10 5 5}
\begin{pspicture}(-2,-2)(2,3)\psSolid[object=cube,action=draw]\end{pspicture}
\begin{pspicture}(-2,-2)(2,3)
\psSolid[object=cube,action=draw*,fillcolor=red!20]
\end{pspicture}
\begin{pspicture}(-2,-2)(2,3)
\psSolid[object=cube,action=draw**,fillcolor=red!20]
\end{pspicture}
```

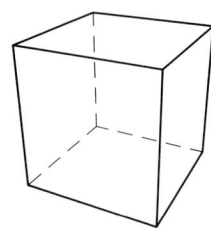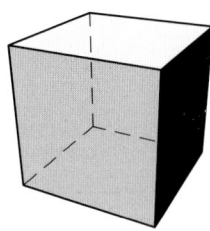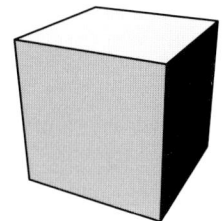

23-06

---

[6]also see http://paulbourke.net/dataformats/obj/.
[7]also see http://paulbourke.net/dataformats/oogl/#OFF.

Grids

To specify the number of polygon faces to be created, you usually use the ngrid option. Alternatively the mode option provides a shortcut for the following objects: cube, tore, sphere, cylindre, cylindrecreux, cone, tronccone, troncconecreux, conecreux, calotesphere, and calotespherecreuse. Only the values 0...4 are valid; the default is 2. The higher the value, the finer the grid. For a cube, only 3 and 4 have any meaning. The following examples show the effect of each value for mode:

```
\usepackage{pst-solides3d}
\psset{lightsrc=10 5 0,viewpoint=50 20 -40 rtp2xyz,Decran=13,incolor=white,
    fillcolor=magenta!50,r0=5,r1=2,h=5,object=troncconecreux}
\begin{pspicture}(-1.4,-1.5)(1.4,1.5)\psSolid[mode=0]\end{pspicture}
\begin{pspicture}(-1.4,-1.5)(1.4,1.5)\psSolid[mode=1]\end{pspicture}
\begin{pspicture}(-1.4,-1.5)(1.4,1.5)\psSolid[mode=2]\end{pspicture}
\begin{pspicture}(-1.4,-1.5)(1.4,1.5)\psSolid[mode=3]\end{pspicture}
\begin{pspicture}(-1.4,-1.5)(1.4,1.5)\psSolid[mode=4]\end{pspicture}
```

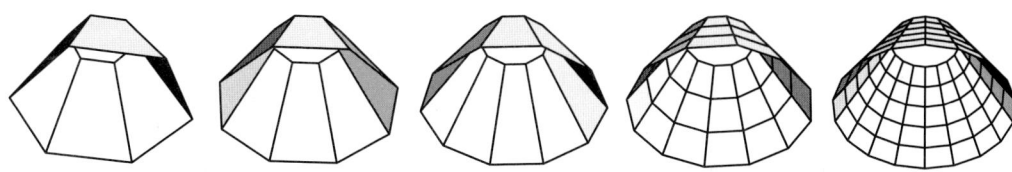

Colours

hue, inhue, and inouthue alter the colour gradients of the individual polygon lines. These parameters can be assigned 2, 4, or 6-8 values; in the first (easiest) case the two values determine the gradient's range for the H value in the HSB colour model – hue=h_0 h_1 with $0 \le h_0 < h_1 \le 1$.

```
\usepackage{pst-solides3d}
\psset{viewpoint=50 50 20 rtp2xyz,Decran=20,linewidth=0.01}
\begin{pspicture}(-2.25,-1.5)(2.5,1)
    \psSolid[object=grille,base=-3 5 -3 3,hue=0 1]
\end{pspicture}
%
\begin{pspicture}(-2.25,-1.5)(2.5,1)
    \psSolid[object=grille, base=-3 5 -3 3,hue=0 0.3]
\end{pspicture}
%
\begin{pspicture}(-2.25,-1.5)(2.5,1)
    \psSolid[object=grille,base=-3 5 -3 3,hue=0.5 0.6]
\end{pspicture}
```

  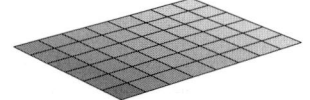

When specifying four values, hue=h_0 h_1 s b, the first two are the hue range as described above, s specifies the value for the saturation, and b the value for the brightness.

```
\usepackage{pst-solides3d}
\psset{viewpoint=50 50 20 rtp2xyz,Decran=20,linewidth=0.01}
\begin{pspicture}(-2.25,-1.5)(2.5,1)
  \psSolid[object=grille,base=-3 5 -3 3,hue=0 1 0.8 0.7]
\end{pspicture}
%
\begin{pspicture}(-2.25,-1.5)(2.5,1)
  \psSolid[object=grille, base=-3 5 -3 3,hue=0 1 0.5 1]
\end{pspicture}
%
\begin{pspicture}(-2.25,-1.5)(2.5,1)
  \psSolid[object=grille, base=-3 5 -3 3,hue=0.3 0.6 0.5 0.7]
\end{pspicture}
```

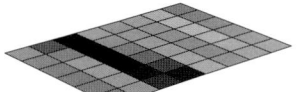 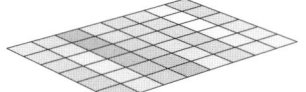 

23-04

The longer options let you use any colour model. Six values designate the minimums and maximums for RGB or HSB; you have to state the model as well to use hsb as otherwise RGB is assumed by default. The ordering of the values is: hue=h_0 s_0 b_0 h_1 s_1 b_1 (hsb) or alternatively hue=r_0 g_0 b_0 r_1 g_1 b_1. When designating eight parameters, CMYK is assumed automatically: hue=c_0 m_0 y_0 k_0 c_1 m_1 y_1 k_1.

```
\usepackage{pst-solides3d}
\psset{viewpoint=50 50 20 rtp2xyz,Decran=20,linewidth=0.01}
\begin{pspicture}(-2.25,-1.5)(2.5,1)
  \psSolid[object=grille,base=-3 5 -3 3,hue=0 0.8 1 1 1 0.7 (hsb)]
\end{pspicture}
%
\begin{pspicture}(-2.25,-1.5)(2.5,1)
  \psSolid[object=grille, base=-3 5 -3 3,hue=1 0 0 0 0 1]
\end{pspicture}
%
\begin{pspicture}(-2.25,-1.5)(2.5,1)
  \psSolid[object=grille, base=-3 5 -3 3,hue=1 0 0 0 0 1 0]
\end{pspicture}
```

  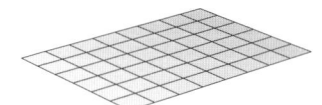

23-06

The final possible way is the explicit specification of two colour names, which have to be put in parentheses and need to be defined beforehand by the system or the user – hue=(colour1) (colour2). You can use the standard colours (cf. Section 2.3 on page 8) as

23.6 pst-solides3d — perspective 3D views

well as all of the colour names requested through the PSTricks package options dvipsnames
or svgnames. Additionally, you can preassign custom colours (using the appropriate numbers)
to the internal colour options color1, color2, color3, and color4. The xcolor notation is
valid. You can also the deactivatecolor option locally to prevent the filling of the polygon
faces.

```
\usepackage[dvipsnames,svgnames]{pstricks} \usepackage{pst-solides3d}
\psset{viewpoint=50 50 20 rtp2xyz,Decran=20,linewidth=0.01}
\begin{pspicture}(-2.5,-1.5)(2.5,1)
\psSolid[object=grille,base=-3 5 -3 3,hue=(Yellow) (CadetBlue)]
\end{pspicture}
%
\begin{pspicture}(-2.5,-1.5)(2.5,1)
\psSolid[object=grille,base=-3 5 -3 3,color1=red!50,color2=green!20,hue=(color1) (color2)]
\end{pspicture}
%
\begin{pspicture}(-2.5,-1.5)(2.5,1)
\psSolid[object=grille,base=-3 5 -3 3,hue=(Yellow) (CadetBlue),deactivatecolor]
\end{pspicture}
```

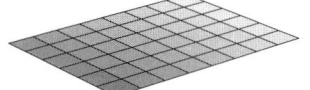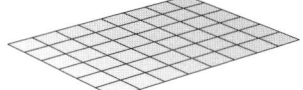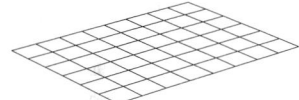

```
\usepackage{pst-solides3d}

\psset{lightsrc=45 15 20,viewpoint=50 20 20 rtp2xyz,Decran=25}
\begin{pspicture}(-2,-1.5)(2,2)
\psSolid[object=cube,a=3,ngrid=3,hollow,
    inouthue=0 1 0.5 1,rm=36 1 44 {} for]
\end{pspicture}
```

```
\usepackage{pst-solides3d}
\begin{pspicture}(-7,-7)(10,12)
\psset[pst-solides3d]{viewpoint=20 5 10,Decran=30,lightsrc=20 10 5}
\psSolid[object=grille,base=-2 2 -2 2,linecolor=white](0,0,-2)
\defFunction{cone}(u,v){u v Cos mul}{u v Sin mul}{u}
\psSolid[object=surfaceparametree,base=-2 2 0 2 pi mul, inhue=0.8 0.2,hue=0.8 0.2,
    function=cone,linewidth=0.01,ngrid=25 40]
\gridIIID[Zmin=-2,Zmax=2](-2,2)(-2,2)[3,0.5,1]
\end{pspicture}
```

23 Three-dimensional figures

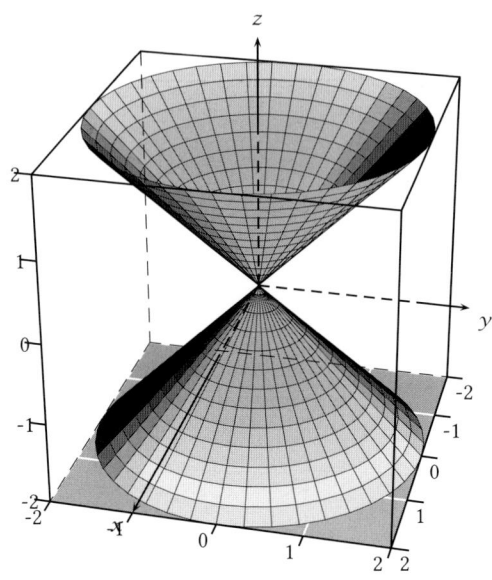

23-06-81

Deletion of surfaces

Using the `affinage` option for objects with more than one surface achieves the effect of looking inside the object; `affinagecoeff` specifies the relative degree of the opening. For the effect to work, you must remember to fill the inside with a different colour through `incolor`.

```
\usepackage{pst-solides3d}
\psset{Decran=6,viewpoint=10 5 5}
\begin{pspicture}(-2,-2)(2,3)
\psSolid[object=cube,action=draw**,numfaces=all,fontsize=80,fillcolor=green!20,
   incolor=blue!30]
\end{pspicture}
\begin{pspicture}(-2,-2)(2,3)
\psSolid[object=cube,action=draw**,affinage=4,fillcolor=green!20,incolor=blue!30,hollow]
\end{pspicture}
\begin{pspicture}(-2,-2)(2,3)
\psSolid[object=cube,action=draw**,affinage=4,affinagecoeff=1,fillcolor=green!20,
   incolor=blue!30,hollow]
\end{pspicture}
```

 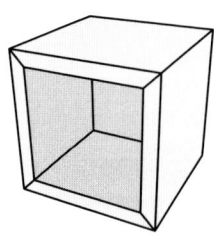 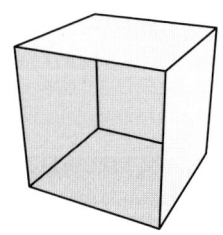

23-06

23.6 pst-solides3d — perspective 3D views

```
\usepackage{pst-solides3d}
\psset{Decran=8,viewpoint=10 5 5}
\begin{pspicture}(-2,-2)(2,3)
\psSolid[object=cube,action=draw**,a=3,ngrid=3,numfaces=all,fontsize=10,
    fillcolor=green!20,incolor=blue!30]
\end{pspicture}
\begin{pspicture}(-2,-2)(2,3)
\psSolid[object=cube,action=draw**,a=3,ngrid=3,affinage=39 40 41,fillcolor=green!20,
    incolor=blue!30,hollow]
\end{pspicture}
\begin{pspicture}(-2,-2)(2,3)
\psSolid[object=cube,action=draw**,a=3,ngrid=3,affinage=39 40 41,affinagecoeff=1,
    fillcolor=green!20,incolor=blue!30,hollow]
\end{pspicture}
```

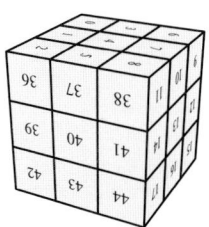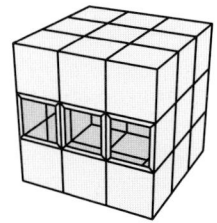

The rm option masks individual surfaces, usually replacing it with a white area. Surfaces that are behind it are not drawn because they are formally invisible. In contrast to affinage, it always removes the complete surface. The numbering of surfaces only refers to the visible surfaces; it can therefore change if particular surfaces that would normally be visible are masked. The hollow option is another way to look inside objects with more than one face (though this option has no effect when also using action==draw**, cf. Table 23.11 on page 418). Here also you must assign a different colour for the inside through incolor or inouthue. It's a good idea to turn off the numbering of surfaces when using hollow as otherwise not visible faces are numbered, which can be very confusing.

```
\usepackage{pst-solides3d}
\psset{Decran=15,viewpoint=10 -15 5}
\begin{pspicture}(-2,-1)(1.5,1)
\psSolid[object=cube,a=3,ngrid=3,inouthue=0 1 0.25 1,numfaces=all]
\end{pspicture}
\begin{pspicture}(-2,-1)(1.5,1)
\psSolid[object=cube,a=3,ngrid=3,inouthue=0 1 0.25 1,numfaces=all,rm= 27 1 35 {} for]
\end{pspicture}
\begin{pspicture}(-2,-1)(1.5,1)
\psSolid[object=cube,a=3,ngrid=3,hollow,inouthue=0 1 0.25 1,
   rm= 27 28 29 30 31 32 33 34 35]
\end{pspicture}
```

23 Three-dimensional figures

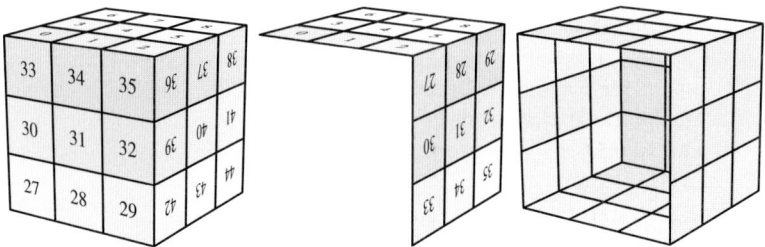

The rm option expects a list of face numbers. This can be in the form of corresponding PostScript code for longer sequences; the above list for example could also have been given as rm=27 1 35 {} for or rm=9 {27} repeat. The order of the elements is irrelevant as they are sorted descending internally before the corresponding faces are deleted. Therefore the following specifications are equivalent:

```
rm=27 28 29 30 31 32 33 34 35
rm=35 -1 27 {} for
rm=35 34 33 32 31 30 29 28 27
rm=27 1 35 {} for
rm=27 27 27 27 27 27 27 27 27
rm= 9 {27} repeat
```

Flattening edges

You can "cut" any edge of an object symmetric to the centre of the object using the chanfrein option. What had been one edge then results in two new edges and an additional face. How much is removed is determined relatively through the value of chanfreincoeff (which takes a value in $0\dots 1$).

```
\usepackage{pst-solides3d}
\psset{Decran=20,lightsrc=10 0 10,viewpoint=50 -20 30 rtp2xyz}
\begin{pspicture}(-2,-2)(2,2)
\psSolid[object=cube,a=5,fillcolor=red!30]
\end{pspicture}
\begin{pspicture}(-2,-2)(2,2)
\psSolid[object=cube,a=5,fillcolor=red!30,chanfrein,chanfreincoeff=0.6]
\end{pspicture}
\begin{pspicture}(-2,-2)(2,2)
\psSolid[object=dodecahedron,a=5,fillcolor=cyan!30,chanfrein,chanfreincoeff=.7]
\end{pspicture}
```

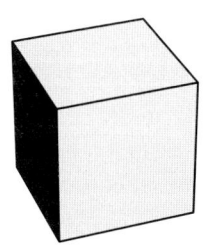
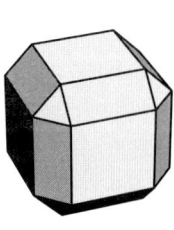
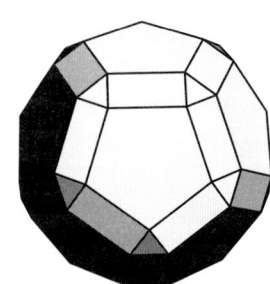

Transformations

We discussed transformations in Section 23.6.6 on page 408, and example ?? on page ?? used transform, but let's look at that option in a bit more detail. In the following example the yellow (right) cube is the original, with its centre at $P(-2,0,0)$. The small cube was created from the large one by translation of the centre to $P(-1,0,3)$ and scalar multiplication of the corners by a factor of 0.5. The wire model of the cube is the original one translated by the vector $V(3,-2,0)$.

When defining the transformation, assume that the current value of the three-dimensional point – x, y, and z – is on top of the stack. then ensure that *after* the PostScript operations there are still three values on the stack in the same order.

```
\usepackage{pst-solides3d}
\psset{viewpoint=20 60 20 rtp2xyz,lightsrc=10 15 7,Decran=20}
\begin{pspicture}(-5,-5)(6,5)
\psSolid[object=grille,base=-3 3 -3 3,fillcolor=red!50]
\axesIIID(4,4,3)
\psSolid[object=cube,fillcolor=yellow!50,a=2,ngrid=3](-2,0,0)
\psSolid[object=cube,fillcolor=green!50,a=2,transform={ 0.5 mulv3d },ngrid=3](-1,0,3)
\psSolid[object=cube,transform={ 3 -2 0 addv3d },action=draw,a=2,ngrid=3](-2,0,0)
\end{pspicture}
```

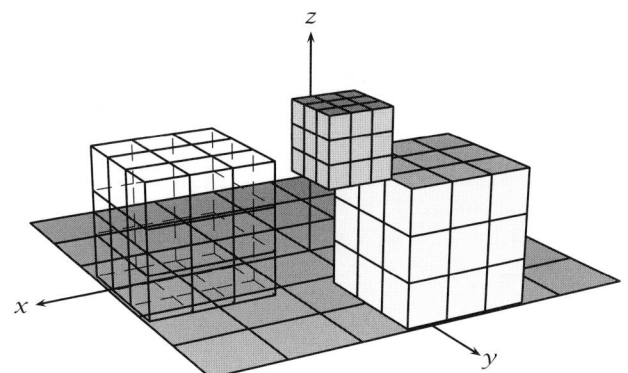

For vector operations, all PostScript functions are available; here we only mention some of the internal functions – addv3d, mulv3d, scale0point3d, and rotate0point3d. More are explained in the documentation of the solides3d.pro prologue file.

```
\usepackage{pst-solides3d}
\psset{viewpoint=20 60 20 rtp2xyz,lightsrc=10 15 7,Decran=20}
\begin{pspicture}(-5,-5)(6,5)
\psSolid[object=grille,base=-3 3 -3 3,fillcolor=red!50]
\axesIIID(4,4,3)
\psSolid[object=cube,a=2,ngrid=3,fillcolor=yellow!50](-2,0,0)
\psSolid[object=cube,a=2,ngrid=3,transform={.75 3 .5 scale0point3d}](2,0,1)
\psSolid[object=cube,a=2,ngrid=3,transform={ 3 -2 0 addv3d },action=draw](-2,0,0)
\end{pspicture}
```

23 Three-dimensional figures

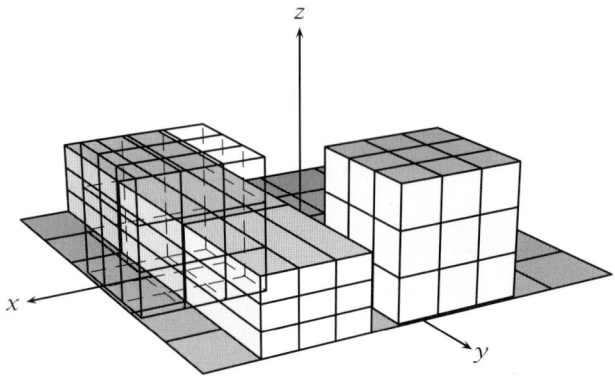

You can also use the \pstVerb command to define a custom PostScript function that can then be referred to when doing a transformation. This is a good way to achieve distortions, for example torsions.

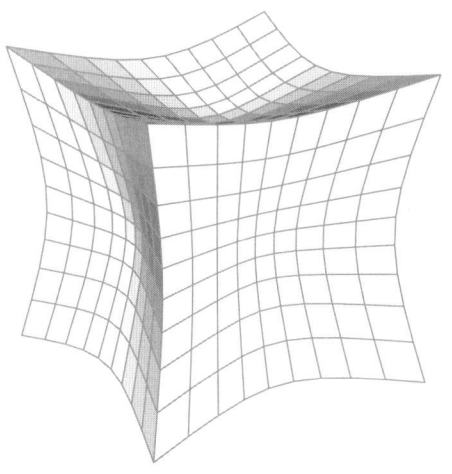

```
\usepackage{pst-solides3d}

\psset{viewpoint=20 60 20 rtp2xyz,
    lightsrc=10 15 7,Decran=20}
\pstVerb{
    /distort {
        4 dict begin     % keep local
        /M defpoint3d    % save as vector
        /a .5 def /b 1 a 3 sqrt mul sub def
        /k M norme3d a mul b add def
        M k mulv3d
        end } def }%
\begin{pspicture}(-3,-4)(3,3)
\psset{linewidth=.02,linecolor=gray}
\psSolid[object=cube,a=3,ngrid=9,
    transform=distort]%
\end{pspicture}
```

The following example begins with a prism of height 10 and side length 1. The sides are divided into grids of 20×2 each. The PostScript function torsion first saves the current point in M and then recalls the coordinates and only saves the z coordinate. After that the current point is put on the stack again; after that the angle values 0 0 and $z \times 18$ follow. They are used for the rotation about the z axis. Because z is at most 10, the torsion of the prism is in total $180°$.

```
\usepackage{pst-solides3d}
\psset{viewpoint=50 50 20 rtp2xyz,lightsrc=25 37 17,Decran=30}
\begin{pspicture}(-1.5,-1)(1.5,6)
\psSolid[object=grille,base=-2 2 -2 2,ngrid=8]
\psSolid[object=prisme,h=10,ngrid=20 2,hue=0 1 0.4 5,
    base=.5 0 .5 .5 0 .5 -.5 .5 -.5 0 -.5 -.5 0 -.5 .5 -.5]
\end{pspicture}
```

```
%
\begin{pspicture}(-1.5,-1)(1.5,6)
\psSolid[object=grille,base=-2 2 -2 2,ngrid=8]
\pstVerb{
  /torsion {     % x y z are on the stack
    2 dict begin % keep everything local
    /M defpoint3d % save x y z coordinates
    M             % put x y z back on the stack
    /z exch def   % save z coordinate
    pop pop       % delete x y
    M                      % put x y z on the stack
    0 0 z 18 mul    % put 0 0 18*z on the stack
    rotateOpoint3d % rotate point
    end
  } def }%
\psSolid[object=prisme,h=10,ngrid=20 2,transform=torsion,hue=0 1 0.4 5,
  base=.5 0 .5 .5 0 .5 -.5 .5 -.5 0 -.5 -.5 0 -.5 .5 -.5]
\end{pspicture}
```

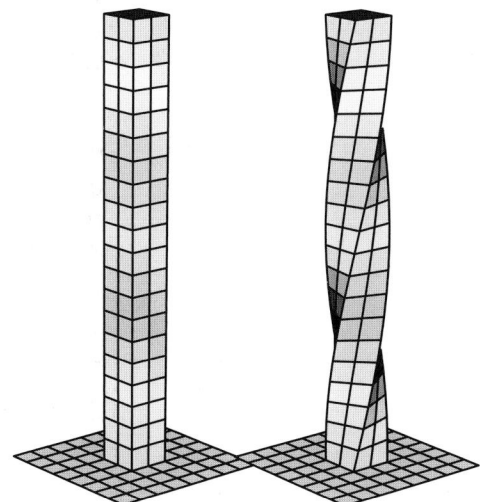

23.6.10 Definition of new objects

In the following example, a special base is created by combining a polyline and a two-dimensional function, which together build a close path. The view of the base side is achieved by a simple rotation about the x axis with RotX=90.

```
\usepackage{pst-solides3d} \psset{lightsrc=10 20 30,viewpoint=50 60 25 rtp2xyz,Decran=25}
\begin{pspicture}(-5,-2)(3,4)  \defFunction[algebraic]{G}(t){ 2*cos(t) }{ 2*sin(t) }{}
\psSolid[object=grille,base=-6 6 -4 4,action=draw,linecolor=black!20]
\psSolid[object=prisme,h=8,fillcolor=yellow!20,RotX=90,hollow,% show inside
  ngrid=8,incolor=red!30,resolution=19,% for courbeR2+
  base=2 0 3 0 3 3 -3 3 -3 0 -2 0 % x y ...
```

23 Three-dimensional figures

```
        Pi 0 { G } CourbeR2+](0,4,0)
\axesIIID[showOrigin=false](3,1.5,3)(5.5,5,5.5)
\psSolid[object=grille,base=-3 3 0 3,RotX=90,action=draw](0,4,0)
\end{pspicture}
```

```
\usepackage{pst-solides3d}
\begin{pspicture}(-7,-2)(7,4)
\psset{lightsrc=80 30 30,viewpoint=1000 60 20 rtp2xyz,Decran=1000}
\psset{solidmemory}
\defFunction[algebraic]{Func}(t){2+2*cos(t)}{2*tan(t/2)}{2*sin(t)}
\defFunction[algebraic]{Func'}(t){-2*sin(t)}{2*(1+tan(1/2*t)^2)}{2*cos(t)}
\psSolid[object=courbe,range=-2.8 2.6,ngrid=72 12,function=Func,name=H1,
   hue=0 1 0.7 1,action=none,r=1]
\psSolid[object=cylindrecreux,h=20,r=1,RotX=90,incolor=green!30,action=none,name=C1,
   ngrid=36 36](2,10,0)
\psSolid[object=fusion,base=H1 C1]
\composeSolid
\end{pspicture}
```

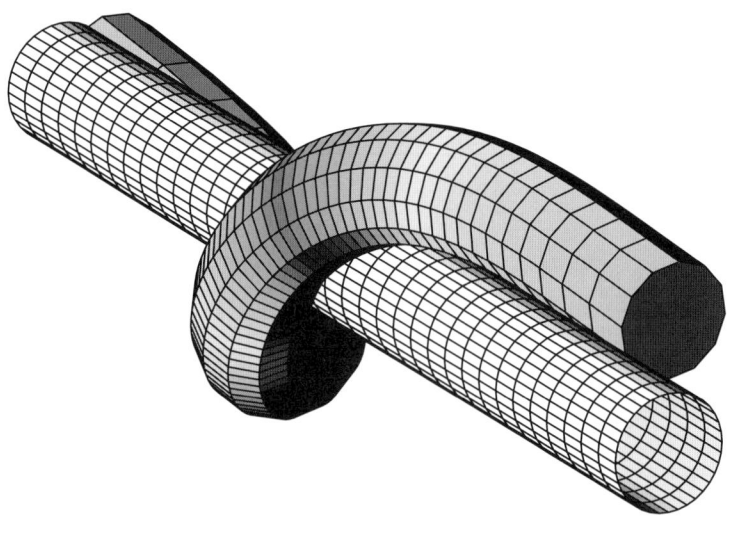

23.6 pst-solides3d – perspective 3D views

Besides the standard objects summarized in Section 23.6.1 on page 395, you can create new objects by specifying the corners and the resulting surfaces or alternatively for prisms by specifying the base. When doing this, you assign the object option the value new. The corners are specified through the optional argument sommets and the surfaces through faces. You can also specify the base of prisms using two-dimensional functions, as shown above in the first example of this section.

You can also create wire models by defining the corners and the faces. Here PostScript needs to know which is the front and the back of the face, which is specified through the rotational direction of the face's direction vector. This is determined with the "right-hand-rule" – the thumb is the direction vector of the outer/front faces and the fingers are the rotational direction. We'll illustrate this for a quadrangle.

```
\usepackage{pst-solides3d}
\psset{viewpoint=50 20 25 rtp2xyz,Decran=35}
\begin{pspicture}(-2.2,-1.5)(2,2)
\psSolid[object=new,action=draw,
   sommets=-2 -2 0  -2 2 0   2 2 0   2 -2 0,faces={[0 3 2 1]},num=all,show=all]
\axesIIID(2,2,0)(3.5,3,2)
\end{pspicture}
\begin{pspicture}(-2.2,-1.5)(2,2)
\psSolid[object=new,fillcolor=red!30,incolor=blue!50,
   sommets=-2 -2 0  -2 2 0   2 2 0   2 -2 0,faces={[0 3 2 1]}]
\axesIIID(2,2,0)(3.5,3,2)
\end{pspicture}
\begin{pspicture}(-2.2,-1.5)(2,2)
\psSolid[object=new,fillcolor=red!30,incolor=blue!50,
   sommets=-2 -2 0  -2 2 0   2 2 0   2 -2 0,faces={[0 1 2 3]},hollow]
\axesIIID(2,2,0)(3.5,3,2)
\end{pspicture}
```

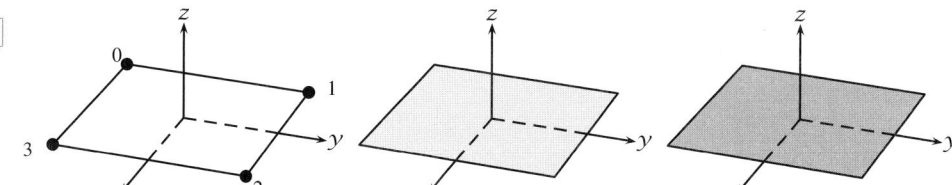

The left figure in the example above shows the internal numbering of the points. The centre figure defines the face through faces={[0 3 2 1]} such that the thumb of the right hand points towards us.[8] The z axis is therefore equal to the direction vector so the visible surface corresponds to "outside" and is filled with fillcolor=red!30, as specified. In the right example, the rotational direction of the rectangle changed; [0 1 2 3] points in the opposite direction and the direction vector is therefore contrary to the z axis. The face visible this time corresponds to "inside" and is filled with incolor=blue!20. Note that this filling only occurs as inside faces were made visible through the hollow option.

---

[8]The braces with {[0 3 2 1]} are important to protect the square brackets within – otherwise the righthand one would be interpreted as the end of the options of \pssolid, which would result in an error.

23 Three-dimensional figures

```
\usepackage{pst-solides3d}
\psset{viewpoint=50 20 30 rtp2xyz,Decran=30}
\begin{pspicture}(-3,-1.5)(3,3.5)
\psSolid[object=new,action=draw,sommets=
    2 4 3   -2 4 3   -2 -4 3   2 -4 3   2 4 0   -2 4 0   -2 -4 0   2 -4 0   0 4 5   0 -4 5
    1 0 3.5   1 -1 3.5   1 0 6   1 -1 6   0 0 4.5   0 -1 4.5   0 0 6   0 -1 6
        2 0 0   2 0 2   2 1 2   2 1 0,
   faces={[0 4 5 1][0 1 2 3][7 6 5 4][0 3 7 18 19 20 21 4][3 9 2][1 8 0][8 9 3 0]
       [9 8 1 2][6 7 3 2][2 1 5 6][10 12 13 11][11 15 17 13][12 13 17 16][12 10 14 16]
       [14 16 17 15][18 21 20 19]},num=all,show=all,numfaces=all]
\axesIIID[showOrigin=false](2,4,5)(5,5,7)
\end{pspicture}
\begin{pspicture}(-3,-1.5)(3,3.5)
\psSolid[object=new,action=draw**,sommets=
    2 4 3   -2 4 3   -2 -4 3   2 -4 3   2 4 0   -2 4 0   -2 -4 0   2 -4 0   0 4 5   0 -4 5
    1 0 3.5   1 -1 3.5   1 0 6   1 -1 6   0 0 4.5   0 -1 4.5   0 0 6   0 -1 6
        2 0 0   2 0 2   2 1 2   2 1 0,
   faces={[0 4 5 1][0 1 2 3][7 6 5 4][0 3 7 18 19 20 21 4][3 9 2][1 8 0][8 9 3 0]
       [9 8 1 2][6 7 3 2][2 1 5 6][10 12 13 11][11 15 17 13][12 13 17 16][12 10 14 16]
       [14 16 17 15][18 21 20 19]},fillcolor=black!10,incolor=blue!30,
       fcol=24 (Goldenrod) 6 (Apricot),rm=15,hollow]
\axesIIID[showOrigin=false](2,4,5)(5,5,7)
\end{pspicture}
```

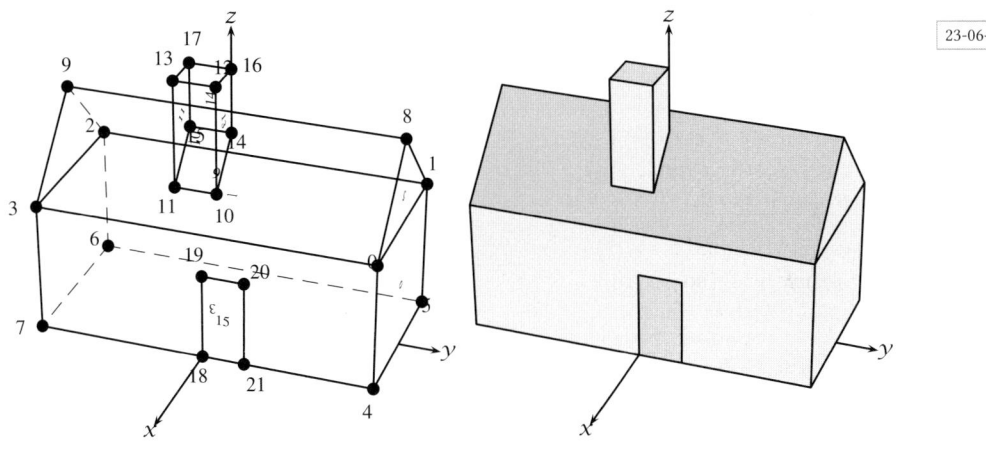

23.6.11 Complex objects

In all the examples given so far, objects have been placed one after another and therefore concealed earlier objects where they have overlapped. The principle of hidden lines or faces wasn't important. However, pst-solides3d can deal differently with overlapping objects when specified accordingly. The solidmemory option means that all objects are collected rather than being drawn immediately, awaiting output at the end with the \composeSolid[9]

---

[9] Internally they are extracted from PSTricks so that they can be referred to at any time by the object name.

command, which is executed by default with the \end{pspicture}. In general this makes it necessary to assign names to all "collected" objects with name=... and action=none.

The following example creates a cylinder inside a ring. Both the ring and the cylinder obstruct parts of the surface of the other object. To make this happen, first of all the entire surfaces of *both* objects have to be saved and then a combination of the two is output.

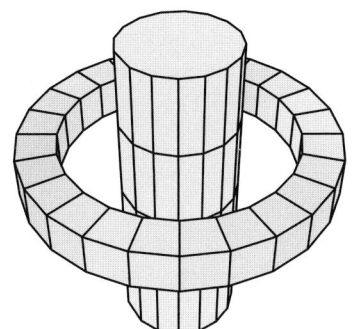

```
\usepackage{pst-solides3d}

\begin{pspicture}[solidmemory,
    Decran=10](-6,-5)(6,4)
\psSolid[object=anneau,h=6,hue=0 1 0.2 0.9,
    R=4,r=3,h=1,action=none,name=Ring](0,0,-1)
\psSolid[object=cylindre,h=8,fillcolor=blue!20,
    r=1.5,ngrid=4 16,action=none,
    name=Cylinder](0,0,-6)
\psSolid[object=fusion,action=draw**,
    base=Ring Cylinder]
\end{pspicture}
```

The order of the objects isn't important here; they are sorted internally anyway before output to prevent obstructed surfaces and lines from being drawn. The objects are created in the usual manner, but with action=none so that no immediate output occurs, but the created PostScript code is still available internally through the arbitrarily chosen names *Ring* and *Cylinder*. The object created last, fusion, is then assigned these names through the base option. This makes the internal sorting of all surfaces and subsequent output possible – once action is assigned the value draw**.

The plane in the cover picture of the German version was used as separation plane for the two cylinders. A separation plane, specified through the plansepare option, separates a whole object into two subobjects. 0 and 1 are appended to the original object's name. In the following example, *cylinder1* and *cylinder2* are separated into *cylinder10* and *cylinder11* and *cylinder20* and *cylinder21*; they can then be referred to in the usual manner.

```
\usepackage{pst-solides3d}
\begin{pspicture}[solidmemory](-8,-5)(7,5)
\psset{lightsrc=50 -50 50,viewpoint=100 -30 40,Decran=100}
\psSolid[object=plantype,definition=equation,args={[0 0 1 0] 90},
    base=-6 6 -7 6,ngrid=9 13,name=monplan]
\defFunction[algebraic]{Cyl1}(t){2*cos(t)}{-6}{2*sin(t)}
\defFunction[algebraic]{Cyl2}(t){-6}{2*cos(t)}{2*sin(t)}
\psSolid[object=cylindre,range=0 6.28,h=12,function=Cyl1,axe=0 1 0,
    incolor=black!30,fillcolor=black!10,ngrid=18 18,
    plansepare=monplan,name=cylinder1,action=none]
\psSolid[object=cylindre,range=6.28 0,h=12,function=Cyl2,axe=1 0 0,
    incolor=black!10,fillcolor=black!30,
    plansepare=monplan,ngrid=18 18,name=cylinder2,action=none]
\psSolid[object=fusion,base=cylinder11 cylinder21]% lower halves
\psSolid[object=plan,args=monplan]              % plane
\psSolid[object=fusion,base=cylinder10 cylinder20]% upper halves
\psProjection[object=texte,plan=monplan,linecolor={[cmyk]{0.4,0.6,1,0.2}},
    text=PSTricks with pst-solides3d,fontsize=20,pos=cc](0,-6.5)
```

23 Three-dimensional figures

```
\axesIIID[linewidth=1pt,labelsep=10pt,showOrigin=false](2,6.7,2)(11,8,5)
\end{pspicture}
```

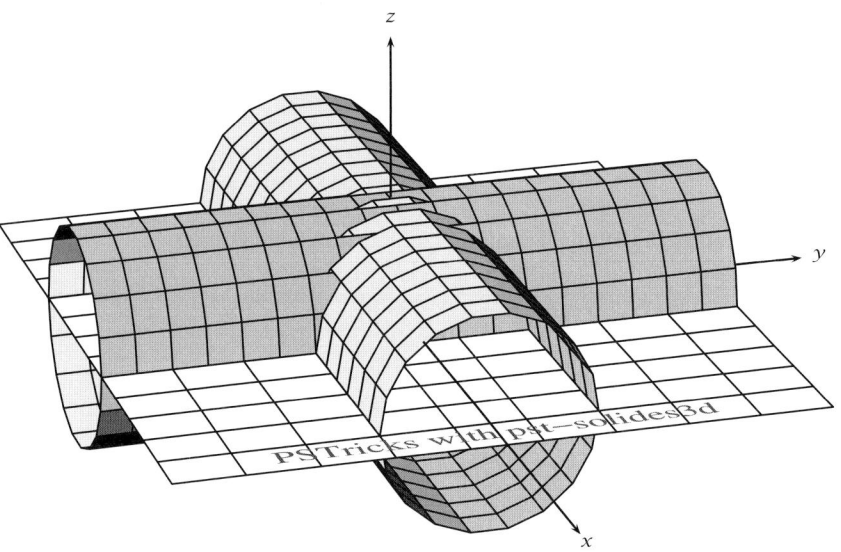

In the following example the vertical cylinder of radius 2 length units and of height 6 length units is split into two parts by the plane with equation $\frac{\sqrt{2}}{2}x + \frac{\sqrt{2}}{2}z = 0$, which in pst-solides3d notation is plansepare={[0.707 0 0.707 0]}[10]. The name in the example was chosen arbitrarily. The y axis is in the plane because of the definition, and the angle between the plane and the other two axes is $45°$ each. The centre of the whole cylinder is at the coordinate origin; the cylinder isn't drawn because of action=none. The two halves are loaded through object=load and the corresponding assignment with load=.... The upper half is additionally rotated by $90°$ about the z axis and translated by 4 length units in the y direction. The lower half stays at the original place.

```
\usepackage{pst-solides3d}
\begin{pspicture}[solidmemory](-4,-5)(7,4)
\psset{viewpoint=50 -40 10 rtp2xyz,Decran=50,linecolor=darkgray,lightsrc=viewpoint}
\psSolid[object=grille,action=draw,base=-3 5 -3 5,linecolor=red](0,0,-3)
\psSolid[object=cylindre,r=2,h=6,ngrid=6 24,plansepare={[0.707 0 0.707 0]},
    name=Cylinder,action=none](0,0,-3)
\psSolid[object=load,load=Cylinder1,fillcolor={[rgb]{0.7 1 0.7}},
    fcol=0 (1 1 0.7 setrgbcolor)]
\psSolid[object=load,load=Cylinder0,RotZ=90,fillcolor={[rgb]{0.7 1 0.7}},
    fcol=0 (1 1 0.7 setrgbcolor)](0,4,0)
\psSolid[object=plan,action=draw,definition=equation,
    args={[0.707 0 0.707 0] 90},base=-2 2 -3 3,planmarks]
\psSolid[object=line,args=0 0 0 0 4 0]% first half y axis
\axesIIID[showOrigin=false](0,6.8,0)(3.5,8,3.5)
\end{pspicture}
```

---

[10] The specification has to be enclosed in braces so that the square brackets don't get confused with the surrounding brackets.

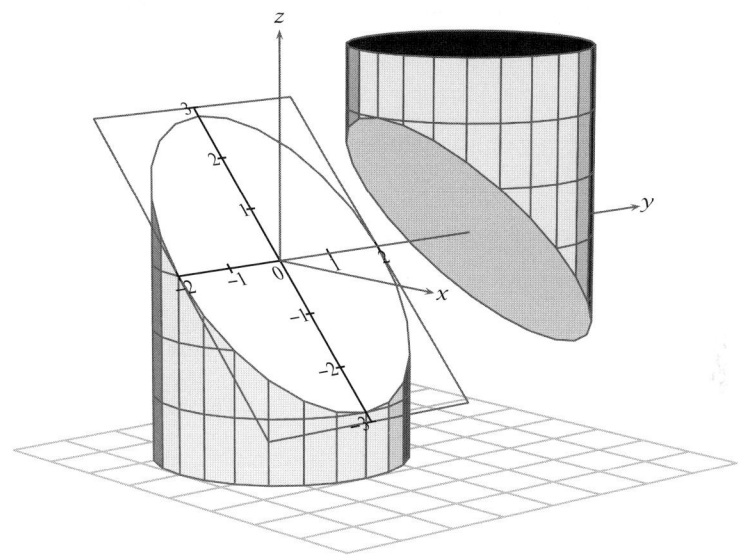

23.7 Examples

```
\usepackage{pst-solides3d}
\begin{pspicture}(-4,-4)(4,4)
\psset{viewpoint=100 20 20 rtp2xyz,Decran=75,solidmemory,lightsrc=viewpoint}
\codejps{ /coeff 0.75 def /r0 4 def /OH coeff r0 mul neg def}%
\psSolid[object=sphere,r=r0,ngrid=9 18,plansepare={[1 0 0 OH]},name=part,action=none]
\psSolid[object=load,load=part1,plansepare={[-1 0 0 OH]},action=none,name=part]
\psSolid[object=load,load=part1,plansepare={[0 1 0 OH]},action=none,name=part]
\psSolid[object=load,load=part1,plansepare={[0 -1 0 OH]},action=none,name=part]
\psSolid[object=load,load=part1,plansepare={[0 0 1 OH]},action=none,name=part]
\psSolid[object=load,load=part1,plansepare={[0 0 -1 OH]},action=none,name=part]
\psSolid[object=load,hue=.1 .8 0.5 1,load=part1](0,0,0)
\end{pspicture}
```

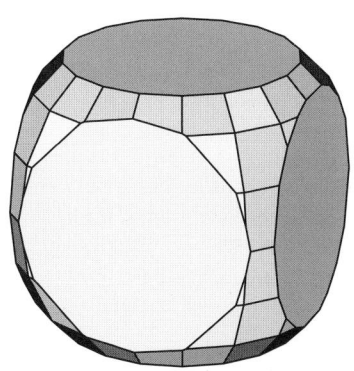

23 Three-dimensional figures

```
\usepackage{pst-solides3d}
\psset{unit=0.45}
\psset{viewpoint=50 -20 30 rtp2xyz,Decran=50}
\def\BASE{0 10 360{/Angle ED 5 Angle cos dup mul mul % x
 3 Angle cos 3 exp Angle sin mul mul } for}% y
\begin{pspicture}(-7,-5.5)(9,6)
\defFunction[algebraic]{F}(t){5*(cos(t))^2}{3*(sin(t))*(cos(t))^3}{}
\psSolid[object=grille,base=-6 6 -6 6,action=draw,linecolor=gray](0,0,0)
\psSolid[object=face,fillcolor=magenta,action=draw*,
  incolor=blue,biface,RotZ=90,base=0 2 pi mul {F} CourbeR2+](0,0,0)
\psSolid[object=face,fillcolor=yellow,action=draw*,incolor=blue,biface,
  base=0 2 pi mul {F} CourbeR2+](0,0,0)
\psSolid[object=face,fillcolor=yellow,action=draw*,incolor=blue,biface,RotY=180,
  base=0 2 pi mul {F} CourbeR2+](0,0,0)
\psSolid[object=face,fillcolor=yellow,action=draw*,incolor=red,biface,RotY=180,RotZ=90,
  base=0 2 pi mul {F} CourbeR2+](0,0,0)
\axesIIID(0,0,0)(6,6,5)
\end{pspicture}
```

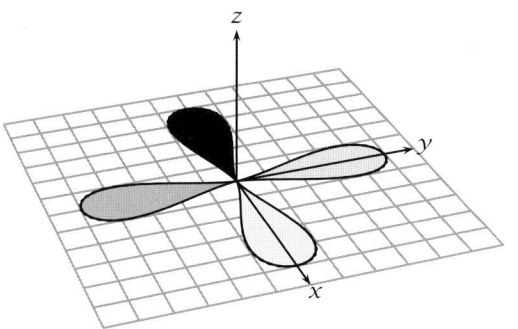

Chapter 24

pst-circ – Creation of circuits

24.1 How it works... 445
24.2 Parameters 446
24.3 The objects 447
24.4 Logical elements 457
24.5 Examples 462

pst-circ, designed for drawing circuit diagrams, is the first package dealt with in this book that relies on "low-level" objects (defined in pst-node and PSTricks) to define new "high-level" objects. The latest version of the package also includes microwave symbols and provides the functionality to draw circuits such as shown in figures 24.2 on page 463 and 24.3 on page 464.

24.1 How it works...

pst-circ is in principle based on pst-node, and puts a graphical object between two defined reference points (nodes). The alignment of the object is only of secondary importance. If it isn't necessary to define a coordinate pair explicitly as a node, you can use the normal $(x|y)$ coordinates instead. The labels are aligned by default with the horizontal axis, but you can rotate and offset them through custom parameters labelangle and labeloffset.

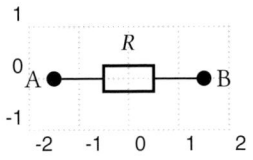

```
\usepackage{pstricks,pst-circ}

\psset{unit=0.7}
\begin{pspicture}[showgrid](-2.1,-1)(2.1,1)
  \pnode(-1.5,0){A}\qdisk(A){3pt}\uput[180](A){A}
  \pnode(1.5,0){B}\qdisk(B){3pt}\uput[0](B){B}
  \resistor(A)(B){$R$}
\end{pspicture}
```

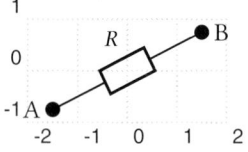

```
\usepackage{pstricks,pst-circ}

\psset{unit=0.7}
\begin{pspicture}[showgrid](-2.1,-1)(2.1,1)
  \pnode(-1.5,-0.75){A}\qdisk(A){3pt}\uput[180](A){A}
  \pnode(1.5,0.75){B}\qdisk(B){3pt}\uput[0](B){B}
  \resistor(A)(B){$R$}
\end{pspicture}
```

24.2 Parameters

This package has so many parameters that it is outside the scope of this book to discuss them all and give examples. Table 24.1 shows a summary, and the examples in the rest of this chapter make use of many of them.

Table 24.1: Summary of the available parameters for pst-circ

name	type	default	meaning
antennastyle	two|three|triangle	two	antenna symbol
couplerstyle	hybrid|directional	hybrid	coupler style
dipoleconvention	type	receptor	engine/generator principle
dipolestyle	type	normal	dipole style
directconvention	boolean	true	direction of current
groundstyle	ads|old|triangle	ads	ground symbol
inputarrow	boolean	false	arrow for input signal
intensity	boolean	false	draw current arrow
intensitylabel	text	\empty	current label
intensitylabeloffset	value	0.5	label offset
intensitycolor	colour	black	colour of current arrow
intensitylabelcolor	colour	black	colour of current label
intensitywidth	value unit	\pslinewidth	line width
intersect	boolean	false	conductor intersection
labelangle	value	0	label rotation angle
labeloffset	value	0.7	label offset
LOstyle	{}|Crystal	{}	oscillator style
output	top|right|bottom|left	top	antenna symbol
OAperfect	boolean	true	ideal operational amplifier
OAinvert	boolean	true	inverting operational amplifier
OAiplus	boolean	false	mark positive connector
OAipluslabel	text	\empty	label of positive connector
OAiminus	boolean	false	mark negative connector
OAiminuslabel	text	\empty	label of negative connector
OAiout	boolean	false	mark output
OAioutlabel	text	\empty	output label
parallel	boolean	false	parallel circuit
parallelarm	value	1.5	conductor length from the intersection of parallel circuits

continued...

... continued

name	value	default	meaning
parallelsep	value	0	additional distance
parallelnode	boolean	false	make nodes for parallel circuits
primarylabel	text	\empty	primary label
tension	boolean	false	draw voltage arrow
tensionlabel	text	\empty	voltage label
tensionoffset	value	1	offset of the voltage arrow
tensionlabeloffset	value	1.2	label offset of the voltage arrow
tensioncolor	colour	black	colour of voltage arrow
tensionlabelcolor	colour	black	colour of voltage label
tensionwidth	value unit	\pslinewidth	line width
transistorcircle	boolean	true	transistor with circle
transistorinvert	boolean	false	swap connectors
transistoribase	boolean	false	base current arrow
transistoricollector	boolean	false	collector current arrow
transistoriemitter	boolean	false	emitter current arrow
transistoribaselabel	text	\empty	current arrow label
transistoricollectorlabel	text	\empty	current arrow label
transistoriemitterlabel	text	\empty	current arrow label
transistortype	type	NPN	PNP/NPN type
secondarylabel	text	\empty	secondary label
transformeriprimary	boolean	false	current arrow
transformerisecondary	boolean	false	current arrow
transformeriprimarylabel	text	\empty	current arrow
transformerisecondarylabel	text	\empty	current arrow
tripolestyle	type	normal	tripole style
variable	boolean	false	variable di- or tripole
logicShowDot	boolean	false	draw connection dots
logicShowNode	boolean	false	draw connection nodes
logicChangeLR	boolean	false	swap left and right
logicWireLength	value	0.5	connector length
logicWidth	value	1.5	width of an element
logicHeight	value	2.5	height of an element
logicNInput	value	2	number of inputs
logicJInput	value	2	number of j-inputs
logicKInput	value	2	number of k-inputs
logictypee	type	and	element type
logicLabelstyle	value unit	\small	label size
logicSymbolstyle	value unit	\large	symbol size
logicNodestyle	value unit	\footnotesize	node size

24.3 The objects

Tables 24.2 to 24.5 in the following sections give a summary of the possible objects (as available in the current version 1.39 of the package). They are grouped according to the following distinction:

Monopole	needs one nodal point
Dipole	needs two nodal points
Multidipole	needs two nodal points, but is internally constructed from several chained dipoles
Tripole	needs three nodal points
Quadrupole	needs four nodal points

In the tables, the objects are given without their options in order to give you a better overview; the options are dealt with in the remainder of this chapter.

Commands are usually in the form:

\object name(node1)(node2)...{identifier}

The last argument (identifier or label) is optional. Some of the tripoles do not have this argument – you have to apply a label manually in these cases.

24.3.1 Monopoles

Monopoles are used as antenna symbols or oscillator symbols in high-frequency engineering.

Table 24.2: List of the predefined circuit symbols for electrical monopoles

identifier	command name	graphic
earth	\newground [settings] {rotation} (node)	
antenna	\antenna [settings] {rotation} (node)	
oscillator	\oscillator [settings] {rotation} (node){L1}{options}	L1

24.3.2 Dipoles

Dipoles are the largest group of objects in the pst-circ package. Apart from \wire, all dipoles take an identifier argument.

Table 24.3: List of the predefined circuit symbols for electrical dipoles

identifier	command name	graphic
battery	\battery	B

continued...

... continued

identifier	command name	graphic
voltage source	\Ucc	Ucc
current source	\Icc	Icc
resistor	\resistor	R
capacitor	\capacitor	C
coil	\coil	L
diode	\diode	D
Zener diode	\Zener	Z
LED	\LED	L
lamp	\lamp	l
switch	\switch	S
connection	\wire	w
arrow line	\tension	V
circle	\circledipole	c
filter	\filter	F
isolator	\isolator	I
multiplier	\freqmult	f ×N
phase shifter	\phaseshifter	P
VCO	\vco	V

continued...

24 pst-circ – Creation of circuits

... continued

identifier	command name	graphic
amplifier	\amplifier	—▷— (A)
detector	\detector	—▷|— (D)
Squid	\SQUID	—⊗— (D)
RelayNOP	\relayNOP	(D)
Suppressor	\Suppressor	—▷|◁— (D)
Arrestor	\Arrestor	—(⫫)— (D)

The \circledipole symbol is particularly useful for depicting voltage and current sources to differentiate them from the battery symbol. Setting labeloffset=0 centres the labels, as illustrated in Table 24.2.

24.3.3 Multidipoles

Multidipoles are in principle just a linear chain of dipoles, which can simplify their creation. For example you could define the equivalent circuit of a coil as a multidipole, instead of defining a new command for it:

```
\usepackage{pstricks,pst-circ}
\psset{unit=0.7}
\begin{pspicture}(0,-0.5)(8,1)
  \pnode(0,0){A} \pnode(8,0){B}
  \multidipole(A)(B)%
    \coil{$L$} \resistor{$R_L$} \capacitor{$C$}.%<-- dot ends the multidipole
\end{pspicture}
```

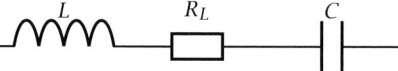

The dot terminates the definition of a multidipole. The number of dipoles is in theory unlimited, though in practice it is limited by the width of the symbol.

24.3.4 Tripoles

Table 24.4 also includes the names of the nodal points, denoted as A, B, and C, to help you understand the syntax of the commands. The order of the nodes is important – all tripoles are called with ...(A)(B)(C). Only the switch command can take an identifier (label); for other tripoles, you have to us the normal \uput command to place labels.

Table 24.4: List of the predefined circuit symbols for tripoles

identifier	command name	graphic
operational amplifier	\OA(A)(B)(C)	
npn transistor	\transistor(A)(B)(C)	
switch	\Tswitch(A)(B)(C){S}	
potentiometer	\potentiometer(A)(B)(C){P}	
mixer	\mixer(A)(B)(C){S}{options}	
circulator	\circulator(A)(B)(C){S}{options}	
automatic gain control	\agc(A)(B)(C){S}{options}	

24.3.5 Quadrupoles

Table 24.5 again gives the nodal points to aid understanding, here designated as *A*, *B*, *C*, and *D*. Again the order is important; quadrupoles are called with ...(A)(B)(C)(D).

24.3.6 Current arrows

You can add a current arrow to any object at its connecting conductors. The following example makes use of all the available parameters for current arrows; the default values for the options

24 pst-circ – Creation of circuits

Table 24.5: List of the predefined circuit symbols for quadrupoles

identifier	command name	graphic
quadripole	\quadripole(A)(B)(C)(D){T}	
transformer	\transformer(A)(B)(C)(D){T}	
coupler	\coupler(A)(B)(C)(D){text}{style}	
optocoupler	\optoCoupler(A)(B)(C)(D){T}	

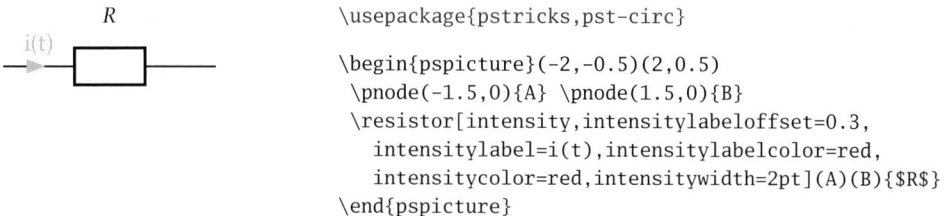

are listed in the documentation of pst-circ. [36]

The direction of the current is determined by the order of the nodes when calling the command. The current arrow therefore points from node1 to node2; however, you can also adjust this through the directconvention=false option.

```
\usepackage{pstricks,pst-circ}

\begin{pspicture}(-2,-0.5)(2,0.5)
 \pnode(-1.5,0){A} \pnode(1.5,0){B}
 \resistor[intensity,intensitylabeloffset=0.3,
    intensitylabel=i(t),intensitylabelcolor=red,
    intensitycolor=red,intensitywidth=2pt](A)(B){$R$}
\end{pspicture}
```

24.3.7 Voltage arrows

You can also add a voltage arrow to any object. The example below again makes use of all the available parameters for voltage arrows; the default values for these options are listed in the documentation of pst-circ. This example also illustrates that the label for the object, which appears above the object by default as in the previous example, can be placed below by modifying the offset.

```
\usepackage{pstricks,pst-circ}
\begin{pspicture}(-2,-0.5)(2,1)
  \pnode(-1.5,0){A}   \pnode(1.5,0){B}
```

```
\capacitor[labeloffset=-0.75,intensity,intensitycolor=red,intensitylabel=i(t),
    intensitylabelcolor=red,intensitylabeloffset=0.3,intensitywidth=2\pslinewidth,
    tension,tensioncolor=green,tensionoffset=0.75,tensionlabel=u(t),
    tensionlabelcolor=green,tensionlabeloffset=1,tensionwidth=\pslinewidth](A)(B){$C$}
\end{pspicture}
```

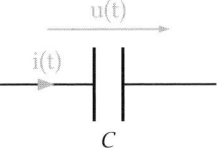

As with current arrows, voltage arrows point from A to B, which formally means that the element is absorbing energy. You can change the direction of the voltage arrow with either of these optional settings: `dipoleconvention=generator` or `dipoleconvention=receptor`. Alternatively you can reverse both the current and voltage arrows at the same time through the `directconvention=false` option.

24.3.8 Parallel circuits

Parallel circuits occur frequently, for example with the equivalent circuit for a capacitor, so pst-circ has some special options for creating these. The following figure shows a simple example, with all parameters included.

```
\usepackage{pstricks,pst-circ}
\begin{pspicture}(-2,-0.5)(2,2)
  \pnode(-2,0){A} \pnode(2,0){B}
  \resistor[labeloffset=0,intensity,intensitycolor=red,intensitylabel=$i_1$,
    intensitylabelcolor=red,intensitylabeloffset=0.3,intensitywidth=2pt,
    tension,tensioncolor=green,tensionoffset=-0.5,tensionlabel=$u_2$,
    tensionlabelcolor=green,tensionlabeloffset=-0.75,tensionwidth=1pt](A)(B){$R$}
  \capacitor[labeloffset=-0.75, parallel,parallelnode, parallelsep=0.2,parallelarm=1.5,
    intensity,intensitycolor=red,intensitylabel=$i_2$,intensitylabelcolor=red,
    intensitylabeloffset=0.3,intensitywidth=2\pslinewidth,
    tension,tensioncolor=green,tensionoffset=0.75,tensionlabel=$u_2$,
    tensionlabelcolor=green,tensionlabeloffset=1,tensionwidth=\pslinewidth](A)(B){$C$}
\end{pspicture}
```

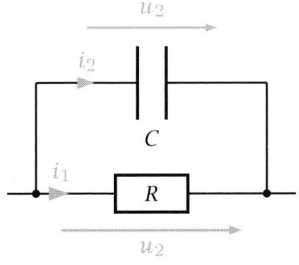

Both objects have the same nodal points, but the second object is arranged above the first object through the `parallel` option. Alternatively you can place the parallel object below the first object with a negative value for parallelarm, for example −2 – the object is drawn at a distance of two length units below. Parallel circuits with three objects are also possible.

24.3.9 Display formats

There are often differences in display formats for symbols, especially between European and American symbols. Almost all can be generated, with the help of various options; they are summarized in Table 24.6.

Table 24.6: Alternative display formats

command	option	graphic
\newground	—	
	groundstyle=old	
	groundstyle=triangle	
\antenna	—	
	antennastyle=three	
	antennastyle=triangle	
\oscillator	—	
	output=left	
	output=bottom	
	output=right	
	inputarrow	
	dipolestyle=crystal	
\resistor	—	

continued...

24.3 The objects

... continued

command	option	graphic
\coil	dipolestyle=zigzag	R resistor zigzag
	—	L coil default
	dipolestyle=rectangle	L rectangle
	dipolestyle=curved	L curved
	dipolestyle=elektor	L elektor
	dipolestyle=elektorcurved	L elektorcurved
\capacitor	—	C capacitor default
	dipolestyle=chemical	C chemical
	dipolestyle=elektor	C elektor
	dipolestyle=elektorchemical	C elektorchemical
\diode	—	D diode default
	dipolestyle=thyristor	D thyristor
	dipolestyle=GTO	D GTO
	dipolestyle=triac	D triac
\coupler	—	coupler default
	couplerstyle=directional	directional
	inputarrow	inputarrow
	quadripoleinput=right[1]	quadripoleinput=right

---

[1] Also needs the inputarrow setting

24.3.10 Variable Resistors, coils, and capacitors

Adding the variable keyword furnishes elements with a diagonal arrow to mark them as a variable object (Figure 24.1).

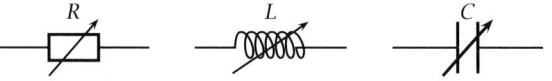

Figure 24.1: Variable objects

24.3.11 Transistors

When drawing an NPN transistor, if you give no further specifications, it is drawn as depicted in Table 24.4. However, the following example shows some of the additional options that are available. The default values for these options are listed in the documentation of pst-circ. The transistorinvert=<boolean> option swaps the emitter and collector connectors. The superordinate intensity option automatically sets all three current arrows for base/emitter/collector to true. You can set the colour for the current arrow and its associated label globally with \psset and the general options intensitycolor=<colour> and intensitylabelcolor=<colour>.

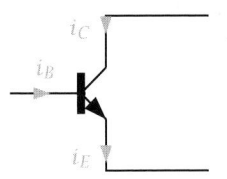

```
\usepackage{pst-circ} \psset{unit=0.7}

\begin{pspicture}(4,3)
\pnode(0,1.5){A}\pnode(4,0){B}\pnode(4,3){C}
\transistor[basesep=1cm,transistorcircle=false,
    transistortype=NPN,transistoribase,transistoricollector,
    transistoriemitter,transistoribaselabel=$i_B$,
    transistoricollectorlabel=$i_C$,
    transistoriemitterlabel=$i_E$,
    intensitycolor=red,intensitylabelcolor=red](A)(B)(C)
\end{pspicture}
```

24.3.12 Operational amplifiers

Table 24.4 shows the default display format for the ideal operational amplifier with infinite amplification. The example below makes use of some of the possible parameters. Again the superordinate option intensity can be used to draw all three current arrows. Similar to transistorinvert, OAinvert swaps the two inputs.

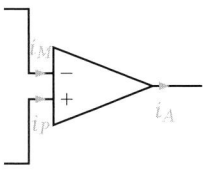

```
\usepackage{pstricks,pst-circ}

\psset{unit=0.7}
\begin{pspicture}(4,3.5)
    \pnode(0,3){A}\pnode(0,0){B}\pnode(4,1.5){C}
    \OA[OAperfect=false,OAiplus,OAiminus,OAiout,
        OAipluslabel=$i_P$,OAiminuslabel=$i_M$,
        OAioutlabel=$i_A$, intensitycolor=red,
        intensitylabelcolor=red](A)(B)(C)
\end{pspicture}
```

24.4 Logical elements

There is a frequently-used alternative display format for operational amplifiers; it is shown in the following example and is achieved through the `tripolestyle=french` option.

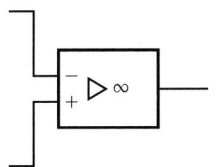

```
\usepackage{pstricks,pst-circ}

\psset{unit=0.7}
\begin{pspicture}(4,3.5)
  \pnode(0,3){A} \pnode(0,0){B} \pnode(4,1.5){C}
  \OA[tripolestyle=french](A)(B)(C)
\end{pspicture}
```

24.3.13 Transformers

The with its options shall be dealt with as the last object. The effect of the options can be seen from the example. Again both current arrows are drawn if the superordinate option `intensity` is set. Furthermore the symbol with rectangular coils, as used in Germany, can be used. The option `dipolestyle=rectangle` is set to achieve this, even if it is a .

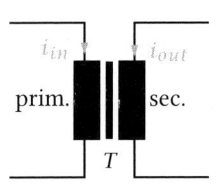

```
\usepackage{pstricks,pst-circ}

\psset{unit=0.7}
\begin{pspicture}(-0.25,0)(4,4)
  \pnode(0,3){A}\pnode(0,0){B}\pnode(4,3){C}\pnode(4,0){D}
  \transformer[dipolestyle=rectangle,primarylabel={prim.},
    secondarylabel={sec.},transformeriprimary,
    transformerisecondary,transformeriprimarylabel=$i_{in}$,
    transformerisecondarylabel=$i_{out}$,intensitycolor=red,
    intensitylabelcolor=red](A)(B)(C)(D){$T$}
\end{pspicture}
```

24.4 Logical elements

The symbols of the logical elements are more or less equivalent to the specifications of the German DIN norm. They are suitable for simple combinations of logical grids.

The syntax of each logical element is identical:

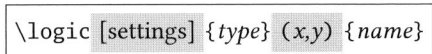

(x,y) specifies the position of the lower left corner of the element. The name must be unique; internally the connection numbers are appended to the name to create node names, which can then be used afterwards to draw arbitrary connections (cf. Section 24.4.11 on page 461).

24.4.1 And

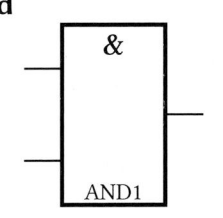

```
\usepackage{pstricks,pst-circ}

\begin{pspicture}(-1,0)(3,2.5)
  \logic{AND1}
\end{pspicture}
```

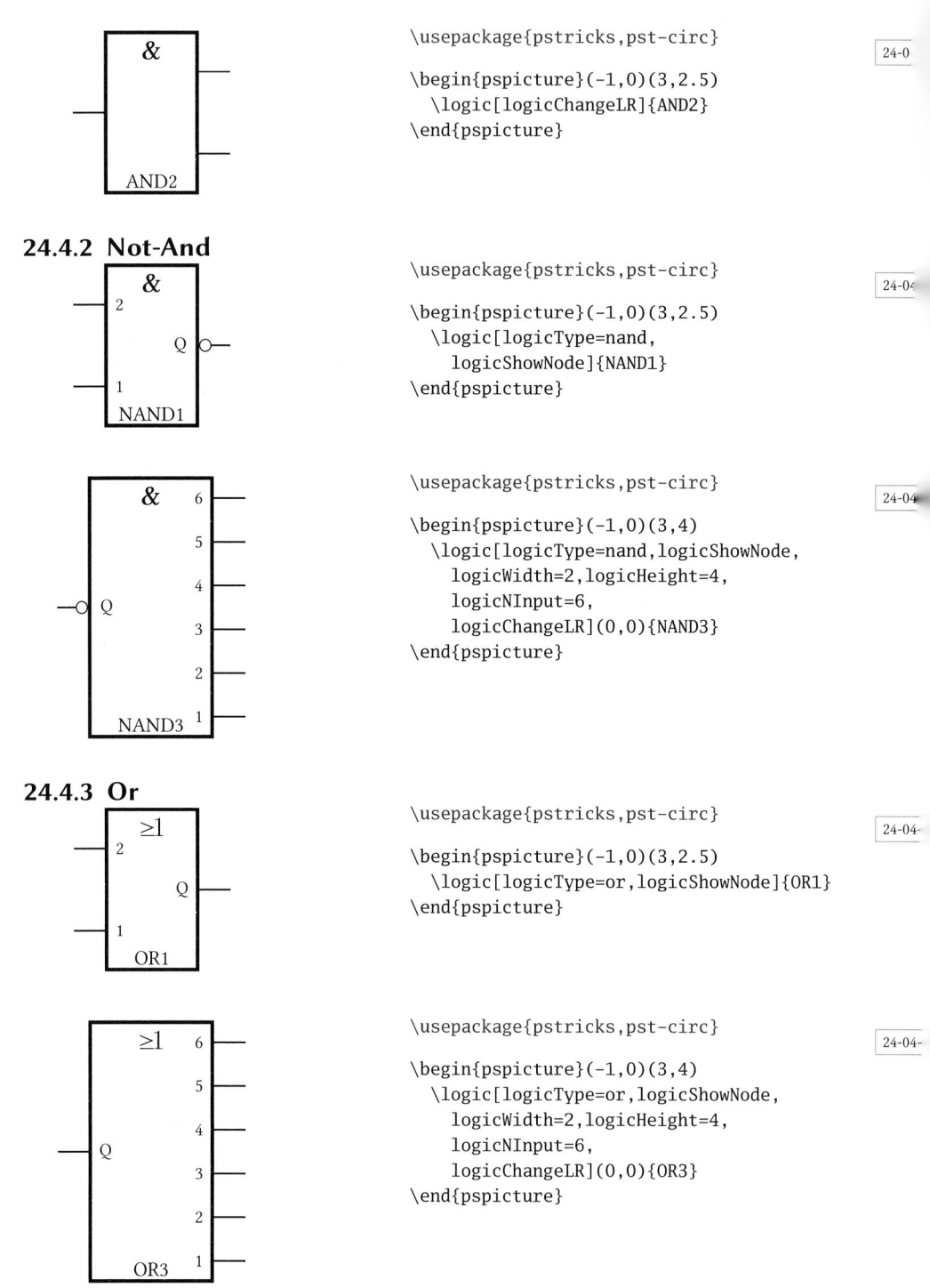

```
\usepackage{pstricks,pst-circ}

\begin{pspicture}(-1,0)(3,2.5)
    \logic[logicChangeLR]{AND2}
\end{pspicture}
```

24.4.2 Not-And

```
\usepackage{pstricks,pst-circ}

\begin{pspicture}(-1,0)(3,2.5)
    \logic[logicType=nand,
        logicShowNode]{NAND1}
\end{pspicture}
```

```
\usepackage{pstricks,pst-circ}

\begin{pspicture}(-1,0)(3,4)
    \logic[logicType=nand,logicShowNode,
        logicWidth=2,logicHeight=4,
        logicNInput=6,
        logicChangeLR](0,0){NAND3}
\end{pspicture}
```

24.4.3 Or

```
\usepackage{pstricks,pst-circ}

\begin{pspicture}(-1,0)(3,2.5)
    \logic[logicType=or,logicShowNode]{OR1}
\end{pspicture}
```

```
\usepackage{pstricks,pst-circ}

\begin{pspicture}(-1,0)(3,4)
    \logic[logicType=or,logicShowNode,
        logicWidth=2,logicHeight=4,
        logicNInput=6,
        logicChangeLR](0,0){OR3}
\end{pspicture}
```

24.4 Logical elements

24.4.4 Not Or

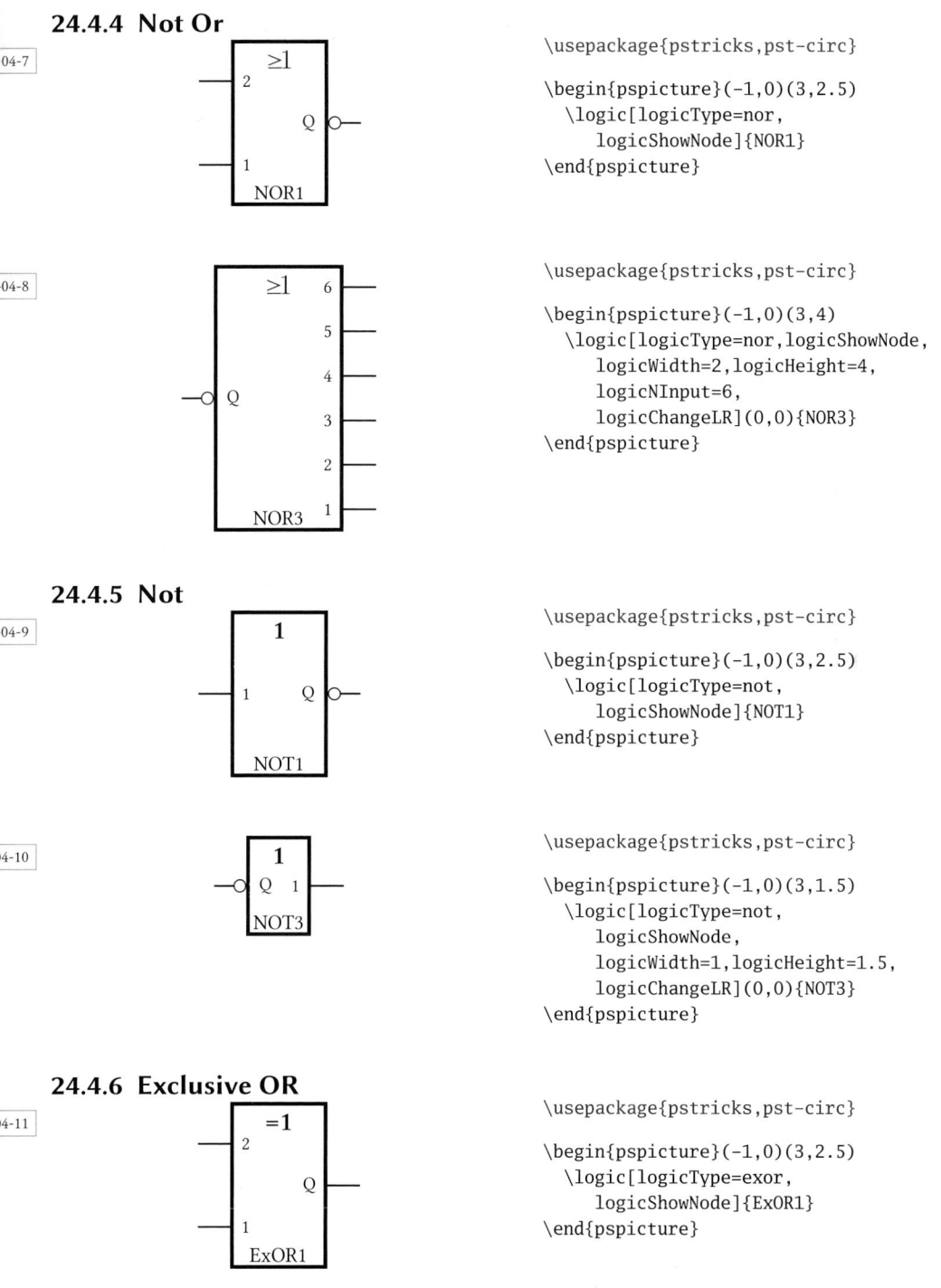

```
\usepackage{pstricks,pst-circ}

\begin{pspicture}(-1,0)(3,2.5)
  \logic[logicType=nor,
    logicShowNode]{NOR1}
\end{pspicture}
```

```
\usepackage{pstricks,pst-circ}

\begin{pspicture}(-1,0)(3,4)
  \logic[logicType=nor,logicShowNode,
    logicWidth=2,logicHeight=4,
    logicNInput=6,
    logicChangeLR](0,0){NOR3}
\end{pspicture}
```

24.4.5 Not

```
\usepackage{pstricks,pst-circ}

\begin{pspicture}(-1,0)(3,2.5)
  \logic[logicType=not,
    logicShowNode]{NOT1}
\end{pspicture}
```

```
\usepackage{pstricks,pst-circ}

\begin{pspicture}(-1,0)(3,1.5)
  \logic[logicType=not,
    logicShowNode,
    logicWidth=1,logicHeight=1.5,
    logicChangeLR](0,0){NOT3}
\end{pspicture}
```

24.4.6 Exclusive OR

```
\usepackage{pstricks,pst-circ}

\begin{pspicture}(-1,0)(3,2.5)
  \logic[logicType=exor,
    logicShowNode]{ExOR1}
\end{pspicture}
```

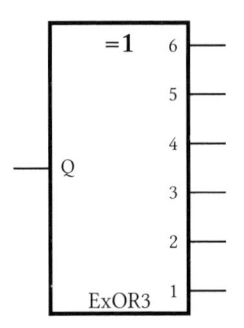

```
\usepackage{pstricks,pst-circ}

\begin{pspicture}(-1,0)(3,4)
    \logic[logicType=exor,logicShowNode,
        logicNInput=6,logicWidth=2,
        logicHeight=4,
        logicChangeLR](0,0){ExOR3}
\end{pspicture}
```

24.4.7 Exclusive NOR

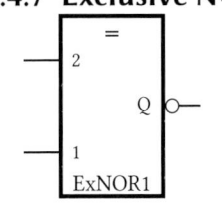

```
\usepackage{pstricks,pst-circ}

\begin{pspicture}(-1,0)(3,2.5)
    \logic[logicType=exnor,
        logicShowNode]{ExNOR1}
\end{pspicture}
```

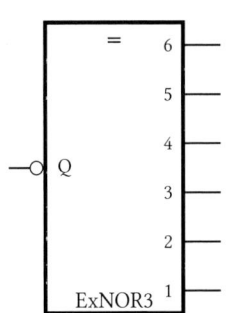

```
\usepackage{pstricks,pst-circ}

\begin{pspicture}(-1,0)(3,4)
    \logic[logicType=exnor,logicShowNode,
        logicNInput=6,logicWidth=2,
        logicHeight=4,
        logicChangeLR](0,0){ExNOR3}
\end{pspicture}
```

24.4.8 RS Flip Flop

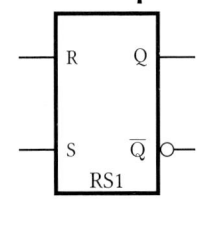

```
\usepackage{pstricks,pst-circ}

\begin{pspicture}(-1,0)(3,2.25)
    \logic[logicShowNode,
        logicType=RS]{RS1}
\end{pspicture}
```

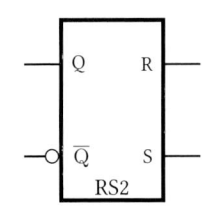

```
\usepackage{pstricks,pst-circ}

\begin{pspicture}(-1,0)(3,2.25)
    \logic[logicShowNode,
        logicType=RS,logicChangeLR]{RS2}
\end{pspicture}
```

24.4.9 D Flip Flop

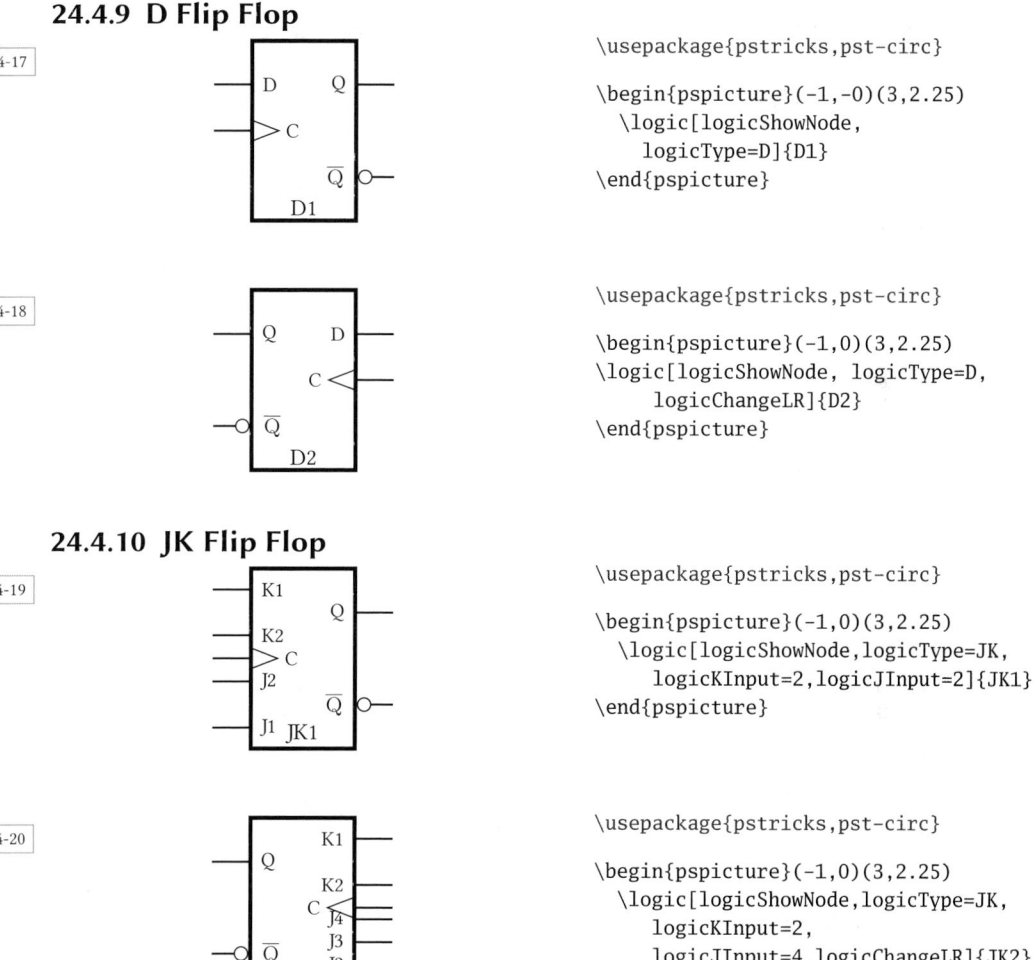

```
\usepackage{pstricks,pst-circ}

\begin{pspicture}(-1,-0)(3,2.25)
  \logic[logicShowNode,
     logicType=D]{D1}
\end{pspicture}
```

```
\usepackage{pstricks,pst-circ}

\begin{pspicture}(-1,0)(3,2.25)
\logic[logicShowNode, logicType=D,
     logicChangeLR]{D2}
\end{pspicture}
```

24.4.10 JK Flip Flop

```
\usepackage{pstricks,pst-circ}

\begin{pspicture}(-1,0)(3,2.25)
  \logic[logicShowNode,logicType=JK,
     logicKInput=2,logicJInput=2]{JK1}
\end{pspicture}
```

```
\usepackage{pstricks,pst-circ}

\begin{pspicture}(-1,0)(3,2.25)
  \logic[logicShowNode,logicType=JK,
     logicKInput=2,
     logicJInput=4,logicChangeLR]{JK2}
\end{pspicture}
```

24.4.11 The node names

Each gate is defined with a unique name internally by appending the connection numbers to the unique element name. For the example below these would be:

NAND11, NAND12, NAND13, NAND14, NAND1Q

If the output is negated, as with almost all flip-flops, `pst-circ` automatically amends the node name with *neg*:

NAND1Q, NAND1Qneg

The internal definition of the nodes means that you can use them afterwards to place objects or create arbitrary connections, as in the following example where red dots are placed at each node.

24 pst-circ – Creation of circuits

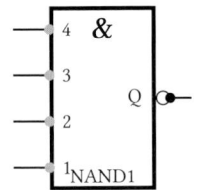

```
\usepackage{pstricks,pst-circ,multido}

\begin{pspicture}(-0.5,0)(3,2.5)
  \logic[logicShowNode,logicLabelstyle=\footnotesize,
    logicType=nand,logicNInput=4]{NAND1}
  \multido{\n=1+1}{4}{%
    \pscircle*[linecolor=red](NAND1\n){2pt}}
  \pscircle*[linecolor=blue](NAND1Q){2pt}
\end{pspicture}
```

24.5 Examples

```
\usepackage{pstricks,pst-circ}
\begin{pspicture}(-1,0)(5,5)
  \psset{logicType=nor,logicLabelstyle=\normalsize,
      logicWidth=1,logicHeight=1.5,dotsize=0.15}
  \logic(1.5,0){nor1} \logic(1.5,3){nor2}
  \psline(nor2Q)(4,0|nor2Q) \uput[0](4,0|nor2Q){$Q$}
  \psline(nor1Q)(4,0|nor1Q) \uput[0](4,0|nor1Q){$\overline{Q}$}
  \psline{*-}(3.50,0|nor2Q)(3.5,2.5)(1.5,2.5)(0.5,1.75)(0.5,0|nor12)(nor12)
  \psline{*-}(3.50,0|nor1Q)(3.5,2)(1.5,2)(0.5,2.5)(0.5,0|nor21)(nor21)
  \psline(0,0|nor11)(nor11)\uput[180](0,0|nor11){R}
  \psline(0,0|nor22)(nor22)\uput[180](0,0|nor22){S}
\end{pspicture}
```

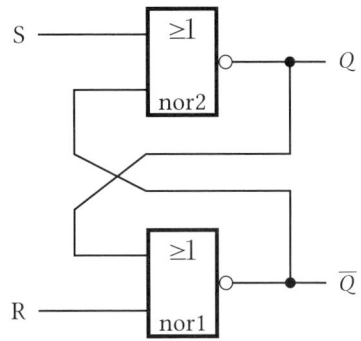

```
\usepackage{pstricks,pst-circ}
\begin{pspicture}(-4,0)(5,7)
  \psset{logicWidth=1,logicHeight=1.4,dotsize=0.15}
  \logic[logicWireLength=0](-2,0.75){A0}  \logic[logicWireLength=0](-2,4.7){A1}
  \ncbar[angleA=-180,angleB=-180,arm=0.5]{A11}{A02}
  \psline[dotsize=0.15]{-*}(-3.5,3.5)(-2.5,3.5) \uput[180](-3.5,3.5){$T$}
  \psline(-3.5,0|A01)(A01)  \uput[180](-3.5,0|A01){$S$}
  \psline(-3.5,0|A12)(A12)  \uput[180](-3.5,0|A02){$R$}
  \psset{logicType=nor, logicLabelstyle=\normalsize}
```

24.5 Examples

```
    \logic(1,1.1){nor1}   \logic(1,4.35){nor2}
    \psline(nor2Q)(4,0|nor2Q)   \uput[0](4,0|nor2Q){$Q$}
    \psline(nor1Q)(4,0|nor1Q)   \uput[0](4,0|nor1Q){$\overline{Q}$}
    \psline{*-}(3,0|nor2Q)(3,4)(1,4)(0,3)(0,0|nor12)(nor12)
    \psline{*-}(3,0|nor1Q)(3,3)(1,3)(0,4)(0,0|nor21)(nor21)
    \psline(A0Q)(nor11)   \psline(A1Q)(nor22)
\end{pspicture}
```

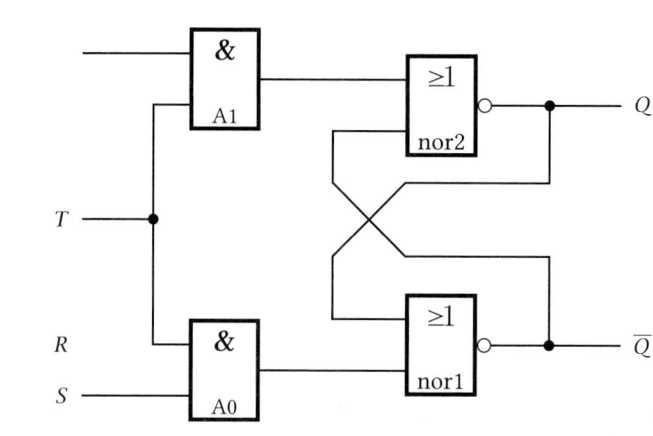

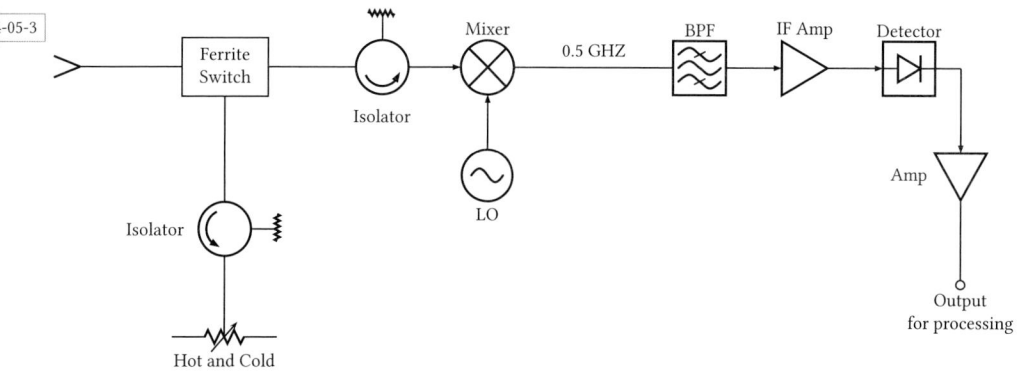

Figure 24.2: Radiometer block diagram (François Boone)

24 pst-circ – Creation of circuits

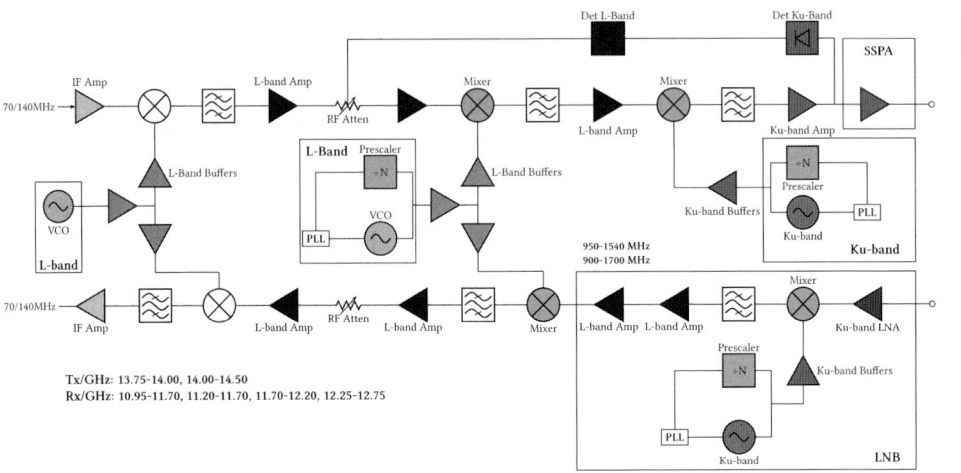

Figure 24.3: Ku band receiver (François Boone)

Chapter 25

pst-geo – Geographic projections

25.1 Installation	466
25.2 Parameters	467
25.3 pst-map2d	476
25.4 pst-map3d	478
25.5 pst-map2dII	487
25.6 pst-map3dII	489
25.7 \mapput and \pnodeMap	491
25.8 Examples	494

pst-geo makes it possible to create many different geographic projections of the earth or parts thereof. There is a fundamental problem, however, with getting coordinates for continents, countries, rivers, etc. as there are only two different databases on the internet that contain more or less all the data of the earth as polylines. The more extensive is the "CIA World DataBank II" (http://www.evl.uic.edu/pape/data/WDB/).The DataBank website states:

> "The CIA World DataBank II is a collection of world map data, consisting of vector descriptions of land outlines, rivers, and political boundaries. It was created by the U.S. government in the 1980s. A highly compressed binary version of the data has been available on the Internet from several sources, but the format of this data is a bit complex and not well documented except by some example C code. Given the continual increase in hard disk sizes and network bandwidth, it's not as vital now to compress the data so much, so I have created plain text versions that are easier to use."

The advantage of this database is also its disadvantage: the amount of data leads to very big PDF files. Unfortunately there is no logical hierarchy for the polylines, so you can't limit the selection of points.

25 pst-geo – Geographic projections

The other data source was at `ftp://ftp.blm.gov/pub/gis/wdbprg.zip`, but is now no longer available online. The disadvantage of this database is that it is only available in encoded format. For `pst-geo`, this database has already been converted into PostScript-compatible data structures and can be used with `pst-geo`. The theoretical background can be found in [74].

`pst-geo` isn't a package name in the normal sense, but actually comprises four packages, each of which achieves different tasks. All of them can display the geographic coordinates of the earth in many different ways. The CTAN: `graphics/pstricks/contrib/pst-geo` directory contains the following files and folders:

```
data . . . . . . . . . . . . . . 2009-08-31
dataII . . . . . . . . . . . . . 2009-08-31
doc. . . . . . . . . . . . . . . 2009-08-31
examples2d . . . . . . . . . . . 2004-05-18
examples3d . . . . . . . . . . . 2008-07-23
pst-map2d.sty. . . . . . . . . . 2007-12-23    1k
pst-map2d.tex. . . . . . . . . . 2009-08-28    11k
pst-map2dII.sty. . . . . . . . . 2007-12-23    1k
pst-map2dII.tex. . . . . . . . . 2009-08-28    14k
pst-map3d.sty. . . . . . . . . . 2007-12-23    1k
pst-map3.pro . . . . . . . . . . 2009-08-11    6k
pst-map3d.tex. . . . . . . . . . 2009-08-28    5k
pst-map3dII.sty. . . . . . . . . 2007-12-23    1k
pst-map3dII.pro. . . . . . . . . 2007-12-23    6k
pst-map3dII.tex. . . . . . . . . 2009-08-28    7k
```

This comprises the four packages (as listed below), each with a TEX-compatible form and a LATEX wrapper file, plus two PostScript prologue (header) files and five more directories.

▷ `pst-map2d` – two-dimensional projection and small database
▷ `pst-map3d` – three-dimensional projection and small database
▷ `pst-map2dII` – two-dimensional projection and big database
▷ `pst-map3dII` – three-dimensional projection and big database

25.1 Installation

The installation of the packages can be done with the structure given above; you have to copy the PostScript-specific prologue files into one of the directories designated for them:[1]

`$TEXMF/dvips/pstricks/`
`$TEXMFLOCAL/dvips/pstricks/`

Only use the local directory if installing `pst-geo` after the installation of the distribution. The two data directories `data` and `dataII` contain compressed files. Programs for decompressing files are available for all operating systems.

---

[1] Depending on the TEX distribution, other directories are possible, too.

25.2 Parameters

Table 25.1 lists the parameters that are available for several or all packages of the `pst-geo` series. The individual parameters are dealt with in the following sections. The continents are always referred to by the the names listed in Table 25.2.

Table 25.1: Summary of the available parameters for the `pst-map2d` package

name	type	default	meaning
path	path	data	path to the database directory
level	value	5	precision
type	1...8	1	map projection method
n	value	1.77245	aspect ratio (for Collignon projection)
limiteL	angle	180	maximum longitude
longitude0	angle	0	reference longitude (for Bonne projection)
latitude0	angle	45	reference latitude (for Bonne projection)
increment	angle	10	difference between the longitudes in degrees
maillage	boolean	true	show longitude and latitude lines
MapFillColor	colour triple	[rgb]{0.99 0.95 0.7}	RGB colour of the continents
Fill	boolean	true	colour land and water
capitals	boolean	false	show capitals
city	boolean	false	show towns
rivers	boolean	true	show rivers
borders	boolean	false	show borders
mapCountry	name	all	country to show towns in
nodeWidth	value unit	1 mm	diameter of the place symbol

europe	Europe and North Pole	asia	Asia and Australia	
africa	Africa and South Pole	namer	North America	
samer	South America	all	all continents	

Table 25.2: Short name for the available continents

25.2.1 path

The `path` parameter is important as it only gets its meaning at PostScript level and therefore can't be found through the TEX file structure. `path` therefore **must** be set correctly for output to occur because the files are only read and processed when the PostScript output or PostScript program is started. This means on one hand that the PostScript file cannot be passed around between different computers because it is useless without the data and on the other hand that corresponding PDF files are several times larger than the PostScript/DVI files because they save the data internally. The advantage is of course that the PDF file can be transferred without the separate data file.

The path has to be relative to the location of the document, or absolute when the PostScript file is called by GhostScript because PostScript doesn't use the TEX directory structure.

Its safest either to set an absolute path or to embed all the data into the TeX document.

```
\usepackage{pstricks,pst-map2d}

\psset{path=pst-geo/data,
    unit=0.25,linewidth=0.1pt,
    rivers=false,increment=25}
\begin{pspicture*}(-9,-9)(10,9)
    \WorldMap[maillage=false]
\end{pspicture*}
```

 With some PostScript to PDF converters you must take care which parameters they use to call GhostScript – if the -dSAFER option is used, problems can arise. This is the case for example for ps2pdfwr, which is used by all ps2pdf versions.

-dSAFER   Disables the "deletefile" and "renamefile" operators and the ability to open files in any mode other than read-only. This is strongly recommended for spoolers, conversion scripts, or other sensitive environments where a badly-written or malicious PostScript program code must be prevented from changing important files.

Even if to open the data files only a *read* is done through (r) file, there can be problems depending on the GhostScript version. Commenting -dSAFER-Option can help if you do get problems. Alternatively you can run GhostScript by hand where <file.pdf> and <file.ps> should be replaced with the real file name:

`gs -q -dNOSAFER ... -sDEVICE=pdfwrite -sOutputFile=<file.pdf> -c .setpdfwrite -f <file.`

25.2.2 level

level sets the precision of the polylines; all positive integers are possible, with lower values increasing precision. With level=10 only about every tenth value is taken into account (though the start and endpoint are always included). The advantages and disadvantages are clear – precise borders or fast calculations; it's up to you to decide on a case-by-case basis which is more important. The following example is the same as the previous one, except for level=5. At this scale the maps look pretty similar, but for larger scales you can distinguish differences between the levels.

```
\usepackage{pstricks,pst-map2d}

\psset{path=pst-geo/data,
    unit=0.25,linewidth=0.1pt,
    rivers=false,
    increment=25}
\begin{pspicture*}(-9,-9)(10,9)
    \WorldMap[level=5,maillage=false]
\end{pspicture*}
```

25.2.3 type

There are several different methods for projecting three-dimensional spherical coordinates onto a two-dimensional Cartesian coordinate system. With the type option, you can choose from eight different projections, as listed in Table 25.3. Each method is briefly discussed below.

type	meaning	type	meaning
1	Mercator	5	cylindric
2	simple Lambert projection	6	Babinet
3	Lambert	7	Collignon
4	Sanson-Flamsteed	8	Bonne

Table 25.3: Summary of the projection methods

Mercator projection

The Mercator projection, named after Gerardus Mercator (1512–1594), is used most frequently, because the *loxodromes*[2] are straight lines after being projected. The x axis corresponds to the equator and the y axis to a longitude θ_0. The problem with the Mercator projection is the considerable distortion of areas in the far north and south of the map. The transformation equations are:

$$x = \theta - \theta_0$$

$$y = \ln\left(\tan\left(\frac{1}{4}\pi + \frac{1}{2}\phi\right)\right) \quad (25.1)$$

$$= \frac{1}{2}\ln\left(\frac{1+\sin\phi}{1-\sin\phi}\right) \quad (25.2)$$

$$= \tanh^{-1}(\tan\phi) \quad (25.3)$$

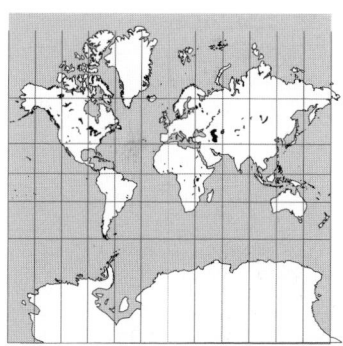

```
\usepackage{pstricks,pst-map2d}

\psset{path=pst-geo/data,
    unit=0.25,linewidth=0.1pt,
    rivers=false,increment=30}
\begin{pspicture*}(-10,-9)(10,9)
    \WorldMap[level=5,type=1]
\end{pspicture*}
```

Simple Lambert projection

The German cartographer Johann Heinrich Lambert (1728–1777) creating the first map of the earth that retained the rectangular form of the Mercator maps while presenting a faithful representation of sizes. This advantage brings with it two disadvantages: the "towel form"

---

[2] A loxodrome (Greek "slant way") connects two points on a sphere such that it always intersects with the meridians at the same angle.

(height to width = 1:3) and the contortion of Europe. In the simplified version of the projection latitudes and longitudes form squares of equal size; this is not the case for the full Lambert projection as shown below.

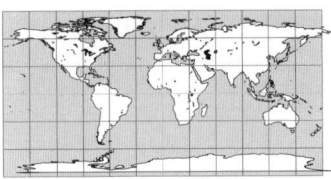

```
\usepackage{pstricks,pst-map2d}

\psset{path=pst-geo/data,
    unit=0.25,linewidth=0.1pt,
    rivers=false,increment=30}
\begin{pspicture*}(-10,-5)(10,5)
    \WorldMap[level=5,type=2]
\end{pspicture*}
```

Lambert projection

The transformation equations are:

$$x = \theta - \theta_0 \qquad\qquad y = \sin\phi \qquad (25.4)$$

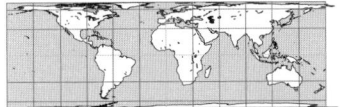

```
\usepackage{pstricks,pst-map2d}

\psset{path=pst-geo/data,
    unit=0.25,linewidth=0.1pt,
    rivers=false,increment=30}
\begin{pspicture*}(-10,-5)(10,5)
    \WorldMap[level=5,type=3]
\end{pspicture*}
```

Sanson–Flamsteed projection

This projection was developed from drafts from the inheritance of Mercator either by the French cartographer Nicolas Sanson (1600–1667) or by the English cartographer John Flamsteed (1646–1719), though most likely in fact by Mercator himself. The onion-shaped map depicts sizes faithfully, but the countries and continents outside the equator zone are heavily contorted. Abandoning the rectangular form of the map means that we lose the perpendicular representation of the north-south direction. The transformation equations are:

$$x = R \times \theta \times \cos\phi \qquad\qquad y = R \times \phi \qquad (25.5)$$

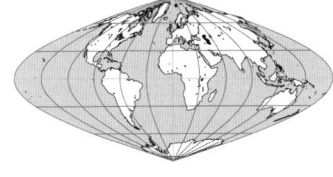

```
\usepackage{pstricks,pst-map2d}

\psset{path=pst-geo/data,
    unit=0.25,linewidth=0.1pt,
    rivers=false,increment=30}
\begin{pspicture*}(-10,-5)(10,5)
    \WorldMap[level=5,type=4]
\end{pspicture*}
```

Cylindric projection

The cylindric projection has the simplest transformation equations, but also severe defects in the representation.

$$x = \theta - \theta_0 \qquad\qquad y = \tan\phi \qquad (25.6)$$

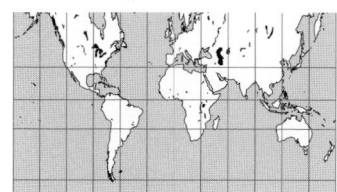

```
\usepackage{pstricks,pst-map2d}

\psset{path=pst-geo/data,
    unit=0.25,linewidth=0.1pt,
    rivers=false,increment=30}
\begin{pspicture*}(-10,-5)(10,5)
    \WorldMap[level=5,type=5]
\end{pspicture*}
```

Babinet projection

This oval map of the earth, which is faithful to sizes, is named after French scientist Jacques Babinet (1794–1872) but was actually created by the German cartographer Ernst Hammer (1858–1929). Again abandoning the rectangular form results in the loss of the perpendicular north-south direction, and bends the latitude circles: everything outside Europe and Africa is heavily contorted.

$$z = \sqrt{1 - \frac{x^2}{16} - \frac{y^2}{4}} \qquad \theta = 2 \times \tan^{-1}\left(\frac{2(2x^2 - 1)}{x}\right) \qquad (25.7)$$

$$\phi = \sin^{-1} xz \qquad (25.8)$$

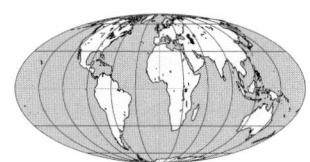

```
\usepackage{pstricks,pst-map2d}

\psset{path=pst-geo/data,
    unit=0.25,linewidth=0.1pt,
    rivers=false,increment=30}
\begin{pspicture*}(-9,-5)(10,5)
    \WorldMap[level=5,type=6]
\end{pspicture*}
```

Collignon projection

This projection method by Édouard Collignon (1831–1897) was published in 1865 and is a triangular form of the earth with heavy contortion at the edges. It represents sizes faithfully, however.

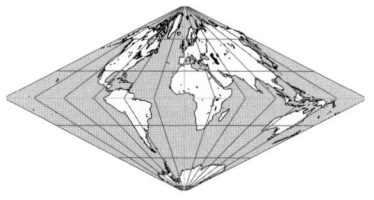

```
\usepackage{pstricks,pst-map2d}

\psset{path=pst-geo/data,
    unit=0.25,linewidth=0.1pt,
    rivers=false,increment=30}
\begin{pspicture*}(-10,-5)(10,5)
    \WorldMap[level=5,type=7]
\end{pspicture*}
```

Bonne projection

This projection, named after the Frenchman Rigobert Bonne (1727–1795), was in fact in use much earlier (around 1500). It also depicts sizes faithfully, but has heavy contortions. It was very popular in the past for large topographic diagrams.

$$x = (\cot \phi_1 + \phi_1 - \phi) \times \sin E \qquad (25.9)$$
$$y = \cot \phi_1 - (\cot \phi_1 + \phi_1 - \phi) \times \cos E \qquad (25.10)$$
$$E = \frac{(\theta - \theta_0) \cos \phi}{\cot \phi_1 + \phi_1 - \phi} \qquad (25.11)$$

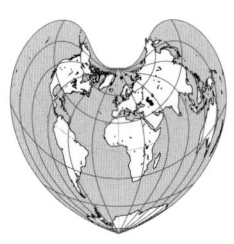

```
\usepackage{pstricks,pst-map2d}

\psset{path=pst-geo/data,
    unit=0.25,linewidth=0.1pt,rivers=false,
    increment=30}
\begin{pspicture*}(-10,-10)(10,3)
    \WorldMap[level=5,type=8]
\end{pspicture*}
```

25.2.4 n

n affects the output for the Collignon projection, controlling the ratio of height to width. The default value of 1.77425 corresponds to $\sqrt{\pi}$.

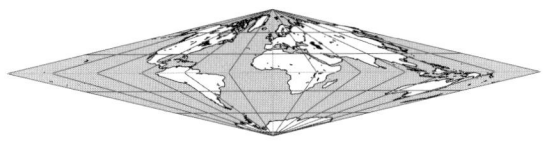

```
\usepackage{pstricks,pst-map2d}

\psset{path=pst-geo/data,unit=0.25,
    linewidth=0.1pt,
    rivers=false,increment=30}
\begin{pspicture*}(-15,-4)(15,4)
    \WorldMap[level=5,type=7,n=1.2]
\end{pspicture*}
```

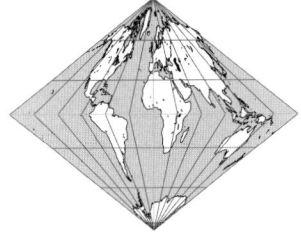

```
\usepackage{pstricks,pst-map2d}

\psset{path=pst-geo/data,
    unit=0.25,linewidth=0.1pt,
    rivers=false,increment=30}
\begin{pspicture*}(-10,-7)(10,7)
    \WorldMap[level=5,type=7,n=2.2]
\end{pspicture*}
```

25.2.5 limiteL

limiteL specifies the value up to which to calculate and draw the longitude lines. The specification refers to the symmetric representation ±limiteL.

25.2 Parameters

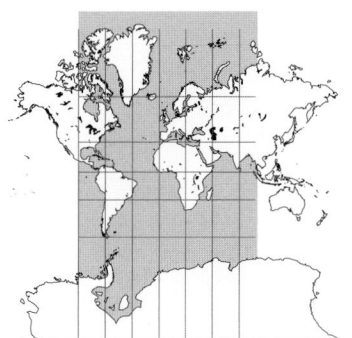

```
\usepackage{pstricks,pst-map2d}

\psset{path=pst-geo/data,
  unit=0.25,linewidth=0.1pt,
  rivers=false,increment=30}
\begin{pspicture*}(-10,-9)(10,9)
  \WorldMap[level=5,limiteL=100]
\end{pspicture*}
```

25.2.6 longitude0 and latitude0

longitude0 and latitude0 specify the perception (or viewing angle) from which the output of the Bonne projection is created. The default values are longitude0=0 and latitude0=45.

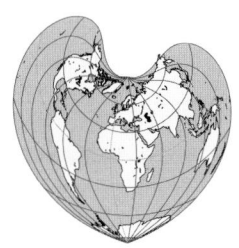

```
\usepackage{pstricks,pst-map2d}

\psset{path=pst-geo/data,
  unit=0.25,linewidth=0.1pt,
  rivers=false,increment=30}
\begin{pspicture*}(-10,-10)(10,3)
  \WorldMap[level=5,type=8,
    longitude0=20]
\end{pspicture*}
```

25.2.7 increment and maillage

increment specifies the angle step between the drawn latitude and longitude lines. maillage=false suppresses all latitude and longitude lines from being output.

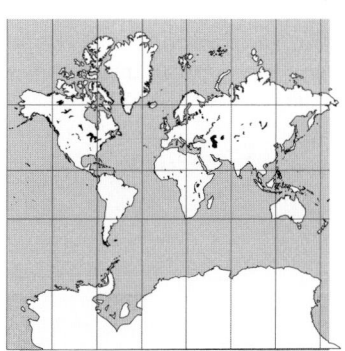

```
\usepackage{pstricks,pst-map2d}

\psset{path=pst-geo/data,
  unit=0.25,linewidth=0.1pt,rivers=false}
\begin{pspicture*}(-10,-9)(10,9)
  \WorldMap[level=5,increment=50]
\end{pspicture*}
```

473

25 pst-geo – Geographic projections

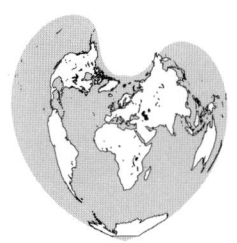

```
\usepackage{pstricks,pst-map2d}

\psset{path=pst-geo/data,
   unit=0.25,linewidth=0.1pt,rivers=false,
   increment=30}
\begin{pspicture*}(-10,-10)(10,3)
   \WorldMap[level=5,type=8,longitude0=20,%
      maillage=false]
\end{pspicture*}
```

25.2.8 MapFillColor

MapFillColor specifies the fill colour of the continents; you have to assign it an RGB triple separated by spaces.

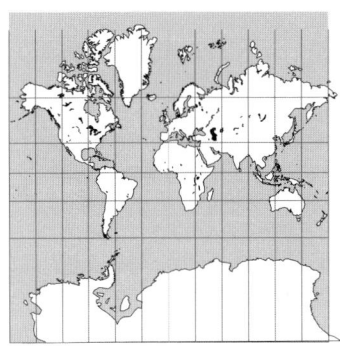

```
\usepackage{pstricks,pst-map2d}

\psset{path=pst-geo/data,
   unit=0.25,linewidth=0.1pt,rivers=false,
   increment=30}
\begin{pspicture*}(-10,-9)(10,9)
   \WorldMap[level=5,
      MapFillColor={[rgb]{0.98 0.98 0.9}}]
\end{pspicture*}
```

25.2.9 Fill

Fill=false inhibits the fill; by default it is set to true.

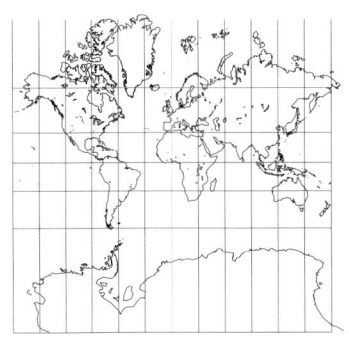

```
\usepackage{pstricks,pst-map2d}

\psset{path=pst-geo/data,
   unit=0.25,linewidth=0.1pt,
   rivers=false,increment=30}
\begin{pspicture*}(-10,-9)(10,9)
   \WorldMap[level=5,Fill=false]
\end{pspicture*}
```

25.2.10 capitals and city

capitals and city are switches to draw the capitals and other big cities and towns. Both are set to false by default. The diameter of the points, set to 3pt, can't be changed in the current version.

25.2 Parameters

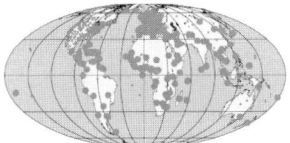

```
\usepackage{pstricks,pst-map2d}

\psset{path=pst-geo/data,linewidth=0.1pt,
    unit=0.3,rivers=false,increment=30}
\begin{pspicture*}(-8.2,-4)(8.2,4)
    \WorldMap[level=5,type=6,capital=true,
        city=true,dotscale=0.25]
\end{pspicture*}
```

25.2.11 rivers and borders

rivers is set to true by default, whereas borders is set to false. Beware of the display becoming cluttered if you set both options to true.

```
\usepackage{pstricks,pst-map2d}

\psset{path=pst-geo/data,unit=0.3,
    linewidth=0.1pt,increment=30}
\begin{pspicture*}(-8.2,-4)(8.2,4)
    \WorldMap[level=5,type=6,
        rivers=false,borders=true]
\end{pspicture*}
```

25.2.12 mapCountry

The mapCountry limits the drawing of town symbols and names to particular countries. However, this only works with the cities.tex file, because it contains the corresponding country for every town. Because of the large number of saved cities, it isn't always easy to achieve automatically the correct placement of the towns with symbol and name – usually manual intervention is required. In the following figure all American cities have been drawn without manual postprocessing so you can see the poor result obtained by automatic placement.

```
\usepackage{pstricks,pst-map2d}
\psset{path=pst-geo/data,level=1,unit=12}
\begin{pspicture*}(-4.3,1.25)(-3.5,2.5)
 \WorldMap[rivers=true,USA=true,maillage=true]
 \def\psNodeLabelStyle{\scriptsize} \psset{mapCountry=USA,nodeWidth=0.5mm}
 \input{cities.tex}
\end{pspicture*}
```

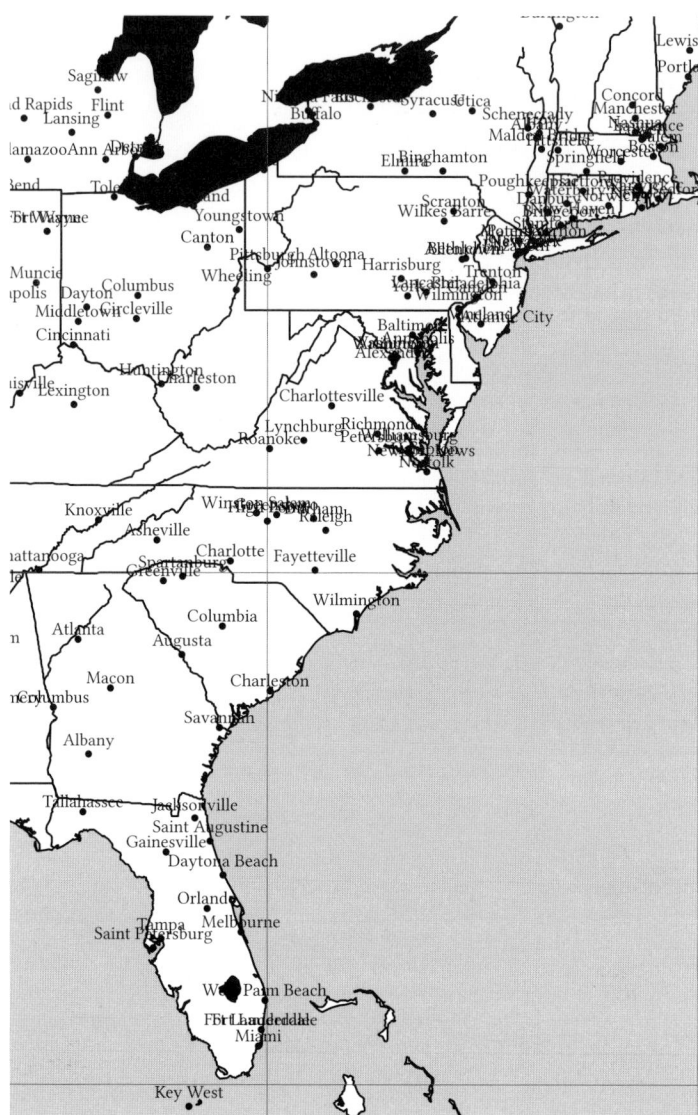

25.3 `pst-map2d`

This package supports all possibilities for two-dimensional projections and is furthermore able to produce relatively small PDF output files with the appropriate parameters. It provides three commands with the following syntax:

25.3 pst-map2d

\WorldMap [settings]
\pnodeMap [settings]
\mapput{distance}[angle](node){text}

\mapput and \pnodeMap are discussed in detail in Section 25.7 on page 491.

25.3.1 Additional parameters

All of the parameters described in the previous section are valid, but there are a few other additional ones available. These are switches that let you specify a certain country (the US, Mexico, or Australia) for drawing, with state boundaries included. This only makes sense if an appropriate unit value for the pspicture* environment has been chosen.

name	type	default	meaning
USA	boolean	false	show USA
AUS	boolean	false	show Australia
MEX	boolean	false	show Mexico

Table 25.4: Summary of the additional parameters for pst-map2d

```
\usepackage{pstricks,pst-map2d}
\psset{path=pst-geo/data,unit=3.7,linewidth=.75pt}
\begin{pspicture*}(-6.5,1)(-3,3)
   \WorldMap[rivers=true,city=true,USA=true,maillage=true]
\end{pspicture*}
```

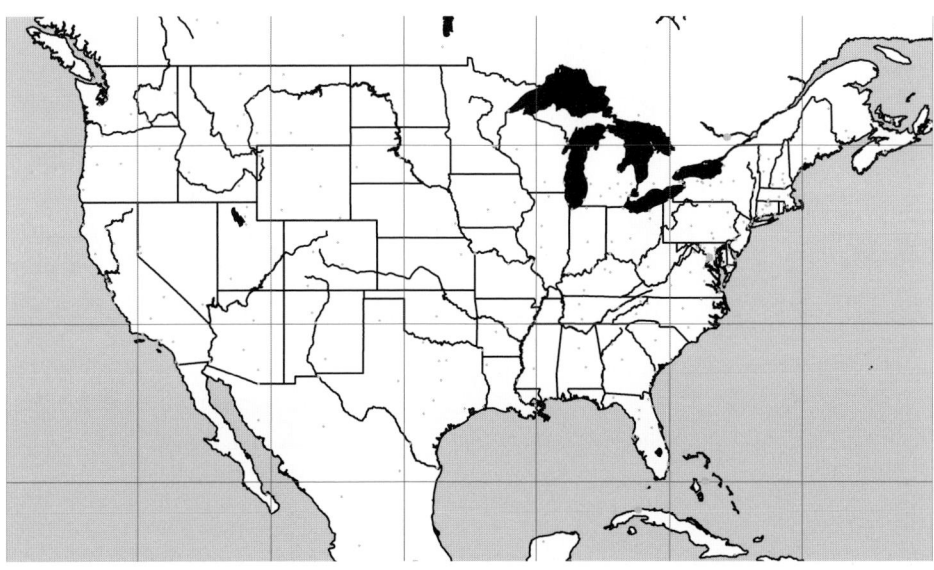

477

25.4 pst-map3d

This package differs from pst-map2d only in that it produces three-dimensional output; this affects some of the parameters however, as detailed below. Several commands are provided with the following syntax:

```
\WorldMapThreeD [settings]
\psGlobeTellure [settings] (longitude,latitude){text}
\psmeridien [settings] {longitude}
\psparallel [settings] {latitude}
\psepicenter [settings] (longitude,latitude)
```

Examples can be found in Section 25.4.2 on page 481.

25.4.1 Parameters

Table 25.5 lists the parameters that are available for the packages of the pst-geo series that produce three-dimensional output. Examples for path, increment, MapFillColor, capitals, city, borders, and maillage were given above in Section 25.2 on page 467. The other parameters are discussed in turn in the following sections.

Table 25.5: Summary of the available parameters for pst-map3d

name	type	default	meaning
path	path	data	path to the database directory
RotX	angle	0	rotation about the x axis
RotY	angle	0	rotation about the y axis
RotZ	angle	0	rotation about the z axis
THETA	angle	0	rotation angle of the coordinate system
PHI	value	45	tilting angle of the coordinate system
Dobs	value	20	centric image distance
Decran	value	25	parallel image distance (scaling factor)
Radius	value	5	earth radius
level	value	5	precision
Day	value	\day	day as a number for \psGlobeTellure
Month	value	\month	month as a number for \psGlobeTellure
Year	year	\year	year as a 4 digit number for \psGlobeTellure
hour	value	12	hour as a number for \psGlobeTellure

continued...

... continued

name	type	default	meaning
increment	angle	10	difference between longitudes in degrees
MapFillColor	colour triple	0.99 0.95 0.7	RGB colour of the continents
capitals	boolean	false	show capitals
capital	boolean	false	show capital
city	boolean	false	show towns
borders	boolean	false	show borders
maillage	boolean	true	show latitude and longitude lines
islands	boolean	true	show islands
borders	boolean	true	show borders
france	boolean	false	show France
capitals	boolean	true	show capitals
usa	boolean	false	show USA
mexico	boolean	false	show Mexico
australia	boolean	false	show Australia
canada	boolean	false	show Canada
citys	boolean	false	show cities
rivers	boolean	true	show rivers
lakes	boolean	true	show lakes
gridmap	boolean	true	gridmap
coasts	boolean	false	show coasts
wfraczon	boolean	false	show fraction zone lines
ridge	boolean	false	show ridge
wmaglin	boolean	false	show maglin lines
circles	boolean	true	show circles
visibility	boolean	true	visibility
blueEarth	boolean	true	plot aarth in blue
daynight	boolean	false	show earth in day–night light
gridmapdiv	value	10	angle increment of a grid
longitudeMeridien	value	0	longitude angle of a meridian
meridienwidth	value unit	1pt	linewidth of a meridien
meridiencolor	colour	red	colour of a meridien
latitudeParallel	value	0	latitude angle
parallelwidth	value unit	1pt	linewidth of a parallel line
parallelcolor	colour	red	line colour of a parallel line
mapcolor	colour	terre	map colour
bordercolor	colour	black	border colour
islandcolor	colour	black	island colour
coastcolor	colour	black	coast color
oceancolor	colour	mer	ocean colour

continued...

... continued

name	type	default	meaning
rivercolor	colour	blue	river colour
wfraczoncolor	colour	red	fraction zone colour
wmaglincolor	colour	darkblue	maglin colour
ridgecolor	colour	red	ridge colour
transfrmcolor	colour	orange	transform colour
trenchcolor	colour	darggreen	trench colour
gridmapcolor	colour	black	gridmap colour
circlecolor	colour	blue	circle colour
circlesep	value	2	circle separation in degrees
circlewidth	value unit	0.5pt	circle linewidth
gridmapwidth	value unit	0.8pt	gridmap linewidth
borderwidth	value unit	0.8pt	border linewidth
coastwidth	value unit	0.8pt	coast linewidth
wfraczonwidth	value unit	0.8pt	fraction zone linewidth
wmaglinwidth	value unit	0.8pt	maglin linewidth
ridgewidth	value unit	2pt	ridgewidth

RotX, RotY, and RotZ

These parameters specify the additional rotation about the respective axis and correspond in their behaviour to the parameters described in Chapter 23.6 on page 391.

```
\usepackage{pstricks,pst-map3d}
\psset{unit=0.5,path=pst-geo/data}
\begin{pspicture}(-7,-7)(7,7) \WorldMapThreeD \end{pspicture}\quad
\begin{pspicture}(-7,-7)(7,7) \WorldMapThreeD[RotX=10,RotY=-40]
\end{pspicture}
```

THETA, PHI, Dobs, and Decran

These parameters refer exclusively to the type of the three-dimensional projection and have all been explained in Chapter 23.6 on page 391.

Radius

`Radius` specifies the radius of the earth in the current unit.

opacity

You can use the `opacity` parameter in order to be able to see the other half of the earth through a semi-transparent globe, as in the example below. Data for the latitude and longitude of a certain place is easily found on the internet, as here for Berlin at $P(13.297, 52.5222)$.

```
\usepackage{pstricks,pst-map3d}
\begin{pspicture}(-4,-4)(4,4)
\psset{RotX=-23,RotZ=30,PHI=46.5833,THETA=0.3333,
   visibility=false,Decran=15,path=pst-geo/data}
\WorldMapThreeD[circles=false,blueEarth=false]
\WorldMapThreeD[circles=false,visibility=true,opacity=0.7]
\psmeridien[visibility=true]{13.297}
\psparallel[visibility=true]{52.5222}
\mapputIIID(13.297,52.5222){Berlin}
\end{pspicture}
```

25-04-2

25.4.2 Examples

Using the `\psGlobeTellure` command and a specification of date and time, you can achieve an output showing day and night for a specific time interval.

25 pst-geo – Geographic projections

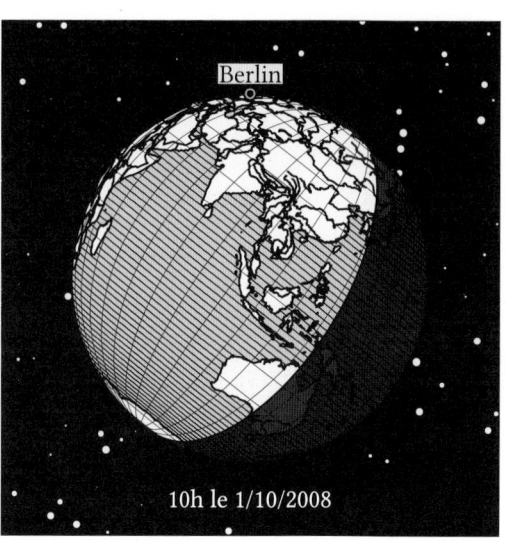

10h le 1/10/2008

```
\usepackage{pst-map3d}

\definecolor{BlueDark}{cmyk}{1,1,0,0.5}
\newpsstyle{Globe}{circles=true,
    gridmap=true,daynight=false}
\newpsstyle{night}{fillstyle=solid,
    fillcolor=BlueDark,linecolor=BlueDark,
    opacity=0.8}
\psset{Radius=5,Decran=100,Dobs=100,
    unit=0.5,path=pst-geo/data}
\begin{pspicture}(-7,-7)(7,7)
\psframe*[linecolor=BlueDark](-7,-7)(7,7)
\psRandomStar[linecolor=yellow!50,
    randomPoints=100](-7,-7)(7,7){%
        \psframe(-7,-7)(7,7)}
\psGlobeTellure[hour=10,Day=1,Month=10,
    Year=2008](13.297,52.5222){Berlin}
\end{pspicture}
```

You can set the maximum radius of the circles in km through Rmax and the number of circles through waves.

```
\usepackage{pstricks,pst-map3d}
\begin{pspicture*}(-0.5\linewidth,-0.45\textheight)(0.5\linewidth,0.5\textheight)
\psset{PHI=45,THETA=5,unit=7.5,path=pst-geo/data}
\WorldMapThreeD[lakes=false,circlesep=0.25,gridmap=false,coasts=false,
    mapcolor={[cmyk]{0.7,0,0.6,0.2}},bordercolor=red,rivers=false,islandcolor=blue]
\WorldMapThreeD[gridmapcolor=yellow,circles=false,lakes=true,gridmapdiv=5,france=true,
    islandcolor=blue,blueEarth=false,bordercolor=red,islands=false,borders=false,
    rivers=true,coasts=true,coastcolor=blue]
\psmeridien{13.30}\psparallel{52.52}
\newpsstyle{NodeLabelStyle}{fillstyle=solid,fillcolor=yellow!50,framesep=0,
    linestyle=none,opacity=0.5}
\input{villesFrance3d}
\newpsstyle{NodeLabelStyle}{fillstyle=solid,fillcolor=red!50,framesep=0,
    linestyle=none,opacity=0.5}
\newpsstyle{psNodeMapStyle}{fillstyle=solid,fillcolor=yellow!50,linecolor=red}
\psset{nodeWidth=0.025\psunit,linecolor=red}
\input{capitales3d}
\psepicenter[circlecolor=red,waves=16,Rmax=2000](13.297,52.5222){Berlin}
\end{pspicture*}
```

25.4 pst-map3d

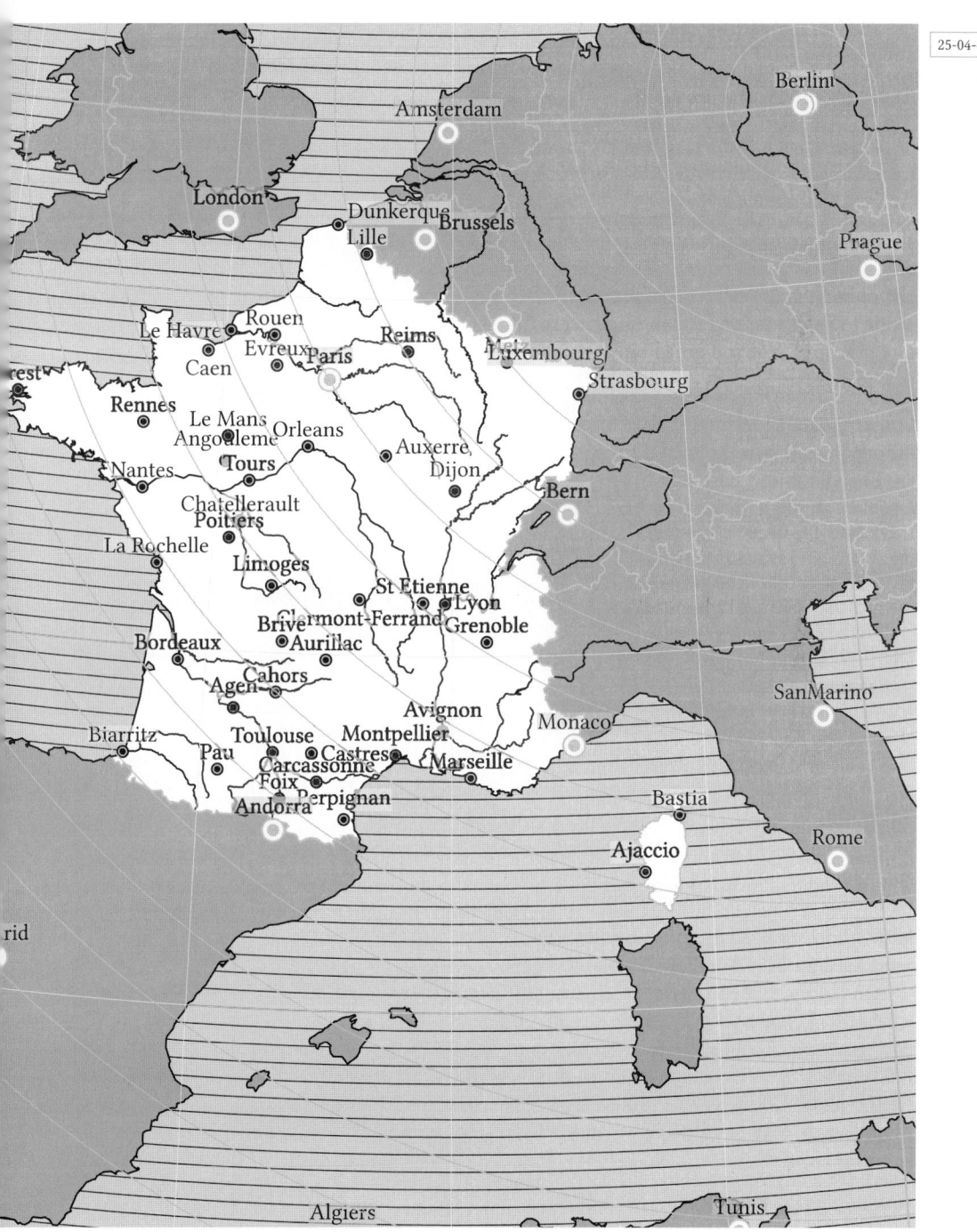

25-04-4

25 pst-geo – Geographic projections

Earthquakes are registered and classified nowadays according to their strength. You can access this data online, for example at http://earthquake.usgs.gov/earthquakes/eqarchives/, which holds records from 1990 onwards. The following figure uses data from http://earthquake.usgs.gov/earthquakes/eqarchives/significant/sig_1990.php.

```
\usepackage{pstricks,pst-map3d}
\psset{unit=0.75,Radius=5,Dobs=200,Decran=200,path=pst-geo/data,PHI=10,
    THETA=120,circlewidth=1.5pt}
\begin{pspicture}(-5,-5)(5,5)
\WorldMapThreeD[circles=false,australia=true]
\psmeridien{95.98}
\psparallel{3.30}
\psepicenter[circlecolor=red!70,waves=4,Rmax=2000](95.98,3.30){Sumatra}
\psmeridien[meridiencolor=red!70]{160}
\psparallel[parallelcolor=red!70]{52.76}
\psepicenter[circlecolor=blue!50](160,52.76){Kamchatka}
\end{pspicture}
```

One of the last earthquakes in Germany was registered on 3rd July 2008 at 12.16 h local time with a magnitude of 2.7 on the Richter scale The epicentre was near Munich, at the coordinates 48.02N and 11.63E, at a depth of approx. 5 km. According to statistical data, the quake was felt in Berlin at a distance of 520 km from the epicentre, so Rmax=600 was chosen for the figure below.

The starred version pspicture∗ has to be used again to achieve automatic clipping of the remaining earth.

```
\usepackage{pst-map3d}
\psset{unit=0.75,Radius=5,Dobs=200,Decran=800,path=pst-geo/data, PHI=50,
    THETA=10,circlewidth=1.5pt}
```

```
\begin{pspicture*}(-5,-5)(5,5)
\WorldMapThreeD[circles=false]%
\psmeridien{11.63}
\psparallel{48.01}
\psepicenter[circlecolor=red!70,waves=4,Rmax=600](11.63,48.02){München}
\mapputIIID(13.297,52.5222){Berlin}
\end{pspicture*}
```

Movements of the earth's tectonic plates and their position are described by data freely available at the Plates Project at http://www.ig.utexas.edu/research/projects/plates/. You can use the ridge option to draw this data as polylines, as in the following example.

```
\usepackage{pst-map3d}
\psset{unit=0.8,RotX=0,Decran=80,Dobs=100,PHI=0,THETA=-100,path=pst-geo/data,
    gridmapcolor=yellow,circles=false,ridge=true}
\begin{pspicture}(-4,-4)(4,4)
\WorldMapThreeD\rput(4,4){Tectonic plates}
\psline[linecolor=red,linewidth=2pt](0,-4.5)(0.8,-4.5)
\uput[0](0.8,-4.5){\color{red}{Ridge}}
\psline[linecolor=darkgreen,linewidth=2pt](2.5,-4.5)(3.2,-4.5)
\uput[0](3.2,-4.5){\color{darkgreen}{Trench}}
\psline[linecolor=orange,linewidth=2pt](5.5,-4.5)(6.3,-4.5)
\uput[0](6.3,-4.5){\color{orange}{Transform}}
\end{pspicture}
\begin{pspicture}(-4,-4)(4,4)\WorldMapThreeD[THETA=100]\end{pspicture}
```

25 pst-geo – Geographic projections

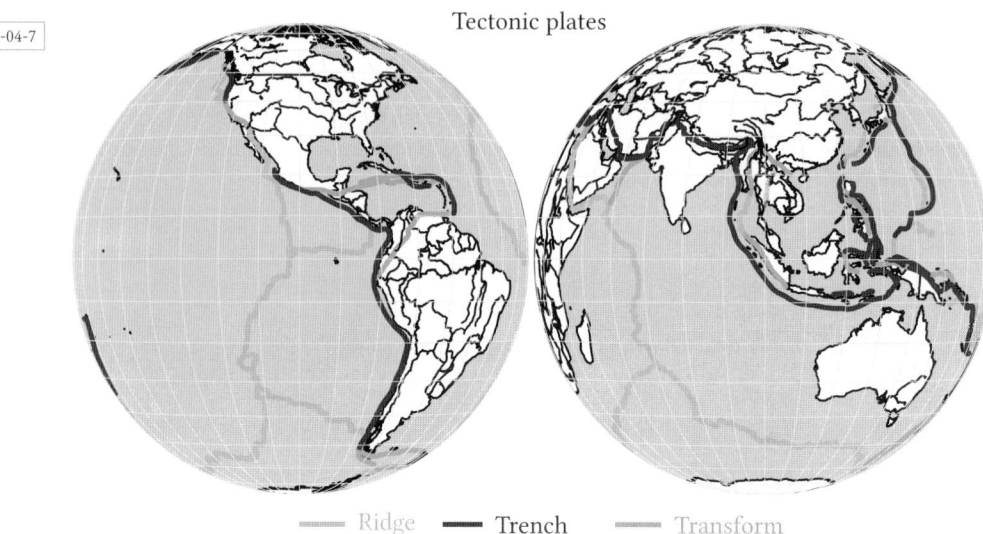

Tectonic plates

━━ Ridge ━━ Trench ━━ Transform

You can also use the optional arguments wfraczon and wmaglin to show the course of tectonic movements and the course of the magnetic lines, respectively.

```
\usepackage{pst-map3d}
\psset{Decran=80,Dobs=100,unit=0.8,path=pst-geo/data,PHI=0,THETA=-90,
  gridmapcolor=yellow,circles=false,wfraczon=true}
\begin{pspicture}(-4,-4)(4,4)
\WorldMapThreeD
\psline[linecolor=red,linewidth=2pt](3.2,-4)(4,-4)\uput[r](4,-4){\color{red}{wzonfrac}}
\end{pspicture}
\begin{pspicture}(-4,-4)(4,4)\WorldMapThreeD[THETA=90]\end{pspicture}
```

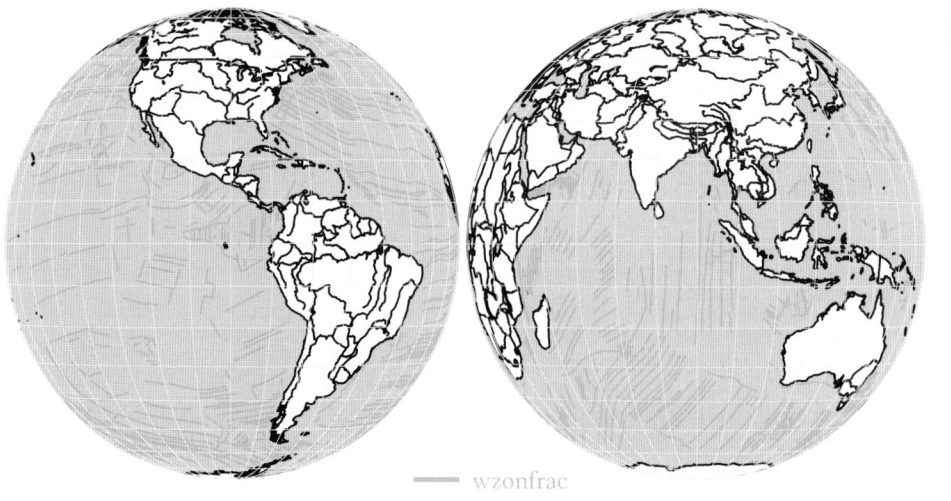

━━ wzonfrac

```
\usepackage{pst-map3d}
\psset{Decran=80,Dobs=100,unit=0.8,path=pst-geo/data,PHI=0,THETA=-90,
  gridmapcolor=yellow,circles=false,wmaglin}
\begin{pspicture}(-4,-4)(4,4)
\WorldMapThreeD
\psline[linecolor=blue,linewidth=2pt](3.2,-4)(4,-4)
\uput[r](4,-4){\color{darkblue}{wmaglin}}
\end{pspicture}
\begin{pspicture}(-4,-4)(4,4)\WorldMapThreeD[THETA=90]\end{pspicture}
```

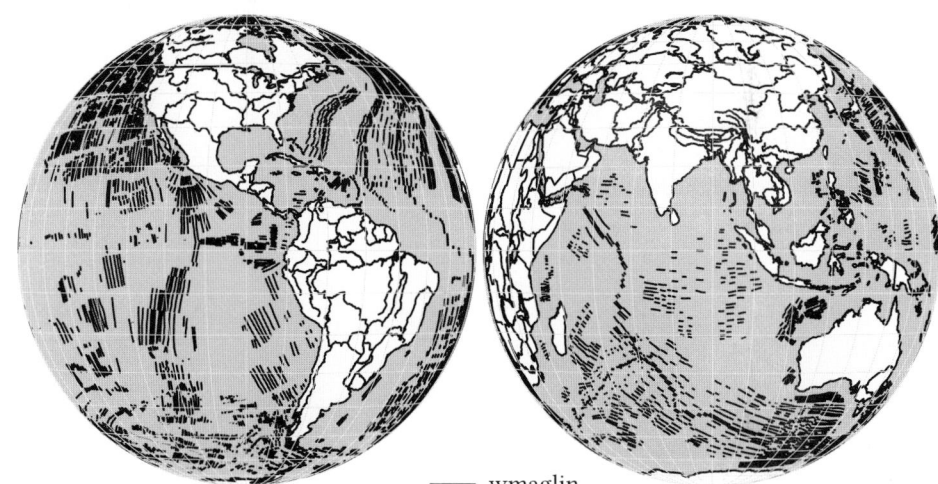

25.5 pst-map2dII

The Roman II suffix on this package name corresponds to the "CIA database II". In practice this package is identical to pst-map2d, but there are a few differences – especially affecting how individual continents can be drawn – because of the way the CIA database is organized.

This package only defines one new command, with the following syntax:

\WorldMapII [settings]

You can also use the \mapput and \pnodeMap commands from pst-map2d, which are discussed in detail in Section 25.7 on page 491.

```
\usepackage{pstricks,pst-map2dII}
\psset{path=pst-geo/dataII,unit=3}
\begin{pspicture*}(-1.75,1.75)(1.75,5.25)
   \WorldMapII[rivers=false,increment=5]
\end{pspicture*}
```

25 pst-geo – Geographic projections

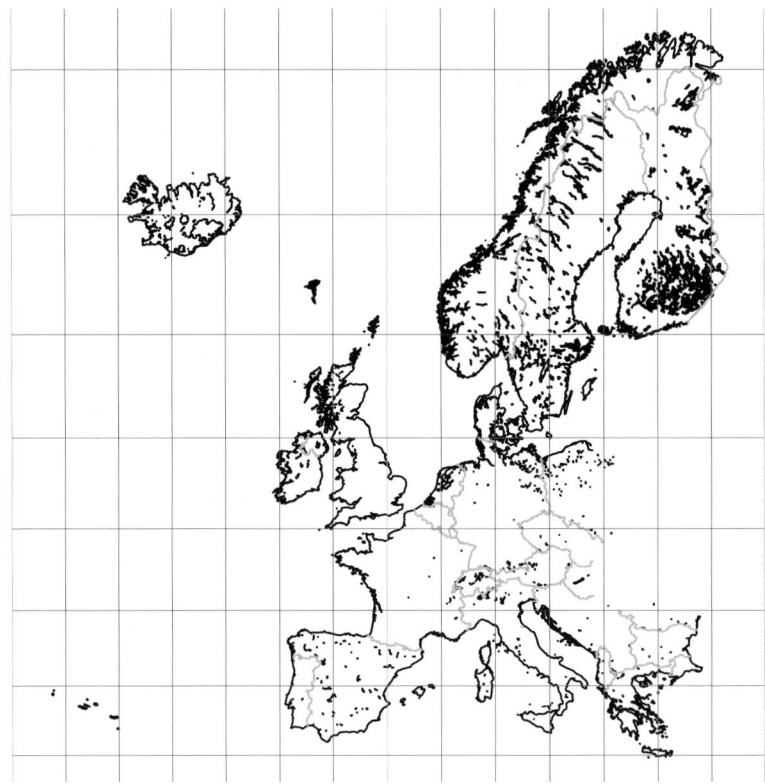

25-05-1

25.5.1 Parameters

Table 25.6 lists the parameters available for pst-map2dII. Most of them were described in Section 25.2 on page 467.

Table 25.6: Summary of the available options for pst-map2dII

name	type	default	meaning
path	path	data	path to the database directory
type	value	1	map projection method
n	value	1.77245	aspect ratio (for Collignon projection)
limiteL	angle	180	maximum longitude
longitude0	angle	0	reference longitude (for Bonne projection)
latitude0	angle	45	reference latitude (for Bonne projection)
increment	angle	10	difference between the longitudes in degrees
level	value	5	precision
capital	boolean	false	show capitals
city	boolean	false	show towns

continued...

... continued

name	type	default	meaning
rivers	boolean	true	show rivers
borders	boolean	false	show borders
maillage	boolean	true	show latitude and longitude lines
europe	boolean	true	select Europe
asia	boolean	false	select Asia
africa	boolean	false	select Africa
namer	boolean	false	select North America
samer	boolean	false	select South America
all	boolean	false	select all continents
mapCountry	boolean	all	select active countries
nodeWidth	boolean	1mm	select all continents

Compared to the `pst-map2d` package, only the special parameters for the US, Mexico, and Australia are missing, but there are additional parameters for the continents; these are all set to `false` by default, except for Europe.

The `level` option has the same meaning as in 25.2.2 on page 468, but can take arbitrary values here. Because of the extremely large size of the database, values of `level=50` or even bigger can be used to keep PDF files smaller, as only every 50th value is taken into account (in addition to the first and the last values in a polyline).

25.6 pst-map3dII

The Roman II suffix on this package name again corresponds to the "CIA database II". In practice this package is identical to `pst-map3d`, but there are a few differences – especially affecting how individual continents can be drawn – because of the way the CIA database is organized.

Again there is only a single command for a world view with the following syntax:

`\WorldMapThreeDII` [settings]

25.6.1 Parameters

Table 25.7 lists the parameters available for `pst-map3dII`. Most of them were described in Section 25.4.1 on page 478.

Table 25.7: Summary of the available options for `pst-map3dII`

name	type	default	meaning
path	path	.	path to the database directory
RotX	angle	0	rotation about the x axis
RotY	angle	0	rotation about the y axis
RotZ	angle	0	rotation about the z axis
THETA	angle	0	rotation angle of the coordinate system

25 pst-geo – Geographic projections

name	type	default	meaning
PHI	value	45	tilting angle of the coordinate system
Dobs	value	20	centric image distance
Decran	value	25	parallel image distance (scaling factor)
Radius	value	5	earth radius
increment	value	10	angle step
level	value	5	precision
capital	boolean	false	mark captials
city	boolean	false	show known cities
maillage	boolean	true	show grid
rivers	boolean	true	show rivers
borders	boolean	true	show country borders
europe	boolean	true	select Europe
asia	boolean	false	select Asia
africa	boolean	false	select Africa
namer	boolean	false	select North America
samer	boolean	false	select South America
all	boolean	false	select all continents

In principle the differences between pst-map2dII and pst-map3dII are the same as between the packages pst-map2d and pst-map3d. As for pst-map2dII, the additional parameters for the continents are all set to false by default, except for Europe.

```
\usepackage{pst-map3dII} \psset{path=pst-geo/dataII,unit=0.75cm}
\begin{pspicture*}(-7,-7)(7,7)
    \WorldMapThreeDII[all=true,rivers=false,level=75]
\end{pspicture*}
```

25.7 \mapput and \pnodeMap

```
\mapput[angle](longitude,latitude)[node name]{name}[country]
\pnodeMap(longitude,latitude){node name}
\def\psNodeLabelStyle{}
```

The \mapput command provides an easy way to place text (the {*name*} argument) at an arbitrary point in the two-dimensional coordinate system. This command is practically identical to \uput and has the same structure (cf. Section 9.6 on page 106). \pnodeMap defines nodes in the same way as \pnode (cf. Section 16.3.3 on page 237); these nodes can be referred to by \mapput. \psNodeLabelStyle sets the font and font style of the node label globally. These commands are currently only available for the two-dimensional version of the packages.

The advantage of this functionality is that a file with \mapput commands can be created and then read with \input. At this time, such files exist for all European capitals and for all large French and Italian cities. The files all have the same structure:

```
\mapput[90](4.366667,50.850000)[Brussel]{Brüssel}[Belgium]
\mapput(13.416667,52.533333){Berlin}
\mapput(7.433333,46.966667){Bern}
\mapput[0](12.583333,55.683333){Copenhagen}[Denmark]
[...]
```

Specifications in square braces are as usual optional – you can omit them if they aren't needed. You can also add extra labels in these files, or alternatively you can set them explicitly outside the file in the following way:

```
\pnodeMap(-15,50){Atlantic}
\rput{80}(Atlantic){Atlantic}
```

This instruction is simplified to \mapput[80](-15,50){Atlantic} with \mapput. The text is also the node name. The files that already exist live in the data folder of data:

```
capitales.tex    villesItalia.tex    villesFrance.tex
cities.tex       % contains all three
```

The following example shows a map of Italy in the Bonne projection, with Rome as centre of the map.

```
\usepackage{pst-map2dII,graphicx}
\resizebox{0.8\linewidth}{!}{%
\begin{pspicture*}(-10,-138.5)(11,-117.5) % xentre set to Rome
  \psset{path=pst-geo/dataII,level=2,unit=40,
      type=8,latitude0=41.923611,longitude0=12.454167}
  \WorldMapII[maillage=true,linewidth=0.75\pslinewidth,limiteL=190,borders=true,increment=2]
  \pnodeMap(10,38){MerMed}
  \rput{0}(MerMed){\shortstack{\Large\it MAR\\\Large\it MEDITERRANEO}}
  \pnodeMap(15,43){MerAdriatique}
  \rput{-35}(MerAdriatique){\Large\textit{MAR ADRIATICO}}
  \pnodeMap(12,40){MerTyrr}
```

```
        \rput{0}(MerTyrr){{\itshape\Large\shortstack{MAR\\TIRRENO}}}
        \pnodeMap(18,39){MerIonienne}
        \rput{0}(MerIonienne){{\itshape\shortstack{MAR\\JONIO}}}
        \pnodeMap(17.25,40){GolfeTarente}
        \rput{7}(GolfeTarente){\footnotesize\itshape\shortstack{Golfo di\\Taranto}}
        \pnodeMap(14,40){Longitude40}
        \rput{5}(Longitude40){\psframebox[fillstyle=solid,linestyle=none]{%
          \large 40$^{\rm o}$N}}
        \mapput[90](15.25,38.80){Stromboli}\psdot[linecolor=red,dotstyle=triangle](Stromboli)
        \mapput[90](15,37.85){Etna}         \psdot[linecolor=red,dotstyle=triangle](Etna)
        \mapput[90](14.97,38.433){Vulcano}  \psdot[linecolor=red,dotstyle=triangle](Vulcano)
        \pnodeMap(18.5,40.117){Otranto}  \pnodeMap(19.328,40.313){Albania}
        \pnodeMap(12.45,37.8){Marsala}   \pnodeMap(11.03,37.0167){Bon}
        \pcline{<->}(Otranto)(Albania)    \lput*{:U}{70\,km}
        \pcline{<->}(Bon)(Marsala)        \lput*{:U}{140\,km}
        \rput(! 9 40 div -137.5 40 div){%
          \psframebox[fillstyle=solid]{\textsf{\textit{pst-map2dII(2004-05-09)}}}}
        \psset{mapCountry=Italy,nodeWidth=0.5mm} \def\psNodeLabelStyle{\small}
        \input{cities.tex}
\end{pspicture*}}
```

25.7 \mapput and \pnodeMap

Working out what geographic coordinates to specify for the size of the corresponding pspicture environment can be a major difficulty. Remember always use the starred version of the environment to clip all polylines outside the specified rectangle. If, for example, you want to show only the surroundings of the German Ruhrgebiet, everything else on the whole map of Europe is simply clipped; this doesn't prevent the PostScript or PDF file becoming quite large though.

```
\usepackage{pst-map2dII,graphicx} \psset{path=pst-geo/dataII}
\resizebox{.8\linewidth}{!}{\begin{pspicture*}(-7,-75)(10,-55)  \psframe(-7,-75)(10,-55)
  \psset{xunit=25,yunit=25,level=50,type=8,latitude0=48.85,longitude0=2.316667}
  \WorldMapII[maillage=true,linewidth=0.75\pslinewidth,limiteL=190,borders=true]
  \input{capitales.tex} \input{villesFrance.tex}
  \pnodeMap(20,35){MerMed}   \rput{15}(MerMed){\shortstack{MER\\MÉDITERANNÉE}}
  \pnodeMap(35,43){MerNoire}\rput{15}(MerNoire){\shortstack{MER\\NOIRE}}
  \pnodeMap(-15,50){OceanAtlan}\rput{80}(OceanAtlan){OCÉAN ATLANTIQUE}
  \pnodeMap(4,56){MerNoire}  \rput(MerNoire){\shortstack{Mer\\du\\Nord}}
\end{pspicture*}}
```

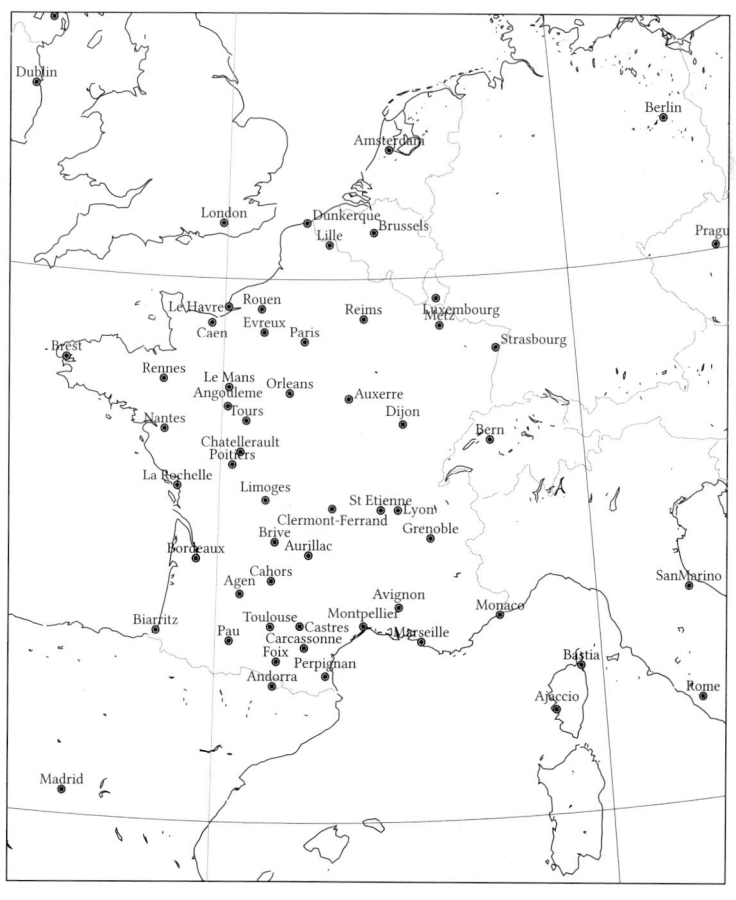

25.8 Examples

```
\usepackage{pstricks,pst-map3dII}
\psset{path=pst-geo/dataII}
\psframebox{%
\begin{pspicture*}(-6.5,-6.5)(6.5,6.5)
    \WorldMapThreeDII[europe=false,samer=true,level=50,RotZ=70,RotY=-20,RotX=-60]
\end{pspicture*}}
```

```
\usepackage{pst-map2dII}
\psset{unit=3,path=pst-geo/dataII}
\begin{pspicture*}(-1.5,-2.5)(3.5,2.5)
  \WorldMapII[europe=false,
    africa=true,level=50,
    maillage=false]
\end{pspicture*}
```

25 pst-geo – Geographic projections

```
\usepackage{pst-map2dII}
\begin{pspicture}*(-5,7)(10,21)
  \psset{unit=4,type=1,level=50,all=true,path=pst-geo/dataII}
  \WorldMapII[maillage=false,linewidth=0.75\pslinewidth,limiteL=190,borders=true]
  \input capitales    \pnodeMap(20,35){MerMed}
  \rput(MerMed){\shortstack{Mer\\M\'editerann\'ee}}  \pnodeMap(35,43){MerNoire}
  \rput(MerNoire){\shortstack{Mer\\Noire}}       \pnodeMap(-15,50){OceanAtlan}
  \rput{90}(OceanAtlan){O c \'e{} a n\hspace{2em} A t l a n ti q u e}
  \pnodeMap(4,56){MerNoire}   \rput(MerNoire){\shortstack{Mer\\du\\Nord}}
\end{pspicture}
```

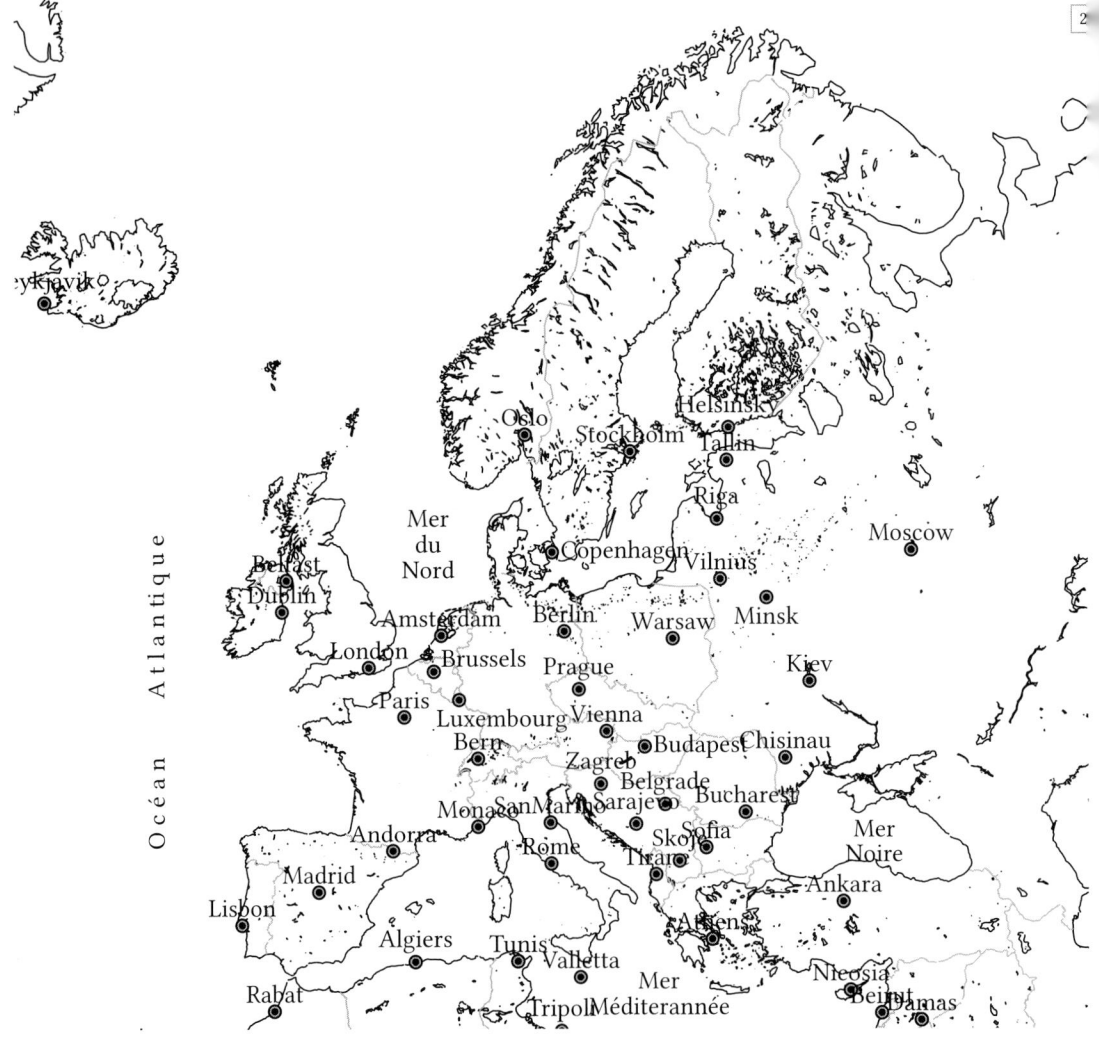

Chapter 26

pst-barcode – Bar codes

26.1 The options. 497
26.2 Types of bar code. 499

The pst-barcode package defines only a single command, which has an unusual PSTricks syntax:

\psbarcode[*TEX options*]{*code*}{*PS options*}{*bar code type*}

The differentiation between TEX and PostScript options is done only for practical reasons as is explained in the following section. The bar code is, as usual for PSTricks, placed in a box of dimension null. If you want to reserve space for it, which will usually be the case, you have to either embed \psbarcode in a pspicture environment or use any other command that reserves space.

The next section discusses the options, and Section 26.2 on page 499 lists the bar code types.

26.1 The options

name	type	default	explanation
transx	value unit	0	horizontal translation
transy	value unit	0	vertical translation
scalex	value	1	horizontal scaling
scaley	value	1	vertical scaling
rotate	angle	0	rotation angle in degrees

Table 26.1: The TEX-specific options for the \psbarcode command

Tables 26.1 and 26.2 show the options available for pst-barcode. Specific PostScript options are available for the first time because the PostScript prologue file pst-barcode.pro can also be used stand-alone to print the bar codes – LaTeX just "borrows" it and `pst-barcode.tex` is only a PostScript interface. This has the advantage that only the PostScript file needs to be maintained. PostScript lengths are always specified without a unit; the unit used internally is as listed in Table 26.2. Individual options are assigned one after another, separated by a space, and where values are assigned to the options, an equals sign is used (cf. the examples in the next two sections).

Table 26.2: The PostScript-specific options for the \psbarcode command

name	type	default	explanation
height	value	1	dimension in inches
textsize	value	10	dimension in pt
textpos	value	-2	dimension in pt; determines the vertical translation of the text
inkspread	value	0.15	dimension in pt; determines the width of the bar code lines
showborder	value	–	–
borderwidth	value	0.5	dimension in pt
borderleft	value	10	dimension in pt
borderright	value	10	dimension in pt
bordertop	value	1	dimension in pt
borderbottom	value	1	dimension in pt
font	font	/Helvetica	must be a PostScript font
includetext	includetext	–	output code as text as well
includecheck	includecheck	–	activate check digit
includecheckintext	includecheckintext	–	output check digit

26.1.1 Examples for the TeX options

```
\usepackage{pstricks,pst-barcode}
\begin{pspicture}(2.5,1in)\psbarcode{12345678}{includetext}{ean8}\end{pspicture}\quad
\begin{pspicture}(-2.6,-1.5)(0.4,0.2in)
\psbarcode[rotate=180,linecolor=red]{12345678}{includetext guardwhitespace height=0.6}{e
\end{pspicture}\quad \begin{pspicture}(3.8,1in)
\psbarcode[scalex=1.5,scaley=0.5,transy=1]{12345678}{includetext inkspread=0.5}{ean8}
\end{pspicture}
```

26.1.2 Examples for the PostScript options

```
\usepackage{pstricks,pst-barcode}
\begin{pspicture}(3,1.1in)
  \psbarcode{2345678}{includetext guardwhitespace height=0.6}{ean8}
\end{pspicture}
\begin{pspicture}(3,1.1in)
  \psbarcode{2345678}{textsize=15 includetext guardwhitespace height=0.6}{ean8}
\end{pspicture}
\begin{pspicture}(3,1.1in)
  \psbarcode{2345678}{includetext inkspread=0.5}{ean8}
\end{pspicture}
\begin{pspicture}(3,1.1in)
  \psbarcode{2345678}{includetext textpos=0}{ean8}
\end{pspicture}
```

```
\usepackage{pstricks,pst-barcode}
\begin{pspicture}(3,1.1in)
  \psbarcode{12345678}{showborder includetext}{ean8}
\end{pspicture}\quad
\begin{pspicture}(3,1.1in)
  \psbarcode{12345678}{showborder borderwidth=2 includetext height=0.6}{ean8}
\end{pspicture}\quad
\begin{pspicture}(3,1.1in)
  \psbarcode[transy=20pt]{12345678}{showborder borderwidth=1 bordertop=10
    borderbottom=10 includetext height=0.6}{ean8}
\end{pspicture}
```

26.2 Types of bar code

This section lists all the currently possible formats for bar codes, with an example. No TEX options are used here to keep the examples simple. The bar codes available in the current version of the package can be taken from [8].

26.2.1 EAN-13

characters   0123456789
data   12 or 13 digits
options   includetext

If only 12 digits are given, the (initial) check digit is calculated automatically.

```
\usepackage{pstricks,pst-barcode}

\begin{pspicture}(3,1in)
  \psbarcode{9781860742712}{includetext
    guardwhitespace}{ean13}
\end{pspicture}
```

26.2.2 EAN-8

characters   0123456789
data   7 digits
options   includetext

```
\usepackage{pstricks,pst-barcode}

\begin{pspicture}(3,1in)
  \psbarcode{0123456}%
    {includetext guardwhitespace}{ean8}
\end{pspicture}
```

26.2.3 UPC-A

characters   0123456789
data   11 or 12 digits
options   includetext

If only 11 digits are given, the (final) check digit is calculated automatically.

```
\usepackage{pstricks,pst-barcode}

\begin{pspicture}(3,1in)
  \psbarcode{78858101497}{height=0.4
    includetext}{upca}
\end{pspicture}
```

26.2.4 UPC-E

characters   0123456789
data   7 or 8 digits
options   includetext

If only 7 digits are given, the (final) check digit is calculated automatically.

```
\usepackage{pstricks,pst-barcode}

\begin{pspicture}(1.5,1.1in)
  \psbarcode{0123456}{height=0.6
    includetext}{upce}
\end{pspicture}
```

26.2.5 EAN-5
characters   0123456789
data   5 digits
options   includetext

```
\usepackage{pstricks,pst-barcode}

\begin{pspicture}(2,.8in)
  \psbarcode{90200}{includetext
    guardwhitespace}{ean5}
\end{pspicture}
```

26.2.6 EAN-2
characters   0123456789
data   2 digits
options   includetext, guardwhitespace

```
\usepackage{pstricks,pst-barcode}

\begin{pspicture}(1,.75in)
\psbarcode{38}{includetext
   guardwhitespace}{ean2}
\end{pspicture}
```

26.2.7 ISBN
characters   −0123456789
data   9(12) or 10(13) digits
options   includetext, guardwhitespace

If only 9 or 12 digits are given, the ISBN (final) check digit is automatically calculated and output. A 9 or 10 digit number is automatically converted to the new ISBN-13 for output at the bottom of the bar code.

```
\usepackage{pstricks,pst-barcode}
\begin{pspicture}(4.5,1.05in)
  \psbarcode{3-86541-175}{includetext guardwhitespace}{isbn}
\end{pspicture}
\begin{pspicture}(4.5,1.05in)
  \psbarcode{978-38654-1175}{includetext guardwhitespace}{isbn}
\end{pspicture}
```

26 pst-barcode – Bar codes

26.2.8 Code-39

characters	0123456789ABCDEFGHIJKLMNOPQRSTUVWXYZ-.@$*+/%
data	variable number of characters
options	includetext, includecheck, includecheckintext

```
\usepackage{pstricks,pst-barcode}

\begin{pspicture}(5,0.6in)
  \psbarcode{CODE-39}{includecheck
     height=0.4 includetext}{code39}
\end{pspicture}
```

26.2.9 Code-128 and UCC/EAN-128

characters	!"#$%&'\(\)*+,-./0...9:;<=>?@A...Z[\\]^_'a...z{|}~
data	variable number of ASCII characters and special symbols; UCC/EAN-128s must have a FNC 1 symbol followed by the start character.
options	includetext, includecheckintext

You can input any non-printable character through an escape sequence, for example ˆ070 for ACK and ˆ102 for FNC 1. As the caret symbol is the character that begins an escape sequence, if you actually want it to appear in a bar code you have to give it as ˆ062. The check digit is added automatically.

```
\usepackage{pstricks,pst-barcode}
\begin{pspicture}(5,1in)
  \psbarcode{^104^102Count^0991234^101!}{includetext}{code128}
\end{pspicture}
```

26.2.10 Rationalized Codabar
characters   0123456789-$:/.+ABCD
data   variable number of digits and symbols
options   includetext, includecheck, includecheckintext

```
\usepackage{pstricks,pst-barcode}

\begin{pspicture}(4,1in)
  \psbarcode{0123456789}{height=0.5
    includetext}{rationalizedCodabar}
\end{pspicture}
```

26.2.11 Interleaved 2 of 5 and ITF-14
characters   0123456789
data   variable number of digits; an ITF-14 has 14 characters and no check digit
options   includetext, includecheck, includecheckintext

If you give an odd number of digits, the data is padded by prefixing the digit 0 in order to have an even number of digits for determining the check digit (if required).

```
\usepackage{pstricks,pst-barcode}

\begin{pspicture}(5,0.7in)
  \psbarcode{05012345678900}%
    {includecheck
      height=0.7}{interleaved2of5}
\end{pspicture}
```

26.2.12 Code 2 of 5
characters   0123456789
data   variable number of digits
options   includetext

```
\usepackage{pstricks,pst-barcode}

\begin{pspicture}(5,1.2in)
  \psbarcode{0123456789}{includetext
    textpos=37 textfont=Helvetica
    textsize=12 height=0.5}{code2of5}
\end{pspicture}
```

26.2.13 Postnet
characters   0123456789
data   variable number of digits
options   includetext, includecheckintext

The check digit is added automatically.

```
\usepackage{pstricks,pst-barcode}

\begin{pspicture}(6,0.3in)
  \psbarcode{01234567}{includetext
    textpos=-10 textfont=Arial
    textsize=10}{postnet}
\end{pspicture}
```

26.2.14 Royal Mail

characters   01...89AB...YZ
data   variable number of digits and capital letters
options   includetext, includecheckintext

The check digit is added automatically.

```
\usepackage{pstricks,pst-barcode}

\begin{pspicture}(5,0.3in)
  \psbarcode{LE28HS9Z}{includetext}%
    {royalmail}
\end{pspicture}
```

26.2.15 Australian postal service

characters   ABC...XYZabc...xyz01234B6789
data   variable number of digits and letters
options   includetext, includecheckintext

```
\usepackage{pstricks,pst-barcode}

\begin{pspicture}(5,0.5in)
  \psbarcode{1139549554}{includetext}{auspost}
\end{pspicture}
```

26.2.16 Kix (Customer Index) – Dutch Mail

characters   ABC...XYZ01234B6789
data   variable number of digits and capital letters
options   includetext, includecheckintext

```
\usepackage{pstricks,pst-barcode}

\begin{pspicture}(5,0.3in)
\psbarcode{1203AA12}{includetext}{kix}
\end{pspicture}
```

26.2.17 Symbol

These symbols are used as 'FIM' symbols in reply mails of the US Postal Service.

26.2 Types of bar code

```
\usepackage{pstricks,pst-barcode}

\begin{pspicture}(1.75,1)
  \psbarcode{fima}{}{symbol}
\end{pspicture}\quad\begin{pspicture}(1.75,1)
  \psbarcode{fimb}{}{symbol}
\end{pspicture}\\[40pt]
\begin{pspicture}(1.75,1)
  \psbarcode{fimc}{}{symbol}
\end{pspicture}\quad\begin{pspicture}(1.75,1)
  \psbarcode{fimd}{}{symbol}
\end{pspicture}
```

26.2.18 MSI

characters	0123456789
data	variable number of digits
options	includetext, includecheckintext, includecheck

```
\usepackage{pstricks,pst-barcode}

\begin{pspicture}(6,1in)
  \psbarcode{0123456789}%
    {includecheck
     height=0.5 includetext}{msi}
\end{pspicture}
```

26.2.19 Plessey

characters	0123456789ABCDEF
data	variable number of hexadecimal digits
options	includetext, includecheckintext

The check digit is added automatically.

```
\usepackage{pstricks,pst-barcode}
\begin{pspicture}(11,1in)
  \psbarcode{0123456789ABCDEF}{height=0.3 includetext}{plessey}
\end{pspicture}
```

26.2.20 Reduced Space Symbology (RSS)

This is a family of bar codes that contains RSS-14®, RSS Limited®, and RSS Expanded® (http://www.gs1.org/barcodes/).

characters	0123456789
data	variable number of digits

rss14 (databaromni)

```
\usepackage{pstricks,pst-barcode}

\begin{pspicture}(2in,.3in)
\psbarcode{(01)24012345678905}%
   {format=truncated includetext height=0.3}%
   {databaromni}
\end{pspicture}
```

rsslimited (databarlimited)

```
\usepackage{pstricks,pst-barcode}

\begin{pspicture}(2in,.3in)
\psbarcode{(01)15012345678907}{height=0.3}%
   {databarlimited}
\end{pspicture}
```

rssexpanded (databarexpanded)

```
\usepackage{pstricks,pst-barcode}

\begin{pspicture}(2in,.3in)
\psbarcode{(10)12A}{height=0.3}{databarexpanded}
\end{pspicture}
```

26.2.21 Pharmacode

There is a description of the Pharmacode at http://www.laetus.com/.
  characters   0123456789
  data   variable number of digits

```
\usepackage{pstricks,pst-barcode}

\begin{pspicture}(1.5in,.3in)
\psbarcode{117480}{}{pharmacode}
\end{pspicture}
```

26.2.22 Data matrix

There is a description of the data matrix bar code at http://en.wikipedia.org/wiki/Data_matrix_(computer).
  characters   0123456789
  data   variable number of digits

```
\usepackage{pstricks,pst-barcode}

\begin{pspicture}(1in,1in)
\psbarcode{^142^164^186}{rows=48 columns=48}{datamatrix}
\end{pspicture}
```

26.2.23 2D MaxiCode

There is a description of the 2D MaxiCode at http://en.wikipedia.org/wiki/MaxiCode. It is a two-dimensional symbolic code that was developed by United Parcel Service (UPS) to sort packages automatically. Because of the arrangement in a symmetric hexagon, it can be read from virtually any direction. MaxiCode has five alphabets, each of which has 64 characters. Additionally, the following six modes are supported:

- mode 0 - Obsolete and not used in practice.
- mode 2 - For numerical post codes, mostly used within the US.
- mode 3 - For international (alphanumeric) post codes.
- mode 4 - Standard error correction.
- mode 5 - Extended error correction.
- mode 6 - Used for development.

characters   @ABCDEFGHIJKLMNOPQRSTUVWXYZ0123456789
data   variable number of alphanumeric characters

```
\usepackage{pstricks,pst-barcode}

\begin{pspicture}(1in,1in)
\expandafter\psbarcode{[\string\)>^03001^02996152382802%
^029840^029001^0291Z00004951^029UPSN^02906X610^029159%
^0291234567^0291/1^029^029Y^029634 ALPHA DR^029%
PITTSBURGH^029PA^029^004}{mode=2 parse}{maxicode}
\end{pspicture}
```

26.2.24 QR Code

The QR code (*q*uick *r*esponse) is another two-dimensional bar code; it was developed by the Japanese company Denso Wave in 1994. There is a description of the bar code at http://en.wikipedia.org/wiki/QR_Code.

characters   @ABCDEFGHIJKLMNOPQRSTUVWXYZ0123456789
data   variable number of alphanumeric characters

```
\usepackage{pstricks,pst-barcode}

\begin{pspicture}(1in,1in)
\psbarcode{http://www.dante.de}{}{qrcode}
\end{pspicture}
```

26.2.25 Aztec Code

The two-dimensional Aztec code was developed in 1995 by Andy Longacre from the US. There is a description at http://en.wikipedia.org/wiki/Aztec_code.

characters   @ABCDEFGHIJKLMNOPQRSTUVWXYZ0123456789
data   variable number of alphanumeric characters

```
\usepackage{pstricks,pst-barcode}

\begin{pspicture}(1in,1in)
\psbarcode{0123456789}%
   {format=compact layers=3}{azteccode}
\end{pspicture}
```

26.2.26 PDF417

PDF417 is a stacked linear bar code used in transportation, identification cards, and inventory management. The PDF417 symbology was invented by Ynjiun P. Wang in 1991 and it is represented by ISO standard 15438.

    characters   0123456789
    data   variable number of characters

```
\usepackage{pstricks,pst-barcode}

\begin{pspicture}(1in,1in)
\psbarcode{^453^178^121^239}%
   {columns=2 rows=10}{pdf417}
\end{pspicture}
```

Chapter 27

pst-bar – bar charts

27.1 Data 509
27.2 Parameters 509
27.3 Commands 513

pst-bar is the first package for displaying bar charts. At the moment it only provides functionality to create simple histograms, but it is still worth mentioning here. You **must** load the package after the base packages of PSTricks and before any others as it doesn't use the new key-value interface.

27.1 Data

The data file must be a list of comma-separated values, with one complete data set per line and no comma after the last value. For example, three valid lines of a file could be:

```
1300--1349, 1350--1399, 1400--1449, 1450--1499
1, 0.5, 2.0, 0.5
1, 2.0, 1.5, 1.0
```

By default the first line is assumed to contain the labels for the x axis. Each line must have the same number of pieces of data and values may only be numeric. This is not checked by TeX, so problems in your data just lead to errors in the PostScript output, which only become apparent when looking at the output with a PostScript viewer.

27.2 Parameters

Table 27.1 shows a summary of the special parameters that are only valid for pst-bar. Each of these parameters is discussed in turn in the following sections. In the examples in these sections, we used the filecontents* environment so as to output the special data set in the code for the examples.

27 pst-bar – bar charts

Table 27.1: Summary of the additional parameters for pst-bar

name	type	default
header	*boolean*	true
chartstyle	block|stack|cluster	cluster
barstyle	*style*	{}
barcolsep	*value*	0.4
barsep	*value*	0
barlabelrot	*angle*	0

27.2.1 header

If the data file doesn't contain a header line, you must set header to false; otherwise the first line of data will be skipped.

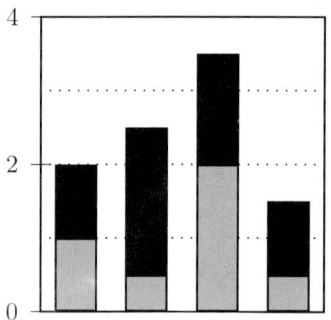

```
\usepackage{pstricks,pst-bar}

\begin{pspicture}(-0.5,-0.1)(4,4)
  \psgrid[xunit=4cm,gridlabels=0,
    subgriddiv=0,griddots=30](0,0)(1,4)
  \psaxes[axesstyle=frame,Ox=0,Dx=1,Dy=2,
    labels=y,ticks=y](0,0)(4,4)
  \readpsbardata[header=false]%
    {\data}{data2T.csv}%
  \psbarchart[barstyle={red,blue},
    chartstyle=stack]{\data}
\end{pspicture}
```

27-02-1

27.2.2 chartstyle

The chartstyle option provides three different styles for the output of the bar charts – cluster, stack, and block. All three are illustrated in the following examples.

cluster

The cluster style puts the individual data sets next to each other – clustered. This only makes sense for a relatively small number of data sets, as for n lines in the data file there are n bars next to each other.

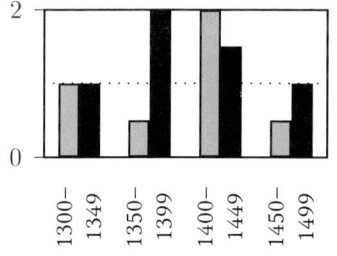

```
\usepackage{pstricks,pst-plot,pst-bar}

\readpsbardata{\data}{data1T.csv}
\begin{pspicture}(-0.5,-1.75)(4,2)
  \psgrid[xunit=4cm,gridlabels=0,
    subgriddiv=0,griddots=30](0,0)(1,2)
  \psaxes[axesstyle=frame,Ox=0,Dx=1,Dy=2,
    labels=y,ticks=y](0,0)(4,2)
  \psbarchart[barstyle={red,blue},
    chartstyle=cluster,
    barlabelrot=90]{\data}
\end{pspicture}
```

27-02-2

stack

The stack style, which was shown already in example 27-02-1 on the preceding page, simply stacks values in the same group on top of each other, i.e. the first value of the second line is put on top of the first value of the first line.

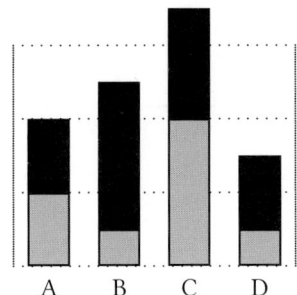

```
\usepackage{pstricks,pst-bar}

\readpsbardata{\data}{data2T.csv}
\begin{pspicture}(-0.5,-1.75)(4,3)
  \psgrid[xunit=4cm,gridlabels=0,
    subgriddiv=0,griddots=30](0,0)(1,3)
  \psbarchart[barstyle={red,blue},
    chartstyle=stack]{\data}
\end{pspicture}
```

block

The third style, block, is more complex. It assumes an even number of lines and pairs them up; the first line of a pair contains the start values and the second line the end values such that two lines together form a data set. If there is an odd number of data sets, the last one is ignored.

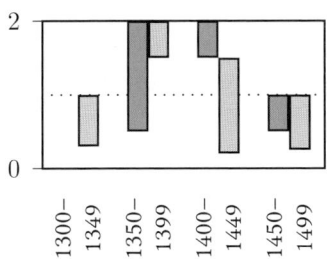

```
\usepackage{pstricks,pst-plot,pst-bar}

\readpsbardata{\data}{data3T.csv}
\begin{pspicture}(-0.5,-1.75)(4,2)
  \psgrid[xunit=4cm,gridlabels=0,
    subgriddiv=0,griddots=30](0,0)(1,2)
  \psaxes[axesstyle=frame,Dy=2,
    labels=y,ticks=y](0,0)(4,2)
  \psbarchart[barstyle={gray,lightgray},
    chartstyle=block,
    barlabelrot=90]{\data}
\end{pspicture}
```

In the example above, the lines of the file are assigned to bars as follows, where the first two are displayed in gray and the latter two in lightgray:

    1–1   0.5–2   2–1.5   0.5–1   ← gray
    0.3–1   1.5–2   0.2–1.5   1–0.25   ← lightgray

Note that the values are assumed to be absolute; the intervals are always in the positive region.

27.2.3 barstyle

Six bar styles are predefined to use the base colours:

```
\newpsbarstyle{red}{fillcolor=red,fillstyle=solid,framearc=0}
\newpsbarstyle{green}{fillcolor=green,fillstyle=solid,framearc=0}
\newpsbarstyle{blue}{fillcolor=blue,fillstyle=solid,framearc=0}
\newpsbarstyle{black}{fillcolor=black,fillstyle=solid,framearc=0}
```

27 pst-bar – bar charts

```
\newpsbarstyle{white}{fillcolor=white,fillstyle=solid,framearc=0}
\newpsbarstyle{gray}{fillcolor=gray,fillstyle=solid,framearc=0}
\newpsbarstyle{lightgray}{fillcolor=lightgray,fillstyle=solid,framearc=0}
\newpsbarstyle{darkgray}{fillcolor=darkgray,fillstyle=solid,framearc=0}
```

You can define additional ones; hatched bar styles are defined in the following example:

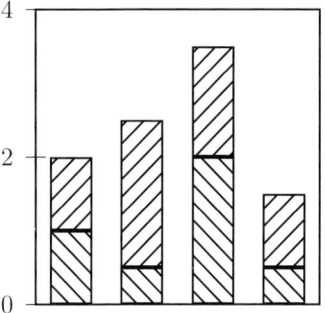

```
\usepackage{pstricks,pst-plot,pst-bar}

\newpsbarstyle{vlines}{fillstyle=vlines}
\newpsbarstyle{hlines}{fillstyle=hlines}
\begin{pspicture}(-0.5,-0.1)(4,4)
  \psaxes[axesstyle=frame,dx=0.75,Ox=0,Dx=1,Dy=2,
    labels=y,ticks=y](0,0)(4,4)
  \readpsbardata[header=false]{\data}{data2T.csv}%
  \psbarchart[barstyle={vlines,hlines},
    chartstyle=stack]{\data}
\end{pspicture}
```

27.2.4 barcolsep

barcolsep is the factor that defines the fraction of space between two data bars and can be set to any arbitrary value.

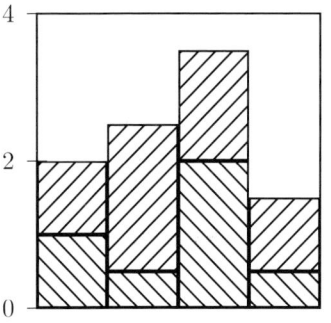

```
\usepackage{pstricks,pst-plot,pst-bar}

\newpsbarstyle{vlines}{fillstyle=vlines}
\newpsbarstyle{hlines}{fillstyle=hlines}
\begin{pspicture}(-0.5,-0.1)(4,4)
  \psaxes[axesstyle=frame,Ox=0,Dx=1,Dy=2,
    labels=y,ticks=y](0,0)(4,4)
  \readpsbardata[header=false]{\data}{data2T.csv}
  \psbarchart[barcolsep=0,barstyle={vlines,hlines},
    chartstyle=stack]{\data}
\end{pspicture}
```

27.2.5 barsep

barsep is the factor that defines the fraction of space between two single connected data sets; it takes effect a level below barcolsep. The default of 0 (no space between values) can be changed arbitrarily.

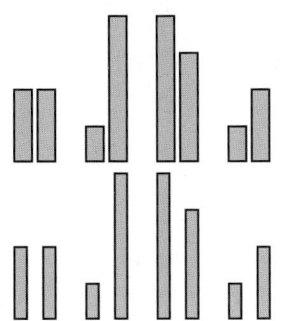

```
\usepackage{pstricks,pst-bar}

\readpsbardata[header=false]{\data}{data2T.csv}
\begin{pspicture}(-0.5,-0.1)(4,2)
    \psbarchart[barsep=0.05,barstyle={red,green},
        chartstyle=cluster]{\data}
\end{pspicture}

\begin{pspicture}(-0.5,-0.1)(4,2)
    \psbarchart[barsep=0.2,barstyle={red,green},
        chartstyle=cluster]{\data}
\end{pspicture}
```

27.2.6 barlabelrot

The x axis
labels are horizontal by default, but you can rotate them by an arbitrary angle about the "lower left" through barlabelrot.

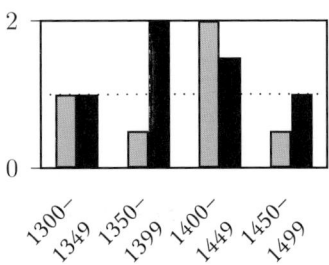

```
\usepackage{pstricks,pst-plot,pst-bar}

\readpsbardata{\data}{data1T.csv}
\begin{pspicture}(-0.5,-1.5)(4,2)
    \psgrid[xunit=4cm,gridlabels=0,
        subgriddiv=0,griddots=30](0,0)(1,2)
    \psaxes[axesstyle=frame,Ox=0,Dx=1,Dy=2,
        labels=y,ticks=y](0,0)(4,2)
    \psbarchart[barstyle={red,blue},
        barlabelrot=45,chartstyle=cluster]{\data}
\end{pspicture}
```

27.3 Commands

The main command is \psbarchart, though there are several additional commands that prepare the data and the layout. The following sections illustrate their use.

27.3.1 \readpsbardata

The \readpsbardata command works similarly to \readdata from the pst-plot package (cf. Section 15.4.2 on page 213), but interprets the data differently. This affects on one hand the header line and on the other hand the line-oriented structure of the file.

\readpsbardata [settings] {*command name*}{*file name*}

Let's look at the following data set, saved in a file called data1.csv:

```
1300--1349, 1350--1399, 1400--1449, 1450--1499
1, 2, 2, 6
1, 0, 4, 1
0, 0, 1, 3
```

27 pst-bar – bar charts

```
0, 0, 0, 2
1, 2, 0, 0
```

The file is read and saved in the \data command with

```
\readpsbardata{\data}{data1.csv}
```

A \show\data writes the saved data into the log file; the header line is not part of \data.

```
> \data=macro:
->[[1 2 2 6 ][1 0 4 1 ][0 0 1 3 ][0 0 0 2 ][1 2 0 0 ]].
l.23 \show\data
```

Because of the comma-separated list (CSV), the number of values per data set can be determined and put into a separate array to be able to process it more efficiently with Post-Script. The whole data is again part of an array. As the header option not being set to false, the first line was treated separately and saved in its own command.

27.3.2 \newpsbarstyle

This command was already mentioned in Section 27.2.3 for calling the predefined styles or defining new ones. Its syntax is:

\newpsbarstyle{*name*}{*definition*}

You can overwrite existing styles too, as in the following example.

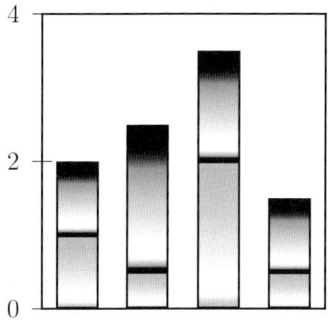

```
\usepackage{pstricks,pst-bar,pst-grad}

\newpsbarstyle{rG}{fillstyle=gradient,
   gradangle=0,gradbegin=red,gradend=white}
\newpsbarstyle{bG}{fillstyle=gradient,gradangle=0,
   gradbegin=blue,gradend=white}
\begin{pspicture}(-0.5,-0.1)(4,4)
\psaxes[axesstyle=frame,Ox=0,Dx=1,Dy=2,
   labels=y,ticks=y](0,0)(4,4)
\readpsbardata[header=false]{\data}{data2T.csv}
\psbarchart[barstyle={rG,bG},chartstyle=stack]{\data}
\end{pspicture}
```

27-03-1

27.3.3 \psbarlabel

The style that is used to place the horizontal labels can be influenced through \psbarlabel. This command is called before placing the text and doesn't have any parameters. It can only be changed by redefining it. The syntax is:

`\renewcommand*\psbarlabel{`*code*`}`

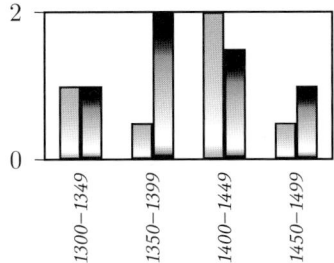

```
\usepackage{pstricks,pst-bar,pst-grad}

\renewcommand*{\psbarlabel}{\small\itshape}
\readpsbardata{\data}{data1T.csv}
\begin{pspicture}(-0.5,-1.75)(4,2)
  \psaxes[axesstyle=frame,Ox=0,Dx=1,Dy=2,
    labels=y,ticks=y](0,0)(4,2)
  \psbarchart[barlabelrot=90,
    barstyle={rG,bG},chartstyle=cluster]{\data}
\end{pspicture}
```

27.3.4 \psbarscale

The syntax for the \psbarscale command is:

`\psbarscale(`*scaling factor*`){`*PostScript code*`}`

The second argument of the \psbarscale command is directly passed to PostScript; it may contain PostScript code. Both specifications exclusively refer to the input data, which can be scaled globally by a factor and for example logarithmized through a PostScript command.

`\psbarscale(2){ 10 mul sqrt ln}`

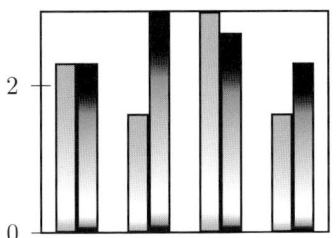

```
\usepackage{pstricks,pst-bar,pst-grad}

\psbarscale(2){10 mul sqrt ln}
\readpsbardata[header=false]{\data}{data1T.csv}
\begin{pspicture}(-0.5,-1.75)(4,2)
  \psaxes[axesstyle=frame,Ox=0,Dx=1,
    Dy=2,labels=y,ticks=y](0,0)(4,3)
  \psbarchart[barlabelrot=90,
    barstyle={redG,blueG},
    chartstyle=cluster]{\data}
\end{pspicture}
```

27.3.5 \psbarchart

The \psbarchart command achieves the actual display. The syntax is:

`\psbarchart [`*settings*`] {`*data command*`}`

You have to use \readpsbardata beforehand to read the external data.

27 pst-bar – bar charts

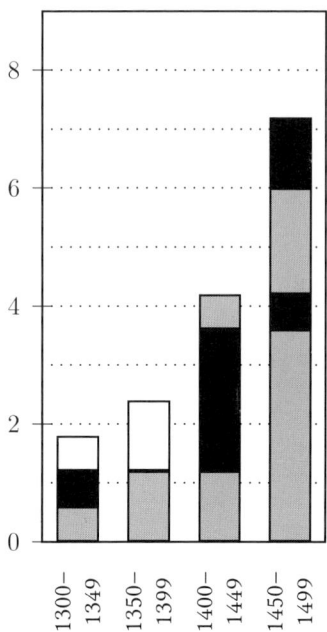

```
\usepackage{pstricks,pst-plot,pst-bar}

\psset{yunit=0.8}
\begin{pspicture}(-0.5,-1.75)(4,9)
  \psgrid[xunit=4cm,
    gridlabels=0,subgriddiv=0,
    griddots=30](0,0)(1,9)
  \psaxes[axesstyle=frame,Ox=0,Dx=1,Dy=2,
    labels=y,ticks=y](0,0)(4,9)
  \psbarscale(0.6){}
  \readpsbardata{\data}{data1.csv}
  \psbarchart[barstyle={red,blue,green,
    black,white},chartstyle=stack,
    barlabelrot=90]{\data}
\end{pspicture}
```

```
\usepackage{pst-bar,pstricks-add}
\psset{unit=0.4cm}
\begin{pspicture}(0,-0.5)(29,8)
  \newpsbarstyle{yellowhatch}{framearc=0.5,fillstyle=hlines*,
    fillcolor=yellow}
  \psaxes[xAxis=false,ticks=y,axesstyle=frame](0,0)(29,8)
  \psbarscale(0.5){2 add}
  \readpsbardata{\data}{temp.dat}
  \psbarchart[barstyle={yellowhatch},barcolsep=0.4]{\data}
\end{pspicture}
```

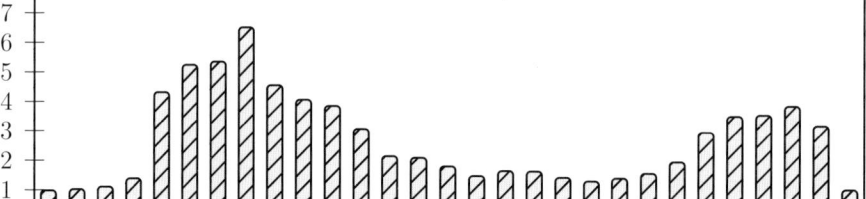

516

Chapter 28

Mathematical functions

28.1 pst-math – Extended PostScript functions 517
28.2 pst-func – Special functions 519

This chapter looks at two packages that provide additional support when drawing mathematical functions. The pst-math package has extensions for dealing with various trigonometric functions, Gaussian curves, and gamma functions. The broader pst-func package assists with polynomials, a wide range of probability distribution functions, and several other specialized mathematical functions.

28.1 pst-math – Extended PostScript functions

This package provides extended mathematical functions at PostScript level (cf. Section 28.1 on page 520). The package doesn't define any TeX commands and is in principle a pure PostScript file, which is loaded as prologue file through \usepackage{pst-math}. The following three sections give a quick example from each family of functions that the package covers; Table 28.1 on page 520 then lists the complete set of new functions available.

28.1.1 Trigonometric functions (normal and hyperbolic)

```
\usepackage{pst-plot,pst-math}
\psset{unit=0.75}
\begin{pspicture*}(-5,-4)(5,5.25)
\psaxes{->}(0,0)(-5,-4)(5,5)
\psset{linewidth=2pt}
\psplot[linecolor=blue]{-5}{5}{ x COSH }
\uput[0](-3.75,4){$\cosh x$}
\psplot[linecolor=red]{-5}{5}{ x SINH }
\uput[0](-3.5,-3){$\sinh x$}
\psplot[linecolor=green]{-5}{5}{ x TANH }
\uput[0](3,1.25){$\tanh x$}
\end{pspicture*}
```

28 Mathematical functions

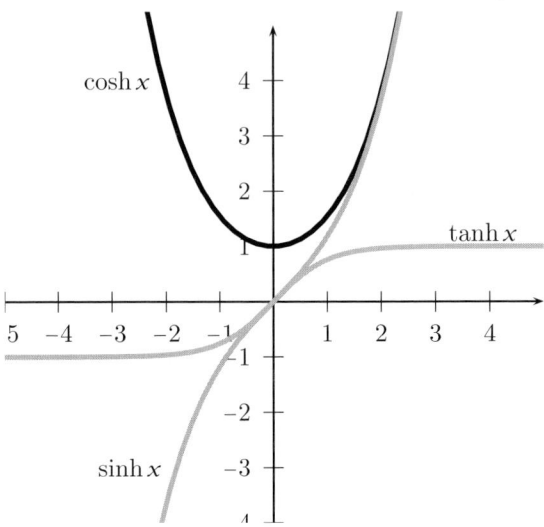

28.1.2 Gaussian Curve

The PostScript function GAUSS expects three parameters on the stack; the x value, the expected value μ, and the standard deviation σ.

$$\text{gauss}: \begin{cases} \mathbb{R} & \to & \mathbb{R} \\ x & \mapsto & \dfrac{1}{\sqrt{2\pi\sigma^2}} \exp - \dfrac{(x-\mu)^2}{2\sigma^2} \end{cases} \qquad (28.1)$$

```
\usepackage{pst-plot,pst-math}
\psset{yunit=5}
\begin{pspicture}(-5,-0.1)(5,0.65)
\psaxes[dy=0.2,Dy=0.2]{->}(0,0)(-5,-.1)(5,0.65)
\psset{linewidth=1pt,plotpoints=200}
\psplot[linecolor=blue]{-5}{5}{x 1 2 GAUSS}
\psplot[linecolor=red]{-5}{5}{x 0 .75 GAUSS}
\end{pspicture}
```

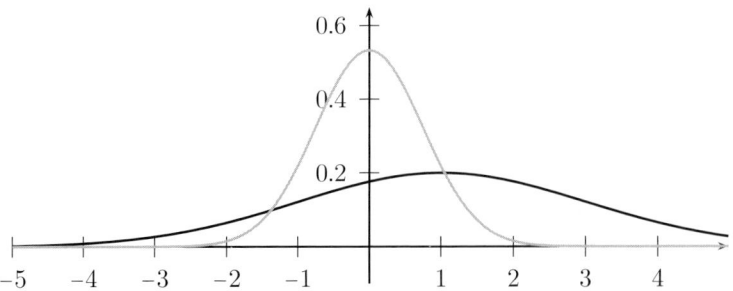

28.1.3 Gamma function and log gamma function

$$\Gamma : \begin{cases} \mathbb{R} \setminus \mathbb{Z} & \to \mathbb{R} \\ x & \mapsto \int_0^\infty t^{x-1} e^{-t}\, dt \end{cases} \qquad (28.2)$$

$$\ln\Gamma : \begin{cases}]0, +\infty[& \to \mathbb{R} \\ x & \mapsto \ln \int_0^t t^{x-1} e^{-t}\, dt \end{cases} \qquad (28.3)$$

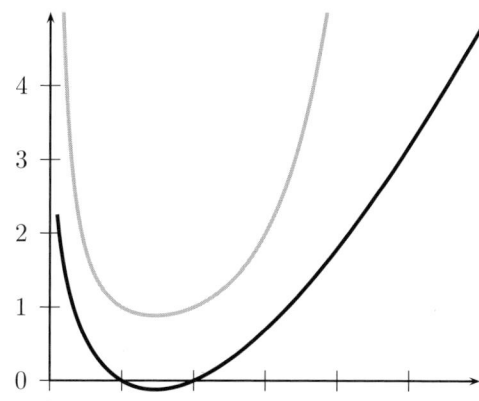

```
\usepackage{pst-plot,pst-math}

\begin{pspicture*}(-0.75,-.5)(6,5)
\psaxes{->}(6,5)
\psset{linewidth=1.5pt,plotpoints=200}
\psplot[linecolor=red]{.1}{6}{x GAMMA}
\psplot[linecolor=blue]{.1}{6}{x GAMMALN}
\end{pspicture*}
```

28.1.4 Summary

Table 28.1 gives a summary of the new mathematical functions of the pst-math package.

Note that the ATAN operator is different from the existing PostScript operator atan – ATAN expects only a single argument on the stack and applies it to the following equation: $\alpha = \left(\arctan \frac{-x}{-1}\right) - 180°$.

28.2 pst-func – Special functions

The pst-func package is in principle based on pst-plot, but contains new commands to deal specifically with plotting the special functions described here. These commands are significantly simpler to use for these functions than the \psplot command itself.

28.2.1 Polynomials

A polynomial of degree n is defined as:

$$f(x) = a_0 + a_1 x + a_2 x^2 + a_3 x^3 + \ldots + a_{n-1} x^{n-1} + a_n x^n \qquad (28.4)$$
$$f'(x) = a_1 + 2a_2 x + 3a_3 x^2 + \ldots + (n-1) a_{n-1} x^{n-2} + n a_n x^{n-1} \qquad (28.5)$$
$$f''(x) = 2a_2 + 6a_3 x + \ldots + (n-1)(n-2) a_{n-1} x^{n-3} + n(n-1) a_n x^{n-2} \qquad (28.6)$$

It is plotted with the \psPolynomial command, with the following syntax:

28 Mathematical functions

Table 28.1: Summary of the functions of pst-math

stack	operator	result	description
num	COS	real	return cos(num)
num	SIN	real	return sin(num)
num	TAN	real	return tan(num)
num	ACOS	angle	return arccos(num) in rad
num	ASIN	angle	return arcsin(num) in rad
num	ATAN	angle	return arctan(num) in rad
num	COSH	real	return cosh(num)
num	SINH	real	return sinh(num)
num	TANH	real	return tabh(num)
num	ACOSH	real	return arcosh(num) in rad
num	ASINH	real	return arsinh(num) in rad
num	ATANH	real	return artanh(num) in rad
num	EXP	real	return the power e^num
num$_1$ num$_2$ num$_3$	GAUSS	real	return the value of the Gaussian curve for num$_1$ with expected value num$_2$ and standard deviation num$_3$
num	SINC	real	return sin(num)/num in rad
num	GAMMA	real	return the Γ function of num
num	GAMMALN	real	return the logarithm of the Γ function of num

`\psPolynomial [settings] {`x_0`}{`x_1`}`

Only the coefficients and the start and end value are needed to plot the polynomial. The special options are summarized in Table 28.2 and are described further in the sections below.

Table 28.2: Summary of the parameters for the `\psPolynomial` command

name	type	default
coeff	a0 a1 a2...	0 0 1
Derivation	value	0
markZeros	boolean	false
epsZero	value	0.1
dZero	value	0.1
zeroLineTo	value	−1
zeroLineStyle	line style	dashed
zeroLineColor	colour	black
zeroLineWidth	value unit	0.5\pslinewidth

coeff

A polynomial is completely determined by specifying its coefficients. You **must** give them in order, a_0 a_1 a_2..., separated by a space. The number of coefficients is only limited by the amount of memory available on the system. The default value is coeff=0 1, which

28.2 pst-func – Special functions

corresponds to the equation of the straight line $y = a_0 + a_1 x = x$.
The following example shows the graphs of these functions:

$$f(x) = 6 + 3x - x^2 \tag{28.7}$$
$$g(x) = 2 - x - x^2 + 0.5x^3 - 0.1x^4 + 0.025x^5 \tag{28.8}$$
$$h(x) = -2 + x - x^2 + 0.5x^3 + 0.1x^4 + 0.025x^5 + 0.2x^6 \tag{28.9}$$

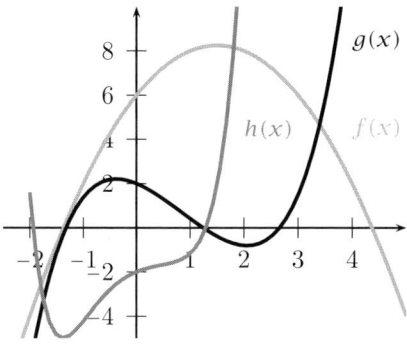

```
\usepackage{pstricks,pst-func}
\psset{yunit=0.3cm,xunit=0.75cm}
\begin{pspicture*}(-2.5,-5)(5,10)
  \psaxes[Dy=2]{->}(0,0)(-2.5,-5)(5,10)
  \psset{linewidth=1.5pt}
  \psPolynomial[coeff=6 3 -1,
     linecolor=red]{-3}{5}
  \psPolynomial[coeff=2 -1 -1 .5 -.1 .025,
     linecolor=blue]{-2}{4}
  \psPolynomial[coeff=-2 1 -1 .5 .1 .025 .2,
     linecolor=magenta]{-2}{4}
  \rput[lb](4,4){\textcolor{red}{$f(x)$}}
  \rput[lb](4,8){\textcolor{blue}{$g(x)$}}
  \rput[lb](2,4){\textcolor{magenta}{$h(x)$}}
\end{pspicture*}
```

Using the starred version of the pspicture environment limits the vertical size of the graph: the polynomials are calculated across the whole interval, but then function values that are too large are trimmed by the activated clipping function.

Derivation

The default is the function itself, which corresponds to the 0th derivation. The coefficients always have to be those of the non-derived function. When creating several graphs, the command has to be called accordingly often, as seen in the following example. The Derivation option lets you plot the derivation of a polynomial without having to specify the coefficients for this derivation.

```
\usepackage{pstricks,pst-func}
\psset{yunit=0.5cm,xunit=1.25}
\def\coeff{-2 1 -1 .5 .1 .025 .2}
\begin{pspicture*}(-3,-5)(3,10)
\psaxes[Dy=2]{->}(0,0)(-3,-5)(3,10)
\psset{linewidth=1.5pt}
\psPolynomial[coeff=\coeff,linecolor=magenta]{-2}{4}
\psPolynomial[coeff=\coeff,linecolor=red,linestyle=dashed,Derivation=1]{-2}{4}
\psPolynomial[coeff=\coeff,linecolor=blue,linestyle=dotted,Derivation=2]{-2}{4}
\rput[lb](2,4){\color{magenta}$h(x)$}
\rput[lb](1,1){\color{red}$h^{\prime}(x)$}
\rput[lb](-1,6){\color{blue}$h^{\prime\prime}(x)$}
\end{pspicture*}
```

28 Mathematical functions

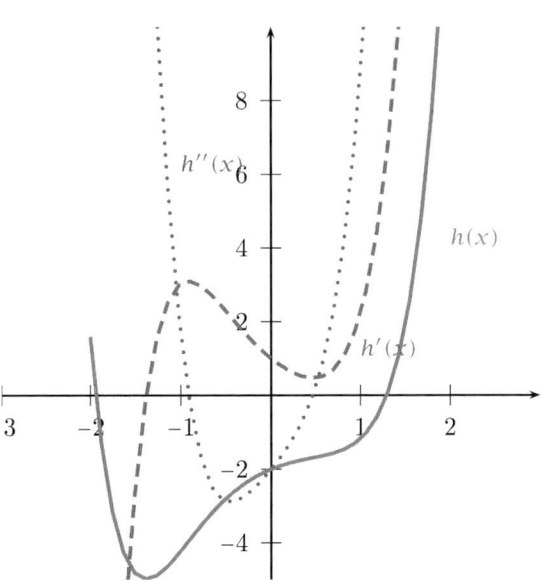

Determine and mark nulls

The rest of the parameters listed in Table 28.2 deal with determining and marking the points where the function evaluates to zero.

markZeros   This Boolean variable determines whether nulls are marked. The calculation of the nulls is done with the Newton method, which always finds a null if it exists and the function changes sign at this place. You can change the default dot marker through the dotstyle or dotscale parameters. This can be important as the nulls are marked before the curve is drawn, so the marks could disappear behind the graph.

epsZero   The difference between two nulls is called epsZero. It is used to test whether a found null has been calculated before. You can choose any arbitrarily small number as the value for this parameter but the smaller it is, the longer the compilation time.

dZero   Step of the x values used to search for nulls with the Newton method. This value, too, can be arbitrarily small.

zeroLineTo   Draws a line from the null of the current function or derivation to the "zeroLineTo" derivation.

zeroLineWidth   Line width with which the lines from the null to the value of the specified function or derivation are drawn.

zeroLineStyle   Line style with which the lines from the null to the value of the specified function of derivation are drawn. This has to be one of the PSTricks line styles (cf. Section 4.1.3 on page 45).

zeroLineColor   Line colour with which the lines from the null to the value of the specified function or derivation are drawn.

```
\usepackage{pstricks,pst-func}
\psset{yunit=0.4cm,xunit=0.8cm}
\begin{pspicture*}(-2,-5)(4,10)
  \psaxes[Dy=2,labelFontSize=\scriptstyle]{->}(0,0)(-3,-5)(4,10)
  \psset{linewidth=1pt,dotstyle=x}
  \psPolynomial[dotscale=2,Derivation=1,coeff=2 -1 -1 .5 -.1 .025,linecolor=red]{-2}{4}
  \psPolynomial[zeroLineTo=1,markZeros,dotscale=2,coeff=2 -1 -1 .5 -.1 .025,
               linecolor=blue]{-2}{4}
  \rput[lb](4,8){$g(x)$}
\end{pspicture*}
\quad
\begin{pspicture*}(-2,-5)(4,10)
  \psaxes[Dy=2,labelFontSize=\scriptstyle]{->}(0,0)(-3,-5)(4,10)
  \psset{linewidth=1pt}
  \psPolynomial[markZeros,dotscale=2,coeff=2 -1 -1 .5 -.1 .025,linecolor=cyan]{-2}{4}
  \rput[lb](4,8){$g(x)$}
\end{pspicture*}
```

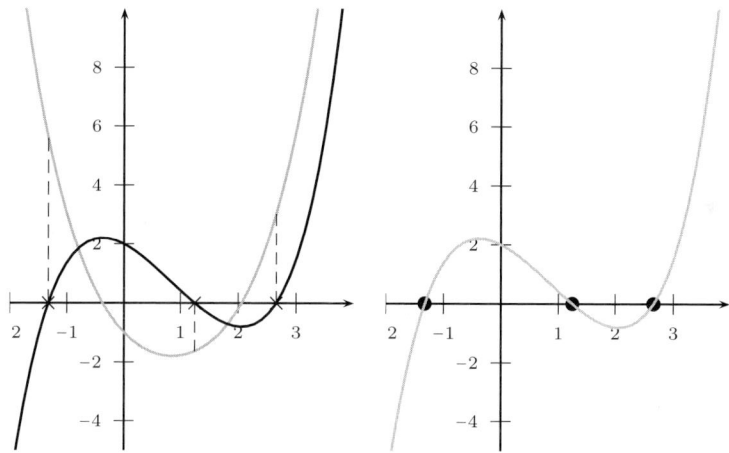

```
\usepackage{pstricks,pst-func}
\psset{xunit=1.25,yunit=0.75}
\begin{pspicture*}(-4,-5)(4,5)
  \psaxes[labelFontSize=\scriptstyle]{->}(0,0)(-4,-5)(4,5)
  \psset{dotscale=2,dotstyle=x,zeroLineStyle=dotted,zeroLineWidth=1pt}
  \psPolynomial[markZeros,linewidth=2pt,coeff=-1 1 -1 0 0.15]{-4}{3}
  \psPolynomial[markZeros,linecolor=red,linewidth=1pt,linestyle=dashed,
               coeff=-1 1 -1 0 0.15,Derivation=1,zeroLineTo=0]{-4}{3}
  \psPolynomial[markZeros,linecolor=magenta,linewidth=1pt,linestyle=dotted,
               coeff=-1 1 -1 0 0.15,Derivation=2,zeroLineTo=0]{-4}{3}
\end{pspicture*}
```

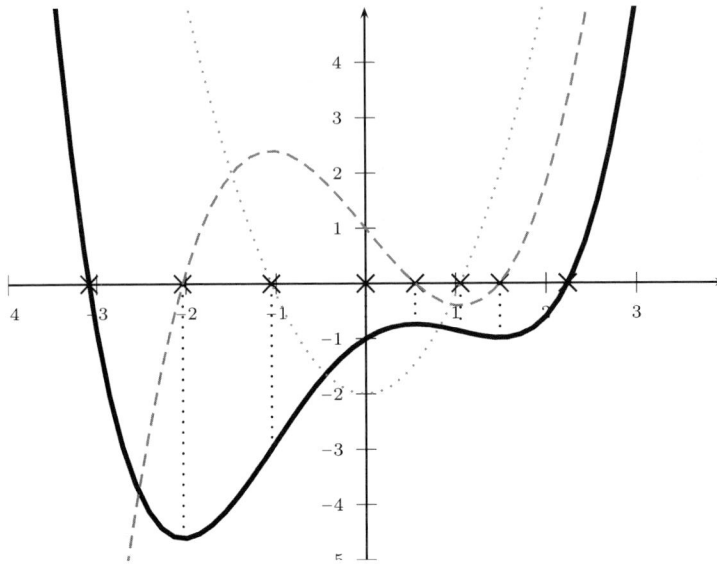

28.2.2 Higher-order Bezier curves

The \psBezier[1] command can output Bezier splines of order 1 to 9, where $n + 1$ pairs of values have to be given as interpolation points. For these interpolation points or control points $P_0, P_1, \ldots, P_n$, the corresponding Bezier curve or Bernstein-Bezier curve is:

$$C(t) = \sum_{i=0}^{n} P_i B_{i,n}(t) \qquad (28.10)$$

Here $B_{i,n}(t)$ is the Bernstein polynomial $B_{i,n}(t) = \binom{n}{i} t^i (1-t)^{n-i}$ with $t \in [0,1]$. The Bezier curves always start at the first interpolation point and end at the last.

\psBezier# [settings] $(x_0, y_0)(x_1, y_1) \ldots (x_n, y_n)$

stands for the order of the curve. The number of internal interpolation points for the calculation of the Bezier curve is determined by the plotpoints parameter, from the pst-plot package (cf. Section 15.2.1 on page 198). The default value here is set to 200.

```
\usepackage{pstricks,pst-func}
\psset{showpoints=true,linewidth=1.5pt,unit=0.5}
\begin{pspicture}(-2,-1)(2,2)% order 1 -- linear
   \psBezier1{<->}(-2,0)(-2,2)\end{pspicture}\quad
\begin{pspicture}(-2,-1)(2,2)% order 2 -- quadratric
   \psBezier2{<->}(-2,0)(-2,2)(0,2)\end{pspicture}\quad
\begin{pspicture}(-2,-1)(2,2)% order 3 -- cubic
   \psBezier3{<->}(-2,0)(-2,2)(0,2)(2,2)\end{pspicture}\quad
```

---

[1]Note the capital B – there is also \psbezier from the standard PSTricks package.

```
\begin{pspicture}(-2,-2)(2,2)% order 4 -- quartic
  \psBezier4{<->}(-2,0)(-2,2)(0,2)(2,2)(2,0)\end{pspicture}\quad
\begin{pspicture}(-2,-2)(2,2)% order 5 -- quintic
  \psBezier5{<->}(-2,0)(-2,2)(0,2)(2,2)(2,0)(2,-2)\end{pspicture}

\begin{pspicture}(-2,-2)(2,2)% order 6
  \psBezier6{<->}(-2,0)(-2,2)(0,2)(2,2)(2,0)(2,-2)(0,-2)\end{pspicture}\quad
\begin{pspicture}(-2,-2)(2,2)% order 7
  \psBezier7{<->}(-2,0)(-2,2)(0,2)(2,2)(2,0)(2,-2)(0,-2)(-2,-2)\end{pspicture}\quad
\begin{pspicture}(-2,-2)(2,2)% order 8
  \psBezier8{<->}(-2,0)(-2,2)(0,2)(2,2)(2,0)(2,-2)(0,-2)(-2,-2)(-2,0)\end{pspicture}
  \quad
\begin{pspicture}(-2,-2)(2,2)% order 9
  \psBezier9{<->}(-2,0)(-2,2)(0,2)(2,2)(2,0)(2,-2)(0,-2)(-2,-2)(-2,0)(0,0)
\end{pspicture}
```

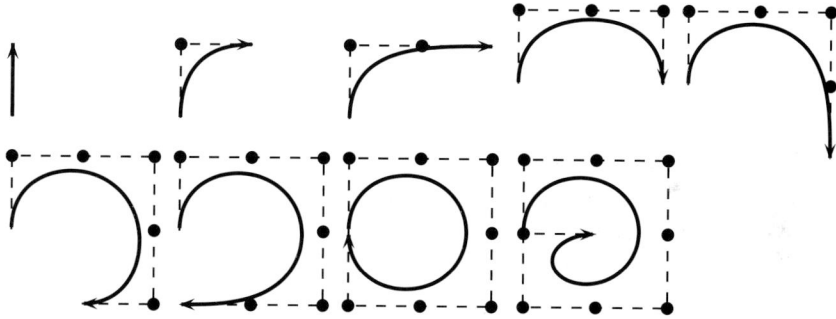

28.2.3 \psBernstein

Bernstein polynomials are defined by

$$B_{i,n}(t) = \binom{n}{i} t^i (1-t)^{n-i} \qquad (28.11)$$

where $\binom{n}{k}$ is a binomial coefficient and $B_{i,n}(t)$ a Bernstein polynomial of degree n.
The syntax for the \psBernstein command is:

\psBernstein [settings] (tStart,tEnd) (i,n)

The optional values for (tStart,tEnd) are predefined with (0,1). The only new parameter is envelope, which lets you output the envelope of the curve (as in the last two examples below).

28 Mathematical functions

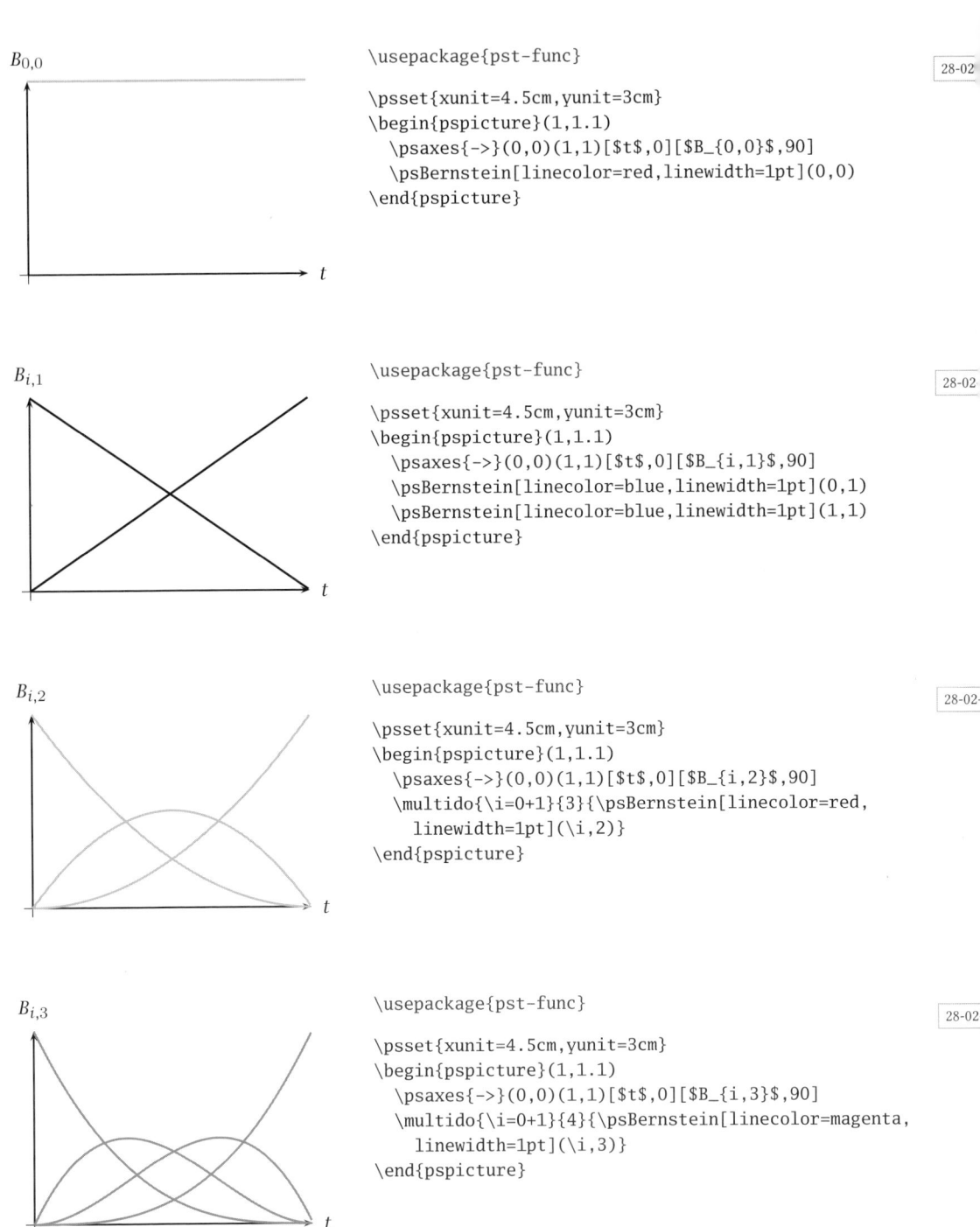

```
\usepackage{pst-func}

\psset{xunit=4.5cm,yunit=3cm}
\begin{pspicture}(1,1.1)
  \psaxes{->}(0,0)(1,1)[$t$,0][$B_{0,0}$,90]
  \psBernstein[linecolor=red,linewidth=1pt](0,0)
\end{pspicture}
```

```
\usepackage{pst-func}

\psset{xunit=4.5cm,yunit=3cm}
\begin{pspicture}(1,1.1)
  \psaxes{->}(0,0)(1,1)[$t$,0][$B_{i,1}$,90]
  \psBernstein[linecolor=blue,linewidth=1pt](0,1)
  \psBernstein[linecolor=blue,linewidth=1pt](1,1)
\end{pspicture}
```

```
\usepackage{pst-func}

\psset{xunit=4.5cm,yunit=3cm}
\begin{pspicture}(1,1.1)
  \psaxes{->}(0,0)(1,1)[$t$,0][$B_{i,2}$,90]
  \multido{\i=0+1}{3}{\psBernstein[linecolor=red,
    linewidth=1pt](\i,2)}
\end{pspicture}
```

```
\usepackage{pst-func}

\psset{xunit=4.5cm,yunit=3cm}
\begin{pspicture}(1,1.1)
  \psaxes{->}(0,0)(1,1)[$t$,0][$B_{i,3}$,90]
  \multido{\i=0+1}{4}{\psBernstein[linecolor=magenta,
    linewidth=1pt](\i,3)}
\end{pspicture}
```

28.2 pst-func – Special functions

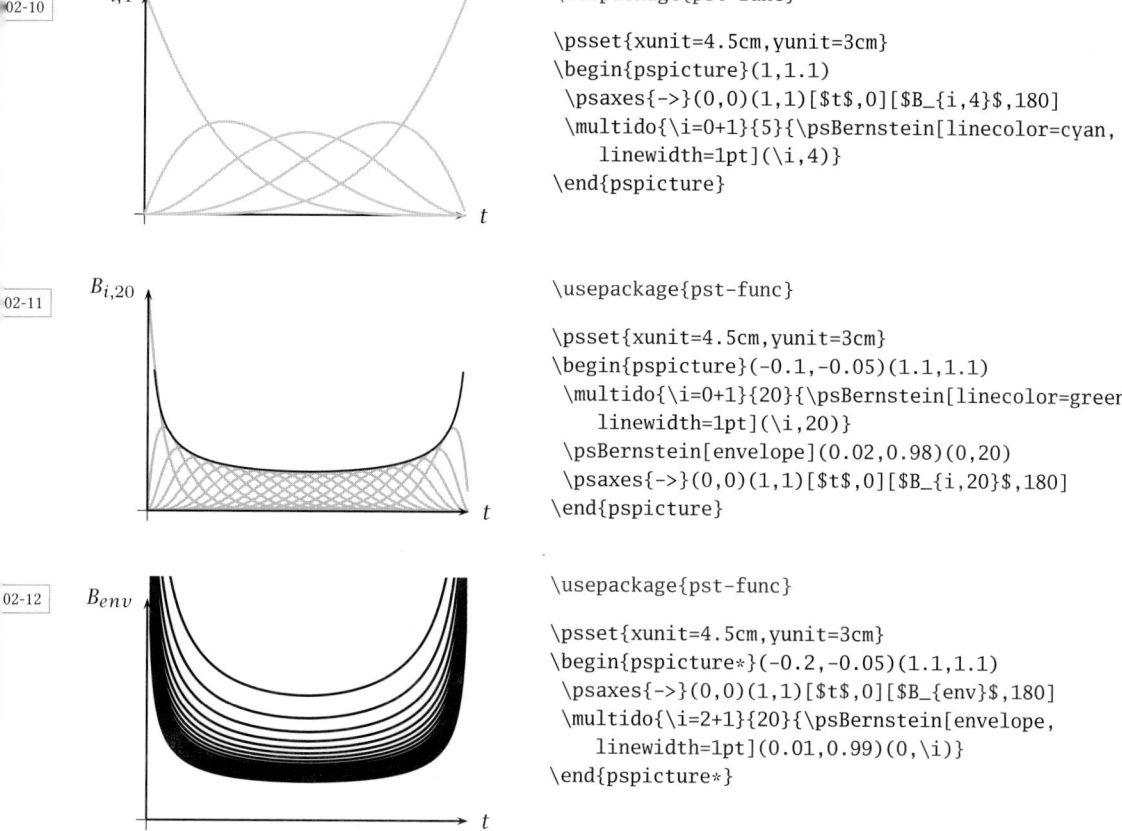

28.2.4 Fourier sums

A Fourier sumhas the form:

$$s(x) = \frac{a_0}{2} + a_1 \cos \omega x + a_2 \cos 2\omega x + a_3 \cos 3\omega x + \ldots + a_n \cos n\omega x$$
$$+ b_1 \sin \omega x + b_2 \sin 2\omega x + b_3 \sin 3\omega x + \ldots + b_m \sin m\omega x \qquad (28.12)$$

The \psFourier command is able to display the graph of such sums. The syntax is similar to that of \psPolynomial; the only difference is that two fields of coefficients have to be specified:

\psFourier[*cosCoeff=a0 a1…, sinCoeff=b1 b2…*]{x_0}{x_1}

You have to give the coefficients in the order a_0 a_1 a_2 … and b_1 b_2 b_3 …, separated by a space. The default is cosCoeff=0,sinCoeff=1, which corresponds to the normal sine function. You can only specify the constant term through the cosCoeff=*a0* option, not through sinCoeff.

28 Mathematical functions

```
\usepackage{pstricks,pst-func}
\begin{pspicture}(-5,-4)(5,5)
\psaxes{->}(0,0)(-5,-3.5)(5,5)
\psset{plotpoints=500,linewidth=1.5pt}
\psFourier[linecolor=red]{-4.5}{4.5}
\psFourier[sinCoeff=-.5 1 1 1 1 ,cosCoeff=-.5 1 1 1 1 1,linecolor=blue]{-4.5}{4.5}
\end{pspicture}
```

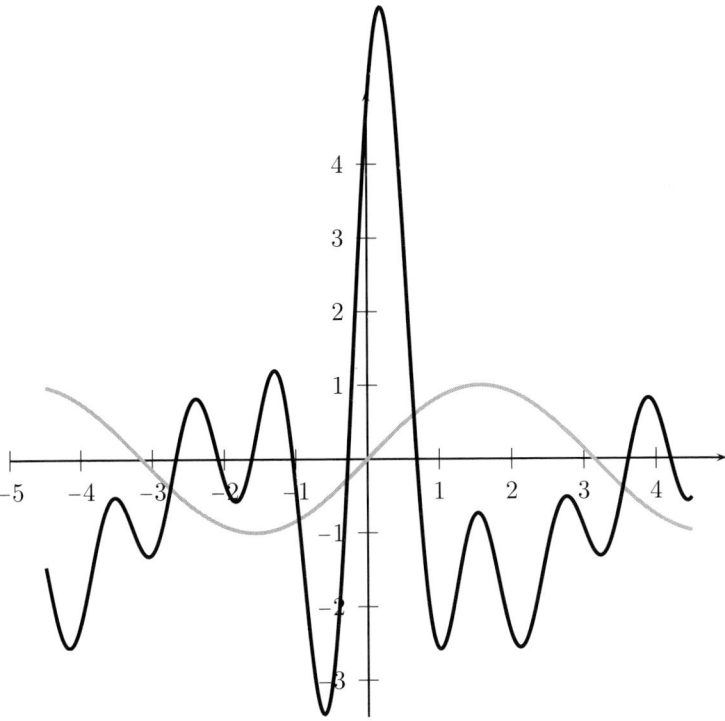

28.2.5 Integral sine and cosine

The general definitions for the integral sine and the integral cosine are:

$$\text{Si}(x) = \int_0^x \frac{\sin t}{t} dt \tag{28.13}$$

$$\text{si}(x) = -\int_x^\infty \frac{\sin t}{t} dt = \text{Si}(x) - \frac{\pi}{2} \tag{28.14}$$

$$\text{Ci}(x) = -\int_x^\infty \frac{\cos t}{t} dt = \gamma + \ln x + \int_0^x \frac{\cos t - 1}{t} dt \tag{28.15}$$

The syntax of the individual commands is:

\psSi [settings] $\{x_0\}\{x_1\}$	\pssi [settings] $\{x_0\}\{x_1\}$
\psCi [settings] $\{x_0\}\{x_1\}$	\psci [settings] $\{x_0\}\{x_1\}$

28.2 pst-func – Special functions

```
\usepackage{pstricks,pst-func}
\psset{xunit=0.75}
\begin{pspicture}(-0.25,-2)(15,2) \psaxes[dx=1cm,Dx=2]{->}(0,0)(-0.25,-2)(15,2)
  \psplot[plotpoints=500]{0.01}{14.5}{ x RadtoDeg sin x div }
  \psSi[plotpoints=500,linecolor=red,linewidth=1pt]{0.01}{14.5}
  \pssi[plotpoints=500,linecolor=blue,linewidth=1pt]{0.01}{14.5}
  \rput(5,1){\color{red}$Si(x)=\int\limits_{0}^x \frac{\sin(t)}{t}\dt$}
  \rput(4.5,-1.5){\color{blue}$si(x)=-\int\limits_{x}^{\infty}
     \frac{\sin(t)}{t}\dt=Si(x)-\frac{\pi}{2}$}
  \rput(8,.5){$f(x)= \frac{\sin(t)}{t}$}
\end{pspicture}
```

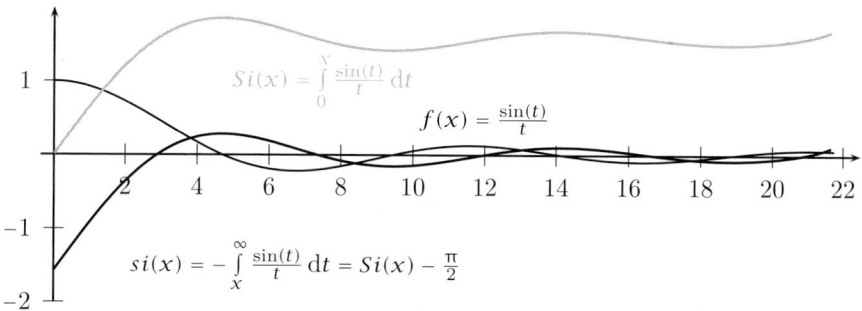

28.2.6 Bessel functions

The solutions of the Bessel differential equation are called Bessel functions and play an important role in the natural sciences. The Bessel function of order n in sum form is defined by:

$$J_n(x) = \frac{1}{\pi}\int_0^\pi \cos(x\sin t - nt)dt = \sum_{k=0}^\infty \frac{(-1)^k}{k!\Gamma(n+k+1)}\left(\frac{x}{2}\right)^{n+2k} \quad (28.16)$$

The syntax of the corresponding command is:

`\psBessel [settings] {order}{x_0}{x_1}`

There are two additional parameters for the Bessel function:

name	type	default
constI	value	1
constII	value	0

These two "constants" have the following meaning: $f(t) = \text{constI} \times J_n + \text{constII}$. The first constant has a multiplicative effect and the second has an additive effect; this allows you to manipulate the output of the Bessel function arbitrarily. Both `constI` and `constII` have to be valid PostScript expressions, for example

`\psset{constI=2.3,constII=t RadtoDeg sin 1.2 mul 0.37 add}`

28 Mathematical functions

The function itself is plotted internally with the \parametricplot command (cf. Section 15.3.2); because of this only the variable name t is valid here. The PostScript function DegtoRad is defined in the PSTricks prologue file.

With both constants defined as above:

$$f(t) = 2.3 \times J_n + 1.2 \times \sin t + 0.37 \qquad (28.17)$$

The number of calculation steps has to be set to at least 500 (with the plotpoints parameter, cf. Section 15.2.1 on page 198) to achieve a sufficient level of precision for the display. You can of course make it much larger, though this results in a longer compilation time.

```
\usepackage{pstricks}
\usepackage{pst-func}
\psset{xunit=0.25,yunit=5}
\begin{pspicture}(-12,-.65)(12,1.1)
  \rput(13,0.8){$\displaystyle
    J_n(x)=\frac{1}{\pi}\int_0^\pi\cos(x\sin t-nt)\mathrm{d}t$}
  \psaxes[Dy=0.2,Dx=4]{->}(0,0)(-26,-.6)(26,1.05)
  \psset{linewidth=1pt}
  \psBessel[linecolor=red]{0}{-25}{25}
  \psBessel[linecolor=blue]{1}{-25}{25}
  \psBessel[linecolor=magenta]{3}{-25}{25}
\end{pspicture}
```

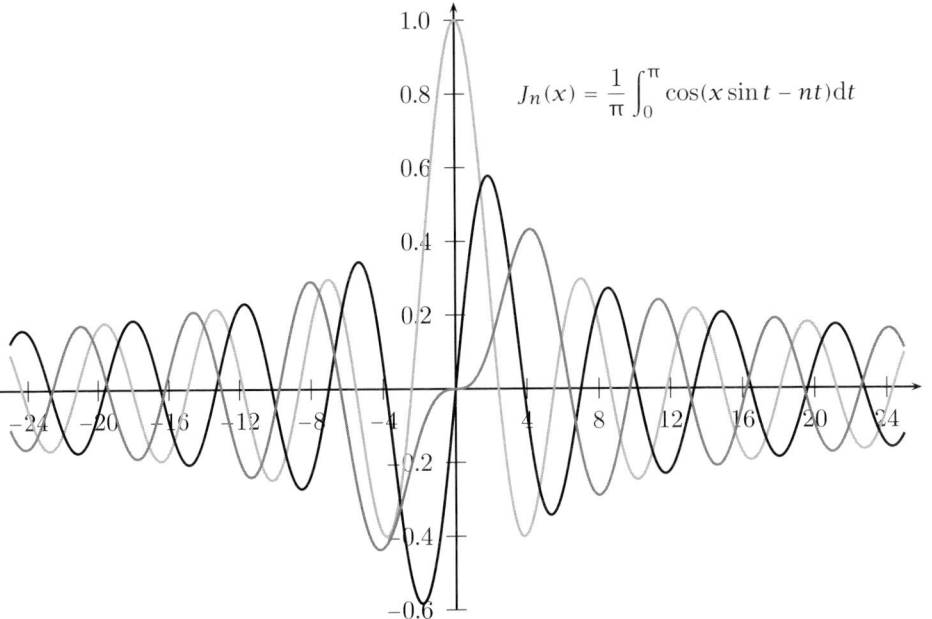

530

28.2.7 Output function values

The `\psPrintValue` command allows you to output arbitrary function values. The calculation happens in PostScript, so you have to give the description of the function in PostScript notation (cf. Section 15.3 on page 203). The syntax for the command is:

`\psPrintValue` [settings] {*PostScript code*}

There are three special parameters, all of which take effect in PostScript:

name	type	default	meaning
PSfont	PS font	Times	only PostScript font names are valid, for example Times-Roman, Helvetica, Courier, AvantGard, Bookman
fontscale	value	10	specification in pt
valuewidth	value	10	the width of the box for the real number – no output occurs if the width is too small

```
\usepackage{pstricks,pst-func}
\psset{fontscale=10}
\makebox[2em]{x(deg)}       \makebox[5em]{$sin x$}
\makebox[5em]{$cos x$}      \makebox[5em]{$\sqrt x$}
\makebox[7em]{$sin x+cos x$}\makebox[6em]{$sin^2 x+cos^2 x$}\\[3pt]
\multido{\iA=0+10}{12}{%
  \makebox[1em]{\iA}
  \makebox[5em]{\psPrintValue[PSfont=Helvetica]{\iA\space sin}}
  \makebox[5em]{\psPrintValue[PSfont=Courier,fontscale=10]{\iA\space cos}}
  \makebox[5em]{\psPrintValue[valuewidth=15,linecolor=blue,
    PSfont=AvantGarde]{\iA\space sqrt}}
  \makebox[7em]{\psPrintValue[PSfont=Times-Italic]{\iA\space dup sin exch cos add}}
  \makebox[6em]{\psPrintValue[PSfont=Palatino-Roman]{
    \iA\space dup sin dup mul exch cos dup mul add}}\\}
```

x(deg)	$\sin x$	$\cos x$	$\sqrt{x}$	$\sin x + \cos x$	$\sin^2 x + \cos^2 x$
0	0.0	1.0	0.0	1.0	1.0
10	0.173648	0.984808	3.16228	1.15846	1.0
20	0.34202	0.939693	4.47214	1.28171	1.0
30	0.5	0.866025	5.47723	1.36603	1.0
40	0.642788	0.766044	6.32456	1.40883	1.0
50	0.766044	0.642788	7.07107	1.40883	1.0
60	0.866025	0.5	7.74597	1.36603	1.0
70	0.939693	0.34202	8.3666	1.28171	1.0
80	0.984808	0.173648	8.94427	1.15846	1.0
90	1.0	0.0	9.48683	1.0	1.0
100	0.984808	-0.173648	10.0	0.81116	1.0
110	0.939693	-0.34202	10.4881	0.597672	1.0

28 Mathematical functions

 Since \psPrintValue only works on the PostScript side, it is nothing but a box of null dimension as far as TEX is concerned, so space must be reserved explicitly for it; this was done in the previous example with the \makebox command.

28.2.8 Distribution functions

The next few sections cover commands for plotting probability distributions. If the distribution is discrete, you can use the markZeros option to display the function as a histogram instead of a polyline. Other options used in conjunction with markZeros change the format of the histogram: printValue outputs the corresponding value labels above the histogram bar and rotated by $90°$; barwidth gives the factor (without unit) for the relative width of the rectangles. These options for use with discrete distributions are summarized below; the options given in Section 28.2.7 on the previous page for the \psPrintValue command are also valid.

name	type	default	meaning
markZeros	boolean	true	draws a histogram instead of a polyline
printValue	boolean	false	output value
barwidth	value	1	specification of the width of the rectangles as a factor (not valid for the normed distribution functions)

Examples of displaying distribution functions as histograms are given below in the sections on binomial distributions and the Poisson distribution.

Binomial distributions

The binomial distribution is the discrete probability distribution $P_p(n|N)$ for exactly n of N Bernoulli experiments[2], where for every experiment a probability of p and a counter probability of $q = 1 - p$ is assumed. Therefore for the binomial distribution the following applies:

$$P_p(n|N) = \binom{N}{n} p^n q^{N-n} \qquad (28.18)$$

$$= \frac{N!}{n!(N-n)!} p^n (1-p)^{N-n}, \qquad (28.19)$$

where $\binom{N}{n}$ is the binomial coefficient and p the probability. [89]

The two binomial distributions are created within the x interval $[0, 1]$ (though you can change the scale through the unit options); \psBinomialN is the normed distribution. The syntax for the commands is:

\psBinomial [settings] {N}{probability p}
\psBinomialN [settings] {N}{probability p}

There are some restrictions on the number N of maximum experiments, which depend on the chosen probability p. In general, expect problems for values of $N > 100$ because PostScript doesn't have the required precision for floating point numbers.

---

[2] Jakob Bernoulli, 1655–1705.

The following three examples use the \psBinomial command for the normal binomial distribution.

```
\usepackage{pstricks,pst-func}
\psset[pst-func]{barwidth=1}
\psset{xunit=1cm,yunit=5cm}
\begin{pspicture}(-1,-0.15)(7,0.5)
\psaxes[Dy=0.2,dy=0.2\psyunit]{->}(0,0)(-1,0)(7,0.5)
\uput[-90](7,0){$k$} \uput[90](0,0.5){$P(X=k)$}
\psBinomial[markZeros,printValue,fillstyle=vlines]{6}{0.4}
\end{pspicture}
```

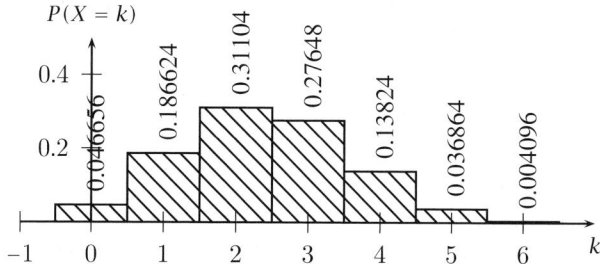

```
\usepackage{pstricks,pst-func}
\psset{xunit=1cm,yunit=10cm}
\begin{pspicture}(-1,-0.1)(8,0.4)
\psaxes[Dy=0.2,dy=0.2\psyunit]{->}(0,0)(-1,0)(8,0.4)
\uput[-90](8,0){$k$} \uput[90](0,0.4){$P(X=k)$}
\psBinomial[linecolor=red,markZeros,printValue,fillstyle=solid,
        fillcolor=blue,barwidth=0.2]{7}{0.6}
\end{pspicture}
```

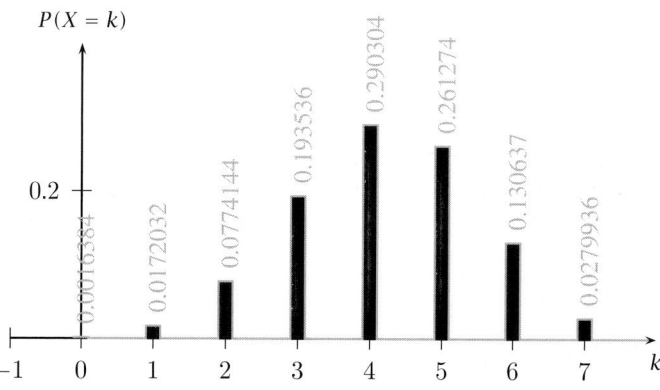

```
\usepackage{pstricks,pst-func}
\psset{xunit=0.25cm,yunit=10cm}
\begin{pspicture*}(-1,-0.1)(51,0.52)
```

```
\psaxes[Dx=5,dx=5\psxunit,Dy=0.2,dy=0.2\psyunit]{->}(50,0.5)
\uput[-90](50,0){$k$} \uput[0](0,0.5){$P(X=k)$}
\psBinomial[markZeros,linecolor=red]{4}{.5} \psset{linewidth=1pt}
\psBinomial[linecolor=green]{5}{.5} \psBinomial[linecolor=blue]{10}{.5}
\psBinomial[linecolor=red]{20}{.5}  \psBinomial[linecolor=magenta]{50}{.5}
\psBinomial[linecolor=cyan]{75}{.5}
\end{pspicture*}
```

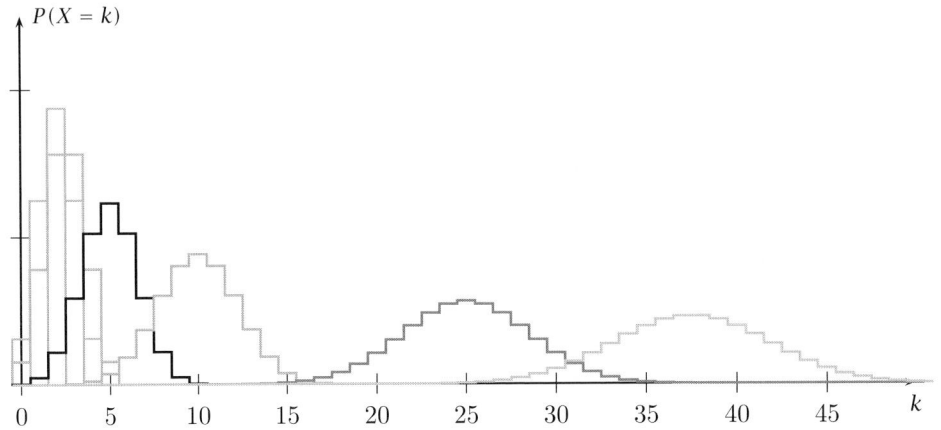

The normal binomial distribution has mean $\mu = E(X) = N \times p$ and standard deviation (variance) $\sigma^2 = \mu \times (1 - p)$. The normed binomial distribution, however, has the mean 0. Instead of $P(X = k)$, $P(Z = z)$ with $Z = \dfrac{X - E(X)}{\sigma(X)}$ and $P \leftarrow P \times \sigma$ are used. Both binomial distributions use a recursive definition:

$$P(k) = P(k-1) \times \frac{N - k + 1}{k} \times \frac{p}{1 - p} \qquad (28.20)$$

The following five examples use the \psBinomialN command for the normal binomial distribution.

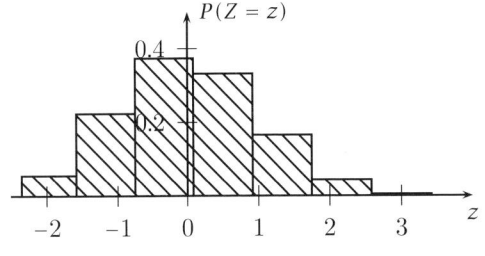

```
\usepackage{pstricks,pst-func}

\psset{yunit=5cm}%
\begin{pspicture}(-2.5,-0.15)(4,0.55)
    \psaxes[Dy=0.2,dy=0.2\psyunit]%
        {->}(0,0)(-2.5,0)(4,0.5)
    \uput[-90](4,0){$z$}
    \uput[0](0,0.5){$P(Z=z)$}
    \psBinomialN[markZeros,
        fillstyle=vlines]{6}{0.4}
\end{pspicture}
```

```
\usepackage{pstricks,pst-func}
\psset{yunit=10}\begin{pspicture*}(-6,-0.07)(6.1,0.55)
    \psaxes[Dy=0.2,dy=0.2\psyunit]{->}(0,0)(-6,0)(6,0.5)
```

```
  \uput[-90](6,0){$z$} \uput[0](0,0.5){$P(Z=z)$}
  \psBinomialN{125}{.5}\psBinomialN[markZeros,linewidth=1pt,linecolor=red]{4}{.5}
\end{pspicture*}
```

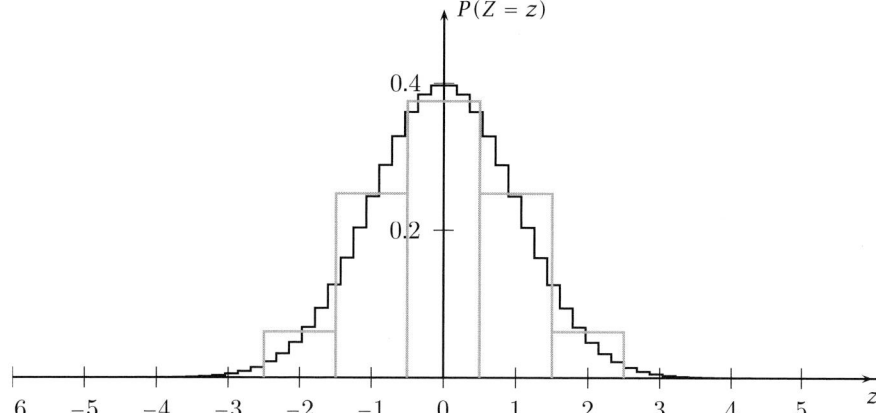

```
\usepackage{pstricks,pst-func}
\psset{yunit=10}\begin{pspicture*}(-6,-0.07)(6.1,0.52)
  \psaxes[Dy=0.2,dy=0.2\psyunit]{->}(0,0)(-6,0)(6,0.5)
  \uput[-90](6,0){$z$} \uput[0](0,0.5){$P(Z=z)$}
  \psBinomialN[markZeros,linecolor=red]{4}{.5}\psset{linewidth=1pt}
  \psBinomialN[linecolor=green]{5}{.5}\psBinomialN[linecolor=blue]{10}{.5}
  \psBinomialN[linecolor=red]{20}{.5} \psBinomialN[linecolor=gray]{50}{.5}
\end{pspicture*}
```

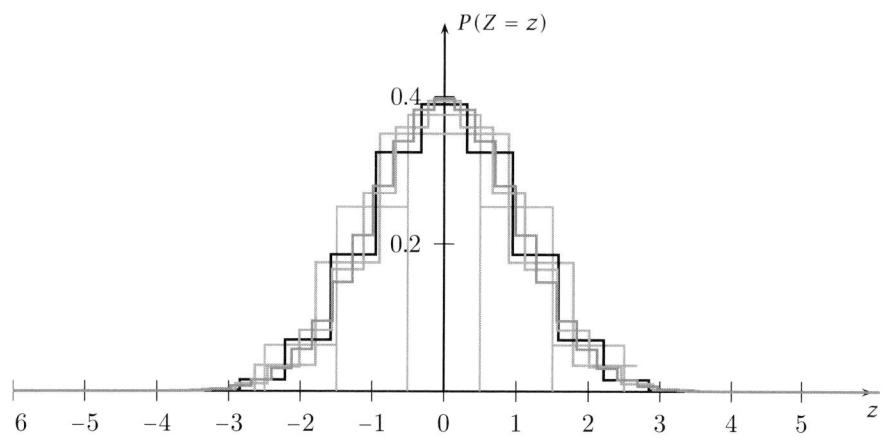

For the normed binomial distribution \psBinomialN, you can alternatively choose plotstyle=curve to allow a better comparison with the normal distribution. The showpoints option is also available in this case.

28 Mathematical functions

```
\usepackage{pstricks,pst-func}
\psset{yunit=10cm}
\begin{pspicture*}(-4,-0.06)(4.1,0.57)
\psaxes[Dy=0.2,dy=0.2\psyunit]{->}(0,0)(-4,0)(4,0.5)
\uput[-90](4,0){$z$} \uput[90](0,0.5){$P(Z=z)$}
\psBinomialN[linecolor=red,fillstyle=vlines,showpoints=true,markZeros]{36}{0.5}
\psBinomialN[linecolor=blue,showpoints=true,plotstyle=curve]{36}{0.5}
\end{pspicture*}\\[10pt]
\psset{yunit=10cm}
\begin{pspicture*}(-4,-0.06)(4.2,0.57)
\psaxes[Dy=0.2,dy=0.2\psyunit]{->}(0,0)(-4,0)(4,0.5)
\uput[-90](4,0){$z$} \uput[90](0,0.5){$P(Z=z)$}
\psBinomialN[linecolor=red]{10}{0.6}
\psBinomialN[linecolor=blue,showpoints=true,plotstyle=curve]{10}{0.6}
\end{pspicture*}
```

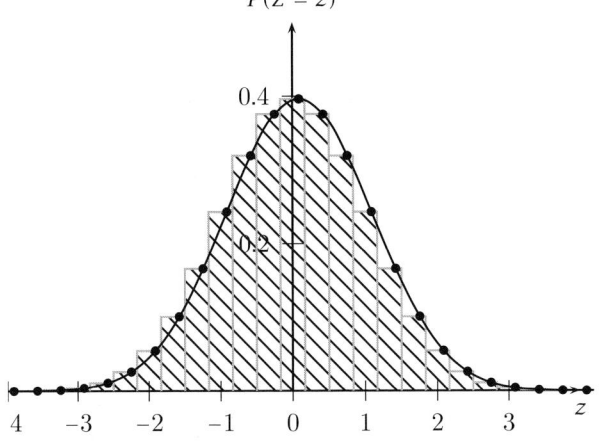

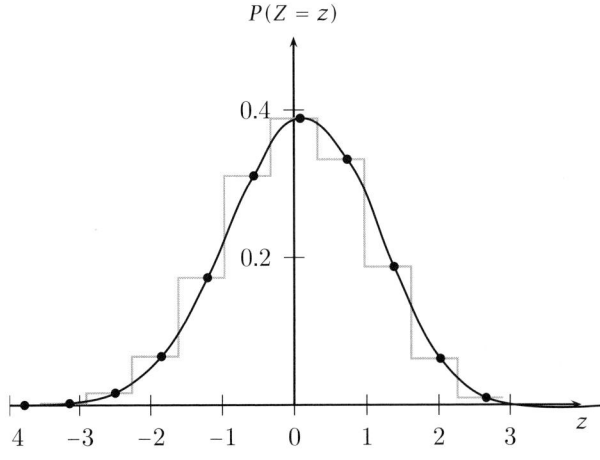

Poisson distribution

For a Poisson process the probability of n successes for N experiments is given by the limit of the binomial distribution [89]:

$$P_p(n|N) = \frac{N!}{n!(N-n)!} \times p^n(1-p)^{N-n} \tag{28.21}$$

The expected number of successes (λ) can be expressed as:

$$\lambda = N \times p \tag{28.22}$$

If we look at the distribution as a function of λ instead of the number of experiments N for fixed p, Equation becomes 28.21

$$P_{\frac{\lambda}{n}}(n|N) = \frac{N!}{n!(N-n)!}\left(\frac{\lambda}{N}\right)^n\left(\frac{1-\lambda}{N}\right)^{N-n} \tag{28.23}$$

If now the number of experiments becomes very large ($N \to \infty$), the distribution tends to:

$$P_\lambda(X=k) = \frac{\lambda^k}{k!}e^{-\lambda}$$

With $p = \frac{\lambda}{n}$ the value of a Poisson-distributed random variable at position k is the following limit:

$$\lim_{n\to\infty} P(X=k) = \lim_{n\to\infty} \frac{n!}{(n-k)!\,k!}\left(\frac{\lambda}{n}\right)^k\left(1-\frac{\lambda}{n}\right)^{n-k} \tag{28.24}$$

$$= \lim_{n\to\infty}\left(\frac{(n-k)! \times (n-k+1)\cdots(n-2)(n-1)n}{(n-k)!\,n^k}\right) \times \tag{28.25}$$

$$\left(\frac{\lambda^k}{k!}\right)\left(1-\frac{\lambda}{n}\right)^n\left(1-\frac{\lambda}{n}\right)^{-k} \tag{28.26}$$

$$= \frac{\lambda^k}{k!} \times \underbrace{\lim_{n\to\infty}\left(\frac{n}{n}\times\frac{n-1}{n}\times\frac{n-2}{n}\times\ldots\times\frac{n-k+1}{n}\right)}_{\to 1} \times \tag{28.27}$$

$$\underbrace{\left(1-\frac{\lambda}{n}\right)^n}_{\to e^{-\lambda}}\underbrace{\left(1-\frac{\lambda}{n}\right)^{-k}}_{\to 1} \tag{28.28}$$

$$= \lambda^k e^{\frac{-\lambda}{k!}} \tag{28.29}$$

This is called the Poisson distribution. Its corresponding command has the following syntax:

```
\psPoisson [settings] {N}{λ}
```

```
\usepackage{pstricks,pst-func}
\psset{xunit=0.8cm,yunit=20cm}
\begin{pspicture}(-1,-0.05)(14,0.25)
\uput[-90](14,0){$k$}
\uput[90](0,0.2){$P(X=k)$}
\psPoisson[linecolor=red,markZeros,fillstyle=solid,
```

28 Mathematical functions

```
    fillcolor=blue!10,printValue,valuewidth=20]{13}{6} % N lambda
\psaxes[Dy=0.1,dy=0.1\psyunit,labelFontSize=\scriptstyle]{->}(0,0)(-1,0)(14,0.2)
\end{pspicture}
```

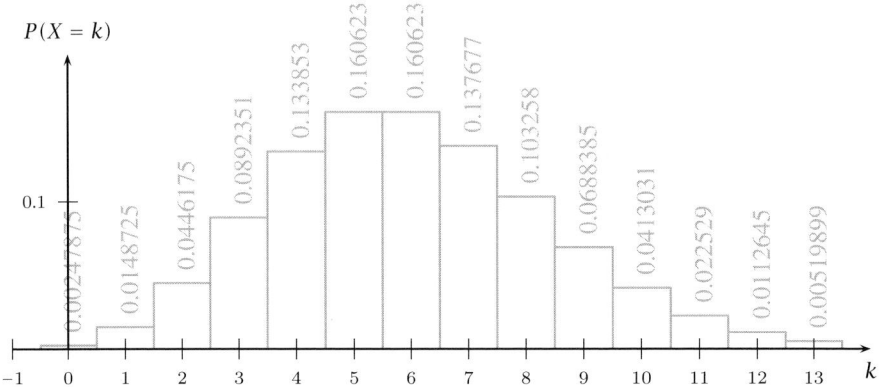

Gaussian distribution

The Gaussian or normal distribution[3] is an important type of continuous probability distribution as many natural and economic processes can be described by it. The Gaussian distribution is in general defined as:

$$f(x) = \frac{1}{\sigma\sqrt{2\pi}} e^{-\frac{(x-\mu)^2}{2\sigma^2}} \qquad (28.30)$$

The commands for the distribution and its integral have the following syntax:

| `\psGauss [settings] {`x_0`}{`x_1`}` | `\psGaussI [settings] {`x_0`}{`x_1`}` |

There are three special parameters:

name	type	default
sigma	value	0.5
mue	value	0
Simpson	value	5

sigma (σ) is the standard deviation and mue (μ) the expected value; you can change the default value for either in the usual manner with \psset. The Simpson method[4] is employed for the numeric integration of the Gaussian distribution: the number of interpolation points for the numeric integration is specified through the plotpoints parameter, which is set to 50 by default; independent of that the number of partial intervals per step, and therefore the precision, is specified through the Simpson parameter, which is set to 5 by default – it is unlikely that you will need to change the default value.

---

[3] Carl Friedrich Gauß, 1777–1855.
[4] Thomas Simpson, 1710–1761.

```
\usepackage{pstricks,pst-func,amsmath}
\psset{yunit=4cm,xunit=3}
\begin{pspicture}(-2,-0.15)(2,1.25)
  \psaxes[Dy=0.25]{->}(0,0)(-2,0)(2,1.2)
  \uput[-90](2,0){x}\uput[0](0,1.2){y}
  \rput[lb](0.6,0.5){$\sigma=0.5$}\rput[lb](1,0.5){$\sigma=1$}
  \rput[lb](-2,0.5){$f(x)=\dfrac{1}{\sigma\sqrt{2\pi}}\,
    e^{-\dfrac{(x-\mu)^2}{2\sigma{}^2}}$}
  \psGauss[linecolor=red,linewidth=2pt]{-2}{1.75}
  \psGaussI[linewidth=1pt,yunit=0.75]{-2}{1.75}
  \rput[lb](1,0.9){$\int f(x)\,\mathrm{d}x$}
  \psGauss[linecolor=cyan,mue=0.5,linewidth=2pt]{-2}{1.75}
  \psGauss[sigma=1,linecolor=blue,linewidth=2pt]{-2}{2}
\end{pspicture}
```

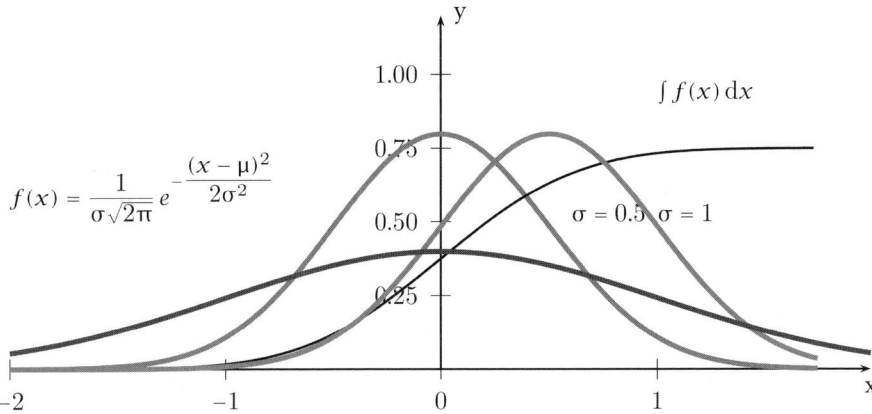

Gamma distribution

The Gamma distribution is a continuous probability distribution on the set of positive real numbers. It is a direct generalization of the exponential function on one hand and the Erlang distribution for non-integer parameters on the other hand. The Gamma distribution has two parameters α and β and is defined as:

$$f(x) = \frac{\beta(\beta x)^{\alpha-1} e^{-\beta x}}{\Gamma(\alpha)} \qquad \text{for } x > 0 \text{ and } \alpha, \beta > 0 \qquad (28.31)$$

The command has the following syntax:

\psGammaDist [settings] {x_0}{x_1}

The =alpha and =beta parameters are set to $\alpha = 0.5$ and $\beta = 0.5$ by default.

```
\usepackage{pst-func}
\psset{xunit=1.2cm,yunit=10cm,plotpoints=200}
\begin{pspicture*}(-0.75,-0.07)(9.5,0.85)
  \psGammaDist[linewidth=1pt,linecolor=red]{0.01}{9}
```

```
\psGammaDist[linewidth=1pt,linecolor=blue,alpha=0.3,beta=0.7]{0.01}{9}
\psGammaDist[linewidth=1pt,linecolor=green,alpha=2,beta=2]{0.01}{9}
\psGammaDist[linewidth=1pt,linecolor=cyan,alpha=2,beta=1]{0.01}{9}
\psaxes[Dy=0.1]{->}(0,0)(9.5,.8)
\end{pspicture*}
```

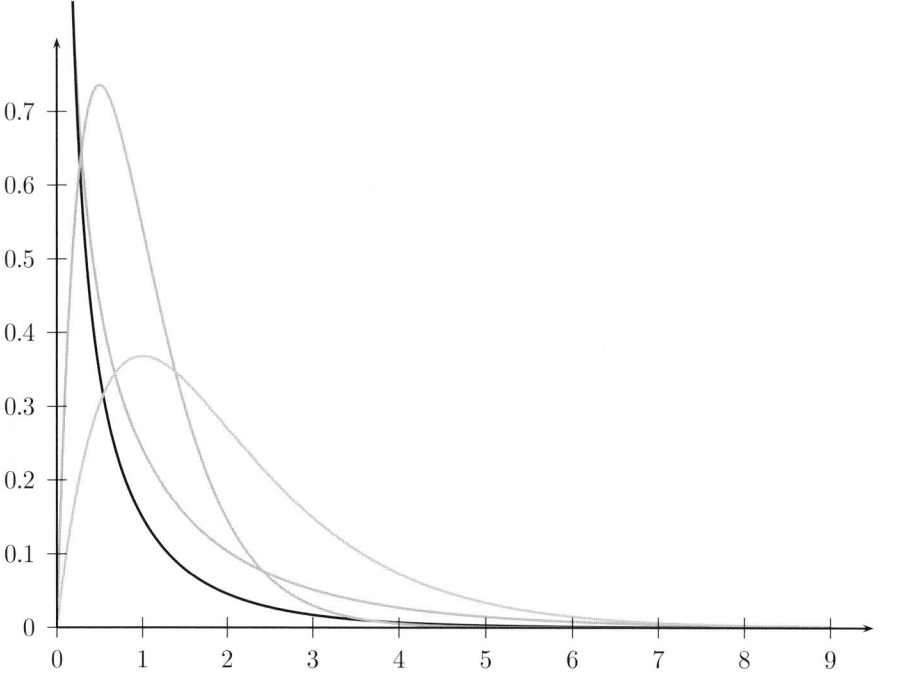

χ^2 distribution

The χ^2 distribution is a continuous probability distribution (sample distribution) on the set of positive real numbers. It is used to estimate distribution parameters.

The χ^2 distribution with the parameter ν corresponds to the Gamma distribution with $\alpha = \nu/2$ and $\beta = 1/2$.

\psChiIIDist [settings] {x_0}{x_1}

The =nue parameter is set to $\nu = 1$ by default.

```
\usepackage{pst-func} \psset{xunit=1.1cm,yunit=9cm,plotpoints=200}
\begin{pspicture*}(-0.75,-0.06)(9.5,.65)
  \multido{\rnue=0.5+0.5,\iblack=0+10}{10}{%
    \psChiIIDist[linewidth=1pt,linecolor=black!\iblack,nue=\rnue]{0.01}{9}}
  \psaxes[Dy=0.1]{->}(0,0)(9.5,.6)
\end{pspicture*}
```

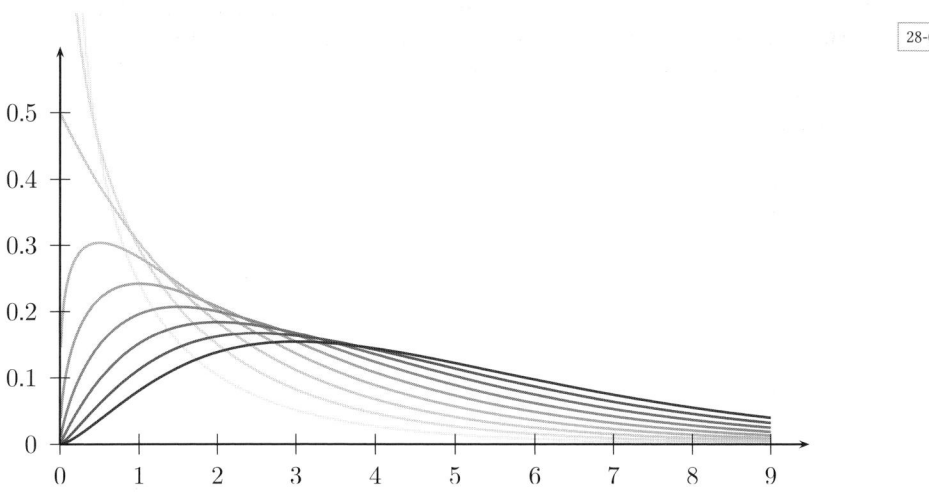

Student's *t* distribution

This statistical distribution was published by William Gosset (1876–1937) in 1908 under the pseudonym "student", hence its unusual name. The *t* distribution with the parameter ν has the following density function:

$$f(x) = \frac{1}{\sqrt{\nu\pi}} \times \frac{\Gamma[(\nu+1)/2]}{\Gamma(\nu/2)} \times \frac{1}{[1+(x^2/\nu)]^{(\nu+1)/2}} \quad \text{for } -\infty < x < \infty \text{ and } \nu > 0 \quad (28.32)$$

The corresponding command has the following syntax:

`\psTDist [settings] {x_0}{x_1}`

The =nue parameter is set to ν = 1 by default.

```
\usepackage{pstricks,pst-func}
\psset{xunit=1.25cm,yunit=10cm}
\begin{pspicture}(-6,-0.1)(6,.5)
  \psaxes[Dy=0.1]{->}(0,0)(-4.5,0)(5.5,0.5)
  \psset{linewidth=1pt,plotpoints=100}
  \psGauss[mue=0,sigma=1]{-4.5}{4.5}
  \psTDist[linecolor=blue]{-4}{4}
  \psTDist[linecolor=red,nue=4]{-4}{4}
\end{pspicture}
```

28 Mathematical functions

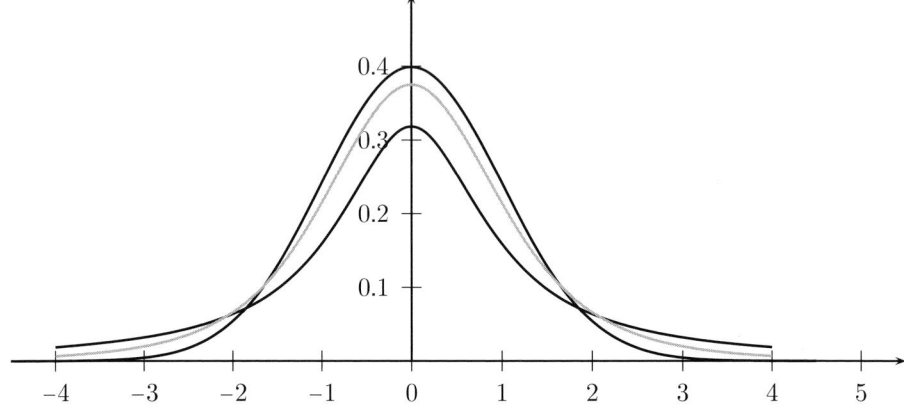

F distribution

The F distribution (after Ronald Aylmer Fisher, 1890–1962) is the probability distribution of a continuous random variable n and results from the quotient of two χ^2-distributed random variables. The F distribution is suitable as a test for determining whether the populations of two samples have the same variance.

The F distribution with the parameters μ and ν has the following density function:

$$f_{n,m}(x) = \frac{\Gamma[(\mu+\nu)/2]}{\Gamma(\mu/2)\Gamma(\nu/2)} \times (\mu/\nu)^{\mu/2} \frac{x^{(\mu/2)-1}}{[1+(\mu x/\nu)]^{(\mu+\nu)/2}} \quad \text{for } x > 0 \text{ and } \mu, \nu > 0 \quad (28.33)$$

The corresponding command has the following syntax:

\psFDist [settings] {x_0}{x_1}

The =mue and =nue parameters are set to $\mu = 1$ and $\nu = 1$ by default.

```
\usepackage{pstricks,pst-func}
\psset{xunit=2cm,yunit=10cm,plotpoints=100}
\begin{pspicture*}(-0.5,-0.07)(5.5,0.8)
 \psline[linestyle=dashed](0.5,0)(0.5,0.75)
 \psline[linestyle=dashed](! 2 7 div 0)(! 2 7 div 0.75)
 \psset{linewidth=1pt}
 \psFDist{0.1}{5}
 \psFDist[linecolor=red,nue=3,mue=12]{0.01}{5}
 \psFDist[linecolor=blue,nue=12,mue=3]{0.01}{5}
 \psaxes[Dy=0.1]{->}(0,0)(5,0.75)
\end{pspicture*}
```

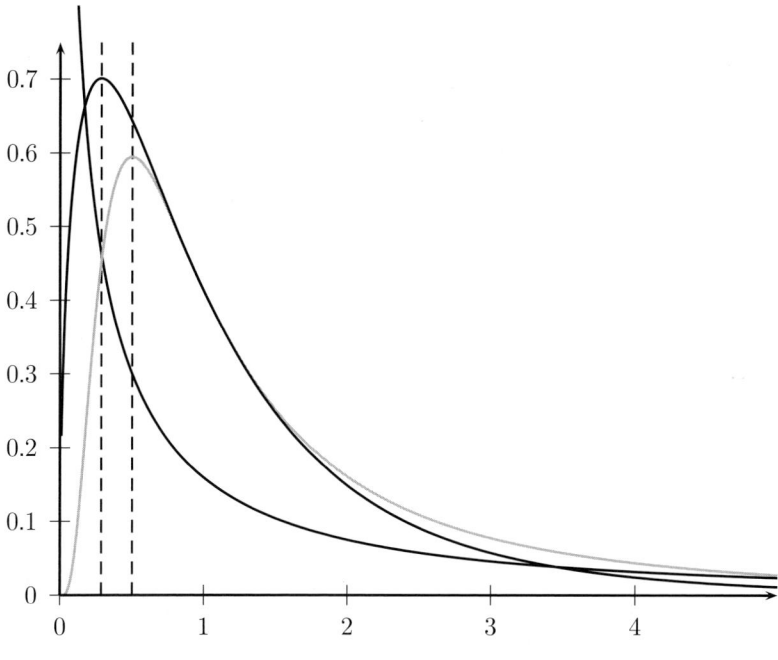

Beta distribution

The Beta distribution is a continuous probability distribution over the interval $[0, 1]$ and is related to the Gamma distribution. It has two free parameters, usually called α and β. The probability function $P(x)$ is defined as:

$$P(x) = \frac{(1-x)^{\beta-1} \times x^{\alpha-1}}{B(\alpha, \beta)} \tag{28.34}$$

$$= \frac{\Gamma(\alpha + \beta)}{\Gamma(\alpha)\Gamma(\beta)} (1-x)^{\beta-1} x^{\alpha-1} \quad \alpha, \beta > 0 \tag{28.35}$$

The corresponding command has the following syntax:

`\psBetaDist [settings] {x_0}{x_1}`

The alpha and beta parameters are set to $\alpha = 1$ and $\beta = 1$ by default.

```
\usepackage{pstricks,pst-func}
\psset{xunit=8cm,yunit=3cm}
\begin{pspicture*}(-0.1,-0.2)(1.1,2.10)
  \multido{\rbeta=0.25+0.25,\iblack=0+5}{20}{%
    \psBetaDist[linewidth=1pt,beta=\rbeta,linecolor=black!\iblack]{0.01}{0.99}}
  \psaxes[Dy=0.2,Dx=0.1]{->}(0,0)(1,2.01)
\end{pspicture*}
```

28.2.9 Lamé curve, a superellipse

A *superellipse*, first given by Gabriel Lamé (1795–1870) in 1818, is defined as follows in Cartesian coordinates:

$$\left|\frac{x}{a}\right|^r + \left|\frac{y}{b}\right|^r = 1 \tag{28.36}$$

Alternatively in parameter form it is:

$$x = a \times \cos^{\frac{2}{r}} t \tag{28.37}$$

$$y = b \times \sin^{\frac{2}{r}} t \tag{28.38}$$

A superellipse with $a = b$ is called a Lamé curve or Lamé oval. The following table lists some special cases of Lamé curves for certain values of r. [89]

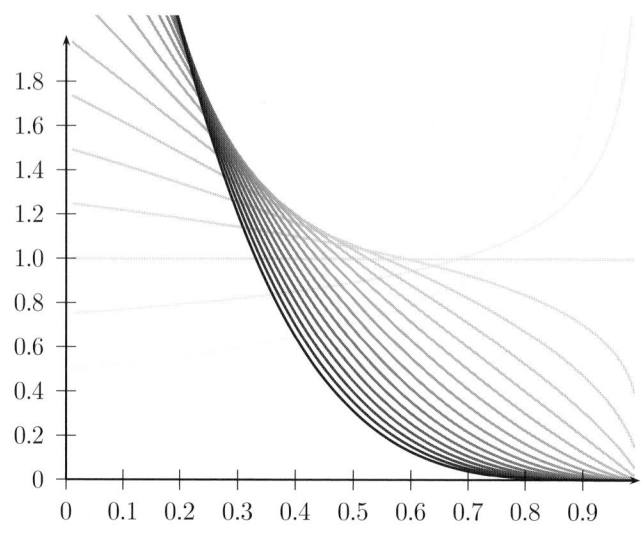

r	Lamé type	example	r	Lamé type	example
$\frac{2}{3}$	astroid		1	diamond	
2	ellipse		$\frac{5}{2}$	Piet Hein's "superellipse"	

For the case where r is rational, the curve is an algebraic superellipse and in the case of r being irrational, a transcendental. For even integers $r = 2, 4, \ldots$, the ellipse approaches a rectangle.

The syntax of \psLame is:

28.2 pst-func – Special functions

`\psLame [settings] {r}`

Internally the Lamé curve is calculated in parameter form with $0 \leq t \leq 2\pi$. The radiusA and radiusB parameters are set to $a = 1$ and $b = 1$ by default.

```
\usepackage{pstricks,pst-func,multido}
\definecolorseries{col}{rgb}{last}{red}{blue} \resetcolorseries[41]{col}
\psset{unit=.5}
\pspicture(-9,-9)(9,9)
  \psaxes[Dx=2,Dy=2,tickstyle=bottom,ticksize=2pt]{->}(0,0)(-9,-9)(9,9)
  \multido{\rA=0.2+0.1,\iA=0+1}{40}{%
    \psLame[radiusA=8,radiusB=7,linecolor={col!![\iA]},linewidth=.5pt]{\rA}}
\endpspicture
```

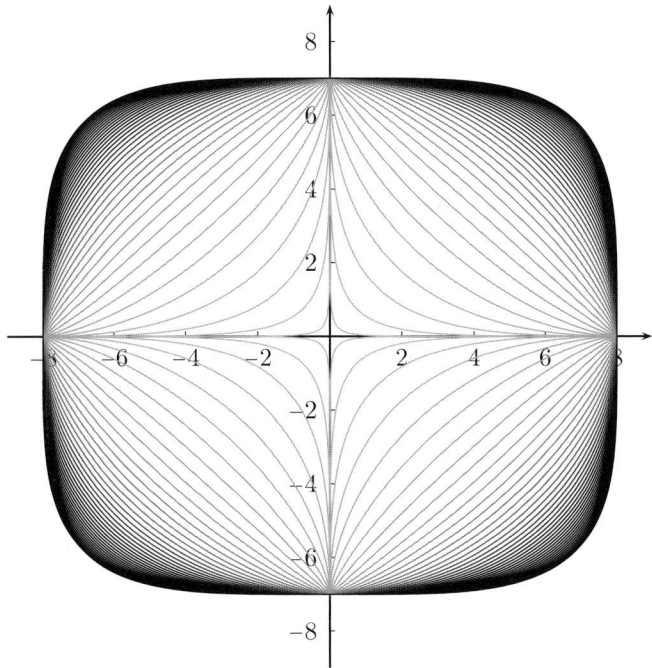

28.2.10 \psThomae – a "popcorn function"

The Thomae function (Carl Johannes Thomae, 1840–1921) is also called the popcorn function or the raindrop function (because of its appearance) or the Riemann function. It is a modified Dirichlet function and is defined as:

$$f(x) = \begin{cases} \frac{1}{q} & \text{if } x = \frac{p}{q} \text{ is a rational number} \\ 0 & \text{if } x \text{ is irrational} \end{cases} \quad (28.39)$$

It is assumed that $gcd(p, q) = 1$ and $q > 0$ to make the function non-negative and therefore defined everywhere. The corresponding command has the syntax:

28 Mathematical functions

```
\psThomae [settings] {x_0,x_1}{number of points}
```

$\{x_0, x_1\}$ is the interval to output; both values must be positive and x_1 must be larger than x_0.

```
\usepackage{pstricks,pst-func,multido}
\psset{unit=4cm}
\begin{pspicture}(-0.1,-0.2)(2.5,1.15)
    \psaxes{->}(0,0)(2.5,1.1)
    \psThomae[dotsize=2.5pt,linecolor=red](0,2){300}
\end{pspicture}
```

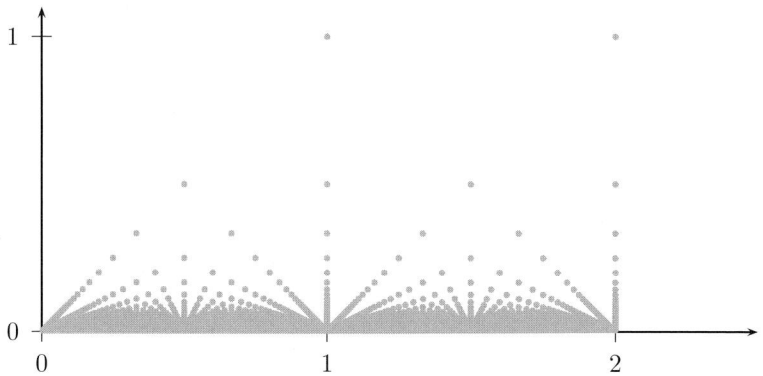

28-02-3

28.2.11 \psplotImp – Plotting of implicitly-defined functions

For a given definition interval x to y, the \psplotImp command steps through all function values $f(x, y)$ in 1pt steps and determines potential sign changes – from $f(x, y) < 0$ to $f(x, y) > 0$ or vice versa. In this case the point (or pixel) has to be part of the implicitly-defined function $f(x, y) = 0$. The whole domain is traversed first line by line and then column by column. This can lead to lengthy calculation times: for example for a section of 400×300 pixels $= 120,000$ function calls have to be made. The transformation of PostScript coordinates to screen coordinates is done internally; you don't have to worry about doing this.

```
\psplotImp [settings] (x_Min, y_Min)(x_Max, y_Max){function f(x,y) = 0}
```

The function $f(x, y) = 0$ has to be specified in the usual PostScript notation (cf. Section 15.3 on page 203) or alternatively you can give it in algebraic form by using the algebraic option, The variables must be called x and y, or if you set the polarplot option, then the variables must be called r and ϕ (cf. Example 28-02-38 on page 548) – the algebraic option is also available in this case. It's a good idea to use the starred version of the pspicture environment when dealing with implicitly-defined functions, as that way a larger interval can be chosen for \psplotImp, which increases the probability of the aforementioned sign changes being captured.

28.2 pst-func – Special functions

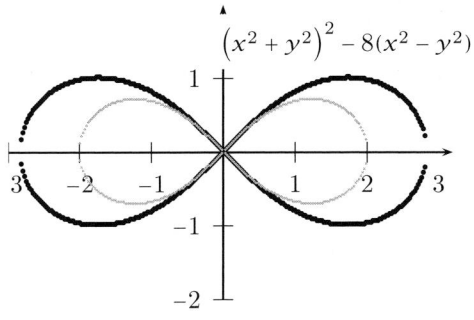

```
\usepackage{pstricks-add,pst-func}

\begin{pspicture*}(-3,-2.2)(3.5,2.5)
\psaxes{->}(0,0)(-3,-2)(3.2,2)
\psplotImp[linewidth=2pt](-5,-2.2)(5,2.4){
  /xqu x dup mul def /yqu y dup mul def
  xqu yqu add dup mul 2 dup
  add 2 mul xqu yqu sub mul sub }
\rput*(2,1.5){%
  $\left(x^2+y^2\right)^2-8(x^2-y^2)=0$}
\psplotImp[linewidth=1pt,linecolor=red,
  algebraic](-5,-2.2)(5,2.4){%
    (x^2+y^2)^2-4*(x^2-y^2) }% Lemniskate a=2
\end{pspicture*}
```

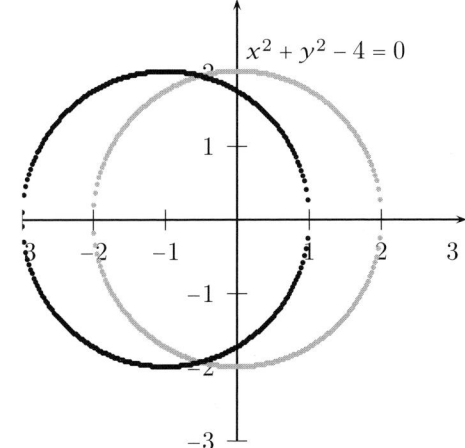

```
\usepackage{pstricks-add,pst-func}

\begin{pspicture*}(-3,-3.2)(3.5,3.5)
\psaxes{->}(0,0)(-3,-3)(3.2,3)
\psplotImp[linewidth=2pt,
  linecolor=red](-5,-2.1)(5,2.1){
  x dup mul y dup
  mul add 4 sub }% circle r=2
\uput[45](0,2){$x^2+y^2-4=0$}
\psplotImp[linewidth=2pt,
  linecolor=blue,
  algebraic](-5,-3)(4,2.4)%
  { (x+1)^2+y^2-4 }
\end{pspicture*}
```

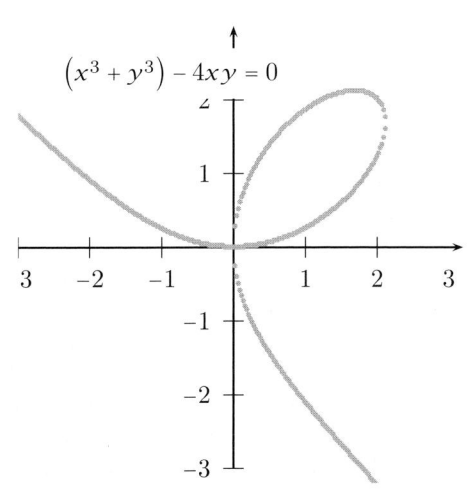

```
\usepackage{pstricks-add,pst-func}

\begin{pspicture*}(-3,-3.2)(3.5,3.5)
\psaxes{->}(0,0)(-3,-3)(3.2,3)
\psplotImp[linewidth=2pt,
  linecolor=green](-6,-6)(4,2.4){
  x 3 exp y 3 exp add
  4 x y mul mul sub }
\uput*[45](-2.5,2){%
  $\left(x^3+y^3\right)-4xy=0$}
\end{pspicture*}
```

547

28 Mathematical functions

```
\usepackage{pstricks-add,pst-func}
\psset{unit=0.8}
\begin{pspicture*}(-5,-3.2)(5.5,4.5) \psaxes{->}(0,0)(-5,-3)(5.2,4)
\psplotImp[algebraic,linecolor=red](-6,-4)(5,4){ y*cos(x*y)-0.2 }
\psplotImp[algebraic,linecolor=blue](-6,-4)(5,4){ y*cos(x*y)-1.2 }
\end{pspicture*}
```

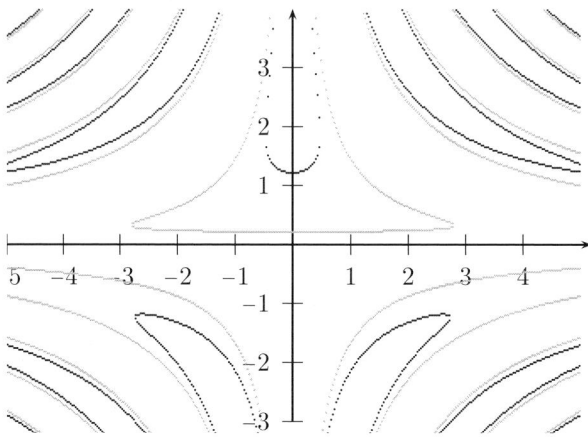

```
\usepackage{pstricks-add,pst-func,multido}
\begin{pspicture*}(-5,-2)(5.5,2)
  \pscircle(0,0){1}\psaxes{->}(0,0)(-5,-1.5)(5.5,2)
  \multido{\rA=0.01+0.2}{5}{%
    \psplotImp[linewidth=1pt,linecolor=blue,polarplot](-6,-6)(5,2.4){
        r dup mul 1.0 r div sub phi sin dup mul mul \rA\space sub }}
  \rput[lb](0.5,1.3){$f(r,\phi)=\left(r^2-\frac{1}{r}\right)\times\sin^2\phi=0$}
\end{pspicture*}
```

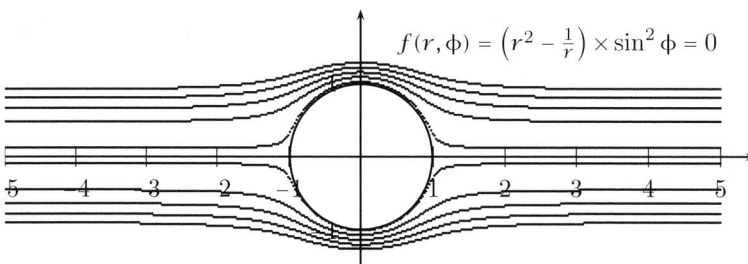

28.2.12 \psVolume – Rotation of a function about the x axis

The \psVolume command creates a symmetric body by rotating a function $f(x)$ about the x axis. The syntax is:

\psVolume [settings] (x_{Min}, x_{Max}){intervals}{$f(x)$}

28.2 pst-func – Special functions

You can give $f(x)$ either in the usual PostScript notation (cf. Section 15.3 on page 203) or in algebraic form by using the algebraic option.

```
\usepackage{pstricks-add,pst-func}
\psset{unit=0.75}%
\begin{pspicture}(-0.5,-2)(5,2.5)\psaxes{->}(0,0)(0,-2)(3,2.5)
\psVolume[fillstyle=solid,fillcolor=magenta!30](0,4){1}{x sqrt}\psline{->}(4,0)(5,0)
\end{pspicture}
\begin{pspicture}(-0.5,-2)(5,2.5)\psaxes{->}(0,0)(0,-2)(3,2.5)
\psVolume[fillstyle=solid,fillcolor=red!40](0,4){2}{x sqrt}\psline{->}(4,0)(5,0)
\end{pspicture}
\begin{pspicture}(-0.5,-2)(5,2.5)\psaxes{->}(0,0)(0,-2)(3,2.5)
\psVolume[fillstyle=solid,fillcolor=blue!40](0,4){4}{x sqrt}\psline{->}(4,0)(5,0)
\end{pspicture}
```

```
\usepackage{pstricks-add,pst-func}
\psset{xunit=1.5}
\begin{pspicture}(-0.5,-4)(3,4)
  \psaxes{->}(0,0)(0,-4)(3,4)
  \psVolume[fillstyle=solid,fillcolor=cyan!40](0,1){4}{x}
  \psVolume[fillstyle=solid,fillcolor=yellow!40](1,2){4}{x dup mul}
  \psline(2,0)(3,0)
\end{pspicture}\qquad
%
\begin{pspicture}(-0.5,-4)(3,4)
  \psaxes{->}(0,0)(0,-4)(3,4)
  \psVolume[fillstyle=solid,fillcolor=cyan!40](0,1){20}{x}
  \psVolume[fillstyle=solid,fillcolor=yellow!40](1,2){20}{x dup mul}
```

```
\psline(2,0)(3,0)
\end{pspicture}
```

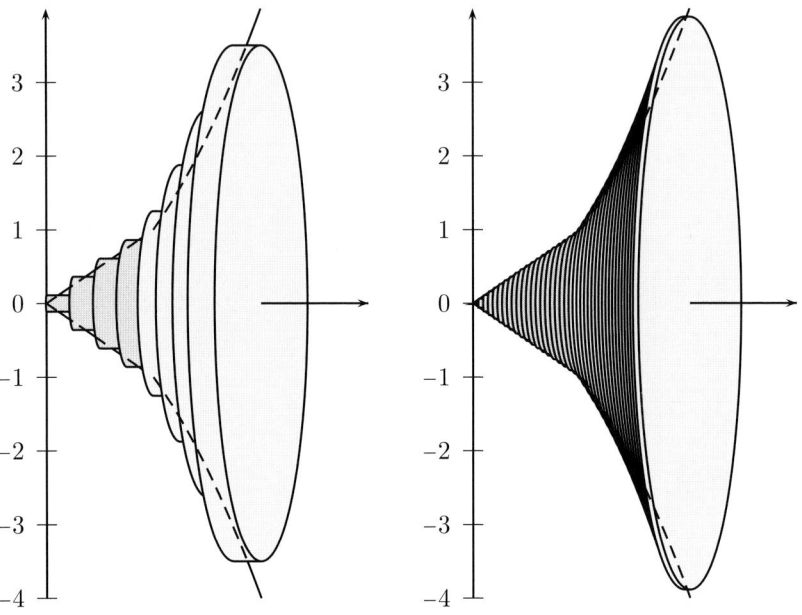

Chapter 29

pst-eucl – Euclidean geometry

29.1 Parameters 551
29.2 Commands 563
29.3 Examples 580

The `pst-eucl` package provides the functionality to calculate many points based only on the specification of a few nodes [64]. For example, from the known three points of a triangle, you can determine the perpendicular bisector of a side, the bisectrix, etc.

Node names are set in math mode by default. They may have an index, but only in the simple notation x_n. Several characters as an index are not possible within the current version.

There are many optional parameters, some of which aren't available for all commands. We cover all of them in the following section, but then give a short list of the available options with the description of the individual commands.

29.1 Parameters

Table 29.1 shows a summary of the special parameters for `pst-eucl`.

Table 29.1: Summary of the parameters for `pst-eucl`

name	type	default	explanation
PointSymbol	symbol	default	point symbol
PointSymbolA	symbol	undef	first point symbol of a series
PointSymbolB	symbol	undef	second point symbol of a series
PointSymbolC	symbol	undef	third point symbol of a series
PointName	name	default	label

continued...

... continued

name	type	default	explanation
PointNameA	symbol	undef	first label of a series
PointNameB	symbol	undef	second label of a series
PointNameC	symbol	undef	third label of a series
PtNameMath	Boolean	true	parameter to activate math mode
PointNameSep	value	default	label distance
PosAngle	angle	undef	rotation of a label
PosAngleA	value	undef	position of the angle at point A
PosAngleB	value	undef	position of the angle at point B
PosAngleC	value	undef	position of the angle at point C
SegmentSymbol	symbol	MarkHashh	symbol for a segment
SegmentSymbolA	symbol	MarkHashh	first symbol of a series
SegmentSymbolB	symbol	MarkHash	second symbol of a series
SegmentSymbolC	symbol	MarkHashhh	third symbol of a series
Mark	symbol	undef	connecting line between label and angle
MarkAngle	angle	undef	angle value
RightAngleSize	value	0.4	size of the rectangle or the arc for the right angle
RightAngleType	type	default	type of marking for the right angle (german|suisseromand)
MarkAngleRadius	value	.4	radius of the symbol for the right angle
LabelAngleOffset	angle	0	angle of offset of the angle label
LabelSep	value	1	distance between line and angle label
LabelRefPt	side	c	reference point
CurveType	type	none	
RotAngle	value	60	rotation angle
TransformLabel	value	none	
CodeFig	Boolean	false	
CodeFigA	Boolean	undef	
CodeFigB	Boolean	undef	
CodeFigAarc	Boolean	true	sense of direction of an arc, starting at the intersection point of two circles
CodeFigBarc	Boolean	true	the same for the other circle
CodeFigColor	colour	cyan	line colour
CodeFigStyle	line style	dashed	line style
HomCoef	value	0.5	intersection angle
DrawCirABC	Boolean	true	circumference
Radius	value	none	radius
RadiusA	value	undef	radius of the first circle
RadiusB	value	undef	radius of the second circle
Diameter	value	none	diameter
DiameterA	value	undef	diameter of the first circle
DiameterB	value	undef	diameter of the second circle

continued...

29.1 Parameters

... continued

name	type	default	explanation
DistCoef	value	none	coefficient of distance/vector
AngleCoef	value	none	angle coefficient
CurvAbsNeg	Boolean	false	change of direction
GenCurvFirst	value	none	
GenCurvLast	value	none	
GenCurvInc	value	1	

29.1.1 PointSymbol, PointSymbolA, PointSymbolB, and PointSymbolC

PointSymbol just defines the point symbol; it's only used with the \psdot command (cf. Section 6.1.1 on page 69) or other commands that are based on it. The default is "*", which corresponds to a filled circle. You can also set each point seperately using PointSymbolA, PointSymbolB, or PointSymbolC. If none of these is specified, the same applies to all three points A,B,C.

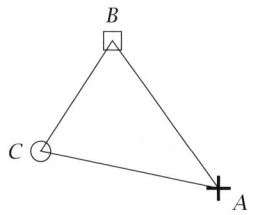

```
\usepackage{pst-eucl}

\psset{dotscale=3}% only for demo
\begin{pspicture}(-1.5,-1.5)(1.5,1.5)
\pstTriangle[PosAngleB=90, PosAngleC=180,
    PointSymbol=square,PointSymbolA=+,PointSymbolC=o,
    linecolor=blue,linewidth=.5\pslinewidth]
    (1.5,-1){A}(0,1){B}(-1,-.5){C}
\end{pspicture}
```

29.1.2 PointName, PointNameA, PointNameB, and PointNameC

PointName defines the label and applies it to all three points. You can also label each point seperately using PointNameA, PointNameB, or PointNameC.

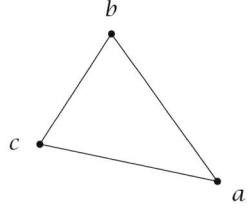

```
\usepackage{pst-eucl}

\begin{pspicture}(-1.5,-1.5)(1.5,1.5)
\pstTriangle[PosAngleB=90, PosAngleC=180,
    PointNameA=a,PointNameB=b=+,PointNameC=c,
    linecolor=blue,linewidth=.5\pslinewidth]
    (1.5,-1){A}(0,1){B}(-1,-.5){C}
\end{pspicture}
```

29.1.3 PointNameSep

PointNameSep defines the distance of the label from the node point and defaults to the dynamic length 1em.

553

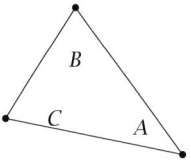

```
\usepackage{pst-eucl}

\begin{pspicture}(-1.5,-1.5)(1.5,1.5)
\pstTriangle[PosAngleB=90, PosAngleC=180,
    PointNameSep=-2em, linewidth=.5\pslinewidth]
    (1.5,-1){A}(0,1){B}(-1,-.5){C}
\end{pspicture}
```

29.1.4 PosAngle, PosAngleA, PosAngleB, and PosAngleC

PosAngle specifies the rotation of a label about the defined node. It applies to all three points unless you specify individual rotations through PosAngleA, PosAngleB, or PosAngleC. The default is a position on the bisectrix.

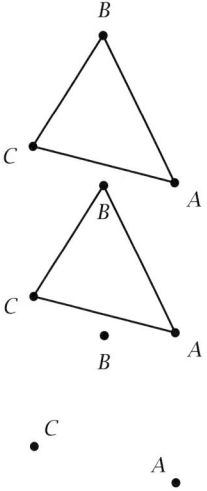

```
\usepackage{pst-eucl}

\begin{pspicture}(-1,-1)(1,1)
    \pstTriangle(1,-1){A}(0,1){B}(-1,-.5){C}
\end{pspicture}

\begin{pspicture}(-1,-1)(1,1)
    \pstTriangle[PosAngleB=-90]%
        (1,-1){A}(0,1){B}(-1,-.5){C}
\end{pspicture}

\begin{pspicture}(-1,-1)(1,1)
    \pstGeonode[PosAngle={135,-90,45}]%
        (1,-1){A}(0,1){B}(-1,-.5){C}
\end{pspicture}
```

For the \pstGeonode command, you can specify separate rotations for each point with a single assignment to PosAngle; the specification must be given as a list, which has to be complete and in the same order as the nodes that follow.

29.1.5 SegmentSymbol, SegmentSymbolA, SegmentSymbolB, and SegmentSymbolC

SegmentSymbol marks a line between two points with a defined symbol. It applies to all three points, unless something else is specified through SegmentSymbolA, SegmentSymbolB, or SegmentSymbolC. All predefined symbols are shown in Table 29.2.

29.1 Parameters

Table 29.2: Summary of all predefined segment symbols

output	SegmentSymbol	output	MarkAngle
—/—	\pstslash		
—//—	\pstslashh		
—///—	\pstslashhh		
—/—	\MarkHash	—/—	30°
—//—	\MarkHashh	—//—	50°
—///—	\MarkHashhh	—⫯⫯⫯—	80°
—×—	\MarkCros		
—✕—	\MarkCross		

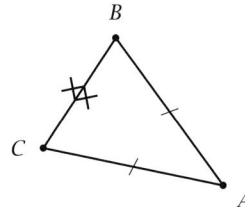

```
\usepackage{pst-eucl}

\begin{pspicture}(-1.5,-1.5)(1.5,1.5)
  \psset{SegmentSymbol=pstslash}
  \pstTriangle[PosAngleB=90, PosAngleC=180,
    linecolor=blue,linewidth=.5\pslinewidth]
    (1.5,-1){A}(0,1){B}(-1,-.5){C}
  \psset{SegmentSymbol=pstslash}
  \pstSegmentMark{A}{B} \pstSegmentMark{A}{C}
  \pstSegmentMark[SegmentSymbol=MarkCross]{C}{B}
\end{pspicture}
```

29.1.6 Mark and MarkAngle

The Mark option specifies the marker line for angles; Mark=MarkHash selects a simple line (see Table 29.2). The MarkAngle option rotates this line arbitrarily about its geometric centre. This isn't usually necessary; the optimal position of the line is determined automatically. Table 29.2 shows the behaviour of this option, which is only defined for a certain types of line. The default angle is 45°.

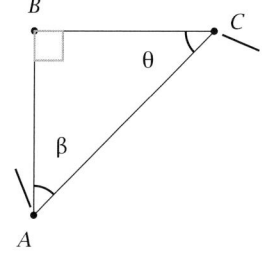

```
\usepackage{pst-eucl}

\begin{pspicture}(-1.5,-1.5)(1.5,1.5)
  \psset{SegmentSymbol=pstslash}
  \pstTriangle[PosAngleB=90,
    linecolor=blue,linewidth=.5\pslinewidth]
    (-1.25,-1.25){A}(-1.25,1.25){B}(1.25,1.25){C}
  \pstRightAngle[linecolor=red]{C}{B}{A}
  \pstMarkAngle[Mark=MarkHash]{B}{C}{A}{$\theta$}
  \pstMarkAngle[Mark=MarkHash]{C}{A}{B}{$\beta$}
\end{pspicture}
```

29.1.7 RightAngleSize and RightAngleType

The RightAngleSize and RightAngleType options specify the size and the type of a right angle. The default type is suisseromand, which is applicable for Anglo-American countries. In Germany and some other countries the german style (an arc with a dot) is preferred.

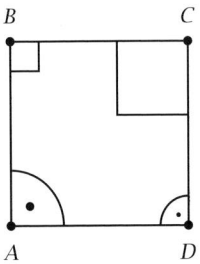

```
\usepackage{pst-eucl}

\begin{pspicture}(-1.5,-1.5)(1.5,1.5)
  \psset{linecolor=black,CodeFig=true}
  \pstGeonode[PosAngle={-90,90,90,-90}](-1.25,-1.25){A}%
    (-1.25,1.25){B}(1.25,1.25){C}(1.25,-1.25){D}
  \pstLineAB{A}{B} \pstLineAB{B}{C}
  \pstLineAB{C}{D} \pstLineAB{D}{A}
  \pstRightAngle{A}{B}{C}
  \pstRightAngle[RightAngleSize=1]{B}{C}{D}
  \pstRightAngle[RightAngleType=german]{C}{D}{A}
  \pstRightAngle[RightAngleType=german,
    RightAngleSize=.75]{D}{A}{B}
\end{pspicture}
```

29.1.8 MarkAngleRadius

MarkAngleRadius works similarly to RightAngleSize, but for arbitrary angles and therefore independent of the type. The arc is always drawn and the label has to be specified.

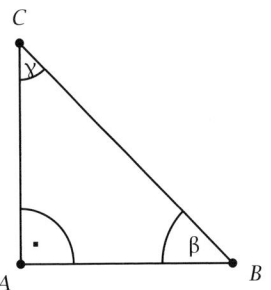

```
\usepackage{pst-eucl}

\begin{pspicture}(3,3.2)
\pstTriangle[PosAngle=-90, PosAngleC=90]
  (0,0){A}(3,0){B}(0,3){C}
\pstMarkAngle[MarkAngleRadius=.75, LabelSep=.3]
  {B}{A}{C}{\psscalebox{2}{$\cdot$}}
\pstMarkAngle[MarkAngleRadius=.5, LabelSep=.4]
  {A}{C}{B}{$\gamma$}
\pstMarkAngle[MarkAngleRadius=1, LabelSep=.6]
  {C}{B}{A}{$\beta$}
\end{pspicture}
```

29.1.9 LabelAngleOffset, LabelSep, and LabelRefPt

LabelAngleOffset is the angular offset of the label in degrees, whereas LabelSep is the linear offset as a length. The specified rotation and translation are applied to the point that represents the centre of the label unless an alternative reference point is specified through LabelRefPt. The reference points may be the usual points of a TeX box (cf. Table 9.1).

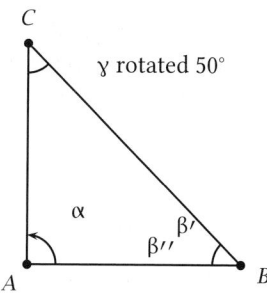

```
\usepackage{pstricks,pst-eucl,textcomp}

\begin{pspicture}(3,3.2)
\pstTriangle[PosAngle=-90, PosAngleC=90]
    (0,0){A}(3,0){B}(0,3){C}
\pstMarkAngle[arrows=->]{B}{A}{C}{$\alpha$}
\pstMarkAngle[LabelAngleOffset=50,LabelRefPt=l]
    {A}{C}{B}{$\gamma$ rotated 50\textdegree}
\pstMarkAngle[LabelSep=1,LabelRefPt=lb]
    {C}{B}{A}{$\beta\prime$}
\pstMarkAngle[LabelSep=1,LabelRefPt=rt]
    {C}{B}{A}{$\beta\prime\prime$}
\end{pspicture}
```

29.1.10 CurveType

CurveType specifies whether nodes are connected by a line, curve, or polygon; you can assign it the values listed in Table 29.3. For arrows, the same conventions as for normal PSTricks lines and curves apply.

Table 29.3: Possible values for the CurveType option

type	option	explanation
open	polyline	option arrows is active, line may have arrows at the ends
open and curved	curve	option arrows is active, line type is bezier
closed	polygon	closed polyline; option arrows not active, no arrows possible

```
\usepackage{pst-eucl} \SpecialCoor
\begin{pspicture}(-1.5,-1.5)(8,2) \psset{arrowscale=2,arrows=->}
\pstGeonode{O}
\pstGeonode[CurveType=polygon](1.5,0){A}(1.5;51.43){B}(1.5;102.86){C}%
    (1.5;154.29){D}(1.5;205.71){E}(1.5;257.14){F}(1.5;308.57){G}
\pstGeonode[CurveType=curve,linestyle=dashed,linewidth=2pt]%
    (0,1){M}(4,2){N}(6,-1){P}(8,2){Q}
\pstGeonode[CurveType=polyline,linestyle=dotted,linewidth=2pt]%
    (2,0.5){R}(4,-1){S}(6,2){T}(8,-1.5){U}
\end{pspicture}
```

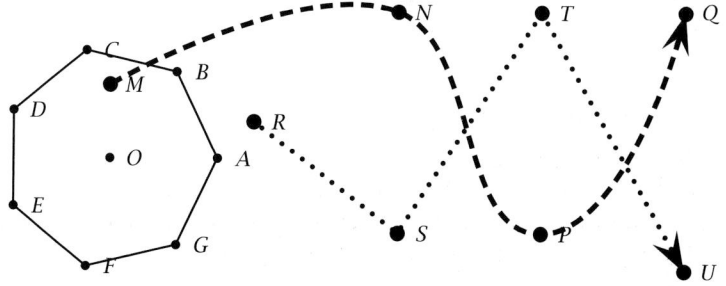

29.1.11 RotAngle

RotAngle determines the angle by which something is rotated with the \pstRotation command.

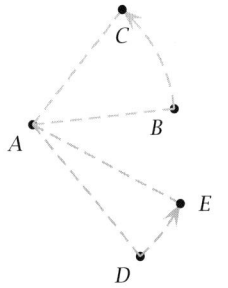

```
\usepackage{pst-eucl}

\begin{pspicture}(-1.5,-2)(1,1)
\psset{arrowscale=2,CodeFig=true}
\pstGeonode[PosAngle=-135](-1.5,-.2){A}(.5,0){B}(0,-2){D}
\pstRotation[PosAngle=-90, RotAngle=45]{A}{B}[C]
\pstRotation[AngleCoef=.5, RotAngle=\pstAngleAOB{B}{A}{C},
    CodeFigColor=red]{A}{D}[E]
\end{pspicture}
```

29.1.12 TransformLabel

You can use the TransformLabel option to place a label; it is usually placed on the line of the bisectrix if nothing else is specified through the LabelAngleOffset option.

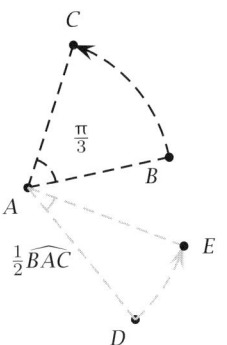

```
\usepackage{pst-eucl}

\begin{pspicture}(-2,-2)(2,2)
\psset{arrowscale=2, CodeFig=true}
\pstGeonode[PosAngle=-135](-1.5,-.2){A}(.5,.2){B}(0,-2){D}
\pstRotation[PosAngle=90, RotAngle=60,
    CodeFigColor=blue,
    TransformLabel=\frac{\pi}{3}]{A}{B}[C]
\pstRotation[AngleCoef=.5, RotAngle=\pstAngleAOB{B}{A}{C},
    LabelAngleOffset=-45,
    TransformLabel=\frac{1}{2}\widehat{BAC}]{A}{D}[E]
\end{pspicture}
```

29.1.13 CodeFig, CodeFigAarc, CodeFigBarc, CodeFigColor, and CodeFigStyle

For all transformations, usually only the end node or end nodes are calculated and displayed. However, you can switch on the CodeFig option to make the transformation visible through a line (translation) or an arc (rotation). CodeFigColor specifies the colour for the line/arc; the default is cyan. CodeFigStyle specifies the line style and may take the usual PSTricks values (cf. Section 4.1.3 on page 45); the default is dashed. Setting CodeFig=false omits the drawing completely.

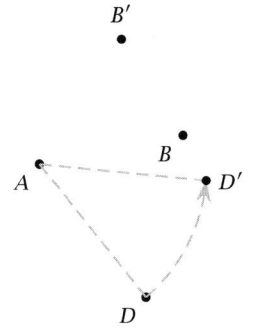

```
\usepackage{pst-eucl}

\begin{pspicture}(-2,-2)(1.5,2)
  \psset{arrowscale=2}
  \pstGeonode[PosAngle=-135]%
      (-1.5,-.2){A}(.5,.2){B}(0,-2){D}
  \pstRotation[PosAngle=90,RotAngle=45,
      CodeFigColor=blue]{A}{B}[B']
  \pstRotation[RotAngle=\pstAngleAOB{B}{A}{B'},
      LabelAngleOffset=-45,CodeFig=true,
      arrowscale=2]{A}{D}[D']
\end{pspicture}
```

The `CodeFigAarc` and `CodeFigBarc` options are similar, but refer to circle commands and therefore let you display circles whose centre was determined through two intersection points with another circle. These options are used to determine the rotation direction of the arc; clockwise or counterclockwise starting from the first point.

```
\usepackage{pst-eucl}
\begin{pspicture}(0,-2)(5,2) \psset{linewidth=1.5pt}
  \pstGeonode[PosAngle={0,-90,0,90}](1,-1){O}(2,1){A}(2,0.1){B}(2.5,1){C}
  \pstInterCC[PosAngleA=135,CodeFigA=false,CodeFigAarc=false,
      CodeFigB=true,CodeFigBarc=true,CodeFigColor=blue]{O}{A}{C}{B}{D}{E}
\end{pspicture}
\begin{pspicture}(0,-2)(5,2) \psset{linewidth=1.5pt}
  \pstGeonode[PosAngle={0,-90,0,90}](1,-1){O}(2,1){A}(2,0.1){B}(2.5,1){C}
  \pstInterCC[PosAngleA=135,CodeFigA=true,CodeFigAarc=true,CodeFigStyle=dotted,
      CodeFigB=true,CodeFigBarc=true,CodeFigColor=red]{O}{A}{C}{B}{D}{E}
\end{pspicture}
```

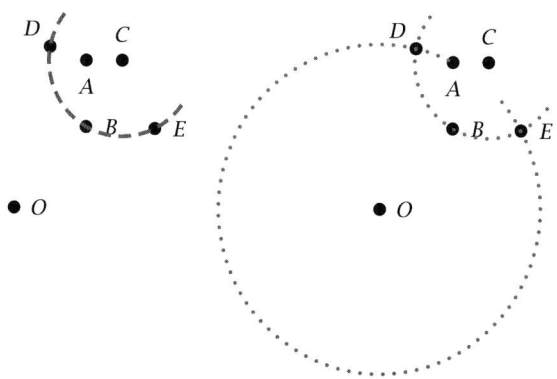

29.1.14 HomCoef

The HomCoef option specifies the stretch factor for a centric stretching; it may also be negative.

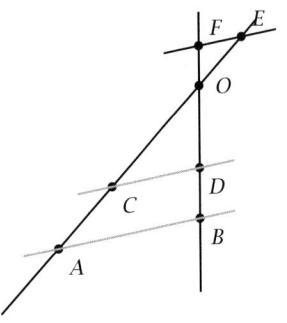

```
\usepackage{pst-eucl}

\begin{pspicture}(-2,-2)(1.5,2)
  \pstGeonode[PosAngle={0,-45}]%
    (.5,1){O}(-1.5,-1.2){A}(.5,-.8){B}
  \pstHomO[HomCoef=.62, PosAngle=-45]{O}{A,B}[C,D]
  \pstHomO[HomCoef=-.3, PosAngle=45]{O}{A,B}[E,F]
  \pstLineAB[nodesep=-1.2]{A}{O}\pstLineAB[nodesep=-1]{B}{O}
  \psset{linecolor=red, nodesep=-.5}
  \pstLineAB{A}{B}\pstLineAB{C}{D}
  \pstLineAB[linecolor=blue,nodesep=-.5]{E}{F}
\end{pspicture}
```

29.1.15 DrawCirABC

If you set the DrawCirABC option to false when using the \pstCircleABC command, this prevents the display of the calculated circumference. The default is DrawCirABC=true. In the following example, the centre points do not appear exactly at the same position. This is because of rounding errors.

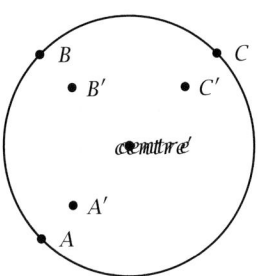

```
\usepackage{pst-eucl}

\begin{pspicture}(-1.5,-1.5)(1.5,1.5)
  \pstGeonode(-1.25,-1.25){A}(-1.25,1.25){B}(1.25,1.25){C}
  \pstCircleABC{A}{B}{C}{centre}\qdisk(centre){2pt}
  \pstGeonode(-.8,-.8){A'}(-.8,.8){B'}(.8,.8){C'}
  \pstCircleABC[DrawCirABC=false]{A'}{B'}{C'}{centre'}
  \qdisk(centre'){2pt}
\end{pspicture}
```

29.1.16 Radius, RadiusA, RadiusB, Diameter, DiameterA, and DiameterB

The Radius, RadiusA, and RadiusB options, and similarly Diameter, DiameterA, and DiameterB specify the radius (or diameter) when drawing a circle and when determining the intersection points of two circles through the \pstInterCC command (cf. Section 29.2.26). In the following example, only the first two points O and M are specified. The first circle with the centre O (line 3) has a radius of two length units. After that the intersection points of the two circles with RadiusA=\pstDistVal{2} and DiameterB=\pstDistAB{O}{M} are determined.

To assign values to the options, you have to use the \pstDistVal and \pstDistAB commands, with additional multiples or parts thereof added through the DistCoef option (cf. Section 29.2.1 on page 563).

29.1 Parameters

```
\usepackage{pst-eucl}
\begin{pspicture}(10,4)
  \pstGeonode[PosAngle=-90](2,2){O}(10,1){M}    \pstMiddleAB{O}{M}{O'}
  \pstCircleOA[Radius=\pstDistVal{2}]{O}{}
  \pstInterCC[RadiusA=\pstDistVal{2},DiameterB=\pstDistAB{O}{M},linewidth=2pt,
      CodeFigA=true,CodeFigB=true,CodeFigAarc=false,PosAngleB=45]{O}{}{O'}{}{A}{B}
  \psset{linecolor=red,nodesep=-1}\pstLineAB{M}{A}\pstLineAB{M}{B}
\end{pspicture}
```

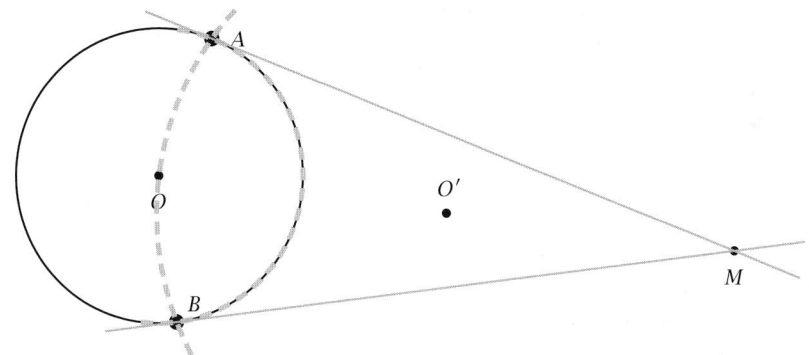

29.1.17 DistCoef

The DistCoef option is used to specify the dilation factor for the translation of a point, with reference to the length of a parallel line. In the following example $\overrightarrow{CC'} = 1.4\overrightarrow{AB}$ applies, which is printed with the CodeFig keyword setting.

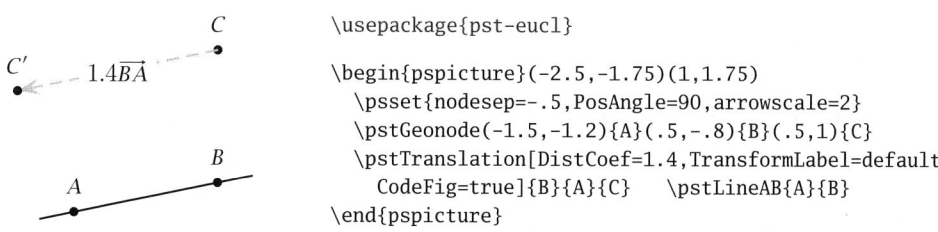

```
\usepackage{pst-eucl}

\begin{pspicture}(-2.5,-1.75)(1,1.75)
  \psset{nodesep=-.5,PosAngle=90,arrowscale=2}
  \pstGeonode(-1.5,-1.2){A}(.5,-.8){B}(.5,1){C}
  \pstTranslation[DistCoef=1.4,TransformLabel=default,
      CodeFig=true]{B}{A}{C}    \pstLineAB{A}{B}
\end{pspicture}
```

Remember that the assignment to DistCoef has to be done **before** the options that affect the distance – for example Radius=\pstDistAB{A}{B} – in the parameter list. Otherwise DistCoef has no effect.

29.1.18 AngleCoef

The AngleCoef option specifies the stretch factor for the rotation of a point, with reference to a given arc. In the following example $\widehat{CE} = 1.4\widehat{CB'}$ applies, where B' results from the extension of the line $\overline{AB}$ to the arc.

29 pst-eucl – Euclidean geometry

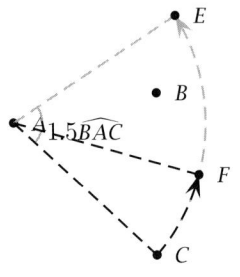

```
\usepackage{pst-eucl}

\begin{pspicture}(-2,-2)(2,1.25)%
    \psset{arrowscale=2}
    \pstGeonode(-1.5,-.2){A}(.5,.2){B}(0.5,-2){C}
    \pstRotation[AngleCoef=1.4,RotAngle=\pstAngleAOB{C}{A}{B},
        CodeFigColor=red,CodeFig=true,
        TransformLabel=1.5\widehat{BAC}]{A}{C}[E]
    \pstRotation[AngleCoef=0.5,RotAngle=\pstAngleAOB{C}{A}{B},
        CodeFigColor=blue,CodeFig=true]{A}{C}[F]
\end{pspicture}
```

Again the assignment to AngleCoef must be done **before** the options that affect the angle – for example RotAngle=\pstAngleAOB{A}{B}{C} – in the parameter list. Otherwise AngleCoef has no effect.

29.1.19 CurvAbsNeg

By default, the positive direction of a circle is counterclockwise, but you can change it to clockwise through the CurvAbsNeg option. In the following example the length of the arc between nodes A and M_1 is defined to be 5 length units. The second node M_2 is now determined by clockwise rotation because of CurvAbsNeg=true. The arc length $\widehat{AM_2}$ is exactly the distance $\overline{AM_1}$.

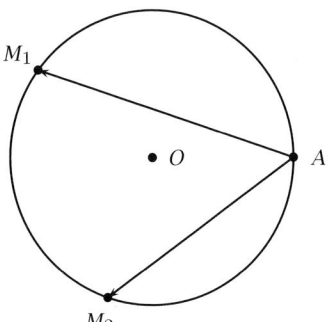

```
\usepackage{pst-eucl}

\begin{pspicture}(-2,-2)(2,2)%
    \pstGeonode(0,0){O}(2,0){A} \pstCircleOA{O}{A}
    \pstCurvAbsNode{O}{A}{M_1}{\pstDistVal{5}}
    \pstCurvAbsNode[CurvAbsNeg=true]%
        {O}{A}{M_2}{\pstDistAB{A}{M_1}}
    \pstLineAB[arrows=->]{A}{M_1}
    \pstLineAB[arrows=->]{A}{M_2}
\end{pspicture}
```

29.1.20 GenCurvFirst, GenCurvLast, and GenCurvInc

The GenCurvFirst, GenCurvLast, and GenCurvInc options determine the behaviour of the \pstGenericCurve command. Different from the current node names, the first one (GenCurvFirst) and the last one (GenCurvLast) can be specified arbitrarily. In the example first all nodes are determined with the \multido command and then given a name M_i. After that the nodes are connected with \pstGenericCurve starting at node A in 20 steps for i. The step results from the step for the \multido command of $20°$. It is used as part of the node name at the same time such that it can be referred to easily later.

562

29.2 Commands

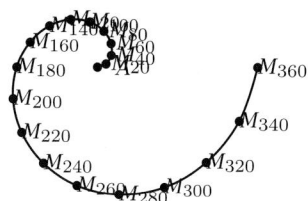

```
\usepackage{pst-eucl}

\begin{pspicture}(-1,-2.5)(2.5,1)
    \psset{unit=.00625}   \pstGeonode{A}
    \multido{\n=20+20}{18}{%
        \pstGeonode[PointName=M_{\n}](\n;\n){M_\n}}
    \pstGenericCurve[GenCurvFirst=A,GenCurvInc=20,
        linecolor=blue]{M_}{20}{360}
\end{pspicture}
```

29.2 Commands

29.2.1 Lengths and angles

For certain options, you can only assign lengths through one of the following commands that calculate the distance specified symbolically by node names.

```
\pstDistAB{A}{B}
\pstDistVal{A}
\pstAngleAOB{A}{O}{B}
```

The first command determines the distance between two given points or nodes; therefore the following expression results in a circle with a radius corresponding to the distance $\overline{AB}$.

`\pstCircleOA[Radius=\pstDistAB{A}{B}]{A}{}`

The second command determines a length from a numeric value, using the current length unit. Both lengths are multiplied internally by the value of the DistCoef option, which you can use to enlarge or shrink the drawing by assigning it values other than 1. The third command works similarly to the first, only the angle at the apex B with the arms A and C is determined by rotating the first arm counterclockwise into the second arm. Internally the angle is multiplied by AngleCoef which similarly allows you to influence the drawing.

Note that you can use the DistCoef option as part of \pstDistAB and \pstDistVal as well as the higher command. In the latter case the specification of DistCoef must precede the distance command; otherwise DistCoef has no effect. The same applies to the AngleCoef option.

29.2.2 \pstGeonode

The base command, \pstGeonode, expects a list of node coordinates and corresponding names of arbitrary length as its arguments:

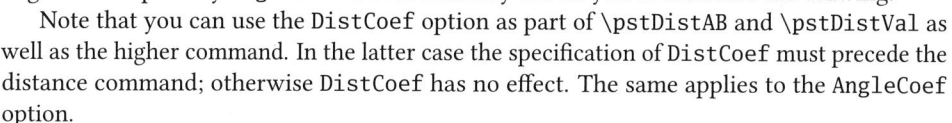

If the first coordinate pair is missing, the coordinate origin $(0,0)$ is assumed. It's safer to specify these coordinates though, in order to avoid misunderstandings. All nodes defined through \pstGeonode can be used in the usual way (cf. Chapter 16 on page 225), i.e. all node connections known from pst-node are also available for pst-eucl.

29 pst-eucl – Euclidean geometry

The following word was defined as a node with the name ZZ, so that connecting it to the following example is easy.

```
\usepackage{pst-eucl}
```

The following word \rnode{ZZ}{was} defined as a
node with the name \emph{ZZ}, so that
connecting it to the following example is easy.

```
\begin{pspicture}[showgrid](-2,-1.7)(1.5,2.2)
  \pstGeonode(-1.5,-1.5){A}(-1.5,-1){B}%
    (0,1.5){C}(1.5,0){D}
  \pstGeonode[PosAngle=-90,PointSymbol=x]{A'}
  \pstGeonode[PtNameMath=false,% no math mode
    PointSymbol=pentagon](0,-1){B'}
  \ncline{D}{A}\nccurve[arrows=->,angleB=-90]{ZZ}{B'}
\end{pspicture}
```

The valid parameters for \pstGeonode are PointName, PointNameSep, PosAngle, PointSymbol PtNameMath.

29.2.3 \pstOIJGeonode

\pstOIJGeonode differs from the base command only in that the coordinates don't have to refer to an orthogonal coordinate system. Rather \pstOIJGeonode expects two additional specifications for the direction of the two axes, such that you can use oblique coordinate systems as well. The prerequisite, however, is that three points O, I, J exist – the origin and two more, distinct points. Then \pstOIJGeonode refers its coordinates to the axes $\overline{OI}$ and $\overline{OJ}$, based on the current PSTricks units.

\pstOIJGeonode [settings] $\{A_1\}(x_2,y_2)\{A_2\}\ldots(x_n,y_n)\{A_n\}$
\pstOIJGeonode [settings] $(x_1,y_1)\{A_1\}(x_2,y_2)\{A_2\}\ldots(x_n,y_n)\{A_n\}$

If the first coordinate pair is missing, the coordinate origin $(0,0)$ is assumed. Again it's best to put in all coordinate pairs to avoid misunderstandings.

```
\usepackage{pst-eucl}
\psset{unit=.5}
\begin{pspicture*}(-4,-4)(4,4)
\pstGeonode[PosAngle={-135,-90,180}]{O}(1,0.5){I}(0.5,2){J}
\pstLineAB[nodesep=10]{O}{I}  \pstLineAB[nodesep=10]{O}{J}
\multips(-5,-2.5)(1,.5){11}{\psline(0,-.15)(0,.15)}
\multips(-2,-8)(.5,2){9}{\psline(-.15,0)(.15,0)}
\psset{linestyle=dotted}
\multips(-5,-2.5)(1,.5){11}{\psline(-10,-40)(10,40)}
\multips(-2,-8)(.5,2){9}{\psline(-10,-5)(10,5)}
\psset{PointSymbol=x,dotscale=2,linestyle=solid}
\pstOIJGeonode[PosAngle={-90,0},CurveType=curve,linewidth=2pt,linecolor=red]%
    (3,1){A}{O}{I}{J}(-2,1){B}(-1,-1.5){C}(2,-1){D}
\end{pspicture*}
```

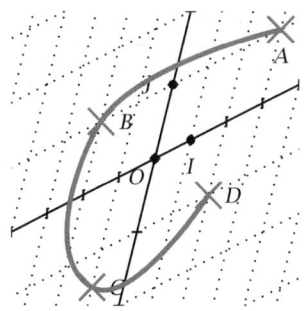

29.2.4 \pstSegmentMark

\pstSegmentMark lets you mark a symbol on any arbitrary line segment specified by two points.

`\pstSegmentMark [settings] {A}{B}`

Table 29.2 on page 555 lists the allowed symbols, which you set through the SegmentSymbol option. The line width of the symbols is the same as the width of the line segment, unless it is a symbol itself.

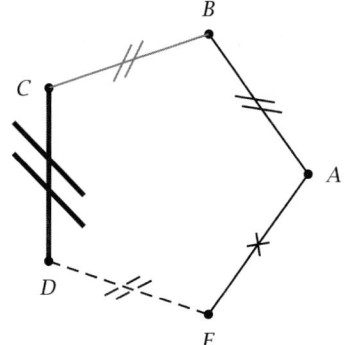

```
\usepackage{pst-eucl}

\begin{pspicture}(-2,-2)(2,2)
    \pstGeonode[PosAngle={0,90,180,-90}]%
        (2,0){A}(2;72){B}(2;144){C}(2;216){D}(2;288){E}
    \pstSegmentMark{A}{B}
    \pstSegmentMark[linecolor=red]{B}{C}
    \pstSegmentMark[linewidth=2pt]{C}{D}
    \pstSegmentMark[linestyle=dashed]{D}{E}
    \pstSegmentMark[SegmentSymbol=MarkCros]{E}{A}
\end{pspicture}
```

29.2.5 \pstTriangle

\pstTriangle is just a combination of \pstGeonode and \psline commands put together as a shortcut for drawing of triangles.

`\pstTriangle [settings] {A}(x_B, y_B){B}(x_C, y_C){C}`
`\pstTriangle [settings] (x_A, y_A){A}(x_B, y_B){B}(x_C, y_C){C}`

If the first coordinate pair is missing, the origin $(0,0)$ is assumed.

29 pst-eucl – Euclidean geometry

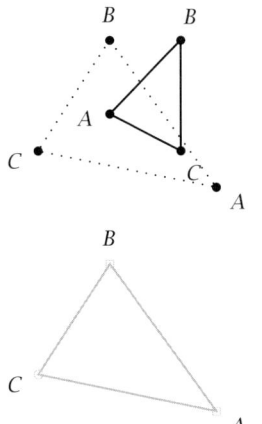

```
\usepackage{pst-eucl}

\begin{pspicture}(-1.5,-1.5)(1.5,1.5)
    \pstTriangle{A}(1,1){B}(1,-.5){C}
    \pstTriangle[linestyle=dotted](1.5,-1){A}(0,1){B}(-1,-.5){C}
\end{pspicture}

\begin{pspicture}(-1.5,-1.5)(1.5,1.5)
    \pstTriangle[PointSymbol=square,PointSymbolC=o,
      linecolor=red](1.5,-1){A}(0,1){B}(-1,-.5){C}
\end{pspicture}
```

The valid parameters for \pstTriangle are PointName, PointNameSep, PosAngle, PointSymbo, PointNameA, PosAngleA, PointSymbolA, PointNameB, PosAngleB, PointSymbolB, PointNameC, PosAngleC, and PointSymbolC.

29.2.6 \pstMarkAngle

This command marks an angle in the usual mathematical notation.

\pstMarkAngle [settings] {A}{B}{C}{label}

The apex of the angle is the second of the three points specified and the orientation results from the order of the points, from first to last. Therefore {A}{B}{C} means an arc from arm A to arm C counterclockwise. The label is placed on the bisectrix at a distance of 1 length unit by default.

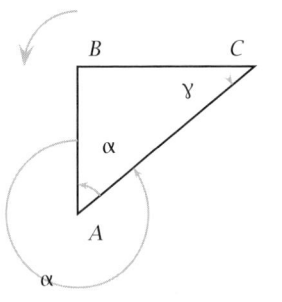

```
\usepackage{pst-eucl}

\begin{pspicture}(-1,-1)(2.5,2)
    \pstGeonode[PointSymbol=none,
      PosAngle={-45,45,135}]{A}(0,2){B}(2.5,2){C}
    \pspolygon(A)(B)(C)
    \psset{arrows=->,linecolor=red}
    \pstMarkAngle{C}{A}{B}{$\alpha$}
    \pstMarkAngle[MarkAngleRadius=1]{B}{A}{C}{$\alpha$}
    \pstMarkAngle[linestyle=dotted]{B}{C}{A}{$\gamma$}
    \pstMarkAngle[arrowscale=2,MarkAngleRadius=-0.75]{A}{B}{C}{}
\end{pspicture}
```

The valid parameters for \pstMarkAngle are MarkAngleRadius, LabelAngleOffset, and Mark.

29.2.7 \pstRightAngle

\pstRightAngle is a special case of the \pstMarkAngle command. The format for the mark depends on which type is specified (cf. Section 29.1.7 on page 556).

29.2 Commands

`\pstRightAngle` `[settings]` `{A}{B}{C}`

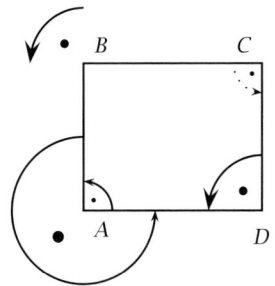

```
\usepackage{pst-eucl}

\begin{pspicture}(-1,-1)(2.5,2)
  \pstGeonode[PosAngle={-45,45,135,-90},
    PointSymbol=none]{A}(0,2){B}(2.5,2){C}(2.5,0){D}
  \pspolygon(A)(B)(C)(D)
  \psset{RightAngleType=german,arrows=->}
  \pstRightAngle{D}{A}{B}
  \pstRightAngle[RightAngleSize=1]{B}{A}{D}
  \pstRightAngle[linestyle=dotted]{B}{C}{D}
  \psset{arrowscale=2}
  \pstRightAngle[RightAngleSize=-0.75]{A}{B}{C}
  \pstRightAngle[RightAngleSize=0.75]{C}{D}{A}
\end{pspicture}
```

The valid parameters for \pstRightAngle are RightAngleSize and RightAngleType.

29.2.8 \pstLineAB

\pstLineAB corresponds exactly to the \ncline command (cf. Section 16.4.1 on page 241). Therefore the nodesep, nodesepA, and nodesepB options are available to extend or shorten the lines.

`\pstLineAB` `[settings]` `{A}{B}`

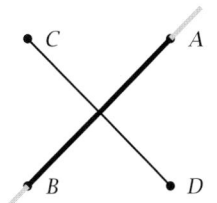

```
\usepackage{pst-eucl}

\begin{pspicture}(-1.5,-1.5)(1.5,1.5)
  \pstGeonode(1,1){A}(-1,-1){B}(-1,1){C}(1,-1){D}
  \pstLineAB{C}{D}
  \psset{linecolor=blue,linewidth=2pt}
  \pstLineAB[nodesep=-0.6,linecolor=lightgray]{A}{B}
  \pstLineAB{A}{B}% overwrite line
\end{pspicture}
```

29.2.9 \pstCircleOA and \pstCircleAB

The \pstCircleOA command expects the centre point as the first node and an arbitrary point on the circle as the second node, thus determining the radius. \pstCircleAB expects two points on the circle that are opposite one another, so that $\overline{AB}$ is the diameter.

`\pstCircleOA` `[settings]` `{A}{}`	`\pstCircleOA` `[settings]` `{O}{A}`
`\pstCircleAB` `[settings]` `{A}{B}`	`\pstCircleAB` `[settings]` `{A}{B}`

Remember that you have to assign the radius and diameter through one of the length commands, as given in Section 29.2.1 on page 563, and that you can enlarge or shrink them with DistCoef (if specified beforehand).

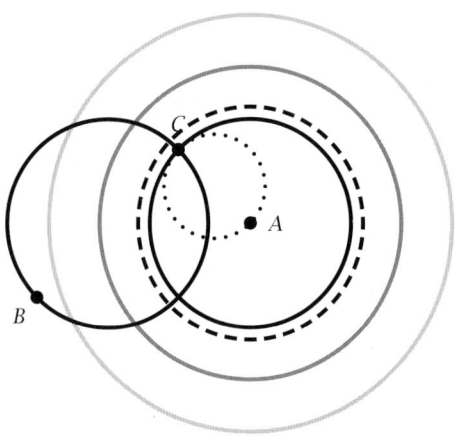

```
\usepackage{pst-eucl}

\begin{pspicture}(-2.5,-2.5)(4,2.5)
  \psset{linewidth=2\pslinewidth}
  \pstGeonode[PosAngle={0,-135,90}]%
    (1,0){A}(-2,-1){B}(0,1){C}
  \pstCircleOA{A}{C}
  \pstCircleOA[linestyle=dashed,
    DistCoef=0.5,Radius=\pstDistAB{A}{B}]{A}{}
  \pstCircleOA[linecolor=cyan,
    Radius=\pstDistAB{B}{C}]{A}{}
  \pstCircleOA[linecolor=magenta,
    DistCoef=0.75,Radius=\pstDistAB{B}{C}]{A}{}
  \pstCircleAB{B}{C}
  \pstCircleAB[linestyle=dotted]{A}{C}
\end{pspicture}
```

29.2.10 \pstArcOAB and \pstArcnOAB

\pstArcOAB draws arcs of the circle with centre O, starting at point A round as far as the angle that results from $\angle AOB$. The second point B does not need to be part of the circle itself; the reference is the connecting line $\overline{AB}$. The second command with the usual PSTricks suffix "n" draws the arc in the mathematically negative direction (clockwise).

```
\pstArcOAB [settings] {O}{A}{B}
\pstArcnOAB [settings] {O}{A}{B}
```

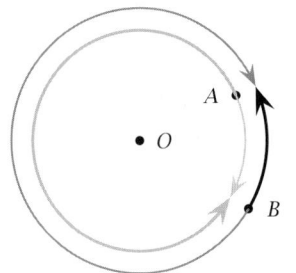

```
\usepackage{pst-eucl}

\begin{pspicture}(-2,-2)(2,2)
  \pstGeonode[PosAngle={0,180,0}]{O}(1.5;24){A}(1.8;-31){B}
  \psset{arrows=->, arrowscale=2}
  \pstArcOAB[linecolor=red, linewidth=1.5\pslinewidth]{O}{A}{B}
  \pstArcOAB[linecolor=blue, linewidth=1.5\pslinewidth]{O}{B}{A}
  \pstArcnOAB[linecolor=cyan]{O}{A}{B}
  \pstArcnOAB[linecolor=magenta]{O}{B}{A}
\end{pspicture}
```

29.2.11 \pstCurvAbsNode

\pstCurvAbsNode lets you determine a point on a circle based on a start point on the circle and the length of an arc.

```
\pstCurvAbsNode [settings] {O}{A}{name}{arc length}
```

In the following example, first the node M_1 is determined by setting the length of the arc to point A as 5.5 length units. Then M_2 is determined by setting the length of the arc from A to M_2 to be the same as the straight-line distance between A and M_1 – i.e. the two dashed lines are the same length.

29.2 Commands

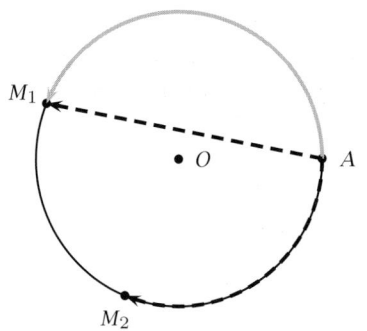

```
\usepackage{pst-eucl}

\begin{pspicture}(-2.5,-2.5)(2.5,2.5)
    \pstGeonode{0}(2,0){A}  \pstCircleOA{0}{A}
    \pstCurvAbsNode{0}{A}{M_1}{\pstDistVal{5.5}}
    \pstArcOAB[linecolor=red,linewidth=1.5pt,
        arrows=->]{0}{A}{M_1}
    \pstCurvAbsNode[CurvAbsNeg=true]{0}{A}{M_2}{%
        \pstDistAB{A}{M_1}}
    \psset{linecolor=blue,linestyle=dashed,
        linewidth=1.5pt,arrows=->}
    \pstArcnOAB{0}{A}{M_2}  \pstLineAB{A}{M_1}
\end{pspicture}
```

If nothing else is specified through the options, the node name is also used as the label and is aligned radially outside the circle. Remember that the assignment of the length of the arc must be done using one of the length commands as given in Section 29.2.1 on page 563, and that you can enlarge or shrink the length with DistCoef (if specified beforehand).

The valid parameters for \pstCurvAbsNode are PointSymbol, PosAngle, PointName, PointNameSep, PtNameMath, and CurvAbsNeg.

29.2.12 \pstGenericCurve

\pstGenericCurve allows connections from a root node to the following nodes in a series.

\pstGenericCurve [settings] {base}{n_1}{n_2}

The nodes all have the same base name prefix, but are indexed with consecutive numbers, starting from n_1 and increasing in steps of size GenCurvInc until n_2 is reached. Now a loop can be used to create a continuous polyline by incrementing the index, as shown already in the example in Section 29.1.20 on page 562.

29.2.13 \pstSymO

\pstSymO is the first and the simplest of the transformation commands; it performs point mirroring.

\pstSymO [settings] {O}{$M_1, M_2, \ldots, M_n$}[$M'_1, M'_2, \ldots, M'_m$]

You can specify several points to be mirrored, with the option of also specifying names for the nodes of the mirrored points. If node names aren't specified, the original name is suffixed with a prime, as shown in the following example with point B. The optional list of names of the mirrored nodes doesn't have to be complete.

29 pst-eucl – Euclidean geometry

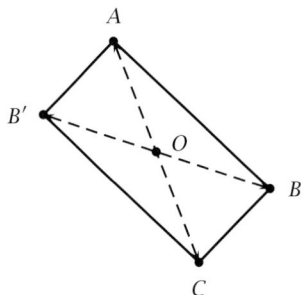

```
\usepackage{pst-eucl}

\begin{pspicture}(-2,-2)(2,2)
  \pstGeonode[PosAngle={20,90,0}]%
    {O}(-.6,1.5){A}(1.6,-.5){B}
  \pstSymO[CodeFigColor=blue,
    PosAngle={-90,180}]{O}{A, B}[C]
  \pspolygon[linewidth=1pt](A)(B)(C)(B')
  \pstLineAB[linestyle=dashed]{<->}{A}{C}
  \pstLineAB[linestyle=dashed]{<->}{B}{B'}
\end{pspicture}
```

The valid parameters for \pstSymO are PointSymbol, PosAngle, PointName, PointNameSep, PtNameMath, CodeFig, CodeFigColor, and CodeFigStyle.

29.2.14 \pstOrtSym

\pstOrtSym determines the orthogonal or axial symmetric points, usually also referred to as line mirroring. The line to be mirrored has to be specified through two points A and B.

\pstSymO [settings] $\{A\}\{B\}\{M_1, M_2, \ldots, M_n\}[M'_1, M'_2, \ldots, M'_m]$

The specification of the names of the nodes of the mirrored points is optional again.

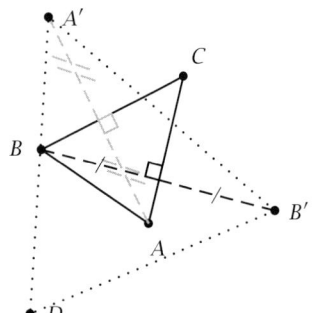

```
\usepackage{pst-eucl}

\psset{unit=.5}%
\begin{pspicture}(0,-2)(8,7)
  \pstTriangle(1,3){B}(5,5){C}(4,1){A}
  \pstOrtSym{A}{B}{C}[D]  \psset{CodeFig=true}
  \pstOrtSym[CodeFigColor=red]{C}{B}{A}
  \pstOrtSym[SegmentSymbol=pstslash,dotsep=3mm,
    linestyle=dotted,CodeFigColor=blue]{C}{A}{B}
  \pspolygon[linestyle=dotted,linewidth=1pt](A')(B')(D)
\end{pspicture}
```

The valid parameters are the same as for the previous command, \pstSymO.

29.2.15 \pstRotation

\pstRotation rotates a point M by the angle RotAngle, where O is the reference point. Again several original points can be given and the list of names of the image points is optional.

\pstRotation [settings] $\{O\}\{M_1, M_2, \ldots, M_n\}[M'_1, M'_2, \ldots, M'_m]$

Alternatively you can specify the rotation angle through the \pstAngleABC command (cf. Section 29.2.1 on page 563).

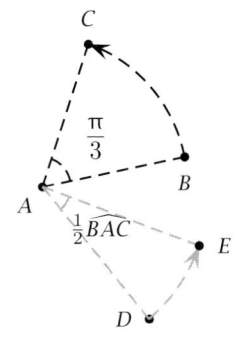

```
\usepackage{pst-eucl}

\begin{pspicture}(-2,-2)(1,2)
\psset{arrowscale=2}
\pstGeonode[PosAngle={-135,-90,180}]%
    (-1.5,-.2){A}(.5,.2){B}(0,-2){D}
\pstRotation[PosAngle=90,RotAngle=60,CodeFig=true,
    CodeFigColor=blue,
    TransformLabel={\displaystyle\frac{\pi}{3}}]{A}{B}[C]
\pstRotation[AngleCoef=.5,RotAngle=\pstAngleAOB{B}{A}{C},
    CodeFigColor=red,CodeFig=true,
    TransformLabel=\frac{1}{2}\widehat{BAC}]{A}{D}[E]
\end{pspicture}
```

The valid parameters for \pstRotation are RotAngle, PointSymbol, PosAngle, PointName, PointNameSep, PtNameMath, RotAngle, and AngleCoef.

29.2.16 \pstTranslation

\pstTranslation makes the simple translation of one or more points possible. The reference point is the vector $\vec{AB}$, which specifies the direction as well as the size of the translation. This means you can easily create a line parallel to a given line.

\pstTranslation [settings] $\{A\}\{B\}\{M_1,M_2,\ldots,M_n\}[M'_1,M'_2,\ldots,M'_m]$

Apart from the specification of two points as a vector for defining the translation, the syntax for this command is identical to the previous ones. You can use DistCoef to dilate or compress the translation by $|\text{DistCoef}\vec{AB}|$.

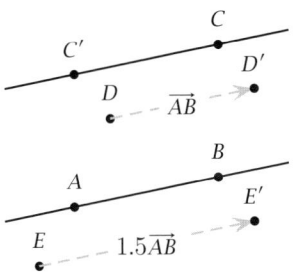

```
\usepackage{pst-eucl}

\begin{pspicture}(-2,-2)(2,1.5)
    \psset{nodesep=-1,PosAngle=90,arrowscale=2}
    \pstGeonode(-1.5,-1.2){A}(.5,-.8){B}(.5,1)%
        {C}(-1,0){D}(-2,-2){E}\pstTranslation{B}{A}{C}
    \psset{CodeFig=true,TransformLabel=default}
    \pstTranslation{A}{B}{D}
    \pstTranslation[DistCoef=1.5]{A}{B}{E}
    \pstLineAB{A}{B}  \pstLineAB{C}{C'}
\end{pspicture}
```

The valid parameters for \pstTranslation are PointSymbol, PosAngle, PointName, PointNameSep, PtNameMath, and DistCoef.

29.2.17 \pstHomO

The name of the \pstHomO command is derived from homothety, which, as an area of geometry, maps straight lines as parallel lines to themselves. In principle it is a centric dilation.

29 pst-eucl – Euclidean geometry

`\pstHomO [settings] {O}{M`$_1$`,M`$_2$`,...,M`$_n$`}[M`$'_1$`,M`$'_2$`,...,M`$'_m$`]`

You can specify an arbitrary number of points. If names aren't given for the image nodes, they are suffixed with a prime as usual; in the following example, only two image points ([D,E]) are specified, so $A \to D$, $B \to E$, and $C \to C'$. Specifying a value other than 1 for the HomCoef coefficient extends or shortens the line.

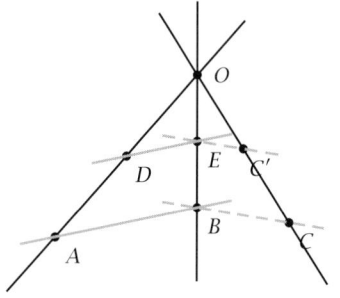

```
\usepackage{pst-eucl}

\begin{pspicture}(-2,-2)(2,2)
  \pstGeonode[PosAngle={0,-45}]%
    (.5,1){O}(-1.5,-1.2){A}(.5,-.8){B}(1.8,-1){C}
  \pstHomO[HomCoef=0.5,PosAngle=-45]{O}{A,B,C}[D,E]
  \psset{linecolor=blue,nodesep=-1}
  \pstLineAB{A}{O}\pstLineAB{B}{O}\pstLineAB{C}{O}
  \psset{linecolor=red,nodesep=-.5,linewidth=1pt}
  \pstLineAB{A}{B}\pstLineAB{D}{E}
  \psset{linestyle=dashed}
  \pstLineAB{B}{C}\pstLineAB{E}{C'}
\end{pspicture}
```

The valid parameters for `\pstHomO` are `PointSymbol`, `PointName`, `PosAngle`, `PointNameSep`, `PtNameMath`, and `HomCoef`.

29.2.18 \pstProjection

`\pstProjection` performs the parallel projection of a point to a straight line $\overline{AB}$. The shortest distance from the point to the line is determined. You can specify an arbitrary number of points. If names aren't given for the image nodes, they are suffixed with a prime as usual.

`\pstProjection [settings] {A}{B}{M`$_1$`,M`$_2$`,...,M`$_n$`}[M`$'_1$`,M`$'_2$`,...,M`$'_m$`]`

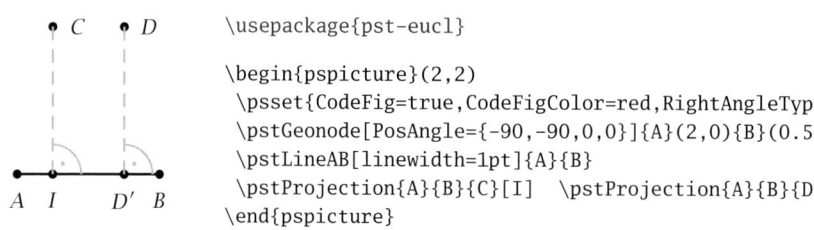

```
\usepackage{pst-eucl}

\begin{pspicture}(2,2)
  \psset{CodeFig=true,CodeFigColor=red,RightAngleType=german}
  \pstGeonode[PosAngle={-90,-90,0,0}]{A}(2,0){B}(0.5,2){C}(1.5,2){D}
  \pstLineAB[linewidth=1pt]{A}{B}
  \pstProjection{A}{B}{C}[I]  \pstProjection{A}{B}{D}
\end{pspicture}
```

This command makes it easy to mark the height of a triangle. The result of the projection itself does not have to be on the line, which is clearly visible for the heights h_c and h_a.

572

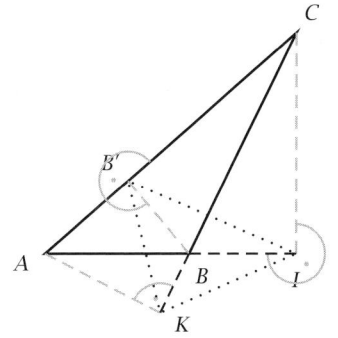

```
\usepackage{pst-eucl}

\begin{pspicture}(-2,-2)(2,2)
\psset{PointSymbol=none,CodeFig=true,
  CodeFigColor=red,RightAngleType=german}
\pstTriangle[linewidth=1pt]%
    (-2,-1){A}(1.5,2){C}(0,-1){B}
\pstProjection{A}{B}{C}[I] \pstProjection{A}{C}{B}
\pstProjection{C}{B}{A}[K]
\pspolygon[linestyle=dotted,linewidth=1pt](I)(B')(K)
\pstLineAB[linestyle=dashed]{B}{I}
\pstLineAB[linestyle=dashed]{B}{K}
\end{pspicture}
```

The valid parameters for \pstProjection are PointSymbol, PosAngle, PointName, PointNameSep,
PtNameMath, CodeFig, CodeFigColor, and CodeFigStyle.

29.2.19 \pstMiddleAB

The \pstMiddleAB command determines the centre of a given line $\overline{AB}$. The name of the new node is placed underneath the line by default.

```
\pstMiddleAB [settings] {A}{B}{node name}
```

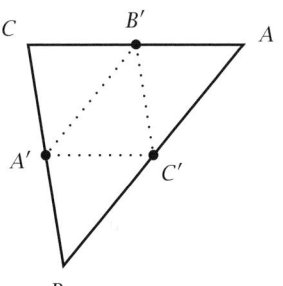

```
\usepackage{pst-eucl}

\begin{pspicture}(-2,-2)(2,2)
  \psset{linewidth=1pt}
  \pstTriangle[PointSymbol=none]%
      (1.5,1.5){A}(-1,-1.5){B}(-1.5,1.5){C}
  \pstMiddleAB{A}{B}{C'} \pstMiddleAB{C}{A}{B'}
  \pstMiddleAB{B}{C}{A'}
  \pspolygon[linestyle=dotted](A')(B')(C')
\end{pspicture}
```

The valid parameters for \pstMiddleAB are PointSymbol, PointName, PointNameSep, PtNameMath,
PosAngle, SegmentSymbol, CodeFig, CodeFigColor, and CodeFigStyle.

29.2.20 \pstCGravABC

The \pstCGravABC command determines the centre of area of a triangle; this corresponds to the intersection point of the medians.

```
\CGravABC [settings] {A}{B}{C}{node name}
```

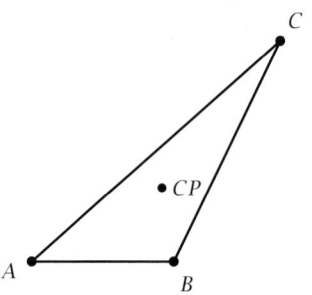

```
\usepackage{pst-eucl}

\begin{pspicture}(-2,-2)(2,2)
    \pstTriangle[linewidth=1pt]%
        (-2,-1){A}(1.5,2){C}(0,-1){B}
    \pstCGravABC{A}{B}{C}{CP}
\end{pspicture}
```

The valid parameters for \pstCGravABC are PointName, PointNameSep, PosAngle, PointSymbol and
PtNameMath.

29.2.21 \pstCircleABC

The \pstCircleABC command determines the centre of the circumcircle of a triangle.

\pstCircleABC [settings] {A}{B}{C}{node name}

With DrawCirABC=true the circle is also drawn; otherwise only the centre is determined.
Drawing the centre can also optionally be suppressed.

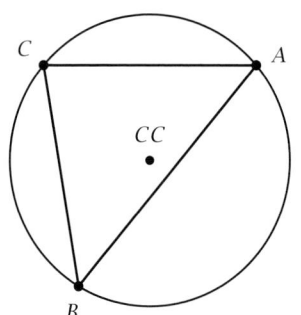

```
\usepackage{pst-eucl}

\begin{pspicture}(-2,-2)(2,2)
    \pstTriangle[linewidth=1pt]%
        (1.5,1.5){A}(-1,-1.5){B}(-1.5,1.5){C}
    \pstCircleABC[PosAngle=90,
        DrawCirABC=true]{A}{B}{C}{CC}
\end{pspicture}
```

We can show the whole construction of the centre through the CodeFig option (the marker symbols can be changed as shown in Section 29.1.5 on page 554).

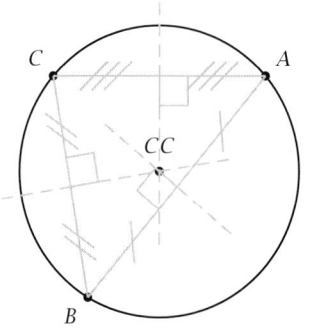

```
\usepackage{pst-eucl}

\begin{pspicture}(-2,-2)(2,2)
    \pstGeonode[PosAngle={45,-135,135}]%
        (1.5,1.5){A}(-1,-1.5){B}(-1.5,1.5){C}
    \pstCircleABC[PosAngle=90,DrawCirABC=true,
                CodeFig=true]{A}{B}{C}{CC}
\end{pspicture}
```

The valid parameters for \pstCircleABC are PointName, PointNameSep, PosAngle, PointSymbol, PtNameMath, DrawCirABC, SegmentSymbolA, SegmentSymbolB, SegmentSymbolC, CodeFig, CodeFigColor, and CodeFigStyle.

29.2.22 \pstMediatorAB

The \pstMediatorAB command determines the perpendicular bisector of the side $\overline{AB}$.

\pstMediatorAB [settings] {A}{B}{node name M}{node name N}

node name M is the name of the node placed at the centre of the line $\overline{AB}$ and node name N is the name of the new auxiliary node placed $0.5\overline{AB}$ from this line along the perpendicular bisector. The order of the nodes A and B determines on which section of the perpendicular bisector the auxiliary node is placed (above or below $\overline{AB}$): the latter of the two points is rotated by 90° counterclockwise to determine the new node's position on the perpendicular bisector.

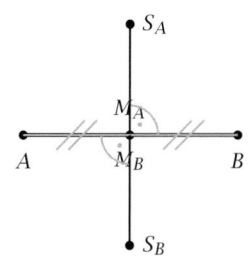

```
\usepackage{pst-eucl}

\begin{pspicture}(-1.5,-1.5)(1.5,1.5)
    \psset{CodeFig=true,CodeFigColor=red,
        RightAngleType=german}
    \pstGeonode[PosAngle={-90,-90}]%
        (-1.5,0){A}(1.5,0){B}
    \pstLineAB[linewidth=1.5pt]{A}{B}
    \pstMediatorAB{A}{B}{M_A}{S_A}
    \pstMediatorAB{B}{A}{M_B}{S_B}
\end{pspicture}
```

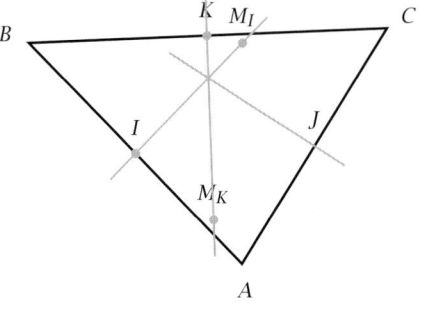

```
\usepackage{pst-eucl}

\begin{pspicture}(5,5)
    \pstTriangle[PointSymbol=none,
        linewidth=1pt](3,1){A}(0,4){B}(5,4.2){C}
    \psset{RightAngleType=german,PosAngle=90,
        linecolor=red,CodeFigColor=red,nodesep=-0.5}
    \pstMediatorAB{B}{A}{I}{M_I}
    \pstMediatorAB[PointSymbol=none,
        PointNameB=none]{A}{C}{J}{M_J}
    \pstMediatorAB[PosAngleA=45]{C}{B}{K}{M_K}
\end{pspicture}
```

The valid parameters for \pstMediatorAB are PointName, PointNameSep, PosAngle, PointSymbol, PtNameMath, CodeFig, CodeFigColor, CodeFigStyle, and SegmentSymbol, where the options A and B are different if the individual option allows for it. A then refers to the centre of the line and B to the perpendicular bisector.

29.2.23 \pstBissectBAC and \pstOutBissectBAC

The \pstBissectBAC command determines the bisectrix, where \pstOutBissectBAC refers to the complementary angle. $\alpha + \beta = 180°$ applies here.

\pstBissectBAC [settings] {B}{A}{C}{node name}
\pstOutBissectBAC [settings] {B}{A}{C}{node name}

The apex of the angle must correspond to the second point – point A in the definition above. This is also clear from the name of the command. The distance of the new point along the bisectrix is determined from the counter-clockwise rotation of the first of the three points.

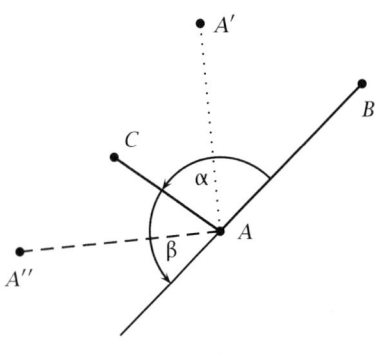

```
\usepackage{pst-eucl}

\begin{pspicture}(-2,-1)(2,2.5)
  \pstGeonode[PosAngle={0,-75,45}]%
    {A}(2,2){B}(-1.5,1){C}
  \pstLineAB[nodesepA=-2]{A}{B}
  \pstLineAB[linewidth=1pt]{A}{B}
  \pstLineAB[linewidth=1pt]{A}{C}
  \psset{MarkAngleRadius=1,LabelSep=0.75,
    LabelAngleOffset=15}
  \pstMarkAngle[arrows=->]{B}{A}{C}{$\alpha$}
  \pstSymO[PointSymbol=none,PointName={}]{A}{B}
  \pstMarkAngle[arrows=->]{C}{A}{B'}{$\beta$}
  \pstBissectBAC[linestyle=dotted]{B}{A}{C}{A'}
  \pstOutBissectBAC[linestyle=dashed,
    PosAngle=-90]{B}{A}{C}{A''}
\end{pspicture}
```

The valid parameters for \pstBissectBAC and \pstOutBissectBAC are PointSymbol, PosAngle, PointName, PointNameSep, and PtNameMath.

29.2.24 \pstInterLL

\pstInterLL determines the intersection of two straight lines. It is assumed that the two lines aren't parallel, but if this were the case the command would return the coordinate origin.

\pstInterLL [settings] {A}{B}{C}{D}{node name}

The command expects two points on each line (A and B on one, and C and D on the other); the intersection doesn't need to lie within the given line segments.

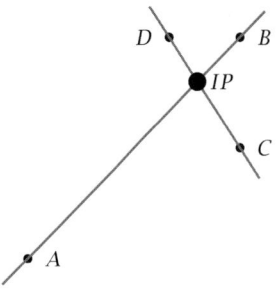

```
\usepackage{pst-eucl}

\begin{pspicture}(-2,-2)(2,2)
  \pstGeonode[PosAngle={0,0,0,180}]%
    (-1.5,-1.5){A}(1.5,1.5){B}(1.5,0){C}(.5,1.5){D}
  {\psset{linecolor=blue,nodesep=-.5,
    linewidth=1pt}
  \pstLineAB{A}{B}\pstLineAB{C}{D}}
  \pstInterLL[dotscale=2,
    labelsep=10pt]{A}{B}{C}{D}{IP}
\end{pspicture}
```

The valid parameters for \pstInterLL are PointSymbol, PosAngle, PointName, PointNameSep, and PtNameMath.

29.2 Commands

29.2.25 \pstInterLC

\pstInterLC determines the intersection points of a straight line and a circle, assuming they exist.

\pstInterLC [settings] {A}{B}{O}{C}{IP₁}{IP₂}

The command expects two points on the line (A and B) and the centre of the circle (O) and an additional point on its circumference (C). {C} can be omitted if instead you assign a value for Radius or Diameter, which can also be modified using the DistCoef option (cf. Section 29.2.1 on page 563).

The position of the two intersection points is chosen so that the vector $\overrightarrow{IP_1 IP_2}$ is not the opposite of the vector $\overrightarrow{AB}$. If the order of the two points of the line is swapped, the labels on the intersection points would be swapped as well.

```
\usepackage{pst-eucl}

\begin{pspicture}(-2,-2)(2,2)
    \pstGeonode[PosAngle=150]{O}(0,1.5){A}
    \pstCircleOA[linecolor=red]{O}{A}
    \pstGeonode(0,2){B}(2,-2){C} \pstLineAB{B}{C}
    \pstInterLC[PosAngle={10}]{B}{C}{O}{A}{D}{E}
    \pspolygon[fillcolor=black!10,
        fillstyle=solid](O)(D)(E)
\end{pspicture}
```

The valid parameters for \pstInterLC are PointSymbol, PosAngle, PointName, PointNameSep, PtNameMath, PointSymbolA, PosAngleA, PointNameA, PointSymbolB, PosAngleB, PointNameB, Radius, and Diameter.

29.2.26 \pstInterCC

\pstInterCC determines the intersection of two circles.

\pstInterCC [settings] {O₁}{A}{O₂}{B}{IP₁}{IP₂}

The command expects the centre of the circles ({O₁} and {O₂}) and an additional point on each circle's circumference ({A} and B). The specification of A and B can be omitted if you specify the size of the circles through the radius or diameter options instead.

Each of the following examples draws the same two nodes and connecting line, even though the circles themselves are only actually drawn in the righthand example.

```
\usepackage{pst-eucl}
\begin{pspicture}(-2,-2)(2,2)
    \pstGeonode[PosAngleA={180,0}](-0.5,0){O1}(0.5,0){O2}
    \pstInterCC[PosAngleA=90,PosAngleB=-90,Radius=\pstDistVal{1.5}]{O1}{}{O2}{}{IP1}{IP2}
    \pstLineAB[arrows=<->]{IP1}{IP2}
\end{pspicture}\hfill
\begin{pspicture}(-2,-2)(2,2)
```

29 pst-eucl – Euclidean geometry

```
\pstGeonode[PosAngleA={180,0}](-0.5,0){01}(0.5,0){02}
\pstInterCC[PosAngleA=90,PosAngleB=-90,Radius=\pstDistVal{1.5},
   CodeFig]{01}{}{02}{}{IP1}{IP2} \pstLineAB[arrows=<->]{IP1}{IP2}
\end{pspicture}\hfill
\begin{pspicture}(-2,-2)(2,2)
\pstGeonode[PosAngle={180,0}](-0.5,0){01}(0.5,0){02}
\pstCircleOA[linecolor=red,Radius=\pstDistVal{1.5}]{01}{}
\pstCircleOA[linecolor=blue,Radius=\pstDistVal{1.5}]{02}{}
\pstInterCC[PosAngleA=90,PosAngleB=-90,Radius=\pstDistVal{1.5}]{01}{}{02}{}{IP1}{IP2}
\pstLineAB[arrows=<->]{IP1}{IP2}
\end{pspicture}
```

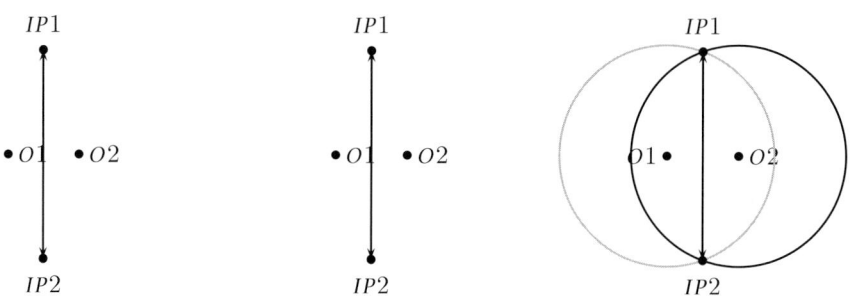

The valid parameters for \pstInterCC are Radius, Diameter, and CodeFig.

29.2.27 \pstInterFF

The \pstInterFF command determines the intersections of the graphs of two functions.

\pstInterFF [settings] {$f(x)$}{$g(x)$}{x_0}{M}

$f(x)$ and $g(x)$ are functions given in PostScript notation (cf. Section 15.3 on page 203), x_0 is the start value for determining the nulls $f(x) - g(x) = 0$. The method after Newton is used, but this doesn't guarantee finding nulls – that's heavily dependent on the functions and especially on the start value. The command only finds the first null, but it can be applied repeatedly with different start values to find more of them. This assumes some knowledge about the trend of the functions however.

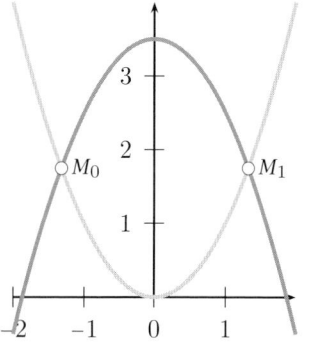

```
\usepackage{pstricks,pst-plot,pst-eucl}

\begin{pspicture}(-2,-.5)(2,4)
\psaxes{->}(0,0)(-2,0)(2,4)
\psset{linewidth=2\pslinewidth}
\psplot[linecolor=lightgray]{-2}{2}{x 2 exp}
\psplot[linecolor=gray]{-2}{2}{x 2 exp neg 3.5 add}
\psset{PointSymbol=o}
\pstInterFF{x 2 exp neg 3.5 add}{x 2 exp}{1}{M_1}
\pstInterFF{x 2 exp neg 3.5 add}{x 2 exp}{-2}{M_0}
\end{pspicture}
```

29.2.28 \pstInterFL

The \pstInterFL command is a special case of the commands given above: it finds the intersection points the graph of a function $f(x)$ with a straight line (given by two points, $\{A\}$ and $\{B\}$).

\pstInterFL [settings] $\{f(x)\}\{A\}\{B\}\{x_0\}\{M\}$

Again you can apply the command repeatedly to find more than one null; the choice of start point x_0 is crucial for which null the Newton method finds.

```
\usepackage{pstricks,pst-plot,pst-eucl}
\psset{unit=.75}
\def\F{x 3 exp 3 div x sub 2 3 div add .0001 add}
\begin{pspicture}(-3,-2)(3,4)
  \psaxes{->}(0,0)(-3,-1)(3,4)
  \psplot[linewidth=2\pslinewidth,linecolor=gray]{-2.5}{2.5}{\F}    \psset{PointSymbol=*}
  \pstGeonode[PosAngle=-45](0,-.2){N}\pstGeonode(2.5,1){M}
  \pstLineAB[nodesepA=-3cm,linecolor=red]{N}{M}
  \psset{PointSymbol=o}\pstInterFL{\F}{N}{M}{2}{A}
  \pstInterFL[PosAngle=90]{\F}{N}{M}{0}{A'}
  \pstInterFL{\F}{N}{M}{-2}{A''}
\end{pspicture}
```

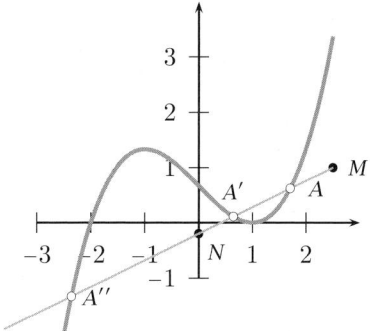

29.2.29 \pstInterFC

The \pstInterFC command determines the intersection points of a circle (given by the centre and a point on its circumference) and the graph of a function.

\pstInterFC[option]$\{f(x)\}\{O\}\{A\}\{x_0\}\{M\}$

As usual $\{A\}$ can be omitted if you instead assign a value for Radius or Diameter, which can also be modified through the option DistCoef (cf. Section 29.2.1 on page 563). Also, as expected, the start value x_0 determines which of the intersection points is found.

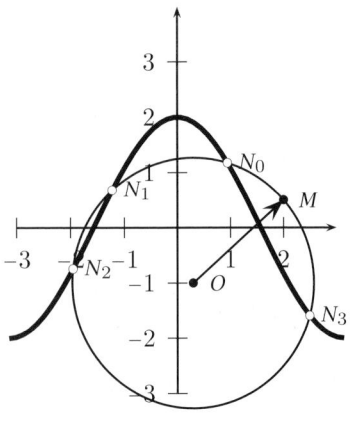

```
\usepackage{pstricks,pst-plot,pst-eucl}

\psset{unit=.75}
\begin{pspicture}[shift=-.5](-3,-4)(3,4)
    \def\F{x 180 mul 3.1415926 div cos 2 mul}
    \pstGeonode(0.3,-1){O}\pstGeonode(2,.5){M}
    \ncline[linecolor=blue, arrowscale=2]{->}{O}{M}
    \psaxes{->}(0,0)(-3,-3)(3,4)
    \psplot[linewidth=2pt]{-3.14}{3.14}{\F}
    \psset{PointSymbol=*}
    \pstCircleOA{O}{M}
    \psset{PointSymbol=o}
    \pstInterFC{\F}{O}{M}{1}{N_0}
    \pstInterFC{\F}{O}{M}{-1}{N_1}
    \pstInterFC{\F}{O}{M}{-2}{N_2}
    \pstInterFC{\F}{O}{M}{2}{N_3}
\end{pspicture}
```

29.3 Examples

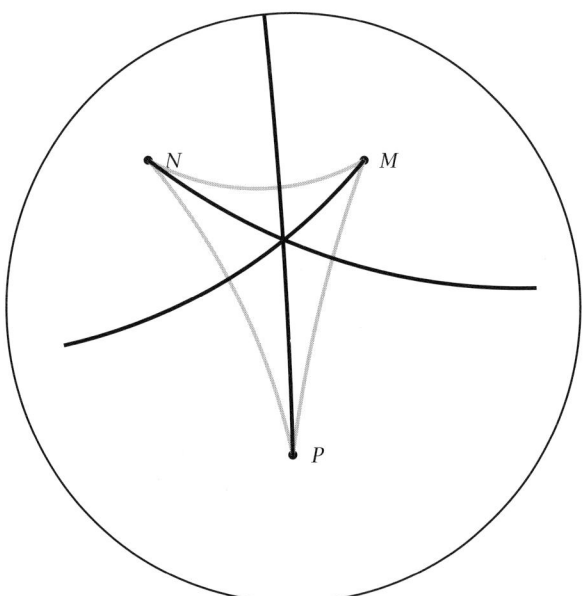

Figure 29.1: Hyperbolic geometry using the example of a simple triangle
(Dominique Rodriguez)

Chapter 30

pstricks-add – Extended basic functions

30.1 Mathematical functions at TEX level 581
30.2 New commands. 584
30.3 Node types and lines 596
30.4 Commands and options to plot data and functions 601

The pstricks-add package is in character "latent dynamic" – it basically comprises the things that appeared on the PSTricks mailing list as bug fixes or extensions that users had requested. Over time, the ones that emerge to be useful after a period of testing will be moved into the respective packages. This happens in years rather than months; therefore it is sensible to give this package its own chapter. In some cases you'll find these commands included (now or later) in other packages, but you'll always be able to find their description in this book with the help of the index. A significant part of the package has already been covered in appropriate places, for example arrows, axis tics, or node connections. In particular, Chapter 15.1.11 on page 176 dealt with using pstricks-add in connection with coordinate axes. In this chapter we only cover the things that haven't been explained before.

In contrast to the usual way packages are presented in this book, the pstricks-add-specific parameters aren't given in a single section at the beginning of the chapter because they are from a wide range of topics and it therefore makes sense to sort them by content.

Note that the pstricks-add package makes many changes to existing packages – remember to load it as the last of the PSTricks-specific packages.

30.1 Mathematical functions at TEX level

These are intended only for internal use by the package, but you can use them for custom commands as well. However, it's a good idea to rename the commands you are using so that you don't have to use the \makeatletter...\makeatother combination all the time. Here is an example of how to rename a command:

30 pstricks-add – Extended basic functions

```
\makeatletter
\let\pstdivide\pst@divide
\makeatother
```

In the following examples a \makeatletter was put into the preamble for the sake of simplicity.

30.1.1 \pst@divide

This command is already part of pstricks. It expects two lengths of arbitrary unit and returns a floating-point number without unit.division Which unit you use isn't important as long as dividend and divisor have the same unit.

\pst@divide{*dividend*}{*divisor*}{*result command*}

The value returned is stored in the result command and you can call it afterwards for output or for use in further calculations.

The last three divisions below are assigned the same values though the units are changed for each example; in the last example the units within the division are not the same for dividend and divisor, which leads to a different result.

5.66666	`\usepackage{pstricks-add}\makeatletter`	30-01-1
-0.17647		
0.17647	`\pst@divide{34pt}{6pt}\quotient \quotient\\`	
0.0062	`\pst@divide{-6cm}{34cm}\quotient \quotient\\`	
	`\pst@divide{-6in}{-34in}\quotient \quotient\\`	
	`\pst@divide{-6pt}{-34cm}\quotient \quotient% wrong!!!`	

30.1.2 \pst@mod

\pst@mod performs the modulo function, returning the remainder of after subtracting the highest possible multiple of a specified integer.

\pst@mod{*number*}{*number*}{*result command*}

The first number is the value to be remaindered, and the second number is the value to be subtracted at its highest multiple. Both numbers have to be integer numbers and are given without a unit.

4	`\usepackage{pstricks-add}\makeatletter`	30-01-2
1		
-1	`\pst@mod{34}{6}\modulo \modulo\\`	
-1	`\pst@mod{25}{-6}\modulo \modulo\\`	
	`\pst@mod{-25}{6}\modulo \modulo\\`	
	`\pst@mod{-25}{-6}\modulo \modulo`	

30.1.3 \pst@max

The \pst@max command determines the larger of two numbers and returns it in a count register. The numbers are given without units (cf. \pst@maxdim below for handling numbers with units).

```
\pst@max{number}{number}{result counter}
```

Because of the return type, to output the contents of the counter in the text you have to use the \the command.

-6
11
	`\usepackage{pstricks-add}\makeatletter`
	
	`\newcount\maxNo`
	`\pst@max{-34}{-6}\maxNo \the\maxNo\\`
	`\pst@max{0}{11}\maxNo \the\maxNo`

30.1.4 `\pst@maxdim`

`\pst@maxdim` determines the larger of two dimensions taking the units into account, which may be different.

```
\pst@maxdim{dimension}{dimension}{dimension register}
```

Dimension is used here in the TeX sense: value and unit. The result is always returned in the unit pt.

1234.0pt
967.39369pt
	`\usepackage{pstricks-add}\makeatletter`
	
	`\newdimen\maxDim`
	`\pst@maxdim{34cm}{1234pt}\maxDim \the\maxDim\\`
	`\pst@maxdim{34cm}{123pt}\maxDim \the\maxDim`

30.1.5 `\pst@mindim`

`\pst@mindim` determines the smaller of two dimensions taking the units into account, which may be different.

```
\pst@mindim{dimension}{dimension}{dimension register}
```

Dimension is used here in the TeX sense: value and unit. The result is always returned in the unit pt.

967.39369pt
123.0pt
	`\usepackage{pstricks-add}\makeatletter`
	
	`\newdimen\minDim`
	`\pst@mindim{34cm}{1234pt}\minDim \the\minDim\\`
	`\pst@mindim{34cm}{123pt}\minDim \the\minDim`

30.1.6 `\pst@abs`

`\pst@abs` returns the absolute value of a number or a counter register. The number is given without unit (cf. `\pst@absdim` below for handling numbers with units).

```
\pst@abs{number}{result counter}
```

34
4
	`\usepackage{pstricks-add}\makeatletter`
	
	`\newcount\absNo`
	`\pst@abs{-34}\absNo \the\absNo\\`
	`\pst@abs{4}\absNo \the\absNo`

30.1.7 \pst@absdim

\pst@absdim also determines the absolute value, but for a dimension with a unit.

\pst@absdim{*dimension*}{*dimension register*}

The result is returned in pt regardless of the input unit; the output can therefore differ from the input also in terms of the actual number, as shown in the following example.

34.0pt
967.39369pt
0.00006pt

```
\usepackage{pstricks-add}\makeatletter

\newdimen\absDim
\pst@absdim{-34pt}\absDim \the\absDim\\
\pst@absdim{-34cm}\absDim \the\absDim\\
\pst@absdim{4sp}\absDim \the\absDim
```

30.2 New commands

30.2.1 \psrotate – Rotate objects

The \rput command (cf. Section 9.4 on page 105) already has an optional argument for rotating arbitrary objects; the rotation centre is automatically the centre coordinates of the command itself. However, the \psrotate command, lets you define the rotation centre; otherwise to do this would require nested calls of the \rput command.

\psrotate [*settings*] (*x*, *y*){*angle*}{*object*}

```
\usepackage{pstricks-add}
\psset{unit=0.75}
\begin{pspicture}(-0.5,-2)(6.5,4)
  \psaxes{->}(0,0)(-0.5,-2)(6.5,4.5)
  \psdots[linecolor=red,dotscale=1.5](2,1)
  \psarc[linecolor=red,linewidth=.1pt,arrowscale=2,showpoints]{->}(2,1){3}{0}{60}
  \psset{linewidth=1pt}
  \pspolygon[linecolor=blue](1,1)(5,1)(6,-1)(2,-2)
  \psrotate(2,1){60}{\pspolygon[linestyle=dashed](1,1)(5,1)(6,-1)(2,-2)}
\end{pspicture}
```

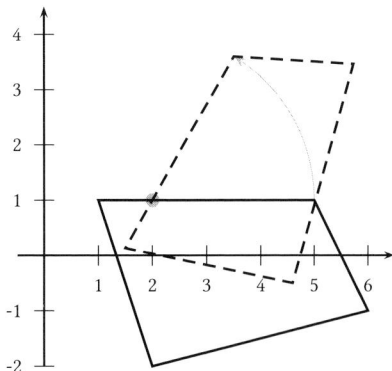

30.2 New commands

In conjunction with the `multido` package and the command of the same name, you can now create animations that show rotating bodies against time t. The following example shows a stick rotating about its gravity axis and additionally the course of one of the end points (idea of Manuel Luque). In the animation itself only one stick at a time would be seen.

```
\usepackage{pstricks-add}
\def\majorette{\psline[linewidth=0.5mm](0,2)\pscircle[fillstyle=solid]{0.1}
  \pscircle[fillstyle=solid](0,2){0.1}}
\psset{unit=0.8}
\begin{pspicture}(0,-6)(15,5)
\psaxes[linewidth=0.5pt]{->}(0,0)(0,-5)(15,5)
\pstVerb{/V0 10 def /Alpha 45 def}% v0 and starting angle
\multido{\nT=0.0+0.05,\iA=0+40}{41}{%
  \pstVerb{ /nT \nT\space def }
  \rput(!V0 Alpha cos mul nT mul -9.81 2 div nT dup mul mul
        V0 Alpha sin mul nT mul add){%
    \psrotate(0,1){\iA}{\majorette\psdot[linecolor=red](0,1)
                                  \psdot[linecolor=green](0,2)}
}}% ende \multido
\parametricplot[linecolor=red]{0}{2}{% centre of grvity
  V0 Alpha cos mul t mul -9.81 2 div t dup mul mul
  V0 Alpha sin mul t mul add 1 add}
\parametricplot[linecolor=green,plotpoints=360]{0}{2}{% s=f(x,y)
  V0 Alpha cos mul t mul 800 t mul sin sub % x(t)
  -9.81 2 div t dup mul mul
  V0 Alpha sin mul t mul add 1 add 800 t mul cos add }%y(t)
\end{pspicture}
```

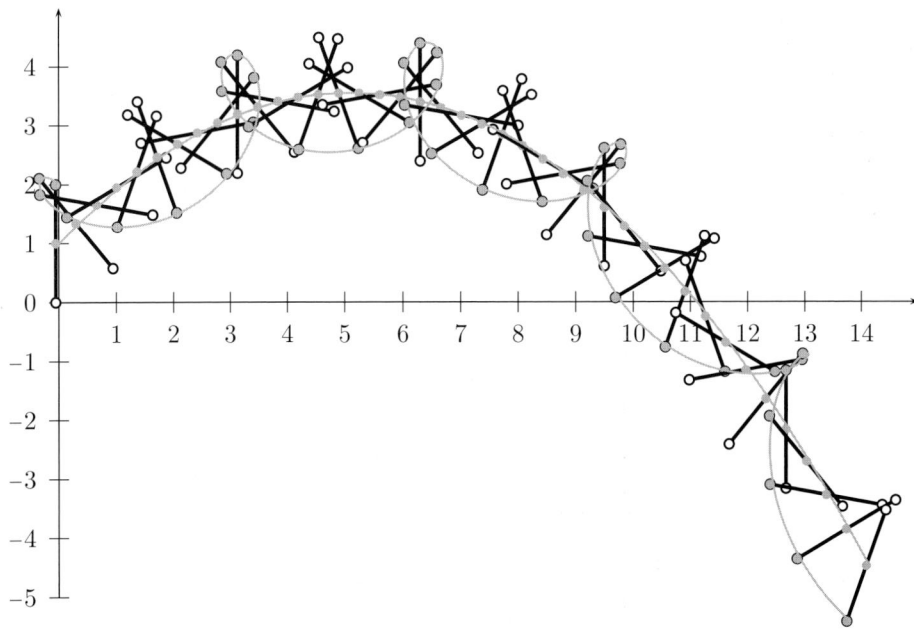

30.2.2 \psHomothetie – Centric dilations

The \psHomothetie command performs centric dilations of arbitrary objects according to an arbitrary dilation factor. The command expects three required parameters: the centre of the dilation, the dilation factor, and the object.

\psHomothetie [settings] (x_C, y_C) {dilation factor} {object}

In the following example the dark-coloured "Jana" is written as a normal command with its centre at the coordinate origin. After that this original text is dilated twice with the centre of the dilation at (0,-1), once with factor 2 (blue "Jana") and once with factor -1.5 (red "Jana"). The dashed auxiliary lines intersect at the centre of the dilation.

```
\usepackage{pst-text,pstricks-add}
\def\Jana{\rput(0,0){\pscharpath{\RM Jana}}}\DeclareFixedFont{\RM}{T1}{ptm}{b}{n}{3cm}
\begin{pspicture}[showgrid](-5,-4)(5,4)
{\psset{fillcolor=black!60,fillstyle=solid}\Jana
\psHomothetie[linecolor=blue,fillcolor=blue!30,opacity=0.6](0,-1){2}{\Jana}
\psHomothetie[linecolor=red,fillcolor=red!30,opacity=0.6](0,-1){-1.5}{\Jana}}
\psline[linestyle=dashed](-5,3)(4,-4.2)\psline[linestyle=dashed](5,2)(-3.6,-3.2)
\psdot(0,-1)
\end{pspicture}
```

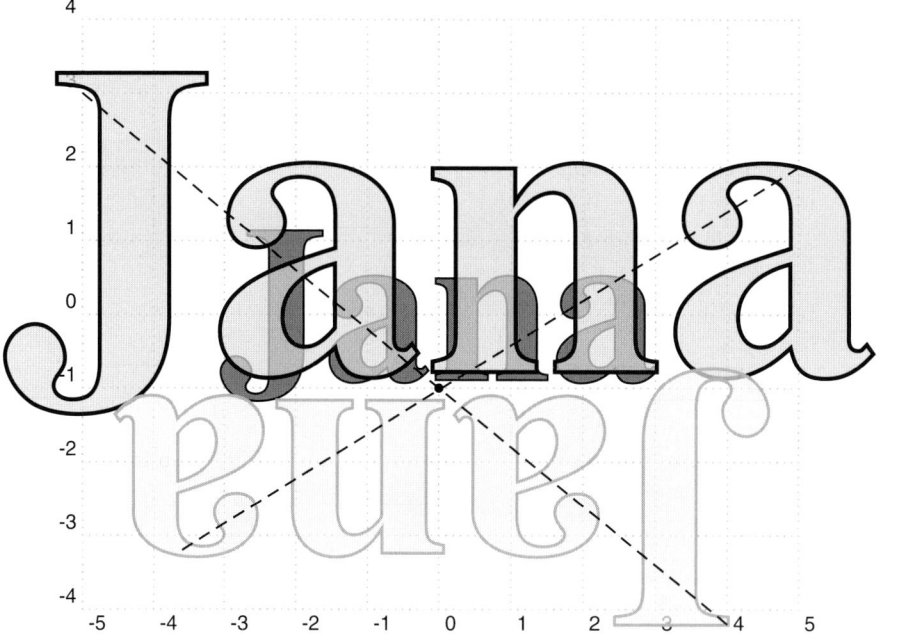

30.2.3 \psChart – Pie charts

The syntax for the \psChart command is:

30.2 New commands

`\psChart [settings] {`*comma-separated list*`}{`*comma-separated list*`}{`*radius*`}`

The first comma-separated list must have at least one value, and in general at least two. These values can sum to anything but to construct the pie chart this sum is equated to 360°; the sizes of the individual pie slices are calculated based on this ratio. The slices are drawn counterclockwise from the positive x axis and are numbered automatically starting with 1 for the first slice. The second comma-separated list contains the index numbers of the slices that are to be highlighted by moving them radially from the centre; this list can be empty. The `\psChart` command defines three nodes for each slice, which you can refer to later. These nodes are all on the bisectrix and are placed (by default) at distances of $0.75r$, r, and $1.5r$ from the tip of the element (cf. Table 30.1 below for the parameters to change these distances). For highlighted elements, the nodes are a bit further away. Names for the nodes are allocated internally: `psChartI?` for the inner node, `psChart?` for the middle node, and `psChartO?` for the outer node, where `?` stands for the index number of the slice.

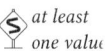

at least one value

Inner and Outer nod

Table 30.1 shows the special parameters available for this command, in addition to the general optional parameters.

Table 30.1: Summary of additional parameters valid for the \psChart command

name	description	type	default
chartSep	distance of a highlighted slice from the centre	value unit	10pt
chartColor	choice of greyscale or coloured slices	gray|color	gray
userColor	comma-separated list of user-defined colour names	$colour_0, colour_1, \ldots, colour_n,$	{}
chartNodeI	relative distance (referring to the radius) from the centre to the inner node	value	0.75
chartNodeO	relative distance (referring to the radius) from the centre to the outer node	value	1.5

The centre of the pie chart is the coordinate origin (0,0) by default, though you can move the diagram to an arbitrary position in the usual way with the `\rput` command (cf. Section 9.4 on page 105). Note that the list of colours passed to `userColor` must be put in curly braces, otherwise a comma in the list is read as a delimiter of an option.

translate centre

`chartColor` uses internally-defined sequences of colours or greyscales, which have the names `chartFillColor?` (where `?` again stands for the number of the slice); they are available for custom purposes as well.

```
\usepackage{pstricks-add}
\begin{pspicture}(-3,-3)(3,3)
\psChart{23,29,3,26,28,14}{}{2}
\multido{\iA=1+1}{6}{%
    \psdot(psChart\iA)\psdot(psChartI\iA)\psdot(psChartO\iA)%
    \psline[linestyle=dashed,linecolor=white](psChart\iA)
    \psline[linestyle=dashed](psChart\iA)(psChartO\iA)}
\end{pspicture}\qquad
```

30 pstricks-add – Extended basic functions

```
\begin{pspicture}(-3,-3)(3,3)
\psChart[userColor={red!30,green!30,blue!40,gray,magenta!60,cyan}]%
    {23,29,3,26,28,14}{1,4}{2}
\end{pspicture}
```

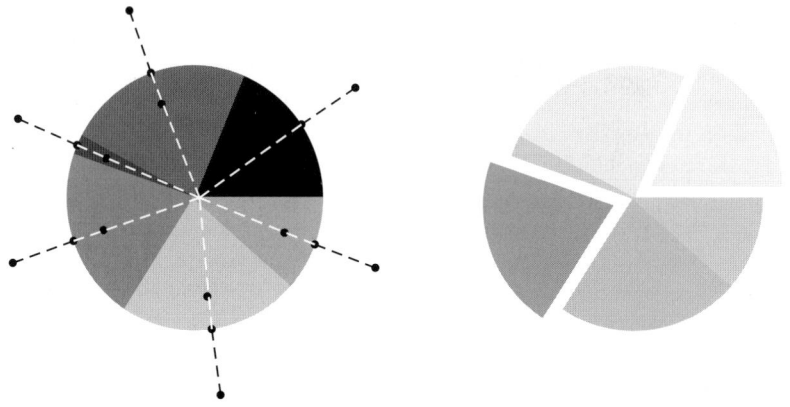

In the following example the internally-defined colour scheme is used to keep the labels in sync with the filling. To achieve this, the colours chartFillColor1 and chartFillColor2 are used for the text while their complementary colours are used for the lines.

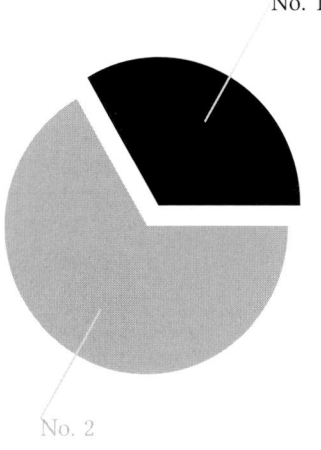

```
\usepackage{pstricks-add}

\begin{pspicture}(-3,-3)(3,3)
\psChart[chartColor=color]{45,90}{1}{2}
\ncline[linecolor=-chartFillColor1,
    nodesepB=-20pt]{psChart01}{psChart1}
\rput[l](psChart01){%
    \textcolor{chartFillColor1}{No. 1}}
\ncline[linecolor=-chartFillColor2,
    nodesepB=-20pt]{psChart02}{psChart2}
\rput[lt](psChart02){%
    \textcolor{chartFillColor2}{No. 2}}
\end{pspicture}
```

30.2 New commands

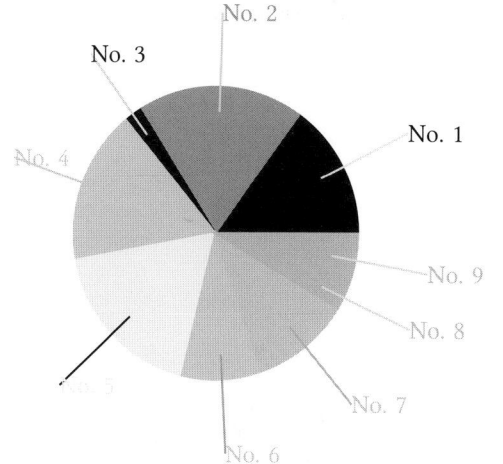

```
\usepackage{pstricks-add}

\begin{pspicture}(-3.25,-3.25)(4.2,3.4)
\psChart[chartColor=color]%
  {23,29,3,26,28,14,17,4,9}{}{2}
\multido{\iA=1+1}{9}{%
 \ncline[linecolor=-chartFillColor\iA,
   nodesepB=-10pt]{psChart0\iA}{psChart\iA}
 \rput[l](psChart0\iA){%
   \textcolor{chartFillColor\iA}{No. \iA}}}
\end{pspicture}
```

```
\usepackage{pstricks-add}
\begin{pspicture}(-3,-3)(3,3)
\psChart{23,29,3,26,28,14}{}{2} \multido{\iA=1+1}{6}{\rput*(psChartI\iA){\iA}}
\end{pspicture}\qquad
\begin{pspicture}(-3,-3)(3,3)
\psChart[userColor={red!30,green!30,blue!40,gray,magenta!60,cyan}]%
     {23,29,3,26,28,14}{1,4}{2}
\end{pspicture}
```

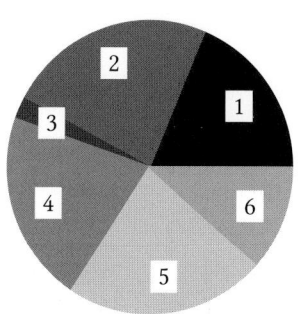 

```
\usepackage{pstricks-add}
\begin{pspicture}(-3,-3)(3,3)
\psChart[userColor={red!30,green!30,blue!40,gray,cyan!50,magenta!60,cyan},
  chartSep=30pt,shadow,shadowsize=5pt]{ 34.5,17.2,20.7,15.5,5.2,6.9}{6}{2}
\psset{nodesepA=5pt,nodesepB=-10pt}
\ncline{psChart01}{psChart1}\nput{0}{psChart01}{1000 (34.5\%)}
\ncline{psChart02}{psChart2}\nput{150}{psChart02}{500 (17.2\%)}
\ncline{psChart03}{psChart3}\nput{-90}{psChart03}{600 (20.7\%)}
\ncline{psChart04}{psChart4}\nput{0}{psChart04}{450 (15.5\%)}
\ncline{psChart05}{psChart5}\nput{0}{psChart05}{150 (5.2\%)}
```

```
\ncline{psChart06}{psChart6}\nput{0}{psChart06}{200 (6.9\%)}
\bfseries\rput(psChartI1){Taxes}\rput(psChartI2){Rent}\rput(psChartI3){Bills}
\rput(psChartI4){Car}\rput(psChartI5){Gas}\rput(psChartI6){Food}
\end{pspicture}
```

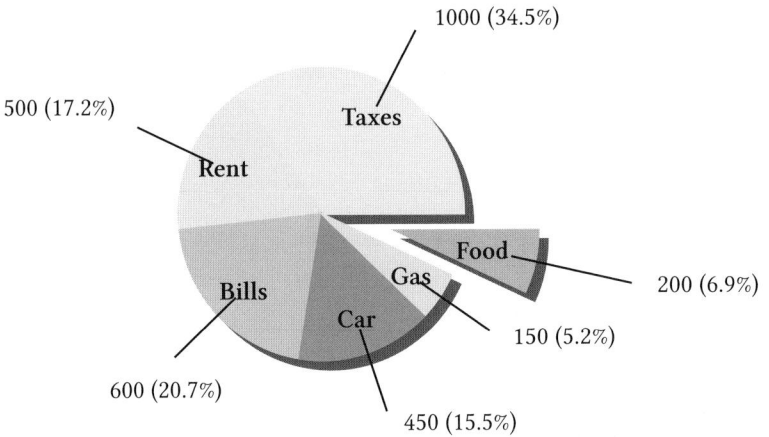

30.2.4 \psbrace

The \psbrace command is only a makeshift solution: the brace is created as a pure polyline so doesn't have the different line widths characteristic of the brace composed of several characters for normal text.

\psbrace * [settings] $(x_1, y_1)(x_2, y_2)$ { text }

If \SpecialCoor is activated (cf. Chapter 12 on page 139), you can use any valid type of coordinates, such as (node name), (x, y), (nodeA|nodeB), …

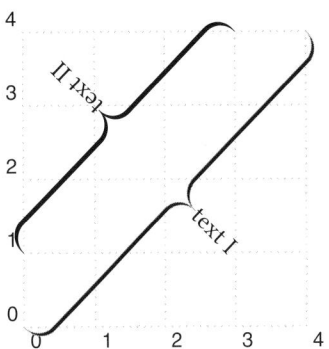

```
\usepackage{pstricks-add}

\begin{pspicture}[showgrid](4,4)
\pnode(0,0){A}
\pnode(4,4){B}
\psbrace[linecolor=red,ref=lC](A)(B){text I}
\psbrace[linecolor=blue,ref=lC](3,4)(0,1){text II}
\end{pspicture}
```

Parameters

In addition to the general parameters such as line colour, line width, etc. there are some special options, which are summarized in Table 30.2 and illustrated in the following figure.

30.2 New commands

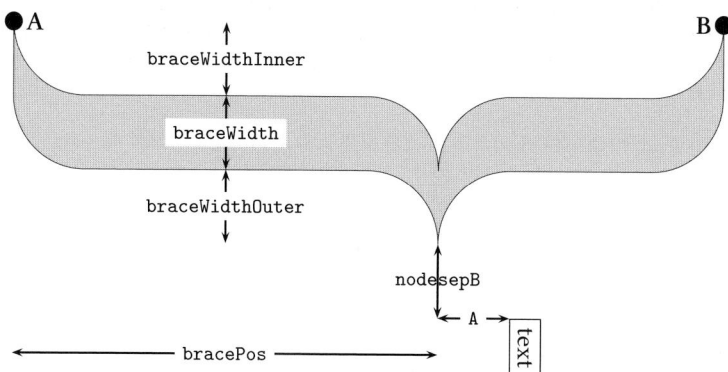

A positive value for nodesepA and nodesepB moves the text towards the top right for positive values and towards the bottom left for negative values. This is independent of any rotation of the text.

Table 30.2: Summary of the special parameters for the \psbrace command

name	meaning	type	default
braceWidth	absolute width of the brace	value unit	2\pslinewidth
braceWidthInner	"inner" distance (ends to brace)	value unit	10\pslinewidth
braceWidthOuter	"outer" distance (tip to brace)	value unit	10\pslinewidth
bracePos	relative position of the tip from end A	value	0.5
nodesepA	x distance of the text from the tip	value unit	0 pt
nodesepB	y distance of the text from the tip	value unit	0 pt
rot	rotation angle of the text	angle	0
ref	reference point for the text with any two-letter combination of	l|b|B|r|t|c|C	c
fillcolor	fill colour of the brace	colour	black

By default the text is placed at right angles to the brace, but you can rotate it in any direction with the rot option. Instead of containing text, the argument may be empty or contain any other object, for example an equation.

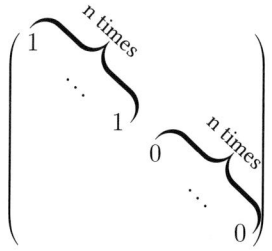

```
\usepackage{pstricks-add,amsmath}

\[\begin{pmatrix}
    \Rnode[vref=2ex]{A}{~1} \\
    & \ddots \\       && \Rnode[href=2]{B}{1} \\
    &&& \Rnode[vref=2ex]{C}{0} \\
    &&&& \ddots \\    &&&&& \Rnode[href=2]{D}{0}~ \\
\end{pmatrix}\]
\psset{linewidth=0.1pt,rot=-90,nodesep=-0.4}\small
\psbrace(B)(A){n times} \psbrace(D)(C){n times}
```

30 pstricks-add – Extended basic functions

```
\usepackage{pstricks-add}
\def\someMath{$\int\limits_1^{\infty}\frac{1}{x^2}\,\mathrm{d}x=1$}
\begin{pspicture}(12cm,2cm)
\psbrace(0,0)(0,2){\fbox{text}}\psbrace[nodesepB=1ex](1.5,0)(1.5,2){\fbox{text}}
\psbrace[ref=1C](3,0)(3,2){\fbox{text}}
\psbrace[ref=lt,rot=90,nodesepB=15pt](4.5,0)(4.5,2){\fbox{text}}
\psbrace[ref=lc,nodesepA=25pt](6,0)(6,2){\someMath}
\psbrace[rot=90,ref=C,nodesepA=10pt](8.5,0)(8.5,2){\someMath}
\psbrace*[rot=90,ref=C,nodesepA=-10pt,linecolor=cyan](11.3,2)(11.3,0){\color{cyan}\someM
\end{pspicture}
```

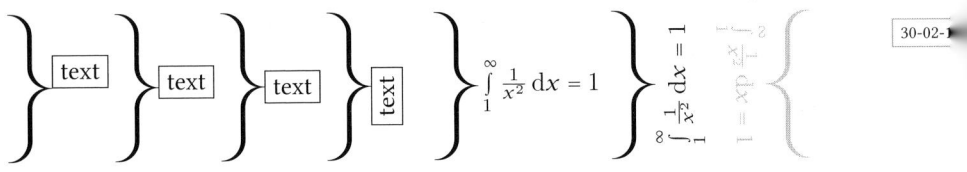

30-02-

```
\usepackage{pstricks-add}
\begin{pspicture}(0,0)(\linewidth,3.5)
 \psbrace[bracePos=0.8,braceWidth=5pt,braceWidthInner=17pt](0,0.5)(.8\linewidth,0.5){%
    \fbox{text}}
 \psbrace[bracePos=0.25,nodesepB=13pt,ref=C](0,2)(.8\linewidth,2){\fbox{text}}
 \psbrace[ref=lC,nodesepA=-3cm,nodesepB=-10pt,rot=-90](.8\linewidth,2.5)(0,2.5){%
    \fbox{some very, very long wonderful text}}
\end{pspicture}
```

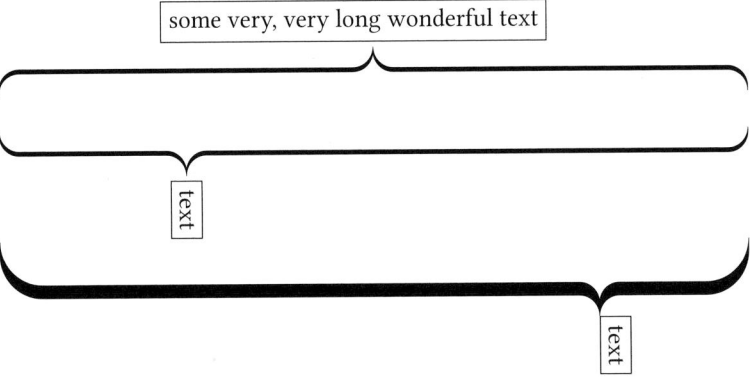

30-02-1

30.2.5 \psdice – Dice views

\psdice creates a two-dimensional view of the side of a dice; the number on the dice is the only required parameter.

\psdice [settings] {*number on the dice*}

The command creates a box of size null and outputs it at the current position of the text if not placed elsewhere through \rput. The default size of the dice is 1cm × 1cm, but you can

30.2 New commands

change that through the unit parameter in the usual manner.

```
\usepackage{pst-func,pstricks-add}
\begin{pspicture}(-1,-1)(8,9)
\multido{\iA=1+1}{6}{\rput(\iA,7.5){\Huge\psdice[unit=0.75,linecolor=red!80]{\iA}}
  \rput(! -0.5 7 \iA\space sub){\Huge\psdice[unit=0.75,linecolor=blue!70]{\iA}}%
  \multido{\iB=1+1}{6}{\rput(! \iA\space 7 \iB\space sub){%
    \rnode[c]{p\iA\iB}{\makebox[1em][l]{\strut\psPrintValue[fontscale=12]{%
      \iA\space \iB\space add}}}}}}
\ncbox[linearc=0.35,nodesep=0.2,linestyle=dotted]{p11}{p66}
\ncbox[linearc=0.35,nodesep=0.2,linestyle=dashed]{p15}{p51}
\rput{90}(-1.5,3.5){first dice} \rput{0}(3.5,8.5){second dice}
\psset{linewidth=1.5pt}
\psline(0.25,0.5)(0.25,8) \psline(-1,6.75)(6.5,6.75)
\end{pspicture}
```

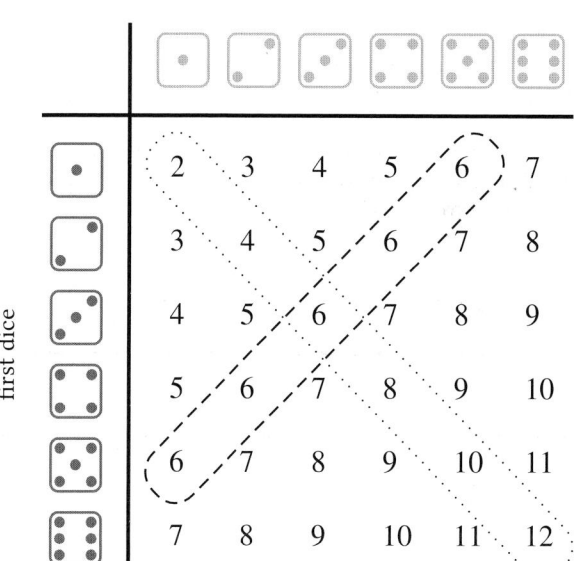

30.2.6 \psCancel environment

The idea for this command came from Stefano Baroni. It works similarly to the \cancel command from the package of the same name, crossing out or overlaying the content of its argument, but you can assign arbitrary objects as this command's argument, including complex figures.

\psCancel * [settings] {object}

All optional parameters for lines and boxes are evaluated by \psCancel. The starred version has the usual effect – the object is filled with the current line colour; transparency is possible through the `opacity` option. The command is especially suitable for presentations to cross out or colour differently equations, figures, or similar with an overlay. You can also make the lines seem transparent through the `strokeopacity` option.

```
\usepackage{pst-func,pstricks-add}
\psCancel{A} \psCancel[linecolor=red]{Tikz :-)} \quad
\psCancel[linecolor=blue,doubleline]{\readdata{\data}{demo1.dat}% see preamble
  \psset{shift=*,xAxisLabel=x-Axis,yAxisLabel=y-Axis,llx=-13mm,lly=-7mm,
    xAxisLabelPos={c,-1},yAxisLabelPos={-7,c}}
  \pstScalePoints(1,0.00000001){}{}
  \begin{psgraph}[axesstyle=frame,xticksize=0 7.5,yticksize=0 25,subticksize=1,
    ylabelFactor=\times 10^8,Dx=5,Dy=1,xsubticks=2](0,0)(25,7.5){5.5cm}{5cm}
  \listplot[linecolor=red, linewidth=2pt, showpoints]{\data}
  \end{psgraph}} \qquad% end of psCancel
\psCancel[linewidth=3pt,linecolor=red,strokeopacity=0.5]{%
  \tabular[b]{c}first line\\second line\endtabular}
```

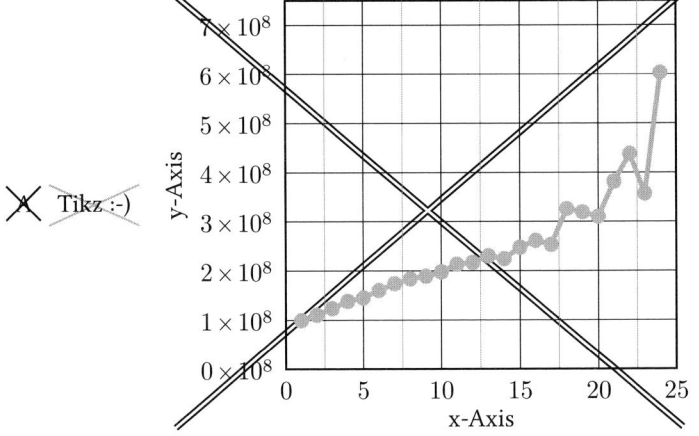

30-02-1

In the following example a transparent and coloured rectangle is put on top of the normal figure; here the starred version `\psCancel*` is used. The size of the rectangle is calculated by the command automatically.

```
\usepackage{pst-func,pstricks-add}
\psCancel*[linecolor=blue!30,opacity=0.5]{\readdata{\data}{demo1.dat}
  \psset{shift=*,xAxisLabel=x-Axis,yAxisLabel=y-Axis,llx=-15mm,lly=-7mm,urx=1mm,
    xAxisLabelPos={c,-1},yAxisLabelPos={-7,c}} \pstScalePoints(1,0.00000001){}{}
  \begin{psgraph}[axesstyle=frame,xsubticks=2,xticksize=0 7.5,yticksize=0 25,
    subticksize=1,ylabelFactor=\times 10^8,Dx=5,Dy=1](0,0)(25,7.5){5.5cm}{5cm}
  \listplot[linecolor=red,linewidth=2pt,showpoints]{\data}
  \end{psgraph}}% end of \psCancel
```

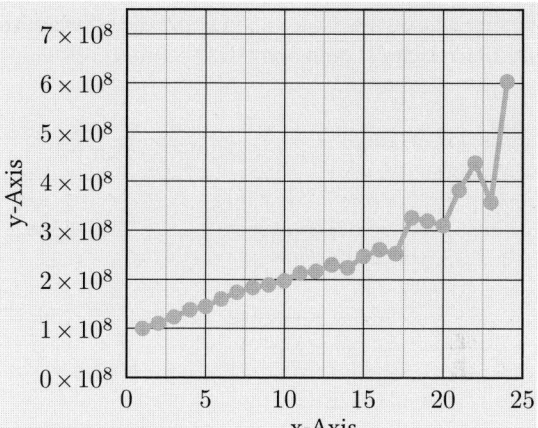

In the last two examples of this section, a transparent and coloured rectangle is put on top of the left figure by using the starred version \psCancel*, and the right figure uses transparent lines by setting the strokeopacity parameter to a value smaller than 1.

```
\usepackage{amsmath,pstricks-add}
\psCancel*[linecolor=red!50,opacity=0.5]{%
  \tabular[b]{c}first line\\second line\endtabular}
\psCancel[linewidth=4pt,strokeopacity=0.4]{\parbox{8cm}{\[
  \binom{x_R}{y_R} = \underbrace{r\vphantom{\binom{A}{B}}}_{\text{scaling}}\times
    \underbrace{\begin{pmatrix} \sin\gamma & -\cos\gamma \\\cos \gamma & \sin \gamma\\
    \end{pmatrix}}_{\text{rotation}} \binom{x_K}{y_K} +
    \underbrace{\binom{t_x}{t_y}}_{\text{translation}} \]} }
```

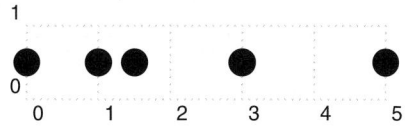

30.2.7 \psforeach

The \psforeach command performs a loop for an individual comma-separated list of values.

\psforeach{*variable*}{*list of values*}{*actions*}

```
\usepackage{pstricks-add}

\begin{pspicture}[showgrid](5,1)
  \psforeach{\nA}{0, 1, 1.5, 3, 5}{%
    \psdot[dotscale=3](\nA,0.5)}
\end{pspicture}
```

595

30 pstricks-add – Extended basic functions

\psforeach accepts any expression for the list of values; the possibilities of \SpecialCoor can be used without further ado. In the following example the points are placed with distances of sqrt(\nA) between them. The "!" sign activates the interpretation of data as PostScript code.

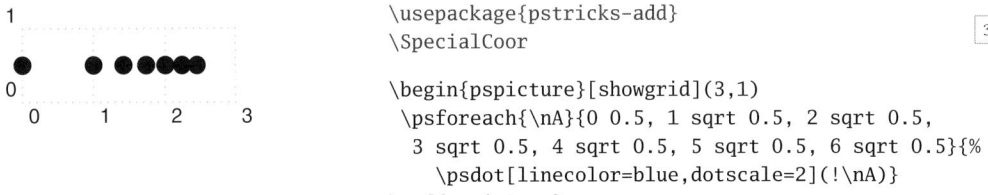

```
\usepackage{pstricks-add}
\SpecialCoor

\begin{pspicture}[showgrid](3,1)
  \psforeach{\nA}{0 0.5, 1 sqrt 0.5, 2 sqrt 0.5,
    3 sqrt 0.5, 4 sqrt 0.5, 5 sqrt 0.5, 6 sqrt 0.5}{%
    \psdot[linecolor=blue,dotscale=2](!\nA)}
\end{pspicture}
```

30.3 Node types and lines

The following node and line commands are all grouped under the "nodes" topic as the results of their calculations are coordinates that are saved in a specified node name.

30.3.1 \psRelNode and \psRelLine

\psRelNode places a node relative to a line given by two nodes or points.

$\boxed{\texttt{\textbackslash psRelNode}(x_0,y_0)(x_1,y_1)\{\textit{dilation factor}\}\{\textit{node name}\}}$

The dilation factor refers to the length of the line $\overline{P_0P_1}$. The node name can't contain any PostScript-specific active characters (cf. Section 16.1 on page 226). Two additional parameters are explained in Table 30.3.

Table 30.3: Summary of the additional parameters for \psRelNode and \psRelLine

name	default	meaning
angle	0	Angle between the given line $\overline{AB}$ and the new one $\overline{AE}$, where E is the end node influenced by the dilation factor.
trueAngle	false	For trueAngle=true, different scale factors aren't taken into account; the specification corresponds to the "visible" angle.

In the following example, the given line $\overline{AB}$ has coordinates $A(3,3)$ and $B(4,2)$. The \psRelNode command places nodes every $30°$, starting from a point dilated by a factor of 2 along $\overline{AB}$. Therefore all new nodes have twice the distance from point A.

30.3 Node types and lines

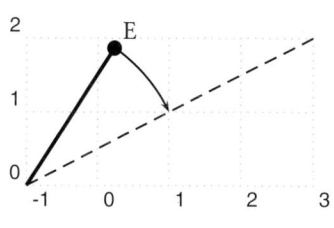

```
\usepackage{pstricks-add}

\psset{unit=0.75}\begin{pspicture}(6,6)
\pnode(3,3){A}\pnode(4,2){B}
\psline[nodesep=-3,
    linewidth=1pt]{*-*}(A)(B)
\multido{\iA=0+30}{12}{%
    \psRelNode[angle=\iA](A)(B){2}{C\iA}%
    \qdisk(C\iA){2pt}\uput[0](C\iA){\iA}}
\psset{linestyle=dashed}
\psline(4,2)(C0)
\psline(3,3)(C30)\psline(3,3)(C60)
\end{pspicture}
```

\psRelLine differs from \psRelNode only in that it also draws the line to the new node.

| \psRelLine [settings] {arrows} $(x_0,y_0)(x_1,y_1)$ {dilation factor}{end node} |

The dilation factor again refers to the distance between the two points $\overline{P_0P_1}$ and the node name must meet the same requirements explained above. In the following example the solid line is half the length of the dashed line and rotated from it by $30°$.

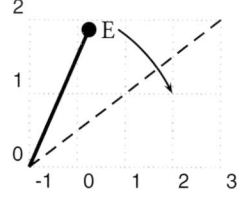

```
\usepackage{pstricks-add}

\begin{pspicture}[showgrid](-1,0)(3,2)
    \pnode(-1,0){A}\pnode(3,2){B}
    \psline[linestyle=dashed](A)(B)
    \psRelLine[linecolor=blue,angle=30,
        linewidth=1.5pt](A)(B){0.5}{E}
    \qdisk(E){3pt}\uput[45](E){E}
    \psarc[nodesep=0]{<-}(-1,0){2.24}{26.57}{56.57}
\end{pspicture}
```

The same example but with different units on the x and y axes yields the same result mathematically, but not optically. The "visible" angle is different from the specification. You can correct this optically by setting the trueAngle option to true, which takes the values of \psxunit and \psyunit into account during the calculation. Note that the determination of the angle for the \psarc command has to be done manually – the second example looks satisfactory.

```
\usepackage{pstricks-add}

\psset{xunit=0.67cm}
\begin{pspicture}[showgrid](-1,0)(3,2)
    \pnode(-1,0){A}\pnode(3,2){B}\psline[linestyle=dashed](A)(B)
    \psRelLine[angle=30,linewidth=1.5pt](A)(B){0.5}{E}
    \qdisk(E){3pt}\uput[0](E){E}
    \psarc[nodesep=0]{<-}(-1,0){2.24}{26.57}{56.57}
\end{pspicture}
```

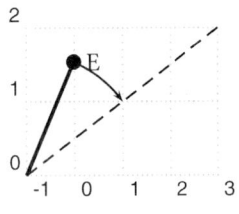

```
\usepackage{pstricks-add}

\psset{xunit=0.67cm}
\begin{pspicture}[showgrid](-1,0)(3,2)
    \pnode(-1,0){A}\pnode(3,2){B}\psline[linestyle=dashed](A)(B)
    \psRelLine[angle=30,trueAngle,linewidth=1.5pt](A)(B){0.5}{E}
    \qdisk(E){3pt}\uput[0](E){E}
    \psarc[nodesep=0]{<-}(-1,0){1.67}{36.73}{66.73}
\end{pspicture}
```

The following two sets of figures are pairwise the same except that in each case the left one is drawn without trueAngle and the right one is drawn with trueAngle. Hence the end nodes in the right figure are all on a circle and everything appears symmetric.

```
\usepackage{pstricks-add}\psset{yunit=0.75cm,xunit=1.1cm}
    \begin{pspicture}[showgrid](-2,-3.4)(3,3.4)
    \pnode(-1,0){A}\pnode(3,2){B}\psline[linecolor=red](A)(B)
    \psRelLine[linecolor=blue,angle=30](-1,0)(B){0.5}{EndNode}\qdisk(EndNode){2pt}
    \psRelLine[linecolor=blue,angle=-30](A)(B){0.5}{EndNode}\qdisk(EndNode){2pt}
    \psRelLine[linecolor=magenta,angle=90](-1,0)(3,2){0.5}{EndNode}\qdisk(EndNode){2pt}
    \psRelLine[linecolor=magenta,angle=-90](A)(B){0.5}{EndNode}\qdisk(EndNode){2pt}
\end{pspicture}\hfill
\begin{pspicture}[showgrid](-2,-3.4)(3,3.4)
    \pnode(-1,0){A}\pnode(3,2){B}\psline[linecolor=red](A)(B)
    \psarc[linestyle=dashed](A){2.4}{-90}{135}  \psset{trueAngle}
    \psRelLine[linecolor=blue,angle=30](-1,0)(B){0.5}{EndNode}\qdisk(EndNode){2pt}
    \psRelLine[linecolor=blue,angle=-30](A)(B){0.5}{EndNode}   \qdisk(EndNode){2pt}
    \psRelLine[linecolor=magenta,angle=90](-1,0)(3,2){0.5}{EndNode}\qdisk(EndNode){2pt}
    \psRelLine[linecolor=magenta,angle=-90](A)(B){0.5}{EndNode}\qdisk(EndNode){2pt}
\end{pspicture}
```

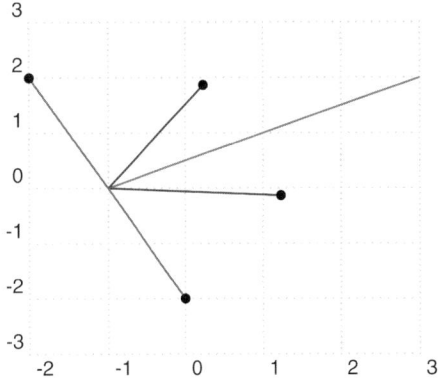
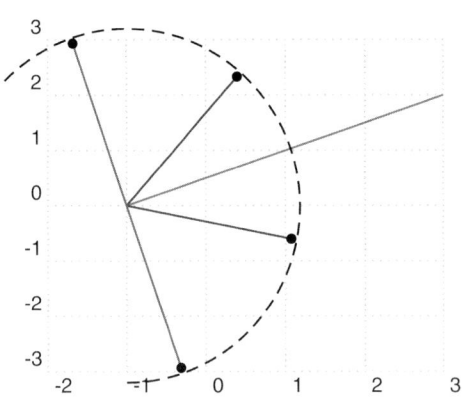

```
\usepackage{pstricks-add}\psset{yunit=1,xunit=2}
\begin{pspicture}[showgrid](-0.5,-1.2)(2.5,3)
\pnode(-1,0){A}\pnode(1,1){B}\multido{\iA=0+10}{36}{%
    \psRelLine[linecolor=blue,angle=\iA](B)(A){-0.5}{E}\qdisk(E){1pt}}
```

```
\end{pspicture}\quad
\begin{pspicture}[showgrid](-0.5,-1.2)(2.5,3)
\pnode(-1,0){A}\pnode(1,1){B}\multido{\iA=0+10}{36}{%
   \psRelLine[linecolor=magenta,angle=\iA,trueAngle](B)(A){-0.5}{E}\qdisk(E){1pt}}
\end{pspicture}
```

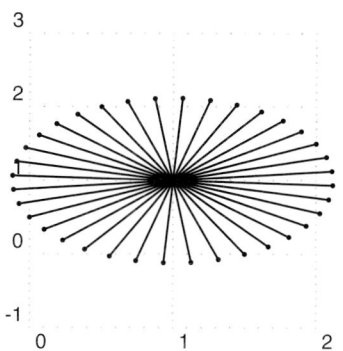
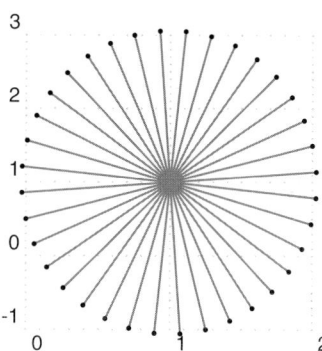

30.3.2 \psParallelLine

Another practical command creates parallel lines, which requires the specification of a reference line and a starting point for the new line.

\psParallelLine [settings] {arrows} $(x_0, y_0)(x_1, y_1)(x_2, y_2)${dilation factor}{end node}

The line drawn is parallel to the line $\overline{P_0 P_1}$, starts at the third point P_2 itself and is of length relative to $\overline{P_0 P_1}$ as specified through the dilation factor. The end node again may not contain any TEX or PostScript-specific active characters.

The following example uses \psParallelLine for the parallel lines on the left and \psRelLine for the crossing lines on the right.

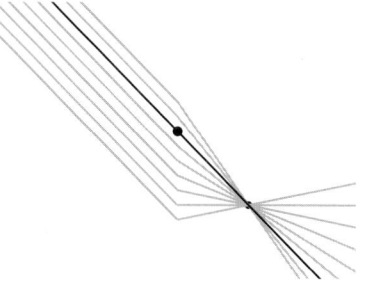

```
\usepackage{pstricks-add}

\psset{unit=0.5cm}\begin{pspicture*}(-5,-4)(5,3.5)
   \pnode(2,-2){F}\qdisk(F){1.5pt}
   \pnode(-5,5){A}\pnode(0,0){O}
   \multido{\nA=-2.4+0.4}{9}{%
      \psParallelLine[linecolor=red](O)(A)(0,\nA){9}{P1}
      \psline[linecolor=red](O,\nA)(F)
      \psRelLine[linecolor=red](O,\nA)(F){9}{P2}}
   \psline[linecolor=blue](A)(F)
   \psRelLine[linecolor=blue](A)(F){5}{END1}
   \qdisk(A){2pt}\qdisk(O){2pt}
\end{pspicture*}
```

30.3.3 \psIntersectionPoint

This command determines the intersection of two lines given by two values each and places a node with the specified name there. It is assumed that the lines are not parallel; there is no way to return an error message from PostScript to TEX.

30 pstricks-add – Extended basic functions

```
\psIntersectionPoint(x0,y0)(x1,y1)(x2,y2)(x3,y3){intersection name}
```

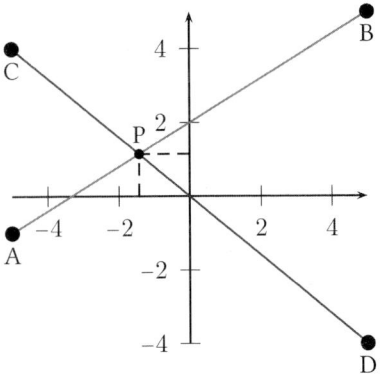

```
\usepackage{pstricks-add}

\psset{unit=0.5cm}
\begin{pspicture}(-5,-4)(5,5)
  \psaxes[dx=2,dy=2,Dx=2,Dy=2]{->}(0,0)(-5,-4)(5,5)
  \psline[linecolor=red](-5,-1)(5,5)
  \psline[linecolor=blue](-5,4)(5,-4)
  \qdisk(-5,-1){3pt}\uput[-90](-5,-1){A}
  \qdisk(5,5){3pt}   \uput[-90](5,5){B}
  \qdisk(-5,4){3pt}  \uput[-90](-5,4){C}
  \qdisk(5,-4){3pt}  \uput[-90](5,-4){D}
  \psIntersectionPoint(-5,-1)(5,5)(-5,4)(5,-4){P}
  \qdisk(P){2pt}    \uput{0.3}[90](P){P}
  \psline[linestyle=dashed](P|0,0)(P)(0,0|P)
\end{pspicture}
```

30.3.4 \psLNode and \psLCNode

\psLNode places a node on a given line $\overline{AB}$ or its extension, depending on the dilation factor. The line $\overline{AC}$ is therefore collinear to the given $\overline{AB}$.

```
\psLNode(x0,y0)(x1,y1){dilation factor}{node name}
```

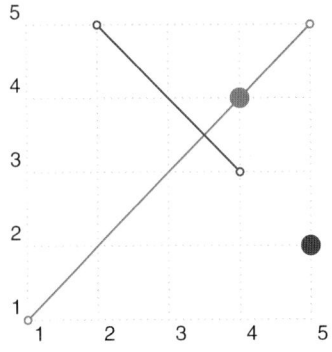

```
\usepackage{pstricks-add}

\begin{pspicture}[showgrid](1,1)(5,5)
  \psset{linecolor=red}
  \psline{o-o}(1,1)(5,5)
  \psLNode(1,1)(5,5){0.75}{P1}\qdisk(P1){4pt}
  \psset{linecolor=blue}
  \psline{o-o}(4,3)(2,5)
  \psLNode(4,3)(2,5){-0.5}{P2}\qdisk(P2){4pt}
\end{pspicture}
```

\psLCNode creates the linear combination of two given points (position vectors), which are each first multiplied by an arbitrary factor and then vector addition yields the new end node. All vectors start at $(0,0)$ by definition.

```
\psLCNode(x0,y0){factor0}(x1,y1){factor1}{node name}
```

30.4 Commands and options to plot data and functions

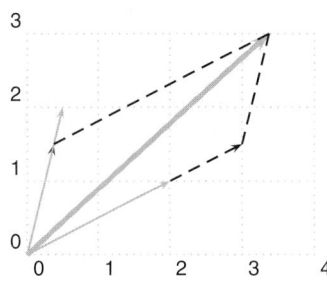

```
\usepackage{pstricks-add}

\begin{pspicture}[showgrid](4,3)
\psline[linestyle=dashed]{->}(3,1.5)
\psline[linestyle=dashed]{->}(0.375,1.5)
\psset{linecolor=red}
\psline{->}(2,1)\psline{->}(0.5,2)
\psLCNode(2,1){1.5}(0.5,2){0.75}{PI}
\psline[linewidth=2pt]{->}(PI)
\psset{linecolor=black,linestyle=dashed}
\psline(3,1.5)(PI)\psline(0.375,1.5)(PI)
\end{pspicture}
```

30.3.5 \nlput and \psLDNode

The \nlput command places a node label at an absolute distance from a given node. All the previous commands only placed labels at relative distances from a node, so \nlput is a sensible extension. Internally the \psLDNode command is used to achieve this; it places a node along the line between two given points or nodes, at an absolute distance from the first point.

\psLDNode(x_0, y_0)(x_1, y_1){*distance*}{*node name*}
\nlput(x_0, y_0)(x_1, y_1){*distance*}{*text*}

\nlput works similarly to \ncput (cf. Section ?? on page ??), only you have to specify the two nodes explicitly here.

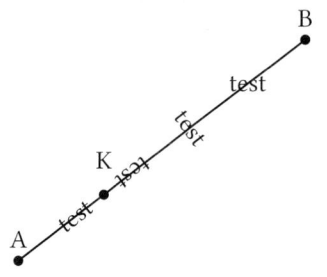

```
\usepackage{pstricks-add}

\begin{pspicture}(5,2)
\pnode(0,0){A}\qdisk(A){2pt}\uput[90](A){A}
\pnode(4,3){B}\qdisk(B){2pt}\uput[90](B){B}
\ncline{A}{B}    \psLDNode(A)(B){1.5cm}{K}
\qdisk(K){2pt}\uput{10pt}[90](K){K}
\nlput[nrot=:U](A)(B){1cm}{test}
\nlput[nrot=:D](A)(B){2cm}{test}
\nlput[nrot=:R](A)(B){3cm}{test}
\nlput(A)(B){4cm}{test}
\end{pspicture}
```

30.4 Commands and options to plot data and functions
30.4.1 psgraph
With psgraph, you can let PSTricks determine axis scale factors itself; you just need to specify the logical and physical dimensions of the box. An environment (LaTeX) and a command (TeX) are defined:

30 pstricks-add – Extended basic functions

```
\begin{psgraph} [settings] {arrows}(x₀,y₀)(x₁,y₁)(x₂,y₂){width}{height}
...
\end{psgraph}
```

```
\psgraph [settings] {arrows}(x₀,y₀)(x₁,y₁)(x₂,y₂){width}{height}...\endpsgraph
```

Here the coordinates (x_1, y_1) and (x_2, y_2) specify the usual PSTricks-specific values of the coordinate system (cf. Figure 15.1 on page 166), while {*width*} and {*height*} specify the physical size of the box. If you don't specify a unit, the current unit is used, which is usually cm. Note that only the arguments are passed on to the \psaxes command; additional instructions must be made beforehand with \psset.

The coordinate pairs behave similarly to the pspicture environment with missing parameters:

▷ if (x_0, y_0) is missing, (x_1, y_1) is assumed as the origin;

▷ if (x_0, y_0) and (x_1, y_1) are missing, $(0,0)$ is assumed for both.

Divisions are required to calculate the current scale; this can lead to problems with very large or very small scales because of the limited floating-point arithmetic in TEX. In these cases, work with the xunit and yunit scale options. You can find examples of this in the documentation of pstricks-add. [88] The special parameters for the psgraph environment are summarized in Table 30.4 on the facing page.

```
\usepackage{pstricks-add}
\readdata{\data}{demo2.dat}\readdata{\dataII}{demo3.dat}
\pstScalePoints(1,1){1989 sub}{}
\psset{llx=-0.5cm,lly=-0.5cm, xAxisLabel=Year,yAxisLabel=Whatever,
    xAxisLabelPos={2in,-0.3in},yAxisLabelPos={-0.3in,1in}}
\psgraph[axesstyle=frame,Dx=2,Ox=1989,subticks=2](0,0)(12,6){4in}{2in}
  \listplot[linecolor=red,linewidth=2pt]{\data}
  \listplot[linecolor=blue,linewidth=2pt]{\dataII}
  \listplot[linecolor=cyan,linewidth=2pt,yunit=0.5]{\dataII}
\endpsgraph
```

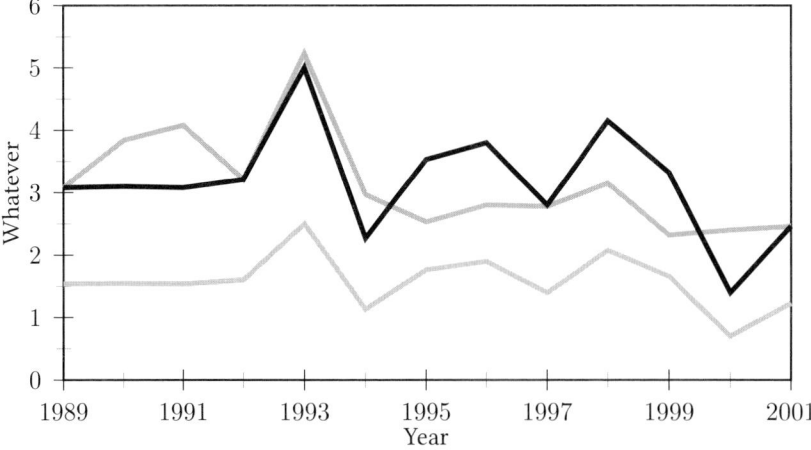

30-04-1

30.4 Commands and options to plot data and functions

Table 30.4: Summary of the special parameters of the psgraph environment

name	default	meaning
xAxisLabel	x	x axis label
yAxisLabel	y	y axis label
xAxisLabelPos	{}	coordinates of the x label
yAxisLabelPos	{}	coordinates of the y label
llx	0pt	trim for "lower left" x
lly	0pt	trim for "lower left" y
urx	0pt	trim for "upper right" x
ury	0pt	trim for "upper right" y

The trim parameters make it possible to reserve additional horizontal and vertical space for fitting in the labels, as the size of the labels isn't taken into account when the scale is determined internally. There is no limit for the values of the trim parameters – but you must set them with \psset **before** using psgraph. Passing them as parameters to psgraph has no effect. The following example is similar to the first one, but takes a different height and width for the figure.

```
\usepackage{pstricks-add}
\psset{llx=-1cm,lly=-1.25cm,urx=0.5cm,ury=0.1in,xAxisLabel=Year,yAxisLabel=Whatever,
  xAxisLabelPos={.4\linewidth,-0.4in},yAxisLabelPos={-0.4in,.5in}}
\readdata{\data}{demo2.dat}\readdata{\dataII}{demo3.dat}
\pstScalePoints(1,1){1989 sub}{}
\psframebox[linestyle=dashed,boxsep=false]{%
\begin{psgraph}[axesstyle=frame,Ox=1989,subticks=2](0,0)(12,6){10cm}{1in}
  \listplot[linecolor=red,linewidth=2pt]{\data}
  \listplot[linecolor=blue,linewidth=2pt]{\dataII}
  \listplot[linecolor=cyan,linewidth=2pt,yunit=0.5]{\dataII}
\end{psgraph}}
```

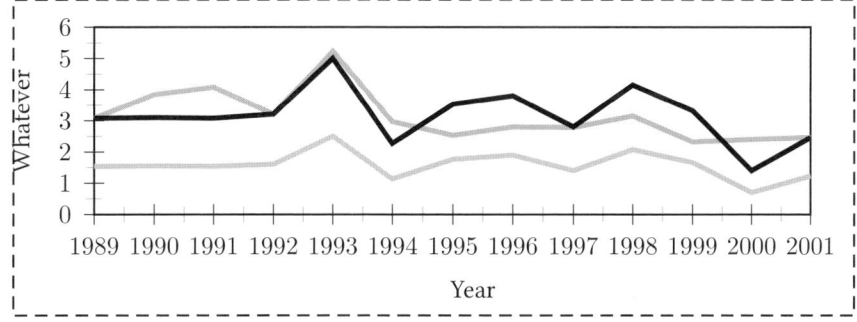

As mentioned earlier, the problem of the limited floating-point arithmetic with TeX may lead to problems with the internal calculation of the scale if very large or very small numbers are involved when determining the scale for the psgraph environment. On the other hand, you can use local scale factors with all PSTricks commands to adjust the scale manually. The following example uses a data set with very large y values:

```
1 99447169
2 110351058
4 138346129
[ ... ]
```

The easiest way to deal with this is to reduce the y values using \pstScalePoints and modify the labels of the y axis accordingly, so the y values are multiplied by 10^{-8}, giving a maximum y value for psgraph of 6.03, and a ylabelFactor of $\times 10^8$ is specified so that the graph is correct.

```
\usepackage{pstricks-add}
\readdata{\data}{demo1.dat} \pstScalePoints(1,1e-8){}{}
\psset{llx=-1cm,lly=-0.3cm}
\begin{psgraph}[axesstyle=frame,xticksize=0 7,yticksize=0 25,subticks=0,
   ylabelFactor={\times 10^8},Dx=5](0,0)(25,7){10cm}{5cm}
    \listplot[linecolor=red,linewidth=2pt,showpoints]{\data}
\end{psgraph}
```

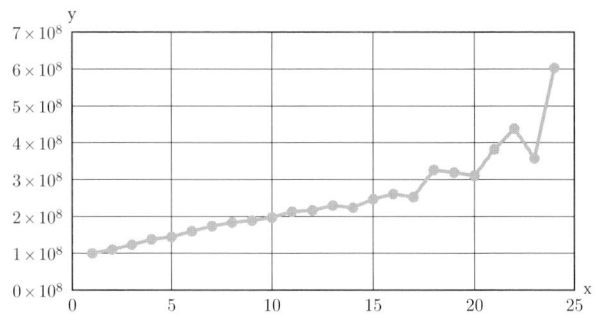

Another problem situation is when x values cover only a very small range. Here, too, we can use the \pstScalePoints command to manipulate the values. In the following example the x values lie between 3.23 and 3.25 – they only vary from the second decimal place onwards:

```
3.2345 34.5
3.2364 65.4
3.2438 50.2
```

So let's tell \pstScalePoints to subtract 3.23 from each x value and then multiply the results by 100.

```
\usepackage{pstricks-add}
\psset{lly=-0.5cm,llx=-1cm}\readdata{\data}{test10.dat}
\pstScalePoints(1,1){3.23 sub 100 mul}{}
\begin{psgraph}[Ox=3.23,Dx=0.01,dx=\psxunit,Oy=30,Dy=10]%
    {->}(0,30)(2.2,70){0.6\linewidth}{3cm}
    \listplot[showpoints,plotstyle=curve,linewidth=1pt]{\data}
\end{psgraph}
```

30.4 Commands and options to plot data and functions

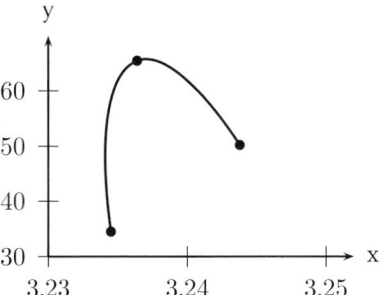

The key points of how we handle the data in this example are summarized below:

3.23 sub 100 mul	the x values become 0.45, 0.64, 1.38; an xMax setting of 2.2 is now appropriate
Ox=3.23	the origin of the x axis is set to the value 3.23
Dx=0.01	the increment of the x labels is set to 0.01
dx=\psxunit	use the calculated scale
Dy=10	the increment of the y label, for dy=1\psyunit

\psgraph saves the calculated scale factors in the \psxunit and \psyunit commands, which can be referenced after that.

30.4.2 \psStep
This command is suitable for displaying upper and lower sums, as known from introductions to analysis.

\psStep [settings] $(x_1, x_2)\{n\}\{function\}$

(x_1, x_2) describes the interval for which the upper sum (StepType=upper), the lower sum (StepType=lower), or the minimum/maximum after Riemann (StepType=Riemann) is to be drawn; the default value for StepType is upper. {n} specifies the number of rectangles. The type of function is arbitrary as long as it can be described in PostScript notation or through the algebraic option.

```
\usepackage{pstricks-add}
\begin{pspicture}(-0.5,-0.5)(10,4) \psaxes{->}(10,4)
  \psplot[plotpoints=100,linewidth=1.5pt,algebraic]{0}{10}{sqrt(x)}
  \psStep[linecolor=magenta,StepType=upper,fillstyle=hlines](0,9){9}{x sqrt}
  \psStep[linecolor=blue,linestyle=dashed,fillstyle=vlines](0,9){9}{x sqrt }
\end{pspicture}
```

30 pstricks-add – Extended basic functions

30-04-5

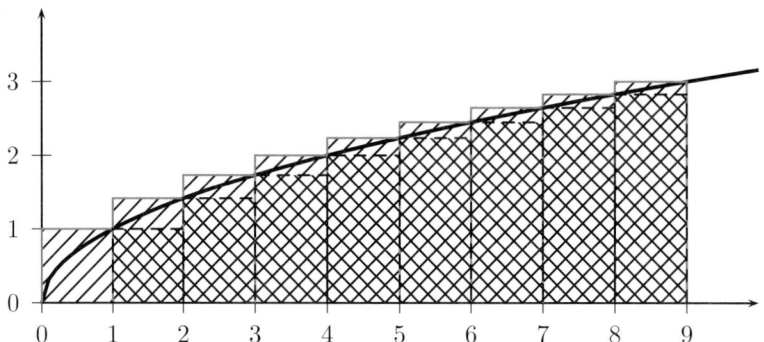

```
\usepackage{pstricks-add}
\psset{plotpoints=200}
\begin{pspicture}(-0.5,-2.25)(10,3)  \psaxes{->}(0,0)(0,-2.25)(10,3)
 \psplot[linewidth=1.5pt,algebraic]{0}{10}{sqrt(x)*sin(x)}
 \psStep[algebraic,linecolor=magenta,StepType=upper](0,9){20}{sqrt(x)*sin(x)}
 \psStep[linecolor=blue,linestyle=dashed](0,9){20}{x sqrt x RadtoDeg sin mul}
\end{pspicture}
```

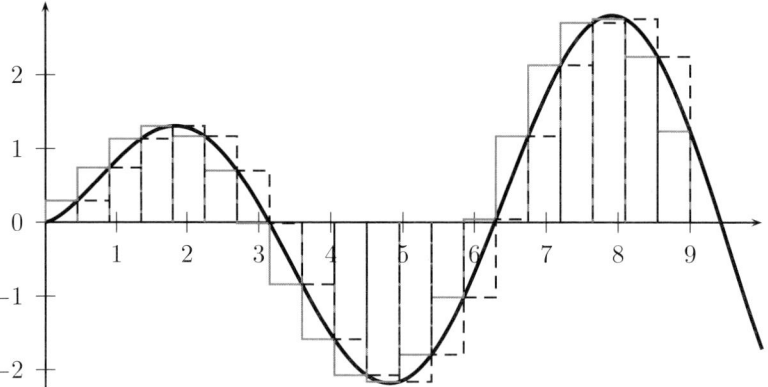

30-04-6

```
\usepackage{pstricks-add}
\psset{yunit=1.25cm}
\begin{pspicture}(-0.5,-1.5)(10,1.5)  \psaxes{->}(0,0)(0,-1.5)(10,1.5)
 \psStep[algebraic,StepType=Riemann,fillstyle=solid,fillcolor=black!10](0,10){50}%
    {sqrt(x)*cos(x)*sin(x)}
 \psplot[linewidth=1.5pt,algebraic]{0}{10}{sqrt(x)*cos(x)*sin(x)}
\end{pspicture}
```

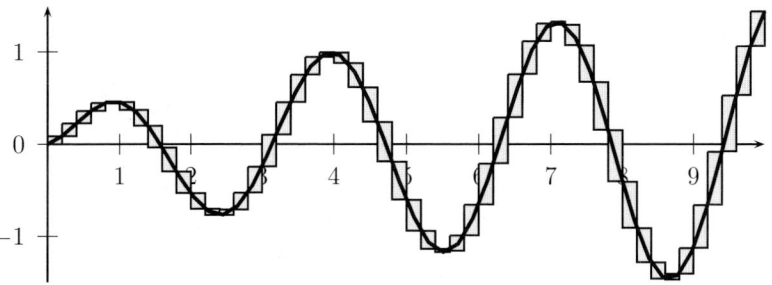

30.4.3 \psplotTangent

The gradient of a function at a point is best illustrated by drawing a short piece of the tangent. You can construct the tangent either by determining the derivative of the function or by determining a sufficiently small secant whose gradient is approximately the same as the gradient of the tangent. Both methods are supported by the \psplotTangent command:

\psplotTangent [settings] {x}{dx}{f(x)}

x	the x value for which the gradient of the function is to be determined
dx	half the length (in the current unit) of the tangent to be drawn
$f(x)$	the function, which is expected in RPN notation (postfix) by default, but can be given in algebraic notation as well through the algebraic option; angles must be specified in degrees for RPN notation, but in radian for algebraic notation

The \psplotTangent command evaluates the function at $x - 0.00005$ and $x + 0.00005$ and then calculates the gradient of this secant, which is approximately the same as the gradient of the tangent. Alternatively if you assign the first derivative of the function to the Derive option, the \psplotTangent command uses this to determine the gradient of the tangent at x. For the derivative function also, angles must be specified in degrees for RPN notation, but in radian if using the algebraic option.

```
\usepackage{pstricks-add}
\def\F{x RadtoDeg dup dup cos exch 2 mul cos add exch 3 mul cos add}
\def\Fp{x RadtoDeg dup dup sin exch 2 mul sin 2 mul add exch
  3 mul sin 3 mul add neg}
\psset{plotpoints=1001,xunit=0.8,yunit=1}
\begin{pspicture}(-7.5,-1.8)(7.5,3.2)
  \psaxes{->}(0,0)(-7.5,-1.8)(7.5,3.2)
  \psplot[linewidth=3\pslinewidth]{-7}{7}{\F}
  \psset{linecolor=red}\multido{\n=-7+1}{8}{\psplotTangent{\n}{1}{\F}}
  \psset{linecolor=magenta}%
  \multido{\n=0+1}{8}{\psplotTangent[linecolor=blue,Derive=\Fp]{\n}{1}{\F}}
\end{pspicture}
```

30 pstricks-add – Extended basic functions

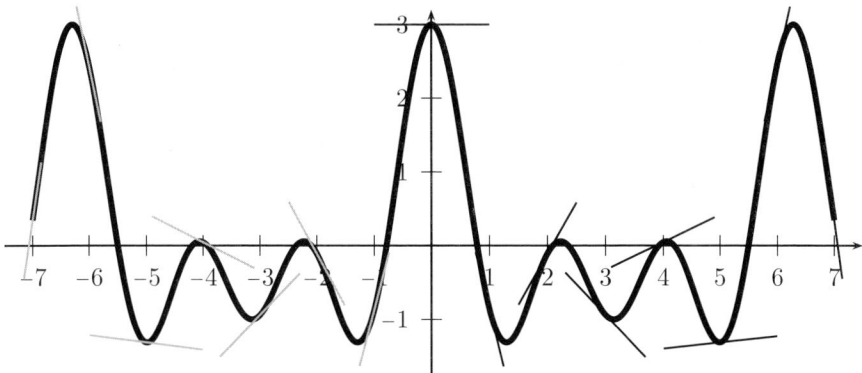

If you have specified the derived function, it is easy then to determine and draw the perpendicular (orthogonal) line to the tangent:

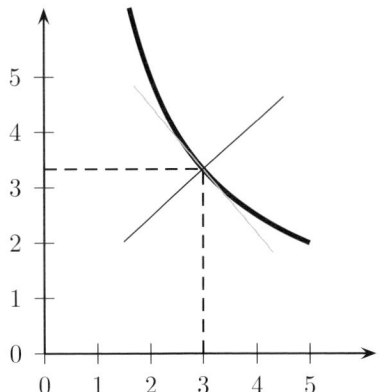

```
\usepackage{pstricks-add}

\def\Func{10 x div}\psset{unit=0.75}
\begin{pspicture}(-0.5,-0.5)(6.25,6.5)
  \psaxes[arrowscale=1.5]{->}(6.25,6.25)
  \psplot[linewidth=2pt,algebraic]{1.6}{5}{10/x}
  \psplotTangent[linewidth=.5pt,linecolor=red,
    algebraic]{3}{2}{10/x}
  \psplotTangent[linewidth=.5pt,linecolor=blue,
    algebraic,Derive=(x*x)/10]{3}{2}{10/x}
  \psline[linestyle=dashed](!0 /x 3 def \Func)%
    (!3 /x 3 def \Func)(3,0)
\end{pspicture}
```

The classic cardioid curve with $\rho = 2(1 + \cos(\theta))$ and $\frac{d\rho}{d\theta} = -2\sin(\theta)$ can be displayed in polar coordinates. The Derive option expects $\frac{d\rho}{d\theta}$ as the derivative, which is then internally used according to the theorem about implicitly-defined functions:

$$\frac{dy}{dx} = \frac{\rho' \times \sin\theta + x}{\rho' \times \cos\theta - y} \quad \text{with } x = r \times \cos\theta \text{ and } y = r \times \sin\theta \tag{30.1}$$

30.4 Commands and options to plot data and functions

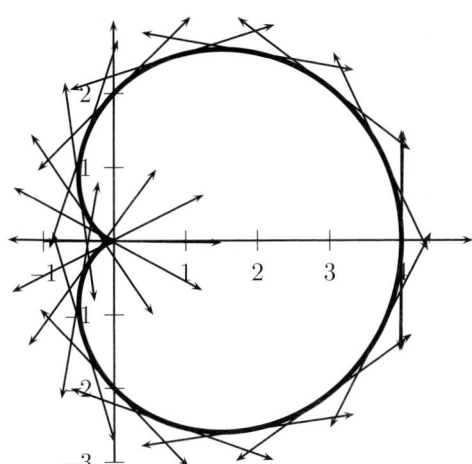

```
\usepackage{pstricks-add}

\begin{pspicture}(-1,-3)(4.75,3)
  \psaxes{->}(0,0)(-1,-3)(5,3)
  \psplot[polarplot,linewidth=2pt,
    algebraic,plotpoints=500]%
    {0}{6.289}{2*(1+cos(x))}
  \multido{\r=0.000+0.314}{21}{%
    \psplotTangent[polarplot,
      Derive=-2*sin(x),algebraic,
      arrows=<->]%
      {\r}{1.5}{2*(1+cos(x))}}
\end{pspicture}
```

The next example looks at a function in parametric representation – the Lissajous figure:

$$x = 3.5\cos(2t) \qquad\qquad y = 3.5\sin(6t) \qquad (30.2)$$

with

$$x' = -7\sin(2t) \qquad\qquad y' = 21\cos(6t) \qquad (30.3)$$

t must be used as the name of the variable. If you are using the algebraic option, you must separate the two parts of the equation with a vertical bar | (as in the second half of the example below).

```
\usepackage{pstricks-add}
\def\Lissa{t dup 2 RadtoDeg mul cos 3.5 mul exch 6 mul RadtoDeg sin 3.5 mul}
\psset{unit=0.75cm}
\begin{pspicture}(-4,-5)(4,5)%  secant gradient
  \parametricplot[plotpoints=500,linewidth=1.5pt]{0}{3.141592}{\Lissa}
  \multido{\r=0.000+0.314}{11}{%
    \psplotTangent[arrows=<->,linecolor=black!40]{\r}{1.5}{\Lissa}}
  \multido{\r=0.157+0.314}{11}{%
    \psplotTangent[arrows=<->,linecolor=black!40]{\r}{1.5}{\Lissa}}
  \rput(0,4.5){secant gradient}
\end{pspicture}\hfill%
%
\def\LissaAlg{3.5*cos(2*t)|3.5*sin(6*t)}
\def\LissaAlgDer{-7*sin(2*t)|21*cos(6*t)}
\begin{pspicture}(-4,-5)(4,5)%  tangent gradient
  \parametricplot[algebraic,plotpoints=500,
    linewidth=1.5pt]{0}{3.141592}{\LissaAlg}
  \multido{\r=0.000+0.314}{11}{%
    \psplotTangent[algebraic,arrows=<->,linecolor=black!40]{\r}{1.5}{\LissaAlg} }
  \multido{\r=0.157+0.314}{11}{%
```

30 pstricks-add – Extended basic functions

```
\psplotTangent[algebraic,arrows=<->,linecolor=black!40,%
    Derive=\LissaAlgDer]{\r}{1.5}{\LissaAlg} }
\rput(0,4.5){tangent gradient}
\end{pspicture}
```

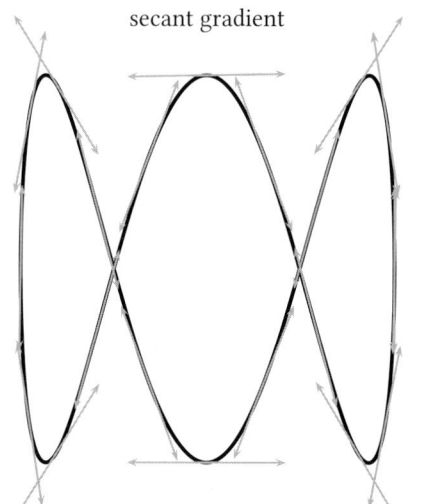
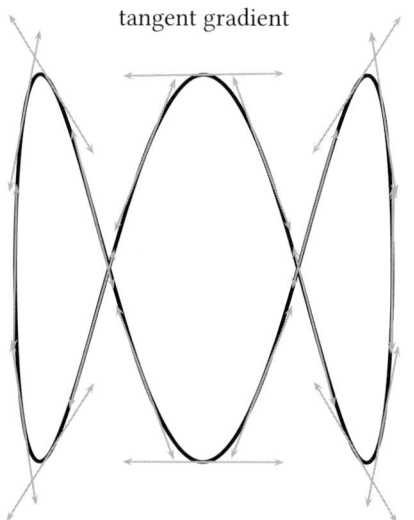

secant gradient

tangent gradient

The calculation of the gradient still works even when the x and y axes have different scale factors. In this case the angle that corresponds to the optical tangent is calculated for each axis, though this is mathematically incorrect.

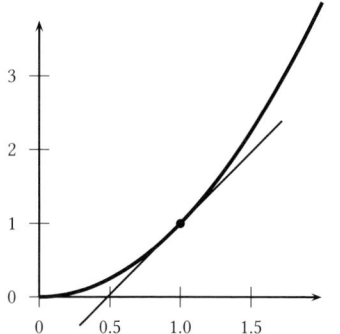

```
\usepackage{pstricks-add}

\psset{xunit=2}
\def\FF{x dup mul} \def\dFF{x 2 mul}
\begin{pspicture}(-0.25,-0.5)(2,4)
    \psaxes[Dx=0.5,Dy=1]{->}(0,0)(2,3.75)
    \psplot[linewidth=1.5pt]{0}{2}{\FF}
    \psplotTangent{1}{1}{\FF}
    \psdot(! 1 /x 1 def \FF)
\end{pspicture}
```

30.4.4 \psplotDiffEqn – Solving of differential equations

A first-order differential equation is given by

$$y' = f(x, y) \quad \text{with } y = y(x) \tag{30.4}$$

To be able to pass the start condition to the command, the following two vectors are defined:

$$Y = [y, y', \ldots, y^{(n-1)}] \qquad Y' = [y', y'', \ldots, y^n] \tag{30.5}$$

The general syntax is:

30.4 Commands and options to plot data and functions

`\psplotDiffEqn [settings] {`x_0`}{`x_1`}{`y_0`}{`$f(x, y, y', \ldots)$`}`

▷ `settings`: parameters specific to `\psplotDiffEqn` (cf. Table 30.5) and any other general options defined before that are sensible, for example `linecolor`.
▷ x_0: start value.
▷ x_1: end value of the definition interval $[x_0; x_1]$.
▷ y_0: vector of start values $y(x_0)\ y'(x_0)\ \ldots$
▷ $f(x, y, y', \ldots)$: the differential equation, interpreted according to the number of start values, for example for a vector of start values of $y_0 = [0\ 1]$ an according second-order differential equation $f(x, y, y')$ results and the `\psplotDiffEqn` command puts the values $y\ y'$ on the PostScript stack.
▷ $x = f(t), y = f(t), x' = f(t), \ldots$: the differential equation in parameter form or as part of a system of differential equations where in RPN notation only the corresponding number of values has to be on the stack while for the algebraic notation the equations have to be separated by the vertical bar.

If using algebraic notation, you must use the individual y variables according to the vector from Equation 30.5: Y→Y[0]; Y'→Y[1]; Y"→Y[2]; …

All new parameters that are only valid for `\psplotDiffEqn` are summarized in Table 30.5:

Table 30.5: Summary of the additional parameters for `\psplotDiffEqn`

name	type	meaning
method	euler|rk4	the solving method; euler (default) or adams as first-order method or rk4 (Runge-Kutta) as fourth-order method
whichabs	index	index of the variable to be plotted on the y axis; x is the default, otherwise a corresponding index of the vector Y has to be given, starting at 0 (cf. Equation 30.5)
whichord	index	index of the variable to be plotted on the x axis; y is the default, otherwise a corresponding index of the vector Y' has to be given, starting at 0 (cf. Equation 30.5)
plotfuncx	PS code	replaces the whichabs option
plotfuncy	PS code	replaces the whichord option
buildvector	boolean	determines how to deal with f: true (default): Y is put on the stack element by element and Y' is given in the same manner false: Y is not put on the stack but Y' has to be returned
algebraic	boolean	activates the algebraic interpretation of the function description; buildvector is ignored in this case

Below are some examples of using the `\psplotDiffEqn` command; you can find more in the package description of `pstricks-add`. [88] The differential equation of a mechanical pendulum is:

$$y'' = -\frac{g}{l}\sin(y) \tag{30.6}$$

If we assume a thread length (l) of 1m, the differential equation is formulated in PostScript as:

% on the stack are the current values y y'
exch RadtoDeg sin -9.81 mul %% Stack: y' -g*sin(y)

Note that when using the algebraic option instead, the PostScript stack is simulated and therefore the corresponding values have to be given in the correct order, separated by a vertical bar. For the pendulum the function is then \def\Func{y[1]|-9.81*sin(y[0])} which puts $y' - 9.81 \sin(y)$ on the stack.

For start conditions $y(0) = 1$ and $y'(0) = 0$, the third parameter of the command must be 1 0. This means that it is a second-order differential equation with two start values. Furthermore we want the differential equation to be calculated in the interval $[0; 3]$.

```
\usepackage{pstricks-add}
\def\Func{exch RadtoDeg sin -9.81 mul}
\psset{yunit=1.5,xunit=2,showpoints}
\begin{pspicture}[showgrid](0,-1.5)(3,2)
  \psplotDiffEqn[linecolor=black!40]{0}{3}{1 0}{\Func}
  \psplotDiffEqn[method=adams,linestyle=dashed]{0}{3}{1 0}{\Func}
  \psplotDiffEqn[method=rk4]{0}{3}{1 0}{\Func}
  \rput[rb](2.9,-0.9){Runge-Kutta (rk4)}\rput[rb](1.9,1.3){Euler}
\end{pspicture}
```

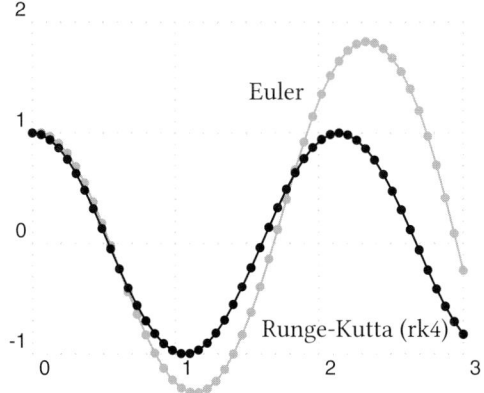

This example uses both options of the method parameter. The difference is clearly visible; the result here should be a cosine function with constant amplitude, so the output in this case from the Euler method is significantly worse than that using the Runge-Kutta method.

A more complicated differential equation is:

$$y'' = -\frac{y'}{4} - 2y \tag{30.7}$$

Formulating it in RPN notation is easier to follow if you note the state of the stack as a comment at each stage:

```
%%% the vector Y=[y y'] is already on the stack %%%
dup              %% y y' y'
3 1 roll         %% y' y y'
```

```
-4 div              %% y' y y'/-4
exch                %% y' y'/-4 y
2 mul               %% y' y'/-4 2y
sub                 %% y' y'/-4-2y
```

Alternatively using the `algebraic` option, the expression is much shorter: `y[1]|-y[1]/4-2*y[0]` where `y[0]` corresponds to y and `y[1]` to y'.

```
\usepackage{pstricks-add}
\psset{xunit=.5,yunit=0.7,plotpoints=500,method=rk4}
\begin{pspicture}(0,-4.25)(24,5.25)
  \psaxes[Dy=2,dx=2]{->}(0,0)(0,-4)(24,5)
  \psplotDiffEqn[linewidth=1.5pt,linecolor=black!40,plotpoints=50]{0}{24}{5 0}%
    {dup 3 1 roll -4 div exch 2 mul sub}
  \psplotDiffEqn[linewidth=1.5pt,linecolor=black,algebraic]{0}{24}{5 0}%
    {y[1]|-y[1]/4-2*y[0]}
  \psplot[linestyle=dashed,linecolor=red]{0}{24}{% theoretic result
    Euler x -8 div exp x 127 sqrt 8 div mul RadtoDeg dup cos
    5 mul exch sin 127 sqrt div 5 mul add mul}
\end{pspicture}
```

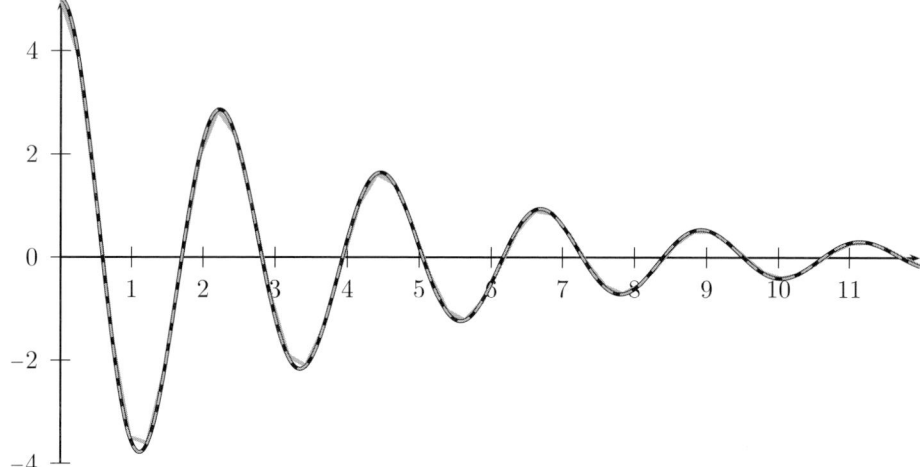

For example start values of $y_0 = 5$ and $y'_0 = 0$ the solution is:

$$y(x) = 5e^{-\frac{x}{8}}\left(\cos(\omega x) + \frac{\sin(\omega x)}{8\omega}\right) \text{ with } \omega = \frac{\sqrt{127}}{8} \quad (30.8)$$

The red dashed line in the example plots this actual function; there is no noticeable difference between this true result and the black curve drawn with `\psplotDiffEqn` using 500 interpolation points and not even that much difference with the light grey curve that has only 40 interpolation points.

Instead of plotting you can create a phase diagram through the `whichabs` and `whichord` options. We plot the deflection y (index 0) on the x axis and the speed as the first derivative of the path with respect to the time y' (index 1) on the y axis.

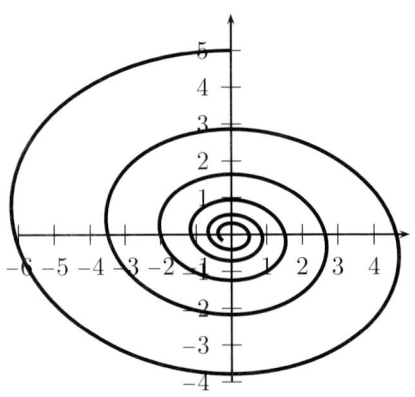

```
\usepackage{pstricks-add}

\psset{unit=0.5cm,plotpoints=500,
    method=rk4}
\begin{pspicture}(-6,-4)(5,6)
    \psaxes{->}(0,0)(-6,-4)(5,6)
    \psplotDiffEqn[linewidth=1.5pt,
        whichabs=1,whichord=0,
        algebraic]{0}{24}{5 0}%
        {y[1]|-y[1]/4-2*y[0]}
\end{pspicture}
```

The spiral of Cornu is also represented as $y = f(y')$. The theory is based on the Fresnel integrals:

$$x = \int_0^t \cos \frac{\pi t^2}{2} \, dt \qquad y = \int_0^t \sin \frac{\pi t^2}{2} \, dt \tag{30.9}$$

with

$$\dot{x} = \cos \frac{\pi t^2}{2} \qquad \dot{y} = \sin \frac{\pi t^2}{2} \tag{30.10}$$

The last two equations are input in algebraic form in the following example:

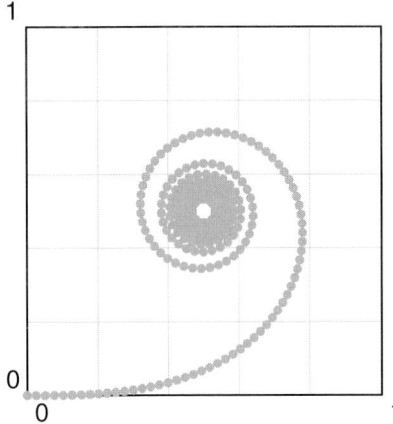

```
\usepackage{pstricks-add}

\psset{unit=5}
\begin{pspicture}(-0.04,-0.04)(1,1)
    \psgrid[subgriddiv=5,
        subgridcolor=lightgray]
    \psplotDiffEqn[whichabs=0,
        whichord=1,linecolor=red,
        method=rk4,algebraic,
        plotpoints=400,
        showpoints]%
        {0}{10}{0 0}%
        {cos(Pi*x^2/2)|sin(Pi*x^2/2)}
\end{pspicture}
```

The next example looks at a proton entering an electromagnetic field at low speed. Its route is described:

$$\vec{E} = E_0 \cos(\omega_1 t) \vec{e}_y \tag{30.11}$$

$$\vec{B} = B \vec{e}_z \tag{30.12}$$

30.4 Commands and options to plot data and functions

Here $a = \dfrac{eE_0}{m}$, $\omega = \dfrac{eB}{m}$, and $\omega_1 = k\omega$.

$$\ddot{x} = \omega \dot{y} \qquad (30.13)$$
$$\ddot{y} = a\cos(\omega_1 t) - \omega \dot{x} \qquad (30.14)$$

and $y(0) = 0$, $\dot{y}(0) = 0$, $a = 1$, $\omega = 2\pi$ applies, as well as $\omega_1 = k\omega$ with the values $k(0, 0.1, 0.2, 1, 5)$, etc.

The start conditions are the quadruple $x\ y\ x'\ y'$; we use $0\ 0\ 0\ 0$ in the example here. Because of the simple mathematical relation, the equations can be determined without numeric integration; they are given here as well.

In the following two figures the functions are described in algebraic notation. For the first solution, four functions have to be described altogether – $\dot{x}, \dot{y}, \ddot{x}, \ddot{y}$. Using $a = 4$ and $k = 0.1$ for this example, we get:

$$\dot{x} = \dot{x} \qquad (30.15)$$
$$\dot{y} = \dot{y} \qquad (30.16)$$
$$\ddot{x} = 2\pi \dot{y} \qquad (30.17)$$
$$\ddot{y} = 4\cos(2\pi x) - 2\pi \dot{x} \qquad (30.18)$$

Both examples depict $\dot{x} = f(x)$, though the second example uses the following parametric equations in the interval $t \in [0, 12]$.

$$x(t) = \dfrac{4}{(2\pi)^2 - (0.2\pi)^2} \times \dfrac{\sin(2\pi \times t)}{0.1} - \sin(2\pi \times t) \qquad (30.19)$$

$$y(t) = \dfrac{4}{(2\pi)^2 - (0.2\pi)^2} \times (\cos(0.2\pi \times t) - \cos(2\pi \times t)) \qquad (30.20)$$

```
\usepackage{pstricks-add}
\psset{unit=5,method=rk4,algebraic,whichabs=0,whichord=1,plotpoints=500,
   linewidth=1pt}
\begin{pspicture}(-1.2,-0.2)(1.2,0.2)
\psgrid[subgriddiv=5,subgridcolor=black!10,gridlabels=7pt](-1.2,-0.2)(1.2,0.2)
\psplotDiffEqn[linecolor=red]{0}{12}{0 0 0 0}%
   {y[2]|y[3]|2*Pi*y[3]|4*cos(0.2*Pi*x)-2*Pi*y[2]}
\end{pspicture}
```

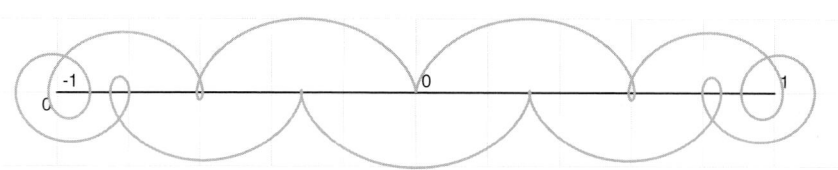

```
\usepackage{pstricks-add}
```

30 pstricks-add – Extended basic functions

```
\psset{unit=5,algebraic,plotpoints=500,linewidth=1pt}
\begin{pspicture}(-1.2,-0.2)(1.2,0.2)
 \psgrid[subgriddiv=5,subgridcolor=black!10,gridlabels=7pt](-1.2,-0.2)(1.2,0.2)
 \parametricplot[plotpoints=500,linecolor=blue]{0}{12}{
    4/((2*Pi)^2-(0.2*Pi)^2)*(sin(0.2*Pi*t)/0.1-sin(2*Pi*t))|%
    4/((2*Pi)^2-(0.2*Pi)^2)*(cos(0.2*Pi*t)-cos(2*Pi*t))}
\end{pspicture}
```

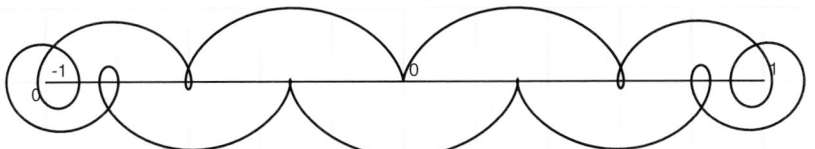

Doubling the parameter *k* to 0.2 achieves the following figure:

```
\usepackage{pstricks-add}
\psset{unit=5,method=rk4,algebraic,whichabs=0,whichord=1,plotpoints=500,linewidth=1pt}
\begin{pspicture}(-1.2,-0.2)(1.2,0.2)
 \psgrid[subgriddiv=5,subgridcolor=black!10,
   gridlabels=7pt](-1.2,-0.2)(1.2,0.2)
 \psplotDiffEqn[linecolor=blue]{0}{12}{0 0 0 0}{%
   y[2]|y[3]|2*Pi*y[3]|4*cos(0.4*Pi*x)-2*Pi*y[2]}
\end{pspicture}
```

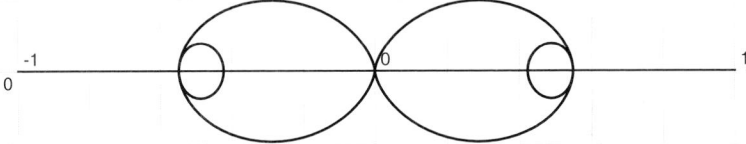

30.4.5 \psMatrixPlot

The \psMatrixPlot command visually represents an $m \times n$ matrix. You must save the data in an external file as shown below; don't forget to include the PostScript name dotmatrix:

```
/dotmatrix [ %     <------------ important line
0 1 1 0 0 0 0 1 1 1
0 1 1 0 1 1 1 0 1 0
[ ... ]
1 0 1 0 0 1 1 1 0 0
] def        %     <------------ important line
```

In general only the specification of the zeroes is important – anything else is interpreted as being greater than zero.

The syntax of the \psMatrixPlot command is

\psMatrixPlot [*settings*] {*rows*}{*columns*}{*file*}

The external file is processed line by line: the first line is also the first line to be output, but then the second line is put **above** the first one, i.e. the output is done by default in reverse order. However, you can change this order through the ChangeOrder option.

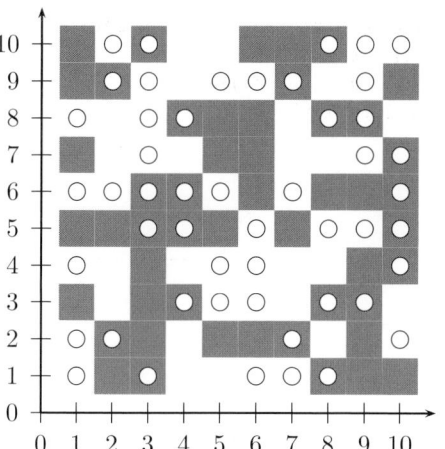

```
\usepackage{pstricks-add}

\psset{unit=0.5}
\begin{pspicture}(-0.5,-0.75)(11,11)
  \psaxes{->}(11,11)
  \psMatrixPlot[dotsize=5.5mm,
    dotstyle=square*,linecolor=magenta]%
    {10}{10}{matrix.dat}
  \psMatrixPlot[dotsize=2.5mm,dotstyle=o,
    ChangeOrder]{10}{10}{matrix.dat}
\end{pspicture}
```

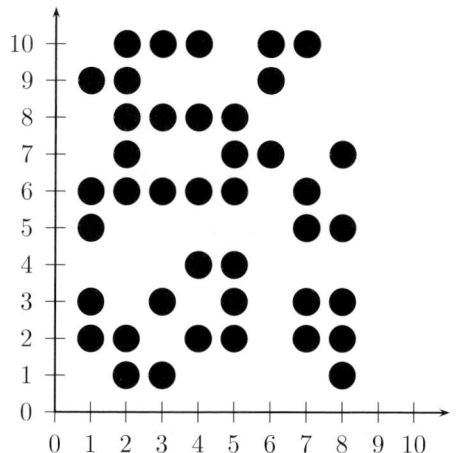

```
\usepackage{pstricks-add}

\psset{unit=0.5}
\begin{pspicture}(-0.5,-0.75)(11,11)
  \psaxes{->}(11,11)
  \psMatrixPlot[dotscale=3,dotstyle=*,
    linecolor=blue]{10}{8}{matrix.dat}
\end{pspicture}
```

30 pstricks-add – Extended basic functions

Chapter 31

pst-labo – Chemical instruments

31.1 Parameters... 619
31.2 Predefined colours and styles.................................. 632
31.3 Commands... 633
31.4 Examples.. 639

pst-labo provides commands for drawing many instruments that are used in chemistry. [24] They often have standardized forms, so using pst-labo saves creating each instrument manually. We discussed the creation of "high-level" objects with PSTricks earlier in Section 14.4 on page 160. All base objects are contained in the file pst-laboObj.tex and are read by pst-labo on startup. They can be used for custom extensions. As well as providing specific commands and associated parameters, pst-labo also defines a range of its own colours and colour styles (cf. Section 31.2 on page 632).

31.1 Parameters

Table 31.1 shows a summary of the parameters that are specific to pst-labo. They are then described in turn in the following sections.

Table 31.1: Summary of the additional parameters for pst-labo

name	values	default	remarks
glassType	tube/ballon/ erlen/becher/ flacon/fioleJauge	tube	type of glass container
bouchon	boolean	false	container with cork
pince	boolean	false	wooden clamp

continued...

31 pst-labo – Chemical instruments

... continued

name	values	default	remarks
tubeDroit	boolean	false	small glass tube
tubeCoude	boolean	false	angled glass tube
tubeCoudeU	boolean	false	double-angled glass tube
tubeCoudeUB	boolean	false	extended version, only for glass types ballon or erlen
etiquette	boolean	false	switch for displaying labels on containers
Numero	text	{}	number for the etiquette option
tubePenche	$-65\ldots 65$	0	tilt angle
tubeSeul	boolean	false	wide/narrow pspicture box
becBunsen	boolean	true	with/without Bunsen burner
barbotage	boolean	false	additional test tube, connected to the actual container via a glass tube
substance	command	\relax	other options: \pstBullesChampagne, \pstFilaments, \pstBilles, \pstBULLES, \pstClous, \pstCuivre
solide	command	\relax	other options: \pstTournureCuivre, \pstClouFer, \pstGrenailleZinc
doubletube	boolean	false	two glass tubes
refrigerantBoulle	boolean	false	condenser
tubeRecourbe	boolean	false	traps gas escaping from a glass container
tubeRecourbeCourt	boolean	false	as above, but no Bunsen burner
recuperationGaz	boolean	false	instrument to capture escaping gases
burette	boolean	true	show/hide burette
niveauReactifBurette	20	$0\ldots 25$	limit to 25 ml
couleurReactifBurette	colour	OrangePale	colour of liquid in burette
AspectMelange	style	DiffusionBleue	
CouleurDistillat	colour	yellow	colour of distillate
phmetre	boolean	false	show pH gauge
agitateurMagnetique	boolean	true	show/hide symbols on mixer
niveauLiquide1	$0\ldots 100$	50	percentage of the height of the container
niveauliquide2	$0\ldots 100$	0	<niveauLiquide1
niveauliquide3	$0\ldots 100$	0	<niveauLiquide2
aspectLiquide1	style	cyan	defined as part of \newpsstyle...
aspectLiquide2	style	yellow	ditto

continued...

31.1 Parameters

... continued

name	values	default	remarks
aspectLiquide3	style	magenta	ditto

31.1.1 glassType

glassType determines the type of the glass container; the normal test tube (tube) is the default. The other options are: ballon, erlen, becher, flacon, and fioleJauge.

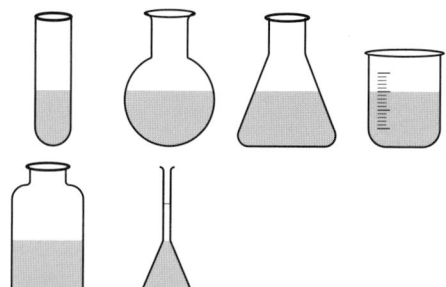

```
\usepackage{pst-labo}

\psset{unit=0.5cm}
\pstTubeEssais[glassType=tube]% default
\pstTubeEssais[glassType=ballon]
\pstTubeEssais[glassType=erlen]
\pstTubeEssais[glassType=becher]
\pstTubeEssais[glassType=flacon]
\pstTubeEssais[glassType=fioleJauge]
```

31.1.2 bouchon

The bouchon option adds a cork or bung to containers.

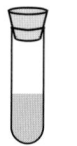
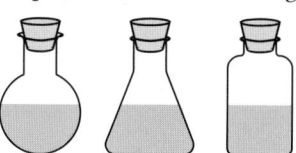

```
\usepackage{pst-labo}

\psset{unit=0.45cm}
\psset{bouchon=true}
\pstTubeEssais[glassType=tube]
\pstTubeEssais[glassType=ballon]
\pstTubeEssais[glassType=erlen]
\pstTubeEssais[glassType=flacon]
```

31.1.3 pince

The pince option adds one of the common wooden clamps to containers.

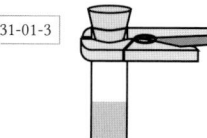
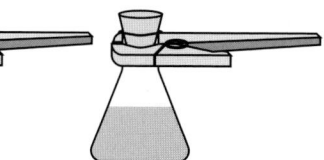

```
\usepackage{pst-labo}

\psset{unit=0.5cm}
\psset{bouchon=true,pince=true}
\pstTubeEssais[glassType=tube]%
\hspace{1.5cm}%
\pstTubeEssais[glassType=erlen]
```

31.1.4 tubeDroit

The tubeDroit option adds a small glass tube to containers; this only makes sense in conjunction with the bouchon=true option – accordingly it is set to that value internally. No vertical space is reserved for the tube, so you must take care of this manually, e.g. with \rule{0pt}{4cm}.

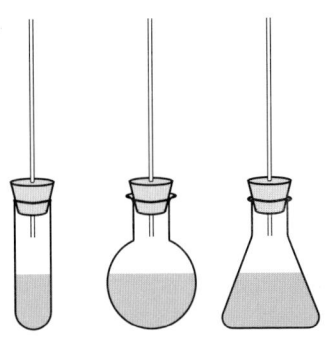

```
\usepackage{pst-labo}

\psset{unit=0.5cm}
\psset{tubeDroit=true}
\rule{0pt}{4cm}%
\pstTubeEssais
\pstTubeEssais[glassType=ballon]
\pstTubeEssais[glassType=erlen]
```

31.1.5 tubeCoude

The tubeCoude option is almost identical to tubeDroit except that the tube bends perpendicular to the starting direction. The required vertical space is therefore significantly smaller.

```
\usepackage{pst-labo}

\psset{unit=0.5cm}
\psset{tubeCoude=true}
\rule{0pt}{2.5cm}%
\pstTubeEssais[glassType=erlen]
```

31.1.6 tubeCoudeU

The tubeCoudeU option is also almost identical to tubeDroit except that the tube is shaped like a rectangular U, so again requires less vertical space.

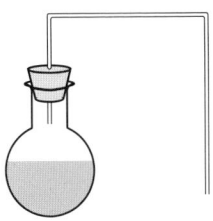

```
\usepackage{pst-labo}

\psset{unit=0.5cm}
\psset{tubeCoudeU=true}
\rule{0pt}{2.5cm}%
\pstTubeEssais[glassType=ballon]
```

31.1.7 tubeCoudeUB

The tubeCoudeUB option, an extension of the U version, is only applicable where the tube can be extended to the floor, for example in the \pstChauffageBallon command.

```
\usepackage{pst-labo}
\psset{unit=0.5cm,glassType=ballon}
\pstChauffageBallon[tubeCoudeU] \pstChauffageBallon[tubeCoudeUB]
```

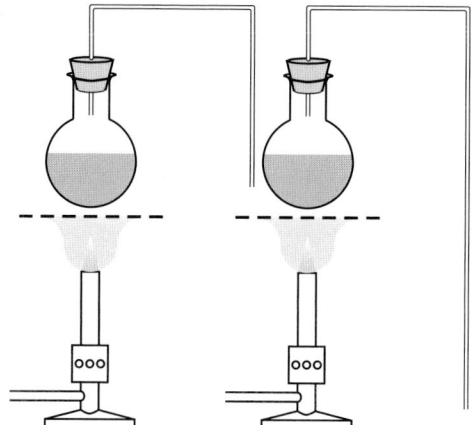

31.1.8 etiquette and Numero

The etiquette option toggles the display of labels created through the Numero option.

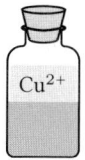

```
\usepackage{pst-labo}

\psset{unit=0.5cm}
\pstTubeEssais[etiquette]
\pstTubeEssais[etiquette,Numero=1]
\pstTubeEssais[glassType=flacon,bouchon,
    etiquette,Numero={\small Cu$^{2+}$}]
```

31.1.9 tubePenche

The tubePenche option lets you arrange chemical instruments at an angle, though the liquid level always remains horizontal. The angle, which must fall within the interval $-65\ldots+65$, is measured counterclockwies from vertical.

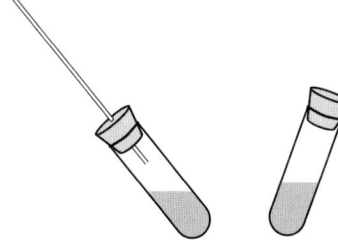

```
\usepackage{pst-labo}

\psset{unit=0.5cm}
\pstTubeEssais[tubeDroit=true,
    tubePenche=40]
\pstTubeEssais[tubePenche=-20,
    bouchon]
```

31.1.10 tubeSeul

tubeSeul reduces the size of the box, which can be helpful if you are only drawing one instrument. In the following example using \psframebox, the right box would have been the same size as the default box on the left if tubeSeul=true hadn't been specified. Not that this option only affects the \pstChauffageTube command and the ballon and tube glass types.

31 pst-labo – Chemical instruments

```
\usepackage{pst-labo}
\psset{unit=0.5cm,glassType=ballon,becBunsen}
\psframebox{\pstChauffageTube[becBunsen,barbotage]}
\psframebox{\pstChauffageTube[tubeSeul=true]}
```

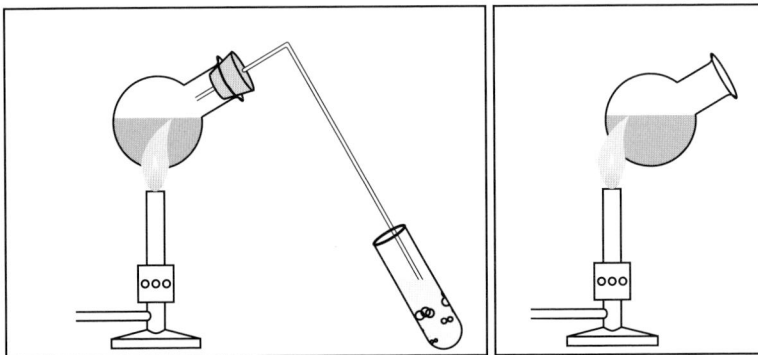

31.1.11 becBunsen

becBunsen is set to true by default for the \pstChauffageTube and the \pstChauffageBallon command. It activates or deactivates the display of the Bunsen burner.

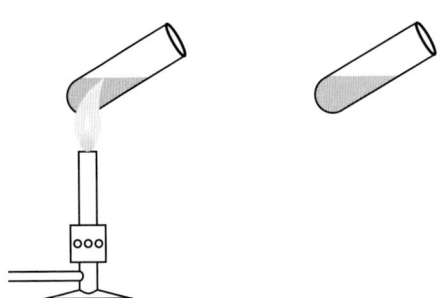

```
\usepackage{pst-labo}
\psset{unit=0.5cm,tubeSeul=true}
\pstChauffageTube
\pstChauffageTube[becBunsen=false]
```

31.1.12 barbotage

The barbotage option creates an additional test tube, connected to the original container via a small glass tube. Don't have the tubeSeul option active when using barbotage or you may not have enough space for the figure (cf. Section 31.1.10 on the previous page).

```
\usepackage{pst-labo}
\psset{unit=0.5cm}
\pstChauffageTube[tubeSeul=true]
\pstChauffageTube[barbotage]
```

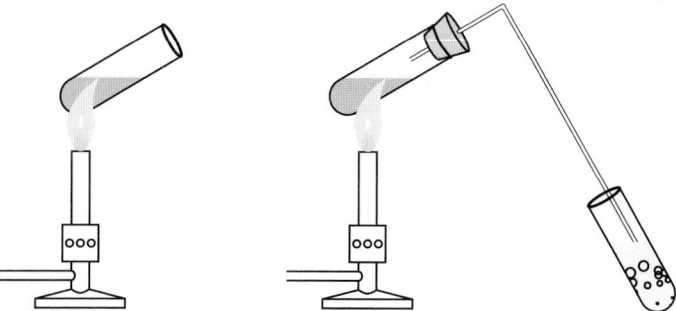

31-01-12

31.1.13 substance

The substance option changes the substance in the containers. The default is a plain blue liquid (\pstBullesChampagne[25]); the other commands designed for use with the solide option are listed in Table 31.2, though you can also use the commands listed in Table 31.3 for the solide option.

command name	default	remarks
\pstBullesChampagne[value]	25	transparent 2D bubbles
\pstFilaments[value]{colour}	5	coloured strands
\pstBilles[value]	50	3D bubbles
\pstBULLES[value]{colour}	20	coloured 2D bubbles

Table 31.2: Summary of the commands for the substance option

\pstFilaments and \pstBULLES require a colour parameter, and all the commands have an optional value that determines the number of iterations for the internal \multido loop, i.e. the number of bubbles or strands. In general there is no limit for this value, but setting it greater than 80 could cause problems with the available TeX memory. If necessary, you can increase the memory by modifying the TeX configuration file. The directory of the configuration file can be found through the following command on a Unix-like system: [1]

```
voss@shania:~> kpsewhich texmf.cnf
/usr/local/texlive/2005/texmf/web2c/texmf.cnf
```

Note that when you do apply the optional value, the whole argument of substance must be enclosed in curly braces as it is already part of another optional parameter: e.g. substance={\pstBULLES[20]{white}}.

The first example below shows each substance command with its default settings (and colour arguments chosen arbitrarily). The second example shows the use of the optional value for the number of iterations.

```
\usepackage{pst-labo}
\psset{unit=0.5cm,glassType=becher}
\pstTubeEssais
```

---

[1] Check the documentation for your TeX installation

```
\pstTubeEssais[substance=\pstBullesChampagne]
\pstTubeEssais[substance=\pstFilaments{red}]
\pstTubeEssais[substance=\pstBilles]
\pstTubeEssais[substance=\pstBULLES{white}]
```

```
\usepackage{pst-labo}
\psset{unit=0.5cm,glassType=becher}
\pstTubeEssais[substance={\pstBullesChampagne[80]}]
\pstTubeEssais[substance={\pstFilaments[20]{black}}]
\pstTubeEssais[substance={\pstBilles[80]}]
\pstTubeEssais[substance={\pstBULLES[20]{white}}]
```

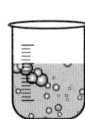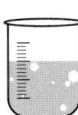

31.1.14 solide

The solide option specifies a solid type of substance in a container. The other commands designed for use with the solide option are listed in Table 31.3, though you can also use the commands listed in Table 31.2 on the preceding page for the substance option.

Table 31.3: Summary of the commands for the solide option

command name	default
\pstTournureCuivre[*value*]	30
\pstClouFer[*value*]	60
\pstGrenailleZinc[*value*]	25

Again remember that if you are applying a different optional value for the number of iterations, you must enclose the whole argument of solide in curly braces.

```
\usepackage{pst-labo}
\psset{unit=0.5cm,glassType=becher}
\pstTubeEssais
\pstTubeEssais[solide=\pstTournureCuivre]
\pstTubeEssais[solide=\pstClouFer]
\pstTubeEssais[solide=\pstGrenailleZinc]
```

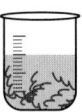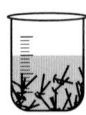

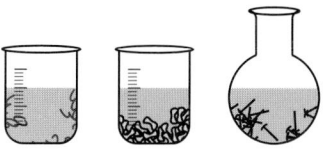

```
\usepackage{pst-labo}

\psset{unit=0.5cm,glassType=becher}
\pstTubeEssais[solide={\pstTournureCuivre[50]}]
\pstTubeEssais[solide={\pstGrenailleZinc[80]}]
\pstTubeEssais[glassType=ballon,
    solide={\pstClouFer[50]}]
```

31.1.15 doubletube

doubletube arranges two glass tubes, and one is fitted with a controller.

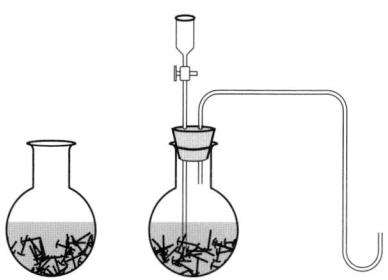

```
\usepackage{pst-labo}

\rule{0pt}{4cm}
\psset{unit=0.5cm,glassType=ballon,
    substance=\pstClouFer}
\pstBallon
\pstBallon[doubletube]
```

31.1.16 refrigerantBoulle

refrigerantBoulle facilitates output of a complex condenser apparatus. If you are adding other objects to this apparatus, note that the geometric centre is the centre of the arrangement.

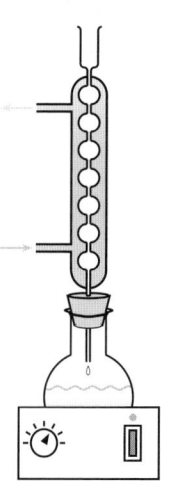

```
\usepackage{pst-labo}

\psset{unit=0.5cm}
\pstBallon[refrigerantBoulles,
    glassType=ballon,
    substance=\pstClouFer]
```

31.1.17 tubeRecourbe

The tubeRecourbe option creates an arrangement designed to collect the gas escaping from a glass container that is being heated by a Bunsen burner. The collection apparatus is provided by the recuperationGaz option (described below).

31 pst-labo – Chemical instruments

```
\usepackage{pst-labo}
\psset{unit=0.5cm,glassType=erlen,recuperationGaz,substance=\pstTournureCuivre}
\pstChauffageBallon
\pstChauffageBallon[tubeRecourbe]
```

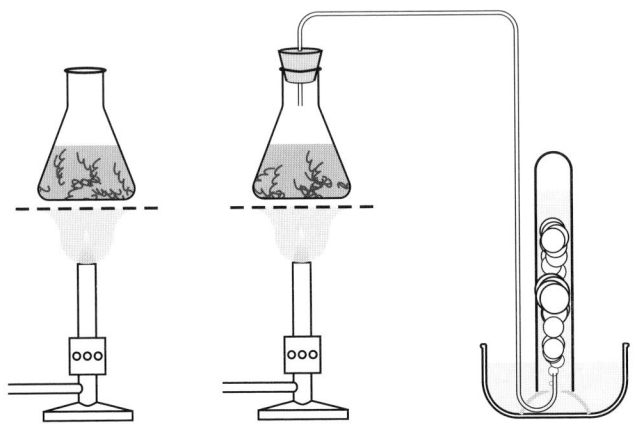

31.1.18 tubeRecourbeCourt

The tubeRecourbeCourt option is like the previous one except that it is shorter as it doesn't have a Bunsen burner.

```
\usepackage{pst-labo}
\psset{unit=0.5cm,glassType=flacon,recuperationGaz,substance=\pstFilaments{red}}
\pstChauffageBallon[tubeRecourbe] \hspace{3cm}
\pstChauffageBallon[tubeRecourbeCourt]
```

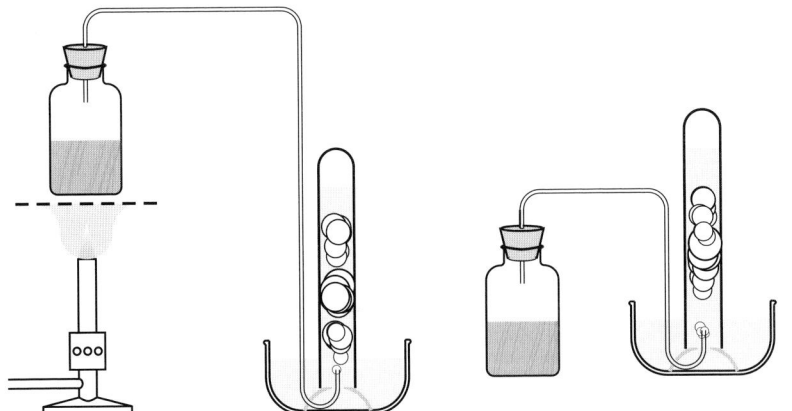

31.1.19 recuperationGaz

recuperationGaz denotes the instrument that captures escaping gases, used in the tubeRecourbe and tubeRecourbeCourt options above.

```
\usepackage{pst-labo}
\psset{unit=0.5cm,glassType=flacon,tubeRecourbe,substance={\pstFilaments[10]{red}}}
\pstChauffageBallon \hspace{2cm}
\pstChauffageBallon[recuperationGaz]
```

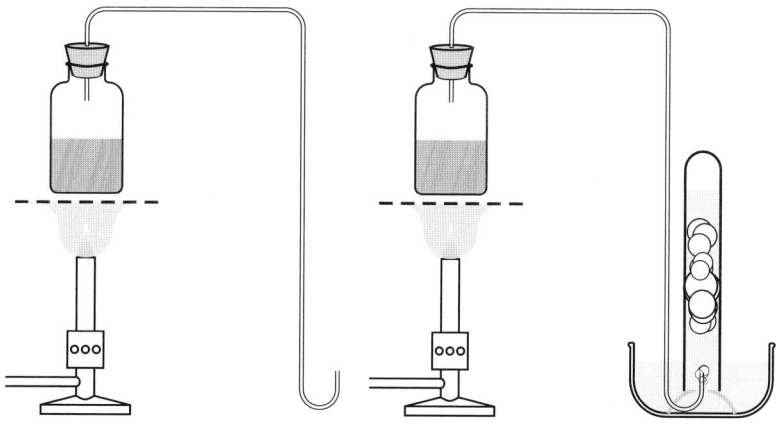

31.1.20 burette

By default, the \pstDosage command creates a burette, but burette=false prevents it from being drawn.

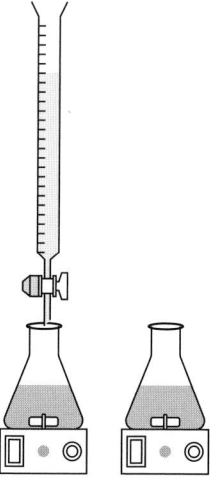

```
\usepackage{pst-labo}

\psset{unit=0.4cm}
\pstDosage[glassType=erlen]
\pstDosage[glassType=erlen,burette=false]
```

31.1.21 niveauReactifBurette and couleurReactifBurette

niveauReactifBurette specifies the liquid level in a burette as a percentage of its height and couleurReactifBurette specifies the colour of the chemical reaction in a burette.

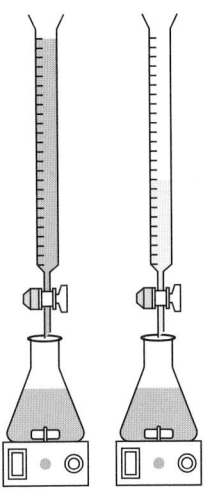

```
\usepackage{pst-labo}

\psset{unit=0.4cm,glassType=erlen,
    niveauLiquide1=60}
\pstDosage[niveauReactifBurette=25,
    couleurReactifBurette=cyan]
\pstDosage[niveauReactifBurette=10]
```

31.1.22 AspectMelange and CouleurDistillat

When using the \pstDistillation command, AspectMelange specifies a colour style for the original chemical substance and CouleurDistillat specifies a pure colour for the distillate. The colour style must be defined beforehand (for styles defined by pst-labo cf. Section 31.2 on page 632; for defining custom styles cf. Section 11.1 on page 121). Colour gradients are possible, and the default style is DiffusionBleue. The default colour for the distillate is yellow.

```
\usepackage{pst-labo}
\psset{unit=0.4cm}
\pstDistillation(-3,-10)(7,6)\quad
\pstDistillation[AspectMelange=Diffusion,CouleurDistillat=red](-3,-10)(7,6)
```

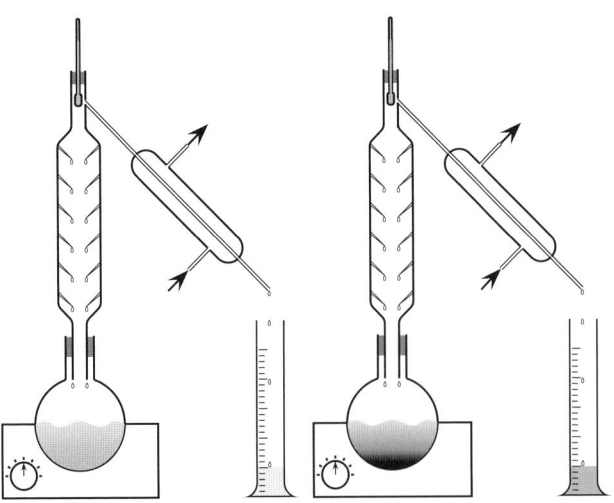

31.1.23 phmetre

phmetre activates the display of a pH-value gauge; this is only available for the \pstDosage command, with glassType=becher.

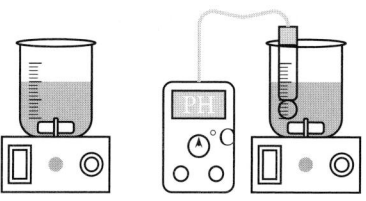

```
\usepackage{pst-labo}

\psset{unit=0.5cm,glassType=becher,
    burette=false}
\pstDosage
\pstDosage[phmetre]
```

31.1.24 agitateurMagnetique

agitateurMagnetique is active by default and denotes the mixer. If deactivated, the symbols aren't drawn though the rectangle remains.

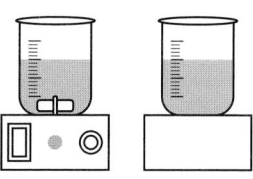

```
\usepackage{pst-labo}

\psset{unit=0.5cm,burette=false,
    glassType=becher}
\pstDosage
\pstDosage[agitateurMagnetique=false]
```

31.1.25 niveauLiquide1, niveauLiquide2, niveauLiquide3, and aspectLiquide1, aspectLiquide2, aspectLiquide3

These six options define height and style of the respective liquids 1, 2, and 3. The style must be defined beforehand (for styles defined by pst-labo cf. Section 31.2 on the next page; for defining custom styles with \newpsstyle cf. Section 11.1 on page 121). Note that depending on the command used, not all options are possible.

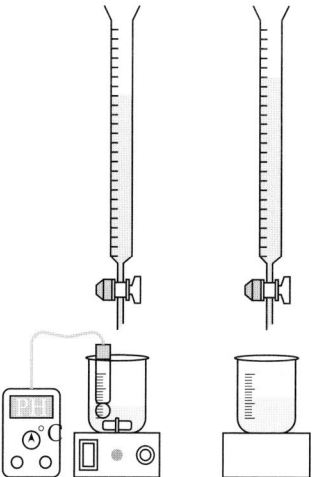

```
\usepackage{pst-labo}

\psset{unit=0.4cm,glassType=becher}
\rule{0pt}{6cm}
\pstDosage[niveauReactifBurette=18,
    niveauLiquide1=30,
    aspectLiquide1=Champagne,%
    glassType=becher,phmetre=true]
\pstDosage[niveauReactifBurette=20,
    niveauLiquide1=40,
    aspectLiquide1=Champagne,%
    glassType=becher,phmetre=false,
    agitateurMagnetique=false]
```

31 pst-labo – Chemical instruments

```
\usepackage{pst-labo}
\begin{pspicture}(3,0)(5,6)
  \rput(4,3){\pstChauffageBallon[becBunsen=true,unit=0.5]}
  \rput(4,4.2){\pstBallon[glassType=becher,xunit=1,yunit=0.5,
    aspectLiquide1=Champagne,runit=0.7]}
  \psset{glassType=tube,tubeDroit=true}
  \rput(4,4){\pstTubeEssais[unit=0.35,niveauLiquide1=70,aspectLiquide1=Diffusion]}
  \rput(4.5,4){\pstTubeEssais[unit=0.35,niveauLiquide1=75,aspectLiquide1=Sang]}
  \rput(3.5,4){\pstTubeEssais[unit=0.35,niveauLiquide1=80]}
\end{pspicture}\hspace{2cm}
\begin{pspicture}(3,0)(5,6)
  \rput(4,3){\pstChauffageBallon[becBunsen=true,unit=0.5]}
  \rput(4,4.2){\pstBallon[glassType=becher,xunit=1,yunit=0.5,
    aspectLiquide1=Champagne,runit=0.7]}
  \psset{tubeDroit=true}
  \rput(3.8,4){\pstTubeEssais[unit=0.35,niveauLiquide1=70,aspectLiquide1=Diffusion]}
  \rput(4.2,4){\pstTubeEssais[unit=0.35,niveauLiquide1=65,aspectLiquide1=Sang]}
  \rput(3.1,4){\pstTubeEssais[unit=0.35,niveauLiquide1=80,tubePenche=10]}
  \rput(4.9,4){\pstTubeEssais[unit=0.35,niveauLiquide1=80,tubePenche=-10]}
\end{pspicture}\hspace{1cm}
\begin{pspicture}(1,3)(5,6)
  \rput(2.5,4){\pstBallon[glassType=ballon,unit=0.5,niveauLiquide1=15]}
  \rput(1.3,5.4){\pstTubeEssais[unit=0.5,niveauLiquide1=95,
  niveauLiquide2=60,niveauLiquide3=30,tubePenche=-60]}
\end{pspicture}
```

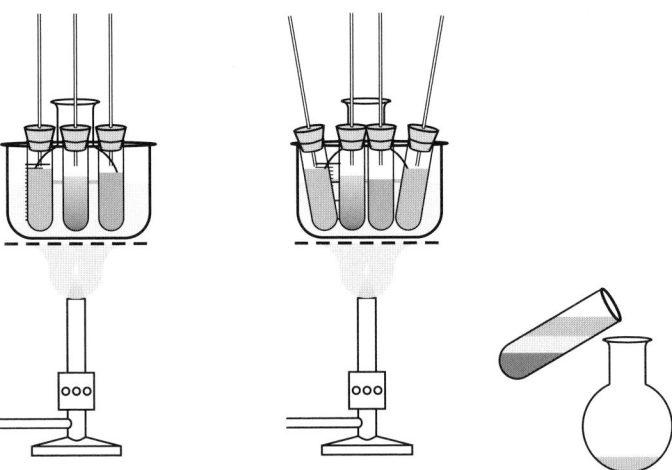

31.2 Predefined colours and styles

This section lists the colours and styles defined by pst-labo. You can overwrite them when defining custom colours or styles (cf. Sections 2.1.1 on page 12 and 11.1 on page 121).

31.3 Commands

```
\definecolor{Beige}{rgb}{.96,.96,.86}        \definecolor{GrisClair}{rgb}{.8,.8,.8}
\definecolor{GrisTresClair}{rgb}{.9,.9,.9}\definecolor{LightBlue}{rgb}{.68,.85,.9}
\definecolor{OrangeTresPale}{cmyk}{0,.1,.3,0}\definecolor{Copper}{cmyk}{0,.9,.9,.2}
\definecolor{OrangePale}{cmyk}{0,.2,.4,0} \definecolor{BleuClair}{cmyk}{.2,0,0,0}
\definecolor{Marron}{cmyk}{0,.3,.5,.3}

\newpsstyle{aspectLiquide1}     {linestyle=none,fillstyle=solid,fillcolor=cyan}
\newpsstyle{aspectLiquide2}     {linestyle=none,fillstyle=solid,fillcolor=yellow}
\newpsstyle{aspectLiquide3}     {linestyle=none,fillstyle=solid,fillcolor=magenta}
\newpsstyle{Champagne}          {linestyle=none,fillstyle=solid,fillcolor=Beige}
\newpsstyle{BilleThreeD}        {linestyle=none,fillstyle=gradient,gradmidpoint=0,
                                 gradend=white,GradientCircle=true}
\newpsstyle{Sang}               {linestyle=none,fillstyle=solid,fillcolor=red}
\newpsstyle{Cobalt}             {linewidth=0.2,fillstyle=solid,fillcolor=blue}
\newpsstyle{Huile}              {linestyle=none,fillstyle=solid,fillcolor=yellow}
\newpsstyle{Vinaigre}           {linestyle=none,fillstyle=solid,fillcolor=magenta}
\newpsstyle{Diffusion}          {linestyle=none,fillstyle=gradient,gradmidpoint=0}
\newpsstyle{DiffusionMelange2}{fillstyle=gradient,gradbegin=white,gradend=red,
                                 gradmidpoint=0,linecolor=red}
\newpsstyle{flammeEtGrille}     {linestyle=none,fillstyle=gradient,gradmidpoint=0,
                                 gradbegin=OrangePale,gradend=yellow}
\newpsstyle{rayuresJaunes}      {fillstyle=hlines,linecolor=yellow,hatchcolor=yellow}
\newpsstyle{DiffusionBleue}     {fillstyle=gradient,gradmidpoint=0,linestyle=none,
                                 gradbegin=green,gradend=cyan}
```

31.3 Commands

31.3.1 \pstTubeEssais

This command creates the simplest chemical instruments and has been used extensively in previous examples. The default without parameters is the normal test tube (glassType=tube).

```
\usepackage{pst-labo}
\psset{unit=0.5} \pstTubeEssais \pstTubeEssais[glassType=becher]
\pstTubeEssais[glassType=erlen,niveauLiquide1=80]
\pstTubeEssais[glassType=flacon]
\pstTubeEssais[glassType=ballon,niveauLiquide1=20,aspectLiquide1=DiffusionBleue]
\pstTubeEssais[glassType=fioleJauge]
```

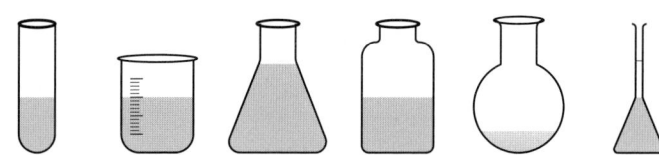

31.3.2 \pstChauffageTube

\pstChauffageTube is an extension of the previous command; it tips the chemical instrument and provides for adding a Bunsen burner, or second tube.

```
\usepackage{pst-labo}
\psset{unit=0.5}
\pstChauffageTube[tubeSeul]
\pstChauffageTube[glassType=ballon,becBunsen=false,tubeSeul,refrigerantBoulles]
\pstChauffageTube[glassType=erlen,becBunsen,pince,tubeSeul]
```

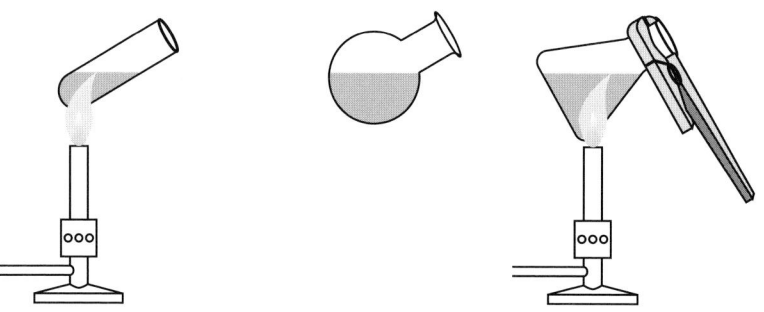

31-03-2

```
\usepackage{pst-labo}
\psset{unit=0.5}
\pstChauffageTube[becBunsen,barbotage,glassType=flacon]
\pstChauffageTube[becBunsen,tubeCoude,glassType=ballon,niveauLiquide1=20,%
    aspectLiquide1=DiffusionBleue,tubeSeul,pince]
```

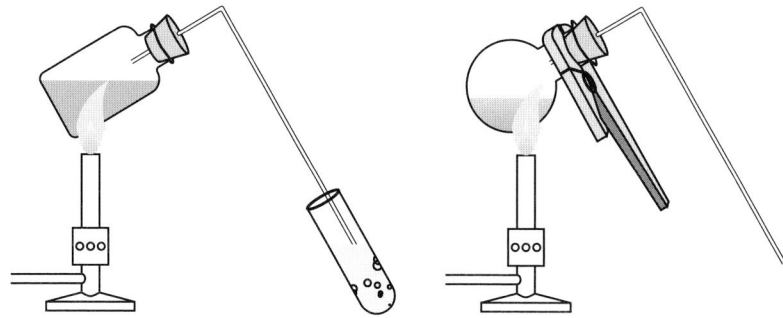

31-03-3

31.3.3 \pstBallon

\pstBallon is almost identical to \pstTubeEssais, but you can assign additional options.

```
\usepackage{pst-labo}
\psset{unit=0.5cm}
\pstBallon\hspace{-0.5cm}
\pstBallon[glassType=erlen]\hspace{-0.5cm}
\pstBallon[glassType=becher,xunit=0.75cm,yunit=0.3cm,aspectLiquide1=Champagne,
    runit=0.4cm]\hspace{-0.5cm}
\raisebox{0.5cm}{\pstBallon[refrigerantBoulles=true]}
```

31.3.4 \pstChauffageBallon

\pstChauffageBallon is an extension of the previous command and adds the Bunsen burner by default.

\usepackage{pst-labo}

\psset{unit=0.5cm} \pstChauffageBallon
\pstChauffageBallon[barbotage,tubeCoudeUB,becBunsen,substance=\pstBilles]\\[20pt]
\pstChauffageBallon[glassType=flacon,recuperationGaz,tubeRecourbeCourt,
   substance={\pstFilaments[10]{red}}]
\pstChauffageBallon[doubletube,recuperationGaz,substance=\pstClouFer]

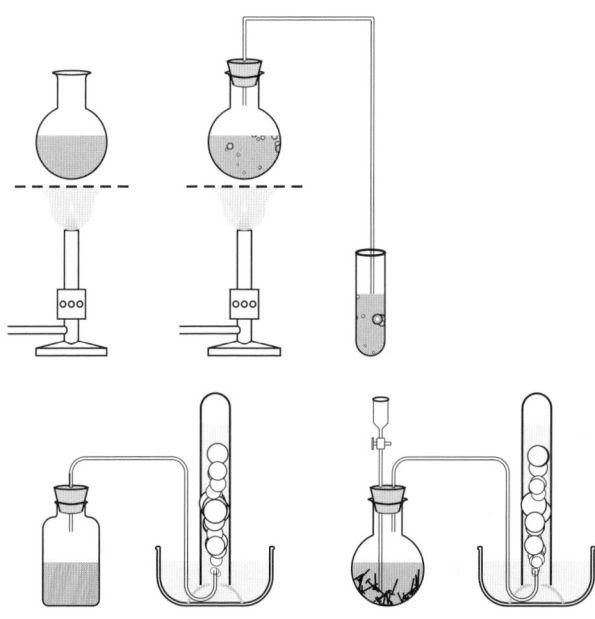

31 pst-labo – Chemical instruments

```
\usepackage{pst-labo}
\psset{unit=0.5cm}
\pstChauffageBallon[glassType=erlen,tubeRecourbe,recuperationGaz,
  substance=\pstTournureCuivre]\hspace{3cm}
\pstChauffageBallon[glassType=becher,aspectLiquide1=Champagne,
  substance=\pstBullesChampagne]\hspace{.25cm}
\pstChauffageBallon[glassType=erlen,substance=\pstBullesChampagne,tubeDroit]
```

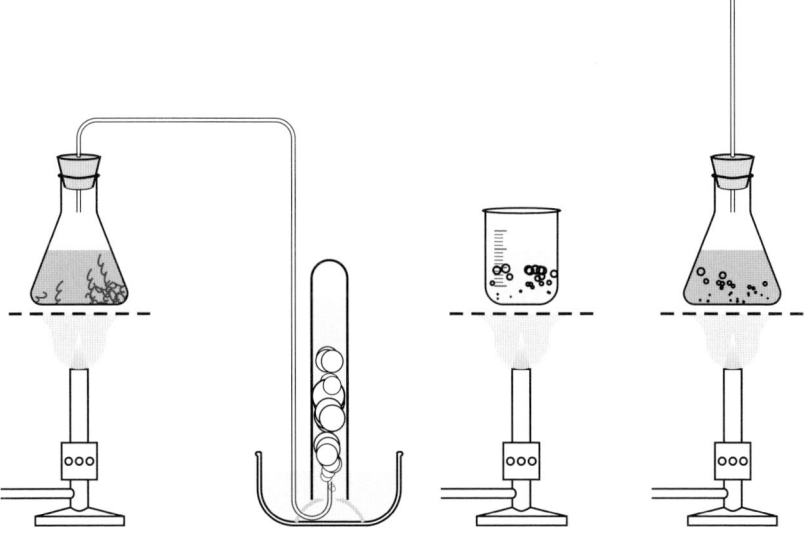

31-03-6

31.3.5 \pstEntonnoir

\pstEntonnoir draws a funnel; it is used with a test tube without parameters, but other combinations are possible as well.

```
\usepackage{pst-labo}
\psset{unit=0.5cm}
\pstEntonnoir
\pstEntonnoir[glassType=becher,tubePenche=-20]
\pstEntonnoir[glassType=flacon,etiquette=true,Numero={\green 37},
  aspectLiquide1=DiffusionBleue,niveauLiquide1=80]
```

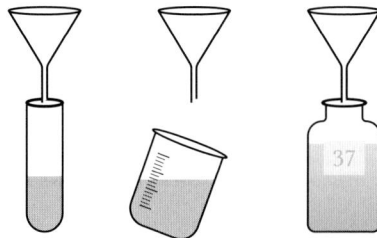

31-03-7

31.3.6 \pstDosage

\pstDosage is usually used along with other instruments. The burette has a maximum capacity of 25 ml; you can change the current height, colour, and type of the substance through the niveauReactifBurette, couleurReactifBurette, and substance options (cf. Sections 31.1.21 on page 629 and 31.1.13 on page 625. You can also add a pH gauge (only if glassType=becher, cf. Section 31.1.23 on page 631) and a mixer (cf. Section 31.1.24 on page 631).

```
\usepackage{pst-labo}
\psset{unit=0.5cm}   \pstDosage \pstDosage[glassType=becher,phmetre=true]
\pstDosage[niveauReactifBurette=10,niveauLiquide1=60,aspectLiquide1=Champagne,
   glassType=flacon,agitateurMagnetique=false]
\pstDosage[glassType=erlen,burette=false]
```

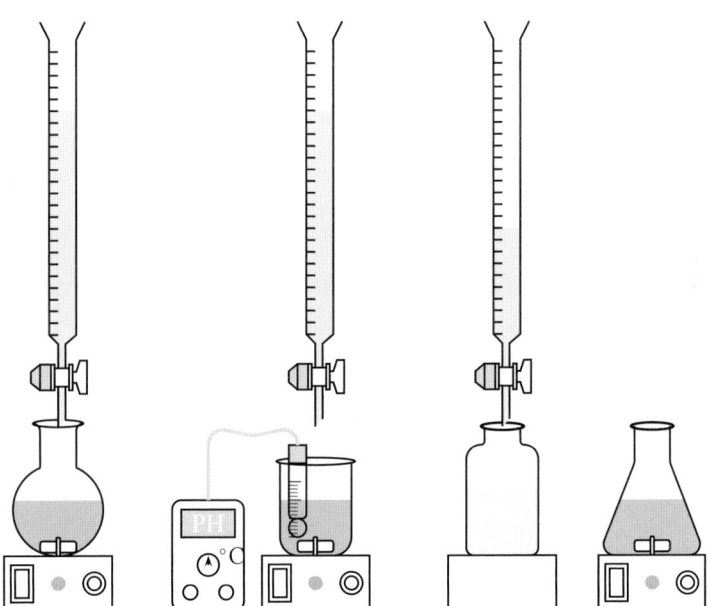

31.3.7 \pstEprouvette

\pstEprouvette draws a normal measuring beaker; you can change the size through PSTricks scale factors.

```
\usepackage{pst-labo}
\pstEprouvette[yunit=0.5cm]
\pstEprouvette[unit=0.6cm,niveauLiquide1=100,niveauLiquide2=60,niveauLiquide3=30]
```

31 pst-labo – Chemical instruments

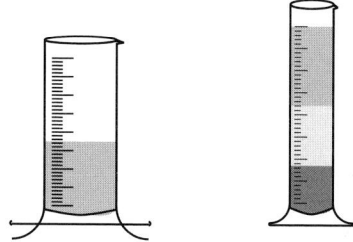

31.3.8 \pstpipette

\pstpipette draws a normal pipette with a scale; you can change the size through the PSTricks scale factors.

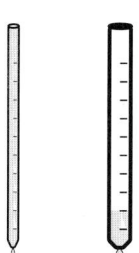

```
\usepackage{pst-labo}

\pstpipette[unit=0.5cm,tubePenche=40]
\pstpipette[yunit=0.5cm]
```

31.3.9 \pstDistillation

\pstDistillation is the only command that expects the size of the pspicture environment as arguments.

```
\pstDistillation
\pstDistillation(x_{ll}, y_{ll})(x_{ur}, y_{ur})
```

If no coordinates are specified, a rectangle of size $(-4, -10)(8, 7)$ is assumed. You can add other objects using the \rput command.

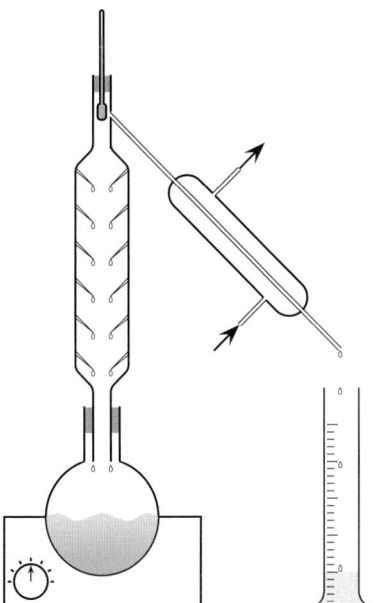

```
\usepackage{pst-labo}

\psset{unit=0.5cm}
\pstDistillation(-3,-10)(7,6)
```

31.4 Examples

Obviously the complexity of the commands increases if the chemical apparatus can't be captured by a standard command. There is and always will be a contradiction between having simple commands and being able to use them universally. Often the simplest commands are sufficient to illustrate texts, as shown in the following example.

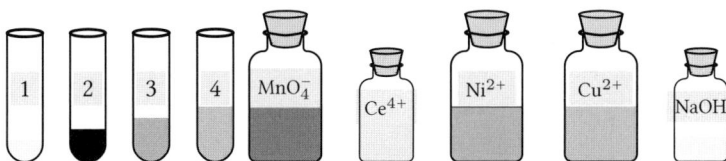

Figure 31.1: Application of \pstTubeEssais

Creating complex examples is much easier when using a coordinate grid created with \psgrid, as demonstrated already in Section 13.2 on page 148 in the context of overlays.

31 pst-labo – Chemical instruments

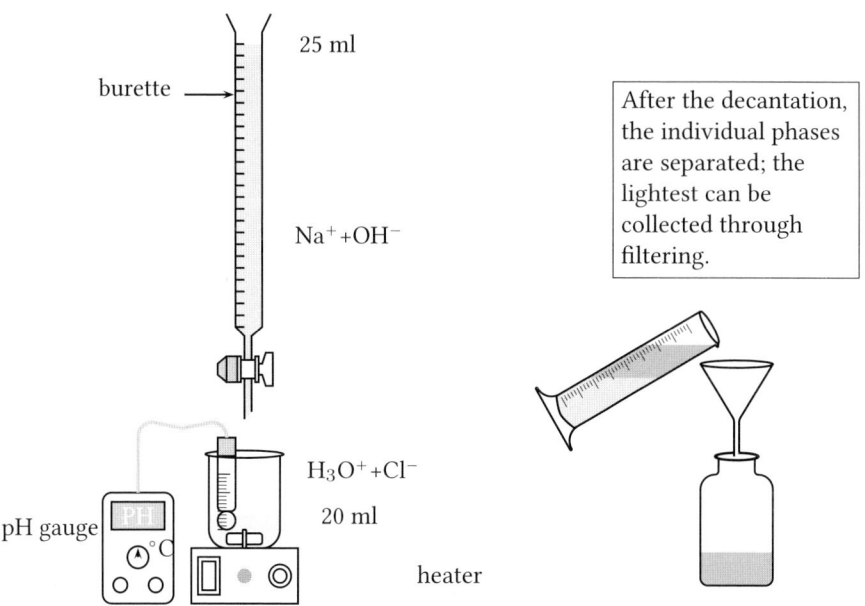

Figure 31.2: Application for \pstDosage (Manuel Luque)

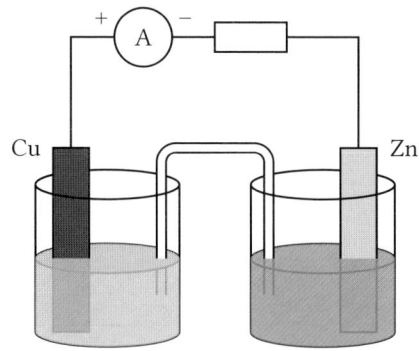

Figure 31.3: Example for an electrolysis (concept by Manuel Luque)

Chapter 32

UML diagrams

32.1 pst-uml 641
32.2 uml 652

PSTricks provides two different packages, pst-uml and uml, for the modelling of software and systems in the Unified Modelling Language.

32.1 pst-uml

The pst-uml package by Maurice Diamantini provides several basic symbols for UML diagrams. The main command, which describes a class, has a simple syntax:

\umlClass [settings] {*title*}{*content*}

The title as well as the actual content may be empty. The box is aligned symmetrically to the base line.

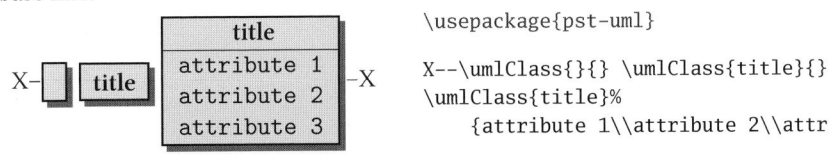

```
\usepackage{pst-uml}

X--\umlClass{}{} \umlClass{title}{}
\umlClass{title}%
    {attribute 1\\attribute 2\\attribute 3}--X
```

Apart from the standard PSTricks options, there are three additional optional parameters available: umlShadow, umlParameter, and umlDoubleRuleSep. The options defined by PSTricks may be overwritten by pst-uml.

umlShadow is Boolean, with default value true. The specification of the shadow refers to the shading of the rectangle as well as the background.

```
\usepackage{pst-uml}

\umlClass{title}{attribute 1\\attribute 2\\
    attribute 3}
\umlClass[umlShadow=false]{title}%
    {attribute 1\\attribute 2\\attribute 3}
```

32 UML diagrams

umlParameter adds the text in its argument above the top-right corner of the box.

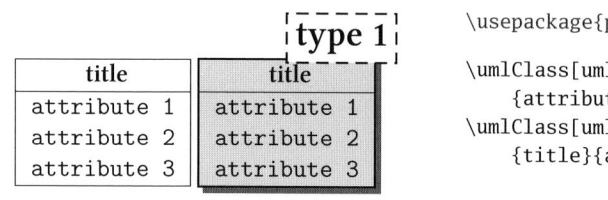

```
\usepackage{pst-uml}

\umlClass[umlShadow=false]{title}%
    {attribute 1\\attribute 2\\attribute 3}
\umlClass[umlParameter=type 1]%
    {title}{attribute 1\\attribute 2\\attribute 3}
```

32-01-3

The content corresponds to a table with one column; you can use all tabular-specific commands like \hline. umlDoubleRuleSep (default is 2mm) controls the distance of separation between two consecutive \hline commands.

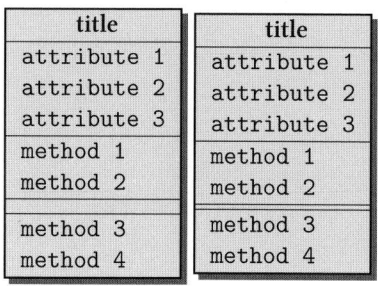

```
\usepackage{pst-uml}

\umlClass{title}%
    {attribute 1\\attribute 2\\attribute 3\\\hline
        method 1\\method 2\\\hline\hline
        method 3\\method 4}
\umlClass[umlDoubleRuleSep=2pt]{title}%
    {attribute 1\\attribute 2\\attribute 3\\\hline
        method 1\\method 2\\\hline\hline
        method 3\\method 4}
```

32-01-4

By default, the width of each box depends on the width of its content, but you can modify the width by putting a line into an additional \makebox command; the line is still centred, but set to a specific width. The title, too, is typeset as a table with one column, so you can only apply \makebox to one line.

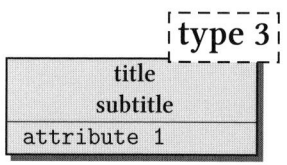

```
\usepackage{pst-uml}

\umlClass[umlParameter=type 3]%
    {\makebox[3cm]{title}\\
        subtitle}{attribute 1}
```

32-01-5

"Actors" are described by the \umlActor command; they are not typeset symmetrically to the base line, but with the actor's feet on it instead.

\umlActor [settings] {name}

```
\usepackage{pst-uml}
\_\umlActor{client}\_\_\umlActor[unit=0.5]{small}\_%
\_\umlActor[umlActorLineWidth=1mm]{Dick}\_\_\umlActor[xunit=0.5,yunit=1.5,
    umlActorLineWidth=1pt]{:-)}\_\_\psframebox{\umlActor{three-\\line\\name}}\_
```

32.1 pst-uml

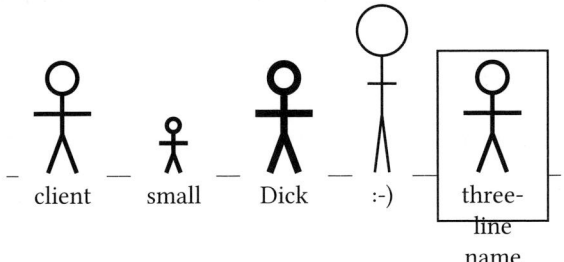

```
\usepackage{pst-uml,graphicx}

\umlClass{\umlStereoType{actor}
    \umlActor{me}}{}
\umlClass{\umlStereoType{actor}
    \raisebox{-0.4\height}{%
        \umlActor{me}}}{}
```

Several commands are provided for state descriptions:

```
\umlState [settings] {title}{content}
\umlStateIn
\umlStateOut
\umlPutStateIn{x_n,y_n}{node name}
\umlPutStateOut{x_n,y_n}{node name}
```

The points made about \umlClass regarding the title and the content also apply here.

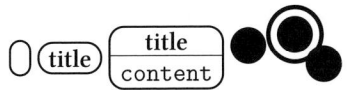

```
\usepackage{pst-uml}

\umlState{}{} \umlState{title}{}
\umlState{title}{content}
\umlStateIn \umlStateOut
\umlPutStateIn{0,0}{Node}
```

As usual you can arrange the symbols arbitrarily within a pspicture environment. Every expression can be centred vertically with a one-column table; thus the following figure is also centred on the base line. You can specify any size for the pspicture environment.

32 UML diagrams

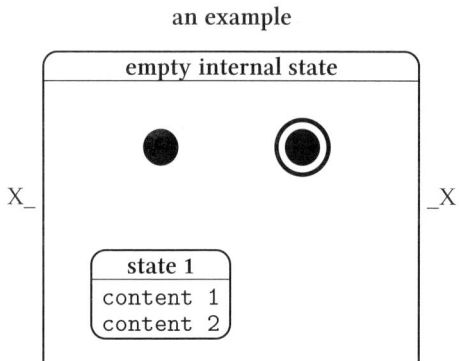

```
\usepackage{pst-uml}

X\_\begin{tabular}{@{}c@{}}
  \begin{pspicture}(-2.75,-2)(2.75,2.75)
  \rput(0,2.75){\textbf{an example}}
  \rput(0,0){\umlState{empty internal state}%
     {\rule{5cm}{0pt}\rule{0pt}{4cm}}}
  \rput(-1,-1){\umlState{state 1}{%
     content 1\\content 2}}
  \rput(-1,1){\umlStateIn}
  \rput(1,1){\umlStateOut}
  \end{pspicture}\end{tabular}\_X
```

Simple nodes are typeset with the \umlCase and \umlCase commands:

\umlCase [settings] {content}

\umlPutCase [settings] {coord n}{node name}{content}

The framesep option is set internally to 0pt, but all other PSTricks options are available.

```
\usepackage{pst-uml}

\umlPutCase{0,0}{A}{node A}%
\umlPutCase[fillcolor=black!20,
   fillstyle=solid,shadow=true]%
   {3,-1}{B}{node B}
\ncline{A}{B}
```

You can create simple remarks with \umlNote, and place them at any arbitrary position through the \rput command:

\umlNote [settings] {content}

The content is a table again and may therefore contain line breaks as well as \hline. The umlAlign parameter controls the horizontal alignment: valid values are l, c, and r, as usual for tables.

```
\usepackage{pst-uml}

\_\umlNote{What I\\
   always\\
   wanted to say\ldots}\_%
\umlNote[fillstyle=solid,fillcolor=black!15,
   umlAlign=r]{What I\\
   always\\
   wanted to say\ldots\\\hline
   was this: nothing :-)}\_
```

The \umlStack command is similar to \umlNote; it takes arbitrary text but doesn't put it inside a frame. Because of this, fill options have no effect on this command.

32.1 pst-uml

`\umlStack [settings] {content}`

The special options for `\umlStack` are summarized in Table 32.1.

Table 32.1: Summary of the parameters for `\umlStack`

name	type	default
umlStackSep	value unit	0
umlStackWidth	value unit	0
umlAlign	l|c|r	c
umlPos	t|c|b	c
umlStackLinesStretch	value	0.85

`umlPos` specifies the vertical alignment of the output and has the same meaning as for a normal `tabular` environment. `umlStackLinesStretch` corresponds to the LaTeX command `\arraystretch`.

32-01-12

```
\usepackage{pst-uml}

\_\umlStack{What I\\
    always\\wanted to say\ldots}\_\_%
\umlStack[umlAlign=r,
    umlPos=b]{What I\\
    always\\wanted to say
    \ldots\\\hline
    was this: nothing :-)}\_
```

32-01-13

```
\usepackage{pst-uml}

\_\fbox{\umlStack[
    umlStackLinesStretch=1.5]%
    {What I\\
    always\\wanted to say
    \ldots}}\_\_%
\umlStack[umlPos=t,
    umlStackSep=10pt]%
    {What I\\always\\
    wanted to say\ldots\\\hline
    was this: nothing :-)}\_
```

You can position the commands described above arbitrarily in the coordinate system with the help of the commands listed below, or with the `\?put` commands of PSTricks.

`\ResetXY`	sets the current point to (0,0)
`\SetX{value unit }`	sets x to value unit
`\SetY{value unit }`	the same for y
`\SetXY{valueX unit }{valueY unit }`	the same for x and y
`\X`	the current x coordinate

645

\Y	the same for *y*
\incrX{*value unit*}	increments the *x* value by *value unit*
\incrY{*value unit*}	the same for *y*
\moveE{*value unit*}	moves *value unit* to the right
\moveN{*value unit*}	the same for up
\moveW{*value unit*}	the same for left
\moveS{*value unit*}	the same for down
\rputXY [*settings*] {*content*}	puts *content* at the current position

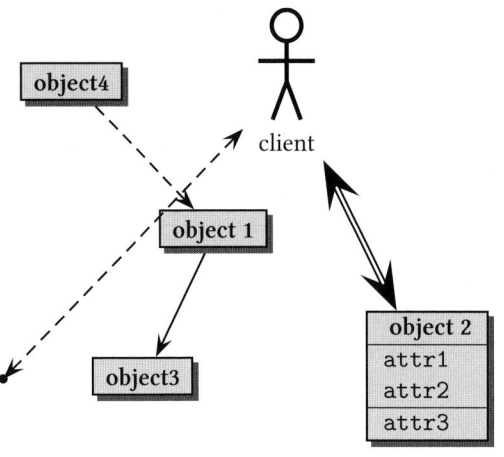

```
\usepackage{pst-uml}

\begin{pspicture}(6,5)
\rput(3,3){\rnode{object1}{%
   \umlClass{object 1}{}}}
\pnode(0,1){pnode1}\psdot(pnode1)
\rput(6,1){\rnode{object2}{%
\umlClass{object 2}{attr1\\attr2\\\hline attr3}}}
\rput(2,1){\rnode{object3}{\umlClass{object3}{}}}
\rput(1,5){\rnode{object4}{\umlClass{object4}{}}}
\rput(4,5){\rnode{client}{\umlActor{client}}}
\ncline{->}{object1}{object3}
\ncline[doubleline=true]{<->}{object2}{client}
\ncline[linestyle=dashed]{<->}{pnode1}{client}
\ncline[linestyle=dashed]{<-}{object1}{object4}
\end{pspicture}
```

```
\usepackage{pst-uml}

\begin{pspicture}(-1.4,-1.4)(1.4,1.4)
   \ResetXY \rputXY{\pscirclebox{1}}
   \moveE{1}\rputXY{\pscirclebox{2}}\moveN{1}\rputXY{\pscirclebox{3}}
   \moveW{1}\rputXY{\pscirclebox{4}}\moveW{1}\rputXY{\pscirclebox{5}}
   \moveS{1}\rputXY{\pscirclebox{6}}\moveS{1}\rputXY{\pscirclebox{7}}
   \moveE{1}\rputXY{\pscirclebox{8}}\moveE{1}\rputXY{\pscirclebox{9}}
\end{pspicture}
```

pst-uml defines the symbols commonly used for UML figures internally. These correspond to the standard PSTricks symbols, but can't be overwritten easily.

umlHerit	→ ▷	→ \pstriangle
umlAgreg	→ ◇	→ \psdiamond
umlCompos	→ ◆	→ \psdiamond[fillcolor=black]

These symbols are accessed through the \ncputicon command.

32.1 pst-uml

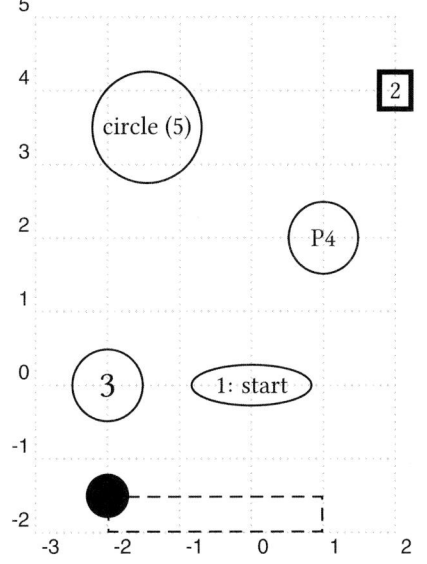

```
\usepackage{pst-uml}

\begin{pspicture}[showgrid=true](-3,-2)(2,5)
  \ResetXY
  \rputXY{\psovalbox{1: start}}
  \SetX{2}\SetY{2}\moveN{2}
  \rputXY{\psframebox[linewidth=2pt]{2}}
  \moveW{4}\moveS{4}\moveE{-10mm}\moveE{1}
  \rputXY{\Large 3}
% current coordinates \X and \Y
  \pscircle(\X,\Y){0.5}
  \moveE{3}\moveN{2}
  \rputXY{\pnode{P4}}\rputXY{P4}
  \rputXY{\pscircle{0.5}}\SetX{-1.5}
  \moveN{1.5}
  \rputXY{\pscirclebox{circle (5)}}
  \SetX{-2}\SetY{-1.5}
  \newlength{\tmpX}\setlength{\tmpX}{\X}
  \newlength{\tmpY}\setlength{\tmpY}{\Y}
  \psaddtolength{\tmpX}{5}
  \psaddtolength{\tmpY}{1}
  \rputXY{\pscircle*{0.3}}
  \rputXY{\psframe[linestyle=dashed]%
    (\tmpX,\tmpY)}
\end{pspicture}
```

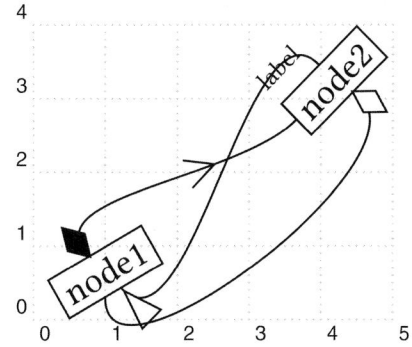

```
\usepackage{pst-uml}

\begin{pspicture}[showgrid=true](5,4)
  \rput[bl]{30}(0.5,0){\rnode{node1}{%
    \psframebox{\Large node1}}}
  \rput[tr]{45}(4.5,4){\rnode{node2}{%
    \psframebox{\Large node2}}}
  \nccurve[angleA=-45,angleB=135]{node1}{node2}
  \ncput[nrot=:U,npos=0.8]{label}
  \ncputicon{umlHerit}
  \nccurve[angleA=-30,angleB=-90]{node2}{node1}
  \ncputicon{umlAgreg}
  \nccurve[angleA=135,angleB=-135]{node1}{node2}
  \ncputicon{umlCompos}
  \ncputicon[nrot=:U,npos=0.7]{umlV}
\end{pspicture}
```

All connections are created using the \nxXXXX commands from pst-node (cf. Section 16.4 on page 241). To simplify their use, pst-uml defines shortcuts referring to the four cardinal directions and the general directions that are added to the names of the connections.

▷ E, W, N, S for east, west, north, and south

▷ H, V for horizontal and vertical

▷ D, X for diagonal and arbitrary

32 UML diagrams

The syntax of all the connection commands is the same:

`\ncXXX [settings] {node1}{node2}`

The connection is always drawn from the first to the second node. For example \SHN means a line from the first node to the south ($\alpha_A = -90°$), then *horizontal* towards the second node and finally north, such that the connection ends in the same angle ($\alpha_B = -90°$). An *X* in the name of the command means that start and target direction are fixed, but the direction of the line segment inbetween is determined by these. The first and last letters of the *XXX* in the connection names always have to be cardinal points, while the middle letter (if present) has to be a general direction. Single letters (cardinal points) are also possible, though a two-segment connection is still produced (cf. Example 32-01-21).

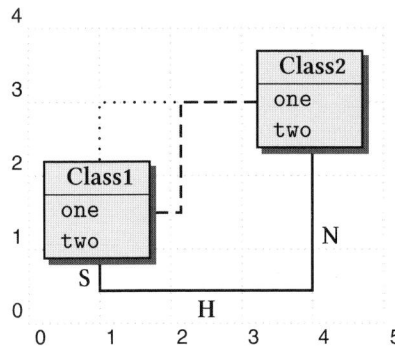

```
\usepackage{pst-uml}

\begin{pspicture}[showgrid=true](5,4)
\rput(1,1.5){\rnode{A}{%
    \umlClass{Class1}{one\\two}}}
\rput(4,3){\rnode{B}{%
    \umlClass{Class2}{one\\two}}}
\end{pspicture}
\psset{linewidth=1pt}%
\ncNE[linestyle=dotted]{A}{B}
\ncEVE[linestyle=dashed]{A}{B}
\ncSHN{A}{B}
\nbput[npos=0.5]{\textbf{S}}
\nbput[npos=1.5]{\textbf{H}}
\nbput[npos=2.5]{\textbf{N}}
```

32-01-19

Depending on the type of the connection, the number of line segments varies from two to four. The example above showed a two-segment connection and two of the three possibile three-segment connections, the U- and Z-shaped ones. Examples of the D-shaped connection and of a connection consisting of the maximum four segments are shown below. Table 32.3 on the next page gives a summary of all possible connection commands.

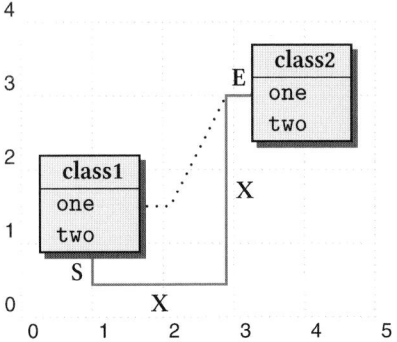

```
\usepackage{pst-uml}

\begin{pspicture}[showgrid=true](5,4)
\rput(1,1.5){\rnode{A}{%
    \umlClass{class1}{one\\two}}}
\rput(4,3){\rnode{B}{%
    \umlClass{class2}{one\\two}}}
\end{pspicture}
\ncEDE[linewidth=1pt,linestyle=dotted]{A}{B}
\ncSXE[linewidth=1pt,linecolor=red]{A}{B}
\nbput[npos=0.5]{\textbf{S}}\nbput[npos=1.5]{\textbf{X}}
\nbput[npos=2.5]{\textbf{X}}\naput[npos=3.5]{\textbf{E}}
```

32-01-20

As the internal specifications use the "cardinal directions", some parameters of the connections can't be overwritten, in particular the values of the angles angleA and angleB (cf. Section 16.2.7 on page 230).

Table 32.3: Summary of the connection commands of the pst-uml package

elements	command name
1	\ncE \ncW \ncN \ncS
2	\ncEN \ncES \ncWN \ncWS \ncNE \ncNW \ncSE \ncSW
3 (U)	\ncEVW \ncWVE \ncSHN \ncNHS
3 (Z)	\ncEVE \ncWVW \ncNHN \ncSHS
3 (D)	\ncEDE \ncWDW \ncNDN \ncSDS
4 (X)	\ncSXE \ncSXW \ncEXS \ncEXN \ncWXS \ncWXN \ncNXE \ncNXW

```
\usepackage{pst-uml,graphicx}
\newcommand{\drawClassi}{%
  \umlClass{class1}{umlClassWidth = 0\\(default) \\\hline
    attribute2 <a wide line> \\\hline attribute3\\\hline method1}}
\newcommand{\drawClassii}{%
  \umlClass[umlClassWidth=4cm,umlParameter={\ T\ }]{class2}{%
    width = 4cm \\\hline attribute2\\\hline method1\\ method2}}
\newcommand{\drawClassiii}{%
  \umlClass[umlClassWidth=2.7]{class3}{attribute1\\ attribute1\\\hline
    method1\\ method2}}
\newcommand{\drawClassiv}{
  \umlClass{class4}{attribute1 \\ attribute2\\\hline method1}}
\newcommand{\drawClassv}{\umlClass[umlClassWidth=0]{class5}{}}
\resizebox{\linewidth}{!}{\begin{pspicture}(18,15)%\psgrid
  \rput(3,13){\rnode{class1}{\drawClassi}} \pnode(17.5,13){pnode1}
  \rput(9,10){\rnode{class2}{\drawClassii}}\rput(2,5){\rnode{class3}{\drawClassiii}}
  \rput(12,5){\rnode{class4}{\drawClassiv}}\rput(5.5,5.5){\rnode{class5}{\drawClassv}}
  \rput(16,11){\rnode{actor1}{\umlActor{actor 1}}}
\end{pspicture}}
\ncline{Class1}{pnode1}\ncputicon[npos=0.7,nrot=:U]{umlV}
\naput{ncline}\naput[npos=1,ref=r]{node "P1"}
\ncSXE[armA=11.5]{pnode1}{Class3}\nbput{SXE (armA=11.5)}\ncputicon{umlV}
\ncputicon[npos=1.9999,nrot=:U]{umlV}\ncputicon[npos=2,nrot=:U]{umlV}
\ncputicon[npos=5,nrot=:U]{umlV}\ncSE{class1}{class2}
\naput[npos=1.5]{\{\ncSE npos=1.5\}}\ncSE[offset=-1]{class1}{class2}
\ncputicon{umlAgreg}\ncputicon[npos=2,nrot=:U]{umlCompos}
\nbput[npos=0.3]{0..*}\naput[npos=1.8]{0..2}\naput[npos=1.4]{ncSE,offset=-1}
\ncSHS[armA=1.5]{class2}{class4}\naput{ncSHS}
\ncSHS[armA=1.5]{class2}{class3}\nbput{ncSHS}
\ncputicon{umlHerit}\ncputicon[npos=3,nrot=:U]{umlV}
\ncSHN[arm=.7]{class3}{Class4}
\naput{ncSHN (3 vers 4)}\ncputicon[npos=1.8,nrot=:U]{umlV}
\ncE{class5}{class4}\naput[npos=0.4]{ncE,npos=0.4}\ncputicon{umlCompos}
\newpsstyle{umlDependance}{linestyle=dashed,arrows=->,arrowscale=3,arrowinset=0.6}
\ncline[style=umlDependance,offset=-0.5]{class3}{class4}
\naput{ncline} \ncputicon{umlV}\nbput[npos=0.15]{1..*}
\ncline[linestyle=dashed]{class2}{actor1}\naput{ncline}\ncputicon{umlAgreg}
\ncputicon[npos=0.7,nrot=:U]{umlAgreg}\ncputicon[npos=1,nrot=:U]{umlCompos}
\nccurve[linestyle=dashed, angleA=75,offsetA=-1,angleB=-45]{Class4}{actor1}
```

32 UML diagrams

```
\ncputicon{umlHerit}\ncputicon[npos=0.7,nrot=:U]{umlHerit}
\ncputicon[npos=1,nrot=:U]{umlHerit}}
```

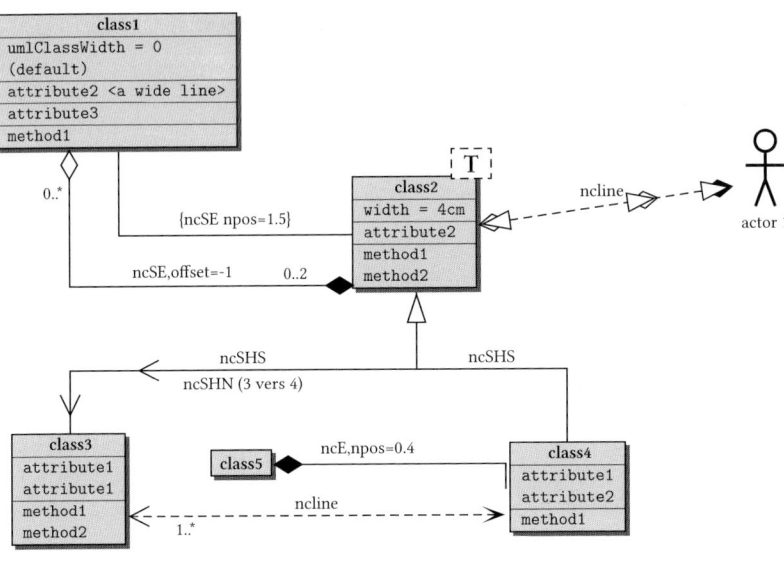

```
\usepackage{pst-uml}
\usepackage[utf8]{inputenc}
\newcommand{\StateGlobal}{%
  \umlState{état global de l'objet \texttt{Graphe}}{\umlEmptyBox{13cm}{16cm}}}
\newcommand{\StateNRSA}{\umlState{non routé \\ sans arêtes}{\space}}
\newcommand{\StateNRI}{\umlState{non routé \\ incomplet}{\space}}
\newcommand{\StateNRC}{\umlState{non routé \\ complet}{\space}}
\newcommand{\StateROU}{\umlState{routé \\ \mbox{}}{\space}}
\newcommand{\StateVisu}{\umlState{Visualisable \\ \mbox{}}{do/superviser()}}
\newcommand{\StateAnu}{%
  \umlState{GrapheAnnulable}{%
    \hspace*{2.25cm}\rmfamily%
    \begin{psmatrix}[colsep=1,rowsep=1.5,mnode=r]
                                          \\[-1.4cm]
      [name=StateInAnu] \umlStateIn    \\[-0.5cm]
      [name=StateNRSA]  \StateNRSA     \\[0cm]
      [name=StateNRI]   \StateNRI      \\[1cm]
      [name=StateNRC]   \StateNRC      \\[0.5cm]
      [name=StateROU]   \StateROU
        &   \umlPutStateOut{0,0}{StateOutAnu}   \\[-1.5cm]
        {}
    \end{psmatrix}\hspace*{1.5cm}
    {\ttfamily\small%
      \ncEXS[offsetA=0.25,offsetB=0.5]{StateNRSA}{StateNRSA}
      \ncput*[npos=1.7]{ajouterSommet}
      \ncWXS[offsetA=-0.25,offsetB=-0.5]{StateNRSA}{StateNRSA}
```

32.1 pst-uml

```
        \ncput*[npos=1.7]{retirerSommet}
        \ncEXS[offsetA=0.25,offsetB=0.5]{StateNRI}{StateNRI}
        \ncput*[npos=1.7]{ajouterArête}
        \ncWXS[offsetA=-0.25,offsetB=-0.5]{StateNRI}{StateNRI}
        \ncput*[npos=1.7]{retirerArête}
        \ncEXN[offsetA=-0.0,offsetB=-0.5]{StateNRI}{StateNRI}
        \ncput*[npos=1.7]{ajouterSommet}
        \ncWXN[offsetA=0.0,offsetB=0.5]{StateNRI}{StateNRI}
        \ncput*[npos=1.7]{retirerSommet}
        \ncEXS[offsetA=0.25,offsetB=0.5]{StateNRC}{StateNRC}
        \ncput*[npos=1.7]{ajouterRoute}
        \ncWXS[offsetA=-0.25,offsetB=-0.5]{StateNRC}{StateNRC}
        \ncput*[npos=1.7]{retirerRoute}
        \ncWXS[offsetA=-0.25,offsetB=-0.5]{StateROU}{StateROU}
        \ncput*[npos=1.7]{réoptimiser}
        \ncline{->}{StateInAnu}{StateNRSA}\naput[npos=0.3]{}
        \ncline{->}{StateNRSA}{StateNRI}\naput[npos=0.3]{ajouterArête}
        \ncline{->}{StateNRI}{StateNRC}\naput[npos=0.3]{graphComplet}
        \naput{graphComplet}
        \ncline{->}{StateNRC}{StateROU}
        \ncput*[npos=0.3]{\umlStack{[ClientPrioritaireSatisfait] DemandeFin}}
        \ncline{->}{StateROU}{StateOutAnu}%
}}}
\resizebox{0.9\linewidth}{!}{%
  \begin{pspicture}(-5,-9.5)(9.5,8)%\psgrid
    \psset{linearc=0.3,armA=1.2,armB=0.8,arrows=->,arrowscale=2,ncurv=2}
    \rput(2.4,-0.75){\rnode{StateGlobal}{\StateGlobal}}\umlPutStateIn{6,5}{StateIn}
    \rput(0,-1){\rnode{StateAnu}{\StateAnu}}\rput(6,-3){\rnode{StateVisu}{\StateVisu}}
    \rput(6,0){\rnode{StateOut}{\umlStateOut}}
    \ttfamily\small
    \ncEXN[offsetA=-0.25,offsetB=-0.5,armA=0.5]{StateVisu}{StateVisu}
    \ncput*[npos=1.7]{zoomer}
    \ncSW[offsetB=-5]{->}{StateIn}{StateAnu}\naput[npos=1.3]{NewGraphAsked}
    \ncEN{->}{StateOutAnu}{StateVisu}\nbput[npos=0.9]{/Sauvegarder}
    \ncline{->}{StateVisu}{StateOut}\ncES[offsetA=3]{->}{StateAnu}{StateOut}
    \naput[npos=0.99]{\umlStack[umlAlign=l]{\ Annuler\\\ /DemanderConfirmation}}
  \end{pspicture}%
}
```

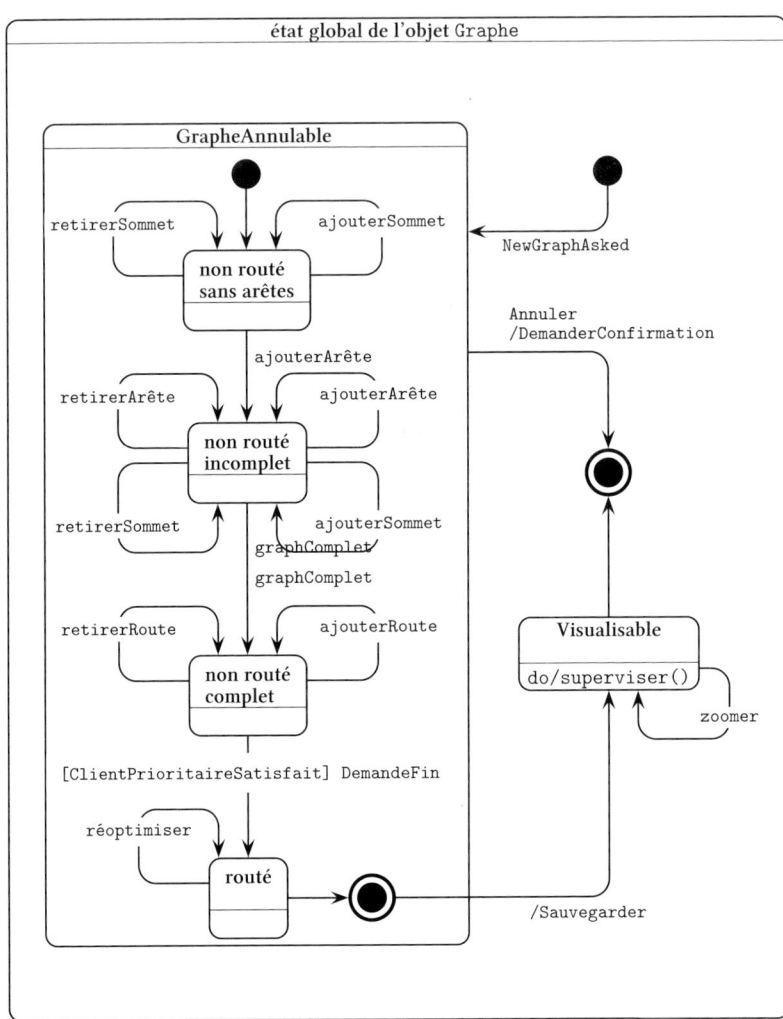

32.2 uml

The uml package by Ellef Fange Gjelstad is not compatible with pst-uml (though it does use some of the same command names). It offers a far more comprehensive set of commands and options – and is therefore somewhat more difficult to use than pst-uml. uml tries to offer an object-oriented interface. The corresponding "inheritance mechanisms" are shown in the following figure, which also provides a first overview of the use of the commands. Each box corresponds to a LaTeX command, here \umlDrawable or \umlElement. Each attribute corresponds to a LaTeX variable (\umlReference) or is a reference itself.

32.2 uml

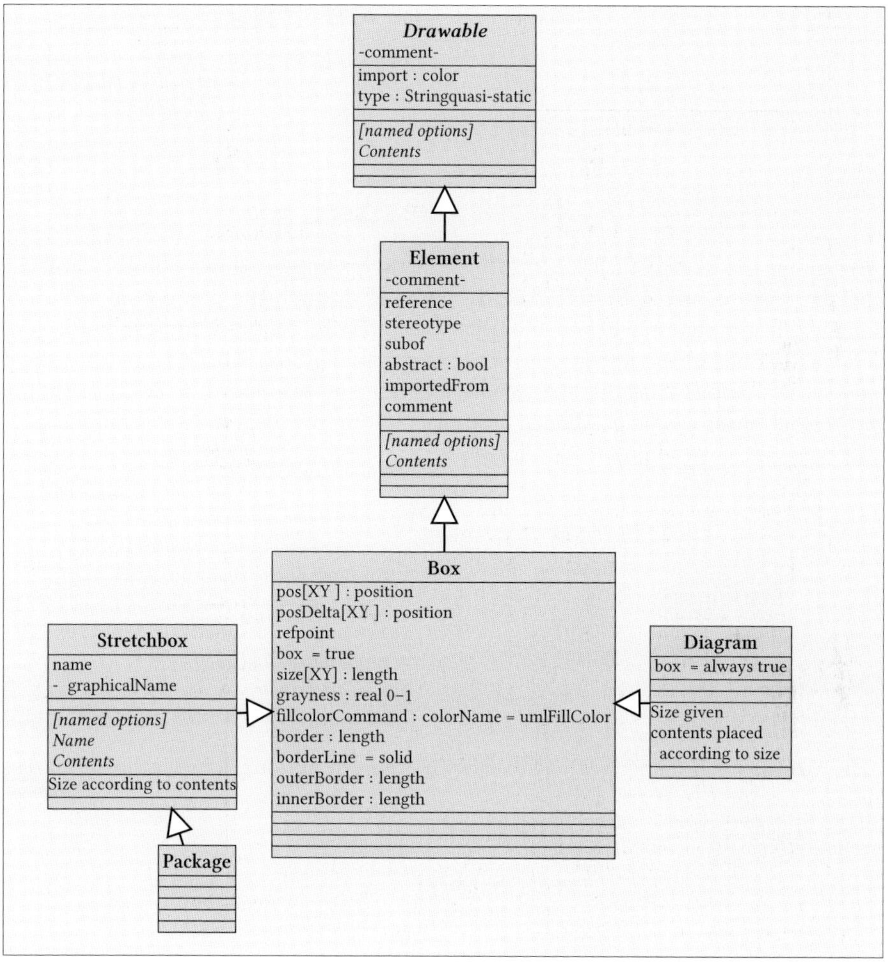

This section's description of uml doesn't follow the object-oriented methodology, but a rather more practical one. It starts with the \umlDiagram command, which takes the place of the pspicture environment and reserves the necessary space within the document.

\umlDiagram [settings] {content}

\umlDiagram is nothing but a \umlBox and thus also inherits all of the options (summarized in Table 32.4 on the next page). You can put anything in the content of the command.

```
\usepackage{uml}

\umlDiagram{content}\\
\umlDiagram[sizeX=3cm,
    sizeY=1cm]{\Large content}
```

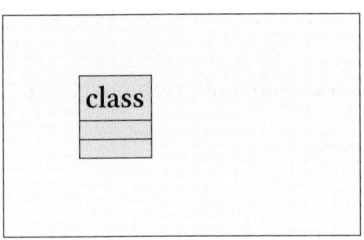

```
\usepackage{uml}

\umlDiagram[sizeX=5cm,
    sizeY=3cm]{\umlClass[refpoint=bl,
    pos={3,3}]{class}{}{}}
```

Assigning the diagram a label (ref=*Dia* in the example) allows you to place objects at specific positions later, by referring to the label through the pos option within other commands. In the example below, the first class refers to the position pos=\umlTop{*Dia*}, which corresponds to the upper edge of the surrounding box. At the same time, the class name becomes another label that the second class can refer to – pos=\umlBottomSep{*class1*}. Thus all other boxes can be positioned arbitrarily within the diagram environment.

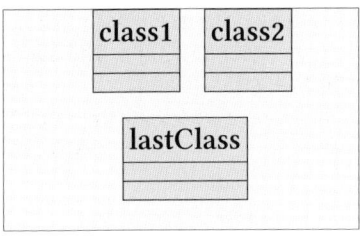

```
\usepackage{uml}

\umlDiagram[ref=Dia,sizeX=4cm,
    sizeY=2cm,innerBorder=5mm]{}
\umlClass[pos=\umlTop{Dia},
    refpoint=rt]{class1}{}{}
\umlClass[pos=\umlRightSep{class1},
    refpoint=lC]{class2}{}{}
\umlClass[pos=\umlBottomSep{class2},
    refpoint=rt]{lastClass}{}{}
```

The \umlBox command creates boxes with different options, which are summarized in Table 32.4.

\umlBox [*settings*] {*content*}
\umlStretchBox [*settings*] {*name*}{*content*}

Table 32.4: Summary of the box options

name	default	description
pos	(*0,0*)	puts the position, usually specified through posX and posY; node and class names are also possible
posX	0	horizontal position
posY	0	vertical position
posDelta	(*0,0*)	relative translation
posDeltaX	0	relative horizontal translation
posDeltaY	0	relative vertical translation
refpoint		reference point – l, r, t, b, or B, and meaningful combinations
grayness	1	background of the box
border	0.4pt	line width of the border

continued...

... continued

name	default	description
borderLine	solid	line style of the border; all PSTricks options are valid (cf. Section 4.1.3 on page 45)
innerBorder	0pt	width of the inner border of the box
sizeX		width of the box
sizeY		height of the box

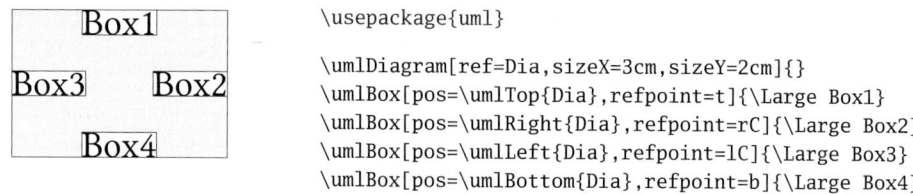

```
\usepackage{uml}

\umlDiagram[ref=Dia,sizeX=3cm,sizeY=2cm]{}
\umlBox[pos=\umlTop{Dia},refpoint=t]{\Large Box1}
\umlBox[pos=\umlRight{Dia},refpoint=rC]{\Large Box2}
\umlBox[pos=\umlLeft{Dia},refpoint=lC]{\Large Box3}
\umlBox[pos=\umlBottom{Dia},refpoint=b]{\Large Box4}
```

\umlStretchBox is a special case of the "normal" box: it adjusts its size according to its content, and can be labelled with a name that can be referenced at the same time. The name must adhere to the conventions of node names (cf. Section 16.1 on page 226).

\umlClassifier is in fact a \umlStretchBox, and can be an instance in the object-oriented language. Furthermore, \umlClassifier is a superclass of \umlClass (discussed below) and is usually separated into *compartments*.

\umlCompartment [settings] {content}
\umlCompartmentline [settings] {content}

name
line 1
line 2
compartment line

```
\usepackage{uml}

\umlClassifier[box=]{name}{%
    \umlCompartment{line 1\\}
    \umlCompartment{line 2\\}
    \umlCompartment{%
        \umlCompartmentline{compartment line}}}
```

The \umlClass command specifies a general class. \umlMethod and \umlAttribute are used inside the arguments for \umlClass. The syntax for the three commands is:

\umlClass [settings] {name}{attributes}{methods}
\umlMethod [settings] {name}{arguments}
\umlAttribute [settings] {name}
\umlArgument [settings] {name}

The following example shows the use of these commands.

```
\usepackage{uml}
\umlClass[reference=AmericanMan,stereotype=Man,importedFrom=America,
    comment=A man from America]{American Man}
    {\umlAttribute[visibility=\#,type=State]{State}
```

```
\umlAttribute[visibility=\#,default=MacDow]{Favourite burger}}
{\umlMethod[visibility=]{Watch TV}{}
\umlMethod[visibility=-,returntype=int]{Vote}{Party party}}
```

«Man»
American Man
From: America
A man from America
State : State
Favourite burger = MacDow
Watch TV()
- Vote(Party party) : int

The `\umlSchema` command is just makes creating classes easier – it doesn't correspond to a particular UML element.

`\umlSchema` [settings] {*name*}{*attributes*}{*methods*}{*arguments*}{*constraints*}{*structure*}

Apart from the optional settings parameter, there are six mandatory ones, though these can be left empty and are then specified in the usual TEX notation. The following example shows what is possible.

Stack
- firstNode : *type* = null
+ push(*type* x)
+ pop() : *type*
type : Metaclass
S:Stack = S.push(x).pop()

Node
data : *type*

```
\usepackage{uml}

\umlSchema[box=]{Stack}{ %attributes
  \umlAttribute[visibility=-,type=\emph{type},
              default=null,]{firstNode}
}{\umlMethod[visibility]{push}{\emph{type} x}% Methods
  \umlMethod[visibility,type=\emph{type}]{pop}{}
}{\umlArgument[type=Metaclass]{type}% Arguments
}{\umlCompartmentline{S:Stack = S.push(x).pop()}% Constraints
}{\umlDiagram[innerBorder=2mm,sizeX=11em,% Structure
     sizeY=5em,ref=StackDiagram,outerBorder=2mm]{%
     \umlClass[pos={.5,.5}, ref=stackNode]{Node}{
       \umlAttribute[visibility=\#,type=\emph{type}]{data}}{}
     \umlRelation[angleA=20,angleB=-20,armA=1em,
                 armB=1em]{stackNode}{stackNode}{%
       \umlLabelA[height=-1ex,fraction=1.5]{stackNode}{1}
       \umlLabelB[height=-5ex,fraction=1.5]{stackNode}{1}}
   }% End of diagram
}% End of Structure/Stack
```

Finally, we should mention the connections. They are referred to either with `\umlRelation` for pure lines with the usual PSTricks styles or with other special commands for connections in the UML sense with special symbols.

`\umlRelation` [settings] {*nodeA*}{*nodeB*}{*label*}

There are several options and special commands for placing labels, which are fully explained in the documentation of the package.

```
\usepackage{uml}
\umlDiagram[box=,sizeX=5cm,sizeY=5cm,ref=relation]{%
  \umlClass[pos=\umlBottomLeft{relation},posDelta={1,1},refpoint=bl,reference=A]{Class A}{}{}
  \umlClass[pos=\umlTopRight{relation},posDelta={-1,-1},refpoint=tr,reference=B]{Class B}{}{}
  \umlRelation{A}{B}{\umlLabelA{AB}{*}\umlLabelB{AB}{1}}
  \umlLabel[fraction=0.5,offset=0]{AB}{centre}
  \umlSubclass[ref=ABsub,angleA=0,armA=5,armAngleA=0,angleB=300,nodesep=1ex]{A}{B}
  \umlComposition[%
    reference=ABComp, % mark
    angleA=120,       % start at A
    arm=3,            % middle line
    armAngleA=80,     % angle of the arm A
    angleB=180,       % start at B
    armAngleB=190     % angle of the arm B
  ]{A}{B} % upper line
  \umlNavigabilityA{ABComp}}% arrow at A
```

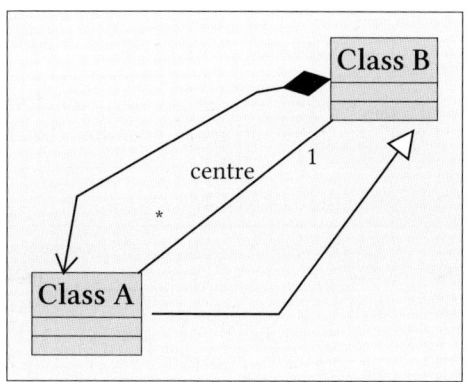

The other special connection commands differ syntax-wise only in that they are missing the last argument of \umlRelation. These commands are:

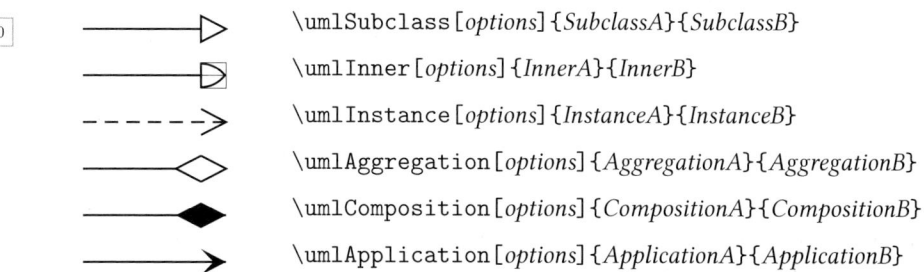

The uml package also defines additional types of connections (relations of relations), which are fully explained in the documentation of the package.

The \umlPackage command doesn't correspond to any particular element in UML notation – it just improves the readability for complex UML diagrams. \umlPackage is formally a \umlBox and therefore inherits all its properties.

32 UML diagrams

`\umlPackage` [settings] {name}{content}

```
\usepackage{uml}
\umlPackage[box=,subof=subof,stereotype=stereo,importedFrom=importedFrom,
    comment=comment]{Package}{%
  \umlDiagram[sizeX=7cm,sizeY=4cm,box=,ref=pack]{%
    \umlClass[pos=\umlBottomLeft{pack},posDelta={2ex,2ex},refpoint=bl]{Book}{}{}
    \umlClass[pos=\umlTopLeft{pack},posDelta={2ex,-2ex},refpoint=tl]{House}{}{}
    \umlClass[pos=\umlTopRight{pack},posDelta={-2ex,-2ex},refpoint=tr]{Person}{}{}
    \umlClass[pos=\umlBottomRight{pack},posDelta={-2ex,2ex},refpoint=br]{Author}{}{}
    \umlAssociation{Book}{House}   \umlLabelB[refpoint=l]{BookHouse}{is in}
    \umlAssociation{Book}{Person}\umlLabelA{BookPerson}{reads}
    \umlSubclass{Author}{Person}   \umlAssociation{Book}{Author}
    \umlLabelA[height=.5ex,refpoint=lb]{BookAuthor}{written}
    \umlAssociation{House}{Person}\umlLabelA{HousePerson}{lives in}
  }% end of \umlDiagram
}% end of \umlPackage
```

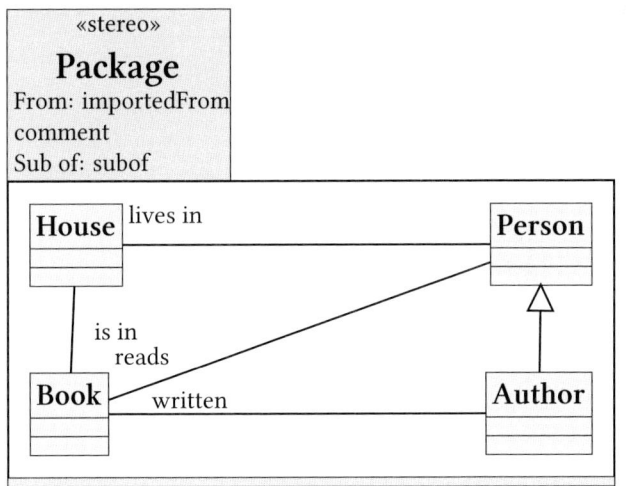

Chapter 33

Further PSTricks packages

33.1 Linguistics 659
33.2 Mathematics. 666
33.3 Natural sciences 683
33.4 Information technology. 724
33.5 Miscellaneous 731
33.6 `multido` 738

This chapter provides brief introductions to packages that have not yet been addressed, grouped by theme; you can find more information in the documentation of the respective packages. Efforts to describe all the packages available for PSTricks (or related to it) is beyond the scope of this book: there is a more or less complete compilation at the official PSTricks site http://PSTricks.tug.org. This page also lists where you can find the packages as not all of them are available at CTAN yet.

33.1 Linguistics

This section looks at several packages for drawing trees: `rrgtrees`, `pst-asr`, `pst-jtree`, and `pst-qtree`. The linguistics in these packages frequently uses symbolic figures that are well suited for PSTricks. A general overview of the possibilities can be found in [71].

33.1.1 rrgtrees – linguistic trees

The `rrgtrees` package by D. J. Gardner provides support for role and reference grammar for human language. It doesn't have a separate TeX version so you can only use it with LaTeX. It requires the standard packages `pst-node` and `pst-tree`.

33 Further PSTricks packages

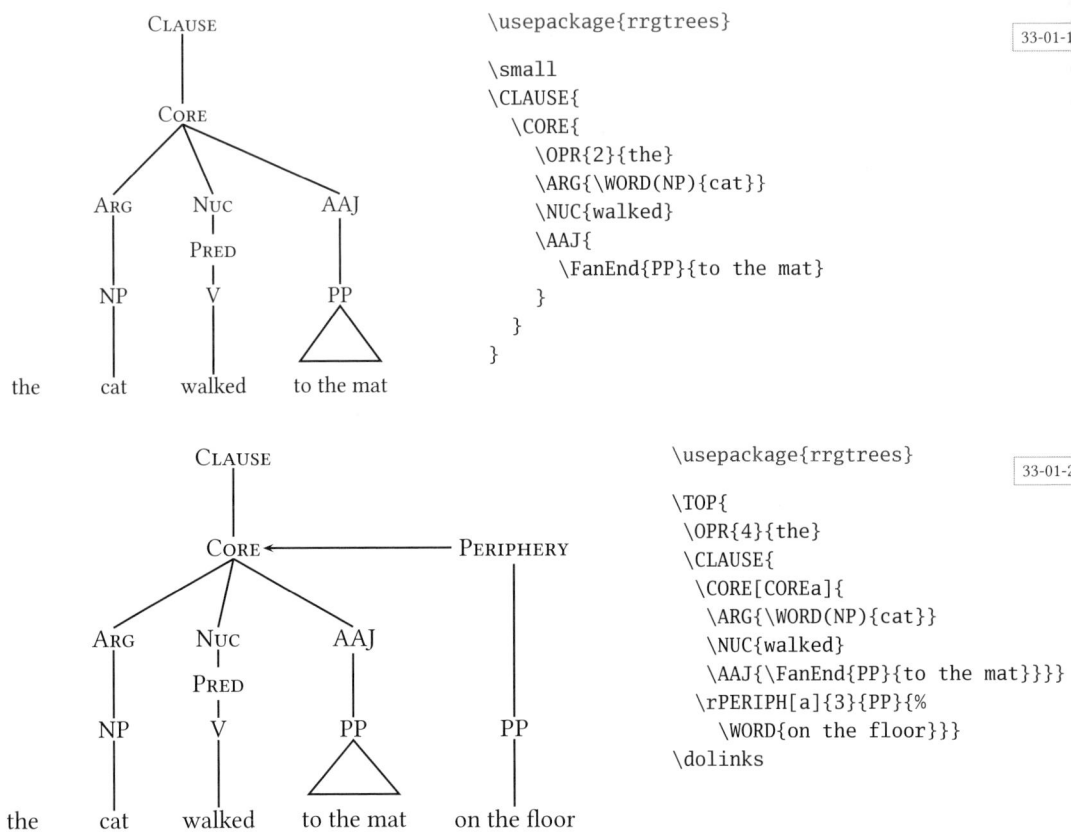

Table 33.2: Summary of the line commands

syntax	description
\CMPL[*name*]{*text*}	
	also \rCMPL; connection to object (default CLAUSE) with right-angled arrow
\LCMPL[*name*]{*length*}{*num*}{*text*}	
	also \RCMPL; connection to object (default CLAUSE) with CMPL-centred length from the target
\lPERIPH[*Extn*]{*num*}{*word*}{*tree*}	
	also \rPERIPH; connection to object COREExtn with right-angled arrow
\LPERIPH[*Extn*]{*length*}{*num*}{*word*}{*tree*}	
	also \RPERIPH; connection to object COREExtn with Periphery-centred length from the target
\lLINK[*extra*]{*name*}{*name*}{*word*}	
	also \rLINK; connection to object with right-angled arrow
\LLINK[*extra*]{*length*}{*name*}{*name*}{*word*}	
	also \RLINK; connects two objects with centred length from the target

Table 33.1: Summary of the tree commands

syntax	description
\TOP{*tree*}	defines a logical tree of dimension zero without drawing the root
\SENTENCE[*name*]{*tree*}	new structural level
\CLAUSE[*name*]{*tree*}	new structural level
\CORE[*name*]{*tree*}	new structural level
\ARG[*name*]{*tree*}	new structural level
\AAJ[*name*]{*tree*}	new structural level
\PP[*name*]{*tree*}	new structural level
\NP[*name*]{*tree*}	new structural level
\NCORE[*name*]{*tree*}	new structural level
\NNUC[*name*]{*tree*}	new structural level
\OPR[*name*]{*num*}{*text*}	inserts *num* levels below the current node
\FanEnd[*name*]{*num*}{*word*}{*text*}	triangle/fan level (without analysis), apex at the word argument
\End[*name*]{*text*}{*tree*}	simpler version of \WORD (obsolete)
\WORD[*name*](*word*){*text*}{*tree*}	creates one or two new levels below the current node
\NUC[*word*]{*text*}{*tree*}	distinguished nucleus
\OP[*name*]{*word*}{*tree*}	projection plane for operator

```
\usepackage{rrgtrees}
\psset{treesep=2ex}
\TOP{
\OPR[DEFa]{5}{the}
\CLAUSE{
  \CORE{
    \CORE[COREa]{
      \ARG{
        \NP{
          \WORD{cat}{
            \OP{N}{\OP{\Nuc\subN}{\OP{\Core\subN}{\OP[cat]{\np}
    }}}}}}
      \LINK{DEFa}{cat}{DEF}
      \OPR[might]{2}{\pnode{IF}might}
      \OPR[not]{2}{not}
      \NUC{forget}{\OP{V}{\OP{\Nuc}{\OP[forgetcore]{\Core}%
    }}}}
    \CMPL[COREb]{3}{to}
    \CORE[COREb]{
      \NUC{eat}{\OP{V}{\OP{\Nuc}{\OP[eatcore]{\Core}}}}
      \OPR[DEFb]{2}{the}
      \ARG{
        \NP{
          \WORD{rat}{
```

33 Further PSTricks packages

```
            \OP{N}{\OP{\Nuc\subN}{\OP{\Core\subN}{\OP[rat]{\np}
          }}}}
          \LINK{DEFb}{rat}{DEF}
}}}}}
\rPERIPH{4}{ADV}{\WORD{tomorrow}} }
\OPJoin{forgetcore}{eatcore}{\OP{\Core}{\OP[a]{\Clause}{%
  \OP[b]{\Clause}{\OP[c]{\Clause}{\OP[d]{\Clause}}}}}
\LINK{might}{b}{MOD}    \LINK{not}{a}{NEG}
\LLINK{8em}{IF}{d}{IF} \LINK{IF}{c}{TNS}
\dolinks
```

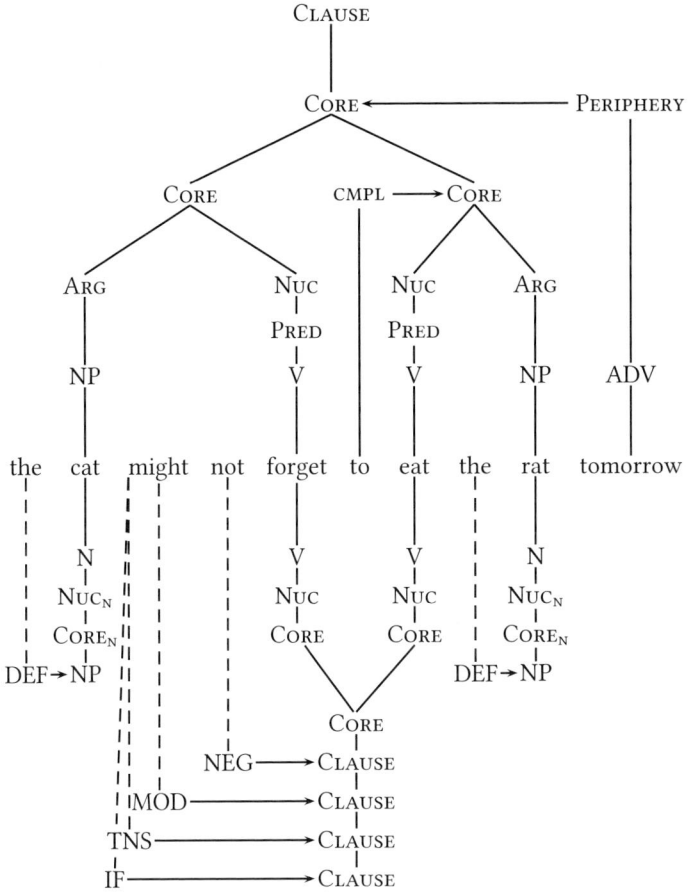

33.1.2 pst-asr – "autosegmental representations"

This package from John Frampton provides several commands for typesetting autosegmental representations that are used in linguistics.

```
\usepackage{pst-asr}
\newpsstyle{dotted}{linestyle=dotted,linewidth=1.2pt,dotsep=1.6pt}
\newpsstyle{crossing}{xed=true,xedtype=\xedcirc,style=dotted}
\newtier{softpal,ant,dist,nasal}   \tiershortcuts
\psset{xgap=1.5in,yunit=3em,ts=0 (Pg),sy=1 ([),ph=-1 (Cg),softpal=.3 (Sg),nasal=-.4 ([),
    ant=-2 ([),dist=-3 ([),tssym=Place,sysym=\textrm{[+cons]},everyph=Coronal}
\DefList{\softpalA{2.5},\antoffset{-.22},\distoffset{.36}} \quad \asr \1{}\1{}\1{}|
\@(\softpalA,softpal){Soft Palate} \-(2,sy) % softpal features
\@(\softpalA,nasal){\textrm{[+nas]}}    \-(\softpalA,softpal) % ant features
\@(\antoffset,ant){\textrm{[-ant]}} \-(0,ph) \-[style=crossing](2,ph)
\@[1](\antoffset,ant){\textrm{[$\alpha$ ant]}} \-(1,ph)
\@[2](\antoffset,ant){\textrm{[-ant]}} \-(2,ph) % dist features
\@(\distoffset,dist){\textrm{[-dist]}} \-(0,ph) \-[style=crossing](2,ph)
\@[1](\distoffset,dist){\textrm{[$\beta$ dist]}} \-(1,ph)
\@[2](\distoffset,dist){\textrm{[+dist]}}  \-(2,ph)
|\endasr
```

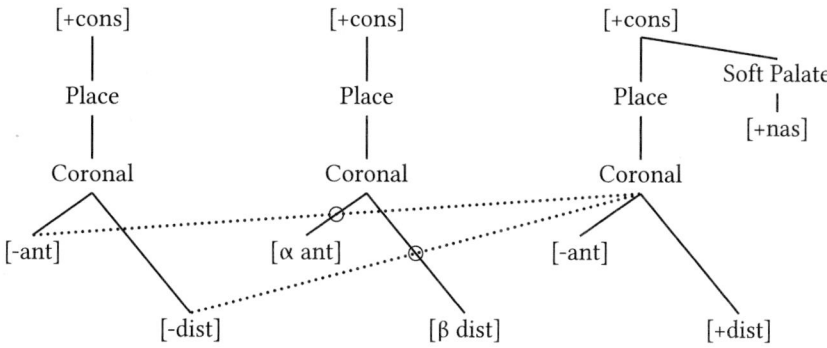

33.1.3 pst-jtree – linguistic trees

The pst-jtree package is, like the previous one, by John Frampton and is a successor to pst-jftree. It provides more general support for linguistic trees, but is pure TeX. LaTeX users can load it, but it can appear quite difficult to use.

```
\usepackage{pst-jtree}
\jtree[xunit=5em,yunit=2em]
\! = {IP}
   <tri>{\triline{sono stati\hfil}}  ^<tri>[triratio=.95]{FP}
   :{F$_{\rlap{$\scriptstyle\rm [+strong]$}}$}!a {Voice$_{\rlap{\scriptsize Pass}}$}
   :{Voice\rlap{$_{\rm Pass}$}}@A2   {$\rm Agr_OP$}
   :{DP}!b   {${\rm Agr_O}'$}
   :[scaleby=.8 1]{$\rm Agr_O$}@A3   [scaleby=.8 1]{VP}
   <tri>[scaleby=.4 .7]{\rnode{A5}{$t_i$}\hskip1ex \rnode{A6}{$t_m$}}.
\!a = <shortvert>{arrestati$_i$}@A1 .  \!b = <shortvert>{alcuni uomini$_m$}@A4 .
```

```
\psset{arrows=->}\nccurve[angleA=225,angleB=-45]{A2}{A1}
\nccurve[angleA=200,angleB=-90,ncurv=1.5]{A3}{A2}\nccurve[angleA=-130,
   angleB=-70]{A5}{A3} \nccurve[angleA=-130,angleB=-70,linestyle=dashed]{A6}{A4}
\endjtree
```

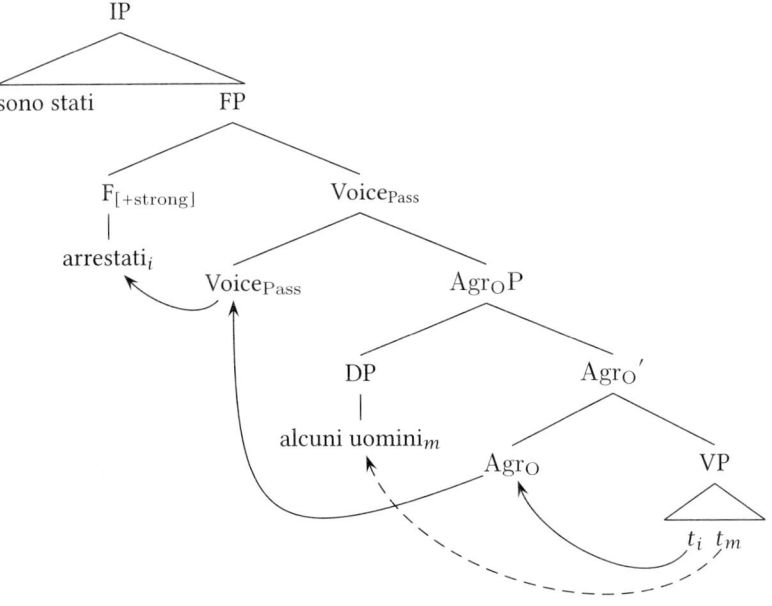

33.1.4 pst-qtree – interface for pst-tree

To make using the standard pst-tree package simpler, David Chiang created a simple interface that utilizes the same syntax for the commands as the qtree package (http://www.ling.upenn.edu/advice/latex/qtree/). Nevertheless its use is not significantly different from the packages previously described.

```
\usepackage{pst-qtree}
\newcommand{\1}{\ensuremath{'}}
\Tree
   [.TP [.NP \rnode{subj1}subj$_i$ ] [.T\1   [.T T+v$_n$+\rnode{V}V$_j$+Apl$_k$ ]
     [.{\it v}P \rnode{io}{ }IO$_l$ [.{\it v}\1 \rnode{subj2}t$_i$
     [.AplP \rnode{v1}t$_n$ [.Apl\1 \rnode{do}DO$_m$ [.{\it v}\1   \rnode{io1}t$_l$
        [.Apl\1 \rnode{apl1}t$_k$ [.VP [.V \rnode{V1}t$_j$ ]\rnode{do1}t$_m$ ] ] ] ] ] ] ]
\psset{linewidth=0.3pt,arrowsize=4pt,angleA=180,angleB=-90}
\nccurve{->}{subj2}{subj1}\nccurve{->}{do1}{do}
\nccurve[linestyle=dashed]{->}{io1}{io}
\nccurve{->}{V1}{apl1}\nccurve{->}{apl1}{v1}\nccurve{->}{v1}{V}
```

33.1 Linguistics

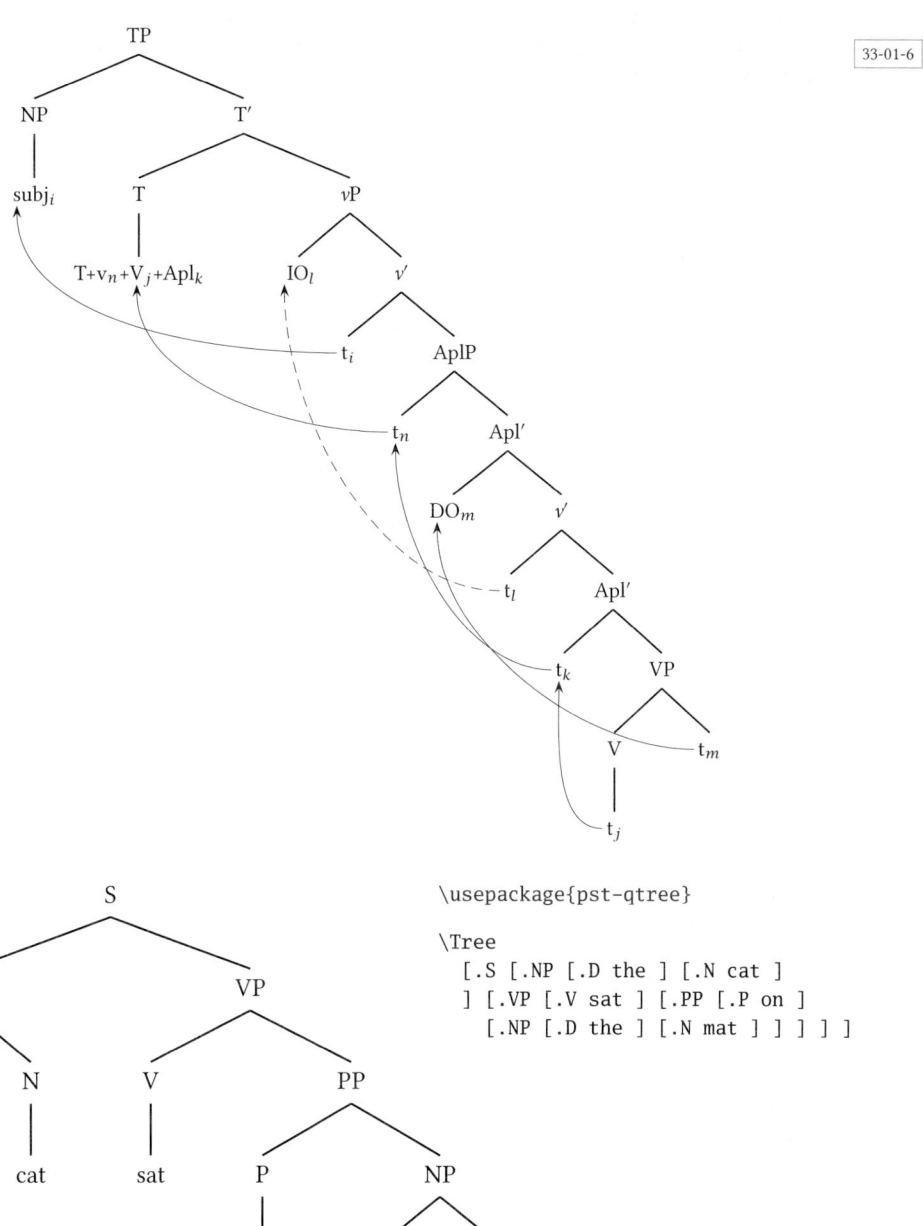

```
\usepackage{pst-qtree}

\Tree
  [.S [.NP [.D the ] [.N cat ]
  ] [.VP [.V sat ] [.PP [.P on ]
  [.NP [.D the ] [.N mat ] ] ] ] ]
```

33.2 Mathematics

This section looks at `infix-RPN` for transforming input into Reverse Polish Notation, `pst-fractal` for drawing fractals, `pst-poly` for drawing polygons, `pst-coxeterp` and `pst-coxcoor` for drawing polytopes, and `makeplot` for plotting data sets.

33.2.1 infix-RPN – "infix–postfix;' transformation

PSTricks is based entirely on PostScript; as we have discussed earlier, all input passed from TeX to PostScript has to be entered in postfix mode (Reverse Polish Notation). If you are unfamiliar with this notation, you can use the `infix-RPN` package by Jean-Côme Charpentier and Christophe Jorssen to transform the infix notation to a PostScript-compatible postfix notation. Don't forget that when your input is an argument of a plot command, the `algebraic` option (cf. Section 15.3.3 on page 207) from the `pstricks-add` package provides the same functionality as `infix-RPN`.

```
\infixtoRPN{infix code}
\RPN
\DeclareNewPSOperator{name}
```

The `\infixtoRPN` command saves the result in the `\RPN` command, which you can then use elsewhere.

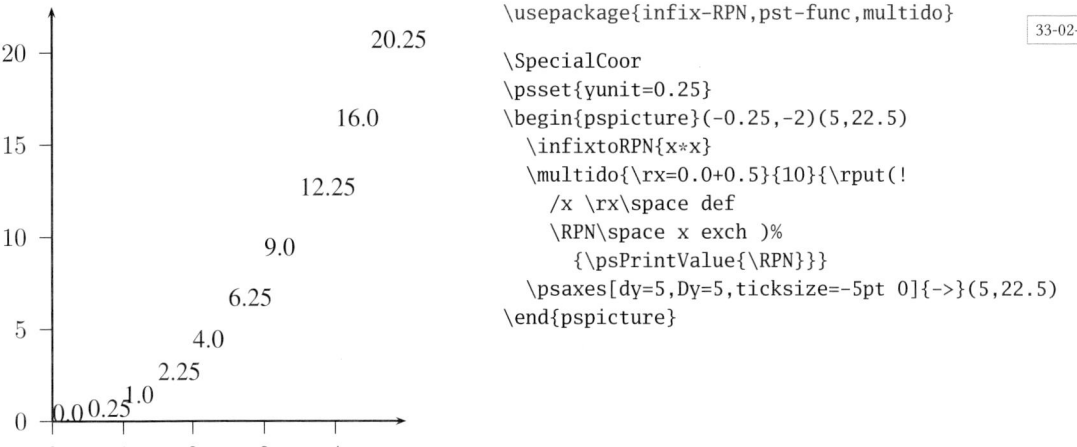

In the example above, `\rput` puts the y values of the normal parabola at the appropriate positions in the coordinate system. To achieve this, we call the `\psPrintValue` command (cf. Section 28.2.7 on page 531), which calculates values before the output. `/x \rx\space def \RPN\space x exch` first defines the variable `\rx` from the `\multido` definition as x, as this is the variable name predefined by `\infixtoRPN{x*x}`. After that, `\RPN` inserts the command in postfix notation, here $x\ x\ mul$. Finally, the x value is pushed onto the stack again and swapped with the function value previously calculated such that the stack now contains the required $x\ y$ pair.

For functions that expect more than one parameter, you have to supply them separated by a comma, as shown here:

33.2 Mathematics

```
                x y atan                        \usepackage{infix-RPN}
                                                \infixtoRPN{atan(x,y)}\RPN
```

You can define additional functions for use with the package through the command \DeclareNewPSOperator. In the following example, the Div operator defined in pstricks.pro is made available:

```
                x y Div                         \usepackage{infix-RPN}
                                                \DeclareNewPSOperator{Div}
                                                \infixtoRPN{Div(x,y)}\RPN
```

The additional pst-infixplot package provides two more commands: \psPlot and \psParametricplot. They work similarly to the commands of pst-plot, but expect the functions to be given in algebraic notation (infix). As mentioned previously, you can also achieve the same result for plot commands through the algebraic option from the pstricks-add package (cf. Section 15.3.3 on page 207).

33.2.2 pst-fractal – fractal graphics

As PSTricks uses PostScript code, you can also create fractal images. However, they usually lead to very large PDF files, especially for images of the Julia or Mandelbrot set, as every pixel has to be saved with its colour value.

The list below shows the commands that are available; they are discussed in turn in the following sections.

\psSier [settings] $(x_0,y_0)(x_1,y_1)(x_2,y_2)$	\psSier [settings] $(x_0,y_0)\{base\}\{recursion\}$
\psfractal [settings] (x_0,y_0) (x_1,y_1)	\psPhyllotaxis [settings] (x,y)
\psFern [settings] (x,y)	\psKochflake [settings] (x,y)
\psAppolonius [settings] (x,y)	\psPTree [settings] (x,y)
\psFArrow [settings] (x,y) $\{fraction\}$	

Sierpinski triangle

The \psSier command uses one of two algorithms, depending on whether you give it three coordinates determining the corners of the triangle or one coordinate pair and the length of one side (in which case it forms an equilateral triangle). The command creates the figure inside a box of size zero so place it inside a pspicture environment to reserve the necessary space. The plotpoints option specifies the number of iterations; the default number is 200.

```
\usepackage{pst-fractal}
\begin{pspicture}(5,5)\psSier[plotpoints=1000](0,0)(2,5)(5,0)\end{pspicture}
\begin{pspicture}(5,5)
\psSier[linecolor=blue!70,fillcolor=red!40](0,0){5cm}{4}
\end{pspicture}
```

33 Further PSTricks packages

Julia and Mandelbrot sets

All arguments of the \psfractal command are optional. The default coordinates are (-1,-1) and (1,1). The type option chooses between a Julia or Mandelbrot set. The special parameters (including type) are summarized in Table 33.3.

Table 33.3: Summary of the parameters for \psfractal

name	description	type	default
type	output type	Julia|Mandel	Julia
baseColor	colour of the convergent area	colour	white
xWidth	physical width of the image	value unit	1cm
yWidth	physical height of the image	value unit	1cm
cx	real start value of the constant c	value	0
cy	imaginary start value of the constant c	value	0
dIter	step for the iteration	value	1
maxIter	maximum value at which an iteration decides whether a series converges	value	255
maxRadius	value at which an iteration is considered to be divergent	value	100

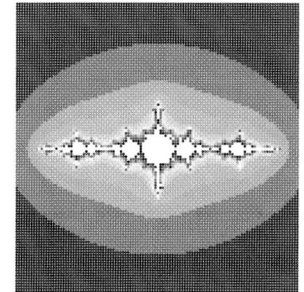

```
\usepackage{pst-fractal}

\psfractal\quad
\psfractal[xWidth=4cm,yWidth=4cm,
    baseColor=white,dIter=20,cx=-1.3](-2,-2)(2,2)
```

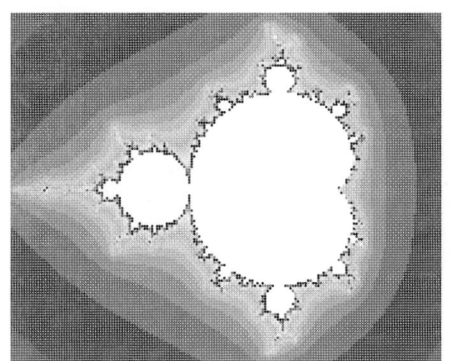

```
\usepackage{pst-fractal}

\psfractal[type=Mandel,xWidth=6cm,
    yWidth=4.8cm,baseColor=white,
    dIter=10](-2,-1.2)(1,1.2)
```

maxIter determines the maximum number of iterations, after which the loop is terminated. Internally, the value is multiplied by dIter so that the step size can be changed arbitrarily.

```
\usepackage{pst-fractal}
\psset{xWidth=5cm,yWidth=5cm}
\psfractal[maxIter=30,cx=-1.3,cy=0](-2,-2)(2,2)\quad
\psfractal[maxRadius=30,dIter=30,cx=-1.3,cy=0](-2,-2)(2,2)
```

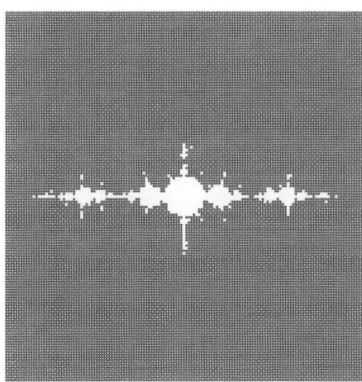 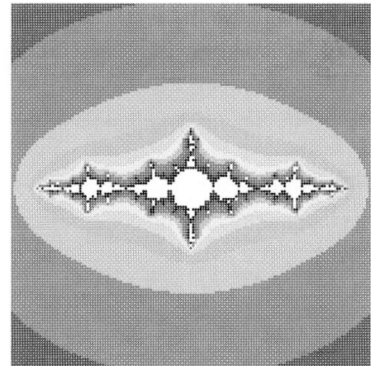

Phyllotaxis

Again all arguments of the \psPhyllotaxis command are optional. If the specification of the centre of the Phyllotaxis image is missing, (0,0) is assumed. Optional parameters are the angle (default 0) of the inner image, the maximum number of iterations maxIter (default 256), and the constant c (default 5).

```
\usepackage{pst-fractal}
\begin{pspicture}(-2.75,-2.75)(2.75,2.75)\psPhyllotaxis\end{pspicture}\quad
\begin{pspicture}(-2.75,-2.75)(2.75,2.75)\psPhyllotaxis[angle=99]\end{pspicture}
```

33 Further PSTricks packages

```
\usepackage{pst-fractal}
\begin{pspicture}(-3,-3)(3,3)\psPhyllotaxis[c=4,angle=111]\end{pspicture}\quad
\begin{pspicture}(-3,-3)(3,3)\psPhyllotaxis[c=6,angle=111,maxIter=100]\end{pspicture}
```

Fern

Again all arguments of the \psFern command are optional. If no centre is specified, (0,0) is assumed. Optional parameters are the scale factor (default value of 10) and the maximum number of iterations maxIter.

```
\usepackage{pst-fractal}
\begin{pspicture}(-1,0)(1,4)\psFern\end{pspicture} \quad
\begin{pspicture}(-3,0)(3,11)\psFern[scale=15,maxIter=100000]\end{pspicture}
```

33.2 Mathematics

Koch curve

Again all arguments of the \psKochflake command are optional. If the starting point is not specified, (0,0) is assumed, which corresponds to the lower left point of the Koch curve. We have highlighted this point with a dot in the following figures – the dot doesn't appear automatically. The special optional parameters scale, maxIter, and angle are available. angle determines the starting angle of the Koch curve.

```
\usepackage{pst-fractal}

\begin{pspicture}[showgrid=true]%
    (-2.4,-0.4)(5,5)
    \psKochflake[scale=10]
    \psdot[linecolor=red,dotstyle=*](0,0)
\end{pspicture}
```

```
\usepackage{pst-fractal}
\begin{pspicture}(-0.4,-0.4)(12,4)
  \psset{fillcolor=lime,fillstyle=solid}
  \multido{\iA=0+1,\iB=0+2}{6}{%
    \psKochflake[angle=-30,scale=3,maxIter=\iA](\iB,2.5)\psdot*(\iB,2.5)
    \psKochflake[scale=3,maxIter=\iA](\iB,0)\psdot*(\iB,0)}
\end{pspicture}
```

33 Further PSTricks packages

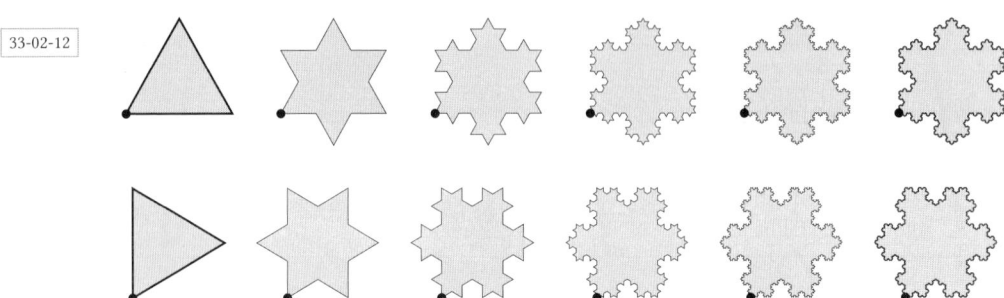

Apollonius circles

Note that the spelling of the \psAppolonius command is different to the spelling of Apollonius. The coordinates of the starting point are again optional, with a default of (0,0). The specific optional parameters are Radius and Color, defaulting to 5 cm and false respectively.

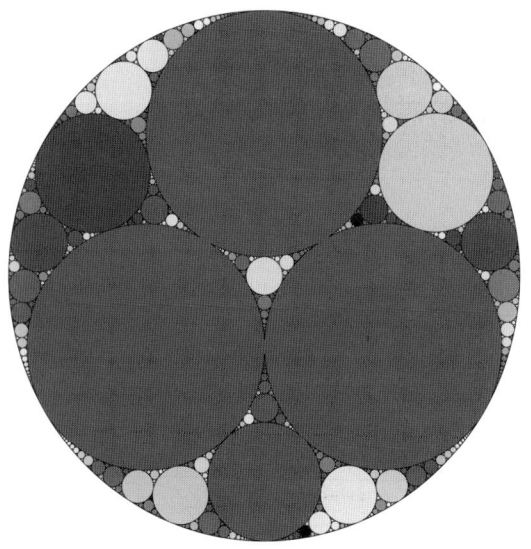

```
\usepackage{pst-fractal}

\begin{pspicture}(-5,-5)(5,5)
    \psAppolonius[Radius=4cm,Color]
\end{pspicture}
```

Trees

There are two different ways of creating fractal "trees": \psPTree and \psFArrow. \psFArrow requires the splitting ratio of the first and second lines. Both commands have an optional argument for the starting point, which defaults to (0,0) if no point is specified. This point is the centre of the lower line, as highlighted with a dot in the first example. The optional parameters listed in Table 33.4 on the next page are available.

Table 33.4: Summary of the parameters for \psPTree and \psFArrow

name	description	type	default
xWidth	width of the base (first line)	value unit	1cm
minWidth	minimum width of the last line	value unit	1pt
c	relative factor for unbalanced trees	0...1	0.5
Color	coloured lines	boolean	false

```
\usepackage{pst-fractal}

\begin{pspicture}(-3,0)(3,4)
  \psPTree\psdot*(0,0)
\end{pspicture}
```

```
\usepackage{pst-fractal}
\begin{pspicture}(-5,-1)(7,8)\psPTree[xWidth=1.75cm,Color=true,c=0.65]\end{pspicture}
```

33 Further PSTricks packages

```
\usepackage{pst-fractal}
\begin{pspicture}(-1,0)(1,3)\psFArrow{0.5}\end{pspicture}\quad
\begin{pspicture}(-2,0)(2,3)\psFArrow{0.6}\end{pspicture}\quad
\begin{pspicture*}(-3,0)(3,3.5)\psFArrow[linewidth=3pt]{0.65}\end{pspicture*}
```

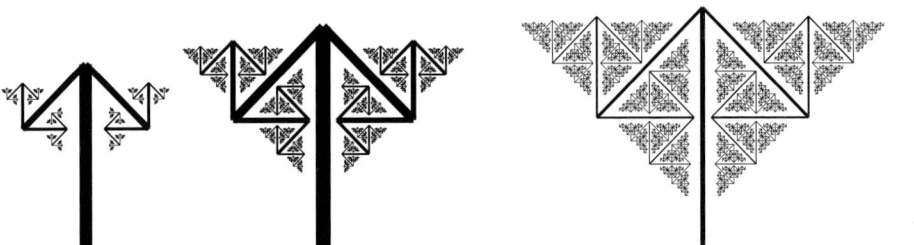

33.2.3 pst-poly – polygons

The pst-poly package by Denis Girou provides a single command to draw polygons or polygon-like geometric figures:

| \PstPolygon [settings] | \PstPolygon* [settings] |

In principle, \PstPolygon simply adds nodes to the corners so that they can be connected. Changing the order of the nodes and the type of connection produces many different geometric figures. The valid options are summarized in Table 33.5. The third and fourth rows of examples show the difference between the starred version, which fills the object with the current line colour, and filling through the fillstyle=solid option.

Table 33.5: Summary of the options available for pst-poly

name	type	default	description
PstPicture	boolean	true	whether the polygon is included in a pspicture environment
PolyRotation	angle	0	rotation angle
PolyNbSides	integer	5	number of corners
PolyOffset	integer	1	step between consecutive nodes; by default none are skipped
PolyIntermediatePoint	value	{}	position of the intermediate point for the connection to the next node, not used if empty
PolyCurves	boolean	false	connection as curve (true) or line (false)
PolyEpicycloid	boolean	false	epicycloid (true) or polygon (false)
PolyName	string	{}	name to achieve similar polygons with different node names

```
\usepackage{pst-poly,multido}
```

```
\multido{\i=3+2}{5}{\PstPolygon[PolyNbSides=\i]\quad}
```

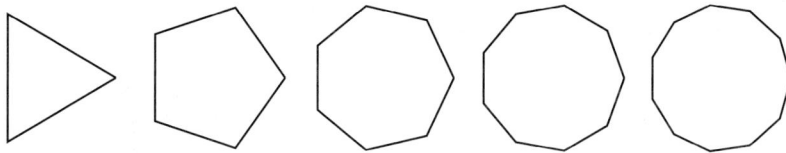

```
\usepackage{pst-poly,multido}
\multido{\i=3+2}{5}{\PstPolygon[PolyOffset=2,PolyNbSides=\i]\quad}
```

```
\usepackage{pst-poly,multido}
\multido{\i=3+2}{5}{\PstPolygon*[linecolor=cyan,PolyOffset=4,PolyNbSides=\i] }
```

```
\usepackage{pst-poly,multido}
\multido{\i=5+2}{5}{\PstPolygon[PolyOffset=7,PolyNbSides=\i,%
  fillcolor=yellow,fillstyle=solid]\quad}
```

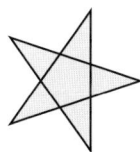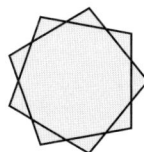

```
\usepackage{pst-poly,multido}
\multido{\i=1+2}{5}{\PstPolygon[PolyOffset=\i,PolyNbSides=5]\quad}
```

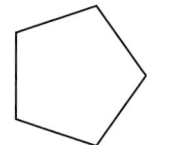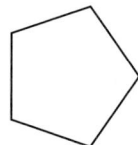

```
\usepackage{pst-poly,multido}
\multido{\i=5+1}{5}{\PstPolygon[PolyCurves,PolyIntermediatePoint=0.1,%
   PolyNbSides=\i]\quad}
```

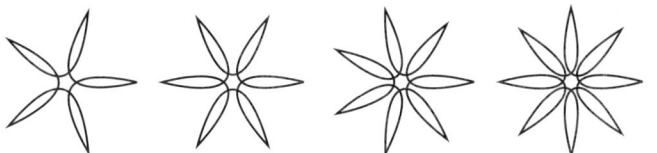

33-02-22

```
\usepackage{pst-poly,multido}
\multido{\i=5+1}{5}{\PstPolygon[PolyCurves,PolyIntermediatePoint=0.2,
   PolyOffset=2,PolyNbSides=\i]\quad}
```

33-02-23

```
\usepackage{pst-poly,multido}
\multido{\i=5+2}{5}{\PstPolygon[PolyCurves,PolyIntermediatePoint=0.15,
    PolyOffset=3,PolyNbSides=\i]\quad}
```

33-02-24

```
\usepackage{pst-poly,multido}
\multido{\n=-1.4+0.5}{5}{%
    \PstPolygon[PolyNbSides=5,PolyOffset=2,PolyIntermediatePoint=\n]\quad}
```

33-02-25

```
\usepackage{pst-poly,multido}
\multido{\n=-1.4+0.5}{5}{\PstPolygon[PolyNbSides=13,PolyOffset=2,%
   PolyIntermediatePoint=\n]\quad}
```

33.2 Mathematics

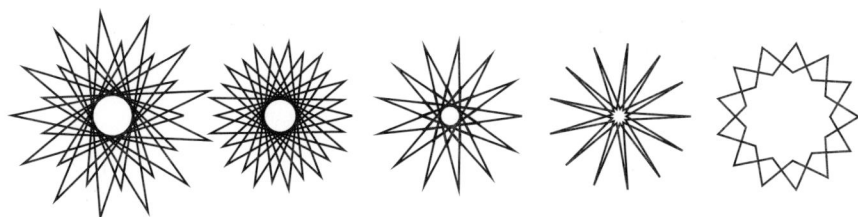

```
\usepackage{pst-poly,multido}
\multido{\n=-1.4+0.5}{5}{%
  \PstPolygon[PolyNbSides=21,PolyOffset=2,PolyIntermediatePoint=\n]\quad}
```

```
\usepackage{pst-poly,multido}
\psset{unit=1.4,linewidth=0.001,PolyNbSides=72,PolyEpicycloid}
% Epicycloid of factor 1 is a cardioid and of factor 2 is a nephroid
\multido{\i=2+1}{3}{\PstPolygon[PolyOffset=\i]\quad}
```

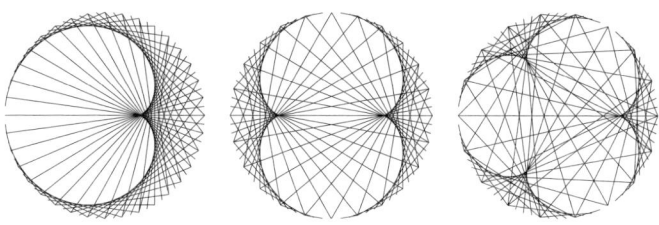

```
\usepackage{pst-poly,multido}
\psset{unit=1.5,linewidth=0.001,PolyNbSides=72,PolyEpicycloid}
\multido{\i=71+1}{3}{\PstPolygon[PolyOffset=\i]\quad}
```

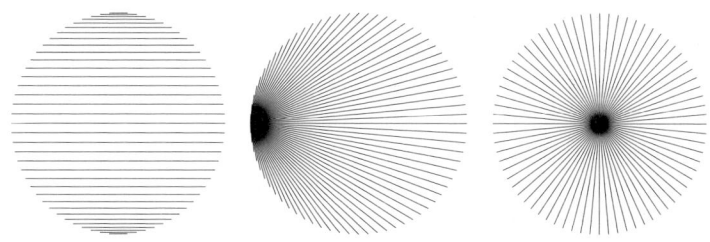

33 Further PSTricks packages

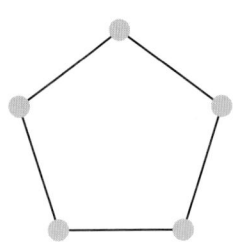

```
\usepackage{pst-poly}

\providecommand{\PstPolygonNode}{%
  \psdots[dotsize=0.2,linecolor=cyan](1;\INode)}
\PstPentagon[unit=1.5]
```

33-02-30

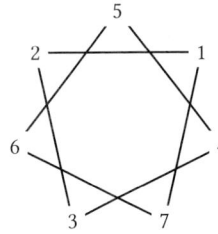

```
\usepackage{pst-poly}

\providecommand{\PstPolygonNode}{%
  \rput*{*0}(1;\INode){\small\the\multidocount}}
\PstHeptagon[unit=1.5,PolyOffset=2]
```

33-02-31

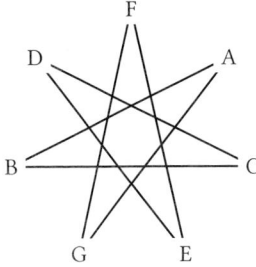

```
\usepackage{pst-poly}

\newcounter{Letter}
\providecommand{\PstPolygonNode}{%
  \setcounter{Letter}{\the\multidocount}%
  \rput*{*0}(1;\INode){\small\Alph{Letter}}}
\PstHeptagon[unit=1.75,PolyOffset=3]
```

33-02-32

```
\usepackage{pst-poly}

\providecommand{\PstPolygonNode}{%
  \SpecialCoor
  \degrees[3]
  \rput{0.5}(0.5;\INode){%
    \pspolygon*(0.5;0.5)(0.5;1.5)(0.5;2.5)}}
\PstTriangle
```

33-02-33

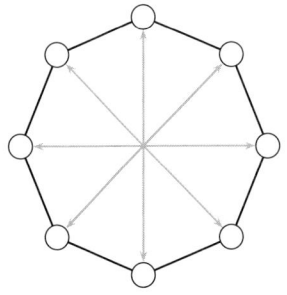

```
\usepackage{pst-poly}

\providecommand{\PstPolygonNode}{%
  \psdots[dotstyle=o,dotsize=0.2](1;\INode)
  \psline[linecolor=red]{->}(0.9;\INode)}
\PstPolygon[unit=1.75,PolyNbSides=8]
```

33-02-34

33.2 Mathematics

```
\usepackage{pst-poly}

\providecommand{\PstPolygonNode}{%
    \psline[linewidth=0.1mm,doubleline=true,
       linecolor=green]{<->}(0;0)(1;\INode)}
\PstHexagon[unit=1.5]
```

```
\usepackage{pst-poly}

\newbox{\Star}\savebox{\Star}{%
    \PstStarFive*[unit=0.15,linecolor=red]}
\providecommand{\PstPolygonNode}{%
    \rput{*0}(1;\INode){\usebox{\Star}}}
\PstNonagon\qquad
\PstDodecagon[linestyle=none]
```

```
\usepackage{pst-poly,multido}
\psset{PolyNbSides=4}
\multido{\nA=0+60}{7}{\pspolygonbox[PolyRotation=\nA,framesep=2mm,doubleline=true,
    linecolor=red,doublecolor=blue]{\magenta Text}}
```

```
\usepackage{pst-poly,multido}
\multido{\nA=3+1}{8}{\pspolygonbox[PolyNbSides=\nA,framesep=10pt,fillstyle=solid,
    fillcolor=cyan,linearc=0.2]{Text}}
```

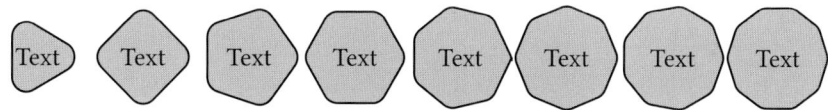

33.2.4 pst-coxeterp and pst-coxcoor – regular polytopes

These two packages were created by Jean-Gabriel Luque and Manuel Luque and are contained in the CTAN pst-cox package. [42] They provide commands for a library of regular polytopes that are based on the works of Harold S. M. Coxeter. The main difference between the packages is that pst-coxeterp draws polytopes based on optional parameters whereas pst-coxcoor recreates predefined ones listed in a library.

The pst-coxeterp package provides six commands:

33 Further PSTricks packages

```
\Polygon [settings]      \Simplex [settings]
\gammapn [settings]      \betapn [settings]
\gammaptwo [settings]    \betaptwo [settings]
```

The polygons are defined through the Q and 0 parameters, where the angle at the centre between the first two corners is $2\frac{P}{Q}\Pi$. The default values are 6 and 1 respectively. The special optional parameters (including P and Q) are summarized in Table 33.6.

Table 33.6: Summary of the options available for pst-coxeterp

name	type	default	description
drawedges	boolean	true	whether to draw edges
drawvertices	boolean	true	whether to draw vertices
drawcenters	boolean	true	whether to draw the centre points of the edges
P	value	6	first parameter (denominator) for the polygon
Q	value	1	second parameter (numerator) for the polygon
dimension	value	3	dimensions of the polytope
colorVertices	colour	green	colour of the corners
colorCenters	colour	red	colour of the centre points of the edges
styleVertices	symbol	o	symbol for the corners
styleCenters	symbol	*	symbol for the centre points of the edges
sizeVertices	value unit	0.05	size of the symbol for the corners
sizeCenters	value unit	0.05	size of the symbol for the centre points of the edges

```
\usepackage{pst-coxeterp}
\begin{pspicture}(-2,-2)(2,2)\Polygon[P=5,Q=2,drawcenters=false]\end{pspicture}
\begin{pspicture}(-2,-2)(2,2)\Simplex[drawvertices=false]\end{pspicture}
\begin{pspicture}(-2,-2)(2,2)\gammapn[unit=0.5,P=4,dimension=4,drawedges=false]
\end{pspicture}
```

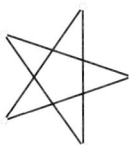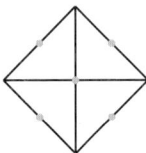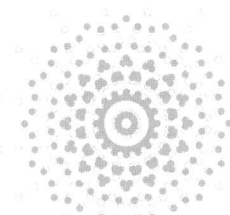

```
\usepackage{pst-coxeterp}
\begin{pspicture}(-2,-2)(2,2)\Polygon[P=5,Q=2]\end{pspicture}
\begin{pspicture}(-2,-2)(2,2)\Simplex\end{pspicture}
\begin{pspicture}(-2,-2)(2,2)\gammapn[unit=0.5,P=4,dimension=4]\end{pspicture}
```

 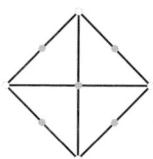 

```
\usepackage{pst-coxeterp}
\begin{pspicture}(-2,-2)(2,2)
\psset{unit=0.5cm,colorCenters=blue,styleCenters=pentagon,sizeCenters=0.2}
\gammapn[P=5,dimension=4]\end{pspicture} \begin{pspicture}(-2,-2)(2,2)
\psset{unit=0.5cm,colorCenters=magenta,sizeCenters=0.1,styleCenters=triangle}
\gammapn[P=5,dimension=4]\end{pspicture}\begin{pspicture}(-2,-2)(2,2)
\psset{unit=0.5cm,colorCenters=red,styleCenters=+,sizeCenters=0.2}
\gammapn[P=5,dimension=4]\end{pspicture}
```

The pst-coxcoor package is, in principle, a PostScript library of polytopes; they are saved in the prologue file pst-coxcoor.pro and you can call them within LaTeX through the \CoxeterCoordinates command.

\CoxeterCoordinates [settings]

The only new parameter is choice. In the current version, this may take integer values between 1 and 80 as the library contains exactly 80 different polytopes. choice=9 results in the following Hessian polytope with 27 corners, 72 sides, and 27 faces...

```
\usepackage{pst-coxcoor}
\begin{pspicture}(-4,-4)(4,4)
\psset{unit=1.5cm,linewidth=0.01mm}\CoxeterCoordinates[choice=9]
\end{pspicture}
```

33 Further PSTricks packages

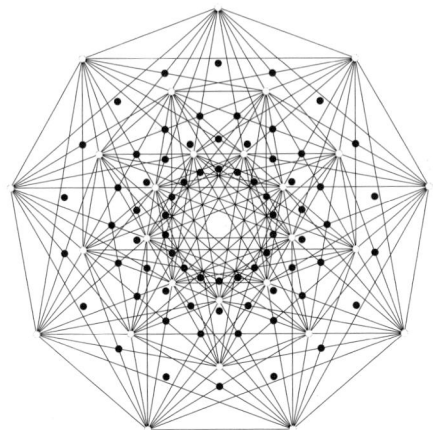

You can find the complete list of all polytopes in the documentation. [42] Here are a few examples:

$2\{3\}3$	$3\{3\}3$	$3\{3\}3$
choice = 1	choice = 2	choice = 3

$3\{\frac{5}{2}\}3$	$5\{\frac{5}{2}\}5$	$2\{\frac{5}{2}\}3$
choice = 37	choice = 38	choice = 39

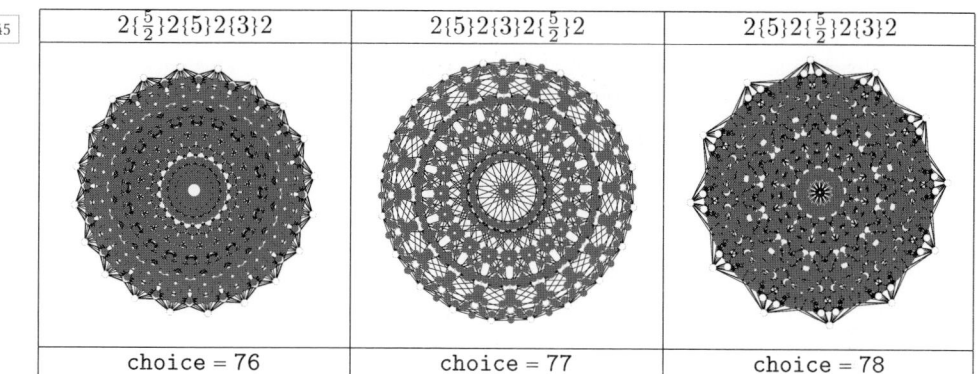

33.2.5 makeplot – plot data sets

The `makeplot` package by Jose-Emilio Vila-Forcen supports plotting data sets created by matlab and then exported (http://www.mathworks.com). The aim is to provide plot routines similar to matlab within PSTricks.

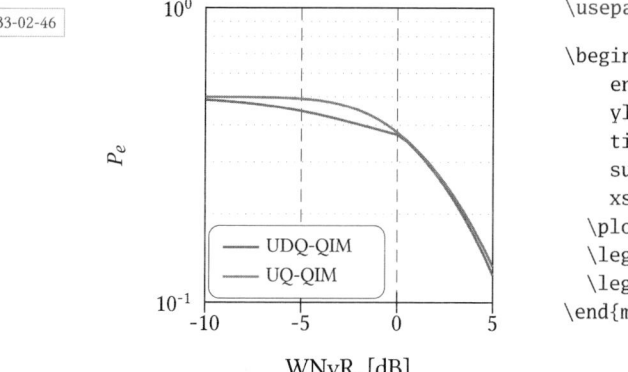

```
\usepackage[color]{makeplot}

\begin{makeplot}[startX=-10,endX=5,startY=-1,
    endY=0,Dx=5,width=40,heightFactor=1,
    ylogBase=10,logLines=y,subticks=10,
    ticklinestyle=dashed,mathLabel=false,
    subticklinestyle=dotted,
    xsubticks=1]{$P_e$}{{WNyR, [dB]}}
\plotFileA{data1.mat}\plotFileB{data2.mat}
\legendDL{24.5}{2} \legendAf{UDQ-QIM}
\legendBf{UQ-QIM}
\end{makeplot}
```

The exported data must conform to an x-y structure and be separated by spaces. Within matlab, this is done through `save <file>.dat values -ascii`. Note that `makeplot` requires the `pstricks-add` package to create the plot (cf. Section 30 on page 581).

33.3 Natural sciences

This section looks at `pst-lens` for creating optical effects, `pst-optic` for drawing optical systems, `pst-optexp` for drawing experimental optics, `pst-diffraction` for drawing diffraction patterns, `pst-magneticfield` for drawing magnetic field lines, `pst-osci` for drawing oscillograms, `pst-spectra` for drawing spectral lines, `pst-stru` for drawing load diagrams, and `pst-pad` for drawing adhesion and friction systems.

33 Further PSTricks packages

33.3.1 pst-lens – optical effects

Magnifying lens effects, provided by the `pst-lens` package by Denis Girou and Manuel Luque, are particularly well suited to highlight parts of text or graphics. This package defines two commands:

```
\PstLens [settings] (x,y) {object}      \PstLensShape{command}
```

If no coordinates are specified for the centre of the lens, $(0,0)$ is assumed. The possible parameters are summarized in Table 33.7.

The principle is always the same; first, the object (text or figure) is typeset as usual. It is advisable to align it at $(0,0)$ through the `lb` (left bottom) option. After that, you can overwrite the object with the lens effect.

Table 33.7: Summary of the options available for `pst-lens`

name	type	default	description
LensMagnification	value	1	magnification factor
LensSize	value unit	1	size of the lens
LensRotation	angle	0	rotation angle of the lens
LensHandle	boolean	true	with or without handle
LensHandleWidth	value unit	0.2	width of the lens handle
LensHandleHeight	value unit	2.5	length of the lens handle from the centre of the lens to the end of the handle (default refers to LensSize=1)
LensStyleHandle	style	LensStyleHandle	style of the lens handle
LensShadow	boolean	true	lens with or without shadow
LensStyleGlass	style	LensStyleGlass	style of the glass of the lens

The following examples all use the arbitrarily-defined `\Wishes` command to write the underlying text:

```
\usepackage{pst-lens}

\def\Wishes{{\rput[lb](0,0){%
    \Large\begin{minipage}{3cm}\centering
    \textbf{All the best,}\\\textbf{Jana},
    \\for the new year\\\Huge 2011!
    \end{minipage}}}}
\begin{pspicture}[showgrid=true](3,3.2)
    \Wishes
\end{pspicture}
```

```
\usepackage{pst-lens}
\begin{pspicture}(0,-1.5)(3,4)
    \Wishes\PstLens[LensMagnification=2](2,2){\Wishes}
\end{pspicture}\hfill
```

```
\begin{pspicture}(0,-1.5)(3,4)
  \Wishes\PstLens[LensMagnification=4](1,2.4){\Wishes}
\end{pspicture}\hfill
\begin{pspicture}(0,-1.5)(3.5,4)
  \Wishes\PstLens[LensMagnification=0.5](1,1){\Wishes}
  \PstLens[LensMagnification=-0.5](2.5,3){\Wishes}
\end{pspicture}
```

33-03-2

```
\usepackage{pst-lens}
\begin{pspicture}(0,-2)(3,3) \Wishes
  \PstLens[LensSize=2,LensRotation=55](1,1){\Wishes}
  \PstLens[LensSize=0.5](3,3){\Wishes}
\end{pspicture}
```

33-03-3

33 Further PSTricks packages

```
\usepackage{pst-lens}

\begin{pspicture}(0,-1)(3,3.8)
  \Wishes\PstLens[%
    LensRotation=80]{\Wishes}
  \PstLens[LensRotation=-108.5](2,2){%
    \Wishes}
\end{pspicture} %
\begin{pspicture}(3,3.5)
  \Wishes \PstLens[%
    LensHandle=false](2,2){\Wishes}
\end{pspicture}
```

33-03-4

```
\usepackage{pst-lens}

\begin{pspicture}(0,-2.5)(3,3.5)
  \Wishes
  \PstLens[LensHandleWidth=0.1]%
    {\Wishes}
  \PstLens[LensHandleWidth=4mm]%
    (2,2){\Wishes}
\end{pspicture} %
\begin{pspicture}(0,-2)(3,3.5)
  \Wishes
  \PstLens[LensHandleHeight=15mm]%
    {\Wishes}
  \PstLens[LensHandleHeight=4]%
    (2,2){\Wishes}
\end{pspicture}
```

33-03-5

The predefined styles for the handle and the glass of the lens are:

```
\newpsstyle{LensStyleHandle}{fillstyle=gradient,gradmidpoint=.5,gradbegin=Brown,
  gradangle=\PstLens@Rotation,gradend=Salmon,linewidth=.5\pslinewidth,framearc=.6}
\newpsstyle{LensStyleGlass}{fillstyle=solid,fillcolor=white,shadow=true,
  shadowcolor=lightgray,shadowsize=0.15,shadowangle=\PstLens@Rotation}
```

The following example defines new styles:

```
\usepackage{pst-lens}
\begin{pspicture}(0,-2.5)(3,3)
 \Wishes
 \newpsstyle{HandleYellow}{linecolor=red,framearc=1,
   fillstyle=solid,fillcolor=yellow}
 \PstLens[LensHandleWidth=0.5,LensStyleHandle=HandleYellow](0,0.5){\Wishes}
 \newpsstyle{HandleCrosshatch}{fillstyle=crosshatch*,fillcolor=white}
 \PstLens[LensStyleHandle=HandleCrosshatch](2,2){\Wishes}
\end{pspicture}
```

33.3 Natural sciences

```
\usepackage{pst-lens}

\begin{pspicture}(0,-0.5)(3,3.1)
  \Wishes
    \PstLens[LensShadow=false](2,2){\Wishes}
\end{pspicture}
```

```
\usepackage{pst-lens}

\begin{pspicture}(3,3.5)
  \Wishes\makeatletter
  \newpsstyle{DarkShadow}{fillstyle=solid,
    fillcolor=white,shadow=true,
    shadowcolor=darkgray,shadowsize=0.2,
    shadowangle=\PstLens@Rotation}
  \makeatother \PstLens[LensRotation=230,
    LensStyleGlass=DarkShadow](2,2){\Wishes}
\end{pspicture}
```

The next two examples employ the \PstLensShape command:

```
\usepackage{pst-lens}
\renewcommand{\PstLensShape}{\psellipse(2,1)}

\psset{LensMagnification=1.5}
\begin{pspicture}(0,-1)(4,3.25)
  \Wishes
  \PstLens(2,2){\Wishes}
\end{pspicture}
```

33 Further PSTricks packages

```
\usepackage{pstricks,pst-lens,pst-3d}
\renewcommand{\PstLensShape}{\psdiamond(1.5,1)}

\psset{LensMagnification=1.5}
\begin{pspicture}(0.8,-1.5)(5.3,3)
  \pstilt{60}{%
    \Wishes\PstLens[LensSize=1.5](2,2){\Wishes}}
\end{pspicture}
```

```
\usepackage{pst-lens,graphicx}
\newcommand\tigerHead{\rput[lb](0,0){\includegraphics[width=4cm]{tiger}}}
\newpsstyle{SimpleGlass}{linestyle=none}\psset{LensStyleGlass=SimpleGlass}
\begin{pspicture}(0,0)(4,4.5) \tigerHead \end{pspicture}\hfill
\begin{pspicture}(-0.5,0)(3,4.5)
  \PstLens[LensHandle=false,LensSize=1.8,LensMagnification=2](1.2,2.3){\tigerHead}
\end{pspicture}\hfill
\newpsstyle{SimpleHandle}{fillstyle=solid,fillcolor=white,framearc=0.5}
\psset{LensStyleHandle=SimpleHandle}
\begin{pspicture}(0,0)(4,4.5)
  \tigerHead
  \PstLens[LensSize=1.5,LensMagnification=4,LensRotation=-45](1.5,2.5){\tigerHead}
\end{pspicture}
```

```
\usepackage{pst-lens,url}
\begin{pspicture*}(-3,-5)(3,4.5)
  \Vorwort
  \PstLens[LensSize=2.5,LensMagnification=2,LensRotation=20](0,1.5){\Vorwort}
\end{pspicture*}\hfill
\begin{pspicture*}(-3,-5)(3,4.5)
  \Vorwort
  \PstLens[LensSize=2,LensMagnification=0.6,LensRotation=-20](0,1.5){\Vorwort}
\end{pspicture*}
```

CELIA: Herein I see thou lov'st me not with the full weight that I love thee. If my uncle, thy banished father, had banished thy uncle, the Duke my father, so thou hadst been still with me, I could have taught my love to take thy father for mine; so wouldst thou, if the truth of thy love to me were so righteously temper'd as mine is to thee.
ROSALIND: Well, I will forget the condition of my estate, to rejoice in yours.
CELIA: You know my father hath no child but I, nor none is like to have; and, truly, when he dies thou shalt be his heir; for what he hath taken away from thy father perforce, I will render thee again in affection. By mine honour, I will; and when I break that oath, let me turn monster; therefore, my sweet Rose, my dear Rose, be merry.
ROSALIND: From henceforth I will, coz, and devise sports. Let me see; what think

33.3.2 pst-optic – optical systems

The pst-optic package by Manuel Luque and the author of this book provides support for geometrical optics as taught in schools and universities. The package has too many options to be described here, so we just give some examples; the documentation of the package provides more detail [43].

```
\usepackage{pst-optic}
\begin{pspicture*}(-7.5,-3)(7.5,2.5)
  \rput(0,0){%
    \lens[lensScale=0.6,X0=-4,nameF=F_1,nameA=A_1,nameB=B_1,%
        nameFi=F'_1,nameAi={ },nameBi={},nameO=O_1,%
        focus=1,OA=-2,lensGlass=true, lensWidth=0.5]}
  \pspolygon[style=rayuresJaunes,linestyle=none](B)(I)(B')(I')(B)
  \Transform
  \rput(0,0){%
    \lens[lensScale=1.2,X0=2,focus=2,nameA=A'_1,spotA=90,nameB=B'_1,spotB=270,%
        nameO=O_2,nameAi=A'_2,spotAi=270,nameBi=B'_2,spotBi=90,nameF=F_2,nameFi=F'_2,%
        lensTwo=true,lensGlass=true,lensWidth=0.5]}
  \pspolygon[style=rayuresJaunes,linestyle=none](B)(I)(B')(I')(B)
\end{pspicture*}
```

33 Further PSTricks packages

33-03-13

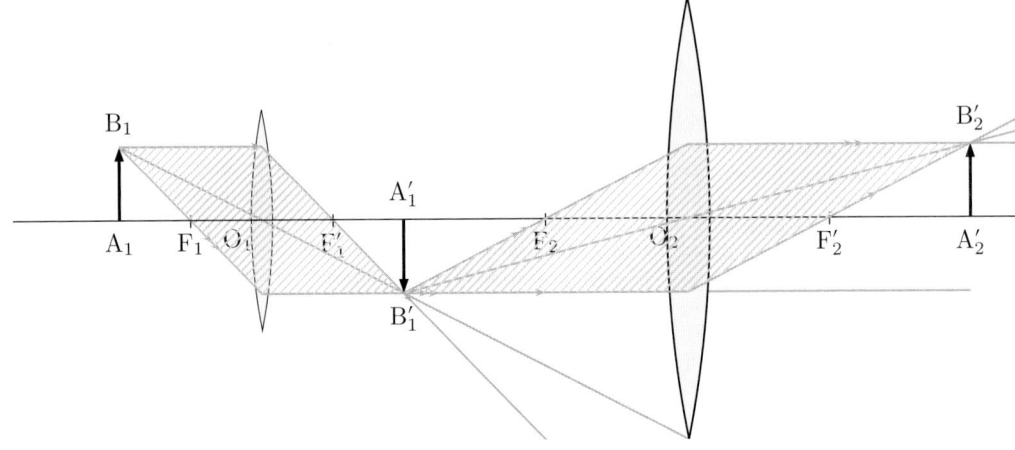

```
\usepackage{pst-optic,graphicx}
\resizebox{\linewidth}{!}{\begin{pspicture}(-7.5,-5.5)(7.5,3)
  \rput(0,0){%
    \lens[focus=1.5,OA=-2,AB=0.5,XO=-5,lensGlass=true,lensWidth=0.4,yBottom=-4,
      yTop=4,drawing=false,lensScale=0.4,nameF=F_1,nameFi=F'_1]
    \psline[linewidth=1pt](xLeft)(xRight)}
  \pnode(! XO 1){UPlens1} \pnode(! XO -1){DOWNlens1} \Transform
  \rput(0,0){%
    \lens[focus=2,XO=3,lensGlass=true,lensWidth=0.4,yBottom=-4,yTop=4,drawing=false,%
      nameF=F_2,nameFi=F'_2,spotF=90,spotFi=90]}
  \psline{->}(A1)(B1)\psline{->}(A'1)(B'1)\uput[270](A1){A}\uput[90](B1){B}
  \uput[270](B'1){$\mathrm{B_1}$}\uput{0.7}[90](A'1){$\mathrm{A_1}$}
  {\psset{linecolor=red}
    \rayInterLens(I11)(B'1){3}{Inter1L2}\rayInterLens(B1)(O1){3}{Inter2L2}
    \rayInterLens(UPlens1)(B'1){3}{Inter3L2}\rayInterLens(DOWNlens1)(B'1){3}{Inter4L2}
    \psline(B1)(I11)(B'1)(Inter1L2)  \psline(B1)(Inter2L2)
    \psline(B1)(UPlens1)(Inter3L2)   \psline(B1)(DOWNlens1)(Inter4L2)
    \psset{length=5}
    \Parallel(B'1)(O)(Inter3L2){B1inftyRigth}\Parallel(B'1)(O)(Inter4L2){B2inftyRigth}
    \Parallel(B'1)(O)(Inter2L2){B3inftyRigth}\Parallel(B'1)(O)(Inter1L2){B3inftyRigth}
    {\psset{length=-5,linestyle=dashed}
    \Parallel(B'1)(O)(Inter3L2){B1inftyLeft}\Parallel(B'1)(O)(Inter4L2){B2inftyLeft}
    \Parallel(B'1)(O)(Inter2L2){B3inftyLeft}\Parallel(B'1)(O)(Inter1L2){B3inftyLeft}
    \pcline[nodesep=6](B'1)(O)}
    \pspolygon[style=rayuresJaunes,linestyle=none](B1)(UPlens1)(Inter3L2)%
      (B1inftyRigth)(B2inftyRigth)(Inter4L2)(DOWNlens1)
    \psline(B1)(UPlens1)(Inter3L2)(B1inftyRigth)
    \psline(B2inftyRigth)(Inter4L2)(DOWNlens1)(B1) }
  \rput(7,0){\eye}
\end{pspicture}}
```

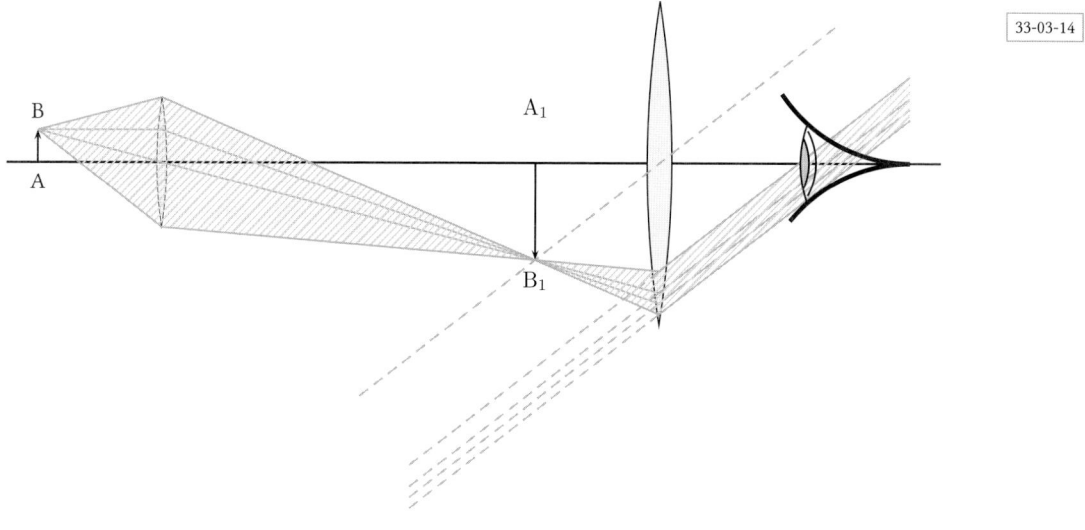

33-03-14

```
\usepackage{pst-optic,graphicx}
\resizebox{\linewidth}{!}{\begin{pspicture}(-8,-3.5)(7,5)
  \rput(0,0){%
    \lens[lensWidth=1,lensGlass=true,lensHeight=6,focus=4,drawing=false,AB=2.5]}
  { \psset{linewidth=0.5pt,linestyle=dashed,arrowsize=5pt,arrows=|<->|}
    \psline(-8,0)(4,0)\pcline(-7.75,-3)(0,-3)\lput*{:U}{2f}
    \pcline(0,-3)(4,-3)\lput*{:U}{f}\pcline(7,0)(7,4)\lput*{:U}{f}
    \pcline(4,5)(5,5)\lput*{:U}{s}\pcline(5.25,2.3)(5.25,2.8)\lput*{:U}{s} }
  \uput[90](0,3){\Large L}\uput[45](-7.7,3){\Large B}\uput[45](-7.7,-2){\Large E}
  \uput[270](3,-0.5){\Large D}\uput[-45](4,0){\Large A=F}\uput[270](3,2){\Large S}
  \uput[90](4,4){\Large Sp}\uput[90](3.5,3.25){\Large B'}
  \uput[0](6.3,2.25){\Large B''}\uput[-90](6,1.1){\Large M}
  \psarc[linewidth=0.5pt](-7.75,2.5){0.5}{-90}{0}\qdisk(-7.55,2.3){1pt}
  \rput{210}(F'){\mirrorTwo}
  { \psset{fillstyle=solid,fillcolor=lightgray}
    \rput{210}(4,2.5){\psframe(-1,0)(1,0.2)}
    \psframe(-8,-3)(-7.75,3)\psframe(3,4)(3.8,4.2)\psframe(4.2,4)(5,4.2)
  }{\psset{linewidth=1pt,linecolor=red,arrows=->,arrowsize=5pt}
    \arrowLine[linecolor=blue,arrowOffset=-0.2](F')(4,2.5){2}
    \arrowLine[linecolor=blue,arrowOffset=-0.2](4,2.3)(6,2.3){1}\qdisk(6,2.3){2pt}
    \psline[linestyle=dashed,arrows=-](F')(5.1,4)
    \psline[linestyle=dashed,arrows=-](5,2.8)(6,2.8)
    \arrowLine(4,4)(F'){3}\arrowLine[linecolor=blue,arrowOffset=-0.2](I)(F'){2}
    \arrowLine(F')(I){2}\arrowLine[linecolor=blue,arrowOffset=-0.3](-7.75,2.5)(I){3}
    \arrowLine(I)(-7.75,2.5){3}}
  \psframe(5.5,1.1)(6.5,3.5)\multido{\r=1.3+0.2}{12}{\psline(6.1,\r)(6.5,\r)}
\end{pspicture}}
```

33 Further PSTricks packages

33-03-15

```
\usepackage{pst-optic}
\psset{unit=0.5}\begin{pspicture}(-1.5,-5.5)(10,5.5)
  \rput(0,0){\beamLight[drawing=false,mirrorDepth=4.75,mirrorWidth=0.1,
    mirrorHeight=10,linecolor=lightgray]}
  \makeatletter \pst@getcoor{Focus}\pst@tempf \psset{linecolor=red}
  \multido{\n=60+5}{18}{\mirrorCVGRay[linecolor=red,mirrorDepth=4.75,
    mirrorHeight=10](Focus)(! /XF \pst@tempf pop \pst@number\psxunit div def
      \n\space cos XF add \n\space sin neg){Endd1}
      \psOutLine[arrows=->,length=.25](Endd1)(Endd1''){Endd2}
    \mirrorCVGRay[linecolor=red,mirrorDepth=4.75,mirrorHeight=10](Focus)(!
      /XF \pst@tempf pop \pst@number\psxunit div def
      \n\space cos XF add \n\space sin ){End1}
    \psOutLine[arrows=->,length=.25](End1)(End1''){End2}}
  \makeatother
\end{pspicture}
```

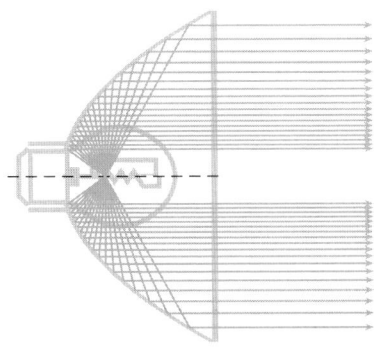

33-03-16

`\usepackage{pst-optic}`

```
\begin{pspicture}(-5,-3)(5,3)
  \pnode(-1,-2.5){A} \pnode(1,-2.5){B} \pnode(1,2.5){C} \pnode(-1,2.5){D}
  \uput[-135](A){A}   \uput[-45](B){B}  \uput[45](C){C}   \uput[135](D){D}
  \pspolygon[fillcolor=lightgray,fillstyle=solid,linecolor=blue](A)(B)(C)(D)
  \refractionRay(-3,-3)(-2,-2)(D)(A){1}{1.5}{END}%       1.
  \psset{linecolor=red,linewidth=2pt,arrowsize=5pt,arrows=->}
  \arrowLine(-3,-3)(END){2}   \ABinterCD(END)(END')(C)(B){Out}
  \arrowLine(END)(Out){1}     \refractionRay(END)(Out)(C)(B){1.5}{1}{Q}
  \arrowLine(Q)(Q'){1}        \psOutLine[length=2](Q)(Q'){End}
  \refractionRay(-3,0)(-2,0)(A)(D){1}{1.5}{END}%         2.
  \psset{linecolor=green,linewidth=2pt,arrowsize=5pt,arrows=->}
  \arrowLine(-3,0)(END){2}    \ABinterCD(END)(END')(C)(B){Out}
  \arrowLine(END)(Out){1}     \refractionRay(END)(Out)(C)(B){1.5}{1}{Q}
  \arrowLine(Q)(Q'){1}        \psOutLine[length=2](Q)(Q'){End}
  \refractionRay(-3,3)(-2,2)(D)(A){1}{1.5}{END}%         3.
  \psset{linecolor=blue,linewidth=2pt,arrowsize=5pt,arrows=->}
  \arrowLine(-3,3)(END){2}    \ABinterCD(END)(END')(C)(B){Out}
  \arrowLine(END)(Out){1}     \refractionRay(END)(Out)(C)(B){1.5}{1}{Q}
  \arrowLine(Q)(Q'){1}        \psOutLine[length=2](Q)(Q'){End}
\end{pspicture}
```

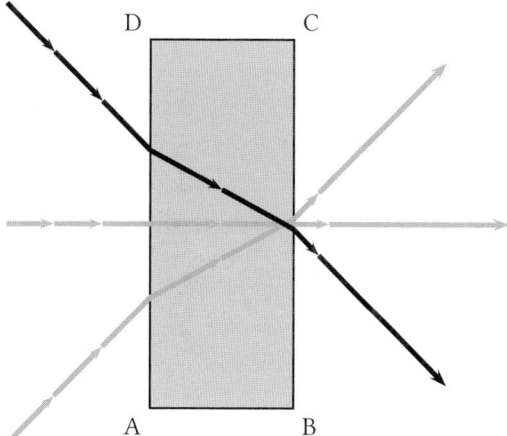

```
\usepackage{pst-optic}
\begin{pspicture}(-7,0.5)(5,5.5)
  \pnode(-3,1){A}\pnode(1,1){B}\pnode(-1,5){C}
  \uput[-135](A){A}\uput[-45](B){B}\uput[30](C){C}
  \pspolygon[fillcolor=lightgray,fillstyle=solid,linecolor=blue](A)(B)(C)
  \psset{linecolor=red,arrowsize=3pt,arrows=->}
  \multido{\rA=0.6+0.2,\rB=1.5+0.2}{7}{%
    \refractionRay(-6,\rA)(-4,\rB)(C)(A){1}{1.5}{END}
    \arrowLine(-6,\rA)(END){2}\ABinterCD(END)(END')(C)(B){Out}
    \arrowLine(END)(Out){1}    \refractionRay(END)(Out)(C)(B){1.5}{1}{Q}
    \psline(Q)(Q')             \psOutLine[length=3](Q)(Q'){End} }
\end{pspicture}
```

33 Further PSTricks packages

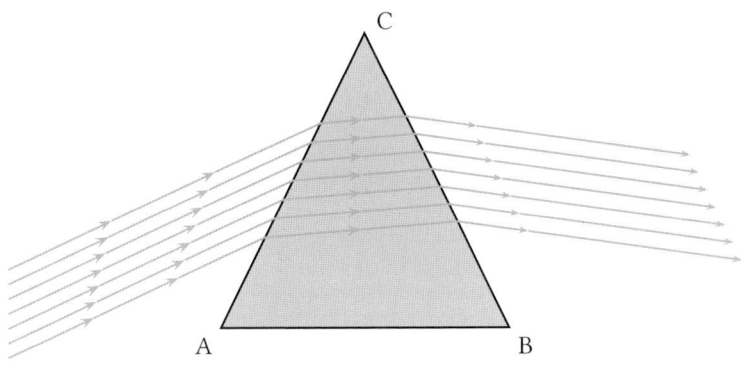

```
\usepackage{pst-optic}
\psset{unit=0.75}
\begin{pspicture}(-8,-2)(8,5.75)
  \pnode(-8,1.5){A}\pnode(8,1.5){B}
  \uput[45](A){A}\uput[135](B){B}
  \pnode(0,0){START}
  \psframe[fillcolor=lightgray,fillstyle=solid,linecolor=blue](-8,-1.5)(B)
  \psset{linecolor=red,arrowsize=3pt,arrows=->}
  \multido{\n=20+5}{29}{%
    \refractionRay(START)(1;\n)(A)(B){1.5}{1}{END}
    \arrowLine(START)(END){2}\arrowLine(END)(END'){1}
    \psOutLine[length=3](END)(END'){Q}\arrowLine(END')(Q){3} }
\end{pspicture}
```

```
\usepackage{pst-optic}
\psset{unit=0.8}
\begin{pspicture*}(-7,-1)(7,7)
  \psprism
\end{pspicture*}
```

33.3 Natural sciences

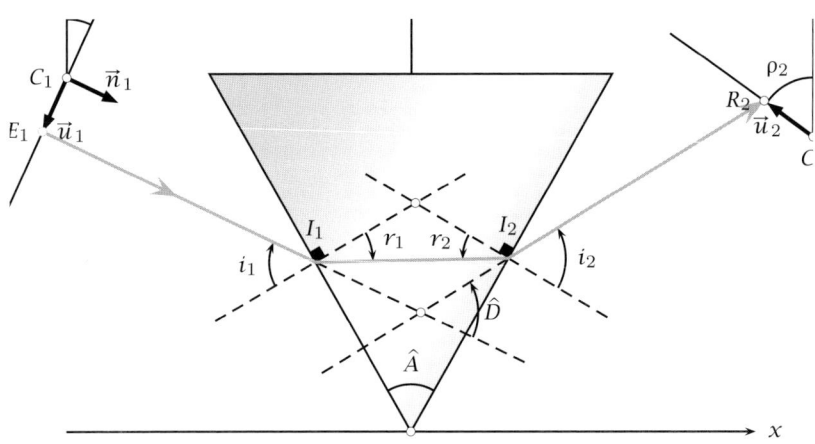

```
\usepackage{pst-optic}
\psset{unit=0.8}
\begin{pspicture*}(-7,-1)(7,7)
  \psprism[notations=false]
\end{pspicture*}
```

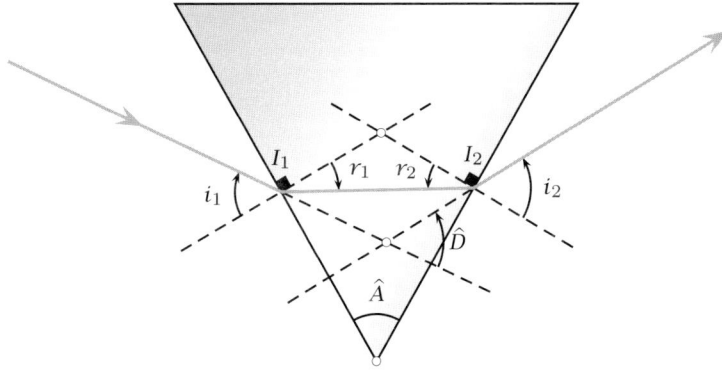

```
\usepackage{pst-optic}
\psset{unit=0.8}
\begin{pspicture*}(-7,-1)(7,7)
  \psprism[k=0.5,lambda=400,rayWidth=1.5pt]
\end{pspicture*}
```

33 Further PSTricks packages

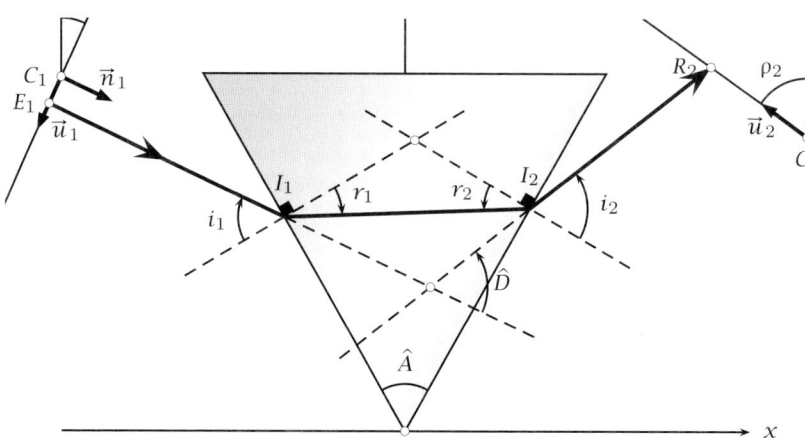

```
\usepackage{pst-optic}
\psset{unit=0.8}
\begin{pspicture*}(-7,-1)(7,7)
  \psprism[k=0.5,lambda=700,rayWidth=1.5pt]
\end{pspicture*}
```

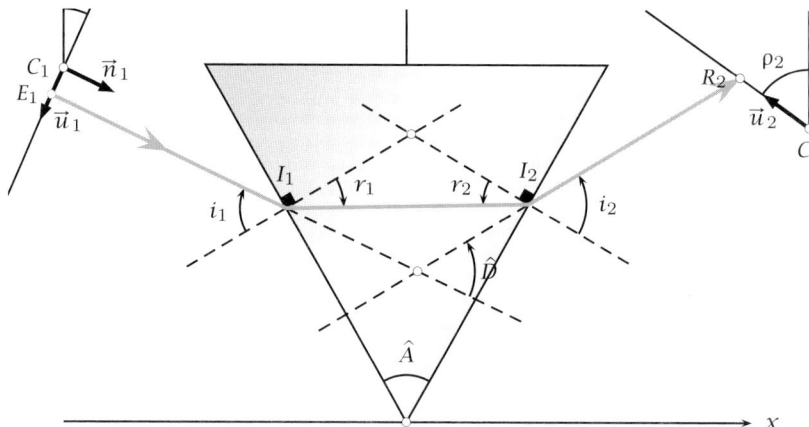

The specification of the wavelength affects the line colour as well as the refraction of the light beam. There is also a \psprismColor command that shows the colour dispersion of white light (cf. Example 36-00-31 on page 781). The following figure shows this for individual light beams; the different refraction is achieved through the specification of the refractivity.

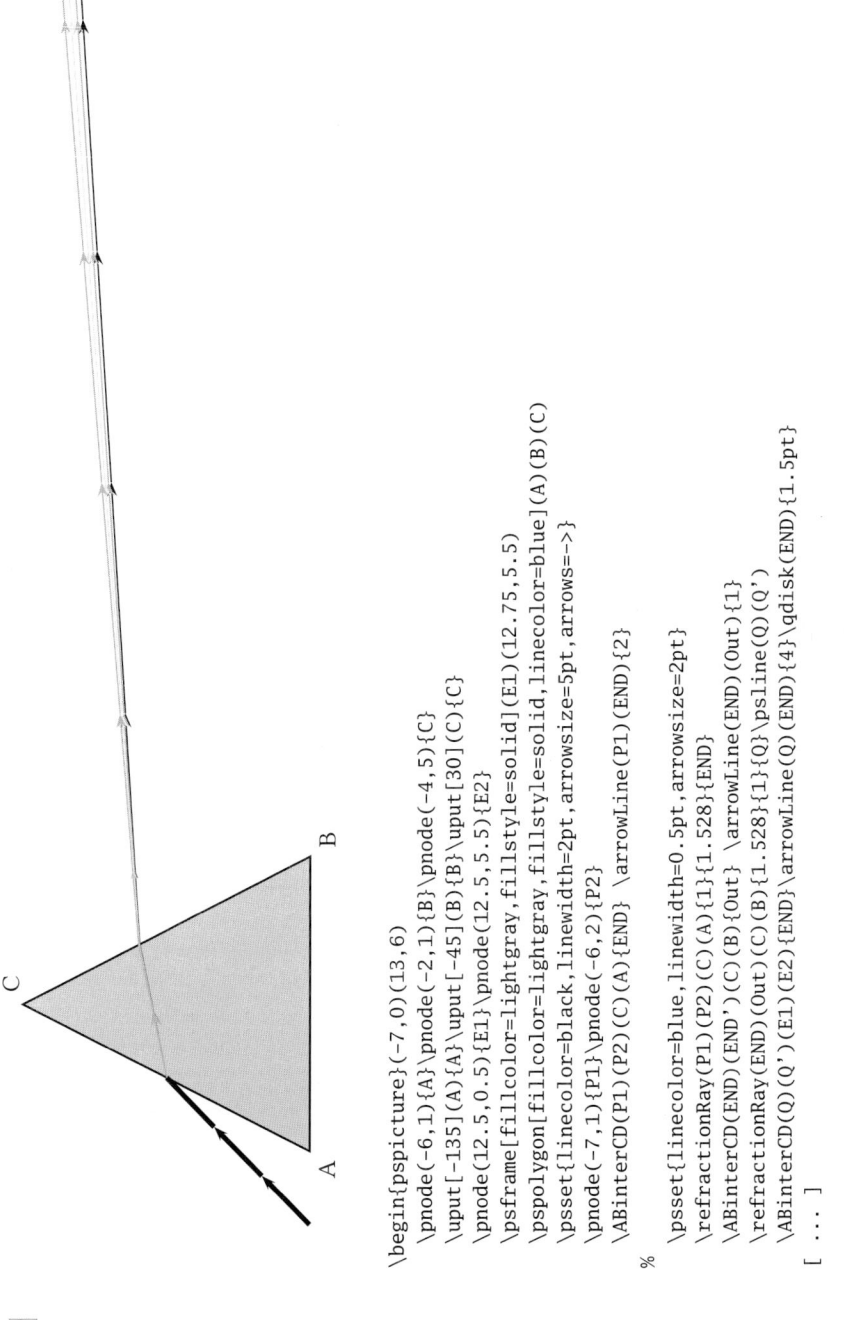

```
\begin{pspicture}(-7,0)(13,6)
\pnode(-6,1){A}\pnode(-2,1){B}\pnode(-4,5){C}
\uput[-135](A){A}\uput[-45](B){B}\uput[30](C){C}
\pnode(12.5,0.5){E1}\pnode(12.5,5.5){E2}
\psframe[fillcolor=lightgray,fillstyle=solid](E1)(12.75,5.5)
\pspolygon[fillcolor=lightgray,fillstyle=solid,linecolor=blue](A)(B)(C)
\psset{linecolor=black,linewidth=2pt,arrowsize=5pt,arrows=->}
\pnode(-7,1){P1}\pnode(-6,2){P2}
\ABinterCD(P1)(P2)(C)(A){END}  \arrowLine(P1)(END){2}
%
\psset{linecolor=blue,linewidth=0.5pt,arrowsize=2pt}
\refractionRay(P1)(P2)(C)(A){1}{1.528}{END}
\ABinterCD(END)(END'){C}(B){Out}  \arrowLine(END)(Out){1}
\refractionRay(END)(Out)(C)(B){1.528}{1}{Q}\psline(Q)(Q')
\ABinterCD(Q)(Q')(E1)(E2){END}\arrowLine(Q)(END){4}\qdisk(END){1.5pt}
[ ... ]
```

33.3.3 pst-optexp – experimental optics[1]

The pst-optexp package by Christoph Bersch is a collection of components that make it easier to describe setups for experimental optics. [7] It was developed with \pst-circ as a guide and thus provides similar, but adapted, concepts to align different optics automatically. The package provides many free beam and fused fibre optics. It also makes it easy to extend this collection with arbitrary custom objects (cf. Example 33-03-29 on page 700). During development, special care was taken to ensure that each component and its labels would be highly configurable.

The free beam components are mainly dipoles, like lenses or retarding discs, which don't change the principal direction of the light – you can place them arbitrarily between two reference nodes. There are also tripoles, like mirrors or beam splitters, which reflect the light and are therefore aligned towards the light. Free beam components can refract and reflect the beam internally several times, as shown by the different prisms. The image is correct as long as two objects are connected (cf. Example 33-03-29 on page 700).

The fused fibre optics are the second category of optical components. They are composed of dipoles, tripoles, and quadrupoles and are aligned similarly to the free beam components.

For all components, you can configure the style of each fibre separately and fit them with, for example, arrows or different curvatures. Especially in the area of optical communications, components are often driven by external signals. Therefore, you can create an additional node for some components that can then be used for external connections with electrical devices. An example of this interaction with pst-circ is shown in example 33-03-28 on the next page.

Future versions of pst-optexp will support widened beams, which will allow for a more complete accounting of the course of the beam in experimental optical setups.

```
\usepackage{pst-optexp, nicefrac}
\begin{pspicture}(10,2)
\psset{optboxwidth=1}\addtopsstyle{Beam}{linewidth=2\pslinewidth}
\pnode(1,1){Start}\pnode(9,1){CCD}\optbox[endbox, labeloffset=0](CCD)(Start){Laser}
\optbox[endbox,labeloffset=0,beam](Start)(CCD){CCD}
\polarization[poltype=perp,abspos=0.5](Start)(CCD)
\optretplate[abspos=1](Start)(CCD){$\nicefrac{\lambda}{2}$}
\lens[lens=0.4 0.4 0.5,abspos=2](Start)(CCD){$L_1$}\lens[abspos=4](Start)(CCD){$L_2$}
\optplate[abspos=6,platelinewidth=3\pslinewidth](Start)(CCD){SLM}
\optplate[abspos=6.5,labelangle=180](Start)(CCD){PF}
\polarization[abspos=6.7](Start)(CCD)\lens[abspos=7](Start)(CCD){$L_3$}
\end{pspicture}
```

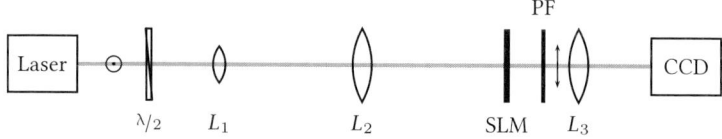

```
\usepackage{pst-optexp, nicefrac}
\begin{pspicture}(-4,-1)(3,3)
\addtopsstyle{Beam}{linewidth=2\pslinewidth,linecolor=red!90!black}
```

---
[1]Thanks to Christoph Bersch for this section.

```
\psset{labeloffset=0.5}
\pnode(-2,0){LaserOut}\pnode(0,0){Grat}\pnode(4;45){Out}\pnode(2.5;67.5){Mvar}
\optbox[optboxwidth=2,labeloffset=0,endbox](Grat)(LaserOut){diode laser}
\mirror[variable,conn=o-](Grid)(Mvar)(Grid){M$_\mathrm{var}$}
\optgrid[beam](LaserOut)(Grat)(Out){grating}
\optretplate[position=0.3,labeloffset=0.8](LaserOut)(Grat){$\nicefrac{\lambda}{4}$}
\rput[l](-3,2){Littman setup}
\end{pspicture}
```

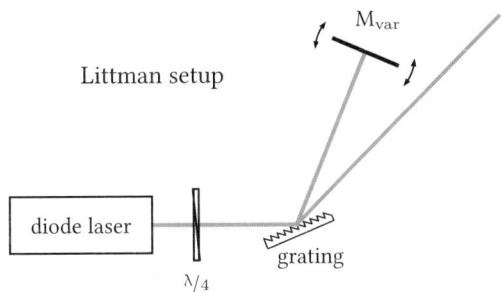

```
\usepackage{pst-optexp}
\begin{pspicture}(8.5,1.6)
\addtopsstyle{Beam}{linecolor=green!90!black}
\pnode(1.6,1){Laser}\pnode(7.6,1){Diode}
\optbox[endbox,labeloffset=0](Diode)(Laser){Laser}%
\optbox[abspos=4,optboxwidth=1,optboxheight=0.6,labeloffset=1,compname=PC,
        conn=o-,angle=-10,rotateref=1,refractiveindex=2.3](Laser)(Diode){Photonic Crystal}
\optdetector[dettype=diode, conn=o-](PCInternN)(Diode|PCInternN){PD}
\defShiftedNode(PCIntern1)(2;170){Angle1}
\psline[linestyle=dashed](PCIntern1)(Angle1)
\psarc{<->}(PCIntern1){1.3}{330}{30}
\psarc[arcsep=1pt]{<->}(PCIntern1){2}{170}{180}
\uput{2.1}[175](PCIntern1){\small $\varphi$}
\end{pspicture}
```

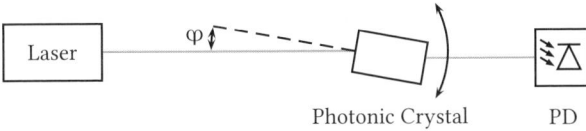

```
\usepackage{pst-circ,pst-optexp,pst-func}
\begin{pspicture}(6.4,3.2)
\addtopsstyle{Fiber}{linecolor=red}
\pnode(2.3,2.3){Lin}
\pnode([Xnodesep=0.5]Lin){Lout}
\pnode([Xnodesep=1.5]Lout){EAMout}
\pnode([Xnodesep=1.5]EAMout){Det}
\optbox[fiber,labeloffset=-0.2,endbox,compname=L,extnode=b](Lout)(Lin){%
```

```
    \psGauss[yunit=0.03,sigma=0.03]{-0.5}{0.5}}
\optbox[fiber,labeloffset=0,optboxwidth=1,compname=EAM,extnode=b](Lout)(EAMout){EAM}
\optfiber[labeloffset=0.3](EAMout)(Det){fibre}
\optdetector(EAMout)(Det){OSA}
\pnode([Xnodesep=-1,offset=-1]LExtNode){Osc}
\pnode(LExtNode|Osc){PSin}
\pnode(EAMExtNode|Osc){PSout}
\oscillator[output=right](Osc){10\,GHz}{}
\phaseshifter[labeloffset=-0.7](PSin)(PSout){$\tau$}
\wire(LExtNode)(PSin)
\wire(EAMExtNode)(PSout)
\end{pspicture}
```

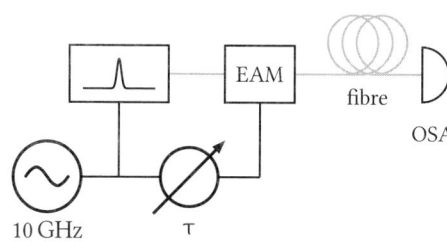

```
\usepackage{pst-optexp}
\makeatletter
\def\LCLV@iii{%
  \psframe[fillstyle=solid,fillcolor=black,dimen=outer](-0.12,-0.5)(0,0.5)
  \psframe[fillstyle=solid,fillcolor=gray!50,dimen=outer](0,-0.5)(0.15,0.5)
  \pnode(-0.12,0){\optexp@nodeA}\pnode(0.15,0){\optexp@nodeB}}
\makeatother
\begin{pspicture}(9,5)
\newOptexpDipole{LCLV}{}
\psset{lens=1.2 0 1}
\pnode(2.4,1){BS1}
\pnode([offset=3]BS1){M1}
\pnode([Xnodesep=5.5]M1){PP}
\pnode(PP|BS1){BS2}
\LCLV[position=0.2, compname=LCLV](BS1)(BS2){LCLV}
\beamsplitter[compname=BS](BS2)(BS1)(M1){BS}
\optretplate(BS1)(M1){P}
\mirror[conn=i-](BS1)(M1)(PP){M}
\lens[position=0.2](M1)(PP){L}
\pinhole(M1)(PP){}
\lens[position=0.2](PP)(M1){L}
\pentaprism[beam](M1)(PP)(BS2){PP}
\beamsplitter(PP)(BS2)(BS1){BS}
\lens(BS2)(BS1){L}
\doveprism[compname=Dove,conn=i-,position=0.27](BS2)(BS1){D}
\drawbeam[conn=b-b]{Dove}{LCLV}
\drawbeam[conn=b-a]{BS}{LCLV}
```

33.3 Natural sciences

```
\psline[arrowscale=1.3, style=Beam]{->}(BS2)([offset=-1]BS2)
\addtopsstyle{Beam}{arrowscale=1.3, ArrowInside=-<}
\optbox[labeloffset=0, endbox, conn=o-](BS1)([Xnodesep=-1]BS1){Nd:YAG}
\end{pspicture}
```

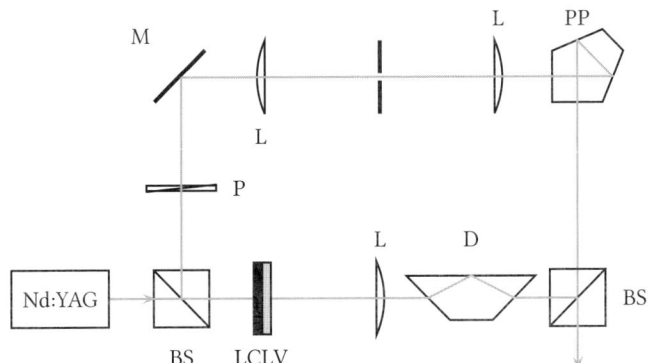

33-03-29

```
\usepackage{pst-optexp, nicefrac}
\begin{pspicture}(8.4,6.3)
 \addtopsstyle{Beam}{linewidth=2\pslinewidth}
 \psset{labeloffset=0.7,labelstyle=\scriptsize,lens=1.2 1.2 0.8,bssize=0.5}
 \pnode(1.5,5.3){Laser}
 \pnode([Xnodesep=2.5]Laser){PBS}\pnode([Xnodesep=2.5]PBS){PBS2}
 \pnode([offset=0.7]PBS2){piezo}  \pnode([offset=-3]PBS){BSFwd}
 \pnode(PBS2|BSFwd){BSBwd}        \pnode([Xnodesep=-2]BSFwd){BS4f}
 \pnode([offset=-1.5]BS4f){M4f3}  \pnode([Xnodesep=1.5]BSBwd){M4f1}
 \pnode([offset=-1.5]M4f1){M4f2}  \pnode([Xnodesep=-1]BS4f){CCD}
 \psline[style=Beam](Laser)(PBS2)(piezo)(BSBwd)(M4f1)(M4f2)(M4f3)(BS4f)(CCD)
 \psline[style=Beam](PBS)(BSFwd)(BS4f)
 \optbox[endbox,labeloffset=0](PBS)(Laser){\parbox{1.5cm}{\centering Nd:YAG\\532\,nm}}
 \lens[lens=0.5 0.5 0.5, position=0.2](Laser)(PBS){MO}
 \pinhole[position=0.3, labelangle=180](Laser)(PBS){PH}
 \lens(Laser)(PBS){L}
 \optretplate[position=0.8](Laser)(PBS){$\nicefrac{\lambda}{2}$}
 \beamsplitter(Laser)(PBS)(BSFwd){PBS}
 \optretplate[position=0.4](PBS)(BSFwd){$\nicefrac{\lambda}{2}$}
 \polarization(PBS)(BSFwd)
 \polarization(PBS2)(BSBwd)
 \lens[position=0.8](PBS)(BSFwd){L}
 \optretplate(PBS)(PBS2){$\nicefrac{\lambda}{2}$}
 \beamsplitter(PBS)(PBS2)(piezo){PBS}
 \optretplate[abspos=0.5](PBS2)(piezo){$\nicefrac{\lambda}{4}$}
 \mirror[mirrortype=piezo, labelangle=90](PBS2)(piezo)(PBS2){PZ}
 \lens[position=0.2](BSBwd)(PBS2){L}
 \crystal[crystalwidth=1,crystalheight=0.5,voltage,lamp,fillstyle=solid,
         fillcolor=yellow!90!black, labeloffset=0.8, beam](BSFwd)(BSBwd){SBN:Ce}
 \beamsplitter(PBS)(BSFwd)(BSBwd){BS}
```

```
\beamsplitter[labelangle=-90](PBS2)(BSBwd)(BSFwd){BS}
\mirror[labeloffset=0.4](BSBwd)(M4f1)(M4f2){M}
\mirror[labeloffset=0.4](M4f1)(M4f2)(M4f3){M}
\lens(M4f3)(M4f2){L}
\mirror[labeloffset=0.4](M4f2)(M4f3)(BS4f){M}
\beamsplitter(M4f3)(BS4f)(CCD){BS}
\optbox[endbox, labeloffset=0, optboxwidth=1](BS4f)(CCD){CCD}
\lens[abspos=0.7](BS4f)(BSFwd){L}
\lens[abspos=0.7](BSBwd)(M4f1){L}
\end{pspicture}
```

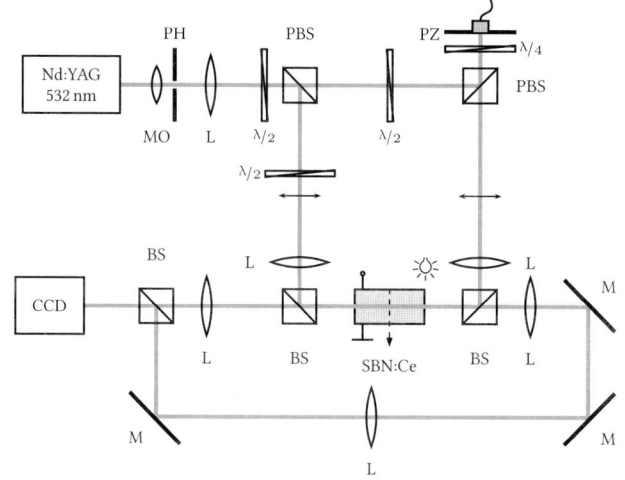

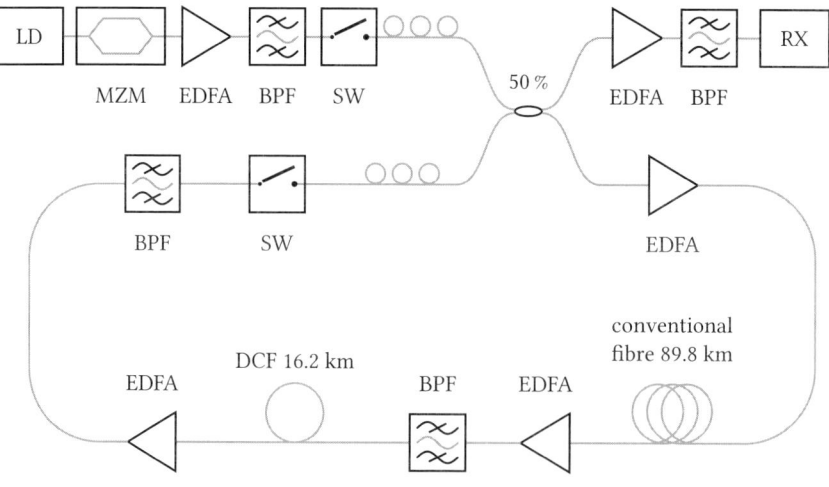

33.3.4 pst-diffraction – diffraction patterns

The pst-diffraction package is, in principle, an extension of pst-optic that calculates diffraction patterns for a monochromatic light source when passing through circular, rectangular, or triangular slits.

Experimental setup

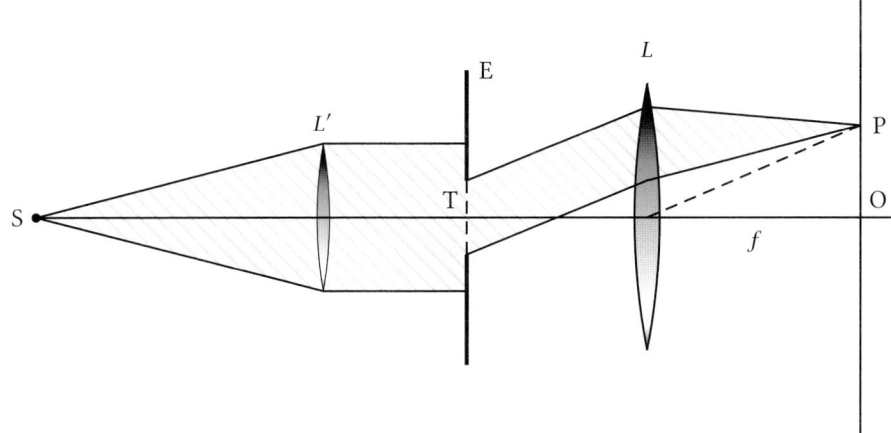

The monochromatic light originating at the point light source S leaves the collecting lens L′ parallel to the axis and reaches the blend E with slit T, where the light is diffracted. Each point of the slit acts as a new punctual light source (Huygens' principle) and an interference pattern (diffraction pattern) is created and made visible on a screen. If the distance between the screen and the blend is sufficiently large, the diffraction is also referred to as Fraunhofer diffraction. In this case, we can assume that all light beams that originated at the slit and reach the screen at the same point P are parallel.

There are three commands: for rectangular, circular, and triangular slits.

```
\psdiffractionRectangle [settings]
\psdiffractionCircular [settings]
\psdiffractionTriangle [settings]
```

The colour

The colour of the light is selected throughout specifying the corresponding wavelength λ (in nanometres); the default is 650. Red for example corresponds to lambda=632. The conversion of the wavelength into the corresponding values of the RGB colour scheme is done internally by PostScript. The code is based on http://www.midnightkite.com/color.html.

Diffraction at a rectangular slit

A rectangle with area $h = k \times a$ is specified through the options a (width) and k (height). The focal length of the lens is specified through f and the resolution is selected through pixel. All lengths refer to the unit m and may be given in exponential notation. The contrast option makes the minor maxima appear more clearly. colorMode=0 creates a black and white image; colorMode=1 creates the reverse. colorMode=2 and colorMode=3 (default) create colour images using the CMYK and RGB colour model, respectively. Table 33.8 summarizes the options and their default values for diffraction at a rectangular slit.

Table 33.8: Summary of the parameters for diffraction at a rectangular slit

name	type	default	name	type	default
a	value	0.2e-3	k	value	1
f	value	5	lambda	value	650
pixel	value	0.5	contrast	value	38
colorMode	0...3	3	IIID	boolean	false

```
\usepackage{pst-diffraction}
\begin{pspicture}(-3,-3)(3,3)
\psdiffractionRectangle[f=2.5]
\end{pspicture}\quad
\begin{pspicture*}(-3,-3)(3,3)
\psdiffractionRectangle[f=4,lambda=550,colorMode=0]
\end{pspicture*}
```

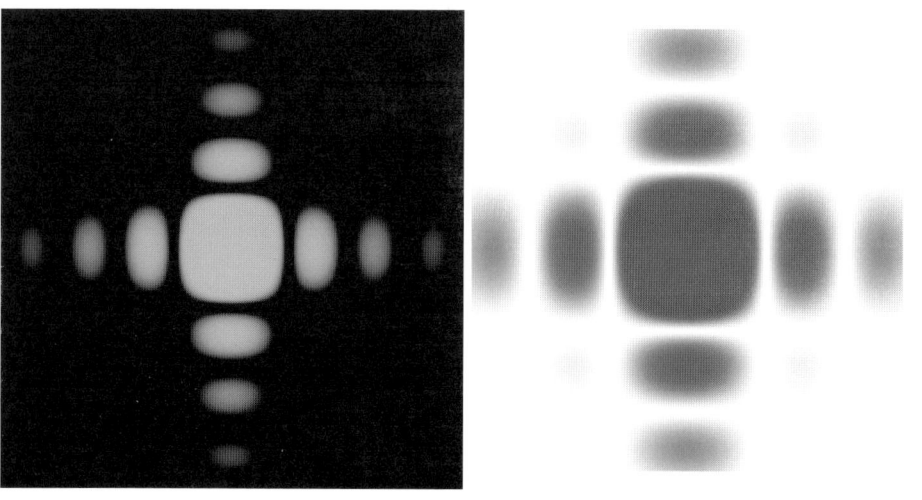

33-03-33

```
\usepackage{pst-diffraction}
\begin{pspicture}(-1.5,-2.5)(3.5,3.5)
\psdiffractionRectangle[IIID,Alpha=30,f=2.5]
\end{pspicture}
```

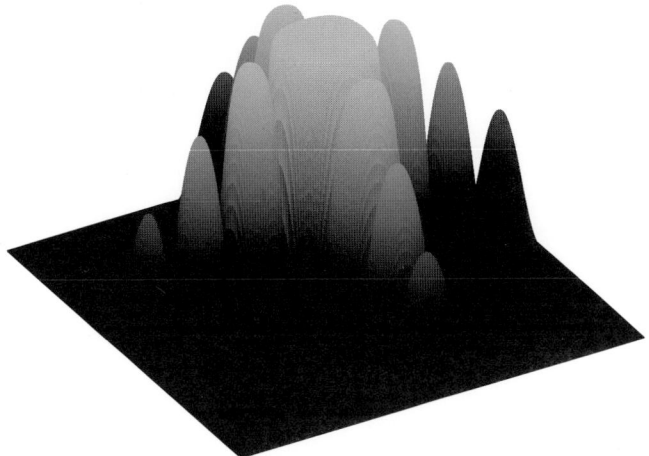

Diffraction at two rectangular slits

The Boolean twoSlit option creates the diffraction pattern of a double slit; this is not active by default. The s option controls the distance between the two slits; its default value is 12×10^{-3} m.

```
\usepackage{pst-diffraction}
\begin{pspicture}(-4.5,-1.5)(4.5,1.5)
\psdiffractionRectangle[a=0.5e-3,k=10,f=10,pixel=0.5,lambda=550,twoSlit,
   s=2e-3,colorMode=0]
\end{pspicture}
```

```
\usepackage{pst-diffraction}
\begin{pspicture}(-2,-1)(4,4)
\psdiffractionRectangle[a=0.5e-3,k=10,f=10,pixel=0.5,lambda=550,twoSlit,
   s=2e-3,colorMode=0,IIID]
\end{pspicture}
```

33 Further PSTricks packages

33-03-36

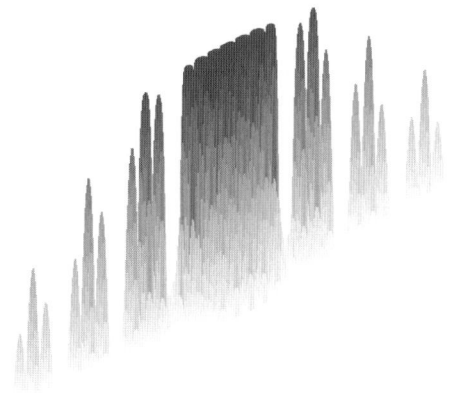

Diffraction at a circular slit

The r option specifies the radius of the hole in the unit m; the default value is r=1e-3 in exponential notation (i.e. r=1 mm).

```
\usepackage{pst-diffraction}
\begin{pspicture}(-3.5,-3.5)(3.5,3.5)
\psdiffractionCircular[r=0.5e-3,f=10, pixel=0.5,lambda=520,colorMode=0]
\end{pspicture}
```

33-03-37

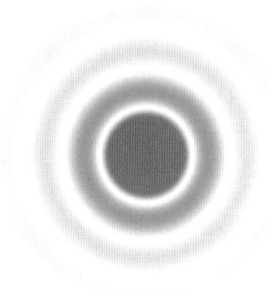

706

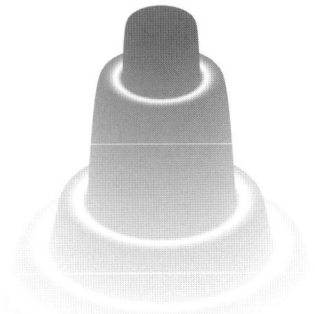

```
\usepackage{pst-diffraction}

\begin{pspicture}(-3.5,-1.5)(3.5,3.5)
\psdiffractionCircular[IIID,r=0.5e-3,
    f=10,pixel=0.5,lambda=520,
    colorMode=0]
\end{pspicture}
```

Diffraction at two circular slits

The only case supported is two holes of the same radius, again specified through the r option. You must also specify half the distance between the centres of the two circles through the d option, which is set to d=3e-3 by default. Again these lengths are specified in the unit m. The twoHole option activates diffraction through two circular slits.

```
\usepackage{pst-diffraction}
\begin{pspicture}(-3,-3.5)(3.5,3.5)
\psdiffractionCircular[r=0.5e-3,f=10,d=3e-3,lambda=515,twoHole]
\end{pspicture}
```

33 Further PSTricks packages

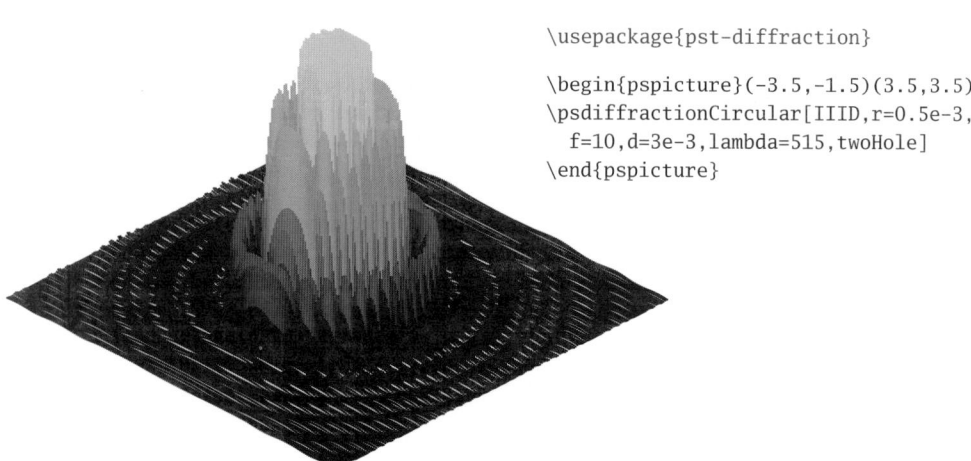

```
\usepackage{pst-diffraction}

\begin{pspicture}(-3.5,-1.5)(3.5,3.5)
\psdiffractionCircular[IIID,r=0.5e-3,
    f=10,d=3e-3,lambda=515,twoHole]
\end{pspicture}
```

The circle in the centre will not contain a striped pattern in every case. The number N of the stripes in the centre is given by $N = 2.44\frac{d}{r}$; therefore this effect can only be observed for $N \geq 2$ or $d = \frac{2r}{1.22}$ (http://www.unice.fr/DeptPhys/optique/diff/trouscirc/diffrac.html).

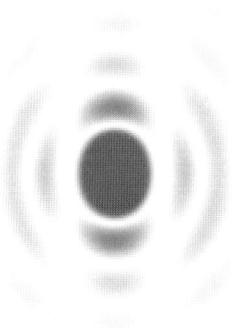

```
\usepackage{pst-diffraction}

\begin{pspicture}(-3,-3.5)(3,3.5)
\psdiffractionCircular[r=0.5e-3,
    f=10,d=4.1e-4,lambda=550,
    twoHole,colorMode=0]
\end{pspicture}
```

```
\usepackage{pst-diffraction}

\begin{pspicture}(-3.5,-1.5)(3.5,3)
\psdiffractionCircular[IIID,r=0.5e-3,
    f=10,d=4.1e-4,lambda=550,twoHole,
    colorMode=0]
\end{pspicture}
```

Diffraction at a triangular slit

The only case supported is an equilateral triangular hole. The slit height h is specified in the unit m; you can calculate it from the length of a side of the triangle s through $h = \frac{\sqrt{3}}{2} s$. The twoHole option is not available with \psdiffractionTriangle.

```
\usepackage{pst-diffraction}
\begin{pspicture}(-2,-2)(2,2)
\psdiffractionTriangle[f=10,h=1e-3,lambda=515,contrast=38]
\end{pspicture}
\quad
\begin{pspicture}(-2,-2)(2,2)
\psdiffractionTriangle[f=10,h=1e-3,colorMode=1,contrast=38,lambda=515]
\end{pspicture}
\quad
\begin{pspicture}(-2,-2)(2,2)
\psdiffractionTriangle[f=10,h=1e-3,colorMode=0,contrast=38,lambda=515]
\end{pspicture}
```

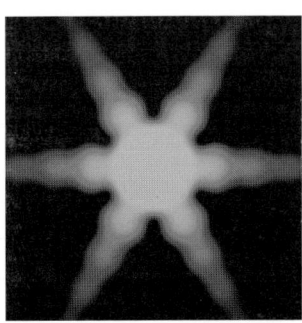  

33.3.5 pst-magneticfield – Magnetic field lines

The pst-magneticfield package, from Manuel Luque, Jürgen Gilg, and the author, aims to trace the shape of field lines of a solenoid. The package provides two commands, one for a two dimensional and one for a three dimensional representation of the magnetic field. The physical parameters are listed in Table 33.9.

```
\psmagneticfield [settings]
\psmagneticfieldThreeD [settings] (x₁,y₁)(x₂,y₂)
```
(with $(x_1,y_1)(x_2,y_2)$)

Table 33.9: Summary of the parameters for pst-magneticfield

name	type	default	description
N	value	6	number of turns
R	value	2	radius
L	value	4	length
pointsB	value	500	maximum number of points on each line of the entire coil
pointsS	value	1000	maximum number of points on lines around turns selected
nL	value	8	number of lines of the entire coil
PasB	value	0.02	differential steps for the lines of the entire coil
PasS	value	0.00275	differential steps for the lines around turns selected
numSpires	list	{}	choice of individual coils to improve the rendering of its layout
nS	value	1	number of field lines around the turns selected
drawSelf	boolean	false	no representation of the solenoid
styleSpire	style	style	colour and thickness of the field lines
styleCourant	style	sensCourant	colour and thickness of the current
AntiHelmholtz	boolean	false	current with the same direction

```
\usepackage{pst-magneticfield}
\psset{unit=0.5cm}
\begin{pspicture*}[showgrid](-7,-8)(7,8)
\psmagneticfield[linecolor={[HTML]{006633}},N=3,R=2,nS=1]
\psframe*[linecolor={[HTML]{99FF66}}](-7,-8)(7,-7)
\rput(0,-7.5){[\Cadre{\textcolor{white}{L=4}},N=3,R=2,nS=1]}
\end{pspicture*}
\begin{pspicture*}[showgrid](-7,-8)(7,8)
\psmagneticfield[linecolor={[HTML]{006633}},L=8,N=3,R=2,nS=1,PasB=0.0025,pointsB=5500]
\psframe*[linecolor={[HTML]{99FF66}}](-7,-8)(7,-7)
\rput(0,-7.5){[\Cadre{\textcolor{white}{L=8}},N=3,R=2,nS=1]}
\end{pspicture*}
```

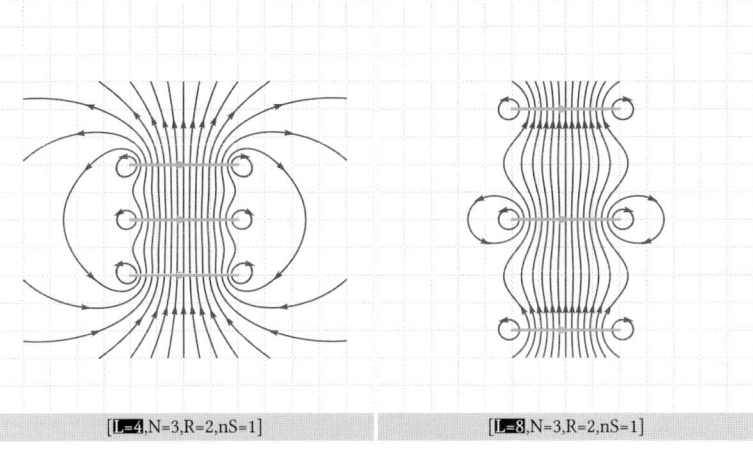

```
\usepackage{pst-magneticfield}
\psset{unit=0.75,AntiHelmholtz,N=2,R=2,pointsB=500,pointsS=1000,PasB=0.02,PasS=0.00275,
    nS=10,nL=2,drawSelf=true,styleSpire=styleSpire,styleCourant=sensCourant,arrowscale=2}
\newpsstyle{gridstyle}{subgriddiv=0,gridcolor=blue!50,griddots=10}
\begin{pspicture*}[showgrid](-7,-6)(7,6)
\psframe*[linecolor={[HTML]{996666}}](-7,7)(7,8)
\psmagneticfield[linecolor={[HTML]{660066}}]
\end{pspicture*}
```

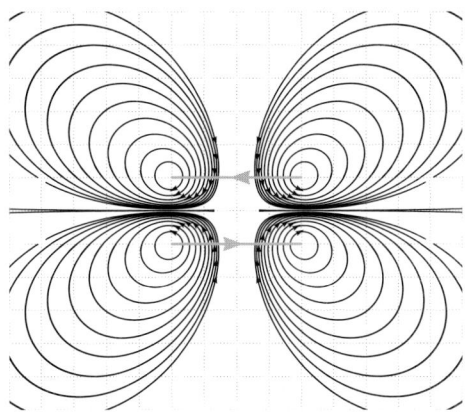

We can change the view of the three-dimensional representation through the viewpoint option of the pst-3d package. There are two predefined styles for the frame – grille and cadre – which can be overwritten.

```
\usepackage{pst-magneticfield}
\psset{unit=0.7cm}
\newpsstyle{grille}{subgriddiv=0,gridcolor=blue!50,griddots=10}
\newpsstyle{cadre}{linecolor=yellow!50}
```

```
\begin{pspicture}(-7,-6)(7,6)
\psmagneticfieldThreeD[N=8,R=2,L=8,pointsB=1200,linecolor=blue,pointsS=1000](-7,-8)(7,8)
\end{pspicture}
```

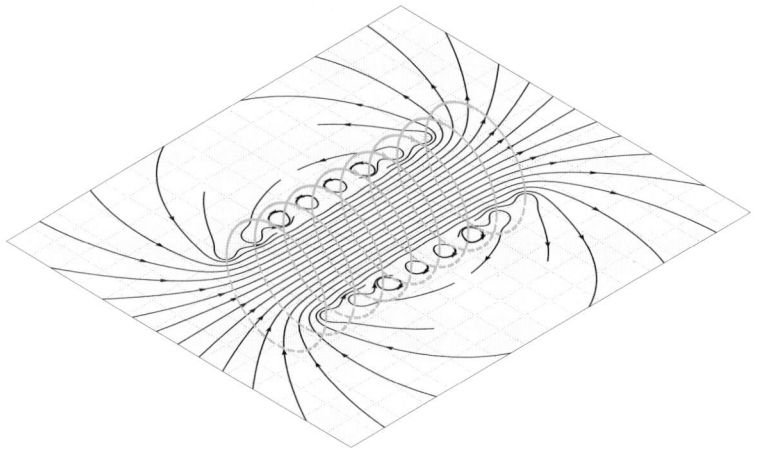

33.3.6 pst-osci – oscillograms

The pst-osci package by Manuel Luque and Christophe Jorssen is structured similarly to pst-labo, and you can likewise create very complex structures with a single command, though this of course means that you have only limited control over the details of the figure. The syntax for the only command is:

\Oscillo [settings]

Internally, the command is included in a pspicture environment. The output needs to be scaled if it should be printed on paper. Everything is controlled by the parameters, summarized in Table 33.10. The most important options are illustrated below through examples.

Table 33.10: Summary of the parameters available for pst-osci

name	type	default	description
period1	value	20	cycle duration T_1 (in ms) of signal 1
periodmodulation1	value	100	cycle duration T_{m1} (in ms) of signal 1
freqmod1	value	0	frequency modulation factor m_1 of signal 1
amplitude1	value	2	amplitude A_1 (in V) of signal 1
CC1	value	0	DC voltage portion c_1 (in V) of signal 1
phase1	value	0	phase shift ϕ_1 (in deg) of signal 1
sensivity1	value	1	input voltage of signal 1 (in V)
damping1	value	0	attenuation λ_1 of signal 1
offset1	value	0	offset signal 1 (in V)
plotstyle1	style	GreenContA	plot style signal 1
Wave1	value	SinusA	signal type (SinusA, RectangleA, TriangleA, LDogToothA, RDogToothA)

continued...

... continued

name	type	default	description
period2	value	20	cycle duration T_2 (in ms) of signal 2
periodmodulation2	value	100	cycle duration T_{m2} (in ms) of signal 2
freqmod2	value	0	frequency modulation factor m_2 of signal 2
amplitude2	value	0	amplitude A_2 (in V) of signal 2
CC2	value	0	DC voltage portion c_2 (in V) of signal 2
phase2	value	0	phase shift ϕ_2 (in deg) of signal 2
sensivity2	value	1	input voltage of signal 2 (in V)
damping2	value	0	attenuation λ_2 of signal 2
offset2	value	0	offset signal 2 (in V)
plotstyle2	style	BlueContB	plot style signal 2
Wave2	value	SinusB	signal type (SinusB, RectangleB, TriangleB, LDogToothB, RDogToothB)
timediv	value	5	time signal on the x axis (in ms)
Fourier	value	100	Fourier analysis
offset3	value	0	offset signal 3 (in V)
plotstyle3	style	RedContLissajou	plot style for XY mode
plotstyle4	style	MagentaContAddSub	plot style for add, sub, or mul
operation	value	\relax	alternative mode as add, sub, or mul
Lissajous	boolean	false	display as Lissajous figure (XY mode)
AllColor	boolean	true	colour or greyscale
combine	boolean	false	overlay the two signals

The output of \Oscillo with default values for its parameters yields the lefthand figure below. The righthand figure is suited for printing on black-and-white printers.

```
\usepackage{pst-osci}
\psscalebox{0.5}{\Oscillo}~
\psscalebox{0.5}{\Oscillo[AllColor=false]}
```

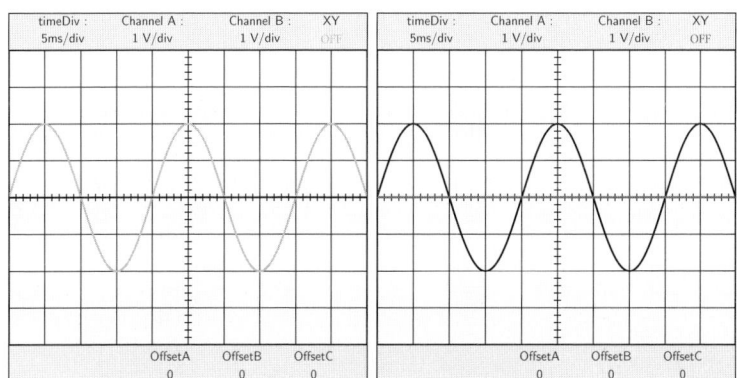

Which predefined plot styles can be used depends on the setting of the AllColor option; the plot styles are therefore a bit different, but can be overwritten at any time. In the list below, lines 1, 3, 5, and 7 refer to the colour output and the others to AllColor=false.

33 Further PSTricks packages

```
\newpsstyle{GreenContA}{linecolor=green,linewidth=0.05,plotpoints=360}
\newpsstyle{BlackContA}{linecolor=black,linewidth=0.05,plotpoints=360}
\newpsstyle{BlueContB}{linecolor=blue,linewidth=0.05,plotpoints=360}
\newpsstyle{DarkgrayContB}{linecolor=darkgray,linewidth=0.06,plotpoints=360}
\newpsstyle{RedContLissajou}{linecolor=red,linewidth=0.05,plotpoints=1000}
\newpsstyle{BlackContLissajou}{linecolor=black,linewidth=0.06,plotpoints=1000}
\newpsstyle{MagentaContAddSub}{linecolor=magenta,linewidth=0.05,plotpoints=1000}
\newpsstyle{DarkgrayDashAddSub}{linestyle=dashed,linecolor=darkgray,%
   linewidth=0.06,plotpoints=1000}
```

If, for example, you want the lines of the signals to be thicker and red (for measuring current), the following styles can be overwritten or newly defined.

```
\usepackage{pst-osci}
\newpsstyle{RedContA}{linecolor=red,linewidth=2pt,plotpoints=360}
\newpsstyle{BlackContA}{linecolor=black,linewidth=2pt,plotpoints=360}
\psscalebox{0.5}{\Oscillo[plotstyle1=RedContA]}~
\psscalebox{0.5}{\Oscillo[AllColor=false]}
```

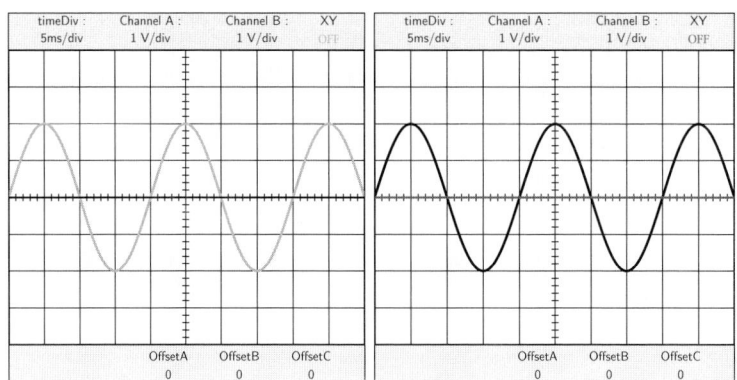

Using the individual options is more or less identical to using a real oscilloscope; not much readjustment is required to put them to paper TEX-style. Here are a few more examples without further discussion; additional information is in the documentation of the package. [34]

```
\usepackage{pst-osci}
\newpsstyle{RedContA}{linecolor=red,linewidth=2pt,plotpoints=360}
\newpsstyle{BlackContA}{linecolor=black,linewidth=2pt,plotpoints=360}
\psscalebox{0.5}{\Oscillo[amplitude1=3,amplitude2=1.5,plotstyle1=RedContA]}~
\psscalebox{0.5}{\Oscillo[amplitude1=3,amplitude2=1.5,phase1=60,phase2=-30,
   AllColor=false]}
```

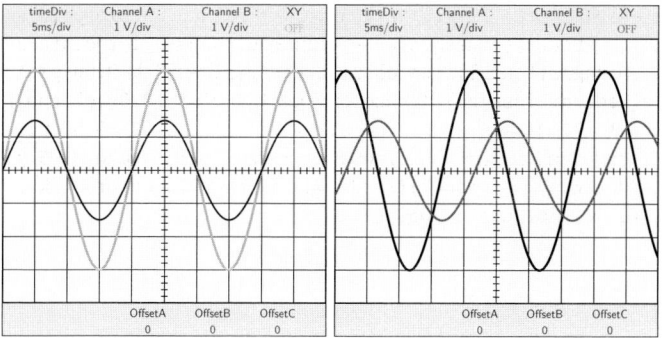

```
\usepackage{pst-osci}
\psscalebox{0.5}{\Oscillo[amplitude2=1.5,period2=50,period1=10,combine,
  operation=mul]}~
\psscalebox{0.5}{\Oscillo[amplitude1=1,amplitude2=2,period2=50,period1=2,
  combine,operation=mul]}
```

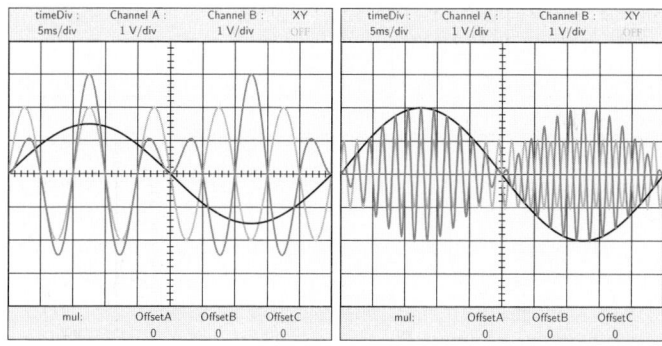

```
\usepackage{pst-osci}
\psscalebox{0.5}{\Oscillo[amplitude1=3.5,phase1=90,amplitude2=3.5,
  period1=50,period2=50,Lissajous=true,damping1=0.01,damping2=0.01]}~
\psscalebox{0.5}{\Oscillo[amplitude1=4,amplitude2=3,period1=25,
  period2=50,Lissajous=true,damping1=0.02,Wave2=\TriangleB]}
```

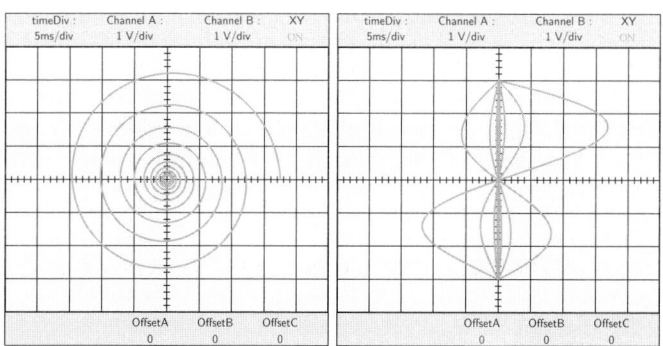

33 Further PSTricks packages

```
\usepackage{pst-osci}
\psscalebox{0.5}{\Oscillo[periodmodulation1=200,freqmod1=5,period1=30,
  timediv=50,plotpoints=1000,amplitude2=2,period2=200]}~
\psscalebox{0.5}{\Oscillo[amplitude1=1,amplitude2=1,CC2=2,
  period2=25,period1=2,combine=true,operation=mul,offset1=5]}
```

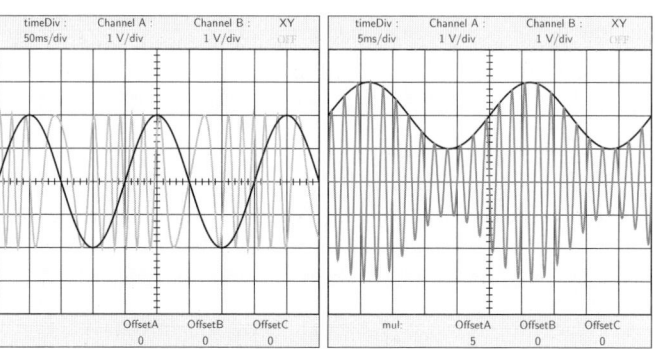

33.3.7 pst-spectra – spectral lines

pst-spectra is a very interesting package created by Arnaud Schmittbuhl for applications in physics and chemistry. It draws spectral lines in various ways. The specifications of the continuous, emission, and absorption spectra are based on a freely-available NASA database (http://cdsweb.u-strasbg.fr/viz-bin/Cat?VI/16). Altogether, the package provides support for 16 880 different visible spectral lines for 99 chemical elements.

Table 33.11: Summary of the parameters for pst-spectra

name	type	default	description
begin	380…780	380	smallest wavelength
end	380…780	780	largest wavelength
gamma	0…1	0.8	gamma colour matching
brightness	0…1	1	CMYK colour contrast
numlines	value	250	number of lines of a spectrum
lines	value list		list of wavelengths
element	name		chemical element
emission	boolean	true	emission spectrum
absorption	boolean	false	absorption spectrum
lwidth	value unit	0.2	line width (in PSTricks unit)
Imin	0…1	0	colour intensity
axe	boolean	false	axis with wavelengths
Dl	value	20	section of two axis ticks in nm
axecolor	colour	black	line colour of the axis
axewidth	value unit	0.05	line width of the axis (in PSTricks unit)

continued…

... continued

name	type	default	description
wlangle	angle	0	angle of the tick labels
wlcmd	command	\small\sf\bf	label style

There is only a single command, which provides many different outputs with the optional parameters listed above. With the default values of all parameters, it draws the continuous spectrum of light.

`\psspectrum` [settings] (x_0, y_0) (x_1, y_1)

Missing optional arguments for the coordinates of the output rectangle are substituted by {0,0}(12,1.5). This yields output of width 12 cm and height 1.5 cm (based on the standard PSTricks unit of 1 cm), as shown in the following example. If only one coordinate pair is specified, the first one automatically becomes {0,0}. Alternatively you can specify {\linewidth},??}, which scales the figure to fill the line width (where ?? is the value specifying the height in the base unit); this only works within a `pspicture` environment, however.

```
\usepackage{pst-spectra}
\psspectrum
```

The naming of the elements follows the usual conventions in the periodic table of the elements (cf. Table 33.1). So to select the emission spectrum of mercury, as in the following example, set `element=Hg`; the charge for cations can also be specified through `Hg2+`. Note that no data is available for the elements in brackets in the table.

Figure 33.1: Periodic table of the elements

H																	He
Li	Be											B	C	N	O	F	Ne
Na	Mg											Al	Si	P	S	Cl	Ar
K	Ca	Sc	Ti	V	Cr	Mn	Fe	Co	Ni	Cu	Zn	Ga	Ge	As	Se	Br	Kr
Rb	Sr	Y	Zr	Nb	Mo	Tc	Ru	Rh	Pd	Ag	Cd	In	Sn	Sb	Te	I	Xe
Cs	Ba	La	Hf	Ta	W	Re	Os	Ir	Pt	Au	Hg	Tl	Pb	Bi	Po	[At]	Rn
[Fr]	Ra	Ac															
			Ce	Pr	Nd	Pm	Sm	Eu	Gd	Tb	Dy	Ho	Er	Tm	Yb	Lu	
			Th	Pa	U	Np	Pu	Am	Cm	Bk	Cf	Es	[Fm]	[Md]	[No]	[Lr]	

33 Further PSTricks packages

```
\usepackage{pst-spectra}
\psspectrum[element=Hg]\\[1.2cm]
\psspectrum[absorption,element=Hg]\\[1.2cm]
\psspectrum[absorption,element=Hg2+]
```

33-03-54

The additional line feed of 1.2cm is required because the spectrum itself was created in a box with a null dimension. Without this line feed, the spectra would be drawn on top of one another. The formal width and height of the spectrum are specified internally (as 12.5 and 1.5 PSTricks units, unless changed through optional coordinates), but these size specifications are only of interest to PostScript. If you want this space to be reserved at the TeX level as well, enclose the \psspectrum command in a pspicture environment (and then you may also refer to the line width, if desired).

```
\usepackage{pst-spectra,pstricks-add} \def\pshlabel{\tiny\bfseries\sffamily}
\begin{pspicture}(0,-0.5)(\linewidth,1.6)
  \psspectrum[element=Mg](\linewidth,1.5)
  \psaxes[linewidth=0.5mm,Ox=380,Dx=20,dx=.855,yAxis=false,ticks=x,ticksize=0 2mm,
    tickwidth=0.5mm,subticks=5,subtickwidth=0.2mm](\linewidth,0.01)
\end{pspicture}
```

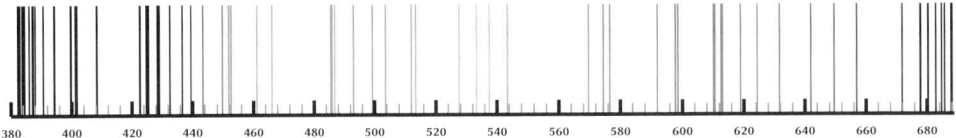

33-03-55

```
\usepackage{pst-spectra,pstricks-add}
\begin{pspicture}(0,-0.75)(\linewidth,4.75)
  \psspectrum[axe,axecolor=red,wlangle=30,Dl=25,wlcmd={\tiny\bfseries},
    element=Zn,lwidth=0.05](1,4.5)(0.5\linewidth,2.5)
  \psspectrum[axe,axecolor=red,wlangle=30,Dl=25,wlcmd={\tiny\bfseries\hspace*{-.35cm}},
    element=Zn+,lwidth=0.05](1,0)(0.5\linewidth,2)
  \rput{90}(.85\linewidth,0){\psspectrum[axe,Dl=50,wlangle=-90,wlcmd={\tiny\bfseries},
    begin=780,end=380,element=Es,absorption](5,2)(0,0)}
\end{pspicture}
```

33.3 Natural sciences

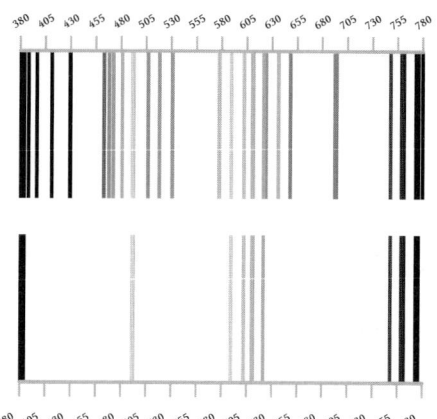
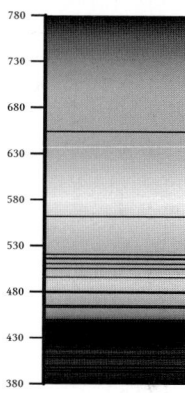

```
\usepackage{pst-spectra,pstricks-add}
\psspectrum[element={Hg,Cd2+,W+},lwidth=0.5pt](\linewidth,1)
```

33.3.8 pst-stru – load diagrams

The `pst-stru` package by Giuseppe Matarazzo and Manuel Luque offers interesting opportunities for civil and structural engineers. You can create many different types of load diagrams by changing the options.

```
\usepackage{pst-stru}
\def\BMdistributed#1#2#3{#2 x sub 0.5 #1 x mul mul mul #3 mul}
\begin{pspicture}(-1,-1.4)(11,2)
  \pnode(0,0){A}\pnode(10,0){B}\rput{0}(A){\hinge}\rput{0}(B){\roller}
  \rput(0,-1){\Large A}\rput(10,-1){\Large B}\psline[linecolor=blue](A)(B)
  \pscustom[linecolor=blue,linewidth=1pt,fillstyle=solid,fillcolor=yellow]{%
    \psplot[linecolor=blue]{0}{10}{\BMdistributed{12}{10}{0.01}}\psline(10,0)(0,0)}
  \psset{arrowsize=1.5mm}\multido{\nStart=0.0+0.2}{51}{%
    \pnode(\nStart,0){E1}\pnode(!/x \nStart\space def x \BMdistributed{12}{10}{0.01}){E2}
    \psline[linecolor=blue,arrowinset=0,arrowsize=1mm]{->}(E2)(E1) }
\end{pspicture}
```

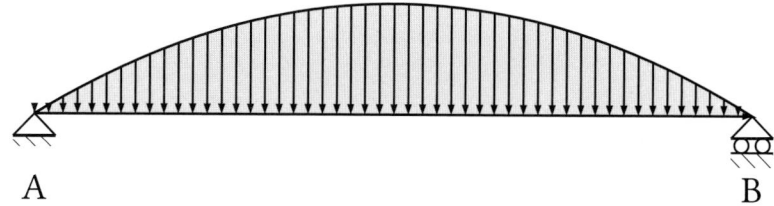

Drawing a triload diagram takes very little effort using the `\triload` command:

33 Further PSTricks packages

```
\usepackage{pst-stru}
\begin{pspicture}(-1,-4)(11,3)\psset{arrowsize=0.8mm,arrowinset=0}
% Total span is (K+1) times L, say AC=(K+1)*L  [K=dimensionless value]
\triload[K=1,P=8,L=5]% k=1 -> AB=BC
\end{pspicture}
```

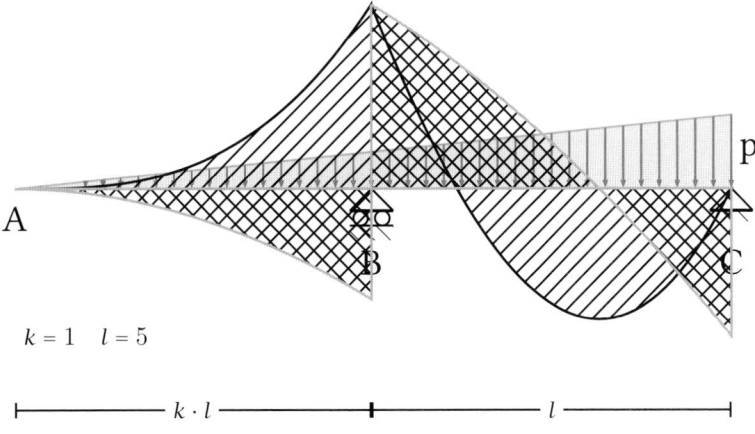

```
\usepackage{pst-stru}
\begin{pspicture}(-1,-6)(11,3) \psset{arrowsize=0.8mm,arrowinset=0}
  \triload[K=0.333,P=8,L=7.5] % k=1/3, like example 6
\end{pspicture}
```

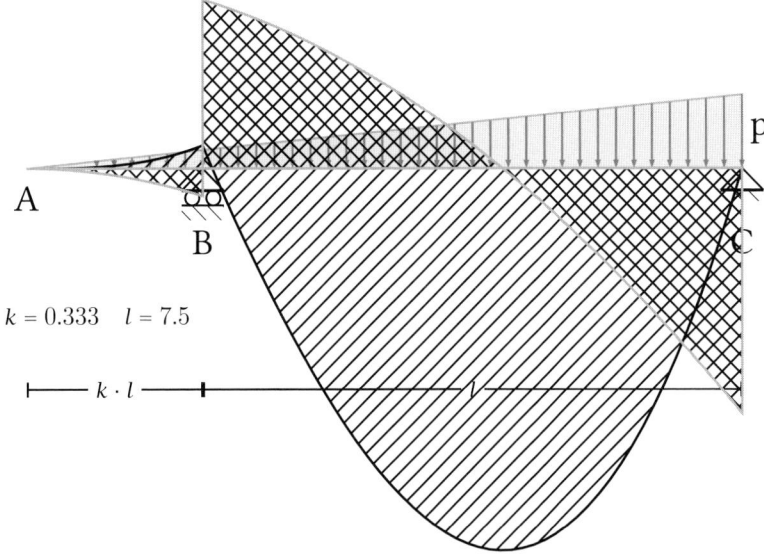

```
\usepackage{pst-stru}
```

```
\begin{pspicture}(-1,-3)(11,5) \psset{arrowsize=0.8mm,arrowinset=0}
  \triload[K=2,P=8,L=3]   % k=2 -> BM always NEGATIVE in the whole structure
\end{pspicture}
```

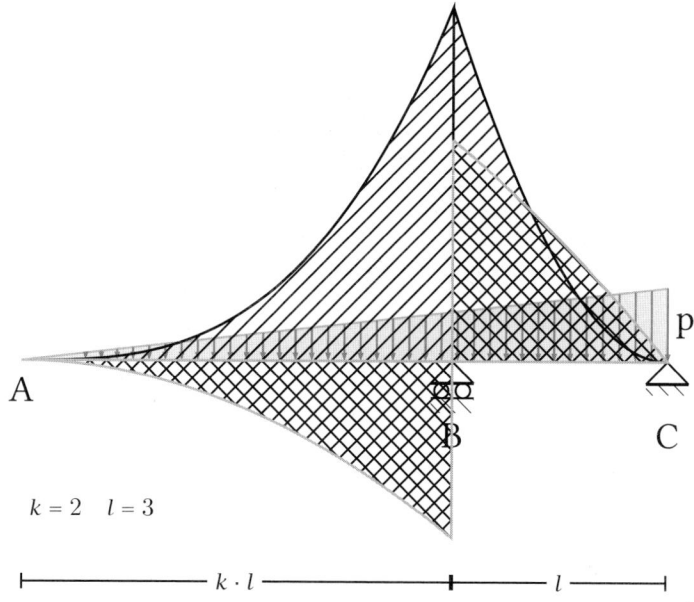

```
\usepackage{pst-stru}

\begin{pspicture}(-1,-3)(12,4)
  \psset{arrowsize=0.8mm,
    arrowinset=0}
  \triload[K=2.5,P=8,L=2]
% k>2 -> Reaction in C downwards
\end{pspicture}
```

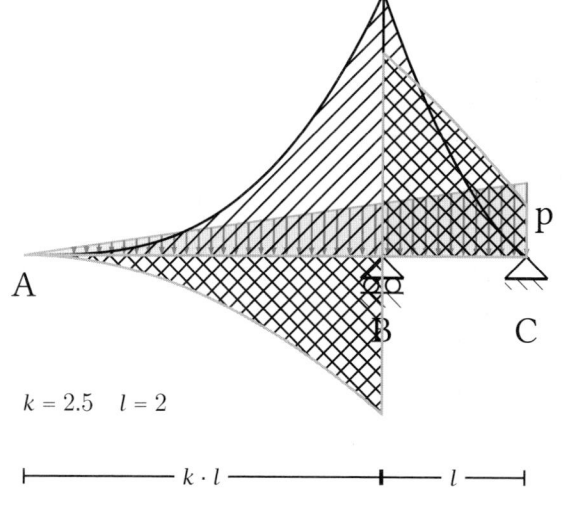

```
\usepackage{pst-stru}
\begin{pspicture}(-1,-4)(9,2) \psset{arrowsize=0.8mm,arrowinset=0}
  \pnode(0,0){A}\pnode(2,0){B}\pnode(8,0){C}\rput{0}(C){\hinge}\rput{0}(B){\roller}
  \psline[linecolor=red,fillcolor=yellow,fillstyle=solid](0,0)(8,0)(8,1)(0,0)
```

```
\multido{\nStart=1.00+0.025}{-37}{%
  \psArrowCivil[RotArrows=0,length=\nStart,start=\nStart,linecolor=magenta](A)(C){}}
\rput(8.3,0.4){\large p}\rput(0,-0.4){\Large A}
\rput(2,-1){\Large B}\rput(8.3,-0.6){\Large C}
\pcline[offset=0,linecolor=blue]{|-|}(0,-3)(2,-3)\lput*{:U}{\bf $\frac{l}{3}$}
\pcline[offset=0,linecolor=blue]{|-|}(2,-3)(8,-3)\lput*{:U}{\bf $l$}
\def\MflettAB#1#2#3{#1 #2 div -.125 mul x mul x mul x mul #3 mul neg}
\pscustom[linecolor=blue,linewidth=1pt,fillstyle=hlines]{
  \psplot[]{0}{2}{\MflettAB{6}{6}{0.15}}\psline[](2,0)(0,0) }
\def\TaglioAB#1#2#3{#1 #2 div -.375 mul x mul x mul #3 mul} %AB
\pscustom[linecolor=green,linewidth=1pt,fillstyle=crosshatch]{
  \psplot[]{0}{2}{\TaglioAB{6}{6}{0.15}}\psline[](2,0)(0,0) }
\def\MflettBC#1#2#3{#1 #2 div -.125 mul x mul x mul x mul
  #1 3.375 div #2 mul x mul add #1 10.125 div #2 mul #2 mul sub #3 mul neg}% BC
\pscustom[linecolor=blue,linewidth=1pt,fillstyle=hlines]{
  \psplot[]{2}{8}{\MflettBC{6}{6}{0.15}}\psline[](8,0)(2,0) }
\def\TaglioBC#1#2#3{#1 #2 div -.375 mul x mul x mul #1 3.375 div #2 mul add #3 mul}
\pscustom[linecolor=green,linewidth=1pt,fillstyle=crosshatch]{
  \psplot[]{2}{8}{\TaglioBC{6}{6}{0.15}}\psline[](8,0)(2,0)(2,1.4) }
\psline[linewidth=1.5pt](0,0)(8,0)   % Printing beam AC after diagrams BM/S
\rput(3,1.6){\em {\scriptsize Shear diagram (green boundary)}}
\rput(3,-1.6){\em {\scriptsize Bending Moment diagram (blue boundary)}}
\rput(2,-1.9){\scriptsize [assumed positive downwards]}
\rput(5,-1){\bf {\large +}}\rput(2.5,0.6){\bf {\large +}}
\rput(7.7,-1.3){\bf {\Large -}}
\end{pspicture}
```

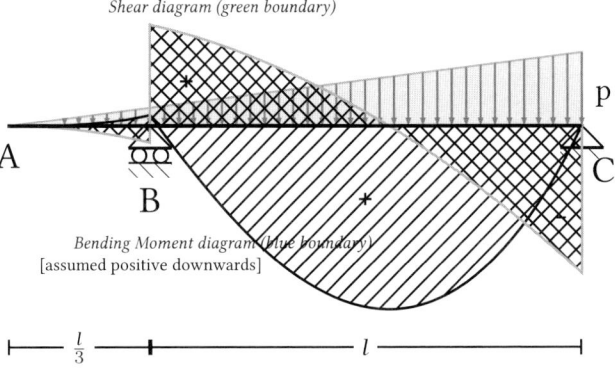

33.3.9 pst-pad – adhesion models

The pst-pad package by Patrick Drechsler is a collection of PSTricks commands to depict adhesion and friction systems, for example, for the JKR or Hertz theory, boundary friction, or elasto-hydrodynamic friction. The commands support bodies of planar, spherical, or elastic form. Additionally, the fluid option determines whether a liquid film exists between the bodies.

```
\PstWallToWall [settings] (x,y)
\PstSphereToWall [settings] (x,y)
\PstPad [settings] (x,y).
```

```
\usepackage{pst-pad}
\begin{pspicture}(4,4)\PstWallToWall(2,2)\end{pspicture}
\begin{pspicture}(4,4)\PstSphereToWall[fluid=false](2,2)\end{pspicture}
\begin{pspicture}(4,4)\PstPad(2,2)\end{pspicture}
```

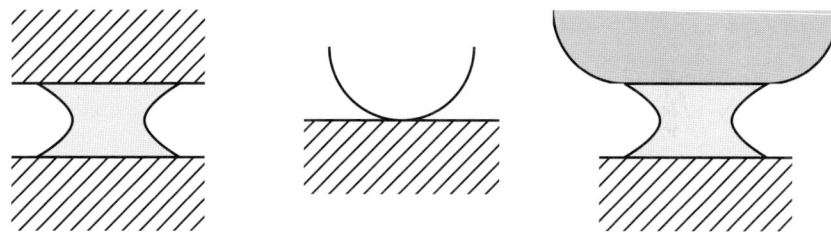

The following example shows the use of the \PstPad command and some of its parameters. The figure created illustrates the meanings of the parameters, giving the default parameter values in blue and below these the actual values used in the example in brown.

```
\usepackage[dvipsnames,svgnames]{pstricks}
\usepackage{pst-pad,graphicx}
\resizebox{0.9\linewidth}{!}{%
\begin{pspicture}(-5,-4)(7.5,4)
\PstPad[FluidMaxRadius=4,FluidMinRadius=3,FluidHeight=1,FSphereHeight=2,
  FSphereFillColor=green!20!white,FluidFillColor=blue!10!white,FluidLineWidth=1.5pt,
  FSphereLineWidth=0.1pt,WallLineWidth=3pt,WallLineColor=blue,
  FSphereLineColor=magenta,FluidLineColor=green!50!black](0,0)
\sffamily\footnotesize%
\psset{linecolor=gray, linewidth=0.2pt} %% "Crosshair" for orientation:
\psline[linestyle=dashed](-5,0)(5,0)
\psline[linestyle=dashed](0,-3)(0,1.5)
%% Node definitions:
\pnode(0,0){center}
\pnode(-4,-2.25){maxradiusLeft}\pnode(0,-2.25){maxradiusRight}
\pnode(-3,0){minradiusLeft}    \pnode(3,0){minradiusRight}
\pnode([nodesep=4.5]center){fluidheightCenter}
\pnode([nodesep=4.5,offset=-1]center){fluidheightBottom}
\pnode([offset=-1]fluidheightBottom){wallThicknessBottom}
\pnode([nodesep=5.2,offset=1]center){fsphereheightBottom}
\pnode([offset=1]fsphereheightBottom){fsphereheightTop}
\psset{arrows=|<->|,linewidth=0.8pt,linecolor=red,arrowscale=1.5}
\rput[l]([nodesep=.2,offset=.2]center){\textbf{(0,0)}}%% Center:
\ncline{minradiusLeft}{center}\nbput{\ParCol{FluidMinRadius}{0.5}{3}}
\ncline{maxradiusLeft}{maxradiusRight}\nbput{\ParCol{FluidMaxRadius}{1}{4}}
\ncline{fluidheightCenter}{fluidheightBottom}\naput{\ParCol{FluidHeight}{.5}{1}}
\ncline{fluidheightBottom}{wallThicknessBottom}\naput{\ParCol{WallThickness}{1}{1}}
```

```
\ncline{fsphereheightBottom}{fsphereheightTop}\nbput{\ParCol{FSphereHeight/2}{2}{2}}
\psline{->}(-.1,2.2)(-.3,1.6)
\rput(-.1,2.6){\ParCol{FSphereFillColor}{"lightgray"}{"green!20!white"}}
\psline{->}(4,2.2)(2.5,.6)
\rput(4,2.6){\ParCol{FluidFillColor}{"yellow"}{"blue!10!white"}}
\psline{->}([offset=.5,nodesep=3]minradiusRight)(minradiusRight)
\rput[l]([offset=-.1,nodesep=3.2]minradiusRight){\ParCol{FluidLineWidth}{1pt}{1.5pt}}
\rput[l]([offset=.8,nodesep=3.2]minradiusRight){%
   \ParCol{FluidLineColor}{"black"}{"green!50!black"}}
\psline{->}(-4.3,2.2)(-3.5,1)\rput(-4.3,2.6){\ParCol{FSphereLineWidth}{1pt}{0.1pt}}
\rput(-4.3,3.4){\ParCol{FSphereLineColor}{"black"}{"magenta"}}
\psline{->}(1.5,-2.25)(1.5,-1)\rput[t](1.5,-2.5){\ParCol{WallLineWidth}{1pt}{3pt}}
\rput[t](1.5,-3.4){\ParCol{WallLineColor}{"black"}{"blue"}}
\end{pspicture}}
```

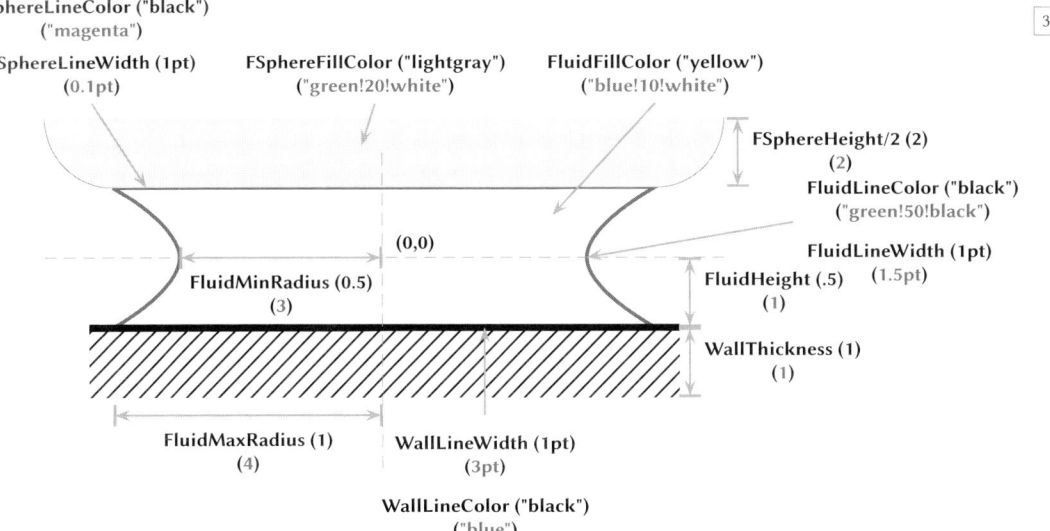

33.4 Information technology

Automata theory, an area of theoretical computer science that originated from cybernetics, describes the study of model computers (automata) and the problems they can solve. Additional keywords are computability and complexity theory. For practical applications, for example when building compilers, the relations can only be depicted symbolically. This also includes the symbolic relations in database and society structures for which several packages exist.

This section looks at `gastex` and `vaucanson-G` for drawing automata systems, `sfg` for drawing information flow charts, `pst-dbicons` for drawing entity relationships, and `pst-pdgr` for drawing pedigrees.

33.4.1 gastex

The gastex package by Paul Gastin for graphs and automata is not a PSTricks-specific package in the true sense, even though it possesses the same structures for passing parameters. Nevertheless we are mentioning it here as it's used in conjunction with other PSTricks packages and commands. gastex does not have any documentation, but there is an example in the documentation part file that is readily accessible.

```
\usepackage[dvipsnames]{pstricks}
\usepackage{gastex}
\psset{unit=2.5pt}
\begin{pspicture}(-35,-37)(85,15)
  \node[Nw=16,linecolor=Yellow,fillcolor=Yellow](A)(-20,0){initial}
  \imark[iangle=200,linecolor=Peach](A)
  \node[Nmr=0,Nw=14,fillgray=0.85,dash={1}0](B)(20,0){\textcolor{RedViolet}{final}}
  \fmark[flength=10,fangle=-30,dash={3 1 1 1}0](B)
  \node[Nadjust=wh,Nadjustdist=2,Nmr=3,Nmarks=r,linecolor=Green](C)(60,-20){%
    $\left(\begin{array}{ccc}2 & 1 & 0\\ -1 & 0 & 1\\ 0 & -1 & 2 \end{array}\right)$}
  \rmark[linecolor=Green,rdist=1.4](C)
  \drawedge[curvedepth=5,linecolor=Red](A,B){\textcolor{Cyan}{curved}}
  \drawedge[ELside=r,ELpos=35](A,B){straight}
  \drawedge[curvedepth=-25,ELside=r,dash={1.5}0](A,B){far}
  \drawloop[ELpos=75, loopangle=150, dash={0.2 0.5}0](A){loopCW}
  \drawloop[loopCW=n,ELside=r,loopangle=30,dash={3 1.5}{1.5}](B){loopCCW}
  \drawqbpedge[ELside=r,ELdist=0,dash={4 1 1 1}0](B,-90,C,180){qbpedge}
  \drawloop[ELpos=70,loopangle=0](C){$b / 01$}
  \drawloop[loopCW=n,ELpos=75,ELside=r,loopangle=-90,sxo=6](C){$a / 01$}
  \drawloop[ELpos=75,loopangle=-90,sxo=-6](C){$b / 10 $}
  \drawloop[loopangle=50](C){$b / 01$}
  \drawloop[ELpos=75,loopangle=148](C){$b / 01$}
\end{pspicture}
```

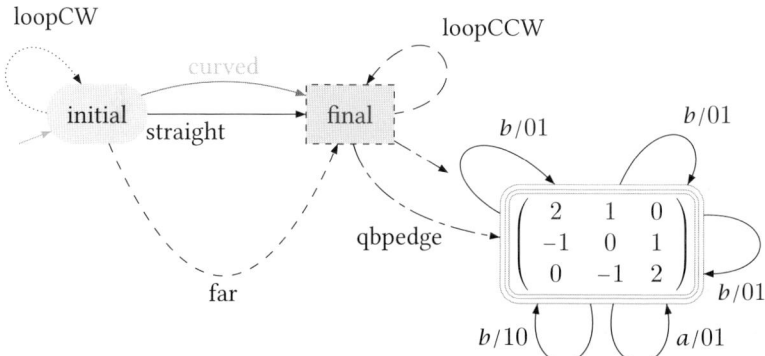

33.4.2 vaucanson-g

vaucanson-g is a similar package to gastex, but vaucanson-g supports more complex structures. The authors, Sylvain Lombardy and Jacques Sakarovitch, haven't put this package on CTAN yet, but it is available from their website http://igm.univ-mlv.fr/~lombardy/

33 Further PSTricks packages

Vaucanson-G/. The philosophy of the package is similar to that of pst-eucl; only a few nodes with physical coordinates are specified and the rest are provided relative to these.

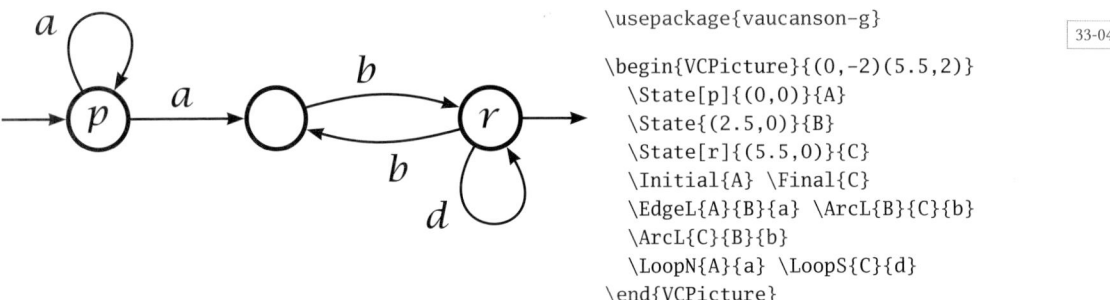

```
\usepackage{vaucanson-g}

\begin{VCPicture}{(0,-2)(5.5,2)}
  \State[p]{(0,0)}{A}
  \State{(2.5,0)}{B}
  \State[r]{(5.5,0)}{C}
  \Initial{A} \Final{C}
  \EdgeL{A}{B}{a} \ArcL{B}{C}{b}
  \ArcL{C}{B}{b}
  \LoopN{A}{a} \LoopS{C}{d}
\end{VCPicture}
```

There is a special adaption for the beamer document class, but note that the instruction on the website to load beamer with xcolor=pst is wrong – this option is now obsolete and no longer supported.

```
\usepackage{vaucanson-g,graphicx}
\resizebox{\linewidth}{!}{\begin{VCPicture}{(-11,-5)(11,12)}
  \PlainState\LargeState\ChgStateLabelScale{0.75}
  \StateIF[p,q]{(-10,-1)}{AB}       \StateIF[q,r]{(-6,-1)}{BC}
  \StateIF[p,r]{(-8,-4.464)}{AC}    \VCPut{(-5,-5)}{$\kappa=[2,0,0]$}
  \StateIF[p]{(8,1.536)}{A}         \StateIF[q]{(6,5)}{B}
  \StateIF[r]{(10,5)}{C}            \VCPut{(8,-0.5)}{$\kappa=[1,0,0]$}
  \StateIF[pq]{(-8,7.536)}{Ab}      \StateIF[qr]{(-6,11)}{Bc}
  \StateIF[pr]{(-10,11)}{Ac}        \VCPut{(-2,11)}{$\kappa=[0,1,0]$}
  \StateIF[p,qr]{(0,-1.464)}{ABc}   \StateIF[q,pr]{(-2,2)}{BAc}
  \StateIF[r,pq]{(2,2)}{CAb}        \VCPut{(3,-2)}{$\kappa=[1,1,0]$}
  \StateVar[pq,pr,qr]{(-8,3)}{AbAcBc}\VCPut{(-8,1)}{$\kappa=[0,3,0]$}
  \StateIF[pr,qr]{(2,8)}{AcBc}      \StateIF[pq,pr]{(0,4.536)}{AbAc}
  \StateIF[pq,qr]{(-2,8)}{AbBc}     \VCPut{(5,9)}{$\kappa=[0,2,0]$}% end phys. coors
  \DimEdge\ChgEdgeLineStyle{dashed} \RstEdgeLineWidth
  \EdgeR{Ab}{AbAc}{}       \EdgeR{Ab}{AbBc}{} \EdgeR{Ac}{AbAc}{}
  \EdgeR{Ac}{AcBc}{}       \EdgeR{Bc}{AbBc}{} \EdgeR{Bc}{AcBc}{}
  \EdgeR{AbAc}{AbAcBc}{} \EdgeR{AbAc}{A}{} \EdgeR{AbBc}{AbAcBc}{}
  \EdgeR{AbBc}{B}{}        \EdgeR{AcBc}{AbAcBc}{}\EdgeR{AcBc}{C}{}
  \EdgeR{A}{ABc}{}         \EdgeR{B}{BAc}{}       \EdgeR{C}{CAb}{}
  \EdgeR{AbAcBc}{ABc}{}  \EdgeR{AbAcBc}{BAc}{} \EdgeR{AbAcBc}{CAb}{}
  \EdgeR{ABc}{AB}{}        \EdgeR{ABc}{AC}{}      \EdgeR{BAc}{AB}{}
  \EdgeR{BAc}{BC}{}        \EdgeR{CAb}{AC}{}      \EdgeR{CAb}{BC}{}
  \RstEdge
  \Initial{Ab}\Final{Ab}\Final[w]{Ac}\Final{Bc}\Initial{AbAc}\Initial{AbBc}
  \Final[s]{AbBc}\Final{AbAc}\Final{AcBc}
  \Initial{AbAcBc}\Final{AbAcBc}\Initial{A}
  \Initial{B}\Final[s]{B}\Final{C}\Initial{ABc}\Initial{BAc}\Initial[s]{CAb}
  \Final[s]{BAc}\Final{CAb}\Initial{AB}\Initial{AC}\Initial[s]{BC}\Final{BC}
  \EdgeR{Ab}{Bc}{a,b}    \EdgeR{Bc}{Ac}{a}     \EdgeR{Ac}{Ab}{a}
  \EdgeL{AbAc}{AbBc}{a} \EdgeL{AbBc}{AcBc}{a} \EdgeL{AcBc}{AbAc}{a}
  \LoopN{AbAcBc}{a}\EdgeL{A}{B}{a}
```

```
\EdgeL{B}{C}{a}\ArcL{A}{C}{b}\ArcL{C}{A}{a}
\LoopN{B}{b}\EdgeL{ABc}{BAc}{a}\EdgeL{BAc}{CAb}{a}\EdgeL{CAb}{ABc}{a}
\EdgeL{AB}{BC}{a,b}\EdgeL{BC}{AC}{a}\EdgeL{AC}{AB}{a}
\end{VCPicture}}
```

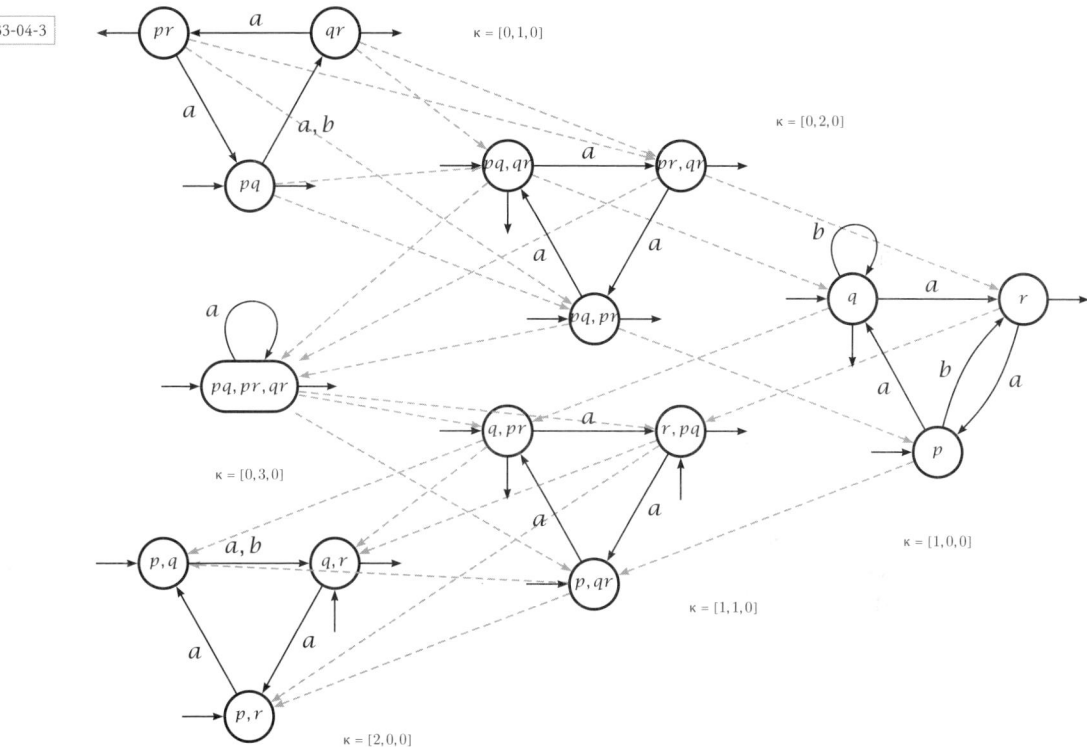

33.4.3 sfg – information flow charts

This package by Hanspeter Schmid draws information flow charts. There is no independent documentation for this package; you can find a description of the commands at the end of the sfg.sty package file.

```
\usepackage{sfg}
\sfgsetunit{0.5cm}
\sfgsetsize{0.12}{0.4}{0.5}{0.3}
\sfgsetcompass
\begin{picture}(27,4)    % branches related to node 2
  \put(6,2){\sfgbranch{3}{0}\S{$\frac{1}{R_1}$}}
  \put(9,2){\sfgbranch{3}{0}\N{\boldmath $Z_2$}}
  \put(18,2){\sfgcurve{-9}{0}{2}\S{$\frac{1}{R_2}$}}
  \put(24,2){\sfgcurve{-15}{0}{-2}\N{$sC_1$}} % branches related to node 3
  \put(12,2){\sfgbranch{3}{0}\N{$\frac{1}{R_2}$}}
  \put(15,2){\sfgbranch{3}{0}\N{\boldmath $Z_3$}}
  \put(0,2){\sfgcurve{6}{0}{2}\N{$1$}}% input, voltage gain, output
```

```
            \put(18,2){\sfgcurve{6}{0}{-2}\S{$\alpha_{\mathrm{V}}$}}
            \put(24,2){\sfgbranch{3}{0}\S{$1$}}
            \put(0,2){\sfgtermnode\S{$V_{\mathrm{in}}$}}     % nodes
            \put(3,2){\sfgnode\S{$I_1$}}
            \put(6,2){\sfgnode\S{$V_1$}}
            \put(9,2){\sfgnode\S{$I_2$}}
            \put(12,2){\sfgnode\S{$V_2$}}
            \put(15,2){\sfgnode\S{$I_3$}}
            \put(18,2){\sfgnode\S{$V_3$}}
            \put(21,2){\sfgnode\S{$I_4$}}
            \put(24,2){\sfgnode\S{$V_4$}}
            \put(27,2){\sfgtermnode\S{$V_{\mathrm{out}}$}}
        \end{picture}
```

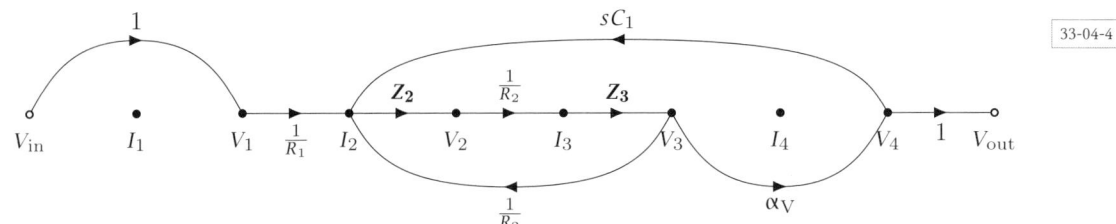

33.4.4 pst-dbicons – ER relations

Wolfgang May created this package for the symbolic description of database models (Entity Relationship). The entities are arranged in a table and then related by node connections. Example 36-00-6 on page 771 illustrates a complex and comprehensive diagram.

```
\usepackage{pst-node,pst-dbicons}
\seticonparams{entity}{shadow=true,fillcolor=black!30,fillstyle=solid}
\seticonparams{attribute}{fillcolor=black!10,fillstyle=solid}
\seticonparams{relationship}{shadow=true,fillcolor=black!20,fillstyle=solid}
\begin{tabular}{cc}
\begin{tabular}{c}
\entity{tblpbl}[tbl\_pbl]\\[2cm]
\entity{tblinst}[tbl\_inst]\\[2cm]
\entity{tbldsc}[tbl\_dsc] \\[2cm]
\end{tabular}\hspace{6em}
\begin{tabular}{c}
~\\[2cm]
\entity{tbllvl}[tbl\_lvl]\\[2cm]
\entity{tblindx}[tbl\_indx]\\[2cm]
\end{tabular}
\attributeof{tblpbl}[3em]{0}{pbljrn}[pbl\_jrn]%attributes
\attributeof{tblpbl}[3em]{90}{pbloth}[pbl\_oth]
\attributeof{tblpbl}[3em]{30}{pblauth}[pbl\_auth]
\attributeof{tblpbl}[3em]{150}{pblyr}[pbl\_yr]
\attributeof{tblpbl}[3em]{180}[key]{pblid}[pbl\_id]
\attributeof{tblinst}[3em]{150}[key]{instprm}[inst\_prm]
```

```
\attributeof{tblinst}[3em]{180}[key]{instid}[inst\_id]
\attributeof{tbldsc}[3em]{180}[key]{dscid}[dsc\_id]
\attributeof{tbldsc}[3em]{150}{dscname}[dsc\_name]
\attributeof{tbldsc}[3em]{220}{dscval}[dsc\_val]
\attributeof{tbldsc}[3em]{270}{dscunit}[dsc\_unit]
\attributeof{tbldsc}[3em]{320}{dscoth}[dsc\_oth]
\attributeof{tbllvl}[3em]{0}[key]{lvlid}[lvl\_id]
\attributeof{tbllvl}[3em]{90}{lvlname}[lvl\_name]
\attributeof{tblindx}[3em]{0}[key]{indxid}[indx\_id]
\attributeof{tblindx}[3em]{30}{indxname}[indx\_name]
\attributeof{tblindx}[3em]{270}{indxrel}[indx\_rel]
\relationshipbetween{tblpbl}{tblinst}{1:m}%relationships
\relationshipbetween{tblinst}{tbldsc}{m:1}
\relationshipbetween{tblinst}{tbllvl}{m:1}
\relationshipbetween{tbldsc}{tblindx}{1:m}
\relationshipbetween{tbllvl}{tblindx}{1:m}
\end{tabular}
```

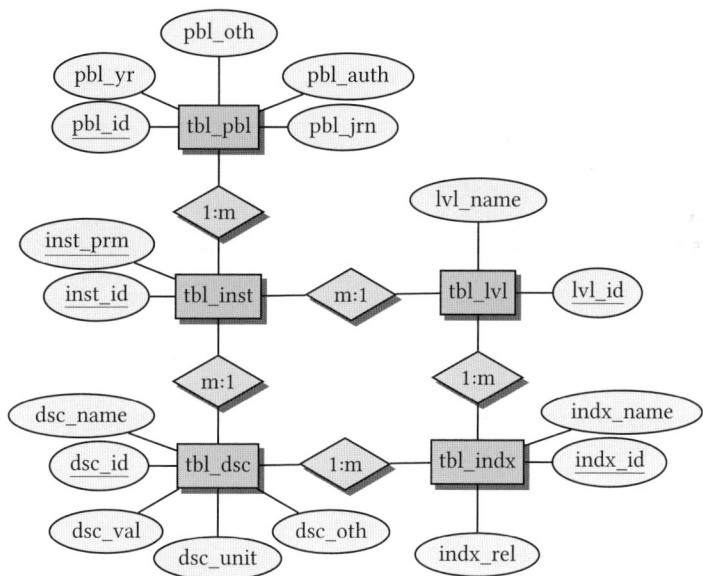

33.4.5 pst-pdgr – pedigrees

The actual meaning of "pedigree" is not the meaning in the context of the package here; in medicine it refers to more than just the relation between individual humans generations. The package authors, Boris Veytsman and Leila Akhmadeeva, provide a detailed description of the theoretical background. [77]

```
\usepackage{pst-pdgr}
\begin{pspicture}(6,6)    \psset{belowtextrp=t,armB=1}
 \rput(2.5,5.5){\pstPerson[male,deceased,belowtext=A:1]{A:1}}
 \rput(3.5,5.5){\pstPerson[female,deceased,belowtext=A:2]{A:2}}
```

```
\pstRelationship[descentnode=A:1_2]{A:1}{A:2}
\rput(1,3.5){\pstPerson[female,affected,belowtext=B:1]{B:1}}
\pstDescent{A:1_2}{B:1}   \rput(2,3.5){\pstPerson[male,belowtext=B:2]{B:2}}
\pstRelationship[descentnode=B:1_2]{B:1}{B:2}
\rput(3.5,3.5){\pstPerson[male,affected,belowtext=B:3]{B:3}}
\pstDescent{A:1_2}{B:3}   \rput(4.5,3.5){\pstPerson[female,belowtext=B:4]{B:4}}
\pstRelationship[descentnode=B:3_4]{B:3}{B:4}
\rput(5.5,3.5){\pstPerson[female,affected,deceased,proband,belowtext=B:5]{B:5}}
\pstDescent{A:1_2}{B:5}   \rput(0.5,1.5){\pstPerson[female,belowtext=C:1]{C:1}}
\pstDescent{B:1_2}{C:1}   \rput(1.5,1.5){\pstPerson[female,belowtext=C:2]{C:2}}
\pstDescent{B:1_2}{C:2}   \rput(2.5,1.5){\pstPerson[female,deceased,
                             belowtext=\parbox{2cm}{\centering C:3\\4/52}]{C:3}}
\pstDescent{B:1_2}{C:3}   \rput(3.5,1.5){\pstPerson[female,affected,belowtext=C:4]{C:4}}
\pstDescent{B:3_4}{C:4}   \rput(4.5,1.5){\pstPerson[male,insidetext=?,belowtext=C:5]{C:5}}
\pstDescent{B:3_4}{C:5}
\end{pspicture}
```

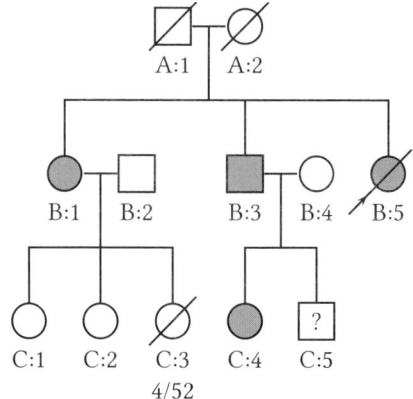

For the illustration of the individual relations, the following symbols are available.

Table 33.12: Symbols of the pst-pdgr package

command	output
person symbols	
\pstPerson[*condition=asymptomatic*]{A}	◇
\pstPerson[*condition=affected, sex=male, evaluated*]{A}	■ *
\pstPerson[*obligatory, female*]{A}	⊙
\pstPerson[*asymptomatic, male, proband*]{A}	⌷ ↗
\pstPerson[*condition=obligatory, sex=male, deceased*]{A}	⌥

continued...

… continued

command	output
\pstPerson[sex=female, adopted, condition=affected, abovetext=Jana]{A}	Jana
\pstPerson[sex=male, condition=affected, belowtext=20 yr, deceased]{A}	28 yr
\pstPerson[unknown, affected, righttext=1 w]{A}	$\overset{A}{1w}$
\pstPerson[sex=male, insidetext=5]{A}	5
\pstPerson[sex=female, condition=affected, insidetext=P]{A}	P
\pstPerson[sex=female, affected, belowtext=SB 2wks, deceased]{A}	$\underset{2wks}{SB}$
abortion symbols	
\pstAbortion[belowtext=male]{A}	male
\pstAbortion[sab, righttext=1w]{A}	1w
\pstAbortion[affected]{A}	
infertility	
\pstChildless[belowtext=vasectomy]{A}	vasectomy
\pstChildless[belowtext=anospermia, infertile]{A}	anospermia

33.5 Miscellaneous

This section looks at pst-light3d for creating 3D light effects, pst-calendar for outputting calendars, and psgo for typesetting game positions.

33.5.1 pst-light3d – 3D light effects

This package is more for play than for work. Nevertheless, it offers functionality that isn't easy to realize even with specialized software. There are two commands, one for textual elements and one for graphical objects.

```
\PstLightThreeDText [settings] {text}
\PstLightThreeDGraphic [settings] {graphical object}
```

The possible options are summarized in Table 33.13. Except for LightThreeDSteps, they are all illustrated in the following examples.

33 Further PSTricks packages

Table 33.13: Summary of the available options for `pst-light3d`

name	type	default	description
LightThreeDXLength	*value unit*	0.2	length of shadow in x direction
LightThreeDYLength	*value unit*	0.3	length of shadow in y direction
LightThreeDLength	*value unit*	–	sets LightThreeDXLength and LightThreeDYLength to the same value
LightThreeDSteps	*integer*	40	number of intermediate steps
LightThreeDAngle	*angle*	45	light incidence angle
LightThreeDColorPsCommand	*PostScript*	2.5 div setgray	arbitrary PostScript code for setting the colour at PostScript level

First, you must specify a font that is available at the required font size as an outline font; otherwise it can't be filled with a colour.

\DeclareFixedFont{command name}{Encoding}{name}{series}{shape}{size}

A possible example is therefore \DeclareFixedFont{\RM}{T1}{ptm}{m}{n}{2cm}. Without any fill instruction, the font is "open" with grey shading.

```
\usepackage{pst-light3d}

\DeclareFixedFont{\RM}{T1}%
    {ptm}{m}{n}{2cm}
\PstLightThreeDText{\RM PSTricks}
```
33-05-1

```
\usepackage{pst-light3d}

\DeclareFixedFont{\SF}{T1}%
    {phv}{m}{n}{2cm}
\PstLightThreeDText[fillstyle=solid,
    fillcolor=cyan]{\SF PSTricks}
```
33-05-2

```
\usepackage{pst-light3d,pst-grad}

\DeclareFixedFont{\RM}{T1}{ptm}{m}{n}{2.5cm}
\psset{linestyle=none,fillstyle=gradient,
    gradbegin={[rgb]{1,0.84,0}},gradend=blue,
    gradangle=90,gradmidpoint=0}
\PstLightThreeDText{\RM\TeX}
```
33-05-3

```
\usepackage{pst-light3d}

\DeclareFixedFont{\RM}{T1}{ptm}{m}{n}{2cm}
\psset{linestyle=none,fillstyle=solid,
    fillcolor={[rgb]{1,0.84,0}}}
\PstLightThreeDText[LightThreeDXLength=0.5]{%
    \RM\TeX}
```
33-05-4

```
\usepackage{pst-plot,pst-light3d}
\psset{xunit=8cm,yunit=2.5cm}
\begin{pspicture}(-0.05,-1)(1,1.2)
  \psaxes[Dx=0.2,Dy=0.4,dy=0.4]{->}(0,0)(0,-1)(1,1.2)
  \psset{plotpoints=500,LightThreeDXLength=0.3,LightThreeDYLength=-0.3}
  \PstLightThreeDGraphic[LightThreeDColorPsCommand=1.5 div 0.05 exch 0.8 sethsbcolor]{
      \psplot{0}{0.95}{x 10 mul 57.296 mul sin}}
  \PstLightThreeDGraphic{\psplot{0}{0.95}{x 40 mul 57.296 mul cos 2 div}}
\end{pspicture}
```

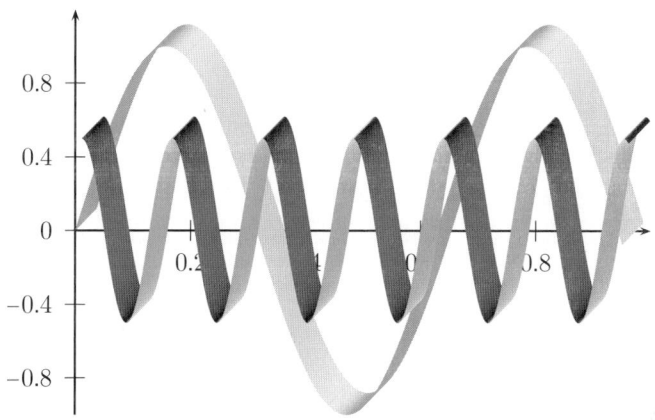

33.5.2 pst-calendar – calendar operations

The pst-calendar package is also by Manuel Luque. It doesn't offer mathematical calendar operations, but functionality to output date sheets. pst-calendar has English (default), French, or German variations; the required language must be activated through the package option if it hasn't been set already for the document class through english, french, or ngerman. Note that there is no special TeX version of this package; if not working with LaTeX, you will have to make special adaptions.

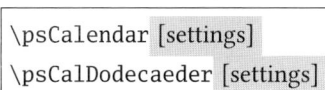

The available parameters are summarized in Table 33.14. Note that the style option requires the name of a month, so its values depend on the specified language.

name	type	default	description
year	integer	\number\year	displayed year
month	1…12	\number\month	displayed month
monthT	1…12	\number\month	mark the current day in the specified month
day	1…31	\number\day	displayed day
style	month	\number\month	month in front for the dodecahedron

Table 33.14: The available parameters for the pst-calendar package

33 Further PSTricks packages

When dates aren't specified, the current date and month is assumed. The output for a complete year can be accomplished with the help of the \multido command, as shown in the next example.

```
\usepackage{pst-calendar}
\multido{\iM=1+3}{4}{%
  \multido{\iMM=\iM+1}{3}{\psscalebox{0.5}{\psCalendar[Year=2011,Month=\iMM]}}\\}
```

There is a slight difficulty in marking holidays, as these are currently based only on the French specification. The corresponding code sequences in the package are easy to recognize, however, and you can change them accordingly.

33.5 Miscellaneous

```
\usepackage{pst-calendar}
\psscalebox{0.5}{\psCalendar}
\psscalebox{0.5}{\psCalendar[Year=2011,Month=3]}
\psscalebox{0.5}{\psCalendar[Year=2011,Day=23,Month=8,MonthUse=8]}
```

	March							March							August					
M	T	W	T	F	S	S	M	T	W	T	F	S	S	M	T	W	T	F	S	S
	1	2	3	4	5	6		1	2	3	4	5	6	1	2	3	4	5	6	7
7	8	9	10	11	12	13	7	8	9	10	11	12	13	8	9	10	11	12	13	14
14	15	16	17	18	19	20	14	15	16	17	18	19	20	15	16	17	18	19	20	21
21	22	23	24	25	26	27	21	22	23	24	25	26	27	22	23	24	25	26	27	28
28	29	30	31				28	29	30	31				29	30	31				

2011   2011   2011

\psCalDodecaeder produces a much nicer output, arranging the months on the sides of a dodecahedron. If you don't specify a month or year, January of the current year is assumed. You can use the style=<month> option to put a different month on the front side.

```
\usepackage{pst-calendar}
\psscalebox{0.2}{\psCalDodecaeder}\hfill
\psscalebox{0.2}{\psCalDodecaeder[Year=2011,Month=3]}\hfill
\psscalebox{0.2}{\psCalDodecaeder[Year=2011,style=april]}
```

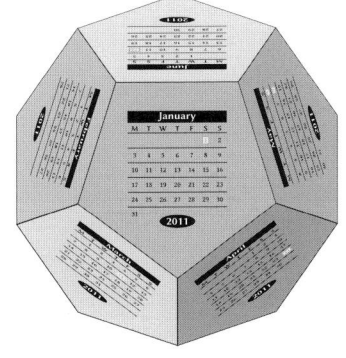  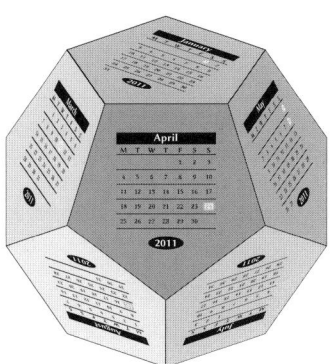

```
\usepackage{pst-calendar}
\psscalebox{0.15}{\psCalDodecaeder[Year=2011,style=february]}\hfill
\psscalebox{0.2}{\psCalDodecaeder[Year=2011,style=march]}\hfill
\psscalebox{0.24}{\psCalDodecaeder[Year=2011,style=july]}
```

33-05-9

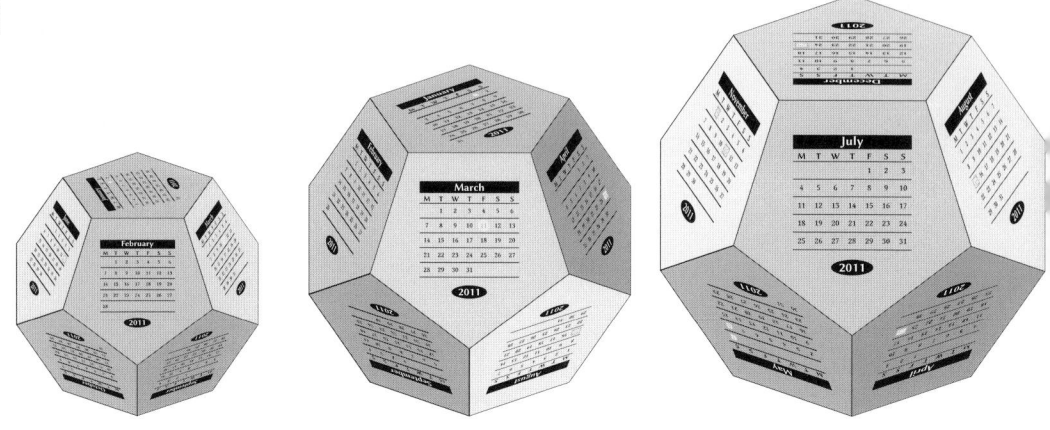

33.5.3 psgo – typesetting of game positions

The psgo package by Victor Bos draws game positions for the game go. The following table summarizes the basic commands for empty positions and for stones.

Table 33.15: Markers for empty positions and for stones

diagram	psgo-*macro*	description	example
⊠	\markma	cross	\markpos{\markma}{b}{2}
△	\marktr	triangle	\markpos{\marktr}{b}{2}
○	\markcr	circle	\markpos{\markcr}{b}{2}
□	\marksq	open square	\markpos{\marksq}{b}{2}
A	\marklb{#1}	label	\markpos{\marklb{A}}{b}{2}
■	\marksl	filled square	\markpos{\marksl}{b}{2}
▨	\markdd	hatched lines	\markpos{\markdd}{b}{2}

continued...

33.5 Miscellaneous

... continued

diagram	psgo-command	description	example
	\markma	cross	\stone[\markma]{black}{b}{2} \stone[\markma]{white}{c}{3}
	\marktr	triangle	\stone[\marktr]{black}{b}{2} \stone[\marktr]{white}{c}{3}
	\markcr	circle	\stone[\markcr]{black}{b}{2} \stone[markcr]{white}{c}{3}
	\marksq	open square	\stone[\marksq]{black}{b}{2} \stone[marksq]{white}{c}{3}
	\marklb{#1}	label	\stone[\marklb{A}]{black}{b}{2} \stone[\marklb{B}]{white}{c}{3}
	\marksl	filled square	\stone[\marksl]{black}{b}{2} \stone[\marksl]{white}{c}{3}
	\markdd	hatched lines	\stone[\markdd]{black}{b}{2} \stone[\markdd]{white}{c}{3}

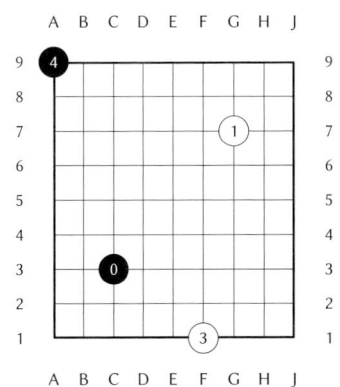

```
\usepackage{psgo}

\psscalebox{0.7}{%
\begin{psgoboard}[9]
\move{c}{3}
\move{g}{7}
\pass
\move{f}{1}
\move{a}{9}
\end{psgoboard}}
```

33 Further PSTricks packages

The two examples shown here illustrate: the first five moves of a game (above), and seven consecutive moves (below).

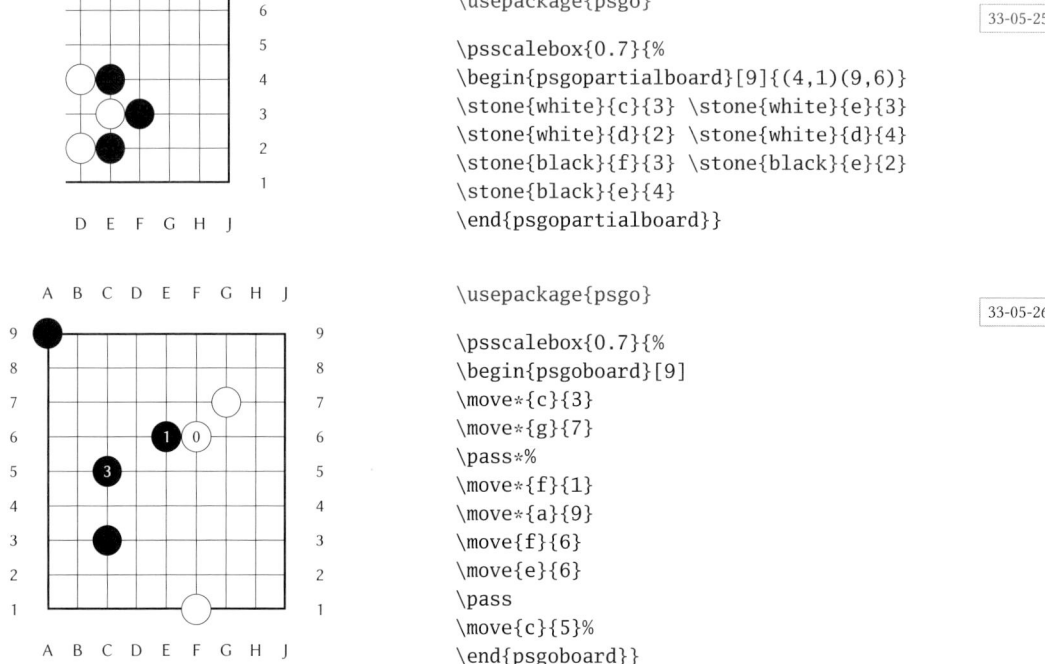

```
\usepackage{psgo}

\psscalebox{0.7}{%
\begin{psgopartialboard}[9]{(4,1)(9,6)}
\stone{white}{c}{3} \stone{white}{e}{3}
\stone{white}{d}{2} \stone{white}{d}{4}
\stone{black}{f}{3} \stone{black}{e}{2}
\stone{black}{e}{4}
\end{psgopartialboard}}
```
33-05-25

```
\usepackage{psgo}

\psscalebox{0.7}{%
\begin{psgoboard}[9]
\move*{c}{3}
\move*{g}{7}
\pass*%
\move*{f}{1}
\move*{a}{9}
\move{f}{6}
\move{e}{6}
\pass
\move{c}{5}%
\end{psgoboard}}
```
33-05-26

33.6 multido

The multido package by Timothy Van Zandt supports the creation of programme loops in an easy way. [94] It's also very useful outside PSTricks applications, which is why the package isn't contained in the PSTricks directory, but in CTAN: /macros/generic/multido. To prevent problems with the fb package, [44] use at least version 1.41 of multido – both define \FP@add and \FP@sub. When using real numbers, relatively large rounding errors may occur; the floating point arithmetic doesn't satisfy all needs. It's a good idea to label the variables clearly so that integers are distinct from real numbers. \multido recognizes the following prefixes:

short form	description
d	lengths (dimension)
n	counters
i	integer number
r	real number

Valid values are, for example, \dA, \nABC, \iAbCd, \rAbCd (cf. example 28-02-38 on page 548). Further information can be found in the documentation. [94]

Chapter 34

Special applications...

34.1 Gouraud shading... 739
34.2 Animations.. 741

34.1 Gouraud shading

The Gouraud shading, introduced in 1971 by Henri Gouraud, is also known as interpolated intensity shading or colour interpolation shading. It is a procedure to shade polygon areas and is, as a scanline rendering procedure, only used on raster output devices like laser printers. It is supported from PostScript level 3 and corresponds to /ShadingType 4. The following extract from pstricks-add.pro shows the implementation of the PostScript part of the \psGTriangle command. Only lines 9–14 and 16–21 are of interest here; they form the array of data and call the PostScript function.

\psGTriangle [settings] $(x_1,y_1)(x_2,y_2)(x_3,y_3)$\{colour1\}\{colour2\}\{colour3\}

```
1   /GTriangle {
2     gsave
3     /mtrx CM def
4     /colorA ED /colorB ED /colorC ED  % save the colours
5     /yA ED /xA ED                      % save the origin
6     xA yA translate
7     rotate                             % \psk@gangle
8     /yB ED /xB ED /yC ED /xC ED        % save other coordinates
9     /ds [                              % save data in a array
10        0 0 0 colorA aload pop         % fd x y xr xg xb
11        0 xB xA sub yB yA sub colorB aload pop
12        0 xC xA sub yC yA sub colorC aload pop
13  %     1 xC xB add yB colorA aload pop  % for use with 4 points ABCD
14     ] def
15     newpath
16     <<
17     /ShadingType 4                    % single Gouraud
```

34 Special applications...

```
18    /ColorSpace [ /DeviceRGB ]
19    /DataSource ds
20    >>
21    shfill
22    closepath
23    mtrx  setmatrix
24    grestore} def
```

The individual application of this command is not particularly interesting, but it can be used to fill areas that are available as a polygon line and can therefore be decomposed into triangles easily.

Not all printers provide PostScript level 3 – a printout won't be successful in every case. The same applies to the PDF viewer xpdf or older versions of acroread, which are also unable to display such a shading.

```
\usepackage{pstricks-add}

\psset{unit=0.5}
\begin{pspicture}(0,-1)(10,10)
  \psGTriangle(0,0)(5,10)(10,0)%
    {red}{green}{blue}
\end{pspicture}
```

34-01-1

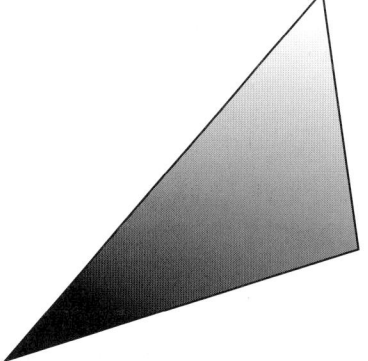

```
\usepackage{pstricks-add}

\psset{unit=0.5}
\begin{pspicture}(0,-1)(10,10)
  \psGTriangle*(0,0)(9,10)(10,3)%
    {black}{white!50}{red!50!green!95}
\end{pspicture}
```

34-01-2

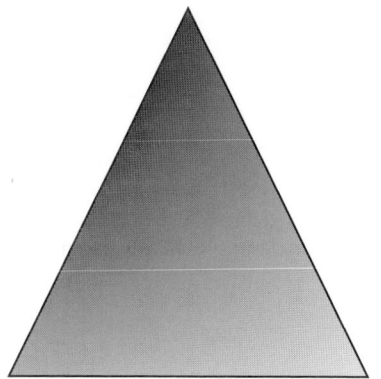

```
\usepackage{pstricks-add}

\psset{unit=0.5}
\begin{pspicture}(0,-1)(10,10)
  \psGTriangle*(0,0)(5,10)(10,0)%
    {red!100!green!84!blue!86}
    {-red!80!green!100!blue!40}
    {-red!60!green!30!blue!100}
\end{pspicture}
```

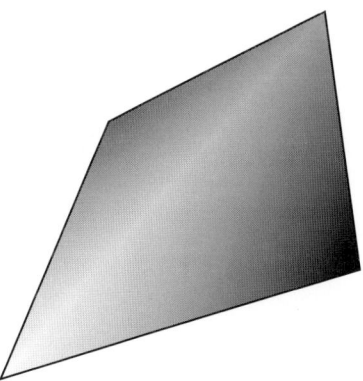

```
\usepackage{pstricks-add}

\psset{unit=0.5}
\begin{pspicture}(0,-1)(10,10)
 \psGTriangle(0,0)(9,10)(10,3)%
    {black!10}{black!50}{black!85}
 \psGTriangle(0,0)(3,7)(9,10)%
    {black!10}{black!65}{black!50}
 \pspolygon(0,0)(3,7)(9,10)(10,3)
\end{pspicture}
```

34.2 Animations

There are several ways to achieve animated PDF or Flash output. In principle, an animation is nothing but a timed sequence of individual pages. The simplest way is to use a presentation class like beamer or powerdot (cf. Chapter 35 on page 747) and a large sequence of slides. These can then be advanced manually or automatically by the Adobe Reader with a set delay, creating the impression of an animation. This section described the three most common methods for creating these slide sequences; the first two ways yield a PDF file and the last one a .swf file.

34.2.1 animate

The animate package by Alexander Grahn provides functionality to create frame sequences easily and automatically adds buttons for start/stop etc. When using PSTricks-generated animations, inline display is usually used.

34 Special applications...

```
\begin{animateinline} [settings] {frame rate}
\multiframe{number}{variables+step}{%
... loop...}
\end{animateinline}
```

The frame rate specifies the mean speed in frames per second; the speed can be changed later through the buttons. It's better to use the animate-specific \multiframe command for animation rather than the usual PSTricks command \multido, which can lead to problems. The following figure is the result of using \multido instead of \multiframe: the partial frames are all put on top of one another.

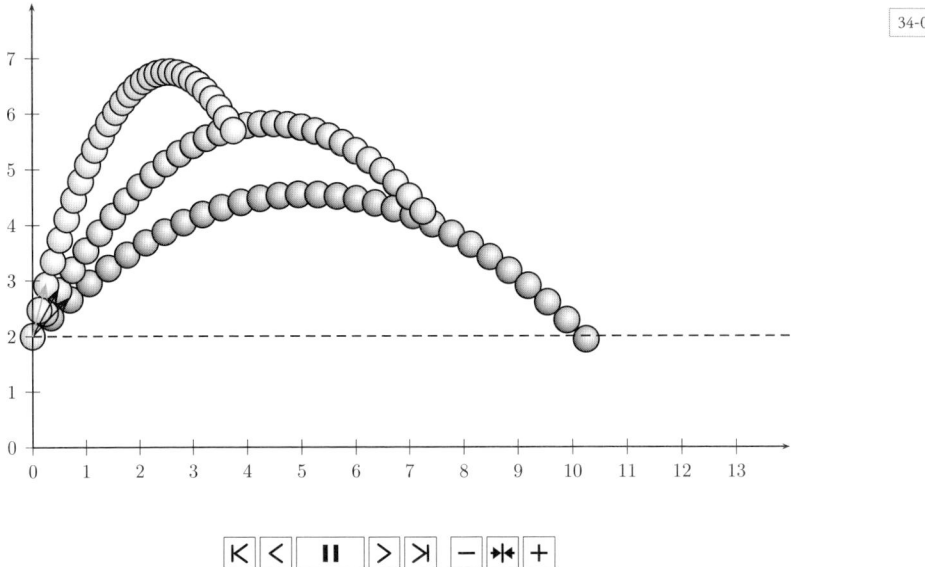

34-02-1

The next figure uses \multiframe – therefore a snapshot at a specific time shows only the current positions of the three balls.

```
\usepackage{pst-plot,pst-slpe,animate}\SpecialCoor
\newcounter{time}\newpsstyle{magenta40}{fillstyle=solid,fillcolor=magenta!40}
\newpsstyle{blue40}{fillstyle=solid,fillcolor=blue!60}
\newpsstyle{Blackball}{fillstyle=ccslope,slopebegin=white,slopeend=black,
    slopecenter={0.6 0.6}}
\newpsstyle{Blueball}{fillstyle=ccslope,slopebegin=white,slopeend=blue,
    slopecenter={0.6 0.6}}
\newpsstyle{Redball}{fillstyle=ccslope,slopebegin=white,slopeend=red,
    slopecenter={0.6 0.6}}
% inclined plane
\newcommand*\VAngle{45 }% starting angle
\newcommand*\VStart{10 }% starting speed in angle direction
\newcommand*\VHeight{2 }% starting height
```

34.2 Animations

```
\def\Vx{\VStart \VAngle cos mul }
\def\Vy{\VStart \VAngle sin mul }
\newcommand*\rBall{0.25 }\newcommand*\mass{1 }
\def\SvonT#1{    % way as function of time, returns x y
  \Vx #1 mul \Vy #1 mul % Sx Sy
  \VHeight add 0.5 9.81 mul #1 dup mul mul sub }
\def\OneShot#1{
  \psaxes{->}(14,8)\psline[linestyle=dashed](0,\VHeight)(14,\VHeight)
  \rput(0,\VHeight){\psline[arrowscale=2]{->}(\VStart mm;\VAngle)}
  \pscircle[style=Blackball](! \SvonT{#1} ){\rBall}
  \def\VAngle{60 }
  \rput(0,\VHeight){\psline[arrowscale=2,linecolor=blue]{->}(\VStart mm;\VAngle)}
  \pscircle[style=Blueball](! \SvonT{#1} ){\rBall}\def\VAngle{75 }
  \rput(0,\VHeight){\psline[arrowscale=2,linecolor=red]{->}(\VStart mm;\VAngle)}
  \pscircle[style=Redball](! \SvonT{#1} ){\rBall}}
\begin{animateinline}[%
  width=0.9\linewidth,begin={\begin{pspicture}(-1.75,-1.25)(14.5,8.5)},
  end={\end{pspicture}},palindrome,controls,autoplay]{10}
\multiframe{49}{nTime=0.0+1.0}{%
   \OneShot{ \nTime\space 20 div }}%
\end{animateinline}
```

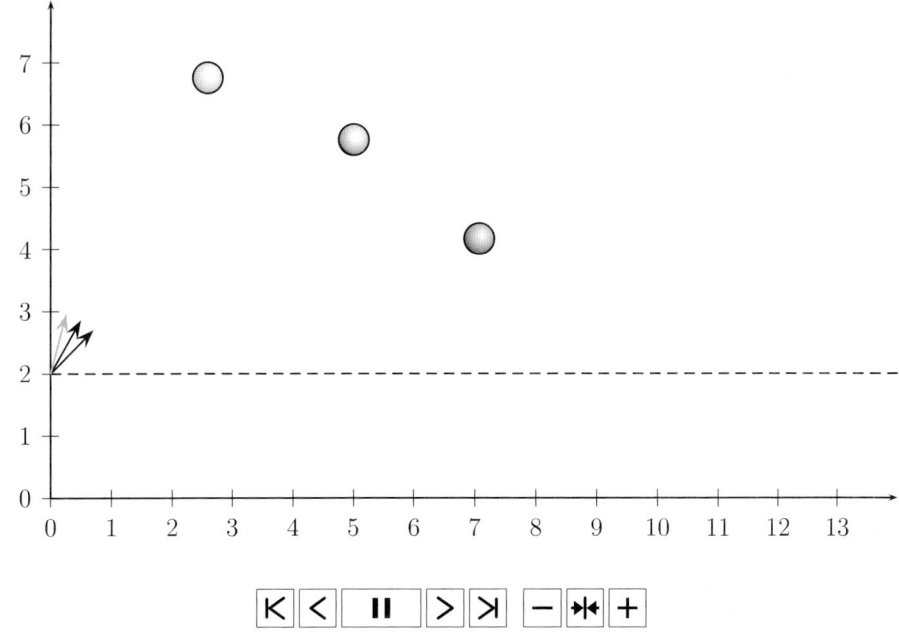

34.2.2 The AcroTEX presentation bundle

Jürgen Gilg showed in [18] how to create PDF animations with the packages of the AcroTEX project by Don Paul Story. The basis is the aeb_pro package, which is available on CTAN. It

34 Special applications...

can create an animated PDF from the PostScript file in conjunction with the commercial Adobe Distiller (version 7.0 or later). Note that you can't use GhostScript together with aeb_pro.

```
\usepackage[
    driver=dvips,
    web={pro},      % the layout style file of AeB
    eforms,         % supports the formfields (push buttons)
    uselayers]{aeb_pro}
\usepackage{pst-3dplot,pstricks-add}
\usepackage[nomessages]{fp}
\DeclareAnime{graph}{10}{37}% call the animations
\newcommand*{\voc}{%
  \animeBld
  \definecolor{APBoceanblue}{rgb}{0.00,0.20,0.74}
  \definecolor{APBcoldblue}{rgb}{0.00,0.48,0.73}
  % viewing angle, line width, line colour, origin
  \psset{Beta=20,Alpha=50,linewidth=0.1pt,linecolor=APBcoldblue,origin={0,0,0}}%
  % figure to animate
  \parametricplotThreeD[xPlotpoints=100](80,\bi)(0,360){%
    t cos 2 mul 4 u sin 2 mul add mul   t sin 2 mul 4 u sin 2 mul add mul   u cos 4 mul}
  \parametricplotThreeD[yPlotpoints=75](0,360)(80,\bi){%
    u cos 2 mul 4 t sin 2 mul add mul   u sin 2 mul 4 t sin 2 mul add mul   t cos 4 mul}
  \parametricplotThreeD[yPlotpoints=1,linecolor=APBoceanblue,linewidth=2pt](0,360)(80,360)
    u cos 2 mul 4 t sin 2 mul add mul   u sin 2 mul 4 t sin 2 mul add mul   t cos 4 mul}%
  \eBld}% end of objects to animate
\psset{unit=0.35}%
\begin{pspicture}(-2,-8)(2,8)
\FPdiv{\myDeltaB}{280}{36}\newcommand*{\bi}{80}%
\multido{\i=1+1}{37}{\voc\FPadd{\bi}{\bi}{\myDeltaB}}% put levels behind one another
\end{pspicture}
\backAnimeBtn{24bp}{12bp}\kern1bp% buttons
\clearAnimeBtn{24bp}{12bp}\kern1bp%
\forwardAnimeBtn{24bp}{12bp}
```

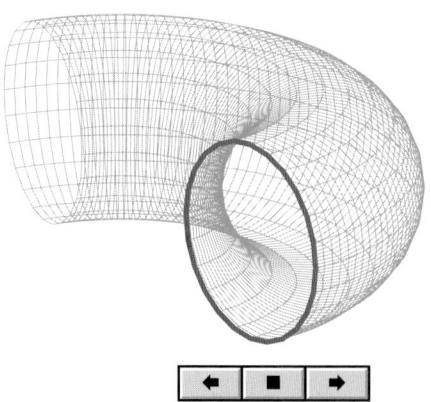

34-02-3

34.2.3 Flash animations

For viewing with a web browser, flash animations are more applicable. A PDF file is created containing one image per page in sequence, which is relatively easy to do with the \multido command. The following TeX file is the basis for the example. Only the first page of the PDF file is displayed here though.

```
\usepackage{pst-solides3d,multido}
\psset{lightsrc=75 -63 17,viewpoint=100 -45 10 rtp2xyz,Decran=50,fontsize=50}
\multido{\iRotZ=0+10}{36}{%
  \begin{pspicture*}(-5,-3)(5,4)
  \psframe(-5,-3)(5,4)\pstVerb{/iRotZ \iRotZ\space def}%
  \psSolid[object=grille,base=-7 7 -7 7,ngrid=1. 1.,action=draw,linecolor=red](0,0,-3.4)
  \defFunction[algebraic]{helix}(u,v)%
    {2*(0.4*cos(v)-1)*cos(u)}{2*(0.4*cos(v)-1)*sin(u)}{0.4*sin(v)+0.3*u}
  \codejps{ /helice -10 10 0 6.28 [60 0.4] {helix} newsurfaceparametree
   {0 0 iRotZ rotate0point3d} solidtransform {0 -4 0 translatepoint3d} solidtransform
   dup solidfacesreverse def
  /helicesym helice dupsolid exch pop {[0 1 0 0] symplan3d} solidtransform
   dup solidfacesreverse def
  /solidgrid false def
  solidlightOn
  helicesym dup [0 1 0.5 1] solidputhuecolors dup (White) inputcolors
  drawsolid**
  .5 setfillopacity [0 1 0 0] eq2plan
  dup [-7 7 -5 3.4] planputrange
  dup [14. 8.4] planputngrid
  newplan dup videsolid
  dup (0.7 0.7 1 setrgbcolor) (0.7 0.7 1 setrgbcolor) inoutputcolors drawsolid**
  helice dup [0 1 0.5 1] solidputhuecolors dup (White) inputcolors drawsolid** }
  \end{pspicture*}
  \newpage}
```

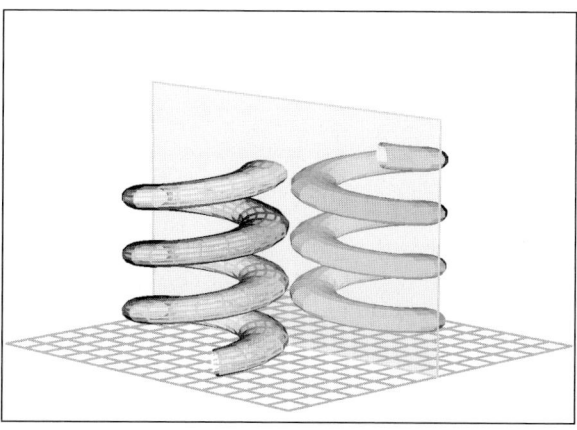

The Perl program popip.pl (http://PSTricks.tug.org/swf/popip.pl) converts the individual pages of the PDF file into .png files.

```
popip -T -f 1.5 -b 10 helice.pdf
```

The script creates a subdirectory `helice` and saves all the .png files in it. In this example, there are exactly 36 .png files, from `helice/image001.png` to `helice/image036.png`; this corresponds to the number of loop iterations. Depending on the complexity of the figure, it may take a very long time to extract the individual pages. Next the .png images are combined into a flash file with the png2swf programme (http://www.swftools.org/).

```
png2swf -r 9 helice/image*.png -o helice.swf
```

You can view the result at http://PSTricks.tug.org/swf/helice.swf.

Chapter 35

PSTricks in presentations

35.1 powerdot 747
35.2 beamer 766

The many features of PSTricks are also useful for presentations. The first package that offered support for this was SLITEX, although it was not particularly easy to use. The next generation seminar and prosper successor packages and document classes were still quite awkward. Nowadays, there are successors that satisfy the requirements for professional presentation: powerdot (by Hendri Adriaens and Christopher Ellison) and beamer (by Till Tantau), both of which are discussed in this chapter. powerdot in particular supports all PostScript functionality – it is in fact based on PSTricks itself.

In principle, you can use PSTricks-specific code in all presentation classes, though as usual pdfLATEX can't be used directly in this case. Ways to achieve PDF output are described in Appendix D on page 851. There is an overview of the presentation classes available for (LA)TEX today on the internet page of Michael Widmann at http://www.miwie.org/presentations/.

35.1 powerdot

The general structure of a presentation with powerdot is in principle the same as for a normal document.

```
\documentclass{powerdot}
\maketitle
\begin{slide}{A slide}
  contents of the first slide
\end{slide}
\section{First section}
\begin{slide}{One more slide}
  contents of the second slide
\end{slide}
```

```
\begin{note}{Personal note}
  The text of the node.
\end{note}
```

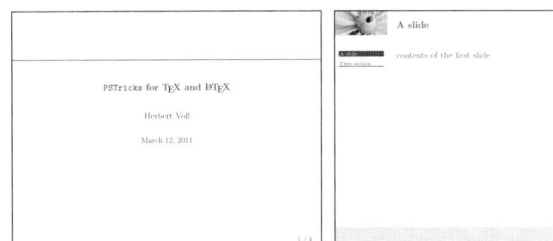

Usually you will want to change the standard layout to one of the styles included with the package. The style examples below include those that are currently available in the powerdot version on CTAN. Most of these styles only define colours, but some of them define additional things like headers and footers. The examples all use the same source except for the definition of the style=<name> and they always display the first and fourth slides.

```
\documentclass[style=aggie]{powerdot}
\usepackage{amsmath,esint}
\title{Example for the style \texttt{aggie}}
\author{Herbert Vo\ss}\pddefinetemplate[slide]{slide}{tocpos}{}
\pdsetup{lf=foot--left,rf=foot--right}
\newcommand*\Q[2]{\frac{\partial #1}{\partial #2}}
\maketitle
\begin{slide}{Example slide}
The first equation of Green:
\begin{align}\label{green}
\underset{\mathcal{G}\quad}\iiint\!\left[u\nabla^{2}v+\left(\nabla u,
   \nabla v\right)\right]d^{3}V=\underset{\mathcal{S}\quad}\oiint u\Q{v}{n}d^{2}A
\end{align}
The equation of Green (\ref{green}) will be proofed later.

\begin{itemize}
  \item A line with \texttt{itemize}.
  \begin{itemize}
    \item A line with \texttt{itemize}.
    \begin{enumerate}
      \item A line with \texttt{enumerate}.
      \begin{description}
        \item[description]-environment
      \end{description}
      \item One more \ldots
    \end{enumerate}
    \item A line with \texttt{itemize}.
  \end{itemize}
  \item A line with \texttt{itemize}.
\end{itemize}
\end{slide}
```

35.1 powerdot

35-01-2

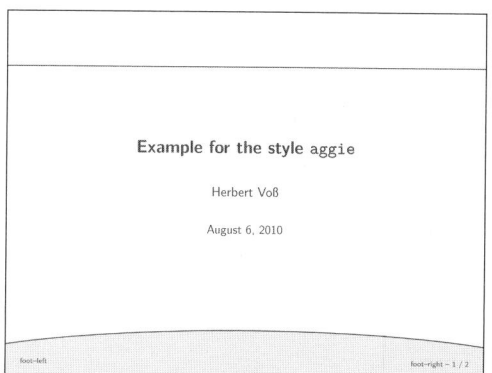

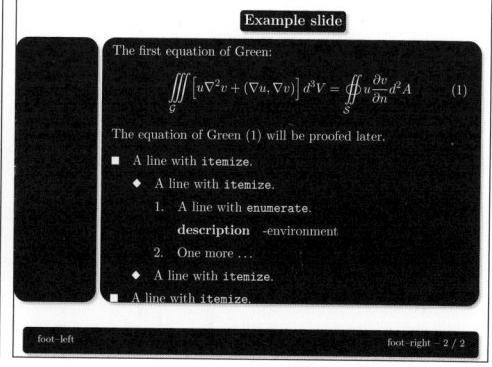

35-01-3

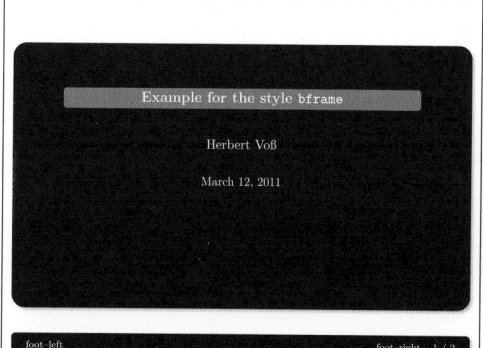

35-01-4

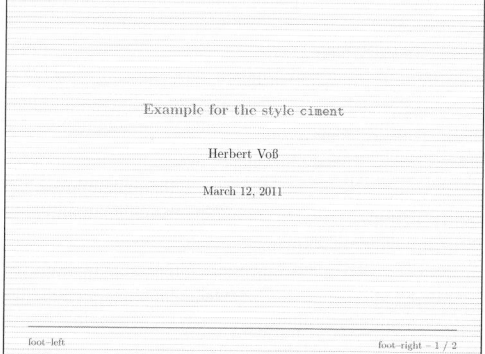

35 PSTricks in presentations

35.1 powerdot

35-01-8

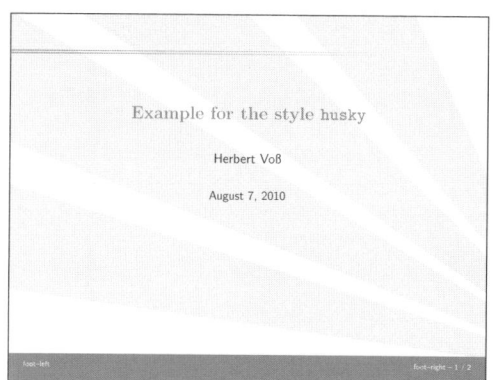

35-01-9

35-01-10

35 PSTricks in presentations

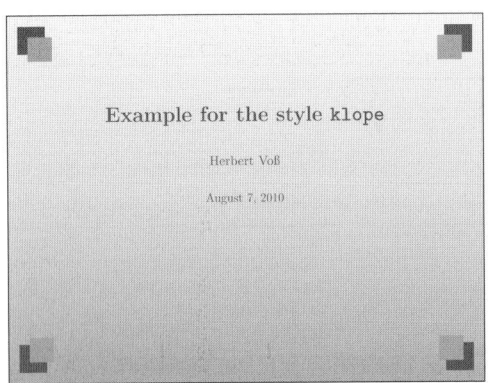
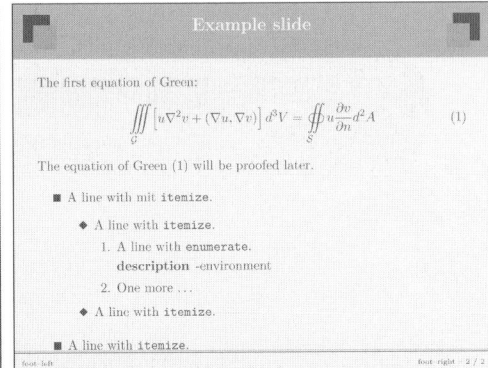
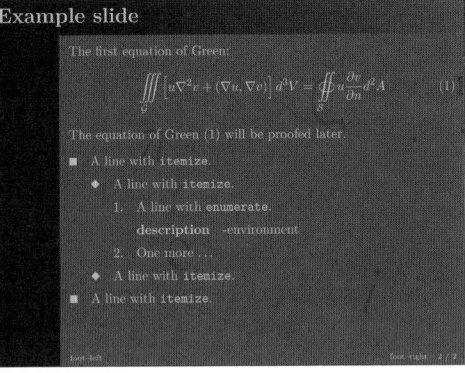

35.1 powerdot

35-01-14

Example for the style sailor

Herbert Voß

March 12, 2011

Example slide

The first equation of Green:

$$\iiint_{\mathcal{G}} \left[u \nabla^2 v + (\nabla u, \nabla v) \right] d^3 V = \oiint_{\mathcal{S}} u \frac{\partial v}{\partial n} d^2 A \qquad (1)$$

The equation of Green (1) will be proofed later.

- A line with itemize.
  □ A line with itemize.
    1. A line with enumerate.
       description -environment
    2. One more ...
  □ A line with itemize.
- A line with itemize.

35-01-15

Example for the style simple

Herbert Voß

March 12, 2011

Example slide

The first equation of Green:

$$\iiint_{\mathcal{G}} \left[u \nabla^2 v + (\nabla u, \nabla v) \right] d^3 V = \oiint_{\mathcal{S}} u \frac{\partial v}{\partial n} d^2 A \qquad (1)$$

The equation of Green (1) will be proofed later.

□ A line with itemize.
– A line with itemize.
  1. A line with enumerate.
     description -environment
  2. One more ...
– A line with itemize.
□ A line with itemize.

35-01-16

Example for the style tycja

Herbert Voß

March 12, 2011

Example slide

The first equation of Green:

$$\iiint_{\mathcal{G}} \left[u \nabla^2 v + (\nabla u, \nabla v) \right] d^3 V = \oiint_{\mathcal{S}} u \frac{\partial v}{\partial n} d^2 A \qquad (1)$$

The equation of Green (1) will be proofed later.

- A line with itemize.
  ◆ A line with itemize.
    1. A line with enumerate.
       description -environment
    2. One more ...
  ◆ A line with itemize.
- A line with itemize.

35 PSTricks in presentations

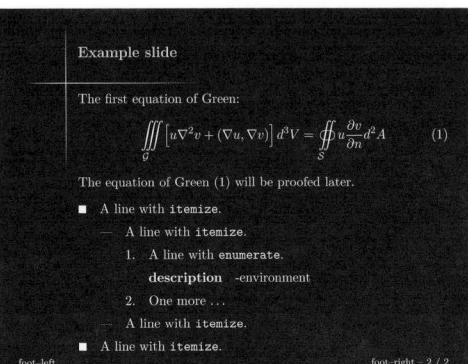

powerdot configures many things through optional arguments for the document class. The following list explains these options. You can set or change most of these afterwards with the \pdsetup command. However, the default values are all sensible, and first-time users won't need to change the parameters.

```
\documentclass[size=12pt,paper=screen,mode=present,display=slidesnotes,
    style=sailor,nopagebreaks,blackslide,fleqn,british]{powerdot}
```

This will create a presentation with:

size=12pt Sets the base font size, similar to other document classes. Possible values are 8pt, 9pt, 10pt, 11pt, 12pt, 14pt, 17pt, or 20pt; the default is 11pt. The extsizes package is used for the non-standard sizes; it should be part of the TeX distribution.

paper=screen Optimizes the paper format for 4/3 screens and sets width and height to 11 inches × 8.25 inches. If you are wanting to print, select paper size a4paper or letter.

mode=present Provides overlays and transition effects; this is the default setting. Other possible values are mode=print for a printout of the slides and mode=handout for a black and white printout of the handouts.

display=slidenotes Includes the notes on the slides. Other possible values are display=slides and display=notes.

style=sailor Specifies the style file.

nopagebreaks When printing the presentation, two slides are put on one page by default. This option prevents the page break and makes other types possible. The option only takes effect when mode=handout.

blackslide Produces an initial black slide. Clicking on this black (empty) slide jumps to the last shown slide. When opening the presentation, the black slide is skipped. This can be helpful for presentations without a title or when using several media.

fleqn All equations are left-aligned.

british Language option; doesn't affect powerdot directly.

You can also use the \pdsetup command to configure the powerdot-specific options such as headers, footers, and transition effects:

```
\pdsetup{lf=\textbf{ZEDAT},rf=\textbf{FU Berlin},trans=Dissolve}
```

lf=ZEDAT defines the left footer.

rf=FU-Berlin defines the right footer.

trans=Dissolve activates the Dissolve transition.

There are special options for inserting a logo:

```
\pdsetup{rf=\textbf{Berlin},logohook=lb,logopos={5pt,5pt},
    logocmd={\includegraphics[height=.5cm]{logofbbw.eps}},trans=Dissolve}
```

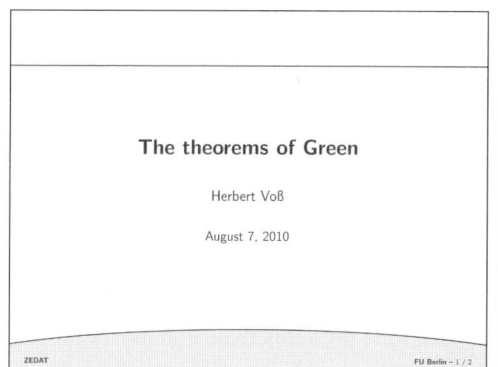
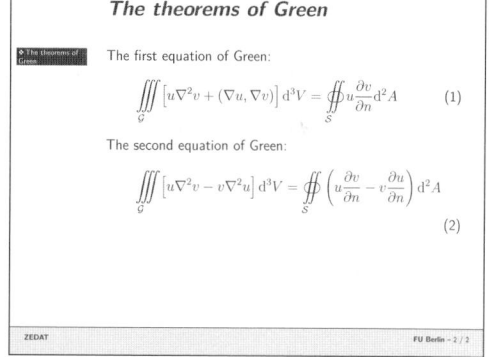

As powerdot uses PSTricks commands to place the individual objects, you can also do this directly yourself. For example, we can place another logo with an \rput command, and by integrating it into the \pddefinetemplate command makes it appear on every slide.

```
\pddefinetemplate[slide]{slide}{}{\rput[lt](15pt,\slideheight){%
    \includegraphics[height=.5cm]{images/zedat2}}}
```

For individual slides, you can use the optional argument of the slide environment, which overwrites the original definition. On the final slide, the lower left logo is missing:

```
\begin{slide}[method=file,logohook=rt,logopos={\slidewidth,\slideheight},
    logocmd={\includegraphics[height=.5cm]{images/UIT}}]{A second logo}
...
\end{slide}
```

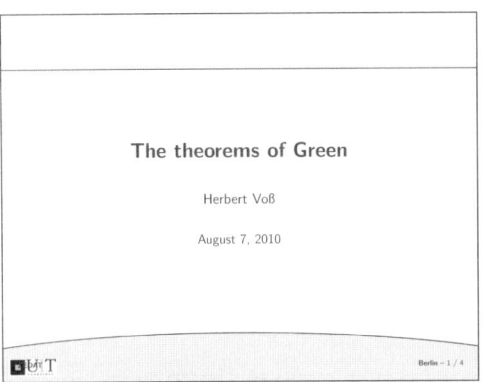
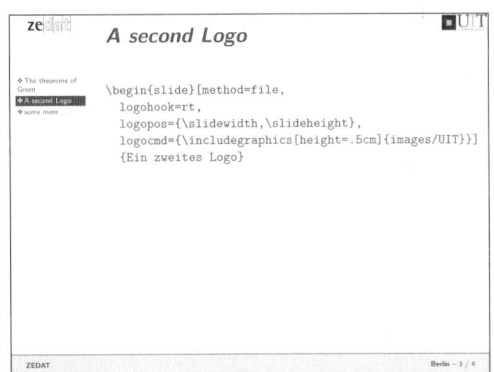

35.1.1 Slides

There are two environments for slides: a general form slide (mentioned already) and a special form wideslide, which uses the whole width of the slide.

```
\begin{slide} [settings] {title} ... \end{slide}
\begin{wideslide} [settings] {title} ... \end{wideslide}
```

Apart from the parameters discussed in the last section, there are two additional ones that are only valid for these two environments: toc and bm. The first defines an alternative entry into the table of contents and the second an alternative entry into the list of bookmarks. If these options aren't specified, the normal title is used.

35.1.2 Overlays

Presentations are generally created by overlaying slides, so the overlay functionality is very important. To control these overlays, powerdot provides the commands described in Table 35.1:

Table 35.1: Commands for controlling the overlays

syntax	description
\pause [settings]	Inserts a stop point (a pause); the following overlays appear only after a button is pressed. The optional argument specifies the number of "waiting" overlays.
\item [settings] <overlays>	The usual LaTeX command for an item in a list. You can specify the number or series of affected overlays optionally in angle brackets, using the notation in Table 35.2 on the next page.

continued...

... continued

syntax	description
\onslide{*overlays*}{...}	The content of the second argument is shown on the overlays specified in the first (optional) argument. \onslide{1,5-7}{foo} makes the text foo only appear on overlays 1 and 5-7 (inclusive). The comma-separated list, using the notation in Table 35.2, can be arbitrarily long. The space required by the second argument is reserved such that subsequent overlays are not shifted.
\onslide+{*overlays*}{...}	Inactive overlays remain visible, but the intensity is lower – by default a light grey.
\onslide*{*overlays*}{...}	Corresponds to the standard case \onslide, but the reserved space is freed when the overlay becomes inactive. This means that subsequent overlays may be shifted accordingly.

Table 35.2: Overlay notation for \item and \onslide with $x, y \in \mathbb{N}$

syntax	description
x	only overlay x
$+x$	only overlay x, counted from the current position (relative)
$-x$	all overlays up to x (inclusive)
$x-$	all overlays from x (inclusive)
$+x-$	same as above, but counted from the current position (relative)
$x-y$	all overlays from x to y (inclusive)
$+x-+y$	same as above, but counted from the current position (relative)

The following examples apply the individual \onslide commands and the notation for which overlays to show (cf. Table 35.2). There are three overlays for each slide; here the first and third are shown in each case. The example text is more or less only the following code, which is the same for all three variations of \onslide.

The first two figures show just the first equation (overlay 1) and the note that appears at the same place it would appear had both equations been shown. The second example is identical, only the inactive overlays are shown with less intensity. In the last example, the starred version of \onslide makes the space an overlay occupies available again when it becomes inactive. Therefore the last overlay appears as the first line.

```
\documentclass[paper=screen,mode=present,display=slidesnotes,
    style=ciment,nopagebreaks,fleqn,ngerman]{powerdot}
\maketitle
\section{\texttt{onslide}}
\begin{slide}{The theorems of Green}
\onslide{1-2}{the first theorem:}
\begin{align}\label{green1}
\underset{\mathcal{G}\quad}{\iiint\!
    \left[u\nabla^{2}v+\left(\nabla u,\nabla v\right)\right]\mathrm{d}^{3}V
```

```
                =\underset{\mathcal{S}\quad}\oiint u\Q{v}{n}\mathrm{d}^{2}A
\end{align}}
\onslide{2}{the second theorem:
\begin{align}\label{green2}
\underset{{\mathcal{G}\quad}}\iiint\!%
        \left[u\nabla^{2}v-v\nabla^{2}u\right]\mathrm{d}^{3}V%
        =\underset{\mathcal{S}\quad}\oiint%
        \left(u\Q{v}{n}-v\Q{u}{n}\right)\mathrm{d}^{2}A
\end{align}}
\onslide{3}{There are no more equations to show!}
\end{slide}

\section{\texttt{onslide+}}
\begin{slide}{The theorems of Green}
\onslide+{1-2}{the first theorem:
\begin{align}\label{green3}
\underset{\mathcal{G}\quad}\iiint\!
        \left[u\nabla^{2}v+\left(\nabla u,\nabla v\right)\right]\mathrm{d}^{3}V
        =\underset{\mathcal{S}\quad}\oiint u\Q{v}{n}\mathrm{d}^{2}A
\end{align}}
\onslide+{2}{the second theorem:
\begin{align}\label{green4}
\underset{{\mathcal{G}\quad}}\iiint\!%
        \left[u\nabla^{2}v-v\nabla^{2}u\right]\mathrm{d}^{3}V%
        =\underset{\mathcal{S}\quad}\oiint%
        \left(u\Q{v}{n}-v\Q{u}{n}\right)\mathrm{d}^{2}A
\end{align}}
\onslide+{3}{There are no more equations to show!}
\end{slide}

\section{\texttt{onslide*}}
\begin{slide}{The theorems of Green}
\onslide*{1-2}{the first theorem:
\begin{align}\label{green5}
\underset{\mathcal{G}\quad}\iiint\!
        \left[u\nabla^{2}v+\left(\nabla u,\nabla v\right)\right]\mathrm{d}^{3}V
        =\underset{\mathcal{S}\quad}\oiint u\Q{v}{n}\mathrm{d}^{2}A
\end{align}}
\onslide*{2}{the second theorem:
\begin{align}\label{green6}
\underset{{\mathcal{G}\quad}}\iiint\!%
        \left[u\nabla^{2}v-v\nabla^{2}u\right]\mathrm{d}^{3}V%
        =\underset{\mathcal{S}\quad}\oiint%
        \left(u\Q{v}{n}-v\Q{u}{n}\right)\mathrm{d}^{2}A
\end{align}}
\onslide*{3}{There are no more equations to show!}
\end{slide}
```

The following four figures show an application of the \item commands, which display individual parts of an equation as node connection with the \onslide command. The first, second, fourth, and last overlay of the first slide are shown. The structure is relatively straightforward.

```
\documentclass[paper=screen,mode=present,display=slidesnotes,
    style=ciment,nopagebreaks,fleqn,ngerman]{powerdot}
\begin{wideslide}{Node example}%
The binding energy in the droplet model consists of the following parts:
```

35 PSTricks in presentations

```
\begin{itemize}[type=0]
\item<3-> the \rnode{b}{surface part,}
\item<2-> the \rnode{a}{volume part,}
\item[]% only dummy
\end{itemize}
\[E =
\onslide{2-}{\rnode[t]{ae}{\psframebox*[fillcolor=darkyellow]{\xstrut a_vA}}+}
\onslide{3-}{\rnode[t]{be}{\psframebox*[fillcolor=lightgray]{\xstrut-a_fA^{2/3}}}+}
\onslide{4-}{\rnode[t]{ce}{\psframebox*[fillcolor=green]{\xstrut-a_c\frac{Z(Z-1)}{A^{1/3}}}}
\onslide{5-}{\rnode[t]{de}{\psframebox*[fillcolor=cyan]{\xstrut-a_s\frac{(A-2Z)^2}{A}}}+}
\onslide{6-}{\rnode[t]{ee}{\psframebox*[fillcolor=yellow]{\xstrut E_p}}}
\]  \medskip \psset{linecolor=darkgray,linewidth=0.5pt,linestyle=solid}
\begin{itemize}[type=0]
\item<4-> the \rnode{c}{Coulomb part,}
\item<5-> the \rnode{d}{symmetry energy,}
\item<6-> and a \rnode{e}{pair building part.}
\end{itemize}
\onslide*{2-}{\nccurve[linecolor=darkyellow,angleA=-90,angleB=90]{->}{a}{ae}}
\onslide*{3-}{\nccurve[linecolor=lightgray,angleB=45]{->}{b}{be}}
\onslide*{4-}{\nccurve[linecolor=green,angleB=-90]{->}{c}{ce}}
\onslide*{5-}{\nccurve[linecolor=cyan,angleB=-90]{->}{d}{de}}
\onslide*{6-}{\nccurve[linecolor=yellow,angleB=-90]{->}{e}{ee}}
\end{wideslide}
```

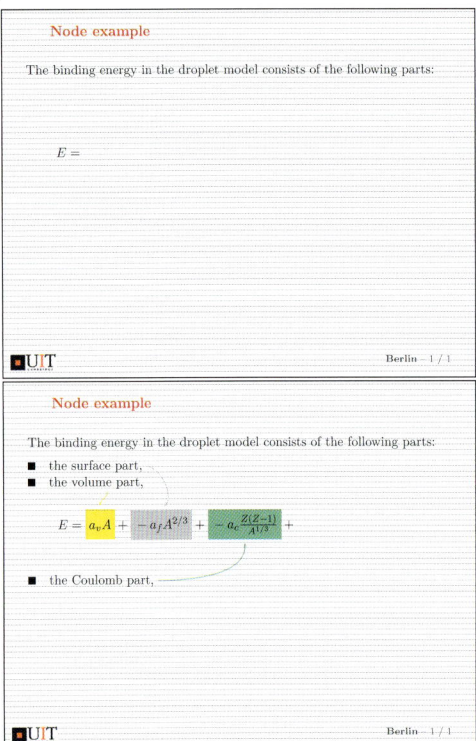
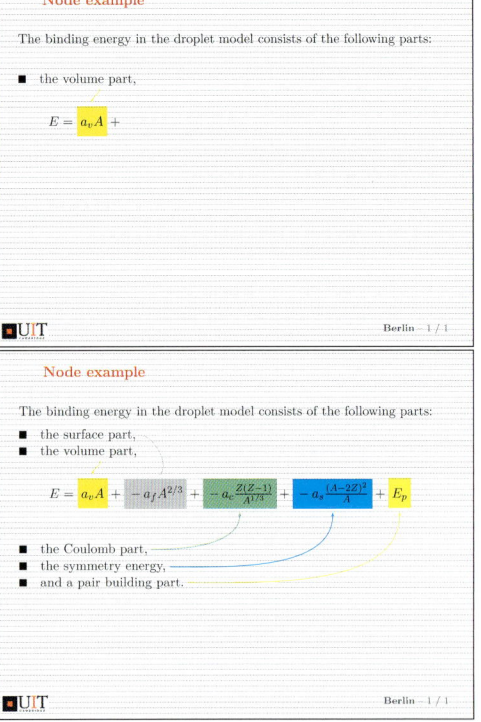

35.1.3 Structure

For the structuring of the content of the presentation and display of a horizontal or vertical overview, powerdot provides the \section command, which is different from the LaTeX \section command.

\section [settings] {*title*}

By default, a separate slide is created for the title and the title is added to the table of contents and list of bookmarks. Table 35.3 lists the available options for further control over this behaviour.

Table 35.3: Parameters for the \section command

option	type	default	description
tocsection	false|true|hidden	true	entry into the table of contents and: for true entry into the superior level of the following slides; for false no entry and normal slide; for hidden the entry only appears on the slides that belong to this section, and otherwise the entry is not visible
slide	boolean	true	own slide or not
template	name		style for the slide

The table of contents is another possibility for structuring the presentation.

\tableofcontents [settings]

The number of sections and slide titles in the table of contents varies, as the space provided for it is limited and depends on the style. Table 35.4 lists the parameters available for configuring the table of contents.

Table 35.4: Parameters for the \tableofcontents command

option	type	default	description
type	0|1	0	entries are only visible if either the slide itself or a slide from the same section is shown; all entries are shown for the value 1, but they change colour if they belong to a slide from a different section
content	all| sections| currentsection| future| futuresections	all	show all sections and slides show only sections show only the current section show only the current and future slides same, but for sections

35.1.4 Two-column mode

The \twocolumn command takes three arguments: an optional one and two mandatory ones for the left and right column respectively.

\twocolumn [settings] {*left*}{*right*}

Without specifying any further options, the following example is created with the style file husky. Inside the *left* and *right* arguments, further commands control the overlays.

```
\documentclass[paper=screen,mode=present,display=slidesnotes,
    style=husky,nopagebreaks,fleqn,ngerman]{powerdot}
\section{Zweispaltenmodus}
\begin{slide}{Example}% exa6.tex -- columns
\twocolumn{%
  \onslide{1-}{%
    The history of \TeX\ started in the last century. The first codes
    were introduced in late 1970 by \textsc{Donald Knuth}. Not that many
    software packages exist, which is to say they are of current age,
    while others are retired ... :-)}
}{%
  \onslide{2-}{\rule{20mm}{25mm}}
    \put(-13,20){{\color{white}\TeX}}~
  \onslide{3}{{\color{red}\rule{20mm}{40mm}}
    \put(-13,20){\LaTeX}}
}
\end{slide}
```

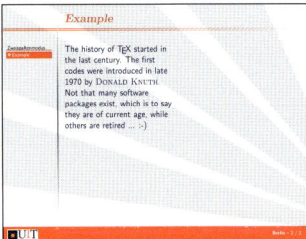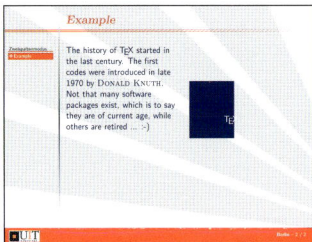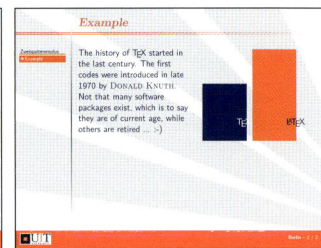

The optional arguments for configuring two-column mode are summarized in Table 35.5 and shown in Figure 35.1 on the next page.

Table 35.5: Parameters for two-column mode

option	type	default	description
lineheight	length	6cm	height of the vertical line between columns
lineprop	style	–	line style in PSTricks notation
lfrheight	length	–	draws a frame of height lfrheight around the left column if the argument is set
lfrprop	style	–	line style for the frame in PSTricks notation

continued...

... continued

option	type	default	description
rfrheight	length	–	equivalent for the right column
rfrprop	style	–	equivalent for the right column
lcolwidth	length	0.47\linewidth	width of the left column
rcolwidth	length	0.47\linewidth	width of the right column
frsep	length	1.5cm	space between normal text and frame (left and right)
colsep	length	0.06\linewidth	space between normal text in columns
topsep	length	0cm	additional space between normal text and the subsequent columns
bottomsep	length	0cm	equivalent for bottom
indent	length	0cm	horizontal indent of the left column

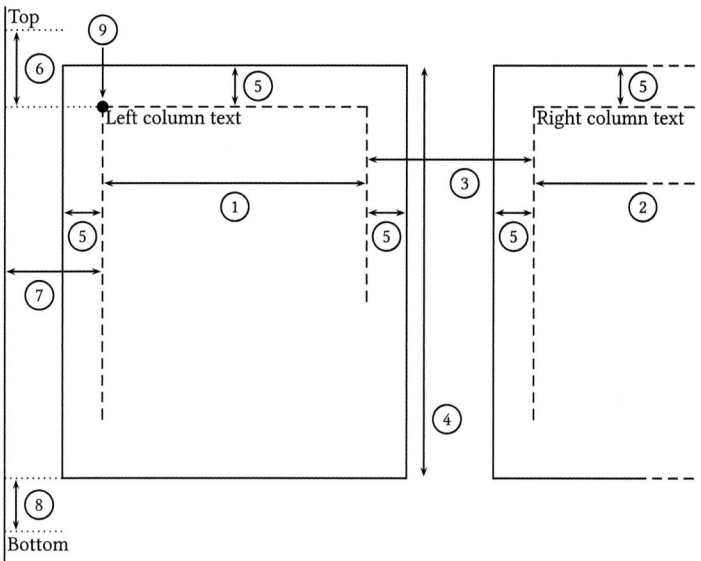

Meaning of the labels

1	lcolwidth	5	frsep
2	rcolwidth	6	topsep
3	colsep	7	indent
4	lfrheight, rfrheight, lineheight	8	bottomsep
		9	reference point

Figure 35.1: Spaces in two-column mode (Hendri Adriaens)

35.1.5 Verbatim mode

Inserting code or similar verbatim material requires special attention, as it isn't always easy to do it in LaTeX. powerdot has three different modes for inserting code, which you can select through the optional method argument of the slide environment. Valid values are:

normal The default mode, which allows for fast translation but only supports verbatim material that has been put into a box outside the slide environment; instead of the verbatim material, the box is inserted into the text.

direct This allows verbatim material, but no overlays on a slide.

file This writes the verbatim material into an external file and reads it back later. This slows down the translation, but allows both overlays and verbatim material.

The following examples illustrate inclusion of a verbatim environment on the first slide and on the second slide an application of the listings package, which reads the example file through \lstinputlisting and outputs it.

```
\documentclass[paper=screen,mode=present,display=slidesnotes,
    style=husky,nopagebreaks,fleqn,ngerman]{powerdot}
\newcommand*\DANTE{{\usefont{OT1}{dante}{m}{n}\selectfont DANTE}}
\usepackage{listings}
\begin{slide}[method=file]{Verbatim-Example}
\small\begin{verbatim}
\newcommand*\DANTE{{\usefont{OT1}{dante}{m}{n}\selectfont DANTE}}
\psshadowbox[shadowsize=14pt]{\Huge\DANTE\reflectbox{\Huge\DANTE}}
\end{verbatim}

\psshadowbox[shadowsize=14pt]{\Huge\DANTE\reflectbox{\Huge\DANTE}}
\end{slide}
\begin{slide}[method=file]{Listings-Example}
\lstinputlisting[basicstyle=\ttfamily\footnotesize,
    firstline=17,lastline=35]{\jobname.ltxpd}
\end{slide}
```

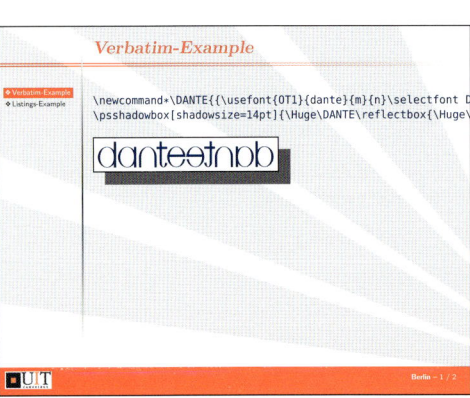

35.1.6 Background picture

A background picture[1] is in essence just a big logo, so can be dealt with as described on page 755.

```
\pddefinetemplate[slide]{slide}{}{\rput[lt](0,0){%
  \includegraphics[width=\slidewidth]{../fuBIB10}}}
```

In this case, the background picture is placed as the background of the whole slide, but this is not always what you want if, for example, there is a navigation bar. To place the background picture only behind the text is a bit more difficult because the coordinates of the lower left corner depend on the style file. You have to do some manual tuning in this case to get it positioned it correctly, as shown in the example below.

```
\documentclass[paper=screen,mode=present,display=slidesnotes,
    style=husky,nopagebreaks,fleqn,ngerman]{powerdot}

\begin{slide}[toc=Text part]{Example 1}
\rput[lt](-0.425cm,0.75cm){%
  \includegraphics[height=0.8\slideheight,width=\slidewidth]{images/fuBIB10}}
\vspace*{\fill}
\begin{center}
\textcolor{black}{\Huge\DANTE}
\end{center}
\vfill~
\end{slide}

\begin{slide}[toc=Folie,logohook=lb,logopos={0,0},
    logocmd={\includegraphics[height=\slideheight]{fuBIB10}}]{Example 2}
\vspace*{\fill}
\begin{center}
\textcolor{black}{\Huge\DANTE}
\end{center}
\vfill~
\end{slide}
```

[1]Source: Free University Berlin, library (Reinhard Görner)

35 PSTricks in presentations

35.1.7 Available space

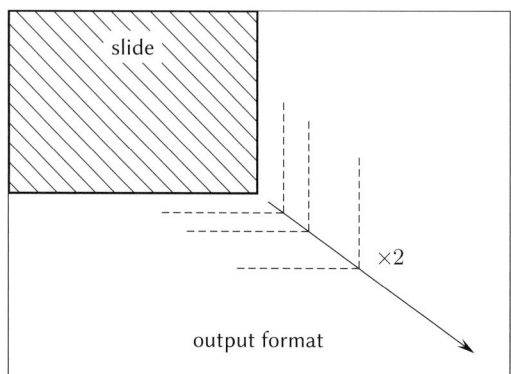

▷ The material on a slide is always scaled by a factor of 2 and output on the requested paper size.

▷ For paper=a4paper ($297\text{mm} \times 210\text{mm}$), the area $148.5\text{mm} \times 105\text{mm}$ is available for a slide.

35.2 beamer

In contrast to powerdot, there is no special support for PSTricks in beamer; it was developed by Till Tantau primarily to work with pdfTeXThe way via latex→dvips→ps2pdf is possible as well, however. beamer has an almost infinite number of options and some quite interesting features. The structure of the individual slides is in principle identical to powerdot.

```
\documentclass[ngerman,xcolor=table,slidestop, smaller, compress,
   hyperref={bookmarks=true,colorlinks}]{beamer}
\begin{frame}
\frametitle{\texttt{pst-3dplot}}
\begin{pspicture}(-4.5,-6.5)(3,3.25)
  \transduration<1-11>{2.5}
  \psset{Alpha=45,Beta=30,linestyle=dashed,unit=0.8cm}
  \visible<+->{\pstThreeDCoor[linestyle=solid,xMin=-5,xMax=5,yMin=-4,yMax=5,zMax=5,IIIDtick
  \visible<+->{\pstThreeDEllipse[linecolor=red](0,0,0)(0,\radius,0)(0,0,\radius)}
  \multido{\iA=15+15,\iB=3+1}{5}{%
     \visible<+->{\pstThreeDEllipse(\radius \iA\space sin mul,0,0)%
        (0,\radius \iA\space cos mul,0)(0,0,\radius \iA\space cos mul)}}
%
  \visible<+->{\pstThreeDEllipse[linestyle=dotted,
     SphericalCoor](0,0,0)(\radius,90,\PhiI)(\radius,0,0)}
  \visible<+->{\pstThreeDEllipse[SphericalCoor,
        beginAngle=-90,endAngle=90](0,0,0)(\radius,90,\PhiI)(\radius,0,0)}
  \visible<+->{\pstThreeDEllipse[linestyle=dotted,
     SphericalCoor](0,0,0)(\radius,90,\PhiII)(\radius,0,0)}
  \visible<+->{\pstThreeDEllipse[SphericalCoor,
        beginAngle=-90,endAngle=90](0,0,0)(\radius,90,\PhiII)(\radius,0,0)}
%
```

```
    \visible<+->{\pscustom[fillstyle=solid,fillcolor=blue]{%
      \pstThreeDEllipse[SphericalCoor,beginAngle=\PhiI,endAngle=\PhiII]%
          (0,0,0)(\radius,90,\PhiII)(\radius,0,0)
      \pstThreeDEllipse[beginAngle=\PhiII,endAngle=\PhiI](\RadIIs,0,0)(0,\RadIIc,0)(0,0,\RadIIc)
      \pstThreeDEllipse[SphericalCoor,beginAngle=\PhiII,endAngle=\PhiI]%
          (0,0,0)(\radius,90,\PhiI)(\radius,0,0)
      \pstThreeDEllipse[beginAngle=\PhiI,endAngle=\PhiII](\RadIs,0,0)(0,\RadIc,0)(0,0,\RadIc)
    }}
\end{pspicture}
\end{frame}
```

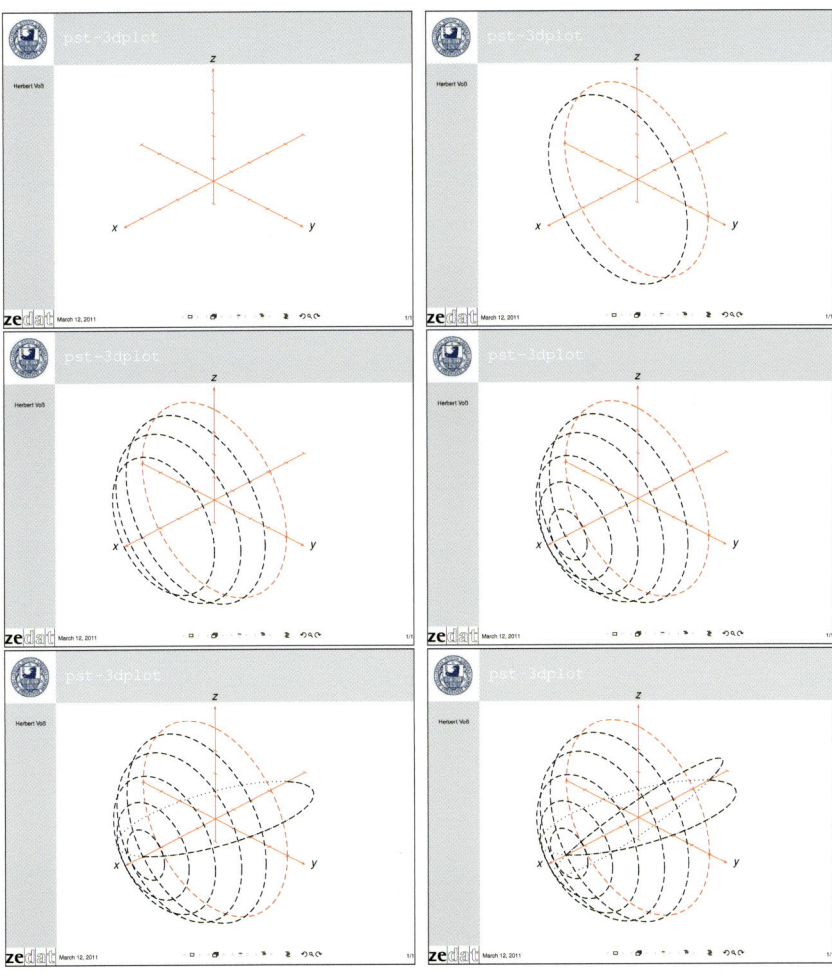

```
\frame[plain]{\setbeamercolor{bodyCol}{fg=white, bg=blue!30}
\titlepage}
\begin{frame}{Bibliografie}{Externe Lösung -- \BibTeX}
\includegraphics[scale=0.75]{images/bibtex-howitworks}
```

```
\end{frame}

\begin{frame}{Bibliografie}{Externe Lösung -- \texttt{biblatex}}
\includegraphics[scale=0.75]{images/biblatex-howitworks}
\end{frame}
```

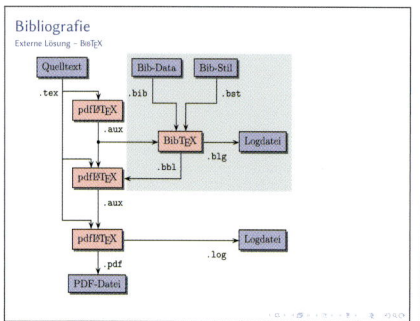 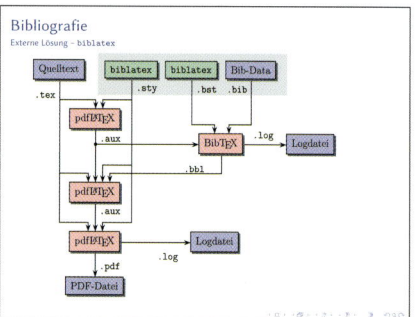

There is a short introduction to the use of the individual commands in [25].

Chapter 36

Examples

The examples in this chapter have been randomly selected with the intention of providing a general overview of what's possible with PSTricks. There are many more examples on the official homepage http://PSTricks.tug.org or on Syracuse: http://melusine.eu.org/syracuse/pstricks/. The source code for the examples is, as usual, available for general download on CTAN or on the PSTricks website.

Figure 36.1: PSTricks written with the symbol font

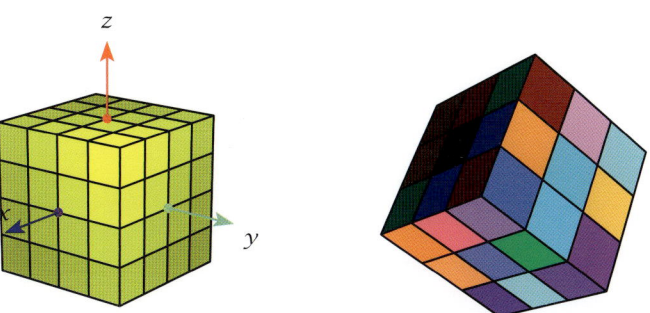

Figure 36.2: Dice (pst-solides3d)

36 Examples

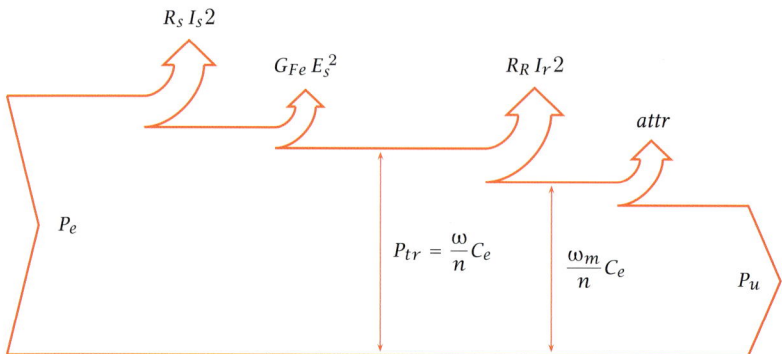

Figure 36.3: Energy diagram of an asynchronous motor

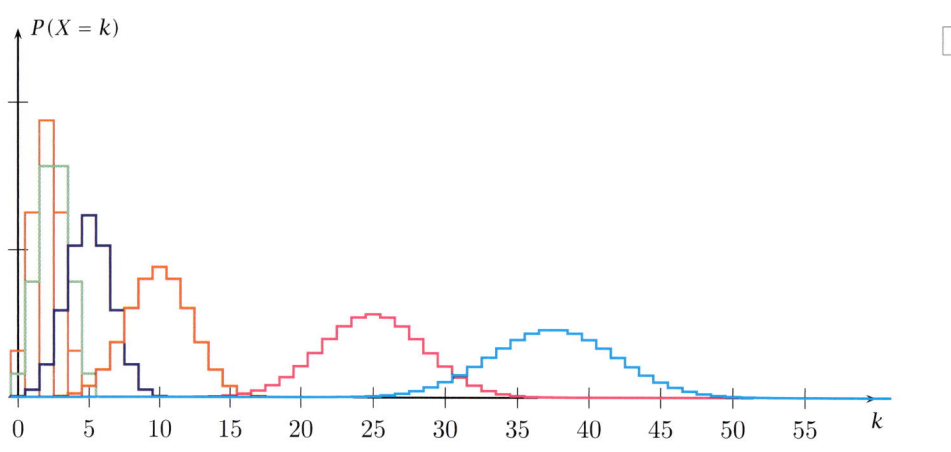

Figure 36.4: Binomial distributions (`pst-func`)

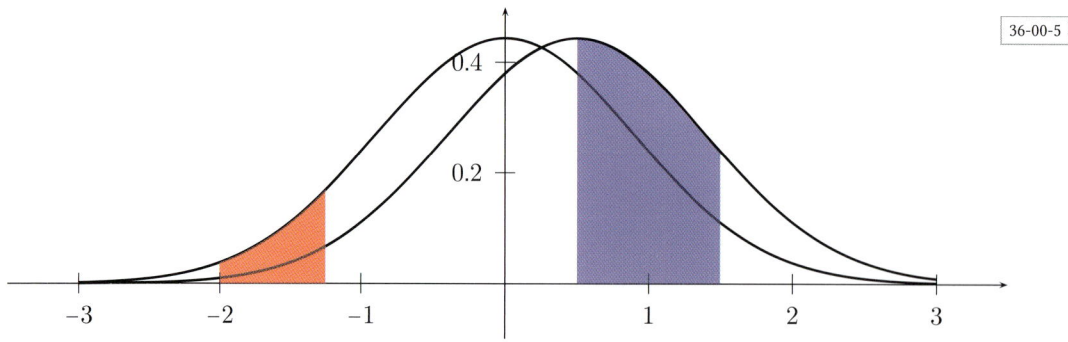

Figure 36.5: Using the `pst-math` package

Examples

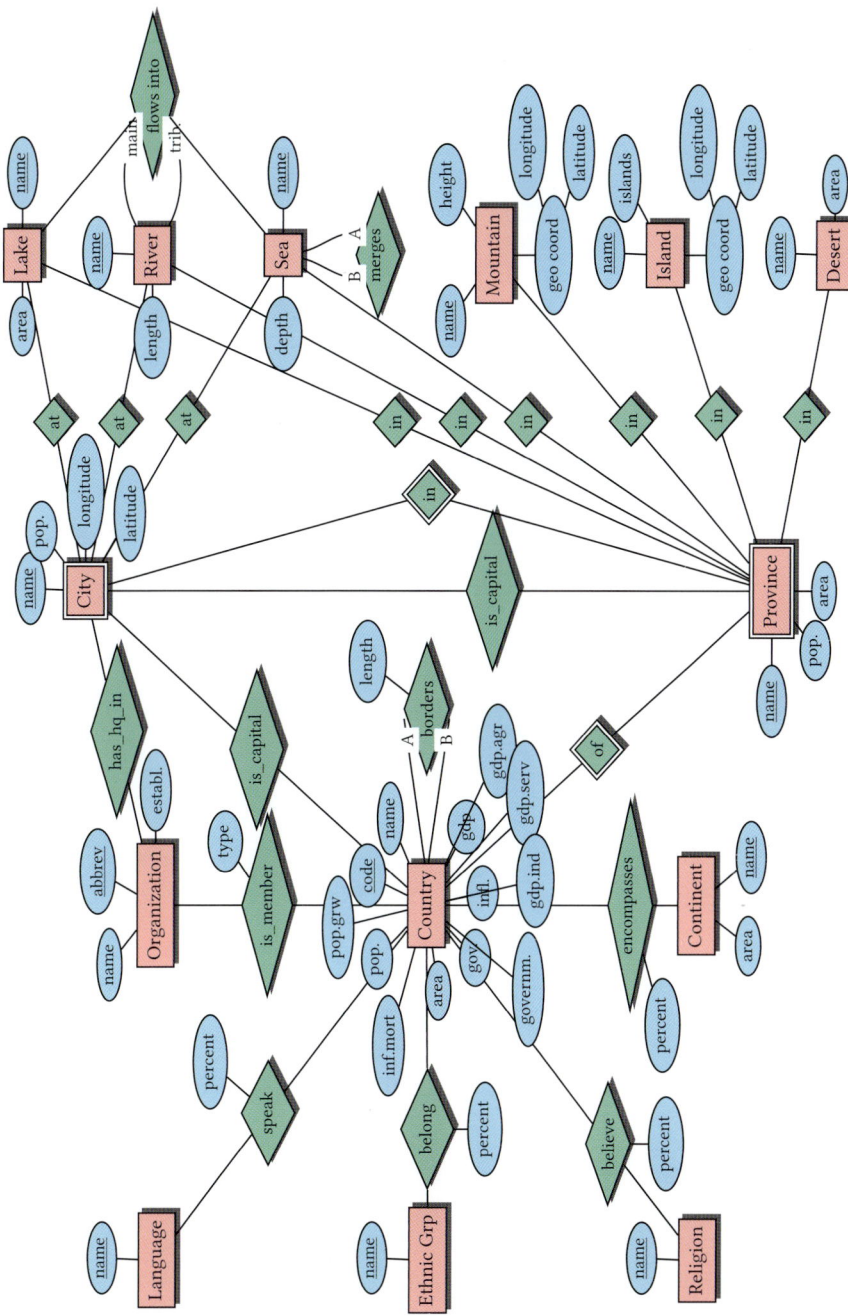

Figure 36.6: Complex example for the pst-dbicons package (Wolfgang May)

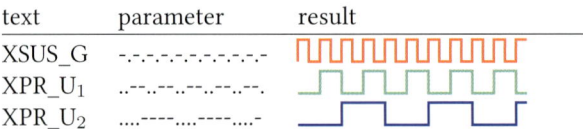

Figure 36.7: Definition of special commands

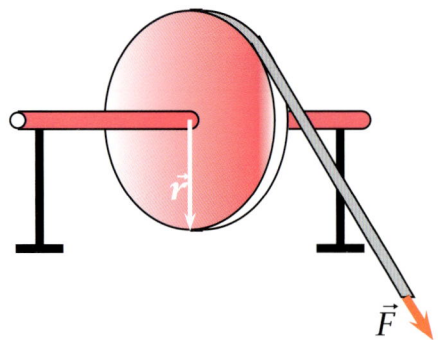

A great many people have never heard the scream of an eagle. The only voice they connect with the kind of the air is a ludicrously feeble squawk, dim with distance, but in his great moments the eagle has a war-cry like that of the hawk, but harsher, hoarser, tenfold in volume. This sound cut into the night in the gulch, and Vic Gregg started and glanced about for echoes made the sound stand at his side; then he looked up, and saw two eagles fighting in the light of the morning. He knew what it meant–the beginning of the mating season, and these two battling for a prize. They darted away. They flashed together with reaching talons and gaping beaks, and dropped in a tumult of wings, then soared and clashed once more until one of them folded his wings and dropped bulletlike out of the morning into the night. Close over Gregg's head, the wings flirted out–ten feet from tip to tip–beat down with a great washing sound, and the bird shot across the valley in a level flight. The conqueror screamed a long insult down the hollow. For a while he balanced, craning his bald head as if he sought applause, then, without visible movement of his wings, sailed away over the peaks. A feather fluttered slowly down past Vic Gregg.

Figure 36.8: Using \rput, \pscircle, and \psarc (Idea by Thomas Siegel)

Figure 36.9: Using \rput, \pscircle, \psarc, and \psellipticarc

Examples

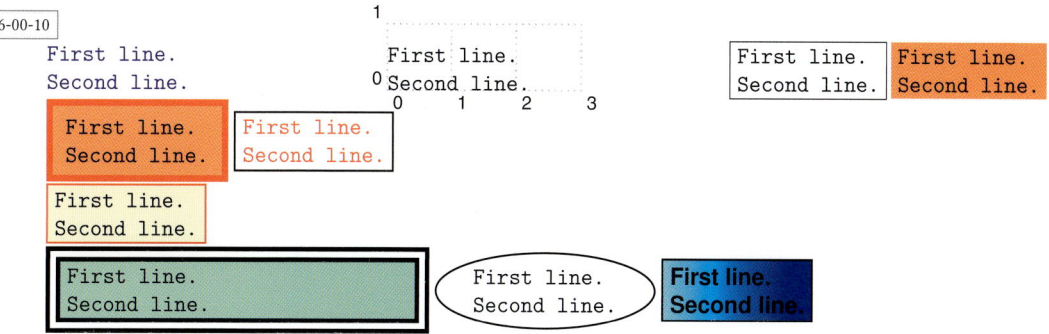

Figure 36.10: Verbatim mode in different boxes (Denis Girou)

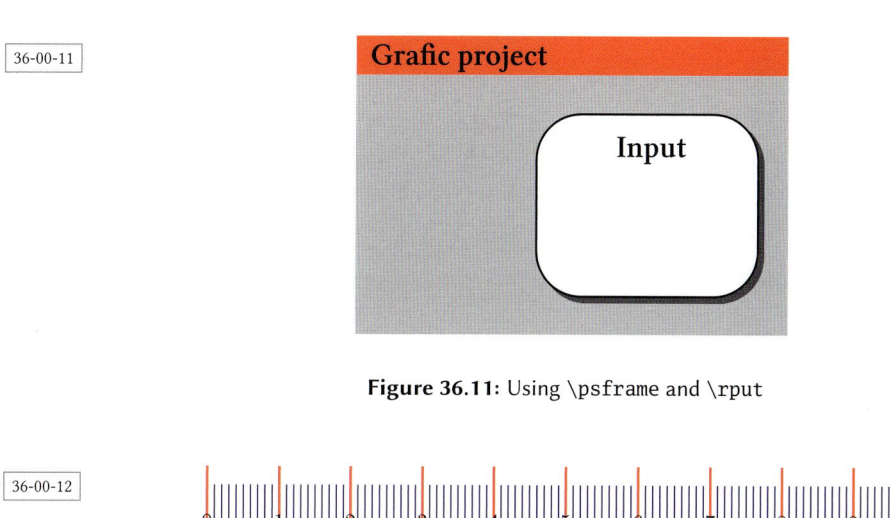

Figure 36.11: Using \psframe and \rput

Figure 36.12: Labelling axes with pst-plot

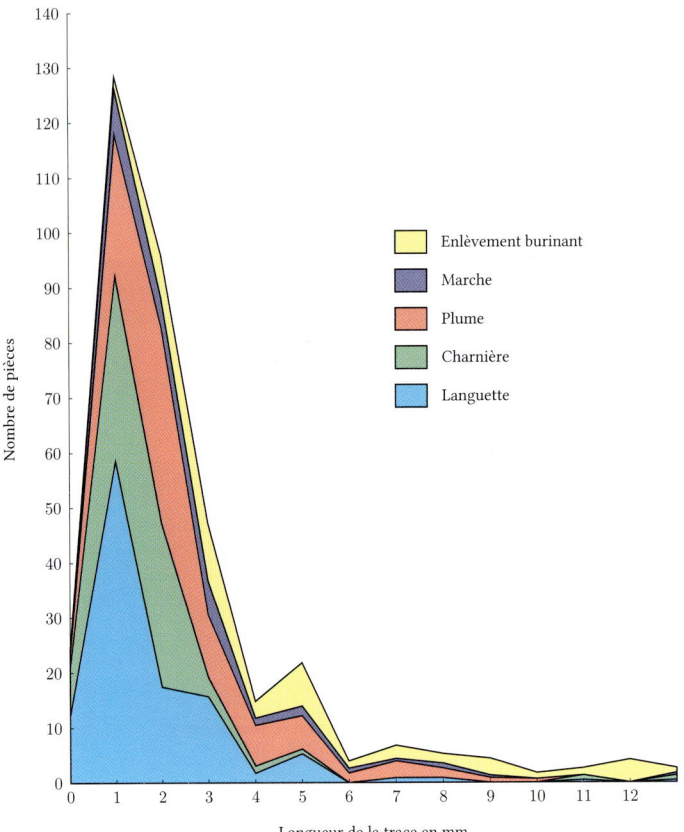

Figure 36.13: Overlays of filled areas

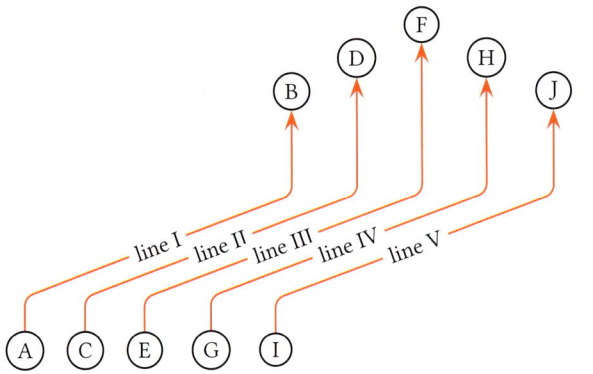

Figure 36.14: Node connections with a constant angle (pst-node)

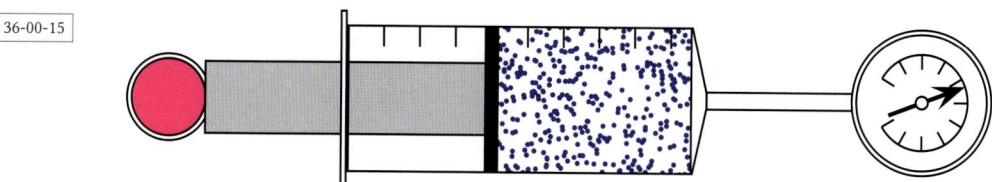

Figure 36.15: Using \psclip and the \random command (pstricks, Manuel Luque)

Figure 36.16: Using the \random command (pst-labo, Manuel Luque).

$$\begin{aligned}
y &= x^2 + bx + c \\
&= x^2 + 2 \cdot \frac{b}{2}x + c \\
&= \underbrace{x^2 + 2 \cdot \frac{b}{2}x + \left(\frac{b}{2}\right)^2}_{\left(x + \frac{b}{2}\right)^2} - \left(\frac{b}{2}\right)^2 + c \\
&= \left(x + \frac{b}{2}\right)^2 - \left(\frac{b}{2}\right)^2 + c \qquad \Big| + \left(\frac{b}{2}\right)^2 - c \\
y + \left(\frac{b}{2}\right)^2 - c &= \left(x + \frac{b}{2}\right)^2 \qquad\qquad\qquad \Big|\text{(Scheitelpunktform)} \\
y - y_S &= (x - x_S)^2 \\
S(x_S; y_S) \quad \text{bzw.} \quad &S\!\left(-\frac{b}{2};\ \left(\frac{b}{2}\right)^2 - c\right)
\end{aligned}$$

Figure 36.17: A grid...

36 Examples

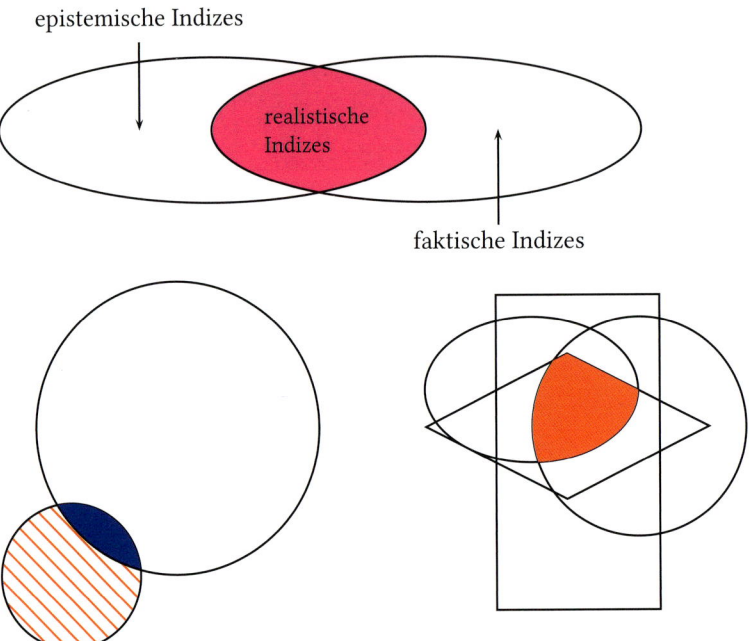

Figure 36.18: Clipping

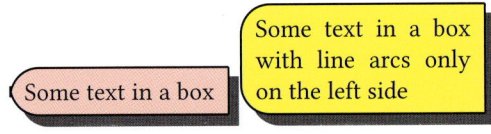

Figure 36.19: Boxes with different corners

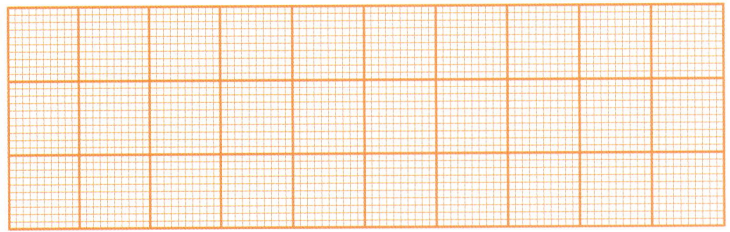

Figure 36.20: Special paper with \psgrid and subgriddiv

36-00-21

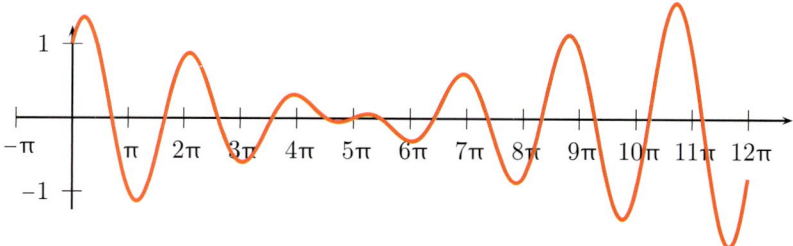

Figure 36.21: Trigonometrical units with `pst-plot`

36-00-22

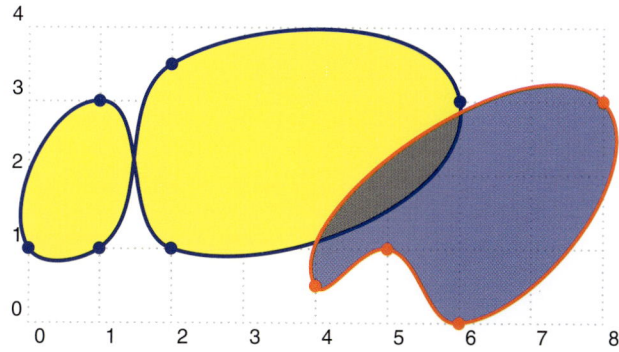

Figure 36.22: Using \psccurve with the eofill fill style

36-00-23

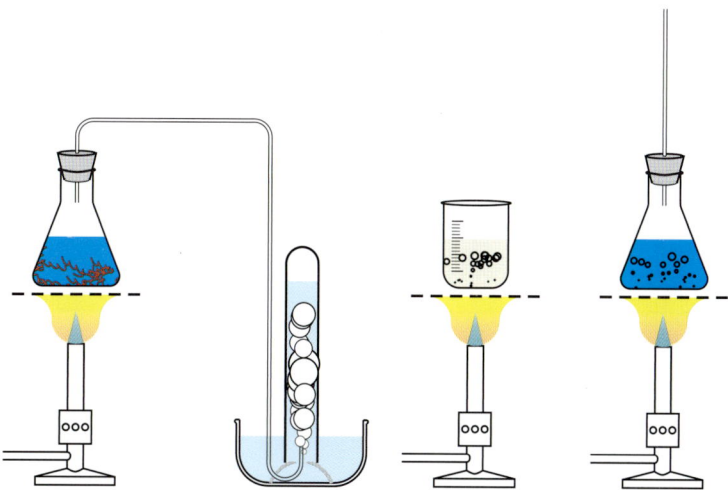

Figure 36.23: Objects from `pst-labo`

36 Examples

Figure 36.24: Transparency

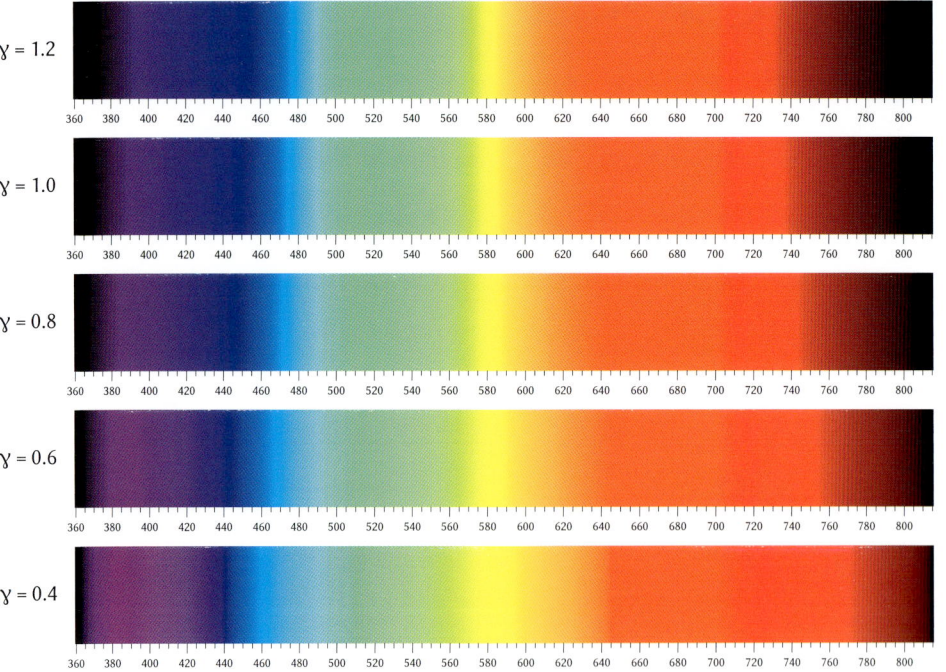

Figure 36.25: Using the wave colour model

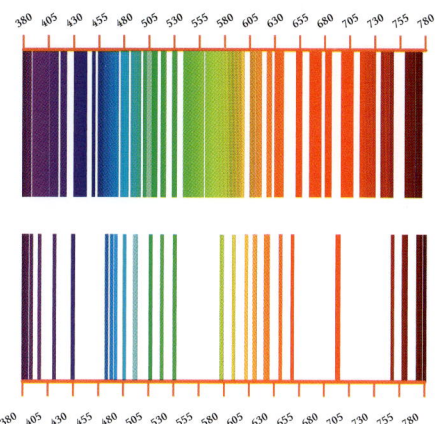
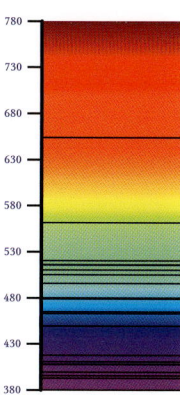

Figure 36.26: Using pst-spectra (Arnaud Schmittbuhl).

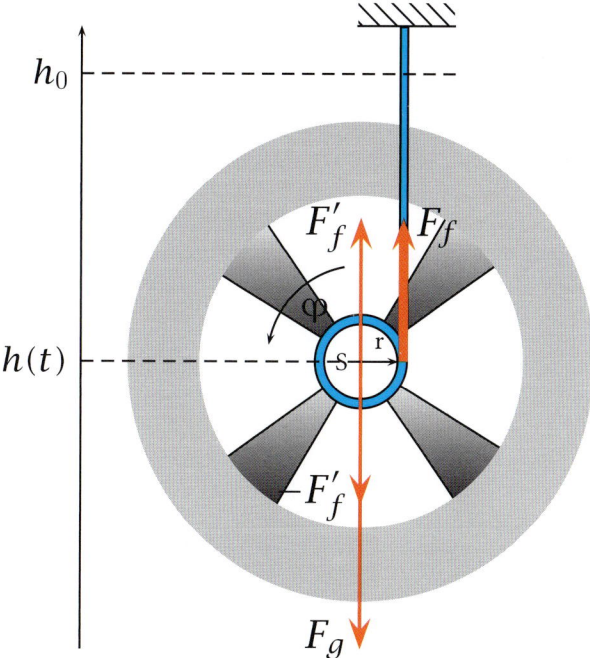

Figure 36.27: Using \multido and \pswedge

36 Examples

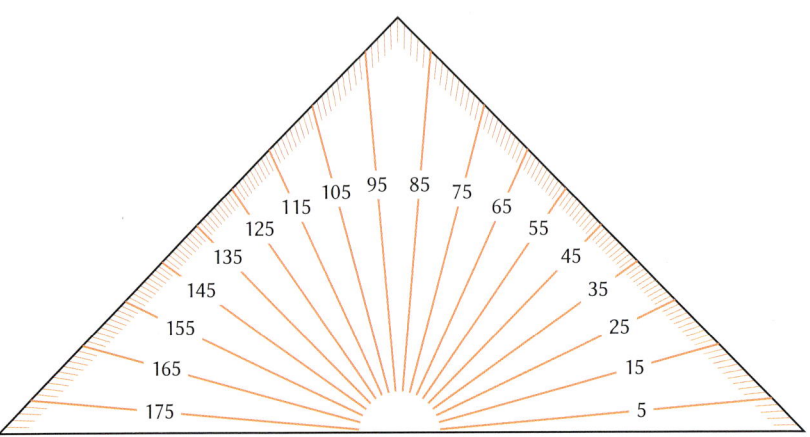

Figure 36.28: Using \pnode and \multido (More examples at http://melusine.eu.org/syracuse/pstricks/rapporteurs/

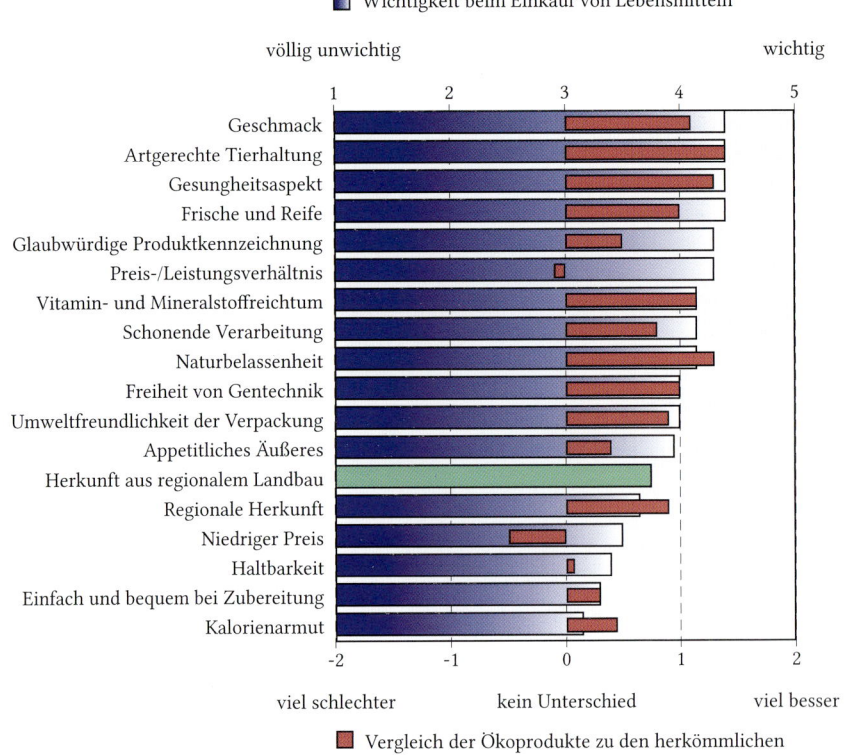

Figure 36.29: Using \multido and pst-grad

Examples

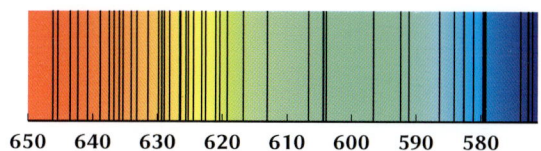

Figure 36.30: Frequency spectra of Neon (pst-spectra, Arnaud Schmittbuhl)

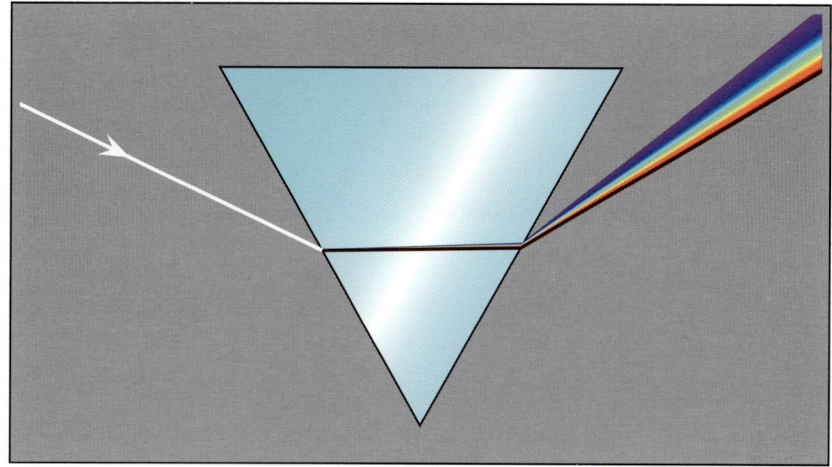

Figure 36.31: Dividing light into its colours (Manuel Luque)

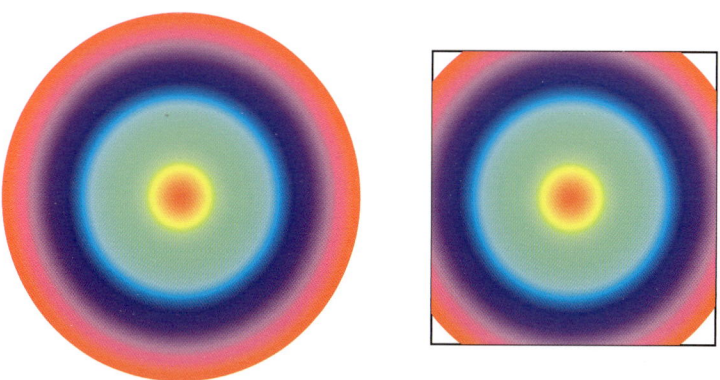

Figure 36.32: \psframe, \psclip, \pscircle, and \multido

36 Examples

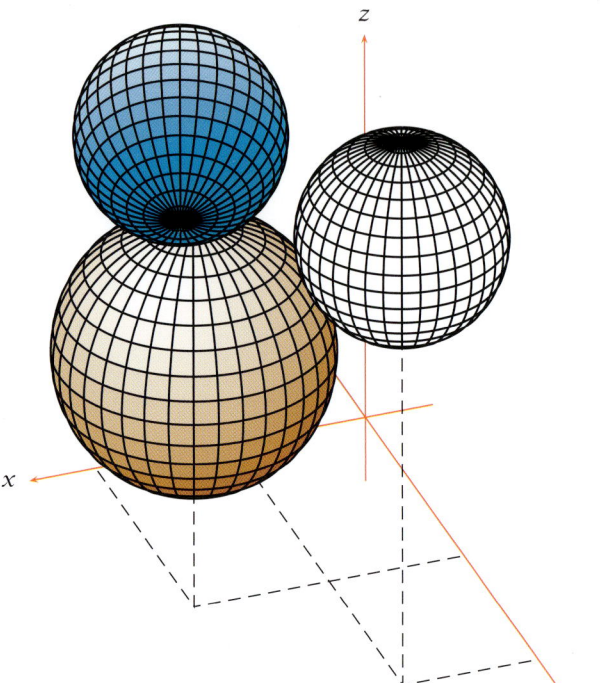

Figure 36.33: Spheres in 3D parallel projection

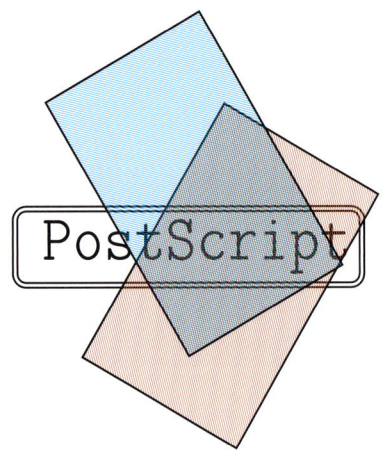

Figure 36.34: Definition of custom fill styles to get a transparency-like filling

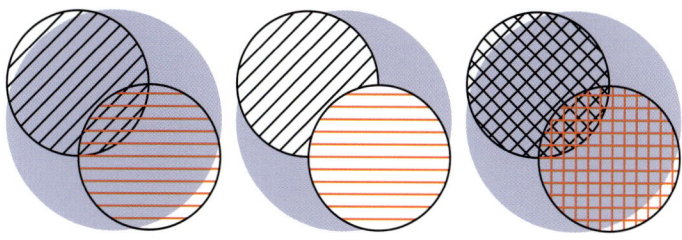

Figure 36.35: \pscircle and fillstyle

Figure 36.36: Using pst-fill (Manuel Luque)

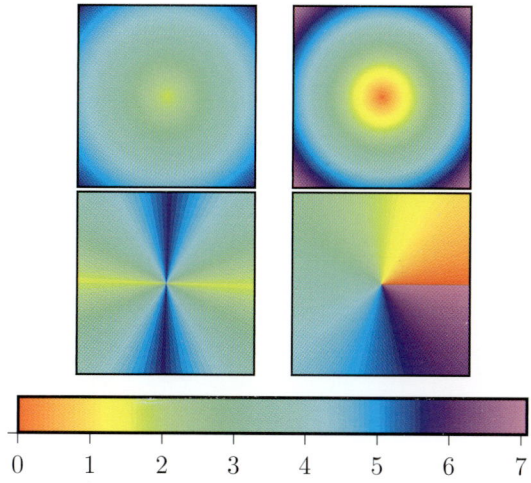

Figure 36.37: Colour slopes with pst-slpe

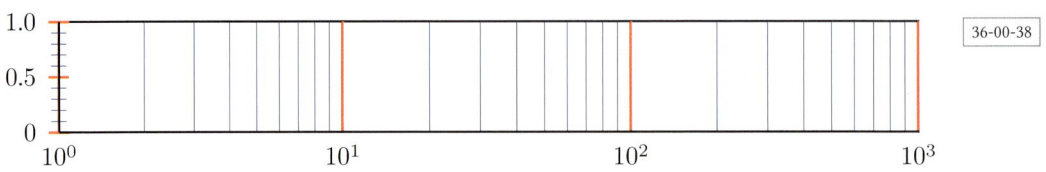

Figure 36.38: Logarithmic axes with `pst-plot`

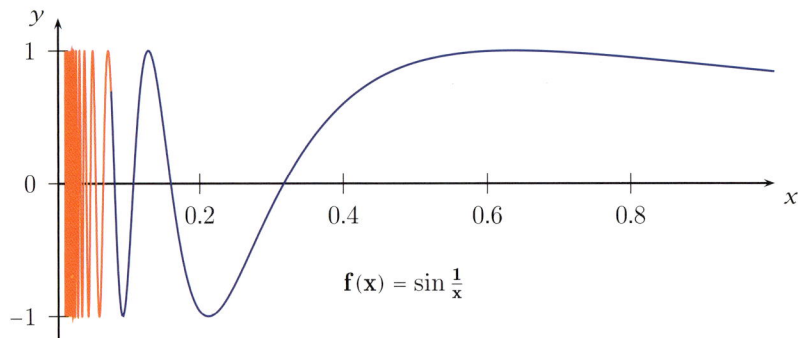

Figure 36.39: Using \psplot with different intervals

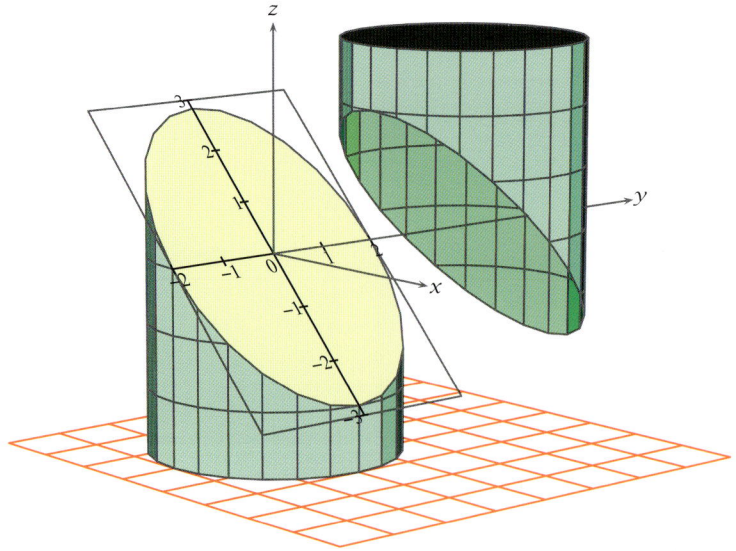

Figure 36.40: Dividing a 3D object into two parts

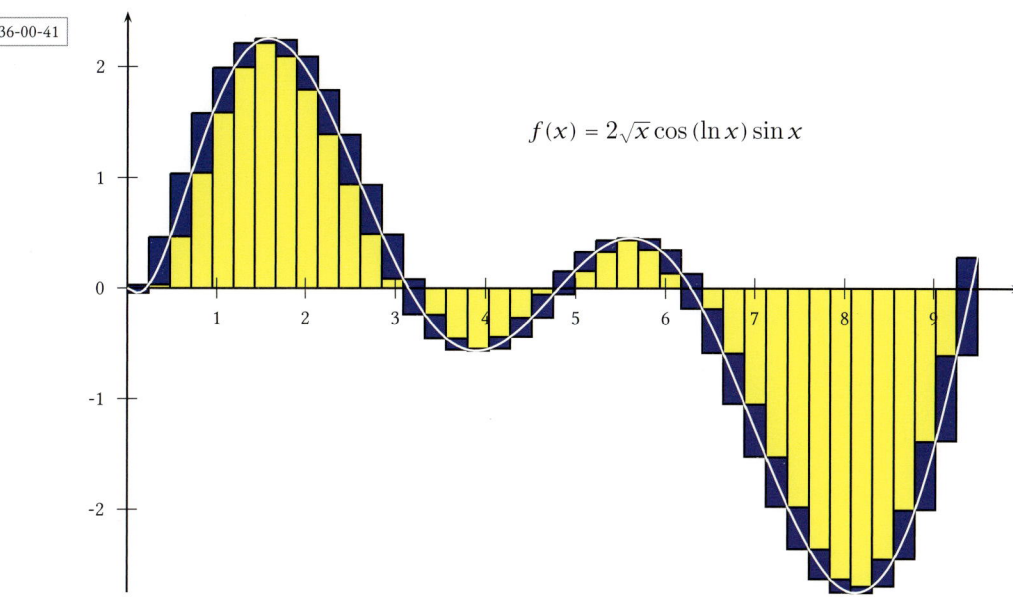

Figure 36.41: Showing the Riemann integral definition using \psStep from the pstricks-add package with the optional setting StepType=Riemann

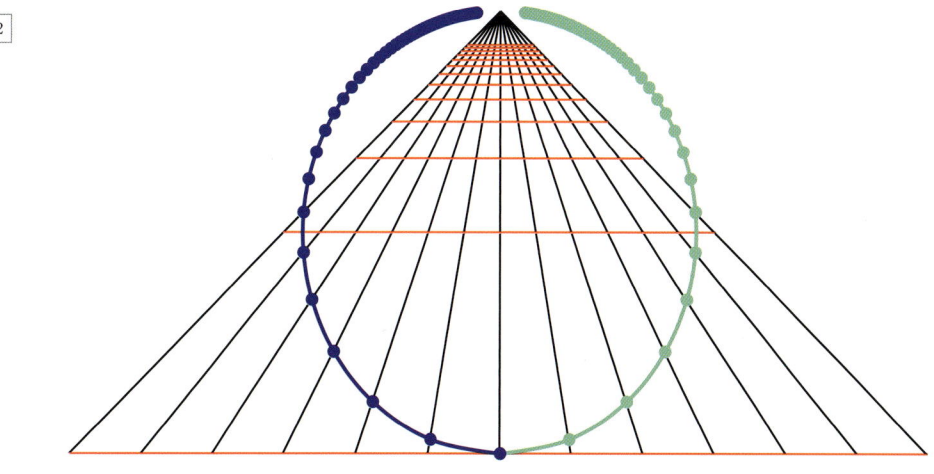

Figure 36.42: "Calculating" with TEX (Chris Sangwin)

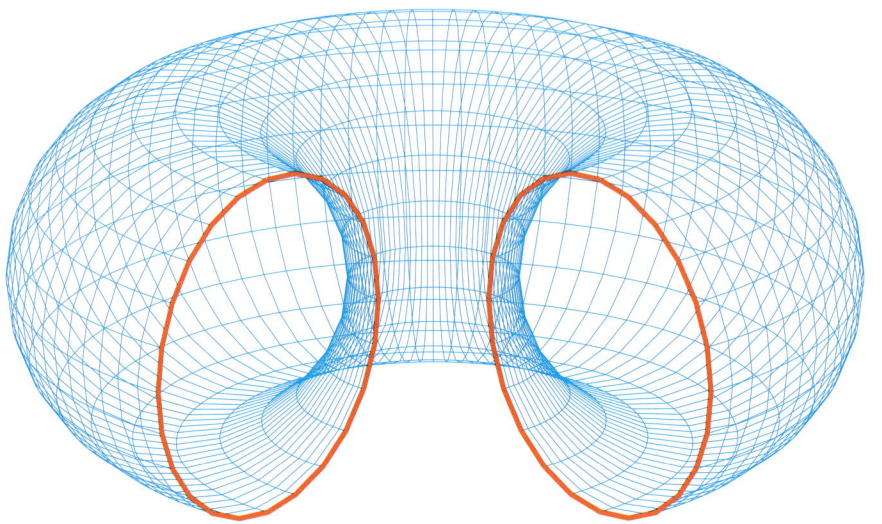

Figure 36.43: Using \parametricplotThreeD from the pst-3dplot package

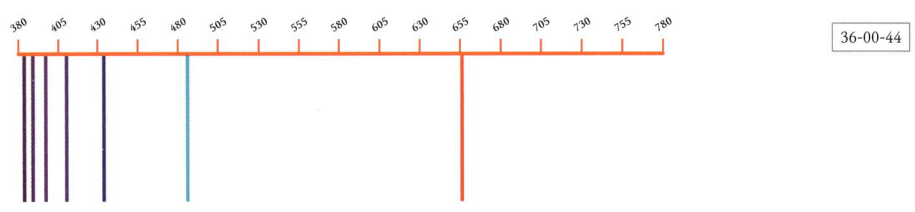

Figure 36.44: The spectrum of Hydrogen (pst-spectra, Arnaud Schmittbuhl)

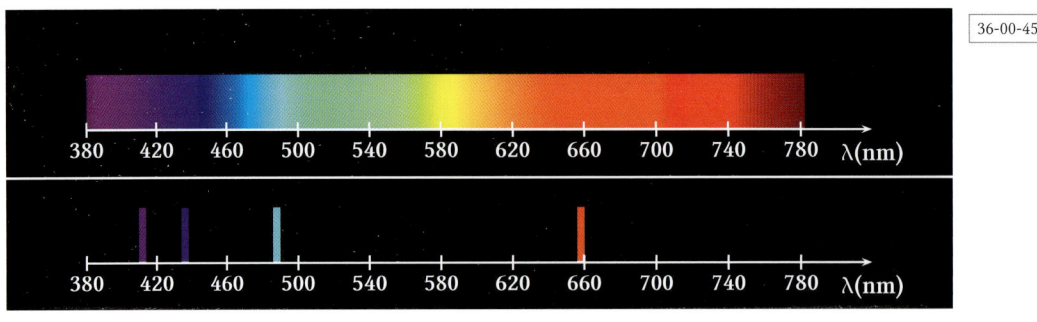

Figure 36.45: The spectrum of Hydrogen (Manuel Luque)

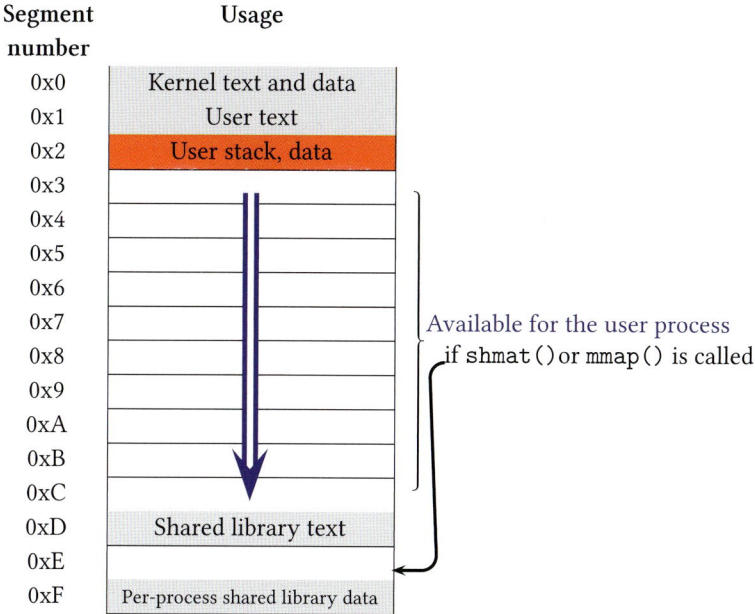

Figure 36.46: Using \ncline and \ncdiag inside a default tabular environment

Figure 36.47: Using pst-lens

Figure 36.48: Colour series with xcolor

36-00-49

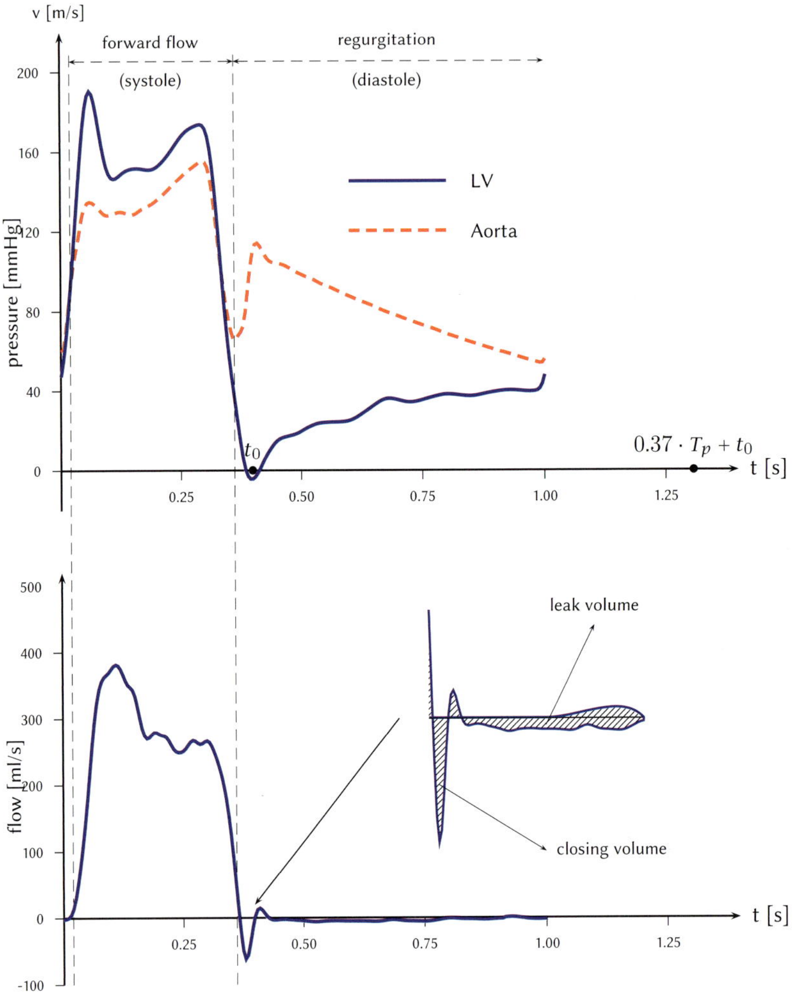

Figure 36.49: A zoom of a data part (Kris Dumont)

36-00-50

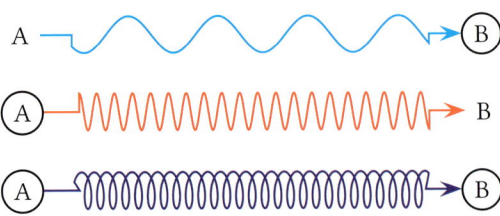

Figure 36.50: Using \circlenode and \nccoil

Examples

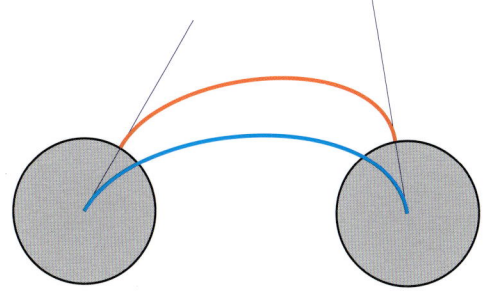

Figure 36.51: Relation between slope and node connection

Figure 36.52: Curves with different styles

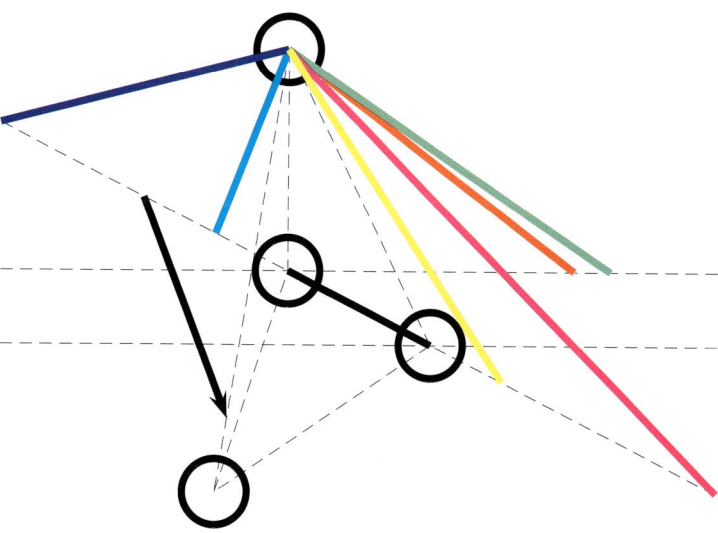

Figure 36.53: Relative node coordinates with [X|Y]nodesep

36 Examples

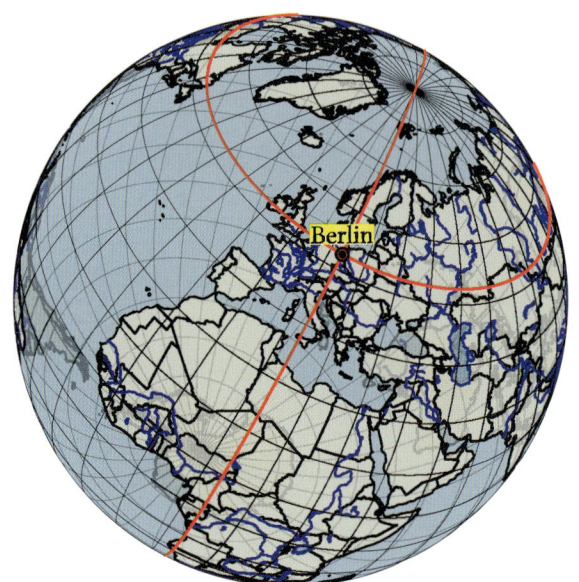

Figure 36.54: A "transparent" earth

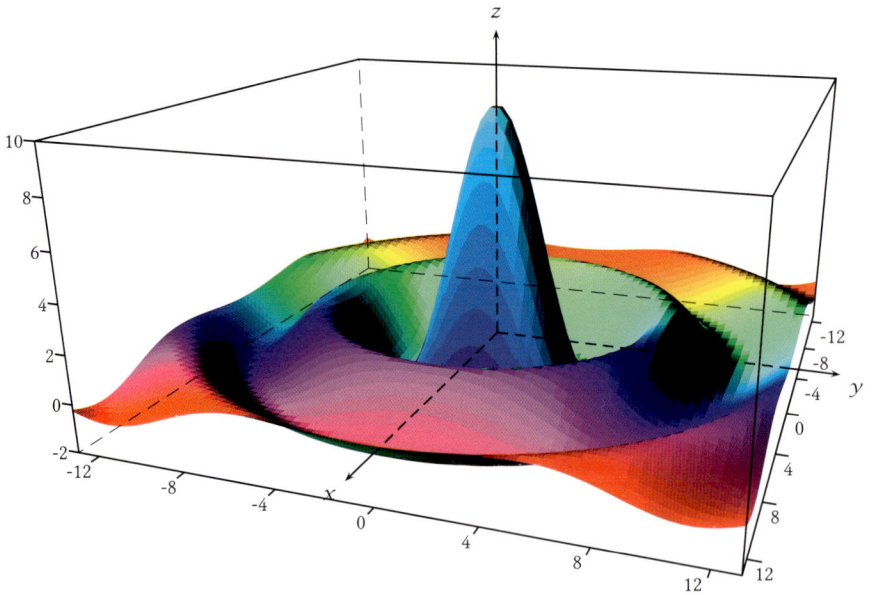

Figure 36.55: Three-dimensional function

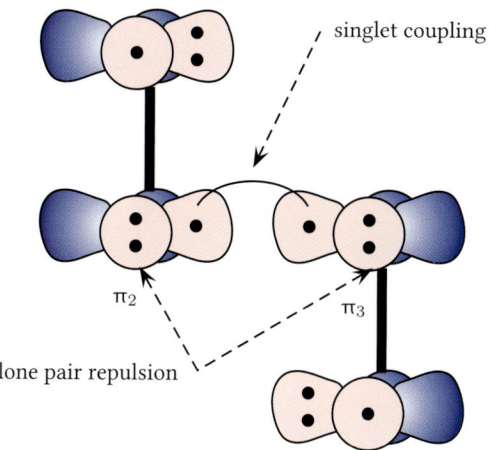

Figure 36.56: Using `psmatrix` and `pst-slpe` (Jorge Luis Llanio)

Figure 36.57: Tiling with `pst-fill` (Denis Girou)

The binding energy in the droplet model consists of the following parts:

- the surface fraction,
- the volume fraction,
- the Coulomb fraction,
- the symmetry energy,
- and a pairing fraction.

$$E = a_v A + -a_f A^{2/3} + -a_c \frac{Z(Z-1)}{A^{1/3}} + -a_s \frac{(A-2Z)^2}{A} + E_p \qquad (1)$$

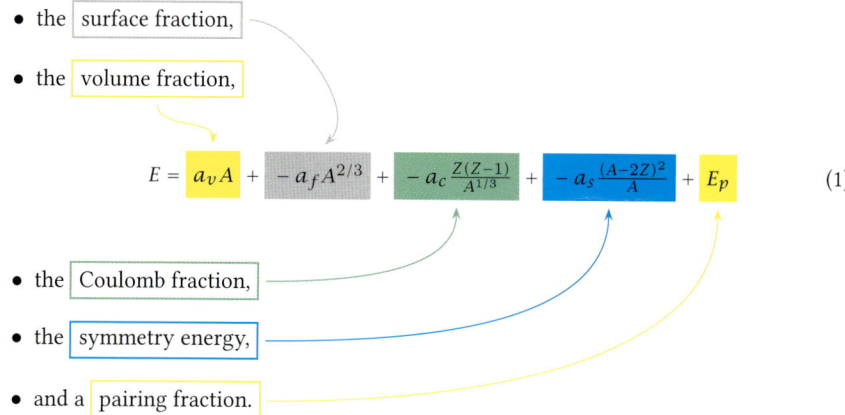

Figure 36.58: Nodes and connections inside math mode

36 Examples

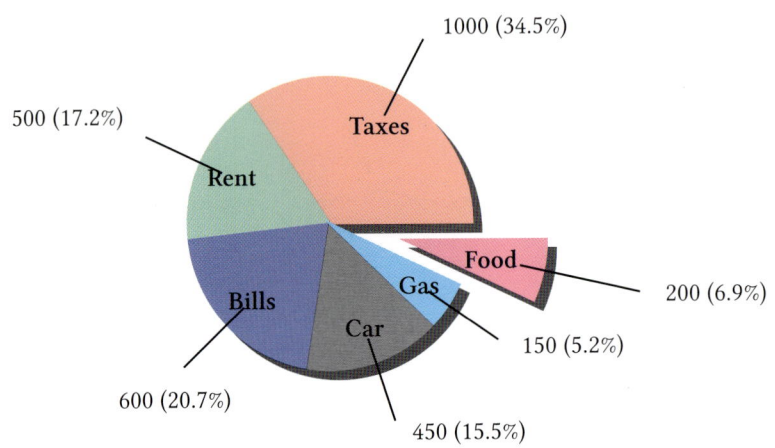

Figure 36.59: A pie chart

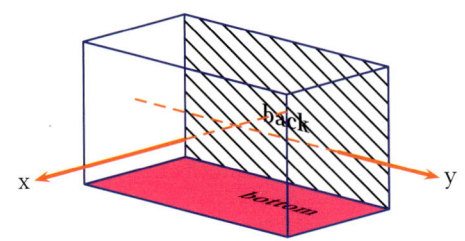

Figure 36.60: Using pst-3dplot

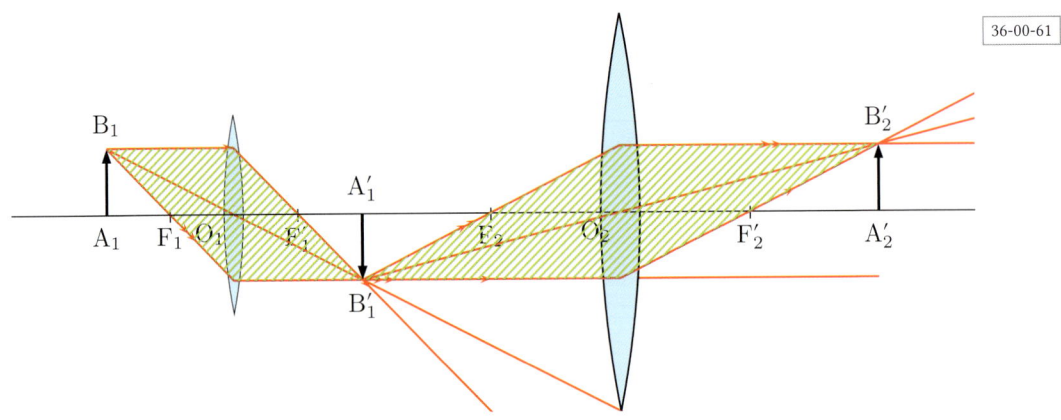

Figure 36.61: Using pst-optic

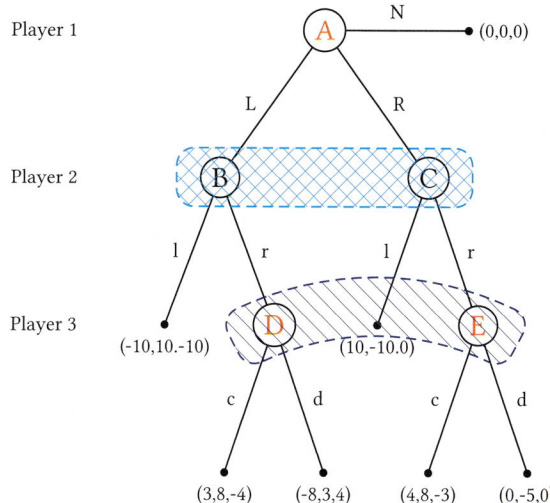

Figure 36.62: Using pst-tree and pst-node (Denis Girou)

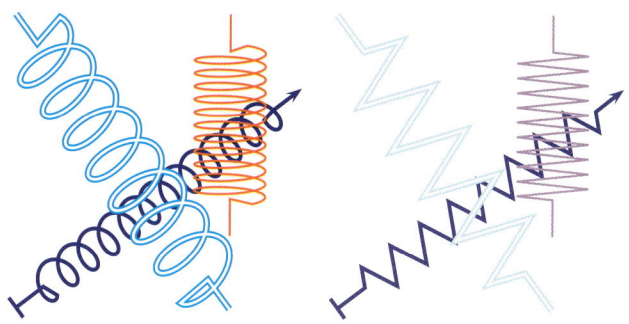

Figure 36.63: Coils and zigzags with pst-coil

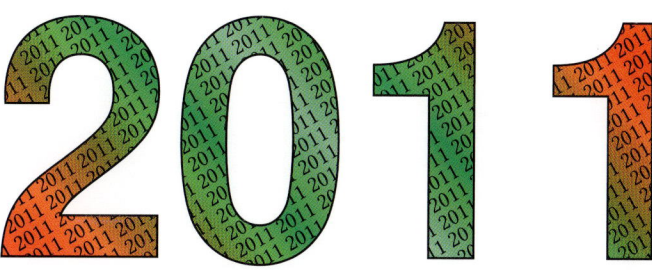

Figure 36.64: Using \pscharpath and \psboxfill

36 Examples

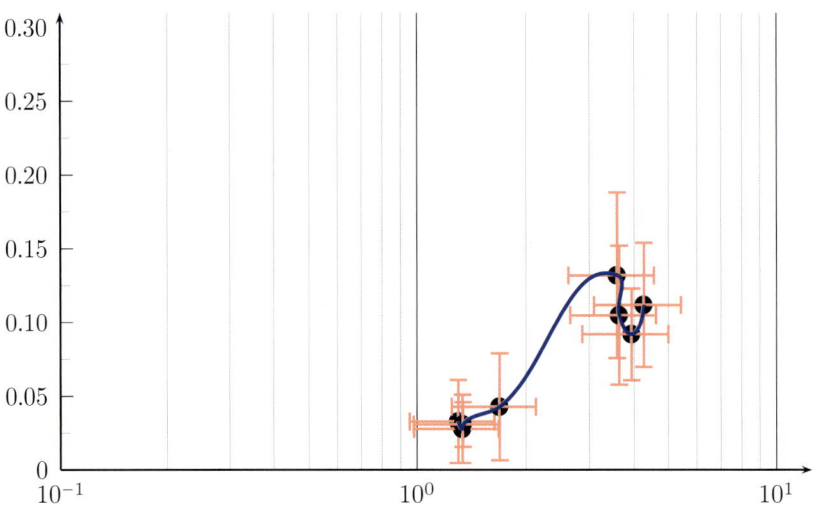

Figure 36.65: Error plotting with data records like x y dx dy

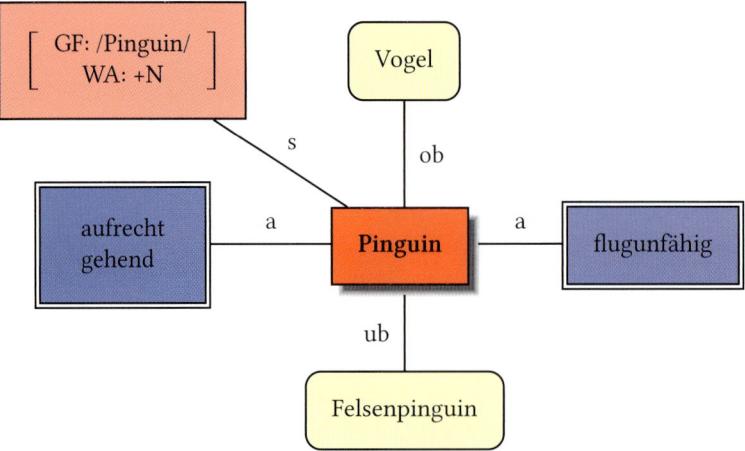

Figure 36.66: Psycholinguistic net of a German word (Christine Römer)

Examples

36-00-67

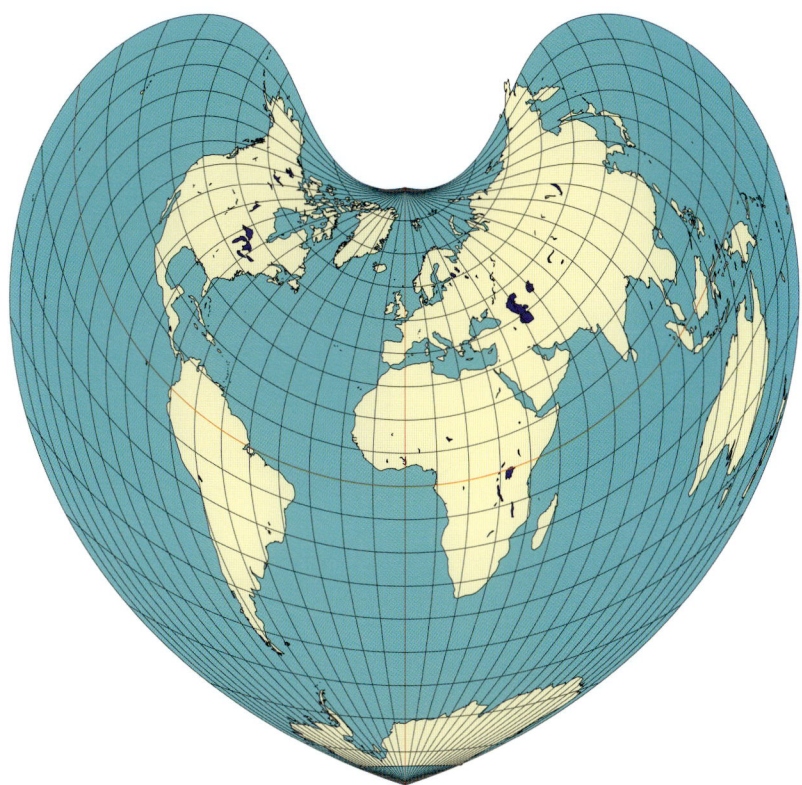

Figure 36.67: "Valentine's day", using `pst-map2d` (Manuel Luque)

36-00-68

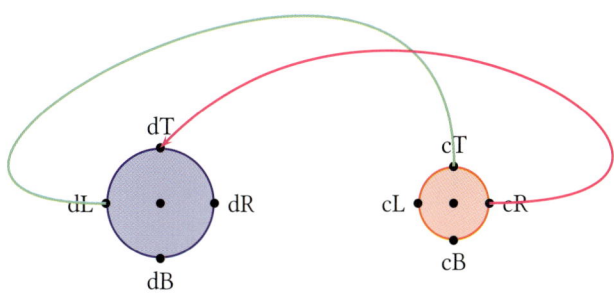

Figure 36.68: Special node connections

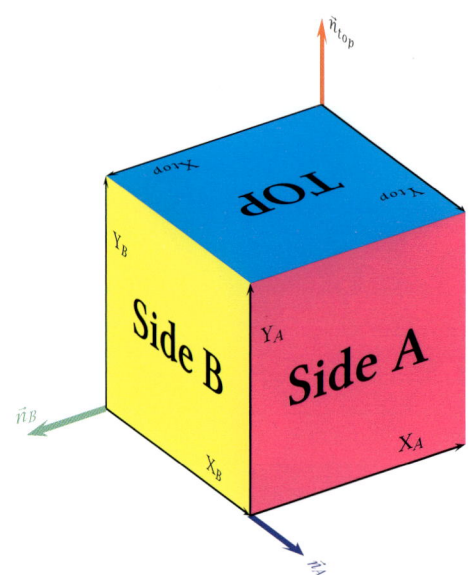

Figure 36.69: Using pst-3d

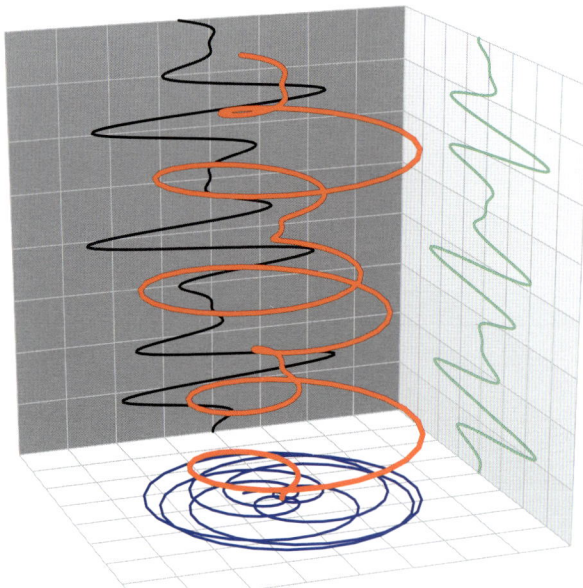

Figure 36.70: Using pst-solides3d

Examples

36-00-71

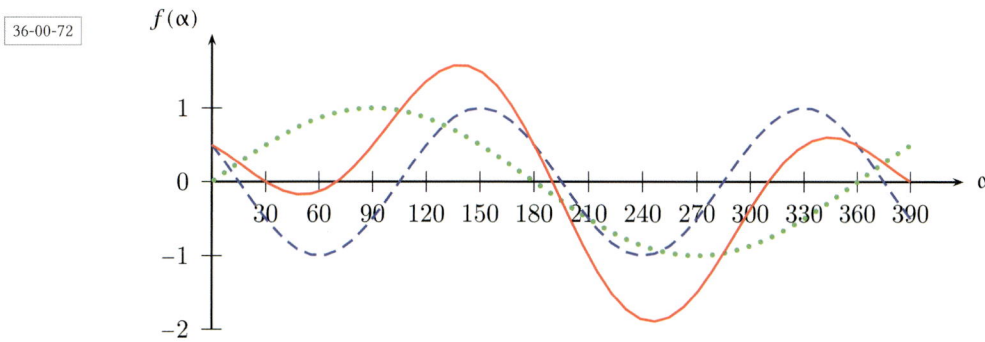

Figure 36.71: Using `pst-calendar`

36-00-72

Figure 36.72: Using `\psplot` from the `pst-plot` package

36 Examples

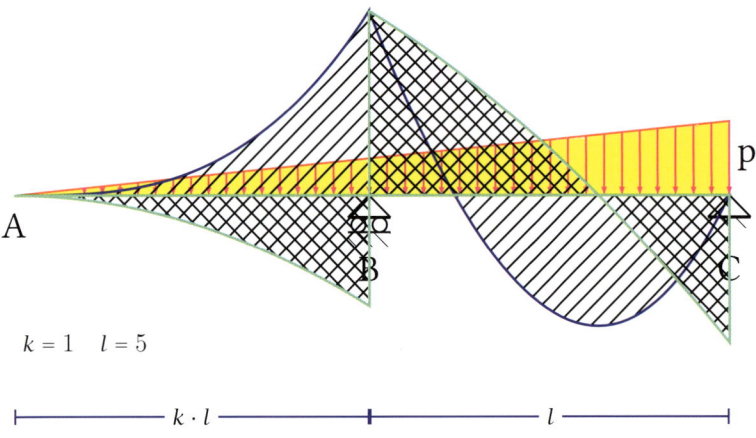

Figure 36.73: Using pst-eucl (Dominique Rodriguez)

Figure 36.74: Using pst-stru (Giuseppe Matarazzo)

Examples

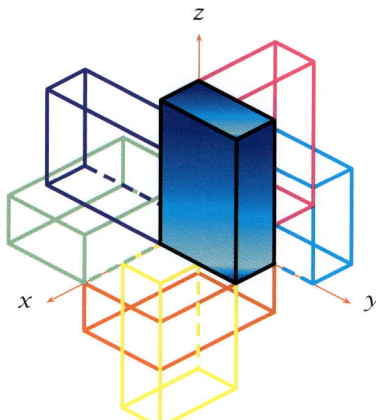

Figure 36.75: Rotation of solids

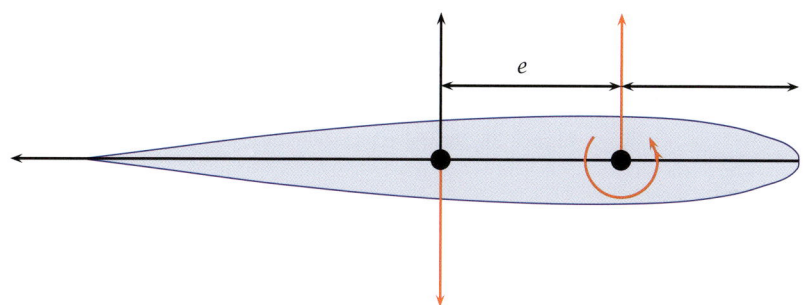

Figure 36.76: Forces on a wing

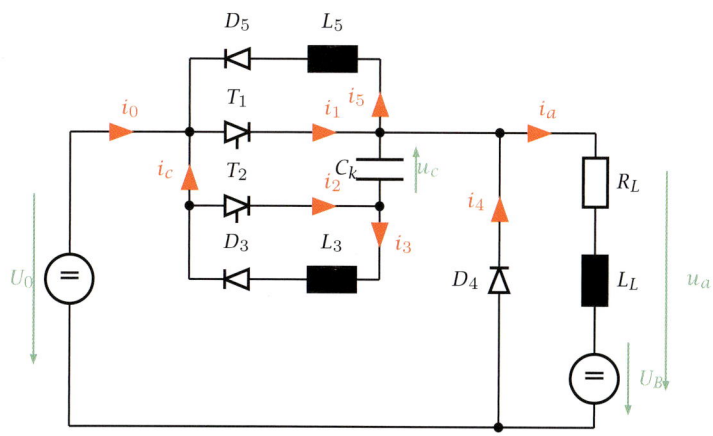

Figure 36.77: Using `pst-circ`

36 Examples

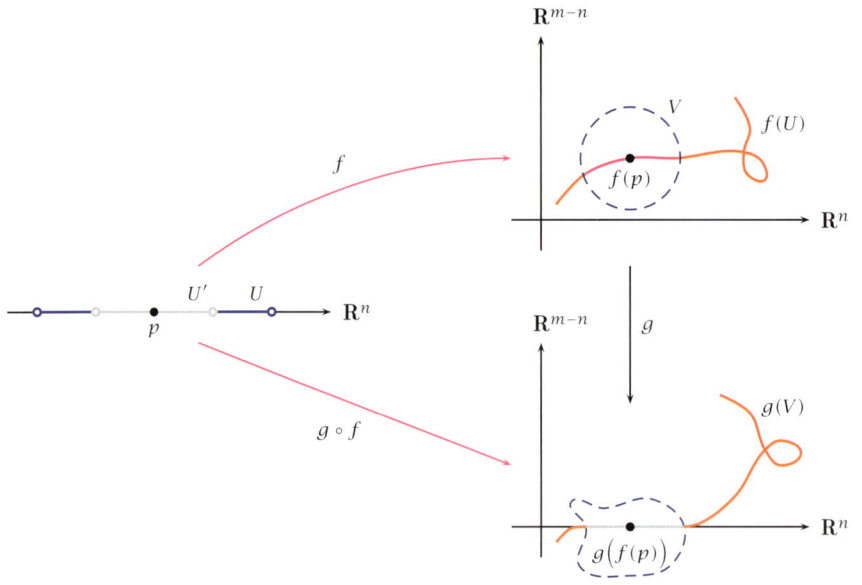

Figure 36.78: Using `pst-solides3d`

Figure 36.79: Using basic commands (Rubens Agapito)

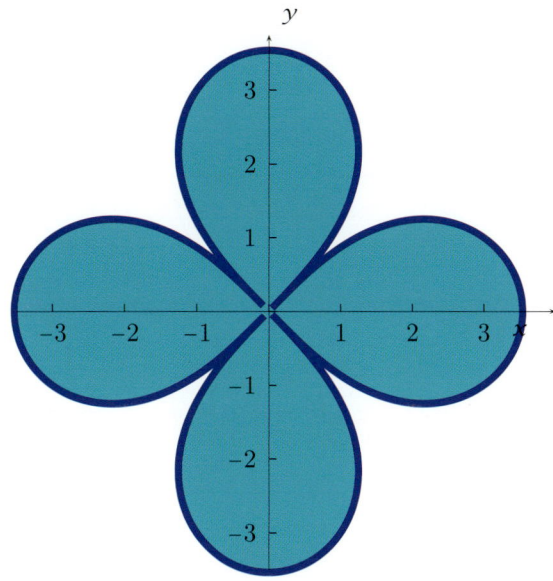

Figure 36.80: The "double" Lemniskate with \psplot and the polar option

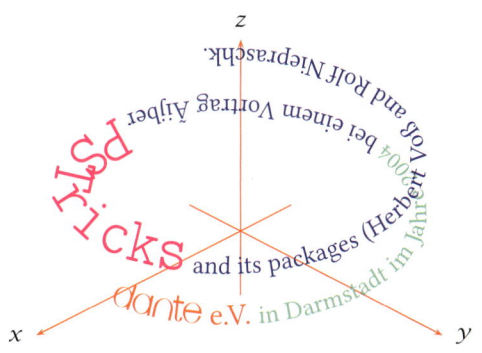

Figure 36.81: Using \pstextpath and \parametricplotThreeD

36-00-82

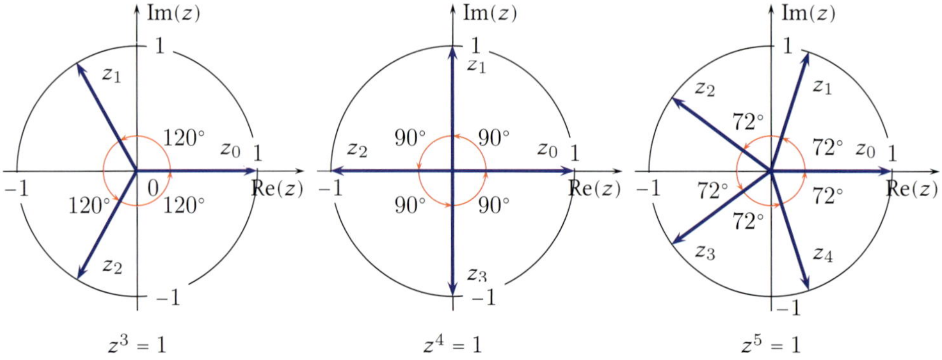

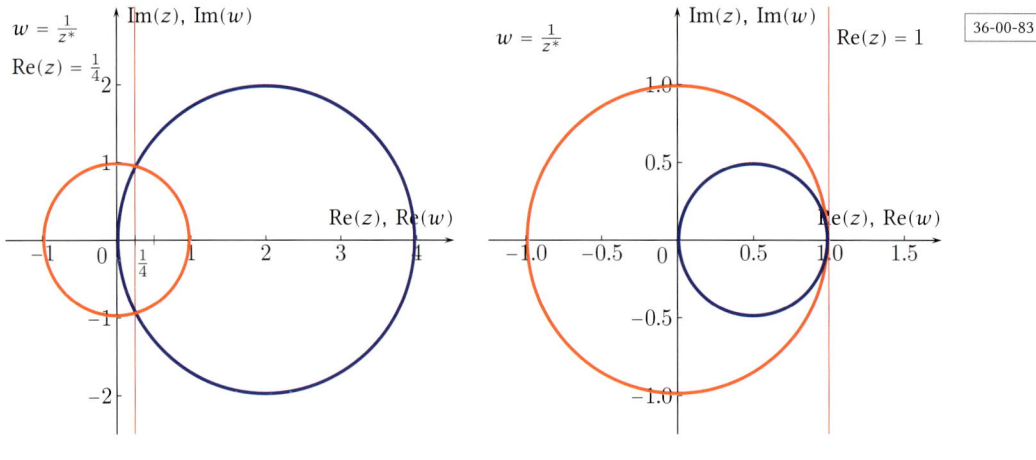

Figure 36.82: Using the basic commands (Ulrich Dirr)

36-00-83

Figure 36.83: Using the basic commands (Ulrich Dirr)

36-00-84

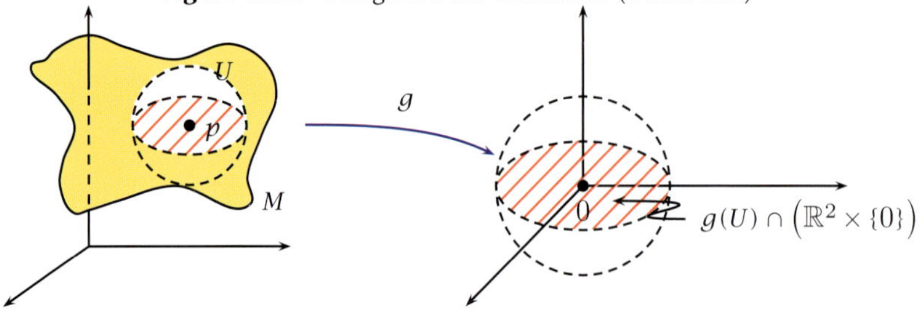

Figure 36.84: Using the basic commands (Rubens Agapito)

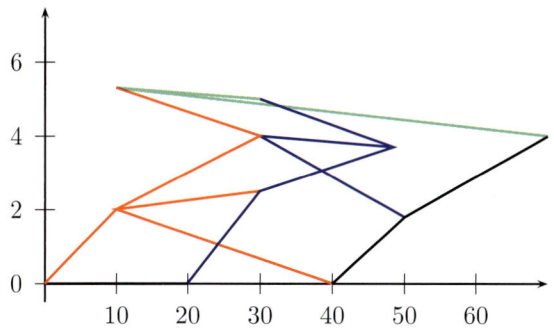

Figure 36.85: Using the \listplot command

Figure 36.86: Using the basic commands to show how the "Quick Sort" works

36-00-87

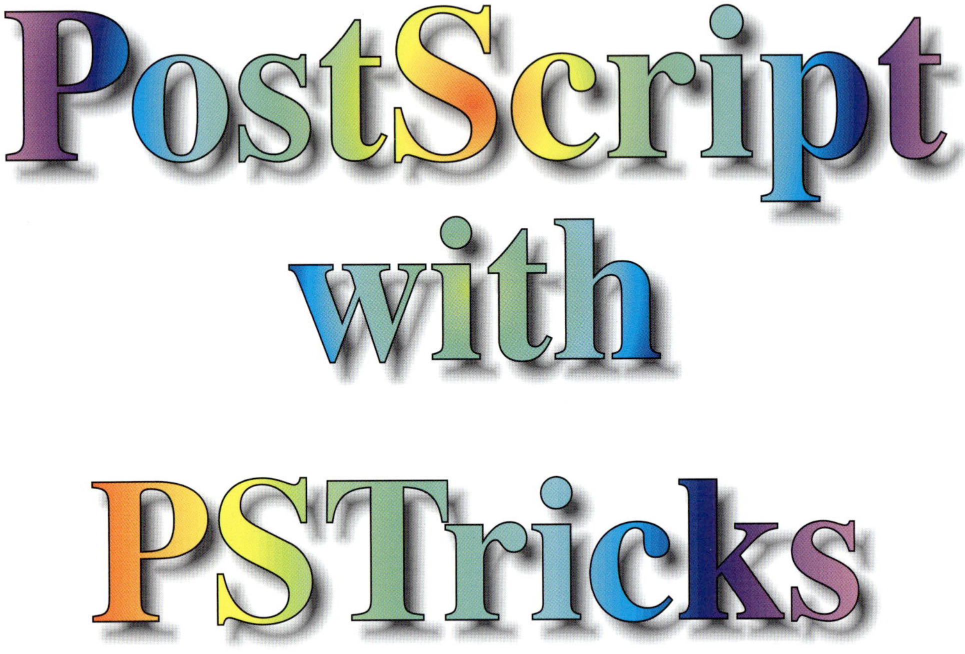

PostScript
with
PSTricks

Figure 36.87: :-)...

36-00-88

$\vec{v}_0$
$\vec{B}$
0
1
-1
-2
0
1
2
3

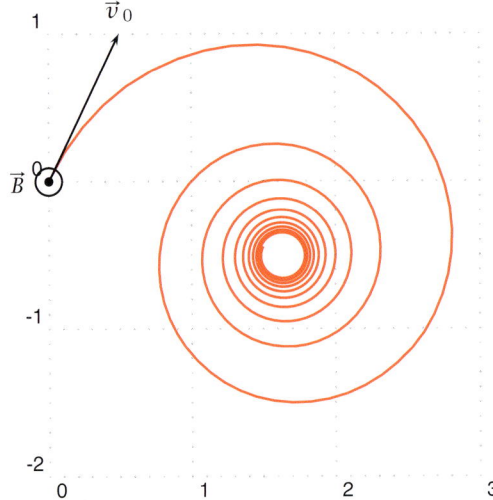

Figure 36.88: Movement of a charged particle in a magnetic field as a solution of the differential equation (pstricks-add, Dominique Rodriguez)

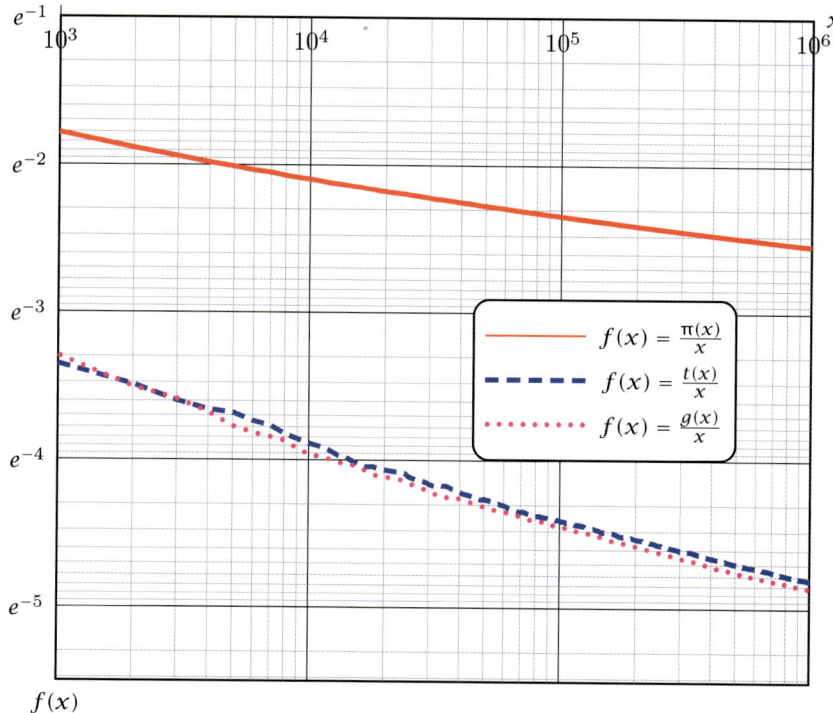

Figure 36.89: Using double logarithmic axes (Lars Kotthoff)

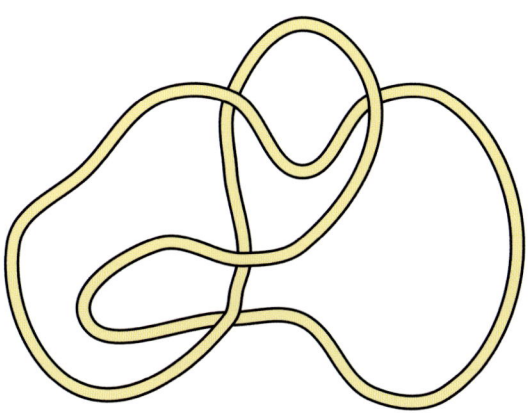

Figure 36.90: Nodes (Jean-Côme Charpentier)

36 Examples

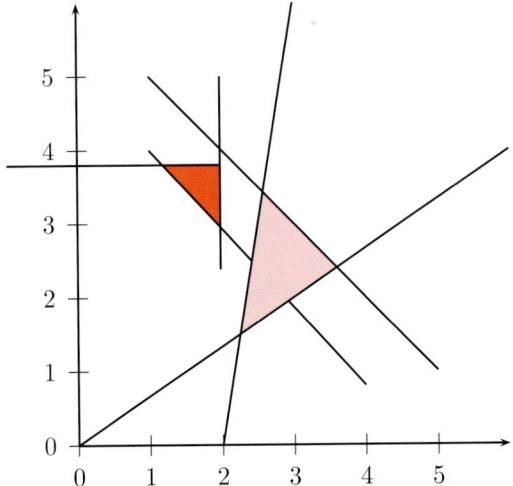

Figure 36.91: Special PSTricks objects

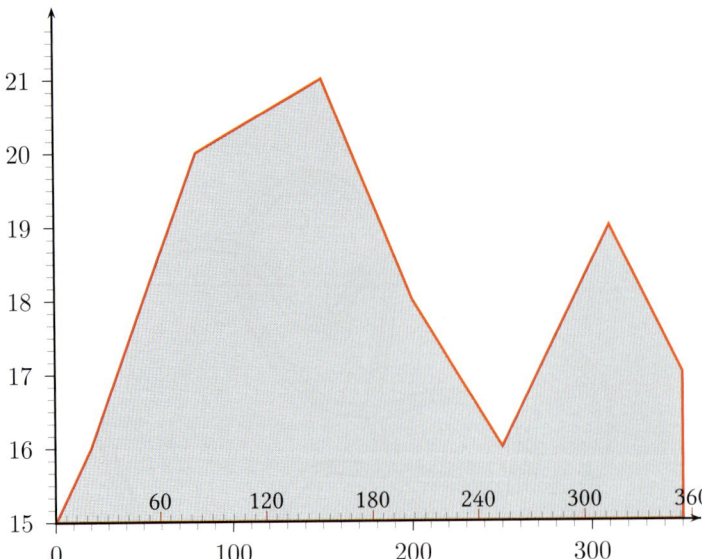

Figure 36.92: Special axes

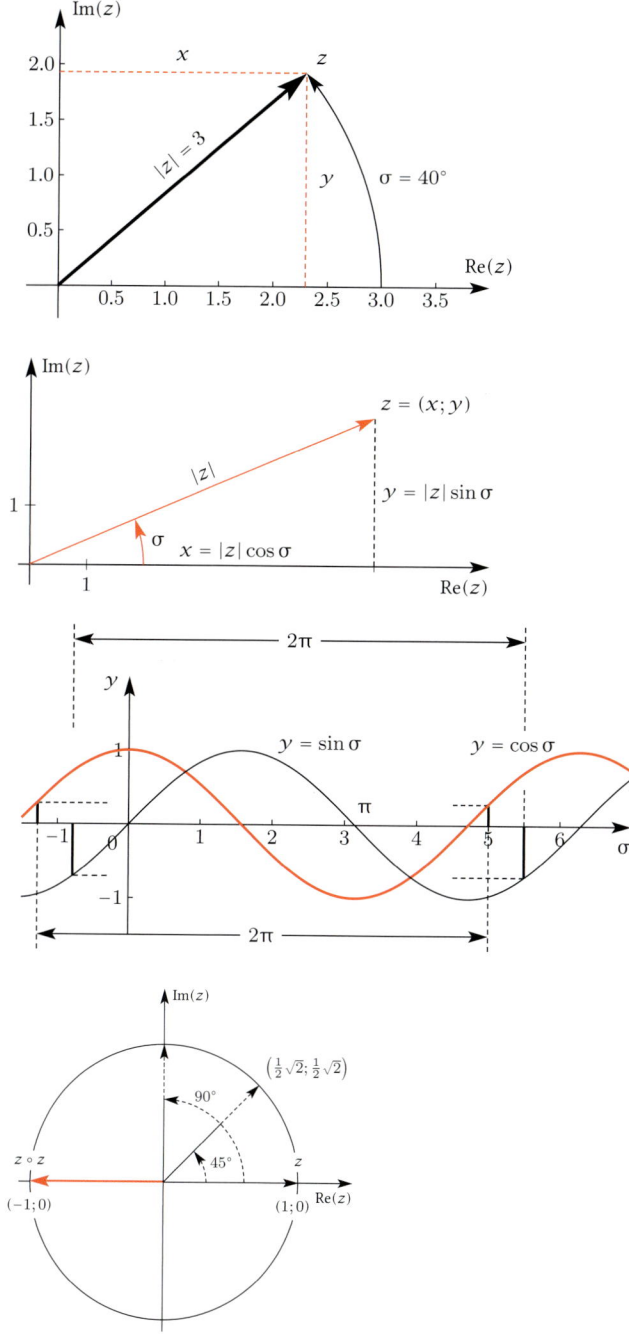

Figure 36.93: Using basic commands (Ulrich Dirr)

36 Examples

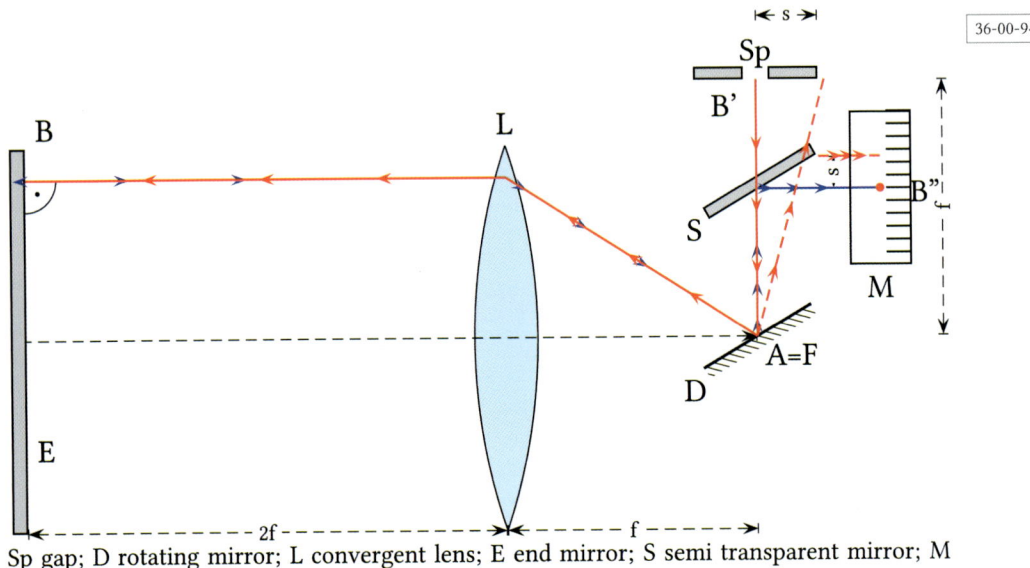

Sp gap; D rotating mirror; L convergent lens; E end mirror; S semi transparent mirror; M unit

Figure 36.94: Using `pst-optic`

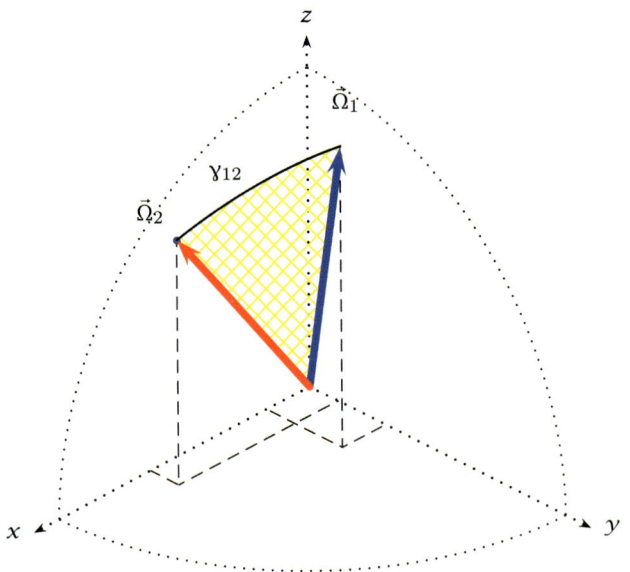

Figure 36.95: Using `pst-3dplot`

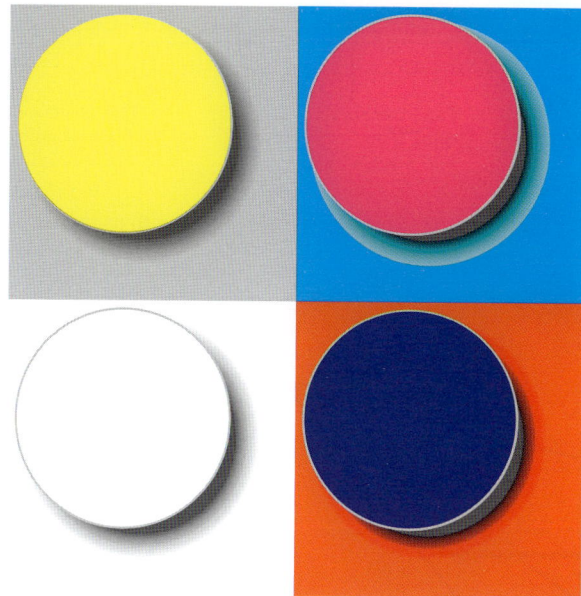

Figure 36.96: Using pst-blur.

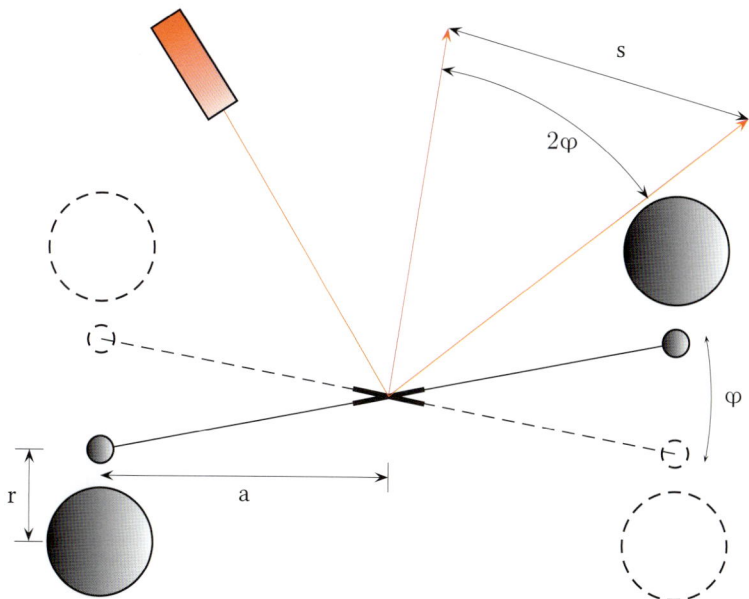

Figure 36.97: Using basic commands

```
if ( Condition ) { Command block 1 } else { Command block 2 }
```

The condition must be true or false

This command is executed if the condition is ≠ 0, which means true.

This command is executed if the condition is = 0, which means false.

Figure 36.98: Commented source code with psmatrix

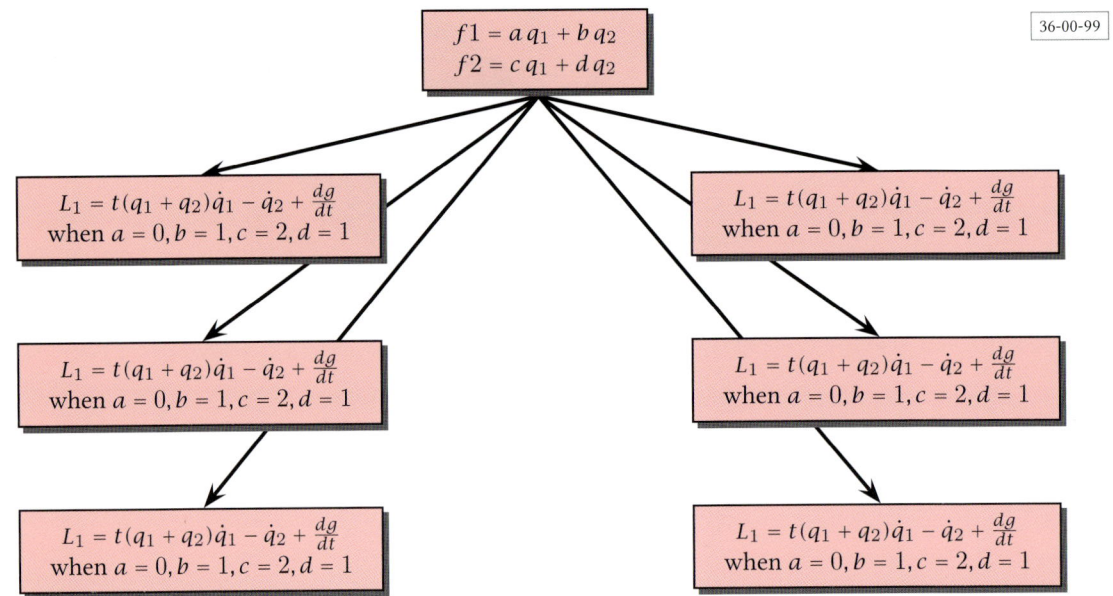

Figure 36.99: Creating hidden lines

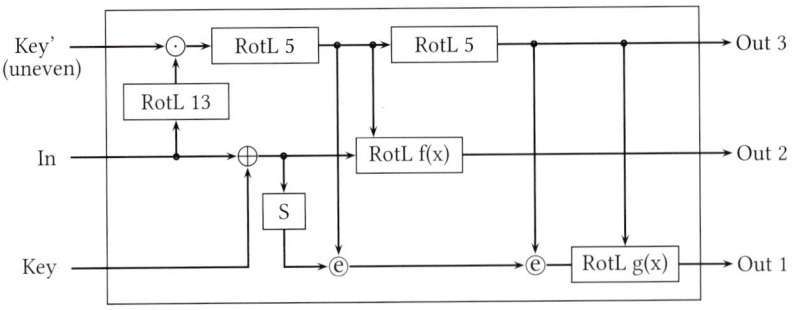

Figure 36.100: Schematic of a Feistel expansion network with the PSTricks standard commands

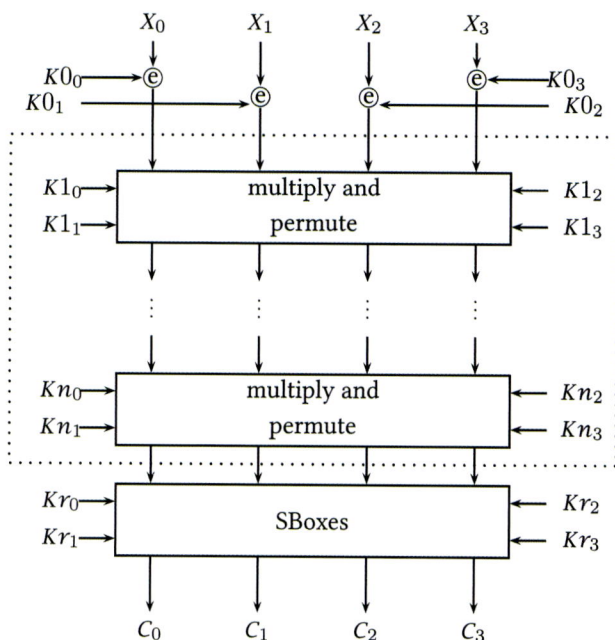

Figure 36.101: The principle of Rijndael, the new AES encryption standard

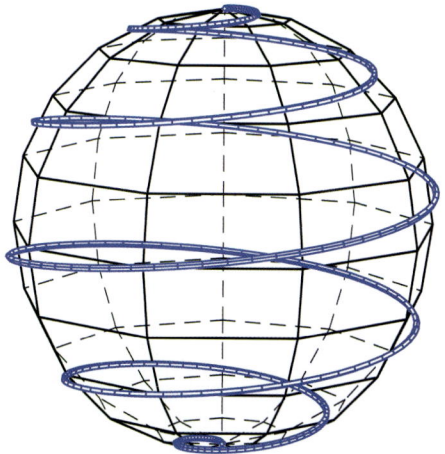

Figure 36.102: A 3D curve on a sphere

36 Examples

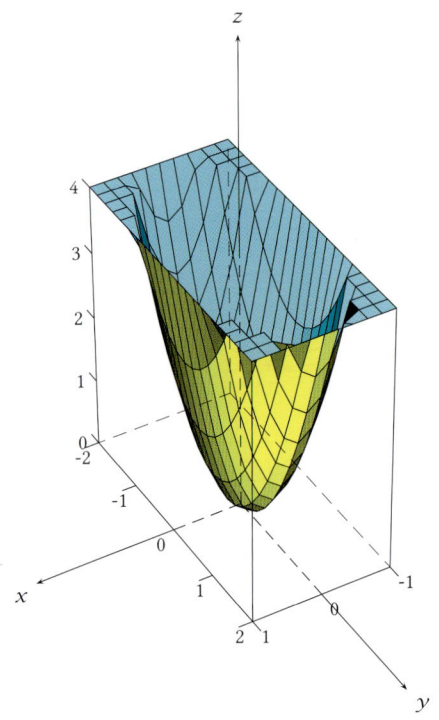

Figure 36.103: 3D function with $z < 4$

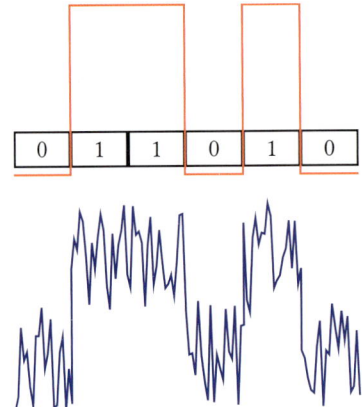

Figure 36.104: A digital signal with random noise

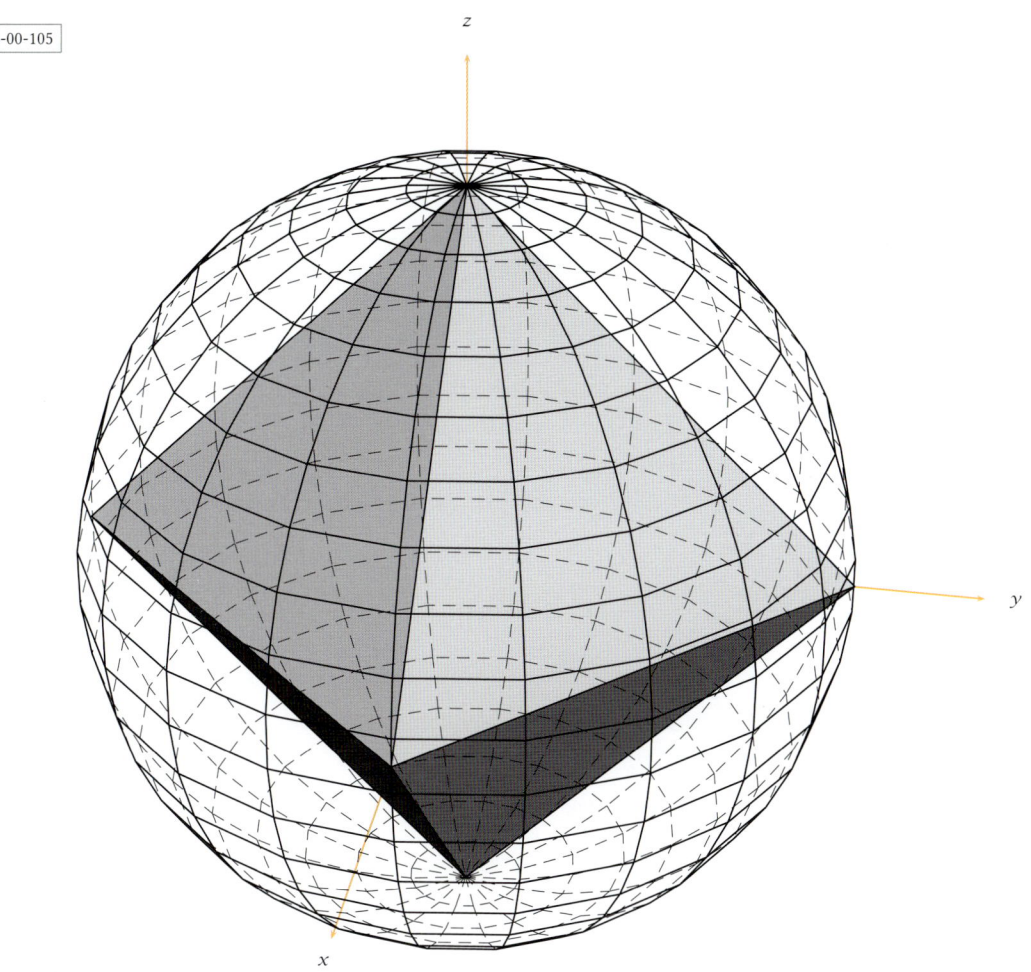

Figure 36.105: A prisma inside a sphere

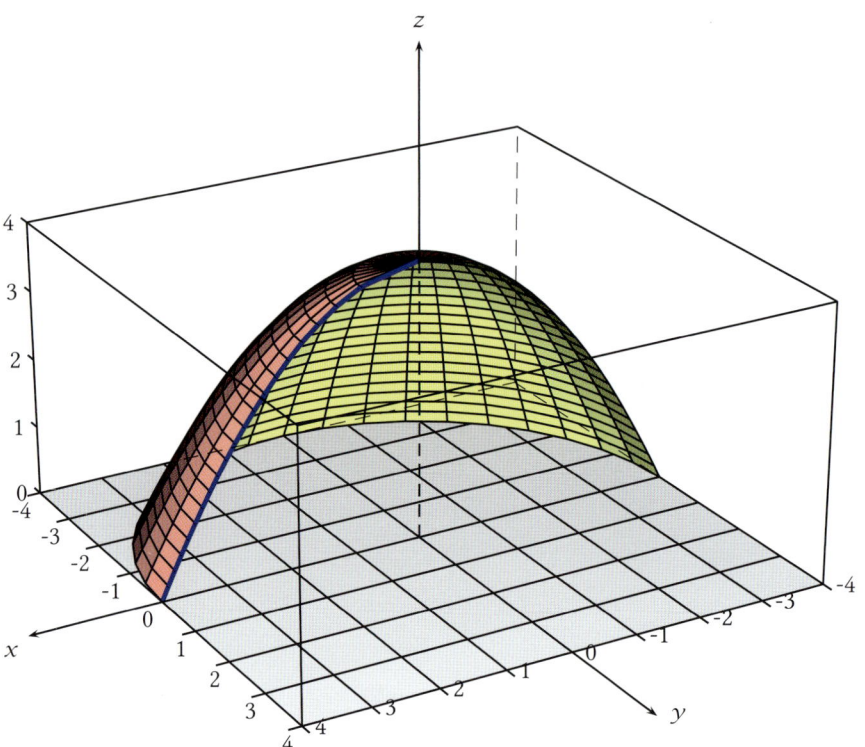

Figure 36.106: An open paraboloid

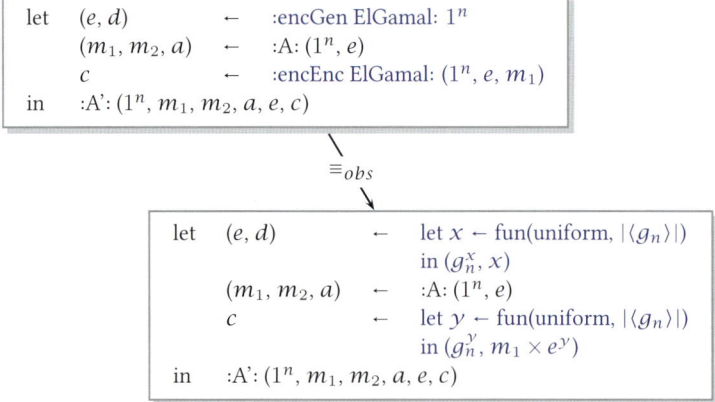

Figure 36.107: Shaded boxes

Examples

36-00-108

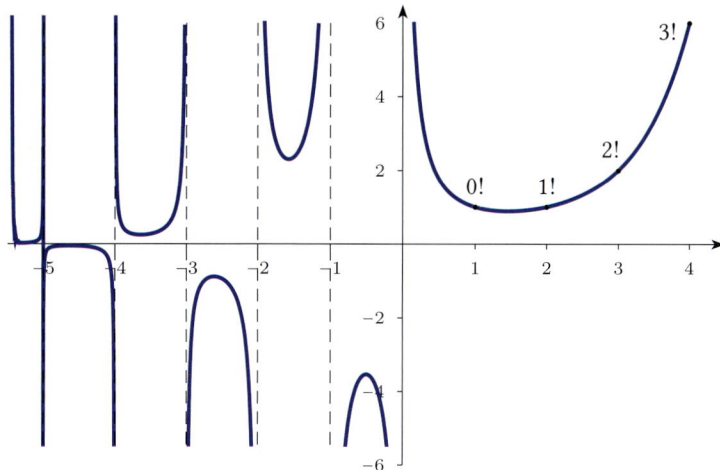

Figure 36.108: The Gamma function

36-00-109

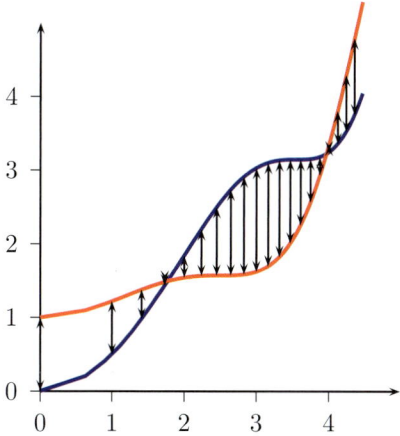

Figure 36.109: A special parametric plot

36 Examples

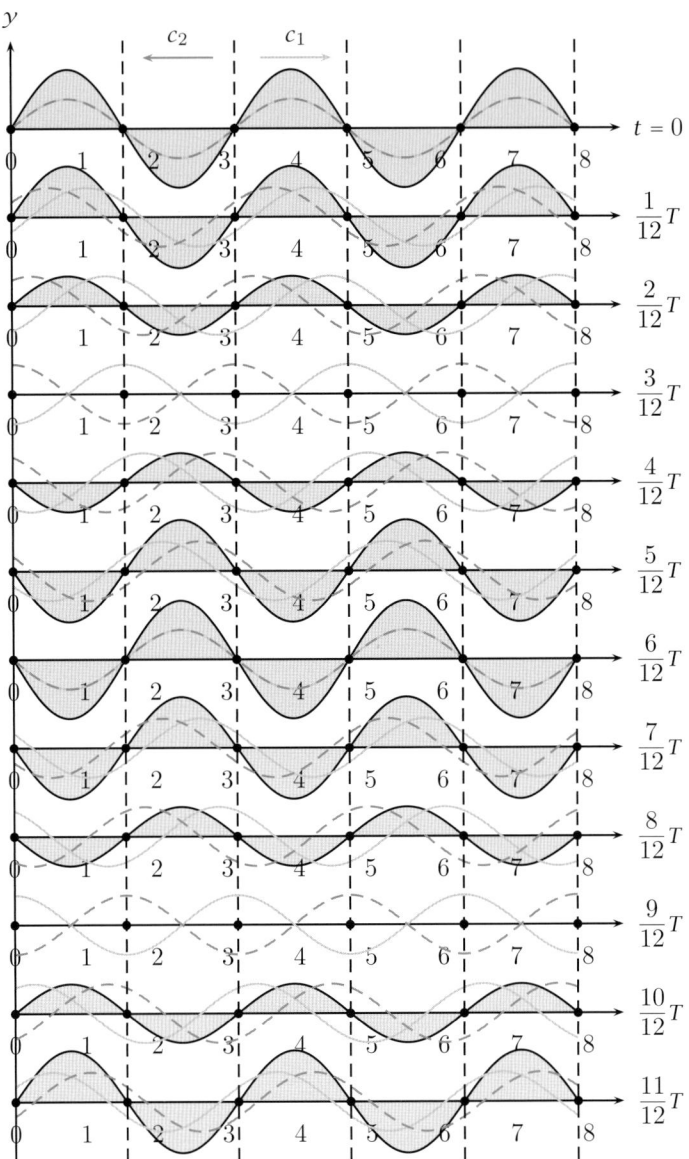

Figure 36.110: Waves (Jürgen Gilg)

Examples

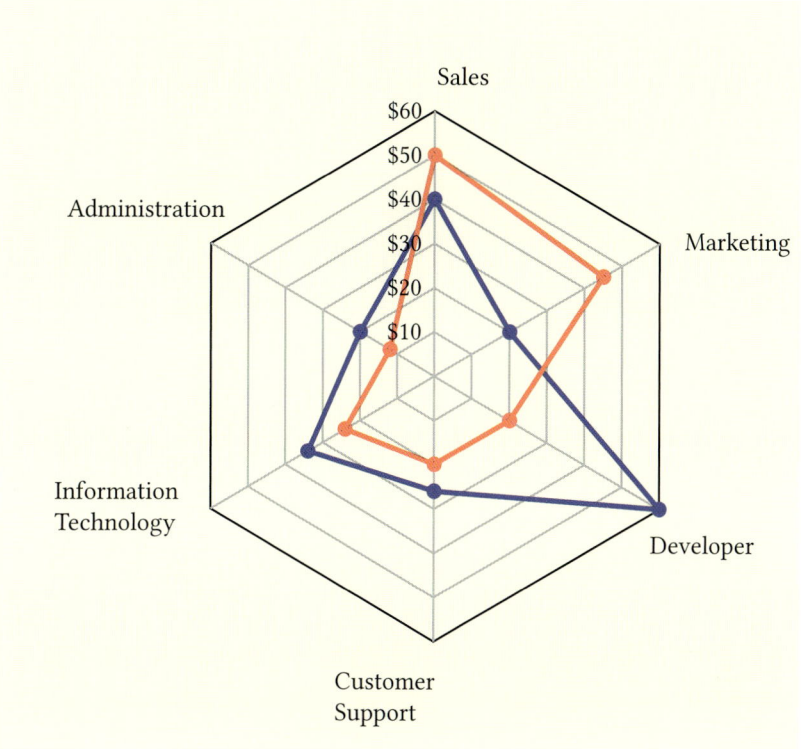

Figure 36.111: A Kiviat diagram

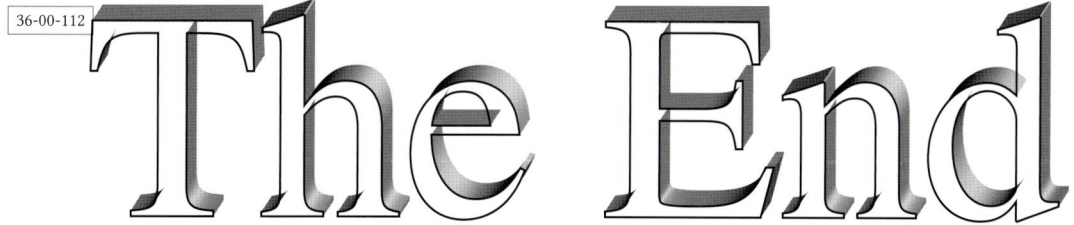

Examples

Anhang A

Tables

A.1 Summary of parameters 819
A.2 Summary of all commands 831

A.1 Summary of parameters

Table A.1: Summary of all parameters

name	type	default	page
Alpha	*angle*	45	361
addfillstyle	none|solid|vlines|vlines*|hlines|hlines*|crosshatch|crosshatch*|boxfill	none	86
angle	*angle*	0	229
angleA	*angle*	0	229
angleB	*angle*	0	229
arcangle	*angle*	8	229
arcangleA	*angle*	8	229
arcangleB	*angle*	8	229
arcsep	*value unit*	0pt	58
arcsepA	*value unit*	0pt	58
arcsepB	*value unit*	0pt	58
arm	*value unit*	10pt	230
armA	*value unit*	10pt	230
armB	*value unit*	10pt	230
ArrowFill	*boolean*	true	100
arrowinset	*value*	0.4	94

continued...

A Tables

... continued

name	type	default	page
ArrowInside	value	{}	100
ArrowInsideNo	value	1	100
ArrowInsideOffset	value	0	100
ArrowInsidePos	value	0.5	100
arrowlength	value	1.4	94
arrows	style	–	92
arrowscale	value1 value2	1	96
arrowsize	value unit value	1.5pt 2	94
AUS	boolean	false	467
axisemph	macro	{}	404
axisnames	{x,y,z}	{x,y,z}	404
axesstyle	axes/frame/none	axes	167
bbd	value unit	{}	276
bbh	value unit	{}	276
bbl	value unit	{}	276
bbllx	value unit	0pt	315
bblly	value unit	0pt	315
bbr	value unit	{}	276
bburx	value unit	0pt	315
bburx	value unit	0pt	315
beginAngle	angle	0	364
Beta	angle	30	361
blur	boolean	false	328
blurbg	colour	white	329
blurradius	value unit	1.5pt	329
blursteps	value	20	330
border	value unit	0pt	51
	value unit	0.4pt	654
borderbottom	value	1	498
bordercolor	colour name	white	51
borderleft	value	10	498
borderLine	line style	solid	654
borderright	value	10	498
borderwidth	value	0.5	498
bordertop	value	1	498
borders	boolean	false	467
boxsize	value unit	0.4cm	231

continued...

A.1 Summary of parameters

... continued

name	type	default	page
bracketlength	value	0.15	95
capitals	boolean	false	467
city	boolean	false	467
coeff	a0 a1 a2...	0 0 1	520
coilarm	value unit	1cm	306
coilarmA	value unit	1cm	306
coilarmB	value unit	1cm	306
coilaspect	angle	45	306
coilheight	value	1	305
coilinc	angle	10	307
coilwidth	value unit	1cm	304
comma	boolean	false	179
Corners	boolean	false	347
CornersColor	colour	black	347
CornersLength	value	0.15	347
cornersize	relative/absolute	relative	51
curvature	value1 value2 value3	1 0.1 0	58
dash	value unit value unit	5pt 3pt	47
Derivation	value	0	521
dimen	outer|inner|middle	outer	49
dipoleconvention	receptor|generator	receptor	446
dipolestyle	normal|zigzag|curved| rectangle|elektor| elektorcurved|triac elektorchemical|GTO chemical|thyristor	normal	446
directconvention	boolean	true	446
dotangle	angle	0	71
dotsize	value unit value	2pt 2	71
dotscale	value1 value2	1	71
dotsep	value unit	3pt	48
dotstyle	style name	*	69
doublecolor	colour name	white	48
doubleline	boolean	false	48
doublesep	value unit	1.25\pslinewidth	48
drawing	boolean	true	361
drawStyle	xLines|yLines| xyLines|yxLines	xLines	366

continued...

A Tables

... continued

name	type	default	page
Dx	value	1	168
			362
dx	value unit	0pt	169
Dy	value	1	168
			362
dy	value unit	0pt	169
Dz	value	1	362
dZero	value	0.1	522
edge	macro	\ncline	274
embedangle	angle	0	344
endAngle	angle	360	364
endfading	1	326	
epsZero	value	0.1	522
fading	boolean	false	326
fansize	value unit	1cm	267
fill	boolean	true	467
fillangle	angle	0	297
fillcolor	colour name	white	80
fillcycle	value	0	297
fillcyclex	value	0	297
fillcycley	value	0	297
fillloopadd	value	0	299
fillloopaddx	value	0	299
fillloopaddy	value	0	299
fillmove	value unit	0pt/2pt	298
fillmovex	value unit	0pt/2pt	298
fillmovey	value unit	0pt/2pt	298
fillsep	value unit	0pt/2pt	297
fillsepx	value unit	0pt	297
fillsepy	value unit	0pt	297
fillsize	auto|{(x0,y0)(x1,y1)}	auto	298
fillstyle	none|solid| vlines|vlines*|hlines|hlines*| crosshatch|crosshatch*|boxfill	none	80
framearc	value	0	50
FrameBoxThreeDBrightnessDistance	0...1	0.15	356
FrameBoxThreeDColorHSB	value value value	0 0 0.5	356
FrameBoxThreeDOn	boolean	true	355
FrameBoxThreeDOpposite	boolean	false	355

continued...

A.1 Summary of parameters

... continued

name	type	default	page
framesep	value unit	3pt	110
framesize	value unit		228
	[value unit]	10pt	
gangle	angle	0	55
gradangle	angle	0	319
gradbegin	colour	gradbegin	318
gradend	colour	gradend	318
GradientCircle	boolean	false	320
GradientPos	(x,y)	(0,0)	320
GradientScale	value	1	320
gradientHSB	boolean	false	320
gradlines	value	500	319
gradmidpoint	value	0.9	319
GraphicsRef	x,y	{}	315
grayness	value	1	654
gridcolor	colour	black	34
griddots	value	0	34
gridlabelcolor	colour	black	35
gridlabels	value unit	10pt	34
GridThreeDNodes	boolean	false	351
GridThreeDXPos	value	0	350
GridThreeDYPos	value	0	350
GridThreeDZPos	value	0	350
GridThreeDXUnit	value	1	350
GridThreeDYUnit	value	1	350
GridThreeDZUnit	value	1	350
gridwith	value unit	0.8pt	33
hatchangle	angle	45	86
hatchcolor	colour name	black	86
hatchsep	value unit	4pt	84
hatchsepinc	value unit	0pt	85
hatchwidth	value unit	0.8pt	85
hatchwidthinc	value unit	0pt	85
headerfile	filename	{}	315
headers	none|all|user	none	315
href	value	0	227
hiddenLine	boolean	false	366
IIIDticks	boolean	false	362
IIIDxticksep	value	−0.4	362

continued...

A Tables

... continued

name	type	default	page
IIIDyticksep	value	-0.2	362
IIIDzticksep	value	0.2	362
IIIDxTicksPlane	xy|xz|yz	xy	362
IIIDyTicksPlane	xy|xz|yz	yz	362
IIIDzTicksPlane	xy|xz|yz	yz	362
increment	angle	10	467
inkspread	value	0.15	498
innerBorder	value unit	0pt	654
intensity	boolean	false	446
intensitycolor	colour	black	446
intensitylabel	text	\empty	446
intensitylabelcolor	colour	black	446
intensitylabeloffset	value	0.5	446
intensitywidth	value	\pslinewidth	446
intersect	boolean	false	446
invisibleLineStyle	line style	dashed	369
labelangle	angle	0	446
labelFontSize	\tiny|\scriptsize|... \scriptscriptstyle| \scriptstyle|...	{}	178
labeloffset	value	0	446
labels	all|x|y|none	all	170
labelsep	value unit	5pt	104
latitude0	angle	45	467
level	value	1	467
levelsep	*value unit	2cm	272
limiteL	value	180	467
liftpen	0|1|2	0	125
linearc	value unit	0pt	50
linecap	0|1|2	0	46
linecolor	colour name	black	45
linejoin	0|1|2	0	45, 364
linestyle	none|solid| dotted|dashed	solid	45
linetype	value	0	52
liftpen	0|1|2	0	52
linewidth	value unit	0.8pt	44
logLines	all|x|y|none	none	190
longitude0	angle	0	467

continued...

A.1 Summary of parameters

... continued

name	type	default	page
loopsize	*value unit*	1cm	230
maillgae	*boolean*	true	467
makeeps	none|new|all|all*	new	315
mapCountry	all|country name	all	467
MapFillColor	*r g b*	0.99 0.95 0.7	467
markZeros	*boolean*	false	522
mathLabel	*boolean*	true	177
MEX	*boolean*	false	467
n	*value*	1.77245	467
nameX	*label*	x	365
nameY	*label*	y	365
nameZ	*label*	z	365
ncurv	*value*	0.67	231
ncurvA	*value*	0.67	231
ncurvB	*value*	0.67	231
nodesep	*value unit*	0pt	229
nodesepA	*value unit*	0pt	229
nodesepB	*value unit*	0pt	229
nodeWidth	*value unit*	1mm	467
normal	*valuex valuey valuez*	0 0 1	343
npos	*value*	{}	234
nrot	*rotation*	0	233
OAinvert	*boolean*	true	446
OAiminus	*boolean*	false	446
OAiminuslabel	*text*	\empty	446
OAiout	*boolean*	false	446
OAioutlabel	*text*	\empty	446
OAperfect	*boolean*	true	446
OAiplus	*boolean*	false	446
OAipluslabel	*text*	\empty	446
offset	*value unit*	0pt	232
offsetA	*value unit*	0pt	232
offsetB	*value unit*	0pt	232
OnlyVisibleFaces	*boolean*	false	346
opacity	*value*	1	88
origin	*xvalue unit ,yvalue unit*	(0pt,0pt)	31
Ox	*value*	0	168
Oy	*value*	0	168
parallel	*boolean*	false	446

continued...

A Tables

... continued

name	type	default	page
parallelarm	value unit	1.5	446
parallelnode	boolean	false	446
parallelsep	value unit	0	446
path	path specification	data	467
plane	xy|xz|yz	xy	365
planecorr	none|normal|xyrot	none	362
plotpoints	value	50	198
plotstyle	dots|line|polygon|curve|ecurve|ccurve	line	198
PolyCurves	boolean	false	674
PolyEpicycloid	boolean	false	674
PolyIntermediatePoint	value	{}	674
PolyName	string	{}	674
PolyNbSides	integer	5	674
PolyOffset	integer	1	674
PolyRotation	angle	0	674
pOrigin	reference point	c	366
pos	(x,y)	(0,0)	654
posX	value 0	654	
posY	value	654	
posDelta	(x,y)	(0,0)	654
posDeltaX	value	0	654
posDeltaY	value	0 654	
PstDebug	0|1	0	299 349
PstPicture	boolean	true	349 674
radius	value unit	0.25cm	228
RandomFaces	boolean	false	346
rbracketlength	value	0.15	95
ref	reference	c	232
refpoint	l|r|t|b|B	l	654
rot	rotation	0	232
rivers	boolean	false	467
Rotation	value	{}	315
RotSequence	xyz|xzy|zxy|zyx|yxz|yzx	xyz	371
rotX	value	0	370
rotY	value	0	370
rotZ	value	0	370
Scale	value1 value2	{}	315

continued...

A.1 Summary of parameters

... continued

name	type	default	page
shadow	boolean	false	51
shadowangle	angle	-45	51
shadowcolor	colour name	darkgray	51
shadowsize	value unit	3pt	51
shapealpha	0|1|2|3	0	83
shift	value unit	0pt	27
shortput	none|nab|tablr|tab	none	234
showborder	-	-	498
showbbox	boolean	false	275
showgrid	boolean	false	29
showpoints	boolean	false	50
showorigin	boolean	true	171
showOrigin	boolean	true	404
sizeX	value		654
sizeY	value		654
slopeangle	angle	0	324
slopebegin	colour	slopebegin	322
slopecenter	x y	0.5 0.5	324
slopecolors	list of colours	0.0 1 0 0	323
		0.4 0 1 0	
		0.8 0 0 1	
		1.0 0 1 0	
slopeend	colour	slopeend	322
sloperadius	value unit	0	325
slopesteps	value	100	324
startfading	0	326	
strokeopacity	value	1	87
subgridcolor	colour	gray	36
subgriddiv	value	5	35
subgriddots	value	0	37
subgridwith	value unit	0.4pt	36
subtickcolor	colour	gray	184
subticks	value	0	182
subticksize	value	0.75	183
StepType	lower|upper	below	605
swapaxes	boolean	false	31
tbarsize	value unit value	2pt 5	95
tension	boolean	false	446
tensioncolor	colour	black	446
tensionlabel	text	\empty	446

continued...

A Tables

... continued

name	type	default	page
tensionlabelcolor	colour	black	446
tensionlabeloffset	value	1.2	446
tensionoffset	value	1	446
tensionwidth	value unit	\pslinewidth	446
thistreefit	value unit	{}	269
thislevelsep	*value unit	{}	272
thistreenodesize	value unit	{}	271
thistreesep	value unit	{}	269
tickcolor	colour	black	184
ticks	all|x|y|none	all	171
ticksize	value unit	3pt	174
	length [length]	-4pt 4pt	181
tickstyle	full|top|bottom	full	172
tndepth	value unit	\dp\strutbox	282
tnheight	value unit	\ht\strutbox	282
tnpos	value unit	{}	281
tnsep	value unit	{}	282
tnyref	number	{}	283
tpos	value	0.5	233
transalpha	value	0.5	739
transistorcircle	boolean	true	446
transistorinvert	boolean	false	446
transistoribase	boolean	false	446
transistoribaselabel	text	\empty	446
transistoricollector	boolean	false	446
transistoricollectorlabel	text	\empty	446
transistoriemitter	boolean	false	446
transistoriemitterlabel	text	\empty	446
transistortype	PNP|NPN	PNP	446
Translation	x, y	{}	315
treeflip	boolean	false	268
treefit	loose|tight	tight	269
treemode	D|U|R|L	D	268
treenodesize	value unit	-1pt	271
treesep	value unit	0.75cm	269
trigLabels	boolean	false	193
trimode	*U|D|R|L	U	111
Tshadowangle	angle	60	334

continued...

A.1 Summary of parameters

... continued

name	type	default	page
Tshadowcolor	colour	lightgray	335
Tshadowsize	value	1	335
type	value	1	467
umlStackSep	value unit	0	645
umlStackWidth	value unit	0	645
umlAlign	lcr	c	645
umlPos	tcb	c	645
umlStackLinesStretch	value	0.85	645
USA	boolean	false	467
viewpoint	valuex valuey valuez	1 -1 1	341
viewangle	angle	0	342
visibleLineStyle	line style	solid	369
vref	value unit	0.7ex	227
xAxis	boolean	true	179
xAxisLabel	anything	{}	601
xAxisLabelPos	$(x,y),(c,y)$ or {}	{}	601
xbbd	value unit	{}	276
xbbh	value unit	{}	276
xbbl	value unit	0	276
xbbr	value unit	0	276
xDecimals	value or {}	{}	180
xlogBase	value or {}	{}	190
xMin	value	-1	361
xMax	value	4	361
Xnodesep	value unit	0pt	229
XnodesepA	value unit	0pt	229
XnodesepB	value unit	0pt	229
xPlotpoints	value	25	363
xsubtickcolor	colour	gray	184
xsubticks	value	0	182
xsubticksize	value	0.75	183
xtickcolor	color	black	184
xticksize	length [length]	-4pt 4pt	181
xyAxes	boolean	true	179
xyDecimals	value or {}	{}	180
xylogBase	value or {}	{}	190
yAxis	boolean	true	179
yAxisLabel	text	{}	601
yAxisLabelPos	$(x,y),(x,c)$ or {}	{}	601

continued...

A Tables

... continued

name	type	default	page
yDecimals	*value* or {}	{}	180
ylogBase	*value* or {}	{}	190
yMin	*value*	-1	361
yMax	*value*	4	361
Ynodesep	*value unit*	0pt	229
YnodesepA	*value unit*	0pt	229
YnodesepB	*value unit*	0pt	229
yPlotpoints	*value*	25	363
ysubtickcolor	*colour*	gray	184
ysubticks	*value*	0	182
ysubticksize	*value*	0.75	183
ytickcolor	*colour*	black	184
yticksize	*value unit [value unit]*	-4pt 4pt	181
zeroLineTo	*value*	false	522
zeroLineStyle	*line style*	dashed	522
zeroLineColor	*colour*	black	522
zeroLineWidth	*value unit*	0.5\pslinewidth	522
zMin	*value*	-1	361
zMax	*value*	4	361

A.2 Content-specific summary of all relevant commands[1]

Basic settings

Picture environment

> \begin{pspicture}(x1,y1)(x2,y2)
> \end{pspicture}

The optional parameter [shift=*dim*] moves the base line up or down.

Unit lengths

> xunit = *dim*   runit = *dim*
> yunit = *dim*   unit = *dim*

unit can be used to set all the values at once.

Colour definitions

> \definecolor[*class*]{*name*}{*model*}{*spec*}
> \colorlet[*name*]{*model*}{*expr*}

Here *spec* is a comma-separated list of values and *expr* is a colour expression. The [dvipsnames], [svgnames], and [x11names] options select predefined colour palettes. More information can be found in the documentation of the xcolor package.

Setting global parameters

> \psset{*key1=value1, key2=value2, ...*}
> \newpsstyle{*name*}{*key1=value1, ...*}

Global parameters can be overridden locally through [*par*] or [style = *name*].

Angle units

> \degrees[*div*]
> \degrees
> \radians

Coordinate representations

> \NormalCoor   \SpecialCoor

Possible coordinate representations (\SpecialCoor)

> (x,y)   (!*code*)   ([*par*]*node*)
> (r;a)   (*node*)   (*coor1*|*coor2*)

Basic graphical elements

Lines, polygons, frames

> \psline[*par*]{*ends*}(x0,y0)(x1,y1)...
> \pspolygon[*par*](x0,y0)(x1,y1)...
> \psframe[*par*](x0,y0)(x1,y1)
> \psdiamond[*par*](x0,y0)(x1,y1)
> \pstriangle[*par*](x0,y0)(x1,y1)

For \psdiamond and \pstriangle, (x0,y0) specifies the centre and (x1,y1) the width and height. The gangle parameter specifies a rotation around the centre. The pst-poly package provides additional polygon commands.

Circles, ellipses, arcs

> \psarc[*par*]{*ends*}(x,y){*rad*}{*ang*}{*ang*}
> \psarcn[*par*]{*ends*}(x,y){*rad*}{*ang*}{*ang*}
> \psellipticarc[*par*]{*ends*}(x,y)(a,b){*ang*}{*ang*}

---
[1] Thanks to Uwe Siart

A Tables

```
\pselliptiarcn[par]{ends}(x,y)(a,b){ang}{ang}
  \pscircle[par](x,y){rad}
  \pswedge[par](x,y){rad}{ang}{ang}
  \psellipse[par](x,y)(a,b)
```

Parameters for lines

```
linewidth   = dim
linecolor   = color
linestyle   = style
linearc     = dim
linecap     = 0/1/2
dash        = dim1 dim2
dotsep      = dim
border      = dim
bordercolor = color
doubleline  = true/false
doublesep   = dim
doublecolor = color
arrows      = ends
```

Possible values for linestyle

| none | solid | dashed | dotted |

Possible values for arrows

-	<<->>	<->	*-*	(-)	[-]
|*-|*	>>-<<	>-<	o-o	)-(	]-[
oo-oo	cc-cc	c-c	C-C	|-|	-

Line endings can also be specified with the optional {ends} parameter in the corresponding commands.
Parameter for line endings

```
arrowsize     = dim num
arrowlength   = num
arrowinset    = num
tbarsize      = dim num
bracketlength = num
```

Dot at every coordinate

```
\psdot*[par](x0,y0)
\psdots*[par](x0,y0)(x1,y1)...
```

Parameters for dots

```
dotstyle = style
dotsize  = dim 'num'
dotscale = num1 'num2'
dotangle = ang
```

Possible values for dotstyle (selection)

*	o	+	x
asterisk	oplus	otimes	|
square	diamond	triangle	pentagon
square*	diamond*	triangle*	pentagon*

For further dotstyles, see pstnews1-15.pdf.
Curves

```
\psbezier[par](x0,y0)...(x3,y3)
\pscurve[par](x0,y0)(x1,y1)...
\psecurve[par](x0,y0)(x1,y1)...
\psccurve[par](x0,y0)(x1,y1)...
```

Text boxes

Framed boxes

A.2 Summary of all commands

\psframebox[*par*]{*stuff*}
\psdblframebox[*par*]{*stuff*}
\psshadowbox[*par*]{*stuff*}
\pscirclebox[*par*]{*stuff*}
\psovalbox[*par*]{*stuff*}
\psdiabox[*par*]{*stuff*}
\pstribox[*par*]{*stuff*}

Parameters for frames and closed paths

```
fillstyle  = style
fillcolor  = color
framearc   = num
framesep   = dim
hatchwidth = dim
hatchcolor = color
hatchangle = ang
hatchsep   = dim
cornersize = relative/absolute
dimen      = inner/middle/outer
```

Possible values for fillstyle

```
none     solid      eofill
hlines   vlines     crosshatch
hlines*  vlines*    crosshatch*
```

The * versions of frames and curves are equivalent to fillstyle = solid. In this case the frames and curves are filled with the colour linecolor.

Placement of objects

Scaling

\psscalebox{*num1 num2*}{*stuff*}
\psscaleboxto(x,y){*stuff*}

Translation and rotation

\rput[*ref*]{*rot*}(x,y){*stuff*}
\multirput[*ref*]{*rot*}(x,y)(a,b){*rep*}{*stuff*}
\psrotateright{*stuff*}
\psrotateleft{*stuff*}
\psrotatedown{*stuff*}

Origin of the coordinate system

origin = {*coor*}

Possible values for *ref*

```
horizontal   vertical
l            t
r            b
             B
```

Labels

\uput{*sep*}[*ang*]{*rot*}(x,y){*stuff*}

Parameters for labels

labelsep = *dim*

Grids

Grid command

\psgrid(x0,y0)(x1,y1)(x2,y2)

Grid parameters

833

A Tables

```
gridwidth      = dim
gridcolor      = color
griddots       = num
gridlabels     = dim
gridlabelcolor = color
subgriddiv     = int
subgridwidth   = dim
subgridcolor   = color
subgriddots    = num
```

Miscellaneous

Connected and closed paths

\pscustom[*par*]{*paths*}

Parameters for connected paths

```
linetype = int
liftpen  = 0/1/2
```

Some commands that can be used inside \pscustom

\closepath	\newpath
\rlineto(x,y)	\curveto(x1,y1)...(x3,y3)
\fill	\rotate={*ang*}
\gsave	\scale={*num1* '*num2*'}
\grestore	\stroke
\lineto(x,y)	\swapaxes
\moveto(x,y)	\translate(x,y)

Clipping objects

\psclip{*clipobjects*}
...
\endpsclip

Shadows

```
shadow      = true/false
shadowsize  = dim
shadowangle = ang
shadowcolor = color
```

Some PostScript operators

add	sub	mul	div
abs	neg	mod	dup
sin	cos	atan	sqrt
exp	ln	log	exch
ceiling	floor	round	truncate

Important numerical values (rounded)

$180°/\pi = 57{,}2958°$ $\pi/180° = 0{,}01745^{\text{rad}/\text{degrees}}$

$\pi = 3{,}14159$ $e = 2{,}71828$

All trigonometric functions expect their arguments to be in degrees. Additional operators and constants are provided by the pst-math package.

multido

Loops

\multido{*variables*}{*rep*}{*stuff*}

Possible variable types are *Integer* (\i), *Dimension* (\d), *Number* (\n), and *Real* (\r). A negative step can be specified like this: \nx=5.30+-1.25.

Fixed point arithmetics

A.2 Summary of all commands

\FPadd{num1}{num2}{command}
\FPsub{num1}{num2}{command}

These commands define *command* and save the result in this command.

pst-text

Typeset text along curves

\pstextpath[justify](x,y){path}{text}

Possible values for *justify*

| l | c | r |

Outline letters

\pscharpath[par]{text}
\pscharclip[par]{text}...\endpscharclip

pst-node

Specifying nodes

\rnode[ref]{name}{stuff}
\Rnode(x,y){name}{stuff}
\pnode(x,y){name}
\cnode[par](x,y){rad}{name}
\Cnode[par](x,y){name}
\circlenode[par]{name}{stuff}
\cnodeput[par]{ang}(x,y){name}{stuff}
\ovalnode[par]{name}{stuff}
\dotnode[par](x,y){name}

Node connections (the number of segments for each connection is shown in parentheses)

\nccurve[par]{arrows}{nodeA}{nodeB}   (0)
\ncline[par]{arrows}{nodeA}{nodeB}   (1)
\ncarc[par]{arrows}{nodeA}{nodeB}   (1)
\nccircle[par]{arrows}{nodeA}{nodeB} (1)
\ncdiagg[par]{arrows}{nodeA}{nodeB}   (2)
\ncdiag[par]{arrows}{nodeA}{nodeB}   (3)
\ncbar[par]{arrows}{nodeA}{nodeB}   (3)
\ncangle[par]{arrows}{nodeA}{nodeB}   (3)
\ncangles[par]{arrows}{nodeA}{nodeB} (4)
\ncloop[par]{arrows}{nodeA}{nodeB}   (5)

Connections between points (number of segments in parentheses)

\pccurve[par]{arrows}(x1,y1)(x2,y2)   (0)
\pcline[par]{arrows}(x1,y1)(x2,y2)   (1)
\pcarc[par]{arrows}(x1,y1)(x2,y2)   (1)
\pcdiagg[par]{arrows}(x1,y1)(x2,y2)   (2)
\pcdiag[par]{arrows}(x1,y1)(x2,y2)   (3)
\pcbar[par]{arrows}(x1,y1)(x2,y2)   (3)
\pcangle[par]{arrows}(x1,y1)(x2,y2)   (3)
\pcangles[par]{arrows}(x1,y1)(x2,y2) (4)
\pcloop[par]{arrows}(x1,y1)(x2,y2)   (5)

Parameters for nodes and connections

```
ncurv  = num    arcangle    = ang
offset = dim    loopsize    = dim
arm    = dim    [XY]nodesep = dim
angle  = ang    radius      = dim
```

The [XY]nodesep, offset, arm, and angle parameters can also be set for each node individually using the *parA* and *parB* versions.

A Tables

Furthermore all line settings apply. The offset is measured from the left side of the path. The radius is the global parameter for \Cnode.

Node labels

\nput[*par*]{*ang*}{*node*}{*stuff*}

Labels for node and point connections

\ncput[*par*]{*stuff*}
\naput[*par*]{*stuff*}
\nbput[*par*]{*stuff*}

The \lput, \aput, \bput, \Aput, \Bput, \Lput, \Mputm and \Rput commands are obsolete, but still supported.

Parameters for labels

nrot = *rot*
npos = *num*

If nrot=:*ang* is specified, the rotation is relative to the direction of the connection (often nrot=:U).

Frames around nodes

\ncbox[*par*]{*nodeA*}{*nodeB*}
\ncarcbox[*par*]{*nodeA*}{*nodeB*}

pst-plot

Axes

\psaxes(x0,y0)(x1,y1)(x2,y2)

Axes parameters

```
ticks     = x/y/all/none
labels    = x/y/all/none
tickstyle = full/top/bottom
ticksize  = dim
showorigin = false/true
axesstyle = axes/frame/none
labelsep  = dim

Ox = num    Dx = num    dx = num
Oy = num    Dy = num    dy = num
```

Ox and Oy are the values of the labels at the origin. Dx and Dy are the increments of the labels. dx and dy are the spacings between the ticks.

Style of axes labels

\renewcommand{\pshlabel}[1]{*commands*#1}
\renewcommand{\psvlabel}[1]{*commands*#1}

Reading data

\readdata{*object*}{*filename*}
\savedata{*object*}{*filename*}

Plotting data

\fileplot[*par*]{*filename*}
\dataplot[*par*]{*object*}
\listplot[*par*]{*object*}

Plotting functions

\psplot{*x1*}{*x2*}{*y(x)*}
\parametricplot{*t1*}{*t2*}{*x(t) y(t)*}

Plot parameters

A.2 Summary of all commands

```
plotstyle  = style
plotpoints = int
```

Possible values for plotstyle

```
dots    line    polygon
curve   ecurve  ccurve
```

pst-grad

Parameters for gradients

```
fillstyle      = gradient
gradbegin      = color
gradend        = color
gradlines      = int
gradmidpoint   = num
gradangle      = ang
gradientHSB    = true/false
GradientCircle = true/false
GradientScale  = num
GradientPos    = coor
```

pst-coil

Coils and zigzag lines

\psCoil[*par*]{*ang1*}{*ang2*}
\pscoil[*par*]{*arrows*}(x1,y1)(x2,y2)
\pszigzag[*par*]{*arrows*}(x1,y1)(x2,y2)

Node connections

\nccoil[*par*]{*arrows*}{*nodeA*}{*nodeB*}
\nczigzag[*par*]{*arrows*}{*nodeA*}{*nodeB*}

Connections between points

\pccoil[*par*]{*arrows*}{*nodeA*}{*nodeB*}
\pczigzag[*par*]{*arrows*}{*nodeA*}{*nodeB*}

Parameters for coils and zigzags

```
coilwidth  = dim
coilheight = num
coilarm    = dim
coilaspect = ang
coilinc    = ang
```

The coilarm parameter can also be set for each end individually as coilarmA or coilarmB.

Default values

```
angle=0                      hatchsep=4pt
arcangle=8                   hatchwidth=0.8pt
arm=10pt                     labelsep=5pt
arrowinset=0.4               linearc=0pt
arrowlength=1.4              linecap=0
arrows=-                     linecolor=black
arrowsize=2pt 3              linestyle=solid
border=0pt                   linewidth=0.8pt
bordercolor=white            loopsize=1cm
cornersize=relative          ncurv=0.67
dash=5pt 3pt                 nodesep=0pt
dimen=outer                  nrot=0
dotangle=0                   offset=0pt
dotscale=1                   plotpoints=50
dotsep=3pt                   plotstyle=line
dotsize=2pt 2                radius=2pt
dotstyle=*                   runit=1cm
```

A Tables

```
doublecolor=white      shadow=false              griddots=0                  subgridwidth=0.4pt
doubleline=false       shadowangle=-45           gridlabelcolor=black        tbarsize=2pt 5
fillcolor=white        shadowcolor=darkgray      gridlabels=10pt             unit=1cm
fillstyle=none         shadowsize=3pt            gridwidth=0.8pt             xunit=1cm
framearc=0             subgridcolor=gray         hatchangle=45               yunit=1cm
framesep=3pt           subgriddiv=5              hatchcolor=black
gridcolor=black        subgriddots=0
```

Anhang B

PostScript

B.1 The mathematical PostScript functions. 839
B.2 The non-mathematical PostScript functions 840
B.3 The PostScript definitions of `pstricks.pro` 844
B.4 The names of the PSTricks dictionaries. 845

B.1 The mathematical PostScript functions

The summary in the table contains all mathematical functions and their properties except for the matrix commands. Here int and real are integers and reals as usual, any may be any type, and num is *real* or *integer*. Additional mathematical functions are provided by the `pst-math` package (cf. Section 28.1 on page 517). The maximal and minimal values for numbers in PostScript are given below; the limits for *real* numbers refer to absolute values.

name	description	use	example
abs	absolute value	*num* abs	−3 abs → 3
add	addition[0]	*num1 num2* add	5 7 add → 12
atan	arc tangent[1]	*real1 real2* atan	2 45 atan→ 2.54
ceiling	round up	*num* ceiling	6.33 ceiling→ 7
cos	cosine[2]	*real* cos	60 cos→ 0.5
cvi	real→integer	*real* cvi	14.13 cvi→ 14
cvr	integer→real	*int* cvr	14 cvr→ 14.00
div	division[3]	*real1 real2* div	100 8 div→ 12.5
dup	duplicate top element	*any* dup	12 dup→ 12 12
exch	exchange[4]	*any1 any2* exch	12 13 exch→ 13 12
exp	exponent	*real1 real2* exp	3 4 exp→ 81.0
floor	round down	*num* floor	6.66 floor→ 6
idiv	integer division	*int1 int2* idiv	100 8 idiv→ 12
ln	natural logarithm	*real* ln	12 ln→ 2.48491

continued...

B PostScript

... continued

name	description	use	example
log	common logarithm	*real* log	1000 log→ 3.00
mod	modulo	*int1 int2* mod	5 3 mod→ 2
mul	multiplication[1]	*num1 num2* mul	5 3 mul→ 15
neg	negative sign	*num* neg	5 neg→ −5
round	round	*real* round	5.7 round→ 6
sin	sine[3]	*real* sin	30 sin→ 0.5
sqrt	square root	*real* sqrt	16 sqrt→ 4.0
sub	subtraction[1]	*real1 real2* sub	17 19 sub→ −2
truncate	truncate decimal part[5]	*real* truncate	−33.33 → −33.00

	integer	real
smallest value	-2^{32}	$\pm 10^{-38}$
largest value	$2^{32} - 1$	$\pm 10^{38}$

Remarks:

[1] If both arguments are integers, the result is integer as well.

[2] Corresponds to $\alpha = \arctan \dfrac{<real1>}{<real2>}$.

[3] The argument must be specified in degrees.

[4] The result is always of type *real*.

[5] The top two stack elements are swapped.

[6] The result remains of the type *real*.

B.2 The non-mathematical PostScript functions

The number of procedures has grown significantly, especially for PostScript level 3. Therefore we list here only a selection of those functions that might be useful in PSTricks.

PS name	stack parameters	function
=	any	Removes the top element from the stack and sends it to standard output.
==	any	Same, but takes the type of the object into account.
aload	*array*	Puts all elements of *array* onto the stack and finally *array* itself.
and	*bool1 bool2*	Both variables are combined with logical AND. If the variables are numbers, they are interpreted as boolean values; 0 corresponds to false.
arc	*x y r α1 α2*	Adds the arc with the specified values to the current path. The angle is measured counter-clockwise. If the starting point of the arc and the current point are not the same, they are connected with a line.

B.2 The non-mathematical PostScript functions

PS name	stack parameters	function
arcn	$x\ y\ r\ \alpha 1\ \alpha 2$	Same, but the arc is drawn clockwise.
arcto	$x_1\ y_1\ x_2\ y_2\ r$	Starting at a point to be determined, an arc is drawn with the specified radius, the current point, and the auxiliary points (x_1, y_1) and (x_2, y_2). Returns the coordinates of the starting point and endpoint on the stack.
array	*int*	Creates an array of length *int* and pushes it onto the stack.
astore	*any any... n* array	Takes the top n elements from the stack and pushes onto the stack an array containing these elements.
begin	*dict*	Pushes *dict* onto the *dictionary stack*.
bind	*proc* bind *proc*	All variables in proc are replaced by their associated values; this yields a speed gain during execution.
charpath	*string bool*	Returns the outline of *string* as path added to the current one.
clear	–	Removes all objects from the user stack.
clip	–	Specifies the new clipping path as the intersection of the current clipping path and the normal path.
closepath	–	Closes the current path and connects the last and the first point.
concat	*matrix*	Combines the six-element *matrix* and the current transformation matrix (CTM).
concatmatrix	*mat1 mat2 mat3*	The six-element matrices *mat1* and *mat2* are multiplied and saved in *mat3*. *mat1* and *mat2* are removed from the stack. The transformation matrix (CTM) is not changed.
copy	*a b... n*	The top n elements of the stack are copied and pushed onto the stack in the same order.
count	*a b...*	Counts the number of elements on the stack and pushes the result onto the stack.
counttomark	mark *a b...*	Counts the number of elements on the stack starting at the mark symbol and pushes the result onto the stack.
currentcmyklcolor	–	Returns the current colour in CMYK encoding.
currentgray	–	Returns the current grey value.
currenthsblcolor	–	Returns the current colour in HSB encoding.
currentlinewidth	–	Returns the current line width.
currentmatrix	*matrix*	Replaces the elements of matrix by the ones of the CTM.
currentpoint	–	Returns the coordinates of the current point.
currentrgblcolor	–	Returns the current colour in RGB encoding.

B PostScript

PS name	stack parameters	function
curveto	x_1 y_1 x_2 y_2 x_3 y_3	Adds a Bezier curve with the endpoint (x_3,y_3) and the interpolation points (x_1,y_1) and (x_2,y_2) to the current path (the current point must exist).
cvn	string	string is converted to /string.
cvs	any string	Creates an identical ASCII string from any.
cvx	any	any is made executable.
def	key value	Associates the key /key with the value in the current dictionary.
end	–	Removes the current dictionary from the dictionary stack.
defaultmatrix	matrix	Writes the default of the CTM to matrix.
dtransform	x y	Transforms the two values to ones in the device coordinate system.
	matrix x y	Same, but uses matrix for the transformation instead of the CTM.
eofill	–	Inner area of the current path is filled with the current colour according to the even/uneven rule.
eq	any1 any2	Compares the two objects for equality.
exec	any	any is executed.
exit	–	Leaves the current loop.
fill	–	Fills the inner area of the current path with the current colour.
findfont	/fontname	Pushes the font dictionary associated with /fontname onto the stack.
for	init inc end proc	Creates a loop starting at init, incremented inc for each iteration, and terminated when end is reached or exceeded.
forall	obj proc	Applies proc for each element of an object of type array, dict, or string.
ge	any1 any2	Compares the two objects for greater than or equal.
get	array n	Pushes the nth element of array onto the stack.
grestore	–	Restores the old graphics state (path, origin, colour,...).
gsave	–	Saves the current graphics state (clipping path, current transformation matrix, dash pattern, device, colour, flatness, font, halftone screen, line width, linecap, linejoin, mitre limit, path, transfer function, and pointer position).
gt	any1 any2	Compares the two objects for greater than.
idtransform	x y	Inversion of the dtransform function.
if	bool proc if	If bool is true, then proc is executed.
ifelse	bool proc1 proc2 ifelse	If bool is true, then proc1 is executed, otherwise proc2.

B.2 The non-mathematical PostScript functions

PS name	stack parameters	function
index	$x_n \ldots x_1\ x_0$ n	The nth element is copied and pushed onto the stack; counting starts at 0.
idtransform	x y	Inversion of the *transform* function.
le	any1 any2	Compares the two objects for *less than/equal*.
length	obj	The length of an object of type array, dict, or string is pushed onto the stack and the object is removed.
lineto	x y	Draws a line from the current point to (x,y). After that, x,y is the new current point.
loop	proc	The procedure is executed until it terminates with the exit command.
lt	any1 any2	Compares the two objects for *less than*.
mark	–	Pushes a *mark* object onto the stack.
moveto	x y	Sets the current point to (x,y), but does not draw a line to it.
newpath	–	Deletes the current path and starts a new one.
not	val	Negates the element on top of the stack.
or	val1 val2	Combines the two values on top of the stack with logical OR.
pop	any	Deletes the element on top of the stack.
pstack	–	All stack elements are printed to standard output without changing the stack itself.
put	array n any	Replaces the nth element of *array* by *any*.
rand	–	A random number ($0 \leq x \leq 2^{32} - 1$) is pushed onto the stack.
rcurveto	$x_1\ y_1\ x_2\ y_2\ x_3\ y_3$	Like *curveto*, but with relative coordinates.
repeat	n proc	Executes the procedure n times.
roll	a b… n j	Takes n objects off the stack and rotates them j times.
rlineto	dx dy	Draws a line from the current point to $(x + dx, y + dy)$; this point becomes the new current point.
rmoveto	dx dy	The same, but no line is drawn.
rotate	angle	Current user coordinate system is rotated counter-clockwise by *angle* degrees.
	angle matrix	The rotation only affects *matrix*, which is pushed onto the stack again after being changed. The rotation is therefore not visible.
scale	x y	Scales the current user coordinate system by x y.
	x y matrix	Similar to rotate.
scalefont	font scale	*font* is scaled by *scale*.
setcmykcolor	c m y k	Sets the current drawing colour.
setdash	array offset	Sets the current line pattern.
setfont	font	Sets the current font.
setgray	val	Sets the current grey value.
sethsbcolor	h s b	Sets the current drawing colour.

B PostScript

PS name	stack parameters	function
setlinecap	int	Sets the *linecap* value.
setlinejoin	int	Sets the *linejoin* value.
setlinewidth	val	Sets the current line width.
setmatrix	matrix	Replaces the CTM by *matrix*.
setrgbcolor	r g b	Sets the current drawing colour.
show	string	Prints *string* at the current position with the current font.
srand	int	Initializes random number generator with *int*.
string	n	Pushes a string of n characters onto the stack.
stroke	–	Draws the current path with the current line width and colour.
transform	x y	Converts (x,y) into the device coordinate system.
	x y matrix	Converts (x,y) into the device coordinate system.
translate	x y	Sets the origin of the user coordinate system to (x,y).
	x y matrix	Similar to *rotate*.
xor	val1 val2	Combines the arguments with exclusive or.
[	–	Pushes a *mark* object onto the stack.
]	[a b ...	Creates an *array* from the stack elements, starting at the last *mark* object, and pushes it onto the stack.

B.3 The PostScript definitions of `pstricks.pro`

The main header file `pstricks.pro` defines several constants and functions that make entering mathematical functions easier, for example for \psplot or \psplotDiffEqn. The following list summarizes the most important ones. Further explanations can be found in the other lists.

Some other packages also have prologue files that define constants. These are usually specific to the application, and therefore are not listed here. Constants and functions from `pstricks.pro` in general can be accessed directly. Otherwise, the respective prologue file must be pushed onto the user dictionary stack, for example

tx@3DDict begin *PostScript code* end

Usually the main dictionary tx@Dict does not have to be loaded explicitly because all PSTricks operations are executed within tx@Dict anyway. However, this does not apply to the dictionaries listed in the following section.

PS name	stack Parameters	function
CM	3×3 matrix	Matrix is replaced by the current transformation matrix.
SLW	value	The top stack element becomes the line width.
CLW	–	Pushes the current line width onto the stack.
CP	–	Pushes the coordinates of the current point onto the stack.
ED	/name value	Saves value as /*name* (exch def).
L	x y	Draws a line to (x,y).

continued...

... continued

PS name	stack Parameters	function
T	$x\ y$	(x,y) becomes the new coordinate origin.
TMatrix	–	Sets TMatrix to {}.
RAngle	–	Sets RAngle to zero.
Atan	$x\ y$	Returns zero if atan is not defined.
ATAN1	x	$\arctan(-x/-1)$
Div	$x\ y$	Returns x if y is equal to zero.
NET	$x\ y$	Sets the origin to -x -y.
Pyth	$x\ y$	$\sqrt{x^2+y^2}$
PtoC	$r\ \alpha$	Converts polar coordinates to Cartesian.
Pi	–	3.14159265359
TwoPi	–	6.28318530718
Euler	–	2.71828182846
RadtoDeg	x	Converts x from radian to degrees.
DegtoRad	α	Converts α from degrees to radian.

B.4 The names of the PSTricks dictionaries

The previos section discussed how to access the individual prologue files. If you want to use a function defined in such prologue without loading the corresponding TEX file, you can load just the prologue with the command \pstheader{*file name*}.

The names of the dictionaries of the prologue files from Section 1 on page 152 are listed alphabetically below. A file may define more than one dictionary.

package name	file name	dictionary name
pstricks	pstricks.pro	tx@Dict
	pst-algparser.pro	tx@CoreAnalyzerDict
		tx@AlgToPs
		tx@AddMathFunc
		tx@Derive
pstricks-add	pstricks-add.pro	tx@addDict
pst-map3d	pst-map3d.pro	tx@map3DDict
pst-map3dII	pst-map3dII.pro	tx@mapII3DDict
pst-3dplot	pst-3dplot.pro	tx@3DPlotDict
pst-bar	pst-bar.pro	tx@BarDict
pst-blur	pst-blur.pro	tx@PstBlurDict
pst-coil	pst-coil.pro	tx@CoilDict
pst-eucl	pst-eucl.pro	tx@EcldDict
pst-fun	pst-fun.pro	tx@FunDict
pst-func	pst-func.pro	tx@FuncDict
pst-fractal	pst-fractal.pro	tx@fractalDict

continued...

B PostScript

... continued

package name	file name	dictionary name
pst-grad	pst-grad.pro	tx@GradientDict
pst-light3d	pst-light3d.pro	tx@LightThreeDDict
pst-node	pst-node.pro	tx@NodeDict
pst-optexp	pst-optexp.pro	tx@OptexpDict
pst-slpe	pst-slpe.pro	tx@PstSlopeDict
pst-solides3d	solides.pro	SolidesDict
pst-spectra	pst-spectra.pro	tx@PstWLDDict
pst-text	pst-text.pro	tx@TextPathDict

Anhang C

Known problems

C.1 pstricks 847
C.2 pst-plot 848
C.3 pst-node 849

As any other software, PSTricks has some bugs which have not been fixed so far because of their complex nature. At least one long-standing bug has been fixed since the last edition. The remaining ones are listed below accompanied with the examples.

C.1 pstricks

C.1.1 Arrows

If arrows are used when a line or curve is drawn, it can affect the way the line is drawn.[1] This can be especially inconvenient for Bezier curves – with arrows, not the coordinates of the point itself, but the coordinates of the beginning of the arrow are considered. The following example clearly shows this fault, which has been emphasised through arrowinset=-4 and the fill option. This can be fixed by modifying the PostScript function /Arrow by setting the current point to (0,0), the end of the line, after drawing the arrow head.

Specifying arrowinset=-4 (an arrow extended backwards) does not make sense in practise and is used here only to make the effect more visible.

```
\usepackage{pstricks}
\psset{unit=1.5,fillstyle=solid,fillcolor=gray!20,arrowinset=-4,showpoints=true}
\begin{pspicture}[showgrid=true](-0.2,-0.5)(4,2.2)
    \psdot*(1,1) \psdot*(3,1)
    \psbezier{->}(1,1)(0,2)(4,2)(3,1) \psbezier{->}(1,1)(0,0)(4,0)(3,1)
\end{pspicture} \quad
\makeatletter\pst@Verb{%
/Arrow { CLW mul add dup 2 div /w ED mul dup /h ED mul /a ED { 0 h T 1 -1
```

---

[1] Thomas Siegel, 1997 (siegel@aix520.informatik.uni-leipzig.de)

C Known problems

```
    scale } if w neg h moveto 0 0 L w h L w neg a neg rlineto
    0 0 moveto % modification by Denis Girou
    gsave fill grestore } def }\makeatother
\begin{pspicture}[showgrid=true](-0.2,-0.5)(4,2.2)
    \psdot*(1,1) \psdot*(3,1)
    \psbezier{->}(1,1)(0,2)(4,2)(3,1) \psbezier{->}(1,1)(0,0)(4,0)(3,1)
\end{pspicture}
```

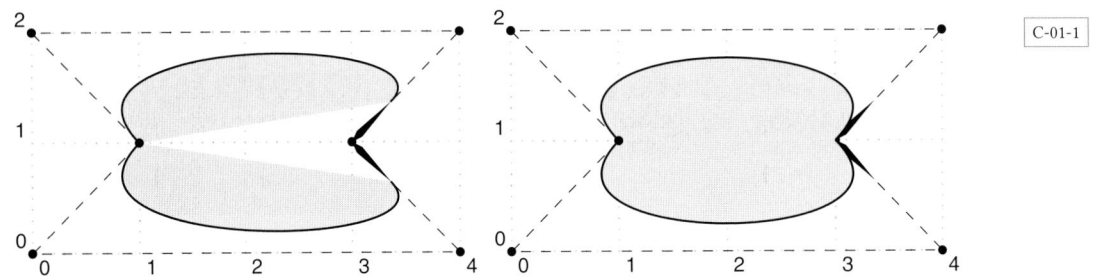

C-01-1

C.2 pst-plot

C.2.1 \savedata

The macro \savedata cannot be used within another macro. There is no error message, but the plot macros will not produce any output. Only the data set which was read last is used because of problems with catcodes.[2] The following examples show this effect clearly. The centre figure shows the same as the left example, but inside a \psframebox macro. Now no plot is created. In the right example, \savedata is used outside \psframebox and the plot is created.

```
\usepackage{pst-plot}
\begin{pspicture}(-1,-1)(2,2)
    \savedata{\test}[-1.09 -0.55 -0.4 -0.1 0 1.02 1.28 0.06 1.51 1.21]
    \dataplot[linewidth=2pt]{\test} \psaxes{->}(0,0)(-1,-1)(2,2)
\end{pspicture}
\psframebox{\begin{pspicture}(-1,-1)(2,2)
    \savedata{\test}[-1.09 -0.55 -0.4 -0.1 0 1.02 1.28 0.06 1.51 1.21]
    \dataplot[linewidth=2pt]{\test} \psaxes{->}(0,0)(-1,-1)(2,2)
\end{pspicture}}
\savedata{\test}[-1.09 -0.55 -0.4 -0.1 0 1.02 1.28 0.06 1.51 1.21]
\psframebox{\begin{pspicture}(-1,-1)(2,2)
    \dataplot[linewidth=2pt]{\test} \psaxes{->}(0,0)(-1,-1)(2,2)
\end{pspicture}}%
```

---

[2] Ivan Maio 1997, (maio@pol88a.polito.it)

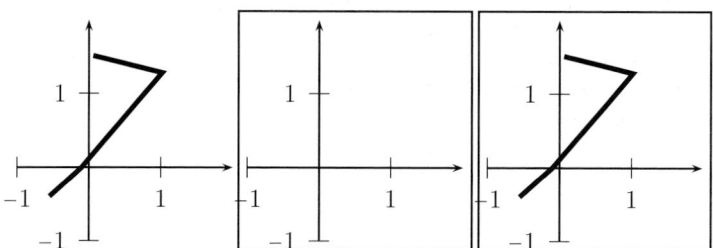

There will be no fix for this bug in the near future. The simple workaround is to use \savedata only outside other macros – this can always be done.

C.3 pst-node

C.3.1 Nodes

Usually, \rput can be used to place arbitrary objects relative to the origin. If the object references defined nodes itself however, \rput does not produce a correct result.[3]

```
\usepackage{pst-node}\SpecialCoor
\begin{pspicture}(5.5,3)
  \qdisk(5,0){2mm} \qdisk(0,2){2mm}\rput(1,1){\psline[linewidth=2pt](5,0)(0,2)}% correct
\end{pspicture}\quad\begin{pspicture}(5.5,2)
  \Cnode*(5,0){f1} \Cnode*(0,2){f2}
  \rput(1,1){\psline[linewidth=2pt](f1)(f2)}% wrong, \rput witout effect
\end{pspicture}
```

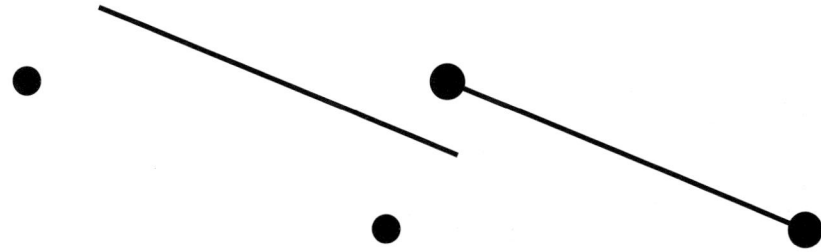

So far, no solution for this problem has been made public. As a workaround, only normal coordinates can be used or the nodes need to take the relative translation of \rput into account. A similar problem arises when putting two labels for a node connection. If one of them uses a node connection itself, the second label is placed incorrectly.[4]

---

[3]Thomas Siegel. 1998 (siegel@aix520.informatik.uni-leipzig.de)
[4]Anthony Doggett, 1999 (adoggett@uiuc.edu)

C Known problems

```
\usepackage{pst-node}\SpecialCoor

\begin{pspicture}(3,-3)
  \newcommand{\correct}{%
    \pnode(0,0){A} \pnode(2,0){B} %
    \psline[linestyle=dashed](A)(B)}
  \pcline[linewidth=2pt](0,0)(3,-3)
  \naput{\correct}\nbput{correct}% correct
  \renewcommand{\correct}{%
    \pnode(0,0){A} \pnode(2,0){B}%
    \ncline[linestyle=dashed]{A}{B}}\hfill
  \pcline[linewidth=2pt](0,0)(3,-3)
  \naput{\correct}\nbput{wrong}% wrong
\end{pspicture}
```

The second label "wrong" should be placed at the same position as "correct". This only works for the label of the dashed line however; instead of below the line, "wrong" is placed above it. There is no fix known or in sight for this bug as well.

C.3.2 Node labels

If the language option french, or the corresponding package, is used, the short forms for placing labels cannot be used. These special characters are marked as active by the french option. This bug does not occur when the babel package with the french option is used.[5]

```
\documentclass{article}
\usepackage{pstricks}
\usepackage{pst-node}
\usepackage{french}
\begin{document}
  \begin{psmatrix}
    E&F\\
    G&H
    \ncline{1,1}{1,2}^w
    \ncline{2,1}{2,2}_f
    \ncline{1,1}{2,1}<u
    \ncline{1,2}{2,2}>v
  \end{psmatrix}
\end{document}
```

This problem can be fixed by placing the PSTricks environment in an arbitrary language environment which does not make those characters active, for example English. Alternatively, the babel package with the french option can be used.

```
\documentclass{article}
\usepackage{pstricks}
\usepackage{pst-node}
\usepackage[french]{babel}
[ ... ]
```

---

[5] Philippe Esperet, 1996 (pesperet@compuserve.com)

Anhang D

PDF output[1]

D.1 ps2pdf 852
D.2 pst-pdf 852
D.3 auto-pst-pdf 855
D.4 pdftricks 855

Most figures can't be processed directly by TEX. Instead, this "foreign" code is encapsulated internally in \special commands. Only the dimensions of the figure must be known when the document is typeset. The contents of the \special commands are then substituted later by visible figures by the output driver. In the case of PostScript code, this substitution takes a lot of effort because PostScript is a powerful programming language and requires a very powerful interpreter for its commands, apart from a few special cases. The output driver built into pdfTEX is not able to fulfil this task. The following sections assume that pdfLATEX is being used, even if the contents usually contain incompatible PostScript code.

To use the PostScript code contained in an EPS figure with a pdfLATEX document, the following steps are necessary:

▷ conversion of the EPS figure into the PDF format –

  epstopdf *figure.eps*

▷ editing of the document (the figure can be included through \includegraphics{*figure*})

  pdflatex *document.tex*

This method is simple, but the amount of effort increases with the number of figures to convert (though the process can be automated with scripts of course). The process of preparing PostScript code is much more difficult if it is not used as a figure file, but directly in the source code of the document, as for example with PSTricks-based packages. If all such figures are included in an auxiliary document, an EPS file can be created with dvips (option -E). This file can then be used as described above. Obviously this is a much more inconvenient way though, which, more importantly, is not without errors.

---

[1]Thanks to Rolf Niepraschk. The section on pst-pdf refers to the article published in *Die TEXnische Komödie*, the journal of the German TEX users group.[50]

D PDF output

D.1 ps2pdf

The ps2pdf program, a special helper based on ghostscript, can be used to easily convert a whole document from PostScript to PDF. In the easiest case, a simple

    ps2pdf file.ps

is enough.

On the other hand, all the additional functionality offered by pdfLaTeX is not available. This method fails very rarely though. ps2pdf can also be used to convert individual figures created with PSTricks to PDF and then to trim the white margin with pdfcrop. For this method, \pagestyle{*empty*} should be used to prevent text in headers or footers.

D.2 pst-pdf

The preview package is very useful when it comes to outputting parts of a document as individual pages. As shown in [50], preview is able to extract arbitrary parts of a document and collect them in a DVI file. The requirement "one object per page" is already met. If the objects are now the PSTricks figures of interest here, the problem PSTricks–PDF can be solved another way.

In the beginning, the pst-pdf package was only meant to make using PSTricks figures in pdfLaTeX easier. Nowadays however, arbitrary PostScript code (e.g. EPS figures) are supported as well. It is easier to use than the predecessor ps4pdf package, where all PostScript fragments had to be given as parameters of a special command. This is not necessary anymore with pst-pdf. The following commands and environments are supported:

▷ The pspicture environment, which is very important for PSTricks.

▷ Most of the other PSTricks commands, also when used outside pspicture; for example \psframebox, pstree. Not supported at the moment are commands with a variable number (greater than three) of parameters in round parentheses, for example \psline. Within pspicture however, this is not a problem.

▷ The \includegraphics command, which loads PostScript files. Interactions with psfrag are possible without restrictions.

▷ The new environment postscript, which may contain arbitrary PostScript code.

 The pst-pdf package requires a current version of the preview package (at least version 0.9).

D.2.1 The process with pst-pdf

In principle, only \usepackage{*pst-pdf*} has to be inserted into the preamble of the document. Then the document is processed as follows (example.tex here):

▷ Create a figure container file example-pics.pdf ("*-pics*" is the default if nothing else is specified) —

  – latex example.tex[2]

  – DVIPS -o example-pics.ps example.dvi

---

[2] preview now creates a special DVI file.

- `ps2pdf example-pics.ps example-pics.pdf`

▷ Create the actual document —

- `pdflatex example.tex`

During the pdfLaTeX run, the definition of the `pspicture` environment and the other PostScript-specific commands is changed: the PDF figure created in the previous step is included automatically.

`\includegraphics[page=n]{example-pics.pdf}`

An internal counter keeps the value n to make sure that the correct page or figure from the figure container file is used. If the content or number of figures changes, the file must be recreated. The file `example-pics.pdf` contains all figures and may also be used for other purposes.

The processing can be made easier by using one of the shell scripts that are included with the package. All of them expect only one parameter – the name of the LaTeX file to translate. They can also be included in existing LaTeX GUIs.

`ps4pdf`	2005-11-02	Unix-like environments, also Cygwin
`ps4pdf.bat`	2005-06-30	Win32+MiKTeX
`ps4pdf.bat.noMiKTeX`	2005-06-01	Win32 without MiKTeX
`ps4pdf.bat.w95`	2005-06-30	Windows98 and older

 If the content, number, or order of figures changes, the figure container file must be deleted and recreated. Otherwise, the old figures are used.

D.2.2 The package options

active Activates extraction mode (DVI output); this is the default for a LaTeX run.

inactive Take no special action, only the `pstricks` and `graphicx` packages are loaded (the default when using VTeX). This option can be used to convert the document with LaTeX into a DVI file and prevent the automatic use of extraction mode.

pstricks Load the `pstricks` package (default).

nopstricks Do not load the `pstricks` package. If `pstricks` is loaded afterwards anyway, the `pspicture` environment is retroactively treated as if the package had been loaded with the `pstricks` option.

draft In pdfLaTeX mode, figures included from the container file are only displayed as frames, which corresponds to the "draft" behaviour of `graphicx`.

final In pdfLaTeX mode, figures included from the container file are displayed entirely (default).

tightpage The dimensions of the figures in the container file correspond to the ones of the respective TeX boxes (default).

notightpage The dimensions of a TeX box that contains a figure are sometimes incorrect as PostScript commands may also draw outside a box. The `notightpage` option causes the figures in the container file to have at least the dimensions of the entire page. To be able to use the figures in a later pdfLATEX run, the container file must be processed to reduce the dimensions of the figures to the visible parts. To achieve this, you can use the pdfcrop[3] or epstool[4] programs.

displaymath The `displaymath`, `eqnarray`, and `$$` mathematical environments are extracted as well and inserted as figures in PDF mode. This way, additional PSTricks extensions can easily be added to the content of these environments.

D.2.3 Environments and commands

pspicture

\begin{pspicture} [settings] $(x_0, y_0)(x_1, y_1)$ ... \end{pspicture}

The environment is not available if `pst-pdf` has been loaded with the `nopstricks` option. It is used as usual in PSTricks. In pdfLATEX mode, the contents are only displayed if the figure container file has been created before.

postscript

\begin{postscript} [settings] ... \end{postscript}

The environment may contain arbitrary code with the exception of floating environments. In pdfLATEX mode, its contents are also taken from the container file. If this file is not present, the required space may be not reserved correctly.

\includegraphics

\includegraphics [settings] {*file name*}

Use as defined in `graphics`/`graphicx`. In addition it is now possible to specify EPS files as arguments also in pdfLATEX mode and display their contents, which is also taken from the container file.

There are further options available to control the behaviour of the \includegraphics and \usepicture commands and the `postscript` environment. Examples can be taken from the documentation of \pst-pdf. [52]

D.2.4 Bounding box

Determining the bounding box is independent of `pst-pdf`, not always easy, and often requires manual intervention. In Example D-03-1 on the facing page the bounding box is too small because of the definition of the `psgraph` environment. It doesn't take the space required for the labels into account such that the figure appears cropped after using `pst-pdf`, which requires that the size of the bounding box is specified correctly.

---

[3]CTAN: `support/pdfcrop/`
[4]`http://www.cs.wisc.edu/~ghost/gsview/epstool.htm`

D.3 auto-pst-pdf

This package depends on pst-pdf, which is loaded by default. auto-pst-pdf simplifies the use because all needed LaTeX runs and conversions are done by the package itself. You just have to run pdflatex with the shell-escape option for TeX Live or enable-write18 for MiKTeX, to allow executing external programs from within pdflatex. By default the package loads pst-pdf with the notightpage option. The following example shows the problem when using the package with the tightpage option, which is the default for the pst-pdf package.

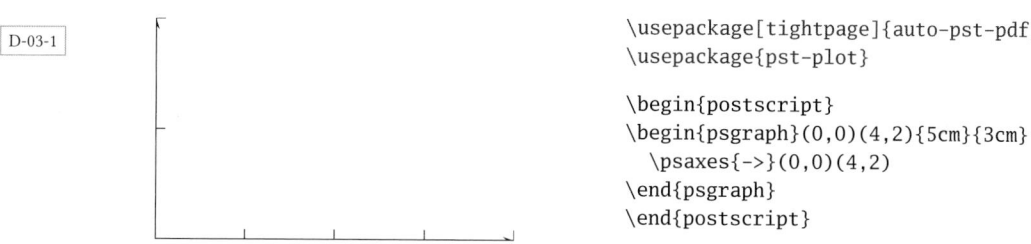

```
\usepackage[tightpage]{auto-pst-pdf}
\usepackage{pst-plot}

\begin{postscript}
\begin{psgraph}(0,0)(4,2){5cm}{3cm}
    \psaxes{->}(0,0)(4,2)
\end{psgraph}
\end{postscript}
```

You can reserve the space required for the labels with the llx and lly or urx and ury options. Alternatively you can use the notightpage optional argument, which is the default for the auto-pst-pdf package. In this case the values for the bounding box aren't taken from the DVI-output, the image is created as a whole page and then cropped with the help of pdfcrop.

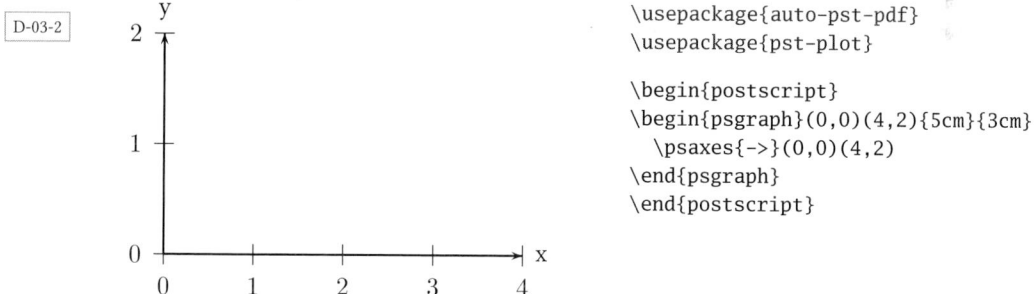

```
\usepackage{auto-pst-pdf}
\usepackage{pst-plot}

\begin{postscript}
\begin{psgraph}(0,0)(4,2){5cm}{3cm}
    \psaxes{->}(0,0)(4,2)
\end{psgraph}
\end{postscript}
```

To include the psgraph environment in preview and therefore pst-pdf or auto-pst-pdf, you can create a local configuration file pst-pdf.cfg with the following command:

\AtBeginDocument{\PreviewEnvironment{psgraph}}

This example can be easily extended. Alternatively you can use the postscript environment; everything inside this environment will be handled by the package and is converted to a PDF image.

D.4 pdftricks

You might think that pdftricks works in a similar way to pst-pdf, but it neither uses the preview package, nor does it offer as much functionality. pdftricks creates separate LaTeX documents for the PSTricks figures encapsulated in pdfpic environments and compiles and includes them separately. In any case, pdftricks is not the PDF version of PSTricks.

D PDF output

In the preamble, all PSTricks packages used in the document must be included in the `psinputs` environment after loading `pdftricks`. Within the document, each PSTricks figure must be encapsulated in the `pdfpic` environment; all commands must be inside that environment as well. New commands can be defined inside `psinputs` for the `pdfpic` environment.

foo

bar

```
\usepackage{pdftricks}
%\usepackage[miktex]{pdftricks}% MiKTeX
\begin{psinputs}
    \usepackage{pstricks}
\end{psinputs}

foo
\begin{pdfpic}
    \begin{pspicture}(3,2)
        \psline{|<->|}(0,0.3)(3,1.9)
    \end{pspicture}
\end{pdfpic}
bar
```

D-04-1

Once this is done, not LaTeX but pdfLaTeX is called.

pdflatex -shell-escape *file*

The `shell-escape` option is required if the created documents that contain the figures are to be compiled and converted automatically, because pdfTeX doesn't allow the execution of external programs otherwise. Depending on the TeX distribution, this option may be different.

To be able to include the figures as PDF files, at least three runs are necessary. You should check the figures afterwards in any case – `pdftricks` uses dvips, which often has problems when determining the size of a figure. [59]

Anhang E

Errors and help

E.1 Frequent errors 857
E.2 Help 858
E.3 Packages 858

E.1 Frequent errors

▷ PSTricks is short for PostScript tricks; this means that almost all DVI viewers do not display it correctly. You should always create the PostScript output and view it with a PostScript viewer.

▷ Parameters, which are set outside a `pspicture` environment through \psset, are global and therefore also affect PSTricks figures afterwards.

▷ When using PiCTeX, the message "No room for a new \dimen" appears. In principle, there is no need to use the package `pictex`, as PSTricks offers much more functionality. If it must be used nevertheless, the FAQ at http://www.dante.de gives several ways to fix the error:

> 6.4.5 When using PiCTeX I get the message 'No room for a new \dimen'. How do I prevent that?

Almost all newer distributions use eTeX or pdfeTeX anyway.

▷ Even though the `center` environment or the \centering command is used, the figure is not centered. This usually happens because the chosen coordinates of the `pspicture` environment are not symmetric and one side is too small or there is too little margin. This can be detected by putting the `pspicture` environment into a \psframebox{...}.

▷ There is too much space above or below the figure. This is similar to the previous point.

▷ The dashed line option has no effect. This is usually caused by old versions of `pstricks.pro` or `pstricks.tex`. Updating those files should fix this; kpsewhich *file* can be used to determine the location:

voss@shania:~> kpsewhich pstricks.pro
/opt/texlive7/texmf/dvips/pstricks/pstricks.pro

```
voss@shania:~> kpsewhich pstricks.tex
/opt/texlive7/texmf/tex/generic/pstricks/pstricks.tex
voss@shania:~>
```

If the new files are saved at the same place, the TeX file structure does not need to be updated.

E.2 Help

The first place to go should always be the documentation of the respective package, which is sometimes very detailed, especially for newer packages, and usually available in PDF form. Another point of contact is the PSTricks mailing list at http://tug.org/mailman/listinfo/pstricks. There is also an archive that goes back to 1997. The usual newsgroup comp.text.tex is also a place where help is available, especially for problems with the TeX distribution.

E.3 Packages

A list of all packages that are currently available is only valid for a certain period of time. You can always find the latest information on CTAN in the PSTricks directory CTAN:/graphics/pstricks/. More information can be found in the TeX catalogue online, which is always updated by the CTAN managers and especially Robin Fairbairns, at http://www.dante.de/CTAN//help/Catalogue/brief.html.

Table E.1: List of all currently known PSTricks packages

name	functionality
pst-3d	basic 3D operations
pst-3dplot	plane-parallel 3D projections
pst-2dplot	Matlab-compatible plots
pstricks-add	extended commands for pstricks/pst-node/pst-plot
pst-abspos	absolute coordinates on a page
pst-am	modulating signals
pst-asr	linguistics – autosegmental representations
pst-bar	bar charts
pst-barcode	bar codes
pst-bezier	Bézier curves
pst-blur	blurred shadows
pst-bspline	special cubix splines
pst-calendar	calendar as table or dodecahedron
pst-circ	circuits
pst-coil	coils and zigzag lines
pst-cox	regular polytopes
pst-dbicons	ER diagrams

continued...

... continued

name	functionality
pst-diffraction	diffraction of light at single and double slits
pst-electricfield	field lines of electrical charges
pst-eps	export PSTricks environments as EPS
pst-eucl	Euclidean geometry
pst-fill	filling with colours and patterns
pst-fr3d	3D boxes
pst-fractal	fractal images
pst-fun	animal and comic characters
pst-func	special mathematic functions
pst-gantt	Gantt charts
pst-geo	geographic projections
pst-gr3d	3D grids
pst-grad	colour gradients
pst-graphicx	using PSTricks with TeX, graphicx, and miniltx
pst-infixplot	postfix–infix
pst-jtree	linguistic trees
pst-knot	special knots
pst-labo	chemical elements and apparati
pst-lens	lens effects
pst-light3d	3D light effects
pst-magneticfield	field lines of Helmholtz coils
pst-math	extended PostScript functions
pst-mirror	objects on a spherical mirror
pst-node	nodes and connections
pst-ob3d	simple 3D objects
pst-optexp	experimental optic systems
pst-optic	optic systems
pst-osci	oscilloscopes
pst-pad	elastic connections
pst-pdf	PostScript–PDF
pst-pdgr	medical pedigrees
pst-platon	Platonic solids in IIID
pst-plot	plot functions and data
pst-poly	polygons
pst-qtree	PSTricks interface for qtree
pst-slpe	extended colour gradients
pst-solides3d	centric 3D projections
pst-soroban	typeset game sequences
pst-spectra	frequency spectra
pst-stru	statics
pst-text	text and character manipulations
pst-thick	very thick lines and curves

continued...

E Errors and help

... continued

name	functionality
pst-tree	trees
pst-uml	UML diagrams
pst2pdf	Perl script to be able to use PDF LaTeX
uml	UML diagrams

PSTricks-based packages

gastex	automata theory
makeplot	plot exported Matlab files
psgo	Go diagrams
RRGtree	linguistic trees for role and reference grammars
multido	loops
sfg	signal flows
vaucanson	automata theory

Bibliography

[1] M. Abramowitz und I. A. Stegun. Handbook of Mathematical Functions with Formulas, Graphs, and Mathematical Tables. National Bureau of Standards Applied Mathematics Series, U.S. Government Printing Office, Washington, D.C., USA, 1964. Corrections appeared in later printings up to the 10th Printing.

[2] H. Adriaens und Ch. Ellison. »The powerdot class«. The successor of the seminar class.
CTAN: /macros/latex/contrib/powerdot

[3] Hendri Adriaens. The xkeyval - package, 2005. An extended key-value-Interface, which is used by all PSTricks packages. CTAN: /macros/latex/contrib/xkeyval/

[4] Hendri Adriaens und Uwe Kern. »xkeyval – new developments and mechanism in key handling«. *TUGboat*, 25(2):194–198, 2004.

[5] Marius Apetri. 3D-Grafik Programmierung. mitp-Verlag, Bonn, 1st edition, 2003.

[6] Donald Arseneau. random – a package for pseudo random numbers, 1995.
CTAN: /macros/generic/misc/random.tex

[7] Christoph Bersch. pst-optexp – a PSTricks package to draw optical setups, 2008. Version 2.0. CTAN: /graphics/pstricks/contrib/pst-optexp/

[8] Terry Burton und Herbert Voß. pst-barcode – a PSTricks package for printing barcodes, 2011. CTAN: /graphics/pstricks/contrib/pst-barcode/

[9] D. P. Carlisle. Packages in the 'graphics' bundle, 1999.
CTAN: /macros/latex/required/graphics/grfguide.tex

[10] D. P. Carlisle und S. P. Q. Rahtz. The keyval - package, 2001. The key-value-Interface.
CTAN: /macros/latex/required/graphics/keyval.dtx

E BIBLIOGRAPHY

[11] Bill Casselman. Mathematical Illustrations – a manual of geometry and PostScript. Cambridge University Press, Cambridge, 1st edition, 2005. Geberal overview of 2D and 3D graphics with PostScript. http://www.math.ubc.ca/~cass/graphics/manual/

[12] David Chiang. `pst-qtree` – Linguistic trees, 2007. Interface for the qtree program. CTAN: /graphics/pstricks/contrib/pst-qtree/

[13] Patrick Drechsler. `pst-pad` – Haftmodelle, 2008. Version 0.3a. CTAN: /graphics/pstricks/contrib/pst-pad/

[14] Chris Ellison und Hendri Adriaens. `powerdot` – a presentation class, 2005. Version 1.3. CTAN: /macros/latex/contrib/powerdot/

[15] »Ghostscript, Ghostview and GSview«. http://pages.cs.wisc.edu/~ghost/

[16] Martin Giese. The `pst-blur` - package, 2005. CTAN: /graphics/pstricks/contrib/pst-blur/

[17] Martin Giese. The `pst-slpe` - package, 2008. CTAN: /graphics/pstricks/contrib/pst-slpe/

[18] Jürgen Gilg. »PDF-Animationen«. *Die TEXnische Komödie*, 17(4):30–37, 2005. Animations with the aeb-Tool of the package acrotex.

[19] Denis Girou. »Présentation de PSTricks«. *Cahier GUTenberg*, 16:21–70, 1994.

[20] Denis Girou. `pst-fill` - a PSTricks package for filling and tiling (Documentation), 2000. CTAN: /graphics/pstricks/generic/

[21] Denis Girou. `pst-fr3d` - a PSTricks package for three dimensional frame boxes, 2001. CTAN: /graphics/pstricks/contrib/pst-fr3d/

[22] Denis Girou. `pst-gr3d` - a PSTricks package for three dimensional grids, 2001. CTAN: /graphics/pstricks/contrib/pst-gr3d/

[23] Denis Girou. `pst-light3d` - a PSTricks package for three dimensional lighten effects, 2005. CTAN: /graphics/pstricks/contrib/pst-light3d/

[24] Denis Girou, Christoph Jorssen, Manuel Luque und Herbert Voß. `pst-labo` – a PSTricks package for chemical Objects, 2005. CTAN: /graphics/pstricks/contrib/pst-labo/

[25] Michel Goossens, Frank Mittelbach, Sebastian Rahtz, Denis Roegel und Herbert Voß. The LATEX Graphics Companion: Illustrating Documents with TEX and PostScript. Tools and Techniques for Computer Typesetting. Addison-Wesley, Reading, MA, 2007. First edition of the Graphics Companion.

[26] Michel Goossens, Sebastian Rahtz und Frank Mittelbach. The LATEX Graphics Companion: Illustrating Documents with TEX and PostScript. Tools and Techniques for Computer Typesetting. Addison-Wesley, Reading, MA, 1997.

[27] Branko Grünbaum und Geoffrey Sheppard. Tilings and Patterns. Freeman and Company, New York, 1987.

[28] Michael C. Grant und David Carlisle. The PSFrag system, version 3, 1996.
CTAN: /macros/contrib/supported/psfrag/pfgguide.tex

[29] Stephen G. Hartke. »A Survey of Free Math Fonts for TEX and LATEX«.
CTAN: /info/Free_Math_Font_Survey/survey.pdf

[30] Alan Hoenig. TEX Unbound: LATEX & TEX Strategies, Fonts, Graphics, and More. Oxford University Press, London, 1998. Introduction into TEX.

[31] Gernot Hoffmann. Equations of Motion for a Masspoint. Fachhochschule Ostfriesland, 2005. This document started as description of the Lagrangian equations for a moving masspoint. Later some methods for terrain interpolation were added.
http://www.fho-emden.de/~hoffmann/masspoint09092002.pdf

[32] Gernot Hoffmann. Function Graphs and Other Applications for PostScript. Fachhochschule Ostfreisland, 2005.
http://www.fho-emden.de/~hoffmann/pstutor22112002.pdf

[33] Zhuhan Jiang. `arrayjob`, 2000. CTAN: /macros/generic/arrayjob/

[34] Christoph Jorssen und Manuel Luque. `pst-osci` – a PSTricks package for oscilloscopes, 2005. CTAN: /graphics/pstricks/contrib/pst-osci/

[35] Christophe Jorssen. `pst-math` - a PSTricks package for mathematical function, 2004. CTAN: /graphics/pstricks/contrib/pst-math/

[36] Christophe Jorssen und Herbert Voß. The `pst-circ` - package, 2010.
CTAN: /graphics/pstricks/contrib/pst-circ/

[37] David Kastrup. The preview Package for LATEX, 2002. CTAN: /support/preview-latex/

[38] David Kastrup. preview-latex, 2003. CTAN: /support/preview-latex/

[39] Uwe Kern. Color extensions with the `xcolor` package, 2006. Version 2.10.
CTAN: /macros/latex/contrib/xcolor/

[40] Nikolai G. Kollock. PostScript richtig eingesetzt: vom Konzept zum praktischen Einsatz. IWT, Vaterstetten, 1989. Summeray of all PostScript commands of level 2.

[41] Hubert Gäßlein und Rolf Niepraschk. The `pict2e` - package, 2004. An extension of the `picture` environment. CTAN: /macros/latex/contrib/pict2e/

[42] Jean-Gabriel Luque und Manuel Luque. The `pst-cox` package, 2008. We describe the LATEX library pst-coxcoor devoted to draw regular complex polytopes.
CTAN: /graphics/pstricks/contrib/pst-cox/

[43] Manuel Luque und Herbert Voß. `pst-optic` – a PSTricks package for optical objects, 2010. CTAN: /graphics/pstricks/contrib/pst-optic/

[44] Michael Mehlich. The `fp` package, 1996. Floating point arithmetic for TEX and LATEX.
CTAN: /graphics/pstricks/generic/

[45] MicroPress Inc. VTEX/Free, 2003. CTAN: /systems/vtex/

E BIBLIOGRAPHY

[46] MicroPress Inc. TeX Fonts, 2004.   http://www.micropress-inc.com/fonts.htm

[47] MicroPress Inc. VTeX/Free v8.23 - the free VTeX distribution for OS/2 and Linux, 2004.   http://www.micropress-inc.com/linux

[48] Frank Mittelbach und Michel Goosens et al. Der LaTeX Begleiter. Pearson Education, München, 2nd edition, 2005.   The general book to LaTeX.

[49] Frank Mittelbach, Michel Goosens, Sebastian Rahtz, Denis Roegel und Herbert Voß. The LaTeX Graphics Companion. Addison-Wesley Publishing Company, Boston, 2nd edition, 2006.   The general book about graphics and TeX and LaTeX

[50] Rolf Niepraschk. »Anwendungen des LaTeX-Pakets preview«. *Die TeXnische Komödie*, 1/2003:60–65, 2003.

[51] Rolf Niepraschk. The ps4pdf Package, 2003.   CTAN: /macros/latex/contrib/ps4pdf/

[52] Rolf Niepraschk. The pst-pdf Package, 2005.
    CTAN: /graphics/pstricks/contrib/pst-pdf/

[53] Rolf Niepraschk und Herbert Voß. »The package ps4pdf: from PostScript to PDF«. *TUGboat*, 22-4:290–292, 2003.

[54] Rolf Niepraschk und Herbert Voß. PSTricks - mehr als nur ein alter Hut. DANTE 2004 in Darmstadt, 2004.   http://userpage.fu-berlin.de/~latex/PSTricks/Darmstadt2004.pdf

[55] Heiko Oberdiek. pdfcrop, 2002.   CTAN: /support/pdfcrop/

[56] Premshree Pillai. infix-postfix.py, 2003.
    http://aspn.activestate.com/ASPN/Cookbook/Python/Recipe/228915

[57] »Mailing list for powerdot.cls«.   http://www.freelists.org/list/powerdot

[58] »PSTricks«.   The PSTricks homepage.   http://PSTricks.tug.org/

[59] CV Radhakrishnan, CV Rajagopal und Antoine Chambert-Loir. Trivial Experiments with psTricks Manipulation, 2003.
    CTAN: /macros/latex/contrib/supported/pdftricks/pdftricks.sty

[60] Sebastian Rahtz. »Most of the PSTricks examples of The LaTeX Graphics Companion«.   CTAN: /graphics/pstricks/doc/lgc/

[61] Sebastian Rahtz. »An introduction to PSTricks, part I«. *Baskerville*, 6(1):22–34, 1996.

[62] Sebastian Rahtz. »An introduction to PSTricks, part II«. *Baskerville*, 6(2):23–33, 1996.   CTAN: /usergrps/uktug/baskervi/

[63] Klaus Richter. Computergrafik und Farbmetrik – Farbsysteme, PostScript, geräteunabhängige CIE-Farben. VDE-Verlag, Berlin und Offenbach, 1st edition, 1996.   An introduction in color systems

[64] Dominique Rodriguez. pst-eucl – a PSTricks package for Euklidian geometry, 2005.   CTAN: /graphics/pstricks/contrib/pst-eucl/

[65] Denis Roegel. MP2GL – prototyping 3D objects with and OpenGL, 2005.
http://www.loria.fr/~roegel/TeX/eurotex2005roegel.pdf

[66] Tomas G. Rokicki. »Advanced special support for dvi drivers«. *TUGboat*, 15(3):205–212, 1994.

[67] Tomas G. Rokicki. »A proposed standard for specials«. *TUGboat*, 16(4):395–401, 1995. A Tom Rokicki draft standard for the contents of TeX special commands.
http://www.tug.org/TUGboat/Articles/tb16-4/tb49roki.pdf

[68] Tomas G. Rokicki. »Dvips: A DVI-to-PostScript Translator, Version 5.66a«, 1997. The user guide for dvips and its accompanying programs and packages such as afm2tfm.
CTAN: dviware/dvips/dvips_man.pdf

[69] Christian Rolland. LaTeX par la pratique. O Reilly, Paris, 1999.

[70] Christian Rolland. L'essentiel de LaTeX et Gnu-Emacs. Manuel de réalisation de documents scientifiques. Dunod, Paris, 2000.

[71] Christine Römer. »PSTricks für linguistische Texte«. *Die TeXnische Komödie*, 20(2):31–52, 2008. Using PSTricks for linguistic texts.

[72] Claus Schönleber und Frank Klinkenberg-Haaß. »Goldene Schnittmuster«. *mc-Extra*, 2:21–25, 1995. http://www.schoenleber.org/penrose/f-d-penrose.html

[73] Ralph-Hardo Schulz, Editor. Mathematische Aspekte der angewandten Informatik. BI-Wissenschaftsverlag, Mannheim, 1st edition, 1994.

[74] J. P. Snyder. »Map Projections–A Working Manual«. *U. S. Geological Survey Professional Paper 1395*, pp. 138–140, 1987.

[75] Ian Stewart. »Ungewöhnliche Kachelungen«. *Spektrum der Wissenschaft*, p. 114, 2001. http://www.wissenschaft-online.de/spektrum/index.php?action=rubrik_detail&artikel_id=5811

[76] LaTeX team. clsguide – documentation of LaTeX class and package writing, 2003. Good overview for package writers CTAN: /macros/latex/base/clsguide.pdf

[77] Boris Veytsman und Leila Akhmadeeva. Drawing Medical Pedigree Trees with TeX and PSTricks, 2006. http://tug.org/pracjourn/2006-4/veytsman

[78] Jean-Paul Vignault, Manuel Luque, Arnaud Schmittbuhl, Jürgen Gilg und Herbert Voß. The pst-solides3d - package, 2011.
CTAN: /graphics/pstricks/contrib/pst-solides3d/

[79] Jana Voß und Herbert Voß. »The plot functions of pst-plot«. *TUGboat*, 22-4:314–318, 2001. http://www.tug.org/TUGboat/Articles/tb22-4/tb72vossplot.pdf

[80] Jana Voß und Herbert Voß. »Die Plot-Funktionen von pst-plot«. *Die TeXnische Komödie*, 2/02:27–34, 2002. http://tug.org/PSTricks/pst-plot/pst-plot.pdf

[81] Herbert Voß. »Three dimensional plots with pst-3dplot«. *TUGboat*, 22-4:319, 2001. http://www.tug.org/TUGboat/Articles/tb22-4/tb72voss3d.pdf

E BIBLIOGRAPHY

[82] Herbert Voß. »Die mathematischen Funktionen von PostScript«. *Die TEXnische Komödie*, 1/02, 2002. A short summery about the mathematical functions of PostScript and using them in TEX with PSTricks. http://tug.org/PSTricks/pst-plot/pst-plot.pdf

[83] Herbert Voß. PSTricks Support for pdf, 2002.
http://PSTricks.tug.org/main.cgi?file=pdf/pdfoutput

[84] Herbert Voß. »VTEX«. *Die TEXnische Komödie*, 1/04:46–51, 2004.

[85] Herbert Voß. LATEX Referenz. DANTE – lehmanns media, Heidelberg/Berlin, 2nd edition, 2010. A referenz of all LATEX macros lengths and counters

[86] Herbert Voß. PSTricks – Grafik für TEX und LATEX. DANTE – lehmanns media, Heidelberg/Hamburg, sixth edition, 2010.

[87] Herbert Voß. The `pst-3dplot` - package, 2011. 3D lines, curves, areas, etc. in parallel projection. CTAN: /graphics/pstricks/contrib/pst-3dplot/

[88] Herbert Voß. The `pstricks-add` - package, 2011.
CTAN: /graphics/pstricks/contrib/pstricks-add/

[89] Eric W. Weisstein. »Binomial Distribution«.
http://mathworld.wolfram.com/BinomialDistribution.html

[90] Michael Wiedmann. References for TEX and Friends, 2005.
http://www.miwie.org/tex-refs/

[91] Zhigang Xiang und Roy A. Plastock. Computergrafik. mitp-Verlag, Bonn, 1st edition, 2003. Introduction into computer graphics.

[92] Timothy Van Zandt. PSTricks - PostScript macros for Generic TEX, Documented Code, 1997. The documented code of the main package `pstricks.tex`.
CTAN: /obsolete/graphics/pstricks/doc/code/

[93] Timothy Van Zandt. The `pst-eps` package, 2001. Export of PSTricks images.
CTAN: /graphics/pstricks/generic/

[94] Timothy Van Zandt. The `multido` package, 2004. Loops inside TEX or LATEX.
CTAN: /graphics/pstricks/generic/

[95] Timothy Van Zandt und Herbert Voß. PSTricks - PostScript macros for Generic TEX, 2011. The official PSTricks homepage. http://PSTricks.tug.org/

[96] Timothy Van Zandt und Denis Girou. »Inside PSTricks«. *TUGboat*, 15:239–246, 1994.

Index of commands and concepts

To make it easier to use a command or concept, the entries are distinguished by their "type" and this is often indicated by one of the following "type words" at the beginning of an entry:

boolean, counter, env., file, file ext., font, font enc., key value, key, length, option, package, program, or syntax.

The absence of an explicit "type word" means that the "type" is either a TeX or LaTeX "command" or simply a "concept".

Use by, or in connection with, a particular package is indicated by adding the package name (in parentheses) to an entry.

An italic page number indicates that the command is demonstrated in a source code snippet or in an example on that page.

When there are several page numbers listed, **bold** face indicates a page containing important information about an entry.

Symbols

* value (pstricks), 28, 69
*D value (pstricks), 110
*L value (pstricks), 110
*R value (pstricks), 110
*U value (pstricks), 110
}, 153
– value (pstricks), 49, *92*
–) value (pstricks), *96*
–« value (pstricks-add), 99
–> value (pstricks), 49, *91*, 91
–» value (pstricks-add), 99
–>> value (pstricks), *91*
–] value (pstricks), 92
–h value (pstricks-add), *98*
–o value (pstricks), *96*
{, 153
/Compatible (PostScript), *83*
/D (PostScript), 213
/Helvetica (PostScript), *216*
/Multiply (PostScript), *83*
/Normal (PostScript), *83*
/Screen (PostScript), *83*
/ShadingType (PostScript), 739
:D value (pst-node), 254
:U value (pst-node), *254*
<– value (pstricks), 91
= (PostScript), 840
= Option (pst-func), 539–542
= value (pst-solides3d), 433
== (PostScript), 840
[(PostScript), 212, 844
[– value (pstricks), 92
\%, *154*
$$ env., 854
\⟨n⟩ame (xcolor), 20
] (PostScript), 844
2D MaxiCode, 507
3D node, 407
3D object, 341
3D package, 348
3D projection, 338

A

a Option
    (pst-diffraction), 703, 704
    (pst-solides3d), 399, 401
a value (pst-tree), 281
a4paper value (powerdot), 766
\AAJ (pst-rrgtrees), *660*, 661
ABcercle value (pst-solides3d), *414*
\ABinterCD (pst-optic), *692*, *697*
abovetext Option (pst-pdgr), 731
abs (PostScript), 208, 839
absolute value (pstricks), 44, *51*, 51
absolute value, 583
absorption Option (pst-spectra), 716, *718*

absorption spectrum, 716
ACOS (PostScript), 520
acos (PostScript), 208
ACOSH (PostScript), 520
acroread program, 740
action Option (pst-solides3d), 393, *402*, *403*, 424, *428*, 428, *432*, *433*, 433, *441*, 441, 442
adams value (pstricks-add), 611, *612*
add (PostScript), 211, 386, 839
add value (pst-osci), 713
addfillstyle Option (pstricks), 80, 86, *87*, *300*, *301*
\addtopsstyle (pstricks), 121
addv value (pst-solides3d), 411
addv3d (PostScript), 435
adhesion system, 722
adopted Option (pst-pdgr), 731
aeb_pro package, 743, 744
affected Option (pst-pdgr), *729*, 731
affected value (pst-pdgr), 730, 731
affinage Option (pst-solides3d), *432*, 432, *433*, 433
affinagecoeff Option (pst-solides3d), *432*, 432, *433*
affinagerm Option (pst-solides3d), 424
afm2tfm program, 865
Africa, 490
africa Option (pst-geo), 467, 489, 490
\agc (pst-circ), 451
agitateurMagnetique Option (pst-labo), 620, *631*, 631
algebraic Option
    (pst-plot), 207, *208–210*, *212*
    (pst-solides3d), 418
    (pstricks-add), 385, 546, *547*, 549, 549, 605, 607, 609, 611–613, *614*, 666, 667
algebraic notation, 207
alignment reference point, 103
all Option (pst-geo), 467, 489, *490*, 490
all value
    (powerdot), 761
    (pst-eps), 315
    (pst-geo), 467
    (pst-plot), 166, 170, 171, 176, 177, 190
    (pst-solides3d), *403*
all* value (pst-eps), 315
AllColor Option (pst-osci), 713, *714*, *715*
\AllColor (pst-osci), *713*
aload (PostScript), 840
Alpha Option (pst-3dplot), 360, **361**, 374
alpha Option (pst-func), 543
\AltClipMode (pstricks), 116
\altcolormode (pstricks), 154
amplifier, 450
\amplifier (pst-circ), 450
amplitude Option (pst-coil), 304, *308*, 308
amplitude1 Option (pst-osci), 712, *714*, *715*
amplitude2 Option (pst-osci), 713, *714*, *715*
amsmath package, 258
and (PostScript), 840
angle, 23, 144

Index of Commands and Concepts (A)

(cont.)
angle Option
    (pst-fractal), 669, 671
    (pst-node), 140, 142, 227, **230**, 230, *231*, 596, *597*
    (pstricks), 106
angleA Option (pst-node), 227, *230*, 230, *231*, 246, 250, 257, 648
angleB Option (pst-node), *230*, 230, *231*, 245, 246, 250, 648
AngleCoef Option (pst-eucl), 553, 561, *562*, 562, 563, 571
angular unit, 23
animate package, 741, 742
animateinline env. (animate), *742*
animeBld env. (aeb_pro), *744*
anneau value (pst-solides3d), *400*, 400, *441*
anospermia value (pst-pdgr), 731
antenna, 448
\antenna (pst-circ), 448, 454, *463*, *464*
antenna symbol, 448
antennastyle Option (pst-circ), 446, 454
AntiHelmholtz Option (pst-magneticfield), 710
apex, 66
apspos Option (pst-optexp), *698*
\Aput (pst-node), 256
\aput (pst-node), 256
arc, 124, 144
arc (PostScript), 840
arc cosine, 32
arc length, 568
arcangle Option (pst-node), 225, 227, **229**, 229, *230*, 242, 251, 251, *252*
arcangleA Option (pst-node), 227, 229, *230*
arcangleB Option (pst-node), 227, *230*, 230
\ArcL (vaucanson-g), *726*
arcn (PostScript), 841
arcsep Option (pstricks), 57, *58*, 58
arcsepA Option (pstricks), 57, *58*
arcsepB Option (pstricks), 57, *58*
arcto (PostScript), 841
area, 79
area border, 121
\ARG (pst-rrgtrees), *660*, 661
args Option (pst-solides3d), *392*, *393*, *396*, 410–415
args value (pst-solides3d), *414*
arm Option (pst-node), 227, *230*, 230, 242, 243
armA Option (pst-node), 227, *230*, 230, 244, 245, 248, 249
armAngle Option (uml), *657*
armB Option (pst-node), 227, *230*, 230, 244, 245, 248, 249
array (PostScript), 212, 841, 843
array env., 258, 261
\arraycolsep rigid length, 260
arrayjob package, 174
\arraystretch, 260, 645
Arrestor, 450
\Arrestor (pst-circ), 450
arrow, 49, 91, 98
    hook, 98

(cont.)
    inner, 99
arrow line, 449
ArrowA (PostScript), *137*
ArrowB (PostScript), *137*
ArrowFill Option (pstricks-add), 100, *102*
arrowinset Option (pstricks), 92, *94*, 94
ArrowInside Option (pstricks-add), 100, *101*, *102*
ArrowInsideNo Option (pstricks-add), 100, *102*
ArrowInsideOffset Option (pstricks-add), 100, *101*, *102*
ArrowInsidePos Option (pstricks-add), 100, *102*
arrowlength Option (pstricks), 92, *94*, 94
\arrowLine (pst-optic), *693*, *694*, *697*
\arrows (pstricks), **137**, *138*
arrows Option (pstricks), 44, 49, *91*, 92, *94–96*, 214
arrowscale Option (pstricks), 92, *96*, 96, *98*, *102*, *182*
arrowsize Option (pstricks), 92, *94*, 94, *96*
ASCII, 842
Asia, 490
asia Option (pst-geo), 467, 489, 490
ASIN (PostScript), 520
asin (PostScript), 208
ASINH (PostScript), 520
aspectLiquide1 Option (pst-labo), 620, *631–634*, *636*, *637*
aspectLiquide2 Option (pst-labo), 620
aspectLiquide3 Option (pst-labo), 621
AspectMelange Option (pst-labo), 620, *630*, 630
astore (PostScript), 841
asymptomatic Option (pst-pdgr), 730
asymptomatic value (pst-pdgr), 730
ATAN (PostScript), 519, 520
Atan (PostScript), 845
atan (PostScript), 519, 839, 845
ATAN1 (PostScript), 845
ATANH (PostScript), 520
\AtBeginDocument, 855
attenuation, 713
attractor, 215
attribute, 652
\attributeof (pst-dbicons), *728*
AUS Option (pst-geo), 477
australia Option (pst-geo), 479
\author
    (beamer), *766*, 767
    (powerdot), *747–757*, *759*, *762*, *764*, *765*
auto value (pst-fill), 298
auto-pst-pdf package, 855
AutoCAD, 5
automatic gain control, 451
automatic mode, 295
AutoSketch, 5
.aux file extension (pst-tree), 274
AvantGarde value (pstricks), 35
axe Option
    (pst-solides3d), 400, 401, *441*

(cont.)
    (pst-spectra), 716
axecolor Option (pst-spectra), 716
axes value (pst-plot), 166, *167*, 167
axesboxed Option (pst-solides3d), *418*, 418, *419*, *420*
\axesIIID (pst-solides3d), *392*, **403**, *404*, *405*
axesstyle Option (pst-plot), 166, *167*, *168*, *174*, *185*, *190*, *337*
axesymdroite value (pst-solides3d), 412
axesympol value (pst-solides3d), 413
axewidth Option (pst-spectra), 716
axis, 166
axis value (pst-plot), 177, 180
axis division, 193
axis style, 184
axisemph Option (pst-solides3d), *404*, 404, *405*
axisnames Option (pst-solides3d), *392*, *393*, *404*, 404, *405*
Aztec code, 507

B

B value (uml), 654
b Option (pst-solides3d), 401
b value
    (pst-tree), 281
    (pst-uml), *645*
    (uml), 654
babel package, 850
Babinet, 469
\backAnimeBtn (aeb_pro), *744*
background colour, 329
ballon value (pst-labo), 619, 620, *621*, 621, 623
bar value (pst-plot), 198, *202*, 202, *203*
bar chart, 509, 510
barbotage Option (pst-labo), 620, *624*, 624, *635*, *636*
barcolsep Option (pst-bar), 510, **512**, 512
barlabelrot Option (pst-bar), 510, 513
barsep Option (pst-bar), 510, **512**
barstyle Option (pst-bar), 510, *512*
barwidth Option
    (pst-func), 532, *533*
    (pst-plot), 198, *202*, 202, *203*
base, 456
base Option (pst-solides3d), *392*, *393*, *396*, 396, *400–402*, *410*, *429–431*, 441
base line, 227, 237, 260, 265, 277, 282, 350
base packages, 8
base unit, 36
baseColor Option (pst-fractal), *668*, 668, *669–674*
baseline, 27, 28
battery, 448
\battery (pst-circ), 448
battery symbol, 450
bbd Option (pst-tree), 267, 276
BBgraf, 391
bbh Option (pst-tree), 267, 276
bbl Option (pst-tree), 267, 276
bbllx Option (pst-eps), 315

bblly Option (pst-eps), 315
bbr Option (pst-tree), 267, 276
bburx Option (pst-eps), 315
bbury Option (pst-eps), 315
beam Option (pst-optexp), *698*
becBunsen Option (pst-labo), 620, *624*, 624, *634*
becher value (pst-labo), 619, *621*, 621, 631
begin (PostScript), 841, 844
begin Option (pst-spectra), 716
beginAngle Option (pst-3dplot), 360, *364*, 364, *370*, 383
below value, 827
belowtext Option (pst-pdgr), *729*, 731
Bernstein polynomial, 524, 525
Bernstein-Bezier curve, 524
Bessel function, 529
Beta Option (pst-3dplot), 360, **361**, 374
beta Option (pst-func), 543
Beta distribution, 543
\betapn (pst-cox), 680
\betaptwo (pst-cox), 680
Bezier curve, 65, 524, 847
Bezier spline, 524
big points, 123
bind (PostScript), 841
binomial distribution, 533, 534, 537
bisectrix, 551, 575
bissectrice value (pst-solides3d), 412
bitmap font, 73
bl value (uml), *654*
blendmode, 83
blendmode Option (pstricks), 83
block value (pst-bar), 510, 511
blue value (pstricks), 45
BlueContB value (pst-osci), 713
blueEarth Option (pst-geo), 479
blur Option (pst-blur), 328, *329–332*
blurbg Option (pst-blur), 328, **329**, 329, 330
blurradius Option (pst-blur), 328, **329**, 329, 330–332
blursteps Option (pst-blur), 328, *330*
bm Option (powerdot), 756
BoldOctogon value (pstricks), 74, 75
Bonne, 469, 491
Bookman–Demi value (pstricks), 35
bookmark, 761
border Option, 355
    (pstricks), 44, **51**, *51*, 124, 250, *251*, 251
    (uml), 654
borderbottom Option (pst-barcode), 498
bordercolor Option
    (pst-geo), 479
    (pstricks), 44, **51**
borderleft Option (pst-barcode), 498
borderLine Option (uml), 655
borderright Option (pst-barcode), 498
borders Option (pst-geo), 467, *475*, 475, *478*, 479, 489, 490
bordertop Option (pst-barcode), 498

Index of Commands and Concepts (C)

(cont.)
borderwidth Option
    (pst-barcode), 498
    (pst-geo), 480
bottom value
    (pst-circ), 454
    (pst-plot), 166, 172, *173*, 173, *174*, 177, 180
bottomsep Option (powerdot), 763
bouchon Option (pst-labo), 619, *621*, 621
bounding box, 276, 313, 314, 324, 349, 854
box, 265
    height, 114
    width, 114
box height, 114
box width, 114, 227
\boxfill (pst-fill), *300*
boxfill value (pstricks), 80, **83**, *83*, 86, *297–300*
boxsep Option (pstricks), 110, *113*
boxsize Option (pst-node), 227, ***231***, 250, 251
bp, 123
\Bput (pst-node), 256
\bput (pst-node), 256
br Option (pstricks), *104, 105*
bracePos Option (pstricks-add), 591
braceWidth Option (pstricks-add), 591
braceWidthInner Option (pstricks-add), 591
braceWidthOuter Option (pstricks-add), 591
bracket width, 95
bracketlength Option (pstricks), 92, *95*, 95, *96*
brightness Option (pst-spectra), 716
bug, 847
bug list, 847
buildvector Option (pstricks-add), 611
Bunsen burner, 624, 628
burette Option (pst-labo), 620, *629*, 629
BUseVerbatim env. (fancyvrb), *773*
BVerbatim env. (fancyvrb), *773*

C

C value (pst-node), 258, 259
c Option
    (pst-fractal), 669, 673
    (pst-solides3d), 401
c value
    (pst-eucl), 552
    (pst-node), 258
    (pst-uml), *644*, 645
C–C value (pstricks), *92*
c–c value (pstricks), *92*
cadre value (pst-magneticfield), 711
calotesphere value (pst-solides3d), 429
calotespherecreuse value (pst-solides3d), 429
calottesphere value (pst-solides3d), *398*
calottespherecreuse value (pst-solides3d), *399*
canada Option (pst-geo), 479
\cancel (cancel), 593
capacitor, 449

\capacitor (pst-circ), 449, *452, 453*, 455, *456*
capital Option (pst-geo), 479, 488, 490
capitals Option (pst-geo), 467, 474, *475*, *478*, 479
cardioid curve, 608
caret symbol, 502
\Cartesian (pstricks), 145
Cartesian coordinate system, 31
Cartesian coordinates, 145
cc-cc value (pstricks), *92*
CC1 Option (pst-osci), 712
CC2 Option (pst-osci), 713
ccslope value (pst-grad), *321*
ccslopes value (pst-grad), *321*, 321, *325*
ccurve value (pst-plot), 198, 200
ceiling (PostScript), 208, 839
center env., 857
\centering, 857
central projection, 338
centre, 573
centre of area, 573
centre of ellipse, 63
centric dilation, 571
cercle value (pst-solides3d), *414*
.cfg file extension, 4
\CGravABC (pst-eucl), 573
chanfrein Option (pst-solides3d), *434*
chanfreincoeff Option (pst-solides3d), *434*
ChangeOrder Option
    (pst-plot), 218, 222
    (pstricks-add), *617*
charpath (PostScript), 841
chartColor Option (pstricks-add), 587
chartstyle Option (pst-bar), ***510***, 510, *511*
\ChauffageBallon (pst-labo), *627*, *628*
check digit, 501
checkfile Option (pst-eps), 315
chemical value (pst-circ), 455
choice Option (pst-cox), 681
CIA database, 487, 489
Circle value (pst-node), 258, 259
circle, 23, 57, 63, 383, 449, 567, 577
    arc, 61, 62, 124, 144, 364, 383, 559, 568
    circle sector, 63
    circle segment, 61
    sector of a circle, 23
circle value (pst-node), 258, 259
circlecolor Option (pst-geo), 480
\circledipole (pst-circ), 449, 450
\Circlenode (pst-node), 259, 277
\circlenode (pst-node), ***239***, 239, *244*, *245*, *247*, 259, 277
\circlenode* (pst-node), 239
circles Option (pst-geo), 479
circlesep Option (pst-geo), 480
circlewidth Option (pst-geo), 480
CircMultiply value (demo), 73
\CircMultiply (demo), *73*
CircPlus value (demo), 73

(C)   Index of Commands and Concepts

(cont.)
\CircPlus (demo), *73*
circular colour gradients, 317
circulator, 451
\circulator (pst-circ), 451
circumcircle, 574
city Option (pst-geo), 467, 474, *475*, *477*, 478, *479*, 488, 490
citys Option (pst-geo), 479
\CLAUSE (pst-rrgtrees), *660*, 661
clear (PostScript), 841
clearAnimeBtn Option (aeb_pro), 744
clip (PostScript), 841
\clipbox (pstricks), **114**, 114, *115*
Clipping, 114
clipping, 25, 115, 121, 295, 521
        path, 292
clipping path, 291
clockwise, 62, 64
closed curve, 68, 124
\closedshadow
        (pst-blur), 328
        (pstricks), 132, ***133***, 133
\closepath (pstricks), *75*, *128*, 128, *133*
closepath (PostScript), 128, 841
cluster value (pst-bar), 510
CLW (PostScript), 844
CM (PostScript), 844
cm value (demo), 96
cm-> value (demo), *96*
cm-cm value (demo), *96*
cm-cp value (demo), *96*
\CMPL (pst-rrgtrees), 660
CMYK, 9, 430, 841
\Cnode (pst-node), *228–231*, 238, **239**, *239*, 259, 277, *849*
\cnode (pst-node), 113, *114*, *229*, *232–236*, **238**, *238*, 238, *244–246*, *254–257*, 277, *311*
\Cnode* (pst-node), 239
\cnode* (pst-node), 238
\cnodeput (pst-node), *239*
\cnodeput* (pst-node), 239
coastcolor Option (pst-geo), 479
coasts Option (pst-geo), 479
coastwidth Option (pst-geo), 480
\code (pstricks), **135**, *135*, 135, *136–138*, **154**, 156, 217
CodeFig Option (pst-eucl), 552, *558*, 558, *559*, 561, 570, *571*, *572*, 573–575, 578
CodeFigA Option (pst-eucl), 552
CodeFigAarc Option (pst-eucl), 552, 559
CodeFigB Option (pst-eucl), 552
CodeFigBarc Option (pst-eucl), 552, 559
CodeFigColor Option (pst-eucl), 552, 558, *570*, 570, *571*, *572*, 573, *575*, 575
CodeFigStyle Option (pst-eucl), 552, 558, *559*, 570, 573, 575
codejps Option (pst-solides3d), *745*
coeff Option (pst-func), 520, *521*, *523*, *524*, *526*, 527

(cont.)
coefficient, 520, 527
coil, 304, 449
\coil (pst-circ), 449, *450*, 455
coilarm Option (pst-coil), *146*, 304, **306**, *306*
coilarm value (pst-coil), 310
coilarmA Option (pst-coil), 304, *306*, 306
coilarmB Option (pst-coil), 304, 306
coilaspect Option (pst-coil), 304, ***306***, 306
coilheight Option (pst-coil), 303, ***305***, *309–312*
coilinc Option (pst-coil), 304, ***307***, 307
coilwidth Option (pst-coil), *146*, 303, **304**, *304*, 305, *311*
collector, 456
Collignon, 469, 472
Color Option (pst-fractal), 672, 673
\color, 9, **10**, ***11***, *12*, *13*, *15*, 313
        (xcolor), 11, *13*, *16*, *18*, *19*, 19
color package, 6, 7, 9, 11, 15, 154, 318, 322
color1 Option (pst-solides3d), 431
color2 Option (pst-solides3d), 431
color3 Option (pst-solides3d), 431
color4 Option (pst-solides3d), 431
\colorbox (xcolor), **15**, 17, ***19***, 19
colorCenters Option (pst-cox), 680
\colorlet (xcolor), ***12***, 12, *13*
colorMode Option (pst-diffraction), 704
colorsets, 13
colortbl package, 10
colorVertices Option (pst-cox), 680
colour, 8, 79, 123
        CMYK, 9
        colour expression, 17
        convert, 20
        definition, 9
        HSB, 9, 317
        model, 20
        PSTricks syntax, 6
        RGB, 9, 317
        xcolor syntax, 6
colour gradients, 13
colour model
        CMYK, 14, 20
        HSB, 14, 20
        HTML, 20
        RGB, 14, 20
colour pattern, 295
Colour series, 13
colours, 45
colsep Option
        (powerdot), 763
        (pst-node), 258, *259*, *260*, 260, *261*, *262*
combine Option (pst-osci), 713
comma Option (pst-plot), 176, *179*, 179
command file, 151
comment Option (uml), *658*
commutative diagrams, 255
compatibility, 5

Index of Commands and Concepts (D)

(cont.)
\composeSolid (pst-solides3d), 440
concat (PostScript), 841
concatmatrix (PostScript), 841
condition Option (pst-pdgr), 730, 731
cone value (pst-solides3d), *393*, *394*, *397*, 429
conecreux value (pst-solides3d), *397*, 429
conn Option (pst-optexp), *698*
connecting line, 279
connection, 449, 648
constI Option (pst-func), 529
constII Option (pst-func), 529
content Option (powerdot), 761
continent, 490
contrast Option (pst-diffraction), 703, 704
\convertcolorspec, 20
    (xcolor), *20*
\coor (pstricks), *136*
coordinate axis, 166, 361
coordinate grid, 35–37
coordinate origin, 24, 132, 167, 168
coordinate plane, 374
coordinate system, 132, 295, 359
    Cartesian, 31, 38, 358
    three-dimensional, 358
    two-dimensional, 358
coordinates, 22, 136, 253
    Cartesian, 145
    polar, 145
coorType Option (pst-3dplot), 375, *376*
copy (PostScript), 841
\CORE (pst-rrgtrees), *660*, 661
Corners Option (pst-ob3d), 346, *347*, 347
Corners=true Option (pst-ob3d), 347
CornersColor Option (pst-ob3d), 346, *347*
cornersize Option (pstricks), 44, **51**, 54
CornersLength Option (pst-ob3d), 346, 347
Cornu, 614
COS (PostScript), 520
cos (PostScript), 208, 211, 839
cosCoeff Option (pst-func), 527
COSH (PostScript), 520
cosine, 32
cosine function, 210
CouleurDistillat Option (pst-labo), 620, *630*, 630
couleurReactifBurette Option (pst-labo), 620, 629, *630*, 637
count (PostScript), 841
counter clockwise, 61
counttomark (PostScript), 841
coupler, 452
\coupler (pst-circ), 452, 455
couplerstyle Option (pst-circ), 446, 455
courbe value (pst-solides3d), *401*, 401, *438*
courbeR2 value (pst-solides3d), *416*
CourbeR2+ (PostScript), *437*
Courier value (pstricks), 35

\CoxeterCoordinates (pst-cox), **681**, 681, *682*, *683*
CP (PostScript), 844
cp value (demo), 96
\cput (pstricks), **108**, 112, 239
\cput* (pstricks), 108
crosshatch value (pstricks), 80, 84–86, 89
crosshatch* value (pstricks), 80
crystal value (pst-circ), 454
CSV, 514
CTM, 841, 842, 844
cube, 347, 422
cube value (pst-solides3d), *394*, *396*, 429
cuboid, 422
current, 205
current arrows, 453
current point, 127
current source, 449, 450
currentcmykcolor (PostScript), 841
currentgray (PostScript), 841
currenthsbcolor (PostScript), 841
currentlinewidth (PostScript), 841
currentmatrix (PostScript), 841
currentpoint (PostScript), 841
currentrgbcolor (PostScript), 841
currentsection value (powerdot), 761
CurvAbsNeg Option (pst-eucl), 553, *562*, 562, 569
curvature Option (pstricks), 57, **58**, 58, *59*, *60*, 199, 200
curve, 57, 58
    closed, 236
curve value
    (pst-eucl), *557*
    (pst-plot), 198, 199, 214
CurveAbsNeg Option (pst-eucl), *569*
curved value (pst-circ), 455
\curveto (pstricks), *129*, 134, **135**, *135*, 135
curveto (PostScript), 212, 842
CurveType Option (pst-eucl), 552, *557*, 557, *564*
cvi (PostScript), 839
cvn (PostScript), 842
cvr (PostScript), 839
cvs (PostScript), 842
cvx (PostScript), 842
cx Option (pst-fractal), 668
cy Option (pst-fractal), 668
cyan value
    (pst-eucl), 558
    (pstricks), *48*, *53*
cylinder, 442
cylindre value (pst-solides3d), *397*, 429, *441*
cylindrecreux value (pst-solides3d), *393*, *394*, *397*, *402*, 429
cylindric projection, 470

D

D (PostScript), 213
D value
    (pst-tree), 266

(pstricks), 110
d Option (pst-diffraction), 707
damping1 Option (pst-osci), 712, *715*, *716*
damping2 Option (pst-osci), 713, *715*, *716*
\dash (pstricks), *48*
dash Option (pstricks), 43, **47**, *47*, *48*, *122*
dashed value
    (pst-3dplot), 369
    (pst-eucl), 558
    (pstricks), 43, *45*, 47, 52, 124, 177, 186, 857
\Data (demo), *213*, 213
data, 212
\data (demo), *514*, 514
data matrix, 506
data set, 358
\dataplot (pst-plot), 165, **212**, ***215***, 215, 218
\dataplot* (pst-plot), 212
\dataplotThreeD (pst-3dplot), ***390***, 390, *391*
\date
    (beamer), *766*, *767*
    (powerdot), *747–757*, *759*, *762*, *764*, *765*
datfile value (pst-solides3d), *403*
Day Option (pst-geo), 478
\day (pst-calendar), 733
day Option (pst-calendar), 733
daynight Option (pst-geo), 479
deactivatecolor Option (pst-solides3d), 431
deceased Option (pst-pdgr), *729*, 730, 731
DeclareAnime Option (aeb_pro), 744
\DeclareFixedFont, 290, *292*, *293*, *586*, *732*
\DeclareNewPSOperator (infix-RPN), **666**, 667
Decran Option
    (pst-geo), 478, 490
    (pst-solides3d), 392, 393, *428*, *429*
\def, 163, 279
def (PostScript), 263, 842, 844
default Option (uml), *656*
default value (pst-eucl), 551, 552
defaultmatrix (PostScript), 842
\defFunction
    (pst-dolides3d), *784*
    (pst-solides3d), **415**, 415, *441–444*
\definecolor (xcolor), **12**, *12*, **13**, *13*, 15, *19*, **20**, *20*, 37
\definecolorseries (xcolor), **13**, *13*, 13, **14**, *14*, **15**, 15, *16*
\definecolorset (xcolor), *13*
\defineTColor (pstricks-add), *89*
definitio Option (pst-solides3d), 411
definition Option (pst-solides3d), *396*, 410–412, *413*, 413, *414*, 414, *415*
definition interval, 203
\DefList
    (pst-asr), *663*
    (pst-qtree), *664*, *665*
deg (PostScript), *156*
degree, 205, 840
\degrees (pstricks), ***23***, 140, 145
DegtoRad (PostScript), 530, 845

(cont.)
delay angle, 205
depth, 103, 271, 282
Derivation Option (pst-func), 520, **521**, *523*
derivative, 607
Derive Option (pstricks-add), *607*, 607, *608*, 608, *609*
derived function, 608
detector, 450
\detector (pst-circ), 450
dia value (pst-node), 258, 259
diamcercle value (pst-solides3d), 414
Diameter Option (pst-eucl), 552, 560, *561*, 577–579
diameter, 304
DiameterA Option (pst-eucl), 552, 560
DiameterB Option (pst-eucl), 552, 560
diamond, 55, 113
\dianode (pst-node), **240**, 259, 277
\dianode* (pst-node), 240
dict (PostScript), 843
differential equation, 529, 610–612
diffraction pattern, 703
DiffusionBleue value (pst-labo), 630, *633*
\dim (pstricks), 135, ***136***, 136
dimen Option (pstricks), 44, ***49***, 49
dimension Option (pst-cox), *680*, 680, *681–683*
\ding (pifont), 69, *106*, *353*
diode, 449
\diode (pst-circ), 449, 455
Dipole, 448
dipole, 448
dipoleconvention Option (pst-circ), 446, 453
dipolestyle Option (pst-circ), 446, 454, 455, *456*, *457*, 457
direct value (powerdot), 764
directconvention Option (pst-circ), 446, 452, 453
directional value (pst-circ), 455
Dirichlet function, 545
display Option (powerdot), 754
displaymath env., 854
\displaystyle, 109, 118, 170, 178
Dissolve value (powerdot), *755*
distance, 272
DistCoef Option (pst-eucl), 553, 560, *561*, 561, 563, 567, 569, *571*, 571, 577, 579
Distiller, 8, 79, 83, 87, 89
dIter Option (pst-fractal), *668*, 668, *669–674*
Div (PostScript), 667, 845
div (PostScript), 839
dividend, 582
division, 582
divisor, 582
D1 Option (pst-spectra), 716
dmax Option (demo), 213
dmin Option (demo), 213
Dobs Option (pst-geo), 478, 490
\DoCoordinate (demo), *213*
documentation, 858

Index of Commands and Concepts (E)

(cont.)
dodecahedron, 735
dodecahedron value (pst-solides3d), *399*
\DontKillGlue (pstricks), 30, 152, **153**
dot, 69, 72
dot value (pst-node), 258, 259
dot matrix, 76
dotangle Option (pstricks), 69, 71, *72*
dotmatrix (PostScript), 616
\dotnode (pst-node), 240, **241**, 259, 277
dots value (pst-plot), *198*
dotscale Option (pstricks), 48, 50, 69, 70, *71*, 71, *72*, *141*, *146*, *213*, 240, *377*, 522, *596*
dotsep Option (pstricks), 44, **48**
dotsize Option (pstricks), 48, 50, 69, *71*, 71, *72*, *73*, 240, *378*
dotstyle Option (pstricks), 69, *71*, *72*, 72, *73*, *377*, 522
dotted value (pstricks), 43, *45*, **48**, 48, 52, 124, 177, 186
doublecolor Option, 355
    (pstricks), 44, **48**, *60*, *61*
doubleline Option, 355
    (pstricks), 44, **48**, *50*, 51, *89*, *108*, 124
doublesep Option (pstricks), 44, **48**, *60*, *61*
doubleset Option (pstricks), 48
doubletube Option (pst-labo), 620, *627*, 627, *635*, *636*
\dp, 42, 148, 281
draw value (pst-solides3d), 393, *428*, 428
draw* value (pst-solides3d), *428*, 428
draw** value (pst-solides3d), *428*, 428, *432*, *433*, 441
drawcenters Option (pst-cox), 680
DrawCirABC Option (pst-eucl), 552, *560*, 560, *574*, 574, 575
drawCoor Option (pst-3dplot), 360, *361*, 361, 377, *378*, *382*, *383*, *385*
\drawedge (gastex), *725*
drawedges Option (pst-cox), 680
drawing Option
    (pst-3dplot), 360, *361*, 361
    (pst-optic), *691*, *692*
\drawloop (gastex), *725*
drawSelf Option (pst-magneticfield), 710
drawStyle Option (pst-3dplot), 360, 366, *367*, *368*, *387*
drawvertices Option (pst-cox), 680
droite value (pst-solides3d), *415*
dtransform (PostScript), 842
dup (PostScript), 211, 386, 839
dvi program, 287
dvips Option (xcolor), 9
dvips program, 9, 11, 12, 155, 156, 209, 287, 290, 313, 314, 766, 851, 856
dvipsnames Option (xcolor), 9
dvipsone program, 156
Dx Option
    (pst-3dplot), 362
    (pst-plot), 166, *168*, 168, *169*, 169, *170*
    (pstricks-add), *610*
Dx value (pst-plot), *174*

dx Option (pst-plot), 166, *169*, 169, *170*
Dy Option
    (pst-3dplot), 362
    (pst-plot), 166, 168, *169*, *170*
Dy value (pst-plot), *174*
dy Option (pst-plot), 166, *169*, 169, *170*
Dz Option (pst-3dplot), 362
dZero Option (pst-func), 520, 522

E

earth, 448, 465
ecurve value (pst-plot), 198, 200
ED (PostScript), 263, 844
edge Option (pst-tree), 267, *274*, 274, 275, *284*, 284
edge length, 422
edge trimming, 424
\EdgeL (vaucanson-g), *726*
edges, 434
elektor value (pst-circ), 455
elektorchemical value (pst-circ), 455
elektorcurved value (pst-circ), 455
element Option (pst-spectra), 716, 717, *718*
ellipse, 57, 63, 64, 113, 359, 383, 544
    3D, 383
    arc, 364
    centre, 383
ellipse sector, 65
embedangle Option (pst-3d), 341, **344**
emission Option (pst-spectra), 716
emission spectrum, 716, 717
emitter, 456
emnode Option (pst-node), 258, **259**
\End (pst-rrgtrees), 661
end (PostScript), 842, 844
end Option (pst-spectra), 716
endAngle Option (pst-3dplot), 360, *364*, 364, 383
endbox Option (pst-optexp), *698*
endfading Option (pst-grad), 322, **326**
\endoverlaybox (pstricks), 147
\endpscharclip (pst-text), 291
\endpsclip (pstricks), 115, 116
\endpsgraph (pstricks-add), 602
\endpsmatrix (pst-node), 258
\endpspicture (pstricks), 24
\endpspicture* (pstricks), 24
\endpsTree (pst-tree), 265
\endskiplevels (pst-tree), 284
\endTeXtoEPS (pst-eps), 314
endX Option (makeplot), *683*
endY Option (makeplot), *683*
english value (pst-calendar), 733
\entity (pst-dbicons), *728*
Entity Relationship, 728
envelope Option (pst-func), 525
eofill (PostScript), 75, 842
eofill value (pstricks), 80, 81, *777*
epicentre, 484

epicycloid, 674
epstool program, 854
epstopdf program, 851
epsZero Option (pst-func), 520, 522
eq (PostScript), 842
eqnarray env., 854
equation value (pst-solides3d), *396*, 410, *413*, *415*
equation notation, 418
equivalent circuit, 450
erlen value (pst-labo), 619, 620, *621*, 621, *634*
error, 8
error message, 67, 68
etiquette Option (pst-labo), 620, *623*, 623
Euler, 612
Euler (PostScript), 845
euler (PostScript), *156*
euler value (pstricks-add), 611
Europe, 490
europe Option (pst-geo), 467, 489, 490, *494*
evaluated Option (pst-pdgr), 730
\everypsbox (pstricks), *118*
exch (PostScript), 263, *612*, 839, 844
exclusive or, 844
exec (PostScript), 842
exit (PostScript), 842, 843
EXP (PostScript), 520
exp (PostScript), 839
expansion, 154
expected value, 518, 538
exponential notation, 204
extsizes package, 754

F

f Option (pst-diffraction), 703, 704
f value (pst-node), 258, 259
face value (pst-solides3d), *401*
faces Option (pst-solides3d), *403*, 403, *439*, 439, *440*
fact (PostScript), 208
fading Option (pst-grad), 322, *326*, 326
false value (powerdot), 761
\FanEnd (pst-rrgtrees), *660*, 661
fansize Option (pst-tree), 266, *267*, 267
Farbe
    black, 8, 10
    blue, 8, 10, 13, 17
    chartFillColor1, 588
    chartFillColor2, 588
    cyan, 8, 10
    darkgray, 8
    gradbegin, 318
    gradend, 319
    gray, 8, 511
    green, 8, 10, 13
    lightgray, 8, 511
    magenta, 8, 10
    red, 8, 10, 13, 17
    white, 8, 10, 133, 373

    yellow, 8, 10
fb package, 738
\fbox, 19, *28*, 28, 109, 118, 313, 314
\fboxrule rigid length, 19
\fboxsep rigid length, 19, 110, 112, 313
fcol Option
    (pst-dolides3d), *784*
    (pst-solides3d), 442–444
\fcolorbox (xcolor), *17*, **19**, *19*
female Option (pst-pdgr), *729*, 730
female value (pst-pdgr), 731
\FHexagon (demo), *299*
figure, 147
\file (pstricks), *137*
file Option (pst-solides3d), *403*
file value (powerdot), 764
filecontents env., 137
filecontents* env., 509
\fileplot (pst-plot), 165, **212**, **214**, 214, *215*, 215
\fileplot* (pst-plot), 212
\fileplotThreeD (pst-3dplot), *390*
Files and File Extensions
    cities.tex, 475
    data1.csv (demo), 513
    dataError.dat (demo), 213
    example-pics.pdf (demo), 852, 853
    example-pics.ps (demo), 852, 853
    example.dvi (demo), 852
    example.tex (demo), 852, 853
    figure (demo), 851
    file.ps (demo), 137
    latex.ltx, 154
    pst-3dplot.pro, *152*, 845
    pst-algparser.pro, *152*, 845
    pst-bar.pro, *152*, 845
    pst-barcode.pro, *152*, 497
    pst-barcode.tex, 498
    pst-blur.pro, *152*, 845
    pst-circ.pro, *152*
    pst-coil.pro, *152*, 845
    pst-coxcoor.pro (pst-cox), 681
    pst-dots.pro, 72, *152*
    pst-dots.pro (pstricks), 74
    pst-eucl.pro, *152*, 845
    pst-fill.tex, 295
    pst-fractal.pro, *152*, 845
    pst-fun.pro, *152*, 845
    pst-func.pro, *152*, 845
    pst-grad.pro, *152*, 846
    pst-laboObj.tex, 619
    pst-light3d.pro, *152*, 846
    pst-map3d.pro, 845
    pst-map3dII.pro, 845
    pst-math.pro, *152*
    pst-mirror.pro, *152*
    pst-node.pro, *152*, 846
    pst-optexp.pro, 846

Index of Commands and Concepts (F)

(cont.)
  pst-pdf.cfg, 855
  pst-slpe.pro, *152*, 846
  pst-spectra.pro, *152*, 846
  pst-text.pro, *152*, 846
  pstricks-add.pro, *152*, 739, 845
  pstricks.con, 4, 155
  pstricks.pro, *152*, 155, 157, 158, 263, 844, 845, 857
  pstricks.pro (pstricks), **156**, 667
  pstricks.sty, 5, 7, 9, 118
  pstricks.sty (pstricks), 79
  pstricks.tex, 7, 9, 118, 857
  pstricks.tex (pstricks), 79
  pstricks97.pro, *152*
  README, 5
  sfg.sty, 727
  solides.pro, *152*, 846
  solides3d.pro (pst-solides3d), 435
  vtex.cfg, 155
  xcolor.pro, 9
Fill Option (pst-geo), 467, *474*, 474
\fill (pstricks), 128, *129*, 129
fill (PostScript), 75, 842
filling, 295
fill area, 86
fill colour, 80
fill style, 79, 80, 84–86, 317
  hiddenStyle, 366
fillangle Option (pst-fill), 296, **297**
fillcolor Option (pstricks), 22, *61*, *80*, 80, *81*, *82*, *88*, 111, 133, 591
fillcolor value (pstricks), 81
fillcycle Option (pst-fill), 296, *297*, 298
fillcyclex Option (pst-fill), 296, **297**, *297*, *298*, *301*
fillcycley Option (pst-fill), 296, **297**, *297*, *298*
fillloopadd Option (pst-fill), 296, *299*, 299, *300*
fillloopaddx Option (pst-fill), 296
fillloopaddy Option (pst-fill), 296
fillmove Option (pst-fill), 296, **298**
fillmovex Option (pst-fill), 296, *298*, 298
fillmovey Option (pst-fill), 296, *298*, 298
fillsep Option (pst-fill), 296, **297**, 297
fillsepx Option (pst-fill), 296, *297*, 297
fillsepy Option (pst-fill), 296, *297*, 297
fillsize Option (pst-fill), 296, **298**, *299*
fillstyle Option
  (pst-grad), 317, *320*, *322*
  (pstricks), 22, *56*, *61*, *80*, 80, 81–87, *123*, 123, *126–128*, *297–300*, *318*, *319*, 320, *336*, *337*, 380, *516*
filter, 449
\filter (pst-circ), 449
findfont (PostScript), *216*, 842
fioleJauge value (pst-labo), 619, *621*, 621
flacon value (pst-labo), 619, *621*, 621
flash animation, 745
flip-flop, 461

(cont.)
floating environment, 257
floating-point arithmetic, 168, 603
floating-point number, 582
floor (PostScript), 208, 839
Flower value (demo), 73
\Flower (demo), *73*
fluid Option (pst-pad), 722
FluidFillColor Option (pst-pad), *723*
FluidHeight Option (pst-pad), *723*
FluidLineColor Option (pst-pad), *723*
FluidLineWidth Option (pst-pad), *723*
FluidMaxRadius Option (pst-pad), *723*
FluidMinRadius Option (pst-pad), *723*
\fmark (gastex), 725
\fnode (pst-node), 228, *229*, **241**, *241*, 241, 259, 277
\fnode* (pst-node), 241
\focalPoint (demo), 161
\focalpoint (demo), 162
focus Option (pst-optic), *689*, *690*
font Option (pst-barcode), 498
fonts
  AvantGard (pst-func), 531
  Bookman (pst-func), 531
  Courier (pst-func), 531
  Helvetica (pst-func), 531
  PSTricksDotFont (pstricks), 72–74
  Symbol (pstricks), 73
  Times-Roman (pst-func), 531
  ZapfDingbats (pstricks), 69, *73*, 73
fontscale Option (pst-func), 531
fontsize Option (pst-solides3d), 410
\footnotesize, 178
for (PostScript), 842
forall (PostScript), 842
formation of shadows, 334
forwardAnimeBtn Option (aeb_pro), 744
Fourier Option (pst-osci), 713
Fourier analysis, 713
Fourier sum, 527
fraction Option (uml), 657
frame Option (pst-plot), 184
frame value (pst-plot), 166, *167*, 167, *185*
framearc Option (pstricks), 44, **50**, *51*, 51, 54, *89*, *111*, *112*, 112
\FrameBoxThreeD (pst-fr3d), *355–357*
FrameBoxThreeDBrightnessDistance Option (pst-fr3d), 355, *356*, 356, *357*
FrameBoxThreeDColorHSB Option (pst-fr3d), 355, 355, *356*, 356, *357*
FrameBoxThreeDOn Option (pst-fr3d), 355, 355, 356, *357*
FrameBoxThreeDopposite Option (pst-fr3d), 355
FrameBoxThreeDopposite Option (pst-fr3d), *355*
FrameBoxThreeDOpposite=true Option (pst-fr3d), 355
framesep Option (pstricks), *110*, 110, *112*, 112
framesize Option (pst-node), 227, 228, *229*, 241
france Option (pst-geo), 479

(cont.)
french value
    (pst-calendar), 733
    (pst-circ), 457
freqmod1 Option (pst-osci), 712
freqmod2 Option (pst-osci), 713
\freqmult (pst-circ), 449
frequency modulation factor, 713
Fresnel, 614
friction system, 722
frsep Option (powerdot), 763
FSphereFillColor Option (pst-pad), 723
FSphereHeight Option (pst-pad), 723
FSphereLineColor Option (pst-pad), 723
FSphereLineWidth Option (pst-pad), 723
full value (pst-plot), 166, 172, 177
full circle, 23, 140
function, 418, 531, 607
    algebraic expression, 207
    derivative, 607
    three-dimensional, 358
    value, 666
function Option
    (pst-coil), 304, *309*, 309
    (pst-solides3d), 401, 402, 410, *438*
function expression, 203
fusion value (pst-solides3d), *402*, 402, *438*, 441
future value (powerdot), 761
futuresections value (powerdot), 761

G

GAMMA (PostScript), 520
gamma Option (pst-spectra), 716
GAMMALN (PostScript), 519, 520
\gammapn (pst-cox), *680*, 680, *681–683*
\gammaptwo (pst-cox), 680
gangle Option (pstricks), 44, 55, *56*, 56
gastex package, 724, **725**, 725
GAUSS (PostScript), *518*, 520
Gaussian, 538
Gaussian distribution, 538
ge (PostScript), 842
GenCurvFirst Option (pst-eucl), 553, 562, *563*
GenCurvInc Option (pst-eucl), 553, 562, 569
GenCurvLast Option (pst-eucl), 553, 562
generator value (pst-circ), 453
geode value (pst-solides3d), *402*
geometry, 571
german value (pst-eucl), 552, 556
get (PostScript), 842
\GetCoordinates (demo), *213*
GhostScript program, 83
ghostscript program, 79, 87, 852
glassType Option (pst-labo), 619, *621*, 621, *622*, *623*, *627*, *631*, 631, *633*, 633, *634*, *636*, 637
glassType=becher Option (pst-labo), 637
glue, 152

gnuplot program, 204
Gouraud shading, 739
grad Option (xcolor), 14
gradangle Option (pst-grad), 318, **319**, *320*
gradbegin Option (pst-grad), *318*, 319
gradbegin value (pst-grad), 318
gradend Option (pst-grad), 318, *319*, 319, *320*
gradend value (pst-grad), 318
gradient, 607, 610
gradient value (pst-grad), 317, **321**
GradientCircle Option (pst-grad), 318, ***320***
gradientHSB Option (pst-grad), 318, ***320***
GradientPos Option (pst-grad), 318, ***320***
GradientScale Option (pst-grad), 318, *320*, 320
gradlines Option (pst-grad), 318, **319**
gradmidpoint Option (pst-grad), 318, *319*
graphics format, 148
GraphicsRef Option (pst-eps), 315
graphicx package, 117, 118, 853
grayness Option (uml), 654
green value (pst-solides3d), 425
GreenContA value (pst-osci), 712
\grestore (pstricks), *129*, 129, *130*, 130, 132, 134
grestore (PostScript), 116, 154–156, *216*, 842
greyscale, 8
grid, 147, 352
grid Option (pst-solides3d), *395*, 418
grid lines, 418
gridcolor Option (pstricks), 33, *34*, 34, *107*
griddots Option (pstricks), 33, *34*, 34, *352*
gridfont Option (pstricks), 35
\gridI (demo), *37*
\gridIIID (pst-solides3d), **405**, 405, *406*, *407*
gridlabelcolor Option (pstricks), 33, *35*, 35
gridlabels Option
    (pst-plot), *215*
    (pstricks), 33, *34*, 34, *108*, *214*, *216*
gridmap Option (pst-geo), 479
gridmapcolor Option (pst-geo), 480
gridmapdiv Option (pst-geo), 479
gridmapwidth Option (pst-geo), 480
gridstyle Option (pstricks), 30
gridstyle value (pstricks), 29, 37
GridThreeDNodes Option (pst-gr3d), *351*
GridThreeDXPos Option (pst-gr3d), 348, *350*, 350
GridThreeDXUnit Option (pst-gr3d), 348, *350*, 350
GridThreeDYPos Option (pst-gr3d), 348, *350*, 350
GridThreeDYUnit Option (pst-gr3d), 348, *350*, 350
GridThreeDZPos Option (pst-gr3d), 348, *350*, 350
GridThreeDZUnit Option (pst-gr3d), 348, *350*, 350
GridThreeNodes Option (pst-gr3d), 348
gridwidth Option (pstricks), 33, *34*, 352
grille value
    (pst-magneticfield), 711
    (pst-solides3d), *392*, *393*, 393, *394*, *396*, 396, *430*
groundstyle Option (pst-circ), 446, 454
\gsave (pstricks), *129*, 129, *130*, 130, 132, 134

Index of Commands and Concepts (H–I)

gsave (PostScript), 116, 154–156, *216*, 842
gt (PostScript), 842
GTO value (pst-circ), 455
guardwhitespace Option (pst-barcode), *499*

H

H value (pstricks-add), 98
h Option
  (pst-diffraction), 709
  (pst-solides3d), 397, 398, 400, 401, *402*, 402
h value (pstricks-add), 98
Hénon, 215
handout, 754
handout value (powerdot), 754
hatchangle Option (pstricks), 80, *81*, 81, *82*, *86*, 86
hatchcolor Option (pstricks), 80, *81*, *82*, 82, *83*, *86*, 86
hatchsep Option (pstricks), 80, 84, *85*, 85, *86*, 87
hatchsepinc Option (pstricks), 80, *85*, 85
hatchwidth Option (pstricks), 80, 85
hatchwidthinc Option (pstricks), 80, 85, *86*
header Option
  (pst-bar), **510**, 514
  (pstricks), 151
header file, 158
headerfile Option (pst-eps), 315
headers Option (pst-eps), 315
height, 103, 271, 282
height Option (pst-barcode), 498, *499*
Helvetica, 35
Helvetica value (pstricks), 35
Helvetica-Narrow value (pstricks), 35
hexagon, 299
Hg value (pst-spectra), 717
hidden value (powerdot), 761
hidden line, 391
hidden line algorithm, 386
hiddenLine Option (pst-3dplot), 360, 386
hiddenLine=true Option (pst-3dplot), 366
hiddenStyle Option (pst-3dplot), 366
high-level command, 160
high-level objects, 445
\hinge (pst-stru), *719*
histogram, 509
\hline (pst-uml), 642, 644
hlines value (pstricks), 80, **82**, 84–86
hlines* value (pstricks), 80
hollow Option (pst-solides3d), *432*, *433*, 433, *437*, *439*, 439
HomCoef Option (pst-eucl), 552, *560*, 560, *572*, 572
homothety, 571
hompol value (pst-solides3d), 412, 413
hooklength Option (pstricks-add), *98*, 98, *99*
hookwidth Option (pstricks-add), *98*, 98, *99*
horizontal mode, 109
horizontale value (pst-solides3d), 411, *415*
hour Option (pst-geo), 478
href Option (pst-node), 227

HSB, 9, 317, 320, 429, 430, 841
HSB colour model, 356
\ht, 42, 42, 148, 281
  (pstricks), 42
hue Option (pst-solides3d), *395*, 425, *429*, 429, *430*, 430, *431*
hyperref package, 10

I

iangle Option (gastex), *725*
\IBox (demo), 148
\Icc (pst-circ), 449
icosahedron value (pst-solides3d), *399*
idiv (PostScript), 839
idtransform (PostScript), 842, 843
if (PostScript), 842
\ifcase, 174
ifelse (PostScript), 842
\ifpsshadow (pstricks), *160*
IfTE (PostScript), 208, *209*, 209
ignoreLines Option (pst-plot), *218*
\ignorespaces (pstricks), *160*
IIID Option (pst-diffraction), 704
IIIDlabels Option (pst-3dplot), 360
IIIDticks Option (pst-3dplot), 360, *362*, 362, *384*
IIIDxticksep Option (pst-3dplot), 362
IIIDxTicksPlane Option (pst-3dplot), 360, 362
IIIDyticksep Option (pst-3dplot), *362*
IIIDyTicksPlane Option (pst-3dplot), 360, *362*, 362
IIIDzticksep Option (pst-3dplot), *362*
IIIDzTicksPlane Option (pst-3dplot), 360, 362
\imark (gastex), *725*
Imin Option (pst-spectra), 716
importedFrom Option (uml), *658*
includecheck Option (pst-barcode), 498, 502, 503, 505
includecheckintext Option (pst-barcode), 498, 502–505
\includegraphics, 42
  (graphicx), *150*, 315, 315, *336*, 688, 852–854
includetext Option (pst-barcode), 498, *499*, 500–505
incolor Option (pst-solides3d), *418–420*, 432, 433
increment Option
  (pst-3dplot), 360, *372*, 372
  (pst-geo), 467, *473*, 473, 478, 479, 488, 490
\incrX (pst-uml), 646
\incrY (pst-uml), 646
indent Option (powerdot), 763
index (PostScript), 843
infertile Option (pst-pdgr), 731
infix, 204, 207, 666
infix-RPN package, 385, 666
\infixtoRPN
  (infix-RPN), **666**, 666, *667*
  (pst-math), 385
inhue Option (pst-solides3d), 429
\Initial (vaucanson-g), *726*
inkspread Option (pst-barcode), 498, *499*

inline mode, 118
inner value
    (pst-plot), 177, 184, *185*
    (pstricks), 44, **49**
innerBorder Option (uml), *653*, 655, *656*, *657*
inouthue Option (pst-solides3d), *420*, *433*
\input, 5, 7, 8
inputarrow Option (pst-circ), 446, 454, 455
insidetext Option (pst-pdgr), 731
integral cosine, 528
integral sine, 528
integration, 538
intensity Option (pst-circ), 446, *452*, *453*, 456, 457
intensitycolor Option (pst-circ), 446, *452*, *453*, *456*, 456, *457*
intensitylabel Option (pst-circ), 446, *452*, 453
intensitylabelcolor Option (pst-circ), 446, *452*, 453, *456*, 456, *457*
intensitylabeloffset Option (pst-circ), 446, *452*, 453
intensitywidth Option (pst-circ), 446, *452*, 453
intercept theorem, 392
interference pattern, 703
intermediate step, 330
interpolated intensity shading, 739
interpolation point, 65, 524
interpolation polynomial, 58, 67, 68
intersect Option (pst-circ), 446
intersection, 51, 576
intersection plane, 425
intersectioncolor Option (pst-solides3d), *394*, *419*
intersectionlinewidth Option (pst-solides3d), *394*, *419*
intersectionplan Option (pst-solides3d), *394*, *419*
intersectiontype Option (pst-solides3d), *419*
interval
    differentiation, 204
inverse function, 32, 204
invisibleLineStyle Option (pst-3dplot), 360, 369
invisibleStyle Option (pst-3dplot), *369*
ISBN, 501
islandcolor Option (pst-geo), 479
islands Option (pst-geo), 479
isolator, 449
\isolator (pst-circ), 449
Italy, 491
\item (powerdot), 756, 757, 759
itemize env., 327

J

\jobname, 274
\jtree (pst-jtree), *663*
    Julia value (pst-fractal), 668
    Julia set, 667

K

K Option
    (pst-pad), *723*

(pst-stru), *720*, *721*
k Option (pst-diffraction), 703, 704
key Option (pst-dbicons), *728*
key-value, 21, 49, 157
\KillGlue (pstricks), 30, 152, **153**
Koch curve, 671
kpsewhich program, 857

L

L (PostScript), 844
L Option
    (pst-magneticfield), 710
    (pst-pad), *723*
    (pst-stru), *720*, *721*
L value
    (pst-tree), 266
    (pstricks), 110
l value
    (pst-node), 258
    (pst-tree), 281
    (pst-uml), 644, 645
    (uml), 654
label, 103, 111, 177, 253
label style, 170
labelangle Option
    (pst-circ), 445, 446
    (pst-optexp), *698*
LabelAngleOffset Option (pst-eucl), 552, 556, 558, 566
labeldistance Option (pstricks), 106
labelFontSize Option (pst-plot), 170, 176, *178*, 178
labeloffset Option
    (pst-circ), 445, 446, 450
    (pst-optexp), *698*
LabelRefPt Option (pst-eucl), 552, 556, *557*
labels Option (pst-plot), 166, *170*, 170, *171*, *172*, 176
LabelSep Option (pst-eucl), 552, *556*, 556
labelsep Option, 404
    (pst-plot), 176, 180, *184*, *185*, *189*, *192*
    (pstricks), 104, 107, 166, 170, *186*, *405*
lakes Option (pst-geo), 479
lambda Option
    (pst-diffraction), 703, 704
    (pst-optic), *695*, *696*
Lambert, 469
lamp, 449
\lamp (pst-circ), 449
Lamé curve, 544
Lamé oval, 544
last Option (xcolor), 14
latex program, 766, 852
latitude, 473
latitude0 Option (pst-geo), 467, *473*, 473, 488
latitudeParallel Option (pst-geo), 479
lattice model, 366
lb Option (pstricks), *104*, 105
lb value (pstricks), 148, 684
\LCMPL (pst-rrgtrees), 660

Index of Commands and Concepts (L)

LColor value (PSTricks), 45
lcolwidth Option (powerdot), 763
LDogToothA value (pst-osci), 712
LDogToothB value (pst-osci), 713
le (PostScript), 843
LED, 449
\LED (pst-circ), 449
left value
    (pst-circ), 454
    (pst-plot), 177, 180
length (PostScript), 843
length register, 23
length unit, 25
\lens
    (pst-optexp), *698*
    (pst-optic), *689–692*
lens Option (pst-optexp), *698*
lensGlass Option (pst-optic), *689*, *690*
LensHandle Option (pst-lens), 684, *686*
LensHandleHeight Option (pst-lens), 684
LensHandleWidth Option (pst-lens), 684, *686*
lensHeight Option (pst-optic), *691*, *692*
LensMagnification Option (pst-lens), 684, 684, 688
LensRotation Option (pst-lens), 684, *685–688*
lensScale Option (pst-optic), *689*, *690*
LensShadow Option (pst-lens), 684, *687*
LensSize Option (pst-lens), 684, *685*, 688
LensStyleGlass Option (pst-lens), 684, *687*
LensStyleHandle Option (pst-lens), 684, *686*
lensWidth Option (pst-optic), *689*, *690*
level Option (pst-geo), 467, **468**, 468, *470–475*, 478, 488, 489, *490*, 490, *491*, *493*
levelsep Option (pst-tree), 267, *272*, 272, *273–275*, 284
lfrheight Option (powerdot), 762, 763
lfrprop Option (powerdot), 762
liftpen Option (pstricks), 44, 52, 125, *126*, 126, 127
light effects, 731
lightintensity Option (pst-solides3d), *395*
lightsrc Option (pst-solides3d), *392*, 392, *394*, 394, *395*, 395, *428*, *429*
LightThreeDAngle Option (pst-light3d), 732
LightThreeDColorPsCommand Option (pst-light3d), 732, *733*
LightThreeDLength Option (pst-light3d), 732
LightThreeDSteps Option (pst-light3d), 731, 732
LightThreeDXLength Option (pst-light3d), *732*
LightThreeDYLength Option (pst-light3d), 732
limiteL Option (pst-geo), 467, *472*, 472, *473*, 488
line, 43, 52
    transparency, 87
line value
    (pst-plot), 198, *199*, 199, 203
    (pst-solides3d), *396*, 412
line beginning, 91
line colour, 22, 86
line distance, 85
line end, 45

(cont.)
line ending, 91
line mirroring, 570
line segment, 233
line style, 124, 288
line type, 52
line width, 44, 85, 94, 95, 128
lineAngle Option
    (pst-node), 244
    (pstricks-add), 244, *245*, 245, *246*
linearc Option, 355
    (pstricks), 44, **50**, *50*, 50, 51, *52*, *53*, 214, *231*, 310
linecap Option (pstricks), 43, 46, *47*, 47, 92
linecolor Option, 355
    (pstricks-add), 611
    (pstricks), 22, 43, **45**, *45*, 48, *52*, *53*, 55, 56, *58–60*, 62, 87, 88, 90, 96, 111, *122*, *123*, 123, *124–128*, *141*, *227*, *252*, *382*, 530
lineheight Option (powerdot), 762, 763
linejoin Option
    (pst-3dplot), 360, 364, *365*
    (pstricks), 43, 45, 46
lineprop Option (powerdot), 762
lines Option (pst-spectra), 716
linestyle Option, 355
    (pstricks), 22, 43, **45**, *45*, 47, *59*, 60, *146*, *565*
\lineto (pstricks), 75, **134**, 134
lineto (PostScript), 212, 307, 843
LineToXAxis value (pst-plot), 198, 201
LineToYAxis value (pst-plot), 198, 201
linetype Option (pstricks), 44, 52, 124
linewidth Option (pstricks), 22, 43, **44**, 44, 48, *58*, 71, 94, 95, *108*, *123*, *125*, *127*, *291*, *547*
linguistics, 659
Linux, 79
\lisplot (pst-plot), *185*
Lissajous Option (pst-osci), 713, *715*, *716*
Lissajous figure, 206, 713
listings package, 764
\listplot
    (pst-plot), 165, *202*, *203*, **212**, **215**, 215, **216**, *216*, *217*, *217*, *218*, 218, *219–222*, 222, *223*, 223
    (pstricks-add), *602–604*
\listplot* (pst-plot), 212
\listplotThreeD (pst-3dplot), 390
\LLINK (pst-rrgtrees), 660
\lLINK (pst-rrgtrees), 660
llx Option (pstricks-add), *602*, *603*, 603, *604*, 855
lly Option (pstricks-add), *602*, *603*, 603, *604*, 855
lly value (pst-plot), *185*
ln (PostScript), 208, 839
load Option (pst-solides3d), 403, 442
load value (pst-solides3d), *403*, 442
local options, 21
log (PostScript), 208, 840
\logic (pst-circ), **457**, *458–462*
logicChangeLR Option (pst-circ), 447, *458–462*

881

(cont.)
logicHeight Option (pst-circ), 447, *458–460*, *462–464*
logicJInput Option (pst-circ), 447, *461*
logicKInput Option (pst-circ), 447, *461*
logicLabelStyle Option (pst-circ), *462–464*
logicLabelstyle Option (pst-circ), 447
logicNInput Option (pst-circ), 447, *462*
logicNodestyle Option (pst-circ), 447
logicShowDot Option (pst-circ), 447
logicShowNode Option (pst-circ), 447, *458–464*
logicSymbolstyle Option (pst-circ), 447
logicType Option (pst-circ), *458–464*
logictypee Option (pst-circ), 447
logicWidth Option (pst-circ), 447, *458–460*, *462–464*
logicWireLength Option (pst-circ), 447, *462*
logixInput Option (pst-circ), *458–460*
logLines Option (pst-plot), 177, *190*, 190, *191*
logLines value (pst-plot), 190
logocmd Option (powerdot), *755*
logohook Option (powerdot), *755*
logopos Option (powerdot), *755*
longitude, 473
longitude0 Option (pst-geo), 467, *473*, 473, *474*, 488
longitudeMeridien Option (pst-geo), 479
loop, 250
loop (PostScript), 843
\LoopL (vaucanson-g), *726*
\LoopN (vaucanson-g), *726*
\LoopS (vaucanson-g), *726*
loopsize Option (pst-node), 227, 230, *231*, *249*, 249
loose value (pst-tree), 267, *270*, 270
L0style Option (pst-circ), 446
low-level commands, 160
lower value (pstricks-add), 605
lower sum, 605
loxodrome, 469
\LPERIPH (pst-rrgtrees), 660
\lPERIPH (pst-rrgtrees), 660
\Lput (pst-node), 256
\lput (pst-node), 256
LR box, 119
LR mode, 109
\lstinputlisting (listings), 764
lt (PostScript), 843
lwidth Option (pst-spectra), 716

M

magenta value (pstricks), *45*
MagentaContAddSub value (pst-osci), *713*
mailing list, 858
maillage Option (pst-geo), 467, *473*, 473, *474*, *478*, *479*, 489, 490
\makeatletter, 157, 263, 581, 582
\makeatother, 157, 263, 581
\makebox, 113, *114*, 642
  (pst-func), 532
makeeps Option (pst-eps), 315

makeplot env. (makeplot), *683*
makeplot package, 666, **683**, 683
\MakeShortNab (pst-node), 235
\MakeShortTablr (pst-node), 235
\MakeShortTnput (pst-tree), 281
\maketitle
  (beamer), *766*, 767
  (powerdot), *747–757*, *759*, *762*, *764*, *765*
male Option (pst-pdgr), *729*, 730
male value (pst-pdgr), 730, 731
Mandel value (pst-fractal), 668
Mandelbrot set, 667
manual mode, 295
mapcolor Option (pst-geo), 479
mapCountry Option (pst-geo), 467, *475*, 475, 489
MapFillColor Option (pst-geo), 467, **474**, 478, 479
\mapput (pst-geo), **477**, 477, 487, **491**, 491
Mark Option (pst-eucl), 552, *555*, 555, 566
mark (PostScript), 841, 843
MarkAngle Option (pst-eucl), 552, *555*, 555
MarkAngleOffset Option (pst-eucl), *557*
MarkAngleRadius Option (pst-eucl), 552, *556*, 556, *566*, 566, *576*
\markcr (psgo), 736, 737
\markdd (psgo), 736, 737
MarkHash value (pst-eucl), 552, 555
MarkHashh value (pst-eucl), 552
MarkHashhh value (pst-eucl), 552
marking, 111
\marklb (psgo), 736, 737
\markma (psgo), 736, 737
\markpos (psgo), 736
\marksl (psgo), 736, 737
\marksq (psgo), 736, 737
\marktr (psgo), 736, 737
markZeros Option (pst-func), 520, 532, *533–537*, *539–543*
math mode, 177
mathematics, 118
  inline mode, 118
  mode, 109, 118
  out-of-line formulae, 118
mathLabel Option
  (pst-plot), 170, 176, *178*, 178
  (pst-solides3d), *404*, 404, *405*
\mathrm, 258
Matlab, 858
matrix, 258
matrix env., 258
maxIter Option (pst-fractal), 668, 669, *670*, 670, 671
maxRadius Option (pst-fractal), 668
mcol Option (pst-node), 258, *260*, 260
mean, 534
measure, 22, 24
median, 573
mediatrice value (pst-solides3d), 412
Mercator, 469
mercury, 717

(cont.)
meridian, 469
`meridiencolor` Option (pst-geo), 479
`meridienwidth` Option (pst-geo), 479
`method` Option
    (powerdot), 764
    (pstricks-add), 611, *612*, 612, *613*, *615*, *616*
MEX Option (pst-geo), 477
`mexico` Option (pst-geo), 479
microwave, 445
`middle` value (pstricks), 44, **49**
minipage env., 19, 109, 292
`minWidth` Option (pst-fractal), 673
\mirror (pst-optexp), *698*
\mirrorCVGRay (pst-optic), *692*
mirroring, 216
mixer, 451
\mixer (pst-circ), 451
`mnode` Option (pst-node), 258, *259*, 259, *260*
`mnodesize` Option (pst-node), 258, *261*, 261
mod (PostScript), 840
mode
    automatic, 295
    horizontal, 109
    manual, 295
`mode` Option
    (powerdot), 754
    (pst-solides3d), *429*
modulo, 175, 582
moiré effect, 89
monitor resolution, 44
monohedral, 295
Monopole, 448
monopole, 448
Month Option
    (pst-calendar), *734*, *735*
    (pst-geo), 478
\month (pst-calendar), 733
month Option (pst-calendar), 733
`monthT` Option (pst-calendar), 733
\move (psgo), *737*, *738*
\moveE (pst-uml), *646*, *647*
\moveN (pst-uml), *646*, *647*
\movepath (pstricks), *134*
\moveS (pst-uml), *646*, *647*
\moveto (pstricks), *75*, **127**, 127, 128, *135*
moveto (PostScript), 212, *216*, 843
\moveW (pst-uml), *646*, *647*
\Mput (pst-node), 256
\mput (pst-node), 256
\mrestore (pstricks), *132*
\msave (pstricks), *132*
mue Option (pst-func), 538, *539*
mul (PostScript), 211, 386, 840
mul value (pst-osci), 713
\multicolumn, 261
Multidipole, 448

\multidipole (pst-circ), *450*
\multido
    (animate), 742
    (multido), *14*, *15*, *44*, *47*, *48*, *61*, *71*, *72*, *90*, 168, 363, *609*, *610*, 666, 738, 742, 745
multido package, 8, 585, 738
\multiframe (animate), 742
multiplication, 203
multiplier, 449
\multips (pstricks), **108**, 108, *141*
\multiput (pstricks), *20*
\multirput (pstricks), **105**, 106, 108
\multirput* (pstricks), 105
\multispan, 261
mulv value (pst-solides3d), 411
mulv3d (PostScript), 435
mv Option (pst-dbicons), *728*

N

N Option (pst-magneticfield), 710
n Option (pst-geo), 467, **472**, 488
n-hedral, 295
nab value (pst-node), 227, 234, 235
`nAdjust` Option (gastex), *725*
`nAdjustdist` Option (gastex), *725*
name Option
    (pst-node), 258, 259, *260–264*, 285
    (pst-solides3d), *402*, 410, 426, *441*, 441
    (pst-tree), 285
`nameB` Option (pst-optic), *689*, *690*
`named` Option (xcolor), 9, 11, 12
`nameF` Option (pst-optic), *689*, *690*
`nameFi` Option (pst-optic), *689*, *690*
`nameO` Option (pst-optic), *689*, *690*
`namer` Option (pst-geo), 467, 489, 490
`nameX` Option (pst-3dplot), 360, *365*, 365
`nameY` Option (pst-3dplot), 360, *365*, 365
`nameZ` Option (pst-3dplot), 360, *365*, 365
\naput (pst-node), *102*, 235, **254**, *254*
\naput* (pst-node), 254
`nArrow` Option (pstricks-add), 99
`nArrows` Option (pstricks-add), 99
`nArrowsA` Option (pstricks-add), 99
`nArrowsB` Option (pstricks-add), 99
\nbput (pst-node), 235, *249*, **254**, *254*, 648
\nbput* (pst-node), 254
\ncangle (pst-node), *230*, *231*, 234, **247**, *247*, 247, *248*, 248, 249, 252
\ncangle* (pst-node), 247
\ncangles (pst-node), *234*, 234, **248**, *248*, 248, 249, 252
\ncangles* (pst-node), 248
\ncarc (pst-node), *225*, *230*, 234, **242**, *242*, 252
\ncarc* (pst-node), 242
\ncarcbox (pst-node), 231, 232, *234*, 234, **251**, *251*, 251, *252*, 252
\ncarcbox* (pst-node), 251
\ncbar (pst-node), *230*, 234, **246**, *246*, 246, 252, 256

\ncbar* (pst-node), 246
\ncbarr
        (pst-node), **246**, 246, *247*, 252
        (pstricks-add), 246, *247*
\ncbox (pst-node), 231, 234, **250**, 250, *251*, 252
\ncbox* (pst-node), 250
\nccircle (pst-node), 234, 249, **250**, 250
\nccircle* (pst-node), 250
\nccirclebox (pst-node), 252
\nccoil (pst-coil), *146*, **311**, *311*
\nccoil* (pst-coil), 311
\nccurve (pst-node), *231*, 231, 234, *239*, **250**, *250*, 250, 252, *257*
\nccurve* (pst-node), 250
\ncdiag (pst-node), 234, **242**, 242, *243*, 243–247, 252
\ncdiag* (pst-node), 242
\ncdiagg (pst-node), 234, **245**, 245, 252, 274
\ncdiagg* (pst-node), 245
\ncE (pst-uml), 649
\ncEDE (pst-uml), 649
\ncEN (pst-uml), 649
\ncES (pst-uml), 649
\ncEVE (pst-uml), 649
\ncEVW (pst-uml), 649
\ncEXN (pst-uml), 649
\ncEXS (pst-uml), 649
\ncline (pst-node), *98*, 98, *99*, *142*, *227*–*229*, *232*, *233*, 234, 235–241, **242**, *242*, *243*, 243, 244, 252, *256*, 259–264, *274*, *564*, *567*, *646*
\ncline* (pst-node), 242
\ncloop (pst-node), 230, *231*, 234, **249**, *249*, 249, 252
\ncloop* (pst-node), 249
\ncN (pst-uml), 649
\ncNDN (pst-uml), 649
\ncNE (pst-uml), 649
\ncNHN (pst-uml), 649
\ncNHS (pst-uml), 649
\ncNW (pst-uml), 649
\ncNXE (pst-uml), 649
\ncNXW (pst-uml), 649
\NCORE (pst-rrgtrees), 661
\ncput (pst-node), 232, 249, **254**, *254*, 254, *255*
\ncput* (pst-node), 254
\ncputicon (pst-uml), 646, *647*, 649, *650*
\ncS (pst-uml), 649
\ncSDS (pst-uml), 649
\ncSE (pst-uml), 649
\ncSHN (pst-uml), *648*, 649
\ncSHS (pst-uml), 649
\ncsin (pst-coil), 311
\ncsin* (pst-coil), 311
\ncSW (pst-uml), 649
\ncSXE (pst-uml), 649
\ncSXW (pst-uml), 649
 ncurv Option (pst-node), 227, **231**, 250
 ncurvA Option (pst-node), 227, ***231***
 ncurvB Option (pst-node), 227, *231*

(cont.)
 ncurveA Option (pst-node), 231
 ncurveB Option (pst-node), 231
\ncW (pst-uml), 649
\ncWDW (pst-uml), 649
\ncWN (pst-uml), 649
\ncWS (pst-uml), 649
\ncWVE (pst-uml), 649
\ncWVW (pst-uml), 649
\ncWXN (pst-uml), 649
\ncWXS (pst-uml), 649
\nczigzag (pst-coil), 311
\nczigzag* (pst-coil), 311
 neg (PostScript), 840
 nEnd Option (pst-plot), 218
 NET (PostScript), 845
 new value
        (pst-eps), 315
        (pst-solides3d), *403*, 403, *439*, ***440***
 NewCenturySchlbk value (pstricks), 35
\newcmykcolor (pstricks), 9
\newcommand, *15*, 37
\newcount, *20*
\newframe (animate), *742*
\newgray (pstricks), 9
\newground (pst-circ), 448, 454
\newhsbcolor (pstricks), 9
\newlength, 6
\newpath (pstricks), *127*, 128
 newpath (PostScript), 127, 843
\newpsbarstyle (pst-bar), *512*, *513*, **514**, *514*–*516*
\newpsfontdot (pstricks), *72*, 74
\newpsfontdotH (pstricks), *72*, 73
\newpsobject (pstricks), 37, ***122***
\newpsstyle
        (pst-osci), *714*–*716*
        (pstricks), 30, *30*, *33*, *89*, *121*, *121*, *122*, *336*, *337*, *366*
\newrgbcolor (pstricks), 9
\newsavebox, *18*, *42*, *148*, *150*
 Newton method, 522
 ngerman value (pst-calendar), 733
 ngrid Option (pst-solides3d), 401, 402, 418, 429, *435*, *436*
 ngrid value (pst-solides3d), 401
 niveauLiquide1 Option (pst-labo), 620, *631*, *632*, *637*
 niveauLiquide1 value (pst-labo), *633*
 niveauLiquide2 Option (pst-labo), 620, *637*
 niveauliquide2 Option (pst-labo), 620
 niveauLiquide3 Option (pst-labo), *637*
 niveauliquide3 Option (pst-labo), 620
 niveauReactifBurette Option (pst-labo), 620, 629, *630*, *637*
 nL Option (pst-magneticfield), 710
\nlput (pstricks-add), *601*
 Nmarks Option (gastex), *725*
 Nmr Option (gastex), *725*
\NNUC (pst-rrgtrees), 661
 node, 140, 203, 310, 445

Index of Commands and Concepts (O)

(cont.)
    centre, 227
    coordinates, 226
    name, 226, 351
\node (gastex), *725*
nodealign Option (pst-node), 258, *260*, 260
\nodeBetween (demo), 237, *238*
nodesep Option
    (pst-node), *142*, 142, *144*, 227, **229**, *229*, 229,
    231–233, 250, 251, 253, 257, *567*, 567, *597*
    (pst-tree), *271*, 275
nodesep value (pst-node), 140, 241
nodesepA Option
    (pst-node), 227, *229*, 229, *257*, 567, 591, *592–595*
    (pstricks-add), 591
nodesepB Option
    (pst-node), 227, *229*, 229, 567, 591, *592–595*
    (pstricks-add), 591
nodeWidth Option (pst-geo), 467, *475*, 489
\noexpand, 226
none Option (pstricks), 380
none value
    (pst-3dplot), 362
    (pst-eps), 315
    (pst-eucl), 552
    (pst-node), 227, 234, 235, 258, 259
    (pst-plot), 166, 167, *168*, 170, *171*, *172*, 172, *174*, 176,
    177, 190
    (pst-solides3d), 428, 441, 442
    (pstricks), 22, 43, 45, 80, 177, 186, 288
normal Option (pst-3d), 341, **343**
normal value
    (powerdot), 764
    (pst-3dplot), 362
normal distribution, 535, 538
normal vector, 343
\NormalCoor (pstricks), **139**, 145
normalize value (pst-solides3d), 411
\normalsize, 178
North America, 490
not (PostScript), 843
notations Option (pst-optic), *695*
notes value (powerdot), 754
\NP (pst-rrgtrees), 661
NPN transistor, 456
npos Option (pst-node), 227, **234**, 234, 253
\nput (pst-node), 232, *233*, 255, **256**, *256*, 280
\nput* (pst-node), 256
nrot Option
    (pst-node), 227, **233**, *234*
    (pstricks), *601*
nS Option (pst-magneticfield), 710
nStart Option (pst-plot), 218
nStep Option (pst-plot), 218, 219
\NUC (pst-rrgtrees), *660*, 661
null, 522
null node, 278

num Option (pst-solides3d), *403*
\number, 733
Numero Option (pst-labo), 620, 623
numfaces Option (pst-solides3d), *432*, *433*
numlines Option (pst-spectra), 716
numSpires Option (pst-magneticfield), 710
Nw Option (gastex), *725*

O

O Option (pst-cox), 680
o value (pstricks), *71*
\OA (pst-circ), 451, *456*, 457
OAiminus Option (pst-circ), 446, *456*
OAiminuslabel Option (pst-circ), 446, *456*
OAinvert Option (pst-circ), 446, 456
OAiout Option (pst-circ), 446, *456*
OAioutlabel Option (pst-circ), 446, *456*
OAiplus Option (pst-circ), 446, *456*
OAipluslabel Option (pst-circ), 446, *456*
OAperfect Option (pst-circ), 446, *456*
.obj file extension (pst-solides3d), 428
object
    closed, 160
    open, 160
object Option (pst-solides3d), *392–394*, *396*, 396, *397*,
    398, 398, *399*, 399, *400*, 400, *401*, 401, *402*, 402,
    403, 403, 410, *428–436*, 439, *440*, 442
object=droite value (pst-solides3d), 412
object=line value (pst-solides3d), 412
object=rightangle value (pst-solides3d), 415
object=texte value (pst-solides3d), 417
objfile value (pst-solides3d), *403*
obligatory Option (pst-pdgr), 730
obligatory value (pst-pdgr), 730
oceancolor Option (pst-geo), 479
octahedron value (pst-solides3d), *399*
Octogon value (pstricks), 74, 75
.off file extension (pst-solides3d), 428
offfile value (pst-solides3d), *403*
offset, 27, 288, 289
offset Option (pst-node), *142*, 142, *143*, *144*, 227, **232**,
    232, 232, 256, 267
offset value (pst-node), 140
offset1 Option (pst-osci), 712
offset2 Option (pst-osci), 713
offset3 Option (pst-osci), 713
offsetA Option (pst-node), 227, 232, *256*
offsetB Option (pst-node), 227, 232, *256*
old value (pst-circ), 454
OnlyVisibleFaces Option (pst-ob3d), *346*
OnlyVisibleFaces=true Option (pst-ob3d), 346
\onslide (powerdot), 757, 759
\onslide* (powerdot), 757
\onslide+ (powerdot), 757
\OP (pst-rrgtrees), 661
opacity Option (pstricks), 80, 83, **87**, *88*, 88, 481, 594
open curve, 124

885

\openshadow (pstricks), *132*, 133
  operation Option (pst-osci), 713
  operational amplifier, 451, 456
\OPR (pst-rrgtrees), *660, 661*
\optbox (pst-optexp), *698*
  optboxwidth Option (pst-optexp), *698*
\optgrid (pst-optexp), *698*
  option, 22
\optoCoupler (pst-circ), 452
  optocoupler, 451, 452
\optplate (pst-optexp), *698*
\optretplate (pst-optexp), *698*
  or (PostScript), 843
  origin Option
          (pst-3dplot), *378*
          (pstricks), 31, 32, 124
  orthoproj value (pst-solides3d), *415*
  orthovecteur value (pst-solides3d), 411
  oscillator, 448
\oscillator (pst-circ), 448, 454
  oscillator symbol, 448
\Oscillo (pst-osci), *712*, *713*, *714–716*
  out-of-line formulae, 118
  outer value (pstricks), 44, *49*
  outerBorder Option (uml), *656, 657*
  outline font, 290, 295
  output Option (pst-circ), 446, 454
  oval, 113
  oval value (pst-node), 258, 259
\ovalnode (pst-node), *240*, 240, *243*, *248*, *253*, 259, 277
\ovalnode* (pst-node), 240
  Overlay, 147
  overlay, 41, 215, 756
\overlaybox (pstricks), 147
  overlaybox env. (pstricks), 147
  Ox Option (pst-plot), 166, *168*, 168
  Oy Option (pst-plot), 166, *168*, 168
  oztex program, 9

P

P Option
          (pst-cox), 680
          (pst-pad), *723*
          (pst-stru), *720, 721*
p value (pst-node), 258, 259
page Option (graphicx), 853
\pagecolor (xcolor), 19
\pagestyle, 313, 852
Pakete
          aeb_pro, 743, 744
          amsmath, 258
          animate, 741, 742
          arrayjob, 174
          auto-pst-pdf, 855
          babel, 850
          color, 6, 7, 9, 11, 15, 154, 318, 322
          colortbl, 10

extsizes, 754
fb, 738
gastex, 724, **725**, 725
graphicx, 117, 118, 853
hyperref, 10
infix-RPN, 385, 666
listings, 764
makeplot, 666, **683**, 683
multido, 8, 585, 738
pdftricks, 855, 856
pict2e, 3
pictex, 857
powerdot, 147, 747, 748, 754, 755
preview, 852, 855
ps4pdf, 852
psfrag, 852
psgo, 731, 736
pst-3d, 8, 334, 335, 338, 348, 358, 711
pst-3dplot, 346, 358, 360, 373, 375, 377, 385
pst-all, 8
pst-asr, 659
pst-bar, 509
pst-barcode, 497
pst-blur, 317, 328, 330
pst-calendar, 731, 733
pst-circ, 160, 445, 448, 698
pst-coil, 8, 303, 309, 310
pst-cox, 679
pst-coxcoor, 666, 679, 681
pst-coxeterp, 666, 679
pst-dbicons, 724
pst-diffraction, 683, 703
pst-eps, 8, 313, 315
pst-eucl, 551
pst-fill, 8, 79, 83, 295, 296, 300, 349, 783
pst-fr3d, 355
pst-fractal, 666
pst-func, 65, 517, 519
pst-geo, 465, 466
pst-gr3d, 348, 351, 352
pst-grad, 8, 79, 317, 321, 780
pst-infixplot, 204, 667
pst-jftree, 663
pst-jtree, 659, 663
pst-key, 162
pst-labo, 619, 630–632, 712
pst-lens, 683, 684
pst-light3d, 731
pst-magneticfield, 683, 710
pst-map2d, 466, 478, 487
pst-map2dII, 466, 488, 490
pst-map3d, 466
pst-map3dII, 466, 489, 490
pst-math, 517, 839
pst-node, 8, 142, 225, 226, 236, 256, 259, 260, 265, 277, 280, 285, 310, 445, 659
pst-ob3d, 346

(cont.)
  pst-optexp, 683, 698
  pst-optic, 683, 689, 703
  pst-osci, 683, 712
  pst-pad, 683, 722
  pst-pdf, 852
  pst-pdgr, 724
  pst-plot, 8, 126, 165, 176, 177, 181, 184, 194, 201, 202, 212, 216, 217, 358, 362, 385, 386, 392, 519, 784
  pst-poly, 666, 674
  pst-qtree, 659
  pst-slpe, 79, 317, 320, 321, 326, 783
  pst-solides3d, 346, 358, 391, 421, 440, 442
  pst-spectra, 683, 716
  pst-stru, 683, 719
  pst-text, 8, 287, 295
  pst-tree, 8, 265, 266, 274, 276, 277, 280, 281, 659, 664
  pst-uml, 641, 652
  pst-vue3d, 391
  pst-xkey, 162
  pstricks, 9, 10, 29, 89, 204, 265, 348, 582, 847
  pstricks-add, 23, 33, 47, 89, 92, 98, 99, 106, 144, 170, 175, 176, 244–246, 385, 581, 602, 666
  qtree, 664
  random, 347
  rotating, 337
  rrgtrees, 659
  setspace, 292
  sfg, 724
  uml, 641, 652
  vaucanson-G, 724
  vaucanson-g, 725
  xcolor, 6, 7, 9–15, 17, 20, 154, 184, 318, 322, 372, 373, 431
  xkeyval, 162
Palatino-Roman value (pstricks), 35
paper Option (powerdot), 766
paper plane, 358
\parabola (pstricks), *32*
paral value (pst-solides3d), 411
parallel Option (pst-circ), 446, 453
parallel projection, 358, 572
parallelarm Option (pst-circ), 446, 454
parallelcolor Option (pst-geo), 479
parallelepiped value (pst-solides3d), *401*
parallelnode Option (pst-circ), 447
parallelsep Option (pst-circ), 447
parallelwidth Option (pst-geo), 479
parameter form, 544
parametric form, 206
parametric representation, 609
\parametricplot (pst-plot), 165, 203, 204, *206*, *207*, *209*, 209, *289*, *294*, *312*, *314*, 530
\parametricplotThreeD (pst-3dplot), **389**, 389, *786*
\parbox, 6, 54, 109, *112*, 112, 113, *114*, 284, 335, 357

(cont.)
PasB Option (pst-magneticfield), 710
PasS Option (pst-magneticfield), 710
\pass (psgo), *737, 738*
path, 287
  closed, 123
path Option
  (pst-geo), **467**, 467, *468–475*, *477*, 478, *480–482*, *484–487*, 488, 489
  (pst-solides3d), 410
path state, 52
pattern, 79, 123, 299
\pause (powerdot), 756
\pcangle (pst-node), 252
\pcangles (pst-node), 252
\pcarc (pst-node), 252
\pcarcbox (pst-node), 252
\pcbar (pst-node), 252
\pcbox (pst-node), 252
\pccoil (pst-coil), 311
\pccoil* (pst-coil), 311
\pccurve
  (pst-node), **252**, *257*
  (pstricks-add), *102*
\pcdiag (pst-node), *244*, 244, **252**, *253*
\pcdiagg (pst-node), 245, *246*, **252**
\pcline (pst-node), 252
\pcloop (pst-node), 252
\pcsin (pst-coil), 311
\pcsin* (pst-coil), 311
\pczigzag (pst-coil), 311
\pczigzag* (pst-coil), 311
\pddefinetemplate (powerdot), 755
PDF, 83
PDF417, 508
pdfLaTeX, 148
pdfcrop program, 852, 854, 855
pdflatex program, 851, 853, 855, 856
pdfpic env. (pdftricks), **855**, *856*
pdftex program, 9
pdftricks package, 855, 856
\pdsetup (powerdot), 754, *755*, 755, *765*
pendulum, 611
penrose value (pstricks), 80, 82, *83*
penrose* value (pstricks), 80, 82
period1 Option (pst-osci), 712, *715*
period2 Option (pst-osci), 713, *715*
periodmodulation1 Option (pst-osci), 712
periodmodulation2 Option (pst-osci), 713
periods Option (pst-coil), 304, *307*, 307, *308*
periods value (pst-coil), 307, 308
perp value
  (pst-optexp), *698*
  (pst-solides3d), 412
perpendicular bisector, 551, 575
perspective view, 391
\phantom, *17*

(cont.)
Pharmacode, 506
phase diagram, 613
phase shift, 205, 713
phase shifter, 449
phase1 Option (pst-osci), 712
phase2 Option (pst-osci), 713
\phaseshifter (pst-circ), 449
PHI Option (pst-geo), 478, 490
phi Option (pst-solides3d), 398, 399, 402
phmetre Option (pst-labo), 620, *631*, 631
Phyllotaxis, 669
Pi (PostScript), *195*, 845
pi (PostScript), *156*
pict2e package, 3
pictex package, 857
picture env., 152
picture pattern, 295
pie value (pst-solides3d), *402*
pie diagram, 23
pince Option (pst-labo), 619, *621*, 621, *634*
pixel Option (pst-diffraction), 703, 704
plan Option
    (pst-3dplot), *366*, 368
    (pst-solides3d), 410
plan value (pst-solides3d), *396*, 396, *413*
plane, 442
plane Option (pst-3dplot), 360, 365, 378
planecorr Option (pst-3dplot), *362*, 362, *378*
planmarks Option (pst-solides3d), *396*, 410, *413*
plansepare Option
    (pst-dolides3d), *784*
    (pst-solides3d), *441*, 441, *442*, 442, *443*, 444
platelinewidth Option (pst-optexp), *698*
Plates Project, 485
plot style, 202
plotfuncx Option (pstricks-add), 611
plotfuncy Option (pstricks-add), 611
plotNo Option (pst-plot), 218, 221, *222*, 222, *223*
plotNoMax Option (pst-plot), 218, 221, *222*, 222, *223*
plotpoints Option
    (pst-fractal), 667
    (pst-func), 524, *531*, 538
    (pst-plot), 165, *198*, 198, 203, 206, *207*, 386, 530
plotstyle Option (pst-plot), *198*, 198, *199–203*, 203, *204–206*, 217
plotstyle1 Option (pst-osci), 712, *714–716*
plotstyle2 Option (pst-osci), 713
plotstyle3 Option (pst-osci), 713
plotstyle4 Option (pst-osci), 713
pmatrix env. (pst-node), *591*
.png file extension, 745, 746
png2swf program, 746
\pnode (pst-node), *142–144*, *148*, *150*, **237**, 237, 259, 277, 491, *850*
\pnodeMap (pst-geo), **477**, 477, 487, **491**, 491, *493*
PNP transistor, 456

(cont.)
point
    current, 127
    three-dimensional, 358
point value (pst-solides3d), *396*, *415*
PointName Option (pst-eucl), 551, *553*, 553, *563*, *564*, 564, 566, 569–577
PointNameA Option (pst-eucl), 552, 553, 566, 577
PointNameB Option (pst-eucl), 552, 553, 566, 577
PointNameC Option (pst-eucl), 552, 553, 566
PointNameSep Option (pst-eucl), 552, 553, *554*, 564, 566, 569–577
pointsB Option (pst-magneticfield), 710
pointsS Option (pst-magneticfield), 710
PointSymbol Option (pst-eucl), 551, *553*, 553, *554*, *555*, 564, 564, *566*, 566, *567*, 569–572, *573*, 573, 574, *575*, 575–577, *578* 580
PointSymbolA Option (pst-eucl), 551, 553, 566, 577
PointSymbolB Option (pst-eucl), 551, 553, 566, 577
PointSymbolC Option (pst-eucl), 551, 553, 566
Poisson distribution, 537
Poisson process, 537
\Polar (pstricks), 145
polar coordinates, 140, 145, 210, 608
    conversion, 141
\polarisation (pst-optexp), *698*
polarplot Option
    (pst-plot), 207, **210**, ***211***, 211
    (pstricks-add), 546, *548*, *549*, 609
poltype Option (pst-optexp), *698*
polycurve, 57
PolyCurves Option (pst-poly), 674, *676*
PolyEpicycloid Option (pst-poly), 674, *677*
\Polygon (pst-cox), 680
polygon, 49, 50, 53, 674
polygon value
    (pst-eucl), *557*
    (pst-plot), 198, 199
    (pstricks), *199*
polygone value (pst-solides3d), 412
polygoneregulier value (pst-solides3d), *401*
polyhedron, 422
PolyIntermediatePoint Option (pst-poly), 674, *676*, *677*
Polyline, 49
polyline, 43, 50, 52, 57, 79, 91, 203
polyline value (pst-eucl), *557*
PolyName Option (pst-poly), 674
PolyNbSides Option (pst-poly), *674*, 674, *675–679*
polynomial, 519
PolyOffset Option (pst-poly), 674, *675–677*
PolyRotation Option (pst-poly), 674
polytope, 679
pop (PostScript), 843
popcorn function, 545
popip.pl program, 745
pOrigin Option (pst-3dplot), 360, *366*, 366

Index of Commands and Concepts (P)

(cont.)
pos Option
  (pst-solides3d), 410
  (uml), *654*, 654, *655*, *658*
PosAngle Option (pst-eucl), 552, *553*, *554*, 554, *559–561*,
  564, 566, *568*, 569, *570*, 570, 571, *572*, 572, 573,
  574, 574, *575*, 575, *576*, 576, *577*, 577, *579*
PosAngleA Option (pst-eucl), 552, 554, 566, 577
PosAngleB Option (pst-eucl), 552, 554, 566, 577
PosAngleC Option (pst-eucl), 552, 554, 566
posDelta Option (uml), 654, *658*
posDeltaX Option (uml), 654
posDeltaY Option (uml), 654
position Option (pst-optexp), *698*
position parameter, 148
post codes, 507
postfix, 204, 207, 607, 666
PostScript, 153
  ArrowA, 137
  ArrowB, 137
  commands, 123
  driver, 44
  error message, 5
  fonts, 35
  Header, 151
  interpreter, 5
  Level 1, 9
  prologue file, 497
postscript env.
  (pst-pdf), **852**, 854
  (pstricks-add), 855
PostScript notation, 546, 549
posX Option (uml), 654
posY Option (uml), 654
potentiometer, 451
\potentiometer (pst-circ), 451
power electronics, 205
powerdot package, 147, 747, 748, 754, 755
\PP (pst-rrgtrees), 661
ppoints Option (pst-coil), 304, *307*, 307
presentation, 594
preview package, 852, 855
\PreviewEnvironment (pst-pdf), 855
primarylabel Option (pst-circ), 447, *457*
print value (powerdot), 754
printValue Option (pst-func), 532, *533–537*, *539–543*
prisme value (pst-solides3d), *400*
prismecreux value (pst-solides3d), *400*
.pro file extension (pstricks), 151
probability distribution, 538
proband Option (pst-pdgr), 730
procedure, 151
projection, 572
prologue, 151
prologue file, 151, 497, 517
\protect, 226, 237
prototile, 295

(cont.)
\providecolor (xcolor), 12, 13
\providecolorset (xcolor), *13*
\providecommand (xcolor), 12
PS
  interface, 498
.ps file extension, 5
ps2pdf program, 79, 89, 391, 468, 766, 852, 853
ps2pdf14 program, 79, 89
ps2pdfwr program, 79, 89, 468
ps4pdf package, 852
\psaddtolength (pstricks), 23
\psAppolonius (pst-fractal), 667, *672*, 672, *673*, *674*
\psarc (pstricks), **57**, *58*, **61**, **62**, *62*, 62, 144, *145*, *146*
\psarc* (pstricks), 62
\psarcn (pstricks), *62*
\psarcn* (pstricks), 62
\psaxes (pst-plot), 7, *25*, 25, *26*, *32*, 35, *40*, 40, *41*, 165, **166**,
  166, 166, *167–175*, **176**, *176*, 176, *178–190*, 190,
  191–193, 193, *194–211*, *213–224*, 392, 602
\psBall (pst-grad), **327**, 327, 328
\psbarchart (pst-bar), *510–513*, 513, *514*, **515**, *515*, *516*
\psbarcode (pst-barcode), **497**, *498–508*
\psbarlabel (pst-bar), 514, 515
\psbarscale (pst-bar), 515
\psBernstein (pst-func), 525, *526*, *527*
\psBessel (pst-func), **529**, *530*
\psBetaDist (pst-func), 543
\psBezier (pst-func), 524
\psbezier
  (pstricks-add), *102*
  (pstricks), 65, 65, *66*, 124, 125, *133*, 134
\psbezier* (pstricks), 65
\psBinomial (pst-func), **532**, *533*
\psBinomialN (pst-func), **532**, 532, **534**, 534, **535**, 535, **536**,
  537
\psblurbox (pst-blur), **330**, 330, *331*
\psboxfill (pst-fill), 86, *87*, *293*, 293, *294*, *299*, **300**, 300,
  301
\psbrace (pstricks-add), **590**, *591–595*
\psbrace* (pstricks-add), 590
\psCalDodecaeder (pst-calendar), **733**, 735
\psCalendar (pst-calendar), **733**, *734*, 735
\psCancel (pstricks-add), 593, 593, *594*
\psCancel* (pstricks-add), 594, 595
\pscbezier (pstricks), 65, *66*
\psccurve
  (pst-node), 236
  (pstricks), **68**, 68, 200
\psccurve* (pstricks), 68
\pscharclip (pst-text), **291**, *292*, *293*, 300
pscharclip env. (pst-text), 291
\pscharclip* (pst-text), 291
pscharclip* env. (pst-text), 291
\pscharpath (pst-text), **290**, *291*, 291, 293, *294*, *586*
\pscharpath* (pst-text), 290
\psChart (pstricks-add), 23, 586, **587**, 587, **588**, 589

889

(P) Index of Commands and Concepts

(cont.)
\psChiIIDist (pst-func), **540**, *541–543*
\psCi (pst-func), 528
\psci (pst-func), 528
\pscircle (pstricks), **43**, 49, 50, 57, 58, **60**, *60*, *61*, **63**, 77, *80–83*, *90*, *121*, *122*, *224*, *288*
\pscircle* (pstricks), 60
\pscirclebox (pstricks), 108, **110**, **112**, 112, 113, 239
\pscirclebox* (pstricks), 112
\pscircleOA (pstricks), 61
\pscircleOA* (pstricks), 61
\psclip (pstricks), **115**, *116*, 116, *293*
 psclip env. (pstricks), *90*, 90, 115
\psCoil (pst-coil), 306, **309**, 309, *310*, 310, *312*
\pscoil (pst-coil), *304–307*, **309**, *309*, 309
\psCoil* (pst-coil), 309
\pscoil* (pst-coil), 309
\pscolhook (pst-node), 258
\pscurve (pstricks), **57**, *58–60*, **67**, *67*, 67, 124, 125, *126*, 126, *127*, 127, 199
\pscurve* (pstricks), 67
\pscustom (pstricks), 52, **62**, 64, 65, 75, 115, *116*, **121**, **122**, *123*, 123, *124*, 124, *125*, 125, *126–128*, 128, *129*, 129, *130*, 130, *131*, 131, *132*, *133*, 133, *134–138*, *217*, *325*
\pscustom* (pstricks), 122
\psdblframebox (pstricks), *112*
\psdblframebox* (pstricks), 112
\psdiabox
 (pst-node), 240
 (pstricks), *113*
\psdiabox* (pstricks), 113
\psdiamond (pstricks), 43, **55**
\psdiamond* (pstricks), 55
\psdice (pstricks-add), 592
\psdiffractionCircular (pst-diffraction), 703
\psdiffractionRectangle (pst-diffraction), 703
\psdiffractionTriangle (pst-diffraction), **703**, *704–709*
\psdot (pstricks), 23, 31, 48, 50, 69, *70*, *71*, **72**, *72*, 72, *73*, *76*, *140*, *141*, *145*, *146*, *213*, 240, *596*, *847*, *848*
\psdot* (pstricks), 72
\psdots (pstricks), 69, **72**, 72, *73*, *76*, 125
\psdots* (pstricks), 72
\psecurve (pstricks), 67, **68**, 200
\psecurve* (pstricks), 68
\psedge (pst-tree), 274, 274, 279, 279
\psedgeDash (pst-tree), 274
\psellipse (pstricks), 49, **63**, 64, 77, 78
\psellipse* (pstricks), 63
\psellipticarc (pstricks), 63, *64*
\psellipticarc* (pstricks), 64
\psellipticarcn (pstricks), *64*
\psellipticarcn* (pstricks), 64
\psellipticwedge (pstricks), **65**
\psellipticwedge* (pstricks), 65
\psepicenter (pst-geo), 478
\psFArrow (pst-fractal), 667, *672*

(cont.)
\psFDist (pst-func), 542
\psFern (pst-fractal), 667, *670*
 PSfont Option (pst-func), 531
\psforeach
 (pstricks-add), **595**, 595, *596*, 596
 (pstricks), *23*
\psFourier (pst-func), **527**, *528*
\psfractal (pst-fractal), 667, **668**, 668, *669–671*
 psfrag package, 852
\psframe (pstricks), 43, *49*, 49, 50, *51*, **54**, *54*, 54, *83–87*, *121*, *122*, *241*, *320*, *322*, *338*, *342–344*
\psframe* (pstricks), 54
\psframebox, 7, 355
 (pst-blur), 330
 (pstricks), *24*, *25*, 25, *26*, 26, **110**, *110*, **111**, *111*, 112, 113, *114*, 118, 119, *275*, *848*, *857*
\psframebox* (pstricks), 111
\psGammaDist (pst-func), *539*
\psGauss (pst-func), **538**, *539*
\psGaussI (pst-func), 538
\psGlobeTellure (pst-geo), **478**, 481
 psgo package, 731, 736
 psgoboard env. (psgo), *737*, *738*
 psgopartialboard env. (psgo), *738*
\psgraph (pstricks-add), **602**, 605
 psgraph env. (pstricks-add), 601, **602**, 602, *603*, 603, *604*, 604, 854, *855*, 855
\psgrid (pstricks), **28**, **29**, *30*, 30, *33*, 33, *34*, **35**, 35, *36*, **37**, *37*, **38**, 38, *39*, *40*, 40, *41*, 41, *42*, *49*, 125, 148, *214*, *216*, 776
\psGTriangle (pstricks-add), **739**, *740*, *741*
\psHexagon
 (demo), 157, 158
 (pstricks), **158**, 159
\psHexagon* (pstricks), 158
\pshlabel (pst-plot), *174*
\psHomothetie (pstricks-add), *586*
 psinputs env. (pdftricks), *856*
\psIntersectionPoint (pstricks-add), *600*
\psKochflake (pst-fractal), 667, *671*
\psLame (pst-func), 544, 544, **545**, *545*
\pslbrace (pstricks), 153
\psLCNode (pstricks-add), **600**, 600, *601*
\psLDNode (pstricks-add), *601*
\psline, 7
 (pstricks-add), 98
 (pstricks), **21**, 22, *26*, *28*, *29*, *41*, 43, 44, 45, 45, *46–48*, **49**, 49, *50*, *51*, **52**, *52*, 52, **53**, *53*, 53, *56*, *58*, *75*, *85–88*, *91*, *92*, *94–96*, **122**, *123*, 123, *124*, 124, *125*, 125, *126*, *134*, *263*, *335*
\psline* (pstricks), **52**, *52*
\pslinecolor (pstricks), 22
\psLineIIID (pst-solides3d), **408**, 408, *409*
\pslinewidth rigid length (pstricks), 44, 46, 94, 95
\psLNode (pstricks-add), *600*
\pslongbox (pstricks), 116, 117

890

Index of Commands and Concepts (P)

(cont.)
\psmagneticfield (pst-magneticfield), *710*, 710, *711*
\psmagneticfieldThreeD (pst-magneticfield), 710
\psmathbox (pstricks), 118
\psmathboxfalse (pstricks), 118
\psmathboxtrue (pstricks), *118*
\psmatrix (pst-node), *98*, *99*, **258**, 258, *259*, *260*, 260, *261–264*, 285
  psmatrix env. (pst-node), 226, 258, 261
\psMatrixPlot (pstricks-add), **616**, 616, *617*
\psmeridien (pst-geo), 478
\psNodeLabelStyle (pst-geo), 491
\psOutLine (pst-optic), *693*, *694*
\psovalbox
    (pst-node), 240
    (pstricks), 110, *113*
\psovalbox* (pstricks), 113
\psoverlay (pstricks), **147**, *148*
\psparabola (pstricks), **66**, *67*
\psparabola* (pstricks), 66
\psparallel (pst-geo), 478
\psParallelLine (pstricks-add), *599*
\psParametricplot (infix-RPN), 667
\psPhyllotaxis (pst-fractal), 667, *669*
\psPi (pst-plot), *194*
\pspicture (pstricks), 24
  pspicture env., 7, 32
    (pst-pdf), 854
    (pstricks), 23, **24**, *24–28*, *29*, *29–31*, *41*, 41, *115*, *122*, 497, 857
\pspicture* (pstricks), 24
  pspicture* env. (pstricks), **24**, 24, 114, *115*, 116, 291, 477, 484
\psPiFour (pst-plot), *194*
\psPiH (pst-plot), *194*
\psPiTwo (pst-plot), *194*
\psPlot (infix-RPN), 667
\psplot (pst-plot), *32*, *78*, *126*, 126, *127*, 127, *128*, *165*, *175*, *178*, *179*, *191*, *192*, *193*, *198*, *200*, *201*, 203, *204*, 204, *205*, *208–210*, 210, *211*, 211, *213*, *517–519*, 519, 844
\psplotDiffEqn (pstricks-add), **611**, 611, *612*, *613*, 613, *614–616*, 844
\psplotImp (pst-func), **546**, 546, *547–549*
\psplotTangent (pstricks-add), **607**, 607, *608–610*
\psplotThreeD (pst-3dplot), *363*, *367*, *368*, *385*, **386**, *386–388*
\psPoint (pst-solides3d), *407*
\psPoisson (pst-func), 537
\pspolygon (pstricks), 43, 49, 50, *52*, **53**, *53*, *58*, *111*, 199
\pspolygon* (pstricks), 53
\pspolygonbox (pst-poly), *679*
\psPolygonIIID (pst-solides3d), *408*
\psPolynomial (pst-func), 519, **520**, *521*, *523*, *524*, 527
\pspred (pst-tree), 274, 279, 280
\psPrintValue
    (pst-func), **531**, 532

(cont.)
    (pstricks-add), 666
\psprism (pst-optic), *694–696*
\psprismColor (pst-optic), 696
\psProjection (pst-solides3d), 409, **410**, 410, *411–417*, 417
\psPTree (pst-fractal), 667, 672
\psRandom (pstricks-add), *77*, *78*
\psrbrace (pstricks), 153
\psRelLine (pstricks-add), **597**, 597, *598*
\psRelNode (pstricks-add), **596**, 596, *597*, 597
\psRotate (pstricks-add), *585*
\psrotate (pstricks-add), *584*
\psrotatedown (pstricks), *116*
\psrotateleft (pstricks), **116**, 116, *338*, *341*
\psrotateright (pstricks), **116**, 116, *117*
\psRotation (pst-eucl), *558*
\psrowhook (pst-node), 258
\psrunit (pstricks), 23
  psscale Option (pstricks), 80, 82
\psscalebox (pstricks), **117**, 117, 118, *713*
\psscaleboxto (pstricks), **117**, 118
\psscan (pst-node), 258
\psset
    (pst-node), 238
    (pstricks), **21**, *21–23*, *26*, *33*, *48*, *53*, 53, *61*, *91*, *145*, *162*, *342*, 857
\pssetlength (pstricks), 23
\psshadow (pst-3d), **334**, 334, *335*
\psshadowbox
    (pst-blur), 330
    (pstricks), *112*
\psshadowbox* (pstricks), 112
\psSi (pst-func), **528**, *529*, *531*
\pssi (pst-func), **528**, *529*
\psSier (pst-fractal), *667*
\pssin (pst-coil), 303, *307*, *308*, 308, *309*, 309, 310
\pssin* (pst-coil), 309
\psSolid (pst-solides3d), 391, *392–394*, **395**, *395*, 395, *409*, 409, *410–417*, 418, 421, *428–444*
\pssolid (pst-solides3d), *396–403*
\psspan (pst-node), **261**, 261, *262–264*
\psspectrum (pst-spectra), **717**, *718*, 718, *719*
\psStep (pstricks-add), **605**, *606*
\pssucc (pst-tree), 274, 279, 280
\psSurface (pst-solides3d), **418**, 418, *419*, 420
  pst-3d package, 8, 334, 335, 338, 348, 358, 711
  pst-3dplot package, 346, 358, 360, 373, 375, 377, 385
  pst-all package, 8
  pst-asr package, 659
  pst-bar package, 509
  pst-barcode package, 497
  pst-blur package, 317, 328, 330
  pst-calendar package, 731, 733
\pst-circ (pst-optexp), 698
  pst-circ package, 160, 445, 448, 698
  pst-coil package, 8, 303, 309, 310

(P) Index of Commands and Concepts

(cont.)
pst-cox package, 679
pst-coxcoor package, 666, 679, 681
pst-coxeterp package, 666, 679
pst-dbicons package, 724
pst-diffraction package, 683, 703
pst-eps package, 8, 313, 315
pst-eucl package, 551
pst-fill package, 8, 79, 83, 295, 296, 300, 349, 783
pst-fr3d package, 355
pst-fractal package, 666
pst-func package, 65, 517, 519
pst-geo package, 465, 466
pst-gr3d package, 348, 351, 352
pst-grad package, 8, 79, 317, 321, 780
pst-infixplot package, 204, 667
pst-jftree package, 663
pst-jtree package, 659, 663
pst-key package, 162
pst-labo package, 619, 630–632, 712
pst-lens package, 683, 684
pst-light3d package, 731
pst-magneticfield package, 683, 710
pst-map2d package, 466, 478, 487
pst-map2dII package, 466, 488, 490
pst-map3d package, 466
pst-map3dII package, 466, 489, 490
pst-math package, 517, 839
pst-node package, 8, 142, 225, 226, 236, 256, 259, 260, 265, 277, 280, 285, 310, 445, 659
pst-ob3d package, 346
pst-optexp package, 683, 698
pst-optic package, 683, 689, 703
pst-osci package, 683, 712
pst-pad package, 683, 722
pst-pdf package, 852
pst-pdgr package, 724
pst-plot package, 8, 126, 165, 176, 177, 181, 184, 194, 201, 202, 212, 216, 217, 358, 362, 385, 386, 392, 519, 784
pst-poly package, 666, 674
pst-qtree package, 659
pst-slpe package, 79, 317, 320, 321, 326, 783
pst-solides3d package, 346, 358, 391, 421, 440, 442
pst-spectra package, 683, 716
pst-stru package, 683, 719
pst-text package, 8, 287, 295
pst-tree package, 8, 265, 266, 274, 276, 277, 280, 281, 659, 664
pst-uml package, 641, 652
pst-vue3d package, 391
pst-xkey package, 162
\pstAbortion (pst-pdgr), 731
pstack (PostScript), 843
\pstAngleABC (pst-eucl), 570
\pstAngleAOB (pst-eucl), 562, **563**
\pstArcnOAB (pst-eucl), 568

(cont.)
\pstArcOAB (pst-eucl), 568
\pstBallon (pst-labo), 627, 634
\pstBilles (pst-labo), 620, 625
\pstBissectBAC (pst-eucl), 575, *576*, 576
\pstBULLES (pst-labo), 620, 625
\pstBullesChampagne (pst-labo), 620, 625
\pstCGravABC (pst-eucl), 573, *574*, 574
\pstChauffageBallon (pst-labo), 622, 624, *629*, *635*, 635, *636*
\pstChauffageTube (pst-labo), **623**, *624*, 624, 633, *634*
\pstChildless (pst-pdgr), 731
\pstCircle (pst-eucl), 560
\pstCircleAB (pst-eucl), 567
\pstCircleABC (pst-eucl), 560, **574**, 574, 575
\pstCircleOA (pst-eucl), 562, **567**, 567, *568*
\pstClouFer (pst-labo), 620, 626
\pstClous (pst-labo), 620
\PstCube (pst-ob3d), *346*, **347**, *347*, 348
\pstCuivre (pst-labo), 620
\pstCurvAbsNode (pst-eucl), **568**, 568, *569*, 569
PstDebug Option
    (pst-fill), 296, **299**, 299
    (pst-gr3d), 348, *349*, 349
    (pst-ob3d), *346*
\PstDie (pst-ob3d), **347**, 347, 348
\psTDist (pst-func), 541
\pstDistAB (pst-eucl), 560, 561, **563**, 563
\pstDistillation (pst-labo), *630*, 630, **638**, 638, *639*
\pstDistVal (pst-eucl), 560, **563**, 563
\pstDosage (pst-labo), **629**, *629–631*, 631, *632*, **637**, *637*
\pstEntonnoir (pst-labo), *636*
\pstEprouvette (pst-labo), *637*
\psTextFrame (pstricks), 43, **54**, 54
\psTextFrame* (pstricks), 54
\pstextpath (pst-text), **287**, *288*, *289*, 290, *291*, 291, *294*
\pstFilaments (pst-labo), 620, 625
\PstFrameBoxThreeDMacro (pst-fr3d), 357
\pstGenericCurve (pst-eucl), 562, 562, *563*, *564*, **569**, 569
\pstGeonode (pst-eucl), 554, 554, 555, *557–562*, **563**, 563, 563, *564*, 564, 565, 565, *566–574*, *576*, *577*, *579*, *580*
\pstGrenailleZinc (pst-labo), 620, 626
\PstGridThreeD
    (pst-fr3d), *355*
    (pst-gr3d), 348, *349–351*, 351, **352**, *352*, 352, *353*, 354
\PstGridThreeDHookEnd (pst-gr3d), **352**, 352, *353*, 353, *354*
\PstGridThreeDHookNode (pst-gr3d), 353
\PstGridThreeDHookXFace (pst-gr3d), *353*
\PstGridThreeDHookYFace (pst-gr3d), 353
\PstGridThreeDHookZFace (pst-gr3d), 353
\PstGridThreeDNodeProcessor (pst-gr3d), *353*
\pstheader, 845
    (pstricks), **151**, 151, *152*
\PstHeptagon (pst-poly), *678*
\PstHexagon (pst-poly), *679*

Index of Commands and Concepts (Q)

(cont.)
\psThomae (pst-func), *546*
\psthomO (pst-eucl), *560*, 571, 572, *572*, 572
\psTilt (pst-3d), **335**, *335*, **336**, 336, *337*, 337, **338**, *341*
\pstilt (pst-3d), **335**, **336**, *336*, *337*, 337, *338*
\pstInterCC (pst-eucl), *559*, **560**, **577**, *577*, 578
\pstInterFC (pst-eucl), **579**, *579*, *580*
\pstInterFF (pst-eucl), *578*
\pstInterFL (pst-eucl), *579*
\pstInterLC (pst-eucl), *577*
\pstInterLL (pst-eucl), *576*
\PstLens (pst-lens), **684**, *685–688*
\PstLensShape (pst-lens), **684**, 687
\PstLightThreeDGraphic (pst-light3d), **731**, *733*
\PstLightThreeDText (pst-light3d), **731**, *732*
\pstLineAB (pst-eucl), *560*, *561*, **567**, *567*, 567, *575*, 576
\pstMarkAngle (pst-eucl), *556*, *557*, **566**, *566*
\pstMediatorAB (pst-eucl), *575*
\pstMiddleAB (pst-eucl), *573*
\PstNonagon (pst-poly), *679*
\pstOIJGeonode (pst-eucl), *564*
\pstOrtSym (pst-eucl), *570*
\pstOutBissectBAC (pst-eucl), 575, **576**, 576
\PstPad (pst-pad), *723*
\PstParaboloid (pst-3dplot), *384*
\PstPentagon (pst-poly), *678*
\PstPerson (pst-pdgr), 730, 731
PstPicture Option
    (pst-gr3d), 348, *349*, 349, 350, 352
    (pst-poly), 674
\pstpipette (pst-labo), *638*
\PstPlanePut (pst-3dplot), 365, *366*, 368
\PstPolygon (pst-poly), *674*, 674, *675–678*
\PstPolygon∗ (pst-poly), 674
\PstPolygonNode (pst-poly), *678*, 679
\pstProjection (pst-eucl), *572*, 573
\pstRadUnit rigid length (pst-plot), *194*
\pstRadUnitInv rigid length (pst-plot), *194*
\psTransformPoint (pst-solides3d), **408**, *409*
\psTree (pst-tree), **265**, 265, *266*
  psTree env. (pst-tree), **265**, 266
\pstree (pst-tree), ***265***, 265, *266*, 266, *267–275*, 275, *276*, *278–286*
\pstRelationship (pst-pdgr), *729*
\pstriangle (pstricks), 43, **55**, ***56***
\pstriangle∗ (pstricks), 56
\pstribox
    (pst-node), 240
    (pstricks), *113*
\pstribox∗ (pstricks), 113
pstricks package, 9, 10, 29, 89, 204, 265, 348, 582, 847
PSTricks object, 159
pstricks-add package, 23, 33, 47, 89, 92, 98, 99, 106, 144, 170, 175, 176, 244–246, 385, 581, 602, 666
\PSTricksOff (pstricks), *152*
\PSTricksOn (pstricks), 152
\pstRightAngle (pst-eucl), 566, ***567***, 567

\pstRotation (pst-eucl), 558, *559*, 562, **570**, 570, *571*, 571
\pstScalePoints
    (pst-plot), 192, ***223***, 223
    (pstricks-add), 604
\pstSegmentMark (pst-eucl), *565*
\PstSphereToWall (pst-pad), 723
\pstSymO (pst-eucl), **569**, *569*, **570**, 570
\pstThreeDBox (pst-3dplot), *369*, *371*, **382**, *382*, *799*
\pstThreeDCircle (pst-3dplot), *383*
\pstThreeDCoor (pst-3dplot), *361–373*, **374**, *374*, *376–378*, *381–391*, *799*
\pstThreeDDot (pst-3dplot), *369*, *370*, **377**, *377*, *378*
\pstThreeDEllipse (pst-3dplot), *364*, *370*, **383**, *383*
\pstThreeDLine (pst-3dplot), ***378***, *381*
\pstThreeDNode (pst-3dplot), 377
\pstThreeDPut (pst-3dplot), *363*, *366*, *372*, **377**, *377*, 377, 384
\pstThreeDSphere (pst-3dplot), *372*, *373*, **385**, *385*
\pstThreeDSquare (pst-3dplot), **381**, *382*
\pstThreeDTriangle (pst-3dplot), *365*, **380**, *381*
\PstTiling (pst-fill), 295
\PSTtoEPS (pst-eps), 314, *315*
\pstTournureCuivre (pst-labo), 620, 626
\pstTranslation (pst-eucl), *561*, **571**, *571*
\pstTriangle (pst-eucl), *553–556*, **565**, 565, **566**, *566*, 570, *573–575*
\pstTubeEssais (pst-labo), *621–623*, *625–627*, *633*, 634
\pstTuveEssais (pst-labo), *639*
\pstunit (pstricks), 123
\pstVerb, 436
    (pstricks), 20, 25, *32*, *152*, **154**, 154, **155**, 155, *156*, 156
\pstverb (pstricks), 123, *152*, **154**, 154–156
\pstverbscale (pstricks), 25, **154**, 156
\PstWallToWall (pst-pad), 723
\psunit (pstricks), **23**, 181
\psverbboxfalse (pstricks), 119
\psverbboxtrue (pstricks), *119*
\psvlabel (pst-plot), *174*
\psVolume (pst-func), 548
\pswedge (pstricks), 49, ***63***, 65
\pswedge∗ (pstricks), 63
\psxunit (pstricks), **23**, 140, 597, 605
\psyunit
    (pst-coil), 308
    (pstricks), **23**, 28, 140, 597, 605
\pszigzag (pst-coil), *304–306*, **309**, *310*, 310, *312*
\pszigzag∗ (pst-coil), 309
pt, 36, 123
PtNameMath Option (pst-eucl), 552, *564*, 564, *569–577*
PtoC (PostScript), 845
\put, *358*, *359*
put (PostScript), 843
\putoverlaybox (pstricks), 147
Pyth (PostScript), 845

Q

Q Option (pst-cox), 680

\qdisk (pstricks), *32*, **61**, *61*, *107*, 125, *146*
\qline (pstricks), **53**, 125
QR code, 507
qtree package, 664
quadripole, 452
\quadripole (pst-circ), 452
quadripoleinput Option (pst-circ), 455
Quadrupole, 448
quadrupole, 451, 457

R

R Option (pst-magneticfield), 710
R value
    (pst-node), 258, 259
    (pst-tree), 266
    (pstricks), 110, *113*
r Option
    (pst-diffraction), 706, 707
    (pst-solides3d), 397–399, 401, 402
r value
    (pst-node), 258, 259
    (pst-tree), 281
    (pst-uml), 644, *645*, 645
    (uml), 654
r0 Option (pst-solides3d), 398, 400, *429*
r1 Option (pst-solides3d), 398, 400, *429*
rad (PostScript), *156*
radian, 141, 175, 193, 207
\radian (pstricks), 23
radian measure, 23
Radius Option
    (pst-eucl), 552, 560, *561*, 577–579
    (pst-fractal), 672
    (pst-geo), 478, **481**, 490
radius, 140
radius Option
    (pst-node), 227, *228*, 228, 229, 238
    (pst-tree), *265*, *266*, *270*, *272*, *282*, *284–286*
RadiusA Option (pst-eucl), 552, 560
radiusA Option (pst-func), 544, *545*, 545, *546*
RadiusB Option (pst-eucl), 552, 560
radiusB Option (pst-func), 544, *545*, 545, *546*, *547*
radslope value (pst-grad), *321*, 321, *325*
radslopes value (pst-grad), *321*, 321, *324*
RadtoDeg (PostScript), *195*, 845
railroad diagram, 249
raindrop function, 545
\raisebox, 28
rand (PostScript), *141*, 843
random package, 347
random number generator, 844
RandomFaces Option (pst-ob3d), 346, *347*, 347
randomi counter (pst-ob3d), 347
range Option (pst-solides3d), 401, 410
RAngle (PostScript), 845
\rayInterLens (pst-optic), *690*
rB Option (pstricks), *105*

rb Option (pstricks), *105*
rb value (pst-node), 232
rbracketlength Option (pstricks), 92, *95*, 95
\rccor (pstricks), *137*
\RCMPL (pst-rrgtrees), 660
\rCMPL (pst-rrgtrees), 660
rcolwidth Option (powerdot), 763
\rcoor (pstricks), 136, **137**, *138*
\rcurveto (pstricks), *135*
rcurveto (PostScript), 843
RDogToothA value (pst-osci), 712
RDogToothB value (pst-osci), 713
\readdata
    (pst-3dplot), 390
    (pst-plot), **212**, **213**, 215, 218, 513
\readpsbardata (pst-bar), *512*, **513**, *513–515*, 515, *516*
receptor value (pst-circ), 453
rectangle, 54
rectangle value (pst-circ), 455, 457
RectangleA value (pst-osci), 712
RectangleB value (pst-osci), 713
recuperationGaz Option (pst-labo), 620, 627, 628, *629*, 635
\red (pstricks), *9*
red value (pstricks), *45*
RedContLissajou value (pst-osci), 713
ref Option
    (pst-node), 227, **232**
    (pstricks), 54, *106*, 106, 277, *586*, *590*, 591, *592–595*
    (uml), *654*, 654, *655*, *657*
reference Option (uml), *655*
\reflectbox (graphicx), 117
refpoint Option (uml), *654*, 654, *655*, *658*
\refractionRay (pst-optic), *692–694*, *697*
refrigerantBoulle Option (pst-labo), 620, 627
refrigerantBoulles Option (pst-labo), *627*
\relationshipbetween (pst-dbicons), *728*
relative value (pstricks), 44, **51**, 51
RelayNOP, 450
\relayNOP (pst-circ), 450
\renewcommand*, 515
repeat (PostScript), 843
\resetcolorseries (xcolor), 13, **14**, *14–16*
\ResetXY (pst-uml), **645**, *646*, 647
resistor, 449
\resistor (pst-circ), 445, *446*, 449, *450*, 452, 454
\resizebox (graphicx), *390*, *391*
resolution Option (pst-solides3d), 410, *437*, *439*
reverse coor, 136
Reverse Polish Notation, *see* RPN, 207
rfrheight Option (powerdot), 763
rfrprop Option (powerdot), 763
RGB, 9, 317, 430, 703, 841
ridge Option (pst-geo), 479, 485
ridgecolor Option (pst-geo), 480
ridgewidth Option (pst-geo), 480
Riemann, 605

Index of Commands and Concepts (S)

(cont.)
Riemann value (pstricks-add), 605, *606*
Riemann function, 545
right value
    (pst-circ), 454, 455
    (pst-plot), 177, 180
rightangle value (pst-solides3d), *415*
RightAngleSize Option (pst-eucl), 552, *556*, 556, *567*, 567
RightAngleType Option (pst-eucl), 552, *556*, 556, *567*, *573*
righttext Option (pst-pdgr), 731
rivercolor Option (pst-geo), 480
rivers Option (pst-geo), 467, *468–470*, 474, **475**, *475*, *477*, 479, 489, 490
rk4 value (pstricks-add), 611, *613*, *614*
\rlineto (pstricks), *134*
rlineto (PostScript), 843
\RM (demo), *586*
rm Option (pst-solides3d), 433, *434*, 434
Rmax Option (pst-geo), 482, 484
rmoveto (PostScript), 843
\rmultiput (pstricks-add), *106*
\rmultiput* (pstricks-add), 106
\Rnode (pst-node), 227, 227, **237**, *237*, 237, *238*, 255, *257*, 257, 259, 277
\rnode (pst-node), 142, *166*, *225*, *232*, **236**, *236*, 236, 237, *242*, *246–253*, *256*, *259*, *272*, *273*, 277, *646*
roll (PostScript), *612*, 843
\roller (pst-stru), *719*
root, 265
rot Option
    (pst-node), 227, 232, *233*
    (pstricks), 54, *106*, 106, *591*, *592–595*
RotAngle Option (pst-eucl), 552, *558*, 558, *562*, 570, *571*, 571
\rotate (pstricks), *131*
rotate (PostScript), *216*, 843
rotate Option (pst-barcode), 497, *498*, *499*
\rotatebox (pstricks), 342
Rotatedown env. (pstricks), *117*
rotatedroite value (pst-solides3d), 412
Rotateleft env. (pstricks), *117*
rotateOpoint3d (PostScript), 435
rotatepol value (pst-solides3d), 412, *413*
Rotateright env. (pstricks), *117*
rotating, 116
rotating package, 337
Rotation Option (pst-eps), 315
rotation, 216, 359
rotation Option (pstricks), 106
rotation angle, 375, 489, 570
rotation centre, 584
rotation order, 371
RotSequence Option (pst-3dplot), 360, 370, *371*, 371, *799*
RotX Option
    (pst-geo), 478, *480–482*, *484–487*, 489

    (pst-solides3d), *402*, 408, *437*, 437, *438*
rotX Option (pst-3dplot), 360, *371*, *799*
RotY Option
    (pst-geo), 478, *480–482*, *484–487*, 489
    (pst-solides3d), 408
rotY Option (pst-3dplot), 360, *371*, *799*
RotZ Option
    (pst-geo), 478, 489
    (pst-solides3d), 408
rotZ Option (pst-3dplot), 360, *371*, *799*
rouge value (pst-solides3d), 425
round (PostScript), 208, 840
rowsep Option (pst-node), 258, *260*, 260, *261*
RPN, 203, 207, 211, 607, 612
\RPN
    (infix-RPN), *666*, 666, *667*
    (pst-math), 385
\Rput (pstricks), **107**, 107, *108*
\rput (pstricks), 28, 54, *58*, *60*, *89*, *92*, 103, *104*, 104, **105**, *105*, 105–108, *115*, *150*, 220, *252*, *257*, 491, 587, 592, *666*, 755, *849*
\Rput* (pstricks), 107
\rput* (pstricks), 105
\rputXY (pst-uml), 646
rrgtrees package, 659
RSS Expanded, 505
RSS Limited, 505
RSS-14, 505
rtp2xyz (PostScript), 391, *429*
ruban value (pst-solides3d), *401*
\rule, *260*, 621
Runge-Kutta, 611, 612
\runit (pstricks), 140
runit Option (pstricks), 23

S

s Option (pst-diffraction), 705
sab Option (pst-pdgr), 731
samer Option (pst-geo), 467, 489, 490, *494*
Sanson-Flamsteed, 469
saturation, 430
\savebox, 18, *42*, *115*, 148
\savedata (pst-plot), 212, 213, 848
SaveVerbatim env. (fancyvrb), *773*
\sbox, *18*, *148*, *150*
Scale Option (pst-eps), 315
scale, 23
\scale (pstricks), **130**, *131*
scale (PostScript), 843
scale Option
    (graphicx), *336*, 337
    (pst-fractal), *670*, 670, *671*, 671
\scalebox (graphicx), 118
scalefont (PostScript), *216*, 843
scaleOpoint3d (PostScript), 435
scalex Option (pst-barcode), 497, *498*, *499*
scaley Option (pst-barcode), 497, *498*, *499*

scaling, 71, 116
scaling factor, 335
scanline rendering procedure, 739
\scriptscriptstyle, 109, 170, 178
\scriptsize, 178
\scriptstyle, 109, 170, 178
secant, 607
secondarylabel Option (pst-circ), 447, 457
\section (powerdot), 761
sections value (powerdot), 761
SegmentColor Option (pst-3dplot), 361, 372, 372, 373, 384, 385
SegmentSymbol Option (pst-eucl), 552, 554, 555, 565, 565, 570, 573, 575
SegmentSymbolA Option (pst-eucl), 552, 554, 575
SegmentSymbolB Option (pst-eucl), 552, 554, 575
SegmentSymbolC Option (pst-eucl), 552, 554, 575
semi axis, 63
sensivity1 Option (pst-osci), 712
sensivity2 Option (pst-osci), 713
\SENTENCE (pst-rrgtrees), 661
series expansion, 210
setcmykcolor (PostScript), 20, 843
\setcolor (pstricks), 138
setdash (PostScript), 843
setfont (PostScript), 216, 843
setgray (PostScript), 216, 843
sethsbcolor (PostScript), 141, 843
setlinecap (PostScript), 844
setlinejoin (PostScript), 45, 364, 844
setlinewidth (PostScript), 844
setmatrix (PostScript), 844
setrgbcolor (PostScript), 20, 844
setspace package, 292
\SetX (pst-uml), 645
\SetXY (pst-uml), 645
\SetY (pst-uml), 645
sex Option (pst-pdgr), 730, 731
sfg package, 724
\sfgbranch (sfg), 727
\sfgcurve (sfg), 727
\sfgnode (sfg), 727
\sfgtermnod (sfg), 727
shading, 740
shadow, 328, 329, 334
shadow Option, 355
    (pst-3d), 334
    (pst-blur), 328
    (pstricks), 44, 52, 112, 112, 113, 124, 329–332
shadow colour, 328, 329
shadow creation, 51
shadow effect, 51
shadowangle Option
    (pst-3d), 334
    (pst-blur), 328
    (pstricks), 44, 52, 133, 133

(cont.)
shadowcolor Option
    (pst-3d), 334
    (pst-blur), 328
    (pstricks), 44, 133, 329, 330
shadowsize Option
    (pst-3d), 334
    (pst-blur), 328, 329
    (pstricks), 44, 54, 133, 133
shape Option (pstricks), 80
shape value (pstricks), 80, 83, 84
shapealpha Option (pstricks), 80, 83
shift Option (pstricks), 27, 28, 29
\SHN (pst-uml), 648
shortput Option (pst-node), 98, 114, 227, 233, **234**, 234, 235, 236
\shortstack, 284
\show, 213, 514
show (PostScript), 216, 844
show Option (pst-solides3d), 403
showBase Option (pst-solides3d), 396, 410
showbbox Option (pst-tree), 267, 276, 276
showborder Option (pst-barcode), 498
showbox Option (pst-tree), 265, 266
showFP Option (demo), 162
showgrid Option (pstricks), 27, 29, 30, 30, 33, 37, 44, 48, 53, 56, 117, 124, 596
showInside Option (pst-3dplot), 384
showOrigin Option (pst-solides3d), 397, 403, 404, 404
showorigin Option (pst-plot), 166, 171, 171, 174, 175, 193
showpoints Option (pstricks), 44, 50, 50, 62, 62, 64, 69, 124, 214, 219–221, 535
sigma Option (pst-func), 538, 539
\Simplex (pst-cox), 680, 680, 681
Simpson, 538
Simpson Option (pst-func), 538
SIN (PostScript), 520
sin (PostScript), 195, 208, 211, 840
SINC (PostScript), 520
sinCoeff Option (pst-func), 527
sincoeff Option (pst-func), 528
sine function, 527
SINH (PostScript), 520
SinusA value (pst-osci), 712
SinusB value (pst-osci), 713
sizeCenters Option (pst-cox), 680
sizeVertices Option (pst-cox), 680
sizeX Option (uml), 653–655
sizeY Option (uml), 653, 654, 655
\skiplevel (pst-tree), 283, **284**
skiplevel env. (pst-tree), 284
\skiplevels (pst-tree), 283, **284**, 284
skiplevels env. (pst-tree), 284
slide, 147
\slide
    (beamer), 766, 767
    (powerdot), 747–757, 759, 762, 764, 765

Index of Commands and Concepts (S)

(cont.)
slide Option (powerdot), 761
slide env. (powerdot), 755, *756*, 764
\slideheight rigid length (powerdot), *755*
slides value (powerdot), 754
\slidewidth rigid length (powerdot), *755*
slope value (pst-grad), ***321***, 321, *323*, 324
slopeangle Option (pst-grad), 322, *324*, 324
slopebegin Option (pst-grad), *322*, 322, *323*, 323
slopebegin value (pst-grad), 322
slopecenter Option (pst-grad), 322, 324, *325*, *326*
slopecolors Option (pst-grad), 322, *323*, 323
slopeend Option (pst-grad), 322, *323*, 323
slopeend value (pst-grad), 322
sloperadius Option (pst-grad), 322, ***325***, *326*
slopes value (pst-grad), ***321***, 321, *323*
slopesteps Option (pst-grad), 322, ***324***
SLW (PostScript), 844
\small, 170, 178
Softfont, 74
solid Option (pstricks), 80
solid value
    (pst-3dplot), 369
    (pstricks), 22, 43, *45*, 80, 88, 177, 186
solide Option (pst-labo), 620, 625, *626*, 626, *627*
SolidesDict (PostScript), 846
solidmemory Option
    (pst-dolides3d), *784*
    (pst-solides3d), *402*, *413*, 440, *441–444*
SolidOctogon value (pstricks), 74, 75
sommets Option (pst-solides3d), *403*, 403, *439*, 439, *440*
South America, 490
space, 153
\space, **153**, *154*
    (pstricks), 157
\special, 5, 123, 135, **151**, 151, 155, 262, 851
\SpecialCoor (pstricks), 58, **139**, 144, 145, 161, 237, 253, 590, 596
spectrum, 718
    absorption, 716
    emission, 716
speed, 613
sphere value (pst-solides3d), *393*, *394*, *398*, 429
spherical coordinates, 370
SphericalCoor Option (pst-3dplot), 360, ***370***
spiral, 614
spotX Option
    (pst-3dplot), 360, *365*, 365
    (pst-solides3d), 406, *419*
spotY Option
    (pst-3dplot), 360, *365*, 365
    (pst-solides3d), 406, *419*
\spotZ (pst-3dplot), *365*
spotZ Option
    (pst-3dplot), 360, 365
    (pst-solides3d), 406, *419*
sqrt (PostScript), 208, 211, 386, 840

(cont.)
square value (pstricks), *71*
\SQUID (pst-circ), 450
Squid, 450
srand (PostScript), 844
stack, 204
stack value (pst-bar), 510, 511
stack element, 840
stack system, 203
standard deviation, 518, 534, 538
startfading Option (pst-grad), 322, **326**
startX Option (makeplot), *683*
startY Option (makeplot), *683*
\State (vaucanson-g), *726*
step, 538
step Option (xcolor), 14
StepType Option (pstricks-add), *605*, 605, *606*
stepX Option (pst-solides3d), 406, *407*, *420*
stepY Option (pst-solides3d), 406, *407*, *420*
stepZ Option (pst-solides3d), 406, *407*, *420*
stereotype Option (uml), *655*, *658*
\stone (psgo), 737
straight line, 577
string (PostScript), 843, 844
\stroke (pstricks), *75*, ***128***, 128
stroke (PostScript), 844
strokeopacity Option (pstricks), 80, 83, ***87***, *88*, 88, 594, 595
strophoid, 206
.sty file extension, 5
style, 121
style Option
    (powerdot), 748
    (pst-calendar), 733, 735
    (pstricks), *89*, 121
style file, 151
styleCenters Option (pst-cox), 680
styleCourant Option (pst-magneticfield), 710
styleSpire Option (pst-magneticfield), 710
styleVertices Option (pst-cox), 680
sub (PostScript), 840
sub value (pst-osci), 713
subgridcolor Option (pstricks), 33, 36, *37*, *107*
subgriddiv Option (pstricks), 33, *35*, 35, *36*, *108*, 776
subgriddots Option (pstricks), 33, *37*, 37
subgridwidth Option (pstricks), 33, *36*, 36
subof Option (uml), *658*
substance Option (pst-labo), 620, *625*, 625, *626*, 626, 637
subtickcolor Option (pst-plot), 177, *184*, 184, *185*, *190*
subticklinestyle Option (pst-plot), 177, 186
subticks Option (pst-plot), 177, 182, *183*, 183, *184–190*, *192*
subticksize Option (pst-plot), 177, *183*, 183, *184–186*, *188*, *189*
subtickwidth Option (pst-plot), 177, *186*, 186, *187*
subtree, 266
subv value (pst-solides3d), 411

(cont.)
suisseromand value (pst-eucl), 552, 556
Sum (PostScript), 208, *210*, 210
sum function, 210
superellipse, 544
Suppressor, 450
\Suppressor (pst-circ), 450
surface value (pst-solides3d), *401*, 401
surface* value (pst-solides3d), *402*, 402
surfaceparametree value (pst-solides3d), *402*, *402*, *431*
\swapaxes (pstricks), *131*
swapaxes Option (pstricks), 31, 32, 124
.swf file extension (pstricks-add), 741
switch, 449, 451
\switch (pst-circ), 449
Symbol value (pstricks), 35
symbol, 69
sympol value (pst-solides3d), 413

T

T (PostScript), 845
t value
    (pst-uml), *645*
    (uml), 654
tab value (pst-node), 227, 234, 235
\tabcolsep rigid length, 112
\tableofcontents (powerdot), 761
tablr value (pst-node), 227, 234, 235
tabular env., *29*, 112, 113, 645
TAN (PostScript), 520
tan (PostScript), 208
tangent, 32, 607, 610
TANH (PostScript), 520
\taput (pst-node), 235, **255**
\taput* (pst-node), 255
tbarsize Option (pstricks), 92, *95*, 95
\tbput (pst-node), 235, **255**
\tbput* (pst-node), 255
\TC (pst-tree), *266–269*, *272*, *274*, *276*, **277**, *278–284*, **285**, 285
\Tc (pst-tree), 277, *278*, *280*, *281*
\TCircle (pst-tree), 277
\Tcircle (pst-tree), *268–270*, *274*, **277**, *284*
tCyan value (demo), *89*
\Tdia (pst-tree), *275*, 277
\Tdot (pst-tree), 277, *278*, *285*, *286*
tectonic plate, 485
\temp (xcolor), 16
template Option (powerdot), 761
\tension (pst-circ), 449
tension Option (pst-circ), 447, *452*, *453*
tensioncolor Option (pst-circ), 447, *452*, *453*
tensionlabel Option (pst-circ), 447, *452*, *453*
tensionlabelcolor Option (pst-circ), 447, *452*, *453*
tensionlabeloffset Option (pst-circ), 447, *452*, *453*
tensionoffset Option (pst-circ), 447
tensionwidth Option (pst-circ), 447, *452*, *453*
tetrahedron value (pst-solides3d), *399*

.tex file extension, 5
\text (amsmath), 258
text Option (pst-solides3d), 410
text mode, 109, 178
\textcolor, 9, **10**, **11**, *12*, *27*
texte value (pst-solides3d), *417*
textfont Option (pst-barcode), *504*
TeXtoEPS env. (pst-eps), *314*
\TeXtoEPS (pst-eps), 314
textpos Option (pst-barcode), 498, *499*
textsize Option (pst-barcode), 498, *504*
\textstyle, 109, 178
textures program, 156
\Tf (pst-tree), **277**, *278*
\Tfan (pst-tree), *267*, **279**, *279*
\the, 583
THETA Option (pst-geo), 478, 489
theta Option (pst-solides3d), 398, 399, 402
thislevelsep Option (pst-tree), 267, 273, *274*, *280*, *285*, *286*
thistreefit Option (pst-tree), 267, 270
thistreenodesize Option (pst-tree), 267, 271
thistreesep Option (pst-tree), 267, *269*, 269, *280*
Thomae function, 545
\thput (pst-node), 254, **255**
\thput* (pst-node), 255
three value (pst-circ), 454
three-dimensional illustration, 333
three-dimensional representation, 305
\ThreeDput
    (pst-3d), **338**, 338, *339*, 339, *342–344*
    (pst-gr3d), 352
thyristor value (pst-circ), 455
Thyristor pair, 205
tickcolor Option (pst-plot), 177, *184*, 184, *185*, *186*
ticklength Option (pst-solides3d), 406
ticklinestyle Option (pst-plot), 177, *182–186*, 186
ticks Option (pst-plot), 166, *171*, 171, *172*, 172, *174*, 176, *183*, 183
ticksize Option (pst-plot), 166, *174*, 174, 176, 177, 181, *182*, 182, *183*, *184*, *188*, *189*, *192*
tickstyle Option (pst-plot), 166, 172, *173*, 173, *174*, 174, 177, 181, 182, 184
tickwidth Option (pst-plot), 177, *184–186*, 186, *187*
\tiershortcuts
    (pst-asr), *663*
    (pst-qtree), *664*, *665*
tight value (pst-tree), 267, 269, 270
tiling, 295
tiling, 83, 123
tilting, 334, 335
tilting angle, 490
timediv Option (pst-osci), 713
Times–Roman value (pstricks), 35
\tiny, 170, 178
\title
    (beamer), *766*, *767*

Index of Commands and Concepts (T)

(cont.)
      (powerdot), 747–757, 759, 762, 764, 765
tl value (pstricks), 103
\tlput (pst-node), 235, **255**
\tlput* (pst-node), 255
TMatrix (PostScript), 845
.tmp file extension (pst-tree), 274
\Tn (pst-tree), *278*
  tndepth Option (pst-tree), 281, 282
  tnheight Option (pst-tree), 281, *282*, 282
  tnpos Option (pst-tree), 281, *282*, 285
  \tnput (pst-tree), 281
  tnsep Option (pst-tree), 281, *282*, 282
  tnyref Option (pst-tree), 281, **283**, 283
  toc Option (powerdot), 756
  tocsection Option (powerdot), 761
\TOP (pst-rrgtrees), *661*
  top value (pst-plot), 166, *173*, 173, 177, 180
  topsep Option (powerdot), 763
  tore value (pst-solides3d), *400*, 429
\Toval (pst-tree), 265, *266*, 268, *271*, *272*, *274*, **277**, *278*
\Tp (pst-tree), 277, *278*
\TPoffset (pst-text), 288
tpos Option
    (pst-node), 227, 233
    (pst-tree), *280*
\TR (pst-tree), *271*, *275*, **277**, 277, *278*, *279*
\Tr (pst-tree), *272*, *273*, **277**, 277, *278*
trans Option (powerdot), *755*
\Transform (pst-optic), *689–691*
transform (PostScript), 844
transform Option (pst-solides3d), 410, *435*, 435, *436*
transformation, 358, 408
transformation equation, 359
transformation matrix, 72, 841
transformer, 451, 452, 457
\transformer (pst-circ), 452, *457*
transformeriprimary Option (pst-circ), 447, *457*
transformeriprimarylabel Option (pst-circ), 447
transformerisecondary Option (pst-circ), 447, *457*
transformerisecondarylabel Option (pst-circ), 447
transformerprimarylabel Option (pst-circ), *457*
transformersecondarylabel Option (pst-circ), *457*
TransformLabel Option (pst-eucl), 552, *558*, 558
transfrmcolor Option (pst-geo), 480
transistor, 451, 456
\transistor (pst-circ), 451, *456*
  transistorbase Option (pst-circ), *456*
  transistorbaselabel Option (pst-circ), *456*
  transistorcircle Option (pst-circ), 447, *456*
  transistorcollector Option (pst-circ), *456*
  transistorcollectorlabel Option (pst-circ), *456*
  transistoremitter Option (pst-circ), *456*
  transistoremitterlabel Option (pst-circ), *456*
  transistoribase Option (pst-circ), 447
  transistoribaselabel Option (pst-circ), 447
  transistoricollector Option (pst-circ), 447

(cont.)
  transistoricollectorlabel Option (pst-circ), 447
  transistoriemitter Option (pst-circ), 447
  transistoriemitterlabel Option (pst-circ), 447
  transistorinvert Option (pst-circ), 447, 456
  transistortype Option (pst-circ), 447, *456*
transition, 754
\translate (pstricks), **130**, 130, *131*, *132*, 132, *133*, 134
translate (PostScript), 844
translatedroite value (pst-solides3d), 412
translatepol value (pst-solides3d), 412
Translation Option (pst-eps), 315
translation, 297, 571
transparency, 79, 87, 326
transx Option (pst-barcode), 497
transy Option (pst-barcode), 497
tree, 265
    connection, 266
    node, 269
    object, 266
    structure, 269
    subtree, 266
treefit Option (pst-tree), 267, 269, *270*, 270
treeflip Option (pst-tree), 266, *269*
treeflip=true Option (pst-tree), 268
treemode Option (pst-tree), 266, *268*, 268, *269*, *272–274*, *278*, *280*, *281*, *283*
treenodesize Option (pst-tree), 267, *271*, 271, *272*, *278*
trees, 255
treesep Option (pst-tree), 266, 269, *270*, 270, *272*, *279*, *282*
trenchcolor Option (pst-geo), 480
\Tri (pst-tree), *278*
tri value (pst-node), 258, 259
triac value (pst-circ), 455
triangle, 55, 111, 113
triangle value
    (pst-circ), 454
    (pstricks), *71*, *72*
TriangleA value (pst-osci), 712
TriangleB value (pst-osci), 713
trigLabelBase Option (pst-plot), 177, *193*, *194*, 194, *195–197*
trigLabels Option (pst-plot), 177, *193*, 193, *194*, *195*, *196*, *197*
trigonometric function, 195
\triline (pst-jtree), *663*
\triload
    (pst-pad), *723*
    (pst-stru), **719**, *720*, *721*
trimode Option (pstricks), 110, 111, *113*, 113
\trinode (pst-node), **240**, 259, 277
\trinode* (pst-node), 240
triple, 22
Tripole, 448
tripole, 451
tripolestyle Option (pst-circ), 447, *457*, 457

(cont.)
 tronccone value (pst-solides3d), *398*, 429
 troncconecreux value (pst-solides3d), *398*, *429*
 tRot value (demo), *89*
 \trput (pst-node), 235, ***255***
 \trput* (pst-node), 255
 true value (powerdot), 761
 trueAngle Option (pstricks-add), 596, 597, *598*, 598
 truncate (PostScript), 208, 840
 Tshadowangle Option (pst-3d), *334*
 Tshadowcolor Option (pst-3d), *334*, 334, **335**, *335*, *336*
 Tshadowsize Option (pst-3d), 334, ***335***
 \tspace (pst-tree), 271, ***279***, 279
 \Tswitch (pst-circ), 451
 \Ttri (pst-tree), 277
 tube value (pst-labo), 619, *621*, 621, 623, 633
 tubeCoude Option (pst-labo), 620, *622*, 622
 tubeCoudeU Option (pst-labo), 620, ***622***, 622
 tubeCoudeUB Option (pst-labo), 620, *622*, 622, *635*
 tubeDroit Option (pst-labo), 620, 621, *622*, *623*
 tubePenche Option (pst-labo), 620, *623*, 623, *638*
 tubeRecourbe Option (pst-labo), 620, 627, *628*, 628
 tubeRecourbeCourt Option (pst-labo), 620, *628*, 628
 tubeSeul Option (pst-labo), 620, 623, *624*, 624
 \tvput (pst-node), 255
 \tvput* (pst-node), 255
 \twocolumn (powerdot), 762
 twoHole Option (pst-diffraction), 707, 709
 TwoPi (PostScript), 845
 twoSlit Option (pst-diffraction), 705
 type Option
  (powerdot), 761
  (pst-fractal), 668
  (pst-geo), 467, 469, *470–473*, 488, *493*
  (uml), *656*
 Type 1, 73
 Type 3, 73

U

 U value
  (pst-tree), 266
  (pstricks), 110, 111
 \Ucc (pst-circ), 449
 uml package, 641, 652
 \umlActor (pst-uml), 642
 umlActorLineWidth Option (pst-uml), *642*
 umlAlign Option (pst-uml), ***644***, 645
 \umlArgument (uml), 655
 \umlAttribute (uml), *655*
 \umlBottom (uml), *655*
 \umlBottomLeft (uml), *658*
 \umlBottomRight (uml), *658*
 \umlBottomSep (uml), *654*
 \umlBox (uml), 653, **654**, *654*, *655*, 657
 \umlCase (pst-uml), 644
 \umlClass
  (pst-uml), ***641***, *642*, *643*, 643, *644*, *648*
  (uml), *654*, **655**, *655*
 \umlClassifier (uml), 655
 \umlCompartment (uml), *655*
 \umlCompartmentline (uml), *655*
 \umlDiagram (uml), ***653***, 653, *654*, *655*, *658*
  umlDoubleRuleSep Option (pst-uml), 641, *642*, 642
 \umlDrawable (uml), 652
 \umlElement (uml), 652
 \umlLeft (uml), *655*
 \umlMethod (uml), 655
 \umlNote (pst-uml), *644*
 \umlPackage (uml), 657, *658*, 658
  umlParameter Option (pst-uml), 641, *642*, 642
  umlPos Option (pst-uml), *645*
 \umlPutCase (pst-uml), *644*
 \umlPutStateIn (pst-uml), 643
 \umlPutStateOut (pst-uml), 643
 \umlReference (uml), 652
 \umlRelation (uml), **656**, 656, *657*, 657
 \umlRight (uml), *655*
 \umlSchema (uml), *656*
  umlShadow Option (pst-uml), *641*
 \umlStack (pst-uml), 644, **645**, 645
  umlStackLinesStretch Option (pst-uml), *645*
  umlStackSep Option (pst-uml), *645*
  umlStackWidth Option (pst-uml), 645
 \umlState (pst-uml), ***643***, *644*
 \umlStateIn (pst-uml), ***643***, *644*
 \umlStateOut (pst-uml), ***643***, *644*
 \umlStereoType (pst-uml), *643*
 \umlStretchBox (uml), *654*, 655
 \umlSubclass (uml), *657*
 \umlTop (uml), *654*, 654, *655*
 \umlTopLeft (uml), *658*
 \umlTopRight (uml), *658*
 undef value (pst-eucl), 551, 552
 Unified Modelling Language, 641
 unit, 24, 35
 unit Option (pstricks), 23, *36*, *60*, *94*, *95*, *108*, 347, 477, 593
 unit circle, 210
 \unitlength, *358*, *359*
 unknown Option (pst-pdgr), 731
 upper value (pstricks-add), *605*, 605, *606*
 upper sum, 605
 \uput (pstricks), *32*, *35*, *58–60*, 103, *105*, 106, **107**, *107*, 107, *142*, *183*, *199*, 255, **491**
 \uput* (pstricks), 107
 urx Option (pstricks-add), *602*, *603*, 603, *604*, 855
 ury Option (pstricks-add), *602*, *603*, 603, *604*, 855
 USA Option (pst-geo), *477*
 usa Option (pst-geo), *479*
 \usebox, *42*, *148*, *150*
 \usemodule (context), 7
 \usepackage, 4, 7, 517
 user value (pst-eps), 315
 user coordinates, 140

Index of Commands and Concepts (V–X)

userColor Option (pstricks-add), 587

V

valuewidth Option (pst-func), 531
variable Option
 (pst-circ), 447, *456*, 456
 (pst-optexp), *698*
variance, 534
vasectomy value (pst-pdgr), 731
vaucanson-G package, 724
vaucanson-g package, 725
VCO, 449
\vco (pst-circ), 449
VCPicture env. (vaucanson-g), *726*
vecteur value (pst-solides3d), *392, 393*, 411
vector, 411
vector value (pst-solides3d), *396*
vector font, 73
\verb, 116, 117, 119
verbatim, 116–119
verbatim env., 116, 764
verticale value (pst-solides3d), 411
viewangle Option (pst-3d), 341, **342**, *343*, 344, 344
viewpoint, 392
viewpoint Option
 (pst-3d), 341, *342*, 342, *343*, 344, 344, *347*, *348*, *349*, 358
 (pst-solides3d), 391, *392*, 392, *393*, 407, *428, 429*
viewpoint value (pst-solides3d), 395, 425
visibility Option
 (pst-geo), 479
 (uml), *655, 656*
visibleLineStyle Option (pst-3dplot), 360, 369
visibleStyle Option (pst-3dplot), 369
vlines value (pstricks), 80, **81**, 81, **82**, 82, 84–86
vlines∗ value (pstricks), 80–82
voltage, 205
voltage arrow, 452
voltage source, 449, 450
vref Option
 (pst-node), *227*, 237
 (pst-tree), 283
\vspace, 266, 287

W

WallLineColor Option (pst-pad), *723*
WallLineWidth Option (pst-pad), *723*
Wave1 Option (pst-osci), 712
Wave2 Option (pst-osci), 713
wavelength, 703
waves Option (pst-geo), 482
\wd, *42*, 42, 148
 (pstricks), 42
wfraczon Option (pst-geo), 479, 486
wfraczoncolor Option (pst-geo), 480
wfraczonwidth Option (pst-geo), 480
whichabs Option (pstricks-add), 611, 613, *614*, 615

whichord Option (pstricks-add), 611, 613, *614*
whitespace, 152
wideslide env. (powerdot), 756
width, 103
winding, 305
\wire (pst-circ), 448, 449
wire frame, 366
wire frame model, 342
\Wishes (demo), 684
wlangle Option (pst-spectra), 717
wlcmd Option (pst-spectra), 717
wmaglin Option (pst-geo), 479, 486
wmaglincolor Option (pst-geo), 480
wmaglinwidth Option (pst-geo), 480
\WORD (pst-rrgtrees), 661
\WorldMap (pst-geo), 468–475, **477**, 477
\WorldMapII (pst-geo), **487**, 493, 495, 496
\WorldMapThreeD (pst-geo), **478**, 480–482, 484–487
\WorldMapThreeDII (pst-geo), **489**, 490, 491, 494
writeobj value (pst-solides3d), *403*, 428
writeoff value (pst-solides3d), 428
writesolid value (pst-solides3d), 424, 428

X

\X (pst-uml), 645
x value (pst-plot), 166, *170*, 170, *171*, 171, *174*, 176, 177, 190
xAxis Option
 (pst-plot), 176, *179*, 179
 (pstricks-add), *516*
xAxisLabel Option
 (pst-plot), 177
 (pstricks-add), *602, 603*, 603, *604*
xAxisLabelPos Option
 (pst-plot), 177
 (pstricks-add), *602, 603*, 603, *604*
xbbd Option (pst-tree), 267, 276
xbbh Option (pst-tree), 267, 276
xbbl Option (pst-tree), 267, 276
xbbr Option (pst-tree), 267, 276
xcolor package, 6, 7, 9–15, 17, 20, 154, 184, 318, 322, 372, 373, 431
xDecimals Option (pst-plot), 176, 180, *181*
xdpoint value (pst-solides3d), *415*
xdvi program, 9, 152
xdvipdfmx program, 156
xEnd Option (pst-plot), 218–220
xkeyval package, 162
xlabelFactor Option (pst-plot), 177, *178*, *192*, 192
xlabelPos Option (pst-plot), 177, *180*, 180
xLines value (pst-3dplot), 360, 366
xlogBase Option (pst-plot), 177, *190*, 190
xlogBase value (pst-plot), 190
xMax Option (pst-3dplot), 360, *361*, 361, 374
xMin Option (pst-3dplot), 360, *361*, 361, 374
Xnodesep Option (pst-node), 227, 229
XnodesepA Option (pst-node), 227, 229

XnodesepB Option (pst-node), 227, 229
xor (PostScript), 844
xpdf program, 740
xPlotpoints Option (pst-3dplot), 360, *363*, 363, 386–388
xStart Option (pst-plot), 218–220
xStep Option (pst-plot), 218, 221
xsubtickcolor Option (pst-plot), 177, 184
xsubticklinestyle Option (pst-plot), *183*, 186
xsubticks Option (pst-plot), 177, 182, *183*
xsubticksize Option (pst-plot), 177, *183*
xsubtickwidth Option (pst-plot), *183*
xThreeDunit Option (pst-3dplot), 360, *363*, 363
xtickcolor Option (pst-plot), 177, 184
xticklinestyle Option (pst-plot), 186
xticksize Option (pst-plot), 176, 181, *182*
xunit Option (pstricks), 23, 35, 145, *193*
xWidth Option (pst-fractal), *668*, 668, *669–673*, 673, *674*
xy value (pst-3dplot), 360, 362, 365
xyAxes Option (pst-plot), 176, 179
xyDecimals Option (pst-plot), 176, 180, *181*
xyLines value (pst-3dplot), 366
xylogBase Option (pst-plot), 177, *190*, 190, *191*
xylogBase value (pst-plot), 190
xyrot value (pst-3dplot), 362
xyz value (pst-3dplot), 360, 371
xyzLight Option (pst-3dplot), 361, ***373***
xz value (pst-3dplot), 360, 362, 365
xzy value (pst-3dplot), 371

Y

\Y (pst-uml), 646
y value (pst-plot), 166, *170*, 170, *172*, 172, *174*, 176, 177, 190
yAxis Option (pst-plot), 176, *179*, 179
yAxisLabel Option
  (pst-plot), 177
  (pstricks-add), *602*, *603*, 603, *604*
yAxisLabelPos Option
  (pst-plot), 177
  (pstricks-add), *602*, *603*, 603, *604*
yDecimals Option (pst-plot), 176, *179*, 180, *181*
Year Option
  (pst-calendar), *734*, *735*
  (pst-geo), 478
\year (pst-calendar), 733
year Option (pst-calendar), 733
yellow value (pstricks), *45*
yEnd Option (pst-plot), 218, 220
ylabelFactor Option
  (pst-plot), 177, 192, *202*
  (pstricks-add), 604
ylabelPos Option (pst-plot), 177, *180*, 180
yLines value (pst-3dplot), 366
ylogBase Option (pst-plot), 177, *186*, 190, *191*, 192

ylogBase value (pst-plot), 190
yMax Option (pst-3dplot), 360, *361*, 361, 374
yMaxValue Option (pst-plot), 207, 211, *212*, 212
yMin Option (pst-3dplot), 360, *361*, 361, 374
Ynodesep Option (pst-node), 144, 227, *229*, 229, 257
YnodesepA Option (pst-node), 227, 229, *257*
YnodesepB Option (pst-node), 227, 229
yPlotpoints Option (pst-3dplot), 360, *363*, 363, *386*, 386, *387*, 387, *388*, 388, *389*
yStart Option (pst-plot), 218, 220
ysubtickcolor Option (pst-plot), 177, 184
ysubticklinestyle Option (pst-plot), 186
ysubticks Option (pst-plot), 177, 182, *183*
ysubticksize Option (pst-plot), 177, *183*
yThreeDunit Option (pst-3dplot), 360, *363*, 363
ytickcolor Option (pst-plot), 177, 184
yticklinestyle Option (pst-plot), 186
yticksize Option (pst-plot), 176, 181, *182*
yunit Option (pstricks), 23, 35, 145
yWidth Option (pst-fractal), *668*, 668, *669–674*
yxLines value (pst-3dplot), 366
yxz value (pst-3dplot), 371
yz value (pst-3dplot), 360, 362, 365
yzx value (pst-3dplot), 371

Z

ZapfDingbats, 69
ZapfDingbats value (pstricks), 35
\Zener (pst-circ), 449
Zener diode, 449
zeroLineColor Option (pst-func), 520, 522
zeroLineStyle Option (pst-func), 520, 522
zeroLineTo Option (pst-func), 520, 522
zeroLineWidth Option (pst-func), 520, 522
zigzag value (pst-circ), 455
zigzag line, 304, 309
Zmax Option (pst-solides3d), *406*, 406, *407*, *418*, *419*
zMax Option
  (pst-3dplot), 360, 361, 374
  (pst-solides3d), 405
Zmin Option (pst-solides3d), *406*, 406, *407*, *418*, *419*
zMin Option
  (pst-3dplot), 360, 361, 374
  (pst-solides3d), 405
zThreeDunit Option (pst-3dplot), 360, *363*, 363
zxy value (pst-3dplot), 371
zyx value (pst-3dplot), 371
Document Classes
  beamer, 9, 726, 741, 747
  exaarticle, 1
  powerdot, 9, 147, 741, 747, 747, 755, 761
  prosper, 9, 747
  seminar, 9, 147, 747

People

Adamson, Joel J., 2
Adriaens, Hendri, 162, 747, 763
Agapito, Rubens, 800, 802
Akhmadeeva, Leila, 729
Arnold, David, 2
Arseneau, Donald, 347
Aylmer Fisher, Ronald, 542

Babinet, Jacques, 471
Baroni, Stefano, 593
Bernoulli, Jakob, 532
Bersch, Christoph, 698
Bonne, Rigobert, 471
Boone, François, 463, 464
Bos, Victor, 736
Burlton, Bruce, 2

Carlisle, David, 9
Casselmann, Bill, 391
Charpentier, Jean-Côme, 666, 805
Chiang, David, 664
Coombes, Gerry, 2
Coxeter, Harold S. M., 679

Daven, Mike, 2
Diamantini, Maurice, 641

Dirr, Ulrich, 146, 211, 802, 807
Doggett, Anthony, 849
Drechsler, Patrick, 722
Dumont, Kris, 788

Ellison, Christopher, 747
Esperet, Philippe, 850

Fairbairns, Robin, 858
Field, Malcom, 2
Flamsteed, John, 470
Frampton, John, 663
Férnandez, Juan-Pablo, 2

Görner, Reinhard, 765
Gardner, D. J., 659
Gastin, Paul, 725
Gauß, Carl Friedrich, 538
Gibney, Shane, 2
Giese, Martin, 317, 328, 329
Gilg, Jürgen, 710, 743, 816
Girou, Denis, 1, 4, 354, 355, 674, 684, 773, 791, 793
Gjelstad, Ellef Fange, 652
Gosset, William, 541
Gouraud, Henri, 739
Grahn, Alexander, 741

Hammer, Ernst, 471
Hein, Piet, 544

Jagger, Catherine, 2
Jorssen, Christophe, 666, 712
Joshi, Manjusha, 2

Kern, Uwe, 9
Khalidi, Vafa, 2
Kotthoff, Lars, 2, 805

Lam, Hubert, 2
Lambert, Johann Heinrich, 469
Lamé, Gabriel, 544
Lombardy, Sylvain, 725
Luis Llanio, Jorge, 791
Luque, Jean-Gabriel, 679
Luque, Manuel, 391, 585, 640, 679, 684, 689, 710, 712, 719, 733, 775, 781, 783, 786, 795

Maio, Ivan, 848
Matarazzo, Giuseppe, 719, 798
May, Wolfgang, 728, 771
Mercator, Gerardus, 469

Niepraschk, Rolf, 851

Nitecki, Zbigniew, 2

O'Connor, Bill, 2

Penrose, Roger, 82

Römer, Christine, 794
Rahtz, Sebastian, 4
Ressler, Eugene, 312
Rodriguez, Dominique, 580, 798, 804
Rokicki, Tom, 287, 290, 865

Sakarovitch, Jacques, 725

Sangwin, Chris, 785
Sanson, Nicolas, 470
Schmid, Hanspeter, 727
Schmidt, Walter, 286
Schmittbuhl, Arnaud, 391, 716, 779, 781, 786
Shepard, Rich, 2
Siart, Uwe, 831
Siegel, Thomas, 772, 847, 849
Simpson, Thomas, 538
Story, Don Paul, 743

Tantau, Till, 747, 766
Taylor, Ciaran, 2

Thomae, Carl Johannes, 545
Todd, Ewan, 293

Van Zandt, Timothy, 1, 4, 738
Veytsman, Boris, 2, 729
Vignault, Jean-Paul, 391
Vila-Forcen, Jose-Emilio, 683

Walia, Lakhinder, 2
Widmann, Michael, 747

Zhuhan, Jiang, 174
Ziegenhagen, Uwe, 56

ALSO PUBLISHED BY UIT

Typesetting tables with LaTeX

Herbert Voss

This is the first-ever book dedicated to typesetting tables in LaTeX. With LaTeX you can create just about any kind of table, from simple to extremely complex. But while the table capabilities in LaTeX are powerful, they can be daunting at first sight or when you require a sophisticated layout. This book describes the additional LaTeX packages that are available to simplify your task, and gives ready-to-run examples of each, to get you working as quickly as possible, and present your data in the most effective way.

With this book you will learn:

▷ How to typeset tables, from basic to advanced.

▷ How to use advanced features, such as color and multi-page tables.

▷ How add-on LaTeX tables packages can simplify or enhance your work.

Contents

1. Introduction to LaTeX's table-handling
2. LaTeX packages for tables
3. Using color in tables
4. Multi-page tables
5. Tips and tricks
6. Examples

Praise for the German Edition

"A concise reference book for those who may already have used LaTeX but aren't aware of the powerful capabilities provided by LaTeX's extra tables packages."

ISBN: 9781906860257
240 pages

ALSO PUBLISHED BY UIT

LaTeX quick reference

Herbert Voss

This book lists all LaTeX macros and environments in a comprehensive reference format. (The packages **array** and **graphicx** are included even though they are not part of standard LaTeX, because they are so widely used.) The book also lists examples of fonts for both plain text and math, making it a convenient graphical resource.

This book will:
- Save you time by quickly giving you the detailed command syntax you require.
- Improve your LaTeX by providing a quick-reference to all the available command options.
- Show you how to choose suitable fonts, using the convenient samples of font output.

Contents
1. The Standard Programs
2. Document Structure
3. Commands for Fine-Tuning your Typography
4. Command List
5. Lengths and Counters
6. Fonts
7. Packages
8. Bibliography

Praise for the German Edition

"An essential resource for LaTeX users"

ISBN: 9781906860219
160 pages

ALSO PUBLISHED BY UIT

Practical TCP/IP

Designing, using, and troubleshooting
TCP/IP networks on Linux and Windows

Niall Mansfield

Reprinted first edition

Key benefits
1. Explore, hands-on, how your network really works. Build small test networks in a few minutes, so you can try anything out without affecting your live network and servers.
2. Learn how to troubleshoot network problems, and how to use free packet sniffers to see what's happening.
3. Understand how the TCP/IP protocols map onto your day-to-day network operation – learn both theory and practice.

What readers have said about this book

"Before this book was released I was eagerly searching for a book that could be used for my Linux-based LAN-course. After the release of this book I stopped my searching immediately"
Torben Gregersen, Engineering College of Aarhus.

"Accuracy is superb – written by someone obviously knowledgable in the subject, and able to communicate this knowledge extremely effectively."

"You won't find a better TCP/IP book!"

"An excellent book for taking your computer networking career from mediocre to top notch."

"Covers TCP/IP, and networking in general, tremendously."

"This book has been touted as the 21st-century upgrade to the classic TCP/IP Illustrated (by Richard W. Stevens). These are big boots to fill, but Practical TCP/IP does an impressive job. In over 800 pages of well-organized and well-illustrated text, there is no fat, but rather a lean and – yes – practical treatment of every major TCP/IP networking concept."

"It's an ideal book for beginners, probably the only one needed for the first and second semesters of a university networking course. ... (But it is not a book just for beginners. ...)"

ISBN: 9781906860363
880 pages

ALSO PUBLISHED BY UIT

The Exim SMTP Mail Server
Official Guide for Release 4

Philip Hazel

Second edition

Email is one of the most widely used applications, and Exim is one of the most widely used mail servers, handling mail for tens of millions of users daily.

Exim is free software. It's easy to configure. It's scalable, running on single-user desktop systems as well as on ISP servers handling millions of users. (It's the default server on many Linux systems, and it's available for countless versions of UNIX.)

Exim is fast, flexible, and reliable. It is designed not to lose messages even if your server machine crashes. It can be used as a secure Internet-facing front-end to other, proprietary, mail systems used internally in your organization.

Exim supports lookups from LDAP servers, SQL databases, and other data sources, letting you automate maintenance and configuration. It can work in conjunction with other tools for virus-checking and spam-blocking, to reject unwanted emails before they even enter your site.

This book will help you deploy Exim as your SMTP email server throughout your organization, and to configure, tune, and secure your Exim systems.

Praise for the First Edition

"The book is simply amazing. I find the format/style/whatever 100 times better than [other documentation]."

"If there's even a whiff of a chance of you having to come into contact with Exim or its runtime configuration, then I can do nothing else but strongly recommend this book. The detail's there in spades, it reads very well, and is a fine complement to the reference manual."

"The book exceeds my expectations."

"Well presented and easy to follow"

"An excellent book that is very well written"

"So well written I learn new things every time I open it"

ISBN: 9780954452971
xviii + 622 pages

ALSO PUBLISHED BY UIT

The Joy of X
The architecture of the X window system

Niall Mansfield

This is a reprint of the 1993 classic, describing the architecture of the X window system – the de facto standard windowing system for Linux, UNIX and many other operating systems. The book has three sections:
1. X in a nutshell – a quick overview.
2. How X works, in detail, and how the user sees it.
3. Using the system, system administration, performance and programming.

The book is written in a clear, uncomplicated style, with over 200 illustrations. For maximum accessibility, it has a flexibile, modular structure that makes it easy to skip to the sections that interest you. The book has been widely recommended as a course text.

Niall Mansfield founded the European X window system User Group. He also wrote *The X window system: a user's guide*, and the widely-acclaimed *Practical TCP/IP*.

Praise for This Book

"User interfaces come and go, but X remains the standard window system across a range of operating systems. Niall's book, The Joy of X, still offers an excellent look into how X works and how to make it work better for you."
Keith Packard, X.org project leader

"If you are new to the X Window System environment, we strongly suggest picking up a book such as The Joy of X"   Eric Raymond, in the *Linux XFree86 HOWTO*

"a great little book called The Joy of X by Niall Mansfield that taught me much of what I know."   Jeff Duntemann's ContraPositive Diary

"My personal touchstone when looking for a broad introduction to all things X is The Joy of X ... by Niall Mansfield"
Peter Collinson

ISBN: 9781906860004
xii + 372 pages

ALSO PUBLISHED BY UIT

Alternative DNS Servers
Choice and deployment, and optional SQL/LDAP back-ends

Jan-Piet Mens

This book examines many of the best DNS servers available. It covers each server's benefits and disadvantages, as well as how to configure and deploy it, and integrate it into your network infrastructure. It describes the different scenarios where each server is particularly useful, so you can choose the most suitable server for your site. A unique feature of the book is that it explains how DNS data can be stored in LDAP directories and SQL databases, often required for integrating DNS into large-organization infrastructures.

Other important topics covered include: performance, security issues, integration with DHCP, DNSSEC, internationalization, and specialized DNS servers designed for some unusual purposes.

Praise for This Book

"The first book to describe NSD and Unbound in excellent detail."
    NLnet Labs, authors of NSD and Unbound

"Finally - a clear, in-depth and accessible guide to using BIND-DLZ! A must read for anyone considering alternate DNS servers."
    Rob Butler, BIND-DLZ project creator and author

"Takes the reader through the process of configuring the program from basics to advanced topics."
    Simon Kelley, author of dnsmasq

"An informative accurate guide for anyone interested in learning more about DNS."
    Sam Trenholme, MaraDNS author

"A valuable source of information for every PowerDNS administrator!"
    Norbert Sendetzky, author of PowerDNS LDAP & OpenDBX back-ends

"Jan-Piet has done a great job describing PowerDNS."
    Bert Hubert, principal author of PowerDNS

ISBN: 9780954452995
xxxvi + 694 pages

ALSO PUBLISHED BY UIT

Typesetting Mathematics with LaTeX

Herbert Voss

From a simple equation to a mathematical treatise, this practical guide offers an in-depth review of the mathematics typesetting aspects of the industry-leading typesetting software, LaTeX. Among the topics discussed in this manual are mathematics in line with normal text, the software's special mathematics mode, color in math expressions, and fonts and math.

Handy features include a list of mathematical symbols for quick-reference, a survey of a wide range of additional mathematics packages—with a particular emphasis on the American Mathematical Society package—and ready-to-run examples to enable users to get going quickly.

This book will:

▷ Save you time by quickly giving you the detailed command syntax you require.

▷ Improve your mathematical typesetting by providing a reference to all the available commands.

▷ Showing the advantages of the packages from the American MAthematical Society

▷ Show you how to choose suitable math fonts, using the convenient samples of font output.

Contents

1. Introduction
2. Math in inline mode with standard LaTeX
3. Math in display mode with standard LaTeX
4. Math elements from standard LaTeX
5. Colour in math expressions
6. AMS packages
7. Symbols
8. TeX and math
9. Other packages
10. Examples
11. Fonts and math
12. Bibliography

ISBN: 9781906860172
290 pages

ALSO PUBLISHED BY UIT

OpenStreetMap
Using and enhancing the free map of the world

Frederik Ramm and Jochen Topf, with Steve Chilton
Second edition

OpenStreetMap is a map of the whole world that can be used and edited freely by everyone. In a Wikipedia-like open community process, thousands of contributors world-wide survey the planet and upload their results to the OpenStreetMap database. Unlike some other mapping systems on the Web, the tools and the data are free and open. You can use them and modify them as you require; you can even download all the map data and run your own private map server if you need to.

This book introduces you to the OpenStreetMap community, its data model, and the software used in the project. It shows you how to use the constantly-growing OSM data set and maps in your own projects.

The book also explains in detail how you can contribute to the project, collecting and processing data for OpenStreetMap. If you want to become an OpenStreetMap "mapper" then this is the book for you.

About the authors: Frederik Ramm and Jochen Topf both joined the OpenStreetMap project in 2006, when they were freelance developers. Since then they have made their hobby their profession – by founding Geofabrik, a company that provides services relating to OpenStreetMap and open geodata.

Praise for the First (German) Edition

> "A must-have for OSM newcomers. The basics are presented well and are easy to understand, and you do not need to be an IT specialist to contribute your first data to OSM after a short time."

> "The book is very well written. It is obvious that the authors have a lot of knowledge and experience ..."

> "A very good OSM introduction. Getting up to speed with OpenStreetMap is much easier if you have read this book."

ISBN: 9781906860110
352 pages + 32 pages of color plates

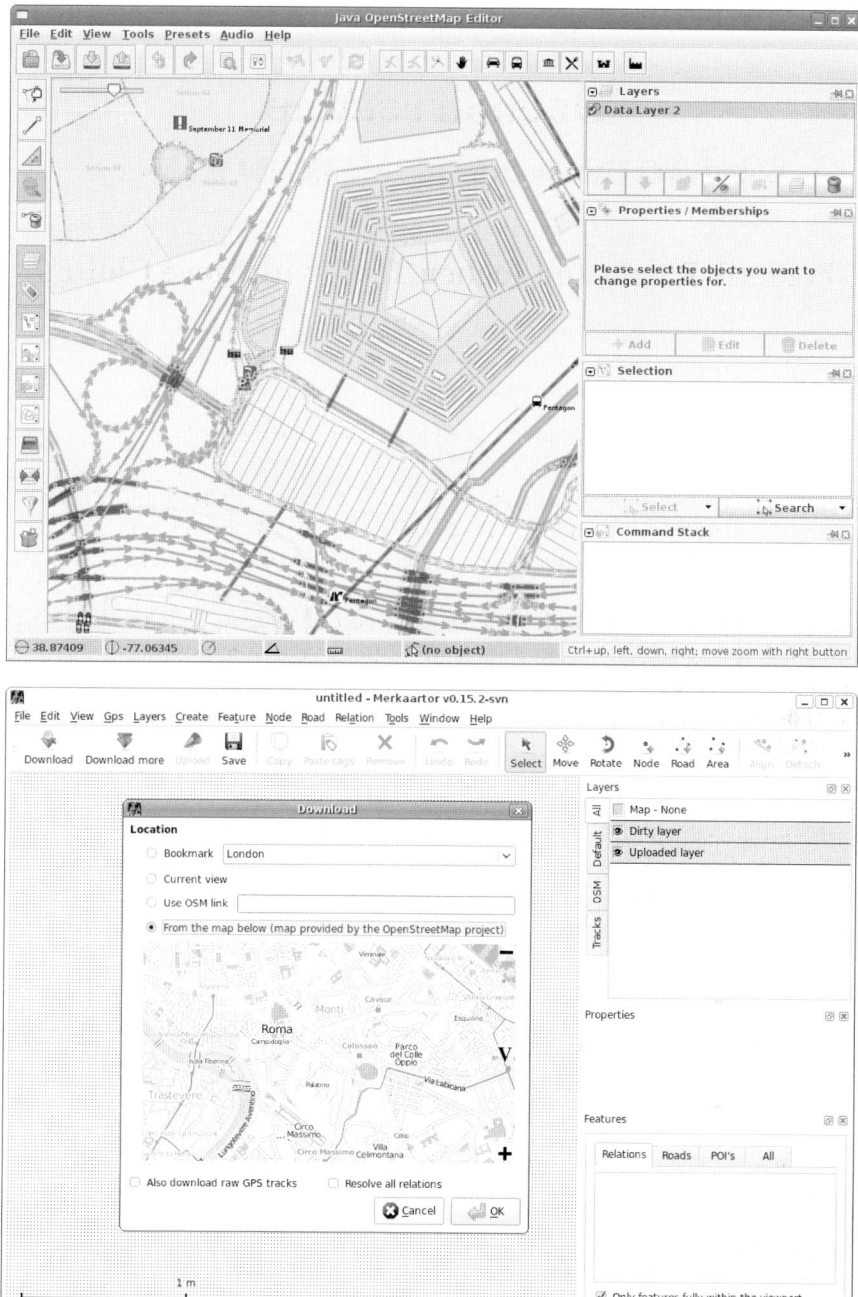

Example illustrations from OpenStreetMap

More about this book

Register your book: receive updates, notifications about author appearances, and announcements about new editions. *www.uit.co.uk/register*

News: forthcoming titles, events, reviews, interviews, podcasts, etc. *www.uit.co.uk/news*

Join our mailing lists: get email newsletters on topics of interest. *www.uit.co.uk/subscribe*

How to order: get details of stockists and online bookstores. If you are a bookstore, find out about our distributors or contact us to discuss your particular requirements. *www.uit.co.uk/order*

Send us a book proposal: if you want to write – even if you have just the kernel of an idea at present – we'd love to hear from you. We pride ourselves on supporting our authors and making the process of book-writing as satisfying and as easy as possible. *www.uit.co.uk/for-authors*

UIT Cambridge Ltd.
PO Box 145
Cambridge
CB4 1GQ
England

Email: *inquiries@uit.co.uk*
Phone: +44 1223 302 041